Mexico

THE ROUGH GUIDE

KT-487-062

There are more than sixty Rough Guide titles covering
destinations from Amsterdam to Zimbabwe

Forthcoming titles include
Bali • Costa Rica • Majorca • Rhodes

Rough Guide Reference Series
Classical Music • World Music

Rough Guide Phrasebooks
Czech • French • German • Greek • Italian • Spanish

Mexico: Rough Guide Credits

Editor:	Samantha Cook
Series editor:	Mark Ellingham
Editorial:	Martin Dunford, Jonathan Buckley, Graham Parker, Jo Mead, Alison Cowan, Amanda Tomlin, Catherine McHale, Annie Shaw, Lemisse al-Hafidh
Production:	Susanne Hillen, Andy Hilliard, Alan Spicer, Judy Pang, Link Hall, Nicola Williamson
Cartography:	Melissa Flack
Finance:	John Fisher, Celia Crowley, Simon Carloss
Marketing and Publicity:	Richard Trillo (UK), Jean-Marie Kelly, Jeffrey Kaye (US)
Administration:	Tania Hummel

Acknowledgments

Thanks on this edition to the staff at the *Mexican Tourist Office* in London and the extremely helpful staff at all the tourist offices in Mexico. Also to all the contributors and readers who made this new edition possible: we received far too many letters to mention you all individually, but please do keep writing. The **researchers** would like to thank Stefan, Renate and Klaus; Olga Ramirez Luna; Cherry Austin; Elizabeth Mistry; Greg Ward; Lotte Friis-Hansen and Jacob Nøhr Schubart; Lily Romina in Bahía de los Angeles; Peter Bak and Trish Henderson; Sebastien Lorquet; the Chiapas tourist offices, particularly Margarita Ruíz in Tuxtla Gutiérrez; Krystyna Deuss of the *Guatemala Indian Centre*; Jamie Marshall; Barbara and Maria from Germany; Peter and Ann Roberts in Orange Walk, Belize; Ned Middleton; Bertie Pringle of *Cosmo Minerals*; the staff and students at the School of Languages and Area Studies at the University of Portsmouth; Carmen Nuñez and Gabriel at the *Hotel Caribe* in Mérida; Jose Chan at *Viajes Rotesa*, Mérida; José at *Don Armandos* in Tulum; Tony Leeman at *Royal Tours* in Cancún; Filomeno Plata Barrios in Frontera; Pedro Alejandro Serrano López at the Campeche tourist office; Odette Chávez at *Komex Tours*; *La Casa de los Amigos* in México; *La Casa de la Cultura* in Tlapacoyan; Daniel López; Silvia Santos and "Hikuri"; Silverio Cruz and "La Farándula"; Lambert, Raúl Rodriguez Yelmi and the street artisans of Jalapa; Martin, Lina and David Aylett; Luciana Dumphries; Sra Lucía Hernandez de la Huerta; Zulma Amador and "La Flota", and finally to the many people in Mexico who make a journey through their country such a pleasure.

John would like to thank all at *Rough Guides* and *Penguin* who put up with the long wait, especially Sam, for editing beyond the call; Kate Berens, who did much of it twice; Gareth Nash, and Sam Kirby for the maps. And as ever to Stretch and, for the first time, to Jake.

This edition published 1995 by Rough Guides Ltd, 1 Mercer Street, London WC2H 9QJ.

Distributed by the Penguin Group:
Penguin Books Ltd, 27 Wrights Lane, London W8 5TZ
Penguin Books USA Inc., 375 Hudson Street, New York 10014, USA
Penguin Books Australia Ltd, 487 Maroondah Highway, PO Box 257, Ringwood, Victoria 3134, Australia
Penguin Books Canada Ltd, 10 Alcorn Avenue, Toronto, Ontario, Canada M4V 1E4
Penguin Books (NZ) Ltd, 182–190 Wairau Road, Auckland 10, New Zealand

Previous edition published in the United States and Canada as *The Real Guide Mexico*.

Typeset in Linotron Univers and Century Old Style to an original design by Andrew Oliver.
Printed in the United Kingdom by Cox & Wyman Ltd (Reading).
Illustrations in Part One and Part Three by Edward Briant; Illustrations on p.1 and p.551 by Henry Iles.

624pp, includes index

A catalogue record for this book is available from the British Library.

ISBN 1-85828-044-3

Mexico

THE ROUGH GUIDE

Written and researched by
John Fisher

with additional research
and accounts by
Pete Eltringham, Paul Whitfield, Anne Barrett,
Silvia Mayer, Mark Whatmore, Daniel Jacobs, Daniel Ribot,
Nic Lazarus, Chris Overington and Mary Farquharson

THE ROUGH GUIDES

LIST OF MAPS

MAP SYMBOLS

REGIONAL MAPS

++++	Railway
——	Main Road
——	Minor Road
- - - -	Track or Trail
——	River
⬯	Lake
— —	Ferry route
-■-■-	International boundary
■■ ■■	Chapter division boundary
∿∿∿	State boundary
⌒⌒	Mountains
▲	Peak
◆	Ancient site
∩	Cave

TOWN MAPS

——	Railway
....	Road
▭▭▭	Steps
▪▪▪▪	Fortified wall
▨	Park
■	Building
✛	Church
⁺⁺⁺	Christian cemetery
▨	Pedestrianized street
ⓘ	Tourist Office
✕	Airport
⬚	Beach

CONTENTS

Introduction x
Temperature and rainfall table xii

Throughout this book the **capital** is referred to as México. Where we refer to the whole country we've left the accent off to make some kind of distinction. For more details see the *Introduction* on p.viii.

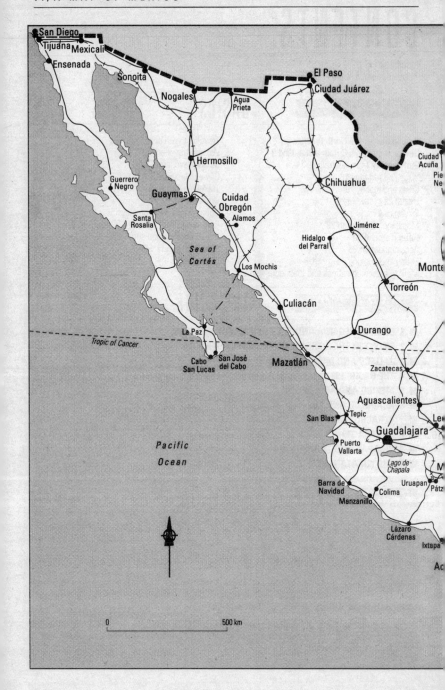

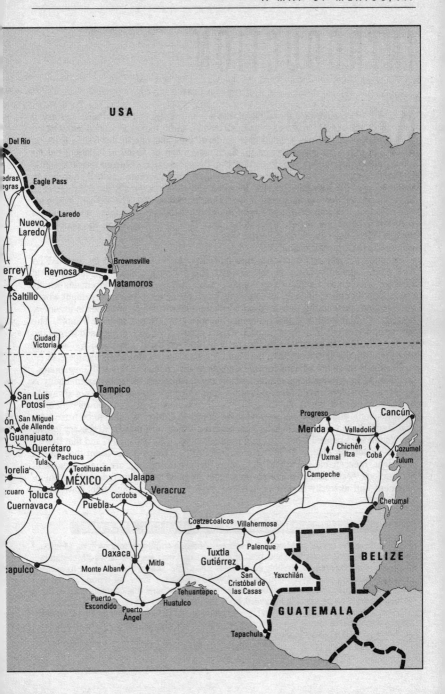

INTRODUCTION

M exico enjoys a cultural blend that is wholly unique: it is an Indian country; it still seems, in places, a Spanish colony, and it has experienced an oil-based boom that has created vast modern cities and one of the fastest growing industrial powers on earth. Each aspect can be found in isolation, but far more often, throughout the Republic, the three co-exist – Indian markets, little changed in form since the Conquest, thrive alongside elaborate colonial churches in the shadow of the skyscrapers of the Mexican miracle. Occasionally the marriage is an uneasy one, but for the most part it works unbelievably well. The people of Mexico reflect it too; there are communities of full-blooded Indians, and there are a few – a very few – Mexicans of pure Spanish descent. The great majority of the population, though, is *mestizo*, combining both traditions and, to a greater or lesser extent, a veneer of urban sophistication.

Despite encroaching Americanism, a tide likely to be accelerated by the **NAFTA free trade agreement**, and close links with the rest of the Spanish-speaking world (leaving aside an avid audience for Mexican soap operas) the country remains wholly distinctive. Its music, its look, its sound, its smell rarely leave you in any doubt where you are, and the thought "only in Mexico" – sometimes in awe, sometimes in exasperation, most often in simple bemusement – is rarely far from a traveller's mind. The strength of Mexican identity perhaps hits most clearly if you travel overland across the border with the United States: this is the only place on earth where a single step will take you from the "First" world to the "Third", a small step that really is a giant leap.

Obviously there are adjustments to be made to any country that is still "developing", and where change has been so dramatically rapid. Although the **mañana** mentality is largely an outsiders' myth, Mexico is still a country where timetables are not always to be entirely trusted, where anything that can break down will break down (when it's most needed), and where any attempt to do things in a hurry is liable to be frustrated. You simply have to accept the local temperament – that work may be necessary to live, but it's not life's central focus, that minor annoyances really are minor, and that there's always something else to do in the meantime. And at times it can seem that there's incessant, inescapable noise and dirt. More deeply disturbing, are the extremes of ostentatious wealth and absolute poverty, most poignant in the big cities where unemployment and austerity measures imposed by the massive foreign debt have bitten

MÉXICO? I THOUGHT WE WERE THERE ALREADY

The name of the capital of Mexico is a source of infinite confusion to travellers. **Mexico City** is not a place on any Mexican map or a name that's ever used: as far as a Mexican is concerned it's **México**, or possibly *El DF* (Day Effé). The country took its name from the city and México, in conversation, almost always means the latter (in writing it's often México DF – the *Distrito Federal* being the administrative zone that contains most of the urban areas). The nation is *la Republica*, or in speeches *la Patria*; very rarely Mexico.

Throughout this book, the capital is referred to as México, the term you'll have to use if you want anyone to understand: where we refer to the country we've left the accent off to make some kind of distinction.

hardest. Nevertheless, it is an easy, a fabulously varied, and an enormously enoyable and friendly place in which to travel – despite the stories you may hear, and the lurid colour spreads of violent crime in Mexican newspapers.

Physically, Mexico resembles a vast horn, curving away south and east from the US border with its final tip bent right back round to the north. It is an extremely mountainous country: two great ranges, the Sierra Madre Occidental in the west and the Sierra Madre Oriental in the east, run down parallel to the coasts, enclosing a high, semi-desert plateau. About halfway down they are crossed by the volcanic highland area in which stand México (ie Mexico City; see box opposite) and the major centres of population. Beyond, the mountains run together as a single range through the southern states of Oaxaca and Chiapas. Only the eastern tip – the Yucatán peninsula – is consistently low-lying and flat.

Where to go

The **north of Mexico**, relatively speaking, is a dull land, arid and sparsely populated outside of a few **industrial cities** – like Monterrey – which are heavily American influenced. The **Baja California** wilderness has its devotees, the **border cities** can be exciting in a rather sleazy way, and there are **beach resorts** on the Pacific, but most of the excitement lies in central and southeastern Mexico.

It is in **the highlands** north of and around the capital that the first really worthwhile stops come, with the bulk of the historic colonial towns and an enticingly spring-like climate year-round. Coming through the heart of the country, you'll pass the silver-mining towns of **Zacatecas** and **Guanajuato**, the historic centres of **San Miguel de Allende** and **Querétaro**, and many smaller places with a legacy of superb colonial architecture. **México** itself is a choking nightmare of urban sprawl, but totally fascinating, and in every way – artistic, political, cultural – the capital of the nation. Around the city lie the chief relics of the pre-Hispanic cultures of central Mexico – the massive pyramids of **Teotihuacán**, the main Toltec site at **Tula**, and **Tenochtitlan**, heart of the Aztec empire, in the capital itself. **Guadalajara**, to the west, is a city on a more human scale, capital of the state of **Jalisco** and in easy reach of **Michoacán**: between them, these states share some of the most gently scenic country in Mexico – thickly forested hills, studded with lakes and ancient villages – and a reputation for producing some of the finest crafts in a country renowned for them.

South of the capital, the states of Oaxaca and Chiapas are mountainous and beautiful, too, but in a far wilder way. The city of **Oaxaca**, especially, is one of the most enticing destinations in the country, with an extraordinary mix of colonial and Indian life, superb markets, and fascinating archeological sites. **Chiapas** is most recently notorious as the centre of the **Zapatista** uprising, but at the time of writing travellers were still visiting with few problems, and the strength of indigenous traditions in and around the market town of **San Cristóbal de las Casas** continue to make it a big travellers' centre. East into the **Yucatán** there is also traditional indigenous life, side by side with a tourist industry based around the magnificent **Maya cities** – **Palenque**, **Chichén Itzá** and **Uxmal** above all, but also hundreds of others – and the burgeoning new Caribbean resorts that surround **Cancún**. The capital, **Mérida**, continues its provincial life remarkably unaffected by the crowds all around.

On the Pacific coast, **Acapulco** is just the best known of the destinations. Northwards, big resorts like **Mazatlán** and **Puerto Vallarta** are interspersed with hundreds of miles of empty beaches; to the south there is still less development, and in the state of Oaxaca are some really exciting shores. Few tourists venture over to the **Gulf Coast**, despite the attractions of **Veracruz** and its mysterious ruins. The scene is largely dominated by oil, the weather too humid most of the time, and the beaches, on the whole, a disappointment.

Climate

To a great extent, the physical terrain in Mexico determines the **climate** – certainly far more than the expected indicators of latitude and longitude. You can drive down the coast all day without conditions changing noticeably, but turn inland, to the mountains, and the contrast is immediate: in temperature, scenery, vegetation, even the mood and mould of the people around you. So generalizations are difficult.

Summer, from June to October, is in theory the **rainy season**, but just how wet it is varies wildly from place to place. In the heart of the country you can expect a heavy but shortlived downpour virtually every afternoon; in the north hardly any rain falls, ever. Chiapas is the wettest state, with many minor roads washed out in the autumn, and in the south and low-lying coastal areas summer is stickily humid too, with occasional spectacular tropical storms. Winter is the traditional **tourist season**, and in the big beach resorts like Acapulco and Cancún, December is the busiest month of the year. Mountain areas, though, can get very cold then: indeed nights in the mountains can be extremely cold at any time of year, so carry a sweater.

In effect there are now tourists all year round – sticking on the whole to the highlands in summer and the coasts in winter. Given a totally free choice, November is probably the **ideal time to visit**, with the rains over, the land still fresh, and the peak season not yet begun. Overall, though, the climate is so benign that any time of year will do, so long as you're prepared for some rain in the summer, some cold in winter, and for sudden changes which go with the altitude at any time.

AVERAGE TEMPERATURE AND RAINFALL

	JAN °F Max Min	Rain inches	MAR °F Max Min	Rain inches	MAY °F Max Min	Rain inches	JULY °F Max Min	Rain inches	SEPT °F Max Min	Rain inches	NOV °F Max Min	Rain inches
Acapulco	88 72	.5	88 72	.2	90 77	0	91 77		90 77	11	90 75	.6
Guadalajara	73 45	.5	82 48	.3	88 57	1	79 59		79 59	7	77 50	.5
La Paz	73 55	.3	79 55	0	91 63	0	97 73		95 73	1	84 63	.5
Mérida	82 64	1	90 68	.5	93 70	3	91 73		90 73	7	84 66	1
México	72 43	.5	81 50	.5	81 55	3	75 55		73 55	5	73 48	.5
Monterrey	68 48	1	79 55	1	88 68	2	93 72		93 72	4	73 54	1
Oaxaca	82 46	2	90 54	1	90 59	5	82 59		81 59	11	82 50	2
San Cristóbal	68 41	2	72 45	2	72 48	7	72 50		70 50	14	68 45	3
Tijuana	68 43	2	70 46	1	73 54	.2	81 61		81 61	.5	73 50	1
Veracruz	77 64	1	79 70	1	86 77	4	88 75		88 77	12	82 70	2

To convert Fahrenheit to Centigrade, subtract 32, multiply by 5 and divide by 9.

PART ONE

THE

BASICS

GETTING THERE FROM NORTH AMERICA

The quickest and easiest way to get to Mexico from Canada and most of the US is to fly. Going by land won't save you much money, if any, but becomes rather more convenient the nearer your home and your destination are to the border. Unless you've got your own boat, getting there by sea is only normally possible on a cruise ship.

BY AIR

There are **flights to Mexico** from just about every major US city, but the cheapest and most frequent fly out of "gateway" cities in the south and west, most commonly **LA**, **Dallas**, **Houston** and **Miami**.

If you live close to the border, it's usually cheaper to cross into Mexico and take an **internal flight** (which you can purchase from your neighbourhood travel agent). If it's a resort that you want, you'll probably find that at least one of the airlines offers an attractive deal including a few nights' lodging (see "Packages and Organized Tours" on p.5).

SHOPPING FOR TICKETS

Barring special offers, the cheapest fare is usually an **Apex** ticket, although this will carry certain restrictions: you have to book – and pay – at least 21 days before departure, spend at least 7 days abroad (maximum stay three months), and you tend to get penalized if you change your schedule. There are also winter **Super Apex** tickets, slightly cheaper than an ordinary Apex, but limiting your stay to between 7 and 21 days. Some airlines also issue **Special Apex** tickets to people younger than 24, often extending the maximum stay to a year. Many airlines offer youth or student fares to **under-25s**; a passport or driving licence is sufficient proof of age, though these tickets are subject to availability and can have eccentric booking conditions. It's worth remembering that most cheap round-trip fares involve spending at least one Saturday night away and that many will only give a percentage refund if you need to cancel or alter your journey, so make sure you check the restrictions carefully before buying a ticket.

You can normally cut costs by going through a **specialist flight agent** – either a **consolidator**, who buys up blocks of tickets from the airlines and sells them at a discount, or a **discount agent**, who wheels and deals in blocks of tickets offloaded by the airlines, and often offers special student and youth fares and a range of other travel-related services, such as travel insurance, rail passes, car rentals, tours and the like. Bear in mind, though, that penalties for changing your plans can be stiff. Remember too that these companies make their money by dealing in bulk – don't expect them to answer lots of questions. Some agents specialize in **charter flights**, which may be cheaper than scheduled flights, but again departure dates are fixed and withdrawal penalties are high (check the refund policy). If you travel a lot, **discount travel clubs** are another option – the annual membership fee may be worth it for benefits such as cut-price air tickets and car rental.

To some extent, the **fare** will depend on the season. Though prices to México (ie Mexico City) and less visited destinations show little if any fluctuation, fares to Mexico are otherwise highest at Easter, from around early June to mid-September and at **Christmas and New Year**, when prices – especially to the resort areas – may run as much as $200 higher than in low season; they drop during the "shoulder" seasons – mid-September to early November and mid-April to early June – and you'll get the best prices during the low season, November through April (excluding Christmas and New Year, of course). Note also that flying at weekends adds $20–60 to the round-trip fare; the

AIRLINES IN NORTH AMERICA

Aero California ☎1-800/237-6225
LA to Cabo San Lucas, Guadalajara, La Paz,
Laredo, Mazatlán and México.

Aeroméxico ☎1-800/237-6639
Atlanta, Dallas, LA, Miami, New Orleans, New
York, Phoenix, San Antonio, San Diego and Tucson
to all destinations in Mexico.

Alaska Airlines ☎1-800/426-0333
LA, Phoenix, San Francisco and Seattle to Cabo,
San Lucas, Mazatlán and Puerto Vallarta.

American Airlines ☎1-800/433-7300
Dallas and Miami to Acapulco, Cancún, León,
México, Monterrey and Puerto Vallarta.

America West Airlines ☎1-800/235-9292
Phoenix to Cabo San Lucas, Mazatlán and México.

Canadian Airlines ☎1-800/665-1177 (Canada);
Toronto to México. ☎1-800/426-7000 (US)

Continental Airlines ☎1-800/525-0280
Houston and San Francisco to Acapulco, Cancún,
Cozumel, Guadalajara, León, Los Cabos, México,
Monterrey and Puerto Vallarta.

Delta Airlines ☎1-800/241-4141
Atlanta, LA, New York and Orlando to México;
also LA to Acapulco, Guadalajara, Ixtapa/
Zihuatanejo, Mazatlán and Puerto Vallarta, and
Atlanta to Monterrey.

Lacsa ☎1-800/225-2272
Houston, LA, Miami, New York and Washington to
México; also New Orleans to Cancún and Mérida.

Mexicana ☎1-800/531-7921
Chicago, Denver, LA, Miami, Newark, San
Antonio, San Francisco and San Jose to all desti-
nations in Mexico.

Taesa ☎1-800/328-2372
Chicago and Oakland to Aguascalientes, Durango,
Guadalajara, México, Morelia and Zacatecas.

United Airlines ☎1-800/538-2929
Chicago, LA, Miami and San Erancisco to México.

US Air ☎1-800/622-1015
Pittsburgh to México.

DISCOUNT TRAVEL COMPANIES IN NORTH AMERICA

Air Brokers International ☎1-800/883-3273
San Francisco-based consolidator.

Air Courier Association ☎303/278-8810
Courier flight broker.

Airtech ☎1-800/575-TECH
Standby-seat broker: for a set price, they guarantee to get you on a flight as close to your preferred
destination as possible, within a week. Mainly
from northeastern US cities.

Council Travel ☎1-800/743-1823
Student travel organization with branches in many
US cities; subsidiary of the Council on
International Educational Exchange (see "Work
and Study").

Discount Travel ☎1-800/334-9294
    International
Discount travel club.

Educational Travel Center ☎1-800/747-5551
Student/youth discount agent.

Encore Travel Club ☎1-800/444-9800
Discount travel club.

International Student Exchange Flights
Student/youth fares,
student IDs. ☎602/951-1177

Last Minute Travel Club ☎1-800/LAST MIN
Travel club specializing in standby flights and
packages.

Now Voyager ☎212/431-1616
Courier flight broker.

STA Travel ☎1-800/777-0112
Worldwide specialist in independent travel with
branches in the New York, LA, San Francisco and
Boston areas.

TFI Tours International ☎1-800/745-8000
New York-based consolidator.

Travel CUTS ☎416/979-2406
Canadian student travel organization with
branches all over the country.

Travelers Advantage ☎1-800/548-1116
Discount travel club.

UniTravel ☎1-800/325-2222
St Louis-based consolidator.

Worldtek Travel ☎1-800/243-1723
Discount travel agency dealing mainly in East
Coast charters.

typical lowest round-trip Apex prices quoted below assume midweek travel in high season.

FROM THE US

Aeroméxico and *Mexicana* fly direct to dozens of destinations in Mexico, and can make connections to many others; the bigger **US airlines** have connections to México and the more popular resorts. Fares are most competitive from **Dallas** and **Houston**, where round-trip flights to México start at $300, rising to $320 to Acapulco and Cancún and $360 to Mérida. From **LA**, figure on $450 to México, $500 to Acapulco and $550 to Mérida or Cancún. Flights from **Miami** to Mérida or Cancún are also good value – hovering between $240 and $280 round-trip – as is *Mexicana's* night service from **San Francisco** and **LA** to Guadalajara and México. Adding a feeder flight from any other city to one of the gateways is easy; New York to México or Cancún shouldn't run to more than $500 for a round trip.

Charter, promotional, student/youth and other **discounted fares** routinely run $100–200 lower than the above.

FROM CANADA

There are few direct scheduled flights from Canada to anywhere in Mexico, although charters are plentiful in the winter. Your options expand greatly if you fly via one US city.

Some typical lowest round-trip Apex fares are (in Canadian dollars): **Montréal** to México $500; to Cancún $600; to Acapulco $820; **Toronto** to México $430; Cancún $550; Acapulco $730; and from **Vancouver** to México $500, to Acapulco or Cancún $700.

PACKAGES AND ORGANIZED TOURS

Hundreds of companies offer good-value **package tours** to Mexican resorts, as do the tour arms of most major North American airlines. Packages are generally only available for the more commercialized destinations, such as Cabo San Lucas, Mazatlán, Puerto Vallarta, Acapulco, Ixtapa or Cancún, and travel agents and the airlines will be extremely reluctant to extend the time-term to permit a bit more independent exploration; If, however, what you want is a week on a Mexican beach, your best bet is to comb the Sunday newspaper travel sections for the latest bargains and then see if your local travel agent can turn up anything better.

Prices vary tremendously by resort, season and style of accommodation, but one week in a better-category hotel in any of the resorts above will generally start at $500 per person. Prices may be slashed to less than that on last-minute deals, available a week or two before the departure date. Christmas and college spring break are the busiest times for Americans travelling to Mexican resorts, so best avoided if possible.

In addition, literally hundreds of **specialist companies** offer tours of Mexico based around

NORTH AMERICAN PACKAGE TOUR OPERATORS

AEM Travel ☎1-800/899-0013
Sightseeing tours.

American Express Vacations
Resort packages, sightseeing ☎1-800/241-1700
tours.

Canadian Holidays ☎1-800/661-8881
Major charter company with departures from Toronto and Vancouver to many Mexican destinations.

Cosmos Tourama ☎1-800/338-7092
Sightseeing tours.

Empire Tours ☎1-800/833-3333
Yucatán sightseeing.

Friendly Holidays ☎1-800/221-9748
Resort packages.

Globus ☎1-800/221-0090
First-class sightseeing.

Gogo Tours ☎1-800/821-3731
Resort packages, sightseeing.

Pleasant Mexico Holidays
Getaways to various beach ☎1-800/448-3333
resorts.

Saga International Holidays
Sightseeing and cruises for ☎1-800/343-0273
seniors.

Suntastic Tours ☎1-800/909-7866
Sightseeing, resort packages.

Suntrips ☎1-800/SUN-TRIP
Resort packages.

Vantage Travel ☎1-800/322-6677
Sightseeing and cruises for seniors.

hiking, biking, diving, bird-watching and the like. See the box below for just a few of the possibilities; a competent travel agent will be able to point out others. (Remember, bookings made through a travel agent cost no more than going through the tour operator – indeed, many tour companies are wholesalers, meaning they only sell through agents.)

For operators that run trips exclusively for seniors, travellers with disabilities and all-women groups, see p.49, p.50 and p.51.

More counter-cultural, and perhaps better value, are overland routes covered by **Green Tortoise Adventure Travel** (☎1-800/227-4766). Converted school buses provide reasonably comfortable transport and sleeping space for up to 35 people; the clientele comes from all over the world, and communal cookouts are the rule.

Most of the tours are designed around departure from the San Francisco headquarters but add-on journeys from Boston, New York and many points along the Pacific Coast are easily arranged on one of *Green Tortoise*'s cross-country services. The only routes that currently include Mexico are the nine- and fourteen-day **overland adventures through Baja** from November to April ($300–450); there are also longer trips through **Mexico to Guatemala** ($400–800).

OVERLAND

There are more than twenty frontier posts along the US–Mexican border. Many of them, however,

---

GREEN TORTOISE SEAT RESERVATION NUMBERS

Green Tortoise main office: PO Box 24459, San Francisco, CA 94124 ☎415/821-0803 or 1-800/227-4766

Boston ☎617/265-8533

LA ☎310/392-1990

New York ☎212/431-3348

Portland ☎503/225-0310

Santa Barbara ☎805/569-1884

Santa Cruz ☎408/462-6437

Seattle ☎206/324-7433

Vancouver ☎604/732-5153

---

are only open during the day, and more-or-less inaccessible without your own transport. The main ones, open 24 hours a day, 7 days a week, are, from west to east:

- San Diego, California – Tijuana, Baja California Norte

- Calexico, California – Mexicali, Baja California Norte

- Nogales, Arizona – Nogales, Sonora

- Douglas, Arizona – Agua Prieta, Sonora

- El Paso, Texas – Ciudad Juárez, Chihuahua

- Laredo, Texas – Nuevo Laredo, Tamaulipas

- Brownsville, Texas –Matamoros, Tamaulipas

NORTH AMERICAN SPECIALIST TOUR OPERATORS

Adventure Center ☎1-800/227-8747
Overland tours.

Backroads ☎1-800/462-2848
Hiking and biking tours.

Baja Expeditions ☎1-800/843-6967
Sea kayaking, bird-watching, snorkelling.

Columbus Travel ☎1-800/843-1060
Copper Canyon rail tours and treks.

Ecosummer Expeditions ☎1-800/688-8605 (US);
☎1-800/465-884 (Canada)
Sea kayaking and whale-watching in Baja.

Journeys ☎800/255-8735
Trekking, Maya ruins.

Landfall Adventure Travel ☎1-800/525-3833
Scuba packages on Cozumel.

Le Boat ☎1-800/922-0291
Yacht charters.

Mountain Travel-Sobek ☎1-800/227-2384
Sea kayaking, whale-watching.

Nature Expeditions International ☎1-800/869-0639
Yucatán archeology.

Suntrek ☎1-800/292-9696
Overland tours in small international groups.

Trek America ☎1-800/221-0596
Overland camping tours.

Trek Holidays ☎403/439 0024 (Canada)
Overland tours.

Tropical Adventures ☎1-800/531-6114
Scuba diving.

BY RAIL

There is no direct connection between US and Mexican passenger **train services** and none cross the border. The nearest they get to each other is at the **El Paso/Ciudad Juárez** crossing, where there are stations in the border towns on both sides. El Paso is on the LA–Dallas line, and connected by *Amtrak*'s Texas Eagle and Sunset Limited services to Dallas, Houston, New Orleans, Miami, Phoenix, LA, St Louis and Chicago. The overnight journey takes 16 hours from Houston, 25 from Miami, 18 from LA, and 44 from Chicago.

Afternoon arrivals on these services give you plenty of time to get across the frontier, have supper in Ciudad Juárez, and board the first-class-only *Division del Norte*, which should in theory get you to México in 36 hours. There is a second-class service next morning, but it's barely worth contemplating.

Other **Mexican services** run from Nogales to México, and from Piedras Negras, Nuevo Laredo and Matamoros to Monterrey, San Luís Potosí and México. However, travelling like this is nothing like as convenient as the bus – and frankly you'd have to be a real train fanatic to go this way (for more on Mexican trains, see "Getting Around" on p.31).

Check current **timetables** with *Amtrak* (☎1-800/USA-RAIL), or *Mexico by Rail* (☎1-800/321-1699). Note that *Amtrak* does not sell tickets for the Mexican rail system.

BY BUS

North American bus travel is pretty grim compared to the relative comfort of *Amtrak*, but you have a wider range of US border posts to choose from. Count on at least 60 hours' journey time from New York to a Texas frontier post

($170), 15 hours from San Francisco to the Baja border ($86) – and at least a further day's travel from either point to México.

Greyhound (for routes and times, plus phone numbers and addresses of local terminals, call ☎1-800/231-2222) runs regularly to all the major **border crossings**, and some of their buses will take you over the frontier and into the Mexican bus station, which saves a lot of hassle. They should also be able to reserve you through tickets with their Mexican counterparts, which is even more convenient but involves a lot of pre-planning. Some Mexican buses similarly cross the border into US bus stations.

A cheap and cheerful alternative to the rigours of *Greyhound* is an overland tour in one of *Green Tortoise*'s summer-of-love style buses (see "Packages and Organized Tours" opposite).

BORDER FORMALITIES

Crossing the border, especially on foot, it's easy to go straight past the **immigration and customs checks**. There's a free zone south of the frontier, and you can cross at will and stay for up to three days. Make sure you do get your tourist card stamped and your bags checked though, or when you try to continue south you'll be stopped after some 20km and sent back to complete the formalities.

BY CAR

Taking **your own car** into Mexico will obviously give you a great deal more freedom, but it has to be said that it's an option fraught with complications. Aside from the border formalities, there is the state of the roads, the style of driving and the quality of the fuel to consider – these problems are dealt with in more detail on p.33.

US **driving licences** are valid in Mexico, but it's a good idea to arm yourself with an International Driving Licence – available for a nominal fee from the *American Automobile Association* (☎1-800/222-4357) – if you run afoul of a Mexican traffic cop for any reason, show that first, and if they abscond with it you at least still have your own more difficult to replace licence. If you are a visitor to the US, driving into Mexico, note that Canadian, British, Irish, Australian, New Zealand and most European driving licences are all valid in the US and Mexico.

GREYHOUND AGENTS ABROAD

UK   Sussex House, London Rd, East Grinstead, W Sussex RH19 1LD (☎01342/317317).

IRELAND   c/o *USIT*, Aston Quay, O'Connell Bridge, Dublin 2 (☎01/679 8833).

AUSTRALIA   c/o *North American Travel Specialists*, Suite 478, High St, Maitland NSW 2320 (☎049/342088).

NEW ZEALAND   *Greyhound Australia Pty Ltd*, Ward Building, cnr Hastings St and Beach St, Mairangi Bay, Auckland 10 (☎09/479 6555).

As a rule, you can drive in **Baja and the Zona Libre** (the border area extending roughly fifteen miles, 24km, into Mexico) without any special formalities. To drive elsewhere in Mexico, however, you must obtain a **vehicle permit** ($10) from the *Delegación de Servicios Migratorios* at the border. This must be paid for using a major credit card, otherwise you'll be asked for a minimum $500 refundable bond plus non-refundable tax and commission. You'll need to show registration and title for the car, plus your driving licence, passport *and* birth certificate. The permits are good for six months. To make sure you **don't sell the car in Mexico** or a neighbouring country, you'll also be required either to post a cash bond equal to the vehicle's book value or give an imprint of a major credit card (*Visa, Mastercard, Diners Club* or *Amex*). Plastic is obviously preferable, although it carries an $11.50 fee, especially as you can only get a refund of a cash deposit at the same border post where you paid it.

With few exceptions, US **auto insurance** policies don't cover mishaps in Mexico. Take out a Mexican policy, available from numerous agencies on either side of every border post. Rates depend on the value of the vehicle, but figure on $10 or so a day. To arrange a policy **before leaving the US**, call *Instant Mexico Insurance Services* (☎1-800/345-4701); *International Gateways* (☎1-800/423-2646); *Oscar Padilla Mexican Insurance* (☎1-800/258-8600); or *Sanborn's Insurance* (☎1-800/222-0158). The last is the acknowledged leader in the field.

To get **discounts** on insurance, it might be worthwhile joining a **travel club** such as *Club Mex* (☎619/585-3033), *Discover Baja Travel Club* (☎1-800/727-BAJA) or *Sanborn's Mexico Club* (see above). These clubs typically also offer discounts on accommodation and free travel advice services. Annual dues are $30–40. For more on general insurance policies, see p.27.

The *American Automobile Association* and *Canadian Automobile Association* produce road maps and route planners for travel to Mexico, and members may qualify for discounted insurance at affiliated border agencies. However, emergency services apply only in the US and Canada.

HITCHING

Hitching into Mexico from the US is not recommended. Quite apart from the obvious safety risks, even if you get a through lift, you need to walk or take a short bus ride across the border; otherwise it will be marked on your tourist card that you came in by car and you may (although it is unlikely) have problems when it's time to leave.

CRUISES

Mexican **cruises** represent a kind of tourism unto themselves – the *Love Boat* has a lot to answer for. Several lines offer seven-day cruises between LA and Acapulco, stopping at Los Cabos, Mazatlán, Puerto Vallarta and Zihuatanejo. Others ply the Caribbean side out of Miami, taking in Cozumel, Playa del Carmen and other Mexican destinations. Prices start at $600 per person (plus airfare to the starting point), and go (way) up from there.

Agencies specializing in cruises include *Cruise Adventures* (☎1-800/545-8118) and *Cruise World* (☎1-800/994-7447).

NORTH AMERICAN CRUISE LINES	
Carnival Cruise Lines	☎1-800/327-9501
Clipper Cruise Lines	☎1-800/325-0010
Commodore Cruise Lines	☎1-800/227-4759
Norwegian Cruise Lines	☎1-800/327-7030
Regency Cruises	☎1-800/388-5500
Royal Caribbean Cruises	☎1-800/327-6700
Starlite Cruises	☎1-800/488-8787

GETTING THERE FROM BRITAIN AND IRELAND

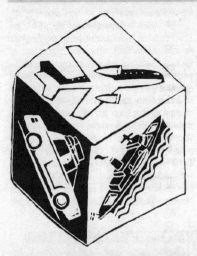

The only direct flight to Mexico from Britain is *BA*'s thrice weekly service from London Heathrow to México (Mexico City). From Ireland, *Aeroflot* fly weekly out of Shannon. If you want to fly from anywhere else, or to any other destination in Mexico, you will have to change planes somewhere.

Another possibility is to fly to the States and continue **overland**, or buy an onward flight over there. New York is usually the cheapest place to get to from London, but it's only halfway to México. LA, then, or Houston, are logical points from which to set off overland: both also have reasonably priced onward flights to a number of Mexican destinations, but if you're going to continue by plane, flying to Miami and on from there to the Yucatán or México may work out cheaper. For more on getting to Mexico from North America, see pp.3–8.

SHOPPING FOR TICKETS

Ticket prices to Mexico are not usually that much lower than to other Latin American destinations, but many US airlines include it in their **air-pass** deal for non-US residents, where you buy coupons at a flat rate for a certain number of flights in North America; these must be bought before you set out, as they are not available in the USA, Canada or Mexico. A typical example is *US Air*'s *Airpass*, costing from £123 for two

flights in winter to £409 for eight in summer, but only available if you fly to the States with *BA* (*US Air*'s partner airline). *American, Continental, Delta, Northwest* and *United* all have similar deals if you cross the Atlantic with them and, even though a deal that takes in Mexico may cost more than one that covers only the USA, these often work out very economical if you plan to visit both countries, or Canada as well.

If you only want to stop over at one place in the States, you should be able to do this for free if it is where you have to change planes. That means choosing an airline which has a hub there. Some airlines have more than one: *Continental* have connections at both Newark (for New York) and Houston, *Delta* at both Atlanta and LA. For some routes, you have no choice but to stop over if your connecting flight is the next day; accommodation is not included in the price of your ticket.

If you simply want a plain return ticket, the best deal you'll get from an airline is usually an **Apex**, which means booking at least two weeks ahead and committing yourself to flight dates that you cannot change without paying a hefty penalty charge. You'll also find that buying a ticket direct from the airline will almost certainly work out a lot more expensive than buying it from a **travel agent** that specializes in discounts (the bucket shops of yore), or one that specializes in Latin America. Remember too that most airlines' **fares** will increase in high season (summer and the runup to Christmas).

DISCOUNT AGENTS

To find **discount agents** in London, see the ads in the *Evening Standard, Time Out* or the free Australasian magazine *TNT* (look for it outside major tube stations). In Manchester, look in *City Life*, and elsewhere try local listings magazines, the classified section of the Sunday broadsheets, or check *Teletext*.

Probably the best first step is to call a specialist in Latin American travel (see p.12), many of which, like *Journey Latin America, South American Experience* and *Trips*, offer flight-only deals as well as organized tours; they may not be the absolute cheapest, but they'll know what they're talking about and may have good deals on, for example, **"open jaw" tickets**, which mean that you can fly in to one Mexican airport and out from another for not much more than a straight return (typically London–México, Cancún–London at around £400, usually with *Continental*). Among the best discount flight specialists, especially if you are a student or under 26, are *STA* and *Campus Travel* in Britain, *USIT* in Ireland (see box for addresses). *Trailfinders* are also worth a try. In any event, it's always worth shopping around, as one firm may have offers that another doesn't have, or be able to get seats that another agent has told you are sold out.

FLIGHTS FROM LONDON

BA's direct flight from Heathrow to México is often the cheapest flight available, depending on the time of year, and *BA* special offers. From a discount agent it can cost less than £300,

although £400 is more likely, rising to £450 in high season. An Apex return bought direct from the airline will usually set you back around £550.

The obvious **alternatives to BA** are *Continental* via Newark or Houston, and *Delta* via Atlanta, which both have daily flights out of Gatwick. Again, prices are seasonal, and somewhat higher from the airline direct (£600–700 return) than from a discount agent, where you might expect to pay around £400–450. A number of other airlines cover the route, sometimes only weekly. North American airlines include *American*, *Canadian*, *Northwest* and *United*; the main European operators are *Air France* via Paris, *Iberia* via Madrid, *KLM* via Amsterdam and *Lufthansa* via Frankfurt. *Aeroflot* also fly to Mexico once a week by a rather indirect route (to Moscow, then back via Shannon and Miami), and

DISCOUNT FLIGHT AGENTS IN BRITAIN AND IRELAND

Campus Travel, 52 Grosvenor Gdns, London SW1W 0AG (☎0171/730 3402).

541 Bristol Rd, Selly Oak, Birmingham B29 6AU (☎0121/414 1848).

39 Queen's Rd, Clifton, Bristol BS8 1QE (☎0117/929 2494).

5 Emmanuel St, Cambridge CB1 1NE (☎01223/324283).

53 Forrest Rd, Edinburgh EH1 2QP (☎0131/668 3303).

166 Deansgate, Manchester M3 3FE (☎0161/273 1721).

13 High St, Oxford OX1 4DB (☎01865/242067).
Student/youth travel specialists, with branches also in YHA shops and on university campuses all over Britain.

Council Travel, 28a Poland St, London W1V 3DB (☎0171/437 7767).
Flights and student discounts.

South Coast Student Travel, 61 Ditchling Rd, Brighton BN1 4SD (☎01273/570226).
Student experts.

STA Travel, 74 Old Brompton Rd, London SW7 3LH (☎0171/937 9962).

25 Queen's Rd, Bristol BS8 1QE (☎0117/929 3399).

38 Sidney St, Cambridge CB2 3HX (☎01223/66966).

75 Deansgate, Manchester M3 2BW (☎0161/834 0668).

Personal callers at 117 Euston Rd, London NW1 2SX; 28 Vicar Lane, Leeds LS1 7JH; 36 George St, Oxford OX1 2OJ; and offices at the universities of Birmingham, London, Kent and Loughborough.
Discount fares, with particularly good deals for students and young people.

Trailfinders, 42–48 Earls Court Rd, London W8 6EJ (☎0171/938 3366).

194 Kensington High St, London W8 7RG (☎0171/938 3232).

22–24 The Priory, Queensway, Birmingham B4 6BS (☎0121/236 1234).

48 Corn St, Bristol BS1 1HQ (☎0117/929 9000).

254–284 Sauchiehall St, Glasgow G2 3EH (☎0141/353 2224).

58 Deansgate, Manchester M3 2FF (☎0161/839 6969).
One of the best-informed and most efficient agents.

Travel Bug, 597 Cheetham Hill Rd, Manchester M8 6EJ (☎0161/721 4000).
Large range of discounted tickets.

USIT, Aston Quay, O'Connell Bridge, Dublin 2 (☎01/679 8833).

10–11 Market Parade, Cork (☎021/270900).

Fountain Centre, College St, Belfast BT1 6ET (☎01232/324073).
All-Ireland student and youth travel specialists.

AIRLINES IN BRITAIN

Aeroflot, 177 Piccadilly, London W1V 9HH (☎0171/355 2233).

Air France, 70 Piccadilly, London W1V 0LX (☎0181/742 6600).

Air UK, Stansted Airport, Essex CM24 1QT (☎0345/666777).

American Airlines, 15 Berkeley St, London W1X 5AE (☎0345/789789).

British Airways, 156 Regent St, London W1R 5TA (☎0345/222111).

Canadian Airlines, 15 Berkeley St, London W1X 5AE (☎0345/616767).

Continental Airlines, Beluah Court, Albert Rd, Horley, Surrey RH11 1XX (☎0800/776464).

Cubana, 49 Conduit St, London W1R 9FD (☎0171/734 1165).

Delta Airlines, Oakfield Court, Consort Way, Horley, Surrey RH6 7AF (☎0800/414767).

Iberia, 11 Haymarket, London SW1Y 4BP (☎0171/830 0011).

KLM, Plesman House, 190 Great South West Rd, Feltham, Middlesex TW14 9RL (☎0181/750 9000).

Lufthansa, 10 Old Bond St, London W1X 4EN (☎0345/737747).

Northwest Airlines, 8 Berkeley St, London W1X 5AD (☎01293/561000).

United Airlines, 193 Piccadilly, London W1V 9LG (☎0181/990 9900; rest of UK ☎0800/888555).

US Air, Piccadilly House, Regent St, London SW1Y 4NB (☎0800/777333).

Virgin Atlantic, 7th floor, Sussex House, High St, Crawley, W Sussex RH10 1BZ (☎01293/562345).

are sometimes the cheapest option, but some travel agents refuse to deal with them as they consider their safety record and reliability to be suspect. Another possibility is *Virgin Atlantic*, which can arrange through tickets to most Mexican destinations with American or Mexican airlines from Miami. *Air UK*, operating out of Stansted, connect in Amsterdam with *KLM's* five weekly flights to México. Also from Stansted, *Cubana* is often the cheapest option (with a year-round price of about £400); however, you'll have to stop over in Havana for at least two days while awaiting your connection (if you do this, don't forget to sort out a Cuban visa before you go).

For **destinations other than the capital**, *Continental* and *American* offer by far the greatest choice, both serving Cancún, Guadalajara, Monterrey and León daily. Other destinations are possible (Acapulco, Cozumel, Los Cabos, Puerto Vallarta and Veracruz), but usually mean overnighting in Houston or Dallas. *Iberia* also fly to Cancún five times weekly via Madrid. Expect to pay around £50 more for these destinations than for México. The exception to this rule is *Cubana*, whose flights to Cancún are even cheaper than those to the capital, but again involve at least one night in Havana (of course, you may consider that a bonus).

Charter flights to Mexico are not that common, but when they do run, it's usually Gatwick to Cancún at Easter or in the summer. If there is a charter, fares can be low, as little as

£250, but your stay will probably be limited to two or four weeks. *STA* usually have good deals; otherwise try *Thomson*, who publish a brochure of their charter flights and prices.

FLIGHTS FROM OTHER BRITISH AIRPORTS

While no airport in Britain offers the same amount of choice as London, most of the major ones have two or three alternatives available. Domestic rail prices being what they are, it may work out cheaper, as well as easier, to fly from an airport nearer home.

From Manchester, many European and American airlines have exactly the same fares as you would pay from London. One such is *Delta*, with daily departures to México, connecting in Atlanta. They do fly to other Mexican destinations, but this involves two changes of plane – at Atlanta and again in LA – and a very long journey. Another possibility is México via Chicago with *American Airlines*, but this means a ten-hour wait between planes. Other Mexican destinations are possible if you stop over in Chicago. To México, you can also fly *KLM* via Amsterdam (usually the cheapest), *Air France* via Paris, or *Lufthansa* via Frankfurt, not forgetting *BA* via London (but with an add-on of around £70 to the London fare). Should you want to stop over in Moscow en route, *Aeroflot* is another possibility, though see the caution above. To fly with *Iberia* to Cancún, you have to overnight in Madrid or Barcelona.

TOUR OPERATORS IN BRITAIN AND IRELAND

Animal Watch, Granville House, London Rd, Sevenoaks, Kent TN13 1DL (☎01732/741612).

Annual whale-watching trip to Baja California, usually with a well-known wildlife photography expert.

Bales, Bales House, Junction Rd, Dorking, Surrey RH4 3HB (☎01306/885991).

Established upmarket operator; escorted tours of central Mexico and the Maya trail.

Cathy Matos Mexican Tours, 61 High St, Barnet, Herts EN5 5UR (☎0181/440 7830).

Wide variety of tailor-made tours including cities, beaches, sightseeing tours, whale-watching and wedding trips.

Cuba Get Travel, 11 South Anne St, Dublin 2 (☎01/6713422).

Cancún beach holidays, or a Cancún–Cuba combination.

Dragoman, 94 Camp Green, Debenham, Stowmarket, Suffolk IP14 6LA (☎01728/861133).

Overland expeditions including México–Guatemala City, México–Alaska, México–Panama and Alaska–Tierra del Fuego via Mexico.

Exodus Expeditions, 9 Weir Rd, London SW12 0LT (☎0181/675 5550).

24-day Ruta Maya tour, or 8-week Panama–México overland trip.

Explore Worldwide, 1 Frederick St, Aldershot, Hants, GU11 1LQ (☎01252/319448).

c/o *Maxwells Travel*, D'Olier Chambers, 1 Hawkins St, Dublin 2 (☎01/677 9479).

Overland tours of the Copper Canyon and Baja California, Indian Mexico and Yucatán or the Maya trail in Mexico, Belize and Guatemala.

First Choice Holidays, First Choice House, Peel Cross Rd, Salford, Manchester M5 2AN.

Beach holidays in Puerto Vallarta on charter flights from Gatwick.

Global Travel Club, 1 Kiln Shaw, Langdon Hills, Basildon, Essex SS16 6LE (☎01268/541732).

Tailor-made Yucatán tours with special emphasis on diving trips, also Maya sites and two-centre holidays with Belize.

Hayes & Jarvis, Hayes House, 152 Kings St, London W6 0QU (☎0181/748 5050).

Beach holidays in Acapulco, Cancún, Cozumel and Playa del Carmen, colonial Mexico tour, Mexican heritage tour, diving holidays in Cozumel.

Journey Latin America, 14–16 Devonshire Rd, London W4 2HD (☎0181/747 8315).

Flights and packages including Aztec and Maya tours, Yucatán and Guatemala budget tours and a trip from Panama to the US border.

Nomadic Thoughts, 23 Hopefield Ave, London NW6 6LJ (☎0181/960 1001).

Tailor-made itineraries for individuals or groups – claim to match all budgets.

Saga Holidays, The Saga Building, Middelburg Square, Folkestone, Kent CT20 1AZ (☎0800/300456).

Holidays for over-50s, including tailor-made tours.

Scuba en Cuba, 7 Maybank Gardens, Pinner, Middlesex HA5 2JW (☎01895/64100).

Diving holidays and diving courses in Cozumel.

South American Experience, 47 Causton St, London SW1 4AT (☎0171/976 5511).

Return and open-jaw flights; tours combining sightseeing with beach resorts, Yucatán with Oaxaca or Guatemala, Copper Canyon Express, Baja California whale-watching, Acapulco, México.

Trek America, Trek House, The Bullring, Deddington, Banbury, Oxfordshire OX15 0TT (☎01869/33877).

c/o *American Holidays*, 39 Pearse St, Dublin 2 (☎01/679 8800).

Camping trips with surfing, windsurfing, horse-riding and diving.

Trips Worldwide, 9 Byron Place, Clifton, Bristol BS8 1JT (☎0117/987 2626).

Tailor-made tours and agents for US operators; flight deals too.

Twickers World, 20–22 Church St, Twickenham TW1 3NW (☎0181/892 8164).

Wildlife and cultural tours (Dec–May) including whale-watching, Baja California and the Copper Canyon.

Twohigs Travel, 8 Burgh Quay, Dublin 2 (☎01/677 2666).

Beach holidays in Cancún and Playa del Carmen.

Unforgettable Moments, 6 Wood St, Ashby de la Zouch, Leicestershire LE65 1EJ (☎01530/413868).

Weddings and honeymoons in Acapulco.

Wildlife Worlwide, 170 Selsdon Rd, South Croydon, Surrey CR2 6PJ.

Whale-watching trips around Baja California Jan–May.

Birmingham, not connected by air to London, is served by *American Airlines*, as well as *Air France*, *KLM* and *Lufthansa*; **Bristol** and **Cardiff** by *KLM*. *Air UK* also fly from a number of airports, notably **Glasgow** and **Edinburgh**, to Amsterdam, where you can pick up the *KLM* flight to México. *KLM* and *Air UK* usually have the best prices. Failing that, most British airports other than Birmingham are served by *BA* flights to London, where you can transfer to *BA*'s México flight.

FLIGHTS FROM IRELAND

Ireland is not tremendously well connected to Mexico, but there is a **direct flight** – once weekly with *Aeroflot* from Shannon. If you don't fancy that, *Delta* fly five times weekly **from Dublin and Shannon** to Atlanta, connecting for México. *BA* also fly from Dublin to meet a connection three times a week in London. You can also make *BA*'s London–México flight by taking *Aer Lingus* from Shannon or **Cork**, but your best bet is probably to fly with them from Dublin to Amsterdam and pick up *KLM*'s twice weekly

afternoon flight to México from there. *Aer Lingus* also fly from Dublin to Paris, where you can pick up *Air France*'s México service three times a week, and to New York where you can easily buy an onward ticket. Although *Lufthansa* and *Iberia* both fly to Dublin, all their connections require an overnight stop. Discount fares from the Republic to Mexico range from IR£430 to IR£570 return.

If you want to reach Mexico **from Belfast**, the cheapest way is probably with *KLM* via Amsterdam, though *BA* may also have good deals via London. Expect to pay £350–450.

PACKAGES AND INCLUSIVE TOURS

In addition to the many **package tours** that offer two weeks in a luxury beach hotel – easily booked through companies like *Thomson*, *Kuoni* or *Sovereign* at any travel agent – a growing number of firms offer alternatives ranging from sightseeing or upmarket cultural tours to overland expeditions, trekking and camping holidays. If you balk at the idea of being shut off from the country in air-conditioned buses and hotels, *Journey Latin America* even offers budget tours that get you around on public transport. Wildlife trips are becoming popular too, with a number of firms offering whale-watching off Baja in season (Jan–April). The Copper Canyon train ride is also a favourite. Other specialist trips include diving, and even getting married and going on honeymoon in Mexico. If none of the published itineraries suits you, a number of firms also offer **tailor-made packages** in which you decide on an itinerary and the travel firm arrange it for you.

These types of tours will work out rather more expensive compared to what you'd pay if you organized everything independently, but they do cut out a lot of hassle, and in the case of cultural and wildlife tours, the presence of an expert guide may justify the expense.

AIRLINE OFFICES IN IRELAND

Aer Lingus, 41 Upper O'Connell St, Dublin (☎01/844 4777).

Aeroflot, Sun Alliance House, Dawson St, Dublin 2 (☎01/679 1453).

British Airways, 60 Dawson St, Dublin 2 (☎0800/626747); 9 Fountain Centre, College St, Belfast BT1 6HR (☎0345/222111).

Delta Airlines, 24 Merrion Square, Dublin 2 (☎0800/768080).

Iberia, 54 Dawson St, Dublin 2 (☎01/677 9846).

KLM, Servisair Ticket Desk, Belfast International Airport, Belfast BT29 4AB (☎0181/750 9000).

Lufthansa, Dublin Airport (☎01/844 5544).

GETTING THERE FROM AUSTRALASIA

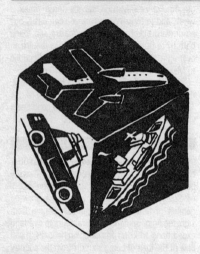

The high season for flights to Mexico from Australia and New Zealand is June to mid-September, together with the Christmas period. From January to May and mid-September to December you can count on paying about $200 less than the fares quoted below.

From **Australia** the cheapest flights – fares quoted are from the eastern cities, from Brisbane to Adelaide – are with *Malaysian Air* (*MAS*) to México via Kuala Lumpur, Taipei and LA (around $1880), and *Japanese Airlines* (*JAL*) to México via LA with an overnight stop in Tokyo ($2050). *United* fly more directly to México via LA for $2300. If you wish to travel around Mexico by air, you could take advantage of the *Air New Zealand–Delta* fare ($2416), which gets you to LA and gives three *Delta* coupons for direct (no stopovers) one-way flights in the *Delta* network, which includes Mexico.

More expensive are the *Qantas–Continental* flights to México via LA ($2500), and *Aerolineas Argentinas* via Auckland and Buenos Aires to México; some flights return to Buenos Aires via Havana ($2475 year-round).

There are two **RTW fares from Australia** that can include Mexico: *Aerolineas Argentinas–KLM* via Auckland, Buenos Aires, México, then on to Amsterdam with a side trip in Europe, and back via Singapore to Australia; and a mileage-based *United Airlines–South African Airways* fare covering any destination that the two airlines fly to – provided that you include the Americas, Europe and South Africa – with no restrictions on stopovers, and backtracking permitted.

From New Zealand it's very much the same situation as outlined above: *United Airlines* (with *Mexicana*), *Air New Zealand* (with *Aeroméxico*) and *Qantas* (with *Continental*) all fly from Auckland via LA at prices starting at around $2500. If you want more exotic stopovers,

AIRLINES IN AUSTRALIA

Air New Zealand, 5 Elizabeth St, Sydney (☎02/223 4666).

Delta, 36 Clarence St, Sydney (☎02/262 1777).

Japanese Airlines, 17 Bligh St, Sydney (☎02/233 4500).

KLM, 5 Elizabeth St, Sydney (☎02/231 6333).

Korean Airlines, Sydney (☎02/262 6000).

MAS, 388 George St, Sydney (☎1-800/269 998 or ☎02/231 5066) .

Qantas, International Square, Jamison St, Sydney (☎02/957 0111 or 236 3636).

South African Airways, floor 9, 5 Elizabeth St, Sydney (☎02/223 4402).

United, 10 Barrack St, Sydney (☎02/237 8888).

AIRLINES IN NEW ZEALAND

Air Caledonie, 229 Queen St, Auckland (☎09/379 4455).

Air New Zealand, cnr Customs St and Queen St, Auckland (☎09/366 2424).

Delta, 87 Queen St, Auckland (☎09/379 3370).

MAS, Swanson Centre, 12–26 Swanson St, Auckland (☎09/373 2741).

Qantas, 154 Queen St, Auckland (☎09/303 2506).

United, 7 City Rd, Auckland (☎09/307 9500).

DISCOUNT TRAVEL AGENTS IN AUSTRALIA

Accent on Travel, 545 Queen St, Brisbane (☎07/832 1777).

Anywhere Travel, 345 Anzac Parade, Kingsford, Sydney (☎02/663 0411).

Brisbane Discount Travel, 360 Queen St, Brisbane (☎07/229 9211).

Discount Travel Specialists, Shop 53, Forrest Chase, Perth (☎09/221 1400).

Flight Centres, Circular Quay, Sydney (☎02/241 2422).
Bourke St, Melbourne (☎03/650 2899).
Other branches nationwide.

STA Travel, 732 Harris St, Ultimo, Sydney (☎02/212 1255 or 281 9866).

256 Flinders St, Melbourne (☎03/347 4711).

Other offices in Townsville, Cairns and state capitals.

Topdeck Travel, 45 Grenfell St, Adelaide (☎08/410 1110).

Tymtro Travel, Suite G12, Wallaceway Shopping Centre, Chatswood, Sydney (☎02/413 1219).

Passport Travel, 320-B Glenferrie Rd, Malvern, Melbourne (☎03/824 7183).

DISCOUNT TRAVEL AGENTS IN NEW ZEALAND

Budget Travel, PO Box 505, Auckland (☎09/309 4313).

Flight Centres, National Bank Towers, 205–225 Queen St, Auckland (☎09/309 6171).

Shop 1M, National Mutual Arcade, 152 Hereford St, Christchurch (☎09/379 7145).

50–52 Willis St, Wellington (☎04/472 8101).

Other branches countrywide.

STA Travel, Traveller's Centre, 10 High St, Auckland (☎09/309 9995).

223 High St, Christchurch (☎03/379 9098).

233 Cuba St, Wellington (☎04/385 0561).

Other offices in Dunedin, Palmerston North and Hamilton.

SPECIALIST AGENTS IN AUSTRALASIA

Adventure World, 73 Walker St, North Sydney (☎02/956 7766).

8 Victoria Ave, Perth (☎09/221 2300).

101 Great Sth Rd, Remuera, Auckland (☎09/524 5118).

4- to 14-day bus and plane sightseeing packages around Mexico. Good flight deals too.

Affordable South America, 288 Queen St, Melbourne (☎03/600 1733).

Tailor-made packages from the sights of México to trekking in the Yucatán.

Contours, 466 Victoria St, N Melbourne (☎03/329 5211).

Wide range of packages from overland camping to deluxe travel and conventional touring: also handles scuba, train rides and personal itineraries.

Destinations Adventure, Premier Building, cnr Queen St and Durham St East, PO Box 6232, Auckland (☎09/309 0464).

Overland expeditions.

Exodus Expeditions, 81a Glebe Point Rd, Sydney (☎1-800/800 724).

Overland truck expeditions, including Maya Empire Highlights through Mexico, Guatemala and Belize; or longer trips between Mexico and Panama.

Mexican Avisa Tours, 697 Pittwater Rd, Dee Why, Sydney (☎02/ 971 4977).

Individual itineraries, including overnight stopovers and multi-week packages.

Peregrine, 258 Lonsdale St, Melbourne (☎03/663 8611).

407 Great Sth Rd, Penrose, Auckland (☎09/525 3074).

Two-week to six-month Dragoman overland truck adventures, taking in Mexico en route to Tierra del Fuego.

South American Adventures, 169 Unley Rd, Unley, Adelaide (☎08/272 2010).

Experienced in handling travel to Mexico, and acts as booking agent for other tour operators.

Aerolineas Argentinas will take you via Buenos Aires for closer to $3000, *MAS* via Kuala Lumpur for around $2700, you could take a flight to LA and a separate fare on from there. An Auckland–LA return, plus a 3-coupon deal with *Delta* (see above), starts at around $2700 on any of the following: *Air Caledonie–Corsair* via Papeete; *Air Pacific* via Fiji; *Korean* via Seoul; and *JAL* via Tokyo. **None of the RTW fares from NZ** includes Mexico, though *United* combines with a variety of Asian carriers for trips via LA, Europe and Asia for around $2700–3400; otherwise try for a tailor-made itinerary with *Aerolineas Argentinas* or any of the airlines mentioned above.

LEAVING MEXICO: A NOTE

If you're **flying out** of Mexico, remember that there's an airport departure tax, equivalent to about $16 payable in pesos or dollars, though if you bought your air ticket outside Mexico, the tax may well have been included in the ticket price. Always remember to check when you buy your ticket.

VISAS AND RED TAPE

Citizens of most Western countries (France and South Africa are exceptions) do not require a visa to enter Mexico as tourists for less than 90 days.

What they do need is a valid passport (a one-year British Visitor's Passport is *not* valid for Mexico) and a **tourist card** (or *FMT – folleto de migración turística*). Tourist cards are free, and if you're flying direct, you should be able to pick one up on the plane, or from the airline before leaving. A good travel agent should be able to arrange one for you too. Otherwise they're issued by Mexican consulates, in person or by post. Every major US city and most border towns have a Mexican consulate; tourist cards and vehicle import forms are also available from all *AAA* offices in California, Arizona, New Mexico and Texas. Finally, failing all those, you *should* be able to get tourist cards at airports or border crossings on arrival. However, if they've run out, you'll have to twiddle your thumbs until the next batch come in, and if your passport is not issued by a rich Western country, you may encounter difficulty in persuading border officials to give you a card; it is therefore far preferable, and easy enough, to get one in advance.

Most people officially need a passport to pick up their tourist card, but for **US and Canadian citizens** all that's required is proof of citizenship (an original birth certificate or notarized copy, for instance, or naturalization papers) along with some form of photo ID (such as a driver's licence). North Americans can even enter Mexico *without* a passport if they carry such documents plus their tourist card with them, but it is not advisable, since officials checking your ID may not be aware of this right.

A tourist card can be valid for up to **90 days**: if you intend to enter and leave Mexico more than once, you could pick up two or three. On the card, you are asked how long you intend to stay: always apply for longer than you need, since getting an extension is a frustrating and time-consuming business. You don't always get the time you've asked for in any case: in particular, at land borders with Belize and Guatemala, you will probably only get 30 days, though they may give you more if you specifically ask. Especially if you are from a poor country, you may also be asked to show sufficient funds for your stay.

A tourist card isn't strictly necessary for anyone only visiting the northern **border towns** and staying less than three days (though you still

MEXICAN CONSULATES AND EMBASSIES ABROAD

The following all issue visas or tourist cards.

USA 1911 Pennsylvania Ave NW, Washington, DC 20006 (☎202/728-1694); 2827 16th St NW, Washington, DC 20036 (☎202/736-1000); and in 50 other US cities.

US/MEXICAN BORDER TOWNS 724 E Elizabeth St, Brownsville, TX 78520 (☎512/542-2051); 331 W 2nd St, Calexico, CA 92231 (☎619/357-3863); 300 E Loyosa St, Del Rio, TX 78840 (☎210/775-2352); 140 Adams St, Eagle Pass, TX 78852 (☎210/773-9255 or 6); 910 E San Antonio St, El Paso, TX 79901 (☎915/533-3644 or 5); 1612 Farragut St, Laredo, TX 78040 (☎210/723-6369); 1418 Beech St, Suite 102–106, McAllen, TX 78501 (☎210/686-0243); 480 Grand Ave, Nogales, AZ 85621 (☎602/287-2521); 730 O'Riety St, Presidio, TX 79845 (☎915/229-3745); 1549 India St, San Diego, CA 92101 (☎619/231-9741).

AUSTRALIA 14 Perth Ave, Yarralumla, Canberra, ACT 2600 (☎06/273 3905); 49 Bay St, Double Bay, Sydney, NSW 2028 (☎02/326 1292).

BELIZE 20 N Park St, Belize City (☎02/30193 or 4).

CANADA 130 Albert St, Suite 1800, Ottawa, ON K1P 5G4 (☎613/233-8988); 200 Mansfield, Montréal, PQ H3A 2Z7 (☎514/288-2502); 60 Bloor St W, Toronto, ON M4W 3B8 (☎416/922-2718); 810-1130 W Pender St, Vancouver, BC V6E 4A4 (☎604/684-3547).

CUBA c/12, #518, Miramar Playa, Havana 6 (☎332679).

GERMANY Kurfürstendamm 72, 10709 Berlin 1 (☎030/3249047); Adenauerallee 100, 53113 Bonn (☎0228/6312226 or 7 or 8); Neue Mainzer Straße 57, 60311 Frankfurt am Main (☎069/2301514); Hallerstraße 70–1, 20146 Hamburg (☎040/458950).

GUATEMALA 13 c/7–30, Zona 9, Guatemala City (☎02/319573); c/o *Farmacía El Cid*, 5 Av/4 Calle, Huehuetenango; 9a Av 6–19, Zona 1, Quezaltenango (☎0961/1312); 3 Av/5 Calle, Retalhuleu.

Consulates in Guatemala often – illegally – charge for tourist cards.

IRELAND 43 Ailesbury Rd, Ballsbridge, Dublin 4 (☎01/260 0699).

NETHERLANDS Nassauplein 17, 2585 EB Den Haag (☎070/3602900); Groothandelsgebow, Statsionplein 45, Rotterdam (☎010/126084).

NEW ZEALAND 111–115 Customhouse Quay, 8th floor, Wellington (☎04/472 5555).

SWEDEN Grevgatan 3, 114 53 Stockholm (☎08/661 2213).

UK 8 Halkin St, London SW1X 8QR (☎0171/235 6393).

---

need a passport or photo ID). In fact, the entire US frontier strip is a duty-free area into which you can come and go more or less as you please; heading farther south, however, beyond this zone, there are checkpoints on every road after about 30km, and you'll be sent back if you haven't brought the necessary documents and been through customs and immigration.

Don't lose the **blue copy** of your tourist card given back to you after immigration inspection. You are legally required to carry it at all times, and if you have to show your papers it's more important than your passport. The blue copy must be handed in on leaving the country – you may not be asked for it at land frontiers with the US, but otherwise anyone trying to leave Mexico without it will certainly encounter hassle and delay.

Should you **lose** your tourist card, or need to have it renewed, head for the nearest office of the immigration department (*Delegación de Servicios Migratorios*); there are downtown branches in the biggest cities, but there, and in the resorts with international flight connections, it's probably easier to go out to the airport. In the case of **renewal**, it's far simpler to cross the border for a day and get a new one on re-entry than apply for an extension; if you do apply, do it as far in advance as possible. And whatever else you may be told, branches of *Sectur* (the tourist office) cannot renew expired tourist cards or replace lost ones – they will only make sympathetic noises and direct you to the nearest immigration office.

Visas, obtainable only through a consulate (in person or by mail), are required by nationals of France and South Africa, and most non-industrialized countries, as well as by anyone entering Mexico to work or to study for more than 180 days. **Business visitors** need a Business Authorization Card available from consulates, and usually a visa too. Anyone **under 18** travelling without both parents needs their written consent (see p.52).

US VISAS

Non-US citizens travelling through the States on the way to or from Mexico, or stopping over there, may need a **US visa**. If there's even a possibility you might stop in the States, unless you are Canadian or from a country on the US visa waiver scheme (see below), obtaining a visa in advance is a sensible precaution. Getting one in Mexico will be a nightmare of queuing and frustration. You can expect a certain amount of queuing wherever you apply in person, but you can always apply by post instead, provided you allow enough time (usually four weeks). A number of countries, including Britain, the Netherlands, Denmark and Germany, but *not* Australia, New Zealand or Ireland, are on a **visa waiver scheme**, designed to speed up lengthy immigration procedures. Visa waiver forms are available from travel agencies, the airline during check-in, or on the plane, and must be presented to immigration on arrival. Be sure to return the part stapled into your passport when you leave

the US: if it isn't returned within the visa expiry time, computer records automatically log you as an illegal alien. If re-entering the US by land from Mexico, you will need to have a form with you in order to be exempt from visa requirements, so make sure you get one in advance.

Many US airports do not have transit lounges, so even if you are on a through flight you may have to go through US immigration and customs. This can easily take two hours, so bear the delay in mind if you have an onward flight to catch.

CUSTOMS

Duty-free allowances into Mexico are three bottles of liquor (including wine), plus 400 cigarettes or two boxes of cigars or a "reasonable quantity" of tobacco for your own use, plus twelve rolls of camera film or camcorder tape. The monetary limit for duty-free goods is US$300. Returning home, note that **it is illegal to take antiquities** out of the country. The penalties for discovery are serious.

EMBASSIES AND CONSULATES IN MEXICO

USA Paseo de la Reforma 305, Colonia Cuauhtémoc, México 06500 (☎5/211-00-42); and in Ciudad Juárez, Guadalajara, Hermosillo, Matamoros, Mazatlán, Mérida, Monterrey, Nuevo Laredo and Tijuana.

CANADA Schiller 529, Colonia Polanco, México 11560 (☎5/724-79-00); and in Acapulco, Cancún, Guadalajara, Mazatlán, Oaxaca, Puerto Vallarta and Tijuana.

UK Aptdo 96 bis, Río Lerma 71, Colonia Cuauhtémoc, México 06500 (☎5/207-20-89); and in Acapulco, Ciudad Juárez, Guadalajara, Mérida, Monterrey, Tampico and Veracruz.

IRELAND Av. San Jeronimo 790-A, Colonia San Jeronimo Lidice, Deleg Contreras, México 10200 (☎5/595-33-33).

NEW ZEALAND José Luis Lagrange 103, 10th floor, Colonia Los Morales, Polanco, México 11510 (☎5/281-54-86).

NETHERLANDS Montes Urales sur 635, Piso 2, Lomas de Chapultetec, México 11000 (☎5/202-84-53 or 202-88-54).

AUSTRALIA Jaime Balmes 11, Plaza Pomanco, Torre B, Piso 10, Colonia Los Morales, México 11510 (☎5/395-99-88).

COSTS AND MONEY

Mexico is not as cheap as it once was, despite the instability of its currency. Although, in general, costs are lower than you'll find at home, compared with the rest of Central or South America, prices here can come as something of a shock.

In the long term, the **NAFTA** free trade treaty with the US and Canada can probably be expected to keep costs (and, one hopes, wages) rising, though prices will fluctuate somewhat as the peso goes down against the dollar, and inflation moves in to fill the gap. As the peso is so unstable, all prices in the *Guide* section of this book are quoted in **US dollars**; be aware however, that these will be affected by unpredictable factors such as inflation and exchange rates. Latest developments and your own common sense will determine how you apply them.

COSTS

The developed tourist resorts and big cities are invariably more expensive than more remote towns, and certain areas, too, have noticeably higher prices – among them the industrialized north, especially along the border, Baja, and all the newly wealthy oil regions. Prices can also be affected by **seasons**: hotel rooms in the peak tourist season – summer, Christmas and Easter where the tourists are mainly Mexican, but November to May in places like Acapulco which attract overseas visitors – are far higher than at other times; and special events will also probably be marked by price hikes. Nonetheless, wherever you go you can probably get by on $150/£100 a week (you *could* reduce that if you hardly travel around, stay only on campsites or in hostels, live on the most basic food and don't buy any souvenirs, but it hardly makes for an enjoyable trip), while on $500/£350 you'd really be living very well.

Accommodation prices range from only a couple of dollars for a beach *cabaña*, through $8–18/£5–12 for a room in a cheap hotel and $25–35/£17–24 in the mid-range, to five-star luxury for anything from $100/£70 up. **Food** prices can also vary wildly, but you should always be able to get a substantial meal in a plain Mexican restaurant for around $4/£3. Most restaurant bills come with 10 percent *IVA* (*Impuesto de Valor Añadido* – VAT) added; this is not always included in prices quoted on the menu. One major expense, if you intend to travel around a lot, may prove to be **transportation**, since distances can be so great. On a per kilometre basis, however, the prices are very reasonable: México to Acapulco for example, a journey of over 400km, costs less than $20/£13 by first-class bus, while a 24-hour journey such as México to Cancún (1800km) works out at around $40/£25. Trains are slightly cheaper.

As always, if you're **travelling alone** you'll end up spending considerably more than you would in a group of two or more people – sharing rooms and food saves a substantial amount. In the larger resorts, you can get "apartments" for up to six people for even greater savings. If you have an international **Student or Youth Card**, you might also take it along for an occasional reduction, but don't go out of your way to obtain one, since most concessions are, at least in theory, only for Mexican students. Cards available include the ISIC card for full-time students and the Go-25 youth card for under-25s, both of which carry health and emergency insurance benefits for Americans, and are available from youth travel firms such as *STA*, who also sell their own card. Even a college photo ID card *might* work in some places.

Tips are hardly ever added to bills, and the amount is entirely up to you – in cheap places if you tip at all it's just the loose change; expensive joints tend to expect their full twelve percent. It is not standard practice to tip cab drivers.

CURRENCY

The new Mexican Peso, or **Nuevo Peso**, introduced in 1993 and usually written N$, is made up of 100 centavos (¢, like a US cent). It is the equivalent of 1000 old pesos. The use of the dollar symbol for the peso is occasionally confusing, as is the fact that some people still talk in old pesos (N$1.50 is more likely to be *mil quinientos* than *uno cincuenta*), but the "N" for *nuevo* is a big help: failing that, common sense and the situation tend to make things obvious. The initials MN (*moneda nacional*) are occasionally used to indicate that it is Mexican, not American money that is being used. In any case, the sign is not *exactly* the same: at least in theory, the Mexican peso symbol has only one vertical bar through it, while that of the gringo dollar has two.

Eventually, the term "Nuevo Peso" will revert to simply peso, as people get used to the new currency: new banknotes with the same design will be released, except without the "Nuevos"; all the banknotes representing the "old" peso will be withdrawn, and the process of substituting the "old" notes for those of the new monetary unit will be completed.

For now, the new peso is issued in bills of N$10, N$20, N$50, N$100, N$200 and N$500, and coins of 5¢, 10¢, 20¢, 50¢, N$1, N$2, N$5 and N$10. A number of coins (especially the huge brass $100 and $1000 coins) and bills ($2000, $5000, $10,000, $20,000, $50,000 and $100,000) featuring the old peso are still in circulation – to deduce their true value, omit the last three zeros. Old peso banknotes are the same as some of the new ones (several series of bills are in circulation), but the coins are rather different.

CURRENCY EXCHANGE

The easiest kind of **foreign currency** to change in Mexico is US dollars cash. US dollar travellers' cheques come second Canadian dollars and other major international currencies such as pounds sterling, yen and deutschmarks are a poor third; and you'll find it hard to change travellers' cheques in those currencies. Quetzales and Belize dollars are best got rid of before entering Mexico (otherwise, your best bet for changing them is with tourists heading the other way).

In general, you'll get the best rates for cash dollars at **banks**, most of which will also change dollar travellers' cheques. Although the banks have all been nationalized, each is run differently.

The *Banco Nacional de Mexico* (known as *Banamex*) is probably the most efficient; *Bancomer*, almost as widespread, is also a possibility, as is the smaller *Banco del Atlantico*. Banks are generally open Monday to Friday from 9.30am until 1.30pm, though sometimes with shorter hours for exchange. The commission varies from bank to bank, while the exchange rate, in theory, is the same – fixed daily by the government. Only larger branches of the big banks, plus some in tourist resorts, are usually prepared to change currencies other than dollars, and even then often at worse rates. **ATM cash dispenser** machines are becoming more and more common in Mexico, and make a useful alternative (see below).

Casas de cambio (money changers) are open longer hours and at weekends, and have varying exchange rates and commission charges; they also tend to have shorter queues and less bureaucratic procedures. It's always worth checking if they're offering better rates than the banks, particularly if the peso is falling. Some money changers give rates for Canadian dollars, sterling and other currencies that are as good as those they give for dollars: again it's worth shopping around, especially if you intend to change a large sum.

If you're desperate, many hotels, shops and restaurants that are used to tourists are prepared to change dollars or accept them as payment, but rates will be very low. There isn't much of a **black market** in Mexico since exchange regulations are relatively loose, and it's not really worth bothering with unless it comes about through personal contacts or you want to do someone a favour.

CASH AND TRAVELLERS' CHEQUES

In touristy places such as Acapulco and Tijuana, **dollar bills** are almost as easy to spend as pesos. The big disadvantage with cash, of course, is that, once stolen or lost, it is gone forever. For that reason, most travellers prefer to bring plastic and/or travellers' cheques (personal cheques are virtually worthless in Mexico). But do bring some dollars cash – sometimes you won't be able to change anything else. It's also a good idea to have a mixture of denominations, including a wad of dollar bills, and to try to bring some pesos ($50/£30-worth, say), just in case you can't for some reason change money on arrival, or would rather not stand in a long line to do so. Although few US banks keep foreign currency on hand, and banks in Britain and Australasia are unlikely to stock Mexican pesos, you should be able to order them from your bank's foreign desk if you give them a few days' notice, or you may find them at specialist exchange desks at the airport.

Travellers' cheques have the advantage over cash that, if you lose them or have them stolen, the issuing company will refund them (they say in 24 hours, but don't count on it) on production of the purchase receipt, which should for that reason be kept safe and separate from the cheques themselves, along with a record of the serial numbers, noting which ones you have already cashed. If your cheques do get lost or stolen, the issuing company will expect you to report the loss forthwith to their local office. You pay 1–2 percent commission to buy the cheques, and occasionally banks or *casas de cambio* in Mexico charge extra for them, but usually the rate and commission are the same as for cash.

When **buying travellers' cheques**, get a sensible mix of denominations (you don't want to have to change a big one on your last day), and stick to the established names – *Thomas Cook, American Express, Visa,* or one of the major American banks – not only because these will be more recognized, but also because there will be better customer service should they be lost or stolen.

CREDIT AND CASH CARDS

Major **credit cards** are widely accepted and handy for emergencies. *Visa* and *Mastercard* are the best; *American Express* and other charge cards are usually only accepted by expensive places, but an *Amex* card is worth it for the other services it offers, such as mail pick-up points and dollar travellers' cheque purchase. Unfortunately credit cards are not accepted in the cheapest hotels or restaurants, or for most bus tickets, but you can use them to get cash advances from banks. Usually there's a minimum withdrawal of around $75 to $100.

In addition, you can get cash 24 hours a day from ATM machines in most towns of any size in Mexico, using credit cards or **ATM cash cards** from home. *Bancomer* machines accept *Visa* and *Mastercard; Banamex* accept these plus debit cards from the *Cirrus* and *PLUS* systems, which allow account holders to withdraw money directly from their accounts back home. You get preferential rates of exchange this way, and there is no minimum withdrawal or commission. In some border towns, some cash machines pay out in US dollars.

Make sure before you leave home that you have a personal identification number (PIN) designed to work overseas. Remember too, that all cash advances on credit cards are treated as loans, with interest accruing daily from the date of withdrawal; there may be a transaction fee on top of this. Finally, be aware that technical hitches are not uncommon – it has been known for machines not to dispense cash, but to debit your account anyway.

WIRING MONEY

Having **money wired** from home is never convenient or cheap, and should be considered a last resort. Funds can be sent via **American Express MoneyGram** (☎1-800/543-4080 in the US and Canada; ☎0171/837 3629 in the UK; ☎01/288 3311 in Ireland; ☎02/379 8243 in Australia; and ☎09/379 8243 in New Zealand), or from the US and Canada via **Western Union** (☎1-800/325-6000). Both companies' fees depend on the amount being transferred, but as an example, wiring $1000/£700 to Mexico will cost around $50/£35. The funds should be available for collection at the local *Amex* or *Western Union* office within minutes of being sent.

It's also possible to have money wired directly from a bank in your home country to a bank in Mexico, although this is somewhat less reliable because it involves two separate institutions. If you take this route, the person wiring the funds to you will need to know the telex number of the bank the funds are being wired to.

INTERNATIONAL LOST CARD OR CHEQUES COLLECT CALL NUMBERS

American Express dial 96 and ask for ☎801/964-9665.

Thomas Cook/Mastercard dial 96 and ask for ☎609/987-7300

Visa dial 96 and ask for ☎415/574-7700.

HEALTH

It is always easier to become ill in a foreign country with a different climate, different food and different germs, still more so in a poor country with lower standards of sanitation than you might be used to. Most travellers, however, get through Mexico without catching anything more serious than a dose of Montezuma's Revenge. You will still want the security of health insurance (see "Insurance" on p.27), but the important thing is to keep your resistance high and to be aware of health risks such as poor hygiene, untreated water, mosquito bites, undressed open cuts and unprotected sex.

PRECAUTIONS

What you eat or drink is crucial: a poor **diet** lowers your resistance. Be sure to eat enough of the right things, including a good balance of protein (meat, fish, eggs or beans, for example), carbohydrates, vitamins and minerals. Eating plenty of peeled fresh fruit helps keep up your vitamin and mineral intake, but it might be worth taking daily multi-vitamin and mineral tablets with you. It is also important to eat enough – an unfamiliar diet may reduce the amount you eat – and get enough sleep and rest, as it's easy to become run-down if you're on the move a lot, especially in a hot climate.

The lack of **sanitation** in Mexico is often exaggerated, and it's not worth being obsessive about it, or you'll never enjoy anything. Even so, a degree of caution is wise – don't try anything too exotic in the first few days, before your body has had a chance to adjust to local microbes, and avoid food that has been on display for a while and is not freshly cooked. You should also steer clear of salads, and peel fruit before eating it. Avoid raw shellfish, and don't eat anywhere that is obviously dirty (easily spotted, since most Mexican restaurants are scrupulously clean) – street stalls in particular are suspect. For advice on **water**, see p.24.

VACCINATIONS

There are no required **inoculations** for Mexico, but it's worth visiting your doctor at least four weeks before you leave to check that you are up to date with your polio, tetanus, typhoid and hepatitis A jabs. North Americans will have to pay for inoculations, available at any immunization centre or at most local clinics. Most GPs in the UK have a travel surgery where you can get advice and certain vaccines on prescription, though they may not administer some of the less common immunizations. Travel clinics are more expensive, but you won't need to make an appointment. In Australasia, vaccination centres are less expensive than doctors' surgeries. Most clinics will also sell travel-associated accessories, including mosquito nets and first-aid kits.

INTESTINAL TROUBLES

Despite all the dire warnings below, a bout of **diarrhoea** ("Montezuma's Revenge" or simply *turista* as it's invariably known in Mexico) is the only medical problem you're at all likely to encounter. No one, however cautious they are, seems to avoid it altogether, largely because there are no reliable preventative measures. It is caused above all by the change in diet and routine and by the fact that the bacteria in Mexican food are different from (as well as more numerous than) those found in other Western diets.

If you go down with a mild dose of the runs unaccompanied by other symptoms, this will probably be the cause. If your diarrhoea is accompanied by cramps and vomiting, it could be food poisoning of some sort. Either way, it will probably pass of its own accord in 24–48 hours without treatment. In the meantime, it is essential to replace the fluid and salts you're losing down the drain, so drink lots of water with oral rehydration salts – *suero oral* – (brand names: *Dioralyte*, *Electrosol*, *Rehidrat*). If you can't get these, dissolve half a teaspoon of salt and three of sugar in a litre of water. Avoid greasy food, heavy spices, caffeine and most fruit and dairy products; some say bananas, pawpaws and prickly pears (*tunas*) are good, while plain yoghurt or a broth made from yeast extract (such as *Marmite* or *Vegemite*, if you happen to have some with you) can be easily absorbed by your body when you have diarrhoea. Drugs like *Lomotil* or *Immodium* plug you up – and thus undermine the body's efforts to rid itself of infection – but they can be a temporary stop-gap if you have to travel.

MEDICAL RESOURCES IN NORTH AMERICA

International Association for Medical Assistance to Travellers (IAMAT), 417 Center St, Lewiston, NY 14092 (☎716/754-4883).

40 Regal Rd, Guelph, ON N1K 1B5 (☎519/836-0102).

Non-profit organization supported by donations. Can provide a list of English-speaking doctors in Mexico, climate charts and leaflets on various diseases and inoculations.

Travel Medicine, 351 Pleasant St, Northampton, MA 01060 (☎1-800/872-8633).

Sells first-aid kits, mosquito netting, water filters and other health-related travel products.

Travellers Medical Center, 31 Washington Square, New York, NY 10011 (☎212/982-1600).

Consultation service on immunizations and treatment.

MEDICAL RESOURCES IN THE UK

British Airways Travel Clinic, 156 Regent St, London W1R 5TA (Mon–Fri 9am–4.15pm, Sat 10am–4pm; ☎0171/439 9584).

Other clinics throughout the country (call ☎0171/831 5333 to find the one nearest to you).

No appointment necessary. Information helpline on ☎0891/224100.

Hospital for Tropical Diseases, Queen's House, 180–182 Tottenham Court Rd, London W1P 9LE (Mon–Fri 9am–5pm; ☎0171/636 6099).

Recorded message service on ☎0839/337722 gives hints on hygiene and illness prevention as well as lists of appropriate immunizations.

Medical Advisory Service for Travellers Abroad (MASTA), c/o London School of Hygiene and Tropical Medicine, Keppel St, London WC1E 7HT (☎0171/631 4408).

Call their "Health Line" on ☎0891/224100 for the latest detailed specific health advice by return post.

MEDICAL RESOURCES IN AUSTRALASIA

Auckland Hospital Vaccinations, Park Rd, Grafton (☎07/797 440; in Auckland use the prefix ☎3).

International Association for Medical Assistance to Travellers (IAMAT), PO Box 5049, 598 Pananui St, Christchurch 5 (☎03/352 9053).

Travel Bug Medical and Vaccination Centre, 161 Ward St, N Adelaide (☎08/267 3544).

Travel Health and Vaccination Clinic, 114 William St, Melbourne (☎03/670 3871).

Travellers' Immunisation Service, 303 Pacific Highway, Sydney (☎02/416 1348).
Branches in Adelaide, Brisbane and Perth.

If symptoms persist for a few days, a course of **antibiotics** may be necessary, but this should be a last resort, following medical advice (see p.26).

MALARIA

Malaria, caused by a parasite that lives in the saliva of *anopheles* mosquitoes, is endemic in many parts of Mexico. Areas above 1000m (such as México) are malaria-free, as are Cancún, Cozumel, Isla Mujeres, and all the beach resorts of the Baja and the Pacific coast. Daytime visits to archeological sites are risk-free too, but low-lying inland areas are risky, especially in **Chiapas**, where the presence of strains resistant to the main drug, chloroquine, is suspected. Few travellers seem to take chloroquine (brand names: *Nivaquin, Resochin, Avloclor, Aralen*), but

it's a good idea to do so, starting about two weeks before you arrive and continuing for six weeks afterwards.

If you go down with malaria, you'll probably know. The fever, shivering and headaches are like severe flu and come in waves, usually beginning in the early evening. Malaria is not infectious, but can be dangerous and sometimes even fatal if not treated quickly. If no doctor is available, take 600mg of quinine sulphate three times daily for at least three days, followed by three *Fansidar* taken together.

The most important thing, however, is to avoid **mosquito bites**. Though active from dusk till dawn, female *anopheles* mosquitoes prefer to bite in the evening, so be especially careful at that time. Wear long sleeves, skirts or trousers, avoid

WHAT ABOUT THE WATER?

In a hot climate and at high altitudes, it is essential to **increase water intake** to prevent dehydration. Most travellers, and most Mexicans if they can, stay off the **tap water**, although a lot of the time it is in fact drinkable, and in practice impossible to avoid completely: ice made with it may appear in drinks unasked for, utensils are washed in it, and so on.

Most restaurants and *licuaderías* use **purified water** (*agua purificada*), but always check; most hotels have a supply and will often provide bottles of water in your room. **Bottled water** (generally purified with ozone or ultra-violet) is widely available, but stick with known brands, and always check that the seal on the bottle is intact since refilling empties with tap water for resale is not unknown (carbonated water is generally a safer bet in that respect).

There are various methods of **treating water** while you are travelling, whether your source is from a tap or a river or stream. **Boiling** it for a minimum of five minutes is the time-honoured method, but it is not always practical, will not remove unpleasant tastes, and is a lot less effective at higher altitudes – including much of central Mexico, where you have to boil it for much longer.

Chemical sterilization, using either chlorine or iodine tablets or a tincture of iodine liquid, is more convenient, but chlorine leaves a nasty aftertaste (though it can be masked with lemon or lime juice), and is not effective in preventing such diseases as amoebic dysentery and giardiasis. **Pregnant** women or people with **thyroid** problems should consult their doctor before using iodine sterilizing tablets or iodine-based purifiers. Inexpensive iodine removal filters are available and are recommended if treated water is being used continuously for more than a month or is being given to babies.

Purification, involving both filtration and sterilization, gives the most complete treatment. Portable water purifiers range in size from units weighing as little as 60g, which can be slipped into a pocket, up to 800g for carrying in a backpack. Some of the best water purifiers on the market are made in Britain by **Pre-Mac**. For suppliers contact:

USA *Outbound Products*, 1580 Zephyr Ave, Box 56148, Hayward, CA 94545-6148 (☎510/429-0096).

CANADA *Outbound Products*, 8585 Fraser St, Vancouver, BC V5X 3Y1 (☎604/321-5464).

UK *Pre-Mac (Kent) Ltd*, 40 Holden Park Rd, Southborough, Tunbridge Wells, Kent TN4 0ER (☎01892/534361).

IRELAND *All Water Systems Ltd*, Unit 12, Western Parkway Business Centre, Lower Ballymount Rd, Dublin 12 (☎01/456 4933).

AUSTRALIA *CCD International*, Radford Park, c/o Vasse Post Office, Busselton, WA 6280 (☎097/554106).

dark colours, which attract mosquitoes, and put repellent on all exposed skin. Plenty of good brands are sold locally. An alternative is to burn coils of pyrethium incense such as *Raidolitos* (these are readily available and burn all night if whole, but are easy to break in transit). Sleep under a net if you can – one which hangs from a single point is best (you can usually find a way to tie a string across your room to hang it from). Special mosquito nets for hammocks are available in Mexico.

Another illness spread by mosquito bites is **dengue fever**, whose symptoms are similar to those of malaria, plus a headache and aching bones. The only treatment is complete rest, with drugs to assuage the fever.

BITES AND CREEPY CRAWLIES

Other biting insects can be a nuisance. These include **bed bugs**, sometimes found in cheap hotels – look for squashed ones around the bed. **Sandfies**, often present on beaches, are small but their bites, usually on feet and ankles, itch like hell and last for days. **Head or body lice** can be picked up from people or bedding, and are best treated with medicated soap or shampoo; very occasionally, they may spread typhus, characterized by fever, muscle aches, headaches and eventually red eyes and a measles-like rash. If you think you have it, seek treatment.

Scorpions are mostly nocturnal and hide during the heat of the day under rocks and in crevices, so poking around in such places when in the countryside is generally ill-advised. If sleeping in a place where they might enter (such as a beach *cabaña*), shake your shoes out before putting them on in the morning, and try not to wander round barefoot. The sting of some scorpions is dangerous and medical treatment should always be sought – cold-pack the sting in the meantime. **Snakes** are unlikely to bite unless accidentally disturbed, and most are harmless in any case. To see one at all, you need to search stealthily – walk heavily and they will usually slither away. If you do get bitten or stung, remember what the snake or scorpion looked like (kill it if you can), try not to move the affected part, and seek medical help: anti-venoms are available in most hospitals.

HEAT AND ALTITUDE PROBLEMS

Two other common causes of problems are **altitude** and the **sun**. The answer in both cases is to take it easy. Especially if you arrive in México (Mexico City), you may find any activity strenuous, and the thin air is made worse by the number of pollutants it contains. The only solution is to allow yourself time to acclimatize. If going to higher altitudes (climbing Popocatépetl, for example), you may develop symptoms of **Acute Mountain Sickness** (AMS), such as breathlessness, headaches, dizziness, nausea and appetite loss. More extreme cases may cause vomiting, disorientation, loss of balance and coughing up of pink frothy phlegm. The simple cure – descent – almost always brings immediate recovery, but never descend too quickly.

Tolerance to the **sun**, too, takes a while to build up: use a strong sunscreen and, if you're walking during the day, wear a hat or stick to the shade. Be sure to avoid dehydration by drinking enough (water or fruit juice rather than beer or coffee), and don't exert yourself for long periods in the hot sun. Be aware that overheating can cause **heatstroke**, which is potentially fatal. Signs are a very high body temperature without a feeling of fever, but accompanied by headaches, disorientation and even irrational behaviour. Lowering body temperature (a tepid shower, for example) is the first step in treatment.

Less serious is prickly heat, an itchy rash that is in fact an infection of the sweat ducts caused by excessive perspiration that doesn't dry off. A cool shower, zinc oxide powder and loose cotton clothes should help.

HIV AND AIDS

Over 20,000 cases of **AIDS (SIDA)** have been reported in Mexico, mostly in the centre of the country, and especially in México. While the problem in Mexico is no worse than in many other countries, it is still a risk and you should take all the usual precautions to avoid it. In particular, to contemplate casual sex without a condom would be madness – carry some with you (preferably from home, but if buying them in Mexico, check the date and remember that heat affects their durability) and insist on using them. They will also protect you from other sexually transmitted diseases.

Should you need an injection or transfusion, make sure that the equipment is sterile (it might be worth bringing a sterile kit from home); any blood you receive should be screened, and from voluntary rather than commercial donor banks. If you have a shave from a barber, make sure a clean blade is used, and don't submit to processes such as ear-piercing, acupuncture or tattooing unless you can be sure that the equipment is sterile.

HEPATITIS AND OTHER DISEASES

Hepatitis A is transmitted through contaminated food and water (someone not washing their hands after going to the toilet and then handling food, for example), or through saliva. It can lay a victim low for several months with exhaustion, fever and diarrhoea, and can even cause liver damage. The new **Havrix** vaccine has been shown to be extremely effective; though expensive (around $100/£70 for a course of two shots), it lasts for up to ten years. The protection given by gammaglobulin, the traditional serum of hepatitis antibodies, wears off quickly, and the injection should therefore be as late as possible before departure: the longer your planned stay, the larger the dose.

Symptoms by which you can recognize hepatitis include a yellowing of the whites of the eyes, general malaise, orange urine (though dehydration can also cause this) and light-coloured stools. If you think you have it, avoid alcohol, try to avoid passing it on, and get lots of rest. More serious is **hepatitis B**, passed on like AIDS through blood or sexual contact. There is a vaccine, but it is only recommended for those planning to work in a medical environment. Otherwise, although it is more contagious than HIV, your chances of getting it are low if you take the same precautions against it.

Typhoid and cholera are spread in the same way as hepatitis A. **Typhoid** produces a persistent high fever with malaise, headaches and abdominal pains, followed by diarrhoea. Vaccination can be by injection or orally, but the oral alternative is more expensive and only lasts a year, as opposed to three for a shot in the arm. **Cholera** appears in epidemics rather than isolated cases – if it's about, you should know. It is characterized by sudden attacks of watery diarrhoea with severe cramps and debilitation. The vaccination offers some protection, but not much; it is not recommended for Mexico unless there is an outbreak of the disease.

Assuming you were vaccinated against **polio** in childhood, only one (oral) booster is needed during your adult life. Immunizations against mumps, measles, TB and rubella are a good idea for anyone who wasn't vaccinated as a child and hasn't had the diseases. You don't need a shot for **yellow fever** unless you're coming from a country where it's endemic (in which case you need to carry your vaccination certificate).

Although **rabies** exists in Mexico, the best advice is just to give dogs a wide berth, and not to play with animals at all, no matter how cuddly they may look. A bite, a scratch or even a lick from an infected animal could spread the disease; wash any such wound immediately but gently with soap or detergent and apply alcohol or iodine if possible. Ideally you should find out what you can about the animal and swap addresses with the owner (if there is one), just in case. If the animal might be infected, act immediately to get treatment – rabies is invariably fatal

> One word of **warning**: in many Mexican pharmacies you can still buy drugs such as *Entero-Vioform* and *Mexaform*, which can cause optic nerve damage and have been banned elsewhere; it is not a good idea, therefore, to use local brands unless you know what they are.

once symptoms appear. There is a vaccine but it is expensive, serves only to shorten the course of treatment you need anyway, and is effective for no more than three months.

GETTING MEDICAL HELP

For minor **medical problems**, head for the *farmacia* – look for a green cross and the *Farmacia* sign. Pharmacists are knowledgeable and helpful, and many also speak some English. They can also sell drugs over the counter (if necessary) which are only available by prescription at home.

For more serious complaints you can get a list of English-speaking **doctors** from your government's nearest consulate (see p.18); big hotels and tourist offices may also be able to recommend someone. Every Mexican border town has hundreds of doctors experienced in treating gringos (dentists, too), since they charge less than their colleagues across the border. Every reasonably sized town should also have a state- or Red Cross-run health centre (*centro de salud*), where treatment is free.

INSURANCE

There are no reciprocal health arrangements between Mexico and any other country, so travel insurance is essential.

First of all, check to see if you are already covered. **Credit and charge cards** (particularly *American Express*) often have certain levels of medical or other insurance included, and travel insurance may also be included if you use a major credit or charge card to pay for your trip. Some **package tours** too may include insurance.

Whatever cover you are going for, always check the **fine print** of a policy. A 24-hour medical emergency contact number is a must, and one of the rare policies that pays medical bills directly is better than one that reimburses you on your return home. The per-article limit for loss or theft should cover your most valuable possession (a camcorder for example) but, conversely, don't pay for cover you don't need — such as too much baggage or a huge sum for personal liability. Make sure too that you are covered for all the things you intend to do. Activities such as climbing, scuba diving and potholing are usually specifically excluded, but can be added for a supplement, usually 20 to 50 percent.

NORTH AMERICAN COVER

North American travellers should certainly check to see if they are already covered for medical care or losses. Canadians are usually covered for medical expenses by their **provincial health plans** (but may only be reimbursed after the fact). Holders of **ISIC** and other student/teacher/ youth cards are entitled to $3000 worth of acci-

dent coverage and 60 days of in-patient benefits for the period the card is valid. Students will often find that their health coverage extends during the vacations and for one semester beyond the date of last enrolment.

In addition, US and Canadian **homeowners' or renters' insurance** often covers theft or loss of documents, money and valuables while overseas, though conditions and maximum amounts vary from company to company.

This is particularly important when you consider that the currently available travel policies don't insure against **theft** of *anything* while overseas, and apply only to items *lost* from, or *damaged* in, the custody of an identifiable, responsible third party (hotel porter, airline, *guardería*, etc.) Even in these cases you will still have to contact the local police to have a complete **report** made out so that your insurer can process the claim.

If you do want a specific travel insurance policy, there's plenty of choice: your travel agent can usually recommend one. Premiums vary, though maximum payouts tend to be meagre, so shop around. The best deals are usually through student/youth travel agencies — *ISIS* policies, for example, cost $48–69 for fifteen days (depending on coverage), $80–105 for a month, $149–207 for two months, right up to $510–700 for a year.

TRAVEL INSURANCE COMPANIES IN NORTH AMERICA

Access America, PO Box 90310, Richmond, VA 23230 (☎1-800/284-8300).

Carefree Travel Insurance, PO Box 310, 120 Mineola Blvd, Mineola, NY 11501 (☎1-800/323-3149).

International Student Insurance Service (ISIS) — sold by *STA Travel*, which has several branches in the US (see p.4).

Travel Assistance International, 1133 15th St NW, Suite 400, Washington, DC 20005 (☎1-800/821-2828).

Travel Guard, 1145 Clark St, Stevens Point, WI 54481 (☎1-800/826-1300).

Travel Insurance Services, 2930 Camino Diablo, Suite 300, Walnut Creek, CA 94596 (☎1-800/937-1387).

For advice on **auto insurance**, see the earlier "Getting There By Car" section.

Most **travel agents** and tour operators will offer you insurance when you book your flight or

---

TRAVEL INSURANCE COMPANIES IN THE UK

Endsleigh Insurance, 97–107 Southampton Row, London WC1B 4AG (☎0171/436 4451).

Columbus Travel Insurance, 17 Devonshire Square, London EC2M 4SQ (☎0171/375 0011). Two weeks' cover starts at around £27; a month costs from £33.75.

Marcus Hearn & Co, 65–66 Shoreditch High St, London E1 6JL (☎0171/739 3444). Good-value policies for long-term travellers: a year's cover will cost around £100, plus £26.50 to include spouse, and £16 for each child under 18.

---

holiday, and some will insist you take it. These policies are usually reasonable value, though as ever you should check the small print. If you feel the cover is inadequate, or you want to compare prices, any travel agent, **insurance broker or bank** should be able to help: some specialists are listed here. If you have a good "all risks" **home insurance** policy, it may well cover your possessions against loss or theft even when overseas, and many private medical schemes also cover you overseas – make sure you know the procedure and the helpline number though.

In **Australia**, *CIC Insurance*, offered by *Cover-More Insurance Services*, Level 9, 32 Walker St, North Sydney (☎02/202 8000), with branches in Victoria and Queensland, has some of the widest cover available and can be arranged through most travel agents. It costs from $140 for 31 days. In **New Zealand** contact any branch of *STA* or *Flight Centres* (see p.15).

MAPS AND INFORMATION

The first place to head for information, and for free maps of the country and many towns, is the Mexican Government Ministry of Tourism (*Secretaría de Turismo*, abbreviated *Sectur*), which runs offices throughout Mexico and in many other countries. If you

---

MEXICAN GOVERNMENT TOURIST OFFICES OVERSEAS

USA 1911 Pennsylvania Ave NW, Washington, DC 20006 (☎202/728-1750).

70 E Lake St, Chicago, IL 60601 (☎312/606 9015).

2707 North Loop West, Houston, TX 7700 (☎713/880-5153).

10100 Santa Monica Blvd, LA, CA 90067 (☎213/203-8191).

405 Park Ave, New York, NY 10022 (☎212/755-7261).

CANADA 1 Place Ville Marie, Montréal, PQ H3B 3M9 (☎514/871-1052).

2 Bloor St West, Toronto, ON M4W 3E2 (☎416/925-0704).

999 W Hastings St, Vancouver, BC V6C 1M3 (☎604/669 2845).

UK 60–61 Trafalgar Square, London WC2N 5DS (☎0171/839 3177).

AUSTRALIA 109 Pitt St, Sydney (☎02/231 3411).

TRAVEL BOOK AND MAP OUTLETS

NORTH AMERICA

British Travel Bookshop, 551 5th Ave, New York, NY 10176 (☎1-800/448-3039 or 212/490-6688).

The Complete Traveler Bookstore, 199 Madison Ave, New York, NY 10016 (☎212/685-9007).

3207 Fillmore St, San Francisco, CA 92123 (☎415/923-1511).

Elliot Bay Book Company, 101 S Main St, Seattle, WA 98104 (☎206/624-6600).

Open Air Books and Maps, 25 Toronto St, Toronto, M5R 2C1 (☎416/363-0719).

Pacific Traveler Supply, 529 State St, Santa Barbara, CA 93101 (☎805/963-4438; phone orders ☎805/965-4402).

Rand McNally, 1201 Connecticut Ave NW, Washington, DC 20036 (☎202/223-6751).

444 N Michigan Ave, Chicago, IL 60611 (☎312/321-1751).

150 E 52nd St, New York, NY 10022 (☎212/758-7488).

595 Market St, San Francisco, CA 94105 (☎415/777-3131).

Plus more than 20 stores across the US; call ☎1-800/333-0136 (ext 2111) for the address of the nearest, or for direct mail maps.

Traveler's Bookstore, 22 W 52nd St, New York, NY 10019 (☎212/664-0995).

Ulysses Travel Bookshop, 4176 St-Denis, Montréal (☎514/289-0993).

World Wide Books and Maps, 1247 Granville St, Vancouver V6Z 1G3 (☎604/687-3320).

UK

Daunt Books, 83 Marylebone High St, London W1M 4AL (☎0171/224 2295).

John Smith and Sons, 57–61 St Vincent St, Glasgow G2 5JF (☎0141/221 7472).

National Map Centre, 22–24 Caxton St, London SW1E 6PD (☎0171/222 4945).

Stanfords, 12–14 Long Acre, London WC2E 9LP (☎0171/836 1321).

For maps by mail or phone order call ☎0171/836 1321.

Thomas Nelson and Sons Ltd, 51 York Place, Edinburgh EH1 3JD (☎0131/557 3011).

The Travellers' Bookshop, 25 Cecil Court, London WC2N 4EZ (☎0171/836 9132).

AUSTRALIA

Bowyangs, 372 Little Bourke St, Melbourne, Vic 3000 (☎03/670 4383).

Hema, 239 George St, Brisbane, Qld 4000 (☎07/221 4300).

The Map Shop, 16a Peel St, Adelaide, SA 5000 (☎08/231 2033).

Perth Map Centre, 891 Hay St, Perth, WA 6000 (☎09/322 5733).

Speciality Maps, 58 Albert St, Auckland (☎09/307 2217).

Travel Bookshop, 20 Bridge St, Sydney, NSW 2000 (☎02/241 3554).

---

know where you're going, it's always worth **stocking up in advance with as many relevant brochures and plans as they'll let you have, since offices in Mexico are frequently closed or have run out.**

Once you're in Mexico, you'll find **tourist offices** (sometimes called *turismos*) run by *Sectur*, but also by state and municipal authorities; quite often there'll be two or three rival ones in the same town. It's quite impossible to gener-

alize about them – some are extremely friendly and helpful, with free information and leaflets by the cart-load; others are barely capable of answering the simplest enquiry.

MAPS

Good **maps** of Mexico are rare. Road maps on a larger scale than the free handouts (though still not exactly detailed) can be bought at any large bookshop: the *Hallwag* 1:2,600,000 is one of the clearest, the *Nelles* 1:2,500,000 better still. *Bartholemew*'s and *HFET*'s 1:3,000,000 maps have coloured contours for altitude, and show other physical features, but are weaker on road details. In the US, route maps can be bought at gas stations (*Mobil* and the *AAA* both produce reasonable ones).

In Mexico, the best are those published by *Patria*, with individual maps of each state, and *Guía Roji*, which also publishes a Mexican Road Atlas and a México street guide. Both are widely available – try branches of *Sanborn's* or large *Pemex* stations.

More detailed, **large-scale maps** – for hiking or climbing – are harder to come by. The most detailed, easily available area maps are produced by *International Travel Map Productions*, whose 1:1,000,000 *Travellers' Reference Map* series includes the peninsulas of Baja California and the Yucatán. *INEGI*, the government map-makers, also produce very good topographic maps on various scales. They have an office in every state capital and an outlet at the airport at México. Unfortunately, stocks can run rather low, so don't count on being able to buy the ones that you want.

GETTING AROUND

Distances in Mexico can be huge, and if you're intending to travel on public transport, you should quickly get used to the idea of long, long journeys. Getting from Tijuana to México, for example, could take nearly two days non-stop. Although public transport at ground level is frequent and reasonably efficient everywhere, taking an internal flight at least once may be worth it for the time it saves.

BY BUS

Within Mexico, **buses** (*camiones* in Mexican Spanish, hardly ever *autobuses*) are by far the most common and efficient form of public transport. There are an unbelievable number of them, run by a multitude of companies, and connecting even the smallest of villages. Long-distance services generally rely on very comfortable and dependable vehicles; remoter villages are more commonly connected by what look like (and often are) recycled school buses from north of the border.

There are basically two classes of bus, first (*primera*) and second (*segunda*), though on major long-distance routes there's often little to differentiate the two. **First-class** vehicles have numbered, reserved seats, videos and air conditioning, but nowadays many **second-class** lines have all these too. The main difference will be in the number of stops – second-class buses call at more places, and consequently take longer to get where they're going – and the fare – about 10 percent higher on first-class services; you may be able to get a discount with a student card, though it is not, it must be said, especially likely. Most people choose first-class for any appreciably long distance, second- for short trips or if the destination is too small for first-class buses to stop, but you should certainly not be put off second-class if it seems more convenient – it may even prove less crowded. Air conditioning is not necessarily a boon – there's nothing more uncomfortable than a bus with sealed windows and a broken air-conditioner; and if it does work, you may need a sweater. The videos, by the way, are often in

English, usually as action-packed as possible, and not restricted to tasteful family viewing. Having the video on means that everyone wants to keep the blinds shut – in fact they shut them much of the time anyway, and it's amazing how soon you adapt to doing the same in a landscape that sometimes doesn't change for hours.

On important routes, especially in the north, there are also **de luxe or pullman buses** with names like *Primera Plus* or *Turistar Plus*, and fares around 30 percent higher than those of first-class buses. They have few if any stops, waitress service and free snacks and drinks on long-distance services, extra-comfortable airline seating, and air conditioning that works – be sure to keep a sweater handy, as it can get very cold. They may also be emptier, which could mean more space to stretch out and sleep. Pullman services almost all have **computerized reservation** services and will usually accept credit cards in payment: these facilities are increasingly common with the bigger regular bus lines too.

Most towns of any size have a modern, centralized **bus station**, known as the **Central Camionera** or **Central de Autobuses**, often a long way from the middle of town. Where there is no unified terminus you may find separate first- and second-class terminals, or individual ones for each company, sometimes little more than bus stops at the side of the road. In almost every bus station there is some form of **baggage deposit** (left luggage) office – usually known as a *guardería, consigna* or simply *equipaje*, and costing about 30¢–$1/20–70p per item per day. Before leaving anything, make sure that the place will be open when you come to collect. If there's no formal facility, staff at the bus companies' baggage dispatching offices can often be persuaded to look after things for a short while.

Always check your route and arrival time, and whenever possible buy tickets from the bus station **in advance** to get the best (or any) seats; count on paying about US$3–4 for every 100km covered. There is very rarely any problem **getting a place** on a bus from its point of origin or from really big towns. In smaller, mid-route places, however, you often have to wait for the bus to arrive (or at least to leave its last stop) before discovering if there are any seats – though the increasing prevalence of computerized ticketing is easing the problem. Often there are too few seats, and without fluent and loud Spanish you may lose out in the fight for the ticket clerk's

attention. Alternatively there's almost always a bus described as **local**, which means it originates from where you are (as opposed to a **de paso** bus, which started somewhere else and is simply passing through), and tickets for these can be bought well in advance.

Weekends, holiday season, school holidays and fiestas can also overload services to certain destinations: again the only real answer is to buy tickets in advance, though you could also try the cheaper second-class lines, where they'll pack you in standing, or take whatever's going to the next town along the way and try for a *local* from there. A word with the driver and a small tip can also sometimes work wonders.

Terms to look out for on the timetable, besides *local* and *de paso*, include *vía corta* (by the short route) and *directo* or *expresso* (direct/non-stop – in theory at least). *Salida* is departure, *llegada* arrival. A decent **road map** will be extremely helpful in working out just which buses are going to pass through your destination.

Though the legendary craziness of Mexican **bus drivers** is something of an exaggeration (and many bus companies have installed warning lights and buzzers to indicate when the driver is exceeding the speed limit), you'll invariably have some hair-raising experiences. **Mechanical breakdown**, however, is a far more common cause of delay than accidents. In recent years the government has been trying to further improve the safety record through regular mechanical checks and also by keeping tabs on the drivers.

BY TRAIN

Rail travel is even cheaper than the bus in Mexico as a rule, but also much slower and rarely on time – that's hours late, not minutes. Nor are trains frequent, with only one or two a day on most lines. Theft on board has become a serious problem as well, and services have for the most part deteriorated, with many of them cut. In general, train travel is only recommended in northern and central Mexico. The most popular journeys include those from the border to México (where sleeper services represent great value), México to Oaxaca, and the amazing Copper Canyon Railway (see p.128). In addition, some new first-class-only trains from the capital (to San Miguel de Allende and Zacatecas, for example) offer airline-style service with meals served at your seat and a reasonably reliable timetable.

See the box above, however, for doubts about the entire future of the Mexican rail system.

Though there are two classes, they're rarely both available on the same train these days. *Locales* (slow trains), will be second-class, while *rapidos*, faster trains with limited stops, are often first-class only. **Second-class** (*segunda*) carriages are invariably crammed to the limit with villagers, their bags, baggage and livestock. It is dirty, hot and uncomfortable, and while it may be fascinating for shorter journeys, is liable to become unbearable if you're going any distance.

First-class (*primera*) varies in standard, but you should at least get a seat. Formerly, there were two types of first-class: *primera general* (ordinary first), less crowded than second but not particularly comfortable; and *primera especial* (special first), with reclining seats in air-conditioned coaches, and windows with blinds. Now these have been consolidated into a single first-class with *primera especial* fares (about three times the price of second-class, and generally a little cheaper than the bus), but the coaches from both the old first-classes, so it's pot luck which you get, although as a rule you can expect to find former *primera especial* coaches on named overnight trains such as *La Oaxaqueña* from México to Oaxaca, *El Tapatío* to Guadalajara, and *El Regiomontano* to Monterrey, as well as the newer business-oriented services.

For **sleepers**, you pay a supplement over the first-class fare. Least expensive are pullman-style carriages with curtained-off bunks – the *cama alta* (upper berth) is slightly cheaper than the *cama baja* (lower berth). Then there is a *camarín*, a tiny private room for either one or two people, or ultimately an *alcoba*, a larger room with private bathroom (big enough for two adults and two small kids). Any of these cost more than the bus, but you won't find cheaper sleeping cars anywhere.

Places must be **reserved** for first-class and sleepers, and this should be done as far in advance as possible (up to a month if you do it in person), especially during holiday periods. Note that sleepers cannot always be booked from smaller stations, so do it in advance at a larger station if you can. **Cancellations** can be made up to 24 hours before departure, for a full refund, and if there are no places on the train you want, cancellations may make them available, but you'll have to ask specifically for cancellations – in México's Buenavista station, they are sold from a separate counter. Second-class tickets are sold only on the day of departure (in places with only one train a day, the *taquilla* often opens for ticket sales just an hour or so before the official departure time, which can of course be several hours before the actual departure time).

During holiday periods you may have to queue for the best part of a day in order to get your ticket. Seats cannot be reserved in second-class, so your best chance for one is to turn up very early at the train's station of origin. If you're picking up the train halfway along its route, expect to stand. Even in first-class, it might be an idea to turn up fairly early, since overbooking is normal.

The **US and Canadian agent** for tickets on Mexican National Railways is *Mexico by Rail* (☎1-800/321-1699).

BY AIR

There are more than fifty **airports** in Mexico with regular passenger flights run by local airlines and several smaller airports with feeder services into them. The two big companies, both formerly state-owned and with international as well as domestic flights, are **Aeroméxico** and **Mexicana**, which between them connect most places to México, usually several times a day. In the last few years, since deregulation, a whole host of smaller, **regional airlines** have sprung up. Of these, *Inter* serves the Yucatán, Chiapas, Oaxaca and Monterrey, *Aviacsa* covers those areas and also Ciudad Juárez, *Aeromar* operates in the Bajío, and *Aero California* mainly in the northwest of the country, especially Baja California, while airlines with names like *Aero Oaxaca* and *Aeromorelos* really speak for themselves. *Taesa* has services mostly in the north, but also operates flights to the Yucatán; *SARO*, in spite of its name (*Servicios Aereos Rutas Oriente*), flies to destinations all over the country from its base at Monterrey (which has become Mexico's second air hub); and new airlines are appearing all the time. Information about the smaller airlines is not usually available in cities not served by them, nor from *Aeroméxico* and *Mexicana* offices, though a good travel agent should be able to help.

Internal air **fares** reflect the popularity of the route: the more popular the trip, the lower the price. Thus the flight from Tijuana to México costs little more than the first-class bus, while the journey from Tijuana to La Paz is three times the bus fare, or twice as much as the rather longer Tijuana–México route. Obviously, fares like the first are a real bargain, but even on more expensive routes they can be well worth it for the time they save. There are few discounts and, while fares are different for each airline (the smaller ones are usually cheaper), the price of a ticket on a particular flight doesn't normally vary, and is usually twice as much for a return as a single. *Mexicana*, *Aeroméxico* and *Inter* offer **multi-flight airpasses**, available only outside Mexico, valid for 2 to 45 days, and with different prices for 2- to 5-flight passes depending on which region of the country is covered. Although they may save you time spent buying air tickets in Mexico, they are not really a great bargain. In the US contact the airlines direct; in the UK, contact *British Airways*.

USEFUL AIRLINE NUMBERS

Aero California: ☎1-800/237-6225 (US)

Aeroméxico: ☎1-800/237-6639 (US)

Aeromorelos ☎951/6-09-74; fax 6-10-02 (Mexico)

Aero Oaxaca ☎951/3-10-95 24-hr tel & fax (Mexico)

Aviacsa ☎800/0-06-22 (toll-free in Mexico)

Inter c/o *Mexicana*; also ☎98/84-20-00; fax 87-43-86 (Mexico)

Mexicana ☎1-800/531-7921 (US); ☎800/0-01-24 (toll-free in Mexico)

SARO ☎1-800/538-7276 (US); ☎800/8-32-24 or 9-03-23 (toll-free in Mexico)

Taesa ☎1-800/328-2372 (US)

BY FERRY

Ferries connect Baja California with a trio of ports on the Pacific mainland: Santa Rosalía to Guaymas, and La Paz to Mazatlán and Topolobampo (for Los Mochis). Passenger fares start at around $15/£10, cars from around $100/£70. There are also smaller boats to islands off the Caribbean coast: from Playa del Carmen and Puerto Morelos to Cozumel, and from Cancún to Isla Mujeres (prices for these start at around $1/70p for foot passengers, $8/£5 for a car). Though not as cheap as they once were, all these services are still pretty reasonable, and make a nice change from the bus.

BY CAR

Getting your car into Mexico **properly documented** (see "Getting There" on p.7) is just the start of your problems. Although most people who drive enjoy it and get out again with no more than minor incidents, driving in Mexico does require a good deal of care and concentration, and almost inevitably involves at least one brush with bureaucracy or the law, although the police have eased up of late, due to instructions from above to stop putting the bite on tourists.

Renting a car in Mexico – especially if you do it just for a day or two, with a specific itinerary in mind – avoids many of the problems and is often an extremely good way of seeing quickly a small area that would take days to get around on public transport. In all the tourist resorts and major cities there are numbers of competing agencies, with local operations usually charging less than the well-known chains. You should check rates carefully, though – the basic cost of renting a VW Beetle for the day may be as little as $15, but by the time you have added insurance, tax and mileage it can easily end up being three or four times that. Weekly rates can be better – around $300/£200 including 1000 free kilometres – and unlimited mileage offers are almost always a bargain. For shorter distances, mopeds and motorbikes are also available in most resorts.

Drivers from the US, Canada, Britain, Ireland Australia and New Zealand will find that their **licences** are valid in Mexico, though an international one is still advisable, especially if yours has no photo on it. You are required to have all your documents with you when driving. Insurance is not compulsory, but you'd be very foolhardy not to take some out.

CAR RENTAL RESERVATION NUMBERS

IN MEXICO

Avis	☎800/7-07-77	**Hertz**	☎5/566-00-99
Budget	☎800/457-65-18	**National (Europcar/Interrent)**	☎5/762-82-50

IN NORTH AMERICA

Avis	☎1-800/331-1084 (US & Canada)	**National (Europcar/Interrent)**	
Budget	☎1-800/527-0700 (US & Canada)		☎1-800/CAR-RENT (US & Canada)
Dollar	☎1-800/421-6868 (US)	**Thrifty**	☎1-800/367-2277 (US)
Hertz	☎1-800/654-3001 (US);		
	☎1-800/263-0600 (Canada)		

IN THE UK AND IRELAND

Avis	☎0181/848 8733 (UK);	**Europcar/Interrent**	☎0345/222525 (UK)
	☎021/281111 (Ireland)	**(National)**	☎01/668 1777 (Ireland)
Budget	☎0800/181181 (UK);	**Hertz**	☎0181/679 1799 (UK);
	☎0903/24759 (Ireland)		☎01/676 7476 (Ireland)

IN AUSTRALASIA

Avis	☎1800/225533 (Australia);	**Hertz**	☎03/698 2555 (Australia);
	☎09/525 1982 (New Zealand)		☎0800/655955 (New Zealand)
Budget	☎1800/132848 (Australia);	**National (Europcar/**	☎1800/331181 (Australia);
;	☎0800/652227 (New Zealand)	**Interrent)**	☎09/275 0066 (Ne Zealand)
Dollar	☎1800/658658 (Australia)	**Thrifty**	☎1800/652008 (Australia);
			☎09/256-1405 (New Zealand)

Fuel can be a problem: the government oil company *Pemex* has a monopoly and sells two types of petrol: *Nova* (leaded) and *Magna Sin* (unleaded), which cost about the same as regular unleaded north of the border. Often, however, *Nova* is the only type available; it's very dirty, and will quickly foul up any car with a highly tuned engine or anything designed to run on unleaded fuel. In response to howls of outrage from US motorists with ruined engines, *Sectur* offices in North America give out lists of supposedly dependable unleaded outlets along major roads, but working, full pumps at these places cannot be counted on and, even though things are improving, using unleaded fuel will confine you to certain routes. Nor is it unknown for *Magna Sin* pumps to dipense *Nova*, so check first. Some drivers of American or Canadian vehicles have got round these problems by disconnecting their catalytic convertors and running on leaded – but this won't do your engine much good (you'll also have to get across the border before you can do it legally, and reattach it before crossing back). Two new brands of fuel called *Nova Plus* and *Extra Plus* have been introduced, but are not easy to come by.

Mexican **roads and traffic**, though, are your chief worry. Traffic circulates on the right, and the normal **speed limit** is 40km/h (25mph) in built-up areas, 70km/h (43mph) in open country, and 110km/h (68mph) on the freeway. Some of the new highways are excellent, and the toll (*cuota*) superhighways are better still, though extremely expensive to drive on. Away from the major population centres, however, roads are often narrow, winding and potholed, with livestock wandering across them at unexpected moments. Get out of the way of Mexican bus and truck drivers (and remember that if you signal left to them on a stretch of open road, it means it's clear to overtake). Every town and village on the road, however tiny, protects its peace by a series of **topes** (concrete or metal speed bumps) across the road. Look out for the warning signs and take them seriously; they are often huge and can be negotiated only at a crawl. Most people suggest, too, that you never drive at night (and not just for road safety reasons: see the box below) – sound advice even if not always practical. Any good road map should provide details of the more common symbols used on Mexican **road signs**, and *Sectur* have a pamphlet on driving in Mexico that features the most common ones. One convention to be aware of is that the first driver to flash their lights at a junction, or where only one vehicle can pass, has right of way, so someone who flashes you is *not* inviting you to go first.

In most large towns you'll find extensive **one-way systems** on both major roads and back streets. Traffic direction is sometimes, but by no means always, indicated by small arrows affixed to lampposts. Poor marking is less of a problem than it sounds; simply note the directions in which the parked cars are facing.

Parking in cities is always going to be a hassle, too – the restrictions are complicated and foreigners are easy pickings for traffic police, who usually remove one or both plates in lieu of a ticket (retrieving them can be an expensive and

time-consuming business). Since theft is also a real threat, you'll usually have to pay extra for a hotel with secure parking. You may well also have to fork over on-the-spot "fines" for traffic offences (real or imaginary). In the capital, cars are banned from driving on one day of every week, determined by their licence number (see p.253).

Unless your car is a basic model VW, Ford or Dodge (all of which are manufactured in Mexico), **parts** are expensive and hard to come by – bring a basic spares kit. **Tyres** suffer particularly badly on burning-hot Mexican roads, and you should carry at least one good spare. Roadside *vulcanizadoras* and *llanteros* can do temporary repairs; new tyres are expensive, but remoulds aren't a good idea on hot roads at high speed. If you have a **breakdown**, there is a free highway mechanic service known as the **Ángeles Verdes** (Green Angels). As well as patrolling all major routes looking for beleaguered motorists, they can be reached by phone via México ☎5/250-01-23 (although they don't actually operate inside the DF, where you should call the *AAM* – equivalent of the *AA* or the *AAA* – on ☎519-34-36). The *Ángeles Verdes* speak English.

Should you have a minor **accident**, try to come to some arrangement with the other party – involving the police will only make matters worse, and Mexican drivers will be as anxious to avoid doing so as you will. Also, if you witness an accident, don't get involved – witnesses can be locked up along with those directly implicated to prevent them from leaving before the case comes up. In any more serious incident, contact your consulate and your Mexican insurance company as soon as possible.

BANDITRY: A WARNING

You should be aware when driving in Mexico, especially in a foreign vehicle, of the danger of bandits. **Robberies and even more serious assaults** of motorists do occur, above all in the northwest and especially in the state of Sinaloa. Sometimes robbers pose as police, sometimes as hitchhikers or motorists in distress, so think twice about offering a lift or a helping hand. They may also try to make you stop by indicating there's something wrong with your vehicle. On the other hand, remember that there are plenty of legitimate **police checkpoints** along the main roads, where you must stop. Roads where there have been regular reports of problems, and where you should certainly try to avoid driving at night, include Hwy-15 (Los Mochis–Mazatlán) and express Hwy-1 in Sinaloa, Hwy-5 (México–Acapulco) in Guerrero, Hwy-75 (Oaxaca–Tuxtepec), Hwy-57 (San Luis Potosí–Matahuela), and near the border, in particular on Hwy-2 (Mexicali–Agua Prieta) and Hwy-40 (Matamoros–Monterrey). The US embassy in Mexico advises never driving after dark.

HITCHING

It's possible to **hitch** your way around Mexico, but it can't be recommended – certainly not in the north. Lifts are relatively scarce, distances vast, risks high, and the roadside often a harsh environment if you get dropped at some obscure turnoff. You may also be harassed by the police, though this depends very much on local policy and on their mood at the time. Many drivers – especially truck drivers – expect you to contribute to their expenses, which you may think rather defeats the object of hitching. The bottom line, really, is that hitching is **not safe**: robbery is not uncommon, and women in particular (but also men) are advised not to hitch alone. You should wait to know where the driver is going before getting in, rather than stating your own destination first, sit by a door and keep your baggage to hand in case you need to leave in a hurry (feigned carsickness is one way to get a driver to stop). Particularly avoid areas frequented by *bandidos*, such as those listed on p.35.

That said, however, over short stretches, to get to villages where there's no bus or simply to while away the time spent waiting for one, you may find yourself hitching and you'll probably come across real friendliness and certainly meet people you wouldn't otherwise. It does help if your Spanish will stretch to a conversation.

LOCAL TRANSPORT

Public transport within Mexican towns and cities is always plentiful and inexpensive, though also crowded and not very user friendly. Usually you'll be relying on **buses**, which pour out clouds of choking diesel fumes (though México has an extensive, excellent **metro** system, and there are smaller metros in Guadalajara and Monterrey); often there's a flat-fare system, but this varies from place to place. Wherever possible we've indicated which bus to take and where to catch it, but often only a local will fully understand the intricacies of the system and you may well have to ask: the main destinations of the bus are usually painted up on the windscreen, which helps.

In bigger places **combis** or **colectivos** offer a faster and perhaps less crowded alternative for only a little more money. These are minibuses, vans or large saloons that run along a fixed route to set destinations, and will pick you up and drop you off wherever you like along the way. You pay the driver for the distance travelled. In México *combis* are known as *peseros*.

Regular **taxis** can also be good value, but beware of rip-offs. Unless you're confident that the meter is working, fix a price before you get in. In the big cities there may be tables of fixed prices posted at prominent spots. At almost every **airport** and some of the biggest bus stations you'll find a booth selling vouchers for the official taxis – sometimes there's a choice of paying more for a private car or less to share – and even though these may cost more than a regular cab, it's worth it for the extra security. In every case you should know the name of a hotel to head for, or they'll take you to the one that pays the biggest commission (they may try to do this anyway, saying that yours is full). Never accept a ride in any kind of unofficial or unmarked taxi.

ACCOMMODATION

Mexican hotels may describe themselves as anything from *paradores*, *posadas* and *casas de huéspedes* to plain *hoteles*: terms which are used more or less interchangeably. A *parador* is totally unrelated to its upmarket Spanish namesake, for example, and although in theory *casa de huéspedes* means a small cheap place like a guest house, you won't find this necessarily to be the case.

Finding a room is rarely difficult – in most old and not overly touristy places the cheap hotels are concentrated around the main plaza (the *zócalo*), with others near the market, train station or bus station (or where the bus station *used* to be, before it moved out of town). In

ACCOMMODATION PRICES

All the accommodation listed in *The Rough Guide to Mexico* has been categorized into one of nine **price bands**, as set out below. The prices quoted are in US dollars and normally refer to the cheapest available rates for two people sharing in high season.

① less than $8	④ $18–25	⑦ $50–75
② $8–12	⑤ $25–35	⑧ $75–100
③ $12–18	⑥ $35–50	⑨ more than $100

bigger cities there's usually a relatively small area in which you'll find the bulk of the realistic possibilities. The more modern and expensive places have very often been built on the outskirts of towns, accessible only by car or taxi. The only times you're likely to have big problems finding somewhere to stay are in coastal resorts over the peak Christmas season, at Easter, on Mexican holidays, or almost anywhere during a local fiesta: at such times it's well worth trying to reserve ahead.

All rooms should have an official **price** displayed, though this is not always a guide to quality – a filthy fleapit and a beautifully run converted mansion may charge exactly the same, even if they're right next door to each other. To guarantee quality, the only recourse is never to take a room without seeing it first – you soon learn to spot which establishments have promise. You should never pay more than the official rate (though just occasionally the sign may not have kept up with inflation) and in the low season you can often pay less. The charging system varies, sometimes it's per person but usually the price quoted will be for the room regardless of how many people occupy it. So **sharing** can mean big savings: *sencillo* (single) generally means a room with one double bed (*cama matrimonial*), which is invariably cheaper than a room with two single beds (*doble* or *con dos camas*), and most hotels have large "family" rooms with several beds, which are tremendous value for groups. In the big resorts there are lots of apartments that sleep six or more and include cooking facilities, for yet more savings. A little gentle haggling rarely goes amiss, and many places will have some rooms which cost less, so ask (*¿Tiene un cuarto mas barato?*).

Air conditioning (*aire acondicionado*) is a feature that inflates prices – often you are offered a choice. Unless it is quite unbearably hot and humid, a room with a simple ceiling fan

(*ventilador*) is generally better. Except in the most expensive places, the air-conditioning units are almost always noisy and inefficient, whereas a fan can be left running silently all night and the draught will also help to keep insects away from the bed. It might seem too obvious to mention, but be careful of the ceiling fans, which are often quite low. Don't stand on the bed, and keep well clear of them when removing any clothes from the upper body. In winter, especially at altitude or in the desert, it will of course be **heating** rather than cooling that you will be interested in – if there isn't any, make sure there's enough bedding and ask for extra blankets if necessary.

When looking at a room, you should always check its **insect proofing**. Cockroaches are common, and there's not much anyone can do about them, but decent netting will keep mosquitoes and worse out and allow you to sleep. If the mosquitoes are really bad you'll probably see where previous occupants have splattered them on the walls. Ditto for bed bugs around the bed.

CAMPSITES, HAMMOCKS AND *CABAÑAS*

There is not usually much alternative to staying in hotels. **Camping** is easy enough if you are hiking in the back country, or happy to simply crash on a beach – beaches cannot be privately owned in Mexico, but robberies are common, especially in places with a lot of tourists. There are very few organized campsites, and those that do exist are first and foremost **trailer parks**, not particularly pleasant to pitch tents in. Of course, if you have a van or RV you can use these or park just about anywhere else – there are a good number of facilities in the well-travelled areas, especially down the Pacific coast and Baja.

If you're planning to do a lot of camping, an **international camping carnet** is a good investment, serving as useful ID and getting you discounts at member sites. It is available from home motoring organizations, in **North America** from *Family Campers and RVers* (US: ☎1-800/245-9755; Canada: ☎1-800/245-9755), and in the **UK** from *Camping and Caravan Club* (☎01203/694995).

In a lot of less official campsites, you will be able to **rent a hammock** and a place to sling it for the same price as pitching a tent (around $3/£2), maybe less, and certainly less if you're packing your own hammock (Mexico is a good place to buy these, especially in and around Mérida).

Beach huts, or **cabañas**, are found at the more rustic, backpacker-oriented beach resorts, and sometimes inland. Usually just a wooden or palm-frond shack with a hammock slung up inside (or a place to sling your own), they often do not even have electricity, though as a resort gets more popular, they tend to transform into sturdier beach bungalows with mod cons and higher prices. At backwaters and beaches too untouristed for even *cabañas*, you should still be able to sling a hammock somewhere (probably the local bar or restaurant, where the *palapa* serves as shelter and shade).

YOUTH HOSTELS

There are 26 **youth hostels** in Mexico, charging around US$5–8 per person for basic, single-sex bunk-room type facilities. A YH card is not usually necessary, but you may pay more without one. **Rules**, in most places, are strict (no booze, 11pm curfew, up and out by 9am) and at holiday periods they're often taken over completely by Mexican groups.

There are hostels in: Aguascalientes, Cabo San Lucas, Campeche, Cancún, Chetumal, Ciudad Obregón, Cuautla, Durango, Guadalajara (two), Guanajuato, La Paz, Mexicali, Monterrey, Morelia, Oaxaca, Playa del Carmen, Quéretaro, San Luis Potosí, Tijuana, Tuxtla Gutiérrez, Veracruz, Villahermosa, Zacatecas and Zihuatanejo. All stay open 365 days a year.

YOUTH HOSTEL ASSOCIATIONS

MEXICO

Comisión Nacional del Deporte (CONADE), Dirección Villas Deportivas Juveniles, Glorieta del Metro Insurgentes, Local C-11, Colonia Juárez, CP 06600, México DF (☎5/530-03-11).

NORTH AMERICA

Hostelling International-American Youth Hostels (HI-AYH), 733 15th St NW, PO Box 37613, Washington DC 20005 (☎202/783-6161).

Canadian Hostelling Association, Room 400, 205 Catherine St, Ottawa, ON K2P 1C3 (☎1-800/663-5777 or 613/237-7884).

UK AND IRELAND

Youth Hostel Association (YHA), Trevelyan House, 8 St Stephen's Hill, St Albans, Herts AL1 2DY (☎01727/845047).

Scottish Youth Hostel Association, 7 Glebe Crescent, Stirling, FK8 2JA (☎01786/451181).

Youth Hostel Association of Northern Ireland, 56 Bradbury Place, Belfast, BT7 1RU (☎01232/324733).

An Óige, 61 Mountjoy St, Dublin 7 (☎01/830 4555).

AUSTRALASIA

Australian Youth Hostel Association, Level 3, 10 Mallett St, Camperdown, NSW 2050 (☎02/565 1699).

Youth Hostel Association of New Zealand, PO Box 436, Christchurch 1 (☎03/379 9970).

EATING AND DRINKING

Whatever your preconceptions about Mexican food, if you've never eaten in Mexico they will almost certainly be wrong. It bears very little resemblance to the concoctions served in "Mexican" restaurants or fast-food joints in other parts of the world – certainly you won't find *chile con carne* outside the tourist spots of Acapulco. Nor, as a rule, is it spicy; indeed, a more common complaint from visitors is that after a while it all seems rather bland.

WHERE TO EAT

Basic meals are served at **restaurantes**, but you can get breakfast, snacks and often full meals at **cafes** too; there are **take-out** and **fast-food** places serving sandwiches, *tortas* (filled rolls) and *tacos* (soft, rolled *tortillas* with a filling), as well as more international-style food; there are establishments serving nothing but wonderful **fruit drinks** (*licuados*) and **fruit salads** (usually identified by a sign saying *Jugos y Licuados*) and there are **street stalls** dishing out everything from *tacos* to orange juice to ready-made crisp vegetable salads sprinkled with *chile*-salt and lime. Just about every **market** in the country has a cooked food section, too, and these are invariably the cheapest places to eat, if not always in the most enticing surroundings. In the big cities and resorts, of course, there are international restaurants too – **pizza** and **Chinese food** are ubiquitous.

When you're **travelling**, as often as not the food will come to you; at every stop people clamber onto buses and trains (especially second-class ones) with baskets of home-made foods, local specialities, cold drinks, or jugs of coffee. You'll find wonderful things this way that you won't come across in restaurants, but they should be treated with respect, and with an eye to hygiene.

WHAT TO EAT

The basic Mexican **diet** is essentially one of corn (*maíz*) and its products, supplemented by beans and *chiles*. These three things appear in an almost infinite variety of guises. Some dishes are hot (ask *¿es picante?*), but on the whole you add your own seasoning from the bowls of home-made *chile* sauce on the table – these are often surprisingly mild, but they can be fiery and should always be approached with caution.

There are at least a hundred different types of **chile**, fresh or dried, in colours ranging from pale green to almost black, and all sorts of different sizes (large, mild ones are often stuffed with meat or cheese and rice to make *chiles rellenos*). Each has a distinct flavour and by no means all are hot, although the most common, *chiles*

SALSA

Since so much Mexican food is simple, and endlessly repeated in restaurant after restaurant, one way to tell the places apart – and a vital guide to the quality of the establishment – is by their **salsa**. You'll always get at least one bowl or bottle per table, and sometimes as many as four to choose from. A couple of these will be proprietary brands (Tabasco-like, usually with great, exotic labels and invariably *muy picante*) but there should always be at least one home-made concoction. Increasingly this is raw, California-style *salsa*: tomato, onion, *chile* and cilantro (coriander) finely chopped together. More common, though, are the traditional cooked *salsas*, either green or red, and almost always relatively mild (though start eating with caution). The recipes are – of course – closely guarded secrets, but again the basic ingredients are tomato (the green Mexican tomato in green versions), onion, and one or more of the hundreds of varieties of *chile*.

jalapeños, small and either green or red, certainly are. You'll always find a *chile* sauce (*salsa*) on the table when you eat, and in any decent restaurant it will be home-made; no two are quite alike. *Chile* is also the basic ingredient of more complex cooked sauces, especially **mole**, an extraordinary mixture of chocolate, *chile*, and fifty or so other ingredients traditionally served with turkey or chicken (the classic *mole poblano*), but also sometimes with *enchiladas* (rolled, filled *tortillas* baked in sauce). Another speciality to look out for is *chiles en nogada*, a bizarre combination of stuffed green peppers covered in a white sauce made of walnuts and cream cheese or sour cream and topped with red pomegranate: the colours reflect the national flag and it's served especially in September around Independence Day, which is also when the walnuts are fresh.

Beans (*frijoles*), an invariable accompaniment to egg dishes – and with almost everything else too – are of the pinto or kidney variety and are almost always served *refritos*, ie boiled up, mashed, and "refried" (though actually this is the first time they're fried). They're even better if you can get them whole in some kind of country-style soup or stew, often with pork or bacon.

Corn, in some form or another, features in virtually everything. In its natural state it is known as *elote* and you can find it roasted on the cob at street stalls or in soups and stews such as *pozole* (with meat). Far more often, though, it is ground into flour for **tortillas**, flat maize pancakes of which you will get a stack to accompany your meal in any cheap Mexican restaurant (in more expensive or touristy places you'll get rolls, *bolillos*). *Tortillas* can also be made of wheatflour (*de harina*), which may be preferable to outsiders' tastes, but these are rare except in the north.

Tortillas form the basis of many specifically Mexican dishes, often described as *antojitos* (appetizers, light courses) on menus. Simplest of these are **tacos**, *tortillas* rolled and filled with almost anything, from beef and chicken to green vegetables, and then fried (they're usually still soft, not at all like the baked taco shells you may have had at home). *Enchiladas* are rolled, filled *tortillas* covered in *chile* sauce and baked; *enchiladas suizas* are filled with chicken and have sour cream over them. *Tostadas* are flat *tortillas* toasted crisp and piled with ingredients – usually meat, salad vegetables and cheese (smaller bite-size versions are known as *sopes*), while *quesadillas* are *tortillas* wrapped around cheese, some-

times with other fillings, and toasted or fried. *Tortillas* torn up and cooked together with meat and (usually hot) sauce are called *chilaquiles*: this is a traditional way of using up leftovers. Especially in the north, you'll also come across *burritos* (large wheatflour *tortillas*, stuffed with anything, but usually beef and potatoes or beans) and *gorditas* (delicious small, fat, corn *tortillas*, sliced open, stuffed and baked or fried).

Cornflour, too, is the basis of **tamales** – found predominantly in central and southern Mexico – which are a sort of cornmeal pudding, stuffed, flavoured, and steamed in corn or banana leaves. They can be either savoury, with additions like prawn or *elote*, or sweet when made with something like coconut.

Meat, except in the north, is not especially good – beef in particular is usually thin and tough; pork, kid and occasionally lamb are better. If the menu doesn't specify what kind of meat it is, it's usually pork – even *bistec* can be pork unless it specifies *bistec de res*. For thick American-style steaks, look for a sign saying *Carnes Hereford* or for a "New York Cut" descrip-

---

VEGETARIAN FOOD IN MEXICO

Vegetarians can eat well in Mexico, although it does take caution to avoid meat altogether. Many Mexican dishes are naturally meat-free and there are fabulous fruits and vegetables. Most restaurants serve vegetable soups and rice, and items like *quesadillas*, *chiles rellenos*, and even *tacos* and *enchiladas* often come with non-meat fillings. Another possibility is *queso fundido*, simply (and literally) melted cheese, served with *tortillas* and sauce. Eggs, too, are served anywhere at any time, and many of the *jugos* shops (see p.41) serve huge mixed salads to which grains and nuts can be added.

However, do bear in mind that vegetarianism as such is not particularly common and a simple cheese and *chile* dish may have some meat added to "improve" it. Worse, most of the fat used for frying is animal fat (usually lard), so that even something as unadorned as refried beans may not be strictly vegetarian (especially as a bone or some stock may have been added to the water the beans were originally boiled in). Even so-called **vegetarian restaurants**, which are increasingly common and can be found in all the big cities, often include chicken on the menu. You may well have better luck in **pizza** places and Chinese or other ethnic restaurants.

tion (only in expensive places or in the north). **Seafood** is almost always fresh and delicious, especially the spicy prawn or octopus cocktails which you find in most coastal areas (*coctel* or *campechana de camaron/pulpo*), but beware of eating uncooked shellfish. **Eggs** – in country areas genuinely free-range and flavoursome – feature on every menu as the most basic of meals, and at some time you must try the uniquely Mexican combinations of *huevos rancheros* or *huevos a la mexicana*.

Traditionally, Mexicans eat a light **breakfast** very early, a **snack** of *tacos* or eggs in mid-morning, **lunch** (the main meal of the day) around two o'clock or later – in theory followed by a siesta, but decreasingly so, it seems – and a late, light **supper**. Eating a large meal at lunch-time can be a great moneysaver – almost every restaurant serves a cut-price **comida corrida**.

Breakfast (*desayuno*) in Mexico can consist simply of coffee (see "Drinking", below) and *pan dulce* – sweet rolls and pastries that usually come in a basket; you pay for as many as you eat. More substantial breakfasts consist of eggs in any number of forms, or at fruit juice places you can have a simple *licuado* (see "Drinking", below) fortified with raw egg (*blanquillo*). Freshly squeezed **orange juice** (*jugo de naranja*) is always available from street stalls in the early morning.

Snack meals mostly consist of some variation on the *taco/enchilada* theme (stalls selling them are called *taquerías*), but **tortas** – rolls heavily filled with meat or cheese or both, garnished with avocado and *chile* and toasted on request – are also wonderful, and you'll see take-out *torta* stands everywhere. Failing that, you can of course always make your own snacks with bread or *tortillas*, along with fillings such as avocado or cheese, from shops or markets. **Sandwiches**, on soft, tasteless bread, meanly filled, and *hamburguesas* are almost always awful.

You can of course eat a full meal in a restaurant at any time of day, but you'd do well to adopt the local habit of taking your main meal at lunchtime, since this is when **comidas corridas** (set meals, varied daily) are served, from around 1 to 5pm: in more expensive places the same thing may be known as the *menu del día* or *menu turístico*. Price is one good reason: often you'll get four courses for $5/£3.50 or less, which can't

be bad. More importantly, though, the *comida* will include food that doesn't normally appear on the menus – home-made soups and stews, local specialities, puddings, and above all vegetables that are otherwise a rarity – a welcome chance to escape from the budget traveller's staples of eggs, *tacos* and beans.

A **typical comida** will consist of "wet" soup, probably vegetable, followed by "dry" soup – most commonly *sopa de arroz* (simply rice seasoned with tomato or *chile*), or perhaps a plate of vegetables, pasta, beans or *guacamole* (avocado mashed with onion, and maybe tomato, lime juice and *chile*). Then comes the main course, followed by pudding, usually fruit, *flan* or *pudin* (crème caramel-like concoctions), or rice pudding. The courses are brought at great speed, sometimes all at once, and in the cheaper places you may have no idea what you're going to get until it arrives, since there'll simply be a sign saying *comida corrida* and the price.

Some places also offer set meals in the **evening**, but this is rare, and on the whole going out to eat at night is much more expensive.

The basic **drinks** to accompany food are water or beer. If you're drinking **water**, stick to bottled stuff (*agua mineral* or *agua de Tehuacán*) – it comes either plain (*sin gas*) or carbonated (*con gas*).

JUGOS AND LICUADOS

Soft drinks (*refrescos*), including Coke, Pepsi, Squirt (fun to pronounce in Spanish), and Mexican brands such as apple-flavoured *Sidral* (which are usually extremely sweet), are on sale everywhere. Far more tempting are the **real fruit juices** and *licuados* sold at shops and stalls displaying the *Jugos y Licuados* sign or sometimes known as *licuaderías*. Juices (*jugos*) can be squeezed from anything that will go through the extractor. Orange (*naranja*) and carrot (*zanahoria*) are the staples, but you should also experiment with some of the more obscure tropical fruits, most of which are much better than they sound. *licuados* are made of fruit mixed with water (*licuado de agua* or simply *agua de . . .*) or milk (*licuado de leche*) in a blender, usually with sugar added. They are always fantastic. *Limonada* (fresh lemonade) is also sold in many of these places, as are *aguas frescas* – flavoured cold

A GLOSSARY OF MEXICAN FOOD AND DRINK TERMS

Basics

Azucar	Sugar	Pescado	Fish
Carne	Meat	Pimienta	Pepper
Ensalada	Salad	Queso	Cheese
Huevos	Eggs	Sal	Salt
Mantequilla	Butter	Salsa	Sauce
Pan	Bread	Verduras/Legumbres	Vegetables

Soups (*Sopas*) and starters

Caldo	Broth (with bits in)	Sopa	Soup
Ceviche	Raw fish salad, marinated in lime juice	De Arroz	Plain Rice
		De Fideos	With Noodles
Consome	Consommé	De Lentejas	Lentil
Entremeses	Hors d'oeuvres	De Verduras	Vegetable

Eggs (*Huevos*)

a la Mexicana	Scrambled with mild tomato, onion and *chile* sauce	Rancheros	Fried and smothered in a hot *chile* sauce
con Jamon	With ham	Revueltos	Scrambled
Motuleños	Fried, served on a *tortilla* with ham, cheese and sauce	Tibios	Lightly boiled
		con Tocino	With bacon

Antojitos

Burritos	Wheatflour *tortillas*, rolled and filled	Molletes	Split *torta* covered in beans and melted cheese, often with ham and avocado too
Chilaquiles	Torn-up *tortillas* cooked with meat and sauce	Quesadillas	Toasted or fried *tortillas* with cheese
Chiles rellenos	Stuffed peppers		
Enchiladas	Rolled-up *tacos*, covered in *chile* sauce and baked	Queso fundido	Melted cheese, served with *tortillas* and *salsa*
Enchiladas suizas	As above, with sour cream	Sopes	Smaller bite-size versions of *tostadas*
Flautas	Small rolled *tortillas* filled with red meat or chicken and then fried	Tacos	Rolled, fried *tortillas* with filling
Gorditas	Small, fat, stuffed corn *tortillas*	Tamales	Cornmeal pudding, usually stuffed and steamed in banana leaves
Machaca	Shredded dried meat scrambled with eggs	Torta	Filled bread roll
		Tostadas	Flat crisp *tortillas* piled with meat and salad

Fish and seafood (*Pescados y mariscos*)

Anchoas	Anchovies	Camarones	Prawns
Atun	Tuna	Cangrejo	Crab
Cabrilla	Sea Bass	Corvina Blanca	White Sea Bass
Calamares	Squid	Dorado	Dolphin Fish (Mahi Mahi)

fish and seafood (*Pescados y mariscos*) continued

Filete Entero	Whole, filleted fish	*Ostion*	Oyster
Huachinango	Red Snapper	*Pez Espada*	Swordfish
Jurel	Yellowtail	*Pulpo*	Octopus
Langosta	Crawfish or Rock lobster	*Robalo*	Bass
Lenguado	Sole	*Sardinas*	Sardines
Merluza	Hake	*Trucha*	Trout

Meat (*Carne*) and Poultry (*Aves*)

Alambre	Kebab	*Costilla*	Rib
Albondigas	Meatballs	*Filete*	Tenderloin/fillet
Barbacoa	Barbecued meat	*Guisado*	Stew
Bistec	Steak (not always beef)	*Higado*	Liver
Cabeza	Head	*Lengua*	Tongue
Cabrito	Kid	*Lomo*	Loin (of pork)
Carne (de res)	Beef	*Milanesa*	Breaded escalope
Carne Adobado	Barbecued/spicily stewed meat	*Pata*	Feet
		Pato	Duck
Carnitas	Spicy pork	*Pavo/Guajolote*	Turkey
Cerdo	Pork	*Pechuga*	Breast
Chivo	Goat	*Pierna*	Leg
Chorizo	Spicy sausage	*Pollo*	Chicken
Chuleta	Chop	*Salchicha*	Hot dog or salami
Codorniz	Quail	*Ternera*	Veal
Conejo	Rabbit	*Tripa/Callos*	Tripe
Cordero	Lamb	*Venado*	Venison

Vegetables (*Legumbres, verduras*)

Aguacate	Avocado	*Frijoles*	Beans
Betabel	Beetroot (often as a *jugo*)	*Hongos*	Mushrooms
Calabacita	Zucchini/courgette	*Lechuga*	Lettuce
Calabaza	Squash	*Lentejas*	Lentils
Cebolla	Onion	*Nopales*	Prickly Pear Fronds, something like Squash
Champiñones	Mushrooms		
Chícharos	Peas	*Papas*	Potatoes
Col	Cabbage	*Pepino*	Cucumber
Coliflor	Cauliflower	*Rajas*	Strips of green pepper
Elote	Corn on the cob	*Tomate ./Jitomate*	Tomato
Espáragos	Asparagus	*Zanahoria*	Carrot

food and drink glossary continues over...

food and drink glossary continued...

Fruits (*Fruta*) and juice

Chabacano	Apricot	*Mamey*	Pink, sweet, full of pips
Ciruelas	Tiny yellow plums	*Mango*	Mango
Coco	Coconut	*Melon*	Melon
Durazno	Peach	*Naranja*	Orange
Frambuesas	Raspberries	*Papaya*	Papaya
Fresas	Strawberries	*Piña*	Pineapple
Granada	Pomegranate	*Platano*	Banana
Grenadilla	Yellow Passion Fruit	*Sandia*	Watermelon
Guanabana	Soursop, like a large Custard Apple	*Toronja/Pomelo*	Grapefruit
		Tuna	Prickly Pear (Cactus Fruit)
Guayaba	Guava	*Uvas*	Grapes
Higos	Figs	*Zapote*	Sapodilla, fruit of the Chicle tree
Limon	Lime		

Sweets

Ate	Quince paste	*Ensalada de Frutas*	Fruit salad
Cajeta	Caramel confection often served with...	*Flan*	Crème caramel
		Helado	Ice cream
Crepas	Pancakes	*Nieve*	Sorbet

Common terms

Asado/a	Roast	*Con Mole*	The most famous of Mexican sauces – it contains *chile*, chocolate and spices – served with chicken or turkey
Al Horno	Baked		
A la Tampiqueña	Meat in thin strips served with guacamole and *enchiladas*		
A la Veracruzana	Usually fish, cooked with tomatoes and onions	*A la Parilla*	Grilled
		Empanado/a	Breaded
Al Mojo de Ajo	Fried in garlic and butter		
Barbacoa or Pibil	Wrapped in leaves and herbs and steamed/cooked in a pit		

drinks, of which the most common are *horchata* (a white and milky extract of tiger nuts), *agua de arroz* (like an iced rice pudding drink – delicious), *agua de jamaica* (hibiscus) or *de tamarindo* (tamarind). These are also often served in restaurants or sold in the streets from great glass jars. Make sure that any water and ice used is purified – street stalls are especially suspect in this regard. Juices and *licuados* are also sold at many ice-cream parlours – *neverías* or *paleterías*. The **ice cream**, also in a huge range of flavours and more like Italian *gelato* than the heavy cream US varieties, can also be fabulous.

COFFEE AND TEA

A great deal of **coffee** is grown in Mexico and in the growing areas, especially the state of Veracruz, as well as in the traditional coffeehouses in the capital, you will be served superb coffee. In its basic form, *café solo* or *negro*, it is strong, black, often sweet (ask for it *sin azúcar* for no sugar), and comes in small cups. For weaker black coffee ask for *café americano*, though this may mean instant (if you want instant, ask for "Nescafé"). White is *café cortado* or *con un pocito de leche*; *café con leche* is delicious, but made with all milk and no water.

Espresso and cappuccino are often available too, or you may be offered **café de olla** – stewed in the pot for hours with cinnamon and sugar, it's thick, sweet and tasty. Outside traditional coffee areas all of the above applies, except that the coffee is often terrible and if you look like a tourist they may automatically assume you want instant.

Tea (*té*) is often available too, and you may well be offered a cup at the end of a *comida*. Usually it's some kind of herb tea like *manzanillo* (camomile) or *yerbabuena* (mint). If you get the chance to try traditional **hot chocolate** ("the drink of the Aztecs"), then do so – it's an extraordinary, spicy, semi-bitter concoction, quite unlike the milky bedtime drink of your childhood.

ALCOHOL

Mexican **beer**, *cerveza*, is excellent – especially compared to the puny US product. Most is light, lager-style *cerveza clara*, fine examples being *Bohémia, Superior, Dos Equis* and *Tecate* (the last normally served with lime and salt); but you can also get dark (*oscura*) beers, of which the best are *Negra Modelo* and *Tres Equis*. Locally bottled beers, such as *Sol* on the east coast or *Pacífico* on the west, are often even better than the national labels. You'll normally be drinking in bars, but if you don't feel comfortable – this applies to women, in particular (for more on which, see later) – you can also get takeouts from most shops, supermarkets, and, cheapest of all, **agencias**, which are normally agents for just one brand.

When buying from any of these places, it is normal to pay a deposit of about 30–40 percent of the purchase price: keep your receipt and return your bottles to the same store. Beer is cheapest of all if, instead of buying 330ml bottles, you go for the 940ml vessels known as "*caguamas*" (turkeys), or in the case of *Pacífico*, "*ballenas*" (whales).

Wine (*vino* – *tinto* for red, *blanco* white) is not seen a great deal, although Mexico does produce a fair number of perfectly good ones. You're safest sticking to the brand names like *Hidalgo* or *Domecq*, although it may also be worth experimenting with some of the new labels, especially those from Baja California, which are attempting to emulate the success of their neighbours across the border and in many cases have borrowed techniques and winemakers from the US.

Tequila, distilled from the maguey cactus in and around the town of Tequila in Jalisco, is of course the most famous of Mexican spirits, usually served straight with lime and salt on the side. Lick the salt and bite into the lime, then take a swig of tequila (or the other way round – there's no correct etiquette). The best stuff is aged (*añejo* or *reposado*) for smoothness; try *Sauza Hornitos*, which is powerful, or *Commemorativo*, which is unexpectedly gentle on the throat.

Mescal (often spelt *mezcal*) is basically the same drink, but made from a slightly different type of maguey, younger and less refined. In fact, tequila was originally just a variety of *mescal*. The worm in the bottom of the *mescal* bottle, a grub which lives only on the maguey, is there to prove its authenticity – the spurious belief that the worm is hallucinogenic is based on a confusion between the drink and the peyote cactus, which is also called *mescal*; by the time you've got down as far as the worm, you won't be in any state to tell anyway.

Pulque, a mildly alcoholic milky beer made from the same cactus, is the traditional drink of the poor and sold in special bars called *puquerías*. The best comes from the state of México, and is thick and viscous – it's a little like palm wine. Unfermented *pulque*, called *aguamiel*, is sweet and non-alcoholic.

Drinking other **spirits**, you should always ask for *nacional*, as anything imported is fabulously expensive. Rum (*ron*), gin (*ginebra*) and vodka are made in Mexico, as are some very palatable brandies (*brandy* or *coñac* – try *San Marcos* or *Presidente*). Most of the **cocktails** for which Mexico is known – margaritas, piñas coladas and so on – are available only in tourist areas or hotel bars, and are generally pretty strong. *Sangrita* is a mixture of tomato and fruit juices with *chile*, often drunk as a mixer with tequila.

For all these, the least heavy atmosphere is in hotel **bars**, tourist areas, or anything that describes itself as a "ladies' bar". Traditional *cantinas* are for serious and excessive drinking, have a thoroughly threatening, macho atmosphere, and are barred to women 99 percent of the time; there's almost inevitably a sign above the door prohibiting entry to "women, members of the armed forces, and anyone in uniform". Big-city *cantinas* are to some extent more liberal, but in small and traditional places they remain exclusively male preserves, full of drunken bonhomie that can suddenly sour into threats and fighting.

MAIL, TELECOMMUNICATIONS AND THE MEDIA

Although on the face of it Mexico has reasonably efficient postal and telephone systems, phoning home can be a hazardous business, while packages tend to go astray in both directions. One thing to watch is the outrageous cost of international phone calls, faxes and telegrams – call collect or use a calling card wherever possible.

MAIL

Mexican **postal services** (*correos*) are reasonably efficient. Air-mail to México should arrive within a few days, but it may take a couple of weeks to get anywhere at all remote. **Post offices** (generally Mon–Fri 9am–6pm, Sat 9am–noon) can offer a **poste restante/general delivery** service: letters should be addressed to **Lista de Correos** at the *Correo Central* (main post office) of any town; all mail that arrives for the *Lista* is put on a list updated daily and displayed in the post office, but held for two weeks only. You *may* get around that by having letter-writers put "*Favor de retener hasta la llegada*" (please hold until arrival) on the envelope. Letters are often filed incorrectly, so you should request a review under all your initials, preferably use only two names on the envelope (in Hispanic countries, the second of people's three usually quoted names is the paternal surname, and the most important, so if three names are used, your mail will probably be filed under the middle one) and capitalize and underline your surname. To collect, you need your passport or some other official ID with a photograph. There is no fee.

American Express also operates an efficient mail collection service, and has a number of offices all over Mexico – most useful in México, where the address for the most central is: c/o American Express, Reforma 234, México 6 D.F. They keep letters for a month, and also hold faxes. If you don't carry their card or cheques, you have to pay a fee to collect your mail, although they don't always ask.

Sending letters and cards is also easy enough, if slow. Anything sent abroad by air should have an airmail (*por avión*) stamp on it or it is liable to go surface. Letters should take around a week to North America, two to Europe or Australasia. Anything at all important should be taken to the post office and preferably registered rather than dropped in a mail box, although the new special airmail boxes in resorts and big cities are supposed to be more reliable than ordinary ones.

Sending **packages** or parcels out of the country is drowned in bureaucracy. Regulations about the thickness of brown paper wrapping and the amount of string used vary from state to state, but most importantly, any package must be checked by customs and have its paperwork stamped by at least three other departments, which may take a while. Take your parcel (unsealed) to any post office and they'll set you on your way. Many stores will send parcels for you, which is a great deal easier. Within the country, you can send a package by bus if there is someone to collect it at the other end.

Telegram offices (*Telegrafos*) are frequently in the same building as the post office. The service is super-efficient, but international ones are very expensive, even if you use the cheaper overnight service. In most cases, you can get across a short message for less by phone or fax. **Faxes** can be sent from (and received at) many long-distance telephone *casetas* (see below): again the cost is likely to be astronomical.

PHONES

Local **phone calls** in Mexico are cheap, and most hotels will let you call locally for free. Coin-operated phones – even those that seem to be in a terrible state usually work for local calls – cost very little. **Internal long-distance** calls can be made from any reasonably new coin-phone, but these are far more expensive. Public phones, which are rapidly being replaced and are usually reliable in big cities, are blue for long distance, or orange for local (and operator-connected) calls only. They'll be very familiar to British readers as they're exactly the same as those in the UK; most long-distance ones also have instructions in English. With either you lift the receiver, insert coins (check for tone; some have a button to get a dial tone) and dial. On long-distance calls, if you haven't put enough in, it will tell you. Some also take **phonecards**, available from telephone offices and stores near the phones that use them (especially in bus and train stations, airports and major resorts). Currently, there are two types of card, which won't work in the same telephones, so make sure you're using the right sort. Many newer public phones say they accept **credit cards**; in practice, however, they often don't.

DIALLING CODES

Calling from long-distance (*Ladatel*) phones, dial:

Mexico interstate: ☎91 + area code + number

US and Canada: ☎95 + area code + number

UK: ☎98 44 + area code (minus initial zero) + number

Ireland: ☎98 353 + area code (minus initial zero) + number

Australia: ☎98 61 + area code (minus initial zero) + number

New Zealand: ☎98 64 + area code (minus initial zero) + number

To **call collect** or **person-to-person**, dial ☎92 for interstate calls within Mexico, ☎96 for the US and Canada, ☎99 for the rest of the world.

Slightly more expensive, but reliable and easy because someone will make the connection for you, are **casetas de teléfono**. There are lots of them, as many locals still don't have phones of their own: they can be simply shops or bars with public phones, indicated by a phone sign outside, in which case you may only be allowed to make local calls, but many are specialist phone and fax places displaying a blue-and-white *Larga Distancia* sign. You're connected by an operator who presents you with a bill afterwards – once connected, the cost can usually be seen clicking up on a meter. There are scores of competing companies, and the new ones, like *Computel*,

---

To call Mexico from abroad, dial:

From US:	☎011 52
From UK, Ireland and New Zealand:	☎00 52
From Australia:	☎0011 52

---

tend to be better – many take credit cards. Prices vary, so if you're making lots of calls it may be worth comparing. There are *casetas* at just about every bus station and airport.

Wherever you make them from, **international calls** are fabulously expensive – the least bad rates are from public call boxes, next from a *caseta*, and madness from a hotel: charges vary a great deal, but don't be surprised to find yourself paying $5 a minute to call the US, £5 a minute to the UK. If you plan to make international calls, by far the best plan is to arm yourself in advance with a **charge card** or **calling card** that can be used in Mexico (see the list below); you'll be connected to an English-speaking operator and will be billed at home at a rate that is predictable (if still high). You should be able to get through to the toll-free numbers from any working public phone.

Next best is to **call collect** (*por cobrar*). In theory you should be able to make an international collect call from any public phone, by dialling the international operator (☎09) or getting in touch with the person-to-person direct dial numbers listed below, though it can be hard to get through. At a *caseta* there may be a charge for making the connection, even if you don't get through, and a hotel is liable to make an even bigger charge.

If you do have to pay for the call on the spot, a phonecard is probably the cheapest option, though even the highest denomination ones won't last long. The modern *casetas* are at least reliable – rates vary more than you'd expect, so shop around.

CALLING CARD NUMBERS

US and UK calling card numbers for **English-speaking operator and home billing**:

AT&T: ☎95-800-462-4240

BT: ☎＊791 (from certain phones only)

Sprint: ☎95-800-877-8000

MCI: ☎95-800-674-7000

MEDIA

As for keeping in touch in other ways, a daily **English-language newspaper**, the *Mexico City News*, is published in the capital and distributed to larger towns nationwide. There are also free bulletins in English that can be picked up in México and anywhere with a sizeable tourist population – either in large hotels or from the tourist office – and *Time* and *Newsweek* are widely available. Few domestic newspapers carry much foreign news, and what there is is mainly North American; they are often lurid scandal sheets, full of corruption and violent crime in full colour. Each state has its own press, however, and they do vary: while most are little more than PRI propaganda, others can be surprisingly independent.

On Mexican **TV** you can watch any number of US shows dubbed into Spanish – it's most bizarre to be walking through some shantytown as the strains of the *Dynasty* theme tune come floating across the air. Cable and satellite are now widespread, and even quite downmarket hotels offer numerous channels, many of them American.

Radio stations in the capital and Guadalajara (among others) have programmes in English for a couple of hours each day, and in many places US broadcasts can also be picked up. The BBC World service in English can be picked up by radios with short wave on 5975KHz in the 49m band, especially in the evening, and on 11,865KHz in the 25m band, especially in the morning. Other possible frequencies include: 6195KHz, 9515KHz and 9640KHz. The *Voice of America* broadcasts on 15,210KHz, 11,740KHz, 9815KHz and 6030KHz.

TRAVELLERS WITH DISABILITIES

Mexico is not well equipped for people with disabilities, but it is improving all the time and, especially at the top end of the market, it should not be too difficult to find accommodation and tour operators who can cater for your particular needs. The important thing is to check beforehand with tour firms, hotels and airlines that they can accommodate you specifically. The box below details organizations that can advise you as to which tour operators and airlines are the most reliable.

If you stick to beach resorts – Cancún and Acapulco in particular – and upmarket tourist **hotels**, you should certainly be able to find places that are, for example, wheelchair-friendly and used to having disabled guests. American chains are very good for this, with *Holiday Inn*, *Sheraton* and *Westin* among those claiming to have the necessary facilities for at least some disabilities.

You'll find that, unless you have your own transport, the best way to **travel** inside the country may prove to be by air, since trains and buses rarely cater for disabled people, and certainly not for wheelchairs. Travelling on a lower budget, or getting off the beaten track, you'll find few facilities. Ramps are few and far between, streets and

pavements not in a very good state, and people no more likely than at home to volunteer help. Depending on your disability, you may want to find an able-bodied helper to accompany you. If you cannot find somebody suitable from among your own friends or family, the organizations listed below may be able to help you get in touch with someone.

CONTACTS FOR TRAVELLERS WITH DISABILITIES

North America

Directions Unlimited, 720 N Bedford Rd, Bedford Hills, NY 10507 (☎1-800/533-5343). *Tour operator specializing in custom tours for people with disabilities.*

Jewish Rehabilitation Hospital, 3205 Place Alton Goldbloom, Montréal, PQ H7V 1R2 (☎514/688-9550, ext 226). *Guidebooks and travel information.*

Mobility International USA, PO Box 10767, Eugene, OR 97440 (☎503/343-1284). *Information and referral services, access guides, tours and exchange programmes. Annual membership $20 (includes quarterly newsletter).*

CONTACTS FOR TRAVELLERS WITH DISABILITIES (continued)

Society for the Advancement of Travel for the Handicapped (SATH), 347 5th Ave, New York, NY 10016 (☎212/447-7284).
Non-profit travel-industry referral service that passes queries on to its members as appropriate; allow plenty of time for a response.

Travel Information Service, Moss Rehabilitation Hospital, 1200 W Tabor Rd, Philadelphia, PA 19141 (☎215/456-9600).
Telephone information and referral service.

Twin Peaks Press, Box 129, Vancouver, WA 98666 (☎1-800/637-2256 or 206/694-2462).
Publisher of the Directory of Travel Agencies for the Disabled ($19.95), listing more than 370 agencies worldwide; Travel for the Disabled ($14.95); The Directory of Accessible Van Rentals and Wheelchair Vagabond ($9.95), loaded with personal tips.

UK

Holiday Care Service, 2 Old Bank Chambers, Station Rd, Horley, Surrey RH6 9HW (☎01293/774535).
Information on all aspects of travel.

Mobility International, 228 Borough High St, London SE1 1JX (☎0171/403 5688).
Information, access guides, tours and exchange programmes.

RADAR, 25 Mortimer St, London W1N 8AB (☎0171/637 5400).
A good source of advice on holidays and travel abroad.

Australasia

ACROD, PO Box 60, Curtain, Canberra, ACT 2605 (☎06/682 4333).
Can offer advice and keeps a list of travel specialists.

Barrier-Free Travel, 36 Wheatley St, North Bellingen, NSW 2454 (☎066/551733).
Consultancy service for disabled travellers, with a flat $50 fee for any number of consultations.

Disabled Persons Assembly, PO Box 10–138, The Terrace, Wellington (☎04/472 2626).
Umbrella group for all organizations dealing with disability in New Zealand.

WOMEN TRAVELLERS

So many oppressive limitations are imposed on women's freedom to travel that any advice or warning seems merely to reinforce the situation. That said, machismo is engrained in the Mexican mentality and although it's softened to some extent by the gentler mores of Indian culture, a degree of harassment is inevitable.

On the whole, any **hassle** will be limited to comments (*piropos*, supposedly compliments) in the street, but even situations that might be quite routine at home can seem threatening without a clear understanding of the nuances of Mexican Spanish. It's a good idea to avoid eye contact – wearing sunglasses helps. To avoid matters escalating, any provocation is best ignored totally. Mexican women are rarely slow with a stream of abuse, but it's a dangerous strategy unless you're very sure of your ground – coming from a foreigner, it may also be taken as racism.

Public transport can be one of the worst places for harassment, especially groping in crowded situations. On the México metro, there are separate women's carriages and passages during rush hours. If you get a seat, you can hide behind a newspaper.

Any problems are aggravated in the big tourist spots, where the legendary "easy" tourists attract droves of would-be gigolos. México can feel heavy, though if you're from a big city yourself, it may not seem that different, and requires the same common sense. Away from the cities, though, and especially in Indian areas, there is rarely any problem – you may as an outsider be treated as an object of curiosity (or even resentment), but not necessarily with any implied or intended sexual threat. And wherever you come across it, such curiosity can also extend to great friendliness and hospitality. On the whole, the further from the US border you get, the easier things will become – though some women have reported that other Latin American countries further south, less used to tourists, are infinitely worse.

The restrictions imposed on **drinking** are without a doubt irksome: women are simply and absolutely barred from the vast majority of *cantinas*, and even in so-called Ladies' Bars "unescorted" women may be looked at askance or even refused service. Carrying a bottle is the only answer, since in small towns the *cantina* may be the only place that sells alcoholic drinks.

There's a growing and radical **feminist movement** in Mexico, largely concentrated in the capital. The main political issue at present is abortion, which is illegal. If you're interested, **contact** the feminist publication *Revuelta*, Vincente Tones 156, Coyoacán, México 21 D.F.; or *Movimento Nacional Para Mujeres*, San Juan de Letran 11–411, México D.F. (☎5/512-58-41), useful for contacts throughout the country.

SPECIALIST HOLIDAY OPERATORS FOR WOMEN IN THE US

The following organizations arrange **all-women holidays in Mexico**; although they deal in "adventure travel", no experience is required, and trips can range from a week to a month.

Alaska Women of the Wilderness, PO Box 773556, Eagle River, AK (☎907/688-2226).

Non-profit making confidence-raising holidays; occasional trips to Baja California.

Outdoor Vacations for Women Over 40, PO Box 200, Groton, MA 01450 (☎508/448-3331).

Adventure trips to Mexico; no previous experience required.

Rainbow Adventures Inc, 15033 Kelly Canyon Rd, Bozeman, MT 59715 (☎406/587-3883).

Adventure travel for women over 30; includes whale-watching in Baja.

SENIOR TRAVELLERS

One of the advantages of retirement is that you are able to take as much time as you like; remember, though, that things you might have taken in your stride years ago, such as sleeping on all-night train and bus journeys, are going to suit you a lot less now. If you are planning any very long journeys on your trip, consider breaking them by stopping off at a few places overnight en route. Pollution and altitude can create real medical risks, especially for anyone with respiratory or cardiac problems: in the capital the combination of the two is particularly severe.

If you are choosing a **sightseeing package tour**, it's a good idea to check on the pace of the itinerary, and consider opting for a slower one with plenty of free time, rather than one that packs the maximum number of sights into the shortest possible period. *Saga* and *Vantage* (see p.5 and p.12) are among firms specializing in holidays for the over-50s. Cruises, on the other hand, may not be as sedate as you might think: many are regarded nowadays as "floating holiday camps," so be particularly careful when selecting one.

US CONTACTS FOR SENIOR TRAVELLERS

American Association of Retired Persons, 601 E St NW, Washington, DC 20049 (☎1-800/424-3410).
Can provide discounts on accommodation and vehicle rental. Membership open to US residents aged 50 or over for an annual fee of $8.

Elderhostel, 75 Federal St, Boston, MA 02110 (☎617/426-8056).
Worldwide network of educational and activity programmes, cruises and homestays for people over 60 (companions may be younger). Programmes generally last a week or more and costs are in line with those of commercial tours.

Gateway Books, 2023 Clemens Rd, Oakland, CA 94602 (☎510/530-0299).
Publishes books for senior travellers.

National Council of Senior Citizens, 1331 F St NW, Washington, DC 20004 (☎202/347-8800).
Group travel and discounts. Annual membership $15.

GAY AND LESBIAN TRAVELLERS

There are no federal laws governing homosexuality in Mexico, and hence it's legal. There are, however, laws enforcing "public morality", which although they are supposed only to apply to prostitution, are often used against gays out cruising. Recently, too, the government of the state of Jalisco has been running an anti-gay campaign.

There are in fact a large number of **gay groups and publications** in Mexico, some of which are listed on p.52. The lesbian scene is nothing like as visible or as large as the gay scene for men, but it's there and growing. There are gay **bars and clubs** in the major resorts and US border towns, and in large cities such as the capital, and also Monterrey, Guadalajara, Veracruz and Oaxaca; elsewhere, private parties are where it all happens, and you'll need a contact to find them.

As far as popular attitudes are concerned, religion and machismo are the order of the day, and prejudice is rife. Even so, soft porn magazines for gay men are sold openly on street stalls and, while you should be careful to avoid upsetting macho sensibilities, you should have few problems if you are discreet. Camp gay men and butch women, incidentally, are known in Mexico as *obvios.*

CONTACTS FOR GAY TRAVELLERS

Ferrari Publications, PO Box 37887, Phoenix, AZ 85069 (☎602/863-2408).
Publishes Inn Places: USA and Worldwide Gay Accommodations *and other gay/lesbian guides.*

Inland Book Company, PO Box 120261, East Haven, CT 06512 (☎203/467-4257).
Publishes Women Going Places, *an international travel guide with an emphasis on lesbian experience.*

International Gay Travel Association, PO Box 4974, Key West, FL 33041 (☎1-800/448-8550).
Trade group that can provide a list of gay-owned or gay-friendly travel agents, accommodation and other travel businesses.

Spartacus Gay Guide, Publisher: *Bruno Gmünder Verlag*, Dessauer Str 1–2, 10963 Berlin, Germany (☎49-30/2611646). Distributors: *Calt Studio*, PO Box 1608, Studio City, CA 91614 (☎818/985-5786); *Inland Book Co.* (see above); *Prowler Press Ltd*, 27 Gloucester St, London WC1N 3XX (☎0181/348 9963); *Edition Habit Press Ltd*, 112 Bronte Rd, Bondi Junction, NSW 2022 (☎02/387 4339).
International gay guide with information on meeting and cruising spots for gay men, but nothing much for lesbians.

HIV and AIDS (SIDA) are as much a threat in Mexico as anywhere else in the world, and the usual precautions are in order. As for **contacts** within Mexico: lesbians can get in touch with *Grupo Lesbico Patlatonalli*, Aptdo Postal 1–4045, Guadalajara, Jalisco; while for gay men, *CIDHOM* (*Colectivo de Información de las Homosexualidades en Mexico*), Aptdo Postal 13–424, México D.F. 03500, can offer information.

TRAVELLING WITH CHILDREN

A minor aged under 18 needs the permission of *both* parents in order to enter Mexico; if travelling alone, they need written permission on a form signed by both parents at the consulate or on official·y notarized affidavits; if travelling with one parent, they need official written permission from the other.

This **law** was introduced in order to prevent parents absconding from the US with their children for the purpose of avoiding court judgements in favour of the other parent. If you are taking your child with you and are not in touch with the other parent, this may cause difficulties, which should be sorted out with the Mexican authorities before leaving home (you'll need proof of sole custody, for example).

Once in the country, you will find that most Mexicans dote on children and they can often help to break the ice with strangers. The main problem, especially with small children, is their extra vulnerability. Even more than their parents, they need protecting from the sun, unsafe drinking water, heat, and unfamiliar food. All that *chile* in particular may be a problem, especially with older kids, who are not used to it. Remember too that diarrhoea can be dangerous for a child: rehydration salts (see p.22) are vital if your child goes down with it. Make sure too, if

(see p.22)

possible, that your child is aware of the dangers of rabies; keep children away from animals and consider a rabies jab.

For touring, hiking or walking, **child-carrier backpacks** such as the *Tomy Lightrider* are ideal, starting at around $75/£50 and can weigh less than 2kg. If the child is small enough, a fold-up buggy is also well worth packing – especially if they will sleep in it (while you have a meal or a drink. . .).

US CONTACTS FOR TRAVELLERS WITH CHILDREN

Families Welcome, 21 West Colony Place, Suite 140, Durham, NC 27705 (☎1-800/767-8252).
Vacations for parents and kids.

Rascals in Paradise, 650 5th St, #505, San Francisco, CA 94107 (☎1-800/U RASCAL).
Scheduled and customized itineraries, built around activities for kids.

Travel with Your Children, 45 W 18th St, New York, NY 10011 (☎212/206-0688).
Publishes Family Travel Times, *a newsletter that comes out ten times a year. The $55 annual subscription includes the use of a call-in advice line.*

WORK AND STUDY

There's virtually no chance of finding temporary work in Mexico unless you have some very specialized skill and have arranged the position beforehand.

Work permits are almost impossible to get hold of. The few foreigners who manage to find work do so mostly in language schools. It might be possible, though not legal, to earn some money as an English instructor by simply advertising in a local newspaper or on notice boards at a university.

The best way to extend your time in Mexico is on a **study programme** or **volunteer** project. An American organization called *Amerispan* selects **language schools** throughout Latin America, including Mexico, to match the needs and requirements of students, and provides advice and support. For further information, call (from the US or Canada) ☎1-800/879-6640; fax 215/829-0418; or write to PO Box 40513, Philadelphia, PA 19106–0513.

EARTHWATCH

Earthwatch matches volunteers with scientists working on a particular project. Recent expeditions in Mexico have included excavations of megafauna in San Miguel de Allende, investigations into pre- and post-Conquest religious architecture in the Yucatán, and a survey of carnivores in the tropical dry forests of Jalisco. Fascinating though this work is, it's not a cheap way to see the country: volunteers must raise around $1000–1500 for each two-week stint as a contribution to the cost of research. For more information:

Earthwatch HQ, 680 Mt Auburn St, PO Box 403, Watertown, MA 02272-9924, USA (☎617/926-8200).

Earthwatch California, Altos Center, Suite F2, 360 S San Antonio Rd, Los Altos, CA 94022, USA (☎415/917-8186).

Earthwatch Europe, Belsyre Court, 57 Woodstock Rd, Oxford OX2 6HU, UK (☎01865/311600).

Earthwatch Australia, 453–457 Elizabeth St, Melbourne 3000, Australia (☎03/600 9100).

US STUDY PROGRAMMES

American Institute for Foreign Study, 102 Greenwich Ave, Greenwich, CT 06830 (☎1-800/727-2437).
Language study and cultural immersion for the summer or school year.

Beaver College Center for Education Abroad, 450 S Easton Rd, Glenside, PA 19038 (☎1-800/755-5607).
Study programmes in Mexico.

Elderhostel, 75 Federal St, Boston, MA 02110 (☎617/426-8056).
See "Contacts For Senior Travellers" p.51.

Global Exchange, 2017 Mission St, #303, San Francisco, CA 94103 (☎415/255-7296).
Educational/research trips.

Institute of International Education, 809 UN Plaza, New York, NY 10017 (☎212/984-5413).
Publishes an annual study-abroad directory.

School for International Training, Kipling Rd. PO Box 676, Brattleboro, VT 05302 (☎802/257-7751).
Accredited college semesters abroad, comprising language and cultural studies, homestay and other academic work.

Unipub, 4611-F Assembly Dr, Lanham, MD 20706 (☎1-800/274-4888; in Canada: ☎1-800/233-0504).
Distributes UNESCO's encyclopedic Study Abroad.

OPENING HOURS AND HOLIDAYS

It's almost impossible to generalize about opening hours in Mexico, for even when times are posted at museums, tourist offices and shops, they're not necessarily strictly adhered to.

The **siesta**, though, is still around, and many places will close for a couple of hours in the early afternoon, usually from 1 to 3pm. The strictness of this is very much dependent on the climate; where it's hot – especially on the Gulf Coast and in the Yucatán – everything may close for up to

four hours in the middle of the day, and then reopen until 8 or 9pm. In the industrial north and highland areas, hours may be the standard nine-to-five.

Museums and galleries, in the most general terms, will be open from about 9am to 1pm and again from 3 to 6pm. Many have reduced entry fees – or are free – on Sunday, but may open only in the morning, and most are closed on Monday. **Archeological sites** are usually open right through the day.

PUBLIC HOLIDAYS

The main **public holidays**, when virtually everything will be closed, are:

Jan 1 New Year's Day
Feb 5 Anniversary of the Constitution
Feb 24 Flag Day
March 21 Benito Juárez Day
Good Friday and Easter Saturday
May 1 Labor Day
May 5 Battle of Puebla

Sept 1 Presidential address to the nation
Sept 16 Independence Day
Oct 12 Dia de la Raza/Columbus Day
Nov 1/2 All Saints/Day of the Dead
Nov 20 Anniversary of the Revolution
Dec 12 Virgin of Guadalupe
Dec 24–26 Christmas

In addition, many places close on **Jan 6** (Twelfth Night/*Reyes*).

Shops tend to keep fairly long hours, say from 9am to 8pm, though again many will close for a couple of hours in the middle of the day. Main **post offices** are open Mon–Fri 9am–6pm, Sat 9am–noon. **Banks** generally open Mon–Fri 9am–1.30pm.

FIESTAS AND ENTERTAINMENT

Stumbling, perhaps accidentally, onto some Mexican village fiesta may prove to be the highlight of your travels. Everywhere, from the remotest Indian village to the most sophisticated city suburb, will take at least one day off annually to devote to partying. Usually it's the local saint's day, but many fiestas have pre-Christian origins and any excuse – from harvest celebrations to the coming of the rains – will do.

Traditional dances and music form an essential part of almost every fiesta, and most include a procession behind some revered holy image or a more celebratory secular parade with fireworks. But the only rule is that no two will be quite the same. The most famous, spectacular or curious are listed at the end of each chapter of this guide, but there are many others and certain times of year are fiesta time almost everywhere.

Carnival, the week before Lent, is celebrated throughout the Roman Catholic world, and is at its most exuberant in Latin America. It is the last week of taking one's pleasures before the forty-day abstinence of Lent, which lasts until Easter. Like Easter, its date is not fixed, but it generally falls in February or early March. Carnival is celebrated with costumes, parades, eating and dancing, most spectacularly in Veracruz and Mazatlán, and works its way up to a climax on the last day, Mardi Gras or Shrove Tuesday, when the only thing the inhabitants of certain other countries can manage is to toss the odd pancake.

The country's biggest holiday, however, is **Semana Santa** – Holy Week – beginning on Palm Sunday and continuing until the following Sunday, which is Easter Day. Still a deeply religious festival in Mexico, it celebrates the resurrection of Christ, and has also become an occasion to venerate the Virgin Mary, with processions bearing her image a hallmark of the celebrations. During *Semana Santa*, expect transport communications to be totally disrupted as virtually the whole country is on the move, visiting family and returning from the big city to their village of origin: you will need to plan ahead if travelling then. Many places close for the whole of Holy Week, and certainly from Thursday to Sunday.

Secular **Independence Day** (Sept 16) is in some ways more solemn than the religious festivals with their exuberant fervour. While Easter and Carnival are popular festivals, this one is more official, marking the historic day in 1810 when Manuel Hidalgo y Costilla issued the *Grito* (Cry of Independence) from his parish church in Dolores, now Dolores Hidalgo, Guanajuato, which is still the centre of commemoration today. You'll also find the day marked in the capital with mass recitation of the *Grito* in the zócalo, followed by fireworks, music and dancing.

The **Day of the Dead** is All Saints or All Souls' Day and its eve (Nov 1–2), when offerings are made to ancestors' souls, frequently with picnics and all-night vigils on their graves. People build shrines in their homes to honour their departed relatives, but it's the cemeteries to head for if you want to see the really spectacular stuff. Sweetmeats and papier-mâché statues of dressed up skeletons give the whole proceedings rather a gothic air.

Christmas is a major holiday, and again a time when people are on the move and transport booked solid for weeks ahead. Gringo influence nowadays is heavy, with Santa Claus and Christmas trees, but the Mexican festival remains distinct in many ways, with a much stronger religious element (virtually every home has a nativity crib). **New Year** is still largely an occasion to spend with family, the actual hour being celebrated with the eating of grapes. Presents are traditionally given on **Twelfth Night** or Epiphany (Jan 6), which is when the three Magi of the bible arrived bearing gifts – though things are shifting into line with Yankee custom, and more and more people are exchanging gifts on December 25. One of the more bizarre Christmas events takes place at Oaxaca, where there is a public display of nativity cribs and other sculptures made of **radishes**. . .

DANCE

The **dances**, complicated and full of ancient symbolism, are often a fiesta's most extraordinary feature. Many of the most famous – including the Yaqui Indian stag dance and the dance of *Los Viejitos* (the little old men) – can be seen in sanitized form at **Ballet Folklórico** performances in México or on tour in the provinces. Many states, too, have regular shows put on by regional *folklórico* companies, and many *indigenos* help make ends meet by putting on their people's traditional dances for tourists. The spectacular *Voladores* flying dance of the Totonacs of Veracruz state, for example, is performed regularly at Papantla and the nearby archeological sites.

But you should try at least once to see dance in its authentic state, performed by enthusiastic amateurs at a village celebration. Some of the most impressive are the plant and animal **Las Varitas** and **Zacamson** dances of the Huastecs in the southeastern corner of San Luis Potosí state, performed for the festivals of San Miguel Arcángel (Sept 28–29) and Virgen de Guadalupe (Dec 12). Information is available from tourist offices. Less indigenous are the **Moros y Cristianos** dances celebrating the victories of the Christian *reconquista* over the Muslim Moors in thirteenth- to fifteenth-century Spain, and widely performed in Mexico to this day. Of more recent origin, the masked dance held on **Mardi Gras** in Huejotzingo, northwest of Puebla, re-enacts nineteenth-century battles between Mexicans and the French troops of Emperor Maximilian.

SPORT

You'll find facilities for golf, tennis, sailing, surfing, scuba diving and deep-sea fishing – even riding and hunting – provided at all the big resorts. Sport **fishing**, especially, is enormously popular in Baja California and the big Pacific coast resorts, while freshwater bass fishing is growing in popularity too, especially behind the large dams in the north of the country. The gentler arts of **diving** and snorkelling are big around the Caribbean, with world-famous dive sites at Cozumel and on the reefs further south. The Pacific coast is becoming something of a centre for **surfing**, with few facilities as yet (though you can rent surfboards in major tourist centres such as Acapulco and Mazatlán) but plenty of Californian surfies who follow the weather south over the winter. The most popular places are in Baja California and on the Oaxaca coast, but the biggest waves are to be found around Lázaro Cárdenas in Michoacán (where, however, local people are not known for their enthusiasm for surfers). A more minority-interest sport for which Mexico has become a major centre is **caving**. With a third of the country built on limestone, there are caverns in most states that can be explored by experienced cavers, potholers or spelunkers.

The Ministry of Tourism publishes a leaflet on participatory sport in Mexico, and can also advise on such things as licences and seasons.

SPECTATOR SPORTS

Mexico's chief spectator sport is **soccer** (*futbol*). Mexican teams have not been notably successful on the international stage, but going to a game can still be a thrilling experience, with vast crowds for the big ones. The capital and Guadalajara are the best places to see a match, with the derby between the two cities a major event in the footballing year. **Baseball** (*beisbol*) is also popular, as is American football (especially on TV). **Jai-alai** (better known as *frontón*, or *pelota*) is Basque handball, common in big cities and played at very high speed with a curved scoop attached to the hand. Points are scored by whacking the ball hard and fast against the end wall, as in squash, but the real scores are made in odds and pesos, since this, for spectators at least, is largely a gambler's sport.

Mexican **rodeos** (*charreadas*), mainly seen in the north of the country, are as spectacular for their style and costume as they are for the events, while **bullfights** remain an obsession: every city has a bullring – México's Plaza México is the world's largest – and the country's *toreros* are said to be the world's most reckless, much in demand in Spain. Another popular bloodsport, usually at village level, is **cockfighting**, still legal in Mexico and mainly attended for the opportunity to bet on the outcome.

Masked wrestling is very popular in Mexico, too, with the participants, Batman-like, out of the game for good should their mask be removed and their secret identity revealed. Nor does the resemblance to comic-book superheroes end with the cape and mask: certain wrestlers, most famously the capital's **Superbarrio**, have become popular social campaigners out of the ring, always ready to turn up just in the nick of time to rescue the beleaguered poor from eviction by avaricious landlords, or persecution by corrupt politicians. For more on wrestling, see p.295.

CRAFTS, MARKETS AND SHOPS

The craft tradition of Mexico, much of it descended directly from arts practised long before the Spanish arrived, is still extremely powerful. Regional and highly localized specialities survive, with villages throughout the republic jealously guarding their reputations – especially in the state of Michoacán and throughout Oaxaca, Chiapas and the Yucatán. There's a considerable amount of Guatemalan stuff about too.

CRAFTS

To buy crafts, there is no need these days to visit the place of origin – craft shops in México and all the big resorts gather the best and most popular items from around the country. On the other hand, it's a great deal more enjoyable to see where the articles come from, and certainly the only way to get any real bargains. The good stuff is rarely cheap wherever you buy it, however, and there is an enormous amount of dross produced specifically for tourists.

FONART shops, which you'll come across in major centres throughout Mexico, are run by a government agency devoted to the promotion and preservation of crafts – their wares are always excellent, if expensive, and the shops should always be visited to get an idea of what is potentially available. Where no such store exists, you can get a similar idea by looking at the best of the tourist shops.

Among the most popular items are: **silver**, the best of which is wrought in Taxco, although

rarely mined there; **pottery**, almost everywhere, with different techniques, designs and patterns in each region; **woollen goods**, especially blankets and *sarapes* from Oaxaca, which are again made everywhere – always check the fibres and go for more expensive natural dyes; **leather**, especially tyre-tread-soled *huaraches* (sandals), sold cheaply wherever you go; **glass** from Jalisco; **lacquerware**, particularly from Uruapán; and **hammocks**, the best of which are sold in Mérida.

A rather limited selection of English-language **books** are sold in all tourist areas and often in major or university bookshops. Branches of *Sanborn's* can always be relied on to carry a good stock. A number of books on Mexican culture and history are available in English, notably the *Panorama* series on history, archeology and art, and the *Minutiae Mexicana* series on wildlife, art and customs. For a rundown on Mexican literature and books about the country, see p.589 in *Contexts*.

Two more recent developments are the markets in pre-Hispanic antiquities and fake **designer labels**. There's no reason why you shouldn't buy a *Gucci* handbag or *Lacoste* shirt in Mexico, as long as you're aware it's unlikely to be the real thing. **Antiquities**, though, should be looked at more carefully: invariably they prove to be worthless fakes, but should you stumble on anything authentic it is illegal to buy or sell it, and even more illegal to try taking it out of the country.

MARKETS

For bargain hunters, the **mercado** (market) is the place to head. There's one in every Mexican town, which on one day of the week, the traditional market day, will be at its busiest with villagers from the surrounding area bringing their produce for sale or barter. By and large, of course, mercados are mainly dedicated to food and everyday necessities, but most have a section devoted to crafts, and in larger towns you may find a separate crafts bazaar.

Unless you're completely hopeless at bargaining, prices will always be lower in the market than in shops, but **shops** do have a couple of advantages. Firstly, they exercise a degree of quality control, whereas any old junk can be sold in the market; and secondly, many established shops will be able to ship purchases home for you, which saves an enormous amount of the frustrating bureaucracy you'll encounter if you attempt to do it yourself.

Bargaining and haggling are very much a matter of personal style, highly dependent on your command of Spanish and to some extent on experience. The old chestnuts (never show the least sign of interest, let alone enthusiasm; walking away will always cut the price dramatically) do still hold true; but most important is to know what you want, its approximate value, and how much you are prepared to pay. Never start to haggle for something you definitely don't intend to buy – it'll end in bad feelings on both sides. In shops there's little chance of significantly altering the official price unless you're buying in bulk, and even in markets most food and simple household goods have a set price (though it may be doubled at the sight of an approaching gringo).

CRIME AND SAFETY

Despite soaring crime rates and dismal-sounding statistics, you are unlikely to run into trouble in Mexico as long as you stick to the trodden paths. Even in México, which has an appalling reputation, there is little more threat than there would be in an average North American or European city. Obviously there are areas of the cities where you wander alone, or at night, at your peril; but the precautions to be taken are mostly common sense and would be second nature at home. Travelling in the Zapatista-controlled areas of the state of Chiapas you will undoubtedly come across guerrillas and the army, but tourists are a target of neither and there should be no trouble.

AVOIDING THEFT

Petty **theft** and **pickpockets** are your biggest worry, so don't wave money around, try not to look too obviously affluent, don't leave cash or cameras in hotel rooms, and do deposit your valuables in your hotel's safe if it has one. Crowds, especially on public city transport, are obvious hotspots: thieves tend to work in groups and target tourists. Distracting your attention, especially by pretending to look for something (always be suspicious of anyone who appears to be searching for something near you), or having one or two people pin you while another goes through your pockets, are common ploys, and can be done faster and more easily than you might imagine. Razoring of bags and pockets is another gambit, as is grabbing of handbags, or anything left unattended even for a split second. When carrying your valuables, keep them out of sight under your clothes. If you are held up, however, don't try any heroics: hand over your money and rely on travellers' cheque refund schemes and credit card hotlines if appropriate. **Mugging** is less common, but you should steer clear of obvious danger spots, such as deserted pedestrian underpasses in big cities – indeed, steer clear of *anywhere* deserted in big cities. At night the beaches in tourist areas are also potentially dangerous.

When **travelling**, keep an eye on your bags (which are safe enough in the luggage compartments underneath most buses). Trains, especially second-class, are a frequent scene of theft. The most dangerous time is when the train stops at a station, since thieves will board and, with luck, have your gear away unnoticed until the train is again on the move. Beware of deliberate distractions. If all the lights suddenly go off at night for no apparent reason, that is also a danger signal.

Drivers are likely to encounter problems if they leave anything in their car. The vehicle itself is less likely to be stolen than broken into for the things inside. To avoid the worst, always park legally (and preferably off the street) and never leave anything visible inside the car. Driving itself can be hazardous, too, especially at night (see p.33).

POLICE

Mexican **police** are, in the ordinary run of events, no better nor worse than any other; but they are very badly paid, and graft has become an accepted part of the job. This is often difficult for foreign visitors to accept, but it is a system, and in its own way it works well enough. If a policeman accuses you of some violation (and this is almost bound to happen to drivers at some stage), explain that you're a tourist, not used to the ways of the country – you may get off scot-free, but more likely the subject of a "fine" will come up. Such on-the-spot fines are open to negotiation, but only if you're confident you've done nothing seriously wrong and have a reasonable command of Spanish. Otherwise pay up and get out.

In the event of trouble, dial ☎06 for the **Police emergency** operator. Most phone booths give the number for the local **Red Cross** (*Cruz Roja*).

These small **bribes** are known as *mordidas* ("little bites"), and they may also be extracted by border officials or bureaucrats (in which case, you *could* get out of paying by asking for a receipt, but it won't make life easier). In general, it is always wise to back off from any sort of confrontation with the police and to be extremely polite to them at all times.

Far more common than the *mordida* is the **propina**, or tip, a payment that is made entirely on your initiative. There's no need to do this, but it's remarkable how often a few pesos can oil the wheels, complete paperwork that would otherwise take weeks, open doors that were firmly locked before, or even, in other situations, find a seat on a previously full bus. All such transactions are quite open, and it's up to you to literally put your money on the table.

Should a crime be committed against you – in particular **if you're robbed** – your relationship with the police will obviously be different, although even in this eventuality it's worth considering whether the lengthy hassles you'll go through make it worth reporting. Some insurance companies will insist on a police report if you're to get any refund (see p.27) – in which case you may practically have to dictate it to the officer and can expect little action – but others will understand the situation. *American Express* in México, for example, may accept without a murmur the fact that your cheques have been stolen but the theft was not reported to the police. The department you need in order to *presentar una denuncia* (report the theft officially) is the Procuraduría General de Justicia.

The Mexican **legal system** is based on the Napoleonic code, which assumes your guilt until you can prove otherwise. Your one phone call should you be jailed should be to your consulate – if nothing else, they'll arrange an English-speaking lawyer. You can be held for up to 72 hours on suspicion before charges have to be brought. Mexican **jails** are grim, although lots of money and friends on the outside can ameliorate matters slightly.

DRUGS

Drug offences are the most common cause of serious trouble between tourists and the authorities. Under heavy pressure from the US to stamp out the trade, Mexican authorities are particularly happy to throw the book at foreign offenders.

A good deal of **marijuana** (known as *mota*) – that famous Acapulco Gold, as well as weed from the Yucatán, Oaxaca and, more locally renowned, Michoacán – continues to be cultivated in Mexico, despite US-backed government attempts to stamp it out (at one time, imports of Mexican marijuana were having such a deleterious effect on the US trade balance that the DEA had crops sprayed with paraquat). Cannabis is **illegal**, and foreigners caught in possession are dealt with harshly; for quantities reckoned to be dealable you can wave goodbye to daylight for a long time, but even for possession of small quantities, unless you are nifty with the *mordidas*, you can expect a lengthy jail sentence, no sympathy and little help from your consulate.

Other naturally occurring drugs – Mexico has more species of psychoactive plants than anywhere else in the world – still form an important part of many Indian rituals. Hallucinogenic **mushrooms** can be found in many parts of the country, especially in the states of Oaxaca and in Chiapas, while the **peyote** cactus from the northern deserts is used primarily by the Huichols, but also by other indigenous peoples. It is theoretically illegal, but the authorities turn a blind eye to native use, and even tourists are unlikely to get into much difficulty over personal use (though raids on guesthouses in *peyote* country have been known).

Heroin has never been a serious problem inside Mexico, but **cocaine** is a different story, with the country a major staging post on the smuggling route from Colombia to the US, and well-connected gangs involved in the trade, especially in Guadalajara. Use of cocaine, even crack, is becoming as serious a problem here as it is all over the Caribbean. Best advice as far as this unpleasant trade goes is to steer well clear.

DIRECTORY

ADDRESSES In Mexico addresses are frequently written with just the street name and number (thus: Madero 125), which can lead to confusion as many streets are known only as numbers (c/ 17). *Calle* (c/) means Street; *Avenida*, *Calzada* and *Paseo* are other common terms – most are named after historical figures or dates. An address such as Hidalgo 39 8° 120, means Hidalgo no. 39, 8th floor, room 120 (a ground-floor address would be denoted PB for *Planta Baja*). Many towns have all their streets laid out in a numbered grid fanning out from a central point – often with odd numbered streets running east–west, even ones north–south. In such places a suffix – Ote. (for *Oriente*, East), Pte. (for *Poniente*, West), Nte. (for *Norte*, North), or Sur (South) – may be added to the street number to tell you which side of the two central dividing streets it is.

AIRPORT TAX A departure tax is payable when flying out of Mexico (the equivalent of US$16). This is included in the price of most air tickets, but be sure to check when buying.

BEGGARS When you consider that there's no social security worth mentioning and that most Mexicans are very generous towards them, beggars are surprisingly rare in Mexico. What you will see, though, are people selling worthless trinkets, or climbing onto buses or trains, singing a song, and passing the hat.

ELECTRICITY Theoretically 110 volts AC, with simple two-flat-pin rectangular plugs, so most North American appliances can be used as they are. Travellers from the UK, Ireland, Australasia and Europe should bring along a transformer and a plug adapter. Cuts in service and fluctuations in the current do occur, and in cheap hotels any sort of appliance that draws a lot of current may blow all the fuses as soon as it's turned on.

FILM AND CAMERA EQUIPMENT Film is manufactured in Mexico and, if you buy it from a chain store like *Woolworth's* or *Sanborn's* rather than at a tourist store costs no more than at home (if you buy it elsewhere, be sure to check the date on the box, and be suspicious if you can't see it). Up to twelve rolls of film can be brought into Mexico, and spare batteries are also a wise precaution. Any sort of camera hardware, though, will be prohibitively expensive.

TIME ZONES Three time zones exist in Mexico. Most of the country is on GMT−6 year-round. In winter, this is the same as US Central Standard Time, but an hour behind when the US and Canada are on Daylight Saving. Baja California Sur and the northwest coastal states of Sonora, Sinaloa and Nayarit are on GMT−7, the same as Mountain Standard Time in the winter, an hour

behind it in summer. Confusingly, Baja California Norte *does* observe Daylight Saving Time, making it GMT−7 in summer and GMT−8 in winter, so you won't need to change your watch if crossing the border from California at any time of year.

In principle then, most of Mexico is six hours behind the British Isles, 14 hours behind western Australia, 16 behind eastern Australia, and 18 behind New Zealand, but summer time in those places will add an hour to the difference, as will travel into the northwestern states mentioned above.

TOILETS Public toilets in Mexico are almost always filthy, and there's never any paper (though someone may sell it outside). They're known usually as *baños* (literally bathrooms) or as *excusados, sanitarios* or *servicios*. The most common signs are *Damas* (Ladies) and *Caballeros* (Gentlemen), though you may find the more confusing *Señoras* (Women) and *Señores* (Men). Always carry some toilet paper with you: it's easy enough to buy in Mexico, but it's never there when you need it.

Poor Mexico – so far from God, so close to the United States.
– Mexican proverb

PART TWO

THE

GUIDE

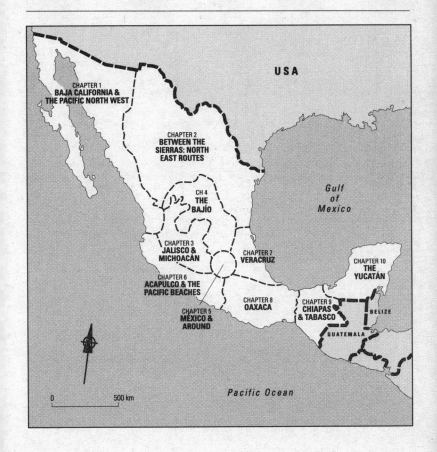

USA

CHAPTER 1
**BAJA CALIFORNIA &
THE PACIFIC NORTH WEST**

CHAPTER 2
**BETWEEN THE
SIERRAS: NORTH
EAST ROUTES**

CH 4
**THE
BAJÍO**

*Gulf
of
Mexico*

CHAPTER 3
**JALISCO &
MICHOACÁN**

CHAPTER 7
VERACRUZ

CHAPTER 10
**THE
YUCATÁN**

CHAPTER 6
**ACAPULCO & THE
PACIFIC BEACHES**

CHAPTER 8
OAXACA

CHAPTER 9
**CHIAPAS
& TABASCO**

BELIZE

CHAPTER 5
**MÉXICO &
AROUND**

GUATEMALA

0   500 km

Pacific Ocean

CHAPTER ONE

BAJA CALIFORNIA AND
THE PACIFIC NORTHWEST

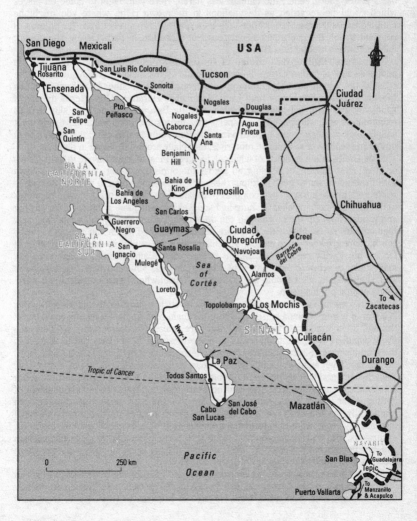

Mexico's northwest is something of a bizarre – and initially uninviting – introduction to the country. Aspects of what you see here will be echoed constantly as you travel further south, yet in many ways it's resolutely atypical: at once desert and the country's most fertile agricultural area, wealthy and heavily Americanized, yet drab and apparently barren. Nor is the climate exactly welcoming – although the ocean and local conditions help produce one or two milder spots, summer temperatures can hit 50°C, while winter nights in the desert are often really chilly.

Travelling overland from west coast USA you're clearly going to come this way, but on the whole the best advice is to hurry through the northern part at least: once you've crossed the invisible line of the Tropic of Cancer there's a tangible change – the country is softer and greener, the climate less harsh. Here you begin to come on places which could be regarded as destinations in their own right, where you might be tempted to stay some time, rather than as a night or two's relief from the rigours of constant travel: the enormous all-out resort of **Mazatlán** in particular, or the quieter Pacific beaches around **San Blas**.

There's a straightforward **choice of routes**: down from Tijuana through the Baja peninsula and on by ferry from La Paz; or around by the mainland road, sticking to the coast all the way or possibly cutting up into central Mexico, either by railway from Los Mochis to Chihuahua, or by road from Mazatlán to Durango. The latter is quicker if your only aim is to get towards México, but the Baja route is perhaps slightly less monotonous and, surprisingly, cheaper – the ferries are good value if you go as a simple deck passenger. If you're **driving**, the Baja route is also safer: there have been numerous reports of assaults on motorists, especially around Culiacán in Sinaloa.

Baja California has plenty of fanatical devotees, most of whom arrive in light planes or in vehicles capable of heading off across the punishing desert tracks, laden down with fishing and scuba gear. Without these, it's impossible to get to most of the peninsula's undeniable attractions – completely isolated beaches, prehistoric cave paintings in the hilly interior, excellent fishing and snorkelling, and some great spots for surfing and windsurfing. On the bus all you can do is pound down Hwy-1, still a relatively new road and low on facilities. Still, there are beautiful beaches which you can get to in the south, more crowded ones around Tijuana in the north, and if you're heading straight for the big Pacific resorts – Mazatlán, Puerto Vallarta and on towards Acapulco – it makes a lot of sense to come this way. Early in the year you can witness extraordinary scenes at Scammon's Lagoon, near Guerrero Negro, when hordes of **whales** congregate just offshore to spawn.

On the **mainland route**, too, most people stick rigidly to the highway – over 2000km of it from Tijuana to Tepic, where the main road finally leaves the coast to cut through the mountains to Guadalajara. But here at least you're not forced to; it's a relatively populous area, and from towns all along the route local buses run to villages in the foothills of the Sierra Madre or down to beaches along the Sea of Cortés and, later, the Pacific. Then again you can leave the coast entirely, heading inland by road or rail over the mountains. On the whole though, the equation is simple: the further south you travel, the more enticing the land becomes. For the first stages it's a question of getting as far in one go as you can stand: try to make it as far as Guaymas, or even Alamos. By the time you reach Mazatlán the pace becomes more relaxed and you'll increasingly come on things to detain you: village fiestas, tropical beaches, mountain excursions. **Beyond Tepic** you're faced with the choice of following the mainstream and heading inland towards the central highlands, or sticking to the coast, where there's a good road all the way to Acapulco and beyond.

As everywhere, **buses** are the most efficient and fastest form of transport: they run the entire length of the coast road, and from Nogales or Tijuana to México, frequently down through Baja. The **train**, from Nogales or Mexicali to Guadalajara, is perhaps

---

BORDER CHECKS

Crossing the border, do not forget to go through **immigration and customs** checks. As everywhere, there's a free zone south of the frontier, and you can cross at will. Try to continue south, though, and you'll be stopped after some 20km and sent back to get your tourist card stamped. You can drive throughout Baja without special papers but if you're planning to continue on the ferries across to the mainland you need to get the formalities dealt with at the border: attempting to rectify your error in La Paz or Santa Rosalía is fraught with difficulties.

---

more comfortable if you're making the journey non-stop. There are also a number of **flights** taking advantage of deregulated airspace to link the major towns all the way down the coast. Flights **to México** can be especially competitive. Even on less used and therefore more expensive routes, an hour-long flight can be a tempting alternative to a ride of ten hours or more: from Tijuana to La Paz or Culiacán, for example.

If you're **driving**, it's very much quicker to go via Nogales. Even if you're coming from Mexico's west coast, you'll save considerably by taking US highways via Tucson. Heading down through Baja you could be delayed for a day or two trying to get your car onto a ferry – book ahead if at all possible. **Hitching** should be regarded here only as a last resort: long-distance traffic moves fast and is reluctant to stop, and it's exceedingly hot if you get stranded by the roadside. The north is also the area where most of the "disappearing gringo" horror stories originate.

TIJUANA AND THE BAJA PENINSULA

The early Spanish colonists believed Baja California to be an island and, after failing to find any great riches or to make much impact in converting the Indians, they left it pretty much alone. There's little of historic interest beyond a few old mission centres, and almost all you see dates from the latter half of this century, in particular since Hwy-1 was opened in 1973. Development has continued apace: in the south new resorts are springing up all the time, while what in the early nineteenth century was simply Aunt Joanna's ranch (*El Rancho de Tia Juana*) became the border in 1848 and has not looked back since: **Tijuana** now ranks as Mexico's fourth city. Prohibition in the US was the biggest individual spur, but the city has never been slow to exploit its neighbour's desires, whether they be for sex, gambling or cheap labour.

Tijuana

TIJUANA is *the* Mexican border town – with every virtue and vice that this implies. Over 36 million people cross the border every year – the vast majority of them staying only a few hours – so it can boast with some justification of being the "World's Most Visited City". Which is not to say it's somewhere you should plan to hang around; but if you want to stop off before starting the long trek south, Tijuana is certainly the most practical choice. There's no shortage of reasonable hotels although, as you'd expect, most things are far more expensive than they are further south.

Above all the town is geared towards dealing with hordes of day-trippers, which means hundreds of tacky souvenir stands, cheap doctors, dentists and auto-repair shops, and countless bars and restaurants, pricey by Mexican standards but cheaper

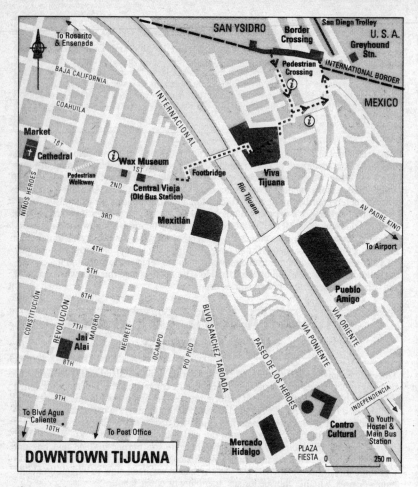

DOWNTOWN TIJUANA

than anything you'll find in San Diego. One thing you won't find much of any more – at least not anywhere near the centre of town – is the prostitution and the sex shows for which the border towns used to be notorious. This is partly the result of a conscious attempt to clean the city up, partly due to the changing climate in the US: indeed in many places, though not visibly here, the traffic now runs in the other direction with vast billboards on the American side of the border offering lurid invitations to "Total nudity – 24 hours a day". Tijuana does still thrive on **gambling** though, with greyhound racing every evening; jai alai from 8pm every night except Wednesday in the huge downtown *Frontón Palacio*; and **bullfights** throughout the summer (May–Sept) at two rings, one right on the coast, the other a couple of kilometres southeast of the centre. At the off-track betting lounges all around Tijuana you can place money on just about anything that moves and monitor progress on the banks of closed-circuit TVs.

The parts of the city most tourists don't see fit less easily into expectations. **Modern Tijuana** is among the wealthiest cities in the Mexican republic, buoyed up by the region's duty-free status and by *maquiladora* assembly plants (raw or semi-assembled materials are brought across the border duty-free, assembled by cheap Mexican labour, and re-exported with duty levied only on the added value). How the NAFTA treaty affects this remains to be seen, but chances are it means further boom times for Tijuana's industrial zone. Downtown – though beyond the areas where most tourists venture – the modern concrete and glass wouldn't look amiss in southern California. The flip side of the boom lies along the border, where shantytowns sprawl for miles: housing for the labourers and also more traditionally the final staging point for the bid to disappear north.

Arrival

As in so many places in Mexico, Tijuana's **long-distance bus station** is miles from the centre; almost thirty minutes on the local bus. These blue-and-white buses (look for "Central Camionera") run through the centre on 2nd and pass the border on the way to the terminal; take them in preference to taxis, which, quite legally, charge extortionate fares. **Taxis** to other points in Tijuana are not so bad, provided the meter is working, but you'll still save a lot by finding out which bus to take. The **airport** is slightly closer in than the bus station and frequent buses run from there into town.

The border

If you have the right documentation, crossing the border (known as *la Linea*, the Line) is normally a breeze, though you may have to wait in line, and US immigration can be pretty intimidating if you're entering the US. Heading into Mexico, the main worry is to remember to have your tourist card stamped at *Migración* – people only visiting Tijuana, Ensenada and San Felipe don't need to do this. The border is open 24 hours a day.

On the US side, **San Ysidro**, there's excellent local transport into downtown **San Diego** – buses ($1.50) and trams (the "San Diego Trolley"; 5am–1pm & hourly through Sat night; $1.75) run every few minutes – and plenty of alternatives if you're heading further north. Vans and minibuses, as well as *Greyhound* and other services, run almost constantly to **Los Angeles**; the *Greyhound* terminal is right by the border. San Ysidro itself, at least around the border, has little to offer: there's *McDonalds* and *Burger King*, a few second-hand clothes stores, money exchange places and motor insurance offices, and a number of car parks charging $3–7 a day. There are also a few motels – closest to the border are the *Gateway Inn* (☎619/428-2251; ⑥) and *Holiday Lodge* (☎619/428-1105; ⑤).

On the **Mexican side** it's only a short walk downtown – through the *Viva Tijuana* shopping mall, over the footbridge, and along 1st to Revolución. Alternatively you can get downtown (look for "Centro" or "Revolución") or to the bus station (blue-and-white bus marked "Buena Vista/Central Camionera") from the public bus and taxi terminal right by the entrance to *Viva Tijuana*.

It's also possible to **cross the border by bus**, though it usually costs more and sometimes takes longer than walking over and picking up transport the other side. For example, *Mexicoach* (Revolución and 7th) and *Transportes Diamante* (Revolución just below 1st) both run shuttles to San Ysidro ($1); *Mexicoach* also operates a shuttle service between the border and Revolución.

Information

Tijuana has three very helpful **tourist offices**. The first two are right at the frontier: one office for pedestrians, another for drivers (insurance available) – well worth stopping at to pick up a free map and a few leaflets. There's another branch right in the centre of downtown at Revolución and 1st (daily 9am–7pm; ☎66/88-16-85), while on the opposite corner you'll find the **Tourism Protection Office** (daily 9am–7pm; ☎66/85-05-55). This is the office to head for if you become a victim of crime, a rip-off, or simply want to make a complaint (with so many tourists, Tijuana feels safe enough, but there's plenty of petty crime; they might also have some maps and general information).

Changing money should be no problem either, with *casas de cambio* on virtually every corner. Most offer good rates – almost identical to those north of the border – though few of them accept travellers' cheques, and if they do, charge a heavy commission. For cheques you're better off with a **bank**, most of which are on Constitución, a block over from Revolución. There's also an **American Express** office in *Viajes Carrusel* (Mon–Fri 9am–6pm, Sat 9am–noon) way out on Sanchez Taboada at Clemente Orozco, but the rates are poor. Dollars are accepted almost everywhere anyway – again the rates are usually fair, but always check.

The **post office** is at Negrete and 11th (Mon–Fri 8am–7pm, Sat & Sun 9.30am–1pm), though to send international mail or make long-distance **phone** calls, you're better off crossing the border.

Accommodation

By comparison with the rest of Mexico, **accommodation** in Tijuana is overpriced and low-quality, but at least there's plenty of choice. Watch out for noise and security if you're staying in the centre. None of the budget places along 1st heading west from Revolución is recommended – particularly not for lone women – as most of your fellow guests will only be staying for an hour or less. The more expensive hotels, mostly further out, are better value, but there's little point staying at these unless you're here on business.

Inconveniently sited (about 30–40min walk from the centre), the **youth hostel**, off Av. Padre Kino by Cuauhtémoc Bridge (☎66/84-75-10; members $5, non-members $7), has small soulless dorms; but at least it's cheap and clean. Buses from the Central Camionera pass close by.

Caesar, Revolución 1079 at 5th (☎66/88-05-50). Classy old place with uniformed staff. The restaurant claims to have invented the Caesar salad. Has seen better days, but surprisingly good value. ⑤.

Catalina, 5th at Madero (☎66/85-97-48). Old but modernized hotel with clean, spacious en suite rooms. ④.

Geni, Revolución 417, below 1st. Basic, but acceptable and relatively cheap. ④.

Grand Hotel Tijuana, Agua Caliente 4500 (☎66/81-70-00). 23-storey twin towers mark Tijuana's fanciest hotel. ⑨.

Lucerna, Paseo de los Heroes at Rodríguez (☎66/34-20-00). Closer in and slightly more characterful than most of the pricey hotels. Pool. ⑦.

Motel Diaz, Revolución 650, below 1st (☎66/85-71-48). Unit-style motel, worth the money if you need parking. *Motel Alaska*, opposite, is similar but bigger. ④.

Nelson, Revolución 721 at 1st (☎66/85-43-02). Pleasant, old-fashioned, respectable hotel in ideal, though noisy, location. Colour TV and cable. ④–⑤.

ACCOMMODATION PRICES

All the accommodation listed in this book has been categorized into one of nine price bands, as set out below. The prices quoted are in US dollars and normally refer to the cheapest available room for two people sharing in high season. For more details see p.37.

① less than $8	④ $18–25	⑦ $50–75
② $8–12	⑤ $25–35	⑧ $75–100
③ $12–18	⑥ $35–50	⑨ more than $100

Plaza de Oro, Revolución 588, below 1st (☎66/38-41-12). Comfortable, modern place with cable TV but little character. ⑤.
St Francis, 2nd between Revolución and Madero (☎66/85-49-03). Clean and old-fashioned. ④.
Villa de Zaragoza, Madero 1480 at 7th (☎66/85-18-32). Modern, upmarket, US-style motel. ⑥.

Downtown Tijuana

If you're here to shop, drink and shake your stuff, you won't need to wander far off the few blocks of Avenida Revolución between 1st and about 8th streets. Here there's an uninterrupted stream of bars, dance clubs, malls, markets and souvenir stalls, and more or less permanent crowds. If you're after anything else, you're in the wrong town, though there are a few purpose-built attractions to occupy some time. Buses between the centre and the border pass the **Centro Cultural** (☎66/84-11-11, ext 301), a spectacularly threatening globe of a complex that resembles nothing so much as a huge nuclear reactor dumped in the city centre. Designed by Pedro Ramírez Vázquez – the architect responsible for México's Aztec stadium and Anthropological Museum – it is said to represent the earth breaking out of its shell. Inside, the **Cine Planetario** (Mon–Fri 3–9pm, Sat & Sun 11am–9pm; $5) hosts a multimedia spectacular on its giant Cinemax movie screen; the programme changes every six months or so. English-language films are planned. There are also regular exhibitions and shows, a restaurant, and the inevitable shopping arcade, along with a **museum** (daily 11am–8pm; $1, free with exhibition or movie), which is not at all bad as an introduction to Mexican culture and art, despite the fact that almost everything you see is a reproduction.

Lesser attractions include **Mexitlán** (mid-May to mid-Sept daily 10am–10pm; mid-Sept to mid-May Wed–Fri 10am–6pm, Sat & Sun 9am–9pm; $3), a miniature Mexican theme park with models of famous Mexican buildings, folklore performances, and more restaurants and shops, which is hard to miss as you approach town from the border; a new and very tacky **wax museum** at Madero and 1st (don't waste your money); and various modern **shopping malls**. Most of these are given over to a mix of duty-free goods and stalls selling souvenirs, fake designer clothing and jewellery – two of the biggest are *Viva Tijuana*, which you'll walk through on the way to the centre if you cross the border on foot, and *Pueblo Amigo*.

Eating

With all the crowds passing through Tijuana you might expect some great restaurants, but you'd be disappointed. On the main drag everything is aimed at tourists: Mexican restaurants US-style, almost all of them with loud music and "party" atmosphere. *Plaza Fiesta*, opposite the Centro Cultural, has a wide variety of restaurants and fast-food places; you'll find a similar, though smaller range in any of the shopping plazas.

Plainer Mexican food can be found in the surrounding streets, especially on Madero and Constitución, but despite the fact that migrants from all over Mexico bring their cuisine with them, naming their *loncheria* or *taqueria* after their home state, there's nothing very exciting even here.

Antojitos Bíbi's, in the Mercado Hidalgo. Clean and inexpensive place for simple meals all day. Handy for the Centro Cultural.

Café Français, 7th between Revolución and Constitución. Delicious pastries and a dozen types of coffees and infusions.

Café Revolución, Madero between 4th and 5th. Basic but good Mexican restaurant hung with photos depicting heroes of the Revolution.

Makko Sushi Bar, Plaza Fiesta. Tempura and sushi in spartan surroundings. Closed Sun.

Hotel Nelson, Revolución and 1st. Decent value tourist-oriented Mexican place.

Pipirin, Constitución between 2nd and 3rd. Bargain sit-down *taco* joint.

Punto Café, Plaza Fiesta. Trendy but low-key place with outside seating, magazines to flick through and good coffee.

Tía Juana Tilly's, Revolución 1420 at 7th. Slick, predictably Tex-Mex restaurant with terrace, linked to the jai alai hall. Bow-tied waiters, main courses (steaks, chicken, seafood) around $7–12.

Tortas Ricardo's, Madero at 7th. A massive range of Mexican dishes served in American diner surroundings. Open late.

Vittorio's, Revolución 1687 at 10th. Full range of well-prepared Italian dishes as well as Mexican staples. Good pizza and great espresso. Inexpensive to moderate.

Drinking and nightlife

Apart from a few exclusive **nightclubs** – which operate as restaurants during the day – out beyond the Centro Cultural, all the action in Tijuana happens close to Revolución, where numerous places pump out soft rock or dance-oriented rap. English is the lingua franca, dollars are the currency of choice, and the playlist is solidly North American. Most places are open until around 2am and have a small cover charge, but on slower weeknights this is waived and drinks are offered two for the price of one: walk along Revolución and pick the liveliest-looking joint on the night. More traditional **Mexican bars**, as well as those featuring "exotic dancers", cluster around 1st and Constitución and on Revolución at 6th.

Casa Club, 7th between Negrete and Madero. Unassuming, safe place to drink and listen to live Latin sounds.

The Cave, Revolución 1137 between 5th and 6th. Much the same as all the other tourist-oriented places but at ground level so you can see what you are letting yourself in for.

Diamante Disco, Revolución and 1st. The least intimidating of the seedy Latin bars but still not recommended for unaccompanied women.

People's Sports and Rock, Revolución 786 at 2nd. Consistently one of the better "fun" bars, with a slightly harder edge to the music. Be prepared for the bar staff moving to pour tequila down your throat in an effort to loosen the purse strings.

Las Pulgas, Revolución 1127 opposite jai alai. Modern Latin disco with a huge dance floor.

Salón de Baile, 6th between Revolución and Madero. Don't be put off by the lurid wall paintings, this is the real thing: a traditional dancehall with an almost Caribbean feel playing *salsa, cumbia* and *norteño*. Look for the big red star.

Listings

Airlines *Aeroméxico*, Revolución 1236 (☎66/85-44-05); *Aero California*, Paseo de los Heroes 95, Plaza Río Local C-20 (☎66/84-28-76); *Mexicana* at the airport (☎66/83-28-50); and *TAESA*, Paseo de los Heroes 9288-B1 (☎66/84-84-84).

Consulates *Australia/Canada*, German Gedovius 5-202, Zona Río (☎66/884-04-61); *UK*. Salinas 1500 (☎66/85-73-23); *USA*, Tapachula 96 (☎66/881-74-00).

Left luggage Bags can be left at the Central Camionera (6am–10.30pm), in lockers over the border in the *Greyhound* station (24hr), or next door at *Pro-Pack* (Mon–Sat 9am–6pm).

Rosarito

If you want to escape the pace and noise of Tijuana for a while, head for **ROSARITO**, about 45 minutes' bus ride on the old road to Ensenada. **Beaches** in Tijuana itself are invariably crowded and dirty: Rosarito, while scarcely less popular, has a far longer, sandier strand and a much more restful atmosphere. It's not particularly attractive – the beach is grey, windswept, and none too clean, lined with condo developments and hotels – but it does make for a worthwhile afternoon. You could even stay out here; the motels lining the road are better value than those in town.

MOVING ON FROM TIJUANA

Heading for **the US**, you can pick up *Greyhound* **buses** (roughly hourly 6am–6pm) as you arrive at the Central Camionera (☎66/26-17-01 for all companies) and avoid stopping in Tijuana altogether. The *Greyhound* goes on to pick up in central Tijuana from the old bus station, Central Vieja (see below), then crosses the border, stopping for passengers at San Ysidro. Slightly more expensive, *Transportes Intercalifornias* run 9 times daily from the airport, Camionera Central, the centre of town, and either side of the border to LA .

The Central Camionera handles departures for almost all **Mexican destinations**, with numerous departures to the west coast and to a lesser extent down Baja. Catch the blue-and-white buses marked "Buena Vista" or "Central Camionera". The **Central Vieja** bus station, at Madero and 1st, handles buses to Rosarito (hourly 8am–8pm).

Though they vary greatly depending on demand, **flights** to the rest of Mexico, and particularly to México (4 daily; 2hr 30min), can be surprisingly cheap from Tijuana, sometimes dropping to around $100 or much the same price as a first-class bus. Flights to other destinations are less competitive: typically $100 to Guadalajara, $135 to Acapulco, and $220 to La Paz. *Viajes La Mesa* at Madero and 1st (☎66/88-15-11) can help with bookings but it pays to shop around for the best prices; the **airport** (☎66/82-39-03) can be reached on buses marked "Aeropuerto" from Madero and 2nd.

Practicalities

To **get to** Rosarito from Tijuana, take one of the *colectivo* taxis that leave from Madero between 4th and 5th, or head for the old bus station at Madero and 1st, from where buses leave every hour or so; to get back, just flag down a bus or *colectivo* on Rosarito's main street.

Towards the southern end of the main strip, there's a **tourist office** (daily 9am–7pm; ☎661/2-02-00) tucked in behind a police compound and opposite the cheapest of the **motels**, *Villa Nueva* (no phone; ④). For somewhere slightly smarter, right on the beach with ocean views, try the *Hotel Los Pelicanos* (☎661/2-04-45; ⑤–⑦) by the large terracotta-coloured hotel block, or *Hotel California* (☎661/2-25-50; ⑤), just south of the tourist office. The style and charm that made the *Rosarito Beach Hotel* (☎661/2-01-44; ⑦) a Hollywood favourite during the prohibition years has now largely been obliterated by modern development, but the older rooms still have some character. Along the single street behind the beach is a row of restaurants, cafes and bars, some of them pretty good, in particular, the **fish restaurants** and a couple of cafes that serve decent cappuccino and cakes. The party-time focus is *Papas and Beer*, four blocks south of the tourist office, where beach volleyball and knocking back as much Corona as possible is the order of the day.

If you're **continuing south** to Ensenada and beyond, you can pick up long-distance buses (hourly or more) at the *autopista* toll booth 1km south of the tourist office, past the *Rosarito Beach Hotel*. The coast road down through Rosarito – now supplanted by the motorway to Ensenada – is an attractive drive, lined with seaside villas and condos.

Ensenada, San Felipe and the road south

ENSENADA, just a couple of hours on from Tijuana by the toll road, is favoured by sophisticated Californians "in the know" about where to go in Mexico. It's cheaper, raunchier, less totally geared to visitors, but still with a pretty clear idea of the value of the Yankee dollar. No more attractive than Tijuana, it does at least have some life of its own as a major port and fish processing centre, and at weekends it's packed with party-ing southern Californians.

Almost all the action is squeezed into a few streets around the harbour: seafront Boulevard Costero (aka Lázaro Cárdenas), Avenida Mateos (or c/1), which runs parallel, and as far inland as Avenida Juárez (c/5). Here you'll find scores of souvenir shops and outfits offering sport fishing trips, as well as most of the bars, hotels and restaurants. For most visitors, local action involves eating, drinking, shopping and little else. If you do want to explore further you could check out the view from the Chapultepec Hills, overlooking town from the west, or visit the *Bodegas de Santo Tomás* **winery**, one of Baja's largest, which offers regular tours and tastings at Miramar 666 between c/6a and 7a (tours daily 11am, 1pm & 3pm; $2; ☎617/8-33-33). Most of the wines are only passable; if it isn't offered, ask to try the white sherry.

Ensenada also attracts its share of surfers and beach boys, of course, though as you'll find throughout Baja it really pays to have your own transport. The best **beaches** are at **Estero**, some 10km to the south, off the main road. Occasional local buses run past these to perhaps the most startling attraction in the area, **La Bufadora**, a natural blow-hole or geyser, where the action of wind, waves and an incoming tide periodically forces a huge jet of sea water up through a small vent in the roof of an undersea cavern, in ideal conditions attaining 25–30m. This is more than 20km off the main road, and reached during daylight hours on yellow-and-white buses that leave roughly hourly from the Tres Cabezas park on Costero at the bottom of Riveroll.

Ensenada practicalities

The **bus station** (plus *guardería*) is at c/11 and Av. Riveroll: turn right and head down Riveroll to reach the bay – head left when you reach Mateos for the centre of town. There's a second, smaller station a couple of blocks down Riveroll between c/8 and c/9, which handles frequent services to Tijuana. The **tourist office** (daily 9am–7pm; ☎617/8-24-11) is on Costero at the corner of Gastelum, where the main road enters town.

Accommodation

If you're hoping for somewhere to **stay** at the weekend – the best time to be here, if only for the nightlife – you'd be well advised to book, or arrive early; during the week there should be no problem. Most of the hotels are on Mateos and Costero between Riveroll and Espinoza; though **rates** in general are high, the cheaper places tend to be on Mateos.

Bahía, Mateos between Riveroll and Alvarado (☎667/8-21-01). Huge, popular place with big range of rooms. ⑤.

Cortez Motor Hotel, Mateos 1089 at Castillo (☎667/8-23-07). Comfortable *Best Western* motel with pool and decent restaurant. ⑦.

Misión Santa Isabel, Castillo 1100 at Costero (☎667/8-36-16). Modern colonial-style motel, with pool and restaurant *El Campanario*. ⑦.

Motel America, Mateos at Espinoza (☎667/6-13-33). No frills, but OK. Some kitchenettes. ④.

Motel Pancho, Alvarado 211 at c/2a (☎667/8-23-44). Cheapest in town, basic but clean. ③–④.

Travelodge, Blancarte 130 at Mateos (☎667/8-16-01). Another good, central motel with pool and a pricey French-Mexican restaurant, *El Rey Sol*. ⑧.

Eating and drinking

Places to **eat and drink** are near the hotels, and there's plenty of choice. One unavoidable attraction is *Hussongs Cantina*, Ruiz 113, whose bumper stickers and T-shirts are seen throughout California; one of a cluster of places around the corner of Ruiz and Mateos, it manages to remain pretty sleazy for all its fame and popularity. Most of the other places in the vicinity seem to be owned by the Hussong empire, too, but few are as popular as the original. Exceptions include *El Charro*, Mateos 486, a good place to soak up some of the beer, with roast chicken and plain Mexican food at reasonable prices, till late, and *Las Brasas*, nearby, which is similar and also good. The bohemian *Café Café*, Mateos and Gastelum, is considerably more low-key, with backgammon and, at weekends, live folk, jazz or blues from both Californias. Thursday night is currently art-house film night.

The stalls at the **fish market**, by the harbour, sell fish tacos and other seafood at a fraction of the price of the fancy restaurants that line Costero. If you do want to sit down and don't mind missing out on the views for excellent, plain seafood, try *Mariscos Playa Azul*, Riveroll 113. *Señor Salud*, Espinoza and c/9a, is a bit of a walk, but its salads, fruit, juices and veggie dishes make a welcome change. Among the numerous **Chinese restaurants** is *China Land*, at Riveroll 1149, by the bus station.

San Felipe

With so few places in northern Baja boasting a decent beach and reasonable public transport, the prospect of **SAN FELIPE**, a growing Sea of Cortés resort on a dead-end road 200km south of Mexicali, may seem attractive. But its appeal is limited: the entire bay is strung with RV parks and the dunes between here and the encircling folded ridges of the San Pedro Martin mountains reverberate to the screaming engines of dune buggies and balloon-tyred trikes. If you are planning to continue south down Baja, then do just that. But San Felipe does have good swimming – at least at high tide – and if you are confined to the north, it's the best place to rent a catamaran or just relax for a day or so.

San Felipe first came to the attention of fishermen who, in the early 1950s, took advantage of the new tarmac road – built to serve the American radar station to the south on what is now called Punta Radar – to exploit the vast schools of tortuava, a species now fished onto the endangered list. Since the 1980s, the fishing village has grown to accommodate the November to April influx of vacationers from north of the border and college students on Spring Break. Apart from lying on the beach, you can rent **dirt bikes** and trikes from a couple of places along the malecón (around $20 an hour), **catamarans** (similar price; just ask along the beach wherever you see one), or indulge in a little **sport fishing** on tours from a couple of places at the northern end of the malecón.

If the road through the cactus desert south of here to Hwy-1 ever gets improved to the point that it can be negotiated by low clearance vehicles, this could become an interesting alternative route to southern Baja, but for the moment the hamlet of **Puertecitos**, 85km south (no public transport), is as far as ordinary cars can get – and even then with difficulty.

Practicalities

Buses from Mexicali (4 daily; 3hr) and Ensenada (2 daily; 3hr 30min) arrive 1km inland: turn left out of the bus station and right down Manzanillo to get to Av. Mar de Cortez, which runs parallel to the sea. At the junction, the **tourist office** (Mon–Fri 8am–7pm, Sat 9am–3pm, Sun 10am–1pm; ☎657/7-11-55) gives out a map of the town but little else. North from here along Cortez there's a *farmacia* where you can change money (Mon–Fri 9am–6pm) and, beyond, a *Bancomer* but no ATM. The **post office** is on Mar Blanco just off Chetumal, five blocks inland. **Hotels** in San Felipe are not particularly cheap, though there are a couple of decent reasonably priced places: *La Hacienda*, Chetumal 125 (☎657/7-15-70; ⑤), is marginally best than *Chapala Motel*, Mar de Cortez 142 (☎657/7-12-40; ⑤), but the best of all is *El Capitan Motel*, Mar de Cortez 298 (☎657/7-13-03; ⑥), with pool, TVs and a/c. **Camping** is best at the RV parks to the north of town, notably *Ruben's R.V. Trailer Park*, Golfo de California (☎657/7-10-91; $12), or you can just sleep on the beach around the bottom of Chetumal, where there are showers and toilets.

DIVING AND FISHING AROUND BAJA CALIFORNIA

Nowhere in Baja California is more than 90km from either the Pacific Ocean or the Sea of Cortés, both bodies of water that support an abundance of **sea life**. The unmatched variety of marine environments makes the Sea of Cortés in particular one of the richest seas in the world, with over 800 species of fish and more than twice as many shellfish. Throughout the peninsula you'll see RVs and off-road vehicles laden down with fishing tackle, dinghies and scuba gear, headed for remote fish camps or sheltered bays to launch the dive boat. Opportunities for less well-prepared visitors are limited but the bigger towns, particularly around **Cabo San Lucas** and **San José del Cabo**, are seething with operators eager to take you out.

The most popular **diving** areas in the north are **Islas Los Coronados**, off Tijuana but only served by organized trips from San Diego north of the border; and **Punta Banda** and **Islas de Todos Santos**, off Ensenada. In the south, where the waters are a good deal warmer and the fish dramatically colourful, the best spots are the coast off **Santa Rosalía**, **Bahía de Concepción** south of Mulegé, **La Paz** and **Los Cabos**. The ideal combination of water clarity and warmth occurs from August to November. There are a number of regulations governing sport fishing in Mexico; check with a tourist office for a rundown.

Not surprisingly, **seafood** is the staple diet here, with numerous stands selling shellfish cocktails and several restaurants along the front. Head for *The Bearded Clam* at the northern end of the beachfront malecón, or *The Red Lobster* at *La Hacienda* hotel.

On to the 28th parallel

Beyond Ensenada you're heading into Baja California proper – barren and god-forsaken. At times the road runs along the coast, but for the most part the scenery is dry brown desert, with the peninsula's low mountain spine to the left and nothing but sand and the occasional scrubby cactus around the road. The towns are generally drab, dusty and windswept collections of single-storey shacks which belie their supposed wealth. At **SANTO TOMÁS**, 45km from Ensenada, the *El Palomar* motel (☎667/8-23-55; ⑥), with pool, trailer park and restaurant, makes a good place to break the journey; the town itself is known for its wine and a deserted Dominican mission. If you can get off the highway, the attractions of the desert and its extraordinary vegetation become clearer. Sixty-five kilometres past Santo Tomás, just beyond Colonet, a road turns inland towards the **Parque Nacional San Pedro Martír**. The side road, unsurfaced but in good condition, winds almost 100km up into the Sierra, which includes Baja's highest peaks at over 3000m – snowy in winter. As you climb, the land becomes increasingly green and wooded, and at the end of the road astronomical observatories take advantage of the piercingly clear air. There are breathtaking views in every direction. Numerous ill-defined trails wind through the park, but again, there's no public transport and you need to be fully equipped for wilderness camping.

San Quintín

SAN QUINTÍN is the first town of any size south of Ensenada, and even here, though there are a couple of big hotels, most of the buildings look temporary. **Bahía San Quintín**, however, is undeniably attractive, with five cinder-cone volcanoes as a back-drop to a series of small sandy beaches, and endless fishing (though not without a permit) and superb clamming that draw campers and RV drivers. The closest of the beaches are some 5km from the highway and there's no transport to reach them.

Buses from Ensenada stop at **Lázaro Cárdenas**, 5km south of town. If you want to **stay**, the *Hotel La Pinta* (☎667/6-26-01; ⑦) is the luxury option, right on the beach 3km off the highway, some 8km south of Lázaro Cárdenas. More realistic alternatives include *Cielito Lindo* (⑥), close to *La Pinta* and *Molino Viejo* (⑤–⑥) – from where fishing trips can be organized – on the bay; or one of the motels in town: *Las Hadas* (③) or *Romo* (☎667/5-23-96; ③), which also has a decent **restaurant**. There are also plenty of camping spots around the bay if you come equipped, and RV sites at the *Molino Viejo*.

El Rosario and Cataviña

Some 60km beyond San Quintín, the highway passes through **EL ROSARIO**, the original site of a Dominican mission. Founded in 1774, the mission was forced by a shortage of water in 1802 to move downstream 3km to **El Rosario de Abajo**, where you can see the ruins: nowadays, however, it's little more than a BMX track for the local kids, and definitely not worth getting off the bus for. These days, El Rosario is just another staging point, and modern El Rosario de Arriba consists of just a couple of filling stations and a few restaurants and **motels**. *El Rosario* (③), as you come into town, is good value, if rather noisy, with trucks roaring down the hill throughout the night, while the *Motel Sinai* (☎616/5-88-18; ⑤), at the southern edge, is quieter and more expensive. There's a rather rocky beach 12km south at Punta Baja.

Beyond El Rosario, the road turns sharply inland, to run down the heart of the peninsula for some 350km to Guerrero Negro. It's a bizarre landscape of cactus – particularly yucca, *cirios*, unique to this area, and *cardones*, which can grow over 15m tall – and rock, with plenty of strange giant formations; much of it is protected in the **Parque Natural del Desierto Central de Baja California**. In the heart of this area is **CATAVIÑA**, a dozen or so buildings strung along the highway, complete with luxury hotel *La Pinta* (⑨), trailer park and restaurants. There's cheaper accommodation at *Rancho Santa Ines*, a couple of kilometres south (③), which offers dorm beds and cold showers. If you do stop, take time to look at some of the giant boulders; not far off the highway at Km 171, just before Cataviña, is **La Cueva Pintada**, a tiny cave beneath a huge rock decorated with ancient paintings – circles, dots, sunbursts and stick figures.

Bahía de los Angeles

The turn-off for **BAHÍA DE LOS ANGELES**, a growing resort on the Sea of Cortés, is about 110km farther on. Still a small place, some 70km off Hwy-1, Bahía has a sheltered bay full of marine life hemmed in by contorted mountains. There's little else but a few hotels, cafes and fishing boats; many visitors arrive here by light plane. While here, visit the small bilingual **museum** (daily 9am–noon & 3–5pm; free) marked by a narrow-gauge locomotive, a relic of the gold and copper mines that first attracted Europeans to the area. Mining history and that of the local *ranchero* life is well covered, along with details of sea life in the bay. The **Isla Angel de la Guarda**, out in the bay, is the biggest island in the Sea of Cortés and the destination of numerous diving and fishing trips. There are no official rental places for **scuba**, **snorkelling** or **fishing gear**, but the hotels can organize things and you should be able to strike a deal by asking around.

There's a frontier feeling in Bahía: the **weekly bus** is met by people eager for their only mail delivery, and the town has just one communal phone (☎665/0-32-06). The **bus**, which at the time of writing was still in new and poorly patronized service, leaves Ensenada on Saturday at 8am, arriving in Bahía nine hours later; the return bus to Ensenada leaves on Sunday at 4pm and will drop you an hour later at Punta Prieta on Hwy-1, in time for you to pick up a southbound bus before dark.

Of Bahía's three **hotels**, the fanciest is *Villa Vitta* (from USA: ☎619/741-9583; ⑥), which has a pool; *Casa Diaz* (from USA: ☎619/278-9676; ⑤) and *Las Hamacas* (⑤) are slightly less so. *Guillermo's Trailer Park* and *La Playa RV Park* both have **camping**, and are seldom packed; for free camping, walk to the beaches to the south. You can eat at any of these places, but for location the restaurant at *Guillermo's* has the edge.

Guerrero Negro: watching the whales

Continuing on the main highway, there's little between Cataviña and the 28th parallel, where an enormous metal monument, and a hotel, mark the border of Baja California Norte and **Baja California Sur**; you'll have to put your watch forward an hour when you cross, unless Baja California Norte is on Daylight Saving Time (April–Oct), in which case there's no change. **GUERRERO NEGRO**, just across the border, offers little in the way of respite from the heat and aridity that has gone before. Flat and fly-blown, it's an important centre for salt production, surrounded by vast salt pans and stark storage warehouses. At most times of year you'll want to do no more than grab a drink and pass straight through. In January and February, though, Guerrero Negro is home to one of Mexico's most extraordinary natural phenomena, when scores of **California gray whales** congregate to spawn just off the coast.

The whales, which spend most of their lives in the icy Bering Sea around Alaska, can be watched (at remarkably close quarters; the young are sometimes left stranded on the beaches) from an area within the **Parque Natural de la Ballena Gris**, which surrounds the Laguna Ojo de Liebre. The laguna is also known as **Scammon's Lagoon** after the whaling captain Charles Melville Scammon, who first brought the huge potential of the bay to the attention of rapacious whalers in 1857 – the town itself gets its name from the *Black Warrior*, an overladen whaling barque that sank here a year later.

At the right times of the year (Jan and Feb above all, but there may be whales from Dec until May) there are **organized trips**, and an observation tower that guarantees at least a distant sighting. You'll need to check locally to find out exactly what the current situation is with tours and **boat trips**, however, as every year there's talk of restricting numbers or banning boats altogether. If you can take one, then do so – it's an exceptional experience, and many visitors actually get to touch the whales, which often come right up to the vessels as they float in the lagoon, engines stopped. Whale-watching trips are mainly run from *Don Miguelito's* and *Mario's* (see below): both charge around $30 per person for a four-hour trip, including all costs and a drink or two.

To get to the shore **with your own vehicle** (it needs to be sturdy), head south from town until you see the park sign; from here a poor sand track leads 24km down to the lagoon. Midway there's a **checkpoint** where you must register your vehicle and its occupants, and at the park entrance a **fee** of around $3 is charged. To see the whales **from the shore** you'll need to get up early or stay late, as they move out to the deeper water in the middle of the day.

Practicalities

If you want to **stay** in Guerrero Negro, you can choose from numerous hotels and motels strung out along the main drag. Perhaps the best is the *Motel Cabañas Don Miguelito* (☎685/7-02-50; ④), to the right as you enter town, with clean rooms with TV, RV spaces, and a good seafood restaurant. Further into town, the *Motel Las Dunas* (☎685/7-00-55; ③) is simple and friendly, as is *Las Ballenas* (☎685/7-01-16; ③), up a side road next to *Mario's* (see below); the *Hotel San Ignacio* (☎685/7-02-70; ⑤) is probably not worth the extra. You can also **camp** on nearby beaches for free – it's usually allowed even inside the Parque Natural, though you need your own transport to get there.

There are plenty of **restaurants** along the main street, though only a few ever seem to be open at any one time. *Malarrimo*, next to *Don Miguelito's*, has good seafood and is another place to check about whale-watching trips; *El Asadero Norteño* serves meaty northern specialities; *Mario's*, next to the *Motel El Morro*, is good for breakfast and the basics; while *El Taco Feliz* dishes up delicious seafood snacks. You can also buy your own fresh produce from the small **market**.

Buses from Guerrero Negro's bus station, near the hotels, are irregular. The five services (one local) which head north to Tijuana, and the one to Mexicali, leave at night or early morning; southbound services – five, one local, running all the way to La Paz – depart either early in the morning or in the late afternoon and evening.

San Ignacio and cave paintings

Leaving Guerrero Negro, the highway heads inland again for the hottest, driest stage of the journey, across the Desierto Vizcaíno. In the midst of this landscape, **SAN IGNACIO** comes as an extraordinary relief. At the very centre of the peninsula, this is an oasis in every sense of the word; not only green and shaded but, with some of the few colonial buildings in Baja, a genuinely attractive little town. The settlement was founded by the Jesuits (and named after their founder) in 1728, but the area had always been populated by Guaicura Indians, attracted by the tiny stream, the only fresh water for hundreds of miles. San Ignacio's **church**, built when the place was first settled, is probably the best example of colonial architecture in the whole of Baja California, and there are other ancient buildings around it and the shaded plaza. Early missionaries were responsible too for the palms which give the town its special character, and as well as dates, the town also produces limes, grapes and olives.

In the bleak sierras to the north and south are any number of **caves**, many of them decorated with **ancient paintings**. Not much is known about the provenance of these amazing designs, beyond the fact that they were painted at different periods and bear little resemblance to any other known art in this part of the world. Indian legend, as related to the earliest colonists, has it that they are the product of a race of giants from the north. Certainly many of the human figures – most paintings depict hunters and their prey – are well over 2m tall. They are, however, extremely hard to visit, reached only by tracks or mule paths and almost impossible to find without a guide. If you're determined, join one of the **tours** arranged from the hotels in town, though these can be pricey. At the beginning of the year, the same guides also offer **whale-watching** trips to the nearby **Laguna San Ignacio**, which some say is a better location even than Guerrero Negro.

Practicalities

The centre of San Ignacio lies almost 3km off the main highway where all the **buses** stop. Upon arrival you may be lucky enough to pick up a taxi, otherwise it's a thirty-minute walk through the palms. Along the way you pass a number of places you could **free camp**, worth considering since there are no budget **hotels**: *La Posada Motel* at Carranza 22 (☎685/4-00-13; ⑤), southeast of the zócalo, is the cheapest, *La Pinta* (☎667/6-26-01; ⑦) the luxury alternative. Some of the **trailer parks** along the highway and on the road into town have camping space; the most useful, *El Padrino*, almost opposite *La Pinta*, charges $3–4 per person. Of the many **places to eat** around the central plaza, *Restaurant Chalita* is a traditional Mexican choice, *Tota's* somewhat more Americanized. Other facilities in town don't stretch beyond the one **bank** (Mon–Fri 8.30–11am).

Santa Rosalía

The highway emerges on the east coast at **SANTA ROSALÍA**, terminal for the ferry to Guaymas (see p.98). An odd little place, wedged in the narrow valley of the Arroyo de Santa Rosalía, the town was built as a port to ship copper from the nearby French-run mines of the El Boleo company. Nowadays the mines are virtually played out and the smelters stand idle, though much of the paraphernalia still lies around town, including parts of a rusting narrow-gauge railway. Currently there is a plan to employ modern techniques to extract the last of the ore from the five million tonnes of tailings, which will provide a much needed financial boost to a community that struggles by on revenue from fishing and the plaster mines on the Isla de San Marcos to the south.

The town itself has something of a temporary look, many of its buildings strikingly un-Mexican in aspect. The workers' houses in the valley resemble those in the Caribbean, with low angled roofs over hibiscus-flanked porches, while grander colonial residences for the managers rim the hill to the north. Look out especially for the church on Obregón, a prefabricated iron structure designed by Eiffel and exhibited in Paris before it was shipped here.

Practicalities

Highway-One runs along the coast, passing between Santa Rosalía's harbour and Parque Morelos. Five streets – avenidas Obregón, Constitución, Carranza, Sarabia and Montoya – run perpendicular to the coast, crossing the numbered calles.

Santa Rosalía's **bus station** lies ten minutes' walk south of Parque Morelos, just beyond the ferry terminal. All buses are *de paso*: northbound call in the very early morning, while those heading south stop mostly in the late morning and late evening. **Ferries** leave twice a week (Wed & Sun at 8am) for the seven-hour trip to Guaymas. Tickets – which cost $14 for a reclining seat, twice that for a four-berth cabin, nothing for a bike and $105 for a small car – go on sale at the terminal from 6am on the day of departure, but check times and reserve in advance (☎685/2-00-13), or buy your ticket

---

SANTA ROSALÍA'S COPPER MINES – A LITTLE HISTORY AND A WALK

While walking in the hills in 1868, one José Villavicencio chanced upon a **boleo**, a blue-green globule of rock that proved to be just a taster of a mineral vein containing more than 20 percent copper. By 1880 the wealth of the small-scale mining concessions came to the notice of the **Rothschilds**, who provided finance for the French El Boleo company to buy the rights and found a massive extraction and smelting operation. Six hundred kilometres of tunnels were dug, a foundry was shipped out from Europe, and a new wharf was built to transport the smelted ore to Washington state for refining. Ships returned with lumber for the construction of a **new town**, laid out with houses built to a standard commensurate with their occupier's status within the company. Water was piped from the Santa Agueda oasis 15km away and labour was brought in: Yaqui Indians from Sonora as well as two thousand Chinese and Japanese who, finding that Baja was too arid to grow rice, soon headed off to the Mexican mainland. By 1954 falling profits from the nearly spent mines forced the French to sell the mines and smelter to the Mexican government who, though the mines were left idle, continued to smelt ore from the mainland. By the early 1990s this too had stopped.

If you fancy a **short desert walk**, pick a cool part of the day and make a circuit of what remains of the mining equipment and the tunnels that riddle the hills to the north. None of the mines is fenced, so take a torch and explore cautiously. Following c/Altamirano from Eiffel's church, you reach the massive kilometre-long above-ground duct, built of furnace slag, which once conveyed fumes from the smelter to the hilltop stack. You can walk along the top of it to the chimney for a superb view of the town and surrounding desert. From here, choose one of the numerous paths which head away inland to a series of gaping maws in the hillside. Either return the same way, pick your way straight down to the town or, with enough time, continue among the low cactus on the mesa, working your way down to the top end of Santa Rosalía.

from a travel agent, as the timetable may change. Car drivers should ensure that their papers are in order for the mainland (see "Border Checks" on p.67).

After the resorts to the north, it comes as some relief to find that Santa Rosalía has some good-value **hotels**. The budget option is the faded but friendly *Playa* on c/1 (②), though you may prefer to pay a little more to stay at the popular *Blanco y Negro* (☎685/ 2-00-80; ③), just off the southwest corner of Plaza Juárez four blocks in from the waterfront. The *Olvera* (☎685/2-00-57; ③), and the *Hotel del Real* (☎685/2-00-68; ④) are both on Parque Morelos; the latter is really just as good as the new, upmarket *Minas de Santa Rosalía* (☎658/2-10-60; ⑤) on Constitución at 10th. It may be worth asking if the beautiful colonial *Hotel Francés*, on the hill to the north of town, is running again: it operates sporadically but was closed at the time of writing. The *El Morro* (☎685/2-04-14; ⑤), on the highway a short way south of town, offers more comfort, with sea views, pool and restaurant, and a good beach nearby.

Sadly, no French **restaurants** remain as a reminder of the town's beginnings, but the *Panaderia El Boleo* produces some of the best baked goods in these parts, even if the baguettes aren't as crisp as the real thing. Restaurants in general aren't up to very much, though you can eat well enough at the expensive *Turco's Pollito*, Obregón at c/ Playa (between c/2 and c/3), and dine on good seafood at *El Cachano* on Constitución at 5th. Several cheaper places are scattered along Obregón, and a van on 4th between Constitución and Obregón sells great fish and seafood *tacos*.

The **banks** are both on Constitución: *Bancomer* changes cheques until noon, *Banamex* accepts only bills until 1pm. The **post office** is on Constitución at c/2 and there's a **phone** outside the *Hotel del Real*.

Mulegé and around

Some 60km to the south lies **MULEGÉ** ("Moo-leh-HAY"), a small village on the site of an ancient mission. Like San Ignacio it's a real oasis, and there's a definite feel of the tropics, too: a laid-back atmosphere helped by some superb beaches strung out along the coast to the south. Yet again you'll miss out on the best of them without some means of getting about, but here hitching is at least a realistic possibility (many visitors commute to the beaches daily, particularly during the high season from mid-Oct to April).

Other than as a springboard for the beaches to the south, the main reason to stop here is to take one of the **tours to the cave paintings** out in the Sierra de Guadalupe. This range boasts the densest collection of rock art in Baja, as well as some of the most accessible, requiring as little as five hours. Getting a group together to cut costs shouldn't prove a problem in high season, but you still need to shop around as the tours differ considerably. Salvador Castro at the *Las Casitas* hotel usually runs trips on Wednesday and Saturday, requiring a minimum of eight people, whereas Kerry Otterstrom, usually found at *El Candil*, runs more adventurous trips to order for as few as four people. Expect to pay $12–15 each.

Snorkelling and diving trips in Bahía Concepción (see below) are also available from Mulegé at *Mulegé Divers*, Madero 45 (Mon–Sat; ☎685/3-01-34). A beginner's resort course costs $60, a snorkelling trip $25.

Bahía Concepción

There's good diving and fishing immediately around Mulegé, but the best beaches are laid out along the shore of **Bahía Concepción**, between 10km and 50km south. The better stretches of sand include **Playa Punta Arena**, some 16km down the highway followed by 2km on a dirt road, where there are some basic *palapa* shelters to rent. **Playa Santispac**, some 5km further on, is right on the highway and easy to get to – despite the early stages of development and occasional crowds of RVs, it still has plenty of room to camp (for a fee) and enough life to make staying here longer-term a realistic option. *Baja Tropicales* at *palapa* 17 organizes good-value kayaking and snorkelling trips. Further south there are fewer facilities for anything other than self-sufficient camping: **Playa El Requesón** is one of the last and best opportunities for this, though with no fresh water.

Mulegé practicalities

From the **bus stop** it's a ten-minute walk into Mulegé: follow the side road, take the right fork onto Martinez then second right onto Zaragoza and the plaza. Bus travellers may have difficulty getting out of the place – for details of timetables, ask at the small cafe with the "ABC" sign near the bus stop. You have to hope there's room on one of the *de paso* services on the highway, as none originate here. Heading south there are no afternoon buses, all services currently passing between 9pm and noon; northbound buses mostly pass in the afternoon or very early morning.

If you want to **stay** in Mulegé, you've a choice of cheap and very basic *casas de huéspedes* or relatively upmarket hotels. The *Hacienda* (☎685/3-02-21; ⑤), on Madero just off the plaza, is the pick of the latter, with a small pool, though *Las Casitas*, Madero 50 (☎685/3-00-19; ⑤), the former home of Mexican poet José Gorosave, is almost as good. There's also the bright new *Motel Siesta* (☎685/3-05-55; ⑤), on the road in from the bus stop, and *Rosita* (no phone; ④), which has kitchenettes but no pans. Budget alternatives include the *Casa de Huéspedes Nachita* (☎685/3-01-40; ②) and the slightly more comfortable *Manuelita* (☎685/3-01-75; ②), both on Moctezuma, the left fork as you head into Mulegé from the highway, and, slightly better, *Canett* (☎685/3-02-72; ②), on Madero beyond the church. **Campers** should head 1km south of the bus stop (or along the dirt road on the south side of the river from Mulegé) to *Huerta Saucedo RV Park* – also called *The Orchard* (☎685/3-03-00) – where two can pitch a tent for $6 and guests can rent canoes on the Mulegé river.

Eating and drinking options are as polarized as the accommodation. The majority of the North American long-stayers and a good many Mexicans gravitate towards the decent but pricey restaurant and bar at *Las Casitas* or the less formal and slightly cheaper *El Candil* on the plaza. To eat less expensively you are limited to *taco* stands and *El Pollo Salvaje*, just south of the plaza, or a slice of pizza at *Donna Moe's* next to *El Candil*. *Las Casitas* also acts as an informal tourist office for information on other local attractions.

Mulegé has no banks, only a **casa de cambio** with poor rates (daily 9am–1pm & 3–7pm) on the road in, and a small **post office** with a long-distance phone outside on Martinez.

Loreto

LORETO, the next town down the coast, is a far bigger place, on the site of the earliest permanent settlement in the Californias. Founded in 1697 as the head of the Jesuit missions to California, and later taken over by the Franciscans, it was in practice the administrative capital of the entire territory for some 150 years until a devastating earthquake struck in 1829. More recently it has been a popular escape for fishing and scuba enthusiasts, and nowadays it's enjoying something of a renaissance, boosted by the development of southern Baja California as a whole. A super-resort along the lines of Cancún was planned some 10km south of town – an airport laid out, roads and electricity put in – but for a long time things went no further as priorities were switched elsewhere. As of now there's the *Stouffer Presidente* hotel, a tennis centre and the beginnings of construction on further stages, but mostly **Nopoló** (as the result will be known) seems deserted. The main upshot seems to be that downtown Loreto itself has been spruced up in expectation, and that prices have risen accordingly. There is, however, the tidy, if impersonal malecón, Boulevard Lopez Mateos, backing the tolerable **town beach**, and, with transport, you can reach some more great stretches of sand a few miles to the south – good camping territory too.

The original **mission church** is still standing and, though heavily restored after centuries of earthquake damage, its basic structure – solid, squat and simple – is little changed. The inscription over the door, which translates as "The head and mother church of the missions of upper and lower California" attests to its former importance, as does the Baroque altarpiece originally transported here from México. Next door a small **museum** (Wed–Fri 9am–1pm & 1.30–4pm, Sat & Sun 8am–2pm; $3) chronicles the early conversion and colonization of California.

From Loreto's **bus station** it's a fifteen-minute walk east along Salvatierra to the mission church and central plaza, and a further five minutes in the same direction to the beach. Along the way you pass the best of the town's budget **hotels**, *Motel Salvatierra* (☎113/5-00-21; ④), better value than *Casa de Huéspedes San Martín* (☎113/5-04-42; ③) on Juárez, two blocks north of the plaza. The other hotels are relatively expensive, but not bad value for what you get, catering as they do mainly for diving buffs and people who know the area well. If you can afford it, make for the beachfront *Oasis* (☎113/5-02-11; ⑧ full board), three blocks south of the plaza, which has a pool and all the trappings. Otherwise the most pleasant is the colonial-style *Misión de Loreto* (☎113/5-00-48; ⑥), Lopez Mateos 1 on the waterfront east of the plaza. **Campers** should head towards the beaches north of town for a free spot, or walk 1km south along Madero to *Villas de Loreto* (☎113/5-05-86; $10 for two camping; rooms ⑤), which has a pool and rents out windsurfers, kayaks and bicycles.

Finding simple Mexican **food** is no problem at *taco* stands along Salvatierra or at fancier places around the plaza, notably *Café Olé*, which does good-value breakfasts and *antojitos*. *Embarcadero* on the waterfront turns out tasty seafood, or try the cinnamon rolls and excellent, if pricey, pizza at *Tiffany's Pisa Parlour* on Hidalgo south of the plaza. The **post office** and a **Bancomer**, which changes cheques until noon, can be found on the plaza.

From Loreto five buses head north daily (all in the afternoon and early evening) and another handful run south (8am–midnight) to La Paz, five long hours away. If you're confined to the main road there's really nothing to detain you. **Puerto Escondido**, on the coast just before the highway turns west inland, is another spot slated for upmarket development, but for the moment, at least, offers just a shop, a restaurant, and the opportunity to camp on the beach. **Ciudad Constitución**, about halfway to La Paz, is a large, modern town with plenty of facilities but nothing else to stop for.

La Paz

Everyone ends up in **LA PAZ** eventually, if only to get the ferry out, and it seems that most of the population of Baja California Sur is gravitating here too. The outskirts are an ugly sprawl, their development outpacing the spread of paved roads and facilities. But the town centre, modernized as it is, has still managed to preserve something of its quiet colonial atmosphere and small-town pace. Down by the sea you can stroll along the waterfront malecón, and for once the beach in town looks inviting enough to swim from – though there are no guarantees on the cleanliness of the water.

The Bay of La Paz was explored by **Cortés** himself in the first years after the Conquest – drawn, as always, by tales of great wealth – but he found little to interest him and, despite successive expeditions, at first merely rapacious, later missionary, La Paz wasn't permanently settled until the end of the eighteenth century. It grew rapidly,

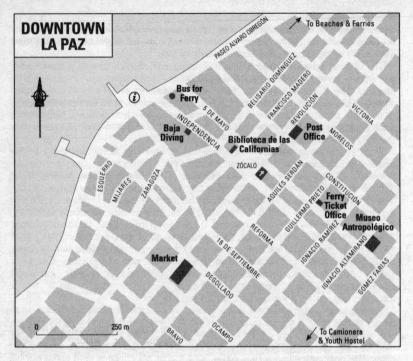

however, thanks to the riches of the surrounding sea, and above all as a pearl fishing centre. American troops occupied the town during the Texan war, and six years later it was again invaded, by William Walker in one of his many attempts to carve himself out a Central American kingdom; by this time it was already capital of the territory of California. The pearl trade has pretty much dried up – a mystery disease wiped out most of the oysters – but since the 1960s La Paz has continued to boom, buoyed up by tourists at first flown in, then boosted by the growing ferry service, and now supplemented by the hordes pouring down Hwy-1.

Arrival

If you arrive in La Paz by bus you'll be stuck at a **bus station** about 5km out in the suburbs at Jalisco and Independencia. Long-distance services often arrive in the middle of the night and you may have no choice but to walk into town, but this is not recommended. During the day you might be lucky enough to pick up one of the irregular buses ("Centro/Camionera"); a taxi should cost around $3. **Ferry** passengers arriving at Pichilingue (see below) are better off – there should be buses to town, and also *colectivo* taxis. From the airport, 12km south, there's a fixed-rate taxi service.

The most useful **tourist office** (Mon–Fri 8am–8pm; ☎112/2-59-39) is in the centre, on the waterfront at 16 de Septiembre, though there is another with the same hours and information on the highway as you enter town. Apart from the **post office** at the corner of Revolución and Constitución, all the facilities, including numerous **banks** and the **American Express** office (Mon–Fri 9am–2pm & 4–6pm, Sat 9am–2pm; ☎112/ 2-83-00) at Esquerro 1679 behind *Hotel Perla*, lie between the zócalo and the waterfront.

Accommodation

Most of the inexpensive **hotels**, where rooms are good value by Baja standards, are within a few blocks of the zócalo; some of the older fancier places are downtown too, but the newer ones tend to be out along the coast. The **youth hostel**, on Forjades (☎112/2-46-15; $6), has inexpensive, impersonal dorms, inconvenient for town but fairly close to the bus station; turn right up Jalisco, left along Isabel La Catolica, taking the right fork when it splits, then next right and right again, perhaps 1km in all. The nearest **campsite** is *El Cardón Trailer Park* (☎112/2-12-61), about 2km out on the road north.

Cabañas Los Arcos, Paseo Obregón 498 (☎112/2-27-44). Popular fishing centre on the bay. Older *cabañas* have more character than newer hotel rooms: both a/c, with pool and all other facilities. ⑧.

Hosteria del Convento, Madero Sur 85 (☎112/2-35-08). Uncannily similar to *Pension California* though less frequented by backpackers. On the site of a former convent. ③.

Miramar, 5 de Mayo and Domínguez (☎112/2-88-85). Good deal if you get a sea view: comfortable a/c rooms with TV. ⑤.

Pension California, Degollado between Madero and Revolución (☎112/2-28-96). Wonderful old building with courtyard and assorted artworks. The plain rooms all have bath and fan. Communal kitchen and laundry. ③.

Perla, Paseo Obregón 1570 at La Paz (☎112/2-07-77). Once *the* place to stay and still a good deal, with a/c, pool and restaurant. ⑤.

Posada San Miguel, Belisario Domínguez, off 16 de Septiembre (☎112/2-18-02). Simple, courtyard rooms in a colonial-style villa. Good value. ③.

San Carlos, Revolución and 16 de Septiembre (☎112/2-04-44). Plain hotel with bare rooms. ②–③.

Yeneka, Madero, near the zócalo (☎112/5-46-88). Eccentric decor but comfortable; with cafe. ④.

The Town

There's not a great deal to see in La Paz and if you're staying for any length of time you should head for the beaches. If you're just hanging around waiting for a ferry, however, you can happily fill a day window-shopping in the centre – hundreds of stores take advantage of the duty-free zone – and browsing around the market. The small **Museo Antropológico** (Mon–Fri 8am–6pm, Sat 8am–2pm; free) at 5 de Mayo and Altamirano is also worth a passing look: exhibits include reproductions of cave paintings and an ethnological history of the peninsula. This is as good as Baja museums get but has no labelling English. More information on all aspects of Baja, some of it English-language, is available in the *Biblioteca de las Californias*, opposite the cathedral on the zócalo.

Beaches ring the bay all around La Paz, but the easiest to get to are undoubtedly those to the south, served by the local bus that runs along Obregón to the ferry terminal at Pichilingue. Perhaps the best of the beaches are **Playa del Tesoro**, shortly before Pichilingue, and **Playa Pichilingue**, a walk of fifteen minutes or so beyond the end of the bus route. Both have simple facilities, including a restaurant. There are plenty of opportunities for fishing and diving, and for boat trips into the bay; just stroll along the malecón to find people offering the latter – the **Isla Espíritu Santo** is a popular destination. *Baja Diving and Service*, 1076 Independencia, just north of Domingúez (☎112/2-18-26), offers good **diving** and snorkelling tours and courses. Reasonably priced kayak trips along the coast and out to the islands, ranging from half a day to overnight, are run by *Kayak Tours* (☎112/5-46-88) who operate from the *Yeneka* hotel.

Eating and drinking

Wandering round La Paz you'll come on dozens of places to **eat** – the seafood, above all, is excellent. There are numerous inexpensive local restaurants near the market, especially on Serdán and 16 de Septiembre.

Bismark II, Altamirano and Degollado. Excellent seafood without having to pay inflated seafront prices.

Café Chante, on the waterfront behind the tourist office. La Paz's attempt at a bohemian cafe. Reasonable cakes and coffee but the TV ruins the ambience.

El Camaron Feliz, opposite *Los Arcos* on the waterfront (☎112/2-90-11). An attractive place to dine on seafood, the location justifying the price.

Pizza La Fabula, Obregón at Independencia and other locations in town. Popular local pizza chain.

El Quinto Sol, Independencia and Belisario Domínguez. Vegetarian and wholefood shop and cafe; juices and *tortas* too.

La Terraza, Obregón 1570 at La Paz. Cafe/restaurant under the *Hotel Perla*. Popular but pricey, spot to watch the world go by.

Moving on from La Paz

La Paz **bus station** (☎112/2-64-76) is also the southern terminus for the peninsula **buses**. Nine regular daily services head north, four of which (currently 10am, 4pm, 8pm & 10pm) go as far as Tijuana, 22 hours away. Buses leave roughly hourly (6am–7pm) for Cabo San Lucas and San José del Cabo; some are routed via Todos Santos, others take the eastern route direct to San José.

Flights leave from the airport, 8km southwest from town (expensive taxis only). For flight details contact *Viajes Perla* travel agency, on the corner of 5 de Mayo and Domingues (Mon–Sat 8.30am–7.30pm, Sun 9am–2pm; ☎112/2-86-66).

THE FERRY FROM LA PAZ

If you're planning to take the **ferry** across the Sea of Cortés to **Mazatlán** or **Topolobampo** (the port for Los Mochis), you should buy tickets as soon as possible: space for cars and cabins – either *Turista* (4 bunks), *Cabina* (2 bunks) or *Especial* (suite) – are often oversubscribed. There's rarely any problem going *Salón* class (entitling you to a reclining seat), for which tickets are only available a day in advance. On balance, for most people, *Salón* is the best option, as the cabins can be freezing if the a/c works and stiflingly hot if not. Sleeping out on deck is best of all.

Departures for the 18hr run to Mazatlán leave daily at 3pm, except Saturday during the off season (the Wed sailing has *Salón* class only); those for the 9–10hr sailing to Topolobampo leave daily except Tues at 8pm.

You can make **reservations** at the downtown ticket office of the operating company, *SEMATUR*, 5 de Mayo and Prieto (Mon–Fri 7am–1pm & 4–6pm, Sat & Sun 8am–1pm; arrive early and be prepared to wait in line; ☎112/5-38-33); direct at the terminal (☎112/2-94-85) or through local travel agents. The **cost** of tickets, which can be paid for with *Visa* and *Mastercard*, ranges from $13 to $135 according to class and destination; bicycles are free.

Before buying tickets, car drivers should ensure they have a **permit to drive** on the mainland. This should have been obtained when crossing the border into Mexico, but if not you may have some joy by taking your vehicle and all relevant papers along to the customs office at the ferry terminal a couple of days before you sail. If for some reason you've managed to get this far without having your **tourist card** stamped, you should also attend to that before sailing – there's an immigration office on c/Muelle, just off the waterfront downtown.

To **get to the ferry** itself, which sails from the terminal at Pichilingue, some 14km away, go to the old bus station on the malecón – straight down Independencia from the zócalo – and, again, get there early. There is only one bus an hour (8am–6pm; $1.30) and you need to leave time for the interminable customs and immigration checks before departure. According to signs at the terminal, it is illegal to take your own food on board, but since the catering is so poor everyone does and nobody seems to mind

Los Cabos

Almost everything beyond La Paz is purpose-built. **LOS CABOS**, the series of capes and beaches around the southern tip of the Baja peninsula, is one of the fastest developing tourist areas in Mexico – heavily promoted by the authorities and a boom area for the big hotel chains and resort builders. Undeniably stunningly beautiful, it's not a place for the penniless traveller to venture unprepared. Not far south of La Paz the highway splits: the fast new road cuts across to the Pacific to run straight down the west coast to **Cabo San Lucas**; the old route trails through the mountains, emerging only briefly above the Sea of Cortés on its long journey to **San José del Cabo**. Neither route offers much to stop for, although there are isolated hotels and developments on beaches all the way around.

Cabo San Lucas

Fifteen years ago **CABO SAN LUCAS**, at the southernmost tip of Baja, was little more than a fishing village occasionally visited by sport fishermen with the means to sail in or fly down. In recent years, however, it has rapidly become the focal point of Los Cabos: condos have sprung up, palms have been transplanted, water has been piped in from San José and everywhere is kept pristine. More like an enclave of the US than part of Mexico, preserving almost nothing that is not geared to tourism, it can be fun for a day or two; though prices are higher than in neighbouring San José (see p.89), there's more of a party atmosphere, with a younger crowd.

Arrival and information

Buses from La Paz (roughly hourly 6am–7pm; 2–3hr) and San José del Cabo (roughly hourly 7am–10pm; 30min) arrive at the junction of Zaragoza and 16 de Septiembre, close to the centre. From the **airport** (see p.89), catch a taxi to San José and a bus from there. Surprisingly, Cabo has no official **tourist office**, just dozens of places dishing out maps and information, and usually throwing in some timeshare patter while they're at it. There's an ATM, and the best **exchange rates**, at *Bancomer* (cheques 8.30am–noon) on Lázaro Cárdenas at Hidalgo; after hours several *casas de cambio* (one by *Giggling Marlin*; see p.89) offer halfway decent rates until 11pm. The **post office** is on Lázaro Cárdenas east of the marina (Mon–Fri 9am–6pm), and there's a US **consul** at Blvd. Marina and Pedregal (☎114/3-35-66).

The Town

The current state of Cabo San Lucas is a pity, because with its great sands and fascinating marine life it could feasibly have been one of the most attractive spots in Baja. Above all there's the huge **rock arch** at Finisterra – Land's End, where the Sea of Cortés meets the Pacific – an extraordinary place, with a clear division between the shallower turquoise waters on the left and the profound blue of the ocean on the right. A colony of sea lions lives on the rocks roundabout. You can't walk to the arch, but there are plenty of trips out here from the **marina**, most of which take in one of the small surrounding beaches, more often than not Playa del Amor, which boasts strands on both seas.

Around the marina, down the nearby streets and along the **Playa Médano**, the town's closest safe beach, hawkers constantly tout trips in glass-bottomed boats, fishing, water skiing, paragliding or bungee jumping, and will rent anything from off-road quad bikes to jet skis and underwater gear. Competition is fierce, prices change and places come and go, so shop around. **Scuba diving** and **snorkelling** are perhaps the most rewarding of these activities, though the best sites (out towards Finisterra) can

---

THE CAPE BEACHES

The highway between Cabo San Lucas and San José del Cabo gives access to a welter of superb beaches, many of them visible from the road. You could just ride along until you see one you fancy, but if you have a preference and are using the bus between the two towns, make sure the driver is prepared to let you off at your desired stop.

Apart from Solmar and Del Amor, all distances are measured east from Cabo San Lucas towards San José del Cabo, 33km away.

Solmar, 1km west. Pacific side beach with strong undertow. Whale-watching Jan–April.

Del Amor, 0km. Boat access beach spanning the two seas out by El Arco.

Médano, 1km. Cabo's beach. Sand, restaurants, bars and abundant aquatic paraphernalia to rent.

Cemeterío, 4km. Beautiful swimming beach.

Barco Varada, 9km. Shipwreck beach. The remains of a Japanese trawler that sank in 1966 is the main diving focus. Rock reefs too.

De las Viudas, 11km. Excellent swimming.

Santa María, 12km. Scuba and snorkelling on rock reefs at both ends. Excellent swimming.

Punta Chileno, 14km. Underwater sports on rock and sand bottom. Very good swimming.

Canta Mar, 16km. Appropriately dubbed "surfing beach". Occasional point breaks.

Punta Palmilla, 27km. Good safe beach used by San José hotel residents needing escape from the strong rip closer to home. Point and reef breaks when surf's up.

Costa Azul, 29km. Consistently the region's best surf beach. Shore break but rocks at low tide.

---

only be reached by boat. Gear rental and trips ranging from a couple of hours' snorkelling ($25) to the full five-day Open Water Scuba Course ($350) can be arranged through *Underwater Diversions* (☎114/3-40-04) in Plaza Marina along Blvd. Marina. Experienced divers shouldn't miss the rim of a marine canyon off Playa del Amor, where unusual conditions at 30m create a "sandfall" with streams of sand starting their 2000m fall to the canyon bottom.

Accommodation

Possibly the best way to enjoy the sands and waters around Cabo San Lucas is to stay in San José and visit for the day on one of the frequent buses. If you do decide to **stay** here for any reason, however, you have the choice of a few good-value places (though none is cheap). If you're here out of season (May–Oct) you may find dramatically reduced rates at one of the swanky beachfront hotels.

Camping on the local Playa Médano is not encouraged by the beachfront restaurateurs, nor is it particularly safe, but you could toss down a sleeping bag on one of the relatively secluded beaches nearby. Local **RV parks** include *Vagabondos del Mar* (☎114/3-02-90), 3km east; *Club Cabo* (☎114/3-33-48), 4km east; and *Faro Viejo* at Abasolo and Mijares in town. For campers, all cost $10–12.

Casa Blanca, Revolución between Morales and Vicario (☎114/3-10-33). Comfortable a/c rooms with bathrooms but nothing special. ④.

Dos Mares, Zapata near Hidalgo (☎114/3-03-30). Good location, TV and tiny pool. Some studios with kitchens. ④–⑤.

Mar de Cortés, Lázaro Cárdenas between Guerrero and Matamoros (☎114/3-00-32). Decent-sized a/c rooms around a pool. Good restaurant too. ⑤.

Solmar Suites, Playa Solmar, 1km west towards Finisterra (☎114/3-35-35; in US: ☎1-800/344-3349). One of the top luxury hotels with all amenities. Expensive, but ask about the 3-nights-plus-meals deals which can be as little as $160 off season. ⑨.

Youth Hostel, *Villa Deportiva Juveniles*, Av. de la Juventud at Morales (☎114/3-01-48). Basic facilities in single-sex dorms. No curfew. From the bus station, turn left, walk 8 blocks up Zaragoza then right onto Juventud and continue 4 blocks. Dorms $6 each, some double rooms. ①–④.

Eating, drinking and nightlife

For reasonably inexpensive **food**, head for Morelos and the streets away from the waterfront. The more touristy places – some of them the most expensive in Baja – cluster around the marina and along Hidalgo. At night, such places compete for the custom of partying visitors by offering **happy hours** (often 6–8pm) and novel cocktails. There's little to choose between them; stroll along and take your pick.

Cabo Wabo, Guerrero between Lázaro Cárdenas and Madero. Van Halen-owned club fashioned in their image. Loud and lively but often with a hefty cover charge.

Café Cabo, Morelos between Niños Héroes and 16 de Septiembre. Breakfast and *antojitos* spot, justifiably popular with both gringos and locals. Closed Sun.

Café del Mundo, marina waterfront. The best coffee in town. Delicious cakes, US papers, magazines and a harbour view.

El Delfín, Playa Médano. Restaurant and bar which, along with its neighbour, *The Office*, pumps out rock classics and offers happy hours (3–5 or 6pm). Ideal for an afternoon drink on the beach but the food is expensive.

Giggling Marlin, Blvd. Marina at Matamoros. A Cabo institution, drawing an older set than most places on the strip. Mostly a place to drink and dance to Latin standards: chances of getting out without hearing *La Bamba* are slim.

Mariscos Mocambo, Morelos at Revolución. Unpretentious seafood restaurant popular with Mexicans.

La Perla, Lázaro Cárdenas between Matamoros and Abasolo. Very inexpensive and thoroughly Mexican place right in the tourist zone. Good Mexican staples and *licuados*.

Tacos Maury, Morelos at 20 de Noviembre. Quality meat and seafood *tacos* with some great *salsas*.

San José del Cabo

SAN JOSÉ DEL CABO, 33km east of Cabo San Lucas, is the older and altogether more traditional of the two resorts, with at least some trace of a town that once existed as a mission, agricultural centre and small port. Though fast being swamped, the old plaza and the Paseo Mijares (which now leads to a modern hotel zone about 1km seaward) are still more or less intact and there's a small local museum in the *Casa de la Cultura*. To get to the **beaches** it's a considerable walk down Mijares to the hotel zone, and on from there to find empty sand: they stretch for miles so there's no shortage of space.

Practicalities

Alaska, *Mexicana*, *Aero California* and *United* all serve **San José airport**, 5km north of town, flying to several Mexican and US west coast destinations. Expensive van-taxis shuttle into town. The **bus station** is about fifteen minutes' walk from the centre: turn left out of the station along Mijares then, after 1km, left onto Gonzales and to the zócalo – easily spotted by the church towers. Zaragoza crosses Mijares at this point; Obregón and Doblado run parallel to and either side of Zaragoza. The **tourist office**, which hands out free maps, is right at this junction (Mon–Fri 8am–3pm; ☎114/2-04-46), and the **post office**, **banks** and other facilities are all nearby.

The closest thing San José offers to a decent budget **hotel** is the *Hotel Ceci*, Zaragoza 22 (☎114/2-00-51; ③), very close to the centre; noise is the chief problem here. Alternatives include the *San José Inn* on Obregón (no phone; ④), parallel to and north of Zaragoza; *Hotel Diana*, Zaragoza 30 (☎114/2-04-90; ④), with a/c and TV, or the comfortable *Hotel Colli* (☎114/2-07-25; ⑤), on Hidalgo between Zaragoza and Doblado. Down in the hotel zone along the beach you may find bargains out of season, but on the whole these places are expensive and pre-booked. One of the most likely to have affordable space is the motel-type *Fiesta Inn* (☎114/2-00-77; ⑥), with pool and restaurant. If you're **camping**, head for the (pricey) *Brisa del Mar Trailer Park*, on the beachfront southwest of town.

There's a huge variety of upmarket **restaurants** along Mijares downtown, but it's less easy to find places with local prices – look around Zaragoza and Obregón. The best-value traditional Mexican food is served at *Jazmin* on Morelos, one block west of the zócalo; for not much more you can eat seafood in the hotel zone at *Calafia*, Mijares 34. French cuisine is dished up at the excellent *Café Europa* on Mijares and the pricier Belgian-run *Le Bistro* (closed Mon) on Juárez, three blocks south of the zócalo. Down at the beach in Pueblo La Playa, *La Playita* serves wonderful seafood in a breezy *palapa*.

Los Barriles and Todos Santos

On the western side of the peninsula, all the land is rapidly being bought up and converted into residential developments. Neither of the two big attractions here, game fishing and windsurfing, is easily arranged on the spot, however, and there's almost nowhere you can turn up and find an inexpensive room. The largest resort is **LOS BARRILES**, 40km north of Cabo San Lucas, a major **windsurfing** centre taking advantage of the near constant strong breeze in the bay. The wind, best in winter, is brilliant for experienced windsurfers (less so for beginners) and makes this a regular venue for international competitions. Equipment can be rented on the beach. Hotels are expensive, and you almost certainly need to have booked in advance; but you should be able to camp, either at one of the nearby trailer parks, or on the beach.

Todos Santos

On the new road, just north of the Tropic of Cancer, the farming town of **TODOS SANTOS** marks almost exactly the halfway point between Cabo San Lucas and La Paz. It's also the closest thing to an exception to all the rules about the cape region, with some great beaches in easy reach, affordable hotels, and a bus service. The town's charm has already lured a few score gringos to the area and less benign mega-development has been on the cards for some time, so catch it while you can. The best **beaches** – Los Lobos and Pedrito, for example – are a walk of half an hour or so; check that they haven't been buried under a new hotel before setting out.

The highway runs through the middle of Todos Santos as c/Colegio Militar. Here, and on parallel Juárez, are the **bank**, shops, **post office** and telephones. The bus will drop you at the corner of Colegio Militar and Zaragoza. The best **place to stay**, if you can afford it, is the colonial-style *Hotel California* (☎682/5-00-02; ⑥), a block and a half north on Juárez from Zaragoza. Alternatively, try the *Motel Guluarte* (☎682/5-00-06; ④), around the corner on Morelos. If no one is around, ask at the supermarket nearby. There should be no problem camping on Los Lobos and Pedrito beaches; the nearest official **campsite**, the *San Pedrito RV Park*, is some 7km south.

Places to eat are mainly on Colegio Militar: street stalls around the bus stop area and a couple of decent restaurants at the traffic lights a block away. *Caffé Todos Santos* (closed Mon) at Tapete and Centenario, three blocks north and two west from the bus stop, serves first-class cakes and coffee, stuffed sandwiches and, on Friday ("movie night"), pizza bread and salad.

THE MAINLAND ROUTE

On the mainland route through the northwest, it is the extraordinary **desert scenery** that first grabs the attention. Between Tijuana and Mexicali, especially, is a region of awesome barrenness. Continuing south through the states of Sonora and Sinaloa the desert becomes rockier, which, along with the huge cacti, makes for some archetypal Mexican landscapes. Only as you approach Mazatlán does the harshness finally start to relent, and some colour creep back into the land.

Historically, this part of the country was little more favoured than Baja California. The first Spanish explorers met fierce resistance from a number of tribes – the Pima, Seri and Yaqui are still among the least integrated of Mexico's peoples – and it was not until the late seventeenth century that the Jesuit missionary **Padre Kino** established a significant number of permanent settlements. During the dictatorship of Porfirio Díaz new road and rail links were established, and after the **Revolution** (many of whose most able leaders came from the northwest) these communications began to be exploited through irrigation and development programmes that brought considerable agricultural wealth. Today the big **ranchers** of Sonora and Sinaloa are among the richest in Mexico.

El Gran Desierto

If the peninsula of Baja California is desolate, the northern part of the state – to Mexicali and beyond into northern Sonora – is infinitely, spectacularly, more so. The **drive from Tijuana to Mexicali** is worthwhile for the extraordinary views alone, as the mountains suddenly drop away to reveal hundreds of miles of desert and the huge salt lake below. This is "**El Gran Desierto**" and it's a startlingly sudden change: the western escarpment up from Tijuana through **Tecate** (the small border crossing where the beer comes from) and beyond is relatively fertile and climbs deceptively gently, but the rains from the Pacific never get as far as the eastern edge, where the land falls away dizzily to the burnt plain and the road teeters between crags seemingly scraped bare by the ferocity of the sun. The heat at the bottom is incredible, the road down terrifying – its constant precipices made worse by the piles of twisted metal at the bottom of each one of them. By 1996 the new fast toll road should have tamed the route somewhat.

Mexicali

MEXICALI, too, is hot – unbearably so in summer, though winter nights can drop below freezing – but despite its natural disadvantages it's a large, wealthy city, the capital of Baja California Norte and an important road and rail junction for the crossing into the States. There may be an exotic ring to the name but there is nothing exotic about the place, and if you come looking for a movieland border town, swing-door saloons and dusty dirt streets, you'll be disappointed. There's more chance of choking to death on exhaust fumes or getting run over trying to cross the street. Even the name, it turns out, is a fake, a sweet-sounding hybrid of Mexico and California with an appalling bastard sister across the border – **Calexico**.

Though it's less commercial than many of the border towns, and relatively hassle-free, it's not a place you'd choose to spend time, except possibly to prepare for the next stage south, a daunting trip of at least nine hours on the bus to Hermosillo, the first place you might remotely choose to take a break, and a further hour and a half to the much more appealing Guaymas. Mexicali is an increasingly important destination for Mexican migrants looking for work in the *maquiladoras* and, as in Tijuana 160km to the west, the city's hinterland is rapidly being covered by shantytown sprawl.

During October you'll find a few cultural activities – live music, dance, cockfights and the like – taking place as part of the **Fiesta del Sol**; at any other time of year you can fill an hour browsing the local history exhibits at the free **Museo Regional de la Universidad de Baja California**,on Reforma at c/L.

Arrival and orientation

The Mexicali **border crossing** is open 24 hours and, except at morning and evening rush hours, is usually relatively quiet, the procedures straightforward. Remember to visit *Migración* if you're travelling further on into Mexico. In **Calexico**, Imperial Avenue leads straight to the border, lined with handily placed auto-insurance offices, banks and exchange places that offer almost identical rates to those in Mexicali; the *Greyhound* station is just one block from the frontier on 1st St.

It's possible to get a *Golden State* bus from LA to the **Central Camionera** in Mexicali: the bus only comes as far the border, where they bundle you into a taxi for the rest of the journey. The **airport** lies some 20km to the east. Fixed-price **taxis** and minibuses bring passengers into town.

Broad avenues lead away from the **frontier**: straight ahead is López Mateos, which will eventually take you straight out of town, passing close by the **train and bus terminals** on the way. To the left, off López Mateos and following the covered walkway from the border, you find yourself on Madero, which, along with parallel Reforma, is the main commercial street downtown. The **local bus stand** is at the back of the small market just up from the border – a couple of blocks up López Mateos to the right. **Taxis** wait at ranks around the junction of López Mateos and Madero.

Information

The **tourist information** booth (nominally Mon–Fri 9am–1pm & 3–6pm, Sat 9am–1pm) right by the border seldom seems to be open; the **main office** (Mon–Fri 8.30am–6pm; ☎65/57-25-61) is a very long way down López Mateos at Camelias, a journey not worth making unless you have some special reason. There are several **banks** and *casas de cambio* very close to the border – *Bancomer*, on Madero, is closest, *Banamex* a couple of blocks up Madero near the **post office**.

Accommodation

Most of Mexicali's cheaper **hotels** can be found in the older streets around the border. Not that there are any great bargains here – indeed, if you're looking for somewhere to stay **Calexico** is arguably better value, with several motels charging around $30. Try for example the *Don Juan Motel*, 344 4th St East, between Hefferman and Heber (☎619/357-3231; ⑥), or the *El Rancho* (☎619/357-2458; ⑤) opposite.

In **Mexicali**, there are a couple of cheap and fairly decent places: the **youth hostel**, Coahuila 2050 at Salinas Cruz (☎65/57-61-82; $6) – take the blue-and-white "c/Tercera" or "c/Once" bus from the local bus stand – and *16 de Septiembre*, Altamirano 353 (☎65/52-60-70; ③), just south of Mateos.

The *Hotel del Norte*, Madero 203 just off López Mateos (☎65/52-81-01; ⑥), is one of the first things you see as you cross the border; it looks better than it is. The *Imperial*, Madero 222 (☎65/53-67-33; ⑤), just beyond, and *Plaza*, Madero 366 (☎65/53-63-33; ⑤), in the next block, are simpler places, but better value. For the same price as the *Del Norte*, the *Hotel San Juan Capistrano* (☎65/52-41-04; ⑥), Reforma 646, not much farther from the border, is a far better deal – a rather bland business hotel with a decent restaurant. The *Motel Azteca de Oro*, c/de la Industria 600 (☎65/57-21-85; ④), right by the train station, is comfortable and handy for transport: the Camionera is only about ten minutes' walk away up López Mateos. More **expensive hotels** are mainly on the outskirts, particularly along Juárez – the modern, international-style *Lucerna*, for example, at Juárez 2151 (☎65/66-10-00; ⑦). One exception is the new *Crowne Plaza*, near the Centro Civico on López Mateos at Av. de los Héroes (☎65/57-36-00; ⑨).

Eating

There's plenty to **eat** in the border area too, with lots of stalls and small restaurants around the market and on Madero and Reforma. The restaurant in the *Del Norte* is convenient, and better than the hotel itself, while on Reforma at c/D, about six blocks down, *La Parroquia* serves good Mexican food, albeit a bit touristy. Entirely off the tourist track are the many restaurants and cafes in and around the Centro Civico, on Independencia a couple of blocks from the Central Camionera. The Centro itself has a branch of *Sanborn's*, reliable as ever; *Café Petunias*, at Plaza Cholula 1091 off Calafia, is one of many in this area serving sandwiches, juices, and lunch for office workers and shoppers.

Beyond Mexicali

Beyond Mexicali the road towards central Mexico trails the border westwards, while the rail line cuts south around the northern edge of the Sea of Cortés – between them rises the Sierra del Pinacate, an area so desolate that it was used by American astronauts to simulate lunar conditions. Not far out of Mexicali you cross the border from Baja California into the state of **Sonora**: you'll have to put your watch forward an hour when you cross, unless Baja California Norte is on Daylight Saving Time (April–Oct), in which case there's no change.

There's little to stop for on the road. You'll pass through **San Luis Río Colorado**, something of an oasis with a large cultivated valley watered by the Colorado River, and **Sonoita** (or Sonoyta), a minor border crossing on the river of the same name. Both are pretty dull, though they have plenty of facilities for travellers passing through. Past Sonoita the road cuts inland and turns to the south, hitting the first foothills of the Sierra Madre Occidental, whose western slopes it follows, hugging the coast, all the way to Tepic. At **Santa Ana** it meets the Nogales road, and near the tiny village of **Benjamin Hill** rejoins the rail tracks. If you're travelling north you may well have to change buses at Santa Ana (especially en route to Nogales – there are far more buses to Mexicali) but it's a nothing town and there's little point venturing beyond the bus terminal.

MOVING ON FROM MEXICALI

Mexicali's **Central Camionera** (☎65/57-24-10; *guardería*) is 4km from the border on Independencia at Anahuac, close to the new **Centro Civico** development and not far off López Mateos. To get there, take a "Calle 6" bus from the local bus stand off Mateos. Altogether well over fifty buses a day head **south** (20 to México), and there's at least one local service an hour to **Tijuana**. *Golden State* has an office at the station: 3 buses leave daily for LA via Palm Springs. On the other hand, you'll have far more choice, and save a few dollars, if you walk across the border to Calexico's *Greyhound* station.

The **train station** is just off López Mateos, not quite as far out as the Camionera; buses and *colectivo* taxis heading up Mateos will take you there. The "express", first-class train leaves for **Guadalajara** at 10am daily, arriving some 34 hours later. The second-class slow train leaves at 9.50pm, and takes about ten hours longer – tickets for both are sold at the station an hour or so before departure. You can reserve – advisable for first-class during holidays – by calling ☎65/57-21-01, ext 221.

Flights to México and Acapulco leave daily from the airport 20km east of town.

Puerto Peñasco

On the rail route there's just one place of any size, **PUERTO PEÑASCO**, a shrimping port that, while not particularly attractive, does have good beaches that attract large weekend crowds from across the border (Tucson is only about three hours away). There's a good road down here from Sonoita, and a new one east to Caborca, not far from Santa Ana. If you're on the train it's really not worth breaking the journey – you may well have difficulty getting back on – and the buses are fairly infrequent, with a couple of daily services each to Hermosillo, Mexicali and Nogales. But if you have your own vehicle you may fancy the detour, especially as it's possible to cut east to Caborca and rejoin the main road there. There are plenty of places to stay and to eat, though **rooms** can be a problem at busy weekends. For luxury try the *Hotel Viña del Mar* complex (☎638/3-36-01; ⑥), or there are plain motel rooms at the *Señorial* (☎638/3-20-65; ⑤) and *El Faro* (☎638/3-32-01; ⑤), both just a block or so from the beach. **Seafood** stalls gather at the end of Eusebio Kino, while for more substantial Mexican food you can head for *Los Arcos* on Eusebio Kino at Tamarindos.

Nogales to Hermosillo

Compared to most of the frontier, **NOGALES** (its name means walnut trees, few of which are in evidence) is remarkably pleasant. Despite the fact that the Mexican streets are jammed with curio shops and the US side with hardware, clothes and electrical stores, and that there's the usual contrast between the neatly planned streets on the US side and the houses straggling haphazardly up the hillside in Mexico, this doesn't feel much like a border town. Indeed, the slackening of trade barriers in recent years has seen a marked reduction in small-time cross-border traffic, a process which is likely to continue under NAFTA. There's none of the oppressive hustling and little of the frenetic nightlife which mark Ciudad Juárez, say, or Tijuana.

The **Nogales pass** has been a significant staging post since explorers first passed this way, with evidence of settlements several thousand years BC. After the Conquest it was used by Spanish explorers and surveyors, followed in rapid succession by evangelizing Jesuits (especially the celebrated Padre Kino) and Franciscans on their way to establish missions in California. Nogales itself remained no more than a large ranch, often existing in a state of virtual siege under harassment from the Apaches, until the war with the USA and the ceding of Arizona, New Mexico, Texas and northern California to the Americans in 1848. Thereafter, with the border passing straight through, the town was deliberately developed by both sides to prevent the periodic raids of the other. Yankee troops marched through a few years later, protecting Union supplies shipped in through Guaymas during the Civil War, and there was a constant traffic of rustling and raids from both sides – culminating in the activities of Pancho Villa in the years leading up to the Mexican Revolution. The railway to the coast brought the final economic spur, and the town's chief business remains that of shipping Sonora's rich agricultural produce to the States. Just over the border on the US side an excellent little **museum** of local history (Tues–Fri 10am–noon & 1.30–5pm, Sat 10am–4pm; free), run by the Pimeria Alta Historical Society, records all this, and some of the traditions of the Pima Indians, whose land this traditionally was.

Nogales practicalities

Mexican Nogales is a sleepy, provincial town, not a bad place to rest up and acclimatize for a while, though accommodation is a little pricey. Crossing the border (24hr) is straightforward; remember to have your tourist card stamped by *Migración* if you're heading further south – there's also an office at the bus station where they can do this. Immediately by the border, the small **tourist office** (Mon–Fri 8am–5pm; ☎631/2-64-46) has a limited amount of local information and maps, while just beyond this you're in an area teeming with blanket stalls, cafe and a few hotels. These last are concentrated on two streets leading away from the border: Obregón, which eventually becomes the highway south, and Juárez. There are several **banks**, most with ATMs (some giving US dollars), and *casas de cambio* along López Mateos and Obregón, but if you want to phone or send mail you're better off doing so across the border.

If you're looking for a cheap **place to stay**, there's no need to go any farther: possibilities include the *Imperial*, Internaciónal 79 (☎631/2-14-58; ④), right by the border fence west of the checkpoint and probably as basic as you'd want on your first night in Mexico; the *San Carlos*, Juárez 22 (☎631/2-13-46; ⑤), with more frills, including TV and a/c, and the *Olivia*, Obregón 125 (☎631/2-22-00; ⑤), another step up in class. There are plenty of cafes and **restaurants** in the same area; *Café Olga*, on Juárez just across the border, is a Nogales institution, open 24 hours. Many of the alternatives are far more touristy, with live *mariachi* in the evenings: *El Greco*, Obregón 125, is a good example.

The **bus and train stations** are opposite each other on the highway about 5km south of town – local buses (signed "Central Camionera") run from the border, or take a taxi, which will cost around $10. Southbound departures from the Camionera – which has all the usual facilities including long-distance phones and *guardería* – are very frequent, going as far south as Guadalajara (26hr) and México (34hr). Two **trains** a day head towards Guadalajara, the slow, second-class service at 7am, the heavily booked, first-class train at 3.30pm. On the other side of the border the *Greyhound* station is right by the customs office; buses leave every one or two hours (6.45am–6.45pm) for **Tucson** and **Phoenix**.

Agua Prieta

To the east lies another border crossing, **AGUA PRIETA**, just across from Douglas, Arizona. A quiet town which sees few tourists, it's gradually growing thanks to the *maquiladora* assembly plants on both sides of the border, and to new roads linking the town to **Janos** (for Ciudad Juárez and Nuevo Casas Grandes) and direct to Hermosillo. Despite the fact that these are barely marked on many maps, they're perfectly good paved highways, and Agua Prieta is thus on the only route from central Mexico to the Pacific between the border and Mazatlán. Several buses a day run in each direction. If you're **staying** over, try the *Hotel Plaza* (⑤) on the central plaza – though you may find better value in Douglas, where there's a *Motel 6* among other cheap motels.

Hermosillo

HERMOSILLO, the state capital of Sonora, is a thriving city and a big ranching supply centre. The market overflows with meat and the shops are full of tack gear, cowboy hats and boots. From a distance it's an odd-looking place, surrounded by strange rock forma-

---

THE REMAINS OF PADRE KINO

There's little to see between Nogales and Santa Ana, and still less on the long stretch of desert highway from Santa Ana to Hermosillo. Shortly before Santa Ana, however, you pass through the small town of **Magdalena**, where most buses stop briefly. Here there's a mausoleum containing, under glass, the recently discovered remains of **Padre Kino**. Kino, "Conquistador of the Desert", was a Spanish Jesuit priest who came to Mexico in 1687 and is credited with having founded twenty-five missions and converted at least seven local indigenous tribes – among them the Apaches of Arizona and the Pima, Yuma and Seri of Sonora.

tions and overlooked, right in the centre, by a tall outcrop crowned by radio masts, lit up at night like a helter-skelter. Close up, though, it's less interesting – the boom of the last half-century has wiped out almost everything that might have survived of the old town. And the boom in Sonora this century has been remarkable, helped by the fact that some of the earliest organized **Revolutionaries**, including General Alvaro Obregón, were locals, as were many of the early presidents of Revolutionary Mexico: Obregón himself, Huerta, whom he overthrew, Plutarco Elías Calles and Abelardo Rodríguez. Their many monuments and the streets named after them reflect the local debt.

While it's interesting enough to experience such an archetypal Mexican town, there's no reason to stay long: in any case, Hermosillo, spread-out and car-oriented, is not geared to welcoming visitors, especially those without their own vehicle. If you do have to or want to spend time here, head down to the **beaches** at Bahía de Kino. Short stays can be enlivened by strolling down Serdán past the market, and taking a look at the attractive plaza around the cathedral, across Rosales from the bottom of Serdán.

Arrival and information

Although the city sprawls, **downtown** Hermosillo is relatively compact. The highway comes into town as Blvd. Eusebio Kino, known as Blvd. Rosales as it runs north–south through the centre of town: crossing it, Blvd. Luis Encinas passes the bus station, 3km east of the centre, leaving town to the west, past the airport towards Bahía de Kino. Virtually everything you might want to see lies in an area bounded by these two, as well as Juárez and Serdán, the main commercial street downtown, which runs past the bottom of the distinctive hill known as the Cerro de la Campaña.

From the rather isolated **Central Camionera** (with *guardería*), take a "Ruta 1" microbus, a van (marked "Ranchito") or a "Multirutas" town bus to get downtown. Taxis are expensive and the drivers unwilling to bargain. Almost all the buses passing through Hermosillo are *de paso*, and at times it can be very hard to get on. However, *TBC* (depot outside the Central Camionera and left a few paces) run a local service to Guaymas, Navojoa and, four times daily, to Alamos.

The **train station** is still further out, by the highway; again there should be *colectivos* or buses into town. From the **airport**, a short way out on the road towards Bahía de Kino, you can pick up one of the usual fixed-fare taxis. The **tourist office** (generally Mon–Fri 8am–3pm & 5–7pm, Sat 10am–1pm; ☎62/17-29-64) is in the Palacio Administrativo at Tehuantepec and Comonfort, in the smaller square just off the cathedral square; they generally prove helpful, though they have little printed information and seem to come across few visitors.

Other facilities and shops are mostly on Serdán, including numerous **banks** and *casas de cambio* (there's also a handy *Bancomer*, with ATM, at Matamoros and Sonora, on the plaza a block from the *Monte Carlo* hotel). The **post office** is at the corner of Serdán and Rosales. Should you want to book a flight out, head for *Travesías de Anza*, Serdán 122-B (☎62/12-26-70), a helpful **travel agency**.

Accommodation

All the cheaper **hotels** in Hermosillo are strikingly poor value, but some very pleasant mid-range places cater to businesspeople and the wealthy *rancheros* who come here for the markets. The long-standing budget favourite is the *Monte Carlo*, Juárez at Sonora (☎62/12-08-53; ④–⑤) – about six blocks north of Serdán, and just off Encina by a large plaza. Even here the rooms are little more than acceptable (though they do have good a/c, essential in the summer) and the red-light district starts immediately behind. Of the many very basic *casas de huéspedes* and hotels there, none is recommended, though *Hospedaje Los Faroles* (no phone; ②), on Noriega between Matamoros and Juárez, is certainly cheap.

The *Hotel Niza*, Plutarco Elias Calles 66, just off Serdán near the market (☎62/17-20-28; ⑤), has a better location and cable TV, but is still poor value. Much nicer, if you can afford them, are a couple of businesslike places down on Rosales: the solidly comfortable *Hotel San Alberto*, Serdán and Rosales (☎62/13-18-40; ⑦), and the colonial-style *Hotel Kino*, Pino Suárez 151, just off Rosales near the cathedral plaza (☎62/13-31-31; ⑥), which is really a motel, but with all facilities including a pool. The more expensive hotels, and a number of motels, are almost all in the hotel zone, a long way from the centre on Kino.

Eating

Downtown Hermosillo is surprisingly short of decent **places to eat**: Serdán and the surrounding streets are lined with plenty of juice bars and places that have *tortas* and other snacks for sale, but local people in search of fancier food tend to get in their cars and head for the restaurants situated on the main boulevards or in the hotel zone. All the hotels mentioned above have restaurants which are at least passable, and there are several places on and around the plaza by the *Hotel Monte Carlo*: try *Napy's*, Matamoros 109 between Noriega and Morelia; *La Fabula Pizza*, a branch of a chain at Morelia 34 between Matamoros and Juárez; or the vegetarian restaurant and wholefood shop *Jung* (closed Sun), Niños Héroes 75 between Matamoros and Guerrero.

Bahía de Kino

Offering the nearest beaches to Hermosillo, **BAHÍA DE KINO**, 117km west, is a popular weekend escape for locals and increasingly a winter resort for Americans, many of whom have second or retirement homes down here. There are two settlements around the bay: the old fishing village of **Kino Viejo**, a dusty collection of corrugated-iron huts, passed over by the fruits of development, and newer **Kino Nuevo** – basically a single road strung with one-storey seafront houses, trailer parks, and a couple of hotels and restaurants. There's really not a lot to it, but the beach is good, with miles of sand – and the offshore islets and strange rock formations make the spectacular sunsets still more worth watching.

Practicalities

Buses leave Hermosillo from a small bus station on Sonora, a block and a half east of the *Monte Carlo*. There are about nine a day – currently hourly from 5.40am to 9.30am, then every two hours – with more at busy weekends; they take around two hours. Probably the best-value **place to stay** is the *Motel Kino Bay* (☎62/14-17-32; ⑦), where you'll get a unit with kitchen and all facilities; it's one of the last places on the road, by the *Trailer Park Bahía Kino* (☎624/2-02-16). During the off season you may be able to pitch a tent here and, if you are reasonably discreet and careful with your stuff, free camping on the Kino Nuevo beach is a good possibility. Opposite the trailer park, the *Restaurant Kino Bay* is a good place to make enquiries about the local area, to sample the local seafood, or simply to enjoy a beer and watch the sun go down. The *Hotel Saro* (☎624/2-00-07; ⑦), soon after you enter Kino Nuevo, has similar facilities, and another decent restaurant.

This whole area used to be inhabited by the Seri peoples, and there are still a few communities living roundabout: one such, on the offshore **Isla Tiburón** (Shark Island), was relocated when the island was made into a wildlife refuge. You may come across Seri hawking traditional, and not so traditional, ironwood carvings along the beach in Kino Nuevo and their crafts are widely on sale. The tiny **Museo de los Seris** (Wed–Sun 9am–1pm & 3–6pm; free) on the "plaza" in the middle of Kino Nuevo gives a little more information on Seri history.

Guaymas

Back on the route south the next major stop is **GUAYMAS**, an important port with a magnificent, almost landlocked natural harbour where the mountains come right down to the sea. Although Guaymas claims a proud history – seemingly every adventurer whose eyes ever turned greedily to Mexico sent a gunship into the bay – there's really nothing to see beyond a couple of grandiose *Porfiriano* bank buildings on the main street. Nonetheless, if you have to choose somewhere to stop, this is definitely a more attractive option than Hermosillo, ninety minutes away, or Los Mochis, six hours on.

The Americans, the French and the British have all at one time or another attempted to take the town (only the Americans had any real success, occupying the town in 1847–8), but the most extraordinary invader was a Frenchman, **Conte Gaston Raousset de Bourbon**. Attempting, with the tacit support of the then president, General Santa Ana, to carve out an empire in Sonora, Raousset invaded twice, holding Guaymas for several months in 1852. His second attempt, in 1854, was less successful and ended with most of the pirates, the count included, captured and shot. There are monuments to the hero of that battle – one General Yañez – all over town.

Today, Guaymas is still a thriving fishing and naval centre and makes few concessions to tourism. At the waterfront there's an attractive plaza where you can sit and look out over the deep bay, alive with the comings and goings of ships, and the scores of fishing boats at anchor. In the south of France this would no doubt be surrounded by outdoor waterfront cafes; this being Mexico, the dockside looks more like a building site. Still, it's a pleasant spot, and there are also some good beaches a short bus ride away.

Arrival and information

Virtually everything that happens in Guaymas happens on Serdán, the main drag which brings southbound traffic from the highway into town from the west, and leaves to the east for Ciudad Obregón via the docks and railway station. This is not a good place to arrive by **train**, since the station is 10km away in the neighbouring town of Empalme; buses run between the two (look for "Empalme" buses on Serdán to get out there), but you have to change for a local station bus in Empalme. There's a railway information office where you can check train times at Serdán and c/30.

The **airport**, off the highway west of town, is closer, though here you'll have to rely on taxis for transport. Most people arrive by **bus**, however: the three terminals serving

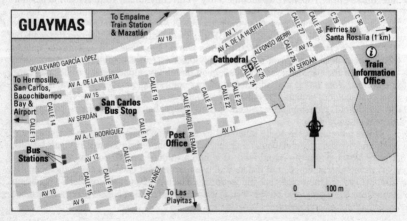

Tres Estrellas, Norte de Sonora, Baldamero Corral (TBC) and *Pacifico* are right opposite each other on c/14 at Rodríguez, a couple of blocks off Serdán and within walking distance of all the action. **Ferries** from Santa Rosalía arrive at the docks 2km east of the centre, easily reached on local buses along Serdán. For departures, see "Moving On from Guaymas" on p.100.

You'll find several **banks** on Serdán: *Bancomer* at c/18, and *Banamex* at c/20 (both with 24hr ATMs); and long-distance **telephones** in *Farmacía Bell*, Serdán at c/22, as well as in the *Tres Estrellas* terminal. The **post office** is on Av. 10 just off c/20 (c/ Miguel Aleman), which runs south from Serdán and round the side of the bay. The **Mercado Municipal**, a block off Serdán on c/20, sells fresh food good for picnics.

Accommodation

From the bus stations, Rodríguez leads towards the centre, the street numbers rising as you go. In the first block you pass what looks like a Venetian castle, but is in fact the town jail. The best of the budget **places to stay** in Guaymas is the *Casa de Huéspedes Lupita*, c/15 no. 125 (☎622/2-84-09; ②–③), right by the prison and just a block from the bus stations. Some rooms have private bath. Couples can get a cheaper bed and bath at *Casa de Huéspedes Esperanza* (no phone; ②) at the junction of c/14 and Av. 9.

For a little more comfort, carry on into town and try the *Hotel Impala*, c/21 at Av. 12, one block off Serdán (☎622/4-09-22; ⑤), an oldish place whose price seems inflated because it has a lift, or the *Hotel Rubi*, Serdán and c/29 at the far end of the waterfront (☎622/2-04-95; ④), better value for simple, quiet courtyard rooms with private bath, TV and a/c. In the other direction, at Serdán and Mesa (c/9), the *Santa Rita Hotel* (☎622/ 4-14-64; ④) is also worth a try (not to be confused with the more expensive motel of the same name). One of the prettiest places to stay is the comfortable hotel-trailer park complex, *Las Playitas* (☎622/1-52-27; ⑤), with pool, pleasant restaurant, and rooms in bougainvillea-covered, traditionally furnished cottages. It's out of town on the coast at nearby Las Playitas (see below; take a taxi, or even the local bus). In San Carlos (see below) the *Creston* (☎622/6-00-20; ⑦) is a good option, also with a pool: rates can be reduced by up to 50 percent out of season (it's on the main road and the bus goes past the door).

Eating

Guaymas has plenty of inexpensive, no-nonsense **places to eat**: *Jax Snacks* at c/14 is handy for the bus terminals and serves pizza, burgers and the like; *Vivenos del Sol*, between c/14 and c/15, though little more than a glorified *taco* stand, has a great Mexican-style help-yourself salad bar; and in the next block the ordinary-looking *Todos Comen* serves good *antojitos* and main meals. Further up, between c/17 and c/18, *Las 1000 Tortas* dishes out tasty *tortas, tacos, quesadillas* and *comidas*; off to the right you'll find *Restaurant Mandarin*, a Mex-Chinese place in the *Hotel Impala*. To sample some of the town's best **seafood** head for *Los Barcos* on the seafront, Av. 11 at c/20, with its huge *palapa* dining area, or the nautically decorated restaurant in the *Las Playitas* complex, where you can dine on huge fishy stews accompanied by live guitar music.

Beaches around Guaymas

The **beach** the locals use is at **MIRAMAR**, an upmarket suburb on Bacochibampo Bay, a few kilometres north of Guaymas. On balance, this is your best bet for swimming, though there is more happening 16km further north at **SAN CARLOS** (somewhat hopefully dubbed "Nuevo Guaymas"), which is on its way to becoming a big resort. So far it has a couple of big resort hotels, a *Club Med*, a yacht marina, a country club with a golf course, and scores of villas and half-completed developments all linked to the main highway north by a long avenue of transplanted palms. There are some lovely places here – bays set about with tall crags weirdly sculpted by the wind – and wonderful sunsets, but access to the shore is difficult, and most of the beaches you can reach are stony. As compensation you can rent all manner of **aquatic gear** or go diving, fishing and sightseeing with *Gary's* (☎622/6-00-49), about 1km south of the marina.

There's a more impressive stretch of sand at **Algodones**, over the hill beyond San Carlos, though there's no public transport out there and it's not exactly walking country. Algodones is where *Catch-22* was filmed and you can still see parts of the set and the runway built for the production.

You may also be told that there are beaches at **LAS PLAYITAS**, on the other side of Guaymas bay. Don't believe it: the *Las Playitas* motel-trailer park has a pool and a good restaurant, but the beach is entirely wishful thinking. If you've a couple of hours to kill, though, it is interesting to take the bus out this way for the ride – you can stay on all the way and eventually ıt will turn round and head back home. You get to see the ship-building industry, the fish-freezing and processing centres, and some fine views of the outer stretches of the wreck-strewn bay.

Buses for Miramar and San Carlos ("Miramar" or "San Carlos") leave every thirty minutes or so from c/19 by the post office, but it's easier to catch them as they head up Serdán, for example at the corner of c/18. It can take up to an hour to reach San Carlos. To get to **Las Playitas**, hop on the bus marked "Parajes" from c/Miguel Aleman.

MOVING ON FROM GUAYMAS

The **ferry to Santa Rosalía** in Baja California leaves from the docks about 2km beyond Guaymas centre – just about any bus heading east on Serdán will take you there. There are currently two sailings a week (Tues & Fri 8am) and you buy tickets from the **terminal** (sales and reservations Mon–Fri 8am–3pm, Sat 8am–1pm; ☎622/2-23-24); check the timetable and reserve in advance if possible – you'll need to if you plan to take a car across. Single **fares** for the 7hr crossing are currently $13 for a reclining seat, $26 sharing a simple 4-berth cabin and $82 for a small car.

Many first-class buses on the Mazatlán–Hermosillo run stick to the main highway, skipping Guaymas. There are, however, second-class buses every thirty minutes or so in both directions and a direct, Hermosillo-sourced *TBC* service to Alamos four times daily at 1.45, 4.45, 6.45 and 8.45pm.

Ciudad Obregón to Alamos

On the main highway, there's little to tempt you to stop between Guaymas and the state border. **CIUDAD OBREGÓN**, founded in 1928 and named after the president, has thrived on the agricultural development which accompanied the plans to utilize the Río Yaqui. Thanks to the irrigation schemes and huge dams upriver it's now a very large and uncompromisingly ugly town. About the only attraction is for fans of cowboy clothing: locally produced **straw stetsons** are among the best and least expensive you'll find anywhere.

NAVOJOA, too, is a rather dull farming town, little more than a string of Americanized motels and restaurants along the highway. Where it scores over Ciudad Obregón is in having a reasonably priced hotel, a good market, and above all in being the jumping-off point for Alamos (see below). Most **buses** (usually *de paso*) pull in to either the *TBC* or *Transportes de Pacifico* stations, near each other around the junction of Guerrero and c/de Ferrocarril, a couple of hundred metres away from the train station. Local buses to Alamos (6.30am–6.30pm; hourly) leave from a separate station, some eight blocks west

THE YAQUI

Between Guaymas and Ciudad Obregón lies the valley of the Río Yaqui, traditional home of the **Yaqui**. The Yaqui were perhaps the fiercest and most independent of the Mexican peoples, maintaining virtual autonomy until the beginning of this century. Rebellions, and at times outright war, against the government of the day were frequent – the most significant coming in 1710 and again, after Independence, in 1852. The last major uprising was in 1928 during the brief presidency of General Alvaro Obregón. Obregón, himself a Sonoran, was assassinated in México but his plans for the development of the northwest laid the basis for peace with the Yaqui: aided, no doubt, by the fact that earlier regimes had shipped rebels out wholesale to work on the tobacco plantations of Oaxaca. Today the Yaqui enjoy a degree of self-rule, with eight governors, one for each of their chief towns, but their cultural and political assimilation is rapid. One surviving element of Yaqui culture is the celebrated **Danza del Venado**, or Stag Dance, not only performed frequently at local festivals in the villages of this area but also at folklore festivals throughout the republic – and it forms one of the centrepieces of the *Ballet Folklórico* in México. The chief dancer wears a deer's head, a symbol of good (the stag being the sacred animal of the Yaqui), and is hounded by one or more coyote dancers, falling eventually, after a gallant struggle, to these forces of evil.

along Guerrero. It takes about fifteen minutes to walk, so in the heat of the day a taxi is well worth the expense. The *Transportes de Pacifico* bus station is handy for one of the town's cheaper **hotels**: the *Aduana* (④) on Ignacio Allende, which has a/c rooms. Unless time is against you, however, you're better off heading straight through to Alamos.

Alamos

The existence of **ALAMOS**, a decaying Spanish colonial town just five hours' drive from the US border and 50km southeast of Navojoa, hasn't escaped the notice of scores of Americans – predominantly "artists" and retirees – who have chosen to settle here over the last forty years or so. The ex-pat community lives in near complete social isolation from the local Mexicans, but the necessary economic interaction at least stops Alamos going the way of so many other ex-mining villages in the region. Though perhaps over-rated – Alamos certainly doesn't compare with the colonial towns of central Mexico – a ride out here to this patch of green, where the Sonoran and Sinaloan deserts meet at the foot of the rugged Sierra Madre Occidental, does make a very pleasant respite from the monotony of the coastal road. It's a great place to do nothing for a while; a tour of the town takes no longer than a couple of hours and there's little else to do but walk and hunt in the mountains (an exceedingly hot exercise in summer).

Coronado was the first European to pass through this area in 1540, spending most of his time trying to subjugate the Mayo and Yaqui, unaware that below his feet lay some of the richest **silver ore** in Mexico. Silver was discovered late in the seventeenth century and Alamos became Mexico's northernmost silver mining town, within a century a substantial city with its own mint on the coastal branch of the Camino Real. With Mexican Independence, control fell into the hands of the Aldama family who, despite initially productive mines, spent the rest of the nineteenth century protecting their piece from political wranglings and petty feuds, and watching over the region's decline. The mint closed in 1896 and even the brief existence of a railway only served to help depopulate a dying town. Alamos languished until the 1940s, when an American, **William Alcorn**, bought numerous houses here and set about selling the property to his countryfolk.

Though Alamos has suffered from its own popularity – most of the ancient stone mansions have been done up by recent wealthy settlers, giving the whole place a somewhat sanitized aspect – it does have a beautiful old arcaded **plaza** and an elegant eighteenth-century **cathedral**. Opposite the arcade on the Plaza de Armas, the mildly diverting **Museo Costumbrista de Sonora** (Mon–Fri 9am–1pm & 3–6pm; $1) illustrates the town's heyday through a mock-up of the mine, and grainy photos of moustachioed workers. More interesting are the town's magnificent old Andalucian-style **mansions**, brooding and shuttered from the outside, but enclosing beautiful flower-filled patios. If poking your head through gaping doorways and visiting the restaurants or bars of houses converted into swanky hotels doesn't satisfy your curiosity, you can take an hour-long **house tour** (Sat 10am; $3) which leaves from by the bank on the Alameda and visits some of the finest, predominantly American-owned homes.

Arrival and information

From Navojoa hourly **buses** run to Alamos (6.30am–6.30pm; 1hr), arriving at the bus station on Morelos by the Alameda. There is a *Bancomer* across the park on Rosales. Follow Rosales east, then Juárez south to reach the Plaza de Armas, the cathedral and the enthusiastic **tourist office** (Mon–Fri 9am–1pm & 3–6pm, Sat & Sun 9am–1pm; ☎642/8-04-50). The **post office** is on the approach into town, opposite the *Dolisa Motel and Trailer Park*.

Moving on from Alamos, there are four daily *TBC* buses (☎642/8-01-75) leaving for Navojoa, Guaymas and Hermosillo in the morning, returning in the late afternoon and evening.

Accommodation

Low-cost accommodation in Alamos is hard to come by, but there are some beautiful moderately priced hacienda-style places, with cool rooms ranged around bougainvillea-draped courtyards. You'll pay 10 to 20 percent less outside the high season (Nov–April). The town also boasts two **trailer parks**: *Dolisa Motel and Trailer Park* (☎642/8-01-31), a convenient though often crowded site at the entrance to town (open all year), and *Acosta Trailer Rancho*, about 1km east of town (Oct–April; ☎642/8-02-64), a secluded park with camping spots and a pool. To get there, follow Morelos east across the usually dry Arroyo La Aduana then turn left at the cemetery.

Casa Encantada, Obregón 2 (☎642/8-57-60). Beautiful 300-year-old mansion, with fully refitted rooms, some with a/c. The same people also run a slightly more expensive establishment across the road, which has a pool, and breakfast included. ⑦.

Casa de los Tesoros, Obregón 10 (☎642/8-00-10). Just along from the *Casa Encantada*, up behind the cathedral, this eighteenth-century former convent now has a pool and beautifully decorated rooms. Ceiling fans for summer, fireplace for winter. Rates includes breakfast. ⑧.

Enríquez, Juárez on the Plaza de Armas (no phone). Alamos' only cheap hotel and not that pleasant, though serviceable. Just one room has a private bath. ②.

Los Portales, Juárez on the Plaza de Armas (☎642/8-02-11). Beautiful restored hacienda, formerly owned by the Aldama family, with pleasant rooms around a broad stone courtyard but no a/c or pool. ⑥.

Eating and drinking

The best **restaurants** in Alamos are at the fancier hotels, in particular the *Casa de los Tesoros* and *Casa Encantada*, which boasts *La Casa de Café*, a great breakfast place for scrumptious coffee and cake in the courtyard, and a restaurant (mid-Oct to March only) offering a moderately priced Mexican buffet on Thursday, Friday and Saturday nights. *Las Palmeras* on the plaza also serves excellent food, and there are a number of run-of-the-mill cheaper places around the **market** that fronts onto the Alameda.

Into Sinaloa: Los Mochis

Continuing down the coast and crossing into the state of Sinaloa, the next place of any size is **LOS MOCHIS**, another modern agricultural centre, broad-streeted and rather dull, but a major crossing point for road, rail and ferry, and above all the western terminus of the incomparable **rail trip** between here and Chihuahua through the Barranca del Cobre (see p.128).

The various modes of transport into and out of this area are infuriating in their failure to connect in any way – even the bus stations are on opposite sides of town. The two **rail**

ARRIVING IN AND MOVING ON FROM LOS MOCHIS

The *Pacifico* and *Norte de Sonora* **bus stations** are next to each other on Morelos between Zaragoza and Leyva. *Tres Estrellas* and *Elite* are based on Santos Degollado, between Juárez and Morelos, within easy walking distance of most downtown hotels and restaurants. The latter two have more first-class departures, but are also busier; finding a seat on mostly *de paso* buses can be a problem, but with departures north and south every thirty minutes or so you shouldn't have too long to wait.

Trains are much less convenient: two currently leave for **Chihuahua** each day, the first-class *Vista Tren* at 6am (arrives Chihuahua 7.50pm) and the second-class train at 7am (arrives Chihuahua 10.25pm), though remember that this line works on **Chihuahua time** – an hour later than local time in Los Mochis – so printed timetables will be one hour ahead of the times quoted here. Make sure you know which you are talking about when you find out when your train is leaving. Fares on the *Vista Tren* are currently $17 to Creel, $32 to Chihuahua; on the second-class train $6 to Creel and $10 to Chihuahua. The **ticket office** at the station opens at 5am for same-day sales for both trains; tickets for the *Vista Tren* can also be bought the previous day at *Viajes Flamingo*, under the *Hotel Santa Anita* in town. The **station** is 3km from the centre and although there are frequent buses (marked "Colonia Ferrocarril") from Zaragoza, between Hidalgo and Obregón, you can't rely on them to get you there in time for the 6am departure or the late evening arrival of trains from Chihuahua.

Taxi fares in Los Mochis are a long-established rip-off, so grin and bear it: if possible, gather a group of people and arrange in advance for a driver to pick you up, as there can be a rush when the train is about to leave. Normally, though, taxis are easy enough to find, especially around the bus stations and *Hotel Santa Anita* – the hotel also lays on a free bus for guests only, connecting with the tourist trains.

The **Nogales–Guadalajara** line doesn't in fact come to Los Mochis at all – its junction with the Chihuahua line is actually near **San Blas**, Sinaloa (not to be confused with the better-known San Blas in Nayarit), some 40km inland, at a station known as **Sufragio**. If you're **coming down from Chihuahua**, you should be able to make a direct connection with the slow train to Guadalajara, but you're probably better off waiting for the first-class train, which passes through in the early hours (6.25am heading north, 2.15am coming south). It's better still if you are on the first-class northbound which, if on schedule, will reach Sufragio just before the Chihuahua-bound *Vista Tren* comes through, though if you miss it there's nothing to do while you wait for the next train. A bus operates every thirty minutes during the day between Sufragio, San Blas and Los Mochis' *Norte de Sinaloa* terminal, at the corner of Zaragoza and Ordoñez.

Buses for the forty-minute journey to Topolobampo, and the **ferries**, operate every fifteen minutes from Cuauhtémoc, between Zaragoza and Prieta. Departures for the 9–10hr **crossing to La Paz** are daily except Sunday at 9am; you can buy tickets as you board, but as ever it's safest to get them, and check the timetable, in advance. The downtown *SEMATUR* office is in the *Viajes Paotam* travel agency at Rendón 519 (Mon–Fri 8.30am–6.30pm, Sat 8.30am–2pm; ☎681/5-82-62), about six blocks north of Hidalgo – take Flores, then turn left at Rendón.

lines, the Los Mochis–Chihuahua and the Nogales–Guadalarjara, have at least attempted to synchronize their schedules, but given the unreliability of timetables on both, this has helped little. The **ferry**, meanwhile, leaves from the port at Topolobampo, 24km away, and although the Chihuahua line goes there, the train doesn't carry passengers beyond Los Mochis. For full details, see "Moving on from Los Mochis".

What all this boils down to is that almost no matter how you arrange things, if you're taking the ferry or train you'll have little choice but to **stay** at least one night here. Don't expect much excitement. The sweltering grid of streets that makes up Los Mochis has no real focus, but what there is of a **town centre** is on Hidalgo, between Prieto and Leyva. From the *Tres Estrellas* station, head right along Juárez then, after four blocks, left onto Leyva; from *TNS* or *Pacifico*, turn left along Morelos and next left onto Leyva.

To kill an afternoon you could pop out to **TOPOLOBAMPO**, a strange place on an almost Scandinavian coastline of green, deeply inset bays – there's water all around but the ocean itself is invisible and the ferry steams in through a narrow channel, appearing suddenly from behind a hill into what seems a landlocked lake. No beaches, unfortunately, but you might persuade a local fisherman to take you out for a ride round the bay and a swim off the boat. The *Sociedad Cooperativa de Servicios Turisticos* runs trips out to the offshore islands, some of which host colonies of sea lions. Should you wish to **stay**, try *Pension Paotam* (☎681/5-19-14; ③).

Practicalities

Frankly, Los Mochis is dull; a place to get out of as fast as possible. There are few concessions to tourism, though you'll find a **tourist office** (Mon–Fri 8am–3pm & 4–7pm; ☎681/2-66-40) in the Unidad Administrativa building, Allende and Cuauhtémoc. You can **exchange currency** at *Banamex* (Mon–Fri until 2pm), at the corner of Prieto and Hidalgo, which also has an ATM. The **post office** is on Ordoñez, between Zaragoza and Prieto (Mon–Fri 9am–6pm, Sat 9am–1pm).

Since they don't have to try too hard to attract customers, most of whom are stuck here, many of the **hotels** in Los Mochis are poor value. The situation with **eating** is equally grim: there are plenty of places around the hotels and the bus terminals, but nowhere really exciting, and hardly anywhere at all if you arrive late.

Accommodation

Of the cheaper **places to stay**, the *Hotel Los Arcos*, Allende 534 Sur at Castro (☎681/2-32-53; ③), is the best: friendly though cramped and with shared bathrooms. The *Hotel Hidalgo*, on Hidalgo Pte. 260 between Prieto and Zaragoza (☎681/2-34-56; ④), is marginally more expensive and usually has space – probably because some of its rooms are pretty foul; check cleanliness and the efficiency of the air conditioning first. Moving up a notch, the *Hotel Catalina*, on Obregón 186 between Allende and Degollado (☎681/2-12-40; ⑤), is not as good as it looks; you'll get better value for a similar price at the *Lorena*, Obregón at the corner of Prieto (☎681/2-02-39; ⑤), or especially the *Montecarlo*, Flores at Independencia (☎681/2-18-18; ⑤), where spacious rooms are set around a colonial-style courtyard. The luxury option is the modernish and rather bland *Hotel Santa Anita*, Leyva and Hidalgo (☎681/8-70-46; ⑧), owned by the same people who operate many of the fancier lodges along the Copper Canyon line. It's often full with tour groups, but is also good for information and making reservations.

Eating

You're not going to do much gourmet dining in Los Mochis. *Mi Cabaña*, on the corner of Obregón and Allende, serves excellent *tacos* and *burritos;* *El Gordo*, a very plain place with good-value *comidas*, is at Zaragoza and Morelos – handy for *Norte de Sonora* and *Pacifico* bus stations. *La Chispa*, Leyva 115 Sur, does particularly good breakfasts

---

and light meals in clean surroundings, as does the a/c *Restaurant Panama Leon*, Obregón 419 between Leyva and Flores, which also serves decent coffee. The reliable Mexican-Spanish *Restaurant España*, Obregón 525 (☎681/2-23-35), has international pretensions and prices to match. *El Taquito*, just over a block up Leyva from here, near the *Santa Anita Hotel*, is also on the expensive and bland side, but clean and reassuring – it claims to be open 24 hours.

Culiacán

Some 200km south of Los Mochis, **CULIACÁN**, the capital of Sinaloa, is a prosperous city with a population of nearly a million, surrounded by some of the richest arable land in Mexico. It appears horribly ugly where it sprawls along the highway, but at its heart it's not too bad – mostly modern, but not unattractive. There's a lot more life in the streets, too, than in any of its near neighbours – probably thanks to the State University in the centre of town. Buses on the main road directly opposite the Camionera will take you to the **Cathedral**, from where you can head three blocks downhill to the **market**. You could pass an hour or so inspecting the artworks in the local **Centro Cultural**, or get to local **beaches** at Atlata or El Tambor, about an hour away by bus. None of this, however, really adds up to any very compelling reason to stop, especially as Mazatlán is only another 200km further south. In any case, it's often extremely hard to get back on a bus, all too many of which are *de paso*.

Practicalities

The several **hotels** right by the Central Camionera all seem to charge the same. Given this, the best choice is the *Salvador*, Leyva Solano 297 (☎67/13-44-62; ⑤), directly opposite. There's better value, and more interesting surroundings, downtown. The *Hotel San Francisco* (☎67/13-58-63; ⑤), Hidalgo Pte. 227, just by the market, is the best choice; you could also try the *Hotel Santa Fe* (☎67/15-17-00; ⑤), at Hidalgo Pte. 243, or the slightly more upmarket, modern and airy *Santa Fe II* (☎67/16-01-40; ⑥), Hidalgo Pte. 321. There's **street food** aplenty round here, and several pizza places, but otherwise not too many restaurants in the centre – the *Restaurant Santa Fe*, Hidalgo Pte. 317, isn't bad, or stick with the bus station restaurant.

Mazatlán

About 20km from **MAZATLÁN** you cross the Tropic of Cancer. It can't be a sudden transformation but somehow it always seems that way: Mazatlán is a tropical town where Culiacán was not, and there's that damp airlessness about it which at first makes breathing seem an effort.

Primarily, of course, Mazatlán is a resort, and a burgeoning one at that, with hotels stretching further every year along the coast road to the north, flanking a series of

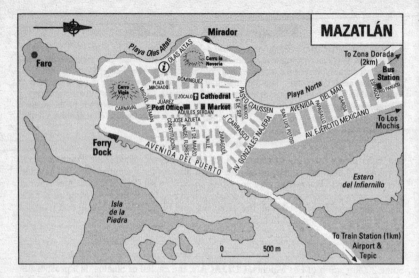

excellent sandy beaches. The new avenues of hotels may be entirely devoted to tourism, but that said, on the whole Mazatlán seems far less dominated by its visitors than its direct rivals Acapulco or Puerto Vallarta. Most holidaymakers stay in the *Zona Dorada*, the "Golden Zone", and penetrate the town itself only on brief forays.

Though heavily dependent on tourism, Mazatlán is also Mexico's largest Pacific port and a thrusting town in its own right, and thanks to its situation on a relatively narrow peninsula, the centre of town has preserved much of its old, cramped and thoroughly Mexican atmosphere. There's not a great deal actually to *do* in Mazatlán – you certainly wouldn't come here for the architecture – but it is a pleasant enough place and the separation of town and tourism means that you can find some remarkably good-value hotels on the streets just a few blocks inland. Mexican families mostly stay here, making the beachfront developments almost exclusively foreign preserves. There's an excellent bus service out along the coast road, so staying in town doesn't mean sacrificing the beach-bum lifestyle: with discretion, non-residents can use the hotel pools and the beaches in front of them. Remember to book accommodation well ahead if you are planning to be here around **Semana Santa**, when Mexicans descend on the city for carnival celebrations.

Arrival, information and city transport

From the **bus station**, head up the hill to the main road and get on just about any bus heading to the right – they'll get you, by a variety of routes, to the **market**, very central and effectively the terminus for local buses. For the *Zona Dorada*, walk downhill from the bus station and catch a "Sábalo" bus heading to the right along the coast road.

Arriving by **ferry** you'll be at the docks, south of the centre: there are buses here, but getting an entire ferry-load of people and their baggage on to two or three of them always creates problems. Taxis are in demand too, so try to be among the first off the boat. If you do get stranded, don't despair: the 1km walk to the centre of the old town isn't too bad. The **train station** is east of town in the Esperanza district; buses run from here to the market, and taxis also meet most arrivals. Mazatlán **airport** is some 20km south of town; there's the regular system of fixed-price vans ($22) and taxis.

Information

Mazatlán's **tourist office** (Mon–Fri 9am–2pm & 4–7pm; ☎69/85-12-20) is at Olas Altas 1300 in the *Banco de México* building; they're helpful, speak English, and have reasonable maps. In the *Zona Dorada*, commercial information booths pop up on almost every corner – selling tours and condos, mostly, but some give friendly free advice too. If you have any trouble – theft, accident and so forth – seek help from what is effectively a **district attorney for tourists** (☎69/14-32-22) at Rodolfo Loaiza 100, in the conference centre-mall complex opposite the *Hotel Los Sabalos* on the main seafront avenue.

Most places in the *Zona* accept **dollars** though often at a poor rate, so you may want to make use of Mazatlán's numerous **casas de cambio**. In the old town the main *Banamex* office on Juárez at Ángel Flores by the zócalo has the longest hours (8.30am–1pm) and good exchange rates. The main **post office**, Juárez and 21 de Marzo (Mon–Fri 8am–5.45pm, Sat 9am–1pm), is nearby, and you can make calls from any number of **long-distance phones** around the town or in the *Larga Distancia* places at Serdán 1512 (24hr), in the bus station or at several sites in the *Zona*.

City transport

Downtown, you can walk just about everywhere, and the rest of the resort is stretched out 15km along the coast road northwards – all linked by a single bus route and patrolled by scores of taxis and little open *pulmonías* (they look like overgrown golf carts but are usually cut-down VW Beetles; cheaper than taxis as long as you fix the fare before getting in).

Accommodation

Almost all Mazatlán's cheaper **hotels** are downtown, within a short walk of the market. There's also a small group around the bus station: convenient for transport and beaches, but not the most appealing part of town. Many have two classes of rooms, with and without a/c. The fancier hotels are all in the *Zona Dorada*, but even here some of the older places, and those on the fringes, can be real bargains out of high season or for longer stays.

If you're in a group it is worth looking round for an **apartment**, which are usually great value. **Trailer parks** tend not to last very long, occupying vacant lots and then moving north to keep ahead of development, so perhaps the best course for campers is to drive or take the bus along the beach unt5il you spot a promising location. Two of the most permanent sites are are *Trailer Park Playa Escondida*, Playa Escondida (☎69/88-00-77), in a quiet location almost at the end of the bus route, so probably safe from development for a few seasons (it also rents bungalows with kitchenettes; ④), and *Trailer Park Rosa Mar*, Cámaron Sábalo 702 (☎69/83-61-87), which is closer to the action.

The old town

Central, Belisario Domínguez between Ángel Flores and Escobedo (☎69/82-18-88). Comfortable a/c rooms with TV in characterless business hotel. ④.

Hotel del Centro, Canizales 705 Pte. (☎69/81-26-73). Large clean rooms all with private bath and some with a/c, close to centre. ③.

Joncol's, Belisario Domínguez 149 just off Paseo Claussen (☎69/81-21-31). Slightly bizarre tile-floored rooms in concrete hotel well past its prime; great position though, good value, and popular with Mexican holidaymakers. ③.

La Siesta, Olas Altas 11 between Ángel Flores and Escobedo (☎69/81-26-40). Lovely old hotel with great sea views (worth the extra money); drawbacks are small rooms and noise till late from *El Shrimp Bucket* restaurant in the inner patio. Off-season rooms for as little as half-price. ④.

Vialta, Jose Azueta 2006, about three blocks north of the market (☎69/81-60-27). Plain but acceptable rooms round a courtyard; some with a/c. ③.

Zaragoza, Zaragoza 217 between Serdán and Juárez (☎69/81-36-66). What you'd expect from almost the cheapest in town, but the bare rooms are clean, with fan and bath, and the whole place feels spacious and cool. ②.

Near the bus station

Economico, Esperanza, (☎69/82-13-00). Suitably named; very basic. ③.

Emperador, Río Panuco, right opposite the bus station (☎69/82-67-24). Convenience is the main attraction, though rooms are clean and comfortable; some with TV and a/c. ④.

Esperanza, Ejército Mexicano (☎69/81-79-25). Marginally cheaper than *Economico* and a little nicer, but avoid the noisy front rooms. Turn left out of the bus station and take the second left. ②.

Motel Acuario, Av. del Mar near the Aquarium (☎69/82-67-24). A short way down towards the *Zona*, the *Acuario*'s rooms are spartan with no a/c, though there is a pool. ④.

Sands Hotel, Av. del Mar 1910 (☎69/82-00-00). Facing the beach, straight down from the bus station. Comfortable, US-style motel with pool and sea views; very good value, especially off-season, when prices drop by $10. ⑤.

Zona Dorada

Apartamentos Fiesta, Ibis 502 (☎69/13-53-55). Well into the *Zona* off Playa Gaviotas, three blocks inland from the *Hotel Balboa Towers*. Basic, good-value apartments and studios in garden setting for four or six people. Normally rented by the week, but in the off season can be rented per night. ②–⑤.

Del Real Suites, Av. del Mar 1020 (☎69/83-19-55). Well-appointed hotel with parking, a/c, cable TV and a pool. Accommodation (considerably cheaper by the week) is either in large suites with kitchenette (sleeping up to 5), smaller suites or kitchen-less rooms. ⑤–⑦.

Inn at Mazatlán, Camarón Sábalo 6291 (☎69/13-55-00). The place to do it in style; a classy hotel-time share complex that oozes chic (at least by Mazatlán standards). Larger apartment units are excellent value for families or small groups. ⑧.

Las Jacarandas, Av. del Mar 2500, at entrance to the *Zona* (☎69/84-11-77). Along with the nearby *San Diego*, an older hotel with a pool that's been left behind by development and can no longer draw the crowds. Fading, but good value; some rooms with a/c and sea views. ④.

Motel Marley, Rodolfo Loaiza 226 (☎69/13-55-33). Comfortable units in small-scale place with great position right on the sand, and a pool. ⑦.

Plaza Gaviotas, Bugambilias 100 (☎69/13-42-33). Pool and good position, but the shabby rooms don't really justify the price, despite the cable TV. ⑤.

The Town

As befits a proper Mexican town, Mazatlán's **zócalo** is very much the commercial heart of the city, harbouring the cathedral (modern and not at all attractive), government offices, the post office, main bank branches and travel agencies. Always animated, it's especially lively on Sunday evening (5–7pm), when there's a free *folklórico* show with singing and dancing. Take time to stroll through the **market**, and in the other direction have a look round the newly restored **Plaza Machado**, surrounded by fine nineteenth-century buildings, including the **Teatro Ángela Peralta**, which often hosts interesting events or exhibitions. As far as sights go, that's about it, though you could also check out the small **Museo de Arqueología**, Sixto Osuna 76 (Tues–Sun 10am–1pm & 4–6pm; $1), just a couple of blocks towards Olas Altas, or the **Aquarium** (daily 10am–6pm; $4), just off Av. del Mar halfway between town and the *Zona Dorada*. There are also some great **views** of town from the top of the Cerro Vigia or Cerro La Nevería; unless you're feeling very energetic, take a *pulmonía* or taxi up. Likewise, the top of the **Faro de Creston** (unrestricted access) at the southern edge of town is a good vantage point, though you'll have to walk up.

The beach

Right in town, **Playa Olas Atlas** is a great place to watch the sun go down or the local kids playing, but not the best place to swim – it's rather rocky and the waves tend to be big. Following the seafront drive from here around the rocky coast under the Cerro La Nevería brings you to the **Mirador** – an outcrop of rock from which local daredevil youths plunge into the sea. At little over 10m, it's nowhere near as spectacular as the high-diving in Acapulco, but dangerous nonetheless. You'll see them performing whenever there are enough tourists to raise a collection, but generally from 10 or 11am – especially in summer and during *Semana Santa* – and again in the late afternoon (around 5pm) when the tour buses come past.

The Zona Dorada

To get to the **northern beaches** from here, you have to go back into the centre of town or continue all the way round to Playa Norte, as the buses don't follow the coast round the Cerro la Nevería. In general, the further north you go the better, and certainly there's no point stopping at the exposed **Playa Norte** unless you happen to be staying right by it. The sands improve greatly around **Sábalo**, a short way into the *Zona Dorada*, where the first of the big hotels went up and where many of them still are. It really depends from here on what you want – the beaches right in front of the hotels are clean and sheltered by little offshore islands (boats sail out to these from various points along the beach), while further on they're wilder but emptier. The more populous area has its advantages – it never gets too crowded (most people stay by their pools and bars) and there's always a lot going on: waterskiing, sailing, parascending behind speedboats, you name it. And if you get bored, there are the hotel pools and bars and any number of tourist watering-holes and shops to pass the time. Among the dozens of *artesanía* markets and shopping malls, **Sea Shell City**, on Rodolfo Loaiza in the heart of the *Zona*, stands out as the kitschest of all – a two-storey emporium of sea shells that describes itself as a museum and is definitely worth a look. Stay on the bus past all this, though, and you eventually get to an area where there's far less development. Along the way you can see just how quickly Mazatlán is spreading, and assess progress on the new marina development by the *Hotel Camino Real*. Towards the end of the bus line, make sure you get off somewhere you can reach the beach – often the only access is through villa or condo developments with gates and security. **Buses** (marked "Sábalo") leave from the market on the Juárez side, and run up Av. del Mar and right through the *Zona* to the last hotel, where they turn around. Those marked "Cerritos" can be picked up along Insurgentes and run past Cerritos, eventually turning around twenty minutes or so out of the *Zona* at Playa Escondida.

In the other direction, you can take a short and inexpensive boat trip (every 10min; 5am–11pm) from the end of the ferry docks to the **Isla de la Piedra**, actually a long peninsula. On the far side there are excellent swimming and snorkelling beaches where you can sleep out or sling a hammock on the terrace of one of the small restaurants. Once a very basic community, the Isla is increasingly included in tour itineraries and can, at times, become positively crowded. Also from the docks, the *Yate Fiesta* three-hour **harbour cruise** leaves daily at 11am (☎69/85-22-37 or 38; $12).

Eating and drinking

As a rule, Mazatlán's more authentic and lower-priced **restaurants** are in the old town; but you can come across bargains in the *Zona* too, as long as you don't mind the menu being in English and the prices in dollars. The sheer number of tourists there means lots of competition and **special offers**; breakfast deals are often the best of all. For rock-bottom prices, seek out the noisy and hectic restaurants on the upper floor of the **market** on the Juárez side.

The old town

Café Pacifico, Constitución 509 at Heriberto Frías. "European pub" that also serves snacks, sandwiches and coffee. A relaxing place to drink (until around midnight) without the macho overtones of many Mexican bars.

La Casa de Ana, Constitución 515. Excellent veggie place with tables under the shady trees around the Plaza Machado. Open daily until 10pm (7pm on Sun); *comidas corridas* noon–5pm.

Restaurant Doney's, Escobedo 610 at 5 de Mayo. Classy and slightly touristy place that's not as pricey as you might think – well worth it for good local food, including a fine *comida corrida*.

Jade, Morelos just off 5 de Mayo. About the only Chinese restaurant in the centre; not at all bad.

El Jardin, right under the bandstand in the zócalo. Cafe with good coffee – great if you don't mind the smell of boot polish wafting in from the stands outside.

Hostería Machado, Constitución 519. Fancy restaurant on the Plaza Machado with a piano player in the evening.

Pastelería Panamá, Juárez and Canizales, between the zócalo and the market. Fast-food style restaurant/cafeteria, good for breakfast.

Royal Dutch, Juárez, between Escobedo and Constitución. Great coffee, cakes and *tortas* served around an arcaded patio, all marked by a windmill sign.

El Shrimp Bucket, in the *Hotel La Siesta*, Olas Altas 11, between Ángel Flores and Escobedo. One of the oldest and best-known restaurants in Mazatlán – and apparently the original of the Carlos Anderson chain – it seems a little faded now, but still has plenty of atmosphere and decent, if pricey food.

Restaurante Vegetariano, Belisario Domínguez at 21 de Marzo. Simpler, cheaper alternative to the *Casa de Ana*, serving lunch only, 12.30–3pm.

Zona Dorada

Casa Loma, Gaviotas 104 (☎69/83-53-98). For that perfect romantic, and expensive, evening, this secluded restaurant in a colonial setting has far more atmosphere than the big hotels. Tends only to be open in peak season, however, and reservations are recommended.

No Name Café, Rodolfo Loaiza opposite the arts and crafts centre. Food and breakfast specials, but mainly a place for cool beer, party atmosphere, and big-screen TV sports. Typical among many.

El Tío Juan, Rodolfo Loaiza at Bugambilias. Again, just one of many similar places; friendly, English-speaking and not bad value if you choose with care or look for special offers. Cheap breakfasts.

Listings

Car rental Dozens of outlets, including *Budget*, Camarón Sábalo 402 (☎69/13-20-00); *National*, Camarón Sábalo 7000 (☎69/13-60-00).

American Express Camarón Sábalo, Plaza Balboa in the *Zona* (Mon–Fri 9am–1pm & 4–6pm; ☎69/13-06-00). Poor rates for cheques, but cardholders can receive mail.

Consulates *Canada*, Hotel Playa Mazatlán, Zona Dorada (☎69/13-73-20); *USA* (representative only), *Hotel Playa Mazatlán* (☎69/13-44-55 and ask for rep).

Language courses *Centro de Idiomas*, Belisario Domínguez 1908 (☎69/82-20-53), offers courses from a week to a month, starting at around $100; they can also arrange accommodation with Mexican families.

Laundry *Lavafacil* opposite the bus station by the *Hotel Fiesta*, and others at regular intervals throughout the *Zona* – in the *Puebla Bonita* complex, for example. Also several downtown.

Medical emergencies *Cruz Verde*, Gutiérrez Najéra and Obregón (☎81-22-25).

Police ☎83-45-10.

Mazatlán to Durango

Leaving Mazatlán, you face the choice of continuing down the coast to Tepic and from there along the main road to Guadalajara, or more Pacific beaches at San Blas and Puerto Vallarta, or cutting **inland to Durango** and the colonial cities of the Mexican

---

MOVING ON FROM MAZATLÁN

Mazatlán's large **bus station** lies on the main west coast route linking Tijuana and Mexicali in the north with Guadalajara and México in the south. The station has all facilities, including *guardería* and long-distance phones, and there are constant departures north and south. The region's major **bus companies** – *Transportes Norte de Sonora* (☎69/81-23-35), *Tres Estrellas de Oro* and *Elite* (both ☎69/81-36-80), and *Transportes del Pacífico* (☎69/82-05-77) – all have *de paso* services roughly hourly in both directions and frequent local buses to **Culiacán** (4hr), **Los Mochis** (7hr), **Tepic** (4hr) and **Guadalajara** (4hr). In addition, two buses daily run direct to **San Blas** (currently 11am & 5pm; 4hr). *Estrella Blanca* (☎69/81-53-81) and *Transportes Frontera* between them cover the route to **Durango** (13 daily; 6hr). To **get to the bus station**, take a "Sábalo" bus along the beachfront from Juárez near the market, then walk the 300m along Espinoza.

The **train station** (☎69/84-67-10) – on the west Mexico main line between Guadalajara and Mexicali/Nogales – lies 3km inland from the centre of Mazatlán and is served by one first-class and one second-class train in each direction. **Timetables** change frequently and trains are often late so check locally, but the northbound first-class train, which is comfortable enough to sleep on, is scheduled to reach **Sufragio** (near Los Mochis) in time to meet the tourist train up to the Copper Canyon and Chihuahua. **Tickets** can only be bought at the station and go on sale an hour before the train departs. **Getting to the station** from town, catch the "Insurgentes" bus on Juárez, or a bus heading down Av. del Mar in the *Zona*.

The **ferry to La Paz** (daily except Sat at 3pm; 18hr) leaves the port at Playa Sur, 1km southeast of the centre: catch the "Playa Sur" bus from Juárez. **Information** and tickets are available from *SEMATUR* (8am–3pm; ☎69/81-70-20) at the port: a *salón* class ticket (available on all boats) qualifies you for a reclining seat ($19), a *turista* class ticket (daily except Wed) gets you a space in a 4-berth cabin ($38), *cabina* ($57) is a two-berth cabin, a small car will cost $135, and bicycles go free. Food on board isn't great and, though there are signs prohibiting bringing your own, no one checks or seems to care.

Direct **flights** leave Mazatlán airport (☎69/82-23-99) – 20km south of the city and only reachable by expensive taxi. These are run by *Aeroméxico* (☎69/14-11-11), *Alaska* (☎69/85-27-30), *Mexicana* (☎69/82-72-22), *Delta* (☎69/82-13-49), *Noroeste* (☎69/14-38-55) and *Saro* (☎69/84-97-68), but you'd do better booking through a **travel agent** such as *Turismo Coral*, 5 de Mayo 1615 (Mon–Fri 8am–2pm & 3–6.30pm; ☎69/81-32-90), two blocks west of the zócalo.

---

heartland. This road, the first to penetrate the Sierra Madre south of the border, is as wildly spectacular as any in the country, twisting and clawing its way up to the Continental Divide at over 2500m. New vistas open at every curve as you climb from tropical vegetation, through temperate forests of oak, to the peaks with their stands of fir and pine. It can get extremely cold towards the top, so keep plenty of warm clothing to hand to cover the T-shirt and shorts you'll need for the first sweaty hour. Little more than 300km, it's a very slow road, so reckon on six hours to Durango at the least.

Popular with tours from Mazatlán, but quiet otherwise, **CONCORDIA**, 42km inland, is an attractive colonial town with a reputation for making robust wooden furniture, examples of which crop up all over the region. The eighteenth-century Baroque **Church of San Sebastian**, overlooking the shady square, is unique in these parts but otherwise unexceptional, so you might as well press on towards the far grander edifices in the central highlands. For almost four hundred years, **COPALA**, a further thirty minutes on the bus towards Durango and a 1km walk down a side road, was Sinaloa's most important silver mining town. But in 1933 Charles Butters' processing plant closed, putting 600 people out of work; though the locals picked over the remains until the 1970s, the town's decline was already well advanced. The **jungle**, which has already engulfed the crushing mills and separation tanks, is nibbling at the edges of the village, which today largely relies on tourists from Mazatlán for its survival. Once the day-trippers leave, however, the place takes on a languorous air, making it a relaxing, and cool, place to **spend a night** or two. The *Copala Butter Company*, Plaza Juárez (☎69/85-42-25; ④), has beautiful rooms with bath, and a balcony with views of the eighteenth-century church across the central plaza. It also offers **self-catering** bungalows (⑤), sleeping up to four people, and an excellent and reasonably priced **restaurant** – a good thing since there's only one other place in town to eat.

South of Mazatlán: Tepic

Below Mazatlán the main road steers a little way inland, away from the marshy coastal flatlands. There are a few small beach communities along here, and deserted sands, but on the whole they're impossible to get to without transport of your own, and flyblown, exposed and totally lacking in facilities once you get there. The first town of any size, capital of the state of Nayarit and transport hub for the area, is **TEPIC**.

Despite its antiquity – the city was founded by Cortés' brother, Francisco, in 1544 – there's not a great deal to see in Tepic. Appealing enough in a quietly provincial way, for most it's no more than a convenient **stopover** before continuing across the mountains to Guadalajara or a place to switch buses for the coast. And this is probably the best way to treat it, for while the surrounding country can be beautiful, it's largely inaccessible and visited only by anthropologists for whom the mountains of Nayarit, homelands of the Huichol and Cora, are rich in interest.

The eighteenth-century **Cathedral**, on the zócalo, is worth a look, as is the small **Museo Regional** (Mon–Sat 9am–7pm; free), at the corner of Mexico and Zapata,

---

THE HUICHOL

The **Huichol**, some 10,000 of whom live in the isolated mountain regions around the borders of Nayarit, Jalisco, Zacatecas and Durango, are perhaps the indigenous people least affected by the four and a half centuries since the Spanish invasion of Mexico. New roads are bringing apparently inevitable pressure for "development" of their lands, but for now much of their territory remains accessible only by the occasional mule track or via one of many simple landing strips for light aircraft. In these fastnesses they have preserved, little affected by attempts at evangelization, their ancient beliefs, government and social forms.

Religion and ritual play such an intimate and constant part in Huichol lives that it's almost impossible for an outsider to comprehend. Even the simplest action or object or item of dress has ritual significance in a religion based on daily life: Mother Earth and Father Sun; the goddess of rain and the god of corn; the deer for hunters, and peyote for food gatherers. Peyote in particular, for which a group of Huichol have to make an annual cross-country pilgrimage to Real de Catorce (p.215), plays an important part in their ceremonials. Huichol **art** – brightly coloured wool "paintings" – is rich in stylized symbols based in nature: animals, suns, moons and traditional themes of fertility and birth. You can buy these pictures in Tepic and elsewhere, and you may see traditionally dressed Huichol at the market or paying homage in the Church of Santa Cruz in Tepic (the missionaries did have some effect, and two Christs have been absorbed into the Huichol pantheon). There's more chance of seeing Huichol life at **religious festivals** in nearby villages, though you should consider whether you want to add your possibly unwelcome intrusion to that of many others.

Getting to Huichol territory is not easy, despite daily light planes from the airport in Tepic; you'll need permission from the authorities, and of course there are no regular facilities to feed or house visitors, little to see in the collections of mud-floored shacks that make up the villages, and no guarantee that you'll be welcome.

south from the zócalo, with a lovely collection of local pre-Columbian and Huichol arte-facts. A couple of kilometres south on Mexico, the **Ex-Convento de la Cruz de Zacate**, built in the sixteenth century to house a miraculous cross, has today been restored for visitors. Plenty of places sell **Huichol art**: one of the best is upstairs at *Casa Arguet*, Amado Nervo 132, a couple of blocks north of the zócalo.

Practicalities

Tepic's **bus station** lies a couple of kilometres southeast of the centre, but local buses shuttle in and out from the main road outside; similarly, the **train station**, on the main Guadalajara to Nogales line, is 2km east of the centre on Zapata and linked by buses to the centre. The main **tourist office** (daily 9am–3pm) is south of the zócalo on Mexico, just before the Plaza Constituyentes; there's a smaller branch in the Ex-Convento de la Cruz de Zacate.

For just one night it's easiest to put up with the noise and stay by the bus station. Two cheap **hotels** with little to choose between them – the *Nayar* (☎321/3-23-22; ③) and the *Tepic* (☎321/3-13-77; ③) – stand immediately behind the terminal on Martínez. In the centre, try the *Hotel Serita*, Bravo Pte. 112 (☎321/2-13-33; ③), north of the zócalo, or the *Cibrian*, Amado Nervo Pte. 163 (☎321/2-86-98; ⑤), slightly closer, or for more comfort the *Sierra de Alicia*, Mexico Nte. 180 (☎321/2-03-25; ⑥), or the luxury *Fray Junípero Serra*, Lerdo Pte. 23 (☎321/2-22-11; ⑦), right on the zócalo. If you stay out by the bus station you'll want to hop on a bus to the centre anyway, to find something to eat and for something to do in the evening. For **food**, there's plenty of choice around the zócalo and on Mexico: *Altamirano*, Mexico Sur 109, serves substantial traditional Mexican food; *Café Diligencias*, Mexico Sur 29, is a good place to linger over a coffee; while *Acuarios*, Morelos Pte. 139, serves simple vegetarian dishes. Fancier restaurants, other than those in the hotels, are west of here, near the open spaces of the Parque La Loma: try for example *Roberto's*, Insurgentes and Paseo La Loma, on the far side of the park.

San Blas

West of Tepic lies the coastal plain: sultry, marshy and flat, dotted with palm trees and half-submerged under little lagoons teeming with wildlife. Through this you reach **SAN BLAS**, as godforsaken a little town as you could hope to see – at least at first impression. It was an important port in the days of the Spanish trade with the Orient, wealthy enough to need a fortress to ward off the depredations of English piracy, but though there's still an enviable natural harbour and a sizeable deep-sea fishing fleet, almost no physical relic of the town's glory days remains. Popular in winter with Californian surfers, in summer the town is virtually deserted save for legions of fero-cious mosquitoes.

There's an air of abandonment and torpor about San Blas – life is very, very slow, the houses neglected, the beach a mess, and many of the hotels and restaurants seem content to let things go. The other side of this is an enjoyably laid-back travellers' scene, with plenty of people who seem to have turned up years ago and never summoned the energy to leave. Though there's always talk of development, it seems a long way off; the latest hope is ecotourism, which will supposedly attract crowds to explore the wildlife in the marshes and lagoons.

Arrival and information

The majority of the **buses** serving San Blas arrive from Tepic, 65km east, though if you are coming from neighbouring coastal resorts you can save time and hassle by catching either the direct bus from Mazatlán (twice daily) or the service from Puerto

Vallarta (twice daily) via Las Varas along the coast. *Transportes Norte de Sonora* run these and a daily bus to Guadalajara via Tepic.

The **bus station** is on Sonora at the northeastern corner of the zócalo, right in the centre of town. Here Juárez, the main street into town, crosses Heroico Batallón de San Blas, which runs 1km south to the town beach, Playa de Barrego. Services on the zócalo include a small and irregularly open, though helpful, **tourist office** (no phone), a few steps west along Juárez. Though the *Banamex* branch, on Juárez just east of the zócalo, cashes cheques (Mon–Fri 8am–noon) and has an ATM, it is plagued by long queues, poor rates and an occasional surfeit of funds. Change money before you get here or, if pushed, see if the *Pato Loco* store next to the tourist office will change cheques. The **post office** is a block northeast of the bus station at Sonora and Echevarría, and long-distance **phones** can be found in the bus station.

Accommodation

Though there are no luxury **hotels** in San Blas, there's plenty of choice in the lower ranges. Most places are on Juárez or Heroico Batallón. The town is especially well geared to small, **self-catering** groups: "bungalows" and "suites" are apartments with up to six beds, a small kitchen and usually (though you should check) some cooking equipment. Wherever you stay, make sure that the screens are intact and the doors fit or you'll be plagued by biting **insects**.

The *Coco Loco* **trailer park** (☎321/5-00-55) is a shady and grassed camping area close to the beach, a kilometre down Batallón from the zócalo. There's also **free camping** on Playa de Barrego, but the bugs and the availability of good, cheap accommodation make this less than appealing.

Las Brisas, Cuauhtémoc 106, on the way to the beach (☎321/5-01-12). The best and priciest in town – comfortable a/c rooms, pool, garden, and some kitchenettes. Rates include breakfast. ⑦.

Casa María, Batallón at Michoacán (☎321/5-06-32). Budget stand-by, almost overfriendly; rooms with or without bath include use of kitchen; beds in communal rooms at peak times. ②.

Playa Hermosa, right on the beach, about a 30min walk south of the zócalo along Batallón: turn left at the *Coco Loco* trailer park and keep going. Legend has it that this elegant wreck was once a Mafia hotel. Today only 20 of the 100 or more rooms are in use, almost completely bare but clean and, if you don't mind sharing with a few lizards, the faded grandeur is worth any inconvenience. ③.

Portolá, Paredes 118, two blocks northeast of the zócalo (☎321/5-03-86). Immaculate rooms with good kitchenettes for up to 5 people. Resident or not, you can also rent bikes. Five people can pay as little as $30 between them. ④.

Posada del Rey, Campeche 10, not far from the water (☎321/5-01-23). Possibly the most together hotel in San Blas, with tiny pool and bar, and plain but comfortable rooms with a/c and fans. ⑥.

La Quinta California, Batallón (no phone). Good-value apartments with well-equipped kitchens, close to the beach behind *El Herradero Cantina*. ④–⑤.

Suites San Blas, down by the beach (☎321/5-05-05). Especially good value for groups or families – units for up to 6 people with (ill-equipped) kitchen in quiet spot with a pool. $40–45 for 6 people. ⑤.

The Town

When not lying on the pristine **beaches** to the south of San Blas or taking the excellent "jungle boat trip" to **La Tovara springs** (see below, for both), most people seem content just to relax or amble about town. A more focused hour can be spent at **La Contadora**, the ruins of a late eighteenth-century fort which, with the vaulted remains of a chapel, crown the Cerro de San Basilio near the river, a kilometre along Juárez towards Tepic. From here you get great views over the town to the ocean, where the small white island on the horizon is said, by the Huichol, to represent peyote. It marks the symbolic starting point of their annual pilgrimage to the central highlands (see "The Huichol" on p.112), the actual start being on the Isla del Rey, the lighthouse-topped peninsula across the Estero del Pozo channel from San Blas. The pilgrimage begins a couple of weeks before Easter, with feasts and elaborate ceremonies centred around a sacred **cave** below the lighthouse. Remains of the cave can still be seen, though most of it was criminally destroyed by the government in the 1970s to provide rock for a jetty. You can catch a **boat** across to the Isla del Rey from the landing stage at the end of Héroes 21 de Abril.

La Tovara and the jungle boat trip

The **lagoons and creeks** behind San Blas are almost unbelievably rich in bird and animal life – the ubiquitous white herons, or egrets, above all, but hundreds of other species too, which no one seems able to name (any bird here is described as a *garza* – a heron). The best way to catch a glimpse is to get on one of the three-hour trips "into the jungle", the *lancha* negotiating channels tunnelled through dense mangrove, flighting herons and frightening sunbaking turtles. Best time to go is at dawn, before other trips have disturbed the animals, when you might even glimpse a caiman along the way. Most trips head for **La Tovara**, a cool freshwater spring that fills a beautiful clear pool perfect for swimming and pirouetting off the rope swing. Eat at the fairly pricey *palapa* restaurant or bring your own picnic.

Trips leave from the river bridge 1km inland from the zócalo along Juárez, and can often be arranged the night before when boat owners prowl the hotels and restaurants for custom: get a group together for the best prices. The officially posted rates (around $54 for four; $10 per extra person) should be regarded as a maximum: off-season prices could be as little as half this. You may also want to consider negotiating something longer than the standard three hours, giving more time for swimming and wildlife-spotting en route. Shorter jungle boat trips leave from Matanchén (see below) but the longer boat ride from San Blas justifies the marginally higher cost.

Beaches

By far the best of San Blas' beaches are some 4km away around the **Bahía de Matanchén**, a vast, sweeping crescent of a bay entirely surrounded by fine soft sands. At the near end, the tiny community of **Las Islitas** on the Playa Miramar has numerous *palapa* restaurants on the beach, serving up grilled fish and cold beers and, on the point, a group of beautifully situated but expensive cabins for rent. At the far end lie **Aticama** (with more basic shops and places to eat) and the **Playa los Cocos**. In between, acres of sand are fragmented only by flocks of pelicans and the occasional crab. There are plenty of spots where you can camp if you have the gear and plenty of repellent, as well as a trailer park at Los Cocos. The waves here, which rise offshore beyond Miramar and run in, past the point, to the depths of the bay, are in the *Guinness Book of Records* as the longest in the world: it's very rare that they get up enough for surfers to be able to ride them all the way in, but there's plenty of lesser **surfing** potential – surf- and boogie-boards can be rented in Las Islitas or San Blas.

You can walk from San Blas to Matanchén, just about, on the roads through the lagoons – it's impossible to penetrate along the coast, which would be much shorter – but in the heat of the day it's far easier to get one of the buses ("Santa Cruz"), that leave several times a day from the zócalo, or a taxi (bargain fiercely).

Eating and drinking

Seafood is big business in San Blas; as well as the **restaurants** in town, you can buy it at beachfront *palapas* and from stands that spring up daily on the streets. There's also plenty of fruit and healthy offering to cater for the tourists. Down at the beach most places close around sunset and if you want to eat later you'll have to walk into town – a flashlight to guide your way is a worthwhile investment.

El Delfín, at *Hotel Las Brisas*. The best food in town. Sit outside in the evening protected by efficient mosquito screens. Pricey but not outrageous seafood, steak and the like.

La Isla, c/Mercado at Paredes. A must, if only to admire the astonishingly kitsch decor: draped fishing nets festooned with shell pictures, shell mobiles and shell lampshades. Moderately priced meat and seafood dishes of average quality.

McDonald's, Juárez 36. No relation to Ronald, this unpretentious restaurant just off the zócalo is a prime meeting place, particularly among ex-pats who gather here for breakfast. Broad menu and reasonable prices.

Mike's Place, Juárez 36 above *McDonald's*. Quiet drinking midweek but livens up on Friday and Saturday with dancing to anything from Latin to classic rock.

La Tumba de Yako, c/Batallón at Querétaro. Kiosk run by the local surf team, popular for its banana bread and natural yoghurt.

Around San Blas: Santiago Ixcuintla and Mexcaltitlán

North of San Blas, from Hwy-15 you could take the turn-off for **SANTIAGO IXCUINTLA**, a market town where the only real interest lies in the Huichol Centre for Cultural Survival and Traditional Arts (some way from the centre of town at 20 de Noviembre and Constitución). This co-operative venture, aimed at supporting Huichol people and preserving their traditions, raises money by selling quality Huichol art and offering various classes. From Santiago a road leads straight down to the coast and the **Playa Los Corchos**, a perfect stretch of sand lined with palm trees, by the mouth of the Río Grande de Santiago. Santiago has a few cheap hotels, but no other formal facilities – you might, however, find someone prepared to let you have a room, or at least space to sling a hammock under the verandah of one of the beach bars.

To the right beyond Santiago, another road leads across the lagoon to the extraordinary islet of **MEXCALTITLÁN**. The little town here must look something like a smaller version of Aztec Tenochtitlán before the Spanish arrived, laid out in radiating spokes from the centre of the round island. Local transport is by canoe along a series of tiny canals crossed by causeways, and indeed the place is one candidate for the site from which the Aztecs set out on their long trek to the Valley of Mexico. Mexcaltitlán sees very little tourism, but you should be able to find a guide to paddle you around the island, a room at the single **hotel** (④) near the church, and somewhere to eat. If you're in the area around the end of June you should definitely try to visit the island fiesta, on June 29, when there are canoe races around the lagoons and rivers.

Tepic to Guadalajara: Ixtlán

Between Tepic and Guadalajara it's a long climb over the Sierra Madre, with an excellent new toll road much of the way. **IXTLÁN DEL RÍO** is the first place you might be tempted to stop – the only other is Tequila (see p.177). Ixtlán was made famous by Carlos Castaneda's *Journey to Ixtlán*, attraction enough for a few – it's hard to believe that many find what they're after, though, for this is an exceptionally ugly little strip of ribbon development along the highway, beset by constant traffic noise from huge trucks and permanent jams. What it does offer is plenty of hotels and restaurants: if you do want to **stay**, try the *Hidalgo* (④) or the *Santa Rita* (④), two of the more central places on the highway. The *Río Viego*, very near the plaza, is a decent **restaurant**.

Disappointing as it may be in spiritual matters, Ixtlán does have one worthwhile attraction in its **archeological site**, a couple of kilometres east. The site is right by the highway and rail line: there are local buses, and second-class services on the main road should stop. Though not very impressive in comparison with the great sites in central and southern Mexico, this is one of the largest and most important in the west, with numerous heavily restored buildings of plain, unadorned stone. The site itself (dawn–dusk) has a series of rectangular buildings forming plazas, each centring on an altar. The finest structure, and the most thoroughly restored, is an unusual circular temple surrounded by a circular wall. The sides, which now slope out slightly, were originally vertical, so that the cylindrical building looked like a brazier: circular temples like this are usually associated with **Quetzalcoatl** in his guise of Ehecatl, God of Wind, but here the brazier shape may also refer to **Huehueteotl**, the Old God or God of Fire. Perhaps most impressive of all is the sheer size of the place. What you can see is extensive, but the site in total is said to cover an area five times larger – and this is an "insignificant" culture of which relatively little is known. Outside the site it's easy to spot piles of stones in the farm at the back and odd humps in the surrounding fields; at one point the site fence cuts through an obvious mound.

fiestas

February

3rd DÍA DE SAN BLAS. The feria in **San Blas** (Nayarit) starts on January 30th, with parades, dancing, fireworks and ceremonial.

CARNIVAL (the week before Lent, variable Feb–March) is celebrated with particular gusto in **La Paz** (Baja California Sur), **Ensenada** (Baja California Norte) and **Culiacán** (Sinaloa). The best carnival in the north, though, is at **Mazatlán** (Sin.).

March

19th DÍA DEL SEÑOR SAN JOSÉ. Saint's day celebrations in **San José del Cabo** (B.C.S.) with horse races, cockfights and fireworks, and in the hamlet of San José near **Guaymas** (Sonora), where the religious fervour is followed by a fair.

PALM SUNDAY (week before Easter) sees dramatizations of biblical episodes in **Jala** (Nay.), an ancient little town between Tepic and Guadalajara.

HOLY WEEK is widely honoured. High points include passion plays in **Jala** (Nay.), processions and native dances in **Rosamorada** (Nay.), north of Tepic on the main road, and, in the Yaqui town of **Cocorit** (Son.) near Ciudad Obregón, pilgrimages and Yaqui dances including the renowned *Danza del Venado*. This can also be seen in **Potam** (Son.), on the coast near here, along with curious ancient religious rites and the burning of effigies of Judas.

May

3rd DÍA DE LA SANTA CRUZ celebrated in **Santiago Ixcuintla** (Nay.), north of Tepic, a fiesta rich in traditional dances.

June

1st Maritime celebrations in the port of **Topolobampo** (Sin.) with parades and a fair.

24th DÍA DE SAN JUAN. **Guaymas** (Son.), **Navojoa** (Son.) and **Mochicahui** (Sin.), a tiny village near Los Mochis, all celebrate the saint's day with processions and, later, with native dancing. In **Navojoa** there's a *feria* that carries on to the beginning of July.

29th In **Mexcaltitlán** (Nay.) a religious fiesta in honour of St Peter, with processions in boats round the islet.

July

First Sunday *Romería* in **Tecate** (B.C.N.), extremely colourful, with cowboys, carnival floats and music.

25th DÍA DE SANTIAGO. Bizarrely celebrated in **Compostela** (Nay.), south of Tepic, where the men ride around on horses all day – the women take over their mounts the following morning and then do the same. Also boasts a fair with fireworks.

September

8th Formal religious processions in **Jala** (Nay.) with traditional dress and regional dances.

16th INDEPENDENCE DAY is a holiday everywhere in the country, and especially lively along the border. **Tijuana** (B.C.N.) has horse and motor races, *mariachi*, dancing, gambling and fireworks, while the much smaller crossing of **Agua Prieta** (Son.) has a more traditional version of the same, with parades and civic ceremonies.

28th DÍA DE SAN MIGUEL. A pilgrimage to Boca, a community located very close to **Choix** (Sin.), on the railway from Los Mochis. There's dancing and a number of parades in Choix, with a procession to Boca.

October

4th DÍA DE SAN FRANCISCO is the culmination of two weeks' fiesta in **Magdalena** (Son.), attended by many Indians (Yaqui and Sioux among them) who venerate this missionary saint. Traditional dances.

First Sunday In **Guasave** (Sin.), between Los Mochis and Culiacán, a pilgrimage to the Virgen del Rosario, with many dance groups.

Last Sunday Repetition of events in **Guasave** and, in **Ixtlán del Río** (Nay.), hundreds of pilgrims arrive to observe the DÍA DE CRISTO REY – more dancing.

November

2nd DAY OF THE DEAD celebrations everywhere – **Navojoa** (Son.) is one of the more impressive.

December

First Sunday Lively festival honouring El Señor de la Misericordia in **Compostela** (Nay.).

8th DÍA DE LA INMACULADA CONCEPCIÓN celebrated by the pilgrims who converge on **Alamos** (Son.), and in **Mazatlán** (Sin.), with parades, music and dancing. **La Yesca**, in a virtually inaccessible corner of Nayarit east of Tepic, has religious ceremonies and a *feria* attended by many Huichol people which lasts till the 12th.

12th DÍA DE LA VIRGEN DE GUADALUPE. In **Navojoa** (Son.), the climax of ten days of activities comes with a procession. **Tecate** (B.C.N.) and **Acaponeta**, on the main road in northern Nayarit, both have lively and varied fiestas.

travel details

Buses

Services on the main highways south from Tijuana or Nogales are excellent, with constant fast traffic and regular express services, if you want them, from the border all the way to México. Be warned, though, that *de paso* buses can be hard to pick up along the way, especially in Hermosillo, Culiacán and Los Mochis. Baja California has far fewer services. Chief operators are *Tres Estrellas de Oro* – arguably the most reliable company – *Transportes del Pacifico* and *Transportes Norte de Sonora* (*TNS*), with dozens of second-class companies serving lesser destinations. For long distances and on the busiest routes you might consider one of the pullman services run by companies like *Elite*, with airline-style seats, drinks, video and icily effective air conditioning. The following frequencies and times are for f**irst-class services**. Second-class buses usually cover the same routes, running 10–20 percent slower.

Cabo San Lucas to: La Paz via San José del Cabo (6 daily; 3–4hr); La Paz via Todos Santos (8 daily; 2hr); San José del Cabo (roughly hourly; 30min); Todos Santos (8 daily; 1hr).

Ensenada to: Bahía de Los Angeles (one weekly, Sat 8am; 7hr); Guerrero Negro (7 daily; 8hr); La Paz (4 daily; 20hr); Loreto (6 daily; 15hr); Mexicali (4 daily; 4hr); San Felipe (2 daily; 3hr 30min); Tijuana (hourly; 1hr 30min).

Guaymas to: Hermosillo (every 30min; 1hr 30min); Los Mochis (every 30min; 5hr); Mexicali (every 30min; 11hr); Navojoa (every 30min; 3hr); Nogales (hourly; 5hr 30min); Tijuana (every 30min; 14hr).

Guerrero Negro to: Ensenada (7 daily; 8hr); La Paz (4 daily; 12hr); San Ignacio (7 daily; 3hr); Santa Rosalía (7 daily; 4hr); Tijuana (7 daily; 10hr).

Hermosillo to: Bahía de Kino (9 daily; 2hr); Guaymas (every 30min; 1hr 30min); Mexicali (every 30min; 9–10hr); Nogales (hourly; 4hr); Tijuana (every 30min 12–13hr).

La Paz to: Cabo San Lucas via Todos Santos (8 daily; 2hr); El Rosario (4 daily; 16hr); Ensenada (4 daily; 20hr); Guerrero Negro (4 daily; 12hr); Loreto (4 daily; 5hr); Mulegé (4 daily; 7hr); San Ignacio (4 daily; 9hr); San José del Cabo via eastern route (6 daily; 3–4hr); Santa Rosalía (4 daily; 8hr); Tijuana (4 daily; 22hr); Todos Santos (8 daily; 1hr).

Los Mochis to: Guaymas (every 30min; 17hr); Mazatlán (every 30min; 7hr); Navojoa (every 30min; 2–3hr); Tijuana (every 30min; 19hr); Topolobampo (every 15min; 40min).

Mazatlán to: Culiacán (every 30min; 4hr); Durango (13 daily; 6hr); Guadalajara (every 30min; 9hr); Los Mochis (every 30min; 7hr); San Blas (2 daily; 4hr); Tepic (every 30min; 4hr); Tijuana (every 30min; 26hr).

Mexicali to: Ensenada (4 daily; 4hr); Guaymas (every 30min; 11hr); Hermosillo (every 30min; 9–10hr); San Felipe (4 daily; 3hr); Tijuana (every 30min; 3hr).

Navojoa to: Ciudad Obregón (every 30min; 1hr 30min); Guaymas (every 30min; 3hr); Los Mochis (every 30min; 2–3hr); Tijuana (every 30min; 17hr).

Nogales to: Agua Prieta (2 daily; 3–4hr); Guaymas (hourly; 5hr 30min); Hermosillo (hourly; 4hr).

San Blas to: Mazatlán (2 daily; 4hr); Puerto Vallarta (2 daily; 3–4hr); Santiago Ixcuintla (3 daily; 1hr); Tepic (hourly; 1hr 30min).

Santa Rosalía to: Guerrero Negro (7 daily; 4hr); La Paz (4 daily; 8hr); Loreto (8 daily; 3hr); Mulegé (8 daily; 1hr); San Ignacio (7 daily; 1hr); Tijuana (4 daily; 14hr).

Tepic to: Guadalajara (every 30min; 5hr); Mazatlán (every 30min; 4hr); Puerto Vallarta (hourly; 3–4hr); San Blas (hourly; 1hr 30min); Tijuana (every 30min; 30hr).

Tijuana to: Culiacán (every 30min; 22hr); El Rosario (4 daily; 6hr); Ensenada (hourly; 1hr 30min); Guadalajara (every 30min; 35hr); Guaymas (every 30min; 14hr); Guerrero Negro (7 daily; 10hr); Hermosillo (every 30min; 12–13hr); La Paz (4 daily; 22hr); Loreto (4 daily; 17hr); LA (12 daily; 4hr); Los Mochis (every 30min; 19hr); Mazatlán (every 30min; 26hr); Mexicali (every 30min; 3hr); Mulegé (4 daily; 15hr); Navojoa (every 30min; 17hr); San Ignacio (4 daily; 13hr); Santa Rosalía (4 daily; 14hr); Tepic (every 30min; 30hr).

Trains

The main line through northwestern Mexico runs from Nogales to Guadalajara, connecting with the Sonora–Baja California line to Mexicali at Benjamin Hill (Son.), and with the amazing Chihuahua–Los Mochis Copper Canyon railway at Sufragio (Sin.). Two trains – one first-class, the other second – run in each direction each day. Remember that on both lines timetables are confused by the hour's difference between the region covered in this chapter and the rest of Mexico. The Los Mochis–Chihuahua *Vista Tren* departs Los Mochis daily 6am, regular train at 7am local time.

Planes

Almost every town of any size has an airport, with flights, not necessarily direct, to México. Busiest are Tijuana – with half a dozen flights a day to the capital by a variety of routings and a couple direct to Guadalajara – and La Paz, with flights to México and many towns along the mainland coast. Mazatlán is the busiest of all. *Aero California* is the biggest of the new local operators, though *Mexicana* and *Aeroméxico* operate flights to major Mexican cities, often at prices little higher than the equivalent cost of the bus.

La Paz to: Guadalajara (1 daily); Los Angeles via Loreto (1 daily); México (1 daily); Tijuana (2 daily); Tucson (1 daily).

Mazatlán to: Denver (3 per week); La Paz (1 daily); Los Angeles (3 daily); México (4 daily) and Tijuana (2 daily).

Ferries

All ferries linking Baja to the mainland were, until recently, state-run and subsidized, their primary function being to help the development of the peninsula. As part of the government's privatization programme they were sold off to a Japanese concern which runs them on a commercial basis. Accordingly, prices have risen for all users. Private vehicles do not have a high priority, and at times may have to wait days for space. Even foot passengers face extremely long queues: best arrive at the office well before it opens on the morning of departure (morning before for early ferries) – most offices are open 8.30am–1pm.

La Paz to: Mazatlán (daily except Sat/daily during holiday periods; 18hr); Topolobampo (daily except Tues; 9–10hr).

Santa Rosalía to: Guaymas (2 weekly; 7hr).

CHAPTER TWO

BETWEEN THE SIERRAS: NORTHEAST ROUTES

The central and eastern routes into Mexico are considerably shorter than the west coast road, and, though they don't have the beaches, they do offer direct access to the country's colonial heart and much of interest along the way. The high plain between the flanks of the Sierra Madre is also cool – often uncomfortably so in winter – and the highways crossing it are fast.

You'll find most interest heading down from **Ciudad Juárez**: an important archeological site at **Casas Grandes**, and in **Chihuahua** and **Durango** a foretaste of the majesty of the colonial cities to come in the country's heartland. There are historic connotations too: this was the country most fiercely fought for in the Revolution, and the breeding ground for Pancho Villa's *División del Norte*. The supreme attraction

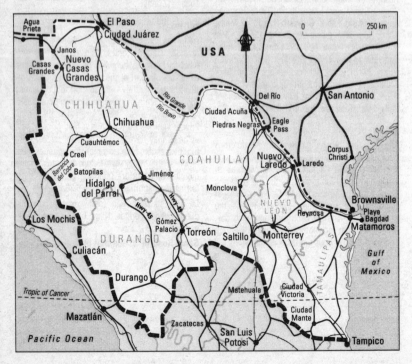

BORDER CHECKS

Crossing the border, do not forget to go through **immigration and customs** checks. As everywhere, there's a free zone south of the frontier, and you can cross at will. Try to continue south, though, and you'll be stopped after some 20km and sent back to get your tourist card stamped.

---

though, must be the train journey through the **Copper Canyon** from Chihuahua to the Pacific coast: a thirteen-hour ride over soaring peaks and around the walls of vast canyons down to the steamy coastal plain. To the east, along the fastest route to the capital, **Monterrey** is a heavily industrialized city that has nevertheless managed to retain its finest sights; nearby **Saltillo** offers escape into tranquil mountains.

Following the **Gulf Coast** is less recommended – steaming hot in summer and not particularly interesting at the best of times. It is, though, the shortest way south, and if you stick it out past the refineries you'll reach the state of Veracruz (see p.365), with its fine beaches and wealth of archeological remains.

THE CENTRAL CORRIDOR

Rapid and efficient bus services run throughout the central area, the best of the main lines probably being *Transportes Chihuahuenses* and *Omnibus de México*, with *Estrella Blanca* mounting a strong challenge as you head south. Non-stop to the capital can take as little as 25 hours. If this is your plan, you might also consider the train, which leaves Ciudad Juárez daily at 10pm, reaching the capital some 36 hours later.

Ciudad Juárez

There's little doubt that the best thing to do on arriving in **CIUDAD JUÁREZ** is to leave. In less than five hours you can reach Chihuahua or, rather closer, Nuevo Casas Grandes, the base for excursions to the archeological site of Casas Grandes. Juárez itself is perhaps the least attractive of all the border towns: modern, sprawling and ugly, as well as extremely confusing to find your way around and, at times, positively intimidating.

Originally a small settlement on the Santa Fe trail known as Paso del Norte, Ciudad Juárez's brief moment of glory came when Benito Juárez established his government here after he had been driven out of the south by Maximilian (you can visit the **house** from which he governed, on 16 de Septiembre). The town changed hands frequently during the Revolution, most notably in 1913, when Pancho Villa, having stolen a train, managed to fool the local commander into expecting reinforcements and steamed into the middle of town with 2000 troops completely unopposed. This was one of the exploits which forged his reputation, as well as giving him access to the border and to arms from the north.

Arrival, orientation and information

The two downtown **bridges over the Río Bravo** are one-way, even for pedestrians. To enter Mexico from El Paso, the large modern one brings you out onto Juárez, the main drag, while the older one, which you should cross to get back to the US, runs from Lerdo. As soon as you cross the border the nature of the place is immediately apparent:

on the US side are blood banks and second-hand clothes emporia, in Mexico cut-rate doctors and dentists and cheap bars. It's all rather sad and sordid. However, if you're staying, this is the place to be, in what's left of the old town. The **market** is a few blocks from the border straight up Lerdo, and in the streets around it are most of the cheaper places to stay and to eat.

If you **drive** across the border, you can avoid downtown Ciudad Juárez altogether by taking the Cordova bridge, a couple of kilometres east of the centre, or the new Zaragoza toll bridge, still further east, which directly connects the US and Mexican highway systems.

Information

The Ciudad Juárez **tourist office** (Mon–Fri 8am–2.30pm & 4–7pm, Sat & Sun 8am–2pm) hides in the basement of the large government office to the right at the end of the bridge. They can fill you in on details of bullfights, *charreadas* and other local entertainments, as well as supplying maps and information about Ciudad Juárez and things you'll be seeing further south. **Banks** are mainly on 16 de Septiembre, as is the **post office**, at the corner of Madero; outside bank hours it's easy enough to change money at *casas de cambio* and tourist shops along Juárez and 16 de Septiembre. In any case many places accept dollars. Make sure you know the current exchange rate before you do any such deals.

Accommodation

None of the hotels in Ciudad Juárez is particularly good value by Mexican standards, but it is still considerably less expensive to stay here than across the border. Over in El Paso, the best budget choice is the atmospheric *Gardner Hotel*, 311 E Franklin St – where John Dillinger stayed in the 1920s – with hostel accommodation and a few private rooms (☎915/532-3661; ③–⑤).

Del Prado, in *Pronaf* centre (☎16/16-88-00). Luxurious, pricey option. ⑦.

Impala, Lerdo Nte. 670 (☎16/15-04-31). Comfortable, clean and modern, right by the border. ⑥.

Juárez, Lerdo Nte. 143 (☎16/15-03-58). A battered and basic budget place. ③.

Koper, Juárez 124 (☎16/15-03-24). Another basic, scruffy hotel, but cheap and central. ③.

Plaza, Ugarte 239 near the cathedral (☎16/2-68-61). Little to recommend it, but great position. ③.

Santa Fe, Lerdo Nte. 673 (☎16/14-02-70). Opposite the *Impala* and similar, though cheaper. Comfortable and convenient for late arrivals. Rooms with a/c and TV, and a 24-hr restaurant. ⑤.

The Town

Probably the best way to kill a few hours in Juárez – especially if you've just arrived in Mexico – is to stroll around downtown. Be careful, however, not to wander far off the main thoroughfares. Where 16 de Septiembre crosses Juárez there's a small **Museo Histórico** (Tues–Sun 10am–6pm; free), tracing the development of the town, in the old

---

ACCOMMODATION PRICES

All the accommodation listed in this book has been categorized into one of nine price bands, as set out below. The prices quoted are in US dollars and normally refer to the cheapest available room for two people sharing in high season. For more details, see p.37.

① less than $8	④ $18–25	⑦ $50–75
② $8–12	⑤ $25–35	⑧ $75–100
③ $12–18	⑥ $35–50	⑨ more than $100

MOVING ON FROM CIUDAD JUÁREZ

Ciudad Juárez enjoys excellent **bus connections** with the whole of north and central Mexico from its modern **Central de Autobuses**. To get there take a local bus (#1A or #1B) from 16 de Septiembre or Guerrero by the market. You could also squeeze into one of the horribly cramped **vans** that operate a shuttle service to and from the border. There are constant departures with one company or another down the main highway to Chihuahua and points beyond, and every couple of hours for Nuevo Casas Grandes (via Janos). If you plan to head straight through, you should be able to get a US bus direct to the terminal (and vice versa).

The **train station** is reached by going straight up Lerdo from the border – there is a bus, but at twelve blocks it's just about walkable. One train leaves for the capital daily at 6.25pm, another sets off for Chihuahua at 6pm daily, and there's a daily 8am departure (except Sun) on the Nuevo Casas Grandes line.

customs building, the *Aduana*. A couple of blocks west of here on 16 de Septiembre you'll find the cathedral and the seventeenth-century mission building, the **Mision de Guadalupe**, around which the town grew up.

If you have more time it's worth making for the **Museo de Arqueología del Chamizal** (Mon–Sat 9am–2pm, Sun 1–8pm; free) in the Parque Chamizal, east of the centre near the river, and the **Museo de Arte y Historia** (Tues–Sun 10am–7pm; 30¢) in the **Pronaf tourist centre** – which also houses a huge, touristy craft market – not far from the bus station (local bus #8 runs there from the centre). Both offer limited introductions to Mexico; the former also has some remarkable pottery from Casas Grandes (see below).

Eating

Places to eat are plentiful around the centre and border area, although new arrivals should probably take it easy on the street food. The fancier options line Juárez near the border. **El Paso** offers better value, however, and if you've been in Mexico some time, you may well want to rush across the border to somewhere like the *San Francisco Grill*, opposite the posh *Paso del Norte* hotel on Pioneer Plaza, which serves not too expensive New American brunches and dinners in an upmarket setting.

Chihuahua Charlies, 2525 Triunfo de la Republica, near the Plaza de Toros. More a glitzy bar than a restaurant, and usually packed with day-trippers on the round-trip trolley rides from El Paso, this is a safe and relatively inexpensive place to eat *enchiladas* and *tortillas* in a lively atmosphere.

Restaurante Martino, Juárez 643. Classy restaurant with high prices and varied cuisine.

Restaurant Norteño, on Juárez just before 16 de Septiembre (opposite the *Hotel Koper*). Good, inexpensive option for plain Mexican food.

Santa Fe, Lerdo Nte. 673. 24-hour hotel restaurant serving *enchiladas* and sandwiches.

Casas Grandes

The archeological site (daily 10am–5pm; $3, free on Sun) at **CASAS GRANDES** – also known as Paquimé – is much the most important, and certainly the most striking, in northern Mexico. Originally an agricultural community of simple adobe houses (similar to those found in Arizona and New Mexico), it became heavily influenced by Meso-American, probably Toltec, culture. Whether this was the result of conquest or, more probably, trade is uncertain, but from around 1000–1200AD, Casas Grandes flourished. **Pyramids** and **ball-courts** were constructed and the surrounding land irrigated by a system of **canals**.

At the same time local craftsmen were trading with points both south and north, producing a wide variety of elaborate ornaments and pottery. Among the finds on the site (almost all of them now in the National Museum of Anthropology in México) were cages in which exotic imported birds were kept to be used for making feathered ornaments; necklaces made from shell, turquoise and semiprecious stones; and other objects of copper, bone, jade and mother-of-pearl. Casas Grandes pottery, with vessels often in the shape of human or animal figures and decorated in geometric patterns of red, black and brown on a white or cream background, was particularly beautiful – remarkably similar objects are still being produced by local indigenous cultures.

The remains of adobe houses – the largest of which have as many as fifty interconnecting rooms – surround the **ceremonial centre**. Originally two or three storeys high, most of the houses survive only as foundations, with an occasional standing wall giving some idea of scale. Much must have been destroyed when the site was attacked, burned and abandoned around 1340 – either by a marauding nomadic tribe such as the Apache or in the course of a more local rebellion. Either way, Casas Grandes was not inhabited again, its people abandoning their already depleted trade for the greater safety of the Sierras. What is left, ruinous and unrestored as it is, remains an impressive monument and unique of its kind in Mexico.

Practicalities: Nuevo Casas Grandes

To **reach the site** you have first to get to Nuevo Casas Grandes. Then take the yellow bus ("Casas Grandes/Col. Juárez") from the train station (you can't miss it) to the plaza in Casas Grandes (about 15min), from where the site is signed – a bare ten-minute walk.

NUEVO CASAS GRANDES itself is not particularly interesting, but is at least a quiet place to **spend the night**. It's very small: you'll see the hotel *California* on the main street, Constitución, as you drive in (☎169/4-11-10; ⑤), and the basic *Juárez* (☎169/4-02-33; ③) is right by the *Transportes Chihuahuenses* and other bus terminals on Obregón. Best of all, the *Motel Piñon*, Juárez Nte. 605 (☎169/4-06-55; ⑤), boasts TV and reliable hot water, and gives occasional tours of the ruins.

If you leave Ciudad Juárez very early you can **visit the site and continue to Chihuahua** in the same day – a route that is only marginally longer and certainly more interesting than the main highway (though rains can take out the road south of Nuevo Casas Grandes). Theoretically one could also get here by **rail**, and then continue to La Junta to join the Chihuahua–Los Mochis railway. But at best there is only one (painfully slow) train a day and, connections being what they are, it would take at least two and possibly three days to complete a journey that can be done in one on the bus.

Chihuahua

Capital of the state of the same name, **CHIHUAHUA** is a big city, an industrial centre, and the transport base for much of the state's mineral and agricultural wealth. There's really no reason to stay here for long, and in poor weather it can be thoroughly depressing. But on a good day Chihuahua can be really attractive, with an ancient centre surrounded by suburbs of magnificent nineteenth-century mansions in the best Gothic horror tradition.

A word about those revolting little short-haired, bug-eyed **dogs** to which the city has given its name. They do come from here originally, but you're most unlikely to see one, presumably because the vicissitudes of a dog's life in Mexico are too great for so pathetic a creature.

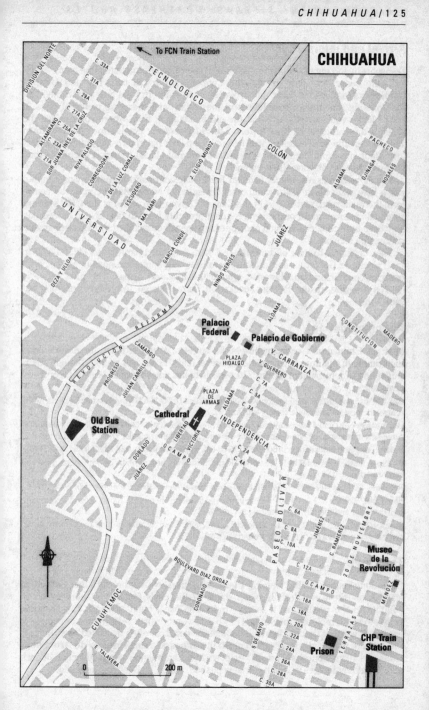

To FCN Train Station

CHIHUAHUA

DIVISION DEL NORTE
C. 33A
C. 31A
C. 29A
TECNOLOGICO
COLON
PACHECO
C. 27A
ALTAMIRANO C. 25A
C. 23A
SOR JUANA INES DE LA CRUZ
C. 21A
RIVA PALACIO
CORREGIDORA
J. DE LA LUZ CORRAL
ESCUDERO
J. MA. MARI
J. ELIGIO MUÑOZ
ALDAMA
OJINAGA
ROSALES
UNIVERSIDAD
GARCIA CONDE
JUAREZ
DEZA Y ULLOA
NIÑOS HEROES
REFORMA
CAMARGO
REVOLUCION
PROGRESO
JULIAN CARRILLO
Palacio Federal
Palacio de Gobierno
ALDAMA
CONSTITUCION
MADERO
PLAZA HIDALGO
V. CARRANZA
PLAZA DE ARMAS
V. GUERRERO
C. 7A
C. 5A
ALDAMA
C. 3A
Old Bus Station
Cathedral
LIBERTAD
VICTORIA
O. CAMPO
INDEPENDENCIA
DORLADO
C. 2A
JUAREZ
C. 4A
PASEO BOLIVAR
C. 6A
C. 8A
JIMENEZ
C. RAMIREZ
C. 10A
20 DE NOVIEMBRE
Museo de la Revolución
BOULEVARD DIAZ ORDAZ
C. 12A
OCAMPO
C. 16A
MENDEZ
CORONADO
C. 18A
CUAUHTEMOC
C. 20A
C. 22A
5 DE MAYO
C. 24A
TERRAZAS
Prison
CHP Train Station
F. TALAVERA
C. 26A
C. 28A
C. 30A

0   200 m

Arrival and information

Transport in and out of Chihuahua is not well co-ordinated, frustrating the many travellers who come here only to take the Copper Canyon rail line. The new **Central Camionera** is miles out, near the airport on Juan Pablo II; local buses from the main road outside run to and from Juárez in the centre, and there are plenty of taxis. If you're lucky you may still arrive at the old bus station, from where you can see the roofs of the cathedral and the tower of the *El Presidente* hotel, also right downtown and, incidentally, with excellent views from its top-floor bar and restaurant. Simply walk towards them. From the airport, the usual system of official transport operates – buy your voucher as you leave the terminal.

The *Ferrocarriles Nacionales* (Ciudad Juárez–México) **train station** is closer in, but still a long walk north of the centre, off División del Norte. Buses run to the centre from the main road. Arriving from the Copper Canyon (see p.128) at the **CHP station**, an equal distance south of the centre, you'll probably want to take a taxi; indeed you may have little choice, since you and your luggage will be grabbed by eager drivers the minute you step out.

There's a small **tourist office** (Mon–Fri 9am–7pm; Sat 10am–2pm; ☎14/10-10-77) in the Palacio de Gobierno, and most other offices and banks are equally central, with branches on Victoria and Libertad around the Plaza de Armas. The **post office** is located opposite, in the Palacio Federal on Plaza Hidalgo (Mon–Fri 8am–7pm, Sat 9am–1pm).

Accommodation

Most of Chihuahua's cheaper **hotels** lie southwest of the Plaza de Armas along Victoria, or in the area between the cathedral and the old bus station, though this is something of a red light district; c/10 especially has a fair number of extremely cheap dives.

Bal Flo, c/5a no. 702 at the junction with Niños Heroes (☎14/16-03-00). A few blocks north of the centre, the best middle-range choice, with a/c. ④.

Del Cobre, c/10 and Progreso, right by the old bus station (☎14/15-17-58). Not much reason to come here nowadays, but good facilities for the price, including a/c and TV. ④.

Palacio del Sol, Independencia 500 (☎14/16-60-00). Top-notch luxury, but a bit further out. ⑧–⑨.

El Presidente, Libertad 9 (☎14/16-06-06). Right downtown, luxury high-rise with views, pool and fancy restaurant. ⑧–⑨.

Reforma, Victoria 809 (☎14/12-58-08). Plain place, less attractive than the nearby *San Juan*. ②.

San Juan, Victoria 823 (☎14/10-26-83). Simple, old-fashioned hotel with rooms around a courtyard; well cared for and friendly. Economical food too. ②–③.

Santa Regina, c/3 no. 107, at Doblado (☎14/15-38-89). Good location just off the pedestrianized central area; rooms a bit depressing despite TV and a/c. ⑤.

The Town

Chihuahua centres on the teeming **Plaza de Armas**, where the city's fine **Cathedral** stands opposite a wonderfully camp statue of the city's founder in the very act of pointing to the ground, as if to say "right lads, we'll build it here". The Baroque, twin-towered temple was begun in 1717 but took more than seven years to complete: work well worth it though; for once the interior detail, so often despoiled elsewhere, is the equal of the facade. In a crypt beneath the cathedral a small **Museo de Arte Sacro** (Mon–Fri 10am–2pm & 4–6pm; $1) displays Mexican religious art, a collection of dark and forbidding images in which Christ is pushed, pulled, stabbed and punched.

Also on the Plaza de Armas is the imposing, but relatively modern, Palacio Municipal – follow Libertad down past this and you'll come to the Plaza Hidalgo, where the **Palacio Federal** and the **Palacio de Gobierno** face each other across the square. The Palacio de Gobierno was originally a Jesuit College, converted to a military hospital after the expulsion of the Jesuits – here Padre Miguel Hidalgo y Costilla and Ignacio Allende, the inspiration and early leaders of the Mexican War of Independence, were executed in 1811, their severed heads sent for public display in Guanajuato (see p.222). The site of the deed is marked (despite the fact that the building has been reconstructed several times since) and you can also visit "Hidalgo's dungeon" where they were held beforehand in the Palacio Federal (Mon–Fri 9am–7pm); inside are various relics of Hidalgo and the Revolution. A golden eagle marks the entrance.

More recent history is commemorated in Chihuahua's premier sight, the **Museo de la Revolución** (daily 9am–1pm & 3–7pm; $1) that occupies Pancho Villa's former home, on c/10. This enormous mansion was inhabited, until her death in the early 1980s, by Villa's "official" widow (there were allegedly many others), who used to conduct personal tours: it has now been taken over by the Mexican army and put on a more official footing. The collection is a fascinating mix of arms, war plans and personal mementoes, including the bullet-riddled limousine in which Villa was assassinated in 1923. Quite apart from the campaign memories, the superbly preserved old bedrooms and bathrooms give an interesting insight into Mexican daily life in the early twentieth century.

The museum is a long way north of the centre. To get there, take a bus (or walk) up Ocampo, and continue two blocks past the huge church and two blocks to the left along Mendez. Also on this northern side of the city, you might want to pop into the extraordinarily elaborate **Museo Quinta Gameros** (Mon–Fri 10am–3pm; $2), at the junction of c/4a and Paseo Bolivar. Just the sort of thing that Villa and his associates were hoping to stamp out, the building was designed by a successful mine owner as an exact replica of a Parisian home. The interior is sumptuously decorated, with stained-glass and ornate woodwork, and, curiously, scenes from Little Red Riding Hood painted on the children's bedroom wall.

Eating and drinking

There's no shortage of good **places to eat** in Chihuahua, from the basic cafes around the old bus station, through the *taco* stalls nearer the centre, to the fancier steak houses and American burger restaurants around the main plazas. Calle Victoria has some of the best options, and tends to stay open late: the *Restaurant Los Arcos* comes recommended, the *Rachasa* is a late-opener serving pasta, coffee and cakes to a young

---

MOVING ON FROM CHIHUAHUA

To get to the **Ferrocarriles Nacionales** train station take a "Villa Colón" or "Granjas Colón" bus from the centre. You'll have to ask someone to tell you where to get off (by the *Motel del Capitan*) because the station is invisible from the road. It's worth going out to the station in advance to buy a ticket if you want *primera reservada*; the *División del Norte* train passes through in the middle of the night in both directions. Alternatively you can book through the tourist office.

The **CHP station**, for the Copper Canyon (see p.128), is an equal distance south of the centre. To get there, take a "Sta. Rosa" or "Col. Rosalia" bus from the centre, get out at the prison (impossible to miss) and walk round behind it to the station. If you're going to get your tickets in the morning you'll have to take a taxi or else walk. The ticket office opens at 6am.

crowd (with a "Ladies Bar" upstairs), while the more expensive *La Parilla* at Victoria 420 specializes in the excellent local meat, with big steaks the order of the day. For something healthier, head for *El Vegetariano* at Libertad and c/13. Convenient breakfast spots include *Mi Café*, Victoria 807, opposite the *Hotel San Juan*, and *Restaurante Txomin* on c/3 in the *Hotel Santa Regina*. Also handy for the *Santa Regina* and downtown is *Dino's Pizza*, Doblado 301.

Chihuahua to Los Mochis – The Copper Canyon Railway

The thirteen hour rail journey that starts on the high plains of Chihuahua, fights its way up to cross the Continental Divide amid the peaks of the Sierra Madre, and finally plunges down to the sweaty Pacific coast at Los Mochis must rate as one of the world's most extraordinary. Not only as an engineering feat (work started at the beginning of the century and was only completed, 73 tunnels and 28 major bridges later, in 1961) but for the breathtaking views as it hangs over the vast canyons of the Urique river. Chief of these is the awesome rift of the **Barranca del Cobre**, with a depth, from mountain top to valley floor, of up to 4000m, and breadth to match. By comparison, the Grand Canyon is a midget.

Even when the bare mountain peaks here are snow-covered, the climate on the canyon floors is semitropical: a fact which the Tarahumara Indians – driven into these mountain fastnesses after the Spanish Conquest – depend on, migrating in winter to the warmth of the deep canyons. The **Tarahumara**, whose population totals some 50,000, live in isolated communities along the line and in the stretch of the mountains known as the Sierra Tarahumara, eking out an existence from the sparse patches of cultivable land. Although as everywhere their isolation is increasingly encroached upon by commercial forestry interests, ranchers and growing numbers of travellers, they remain an independent people, close to their traditions. Their religious life, despite centuries of missionary work, embraces only token aspects of Catholicism and otherwise remains true to its agrarian roots – their chief deities being the gods of the sun, moon and rain. Above all, the tribe are renowned as runners: a common feature of local festivals are the foot races between villages that last at least a day, sometimes several days on end, the runners having to kick a wooden ball ahead of them as they go.

The route

Enormous as the Barranca del Cobre is, bear in mind that **scenically** there's no comparison with the canyons of the southwestern USA, and if you've visited them you may find this a disappointment; certainly you'll get more out of the journey if you get off and do some hiking halfway, or treat it simply as an extraordinary train ride.

The start of the journey, as the tracks run through gentle ranching country towards the base of the mountains, has a character altogether different to what is to come. Many people dismiss these first few hours as dull, but this landscape has its own, albeit less spectacular, appeal. This is pioneer country that wouldn't look out of place in some gentle, romantic Western: verdant grazing land where you see more horses and traps than trucks. The town of **CUAUHTÉMOC**, 130km from Chihuahua, is a chief **Mennonite** centre. You'll come across Mennonites throughout northern Mexico – the men in their bib-and-tucker overalls and straw stetsons, as often as not trying to sell the excellent cheese that is their main produce; the women, mostly silent, wrapped in long, black nineteenth-century dresses with maybe a dash of colour from a headscarf. The sect, founded in the sixteenth century by a Dutchman, Menno Simonis, believe only in the Bible and their personal conscience: their refusal to do military service or take national oaths of loyalty has led to a long history of persecution.

The Mennonites arrived in Mexico early this century, having been driven from Frisia to Prussia, thence into Russia and finally to Mexico by way of Canada – each time forced to move on by the state's demand for military tribute or secular education. These days many are returning to Canada as impoverished emigrants, forced out by limited land and a growing population. Among themselves the Mennonites still speak a form of German, although so corrupted as to be virtually unintelligible to a modern German-speaker.

The mountains

Not far beyond Cuauhtémoc, the train begins to climb in earnest into the first spurs of the Sierra, eventually reaching **Creel**, almost the halfway stage and, at 2300m, close to the highest point of the line. This is the place to stop if you want seriously to explore the Sierra Tarahumara and the canyons; the hotels here are the only reasonably priced options en route. See p.130 for details on staying in Creel and exploring the Sierra Tarahumara, and don't be discouraged by the fact that the journey so far, while beautiful, has not been truly spectacular – the best of the railway lies further on, but Creel gives easy access into some remarkable landscapes.

Stay on the train and you clank onwards to **Divisadero**, where there's a halt of about fifteen minutes to marvel at the view. At first it seems a perverse choice for a stop, with nothing around but the mountain tops and crowds of Tarahumara hawking their crafts and food (delicious *gorditas*). But walk a step down the path and you're standing suddenly on the edge of space. This is the lip of the vast chasm and below you are laid out the depths of the **Barranca del Cobre** and, joining it, the Barranca de Balojaque and the Barranca de Tararecua. There are a couple more – expensive – places to stay here, but for most people it's all too rapidly back on the train for the final stage – six more hours which, from the train fan's point of view, are the most exciting yet.

It was here that the original builders, the *Kansas City, Mexico and Orient Railway Company*, finally gave up on their dream of pushing through a new route from the American Midwest to the Pacific – defeated by the sheer technical complexity of it all – and only in 1953 did the Mexicans start work on the final linking stretch. You can see why. The train zigzags down dizzily, clinging to the canyon wall, plunging into tunnels blasted through the rock, rocking across bridges, only to find itself constantly just a stone's drop below the track it covered twenty minutes earlier. All the time it's getting hotter, until finally the line breaks out of the mountains onto the humid coastal plain as the air-conditioned passengers settle back in their reclining seats and the rest just sweat.

Rail practicalities

The Copper Canyon line is operated by the *Ferrocarril de Chihuahua al Pacifico* (*CHP*, pronounced Shé Pé). There are two **trains** daily: the first-class *Estrella* (also known as the *Vista Tren*, or simply *Primera*), which is primarily a tourist service; and the second-class *Tren Mixto* (or *Tren General*), less than half the price but considerably slower and less comfortable. It's worth taking the *Estrella* service (around $30), not only because it has air conditioning and reserved, reclining seats, but also because the *Tren Mixto* ($10) is slow and, given a tendency to run late, often passes many of the best sections in the dark. During the rainy season, due to landslides that block the track, the service is subject to **delay** and even cancellation without prior warning. Also, cargo trains are often derailed and cause delays on the tracks.

You'll save money by taking along your own **food and drink**, but it's not essential; both are available on the train (though not cheap), and throughout the journey people climb on board or stand on the platforms selling *tacos, chiles rellenos*, fresh fruit, hot coffee or whatever local produce comes to hand.

Tickets from Chihuahua can be booked at the station or, to be sure of a first-class seat, with any travel agency in México. Even better, you can book a four-day tour (around $350 per person) from the capital that includes accommodation and meals (in Creel and Divisadero). You'll have to make your own way to Chihuahua, however. The ticket allows you to stop off and then rejoin the train again while maintaining your reservation throughout the entire journey. It is advisable to break up the journey, not only for its own sake, but also because the trip, even travelling first-class, is very exhausting.

THE CHP TIMETABLE

The timetable is not entirely reliable, and trains frequently run late, but these are the official times.

	Estrella ↑		*Mixto* ↑	
Chihuahua	7am	8.50pm	8am	1.05am
Cuauhtémoc	9.15am	6.30pm	10.40am	10.15pm
Creel	12.25pm	3.15pm	2pm	6.20pm
Divisadero	1.45pm	1.35pm	3.30pm	4.45pm
Bahuichivo	3.30pm	12.15pm	5.30pm	2pm
Sufragio*	8pm	7.45am	10.25pm	9.10am
Los Mochis*	8.50pm	7am	11.25pm	8am

*The train operates, and the timetable is given, in Chihuahua time (Central Standard Time), but Los Mochis and Sufragio are actually an hour ahead of this (Mountain Standard Time). So by local time, the trains leave Los Mochis an hour earlier, at 6am and 7am. If you're changing trains at Sufragio, there's an hour's difference between the timetables of the *CHP* and the *FCP*.

Creel and the Sierra Tarahumara

CREEL is a dusty little place with echoes of the Old West in its log cabins and its street scenes: Indians arriving on foot for supplies, ranchers on horseback, forest managers cruising in shiny new pick-ups. It was named after the state governor, Enrique Creel, son of the US ambassador to Mexico in the 1930s, who founded timber-works in the area. Now just one saw mill remains, and tourism is taking over as the main source of income. Nonetheless, so far it remains an attractive escape, friendly and still relatively quiet.

There's an easy **hike** up the cliff face in town that offers splendid bird's-eye views. Walk through the car park of the *Motel Parador de la Montaña* towards the rear field, and carry on towards the barbed-wire fence by the large boulder. Simply follow the steps carved into the rock face and you quickly reach the top of the cliff. To your right you will see the train station, to your left the early stages of the Copper Canyon and the Tarahumara lands, scattered with **rock formations** that locals insist include frogs, mushrooms, a nativity scene and even the eagle on the cactus of the Mexican flag.

Creel practicalities

Creel does have a small **tourist office**, but the **Jesuit mission shop**, *Artesanías Misión*, on the zócalo near the station, is generally a more useful source of information, selling local maps and guides (Mon–Sat 9.30am–1pm & 3–6pm, Sun 9.30am–1pm).

They also sell Tarahumara **crafts** – blankets, wooden dolls and drums – and photos of the Tarahumara, who on the whole dislike being photographed. Otherwise the village has just about every facility you're likely to need: a **bank** (dollar exchange Mon–Fri 10.30am–noon) and **post office** on the zócalo; long-distance **telephones** in the *Hotel Nuevo*, and a laundry (Mon–Fri 9am–2pm & 3–6pm, Sat 9am–2pm) in the *Pension Creel*, on Lopez Mateos.

The number of good **places to stay** grows every year. Wherever you base yourself, remember that it can get exceedingly cold even on summer nights. *Hotel Nuevo* (④–⑦), right across from the station, is one of the longest established, pricey for what you get, though the best rooms, with fireplaces, can be very nice indeed. *Hotel Korachi* (☎145/6-22-07; ④–⑤), across the tracks, is probably better value, with comfortable rooms and *cabañas*, but the best deal of all must be at *Margarita's*, Mateos 11 (☎145/6-00-45; ①–④), unmarked on the edge of the plaza (if no one accosts when you get off the train, then ask). A night here includes two good meals, plenty of free advice and an abundance of friendly travellers. The hotel also runs the best local tours. For TV, luxury and plenty of hot water, make for *Motel Parador de la Montaña*, Mateos 41 (☎145/6-00-75; ⑦), or take advantage of the courtesy buses that run to one of the luxury **lodges** out in the nearby countryside: *Cabañas Cañon del Cobre* (reservations in Chihuahua: ☎14/16-59-50; Los Mochis: ☎681/5-70-46; ⑦) or the *Copper Canyon Sierra Lodge* (☎681/2-19-29; ⑨), for example.

Around Creel: the Sierra Tarahumara

Just about every hotel in town runs **organized trips** into the surrounding country: try at *Margarita's*, the *Nuevo* or the *Motel Parador*. You could, too, arm yourself with a map and set out to explore independently. Public transport is very irregular at best, but hitching is surprisingly easy to the places that are accessible by road: if you really want to explore, it's best not to have too tight a schedule. Nor should you venture off the beaten track alone, as this can be harsh and unforgiving country. *Margarita's* is a good place to meet up with fellow explorers, or Margarita herself can fix up inexpensive local guides. Rather more expensive, but definitely worth it if you can afford it, is **horseback riding** in the vicinity – again you can do this on an organized trip or simply take a ride out into the country.

Of the nearby attractions, **Basaséachic Falls** are the most famous, protected in the Parque Nacional de Basaséachic. Said to be the highest cascade in North America (310m), this makes a long, but spectacularly rewarding, day's excursion – about four hours driving followed by almost two hours on foot. Unfortunately the falls are virtually impossible to reach except as part of an organized excursion, and these only set off when there are enough takers to justify them. Tours also run to the **Recohuata hot spring**, where you can bathe in steamy sulphurous waters. Much more easily, you can visit **Cusárare**, where there's a smaller fall (about 35m, but still impressive) and an almost entirely original seventeenth-century Jesuit mission church with Tarahumara paintings. This is about 20km south of Creel, on the main road, past some spectacular rock formations.

Also readily accessible is **Lake Arareco**, where you can camp in magnificent surroundings (just follow the tarmac road south for about 7km). A bit further out you'll see some extraordinary rock formations – a huge mountain dotted with bizarrely shaped outcroppings – near **Basihuare** (40km), and from **Kirare** (100km) there are great views of the Batopilas Canyon.

If you'd rather take a stroll in the hills around Creel itself, then head south along the main road and turn left just after the cemetery. Here a rough dirt road will bring you to the **San Ignacio Mission**, less than an hour away. Around the mission are superb pine forest, Indian cave dwellings and a set of weird rock formations known as the "valley of the mushrooms". You can also walk on over the hill to Lake Arareco, which

THE SIERRA TARAHUMARA

A personal account by Paul Harley

I was fortunate to be in Tarahumara country for Holy Week, one of the most important local Indian celebrations (others are the feast of Guadalupe, December 12, and the whole Christmas period up to January 6, Epiphany). I had heard that the celebrations were at their most traditional in **Norogachi**, 80km from Creel and only accessible by hitchhiking, mostly on dirt roads.

For our first lift we shared the back of a forestry worker's truck with an Indian family. We were taken along bumpy dirt roads through spectacular country, then dropped at a tiny village where we eventually picked up a second ride which took us to the shallow river a kilometre or so from Norogachi.

The village is small, dominated by two barracks-like buildings on the plaza, a hospital and a convent school. Adjacent to them stands an adobe church with a corrugated iron roof. There's no hotel, but in a dimly lit shop with saddles hanging over wooden beams, and crates of soft drinks scattered among sacks of maize and beans, a group of men in tattered sombreros broke off their discussion to direct us to the Chavez household. It was an old farmhouse near the edge of the village, run by two widows. They showed us a room in an outbuilding with two primitive beds, a rough table and a dirt floor. One of the doors opened out into the courtyard and the other onto a field of dry, broken earth. Across the field was a yellow cliff face. The widows gave us an oil lamp (the only electricity came from a generator at the hospital) and pointed out the water supply – a tap near the church. Outside the farmhouse was a small hut where they sold *Coca Cola* and cooked food: over our meal of *tortilla* and *frijoles* we met Genevieve, the adopted thirteen-year-old Tarahumara daughter of one of the widows. Apparently, it is common custom for the Tarahumara to give their children up for adoption if they cannot afford to feed them properly. Genevieve went to a Catholic boarding school in Chihuahua and had already forgotten most of her native language. It was clear, when she asked me about my favourite pop groups, that her thoughts veered towards the United States and the modern world. She was taller than most Tarahumara, too, possibly because she enjoyed a better diet in Chihuahua than was available in the village.

The surrounding countryside is arid and mountainous, and the following morning we climbed the nearby cliffs, passing the odd shack with a few chickens and a couple of tethered donkeys. We wandered about seven kilometres that day, stopping at vantage points which gave us long views of the surrounding mountains across the valley where Norogachi was situated. Our walk was regularly punctuated by the sound of drums and occasional glimpses of groups of two or three men heading for Norogachi. When we reached town in the late afternoon we saw a group of seven Tarahumara wearing loin-cloths and tattered check shirts, led by a drummer and a man with a white flag. The cliffs glowed in an intense orange sunset, an electric storm circled nearby, and thunder and lightning accompanied the drums. There was an immense sense of anticipation for the celebrations which would begin on Easter Thursday, next morning.

At cock-crow came the sound of drums, the heartbeat of the fiesta. The village and its largely *mestizo* population had been taken over by the Tarahumara, arriving from their settlements scattered through the sierra. There were groups of as many as thirty and as few as five, all men, dotted around the village preparing – painting their bodies, adjusting turkey feathers in headdresses, practising their dances. Most of them wore headbands, usually red, white loincloths, and on their feet, used to going bare, sandals made from car tyres. When they danced and the unaccustomed burden caused one to trip, the rest of the group would laugh at his discomfort. Some groups smeared their bodies with white paint, others were arrayed with bright polka-dots. The women, who played little part in the celebrations, sat huddled in a corner of the plaza, their blouses a riot of fuschia, crimson, lilac and floral designs. They sat watching, chattering and feeding babies.

The plaza thronged with people. The Indian men were active and purposeful, either dancing or constructing ceremonial arches from pine branches, twelve in all around the village. Finally, all twenty or so groups were ready to dance together. Most were led by a flag and followed by drummers who beat out the rhythm and simultaneously played monotonous tunes on tiny flutes. A typical group of about twenty formed two lines, moving up and down with delicate steps – hop, skip, jump; hop, skip, jump – until at a signal from the leader each line whirled into chaotic circles. During the many processions around the town the pattern of the dance never varied. The townsfolk, loggers and ranchers mostly, looked on bemused, their only involvement attendance at the church services and tagging on behind some of the processions.

It was hard work conversing with the Tarahumara as few of them speak Spanish. Communication for the most part was limited to the exchange of cigarettes for photographs. I did, though, get talking to a group of three young lads who carried a drum with the sun painted on it. They had walked about 25km to the village and had expected more from their settlement to turn up: without them they could not play their full part. They explained the significance of the wooden swords with geometric markings which many groups carried: in this annually re-enacted drama the Pharisees, wearing turkey-feather headdresses, were pitted against the sword-carrying soldiers.

By the church door we encountered a bizarre character who wore a tall headdress of multicoloured paper streamers and who carried an ancient curved sword: he was the Keeper of the Order. Attending him were two men with football rattles who ceremoniously cleared the paths ahead of the numerous processions. The Jesuit priest, a tall, imposing man, stood head and shoulders above those around him. He wore a headband, a brown leather jacket and an air of abstraction, changing for the services into flowing white robes and reverie.

At sunset the dancing intensified and a great mingling of all the dancers took place in the dusty plaza. Darkness descended rapidly but the drums beat on as small groups lit fires and their shadows flickered and danced against the wall of the clinic. The procession that evening was joined by everyone, in an inescapable, starlit atmosphere of power and mystery.

On Good Friday the drumming stopped briefly and a simple cross was erected as people crammed into the church to hear the priest, still immaculately white, still in a state of near trance, and then to process behind him, the men carrying a garish statue of Christ crucified, the women bearing Mary. The dancing continued in the plaza, where a few travelling salesmen did slow business, selling shirts and digital watches. The cool of the church offered some respite from the incessant drumming: inside a constant watch of the altar was maintained by two Indians, each pair relieved so regularly that there must have been some plan in action.

Before the final procession, three Judas effigies appeared. One had a white wooden mask, a hat and a jacket, with a packet of cigarettes in one hand and a beer bottle in the other; another was female, with high-heeled shoes and tight jeans – images of the oppressor. The last procession led to the cemetery, about a mile from town, where the priest delivered a sermon in the Tarahumara language to an assembly of some five hundred people. Back at the church the Indians danced around the altar, briefly but more intensely than ever: it was the clearest sign yet of the absorption of Catholicism into ancient ritual.

On Easter Saturday we got up just in time to see the ritual stabbing of the Judas figures, accompanied by guffaws and cheers and followed by the general consumption of *tesquina*, a local maize beer. The night before, we had missed the ceremonial painting of the *Pascales*, two old characters picked out to be painted all over and fed on *tesquina*. But now we saw them being much ragged as they tottered around unsteadily with fixed grins on their faces.

The festival ended here quite suddenly. By midday all the Indians had left, walking out as they had arrived, beating their drums and carrying their flags. By Saturday afternoon Norogachi had returned to its normal rhythms – no Tarahumara and nothing happening.

is about an hour away. Look out for the rock in the shape of an elephant on the side of the road.

Tours can also be arranged from the Jesuit Mission shop to **San Ignacio Arereco**, a Tarahumara reserve run by the Jesuits, just ten minutes' drive from Creel. There are plenty of crafts on sale here: if you insist on taking photos, make sure you give your subjects a small tip or gift.

Alternative bases: Batopilas, Gnochochi and the lodges

Though Creel is the longest established and best-known place to stay in the Sierra, there are a number of alternative bases, which some feel offer better opportunities for exploring the deep canyons. Four times a week, a bus runs from Creel to the former mining town of **BATOPILAS**, some 150km away (it leaves at 7am, returning the following morning at 4am). Of the many new hotels here, the best is *Monsé's Guest House* (③), with comfy accommodation in a garden setting plus tasty vegetarian meals. He takes travellers' cheques, but be sure to agree the price and exchange rate in advance. The town is a good base for hikes in the canyons, though it's desperately hot much of the year. One of the best excursions is to the "**Lost Cathedral**", a huge crumbling church standing in splendid isolation in a canyon bottom some 7km beyond Batopilas. Another follows the Camino Real for three or four hours to Cerro Colorado.

If you're really desperate to get off the well-trodden paths, then you can leave Creel to the south, along a dramatic mountain highway to the cowboy town of **GNOCHOCHI**. It's a bruising, dusty five-hour bus trip (departing Creel Mon–Sat 7.30am, Sun 1pm), and although the scenery is impressive, skirting the top edge of the great canyons, Gnochochi itself is a disappointing destination. However, there is a surprising number of **hotels**: best are the *Hotel Chaparro* (④), where customers are requested to leave their firearms at reception, and the *Hotel Melina* (⑤). Cheapest is the very basic *Hotel Orpimel* (②), right beside the bus station. To escape Gnochochi there are daily buses to Creel and to Hidalgo del Parral.

Much easier to get to, and far more appealing, are the **lodges** overlooking the canyons near stations along the rail line, all of which offer a variety of organized excursions. At **DIVISADERO** there are the *Cabañas Divisadero Barrancas* (☎14/15-11-99; ⑨), perched right on the canyon lip, and the *Posada Barranca del Cobre* (reservations in Chihuahua: ☎14/16-59-50; Los Mochis: ☎681/5-70-46; ⑨). The best hotel in the area, though, comes after the Divisadero stop, at **BARRANCA DIVISADERO**, where a bus takes you to the *Hotel Mansion Tarahumara* (⑨), a medieval castle in the middle of the canyon. Rates include all meals.

At **BAHUICHIVO** buses will pick you up to take you to the extremely attractive *Misión Cerocahui* (reservations in Chihuahua: ☎14/16-59-50; Los Mochis: ☎681/5-70-46; ⑦), in the mountain village of **CEROCAHUI**.

South to Durango

Below Chihuahua sprawls a vast plain, mostly agricultural, largely uninteresting, broken only occasionally by an outstretched leg of the Sierra Madre Occidental. The train crosses at night, buses hammer through relentlessly and you'd be wise to follow their lead. At **Jiménez** the road divides, Hwy-49 heading straight down through Gómez Palacio and Torreón, while Hwy-45 curves westwards to Durango. The non-stop route for Zacatecas and México is via the former, and the railway too bypasses Durango, but if time is not your only consideration the latter offers far more of interest.

Torreón and **Gómez Palacio** are virtually contiguous – there would be only one city were it not for the fact that the state border runs through the middle: Torreón is in Coahuila, Gómez Palacio in Durango. That said, they're as dull as each other – modern towns anyway, both were devastated by heavy fighting in the Revolution. There's no need whatsoever to stop, though one consolation if you do is that they mark the start of wine-growing country and you can sample the local produce (not the country's best) at various *bodegas*.

Hidalgo del Parral

On the longer route, **Durango** is the first of the Spanish-colonial towns that distinguish Mexico's heartland, and while it's not a patch on some of those further south, it will certainly be the most attractive place you've come to yet. But it's a good ten hours on the bus from Chihuahua, so you might consider breaking the journey in **HIDALGO DEL PARRAL**. Parral, as it's more simply known, is notorious now as the town where General Francisco "Pancho" Villa was assassinated, but it has a much longer history than that, if little to show for it. The stubby hills all around are rich in metals – silver above all, but also lead, copper and some gold – which attracted the Spaniards in the early years after the Conquest. The little mining town of **Santa Barbara**, which still operates some 25km away, was then capital of the province of Nueva Viscaya, a territory that stretched as far north as Texas and southern California: the capital was transferred to Parral after its foundation in 1638.

Mining is still Parral's chief activity and its outskirts are grubbily industrial – at the centre, though, the tranquil colonial plaza features a couple of remarkable buildings put up by prospectors who struck it rich. Chief of these are the **Palacio Pedro Alvarado**, an exuberantly decorated folly of a mansion built in the eighteenth century by a successful silver miner, and, across the river, the **Iglesia de la Virgen del Rayo**. Legend has it that this was constructed by an Indian on the proceeds of a gold mine he had discovered and worked in secret: the authorities tortured him to death in an attempt to find it, but the location died with him. There's also a small museum in the house from which Villa and his retinue of bodyguards were ambushed, but it is seldom open.

Practicalities

Parral's **bus terminal** is inevitably a long way out – take a taxi or local bus to or from the centre, which is itself quite small. There are a few decent **places to stay**, among them the clean and friendly *Hotel San José*, Santiago Mendez 5 (☎152/2-24-53; ⑤), a fancy modern hotel with air-conditioned rooms. Friendly and central, *Hotel Moreira*, Maclovio Herrera and Jesus Barcia (☎152/2-10-70; ⑤), has a decent **restaurant**, while *Hotel Acosta*, near the main plaza on Agustin Barbachano 3 (☎152/2-02-21; ④), is a pleasant old establishment with a 1950s atmosphere. Cheapest of all is the basic but clean *Hotel Los Arcos*, Dr. Pedro de Lille 13 (☎152/3-05-97; ③).

Durango

Although the Sierra Madre still looms on the western horizon, the country around **DURANGO** itself is flat – two low hills marking out the city from the plain. The **Cerro del Mercado**, a giant lump of iron ore that testifies to the area's mineral wealth, rises squat and black to the north, while to the west, the slopes of the **Cerro de los Remedios** are given over to a peaceful city park. The old town shelters between these two, with newer development straggling eastwards and southwards. Durango's **fiesta**, on July 8, celebrates the city's foundation on that day in 1563. Festivities commence several days before and run till July 12 – well worth going out of your way for, though rooms are booked solid.

Arrival and information

Durango's centre may be compact, but the **Central de Autobuses** is a long way out. Virtually any bus on the main road outside will take you downtown, direct to the plaza – look for "Centro/Camionera". In the unlikely event that you arrive by **train**, the station (a fine example of early railway architecture) is only about fifteen minutes' walk from the plaza straight down Constitución, or you can get there on a "Centro" bus by a thoroughly roundabout route.

The **tourist office** is at Hidalgo 208 (Mon–Sat 10am–3pm & 6–9pm, Sun 10am–1pm; ☎181/1-21-39), a couple of blocks west of the Palacio de Gobierno. For **currency exchange** there's a convenient branch of *Bancomer* right by the plaza at the corner of 20 de Noviembre and Constitución.

Accommodation

There's no shortage of **rooms** in Durango, though you should book ahead if you want to visit during the fiesta, when space is at a premium. Cheaper places are almost all pretty grim: if price is your only object, try around the market or near the train station, though even here the better places charge heavily. Of the bare and basic options opposite the station, *Ferrocarril* (③) and *Central* (③) are the best.

Aguirre, Hernandez 715, one block from the train station towards the centre (no phone). Relatively good option, far better than those directly by the station. ③.

Casablanca, 20 de Noviembre 811 (☎181/1-35-99). Big, old-fashioned colonial hotel near the *Duran*. Good value. ③.

Hotel Posada Duran, 20 de Noviembre right beside the cathedral (☎181/1-24-12). The best place to stay in town. An old, slightly faded colonial mansion with large rooms set around the first floor of an inner courtyard – many of them with windows opening out over the plaza. There's a bar downstairs. ③–④.

Oasis, Zarco 317 (☎181/1-45-61). Small, clean rooms with shower, near the market. ②.

Posada San Jorge, Constitución 102 Sur (☎181/3-32-57). Another mansion hotel with comfortable rooms. ④.

Reyes, 20 de Noviembre 220 (☎181/1-50-50). Clean and friendly hotel near the market. ③.

Roma, 20 de Noviembre 705 (☎181/2-01-22). Reliable place near the market. ④.

The Town

Downtown Durango is extremely compact – almost all the monuments cluster in a few streets around the Plaza Principal and the huge covered market nearby. On the plaza itself is the **Cathedral**, its two robust domed towers dwarfing the narrow facade. It's a typical Mexican church in every way: externally imposing, weighty and Baroque, with a magnificent setting overlooking the plaza, and yet ultimately disappointing, the interior dim and by comparison uninspired. Facing it from the centre of the plaza is a bizarre little two-storey bandstand from the top of which the town band plays on Sundays; underneath, a small shop sells expensive local crafts.

Following Av. 20 de Noviembre down from the cathedral (to the left as you face it) brings you to the **Teatro Principal**, a grandiose *Porfiriano* theatre now converted into a cinema. Turn left here onto Bruno Martinez, past the *Teatro Victoria*, and you come out in another plaza, its north side dominated by the porticoed facade of the **Palacio de Gobierno**. Originally the private house of a Spanish mining magnate, this was taken over by the local government after the War of Independence. The stairwells and walls of the two-storeyed arcaded patio inside are decorated with murals by local artists depicting the state's history. On the west side of the square an ancient **Jesuit monastery** now houses the offices of the University of Durango.

From here 5 de Febrero leads back to the **Casa de los Condes**, the most elaborate of the Spanish-style mansions. Built in the eighteenth century by the Conde de Suchil, sometime Spanish governor of Durango, its exuberantly carved columns and wealth of extravagant detail are quite undamaged by time. History has brought some strange functions though: it was the seat of the local Inquisition for some time – and a more inappropriate setting for their stern deliberations would be hard to imagine – while nowadays it operates as a sort of upmarket shopping mall, with most of the rooms off the lower courtyard given over to boutiques. For more exciting shopping, continue on 5 de Febrero to the back of the **market**. Covering a whole block on two storeys, there's just about everything you could want here, from medicinal herbs to farm equipment, as well as a series of little food stalls upstairs.

The University **Museum** is nearby, a couple of blocks up Pasteur to where it crosses Aquiles Serdan; but its displays of local archeology and history are pretty arcane and rarely disturbed by visitors. Better to head back to the plaza from where you can stroll up Constitución, a lively shopping street with several small restaurants, to the little church and garden of Santa Ana, or along to the **Casa de la Cultura** – another old mansion converted into a cultural centre – where there are often interesting temporary exhibitions. A little further afield, take a bus from outside the cathedral ("Remedios/Parque Guadiana") for a walk around the hillside park. From the **Iglesia de los Remedios** at the summit the view takes in the entire city.

Eating

Though **restaurants** abound throughout the central area, particularly along Constitución, none merits particular mention; the very cheapest are the stalls upstairs in the **market**, some of which serve excellent food. *La Terraza*, 5 de Febrero, on the first floor overlooking the plaza opposite the cathedral, is a wonderful setting for a drink – they also serve good pizzas. The *Café Nevería La Bohemia*, 20 de Noviembre 907, serves a wide range of cafe food, European dishes and *comidas*.

Around Durango

The full title of the local tourist office is the *Dirección de Turismo y Cinematografía del Estado de Durango*. Much of their time is spent organizing the vast number of **film** units which come to take advantage of the surrounding area's remarkably constant, clear, high-altitude light, the desert and mountain scenery (Westerns are the speciality), and the relatively cheap Mexican technicians and extras.

If shooting's in progress, the tourist office can normally organize a trip out to watch, and at other times there are excursions to see the permanent sets of **Chupaderos** or **Villa del Oeste**. You can also get to these on the local train line, which goes to **Tepehuanes**, a beautiful run up into the mountains, though the journey is more enticing than the destination and it can be hard to get back. The main road from Parral runs within a few hundred metres of the movie towns, so it's also easy to get there by bus, and to flag one down when you leave – alternatively you get a pretty good view as you pass by.

Perhaps a more exciting day out is to head south to **El Saltito**, a waterfall surrounded by bizarre rock formations which has itself been a frequent film location: the bus can drop you on the road 6km away. On any of these trips, watch out for **scorpions**. There's a genus of white scorpion unique to this area which, though rare – the only place most people see one is encased in the glass paperweights on sale all over the place – has a sting that is frequently fatal.

On **leaving Durango** you face a simple choice: **west** to the Pacific at Mazatlán, over an incredible road through the Sierra Madre (see p.111), which is itself a worthwhile excursion; or **south** to Zacatecas (p.199), the finest of Mexico's colonial cities.

MONTERREY AND THE NORTHEAST ROUTES

The **eastern border crossings**, from Ciudad Acuña to Matamoros, are uniformly dull – dedicated solely to the task of getting people and goods from one country to the other. In this they are at least reasonably efficient, with immigration officials on both sides well used to coping with mass cross-border traffic. In most, Mexican tourist cards are routinely issued at the border, while Mexican consulates in the Texan towns across the Río Grande can handle any problems. If you're walking over the bridges there's a small toll to pay.

Once across the border, you're faced with the choice of pressing on south (generally the best option) or choosing a suitable hotel from the dozens on offer. If you're eager to head on from **Nuevo Laredo**, **Reynosa** or **Matamoros** there are frequent city bus services to the main bus stations, though you have to walk a few blocks to catch them. The bus stations in **Ciudad Acuña** and **Piedras Negras** are in town, within walking distance of the border crossing.

Direct buses get you from the border to México in sixteen to eighteen hours: with the exception of Ciudad Acuña, all the towns mentioned above also have rail links to the south, though few lines are really reliable.

BORDER CHECKS

Crossing the border, do not forget to go through **immigration and customs** checks. As everywhere, there's a free zone south of the frontier, and you can cross at will. Try to continue south, though, and you'll be stopped after some 20km and sent back to get your tourist card stamped.

The Lower Río Grande Valley: Ciudad Acuña to Matamoros

The Río Grande, known to Mexicans as the *Río Bravo del Norte*, forms the border between Texas and Mexico, a distance of more than 1500km. The country through which it flows is arid semi-desert, and the towns along the lower section of the river are heavily industrialized and suffer from appalling environmental pollution. This is the *maquiladora* zone, where foreign-owned assembly plants produce consumer goods, most of them for export to the States. There are few particular attractions for tourists, and most visitors are here for the cheap shopping or simply passing through on their way south.

Ciudad Acuña

The smallest of the border towns, **CIUDAD ACUÑA** (setting of the low-budget Mexican thriller *El Mariachi* and its sequel *El Regreso del Mariachi*) is quiet, relaxed and intensely hot. The zócalo has a small **museum** on one side, with a tiny collection of fossils and artefacts, and rows and rows of deathly dull photographs of local dignitaries.

Though there's little to do in town itself, the area around Acuña offers plenty. Watersports enthusiasts are amply catered for at the **Presa Amistad**, a huge artificial lake straddling the border, while to the west the starkly beautiful mountains, canyons and desert of the interior of Coahuila State invite cautious exploration. The huge and scarcely visited **Parque Internacional del Río Bravo**, opposite Big Bend National Park in Texas, offers superb wilderness but you'll need a well-equipped vehicle to cope with the rugged terrain; there's no public transport.

Practicalities

Arriving over the bridge from Del Rio, Texas, the bus drops you at the **border** post, where there's a map of the town in the modern customs building, together with some limited tourist information. The **bus station**, at the corner of Matamoros and Ocampo, is just five blocks from the border and one from the plaza.

Most shops and restaurants are willing and glad to change your dollars, at a fairly good rate for small amounts. But for proper exchange there's a choice of banks and **casas de cambio**. Of the **banks**, *Bancomer*, Madero 360, off Juárez, has a 24-hour ATM, as does *Banamex*, at the corner of Matamoros and Hidalgo. The **post office** is on Hidalgo 320, past Juárez.

You'll pass several **hotels** as you walk down Hidalgo from the border. The *San Jorge*, Hidalgo 165 (☎877/2-50-70; ⑤), has pleasant, a/c rooms, while *San Antonio*, corner of Hidalgo and Lerdo (☎877/2-51-08; ⑦), is spacious and roomy. The *Alfaro*, Madero 240, between Juárez and Lerdo (no phone; ①), isn't bad if you're desperately low on cash. Also good for one night, especially if you're very tired, is the *Coahuila*, Lerdo 160, one block off Hidalgo (☎877/2-10-40; ③); bear in mind, though, that the bathroom has a tendency to flood and there are no towels provided. You may prefer not to stay in town at all: 30km south of Acuña the road to Piedras Negras (see below) passes through **JIMÉNEZ**, where there are plenty of tranquil spots for **camping** and the new *Hotel Río San Diego* (④) occupies a relaxing position overlooking the river.

One of the most reasonably priced **restaurants** in Acuña is the family run and a/c *Hostería Santa Maria* on Lerdo. Good-value cafes and *loncherías* line Matamoros; the *Café Garcia* has an unusual no-smoking policy.

MOVING ON FROM ACUÑA

Onward transport is more frequent from the towns further south, and it may be easier to head to Piedras Negras, ninety minutes away, and change **buses** there: however, there are a few daily services to **Saltillo** (4hr 30min) and **Monterrey** (8hr) via Monclova, and a couple to México and Torreón. In addition there are frequent runs to Monterrey and Piedras Negras on *Blancos* buses, while *El Aguila* buses go to **Guadalajara** (1 daily), **Zacatecas** (2 daily) and **Chihuahua** (1 daily). The airline-style *Expresso Futura* buses (a/c, reclining seats, toilets and videos) have one daily service each to México, Querétaro and San Luis Potosí.

Piedras Negras

Friendly and hassle-free, with the most laid-back immigration officers you're likely to encounter anywhere in Mexico, **PIEDRAS NEGRAS** is the ideal border town. The unpretentious main square is directly opposite the bridge, with several hotels (though few restaurants) in the immediate vicinity.

Practicalities

The extremely helpful **tourist office** (daily 9am–2pm & 4–7pm), by the main square as you enter Mexico from the US, has free maps of Piedras Negras and Eagle Pass, as well as of other cities in Coahuila. For **currency exchange**, head for *Cambios Coahuila* (Mon–Fri 8.30am–5.30pm), in *Sangar's Shopping Center*, Allende and Xicotencatl (five blocks up Allende from the bus station), or in the market on Zaragoza 107. *Bancomer* (Mon–Sat 9am–5pm), one block from the main plaza on Morelos and Abasolo, has a 24-hour ATM.

Though there's no shortage of **hotels**, most appear to be suffering from years of neglect. One welcome exception is the clean and roomy *Hotel del Centro*, Allende 510, one block from the border (☎878/2-50-30; ④); avoid the *Muzquiz* next door but one. Slightly more expensive, but recommended, is the *Hotel Santos*, Hidalgo 314 at the corner of Matamoros (☎878/2-19-68 or 2-03-64; ⑤). Best of all is the comfortable *Hotel Santa Rosa*, Guerrero 401 on the corner of Morelos (☎878/2-04-00; ⑤). *Autel Rio*, Padre de las Casas 121 and Teran (☎878/2-70-64; ⑨), is very luxurious, with a TV in every room, a swimming pool and plenty of parking space, while *Hotel Reforma*, Zaragoza 507 (☎878/2-03-90; ④), is good for groups, as the rate for a double room is charged for two or more people. For a decent **meal** try the *Café Saloman* on the plaza. The owner speaks English.

MOVING ON FROM PIEDRAS NEGRAS

From the border, the bus station is a fifteen-minute walk along Allende through the town centre. The main companies, *Blancos* and *Aguila*, operate a decent second-class service, with frequent departures to all the major points south. *Blancos* have an office on the main square. *Expresso Futura* buses run to **México**, **Aguascalientes** and **Monterrey**, while *Turistar Ejecutivo* luxury buses serve **México**, **Monclova** and **Querétaro**. *Frontera* second-class buses have frequent departures to **Nuevo Laredo**, three hours away. The *Coahuilense* service to **Saltillo** takes around ten hours.

Turn left after crossing the border, along Zaragoza, for the **train station** and the train to **Saltillo**. The journey takes around ten hours, initially across a parched plain with some wickedly eroded land, then passing through gaps in the mountains; worth taking if you have the time and can afford to travel *Primera Especial*.

Nuevo Laredo

The giant of the eastern border towns, **NUEVO LAREDO** is alive with the imagery and commercialism of the frontier. This is the transport hub of the area, with dozens of departures to México and all major towns in the north, as well as a reliable train service to the capital. Cross-border traffic, legal and illegal, is king here and both bridges are crowded with pedestrians and vehicles 24 hours a day. Mexican insurance offices and sleazy *cantinas* greet you; tired horses hitched to buggies wait dispiritedly for their next load of pasty, overweight tourists.

You'll do best to head straight out: the road **south from Nuevo Laredo** at first crosses a flat, scrub-covered, featureless plain, but after the first hour the scenery begins to improve. Far to the west the peaks of the **Sierra Madre** rise abruptly. Easily the most noticeable plants are the giant yuccas known as **Joshua Trees**; to the early settlers their upraised, spiky branches appeared to resemble Joshua praying in supplication.

Arrival and orientation

As a tourist, entering or leaving Mexico, you'll take *Puente Internacional #1*: there's a small toll, payable in dollars or pesos. Despite the crush, immigration usually proceeds smoothly, though expect long queues crossing to the US in the mornings. The small **tourist office** (daily 8.30am–8pm; ☎871/12-01-04) at the border post is often deserted, but you may be able to pick up leaflets as you pass and there's another, mainly geared to business travellers, eight blocks up Guerrero on the right (same hours). **Street maps** are available from the lobbies of the larger hotels, theoretically for guests only.

Coming from Laredo, Texas, head up Guerrero, past the curio shops, and you'll find everything you're likely to need within seven or eight blocks of the border. Walk past the first square, **Plaza Juárez**, with the cathedral and *Los Arcos* craft market, and head for the main square, the palm-shaded **Plaza Hidalgo**, easily the most pleasant spot in Nuevo Laredo. It seems a pity there are no pavement cafes on the plaza but if you need a meal the air-conditioned *Café Almanza*, on the south side, is reasonably priced and friendly. The plaza is a good place to begin looking for a hotel if you need one, and it's where you catch the bus to the **Central Camionera** (see "Moving on from Nuevo Laredo"). The **post office** is here too, at the rear of the Palacio Municipal. Banks with **ATMs** include *Banamex*, at Reforma and 15 de Septiembre, by the *Gigante* supermarket and *Kentucky Fried Chicken*, and at Guerrero and Canales; *Bancomer*, Reforma and Paseo Colon; and *Serfín*, on the corner of Guerrero and Canales, one block from Plaza Hidalgo.

Accommodation

Although there's no shortage of inexpensive **hotels** in the city centre – especially along Hidalgo – many of them are extremely run-down and frequented by prostitutes and their clients. You may need to stay the night here if you've got an early departure: check what you're getting very carefully before parting with any money.

El Greco, Galeana 619 at the corner of Pino Suárez and Galeana (☎871/12-10-02). Comfortable place with TV, a/c and safe parking. ④.

MOVING ON FROM NUEVO LAREDO

The **Nuevo Laredo International Airport** is a long taxi ride (about $20) out of town. There's actually little international about it, as the only two (very expensive) flights are to Guadalajara and México on *Mexicana*. Nuevo Laredo's huge **Central Camionera** is some distance south of town, but battered city buses (marked "Puente"/"Centro") run frequently between here and the border crossings and Plaza Hidalgo. The restaurant inside the bus station is good but pricey; you'll find cheaper food stalls outside. There's also a *guardería* (Mon–Sat 7am–10pm, Sun 7am–5pm).

The **main bus companies** are *Omnibus de México, Elite, Tamaulipas* and *Turistar*, along with *Transportes Frontera, Transportes del Norte* and *Tres Estrellas de Oro* and many more; you'll have no trouble getting a bus to Monterrey (4hr) or México (16hr), day or night. The luxury *Expresso Futura* bus to **Monterrey** takes only two and a half hours.

Other destinations include Saltillo, Ciudad Victoria, Guadalajara and Zacatecas; there are even a couple of services to Acapulco. If you're **heading into the States** by bus, *Greyhound* tickets are on sale, including the budget *Ameripass*. *Shuttlejacks* offer a cheaper service to San Antonio, Austin and Dallas (one daily, around noon). For the very cheapest way into Texas, leave Nuevo Laredo over the International Bridge and follow the *Quick Travel* sign for a *camionetta* (van) service to San Antonio or Houston.

At the time of writing the *Regiomontano* **train** to México was running only from Monterrey, but it's worth checking if the route has been extended to the border. This is one of the best train services in Mexico, leaving at 7pm and allowing you to travel overnight in a comfortable sleeping car and arrive in the capital at 10am. Another train between Nuevo Laredo and the capital, the *Aguila Azteca*, also known as Train 2, leaves Nuevo Laredo at 6.55pm, calling at Monterrey, Saltillo, San Luis Potosí, San Miguel de Allende and Querétaro, arriving in the capital at 8pm.

To **get to the train station** on foot you face a walk of about twenty minutes; from the border go up Guerrero nine or ten blocks, then turn right along Mina or Gutiérrez for another ten blocks.

Motel Fiesta, Ocampo 559 (☎871/12-47-37). Rooms have TV, a/c and telephone. ⑤.

Nuevo Romano, Doctor Mier 800, one block west from Plaza Hidalgo (☎871/12-26-94). Recently remodelled and refurbished, and good value. Rooms without TV are cheaper. ④.

Sam's, Hidalgo 2903 (☎871/2-59-32). Good-value, reliable place with a range of rooms. ②.

Texas, Guerrero 807, just past Plaza Hidalgo (☎871/12-18-07). Comfortable rooms with fans and bathroom. ③.

Reynosa

A very easy border crossing and excellent transport connections combine to make **REYNOSA** a favourite point to enter Mexico. This sprawling industrial city, filled with car repair shops and *Pemex* plants, has little to detain you, but people are generally friendly and coming and going is simple.

Practicalities

Opposite the bus station is the luxurious *Grand Premier Hotel*, Colon 1304 (☎89/22-48-50; ⑦); the **cheap hotels** are all nearer the centre. From the **bus station**, turn left and along Colon, passing the hotel *San Miguel*, between Colon and Mina (☎89/22-75-27; ⑤). One block beyond Hidalgo is Díaz with more budget hotels. The **train station** is at the end of Hidalgo, just six blocks from the plaza.

You can **change currency** at the *Plaza Premier* shopping centre (daily 9am–6pm), next door to the *Grand Premier Hotel*. There are a number of inexpensive **food stalls** and a *Gigante* supermarket by the bus station, and a well-stocked **market** on Hidalgo, midway between the train station and the plaza.

MOVING ON FROM REYNOSA

Frequent **buses** ply the 9km between Reynosa and **McAllen, Texas** until 11.30pm. The journey takes about forty minutes, including immigration. The *Valley Transit Co.* operates services to **San Antonio, Houston** and **Corpus Christi**.

Buses to the rest of Mexico include services to Matamoros and Ciudad Victoria; Tampico, Tuxpan and Veracruz on the Gulf coast; and even an overnight bus to Villahermosa (24hr). **Rail** connections are of little practical use, with only one train a day in each direction, though you could use it to experience a relatively short Mexican train journey. The *Tamulipeco* train leaves Reynosa for Matamoros at 2.45pm, arriving at 5.10pm, and for Monterrey at 11.25am, arriving at 4pm.

Matamoros

MATAMOROS, across the Río Grande from the southernmost point of the continental USA at Brownsville, is a buzzing, atmospheric town popular with locals and visiting Texans. The busy but compact centre, focused on **plazas** Hidalgo and Allende and the **Mercado Juárez**, on calles 9 and 10, is an accurate introduction to Mexican cities further south. It's also a surprisingly youthful place: the plazas and shopping streets seem to be almost entirely filled with teenagers, and the local youth culture, swollen by American teens beating the Texan age limit on drinking, enlivens the entertainment scene.

Formerly known as Playa Lauro Villar, Matamoros' pleasant **beach**, 35km east of town, was renamed **Playa Bagdad** after the US port of Bagdad which stood at the mouth of the Río Grande. Clean (but watch out for broken glass), and pounded by invigorating surf, it offers the chance for a first (or last) dip in the surf of Mexico's Gulf coast, and is very popular at weekends with Mexican families, who gather in the shade of the *palapas* that stretch for miles along the sand. There are some tiny, decrepit and extremely overpriced **hotels** and lots of **seafood restaurants**, few of which actually seem to have much worth eating. Most locals bring picnics or cook on the public barbecues. Best to treat the trip as a day visit, though you can **camp** for free in the sandhills.

To get there, take a combi marked "Playa" from the Plaza Allende, which drops you off in the car park by the *Administracion*. It takes about an hour, and the office has showers (small charge) and lockers where you can safely store your clothes while you swim.

Arrival and information

Crossing the border is easy enough, and it's possible to walk from Brownsville right into the centre of Matamoros, though fixed-price *peseros*, known as *maxi taxis*, run frequently along Obregón to the centre and the **bus station**, a long way south (look for "Centro" for Plaza Allende, "Puente Internacional" for the border, or "Central" for the bus station). Arriving **by train**, it's possible to walk to the centre along c/9 or c/10, turning left after six blocks along Abasolo; again *maxi taxis* cover the route.

The **tourist office** is a few blocks from the border bridge at Tamaulipas and Obregón (daily 8am–6pm), and you can pick up a variety of leaflets and **maps of Matamoros** from the reception areas of the bigger, more expensive hotels. For **currency exchange**, head for *Banorte*, Morelos between c/6 and c/7. There are also branches of *Bancomer*, corner of Matamoros and c/6; *Banamex*, corner of Matamoros and c/7, one block west off Plaza Hidalgo, and on the plaza itself, *Serfin* (all Mon–Fri 9am–5pm).

Accommodation

Staying in Matamoros is no problem, with hotels in all price categories, including several good budget choices on Abasolo – pedestrianized between c/6 and c/11 – a block north of Plaza Hidalgo. If you're only interested in a comfortable bed for the night near the bus station, then the *Fiesta Gallo* (③) fits the bill, with a decent restaurant too. There has been a recent upsurge in **more expensive** accommodation: if you're in a large group, it can be worthwhile asking for a suite.

Colonial, Matamoros 601 and c/6 (☎891/16-64-42). A bit run-down; rooms equipped with toilet and fan only. ③.

Majestic, Abasolo 89 (☎891/13-36-80). A good budget choice near Plaza Hidalgo. ③.

México, Abasolo 807 between c/8 and c/9 (☎891/12-08-56). Comfortable place whose owner speaks some English. ⑤.

Minerva Paula, Matamoros 125 and c/11 (☎891/16-39-66). Luxury option, with wall-to-wall carpeting, a/c and heating, colour TV with cable, restaurant, phones and parking. ⑥.

Nieto, c/10 no. 1508, between Bravo and Bustamante (☎891/13-08-57). Rooms all with TV and telephone. Parking, swimming pool, and a two-bedroom master suite that sleeps nine. ⑥.

Plaza Riviera, corner of Morelos and c/10 (☎891/16-39-98). Very comfortable refurbished hotel split onto two buildings, one with parking. ⑥.

Ritz, Matamoros 612 and c/7 (☎891/12-11-90). Comfortable a/c hotel; rates include buffet breakfast. Plenty of safe parking and a suite for six people. ⑥.

San Francisco, c/10, between Abasolo and Gonzalez (no phone). By far the best budget hotel in Matamoros, with decent rooms and shared showers. ①.

Eating

Although most **restaurants** in Matamoros are fairly expensive – lots cater for cross-border trade – plenty of places for cheap filling meals line c/10, just off Plaza Allende, and c/9 between Matamoros and Bravo. One of the best is the *Café de México* on Gonzales, between calles 6 and 7. Great coffee and *pan dulce* breakfasts are available from *Los Panchos* on the Plaza Allende, a cafe filled with locals. To order simply sit down and the waiter will bring a basket of *pan dulce* and coffee; just pay at the counter for what you've eaten. For lunch, head for *El Chinchonal*, c/9 and Matamoros, or for an early dinner try *Las Dos Repúblicas*, nearby on c/9, which dishes up huge plates of *tortillas*, *tacos*, *quesadillas* and the like until 8pm.

MOVING ON FROM MATAMOROS

The **Central Camionera** (☎891/12-27-77), equipped with a post office, *guardería* and 24-hour restaurant – as well as a *Gigante* **supermarket** across the road – is well served by buses to the US and to the interior of Mexico.

El Expresso, cheaper than *Greyhound*, runs to Houston (4 daily; 6hr 30min). Reynosa, Monterrey, Ciudad Victoria and México have frequent departures, and there is also a bus to Puebla. Heading **west**, *Transportes Estrella de Oro* serves Mexicali, Guadalajara and Mazatlan, while *Autotransportes de Oriente* covers the **coast route** with buses to Tampico (9 daily; 6hr 30min), Tuxpan (11hr), Veracruz (16hr) and Villahermosa (24hr).

The **train station** is on Hidalgo, just nine blocks north from Plaza Hidalgo. The only train, to Reynosa and Monterrey, currently leaves at 9.20am, arriving at 4pm. The fare for a *primera especial* seat and "lunch" is about the same as a first-class bus ticket.

The Coast Route

The eastern seaboard has so little to recommend it that even if you've crossed the border at Matamoros, you'd be well advised to follow the border road west to **Reynosa** and then cut down to Monterrey (see p.146). Unless you're determined to go straight down through Veracruz to the Yucatán by the shortest route, avoiding México altogether, there seems little point in coming this way. Even the time factor is less of an advantage than it might appear on the map – the roads are in noticeably worse repair than those through the heartland, and progress is considerably slower. Beyond Tampico, it's true, you get into an area of great archeological interest, with some good beaches around Veracruz, but this is probably best approached from the capital. Here in the northeast there's plenty of sandy coast, but access is difficult, beaches tend to be windswept and scrubby, and the whole area is marred by the consequences of its enormous oil wealth: there are refineries all along the coast, tankers passing close offshore, and a shoreline littered with their discards and spillages. It's also very, very hot.

At the time of the Spanish Conquest this area of the Gulf coast was inhabited by the **Huastecs**, who have given their name to the region around Tampico and the eastern flanks of the Sierra Madre Oriental. Huastec settlement can be dated back some 3000 years: their language differs substantially from the surrounding native tongues, but has close links with the Maya of Yucatán. **Quetzalcoatl**, the feathered serpent god of Mexico, was probably of Huastec origin.

The Huastecs were at their most powerful between 800 and 1200 AD, just before the Aztecs rose to dominance, and were still at war with the Aztecs when the Spanish arrived and found willing allies here. After the successful campaign against Tenochtitlán, the Aztec capital, the Spanish, first under Cortès and later the notorious Nuño de Guzmán, turned on the independent-minded Huastecs, decimating and enslaving their former allies.

Ciudad Victoria

CIUDAD VICTORIA, capital of the state of Tamaulipas, is little more than a place to stop over for a night. It's not unattractive but neither is it interesting, and while the surrounding hill country is a paradise for hunters and fishing enthusiasts, with a huge artificial lake, the **Presa Vicente Guerrero**, others will find little to detain them. If you're going to stay in the centre, head, as always, for the zócalo, Plaza Hidalgo, around which most of the town's facilities are concentrated. There are several **hotels** on the plaza itself – *Los Monteros* (☎131/2-03-00; ④), a lovely old colonial building, is probably the best value in town. The cheaper places tend to be a block or two away: try the *Ritz* on Hidalgo (③) or the hotels *Paris* (③) and *Tampico* (③), both on Juárez; cheapest of all is the *San Bernabe* (②), just off the plaza on c/9.

Tampico

Between Ciudad Victoria and **TAMPICO**, very much a tropic port and the country's busiest, the vegetation around the road becomes increasingly lush, green and tropical (the Tropic of Cancer passes just south of Ciudad Victoria, and the Río Pánuco forms the border with the steamy Gulf state of Veracruz). As a treasure port in the Spanish empire, Tampico suffered numerous pirate raids and was destroyed in 1684. The rebuilding finally began in 1823, the date of the cathedral's foundation, and in 1828 Spain landed troops in Tampico in a vain and shortlived attempt to reconquer her New World empire. The discovery of oil in 1901 set the seal on Tampico's rise to prominence as the world's biggest oil port in the early years of this century.

The older parts of town, down by the docks and train station, have a distinct Caribbean feel, with their peeling, ramshackle clapboard houses and swing-door bars. Vivacious and occasionally heavy, Tampico is also a newly wealthy boom town, riding the oil surge with a welter of grand new buildings founded on the income from a huge refinery at the mouth of the Río Pánuco. Downtown, Tampico's dual nature is instantly apparent. Within a hundred metres of each other are two plazas: the **Plaza de Armas**, rich and formal, ringed by government buildings, the cathedral (built in the 1930s with money donated by American oil tycoon Edward Doheny) and the smart hotels; and the **Plaza de la Libertad**, raucous and rowdy, peopled by wandering salesmen and surrounded by cheap bars and hotels.

On the other side of the run-down waterfront and the seamier sides of the city centre lie the affluent new suburbs with their supermarkets and neat planning. Nowhere is this more apparent than in **Ciudad Madero**, Tampico's growing twin town 7km north. You might want to take a trip up there to see the Huastec artefacts in the excellent **Museo de la Cultura Huasteca** (Mon–Fri 10am–5pm) in the *Tecnológico Madero*. Buses run there from Lopez de Lara, three blocks east of the Plaza de Armas.

Tampico's town beach, **Playa Miramar**, is a thirty-minute bus ride from the centre. Here you'll find several small boarding houses, as well as a couple of little restaurants serving good fresh fish. These will also let you use their shower for a small fee. This is good **camping** territory, with a stand of small trees immediately behind the beach, and if you have your own transport you can drive miles up the sand to seek out isolation. Which is one of the chief disadvantages – everyone insists on driving their cars around the beach, most local learners seem to take their first lessons here, and even the bus drives on to the sand to turn round. The other is that the water, so close to the refinery and the mouth of the river, is **heavily polluted**; swimming is not recommended.

Practicalities

Tampico's **bus station** (24-hr *guardería*) is in an unattractive area a long way north of the city. From here, take a bus or rattly *colectivo* downtown. The **tourist office**, hidden away on the eastern side of the Plaza de Armas, on the second floor at Olmos Sur 101 – you reach it on stairs beside an ice cream parlour (Mon–Fri 9am–7pm; ☎121/2-26-78), is helpful enough, but there's little for them to say. Buses back to the Camionera leave from nearby, at the corner of Olmos and Carranza.

One thing you can say for Tampico is that there's no shortage of **hotels**, though most are either expensive or very sleazy. If you don't want the hassle of carrying your bags downtown and searching for a room, then the *Hotel La Central,* at Rosalio Bustamante 224 (☎12/17-09-18; ③), offers very good value; it looks more expensive than it is. *Hotel Santa Elena* (☎12/13-35-07; ⑤), opposite the bus station, is another option, though not great value, with a decent, if pricey, restaurant.

Downtown, many of the cheaper hotels around the docks, train station and market area are brothels. The least expensive and most atmospheric place to stay is around the **Plaza de la Libertad**. The *Capri*, Juárez Nte. 202 (☎12/12-26-80; ②), about four blocks north of the plaza, is the most acceptable of the cheapies. Better still, head for the block of Madero immediately west of the plaza, where you'll spend a little more for the relative comfort of the *Posada del Rey*, Madero Ote. 218 (☎12/14-11-55; ⑤), or the better-value *Plaza*, Madero Ote. 204 (☎12/14-16-78; ⑤); between them is the comfortable business-style *Colonial*, Madero Ote. 210 (☎12/12-76-76; ⑦).

Monterrey and around

Third city of Mexico, capital of Nuevo Leon and the nation's industrial stronghold, **MONTERREY** is a contradictory place. The vast network of factories, the traffic, urban sprawl, pollution and ostentatious wealth that characterize the modern city are relatively recent developments; the older parts retain an air of colonial elegance and the setting remains one of great beauty. Ringed by jagged mountain peaks – which sadly serve also to keep in the noxious industrial fumes – Monterrey is dominated above all by one, the Cerro de la Silla or Saddle Mountain.

In addition to the national and religious holidays, Monterrey celebrates its foundation on September 20, followed by a four-week festival known as the **Feria de Monterrey**. The **Festival Alfonso Reyes** is held in the first two weeks of October, with plenty of music and theatre.

Arrival, information and city transport

Monterrey is the transport hub of the northeast, with excellent national and international connections. Flights from the rest of Mexico and from Dallas land at Mariano Escobedo **international airport**, 6km or so north of the city: if you're arriving here, the best way to get downtown is to buy a taxi ticket from the booth situated near the exit.

Scores of **buses** pull into the enormous Central Camionera, northwest of the centre on Av. Colón, complete with its own shopping centre and post office. To get from the **bus station** to the Gran Plaza, pick up a #1, #7, #17 or #18 bus heading down Pino Suárez and get off at a suitable intersection: Ocampo, Zaragoza or Juárez for example. **Trains** from México and Matamoros arrive northwest of the Central Camionera, on Nieto.

There's almost always someone who can speak English at the exceptionally helpful **tourist office** (Tues–Sun 10am–5pm; ☎83/345-08-70 or 345-09-02), about halfway up the plaza on the corner of Zaragoza and Matamoros as the latter goes under the plaza (look for the "Infotur" sign). They offer a wide variety of maps and leaflets, and information on hotel prices and local travel agencies. Occasionally a student from the local university covers on Mondays. For **tourist information** when dialling from outside Nuevo Leon, call ☎91-800-83-222; from the US: ☎1-800-235-2438.

You can **change money** at any of the several *casas de cambio* on Ocampo, between Zaragoza and Juárez (Mon–Fri 9am–1pm & 3–6pm, Sat 9am–12.30pm). *American Express* **travellers' cheques** can be changed at *Banamex*, Pino Suárez 933 Nte., until 1pm. There are **ATM machines** at the three branches of *Bancomer:* on the corner of

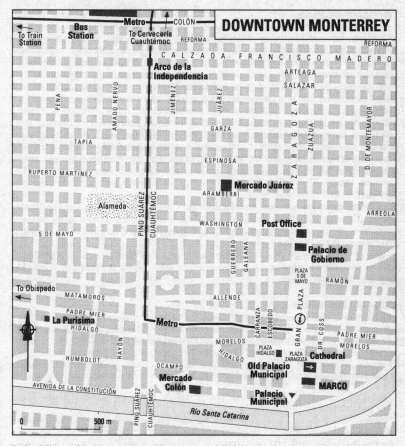

DOWNTOWN MONTERREY

Padre Mier and Juárez; corner of Zaragoza and Hidalgo; and corner of Pino Suarez and Madero (all Mon–Fri 9am–5pm).

City transport

The streets of Monterrey are almost solid with **buses**, following routes that appear incomprehensible at first sight. The city authorities have taken steps to resolve the confusion by putting legible route maps on each bus and numbering all the stops (*paradas*), and the tourist office can provide you with a **timetable** and plan of new bus stops, but it still takes a fair amount of confidence to plunge into the system. The old clangers are slowly being replaced by new panoramic glass vehicles, known as *Panoramicos*. At the time of writing, routes #1, #18, #31, #209 (orbital) and #130, all of which run along Juárez, have new buses. Fares are written on the windscreen.

The **metro** – actually an above-ground monorail – runs on two lines, one east–west along Colon (you see it as soon as you emerge from the bus station), and another north–south from the Gran Plaza. It's simple to use; tickets cost about about 33¢ per journey from the coin-operated ticket machines, and are available for 1, 2, 5 and 11 trips. Each one has a map of the line printed on it.

Accommodation

Accommodation in Monterrey is not especially good value. Most places claim to have hot water, though at certain times there's no water at all due to a shortage; check at the desk for the times when the water's off. The majority of the **budget hotels** are near the bus station, mainly on the other side of Av. Colón, safest crossed on the footbridge. It's not the most pleasant part of town, permanently noisy and crowded, and some way from the centre, but it is convenient for transport, and reasonably safe. You can see several possibilities as you stand outside the bus station, but it's best to penetrate a little further if you want to avc'd the worst of the noise. Amado Nervo, heading south off Colón, has several possibilities, as does narrow Reforma, though the hotel signs are hard to spot above the canopies of the market stalls; places north of Colón are too far from the action to have any particular advantage. The two main north–south streets opposite the bus station, Pino Suárez and Cuauhtémoc, also have numerous budget options, though Pino Suárez has a few sleazy, cockroach-infested places that are best avoided, so look before you book.

Further **downtown**, rooms are of a different class altogether: in modern and "international" hotels, all with air conditioning and many with a pool. Geared up for business travellers, they lower their prices slightly at weekends. There's a good concentration in and around Plaza Hidalgo.

There's **camping** at Villa de Santiago, an hour out of Monterrey. Catch the bus to Alamo from the Camionera and ask the driver to drop you off at Villa de Santiago. The site also caters for RVs.

Near the bus station

Amado Nervo, Amado Nervo 1110 (☎83/375-46-32). Cheapest on this street. ③.

America, Cuauhtémoc Nte. 1114, at Reforma (☎83/374-19-00). Some of the cheapest acceptable accommodation in the area, though the rooms are dark and sparsely furnished. ③.

Conde, Reforma Pte. 427 (☎83/375-71-59). Good value: one of many similar hotels along here. ④.

Estacion, Victoria 1450. Minimal comforts close to the train station; cross the road behind the mounted locomotive then take the third street on the right, with *La Cabana Blanca* restaurant on the corner. ③.

Jandal, Cuauhtémoc Nte. 825, at Salazar (☎83/372-46-06). Best of the more comfortable places, with good a/c rooms with colour TV. ⑥.

Nogales, Nieto, at the train station. Poor value, but handy for late arrivals or early departures. ⑤.

Nuevo Leon, Amado Nervo 1007 (☎83/374-19-00). Pricier than the *Amado Nervo*, but better. ④.

La Posada, Amado Nervo 1138 (☎83/372-39-08). Slightly more upscale place; its restaurant serves a good *comida corrida*. ④.

Reforma, Universidad Nte. 1132, off Reforma just a couple of doors from the *America* (☎83/375-17-86). Rambling hotel where you can be sure of finding a room. ③.

Downtown

Colonial, Hidalgo Ote. 475 (☎83/343-67-91). Much less expensive than anything else in the area, but the tiny rooms don't give value for money. ⑥.

Gran Hotel Ancira, Hidalgo and Escobedo, on Plaza Hidalgo (☎83/343-20-60). Outstanding among the upmarket options, built as a grand hotel before the Revolution and full of period elegance. ⑨.

Royalty, Hidalgo Ote. 402 (☎83/340-98-00). Straightforward, middle-of-the-road business-style hotel. ⑧.

The City

First impressions of Monterrey are unprepossessing – the highway roars through the shabby shantytown suburbs and grimy manufacturing outskirts – but the **city centre** is quite a different thing. Here colonial relics are overshadowed by the office blocks and expensive shopping streets of the *zona commercial*, and by some extraordinary modern architecture – the local penchant for planting buildings in the ground at bizarre angles is exemplified above all by the **planetarium** and the **Instituto Tecnológico**. The city rewards a day of wandering and browsing, but there are just two places worth going out of your way to visit – the old **Obispado**, on a hill overlooking the centre, and the giant **Cuauhtémoc Brewery** to the north.

At its heart, if not the physical centre, is the **Gran Plaza** (officially the Plaza Zaragoza but more commonly known as the Macro Plaza), around which lie the cathedral and government offices. West of here are smart shops, swanky hotels and multinational offices, while just beyond is the dry bed of the **Río Santa Catarina**, now largely given over to playing fields. The first slopes of the Cerro de la Silla rise almost immediately from its far bank.

The Gran Plaza

Monterrey's **Gran Plaza** was created by demolishing some six complete blocks of the city centre, opening up a new vista straight through from the intensely modern City Hall to the beautiful red stone Palacio de Gobierno on what used to be Plaza 5 de Mayo. This is Mexican planning at its most extreme: when the political decision comes from the top, no amount of conservationist or social considerations are going to stand in the way, especially as the constitution's "no re-election" decree makes every administrator determined to leave some permanent memorial.

The result is undeniably stunning, with numerous lovely fountains, quiet parks and shady patios surrounded by museums and state administration buildings. In the evenings people gravitate here for no better reason than a stroll, and there are frequent concerts, dances and other entertainments laid on. At night the whole place is bathed in light when the **Faro del Comercio** flashes out a beam from the top of the Laser Beam Tower, a tall, graceful slab of orange concrete.

The **Cathedral**, with its one unbalanced tower, is a surprisingly modest edifice, easily dominated by the concrete bulk of the new **City Hall**, squatting on stilts at the southern end of the square. Inside there's a small archeological collection, while in the **Palacio de Gobierno** at the other end of the square is a room devoted to local history. The newest building on the plaza, at the junction of Zuazua and Ocampo by the cathedral, is the **Museo de Arte Contemporaneo** or MACRO (Tues, Thurs & Sat 11am–7pm, Wed & Sun 11am–9pm; $4, free on Wed, includes guided tour), a magnificent polished marble setting for a mainly Latin American collection. Off Zaragoza, and again opposite the cathedral, opens the little **Plaza Hidalgo** – a much more traditional, shady place, with old colonial buildings set around a statue of Miguel Hidalgo. The original Palacio Municipal, now superseded by the modern building, is here, acting today as an occasional cultural centre. Otherwise the pavement cafes make a pleasant stopoff – though food is expensive. Pedestrianized shopping streets fan out behind, crowded with window-gazing locals. *Sanborn's*, on Morelos near the plaza, holds a good selection of **English-language books**, magazines and guides.

Of Monterrey's two main **markets** – Juárez and Colón– the latter, on Av. de la Constitución, south of the Gran Plaza, is more tourist-oriented, specializing in local *artesanía*. Incidentally, the best of Monterrey's **flea markets** (*pulgas*; literally fleas) is also held on Constitución: market days are irregular, but ask any local for details.

El Obispado

The elegant **Obispado**, the old Bishop's Palace, tops Chepe Vera hill to the west of the city centre. Its commanding position – affording great views of the city when haze and smog allow – has made it an essential target for Monterrey's many invaders. Built in the eighteenth century, it became by turn a barracks, a military hospital and a fortress:

among its more dramatic exploits, the Obispado managed to hold out for two days after the rest of the city had fallen to the Texan general Zachary Taylor in 1846. The excellent **museum** inside (Tues–Fri 9.30am–5pm; Sat & Sun 10.30am–5pm; $4) records its long history with a little of everything: religious and secular art, arms from the War of Independence, Revolutionary pamphlets, old carriages and displays of regional folkways.

You get to the Obispado along Padre Mier, passing on the way the monumental modern church of **La Purísima**. Take a #R4 bus, alighting where it turns off Padre Mier close to the top; returning to the centre, any bus heading east on Hidalgo will do.

Cervecería Cuauhtémoc

If you're thirsty after all this, a visit to Monterrey's massive **Cervecería Cuauhtémoc** (Tues–Sun 9.30am–9pm; free) is all but compulsory. This is where they make the wonderful *Bohemia* and *Tecate* beers you'll find throughout Mexico (as well as the rather bland *Carta Blanca*) and somehow it seems much more representative of Monterrey than any of its prouder buildings. Inside there's a museum of brewing, a rather incongruous art gallery and a much more congruous Sporting Hall of Fame, commemorating the heroes of Mexican baseball; collectively these are known as the **Museo de Monterrey**, and this is the sign to look for if you want to find the place – guided tours of the brewery itself take place on weekdays at 11am, noon and 3pm. Your reward afterwards is **free beer** in the pleasant gardens outside, where peacocks strut and the blackened tree trunks bear witness to the city's industrial pollution. The *Café Museo*, in the museum, serves an excellent (though meaty) set lunch, with more beer included. Buses #17, #18 and #R1 – the last two leaving from Juárez – run regularly up Cuauhtémoc, past the brewery's main gate.

Eating and drinking

Monterrey's **restaurants** cater to hearty, meat-eating *norteños*, with *cabrito al pastor* or the regional speciality *cabrito asado* (whole roasted baby goat) given pride of place in window displays. You'll find scores of tiny bars and rather sleazy places to eat near the train station – especially at the little market just south of Colon – but up here you might be safer sticking to one of the fast-food joints around the Camionera.

In the **centre** you can eat better, but you also pay more, especially at the dozens of places around the Gran Plaza. There's always *Wendy's* and *McDonald's* if you want to pretend you're not in Mexico. For fresh produce you could do worse than join the locals at the **Mercado Juárez**, north of the Gran Plaza on Aramberri.

As for **nightlife**, in the city centre try *Black Jack*, on the corner of L E Gonzalez and Pablo A Gonzalez. There's live music but drinks are expensive. *Scandal*, on the corner of Rayon and Humoldt, also has live music.

Restaurants

Café San Pedro, Cuauhtémoc. Atmospheric place serving excellent breakfasts: where the locals head for *café con leche* and pastries. There's a free telephone for customers (local calls only).

Fastory, in the *Hotel Fastos* directly opposite the Camionera. 24-hour restaurant; the buffet breakfast (7–10am) is particularly good value.

El Palmito, 2 de Abril 2902. Hefty plates of hot food including *tacos* and *tostadas*. Open daily from around noon until midnight.

La Puntada, Hidalgo Ote. 123. Cheap, authentic, crowded Mexican spot.

Restaurante Vegetariano Superbom, upstairs at Padre Mier and Galeana. Excellent vegetarian *comidas* at lunchtime; they close early evening.

Sanborn's, Morelos near the Plaza Hidalgo. As safe a bet as ever for sandwiches and snacks: great if your stomach's feeling homesick.

Around Monterrey

The tourist office arranges a variety of excursions that allow you to escape the city and discover some of the surprisingly wild and beautiful country that surrounds it. The most impressive of these are to the **Huasteca Canyon**, a mountain ravine some 300m deep, and the **Grutas de Garcia**, off the road to Saltillo. The *grutas* (caves) are easiest reached by tram or funicular from the village of **Villa Garcia**, 9km away; or you can walk (about 30min). This is a popular outing, especially at weekends, with some impressive stalactites and stalagmites and an underground lake at the end of it. Buses run several times daily to Villa Garcia from outside the Camionera, about a block and a half towards the train station; buy your ticket from the *Transportes Monterrey–Saltillo* office or on the bus.

The trip to **Cascada Cola de Caballo** (Horsetail Falls), 35km south of Monterrey, is only really worthwhile after the rains – you can hire horses and *burros* to ride in the hilly Parque Nacional Cumbres de Monterrey, where there are views from the top of the falls and plenty of opportunity for hiking and camping. To get here by bus, take a *Lineas Amarillas* service to **El Cercado**, where *colectivos* wait to take you to the falls: once there, horse buggy rides are available and there are lovely swimming spots. With permission from the *Administracion* you can camp for free. A third alternative is to head up to the **Mesa Chipinque**, a mountain plateau just 18km from Monterrey with famous views back over the city. Here again you can rent horses (from the enormously flash *Motel Chipinque*) to explore the hinterland. If you want an **organized trip** to the caves or falls, try *OSETUR* (☎83/343-66-16), whose very reasonably priced day excursions depart from Ocampo behind the *Gran Hotel Ancira*.

MOVING ON FROM MONTERREY

You'll have no trouble getting an onward bus from the **Central Camionera** at almost any time of day or night; as well as the border destinations (including Ciudad Juárez) and México, there are buses to points all around the country, including Guadalajara and Mazatlán. Monterrey is also a good place to pick up transport into Texas: *Transportes del Norte* has direct connections with the *Greyhound* system; *Autobuses Adame*, on Alamo one block to the right as you leave the Camionera (☎83/331-29-20), runs a daily service to Houston (10hr including immigration checks). There are also slightly less orthodox but much cheaper *camionetas*, running between Monterrey and Houston via the border towns. Their drivers or agents will accost you outside the terminal – the fare is only about a third of the *Greyhound* fare, but you'll be taking a chance as these vehicles are almost certainly not covered by passenger liability insurance.

As for **trains**, *El Regiomontano* (Train 72) leaves for México at 7.50pm, calling at Saltillo and San Luis Potosí, arriving in the capital at 10am; the *Tamulipeco* sets out for Reynosa and Matamoros at 10am; and the *Aguila Azteca* (Train 2) offers a slower service to México, calling at more towns, leaving Monterrey at 11.30pm and arriving some twenty hours later. These journeys are relatively comfortable, with roomettes available on the *Regiomontano* and *primera especial* seats on the *Aguila Azteca*.

Saltillo

Just 85km southwest of Monterrey on a fast road, **SALTILLO**, capital of the state of Coahuila, is the place to head if you can't take the big city's hustle. It's infinitely quieter, with a scattering of beautiful buildings and, at 600m above sea level, feels refreshingly cool and airy.

First though, if you're coming south from Piedras Negras (see p.139), you pass through **MONCLOVA**. It doesn't look much now – aside from the vast steelworks –

but Monclova was for a while the capital of Coahuila, in the days when the state included the whole of Texas. You wouldn't go out of your way to visit, but it can make a useful staging point, some four hours from Piedras Negras, another three on to Saltillo. There are several small **hotels** near the middle of town.

Arrival

Saltillo's new **bus station** is 2km southwest of the centre – there are a couple of small hotels and restaurants directly opposite, but nothing else, and there's no point at all in staying out here unless you plan an extremely early start. Though the station boasts a post office and plenty of phones, there's nowhere to leave luggage. To get downtown, board one of the new **city buses** (marked "Centro/Camionera") that wait outside: get out by the cathedral on the Plaza de Armas, or stay on a couple more stops for the Plaza Acuña, right at the heart of things. The **train station** is much closer in, just a few blocks southwest of Parque Zaragoza, but still a walk of twenty minutes or more – small buses and vans run from here to the centre.

Accommodation

Most of the better-value **hotels** are in the side streets immediately around Plaza Acuña. Head up towards c/Victoria and the cathedral and you pass several: the *Hidalgo* at Padre Flores 217 (☎841/4-98-53; ②), and the *Conde* on Treviño, just above the Plaza Acuña (②), are very basic, rather dingy but clean; on the Plaza Acuña the *Hotel Jardín* (or *de Avila*), Padre Flores 211 (☎841/2-59-16; ③), with a huge sign, is also worth checking. If you can afford a little more and want to savour some **colonial atmosphere**, have a look at the *Urdinola* (☎841/4-09-40; ⑤) at Victoria Pte. 207. The tiled open lobby is dominated by a wide staircase flanked by suits of armour, and fountains play amid the greenery of the courtyard. Out near the **bus station** the clean, modern *Central* (☎841/7-00-04; ②) is the best of the bunch.

The City

There's not a great deal to do in Saltillo, but it's a great place to stroll around and soak up some atmosphere. Two contrasting squares grace the centre of town: the Plaza Acuña marks the rowdy heart of the modern city, surrounded by crowded shopping streets, the market in one corner, a series of little bars and cafes around the square; the old **Plaza de Armas** tells quite another story, sedate, formal and tranquil. This is the formal and cultural centre of Saltillo, shielded from traffic and modern development, illuminated at night and sometimes hosting music performances. Facing the Palacio de Gobierno across a flagged square, the magnificent eighteenth-century **Cathedral** is one of the most beautiful in northern Mexico, with an elaborately carved Churrigueresque facade and doorways, an enormous bell tower and a smaller clock tower.

The town's oldest streets fan out from the square, with some fine old houses still in private hands. One historic building worth seeing out of the many is the carefully preserved old **Ayuntamiento** (town hall) on the corner of Aldama and Hidalgo. The walls of the courtyard and the staircase are adorned with murals depicting the history of Saltillo from prehistoric times to the 1950s.

At the top of c/Victoria, with its shops and cinemas, is the **Alameda**, a shaded, tree-lined park, peopled with students looking for a peaceful place to work: there are several language schools in Saltillo as well as a University and Technical Institute, and, in summer especially, numbers of American students come here to study Spanish.

Saltillo is famous too for its **sarapes**, and there are several small shops (especially on c/Victoria) where you can watch the manufacturing process. These traditional shops tend to offer the best quality – and their prices reflect it – but even if you plan to buy a cheap one, it's a good idea to look here first to get some notion of what to expect.

Sadly the old ways are vanishing fast, and most now use artificial fibres and chemical dyes: all too many of those on sale in the market are mass-produced in virulent clashing colours.

From Saltillo you can head west to Torreón, or south to either San Luis Potosí or Zacatecas. The **direct route to México** is via San Luis, passing through Matehuala (with the possibility of branching off to the mountain ghost town of Real De Catorce) and Querétaro. Going through Zacatecas, though slower, gives you the chance to visit more of the beautiful colonial cities north of the capital. There's little point heading west unless you're aiming for Mazatlán and the Pacific.

Eating and drinking

Restaurants in Saltillo tend to close early and the ones in the centre mainly cater for office workers and students. The *Café Victoria*, on Padre Flores next to the *Hotel Hidalgo*, is good for breakfasts, bulging *tortillas* and *comidas corridas*. There are, as always, plenty of cheap places to eat around the **Mercado Juárez**, which is a decent market in its own right. As a tourist you are treated fairly and not constantly pressured to buy. Around the Plaza de Armas are several more cafes and restaurants, best of them the *Café Plaza*, at the side of the Palacio de Gobierno; there's also a good **pizza** place nearby.

fiestas

Carnival (the week before Lent, variable Feb–March) is at its best in the Caribbean atmosphere of **Tampico** (Tamaulipas) – also in **Ciudad Victoria** (Tam.) and **Monterrey** (Nuevo Leon).

March

19th FESTIVAL DE SAN JOSÉ celebrated in **Ciudad Victoria** (Tam.).

21st Ceremonies to commemorate the birth of Benito Juárez in **Matamoros** (Coahuila), near Torreón.

April

12th Processions and civic festival in honour of the nineteenth-century resettlement of **Tampico** (Tam.), with dress of that era. Celebrations continue for two weeks.

27th FERIA DEL AZUCAR in **Ciudad Mante** (Tam.), south of Ciudad Victoria; very lively with bands, dancing and fireworks.

May

3rd DÍA DE LA SANTA CRUZ. **Tula** (Tam.), between Ciudad Victoria and San Luis Potosí, stages a fiesta with traditional dance. In **Gómez Palacio** (Durango), the start of an agricultural and industrial fair which lasts two weeks.

15th DÍA DE SAN ISIDRO observed in **Guadalupe de Bravos** (Chihuahua), on the border near Ciudad Juárez, with dances all day and parades all night. Similar celebrations in **Matamoros** (Coah.) and **Arteaga** (Coah.), near Saltillo.

FERIA COMERCIAL in **Monterrey** (N.L.), a trade fair leavened with sporting events, bullfights, dances and public spectacles.

June

13th DÍA DE SAN ANTONIO DE PADUA marked in **Tula** (Tam.) by religious services followed by pastoral plays and traditional dances. Colourful native dancing too in **Vicente Guerrero** (Dgo.), between Durango and Zacatecas.

25th DÍA DE SANTIAGO. The start of a week-long fiesta in **Altamira** (Tam.), near Tampico.

July

4th DÍA DE NUESTRA SEÑORA DEL REFUGIO is marked by dancing and pilgrimages in **Matamoros** (Coah.).

8th **Durango** (Dgo.) celebrates its founders' day, coinciding with the *feria* and crafts exhibitions.

23rd FERIA DE LA UVA in **Cuatro Cienegas** (Coah.), a spa town near Monclova.

August

6th Fiesta in **Jiménez** (Chih.) with traditional dances, religious processions and a fair. Regional dancing too in **Saltillo** (Coah.).

9th Exuberant FERIA DE LA UVA in **Parras** (Coah.), between Saltillo and Torreón.

13th **Saltillo** (Coah.) begins its annual *feria*, lively and varied.

September

8th DÍA DE LA VIRGEN DE LOS REMEDIOS is celebrated with parades and traditional dances in **Santa Barbara** (Chih.), near Hidalgo del Parral, and **San Juan del Río** (Dgo.), between here and Durango.

10th Dancing from before dawn and a parade in the evening mark the fiesta in **Ramos Arizpe** (Coah.), near Saltillo.

11th Major *feria* on the border at **Nuevo Laredo** (Tam.).

15th–16th INDEPENDENCE festivities everywhere, the biggest in **Monterrey** (N.L.).

October

25th Joint celebrations between the border town of **Ciudad Acuña** (Coah.) and its Texan neighbour Del Rio. Bullfights and parades.

November

3rd DÍA DE SAN MARTIN DE PORRES is the excuse for a fiesta, with native dances, in **Tampico** (Tam.) and nearby **Altamira** (Tam.).

December

4th **Santa Barbara** (Chih.) celebrates its saint's day.

8th Fiesta with dancing virtually non-stop till the 12th in **Matamoros** (Coah.).

12th DÍA DE NUESTRA SEÑORA DE GUADALUPE is a big one everywhere, especially in **Guadalupe de Bravos** (Chih.), **El Palmito** (Dgo.), between Durango and Parral, **Ciudad. Anahuac** (N.L.) in the north of the state, and **Abasolo** (N.L.), near Monterrey. **Monterrey** itself attracts many pilgrims at this time.

travel details

Buses

Services on the chief routes to and from the frontier (Ciudad Juárez–Chihuahua–Torreón/Durango and from the border to Monterrey– Saltillo–San Luis Potosí/Zacatecas) are excellent, with departures day and night. There are also direct services to México from just about everywhere. The best lines are generally, on the central route, *Omnibus de Mexico* and *Transportes Chihuahuenses*, in the east *Frontera*, *Transportes del Norte* and *Autobuses del Oriente* (*ADO*). *Estrella Blanca*, ostensibly a second-class company, often beats them all for frequency of services and efficiency. What follows should be taken as a minimum.

Chihuahua to: Ciudad Juárez (at least hourly; 5hr); Nuevo Casas Grandes (5 daily; 5hr)

Ciudad Juárez to: Chihuahua (at least hourly; 5hr); Durango (at least hourly; 16hr); Jiménez (at least hourly; 8hr); México (10 daily; 26hr); Nuevo Casas Grandes (8 daily; 4hr); Parral (at least hourly; 10hr); Torreón (at least hourly; 12hr).

Ciudad Victoria to: Matamoros (7 daily; 4hr); Monterrey (6 daily; 4hr 30min); Tampico (10 daily; 4hr).

Durango to: Ciudad Juárez (at least hourly; 16hr); Fresnillo (11 daily; 3hr); Mazatlán (8 daily; 6hr 30min); Torreón (6 daily; 4hr 30min); Zacatecas (11 daily; 4hr 30min).

Matamoros to: Ciudad Victoria (7 daily; 4hr); Tampico (9 daily; 7hr 30min)

Monterrey to: Ciudad Victoria (6 daily; 4hr 30min); Matehuala (12 daily; 5hr); Nuevo Laredo (hourly; 3hr); Reynosa (hourly; 3hr 30min); Saltillo (constantly; 1hr); San Luis Potosí (12 daily; 8hr); Torreón (5 daily; 5hr); Zacatecas (8 daily; 7hr).

Piedras Negras to: Saltillo (9 daily; 7hr).

Tampico to: Ciudad Victoria (10 daily; 4hr); Veracruz (8 daily; 8hr).

Torreón to: Ciudad Juárez (at least hourly; 12hr); Zacatecas (10 daily; 6hr).

Trains

The Copper Canyon railway (see p.128) is the big attraction in this region – one of the few train journeys in Mexico that you might want to take simply for the experience. There are also two main lines heading south from the border to México. From Ciudad Juárez (see p.121) a daily express sets off for the capital, via Chihuahua, Zacatecas and Querétaro, while from Monterrey (with connections to the border at Nuevo Laredo to Reynosa and Matamoros) there are two evening departures, via Saltillo and San Luis Potosí. From the border to the capital takes roughly 15 hours – comfortable if you have some sort of sleeper. As usual with Mexican trains, it's always best to check timetables. Local trains are unreliable, very slow, and rarely a viable alternative to the bus.

Planes

There are frequent flights from most of the major cities to the capital – Chihuahua, Monterrey and Tampico all have several a day. From Monterrey you can also fly to Guadalajara and Acapulco, and there are international services to Dallas, Houston, San Antonio and Chicago. From Nuevo Laredo you can get to the capital and Guadalajara.

CHAPTER THREE

JALISCO AND MICHOACÁN

Separated from the country's colonial heartland by the craggy peaks of the Sierra Madre, the semitropical states of **Jalisco** and **Michoacán** have an unhurried ease of their own. Cursed by a complex landscape – now lofty plain, now rugged sierra – the area is, nevertheless, blessed with supreme fertility and is as beautiful and varied as any in Mexico, ranging from fresh pine woods and cool pastures to lush tropical forest. Both states stretch all the way to the coast, with resorts and beaches that vary from the sophistication of Puerto Vallarta to the simplicity of Playa Azúl: the coastal strip is covered elsewhere in this book, starting on p.327.

Something of a backwater until well into the eighteenth century, the high valleys of Michoacán and Jalisco were left to develop their own strong regional traditions and solid agricultural economy: there's a wealth of local produce, both agricultural and traditionally manufactured, from avocados to tequila, and glassware to guitars. Relative isolation also made the region a bastion of conservatism – in the years following the Revolution the Catholic *Cristero* counter-revolutionary guerrilla movement enjoyed its strongest support here.

Easy-going **Guadalajara** – Mexico's second city – is the area's best-known destination, packed with elegant buildings and surrounded by scenic country. Further afield the land spreads spectacularly green and mountainous, studded with volcanoes and lakes, including **Lake Chapala**, where D H Lawrence wrote *The Plumed Serpent*, and **Pátzcuaro**, probably the most photographed in the republic. There are also some superb colonial relics, especially in the towns of **Morelia** and **Pátzcuaro**, although in the latter it's the majesty of the setting and the richness of Indian traditions that first call for attention. This powerful indigenous culture more than compensates for the paucity of physical remains from the pre-Hispanic era; though the ruins of **Tzintzuntzán** on Lake Pátzcuaro are certainly impressive. **Fiestas** around here – and there are many – are among the most vital in Mexico, and there's a legacy of village handicrafts that survives from the earliest days of the Conquest.

Jalisco and Michoacán are among the most serene states in the country – relaxing, easy to get about, and free of urban hassle. Add to this the fact that Jalisco is the home of **mariachi** and of **tequila** and you've got a region where you could easily spend a couple of weeks exploring without even beginning to see it all.

GUADALAJARA AND JALISCO

Guadalajara dominates the state of **Jalisco** in every way – not just the capital, it is quite simply the main attraction. If you spend any time in the region, you're inevitably going to spend much of it here: it's also very much a transport hub, and would be almost impossible to avoid, even should you wish to. Here the road and train routes from the northwest meet the onward routes to México and the country's central highlands, with a growing web of expensive new *cuota* roads to speed you on your way. To see only Guadalajara, however, would be to miss the real nature of the state, which away from the capital is green, lush and mountainous. **Lake Chapala**, south of the city, offers easy escape and tranquil scenery; in mountain villages like Tapalpa there's fresh air, and rural life still lived at the old tempo; **Tequila** offers . . . well, tequila. The **climate** is for the most part delightfully temperate too. Though the descriptions of Guadalajara as the "city of eternal spring" are somewhat exaggerated, it *is* almost always warm – on much the same latitude as Bombay, yet protected from extremes by its altitude, around 1600m.

Guadalajara

Capital of Jalisco and second city of the Mexican Republic, **GUADALAJARA** has a reputation as a slower, more conservative and traditional place than México, somewhere you can stop and catch your breath. Many claim that this is the most Mexican of Mexican cities, having evolved as a regional centre of trade and commerce, without the imbalances of Monterrey's industrial giants or México's chaotic scale. Being less frenetic than the capital, however, doesn't make it peaceful, and by any standards this is a huge, sprawling, noisy and energetic city. Growth has, if anything, been accelerating in recent years, boosted by the campaign to reduce México's pollution by encouraging people and industry to move to the provinces. Still, it's an enjoyable place to visit and to see something of traditional and modern Mexico, offering everything from museums and colonial architecture through magnificent Revolutionary murals by José Clemente Orozco to a nightlife enlivened by a large student population.

Parks, little squares and open spaces dot Guadalajara, while right downtown around the cathedral are a series of plazas unchanged since the days of the Spanish. This small colonial heart of the city can still, at weekends especially, recall an old-world atmosphere and provincial elegance, and the centre is further brightened by the **Plaza Tapatía** which, driven straight through the heart of some of the oldest parts less than ten years ago, manages to look as if it was always meant to be there. It creates new sight-lines between some of Guadalajara's most monumental buildings and opens out the city's historical core to wandering pedestrians, *mariachi* bands and street theatre. Around this relatively unruffled nucleus revolve raucous and crowded streets more typical of modern Mexico, while farther out still, in the wide boulevards of the new suburbs, you'll find smart hotels, shopping malls and modern office blocks.

A little history

Guadalajara was founded in 1532, one of the fruits of a vicious campaign of Conquest by Nuño de Guzmán – whose cruelty and corruption were such that he appalled even the Spanish authorities, and died in jail in Madrid. The city, named for his birthplace, thrived, being officially recognized by Charles V in 1542 and rapidly becoming one of the colony's most Spanish cities – in part at least because so much of the indigenous population had been killed or had fled during the period of Conquest and suppression. Set apart from the great mining centres of the Bajío, Guadalajara managed to remain relatively isolated, developing as a regional centre for trade and agriculture. The tight reins of colonial rule restrained the city's development and it wasn't until the end of the eighteenth century that things really took off, as the colonial monopolies began to crumble. Between 1760 and 1803 the city's population tripled to reach some 35,000 and a new university was established, as the city became famous for the export of wheat, hides, cotton and wool.

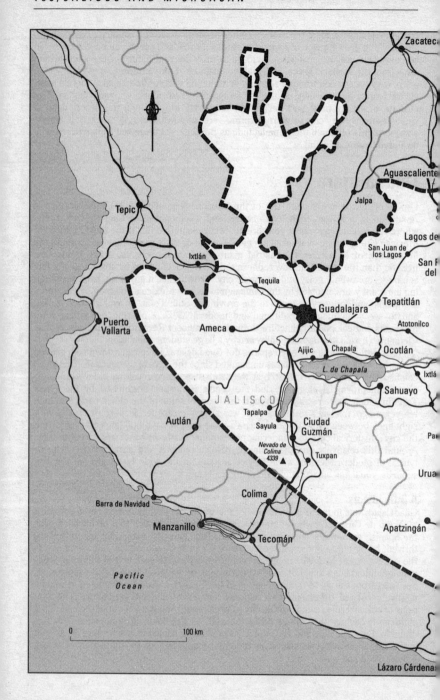

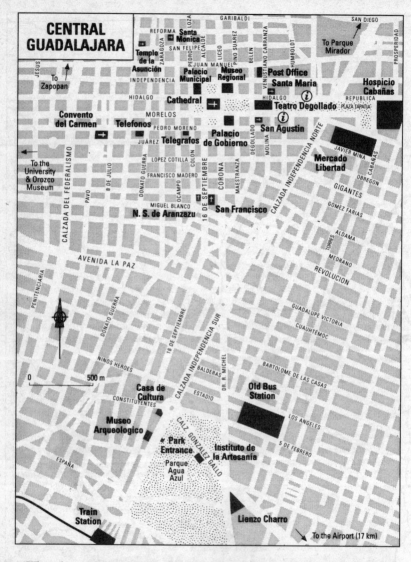

CENTRAL GUADALAJARA

When the empire finally fell apart, Guadalajara supported Hidalgo's Independence movement and became briefly his capital, to be rewarded when the break with Spain finally came by being named capital of Jalisco. By the beginning of this century it was already the second largest city in the republic, and in the 1920s the completion of the rail link with California provided the final spur for development. More recently the exodus from México and attempts at decentralization have swollen numbers here still further.

Arrival

Guadalajara's **airport** is some 17km southeast of the city on the road to Chapala. Facilities include money exchange and car rental, and there's also the usual system of fixed-price taxis and vans to get you downtown (around $10 per person – vouchers are sold inside the terminal). A much cheaper bus service (6am–9pm; every 30min) also runs to and from the old bus station – the Camionera Vieja (see below) – in the centre of town, from where you can hop on a bus to the centre.

Right out in the city's southeastern suburbs, Guadalajara's **Central Camionera** is one of Mexico's newest and largest bus stations, with seven separate terminals strung out in a wide arc, as well as its own shopping centre (*Nueva Central Plaza*) and hotel (see "Accommodation"). Each of the terminals has an extremely helpful information desk – they'll advise exactly which **bus into town** to take to get where you're going, and can also book accommodation. Local buses and *combis* stop outside each terminal, most of them finishing their journey near the church of San Francisco around the junction of Corona and Prisciliano Sanchez, something of a hub for city buses. From here you can easily walk to the hotels around Madero and López Cotilla; it's slightly farther to those near the market.

Some second-class buses from local destinations, including Tequila, Tapalpa and the villages on the shores of Lake Chapala, as well as the airport service, use the **Camionera Vieja**, the old downtown terminal, surrounded by cheap hotels and only a short bus ride up Calzada Independencia from the centre. If you're coming from somewhere only an hour or two away, it can be worth the slightly less comfortable second-class journey for the convenience of this much more central point of arrival.

The **train station** is a couple of kilometres south of the centre at the bottom of Calzada Independencia. It's quite well organized, and to get into town you need simply pick up one of the taxis waiting outside or one of the buses – #142 for example – that head up Independencia towards the centre.

Information

The helpful state **tourist office** is at Morelos 102 (☎36/614-43-65), the slightly less useful federal one at Degollado 50 (☎36/614-86-65), both in Plaza Tapatía. In addition, there are information booths at the Camionera and the airport, as well as a free tourist information phone line (☎36/658-22-22). You can also pick up information about what's on from a number of free **English-language publications**, such as the *Guadalajara Weekly* and *Ver y Oír,* which are available at the tourist offices or in hotel lobbies.

Although any of the banks throughout the centre – the cluster including *Banamex* and *Bancomer* around Corona and Juárez, for example – offer **currency exchange**, *casas de cambio,* many of them around the corner of Maestranza and López Cotilla, are quicker, open longer and offer almost identical rates. After hours, the bigger hotels will usually change money at a considerably worse rate.

Guadalajara's main **post office** (Mon–Fri 8am–7pm, Sat & Sun 9am–1pm) is at Venustiano Carranza 16, the junction with Independencia, and there's a **Telmex** long-distance office at Donato Guerra 72, between Juárez and Moreno (daily 8.30am–9pm). More convenient is the private phone and fax firm *Computel,* which has offices in the bus and trains stations and at 16 de Septiembre 599, Federalismo Sur 81 and Corona 181 (Edificio Mulbar). There are also plenty of **public phones**, including some relatively quiet ones around the Plaza Tapatía.

Car rental agencies can be found at the airport, and downtown they're concentrated on Av. Niños Héroes near the *Sheraton* (not far from the Parque Agua Azul); those here include *Alaniz,* Niños Héroes 961-B (☎36/614-63-93); *Budget,* Niños Héroes 934

(☎36/614-10-53); *National,* Niños Héroes 961-C (☎36/614-71-75, or at the airport ☎36/689-02-87); and *Quick Rent a Car,* Niños Héroes 954 (☎36/614-60-52).

Orientation

The **centre** of the old city is a relatively compact grid around the junction of **Morelos** and **16 de Septiembre**, by the huge bulk of the **Cathedral**; east of here Morelos leads to the **Plaza Tapatía** and the **Mercado Libertad**, while to the west are busy shopping streets. **Juárez**, a couple of blocks south, is actually the main east–west thoroughfare in the centre, heading out to the west past the **University** (where it becomes Vallarta), and crossing avenidas **Chapultepec** and **Americas** in an upmarket residential area. Further west still, it crosses **López Mateos**, a main through-route which heads south past the **Plaza del Sol**, a shopping centre surrounded by big hotels, restaurants and much of Guadalajara's best, but quite expensive nightlife, eventually heading out of the city as the main road towards Colima and the coast.

The main north–south arteries in the centre are the **Calzada Federalismo**, along which the *tren ligero* runs, and **Calzada Independencia**, which runs from the train station, up past the **Parque Agua Azul**, the old bus station, the market and Plaza Tapatía, and eventually out of the city to the **Parque Mirador**. Finally **Revolución** leads off Independencia towards the southeast – to Tlaquepaque, the new bus station and Tonalá. If you fancy taking a **city tour** to get your bearings, try *Panoramex,* Federalismo 948 (☎36/610-51-66).

City transport

Guadalajara is a very big city, but getting around is not too difficult once you've got the hang of the comprehensive system of public transport. In the city centre most of the main attractions are within walking distance of each other, and elsewhere using public transport is relatively straightforward as almost all **buses** are funnelled through the centre on a few main roads and have their destinations written on their windscreens. The sheer number of buses and the speed at which they move can make things slightly more difficult however, especially at peak hours when you may have to fight to get on: if possible, get a local to show you exactly where your bus stops. The new **tren ligero** or metro system, with one north–south and one east–west line, is designed for local commuters, and you're not likely to use it.

Taxis are also reliable if you're in a hurry, and for a group don't work out too expensive as long as you establish a price at the outset; many downtown taxi ranks post a list of fixed prices. From the centre to the Plaza del Sol, Nueva Camionera or Zapopan should cost around $10: slightly less to Tlaquepaque, twice as much to the airport.

SOME USEFUL BUS ROUTES		
All of these also run in the opposite direction: the #600 numbers are minibuses.		
#55	Plaza del Sol–Centro–Tonalá	#616	Nueva Camionera–Camionera Vieja
#124	Nueva Camionera–Centro–Camionera Vieja		
		#629	Centro–Av. Vallarta–Minerva Circle
#142	Centro–FFCC (train station)		
#190	Centro–Zapopan	#647	Centro–Tlaquepaque
#275	Nueva Camionera–Tonalá–Tlaquepaque–Centro–Zapopan	Trolley bus	Plaza del Sol–Centro–Tlaquepaque

Accommodation

Most of Guadalajara's **cheap hotels** are around the old bus station or in the streets south of the Mercado Libertad, areas which are noisy and none too appealing. The more **expensive** establishments, meanwhile, tend to be a long way out in the west of the city. In either case there are alternatives in the centre, within walking distance of the historical heart of the city, and if you can find space this is definitely the place to be.

Guadalajara's **youth hostel** is at Alcalde 1360 (☎36/624-65-15; $5), a short ride (bus #54) north of the city centre along Alcalde. It's a big place with sparse single-sex dorms – call to reserve. If you arrive late at night at the **Camionera Central** and all you want to do is sleep, there's a hotel right by the entrance: *El Parador* (☎36/659-01-42; ⑤) is modern and soulless, but has a pool and reasonably soundproof rooms with TV.

ACCOMMODATION PRICES

All the accommodation listed in this book has been categorized into one of nine price bands, as set out below. The prices quoted are in US dollars and normally refer to the cheapest available room for two people sharing in high season. For more details, see p.37.

① less than $8	④ $18–25	⑦ $50–75
② $8–12	⑤ $25–35	⑧ $75–100
③ $12–18	⑥ $35–50	⑨ more than $100

In the centre

Continental, Corona 450 (☎36/614-11-17). Modern but smaller and cheaper than many of the business hotels, just down the road from the fancy, high-rise *Aranzazú*. ⑥.

Don Quixote, Héroes 91 at Degollado (☎36/658-12-99). Friendly, small hotel with rooms around a colonial-style courtyard. ⑥.

Fenix, Corona 160 (☎36/614-57-14; fax 613-40-05). Large, modern building in the centre of things: it's a *Best Western*, which probably explains its popularity, but it's somewhat overpriced. ⑦.

Francés, Maestranza 35 (☎36/613-11-90; fax 658-28-31). Just off the plaza behind the cathedral, this beautiful colonial building is much the most atmospheric and appealing of Guadalajara's expensive hotels. ⑦.

González, González Ortega 77 (☎36/614-56-81). Clean, simple, friendly and very good value: popular travellers' haunt. ②.

Hamilton, Madero 381, between Galeana and Ocampo (☎36/614-67-26). Small, dark rooms but clean and friendly, a popular spot with backpackers and young Mexican couples. ③.

Jorge Alejandro, Hidalgo 656 (☎36/658-11-79). Spotless and comfortable central hotel in a recently renovated colonial building. ⑤.

De Mendoza, Carranza 16, at Hidalgo (☎36/613-46-46; fax 613-73-10). Plush establishment in a refurbished colonial convent; all amenities including pool. ⑧.

Posada Regis, Corona 171, near López Cotilla (☎36/613-30-26). Bizarre old building: central but quiet (get an inside room) with high-ceilinged rooms around a peaceful, covered courtyard. ⑤.

Posada San Pablo, Madero 218 at Corona (☎36/613-33-12). Hard to spot; clean rooms around a dark, covered courtyard with flowers, birds and friendly old dog. ③.

San Francisco Plaza, Degollado 267 at Héroes (☎36/613-30-26). Nice old place around a series of courtyards: better value than *Don Quixote* opposite. ⑥.

Around the Mercado Libertad

Ana-Isabel, Javier Mina 164 (☎36/617-79-20). Next door to the *Mexico 70* and the better of the two, with clean rooms with TV. Worth bargaining if they're not full; but this is a very noisy area. ④.

Chapala, José María Mercado 84 (☎36/617-71-59). Around the corner from the *Ana-Isabel*, clean and simple, but a touch dark. ③.

Maya, López Cotilla 39 at Huerto (☎36/614-54-54). Bare but decent rooms in a rough, noisy area, but better than on Javier Mina, with the benefits of a garage and restaurant. ④.

Occidental, Huerto at Villa Gómez, just off Independencia behind the *Avenida* (☎36/613-84-08). Simple, good-value rooms with shower; there's a garage and a restaurant for cheap *comidas*. ③.

South: Calzada Independencia and the Camionera Vieja

Canada, Estadio 77 (☎36/619-40-14). One of dozens surrounding the Camionera Vieja, this large place is pretty good value with the bonus of the excellent *Restaurante Ottawa*. Some better, pricier rooms. ③.

Costa Brava, Independencia Sur 739, near Los Angeles (☎36/619-23-27). New, friendly hotel. The slightly more expensive rooms have TV. ③.

La Estacion, Independencia Sur 1297 (☎36/619-61-41). Right beside the station just where Independencia goes under the train tracks. Stay here only if you have a very early train to catch. ④.

Flamingos, Independencia Sur 725 (☎36/619-99-21). Next door to the *Costa Brava*: bigger, rougher, and cheaper. ②.

Leon, Independencia Sur 557 (☎36/619-61-41). Basic, bare and the least expensive of all. ②.

San José, 5 de Febrero 116 at Dr Michel (☎36/619-27-26). The smartest of the places round the Camionera, though inevitably noisy. ④.

The City

Any tour of Guadalajara starts almost inevitably at the **Cathedral**, which, with the Sagrario or sacristry beside it, takes up an entire block at the very heart of the **colonial centre**, bordered by four plazas. At weekends and on warm evenings the plazas are packed, the crowds entertained by an array of street performers and wandering musicians; and there are frequently bands playing during the day too. All around is the traffic, noise and bustle of the busiest commercial areas of downtown Guadalajara: to the east the crowds spill over into Plaza Tapatía and its upmarket shops, beyond which is the complete contrast of the old market; unmodernized shopping streets to the west are no less busy.

Venture a little farther and the atmosphere changes again. Guadalajara's rapid expansion has swallowed up numerous communities that were once distinct villages but are now barely distinguishable from the suburbs around them. Heading **west** the university area blends into chic suburbia and some of the city's most expensive real estate. **East**, Tlaquepaque and Tonalá are the source of some of the area's finest handicrafts. And finally to the **north**, Zapopan has a huge, much revered church and a museum of indigenous traditions, while the Barranca de Oblatos offers stunning canyon views and weekend picnic spots.

The Cathedral

With its pointed, tiled twin towers, Guadalajara's **Cathedral** is a bizarre but effective mixture of styles. Building work began in 1561 and wasn't finished until more than a century later – since then, extensive modifications, which effectively disguise the fact that there was ever a plan behind the design, have included a Neoclassical facade and new towers (the originals collapsed in an 1818 earthquake). The interior is best seen in the evening, when the light from huge chandeliers makes the most of its rich decoration; the picture of the Virgin in the sacristy is attributed to the Spanish Renaissance artist Murillo.

Flanking the cathedral is a series of bustling plazas, often the scene of demonstrations and impromptu street performances. The **Plaza de los Laureles**, planted with laurel trees and with a fountain in the centre, faces the main west entrance, while to the north, by the porticoed **Presidencia Municipal** (less than fifty years old, though you wouldn't know it), lies the **Rotonda de los Jaliscienses Ilustres** in the centre of another plaza. This Neoclassical circle of seventeen Doric columns is the latest architectural expression of Jaliscan pride and commemorates the state's martyred heroes.

The Museo Regional

Across the plaza north of the cathedral, the **Museo Regional** (Tues–Sun 9am–3.45pm; $5, free on Sun) is housed in an eighteenth-century colonial mansion – originally a religious seminary, later a barracks and then a school. It's a supremely elegant setting for an extensive and diverse collection. Downstairs, you start in a section devoted to regional **archeology** – from stone tools and the skeleton of a mammoth through to the finest achievements of the western Mexican cultures in pottery and metal-working. The peoples of the west developed quite separately from those in southern and central Mexico, and there is considerable evidence that they had more contact with South and Central American cultures than with what would now be regarded as their compatriots. The deep **shaft tombs** displayed here are unique in Mexico, but were common down the west coast into Peru and Ecuador. Later the Tarascan kingdom, based around Pátzcuaro (see p.184), came almost to rival the strength of the Aztecs – partly due to their more extensive knowledge and use of metals. Certainly the Aztecs tried, and failed, to extend their influence over Tarascan territory, though following Cortés' destruction of Tenochtitlán the Tarascans submitted relatively peacefully to the Conquistadors.

Upstairs, along with rooms devoted to the state's **modern history** and ethnography, is a sizeable gallery of colonial and modern art. Most remarkable here is the large collection of **nineteenth-century portraiture**, a local tradition that captures relatively ordinary Mexicans in a charmingly naive style – nowadays they'd be snapshots for the family album, and indeed many have the forced formality familiar from early photography.

The Palacio de Gobierno and the Orozco Murals

On the other side of the cathedral, south of the Sagrario, the **Plaza de Armas** centres on an elaborate kiosk – a present from the people of France – where the state band plays every Thursday and Sunday evening. Dominating the eastern side of the square is the Baroque frontage of the **Palacio de Gobierno**. Here Padre Miguel Hidalgo y

JOSÉ CLEMENTE OROZCO

José Clemente Orozco (1883–1949) was a member, along with Diego Rivera and David Siqueiros, of the triumvirate of brilliant Mexican artists who emerged from the Revolution and who transformed painting here into an enormously powerful and populist political statement, especially through the medium of the giant mural. Their chief patron was the state – hence the predominance of their work in official buildings and educational establishments – and their aim was to create a national art that drew on native traditions. Almost all their work is consciously educative, rewriting – or, perhaps better, rediscovering – Mexican history in the light of the Revolution, casting the Imperialists as villains and drawing heavily on pre-Hispanic themes. Orozco, a native of Jalisco (he was born in Zapotlán, now Ciudad Guzmán), was perhaps the least overtly political of the three: certainly his later work, the greatest of which is here in Guadalajara, often seems ambiguous. As a child he moved to Guadalajara and then México, where he was influenced by the renowned engraver Posada (see p.212), and most of his early work is found in the capital, where he painted murals from 1922–27. There followed seven years in the USA, but it was on his return that his powers as an artist reached a peak, in the late 1930s and 1940s, above all in his works at the Hospicio Cabañas and the University of Guadalajara.

Costilla (the "father of Mexican Independence") proclaimed the abolition of slavery in 1810 and here, in 1858, Benito Juárez was saved from the firing squad by the cry of "*Los Valientes no asesinan*" – the brave don't kill. Both these events are commemorated inside, but the overwhelming reason to penetrate into the arcaded courtyard is to see the first of the great **Orozco murals** on the stairway.

The mural here is typical of his work – Hidalgo blasts through the middle triumphant, brandishing his sword against a background of red flags and the fires of battle. Curving around the sides of the staircase, scenes depict the Mexican people's oppression and struggle for liberty, from a pre-Conquest Eden to post-revolutionary emancipation. Upstairs in the domed Congress hall a smaller Orozco mural also depicts Hidalgo, this time as *El Cura de Dolores* (the priest from Dolores), legislator and liberator of slaves.

Plaza de la Liberacion

The largest of the four squares is the **Plaza de la Liberacion**, where the back of the cathedral looks across at the **Teatro Degollado**. Built in the mid-nineteenth century and inaugurated during the brief reign of Maximilian, the theatre is an imposing, domed Neoclassical building, with a Corinthian portico on whose pediment is a frieze depicting the Muses. It still stages a full programme of drama and concerts, as well as the Sunday morning *folklórico* dances – details are posted up around the entrance. The impressively restored interior alone justifies the price of a show ticket: above all the frescoed ceiling illustrating scenes from Dante.

On either side of the theatre are two small churches, **Santa María** and **San Agustín**, each all that remains of a former monastery. San Agustín has a fine Baroque facade; relatively plain Santa María is one of the oldest in the city, built in the seventeenth century on the site of the city's first cathedral. Next door, one of the old monastic buildings is now the **Palacio de Justicia**.

East along the Plaza Tapatía: the Hospicio Cabañas

At the back of the theatre you're at the beginning of the new **Plaza Tapatía**, with a view all the way down to the Hospicio Cabañas. The plaza is almost entirely lined with swish department stores and glossy office buildings, but for all that the pedestrianized area, dotted with modern statuary and fountains, is an undeniably attractive place to wander and window-shop. It takes its name from *tapatío* – an adjective used to describe anything typical of Guadalajara, supposedly derived from the capes worn by Spanish grandees. Guadalajarans themselves are often referred to as *Tapatíos*.

At the far end of the plaza, the **Hospicio Cabañas** (Tues–Sat 10am–6pm, Sun 10.15am–3pm; $5, free on Sun) was founded as an orphanage by the bishop Juan Cabañas y Crespo in 1801 and took nearly fifty years to complete, during much of which time it operated as a barracks. It was an orphanage again, however, when **Orozco** came to decorate the chapel in 1939. The Hospicio is a huge and beautiful building, with no fewer than twenty-three separate patios surrounded by schools of art, music and dance; an art cinema/theatre; various government offices, and a small cafeteria. The chapel, the **Capilla Tolsa**, is a plain and ancient-looking structure in the form of a cross, situated in the central patio right at the heart of the building. The **murals**, in keeping with their setting, are more spiritual than those in the government palace, but you certainly couldn't call them Christian – the Conquistadors are depicted as the Horsemen of the Apocalypse, trampling the native population beneath them. The Man of Fire – who leads the people from their dehumanizing, mechanized oppression – has a symbolic role as liberator, which is clearly the same as that of Hidalgo in the palace murals: in this case he is a strange synthesis of Christian and Mexican deities, a Christ-Quetzalcoatl figure. There are benches on which you can lie back to appreciate the murals, and also a small **Museo José Clemente Orozco** (same hours as the main building) with sketches, cartoons and details of Orozco's life.

Almost alongside the Hospicio is the vast **Mercado Libertad**, which locals claim is the world's largest market under one roof. It's an entirely modern building, but not in the least a modern market – as well as the touristy souvenir stalls you'll find *curanderas* offering herbal remedies, little stalls selling basic foods and vast piles of colourful fruit, vegetables, chocolate and spices, and traditional leather goods, from saddles to clumpy working boots. It's huge, chaotic and engrossing, but before you buy crafts here, it's worth paying a visit to the **Instituto de la Artesanía** in the Parque Agua Azul, or to the expensive boutiques in Tlaquepaque, to get some idea of the potential quality and value of the goods (for both, see below).

South of the Plaza de Armas
South from the Plaza de Armas, the churches of **San Francisco** and **Nuestra Señora de Aranzazu** face each other across Av. 16 de Septiembre. San Francisco lies on the site of what was probably Guadalajara's first religious foundation – a Franciscan Monastery established in the years just after the Conquest. The present church was begun in 1684 and has a beautiful Baroque facade. Aranzazu, by contrast, is entirely plain on the outside, but conceals a fabulously elaborate interior, with three wildly exuberant, heavily carved and gilded Churrigueresque retablos. The **Jardín de San Francisco**, which would be pleasantly peaceful were it not for the number of local buses rattling by, lies across from these two.

Parque Agua Azul
Several different buses ("Parque Agua Azul") run down from here to the **Parque Agua Azul** (Tues–Sun 10am–6pm; $2). Again, you couldn't really describe the park as peaceful: there's always some kind of activity going on and the green areas are permanently packed with kids enjoying the zoo, miniature train rides and playgrounds. An outdoor concert bowl (the *concha*) hosts popular free performances on Sundays, and weekends see football games too, and constant crowds. Nonetheless, by Guadalajara standards it's a haven of peace, especially during the week, and the entrance fee includes attractions such as a dome full of butterflies; exotic caged birds, including magnificent toucans; a palm house also full of tropical birds; and a strange, glass-pyramid orchid house.

Perhaps the greatest attraction of the park, however, is the **Instituto de la Artesanía Jaliscience** (Mon–Fri 10am–7pm, Sat 10am–4pm, Sun 10am–2pm; free; outside park hours entered directly from the street). A showcase for regional crafts that is as much a museum as a shop, this is just plain fabulous, with examples of all sorts of local *artesanía* – furniture, ceramics, toys, glassware, clothing – all of the highest quality. Not surprisingly it's expensive, but for what you get the prices are not unreasonable. Across the road from the park entrance, the **Casa de la Cultura** (Mon–Sat 9am–9pm; free) is by contrast a disappointment: extensively covered in ultra-modern murals and frescoes, it houses a permanent exhibition of modern art, the State Library, and an information service for cultural events in the city. But it's much less interesting than this makes it sound. Equally a let-down is the **Museo Arqueológico** (daily 10am–2pm; free), a low, modern building at the back of the Casa de la Cultura. It rarely seems to be open even when it's meant to be, and the small collection of relics of western cultures inside is really only of specialist interest.

West of the Plaza de Armas
The area to the west of the cathedral is a great part of the city to wander around. In this direction there has been far less modernization, and the busy shopping streets, many of them closed to traffic, turn up fascinating glimpses of traditional Mexican life and plenty of odd moments of interest. There's a small general **market** at Santa Monica and Hidalgo. A little farther out, the university area is quieter than the centre, the streets broader, and there's also a younger atmosphere, with plenty of good restau-

rants and cafes, while farther out still are expensive residential areas, interesting in their own way for the contrast with crowded downtown.

The old **Telegrafos** building – also known as the Ex-Templo de la Compañía and now a university library (Mon–Sat 9am–9pm; free) – lies just west of the Plaza de Armas at the junction of Pedro Moreno with Colón. Originally a church, the building later became a university lecture hall, during which time the nineteenth-century Neoclassical facade was added and it was decorated with **murals** by David Siqueiros and Amado de la Cueva. Later still it housed the telegraph offices. The murals here, depicting workers, peasants and miners in a heroic-socialist style, provide an interesting contrast to Orozco's work. Outside there's an attractive little plaza, and the pedestrianized streets make a pleasant escape from the traffic, if not the crowds.

Immediately to the north are several examples of the beautiful, little-known Baroque churches that stud Guadalajara. The closest is the **Templo de Santa Monica**, on Santa Monica between San Felipe and Reforma, with fabulously rich doorways and an elegant, plain stone interior. The nearby **Templo de San Felipe Neri**, San Felipe at Contreras Medellin, is a few years younger – dating from the second half of the eighteenth century – and more sumptuously decorated still, with a superb facade and lovely, dilapidated tower overgrown with a tangle of plants. Both of these churches have extravagantly decorated rain spouts – in the form of dragons on San Felipe. A block along Contreras Medellin at the corner of Juan Manuel, the **Templo de las Capuchinas** is by contrast a completely plain, fortress-like structure; inside, though, it's more interesting, with paintings and a lovely vaulted brick roof. Between these two, Contreras Medellin is lined with old printing shops, *imprentas*, where you can see the clanking, ancient presses at work. Back on the main route west, at Juárez and 8 de Julio, the ex-**Convento del Carmen** was one of the city's richest monasteries, but its wealth has largely been stripped, leaving an austere, white building of elegant simplicity. Modern art exhibitions, dance events and concerts are regularly staged here.

The University to the Plaza del Sol

If you're heading any farther west you may want to take a bus or taxi (anything heading for the Plaza del Sol should pass all the areas below, or look for "Par Vial"), although the **University** is still just about in walking distance of the centre: a stroll of thirty minutes or so. Here you can see more of Orozco's major murals, among the first he painted in Guadalajara – head for the central hall (the *Paraninfo*) of the main building, at Juárez and Díaz de León (aka Av. Tolsa), to see the frescoed dome and front wall. Again, the theme fits the setting: in this case the dome shows the glories and benefits of education, while the wall shows the oppressed masses crying out for books and education, which are being denied them by fat capitalists and the army. Behind the university buildings, across López Cotilla, the **Templo Expiatorio**, a modern neo-Gothic church (still not entirely complete), features some innovative stained-glass and an attractive altar. A couple of blocks further down Díaz de León you'll find the **Instituto Cultural Norteamericano**. Basically a language school, the institute has English-language magazines lying around and a cafe at the back. You may not be supposed to wander in off the streets, but no one seems to mind.

Beyond the university, Juárez changes its name to Vallarta, and the character of the street changes rapidly too. Within ten blocks, around the major junction of **Vallarta and Chapultepec**, you find yourself in a very different city, a far quieter place of broad avenues, expensive shops and pleasant restaurants, with drive-in burger joints and big houses in the back streets. Many of the airlines have their offices out here, along with *American Express* and several consulates; there's a large branch of *Sanborn's* at Vallarta and General Martín. Further out, Vallarta crosses the major artery of López Mateos at the Minerva Circle, an intersection marked by a triumphal arch.

Continuing down Vallarta, the **Tequila Sauza** bottling plant at no. 3273 offers guided tours on weekday mornings and a bar that serves excellent inexpensive tequila cocktails. Inside the plant, in true Guadalajaran style, a mural depicts an idealized history of Tequila and its delights. There are currently plans to move the bottling plant to Tequila (see p.177), where the stuff is actually brewed, so check with the tourist office first.

Most buses, in any event, turn left at the Minerva Circle down López Mateos Sur towards the **Plaza del Sol**, a vast commercial development said to be one of the largest in Latin America. There's an enormous shopping centre, as well as new administrative offices, and inside a couple of good cafes, an ice-cream parlour and, in the evenings, several disco/clubs. Also on López Mateos are numerous big hotels and theme restaurants. All very much the modern face of suburban Mexico.

San Pedro Tlaquepaque and Tonalá

The most celebrated of Guadalajara's suburbs, **SAN PEDRO TLAQUEPAQUE** is famous for its *artesanías* and for its **mariachi** bands. Once a separate town, some 5km southeast of the centre, it has long since been absorbed by urban sprawl, and its traditional crafts taken over almost entirely by tourism; the streets are lined with shops selling, for the most part, pretty tacky goods at thoroughly inflated prices. Nevertheless, it's worth seeing, and there are still quality pieces among the dross – notably some of the ceramic and glassware on which the place's reputation was originally based.

To see some of the best, visit the small **Museo Regional de la Ceramica** (Tues–Sat 10am–4pm, Sun 10am–1pm; free) at Independencia 237, which has displays of pottery not only from Tlaquepaque but from all over the state, and especially Tonalá (see below). Most of what's on show is for sale – the place is more store than museum – but there's also a traditional kitchen complete with all its plates, pots and pans, and displays of the individual works of some of the finest craftsmen, while the building is a fine old mansion in its own right. Almost all of the fancier **shops** are nearby on Independencia, many of them again occupying colonial-era houses that are interesting in themselves. It's a pleasant place to window-shop, on a street closed to traffic. Among the more worthwhile stores are *La Rosa de Cristal* at no. 232, where you can see glassblowing daily from 9.30am to 2pm, and *Sergio Bustamante* at 236, opposite the museum, where there are flamingos and peacocks in the patio to go with Sergio's famous fantastical figures in papier mâché and bronze – lovely to look at, even if the price and size are such that you won't be buying. Opposite each other immediately below the museum are *La Casa Canela* (no. 258; Mon–Fri 10am–2pm & 3–7pm, Sat 10am–3pm) and *Antigua de Mexico* (no. 255), two more lovely houses that sell upmarket fabrics, furniture and antiques to a mainly Mexican clientele. Juárez, parallel to Independencia, has fewer – but slightly less touristy – stores.

A more compelling reason to make the trip out to Tlaquepaque, though, is to stop off at **El Parian**, an enclosed plaza that is in effect the biggest bar you've ever seen. Since the shops all close down for a siesta anyway, you have every excuse to hang out here for a couple of hours. There are actually a dozen or so separate establishments around this giant courtyard, but since everyone sits outside, the tables tend to overlap and strolling serenaders wander around at random, it all feels like one enormous continuum. They all charge much the same too, and offer the same limited range of food – basically *birria, quesadillas* and *queso fundido* – plus lots to drink: prices seem reasonable on the menu, but watch out for the cost of the drinks and for added service charges. At the weekend, particularly Sunday afternoons, you'll see *mariachi* at its best here, when the locals come along and offer their own vocal renditions to the musicians' backing. On weekdays it can be disappointingly quiet.

You'll find El Parian at the top of Independencia, right by the main plaza. There are a couple of fine colonial churches here too, and several **banks** in case you've been carried away by the shopping experience. And if you've had too good a time to struggle home, or you really take the purchasing seriously, you can **stay** right here at the *Posada en el Parian*, Independencia 74 (✆65/35-21-89; ③). There's a small local **Mercado Municipal** just by El Parian, off Independencia, and numerous fancy **restaurants** on Independencia if El Parian is not for you.

Pottery is slightly cheaper at **TONALÁ**, a ceramics manufacturing centre some 8km beyond Tlaquepaque, but the trip is really only worthwhile if you are seriously planning to shop. Market days are Thursday and Sunday, when things are considerably more animated and the village is crammed with salespeople and shoppers, but be warned that ceramics sold on stalls tend to be rejects from the shops.

To get to San Pedro Tlaquepaque from the centre of town, take a bus heading south on Calzada Independencia (look for "San Pedro" or "Tlaquepaque") or a trolleybus south on Federalisimo. Some of these buses continue to Tonalá, and both Tlaquepaque and Tonalá are on the route of many of the buses between the new bus station and the centre.

Zapopan

ZAPOPAN, some 6km northwest of the city centre, is served by many of the same buses at the opposite extremity of their routes. The **Basilica de la Virgen de Zapopan** here is one of the most important churches in the city, much revered by the Huichols. Pope John Paul II gave a mass in the giant plaza in front of the church during a visit to Mexico in 1979; a statue commemorates the event. The Baroque temple houses a miraculous image of the Virgin that was dedicated to the local Indians by a Franciscan missionary, Antonio de Segovia, after he had intervened in a battle between them and the Conquistadors. Since then it has been constantly venerated and is still the object of pilgrimages, especially on October 12, when it returns from the cathedral to the church in a massive procession, having toured, and been displayed in, all the churches in Guadalajara. This is one of the highlights of the city's *Fiestas de Octubre*.

Beside the church a small **museum** (daily 9.30am–1pm & 3.30–6pm; free) exhibits clothes and objects relating to Huichol traditions, as well as a photographic display of their modern way of life. They also sell Huichol crafts, including intricate embroidery.

Barranca de Oblatos

Also to the north of the city, out at the end of Calzada Independencia, the **Barranca de Oblatos** is a magnificent 600m canyon, along the edge of which a series of parks offer superb views and a welcome break from the confines of the city. The **Parque Mirador** ("Parque Mirador" bus north along Independencia) is a popular family spot with picnic areas and excellent views, while the **Parque Barranca de Oblatos** (bus #603A from Vicente Guerro at the southwest corner of the Hospicio Cabañas) is more of a student haunt, with swimming pools, picnic areas and plenty of young lovers. Also on the edge of the canyon, the new city **zoo** (Tues–Fri 10am–5pm, Sat & Sun 10am–6pm; bus #60 north on Independencia) has superb views from its northern end, along with a relatively well-kept selection of Mexican and international wildlife.

Eating and drinking

They take their food seriously in Jalisco, and Guadalajara boasts literally hundreds of **places to eat**. Among the local specialities dished up at street stalls, bars and the markets are *birria*, beef or lamb in a spicy but not particularly hot sauce, served with *tortillas* or in *tacos*; roast goat, and *pozole*, a stew of pork and hominy (ground maize). In the centre there seems to be more choice west of the cathedral, where traditional cafes and restaurants line **Juárez**; the **university** area also offers good food, especially during semester. For cheap, basic meals, the area around the old bus station is crowded with possibilities, none wildly exciting, while upstairs in the **Mercado Libertad** seemingly hundreds of little stands each display their own specialities to lure you over. Though there are plenty of more **expensive** places round the centre, they tend to be rather dull: in the evenings, locals are far more likely to be found out in the suburbs, or enjoying a raucous night at one of many theme restaurants on López Mateos Sur, a $10 taxi ride from the centre.

A couple of good **panaderías**, for bread and cakes for a picnic, are *Pan Estilo Mexico*, Santa Monica 96 at Independencia, and *Pasteleria Luvier*, Colón 183 at Madero.

Downtown cafes and licuados

Buho's Cafe-Arte Restaurante, Madero 361 at Galeana. Upstairs in an internal courtyard, a pleasant escape for good breakfasts and cheap *comidas*.

Cafe D'Val, Pedro Moreno 696. One of Guadalajara's many busy cafes where men come to chat and play chess. Great coffee, moderately priced light meals, sandwiches and Mexican snacks.

Cafe Madoka, Gonzalez Martínez 78, at Juárez. Another big, traditional cafe, serving inexpensive good breakfasts, soups and *antojitos*. You can also just sip a coffee and play a game of dominoes.

Cafe Madrid, Juárez 264. A smaller European-style coffee bar, again good for coffee, breakfasts, *comidas corridas* at lunchtime, and sandwiches.

Cafe Oasis, Morelos, between Colón and Galeana. Bustling place handy for the centre – *tacos*, sandwiches and egg dishes.

Nectar, Hidalgo 426. Superb juice, ice cream and yoghurt bar offering instant refreshment close to the cathedral.

El Palomar, Juárez at 8 de Julio. Bright, friendly upstairs cafe.

Rosie's Cafe, Juárez 440 at Ocampo. Just down the street from the *Copa de Leche*, (see below) with similar balcony tables overlooking the street scene, but rather cheaper.

Villa Madrid, López Cotilla 533, at Gonzalez Martínez. Great *licuados*, fruit salads and yoghurt as well as more substantial dishes.

Downtown restaurants

Copa de Leche, Juárez 414, between Galeana and Ocampo. Something of an institution among well-heeled Guadalajarans, with street-level bar and upstairs restaurant. Classy, good food, interesting scene, but by no means inexpensive.

Denny's, Juárez just below the Plaza de Armas. The place to go for authentic American and Tex-Mex food in authentic plastic a/c surroundings. Open 24hr but not at all cheap.

El Farol, Moreno 466 at Galeana, upstairs. Pleasant, reasonably priced old restaurant with good *tamales* and *tacos* – try for a table by the window.

Lido, Miguel Blanco and Colón. Spanish-style bar and restaurant, serving good, moderately priced Mexican *moles*, sandwiches, snacks and bull's testicles.

El Mesón del Romeral, Juárez at Pavo. Excellent restaurant serving big breakfasts and good *comidas*.

Naturalismo, 8 de Julio 138. Veggie place serving a very good *comida corrida* and selection of salads, soups and meals. Closed Sun.

Nuevo Faro, López Cotilla 24. Simple restaurant with great value *comidas corridas*.

Patio de la Merced, Hidalgo 426, behind *Nectar*. Fast food with a Mexican twist, including burgers, pizza, *tacos* and *burritos*.

Portal San Angel, corner of the large plaza in front of the Hospicio Cabañas. A good spot to take a break while sightseeing. Fairly standard international menu with reasonably priced *comida corrida*.

La Rinconada, Morelos 86 Plaza Tapatía. Colonial setting serving seafood, US-style steaks and a range of Mexican specialities including *birria* and ox tongue in a spicy Veracruz sauce. Expensive.

Sanborn's, 16 de Septiembre and Juárez. Plush restaurant with a wide selection of international and Mexican food.

Sandy's, Colón 39, at Moreno. Balcony tables overlook the crowds of shoppers; simple Mexican food.

Tacos El Pastor, Juárez 424, by the *Copa de Leche*. Fast, flavoursome *tacos*; popular and cheap though some choices (like *oreja* or *cabeza*) are probably best avoided.

La Terraza, Hidalgo 436 near the cathedral, upstairs. Bar and restaurant, popular in the evenings when there is often live music. Better music than food, with a large, inexpensive menu that includes hamburgers, *burritos, flautas* and *comidas*.

University and farther out

Los Caporales, López Mateos Sur 5290 (☎36/631-41-39). Traditional music and dance performances while you eat most nights, plus rowdy atmosphere and plenty of tequila – popular for birthday parties and celebrations.

Cazuelas Grill, López Mateos Sur 3755 (☎36/631-57-80). Slightly tamer, more traditional version of *Los Caporales*.

La China Poblana, Juárez 887, by the university. Reasonably priced traditional dishes including *mole* and *chiles en nogada*.

La Choza Grill, Calzada Federalismo at López Cotilla. Smaller, city-centre version of the big places out on López Mateos. Pricey meat and seafood dishes.

Ciao Ciao Pizza, López Cotilla 749 at Penitenciaria. Student pizza parlour.

Guadalajara Grill, López Mateos Sur 3771 (☎36/631-56-22). Part of the *Carlos'n'Charlie* chain: Tex-Mex food, loud music, party atmosphere and dancing.

Los Itacates, Chapultepec 110, near Vallarta (☎36/825-11-06). Traditional Mexican food. Bigger, more expensive and better-known than *Tradiciones*, but no better.

Restaurant-Bar Tradiciones, Morelos 1701-3, just off Chapultepec. Lovely place serving traditional Mexican food; great value *comidas*. Popular with locals.

Entertainment and nightlife

Though it has perked up in recent years, Guadalajara's nightlife is still not exactly hot. Most of the fashionable, younger places tend to be a long way out – the Plaza del Sol complex, for example, houses a couple of clubs, as do many of the big hotels out this way. Any of them will knock a severe hole in your wallet.

On the other hand you needn't spend anything at all in the **Plaza de Mariachis**, a little area hard by the Mercado Libertad and the Church of San Juan de Dios, where *mariachi* bands hang around or stroll between bars, playing to anyone prepared to cough up for a song. If they play for you personally you'll have to pay (check how much before they start) but there are usually several on the go anyway. You'll also find *mariachi* bands out in Tlaquepaque.

Lively downtown **bars** tend to be a tad sleazy, though those listed below are worth a try.

Bars

Copenhagen 77, López Cotilla and Marcos Castellanos, in the university area. Bar-restaurant with live jazz 8.30pm–12.30am.

Duran, Duran, Madero 289. Dark bar and disco that fills up at the weekends but is dead otherwise.

Terraza del Oasis, Hidalgo 436. Upstairs restaurant and bar, always packed on Fri and Sat when you can hear live music in the evenings.

Las Yardas, Juárez 37. Very 1970s, with coloured lights and dark corners. Live music 5–10pm.

Performing arts

There's a regular programme of **theatre and dance** in the beautiful Teatro Degollado and a series of events put on by the state Fine Arts department in the former Convento del Carmen and other sites around the city. You can pick up details from the tourist office, or in the listings sections of *Guadalajara Weekly* or *Ver y Oír*.

Guadalajara's **ballet folklórico** – two hours of impressive traditional dance performed by the university dance troupe – is staged in the Teatro Degollado every Sunday at 10am (except when the company's on tour) and is definitely worth getting up for: tickets, from around $3 to $15, are sold at the theatre ticket office (daily 10am–1pm & 4–7pm; ☎36/613-11-15). The state dance company performs a similar ballet, though its reputation isn't as good, in the *Cine-Teatro Cabañas* in the Hospicio Cabañas every Wednesday at 8.30pm. Tickets go for around $5 from the Hospicio (details ☎36/618-60-03, ext 22). The *Cine-Teatro Cabañas* also has live music at least once a week, as well as many other events.

Less formally, you'll find **bands** playing and crowds gathered somewhere round the central plaza complex every weekend and often during the week too (most Tuesdays and Thursdays), and there's always entertainment of some kind laid on in the Parque Agua Azul.

The entire month of October in Guadalajara is dominated by the famous **Fiestas de Octubre**, with daily events including *charreadas* (rodeos) and processions (the biggest on the 12th) and fireworks each night. In **Tlaquepaque** the big day is June 29th: endless *mariachis*, dances, and a mass procession.

Sport

Jaliscans pride themselves on their equestrian skills and other entertainments include, in the summer, regular *charreadas* in the Lienzo Charro, out on the road to the airport near the Parque Agua Azul (for details call ☎36/619-32-32), and in winter **bullfights** in the Plaza Nuevo Progreso (ticket office Morelos 229; ☎36/613-26-94), a long way north on Calzada Independencia. Right opposite this is the mighty Estadio Jalisco (☎36/637-06-69), the enormous **football** stadium where FC Guadalajara (*Las Chivas*) play their home soccer matches, familiar to many from the 1970 and 1986 World Cups.

MOVING ON FROM GUADALAJARA

For transport to the **airport** from the centre of town (around $10 per person) call ☎36/619-05-56, or take a regular taxi for around $20. Buses from the Camionera Vieja also do the run every thirty minutes or so. There are constant **flights** to México, as well as departures to most other Mexican cities, and direct connections to many US, Canadian and Central American destinations.

Long-distance buses all leave from the new Central Camionera, way out in suburbia. To get there from the centre, take a #102, #275 or #275A from Prisciliano Sanchez at Corona, or one of the buses marked "Nueva Central" heading south along Independencia or 16 de Septiembre. The station is huge and can be confusing, though each of the seven terminals has an information booth that can help with advice on where to catch your bus. Very broadly, each terminal serves a different area, but since they're organized by bus company rather than route, it's not quite that simple – there are buses to México from just about every terminal, for example. In general, make for **terminals 1 and 2** for destinations in Jalisco, Colima and Michoacán, plus many of the pullman services to México, México via Morelia and many towns in the Bajío; **3 and 4** serve the north and north-west, with buses to the US border and up the Pacific coast, plus points en route; **5** for eastbound services towards San Luis Potosí and Tampico, as well as some more local services; **6** for the Bajío, the northeast and many local second-class buses; **7** for the north and northeast again, as well as México. If you're heading for somewhere just an hour or so away – Chapala or Tequila, say – it's usually quicker and easier to take a second-class bus from the **Camionera Vieja**, downtown.

Daily **trains** run to México (first-class only at 9pm, arriving 12hr later) and north to Nogales and Mexicali (first-class at 9.30am, second-class at noon). You can get tickets and information from the station, or the downtown reservation office at *Turismo Macull*, López Cotilla 163 (Mon–Fri 9am–2pm & 4–7pm, Sat 9am–2pm; ☎36/614-70-14). There are plenty of **travel agencies** around the centre, including in the lobbies of all the big hotels, or head for *American Express* or *Thomas Cook/Wagons Lits* (see "Listings" overleaf).

Listings

Airlines *Aerocalifornia*, López Cotilla 1423 (☎36/626-19-01); *Aeroméxico*, Corona 196 (☎36/614-54-00); *American*, Vallarta 1526 (☎36/630-03-49); *Continental*, at the airport (☎36/689-04-33); *Delta*, López Cotilla 1701 (☎36/630-31-30); *Mexicana*, Mariano Otero 2353 (☎36/613-50-97); *United*, Vallarta 1461 (☎36/615-44-08).

American Express Vallarta 2440 (Mon–Fri 9am–7pm, Sat 9am–1pm; ☎36/630-02-00).

Bookstores In English, from *Sanborn's*, Juárez between 16 de Septiembre and Corona, and at Vallarta 1600, or *Sandi Bookstore*, Tepeyac 718 in Colonia Chapalita; many of the larger bookstores around the centre also have a small selection of English-language books.

Consulates *Canada*, Hotel Fiesta Americana, Local 30, Aurelio Aceves 225 (☎36/615-86-65 or 825-34-34, ext 3005); *Denmark*, López Mateos 477 (☎36/65-02-93); *Germany*, Corona 202 (☎36/613-96-23); *Holland*, Calzada Lázaro Cárdenas 601 (☎36/811-26-41); *Norway*, Pavo 135 (☎36/614-75-76); *Sweden*, Guadalupe Montenegro 1697 (☎36/615-16-02); *UK*, Calzada Gonzales Gallo 1897 (☎36/625-16-16); *US*, Progreso 175 (☎36/625-27-00).

Laundry Aldama 125, off Independencia a few blocks south of the Mercado Libertad (Mon–Sat 9am–8pm).

Markets The giant Mercado Libertad is just one – every city *barrio* has its own. They include the very touristy Mercado Corona near the cathedral, and craft markets in Tlaquepaque and Tonalá. The Sunday flea market *El Baratillo* is vast, sometimes stretching a mile or more along Javier Mina, starting a dozen blocks east of the Mercado Libertad.

Pharmacy *Farmacía de Descuento*, in the centre at Pedro Moreno 518, is open 24 hours.

Thomas Cook Vallarta 1447 (☎36/826-84-66 or 825-80-33).

Lake Chapala and around

The largest lake in Mexico, **Lake Chapala** lies just over 50km south of the city. Some 30,000 Americans and Canadians are said to live in and around Guadalajara, and a sizeable proportion of them have settled on the lakeside – particularly in **Chapala** and in the smaller village of **Ajijic**. English is spoken widely, and there's even an English newspaper produced down here. This mass presence has rendered the area rather expensive and in many respects somewhat sanitized, but it cannot detract from the beauty of the lake itself, and at weekends and holidays day-trippers from the city help create an enjoyable party atmosphere.

Chapala

CHAPALA, on the shore of the lake, is a sleepy, even dull community most of the time, but can become positively festive on sunny weekends, when thousands come to eat, swim (though the water is none too clean) or take a boat ride, visiting one of the lake's islands. Shoreline restaurants all offer the local speciality, *pescado blanco*, famous despite its almost total lack of flavour, and street vendors sell cardboard plates of tiny fried fish from the lake, very like whitebait. Head to the left along the promenade, past streets of shuttered nineteenth-century villas, and you'll find a small crafts market.

Practicalities

Buses leave the old bus station in Guadalajara for Chapala throughout the day (hourly; 1hr). From Chapala, regular services run on to Ajijic and Jocotepec (and from there back to Guadalajara by a more direct route along the highway to the coast). The *Nido*, Madero 202 (☎376/5-21-16; ⑤), is the town's oldest **hotel**, still rich with turn-of-the-century resort atmosphere. It's a good spot for a meal, the walls of the restaurant decorated with old black-and-white photographs of Chapala. A little less expensive is the *Hotel Candileras*, López Cotilla 363 (☎376/5-22-79; ④), a friendly little place just off the plaza. If you plan to stay for a while, ask about the special monthly rates at the hotels; houses and apartments are advertised on the noticeboard in the *Farmacía Morelos*, on the corner of Galeana and Madero.

Ajijic

Though just 6km west of Chapala, **AJIJIC** has a completely different atmosphere. Undeniably picturesque, it's a smaller, quieter and more self-consciously arty place, with numerous little crafts shops – you get the distinct feeling that the ex-pats here resent the intrusion of outsiders, regarding themselves as writers or artists *manqués*, hoping to pick up some of the inspiration left behind by D H Lawrence and more recent residents like Ken Kesey. In truth, there's little evidence that Lawrence liked the place at all (though he may have disliked it less than he did the rest of the country), but then he can't have had much time to appreciate it, since in just eight weeks here he turned out an almost complete 100,000-word first draft of *The Plumed Serpent* (or *Quetzalcoatl* as it was then titled). Sybille Bedford, too, passed through with barely more than a glance:

> After another hour we came to a much larger village with proper mud houses and a market place. For three hundred yards, potholes were agreeably replaced by cobble-stones. "Now what about this place?"
> "Ajijic," said the driver.
> "I dare say," said E.

Bedford, though, was on her way to the idyllic colonial backwater of her *Visit to Don Otavio* further round the lake – an experience so exquisite that anything else would be likely to pall beside it. Still, she probably had the right idea about Ajijic: it may be a wonderful place to retire, with a thriving ex-pat social and cultural life, but as a visitor you're likely to have exhausted its charms in a couple of hours, which is quite long enough to have wandered by the lake, seen the little art galleries, read the noticeboards and been shocked by the price of everything.

Practicalities

There are a number of luxurious but rather expensive **hotels** in Ajijic, as well as apartments and houses to rent for longer stays; check out the noticeboards in shops and galleries. The *Posada Ajijic* (☎376/5-33-95; ⑤), just outside the village, is a comfortable, welcoming place with lovely gardens and views of the lake. For anyone on a budget the *Hotel Mariana*, Guadalupe Victoria 10 (☎376/5-38-57; ④), is probably the best bet, although it does look a little weary these days. There's also good food: the *Posada* offers pricey but excellent dining in a wonderful lakeside setting, with a lunchtime buffet, while numerous places in the village cater to ex-pat appetites with healthy sandwiches and juices.

San Juan Cosola and Jocotepec

Five kilometres or so along the lakeshore to the west, **SAN JUAN COSOLA** is a lakeside resort of a different kind, where a small cluster of hotels offers visitors the chance to bask in natural thermal waters said to have healing properties. The *Motel Balneario* (☎376/1-03-02; ⑤), right beside the lake, is the cheapest, most popular, and the only one open to day-trippers (who pay a small fee to use the pools). Opposite, *Condominias Cosala* (☎376/9-13-76; ⑦) has rooms with TV, around a pool, while on the road the *Villas Buenaventura* (⑧) offers upmarket suites with two bedrooms, a kitchen and naturally heated jacuzzi.

The last major community along the north shore of the lake, **JOCOTEPEC** is the largest but with fewer tourists and foreign residents than the others. Its chief claim to fame is the manufacture of *sarapes* with elaborately embroidered motifs. You can buy them all around the main square, or at the Sunday market. *El Meson de los Naranjitos* here is a former staging inn that now houses a bar, restaurant and a small shopping complex. By far the nicest **place to stay** is at *Los Dos Bed and Breakfast*, c/Rico 191 (☎376/3-06-57; ⑥), owned by artists, where you can laze by the pool surrounded by lush tropical plants.

Buses between Jocotepec and Guadalajara run on two routes, either along the lakeshore via Chapala, or more directly via the highway from the coast.

South towards the coast: Tapalpa

Some of the most delightful alpine scenery in the country lies southwest of Lake Chapala, on the road to Colima. You'll miss much of it if you stick to the super-efficient new toll road – though even that has its exciting moments in the mountains: the following places are all reached from the far slower, far more attractive old road. For a couple of days' relaxation amid upland pastures and pine forests – perfect rambling country – the town of **TAPALPA** makes an ideal base. With its ancient, wooden-balconied houses and magnificent surroundings of ranch country and tree-clad hills, it's beginning to be discovered as a weekend escape from the city, and can get quite crowded, but for the moment its charm is little affected. It's a place to appreciate the cool, fresh air, to walk, and to wind down.

Though there's a village feel around the plaza, with its eighteenth-century wooden *portales* and two impressive churches, this is actually a fair-sized place, and messy development on the outskirts reflects rapid growth. The best **walks** are out on the road towards Chiquilistlán (signed as you enter Tapalpa). Here you rapidly escape into fresh-scented pine forest, passing a romantically ruined *fabrica* – an old water-driven paper mill – and climbing towards a gorgeous valley of upland pasture, studded with wild flowers and with huge boulders that look as if they've been dropped from the sky. About an hour from Tapalpa, this would be a fantastic place to camp, and you probably could with permission, though there are private property signs all along the road. There's good walking in almost any direction from Tapalpa, in fact, and plenty of wildlife, especially birds, to spot; you can also hire **horses** (look for the signs) – a popular ride is to the local waterfall. Be warned that it's very cold in winter, and even the summer nights can get decidedly chilly. They brew their own tequila in the village, which may help keep out the draughts; it's sold from the barrel in some of the older shops and is extremely rough.

Practicalities

For most things, head for the main plaza, where several of the old buildings have been refurbished as restaurants and hotels, and there's even an efficient branch of *Bancomer* (**exchange** Mon–Fri 9am–1.30pm). The cheapest **place to stay** by some way is the *Hotel Tapalpa* (④), above the *Restaurante Tapalpa*, with simple rooms and warm showers; expensive for what you get, but there's little competition. The *Posada la Hacienda* (☎343/2-01-93; ⑤) seems to offer not much more for nearly twice the price, though the rooms are a little fresher. Far nicer – indeed another world – is the *Posada La Fuente* (☎343/2-01-89; ⑤–⑦), a beautiful place whose rooms are rustic in the most comfortable sense: unfortunately you'll need to be in a group – there are apartments for six or four, which can be rented by couples, but only by the week. Also offering high luxury in more regular hotel style is the new *Villa de San José* (☎343/2-04-51; ⑧), just two blocks from the plaza. At the weekend all the rooms can sometimes be taken, but during the week you'll often be the only outsider. There's also a **campsite** a couple of kilometres before Tapalpa on the main road in.

Numerous **restaurants** serve plain country food – you get good steaks and dairy products up here – though many are open weekends only. One of the best is *Paulinos*, with balcony seats over the plaza and simple but excellent food; the *Tapalpa Grill*, below the red church near where the buses stop, is also a good bet for anything from *tortas* to *carnes asadas*.

Second-class **buses** run from Guadalajara's old bus station to Tapalpa (5am–6.30pm, Sun 5am–7pm; hourly); it's advisable to book your return as soon as you arrive, as the late buses are the most popular. In Tapalpa they stop just off the plaza. Only one, early-morning service runs to Ciudad Guzmán, but many more pass by the junction of the main road (El Crucero, some 20km away); it's easy enough to catch a bus, or even hitch, down there.

On to Colima: Ciudad Guzmán

Beyond the turn-off for Tapalpa, the old main road starts to climb in earnest into the Sierra Madre, passing though **Sayula** (the name chosen by Lawrence for his town on Lake Chapala) and the sizeable city of **CIUDAD GUZMÁN**. Ciudad Guzmán, birthplace of José Clemente Orozco, is a busy, thoroughly Mexican little city, with attractive colonnaded streets in the centre, though there seems little reason to stop except to break a journey. If you do visit, don't miss the lovely little **Museo de las Culturas de Occidente** on Dr Angel González, just off Reforma near the top, two blocks from the plaza (Reforma is the street that leads from the highway into town). It's just one room, but there are some lovely figures and animals in the collection of local archeology, and often an interesting temporary display that may include early works by Orozco. As ever, almost everything else is on or around the plaza, where you'll find banks, phones and **places to stay** and eat. The *Hotel Zapotlan* (☎343/2-00-40; ③), on the lower edge of the square, has a beautiful old wrought-iron courtyard, which sadly the rooms don't live up to (there's a variety of rooms at a variety of prices, so take a look around); half a block away, the *Hotel Flamingos* (☎343/2-01-03; ③), Federico del Toro 133, has less character but is clean and quiet. Among the food stalls on the plaza are several **restaurants**, among them *Juanito*, *La Fogata del Ché* and *Pizza Napoles*, all on the bottom edge, and *El Pollero*, opposite the church, where locals go for *licuados* and roast chicken.

Buses to Ciudad Guzmán stop at a station some way out; local bus #25 will drop you just off the main plaza by the smaller Plaza de las Tres Culturas, where there's an interesting church. The bus back to the Central leaves from the corner diagonally opposite, by the *farmacía*.

Between Ciudad Guzmán and Colima (see p.342) the drive becomes truly spectacular, through country dominated by the Nevado de Colima – at 4335m the loftiest and most impressive peak in the west, snowcapped in winter. The new road slashes straight through the mountains via deep cuttings and soaring concrete bridges, while the old one twists and turns above and beneath it as it switchbacks its way through the hills. Both have great views of the Nevado, at least when it's not covered in cloud. If you're on the old road, close your windows as you pass through **Atenquique**, a lovely hidden valley some 25km from Ciudad Guzmán that is enveloped in a pall of stinking fumes from a vast chemical plant. Not far from here, off the road but on the main train line to the coast, **Tuxpan** is a beautiful and ancient little town that is especially fun during its frequent, colourful fiestas.

Tequila

The approach to **TEQUILA**, some 50km northwest of Guadalajara, is through great fields of spiky, blue-grey maguey cactus. It's from these ugly plants that they make the quintessentially Mexican liquor to which the town lends its name, producing it in vast quantities at a series of local distilleries (*pulque* and *mescal* are also made from the maguey). More than 100 million litres of tequila are manufactured annually, and this simple product alone accounts for some three percent of Mexico's export earnings. The town itself is a grubby, rather dusty little place whose scattering of bourgeois mansions and fine church are overwhelmed by the trappings of thriving modern business. But no matter: you don't come here to sightsee, you come to drink. Or at least to visit the distilleries.

They've made tequila here since the seventeenth century and probably earlier, but the oldest and most important surviving **distillery** is *La Perseverancia*, the Sauza operation founded in 1875, where free tours are given by the gatekeeper. To get there, follow c/Ramon Corona from the plaza down beside the *Banco Promex*. If you'd like to learn more, *Sauza* also operate an experimental cactus farm, again open to the public on the edge of town at *Rancho El Indio*, where they have planted some 197 different varieties of maguey. There are plenty of cafes around the plaza in Tequila for less potent drinks.

It's easy enough **to get to Tequila** on regular buses from Guadalajara's old bus station (every 30min; 1hr 30min); there are also tours from Guadalajara run by *Panoramex* (p.162) among others.

Lagos de Moreno and San Juan de los Lagos

Heading east from Guadalajara towards León, Aguascalientes and the Bajío, the old highway runs through **SAN JUAN DE LOS LAGOS**. From its outskirts, about 150km from Guadalajara, San Juan seems like just another dusty little town, but in the centre you'll find an enormous bus station surrounded by scores of hotels. This is thanks to the vast parish church and the miraculous **image of the Virgin** that it contains: one of the most important pilgrimage centres in Mexico. The chief dates of pilgrimage – when the place is crammed with penitents, pilgrims seeking miraculous cures, and others who are just there to enjoy it – are February 2 (**Día de la Candelaria**) and December 8 (**Fiesta de la Inmaculada Concepción**), but celebration spills over, and there are several lesser events throughout the year, notably the first fortnight of August and the entire Christmas period. There's little chance of finding a room at these times and little point in staying long at any other, so it's best to treat San Juan de los Lagos as a day trip from – or stopover between – Lagos de Moreno and Guadalajara (less than an hour from the former, around three hours from Guadalajara).

Lagos de Moreno

Just 45km east of San Juan, **LAGOS DE MORENO** lies right on the intersection where the road from México to Ciudad Juárez crosses the route from Guadalajara to San Luis Potosí and the northeast. Though the town has always been a major staging post, surprisingly few people stop here now and, despite the heavy traffic rumbling around its fringes, it's a quiet and rather beautiful little town, with colonial streets climbing steeply from a small river to a hilltop monastery.

Cross the bridge by the bus station and head to your left along the stream, away from the choking fumes of the main road, and it's hard to believe you're in the same place. The **zócalo** is the place to head, whether you plan to stay a couple of hours or a few days: in the streets around are a massive Baroque church and a scattering of colonial mansions and official buildings, including an unfeasibly forbidding-looking jail that is actually still in use. Once you've seen the centre you can embark on the long climb up to the **hillside church** – the monastery is inhabited by monks, so you can't visit, and the church itself is tumbling down, but it's worth the trek, especially towards sunset, for the views alone.

There are several run-down but comfortable **hotels** near the zócalo. The delightful and friendly *Hotel Plaza* (③), right on the square, has clean rooms around an open courtyard. Also on the square itself, the *Hotel Paris* (☎2-02-60; ④) is a bizarre, stark building with overpriced rooms; the better-value *Hotel Colonial* (☎2-01-42; ⑦), Hidalgo 279, has its own restaurant and a very friendly and helpful manager. The zócalo also boasts a few good **bars** and **places to eat**.

Getting to and from Lagos de Moreno could hardly be easier: there are buses at least every thirty minutes from Guadalajara, León, Aguascalientes, Zacatecas and México.

MICHOACÁN STATE

To the southwest of Jalisco and Guadalajara, **Michoacán** state is one of the most beautiful and diverse in all Mexico – spreading as it does from a very narrow coastal plain, with several tiny beach villages (see Chapter Six), up to where the Sierra Madre Occidental reaches out eastwards into range after range of wooded volcanic heights.

Several of the towns, including the delightfully urbane capital **Morelia**, are utterly colonial in appearance, but on the whole Michoacán's attractions are simpler ones. The land is green and thriving everywhere – in **Uruapán** the lush countryside seems to press in on the town, and is certainly the main attraction – while throughout the state there is a very active native tradition and a strength of Indian culture matched only in the state of Oaxaca. This is thanks largely to Michoacán's first bishop, **Vasco de Quiroga**, one of the very few early Spanish colonists to see the Indian population as anything more than a slave-labour force. The fruits of Quiroga's efforts are most clear in and around **Pátzcuaro**, the beautiful lakeside town that was his base. Here and in the surrounding villages, traditional and introduced crafts from weaving to guitar manufacture have flourished for centuries, and today this region is one of the most important sources of Mexican *artesanías*. Indian traditions also draw large crowds to the lake for the **Day of the Dead** at the beginning of November, one of the most striking of Mexican celebrations.

On the whole, Michoacán is a region that people travel through rather than to. Morelia, Pátzcuaro, Uruapán and other towns lie conveniently on a direct route from Guadalajara to México. You could easily spend several days in each, or weeks trying to explore the state fully, but even in a couple of days passing through you can get a strong flavour.

Some history

When the Spanish first arrived here they found the region dominated by the **Tarascan (Purépecha) kingdom**, whose chief town, Tzintzuntzán, lay on the shores of Lake Pátzcuaro. Their civilization, a serious rival to the Aztecs before the Conquest, had a widespread reputation for excellence in art, metal-working and feathered ornaments. The Tarascans submitted peaceably to the Spanish in 1522 and their leader was converted to Christianity, but this didn't prevent the massacres and mass torture that Nuño de Guzmán meted out in his attempts to pacify the region and make himself a fortune. **Quiroga** was appointed bishop in an attempt to restore harmony – Guzmán's methods going too far even for the Spanish – and succeeded beyond all expectation. Setting himself up as the champion of the Indians, his name is still revered today. He encouraged the population down from the mountains whence they had fled, established settlements self-sufficient in agriculture and set up missions to teach practical skills as well as religion. The effects have survived in a very visible way for, despite some blurring in objects produced for the tourist trade, each village still has its own craft speciality: lacquerware in Pátzcuaro and Uruapán, pottery in Tzintzuntzán, wooden furniture in Quiroga, guitars in Paracho.

Vasco de Quiroga also left behind him a deeply religious state. Michoacán was a stronghold of the reactionary *Cristero* movement, which fought a bitter war in defence of the Church after the Revolution. Perhaps, too, the ideals of Zapata and Villa had less appeal here; Quiroga's early championing of Indian rights against their new overlords meant that the hacienda system never entirely took over Michoacán and, unlike most of the country, the state boasted a substantial peasantry with land it could call its own.

Guadalajara to Uruapán

From Guadalajara the direct **route to México** heads east through the major junction of La Piedad to join the superhighway outside Irapuato. If you can afford to dawdle a little, though, it's infinitely more rewarding to follow the slower, southern road through Zamora and Morelia, taking a couple of days to cut off through Uruapán and Pátzcuaro. From Uruapán a reasonably good road slices south through the mountains to the Pacific coast at Lázaro Cárdenas (see p.346).

Leaving Guadalajara, you skirt the northeastern edge of Lake Chapala before cutting south, heading into Michoacán and reaching **ZAMORA DE HIDALGO**, some 200km away. Though an ancient city, founded in 1540, Zamora today has little intrinsic interest. However, if you're planning to head straight down to Uruapán you may want to change buses here: it is possible to go direct from Guadalajara but there are far more buses to Morelia, and if you get as far as Zamora there's a much more frequent service to Uruapán. There are several small restaurants and a market very close to the bus station, but little to go out of your way for. The old cathedral, unusually Gothic in style, is ruined and often closed; you can while away some time on the pleasant grassy plaza in front.

The turn-off for Uruapán actually comes in the village of **Carapán**, some 40km further on; as an alternative to changing in Zamora, you could get off here and flag down a bus going south. The route, on a road winding through pine-draped hills, is a beautiful one. About halfway along you pass through the village of **PARACHO**, which has been famous for the manufacture of stringed instruments since Quiroga's time. Every house seems to be either a workshop or a guitar shop or both. The instruments vary enormously in price and quality – many are not meant to be anything more than ornamental, hung on the wall rather than played, but others are serious and beautifully handcrafted. Though you'll find them on display and for sale in the markets and *artesanías* museums in Uruapán or Pátzcuaro, if you want to buy, stop off here. Paracho also hosts a couple of fascinating **fiestas**. On Corpus Christi (the Thursday after Trinity, usually late May/early June) you can witness the dance of *Los Viejitos*. This, the most famous of Michoacán's dances, is also one of its most picturesque, with the dancers, dressed in baggy white cotton and old men's masks, alternating between parodying the tottering steps of the little old men (*viejitos*) they represent and breaking into complex routines. Naturally enough, there's a lot of music too. August 8 sees an even more ancient ceremony, whose roots go back to well before the Spanish era: an ox is sacrificed and its meat used to make a complicated ritual dish – *shuripe* – which is then shared out among the celebrants.

Uruapán

URUAPÁN, they say, means "the place where flowers bloom" in the Tarascan language, though *Appleton's Guide* for 1884 tells a different story: "The word Uruapán comes from *Urani*, which means in the Tarasc language 'a chocolate cup', because the Indians in this region devote themselves to manufacture and painting of these objects."

Demand for chocolate cups, presumably, has fallen since then. Whatever the truth, the modern version is certainly appropriate: Uruapán, lower (at just over 1500m) and warmer than most of its neighbours, enjoys a steamy subtropical climate and is surrounded by jungly forests and lush parks.

It's a prosperous and growing town too, with a thriving commerce based on the richness of its agriculture (particularly a vast export market in avocados) and on new light industry. To some extent this has come to overshadow the old attractions, creating ugly new development and displacing traditional crafts. But it remains a lively place with a fine market, an abiding reputation for lacquerware, and fascinating surroundings – especially the giant waterfall and "new" volcano of Paricutín.

Arrival

Most visitors arrive at Uruapán's modern **bus station**, some way from the centre; a local bus (marked "Centro Central") from right outside will take you down to the Jardín Morelos, the plaza in the heart of town, or back again from there. There are also a couple of **trains** a day from Pátzcuaro, Morelia and México, but it's a painfully slow way to travel unless you plan to sleep away the journey (from Uruapán there's a sleeper that leaves around 7pm and reaches México at about 8am). Again, there's a bus into town from the station.

Information

Uruapán's **tourist office** is at Madero 120 (daily 9am–2pm & 4–7pm; ☎452/4-06-33), just a block and a half from the southeast corner of the Jardín Morelos; they have a good map of town. There are numerous **banks** in the streets around the plaza if you need to change money, and a **casa de cambio**, the *Centro Cambiario*, on the south side of the plaza (Mon–Fri 9am–2pm & 4–8pm, Sat 9am–2pm). The **post office** (Mon–Fri 8am–7pm, Sat 9am–1pm) is on Cupatitizio, south of the plaza. There are several long-distance **casetas** on the plaza, and you can call from *Telmex* on Ocampo (Mon–Fri 9am–8pm, Sat 9am–noon).

Accommodation

Uruapán seems to have more than its fair share of **hotels**, most of them conveniently sited around – or at least within walking distance of – Jardín Morelos.

Capri, at the eastern end of the plaza (no phone). Basic and busy, right in the heart of town, with the action of the plaza often spilling over into the lobby. A much better bet than the *Oseguera* next door. ③.

Concordia, Portal Carillo 8 (☎524/4-20-04). On the plaza, modern, clean and efficent: all rooms with TV and phone. ⑤.

Gran Hotel Acosta, Filomena Mata 325 (☎542/3-45-64). Opposite the bus station, this is hardly an ideal spot, but if you're passing through it does offer clean, simple, reasonably priced rooms. ③.

Mansion del Cupatitzio, at the north end of the Parque Eduardo Ruiz (☎542/3-20-60). Uruapán's finest hotel with pool, restaurant and beautiful grounds. ⑦.

Mi Solar, Juan Delgado 10, a block north of the plaza (☎524/4-09-12). Best budget deal in town, with large, clean rooms with sporadic hot water, set around two large courtyards. ③.

Plaza Uruapán, Ocampo 64 (☎542/3-37-00). Big, modern hotel at the western end of the plaza, with good views from the rooms and second-floor restaurant. ⑦.

Regis, Portal Carillo 2 (☎524/3-98-44). Friendly place in a central location: some rooms overlook the plaza. ④.

Victoria, Cupatitzio 11 (☎524/4-25-00; fax 3-96-62). Another fine, modern hotel with a garage and good restaurant. ⑥.

Villa de Flores, E Carranza 15 (☎524/4-28-00). Clean, simple rooms around a beautiful little courtyard filled, as the name suggests, with flowers. ⑤.

The Town

The **Jardín Morelos**, a long strip of tree-shaded open space, is in every sense the heart of Uruapán. Always animated, it's surrounded by everything of importance: shops, market, banks, post office, principal churches and most of the hotels. So this is the place to head first, either to find a hotel or simply to get a feel for the place. On the plaza, too, is the town's one overt tourist attraction, *La Huatapera*. One of the oldest surviving buildings in Uruapán, it has been restored to house the **Museo Regional de Arte Popular** (Tues–Sun 9am–1.30pm & 3.30–6pm; free), an impressive display of crafts from the region, especially Uruapán's own lacquerwork. This small courtyard with its adjoining chapel was built by Juan de San Miguel, the Franciscan friar who founded the town itself. Later it became one of Bishop Quiroga's hospitals and training centres, so its present function seems appropriate. The wares shown are of the highest quality, and are worth a close inspection if you plan to go out hunting for bargains in the market or in the shops around the park. The art of making lacquer is complex and time-consuming, involving the application of layer upon layer of different colours, with the design cut into the background: all too many of the goods produced for tourists are simply given a couple of coats – one for the black background and a design painted on top – which is far quicker and cheaper, but not the same thing at all.

The **market** begins right behind the museum. Walk round to the back and you come first to the **Mercado de Antojitos**, a large open section just half a block south of the plaza, where women serve up meals for stallholders and visitors alike at a series of long, open-air tables. Take a look – this is where you'll find the cheapest, and very often the freshest and best, food in town. The rest of the market sprawls around here, along Corregidora and spreading up Constitución – replete with herbs, fruit, trinkets, shoe stalls and hot-dog stands. It's not a particularly good place to buy **native crafts**, though – the market that sells those is altogether more commercialized, and concentrated in a series of shops along Independencia, which leads up from the plaza to the Parque Nacional. At the top of this street are several small places where you can watch the artisans at work – some are no more than a single room with a display of finished goods on one side and a worktable on the other, others more sophisticated operations. Opposite the entrance to the park is a little "craft market", mostly selling very poor souvenirs.

The Río Cupatitzio and the Parque Nacional Eduardo Ruíz

The **Parque Nacional Eduardo Ruíz** (daily dawn–dusk) is perhaps Uruapán's proudest asset, a luxuriant tropical park in which the Río Cupatitzio rises and through which it flows in a little gorge via a series of man-made cascades and fountains. The river springs from a rock known as *La Rodilla del Diablo* (the Devil's knee), so called, runs the legend, because water gushed forth after the Devil knelt here in submission before the unswerving Christian faith of the drought-ridden population. Alternatively, Beelzebub met the Virgin Mary while out strolling in the park, and dropped to his knees in respect. *Cupatitzio* means "where the waters meet", though it's invariably translated as "the river that sings" – another appropriate, if not entirely accurate, tag.

Some 12km out of Uruapán, the Cupatitzio crashes over the **waterfall of La Tzaráracua**, an impressive 25m plunge amid beautiful forest scenery. This is a popular outing with locals, especially at weekends, and hence easy enough to get to – take one of the buses (marked "Tzaráracua") from Madero at Cupatitzio, a block south of the plaza, or share a taxi. If it seems too crowded here, make for the smaller fall, **Tzararacuita**, about 1km further downstream.

Eating and drinking

The best place to sample local delights at low prices has to be the **Mercado de Antojitos**: otherwise there are several good cheap cafes on Independencia, just off the plaza, all serving a selection of hamburgers, *tacos*, pizzas, sandwiches and superb *licuados*.

Amazonia, Latinoamérica 19. Simple place serving huge plates of tasty barbecued meats, fresh veg and rice.

Cafe Tradicional de Uruapán, Emiliano Carranza 5. Great breakfasts, superb local coffee, ice cream, cakes and *antojitos*.

La Pergola, south side of the plaza at Portal Carrillo 4. Reasonably priced popular restaurant serving a good *comida corrida*, local coffee and a broad international and Mexican menu.

Rincon del Burrito Real, south side of the plaza. The menu claims it's recommended in the most prestigious guides in the world, and now it is, though not very highly. However, it's open till 2am, convenient, and the food is fine as long as you stick to the simple things and avoid the more exotic specialities on the extremely long menu.

Paricutín

An ideal day trip from Uruapán, giving you an unusual taste of the surrounding countryside, is to the "new" **Volcano of Paricutín**, about 20km northwest of town. On February 20, 1943, a peasant working in his fields noticed the earth begin to move and then to smoke. The ground soon cracked and lava began to flow – eventually, over a period of several years, engulfing the village of Paricutín and several other hamlets, and forcing the evacuation of some seven thousand inhabitants. The volcano was active for eight years, producing a cone some 300m high and devastating an area of around twenty square kilometres. Now there are vast fields of cooled lava, black and powdery, cracked into harsh jags, along with dead cone and crater. Most bizarrely, a church tower – all that remains of the buried hamlet of San Juan Parangaricutiro – pokes its head through the surface. During its active life, the volcano drew tourists from around the world, and indeed it's partly responsible for the area's current development; less exciting now, it continues to get a fair number of visitors, though as the years pass the landscape is sure to soften. Such events are not altogether unprecedented – Von Humboldt devoted more than ten pages of his book on New Spain to the volcano of Jorullo, south of Pátzcuaro, which appeared equally suddenly in September 1759 – this was still hot enough, he reported, that "in the year 1780, cigars might still be lighted, when they were fastened to a stick and pushed in . . .". Jorullo is no longer the subject of any interest – indeed no one seems to know quite where it is – so maybe Paricutín, too, will in time become no more than folk memory.

To get to the volcano, start early. Take a bus ("Los Reyes") from the Central Camionera to the village of **ANGAHUAN** (about 40min). The bus drops you on the highway outside the village, from where you should walk to the plaza and turn left – keep going until you pass a superbly carved wooden building on the left and another labelled *Restaurante Angahuan*, after which you take a left turn and head straight on for about 3km. You eventually arrive at the *mirador* (viewing point) at the *Albergue Turistico*, which offers superb views of the volcano and has several six-bunk cabins, each with an open fire (⑤ per cabin; information from the state tourist office; ☎451/5-03-85).

Though the trip to the *Albergue* can be done in a morning, the journey to the crater is more complicated. In Angahuan you should have no problem finding a guide, whether you want one or not. It's not really necessary if you're just going up the hill for a look, though it seems harsh not to allow the locals some profit from their misfortune (although the volcano was not all bad news, its dust proving a fine fertilizer on the fields not actually buried by it). For the longer journey to the centre you do need a guide, and probably a horse too; not an outrageous expense, and certainly well worth it. A short ride out to the buried church takes just thirty minutes; a full ascent of the volcano is a day trip: take some provisions.

Pátzcuaro

PÁTZCUARO is almost exactly halfway between Uruapán and Morelia, some 60km from both, yet strikingly different from either. Much smaller – little more than a village, really, swollen somewhat by the tourist trade – it manages to be at one and the same time a far more colonial town than Uruapán, and infinitely more Indian than Morelia. In this it's perhaps the Mexican town *par excellence*: dotted with Spanish-style mansions and sumptuous churches, yet owing little or nothing in its lifestyle to the colonists. Add to this the fact that it sits by the shore of probably the most beautiful **lake** in Mexico – certainly the most photogenic, especially during Pátzcuaro's famed **Day of the Dead** celebrations (see p.187) – and it's hardly surprising that it acts as a magnet for tourists, Mexicans as well as foreigners. In the vicinity, you can take trips around the lake, visit other, less developed, villages, and see the site of **Tzintzuntzán**, one-time capital of the Tarascan kingdom.

Arrival and information

The new **bus station** in the south of town is about fifteen minutes' walk, or a brief bus ride ("Centro" or "Col. Popular"), from the centre. If you arrive by **train** you'll be further out still, but again a "Centro" bus will take you in. Although the outskirts of Pátzcuaro straggle a kilometre or so down to the lakeshore, and some of the more expensive hotels are strung out along this drive, the centre of Pátzcuaro is very small indeed, focusing on the two main squares, **Plaza Vasco de Quiroga** (or Plaza Grande) and **Plaza Bocanegra** (Plaza Chica).

The **tourist office** (9am–2pm & 4–7pm; ☎434/2-12-14) is discreetly hidden in a courtyard just off the Plaza Quiroga at Ibarra 2–4 (don't be put off by the "clinic" sign; the office shares the courtyard with a medical practice). For **currency exchange** there are plenty of banks on both plazas and *Multidivisas Casa de Cambio* at the corner of c/ Pedro Lloeda and c/Ahumada (Mon–Fri 9am–6pm).

The **post office** is on Obregón 13 (Mon–Fri 8am–7.30pm, Sat 9am–noon); you can **phone and fax** from *Computel* on Plaza Bocanegra.

Accommodation

None of Pátzcuaro's **hotels** – and there are packs of them – is really very cheap, but on the other hand it has some of the best mid-range places you'll find anywhere, and if you're prepared to pay a little extra for a lot more elegance you should get excellent value. Most are on one or other of the plazas, the ritzier establishments surrounding Vasco de Quiroga and a more basic selection around the Plaza Bocanegra. Wherever you stay, check that there will be an adequate **water supply** – Pátzcuaro suffers regular shortages.

During the first two days of November, when the town celebrates the **Day of the Dead** on the lake, there is little chance of getting a room anywhere near Pátzcuaro without prior booking.

Concordia, Portal Juaréz 31, Plaza Bocanegra (☎454/2-00-03). Large, chilly place but probably the best bargain in town. Simple clean rooms, some without bathrooms. ③.

Los Escudos, Portal Hidalgo 73, west side of the Plaza Vasco de Quiroga, next to the Palacio Municipal (☎454/2-01-38). Beautiful colonial building with rooms around two flower-filled courtyards; all have carpet and TV, some their own fireplaces. There's also a superb restaurant. ⑤.

Fiesta Plaza, Plaza Bocanegra (☎454/2-25-15). Big, simple hotel with three floors of rooms set around an open courtyard. ⑥.

Gran Hotel, Plaza Bocanegra (☎454/2-04-43). Clean, friendly hotel with small rooms and a good restaurant. ④.

Hotel Posada de la Basilica, Araga 6 (☎454/2-11-08). Up the hill opposite the basilica. Simple rooms in an old colonial building with superb views across the town's rooftops. ④.

Mansion Iturbe, Portal Morelos 59, north side of Plaza Vasco de Quiroga (☎454/2-03-68). Another colonial mansion retaining plenty of grandeur. ⑥.

Misión San Manuel, Portal Aldama 12 (☎454/2-13-13). The great colonial front hides a modern interior: nevertheless this ex-convent offers comfortable rooms with fireplaces. ⑥.

Posada de la Rosa, Plaza Bocanegra, Portal Juaréz 29 (☎454/2-08-11). Next door to the *Concordia* and the next best budget option; smaller, with rooms around an upstairs courtyard. ③.

Posada de la Salud, Serrato 9 (☎454/2-00-58). Beside the basilica, a short walk from the centre. Beautiful little hotel, peaceful and spotless; some rooms have fireplaces. Good value. ④.

Posada San Rafael, Plaza Vasco de Quiroga (☎454/2-07-70). One of the largest and fanciest with a long modern extension in colonial style behind the genuinely colonial front. ⑥.

The Town

More than anywhere in the state, Pátzcuaro owes its position to Bishop Vasco de Quiroga's affection for the indigenous peoples (you'll find his statue in the centre of the plaza that bears his name). It was he who decided, in the face of considerable opposition from the Spanish in Morelia (then known as Valladolid), to build the cathedral here. And although subsequent bishops moved back to Morelia, a basis had been laid: indeed it's the fact that Pátzcuaro enjoyed a building boom in the sixteenth century and has been something of a backwater ever since that creates much of its charm. Throughout the centre are old mansions with balconies and coats-of-arms, barely touched since those early years.

The plazas

Nothing much worth seeing in Pátzcuaro lies more than a few minutes' walk from **Plaza Vasco de Quiroga** and **Plaza Bocanegra**, named for Gertrudis Bocanegra, a local Independence heroine. The finest of Pátzcuaro's mansions are on the former – especially the seventeenth-century **Casa del Gigante**, with its hefty pillars and crudely carved figures, and another nearby said to have been inhabited by Prince Huitzimengari, son of the last Tarascan king. These, though, are both privately owned and not open to visitors. There are more on the Plaza Bocanegra, but the most striking thing here is the **Biblioteca** (Mon–Fri 9am–7pm, Sat 9am–1pm). This, the former sixteenth-century church of San Agustín, has been converted into a library and decorated with **murals** by Juan O'Gorman depicting the history of Michoacán, and of the Tarascans in particular. As well as a marvellous name, O'Gorman possessed a prodigious talent, and is one of the muralists who inherited the mantle of Rivera and Orozco: his best known-work is the decoration of the interior of Chapultepec Castle in México (see p.273). The paintings here couldn't be described as subtle, but he certainly ensures that the anti-imperialist point is taken – and even O'Gorman manages to find praise for Vasco de Quiroga.

The Basilica

East of the Plaza Bocanegra, Quiroga's cathedral, the **Basilica** or Colegiata, though never completed, is a massive church for such a small town. Even so, it is often full, for the Indians continue to revere Don Vasco's name and the church possesses a miraculous healing image of the Virgin, crafted in the traditional Tarascan method out of *pasta de caña*, a gum-like modelling paste made principally from maize. Services here, especially on saints' days, during fiestas – when the scrubby little **park** around the church becomes a fairground – or on the 8th of each month, when pilgrims gather to seek the Virgin's intercession, are extraordinary: the worshippers in an intense, almost hypnotic fervour.

Museo de Artes Populares

The **Museo de Artes Populares**, at the corner of Quiroga and Lerin, south of the basilica (Tues–Sat 9am–7pm, Sun 9am–3pm; $5, free on Sun), occupies the ancient Colegio de San Nicolas. Founded by Quiroga in 1540, the college is now devoted to a superb collection of regional handicrafts: local lacquer and pottery; copperware from Santa Clara del Cobre; and traditional masks and religious objects made from *pasta de caña* which, apart from being easy to work with, is also very light, and hence easily carried in processions. Some of the objects on display are ancient, others the best examples of modern work, and all in a very beautiful building. Almost opposite, the church of **La Compañia** was built by Quiroga in 1546 and later taken over by the Jesuits. Quiroga's remains and various relics associated with him are preserved here.

Casa de los Once Patios

A short walk south of the art museum, on Lerin, the **Casa de los Once Patios** (daily 9am–7pm, though individual stores may keep their own hours) is an eighteenth-century convent converted into a crafts showhouse, full of workshops and expensive boutiques. As its name suggests, the complex is set around a series of tiny courtyards, and it's a fascinating place to stroll through even if you can't afford the goods. You can watch restored treadle looms at work, admire the intricacy with which the best lacquerware is coddled, and wander at liberty through the warren of rooms and corridors.

El Humilladero and Cerro del Estribo

In the other direction, a thirty-minute walk from the basilica up Serrato, lies the church known as **El Humilladero** (frequent buses, marked "El Panteon", also run there). Probably the oldest in Pátzcuaro, this stands on the site where the last Tarascan king, Tanganxoan II, accepted Spanish authority. "The place of humiliation", then, may seem an appropriate tag with hindsight, though a more charitable view might suggest that Tanganxoan was simply hoping to save his people from the slaughter that had accompanied resistance to the Spanish elsewhere. The chapel itself offers little to see, so you might be better saving your hiking energies for a climb up the **Cerro del Calvario**, the tiny hill just west of town. A few minutes' walk will reward you with a great view of the lake: invisible as long as you stay in town. Leave the Plaza Grande on c/Ponce de León, pass the old customs house and a little plaza in front of the church of San Francisco, and keep straight on till you start climbing the hill. At the top is the little **chapel of El Calvario**, and if you take the road to the right here you can carry on to the much higher **Cerro del Estribo** (Stirrup Hill), about an hour's walk. For the better view with less effort, you could take a taxi, which leaves you at the bottom of 417 steps that climb to the summit.

Eating and drinking

Most of Pátzcuaro's hotels have their own **restaurants**, with fairly standard menus throughout – lots of good-value, if unexciting, *comidas corridas*. One feature of virtually all menus is *pescado blanco*, the rather flabby white fish from the lake, and *sopa tarasca* – a tomato-based soup with *chile* and bits of *tortilla* in it, usually very good. At the other end of the price range there are plenty of opportunities for finding something to eat in the **market**. This used to operate just one day a week in the streets leading up from the Plaza Bocanegra, but nowadays there is some activity every day, though Monday and Wednesday tend to be slow. It's at its most colourful and animated on Friday, when the Indians come in from the country to trade and barter their surplus. Most evenings you can get basic food from the stalls set up in the Plaza Bocanegra. For the best **fish**, you'll want to go down to the lake, where a line of restaurants faces the landing jetty: for details on getting there, see below.

Restaurants and cafes

Cafe Cayuco, just off the Plaza Quiroga. The buzziest place to be in the evenings, often with live music and always serving good drinks and snacks. Open till midnight, daily except Mon.

Dany's, Zaragoza 32, between the plazas. Charming little restaurant serving a selection of moderately priced international and Mexican food in a very civilized atmosphere, complete with crisp tablecloths and wine list.

Hotel Meson del Gallo, on Lerin near the basilica. Considerably more expensive than most, but with a very successfully contrived colonial atmosphere and interesting Mexican food. On Friday nights they host a *Fiesta Mexicana*, with music and regional dancing, which, if you like that sort of thing, is more tastefully done than most.

El Patio, Plaza Quiroga under the arches. Good coffee, reasonably priced breakfasts, Mexican *antojitos*, steaks, sandwiches and, of course, lake fish.

El Lago de Pátzcuaro

Pátzcuaro's other great attraction is, of course, **the lake** itself. It's less than an hour's walk down to the jetty (follow the *embarcadero* signs), and buses and minibuses leave from the Plaza Bocanegra. Those marked "Lago" will drop you right by the boats, while "Santa Ana" buses pass very close by.

With the completion of several new roads, the lake is no longer the major thoroughfare it once was – most locals now take the bus rather than paddle around the water in canoes – but there is still a fair amount of traffic and regular trips out to the closest island, **Janitzio**. Fares are fixed (get your ticket before you board) but there are almost always sundry "extras". Chief of these is a chance to photograph the famous butterfly nets wielded by Indian fishermen from tiny dug-out canoes. It's hard to believe that anyone actually uses these nets for fishing any more – they may be picturesque but they look highly impractical – but there's almost always a group of islanders with an eye for the main chance prepared to put on a show. They lurk in readiness on the far side of the island and only paddle into camera range when a sufficiently large collection has been taken.

Longer **trips around the lake** and visits to the other islands, or private rental of a boat and guide, can be arranged at the *embarcadero*, either through the office there or by private negotiation with one of the boatmen. Prices are high, but not prohibitive if there are a few of you.

The **Day of the Dead** (November 1, and through the night into the 2nd) is celebrated in spectacular fashion throughout Mexico, but nowhere more so than on Lake Pátzcuaro. Although many tourists come to watch, this is essentially a private meditation, when the locals carry offerings of fruit and flowers to the cemetery and hold vigil over the graves of their ancestors all night, chanting by candlelight. It's a spectacular and moving sight, especially earlier in the evening as Indians from the surrounding area converge on the island in their canoes, each with a single candle burning in the bows.

Janitzio

From the moment you step ashore on the island of **Janitzio** you're besieged by souvenir hawkers. Don't be put off though, for the views from the top of the island, which rises steeply from the water to a massive statue of Morelos at the summit, are truly spectacular. Moreover, you can't blame the islanders for wanting to milk their visitors – it's their only conceivable source of income aside from fishing, and they really are poor compared to the inhabitants of the mainland. Up the single steep street, between the stalls selling pottery and crude wooden carvings, a series of little restaurants display their wares out front – most have good fish, and often great bubbling vats of *caldo de pescado*.

Tzintzuntzán

The remains of **TZINTZUNTZÁN** (daily 9am–6pm; $3), ancient capital of the Tarascans, lie 15km north of Pátzcuaro on the lake shore. The site was established around the end of the fourteenth century, when the capital was moved from Pátzcuaro, and by the time of the Conquest the Spanish estimated that there were as many as 40,000 people living here, with dominion over all of what is now Michoacán and large parts of the modern states of Jalisco and Colima. Homes and markets, as well as the palaces of the rulers, lay around the raised **ceremonial centre**, but all that can be seen today is the artificial terrace that supported the great religious buildings (*yacatas*), and the ruins, partly restored, of these temples.

Even if you do no more than pass by on the road, you can't fail to be struck by the scale of these buildings and by their elliptical design, a startling contrast to the rigid, right-angled formality adhered to in almost every other major pre-Hispanic culture in Mexico. Climb up to the terrace and you'll find five *yacatas*, of which two have been partly rebuilt. Originally each was some 15m high, tapering in steps from a broad base to a walkway along the top less than 2m wide. There is no ornamentation, and the *yacatas* are in fact piles of flat rocks, held in by retaining walls and then faced in smooth, close-fitting volcanic stone. The terrace, which was originally approached up a broad ceremonial ramp or stairway on the side farthest from the water, affords magnificent views across the lake and the present-day village of Tzintzuntzán.

Down in the **village**, which has a reputation for producing and selling some of the region's best ceramics, you'll find what's left of the enormous **Franciscan Monastery** founded around 1530 to convert the Tarascans. Much of this has been demolished, and the rest substantially rebuilt, but there remains a fine Baroque church and a huge atrium where the Indians would gather to be preached at. Vasco de Quiroga originally intended to base his diocese here, but eventually decided that Pátzcuaro had the better situation and a more constant supply of water. He did leave one unusual legacy, though – the olive trees planted around the monastery are probably the oldest in Mexico, since settlers were banned from cultivating olives in order to protect the farmers back in Spain. Tzintzuntzán, incidentally, means "place of the hummingbirds". You're unlikely to see one nowadays, but the theory is that there were plenty of them around until the Tarascans – who used the feathers to make ornaments – virtually exterminated them through hunting. **To get to Tzintzuntzán**, take a bus from Pátzcuaro's Central Camionera to Quiroga.

Tinganio

If Tzintzuntzán has piqued your interest, then you might also want to check out the older, pre-Tarascan ruin of **TINGANIO** (daily 9am–6pm), on the outskirts of the village of **Tingambato**, roughly halfway between Pátzcuaro and Uruapán. This was first inhabited around 450–600 AD and greatly expanded, with influence from Teotihuacán, between 600 and 900 AD. The site has been well restored, revealing a small pyramid, a number of sunken communal areas with terraces, and the remains of numerous buildings or houses. Second-class buses between Pátzcuaro and Uruapán stop in Tingambato, where you follow the paved main street through town, under a bridge, and then turn right by a school after a few hundred metres to reach the site.

Quiroga

Due to its position on the main road from Morelia to Guadalajara, **QUIROGA**, 10km beyond Tzintzuntzán, is another village packed with craft markets, but the only genuinely local products seem to be painted wooden objects and furniture. Really it's no more than a stopover, but if you are waiting here, do take time to wander down to the market. There's a regular bus service between Quiroga and Pátzcuaro, and if you're coming **direct from Guadalajara** to Pátzcuaro, this is the most straightforward route (don't miss the views over the lake from the north, shortly before you reach Quiroga). Logically, this would also be the quickest way of doing the journey in reverse, **from Pátzcuaro to Guadalajara**, but things aren't always that simple: there's no guarantee that you're going to be able to get onto one of the fast buses along the main road – most pass though Quiroga full, without stopping. So although it's slightly farther, you'd be much better off going from Pátzcuaro direct to Morelia and from there doubling back towards Guadalajara – that way you're guaranteed a seat.

Morelia

The state capital, **MORELIA** is in many ways unrepresentative of Michoacán. It looks Spanish and, despite a large Indian population, it feels Spanish – with its broad streets lined with seventeenth-century mansions and outdoor cafes sheltered by arcaded plazas, you might easily be in Salamanca or Valladolid. Indeed, Valladolid was the city's name until 1828, when it was changed to honour the local-born Independence hero, José María Morelos. And it has always been a city of Spaniards – one of the first they founded after the Conquest.

That honour fell on two Franciscan friars, Juan de San Miguel and Antonio de Lisboa, who settled here among the Indians in 1530. Ten years later they were visited by the first Viceroy of New Spain, Antonio de Mendóza, who was so taken by the site that he ordered a town to be built, naming it after his birthplace and sending fifty Spanish families to settle it. From the beginning there was fierce rivalry between the colonists and the Indian town of Pátzcuaro. During the lifetime of Vasco de Quiroga it went in favour of the latter, but later the bishopric was moved here, a university

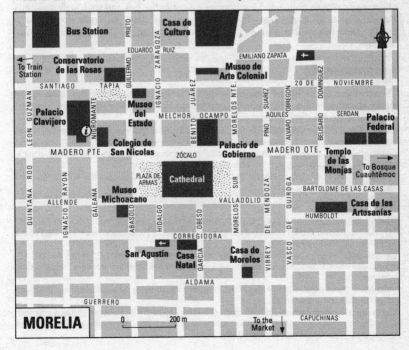

founded, and by the end of the sixteenth century there was no doubt that Valladolid was predominant.

There are specific things to look for and to visit in present-day Morelia, but the city itself outweighs them: it's been declared a "national monument", which allows no new construction that doesn't match perfectly with the old, and it preserves a remarkable unity of style. Nearly everything is built of the same faintly pinkish-grey stone (*trachyte*) which, being soft, is not only easily carved and embellished but weathers quickly, giving even relatively recent constructions a battered, ancient look.

Arrival and information

Morelia's **Central Camionera** is one of the few bus stations in Mexico to remain within walking distance of the city centre; the Plaza de Armas lies just four or five blocks southeast. If you arrive by **train**, you'll have to take a bus to the centre, as the station is 2km west of town on the city's outskirts, on Av. Periodismo; buses stop right opposite the station.

Most of the action in Morelia happens around the **Plaza de Armas** and **Avenida Madero**, the main thoroughfare bordering it to the north. Between the bus station and the centre, the **tourist office**, in the Jardín Ignacio Altamirano on Nigromante, just off Madero Pte. (daily 9am–9pm; ☎451/3-26-54), has a few maps and leaflets. There are plenty of very grand **banks** along Madero Ote., open for exchange on weekday mornings. **Casas de cambio** include *Trocamex*, at Nigromante 132 (Mon–Fri 9am–7pm, Sat 9am–3pm), and *Transacciones*, Allende 40 (Mon–Fri 9am–6pm, Sat 9am–1pm). The **post office** is at Madero Ote. 369 (Mon–Fri 8am–8pm, Sat & Sun 9am–1pm), where *Telmex* has **phone and fax** offices (Mon–Fri 9am–8pm, Sat 9am–noon). Computel also offers long-distance phone and fax from its offices in the bus and train stations and at Portal Galeana 157 (daily 7am–10pm). Getting around town you really don't need to use the local **buses**, though if you do get footsore, plenty of them ply up and down Madero.

Accommodation

Though there are plenty of inexpensive hotels scattered around the **bus station**, it's worth splashing out a little more to stay closer to the centre, where you have the choice of some wonderful fading, colonial hotels.

Casino, Portal Hidalgo 229 (☎451/13-10-03; fax 12-12-52). All rooms with carpet, TV and hot water, set around a small covered courtyard. ⑤.

Catedral, Ignacio Zaragoza 37 (☎451/13-07-83). Rooms around a restaurant in another covered colonial courtyard, although here you certainly pay for the atmosphere. ⑥.

Florida, Morelos Sur 161, southeast of the Plaza de Armas (☎451/12-10-38). Comfortable and clean, all rooms with TV and phone. ⑤.

Posada del Cortijo, Eduardo Ruiz 673 (☎451/2-96-97). Basic but convenient and fairly cheap, opposite the bus station. ④.

Real Victoria, Guadalupe Victoria 245, a block west of the bus terminal (☎451/13-23-00; fax 17-01-71). The broad colonial front conceals a modernized interior: all rooms have phone and TV. Popular with Mexican businesspeople. ⑥.

La Soledad, Ignacio Zaragoza 90, just off the Plaza de Armas (☎451/12-18-90; fax12-21-11). Spectacular colonial building that used to be a convent, with rooms set around a beautiful open courtyard. ⑦.

Valladolid, Portal Hidalgo 241 (☎451/2-00-27). Great position under the colonial arches, but rooms are a little dark and run-down. ④.

Virrey de Mendoza, Madero Pte. 310 (☎451/12-06-33; fax 12-67-19). Fantastic colonial grandeur: even if you can't afford to stay it's worth dropping by to take a look. The rooms are just as impressive as the lobby, with no expense spared. ⑨.

The Town

Avenida Francisco Madero, which runs along the north side of the **Cathedral**, is very much the main street of Morelia, with most of the important public buildings and major shops strung out along it. Everything you're likely to want to see is within easy walking distance of the **Plaza de Armas**.

Around the Plaza de Armas

At the heart of the city, Morelia's massive **Cathedral** boasts two soaring towers that are said to be the tallest in Mexico. Begun in 1640 in the relatively plain Herrerian style, the towers and dome were not completed for some hundred years, by which time Baroque had arrived with a vengeance: nevertheless, it harmonizes remarkably, and for all its size and richness of decoration, the perfect proportions prevent it from becoming overpowering. The interior, refitted towards the end of the last century, after most of its silver ornamentation had been removed to pay for the wars, is simple and preserves, in the choir and sacristy, a few early colonial religious paintings.

Flanking the cathedral, the Plaza de Armas (or de los Martíres) is the place to sit around, in the cafes under its elegant arcaded *portales*, with a coffee and a morning paper (you can buy the *Mexico City News* from the stands here), revelling in the city's leisurely pace. On the southwestern edge of the plaza, at the corner of Allende and Abasolo, the **Museo Michoacáno** (Tues–Sat 9am–7pm, Sun 9am–3pm; $5, free on Sun) occupies a palatial eighteenth-century mansion. The Emperor Maximilian lodged here on his visits to Morelia, and it now houses a collection reflecting the state's diversity and rich history: the rooms devoted to archeology are, of course, dominated by the Tarascan culture, including pottery and small sculptures from Tzintzuntzán, but also display much earlier objects, notably some little obsidian figurines. Out in the patio are two magnificent old carriages, while upstairs the colonial epoch is represented in a large group of religious paintings and sculptures and a collection of old books and manuscripts.

A smaller square, the **Plaza Melchor Ocampo**, flanks the cathedral on the other side. Facing it, the **Palacio de Gobierno** was formerly a seminary – Independence hero Morelos and anti-hero Agustín Iturbide studied here, as did Ocampo, a nineteenth-century liberal supporter of Benito Juárez. It's of interest now for the **murals** adorning the stairway and upper level of the patio: practically the whole of Mexican history is here, and all its heroes depicted. A little further down Madero are several **banks** that are among the most remarkable examples of active conservation you'll see anywhere: all Mexican banks are sumptuous, but they usually go in for steel and glass, marble floors and modern statuary – these are old mansions that have been refurbished in traditional style, and somehow manage to combine reasonably efficient operation with an ambience that is wholly in keeping with the setting.

West and north of the plaza

One block west of the Plaza de Armas, the **Colegio de San Nicolas** is part of the University of Morelia. Originally founded at Pátzcuaro in 1540 by Vasco de Quiroga, and moved here in 1580, the college is the second oldest in Mexico and hence in all the Americas – it now houses administrative offices and various technical faculties. To the side, across Nigromante, is the public library in what was originally the Jesuit Church of **La Compañia**, while next to this is the beautiful **Palacio Clavijero**, converted into government offices. At the bottom of Nigromante, on another charming little plaza, you'll come to the Baroque church of Santa Rosa and, beside it, the **Conservatorio de las Rosas** – a still functioning music academy founded in the eighteenth century. From time to time it hosts concerts of classical music – the tourist office has details.

Also here, at the corner of Santiago Tapia and Guillermo Prieto, is the new **Museo del Estado** (daily 9am–2pm & 4–8pm; free). Inside, the complete furniture and fittings of a traditional *farmacía* have been reconstructed, after which you move, somewhat incongruously, to the prehistory and archeology collections. Mostly this is minor stuff, though there's some fine, unusual Tarascan jewellery, including gold and turquoise pieces, and necklaces strung with tiny crystal skulls. Upstairs there's one room of colonial history and various ethnological exhibits illustrating traditional local dress and lifestyles.

Heading east from here, or north from the Plaza de Armas on Juárez, the **Museo de Arte Colonial** (Tues–Sun 10am–2pm & 4–8pm; free) lies opposite the Plaza de Carmen. Its collection of colonial art is almost entirely regional, and not of great interest. On the north side of the plaza, entered from Morelos, the beautiful old Convento del Carmen now houses the **Casa de la Cultura** (open all day, but museum and most exhibits Mon–Fri 10am–2pm, Sat & Sun 10am–6pm). It's an enormous complex, worth exploring in its own right, with a theatre, cafe, space for temporary exhibitions and classes, and the fascinating little **Museo de la Mascara** (mask museum) scattered around the former monastic buildings.

South and east of the plaza

Directly south of the Casa de la Cultura, and south from the Plaza Melchor Ocampo, on Morelos Sur, the **Casa Museo de Morelos** (Mon–Sat 9am–7pm, Sun 9am–6pm; $4, free on Sun) is the relatively modest eighteenth-century house in which Independence hero José María Morelos y Pavon lived from 1801. It's now a museum devoted to his life and the War of Independence. Nearby, at the corner of Corregidora (the continuation of Alzate) and Garcia Obeso, you can see the house where the hero was born, the **Casa Natal de Morelos** (daily 10am–2pm & 4–7pm; free), which now houses a library and a few desultory domestic objects. This in turn is virtually next door to the **Church of San Agustín**, from where pedestrianized c/Hidalgo runs up one block to the Plaza de Armas and opposite whose attractive facade is a tiny market area, the **Mercado Hidalgo**.

A couple of blocks in the other direction – or take Valladolid directly from the Plaza Ocampo – the **Casa de las Artesanías** (Mon–Sat 9am–8pm, Sun 10am–6pm; free) is possibly the most comprehensive collection of Michoacán's crafts anywhere, almost all of them for sale. The best and most obviously commercial items are downstairs, while

JOSÉ MARíA MORELOS Y PAVON

A student of Hidalgo, **José María Morelos** took over the leadership of the Independence movement after its instigators had been executed in 1811. While the cry of Independence had initially been taken up by the Mexican (Creole) bourgeoisie, smarting under the trading restrictions imposed on them from Spain, it quickly became a mass popular movement. Unlike the original leaders, Morelos (a *mestizo* priest born into relative poverty) was a populist and genuine reformer; even more unlike them, he was also a political and military tactician of considerable skill, invoking the spirit of the French Revolution and calling for universal suffrage, racial equality and the break-up of the hacienda system. Defeat and execution by Royalist armies under Agustín de Iturbide came in 1815 only after years of guerrilla warfare, during which Morelos had come within an ace of taking the capital and controlling the entire country. When Independence was finally gained – by Iturbide, now changed sides and later briefly to be emperor – it was no longer a force for change, rather a reaction to the fact that by 1820 liberal reforms were sweeping Spain itself. The causes espoused by Morelos were, however, taken up to some extent by Benito Juárez and later, with a vengeance, in the Revolution – almost a hundred years after his death.

on the upper floor are a series of rooms devoted to the products of particular villages, often with craftspeople demonstrating their techniques (these are staffed by villagers and hence not always open), and a collection of historic items which you can't buy. It's all housed in what used to be the Monastery of **San Francisco**, whose church, facing onto the little plaza next door, can also be visited.

Finally, in the far east of the city, about fifteen minutes' walk along Madero from the Plaza de Armas, past the Baroque facade of the Templo de las Monjas, is an area of tree-lined walks and little parks on the edge of town, through the middle of which runs the old **aqueduct**. Built between 1785 and 1789, these serried arches brought water into the city from springs in the nearby hills. On the right is the largest of the parks, the **Bosque Cuauhtémoc**, in which there's a small **Museum of Contemporary Art** (Tues–Sun 10am–2pm & 4–8pm; free), featuring a variety of Latin American work, as well as some beautifully laid-out flower displays. To the left, c/Fray Antonio de San Miguel (named for the bishop who built the aqueduct) runs down to the vastly overdecorated **Santuario de Guadalupe**; market stalls, selling above all the sticky local *dulces*, set up here at weekends and during fiestas.

Eating and drinking

For a reasonably priced sit-down meal, the bus station area is the best bet – most of the hotels there also have **restaurants** that serve a fairly standard *comida corrida*. Eating a full meal in any of the cafes on the Plaza de Armas will prove expensive, but they're good for snacks or for a breakfast of coffee and *pan dulce*. In the evenings you can eat outdoors at places set up along traffic-free Hidalgo (between the plaza and San Agustín) and around the Mercado Hidalgo.

Chief of Morelia's specialities are its *dulces*, sweets made of candied fruit or evaporated milk: cloyingly sweet to most non-Mexican tastes, but very popular here. You can see a wide selection at the **Mercado de Dulces y Artesanías**, up Gomez Farias from the bus station and on the left-hand side, around the back of the Palacio Clavijero. As its name suggests, they also sell handicrafts here, but on the whole nothing of any class. Morelians also get through a lot of *rompope* (a drink which you'll find to a lesser extent all over Mexico) – again, it's very sweet, an egg-flip concoction based on rum, milk and egg with vanilla, cinnamon and almond added as flavouring. Finally, as always, there are food stalls and plenty of raw ingredients in the **market**, but Morelia's big Mercado Independencia is on the whole a disappointment, certainly not as large or varied as you'd expect. On Sunday – market day – it perks up a little. Get there by going towards the Plaza San Francisco and then a long six or seven blocks south on Vasco de Quiroga.

Acuarius, in a courtyard off Hidalgo. Vegetarian restaurant – pleasant setting, unadventurous food.

Cafe del Teatro, in the *Teatro Ocampo* on Ocampo and Prieto. Its lush interior makes this one of the most popular spots in town for good coffee and people-watching – try and get a table overlooking the street.

Los Comensales, Zaragoza 148. Pretty courtyard setting complete with caged, squawking birds. The *comida corrida* is good value; splash out a bit more for Mexican specialities, including a tasty chicken in rich, dark *mole*.

Copa de Oro, Juárez at Santiago Tapia. Simple place for fresh *jugos* and *tortas*.

Govinda, Morelos Sur 39. Good, inexpensive (but not very Indian) vegetarian salads, soups, main meals and breakfasts – opens at around 9.30am.

Paraiso, Madero Pte. 103. Facing the cathedral under the arches, a popular and straightforward cafe, good for breakfast, coffee and chat.

Restaurante Cachamay, Zaragoza and Santiago Tapia. Plain place for cheap *comidas*.

El Rey Tacamba, opposite the cathedral. Small, bustling restaurant favoured by townspeople for its good, solid, local food.

Woolworth, Mendoza 60. Excellent selection of celestial hamburgers in the superb setting of a former church.

MOVING ON FROM MORELIA

Moving on from Morelia should present no problem at all: there are **trains** to México (including the sleeper, which leaves here around 11pm and arrives in the capital at 8am), and to Pátzcuaro and Uruapán; and there are buses to just about anywhere in the state and most other conceivable destinations: very frequently to Guadalajara, Pátzcuaro, Uruapán and México: regularly north to Salamanca, for Guanajuato and Querétaro.

The **shortest route to México**, via Zitacuaro and Toluca, is very beautiful – passing through the Mil Cumbres (thousand peaks) – but mountainous and slow. Some buses go round by the faster roads to the north. If only for the scenery, you should try to take the former route – these mountains are the playground of México's middle classes, and there are a couple of places of interest along the way (see below).

Towards México: the Monarch Butterfly Sanctuary

From November to mid-April, between 30 and 100 million Monarch butterflies migrate from the USA and Canada to congregate in the lush mountains of Michoacán and reproduce. It's an amazing sight: in the cool of the morning they coat the trees, turning the entire landscape a rich, velvety orange, while later in the day the increased humidity forces them to the ground, where they form a thick carpet of blazing colour. Although the butterflies sometimes come as far down as the highway, the best place to see them is in the **butterfly sanctuary**, where a guide will show you around and give you a short explanation of their life-cycle and breeding habits (Nov to mid-April daily; small fee; further information from the tourist office in Morelia or the information booth on the highway outside Zitácuaro, towards Toluca; ☎725/3-06-75).

The sanctuary lies in the mountains above the small village of **El Rosario**, north of the Morelia–Toluca highway, about 150km east of Morelia. The turn-off is just before **Zitácuaro**, which is where you should head if you want to reach the sanctuary by public transport: take a bus to the village of **Ocampo**, from where there are buses to the sanctuary itself; alternatively there are tours from Zitácuaro. **Accommodation** in El Rosario is fairly limited; by far the best place to stay is the mining town of **Angangueo**, jammed into the narrow valley just below El Rosario, 10km beyond Ocampo. Here you'll find the comfortable and very friendly *Hotel Don Bruno* (⑥), which has its own restaurant, and the more basic *Casa de Huéspedes El Paso de la Monarca* (②). **Buses** to El Rosario and the sanctuary leave Ocampo at 8am, 12.30pm, 4pm and 6pm, and pass through Angangueo about thirty minutes later. Buses to Ocampo and Angangueo leave hourly from Zitácuaro.

---

fiestas

Both Jalisco and Michoacán preserve strong native traditions and are particularly rich in fiestas: the list below is by no means exhaustive, and local tourist offices will have further details.

January

6th DÍA DE LOS SANTOS REYES (Twelfth Night). Many small ceremonies – **Los Reyes** (Michoacán), south of Zamora and west of Uruapán, has dancing and a procession of the

Magi. **Cajititlán** (Jalisco), on a tiny lake near Guadalajara, also has traditional dances.

8th **San Juan de las Colchas** (Mich.) commemorates the eruption of Paricutín with a dance contest and traditional dress. Many of the homeless villagers moved to this village near Uruapán.

15th **La Piedad** (Mich.). Traditional dances and a major procession for local saint's day.

20th DÍA DE SAN SEBASTIAN. **Tuxpan** (Jal.), a beautiful village between Ciudad Guzmán and

Colima, has traditional dances including the unique *Danza de los Chayacates*. Start of the mass pilgrimages to **San Juan de Los Lagos** (Jal.) which culminate on Feb 2.

February

1st In **Tzintzuntzán** (Mich.) the start of a week-long fiesta founded in the sixteenth century by Vasco de Quiroga.

2nd DÍA DE LA CANDELARIA (Candlemas). Celebrated in **Lagos de Moreno** (Jal.) with pilgrimages, but much more so in nearby **San Juan de Los Lagos** (Jal.), one of the largest in Mexico.

CARNIVAL (the week before Lent, variable Feb–March) is particularly good in **Zinapecuaro** (Mich.), near Morelia, with pretend bulls chasing people through the streets; **Copandaro** (Mich.), also near Morelia on the shores of Lake Cuitzeo, has similar fake bullfights, rodeos and marathon dances; and in **Charapán** (Mich.), near Uruapán, you can see the dance of *Los Viejitos*. All these are best on Carnival Tuesday.

March

PALM SUNDAY (week before Easter) is the culmination of a week's celebration in **Uruapán** (Mich.) – the Indians collect palms from the hills and make ornaments from the leaves, sold here in a big *tianguis*.

HOLY WEEK is observed everywhere. In **Copandaro** (Mich.) they celebrate all week, especially on the Thursday with the ceremony of Washing the Apostle's Feet, and Good Friday when they act out more scenes from Christ's passion. These passion plays are quite common: at **Tzintzuntzán** (Mich.) and the hamlet of Maya near **Lagos de Moreno** (Jal.). In **Ciudad Hidalgo** (Mich.) there's a huge procession.

May

3rd DÍA DE LA SANTA CRUZ. Native dances in **Ciudad Hidalgo** (Mich.), *mariachi* and tequila in **Tequila** (Jal.).

Last Sunday DÍA DEL SEÑOR DE LA MISERICORDIA, fiesta in honour of this highly venerated image in **Tuxpan** (Jal.) – native dances.

CORPUS CHRISTI (variable – the Thursday after Trinity) is celebrated in the neighbouring villages of **Cheran** and **Paracho**, in Michoacán.

June

24th DÍA DE SAN JUAN. **Purepero** (Mich.), between Uruapán and La Piedad, starts a week-long fiesta.

29th DÍA DE SAN PEDRO. In **Tlaquepaque** (Jal.) a highly animated festival with *mariachi*, dancing and processions.

July

First Sunday. Torchlit religious processions in **Quiroga** (Mich.).

22nd DÍA DE MARIA MAGDALENA. Fiesta in **Uruapán** (Mich.) – featuring processions of animals.

26th Culmination of a week-long *feria* in **Acatlán de Juárez** (Jal.), south of Guadalajara: regional dress, dances and fireworks.

28th FIESTAS DEL SEÑOR DEL CALVARIO in **Lagos de Moreno** (Jal.) last until August 6th.

August

8th Very ancient "pagan" fiesta in **Paracho** (Mich.).

15th DÍA DE LA ASUNCION (Assumption) sees a large fair in **Santa Clara del Cobre** (Mich.), near Pátzcuaro, coincide with markets of the renowned hand-made copperware.

September

8th The start of a festival in **San Juan de las Colchas** (Mich.), which lasts to the 22nd, its climax on the 14th.

30th In **Morelia** (Mich.), celebrations for the birthday of Morelos.

October

Guadalajara's FIESTAS DE OCTUBRE run throughout the month.

4th DÍA DE SAN FRANCISCO. Saint's day celebrations culminate in a week of pilgrimages to **Talpa** (Jal.), near Guadalajara, where the faithful come bearing flowers and candles. Celebrated, too, in **Jiquilpa** (Mich.), between Zamora and Lake Chapala, and in **Uruapán** (Mich.), where it's one of the year's biggest.

12th DÍA DE LA RAZA commemorates Columbus's discovery of America. *Feria* in **Uruapán** (Mich.) and, in **Guadalajara**, the highlight of the Fiestas comes with an enormous pilgrimage to the Virgin of Zapopan.

16th Native dances and an all-night procession honour a much revered image of Christ in **Cuitzeo** (Mich.), on Lake Cuitzeo north of Morelia.

21st DÍA DE SAN JOSÉ. In **Ciudad Guzmán** (Jal.), the climax of a lively *feria* which lasts from the 12th to the 23rd.

22nd **Apatzingan** (Mich.), in beautiful mountain country south of Uruapán and the end of the railway through there, has a fiesta which includes dance competitions and rodeos, on the rather flimsy excuse of the anniversary of the 1814 Constitution.

24th–26th The FESTIVAL DE COROS Y DANZAS in **Uruapán** (Mich.). A competition between Tarascan Indian choirs and dance groups. Great.

DÍA DE CRISTO REY. On the last Sunday in October, an ancient series of dances in honour of Christ the King in **Contepec** (Mich.), south of Querétaro, east of Morelia. Also processions and regional costume.

November

2nd DÍA DE LOS MUERTOS (All Souls). The famous Day of the Dead is celebrated everywhere, but the rites in **Pátzcuaro** (Mich.) and on the island of **Janitzio** are the best known in Mexico. Highly picturesque, too, in **Zitácuaro** (Mich.).

December

8th DÍA DE LA INMACULADA CONCEPCIÓN. In **San Juan de Los Lagos** (Jal.), the high point of a massive *feria* that attracts thousands of pilgrims and boasts an enormous crafts market. **Sayula** (Jal.), between Guadalajara and Ciudad Guzmán, also has impressive displays of native dance. In **Tequila** (Jal.), not surprisingly, the celebrations are more earthy, with rodeos, cockfights and fireworks. On the same day **Pátzcuaro** (Mich.) celebrates La Señora de la Salud, an event attended by many Tarascan pilgrims and the scene of Tarascan dances including *Los Viejitos*.

12th DÍA DE LA VIRGEN DE GUADALUPE. Large fiesta in **Jiquilpan** (Mich.) with fireworks and a torchlit procession in which locals dress in the Mexican colours, green, white and red. **Tapalpa** (Jal.) attracts pilgrims from a wide area, with regional dances in front of the church.

23rd In **Aranza** (Mich.), a tiny village near Paracho, they perform pastoral plays on Christmas Eve. On Christmas Eve too, in **Tuxpan** (Jal.), there are very ancient dances and a large religious procession.

travel details

Buses

Relatively densely populated, this area is crisscrossed by thousands of services, local ones between towns and villages, and long-distance runs that call in at all major towns on their routes. It can occasionally be difficult to pick up a *de paso* seat on the latter: they're not normally sold until the bus has arrived. What follows is a minimum, covering the major stops only – it should be assumed that these buses also call at the towns en route.

In general the fastest and most efficient operators are *Omnibus de Mexico* and *Tres Estrellas de Oro*, though there's little to choose between the first-class companies. *Flecha Amarilla* cover many of the local runs and are fairly reliable – *Estrella Blanca* is better but less frequent.

Guadalajara to: Aguascalientes (8 daily; 4hr); Ajijic (hourly; 1hr); Chapala (hourly; 1hr); Colima (7 daily; 5hr); Manzanillo (4 daily; 6hr); México (hourly; 9hr); Morelia (11 daily; 6hr); Pátzcuaro (5 daily; 6hr); Puerto Vallarta (5 daily; 8hr); Tapalpa (hourly; 2hr); Tepic (5 daily; 5hr); Tequila (hourly; 2hr); Uruapán (11 daily; 5hr).

Morelia to: Aguascalientes (4 daily; 7hr); Guadalajara (11 daily; 6hr); Guanajuato (8 daily; 3hr 30min); León (every 30min; 4hr); México (10 daily; 6hr); Pátzcuaro (every 15min; 1hr); Querétaro (hourly; 4hr).

Pátzcuaro to: Guadalajara (5 daily; 6hr); México (hourly; 7hr); Morelia (every 15min; 1hr); Uruapán (every 15min; 1hr).

Uruapán to: Guadalajara (11 daily; 5hr); Lázaro Cárdenas (4 daily; 6hr); Los Reyes (hourly; 1hr); México (9 daily; 6hr); Morelia (every 15min; 2hr); Paracho (every 30min; 40min); Pátzcuaro (every 15min; 1hr).

Trains

Guadalajara is the region's train hub; two trains leave daily for the capital via Querétaro, and there are also daily departures for Nogales and

Mexicali, and a daily departure for Manzanillo travelling through Ciudad Guzmán and Colima. Two trains (first- and second-class) also leave Uruapán for the capital via Pátzcuaro and Morelia.

Planes

Guadalajara to: México (hourly), Central America, Miami, Los Angeles, Houston and several other major US cities.

CHAPTER FOUR

THE BAJÍO

ichly fertile, wild, rugged and scattered with superb colonial towns, the twisting
hills and beautiful valleys of the **Bajío** spread across the central highlands
directly to the north of México. This colonial heartland provided much of the
silver and grain that supported Mexico throughout the years of Spanish rule,
and it's here that the legacy of Spanish architecture remains at its most impressive, in
meticulously crafted towns that – at their cores at least – have changed little over the
centuries.

Coming down by the central or eastern routes you pass, inevitably, through either
Zacatecas or **San Luis Potosí**, which, though they're outside the Bajío proper, are
showcase examples of the region's architectural and historical heritage, sharing all the
attributes of the towns farther south. San Luis, a large modern metropolis, has its share
of monuments, but Zacatecas is far more exciting, an oasis of culture and sophistication
built in mountainous isolation on the wealth of silver.

Farther south, beyond the modern town of **Aguascalientes**, you enter the green
belt of the Bajío proper. This fertile area of central Mexico, stretching almost from
coast to coast and south as far as the capital, has always been the most heavily populated part of the country and it remains much the most consistently developed, both
agriculturally and industrially. If you're heading straight for México you'll bypass
almost everywhere of interest, cutting through the industrial cities of **León** – famous
for its leather – and **Irapuato** before joining the highway past Celaya and Querétaro.
This would be a mistake: crazily ranged up the sides of a ravine, **Guanajuato** is quite
simply one of the country's richest and most scenic colonial towns, with one of its
finest Baroque churches, a thriving student life, and, for good measure, the ghoulish
Museum of Mummies. Other towns are intimately linked with Mexico's Independence
movement: **Dolores Hidalgo** in particular, but also **San Miguel de Allende**, its
gorgeous hillside setting attracting foreign artists and students by the hundred, and
Querétaro, large and industrial, which preserves a fine colonial quarter at its heart.

It's easy enough to **get around** the Bajío – all the towns of interest lie close
together, bus services are excellent, and the **hotels** are some of the best you'll find in
the entire country.

ZACATECAS AND SAN LUIS POTOSÍ

After several hundred miles of bleak desert and dusty cowboy towns, the colonial cities
of **Zacatecas** and **San Luis Potosí** – both state capitals – mark a radical change in
landscape and architecture. There's not a great deal to distract you on the route down
to Zacatecas: a semi-desert landscape punctuated only by the occasional mining town
or ranch where fighting bulls are bred. The one place you might want – or need – to
stop over is **FRESNILLO**, less for any intrinsic interest than as a convenient staging
post, ninety minutes from Zacatecas. It's a quiet town, long deserted by the wealth that

gold-mining once brought, but retains a few fine buildings from its heyday. There are several small hotels, but you'd be best heading straight out on one of the frequent onward bus services. Coming down from Saltillo, the one place of any significance before you reach San Luis Potosí is **Matehuala**, close by the strange ghost town of **Real de Catorce**, its mines and mansions totally deserted.

Zacatecas

ZACATECAS, 2500m up and crammed into a narrow gully between two hills, packs more of interest into a small space than almost anywhere in Mexico and must rank, alongside Guanajuato, as one of the Bajío's finest colonial cities. Its beauty enhanced by the harshness of the semi-desert landscape all around, it remains much as the British Admiralty's *Handbook of Mexico* described it in 1905:

 . . . *irregular, and the streets very narrow, steep, and frequently interrupted by stone steps; where they are paved at all, they are roughly cobbled, and there is no wheeled traffic. There are many churches . . .*

It goes on to warn "that the town is much exposed to winds blowing through the gorge, and pneumonia is prevalent". Most of the streets are now paved and choked with traffic, but otherwise little can have changed: those winds still gust, too, bitterly cold in winter.

All views are dominated by the **Cerro de la Bufa**, with its extraordinary rock cockscomb rearing some 150m above the city; at night it's illuminated, with a giant cross lit up on top. A modern Swiss cable car connects the summit with the Cerro del Bosque (or del Grillo) – a superb ride straight over the heart of the old town. From the Cerro de la Bufa itself there are commanding vistas taking in the entire city, its drab new outskirts and the bare hills all around, pockmarked with old mine-workings. From a height, however, the city's sprawl isn't particularly inviting and it is only when you get down there, among the narrow streets, twisting alleys, colonial fountains, carved doorways and ornate churches, that its real splendour is revealed.

Some history
It didn't take the Spanish Conquistadors long to discover the enormous lodes of **silver** in the hills of Mexico's central highlands, and, after some initial skirmishes with the Zacateco Indians, the city of Zacatecas was founded in 1546. For the next three centuries its mines disgorged fabulous wealth to enrich the Spanish crown and the city; in 1728 the mines here were producing one-fifth of all Mexico's silver. Though local indigenous groups, and bandits, continuously preyed on the town, nothing could deter the fortune-hunters and labourers from around the world – Spanish nobles, African slaves, German engineers, British bankers – drawn by the prospect of all that wealth. The end of the boom, when it came, was brought about more by the political uncertainties of the nineteenth century than by the exhaustion of the mines, some of which still operate today. Throughout nearly a century of war, Zacatecas itself became an important prize: there were major battles here in 1871, when Benito Juárez successfully put down local rebels, and in 1914 when Pancho Villa's **Division del Norte** captured the city, completely annihilating the 12,000-strong garrison with all its baggage and supplies.

Today Zacatecas is booming once more, its business and light industry boosted by the increasing flow of traffic between Mexico and the US. The town's prosperity has ensured a strong streak of civic pride, and many of the old colonial buildings have been lovingly restored, giving the centre a rich and sophisticated air. Little wonder that Zacatecans are now pleading with the United Nations to have the town's colonial core declared a "World Heritage Zone", which would put them on a level with Guanajuato.

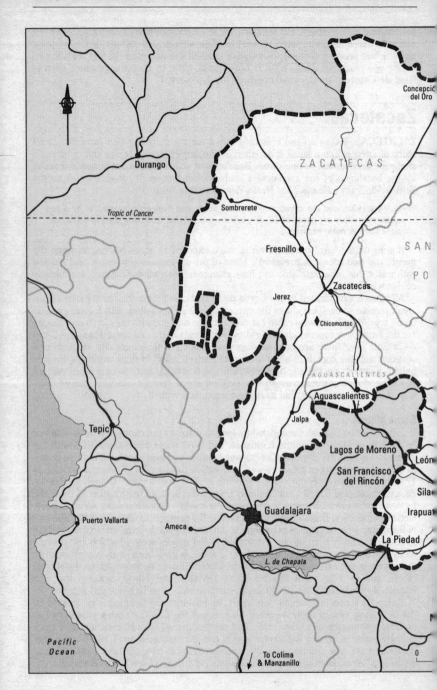

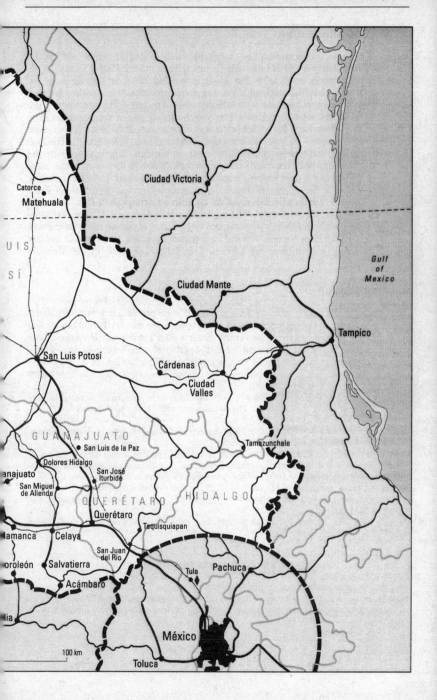

Arrival and information

Zacatecas' brand new **bus station** lies – inevitably – miles out of the centre, north of the ring road. Fortunately it's dead easy to get a bus (#8 and others; 15min) or taxi downtown. Arrive by **train** and you're just about in walking distance – straight up Av. Gonzales Ortega – but it's mostly uphill and again taking a bus or taxi makes life a lot easier. From the **airport** take one of the official *combis*. The Jardín Independencia is the hub of the **local bus** network, and wherever you're heading you're almost certain to be able to get there from here. It's probably the best place to get off the bus if you've come from the bus station too – in reasonable walking distance of most of the accommodation.

Barely marked, the **tourist office** hides away on Hidalgo 603, right opposite the cathedral (daily 8am–8pm; recorded information ☎492/2-66-83); they provide the usual bundle of leaflets and a useful street map. Plenty of **banks** along Hidalgo, including *Banamex* almost at the corner of Juárez, offer currency exchange (Mon–Fri 9am–noon), as does the *Divisa San Luis* **casa de cambio** on Arroyo de la Plata (Mon–Fri 9am–2pm & 4–7pm, Sat 9am–1pm). The **post office** is at Allende 111 (Mon–Fri 8am–7pm, Sat 9am–noon), and there's a convenient *larga distancia* **phone** office on the east side of the Jardín Independencia. Several local **travel agencies** offer tours of the city and to surrounding attractions: try *Cantera Travel* (☎492/2-90-65) in the Mercado Gonzales Ortega mall.

Accommodation

Once you're in the middle of town, finding a **hotel** is no problem unless you're determined to go for rock-bottom prices. The budget options are around the old bus station and on López Mateos, south of the centre, but few offer good value. If you've a little more money to spend, head straight for the superbly elegant establishments in the centre. Nights are cold in Zacatecas, so check you have enough blankets.

Colón, Lopez Velarde 508, at Mateos (☎492/2-89-25). Mid-sized modern hotel, comfortable if uninspiring and some way from the centre. ④.

Condesa, Juárez 5 (☎492/2-11-60). Old-style hotel with huge lobby in a fantastic central location amid the action of Jardín Independencia. The rooms, some with TV, don't live up to expectations, however. ⑤.

Gami, López Mateos 309 (☎492/2-80-05). Large modern establishment: clean, basic and comfortable, if a little noisy and inconveniently situated. ④.

Hostal del Angel, 1 de Mayo 211 (☎492/2-50-26). Hard to find, hidden among the colonial streets opposite the high side of the Mercado Gonzales Ortega mall, this friendly hotel in a simple, colonial building is very cosy and comfortable, offering rooms with TV and bath. ⑥.

Meson de Jobito, Jardín Juárez 143 (☎492/4-17-22). An entire colonial street has been converted into a superb luxury hotel, very pretty and very plush, all rooms a/c, some with jacuzzis. Bar, restaurant and just about everything else. ⑨.

Paraíso Radisson, Hidalgo 703 (☎492/2-61-83). In a palace opposite the Palacio de Gobierno they've installed a bland international hotel. Very comfortable, but a wasted opportunity. ⑧.

ACCOMMODATION PRICES

All the accommodation listed in this book has been categorized into one of nine price bands, as set out below. The prices quoted are in US dollars and normally refer to the cheapest available room for two people sharing in high season. For more details, see p.37.

① less than $8	④ $18–25	⑦ $50–75
② $8–12	⑤ $25–35	⑧ $75–100
③ $12–18	⑥ $35–50	⑨ more than $100

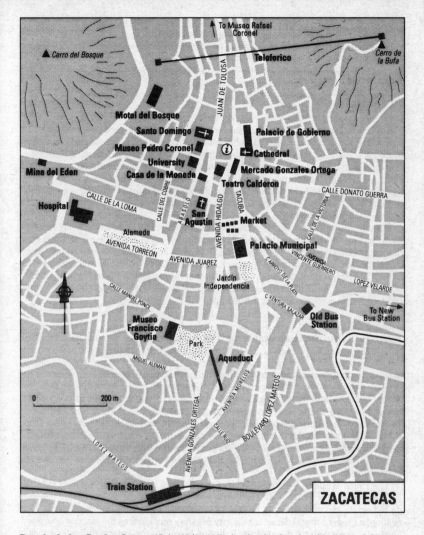

ZACATECAS

Posada de los Condes, Juárez 107 (☎492/2-14-12). Another lovely colonial building, right oppo-site the *Condesa*, but slightly better cared for. ⑤.

Posada de la Moneda, Hidalgo 413, opposite the Mercado Gonzales Ortega (☎492/2-08-81). Brilliant location for pleasant hotel popular with Mexican businesspeople. ⑥.

Posada Tolosa, Juan de Tolosa 811 (☎492/2-51-05). Uphill from the cathedral, beneath the wires of the cable car. Small, friendly hotel with comfortable modern interior behind a colonial front. ⑦.

Quinta Real, Rayón 434 (☎492/2-91-04). Outrageously luxurious hotel with all the comforts. Complex includes the town's ancient bullring and parts of the colonial aqueduct. ⑨.

Río Grande, Calzada de la Paz 513 (☎492/2-53-49). Best budget deal in town, but not easy to find – from old bus station cross López Mateos on the footbridge and walk up the narrow street behind *Refacciones Valdez*. Big, but friendly and clean; all rooms with bath and hot water. ②.

San Carlos, beside the new bus station (☎492/2-57-52). Comfortable, big and modern, but only a good option if you're passing through or leaving very early. ⑥.

Youth Hostel, Parque La Encantada (☎492/2-02-23). Basic, single sex dorms, 11pm curfew, no membership needed. On the #8 bus route. ①.

Zamora, Plaza Zamora, top of c/Ventura Salazar by Jardín Independencia (☎492/2-12-00). Central and cheap, but these are its only virtues. ②.

The Town

Though walking around Zacatecas can be tiring until you get used to the altitude, it's well worth the effort. This is a city of constant surprises, with narrow alleys crowding in on each other as they scramble about the steep-sided ravine, revealing a series of little plazas and glimpses of tiny hidden courtyards. In the beautifully preserved town centre the highlight is undoubtedly the ornate **Cathedral**, and all the other main sights are within walking distance of this. Probably the most rewarding way to enjoy the city is by aimless wandering, particularly in the cool of the evening, when the streets are filled to bursting.

Though the cathedral is the formal heart of the city, life for locals actually revolves more around the **Jardín Independencia**. Just a few paces from the market and from the important junction of Juárez and Hidalgo, this is in effect the city's main plaza, where people gather in the evenings, hang out between appointments and wait for buses. The **Alameda** is a popular spot for an evening *paseo*, the **Plaza Hidalgo** in front of the Palacio de Gobierno is where formal events take place, but the Jardín Independencia is where most of the action is.

Around the cathedral

Zacatecas' flamboyant **Cathedral** is the outstanding relic of the years of colonial glory: built in the pink stone typical of the region, it represents one of the latest, and arguably the finest, examples of Mexican Baroque architecture. It was completed in 1750, its facades stunningly rich and carved with a wild exuberance unequalled anywhere in the country. The interior, they say, was once at least its equal – furnished in gold and silver, with rich wall hangings and a great collection of paintings – but as everywhere, it was despoiled or the riches removed for "safekeeping", first at the time of Juárez's reforms and later during the Revolution; only the structure itself, with its bulky Doric columns and airy vaulting, remains to be admired. On each side of the cathedral there's a small plaza: to the north the formal Plaza Hidalgo, to the south a tiny paved *plazuela*, **Plaza Goytia**, which often hosts lively street theatre and impromptu musical performances.

The **Plaza Hidalgo** is surrounded by more colonial buildings. On the east side, the eighteenth-century **Palacio de Gobierno** was built as a home by the Conde Santiago de la Laguna and subsequently bought by the state government. In keeping with local fashion, a modern mural depicting the city's history embellishes the interior courtyard. Opposite, along with what is now the Radisson hotel, lies the Palacio de Justicia, locally known as the **Casa de la Mala Noche**. According to the legend its builder, Manuel de Rétegui, a mine-owner, was down to his last peso, which he gave away to a starving widow to feed her family. He then spent a long night of despair in the house (*la mala noche* – the bad night), contemplating bankruptcy and suicide, until at dawn his foreman came hammering on the door with the miraculous news that a huge vein of silver had been struck, and they were all rich.

On the other side of the cathedral, the **Mercado Gonzales Ortega** is a strikingly attractive market building, built at the end of the last century. It takes advantage of its sloping position to have two fronts: the upper level opening onto Hidalgo, the lower floor with entrances on Tacuba. Converted into a fancy shopping mall, it's now filled with tourist shops and smart boutiques, as well as some excellent cafes. On Hidalgo opposite the Mercado, the **Teatro Calderón** is a grandiose nineteenth-century theatre. Below the Mercado, head to the right down Tacuba and you'll come to the real **market**, amid a tangle of little alleys and semi-derelict dwellings in which you'll quickly get lost.

Santo Domingo and the Museo Pedro Coronel

Climbing up from the west side of Plaza Hidalgo towards the Cerro del Bosque are streets lined with more mansions – some restored, some badly in need of it, but all deserted now by the mining moguls who built them. The church of **Santo Domingo** stands raised on a platform above the plaza of the same name, just up from the Plaza Hidalgo – its hefty, buttressed bulk a stern contrast to the lightness of the cathedral, though it was built at much the same time. In the gloom of the interior you can just make out the gilded Churrigueresque retablos in the chapels.

Next door the **Museo Pedro Coronel** (Mon–Wed, Fri & Sat 10am–2pm & 4–7pm, Sun 10am–5pm; $4, free on Sun) occupies what was originally a Jesuit monastery attached to the church; they were known collectively as *La Compañía*, after the Company of Jesus. Pedro Coronel Rivera was a local artist, son of Rafael Coronel (see below) and a grandson of Diego Rivera, which perhaps explains how he managed to gather an art collection that reads like a Who's Who of modern art: there are works here by Picasso, Antonio Tapies, Giacometti, Kandinsky, Chagall, Braque, Jean Cocteau, Serge Poliakoff, Dalí, Eduardo Chillida and Miró, as well as sketches by Goya, architectural drawings by Piranesi, Hogarth engravings, and collections of West African and Oriental art, some pre-Columbian antiquities, and a few of Pedro's own works. It's undeniably an amazing collection – astonishing that one person could create it – but it's nothing like as good as the list of names makes it sound. With the exception maybe of a few of the Mirós, these are all very minor works, not particularly well lit or displayed; some of the peripheral collections are actually more interesting. The building itself was converted into a hospital, a barracks and a prison before its recent restoration, and one of the grimmer dungeons has also been preserved as an exhibit.

On the same street, in another converted mansion, is the main building of the Universidad Autonoma de Zacatecas, the **University Rectory** – a good place to check the noticeboards for details of local events. Below this, on c/de Hierro, is the **Casa de la Moneda** – Zacatecas' mint in the days when every silver-producing town in Mexico struck its own coins. There's a small exhibition inside of early coins and the history of the silver industry. Farther along you come to the church of **San Agustín** (Mon–Fri 10am–2pm & 4–5pm, Sat 10am–2pm), an early eighteenth-century temple which, after the Reform Laws, was converted into a casino, while the adjoining monastery became a hotel. They've been restoring it for nearly twenty years now, but it's still not complete, with chunks of statuary and refurbished slabs of frieze scattered around on the floor waiting, rather mournfully, to be put back up. It must have been very beautiful once, and there's still a very un-Mexican simplicity and charm to the place, and a magnificent relief telling the story of St Augustine. A series of before-and-after photographs in the nave explain the work in hand.

Museo Rafael Coronel

Pedro Coronel may have amassed a spectacular art collection, but his father Rafael has a far more beautiful museum, the centrepiece of which is a huge collection of traditional masks, possibly the finest in Mexico. The wonderful **Museo Rafael Coronel** (Mon, Tues & Thurs–Sat 10am–2pm & 4–7pm, Sun 10am–5pm; $3, free on Sun) occupies the **ex-Convento de San Francisco** on the north side of town. Founded in 1593 as a Franciscan mission (the facade is said to be the oldest in the city), it was rebuilt in the seventeenth century and started to deteriorate after the Franciscans were expelled in 1857, damage completed by bombardment during Villa's assault: the building and gardens have now been partially but beautifully restored, and the museum brilliantly integrated with the ruins. There are over 3000 masks on show, with another 2000 in storage. They trace the development of Mexican masks, from some very ancient, pre-Columbian examples to others that are brand new: often there are twenty or more variations on the same theme, and one little room is entirely full of Moors and Christians from the *Danza de los Moros y Cristianos*. As well as the masks, you can see Coronel's collections of ceramics and puppets, and sketches and drawings connected with his wife Ruth Rivera, architect and daughter of Diego Rivera. If you don't fancy the walk to or from town, several bus routes, including #5, #8 and #9, pass close by.

The aqueduct and Museo Francisco Goytia

In quite the other direction you can follow the line of the **aqueduct** that used to carry water to the south of the city. Not much of it remains, but what there is can be inspected at closer quarters from the little **park** on Gonzales Ortega – the continuation of Hidalgo up the hill from the centre. At the back of the park, in what was once the governor's residence, stands a third local artist's museum, the **Museo Francisco Goytia** (Tues–Sun 10am–1.30pm & 5–7.30pm; $4, free on Sun). Goytia was one of Mexico's leading painters early in this century, and this enjoyable little museum houses a permanent exhibition of his work and that of more modern local artists (including Pedro Coronel), as well as temporary displays and travelling art shows.

Mina El Edén

The **Mina El Edén** (daily noon–7.30pm; $4) is perhaps the most fascinating and unusual of all Zacatecas' attractions. The entrance to this old mine is right in the city, up a path behind the modern hospital, from where a small train takes you to the beginning of the sixteenth-century shafts in the heart of the Cerro del Bosque, some 300m below the summit. The guided tour – which takes in only a fraction of the workings – is extraordinary, and some of the statistics terrifying; if the guide is to be believed, fatalities among the workers ran to eight every day at the height of production. It seems perfectly possible when you're down there – level upon level of old galleries fall away for some 1500m beneath you, inaccessible since the mine flooded. When it operated, the miners' only access was via precarious wooden ladders or ropes, carrying their tools down with them, and their product back out. Inside now are an artificial waterfall, subterranean pools, chasms crossed on rickety wooden bridges and, of course, a ghost. Also, where the train stops, you'll find a **disco** (see "Nightlife", below) and a shop where they sell rocks from the mine. The entire hill is honeycombed with tunnels, and in one of them a lift has been installed that takes you up to the slopes of the Cerro del Bosque, about 200m from the lower station of the cable car (you can also enter the mine from this end, though you may have a longer wait for a guide: not all the guides speak English so, wherever you enter, you may have to wait a while for an English-speaking tour). It's a remarkable round trip from the depths of the mine to the top of La Bufa.

To reach the mine, take a bus from the Jardín Independencia up Juárez to the hospital (buses marked "IMSS"), or walk, taking in a pleasant stroll along the **Alameda** and a brief climb.

The cable car

The lower station of the **cable car** (daily 12.30–6pm; $3 return; services can be disrupted by strong winds) is on the slopes of the Cerro del Bosque, beside the *Motel del Bosque* and near the back entrance to El Edén. Once you're used to the altitude, it's an easy climb up from San Agustín, or bus #7 will bring you right to the door. Most people take a return trip up to the top of the Cerro de la Bufa, but walking back down is no great strain. The views down on the houses as you pass right over the city centre are extraordinary.

At the summit of the Cerro de la Bufa, after you've taken in the superb panorama of Zacatecas and its surroundings, visit the little **Capilla del Patrocinio**, an eighteenth-century chapel with an image of the Virgin said to perform healing miracles, and stroll around the observatory, on the very edge of the crags. Also up here, the **Museo de la Toma de Zacatecas** (Tues–Sun 10am–4.30pm; $2, free Sun), full of Revolutionary arms and memorabilia, honours Pancho Villa's spectacular victory in the town.

Behind, in the shadow of that great crest of rock, the **Mausoleo de los Hombres Illustres** is where *Zacatecanos* who have made their mark on history are buried, or at least have their memorials. There are still a few empty places, and it would be a magnificent place to end up – as close to heaven as you could wish, with great views while you're waiting.

Eating, drinking and entertainment

Zacatecas always seems busy, especially in the evenings, and it has a flourishing little **cafe** society, centred on Hidalgo around the Mercado Gonzales Ortega: as well as *La Terraza* and the *Cafe Acropolis* (see below), check out the *Cafe Zas* (Hidalgo 201, where local youth hangs out) and others like the *Cafe Anis* and *Imperio* in the shopping centres. There are also plenty of **restaurants** around central Zacatecas – just about all the hotels have one, for example – or for inexpensive *tacos*, *tostadas* and sandwiches, head back down towards the old bus station: Ventura Salazar is lined with places serving quick snacks. While in Zacatecas, you should sample *tunas*, the succulent green or purple fruit of the prickly pear cactus. In season they're sold everywhere, ready peeled, by the bucket-load, or if you go out into the country you can pick your own (but see the warning on p.210).

Nightlife, especially at weekends during student term-time, is livelier than you might expect. The club inside the mine, open Thursday, Friday and Saturday nights only, with a steep cover charge, certainly has a claim to be unique; *El Elefante Blanco*, by the lower cable car station, is its big rival, with great views over town and similar prices and hours. A couple of **bars** downtown offer quieter alternatives: the *Nueva España*, on the stepped alley down by the side of the Mercado Gonzales Ortega, has a pleasant, pub-like atmosphere; *Paraíso*, opposite in the Mercado building, is much glossier.

Zacatecas has one important **fiesta** at the end of August, which you should definitely try to get to if you're around. The highlight is the battle between Moors and Christians (an import from Spain, where these stylized struggles are common) on the Cerro de la Bufa. August 27 is the main day, but festivities spill over several days before and after, with **bullfights** – the fiercest fighting bulls in all Mexico are bred around Zacatecas – and plenty of traditional carousing.

Restaurants

Acropolis, beside the cathedral in the corner of the Mercado Gonzales Ortega. Very popular cafe serving excellent breakfasts, ice cream, fruit juices and main meals. Daily 8.30am–10pm.

Boca del Rio, Arroyo de la Plata. Popular local seafood restaurant, dishing up bucketfuls of prawns, octopus and fried fish at bargain prices.

Cafe La Terraza, Mercado Gonzales Ortega. Overlooking Tacuba, with great views of the passing action, this is a favourite spot for watching the world go by while drinking beer, supping on a milk shake or snacking on sandwiches, ice cream and *licuados*.

El Jacalito, Juárez 109, under the *Posada de los Condes*. Like the hotel, comforting but bland; standard dishes, club sandwiches.

La Cantera, Tacuba, beneath the Mercado Gonzales Ortega. Touristy "fonda musical"; friendly and lively, serving up good traditional food, local wine and live music.

Meson de la Mina, Juárez 108, by *Hotel Condesa*. Good-value, uncomplicated place, with cafe section at the front, fancier restaurant behind.

Quinta Real, Rayón 434, in the hotel. Pick of the bunch, if only for the setting, if you want an expensive, formal meal.

Restaurante La Bodequilla, Callejon de San Agustín. Small, sophisticated, Spanish-style bar with a smartish, student atmosphere.

Restaurante Calafia, Dr Ignacio Hierro. Intimate fish restaurant with a traditional, reasonably priced Mexican menu.

Restaurante Los Comales, Hidalgo, by the tourist office. Standard local restaurant, unexciting but central.

Restaurante El Tragadero, Juárez 132, by the Alameda. Inexpensive traditional Mexican restaurant.

Taqueria La Cabaña, Jardín Independencia. Always alive with activity, this is one of the town's cheapest and most popular *taco* restaurants. Good basic food, beer and bargain prices.

Viva Pizza, bottom end of the Alameda. Moderately priced US-style pizza.

MOVING ON FROM ZACATECAS

Situated at one of northern Mexico's crucial crossroads, the Zacatecas **bus terminal** is a hive of constant activity day and night. There are very regular long-distance bus services to all parts of **northern Mexico**, with hourly buses to Durango and Chihuahua, some of which push on through to the border at **Ciudad Juárez**. There are also direct buses running to Torreón and Monterrey hourly and twice daily to Mazatlán (you could also catch the first to Durango and a connection from there). Heading **south**, the highway to **México** splits, with hourly buses along either route – the faster, western route runs via Aguascalientes and Léon, while the eastern route runs via San Luis Potosí – the two roads meet again at Querétaro. There are also hourly buses to Guadalajara. To **get to the bus terminal**, take one of the buses marked "Camionera" (#8 and others), which run regularly from the Jardín Independencia.

An overnight **train** service runs to México and there are two daily trains to Chihuahua. You could also **fly** to México on a daily service: the local airport has regular connections to Tijuana and Morelia too, as well as international services to Chicago and Los Angeles.

Around Zacatecas: Guadalupe and Chicomoztoc

It's well worth the trip out to Guadalupe – virtually a suburb of Zacatecas, and within easy striking distance – to see the **Convento de Guadalupe**, a rich, sumptuously decorated monastery, rare in that it has survived the centuries virtually unscathed, and for that reason one of the most important in Mexico. Farther out (you may need a whole day), the ruins of **Chicomoztoc**, a great fortress town in the desert, are in contrast quite unadorned, but nonetheless enormously impressive. If doing it yourself sounds like too much trouble, several travel agents in Zacatecas offer tours to the sites below among others (see p.202).

Guadalupe

Buses run out to **GUADALUPE**, 10km southeast of Zacatecas centre, every few minutes from the corner of López Mateos and Salazar, outside the old bus station. Once there, you can't miss the enormous bulk of the church, with its dome and asymmetric twin towers. You enter through a flagged, tree-studded courtyard; the church doors are straight ahead in the elaborate Baroque facade, while the entrance to the **museum and monastery** (Tues–Sun 9am–1pm & 3–5pm; $4, free on Sun) is to the right. The monastery, founded in 1707 to prepare monks for the difficult task of spreading the faith in northern Mexico, is a vast and confusing warren of a place, with seemingly endless rows of cells opening off courtyards, stairways leading nowhere and mile-long corridors lined with portraits of monks. There are guided tours but it's more enjoyable to wander alone, studying the paintings – which cover every wall – at leisure, possibly tagging on to a group for a few minutes when your paths cross. Locked doors are everywhere, and joining a group helps you get through them, but in theory guards with keys will admit you individually to study the riches of the library or the various chapels. One such locked door admits you from the body of the monastery into the **Coro Alto**, the raised choir at the back of the church, with its beautifully carved and painted wooden choir stalls. Above all, don't miss the **Capilla de Napoles**, whose Neoclassical domed roof is coated in elaborately filigreed gold leaf. Presumably, 150 years ago such sights were not altogether unusual in Mexican churches – today it's the richest you'll see anywhere. If you can't get into the chapel (officially it's only opened on special occasions) you can still look in from the *Coro Alto*.

Next door to the monastery, the **Regional History Museum** (Tues–Sun 10am–4.30pm; free) houses a collection of Indian art and a marginally interesting selection of antique cars and train carriages.

Chicomoztoc

The **ruins of CHICOMOZTOC** (Tues–Sat 9am–5pm; $5, free on Sun), also known, confusingly, as **La Quemada**, lie some 50km south from Zacatecas on the road to Villanueva and Guadalajara. The scale of the complex isn't apparent until you're within it – from the road you can vaguely see signs of construction, but the whole thing, even the one huge restored pyramid, blends so totally into the mountain against which it is built as to be almost invisible. No two archeologists seem able to agree on the nature of the site – its functions or inhabitants – even to the extent that many doubt that it was a fortress, though that much does seem clear from its superb natural defensive position and hefty surrounding walls. Most likely it was a frontier post on the outskirts of some pre-Aztec sphere of domination – probably the Toltecs – charged with keeping at bay the southward depredations of the Chichimeca. Or it could simply be the work of a particularly harsh local ruling class, exacting enough tribute to build themselves these palaces, and needing the defences to keep their own subjects out. Huichol legends seem to support the second theory: there was an evil priest, the story runs, who lived on a rock surrounded by walls and covered with buildings, with eagles and jaguars under his command to oppress the population. The people appealed to their gods, who destroyed the priest and his followers with great heat, warning the people not to go near the rock again. Chicomoztoc was in fact destroyed by fire around 1300 AD and was never reoccupied; even today the Huichols, in their annual pilgrimage from the Sierra Madre in the west to collect peyote around Real de Catorce to the east, take a long detour around this area.

Then again, there are those who say that this is the spot from which the Aztecs set out on their long trek south to the Valley of Mexico and the foundation of Tenochtitlán. Whatever the truth, you'll be in a better position to judge if you've seen it for yourself; in addition to the reconstructed temple, there's a large hall with eleven pillars still standing, a ball-court, the walls, an extensive (but barely visible) system of roads heading out into the valley and many lesser, ruinous structures.

Getting to and from the ruins

It can be a major hassle **getting to Chicomoztoc** from Zacatecas: buses to Guadalajara ("via Corta") pass the turn-off for the site, but don't stop, and even the second-class operators are extremely reluctant to sell you a ticket. If you run into this problem, get a ticket on a second-class bus to **La Quemada** (the nearest village, about an hour's walk from the site) or **Villanueva**, and persuade the driver to let you off at the ruins. You'll then be faced with a twenty-minute walk up a side road to the entrance – a lonely and rather wild place, with the odd rabbit darting across the road at your approach. *Tuna* cacti grow all along here, and it's tempting to pick their fruit to quench your thirst – be warned, though, that the fruits are covered in tiny prickles which take hours to get out of your skin; they're best picked with a pair of heavy gloves and a sharp knife. The site caretaker sells cold drinks from his hut by the entrance.

Getting back from the site is as difficult as the approach, perhaps harder since it's entirely up to any one bus driver whether he ignores you as you try to flag him down, and hitching seems to be totally ineffective. The best bet is to hail all the buses going in either direction – for some reason it's far easier to get to Villanueva and then get on another bus back to Zacatecas. Villanueva's not a bad place to kill a few hours anyway, with several bars and cafes around the old plaza where the buses stop; here too you can change for a fast service **on to Guadalajara**. You *will* get back eventually, even if you have to wait until after dark for the bus that brings local children back from school and stops everywhere.

Aguascalientes

The lively industrial town of **AGUASCALIENTES**, 100km south of Zacatecas, is an important and booming provincial capital. In among the new buildings there are some fine surviving colonial monuments, as well as a couple of excellent **museums** which, while they don't put the city in the top league as a tourist draw, do make it a good place to stop over for a day or two: especially when you take into account its reputation for some of the finest **fiestas** in Mexico – rarely a week goes by without celebration, or at least a band playing in one of the plazas at the weekend – and for the manufacture of excellent wines and brandy.

Arrival, orientation and information

Both the **train station** and the **Central Camionera** are some way from the centre on the city's ring road (Av. Circunvalación): from both there's a frequent bus service into the Plaza de Armas, at the centre of town. Here, and on the adjoining Plaza de la Republica – known jointly as the **Plaza de la Patría** – are all the important public buildings, the cathedral, a handful of banks and government offices, the fancier hotels, and some good restaurants. The **tourist office** is also in the plaza, on the ground floor of the Palacio de Gobierno (Mon–Fri 8am–3pm & 5–8pm, Sat 10am–1pm; ☎491/12-35-11); if they've run out of maps, *Turisste*, at the corner of Nieto and the plaza, sell an excellent one. For long-distance **phones** and **exchange** there's no need to leave the square: you'll see several *larga distancia* signs, while *Banamex*, corner of 5 de Mayo, and *Bancomer*, on Guadalupe Victoria, are both on the north side of the plaza.

Many of the streets around the central plaza are pedestrianized, and most things you'll want to see are in easy walking distance. **North of the plaza**, Juárez and 5 de Mayo run to the market, with Morelos parallel to them to the east. **East** of the plaza the major shopping and commercial thoroughfare of Madero heads towards the train station. **West**, Venustiano Carranza runs past the side of the cathedral and the Casa de le Cultura to the Jardín San Marcos, while to the **south**, José María Chavez runs a couple of blocks to López Mateos, a major through route.

Accommodation

There's little in the way of budget accommodation in Aguascalientes: rooms in the **market area** are cheapest (those listed opposite are a couple of blocks north of the market, six or seven blocks from the centre), while some of the hotels on and around the **Plaza de la Patría** offer real luxury. The **youth hostel**, in a sports complex at Av. de la Convención and Jaime Nuño, Colonia Héroes (☎491/18-08-63; $8), has single-sex dorms and an 11pm curfew. To get there, take bus #20 from outside the bus station.

Colonial, 5 de Mayo 552 (☎491/15-35-77). Comfortable hotel with parking lot. All rooms with TV and phone. ④.

Don Jesús, Juárez 429 (☎491/15-55-98). Basic, big and bare, very near the market, but OK for the price. ③.

Francia, Plaza Principal (☎491/15-60-80). Superb fin-de-siècle-style building: stately and sophisticated with rooms on two floors off a huge well of a lobby with a magnificent chequered floor. Bar, cafe and restaurant. ⑦.

Gomez, Av. Circunvalación and Brasil 602 (☎491/78-21-20). Beside the bus station: not bad if you arrive late or plan to push on early. ④.

Imperial, Plaza Principal (☎491/15-16-50). Very faded elegance, but the best value on the plaza in a fine colonial building. ④.

Río Grande, Plaza Principal (☎491/16-16-66). Modern luxury hotel, offering a little more comfort than the *Francia* but infinitely less style. ⑥.

Roble, 5 de Mayo 540 (☎491/15-39-94). Big, clean and relaxed, with plenty of parking space. ④.

San José, Hidalgo 207, three blocks east from the plaza (☎491/15-14-31). Rooms with fan, TV and bathroom; a little noisy but perfectly comfortable. ④.

Señorial, Colón 104, just of the Plaza Principal (☎491/15-16-30). Simple rooms, but decent value for the location. ④.

The City

The entire centre of Aguascalientes is undermined by a series of tunnels and catacombs carved out by some unknown tribe; unfortunately these are all closed to the public, so the most ancient things you'll actually see here are the colonial buildings around the centre. If you want to visit one of the **hot springs** from which the city takes its name, head for the *Balneario Ojocaliente*, which has a series of pools and bathing chambers, just outside town on the road to San Luis Potosí. To get there, take a blue ("Ruta Madero") bus from the centre.

Around the Plaza de la Patría

The **Plaza de la Patría** is the place to start any exploration of Aguascalientes. In the centre of this enormous area is the **Exedra**, an amphitheatre-shaped space for performances, overlooked by a column topped with a Mexican eagle. Chief of the buildings around it is the **Palacio de Gobierno**, a remarkably beautiful Neoclassical building, built in reddish volcanic rock around an arcaded courtyard with a grand central staircase, and decorated with marvellous murals by the Chilean Oswaldo Barra Cunningham, who learnt his trade from the greatest muralist of them all, Diego Rivera. The first of these, at the back of the ground floor, were painted in 1962, and others span the years from then to now: the most recent are at the front of the building – and there's plenty of room for more.

Next door, the modern **Palacio Municipal** is bland in comparison, while down the other side of the plaza, the eighteenth-century **cathedral** has recently been refurbished to reveal its full glory, in an over-the-top welter of gold, polished marble and gilt. The **Pinacoteca Religiosa**, in an annexe, has a collection of eighteenth-century religious paintings which are well worth a look.

Venustiano Carranza leads down beside the cathedral to the **Casa de la Cultura** (Mon–Fri 7am–2pm & 5–9pm, Sat 9am–2pm; free), a beautiful old mansion given over to music and dance classes and the occasional exhibition. The noticeboard is an excellent place to find out what's on around town, and in the patio there's a small cafe – a tranquil spot to have a drink and a rest or catch up on writing postcards. A little farther down Carranza, on the opposite side, the **Museo Regional de Historia** (Tues–Sun

9am–2pm & 4–8.30pm; $2.50, free on Sun) covers local history from a fossilized mammoth tusk to the Revolution. Among the more interesting exhibits are a display of traditional crafts and a reconstructed *Tienda de Raya*, the company store through which peons became increasingly indebted to their employers, complete with the book recording the generations of debts. Farther west on Carranza, the **Jardín San Marcos** is a long enclosed park, with shady places to sit and rest, flanked by the **Templo del Carmen** to one side and the modern **Casino de la Feria** with its giant *palenque* (where cock fights are staged) just beyond. This is the site of the city's famous fiestas (see opposite). The new **Paseo de la Feria** cuts through to López Mateos, the modern buildings in complete contrast to what went before. Few maps yet show accurate detail of this area, much of which is pedestrianized with the main roads passing underneath in tunnels, but it's worth taking a walk around this way just to see what wealthy modern Mexico can look like: there are numerous upmarket restaurants and clubs, the *Hotel Fiesta Americana*, *Canal 6* TV headquarters, and the *Expo Plaza* by the bullring, with plenty of greenery and post-modern neo-colonial architecture.

Two museums

Though it only occupies a couple of rooms of a small building some way from the centre, the **Museo José Guadalupe Posada** (Tues–Sun 10am–2pm & 4–8pm; free) is one of the main reasons to visit Aguascalientes, almost a place of pilgrimage for his fans. Two rooms, plus another for temporary exhibitions, contain scores of prints, along with the original plates, contemporary photos and biographical information, mainly in Spanish; there is also work by Manuel Manilla, a predecessor of Posada. Many of the prints are for sale. The museum occupies the former priest's house of the

---

POSADA – THE MOST MEXICAN ARTIST

José Guadalupe Posada was perhaps the most Mexican of all artists, his often macabre work familiar even when his name is not: Diego Rivera was not far wrong when he described Posada as "so outstanding that one day even his name will be forgotten". He was born in Aguascalientes in 1852, a baker's son later apprenticed to a lithographer. In 1888

he moved to the capital (having meanwhile lived in León for some time), and started to create in earnest the thousands of prints for which he soon became known. He worked, mainly, for the editor and printer Vanegas Arroyo, and his work appeared on posters but mostly in the satirical broadsheets that flourished despite – or more likely because of – the censorship of the Porfiriano era. Some of his work was political, attacking corrupt politicians, complacent clergy or foreign intervention, but much was simply recording the news, especially the disasters that obsess the Mexican press to this day, or lampooning popular figures, or observing everyday life, with a gleefully macabre eye. Later the events and figures of the Revolution, grotesquely caricatured, came to dominate his work. Although the *calaveras*, the often elegantly clad skeletons that people much of his work, are best known, they are by no means all he did: the museum covers the full range of his work. All of it has a peculiar mix of Catholicism, pre-Columbian tradition, preoccupation with death and black humour that could only be Mexican, and that profoundly affected all later Mexican art. Rivera and Orozco are just two of the greats who publicly acknowl-

edged their debt to Posada. Technically, Posada soon moved on from lithography to engraving in type metal (producing the characteristic hatched effect seen in much of his work) and finally to zinc etching, an extremely rapid method involving drawing directly onto a zinc printing plate with acid-resistant ink, and then dipping it until the untouched areas corroded.

Templo del Señor del Encino, an elegant colonial church of pinkish stone with a pretty tiled dome; inside is the much venerated and miraculous "black Christ" of Encino. To get there, head east from the plaza and take the first right, Díaz de León, south for about seven blocks. In front of the church and museum there's a pleasant, quiet square, at the heart of a peaceful old neighbourhood.

The **Museo de Aguascalientes** (Tues–Sun 10am–2pm & 4.30–7.30pm; $2) lies in the opposite direction, east from the plaza then north on Zaragoza. Its art collection, mostly modern, is none too exciting, though there are lots of works by Saturnino Hernán, a local boy who was a contemporary and friend of Diego Rivera's but who died young and never really achieved much recognition. Opposite the museum, the over the top **Templo de San Antonio**, built around the turn of the century, has a muddled facade with some vaguely discernible Neoclassical elements. Inside, murals provide a blaze of colour.

Eating, drinking and entertainment

Ordinary **restaurants** seem surprisingly thin on the ground in Aguascalientes, though all the large hotels on the plaza have their own: the *Francia* is worth a look for the ambience alone. In addition, plenty of simple places along Juárez serve good, tasty barbecued chicken, and there are *taco* and seafood places in the **market** itself, between Juárez and 5 de Mayo at Alvaro Obregón: the smaller **Mercado de Artesanías**, on Obregón off Juárez, doesn't have much in the way of decent crafts but it does have more eating places without the crush and smell of the market itself. Fancier places to eat line López Mateos, especially just west of the centre towards the Paseo de la Feria. While you're here you should try some of the local **wine** (not always easy except in the more expensive restaurants) or at least the brandy: *San Marco* is the best known, made here and sold all over the republic. The **Patio Domecq** where, supposedly, you can taste local wines and watch some of the processes involved in making them is on López Mateos near the Paseo de la Feria. Opening days – not to mention hours – appear to be utterly random, however.

The most important **fiesta** in the city – famous throughout Mexico – is the ancient **Feria de San Marcos**, celebrated in the Jardín San Marcos during the last couple of weeks of April and the beginning of May. The *Feria de la Uva* in mid-August, celebrating the grape harvest, is almost as popular, with a giant procession (the *Romería de la Asuncion*) on the 15th.

Restaurants

Café La Parroquia, Hidalgo 222. Cool student cafe offering a good selection of Mexican and international food, sandwiches and burgers, along with the obligatory cappuccino.

Jugos Acapulco, Allende 106 between 5 de Mayo and Juárez. Juice bar that also serves *hamburguesas* and meals: good for breakfast.

La Cava del Gaucho, Paseo de la Feria (aka Arturo Pani), near Nieto. One of many fancier restaurants along here, this one Argentine-style, open till 2am with live music.

Kiko's Merendero, Paseo de la Feria at Jardín San Marcos. More bar than restaurant, but food is on offer to soak up the drinks.

Loncheria Max, Madero 331. *Taco* place serving hot food and snacks. Buzzing all night.

Restaurante Mitla, Madero 218. Very popular old-fashioned Mexican restaurant, with white-jacketed waiters serving a good selection of national and local dishes, including seafood and very reasonable *comidas corridas*. Less expensive than it looks.

Pizza Roma, 5 de Mayo next to *Hotel Imperial*. Pizzas and pasta at reasonable prices; fast-food atmosphere.

Restaurante Vegetariano, Ramón López 212. Small, inexpensive place serving tasty wholefood.

Tortas Estilo México, Colón at Plaza de la Patria. Cafeteria/*fuente de soda* with good coffee, *pan dulce* and snacks, plus long-distance phones.

MOVING ON FROM AGUASCALIENTES

Aguascalientes is situated on the main highway between Zacatecas and León and there are hourly **buses** in either direction, many continuing as far as Chihuahua to the north and México to the south (via Irapuato and Querétaro). There are also slower services to Guadalajara and San Luis Potosí. For Guanajuato, you may have to take a bus to León first and a connection from there. To get **to the bus station from the centre**, catch a bus marked "Camionera" from beside the cathedral in Venustiano Carranza .

Aguascalientes is also on the main **train line** between México and Ciudad Juárez. Northbound first-class trains leave Aguascalientes at 6.50am, southbound at 10.30pm. For the hardy there is also a second-class service heading north at 9pm and south at 8am. Buses #19 and #31 run along Madero to the station.

Matehuala and Real de Catorce

Between Saltillo and San Luis Potosí, **Matehuala**, around 260km from Saltillo, 200km before San Luis, is the only place of any size. As such it's an almost inevitable stop, to refuel, rest up and get some food before continuing the journey. Though pleasant enough, with several small hotels and reasonable restaurants, it would be no more than a staging post were it not for the proximity of the ancient and now all but deserted mining town of **Real de Catorce**.

Matehuala

A typically bustling, commercial northern town, **MATEHUALA** is not a place you're likely to be tempted to stay more than one night. The **bus station** is just off the highway on 5 de Mayo, a little over a kilometre south of the centre: if you don't have much luggage it's an easy enough walk, straight up 5 de Mayo and then left on Insurgentes when you reach the centre – you can't miss the grey concrete bulk of the barrel-shaped church on the main plaza (or carry on until you cross Guerrero for Catorce buses). There are also "centro" buses, *peseros* and taxis available most of the time. Though it's far better to stay up the mountain in Catorce, if you have to spend **the night** here, head for the basic *Hotel Matehuala* (☎488/2-06-80; ③), at Bustamante and Hidalgo, a block north of the plaza. Popular with travellers, it's also reasonably handy for the terminus for buses to Catorce. The *Hotel Alamo*, Guerrero 116 (☎488/2-00-14; ③), is even more convenient for this, and slightly cheaper, but considerably less pleasant. Fancier accommodation is almost all out on the highway, where there are several motels like *El Pedregal* (☎488/2-00-54; ⑤). Local **restaurants** include the *Fontinella*, close to the *Matehuala* at Morelos 618, and the *Santa Fe*, Morelos 709 on the plaza. Food at the main bus station is also surprisingly good.

Buses to Catorce, from the local bus station in the centre of town on Guerrero at Méndez, are somewhat irregular, but in theory run every two hours from 6am to 6pm, taking a couple of hours to cover the steep 50km.

Real de Catorce

REAL DE CATORCE (or *Villa Real de Nuestra Señora de la Concepción de Guadalupe de los Alamos de los Catorce*, to give it its full title) is a quite extraordinary place. From a population of some 40,000 at the peak of its silver production (the hills around were reckoned to be the second richest source of precious metals in Mexico, after Guanajuato) it declined to virtually zero by the middle of this century. A few hundred inhabitants hang on now, some prospecting for silver and hoping that the old veins can be reopened, others in the hope that tourism offers a brighter prospect. Meanwhile the town crumbles around them, the inhabited enclave at the centre surrounded by derelict roofless mansions and, as you go farther out, by houses of which only the foundations and an odd segment of wall remain. The mountains around, probably even before they were known to contain silver, have been a rich source of **peyote**. Even now groups of Huichol Indians make the long annual pilgrimage from their homelands in and around northeastern Nayarit to gather the precious hallucinogenic cactus, regarded by them as essential food for the soul, just as corn is essential for the body. This journey, on foot, can take up to a month. Peyote also attracts a number of New Age tourists to Catorce, and some of them live here semi-permanently.

The town is built in a high canyon which you approach, on the road, through a tunnel 2.3km long. It's only broad enough for one vehicle at a time, with a passing place in the middle; as you drive through, the odd mine shaft leads off into the mountain to either side – by one there's a little shrine where a lone candle seems always to be burning. Once in the town, the austere, shuttered stone buildings blend with the bare rocky crags that enclose them – at 2800m the air is cool and clean, but you can't get away from the spirit of desolation that hangs over it all. There's not much to visit – the big Baroque church of **San Francisco**, the Museo Parroquial and the old Casa de la Moneda, where local silver was minted into coin. It's the church that attracts Mexicans to Catorce, or rather the miraculous figure of Saint Francis of Assisi (known as *Panchito*, Pancho being a diminutive of Francisco) which it houses. The walls are covered with handmade retablos giving thanks for cures or miraculous escapes effected by the saint. They are a wonderful form of naive folk art, the older ones painted on tin plate, newer examples on paper or card or even photographs, depicting the most amazing events – last-minute rescues from the paths of oncoming trains, lucky escapes from horrendous car crashes, miraculous avoidance of death or serious injury in more ways than it's comfortable to contemplate – and all signed and dated with thanks to *Panchito* for his timely intervention. October 4, the saint's day, sees thousands of pilgrims crammed into Catorce, and almost no chance of finding anywhere to stay.

The church's **Museo Parroquial** (Tues–Sun 10am–4pm; 50¢) has a small collection of old coins, rusting mine machinery, dusty documents – anything, in fact, that has been found lying among the ruins and looks interesting. Across the square, the **Casa de Moneda** (daily 10am–4pm; free) is a magnificent old mansion whose sloping site means that it has two storeys on one side, three on the other. There's a small exhibit on the history of Catorce upstairs. Having seen these, and maybe checked out the lovely old **Palenque de Gallos** (cockpit) and the ruinous Plaza de Toros, there's nothing to do but wander around, kick up the dust, and climb up into the hills to enjoy the mountain air and look down over the relics.

Practicalities

There are two excellent **hotels** in Real de Catorce, wonderful if you can afford them. Budget accommodation, on the other hand, is mostly very basic: the easiest way to find it is simply to walk up the single main street looking for signs, as the *casas de huéspedes* along here tend to come and go – lots of extra rooms are available in private houses for pilgrims around October 4, for example. *La Providencia* (④) seems permanent, if not very good value. The *Hotel El Real* (⑤), Morelos 20 behind the Casa de Moneda, is the most attractive option, a tastefully converted old house with clean rooms and Indian decorations; the modern *Quinta la Puesta del Sol* (⑤), on Zaragoza a little way above the town, beyond the Palenque de Gallos on the way to the Plaza de Toros and cemetery, offers less atmosphere. It does, however, have satellite TV and great views. All three of these places serve **food**; again *El Real*, with an Italian flavour, is the pick of the bunch and the most expensive. There's just one **phone** in town: if you want to attempt to book any of these places call ☎488/2-37-33.

San Luis Potosí

Situated to the north of the fertile heartland, the sprawling industrial centre of **SAN LUIS POTOSÍ** owes its existence and architectural splendour to a wealth of mineral deposits. Though it can by no means equal the beauty of Zacatecas or Guanajuato, it does have a fine colonial centre and makes a good stop-off if you're heading south from Monterrey towards the Bajío proper.

San Luis was founded as a Franciscan mission in 1592, but it wasn't long before the Spanish discovered rich deposits of gold and silver in the country roundabout and began to develop the area in earnest. They added the name Potosí (after the fabulously rich mines in Bolivia) in the expectation of rivalling the original, but though this was a thoroughly wealthy colonial town, that hope was never fully realized. Unlike its erst-while rivals, however, San Luis still is prosperous – most of the silver may have gone but working mines churn out zinc and lead – with a considerable modern industrial base. As a result, San Luis, while preserving a little-changed colonial heart, is also a large and lively modern city.

Arrival and information

San Luis has two new **bus stations**, linked to each other by a shuttle, on the city's east-ern edge near Hwy-57. Buses to the Alameda, the downtown hub of the local transport network, run from outside the main, second-class terminal on Diagonal Sur – you can buy tickets for all buses from here – while the brand-new first-class terminal lies a couple of blocks to the west. The **train station** is more central, on the north side of the Alameda, within easy walking distance of the centre and most of the accommodation. For maps and general information, head for the **tourist office** (Mon–Fri 8am–8pm, Sat 8am–3pm; ☎481/12-99-06), Venustiano Carranza 325, by the *Hotel Panorama*, just to the west of the Plaza Fundadores.

There are **banks** all around the main plazas, including *Banamex* and the *Banco del Atlántico* at Allende and Obregón, and several *casas de cambio* in the same area – try *La Imperial* at Obregón 407. The **post office** is a little way north of the centre at Morelos and Gonzales Ortega. *Larga distancia* **telephones** are easy to find: among many others there are *Computel* offices in the bus station, at Universidad 700 on the Alameda, and at Carranza 360 opposite the *Hotel Panorama*. The newsstands on Los Bravo, just off the Jardín Hidalgo, often have English-language **newspapers** and magazines.

Accommodation

The cheapest **rooms** are to be found in the run-down area near the bus stations. Unless you're desperately short of cash, though, head for the centre of town – the best places are around the **Alameda**, where there are some very cheap options in the streets beside the station, and near the **Jardín Hidalgo**. There's also a **youth hostel** near the second-class bus terminal at Diagonal Sur (☎481/18-16-17; $8), with single-sex dorms, hot showers and an 11pm curfew: to get there walk left (north) along the main road outside the bus station entrance, and head for the sports grounds.

Alameda, La Perla 3 (☎481/18-65-58). Very basic and rather noisy, but clean, safe and inexpensive. Behind the *Pemex* station on the north side of the Alameda. ②.

Anahuac, Xochitl 140 at Los Bravo (%481/18-65-58). More comfort than most in the station area. ③.

Arizona, Guadalupe Torres 158 (☎481/18-18-48). Modern hotel opposite the second-class bus station; rooms with TV, carpet and comfort: pity about the neighbourhood. ⑤.

Concordia, Morelos 705 at Othon (☎481/12-06-66). Comfortable, old-fashioned business hotel. Parking, and rooms with TV. ⑥.

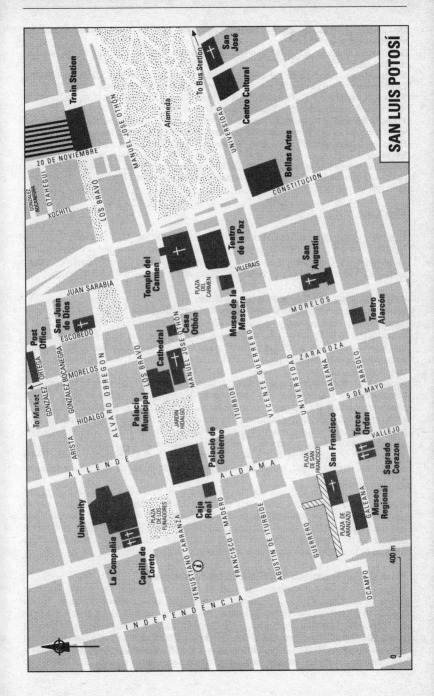

SAN LUIS POTOSÍ

De Gante, 5 de Mayo 140, corner of Jardín Hidalgo (☎481/12-14-92). Central and comfortable but with little atmosphere. ④.

Guadalajara, Jimenez 253 (☎481/12-46-12). Big, modern, faceless hotel with all the standard comforts. ⑤.

Maria Cristina, Juan Sarabia 110 between Othon and Los Bravo (☎481/12-94-08; fax 12-88-33). Large, modern, smart and central, popular with hurried Mexican business people. ⑥.

Panorama, Venustiano Carranza 315, west of Plaza Fundadores (☎481/12-17-77; fax 12-45-91). Slick, central, upmarket business hotel; the plushest in town. ⑦.

Plaza, Jardín Hidalgo 22, on Madero (☎481/12-46-31). Beautiful old building in the heart of the city with a fine, dark lobby and basic but comfortable rooms. Great value for the position. ④.

Principal, Juan Sarabia 145 (☎481/12-07-84). Opposite the *Maria Cristina*, a little dowdy but excellent value. ④.

Progreso, Aldama 415, at Iturbide (☎481/12-03-66). Musty old hotel with stacks of character, basic rooms off a great well of a lobby, plenty of fat men smoking cigars and a lot of "passing trade": not a good spot for lone female travellers. ③.

The City

Despite its uninviting industrial outskirts, the centre of San Luis Potosí is calm and beautiful, set on a tidy grid of largely pedestrianized streets around a series of little colonial plazas, chief among which is the **Jardín Hidalgo**, the old Plaza de Armas, surrounded by state and city government offices and overlooked by the cathedral.

Jardín Hidalgo and the commercial centre

Something of an architectural mishmash, the **cathedral** was built in the early eighteenth century but has been so constantly tinkered with ever since that little remains of the original: certainly it's not the most elegant of the city's churches. Facing the cathedral across the square is the long facade of the **Palacio de Gobierno** (Mon–Fri 8am–9pm, Sat & Sun 8am–2pm; free) with its balustraded roof. This, too, has been substantially refurbished over the years, but at least any alterations have preserved the harmony of its clean Neoclassical lines. Inside, you can visit the suite of rooms occupied by Benito Juárez when San Luis became his temporary capital in 1863. French troops supporting the Emperor Maximilian soon drove him out, but he returned in 1866, and in this building confirmed the death sentence passed on Maximilian (see p.560). There's an absurd waxwork model of Juárez with the Princess Salm Salm, one of Maximilian's daughters, kneeling before him pleading for the emperor's pardon. He refused, "thus" (according to the state government's leaflet) "ending the short-lived empire and strengthening, before all peoples and the entire world, Mexico's prestige as a liberty loving nation".

North of the plaza, Hidalgo, and the streets around it, are the city's main shopping area: the fancy department stores and designer boutiques near the plaza give way to simpler stores as you approach the **Mercado Hidalgo**, a good place for souvenirs and fresh produce. Farther up, continuing along Alhóndiga, the street stalls and stores become increasingly basic until you reach another much larger produce and clothing market, beyond the main road that marks the edge of the central area.

Plaza de San Francisco and Plaza de los Fundadores

Immediately behind the Palacio de Gobierno you can admire the ornate Baroque facade of the **Caja Real** – the old mint – one of the finest colonial mansions in San Luis. It now houses government offices, so you can walk in and take a look during the day: notice the very gentle gradient of the stairway, supposedly to make it easier to lug boxes full of gold and silver up and down. Take a left turn here, along Aldama, and you come to the quiet **Plaza de San Francisco**, a shaded area redolent of the city's colonial history. It's named for the Franciscan monastery whose church, the Templo de

San Francisco, towers over the west side. The monastery itself now houses the **Museo Regional** (Tues–Fri 10am–4.30pm, Sat & Sun 10am–2pm; free), an excellent collection of pre-Hispanic sculpture and other archeological finds, displays of local Indian culture and traditions, and articles relating to the history of the state of San Luis Potosí. There's a fine cloister and, upstairs, access to the lavish **Capilla de Aranzazu**, a Baroque chapel with exceedingly rich Churrigueresque decoration. In the entrance hall and along the stairway leading up is a miscellaneous collection of religious paintings. At the back of the museum the **Plaza Aranzazu** is another pleasant open space.

At the far end of the Plaza San Francisco two more tiny and elaborate churches, **Sagrado Corazon** and the **Templo del Tercer Orden**, stand side by side, with a small, plain presbyterian chapel, seeming terribly incongruous amid all this Baroque grandeur, facing them across Galeana.

One block north on Aldama from the Caja Real, the paved **Plaza de los Fundadores** is a much larger and more formal open space than the Jardín Hidalgo. Nothing much seems to happen here, though, despite the fact that it's dominated by the enormous Neoclassical **State University**. Alongside are two more small churches, **Capilla de Loreto** and **La Compañia**, while the fine arcaded portals of the square continue around the corner into Av. Venustiano Carranza.

Plaza del Carmen, San Agustín and the Alameda

The **Templo del Carmen**, on the little **Plaza del Carmen** up towards the Alameda, is the most beautiful and harmonious of all San Luis' churches. Exuberantly decorated with a multicoloured tiled dome and elaborate Baroque facade, it has an equally flashy interior: in particular, a fantastically intricate retablo attributed to the eighteenth-century eccentric and polymath Francisco Tresguerras. Beside it, where once was a monastery, is the bulky **Teatro de la Paz**, built in the last century under Porfirio Diaz and typical of the grandiose public buildings of that era, though the modern interior fails to live up to the extravagance of the exterior. Directly opposite the theatre you'll find the **Museo de la Mascara** (Tues–Fri 10am–2pm & 4–6pm, Sat & Sun 10am–2pm; free), an impressive exhibition of masks from around the country, including the so-called "giants of San Luis": eight enormous models representing four royal couples (from Africa, Europe, Asia and America), which are flaunted in the streets during the festival of Corpus Christi. It's a compulsive and fascinating place, with everything from pre-Hispanic masks to costumes that are still worn for fiestas and traditional dances. Displays explain – in Spanish – the meaning and continued significance of many of these dances.

South of the museum, the **Templo de San Agustín** faces out onto the tiny Plaza San Agustín. It's another magnificent Baroque exterior, with little to offer if you venture inside. East on Universidad from here, you reach the southern side of the Alameda, where the **Centro de Difusion Cultural** (Tues–Sat 10am–2pm & 5–8pm, Sun 10am–2pm & 6–8pm; free) occupies a concrete building that looks like a modern church. There are changing temporary exhibitions, usually of modern art, here. The **Alameda** itself, ringed by heavy traffic, is crowded with strolling families, photographers, candy sellers, and with people waiting for local buses.

Parque Tangamanga

If urban life is getting you down, the **Parque Tangamanga** in the south of the city offers some escape. In this green expanse there are picnic spots, people jogging, cycling and playing soccer, fitness circuits and a couple of small lakes; inevitably, since this is Mexico, there are also people driving their cars through the middle of it all. It makes a pleasant weekend outing nonetheless, with the added attraction of the **Museo de Arte Popular**, a showcase museum–shop of local crafts, at the bottom of Tatanacho opposite the main entrance to the park.

Eating, drinking and nightlife

San Luis seems to have a surfeit of **places to eat**, with lots of cafes and simple restaurants offering good-value *menus*, though little that's more exciting. The liveliest bars and cafes stretch along Venustiano Carranza, frequented by students and locals. Local specialities to look out for include *enchiladas* and *tacos potosinas* (or *huastecas*), dripping with *salsa* and cheese. There are also lots of *panaderías* (try *La Americana*, Galeana 433 opposite the regional museum) and cake shops (*GloMar*, Plaza Hidalgo 21 by the *Hotel Plaza* is very fancy), especially on Hidalgo and Morelos as they head north from the centre towards the market. The **Mercado Hidalgo** itself includes a host of food stalls, but the place is too packed and noisy for anything other than a hurried snack. *Costanzo* is a wonderful local confectioner, with branches on Carranza at Plaza Fundadores, and at Galeana 420 by the Museo Regional.

Nightlife, at weekends anyway, is pretty lively, with many places on Carranza west of the Plaza Fundadores. *Forum*, Carranza 329 near the *Hotel Panorama*, has live "tropical" music every weekend and a rather older, upmarket crowd; *Museum*, Carranza 763, is more studenty. Other clubs are way out on the outskirts: you'll need a taxi for *Oasis*, for example, out on the main highway.

Cafes and Restaurants

Cafe Florida, Juan Sarabia 235, just off Plazuela San Juan de Dios. Local cafe with great Art Deco interior and good Mexican food. Popular and cheap.

Cafe la Parroquia, Carranza at Plaza Fundadores. Comfortable cafe with family atmosphere and good value *comidas*.

Cafe Pacifico, Los Bravo and Constitución. Very popular cafe/restaurant, open 24hrs, a bustle of gossip, action and reasonably priced food.

Cafe Tokio, facing the Alameda on Othon. Good for a cheap breakfast or for a quick feed at any time, though very much "fast" food.

Mariscos El Sardinero, Othon 355A on Plaza del Carmen. Good seafood restaurant with reasonably priced seafood *comida*.

Restaurant Posada del Virrey, Jardín Hidalgo 3, on the north side. Fine food in fine surroundings – the former home of the Spanish viceroy, with a mildly Mexican menu that includes great seafood.

MOVING ON FROM SAN LUIS POTOSÍ: RÍO VERDE

Most traffic from San Luis is heading south on **Hwy-57** towards México: fast divided highway all the way. Unless you're in a crazy hurry, though, you should definitely turn off into the Bajío proper, to Guanajuato or San Miguel or Dolores Hidalgo, some of the most fascinating towns in the republic. **Hwy-70**, the route east to Tampico and the Gulf of Mexico, can hardly compete for interest, but it does run though the town of **Río Verde**, surrounded by lush fields of maize, coffee and citrus fruits. The town is ringed by thermal springs and has the benefit of a small lake, the **Laguna de la Media Luna**, which is popular with snorkellers and divers. Farther east still the highway comes to **Ciudad Valles**, a busy commercial town some 140km from Tampico and the coast.

Buses from the bus stations cover every conceivable route, with departures for México and Monterrey every few minutes, for Guadalajara, Tampico and the border at least hourly. *Flecha Amarilla* has excellent second-class services to the Bajío: Dolores Hidalgo fourteen times daily, San Miguel every couple of hours, Guanajuato slightly less frequently. Local buses marked "Central" will bring you here from the Alameda.

San Luis is also on the main México–Monterrey **train** line, although the express *Regiomontano* is not exactly convenient: southbound it passes through around 4am, northbound just after midnight. The slow train on this route leaves for México at 11.15am, heading north at 6.30pm. There are also excruciatingly slow trains on a line that goes from Tampico to Aguascalientes, departing for Tampico at 8am, for Aguascalientes at 10.30am.

Tortas de Allende, Allende and Obregón. A chain, but a good one, with *tortas* and snacks.

Tortas del Progreso, Aldama 415 under *Hotel Progreso.* The hotel still has the two original doors labelled "Cantina", which leads to this simple *torta* and *taco* place, entering the *Comedor,* slightly fancier restaurant next door, with good seafood.

Tropicana, Othon 355B on Plaza del Carmen. Juices, yoghurt, *tortas* and health food.

INTO THE BAJÍO

Mexico's broad central plateau narrows and becomes hillier as it approaches the Valley of México. Here in the **Bajío** proper – the states of **Guanajuato and Querétaro** – are its finest colonial cities, founded amid barren land and growing rich on just one thing: **silver.** Before the arrival of the Spanish this was a relatively unexploited area, a buffer zone between the "civilized" peoples of the heartland and the barbarian Chichimec tribes from the north. Though the Aztecs may have tapped some of its mineral wealth, they never began to exploit the area with the greed, tenacity and ruthlessness of the new colonists. After the Conquest the mining cities grew rich, but in time they also grew restive – champing under the heavy hand of control from Spain. The wealthy Creole (Spanish-blooded but Mexican-born) bourgeoisie were free to exploit the land and its people, and forced to pay punitive taxes, but not to rule their own destinies: lucrative government posts and high positions in the Church were reserved exclusively for Gachupines, those actually born in Spain, while the Indians and poor mestizos were condemned either to landless poverty or to almost suicidal labour in the mines.

Unsurprisingly, then, the Bajío was fertile ground for **Revolutionary ideas**. This is *La Cuna de la Independencia* (the Cradle of Independence), where every town seems to claim a role in the break with Spain. In **Querétaro** the plotters held many of their early meetings, and from here they were warned that their plans had been discovered; in **Dolores Hidalgo** the famous *grito* was first voiced by Father Hidalgo, proclaiming an independent Mexico; and from here he marched on **San Miguel de Allende**, picking up more volunteers for his armed rabble as he continued towards a bloody confrontation in **Guanajuato**. Today, despite the total abandonment of the silver mines, both Guanajuato and San Miguel continue to thrive as centres of study, culture and tourism, while Querétaro is a thrusting modern city thanks to its proximity to the capital and position on all the main transport routes; Dolores is less well known, but it too is a thriving market town, and almost a place of pilgrimage for Mexican tourists.

Guanajuato

Shoe-horned into a narrow ravine, **GUANAJUATO** was for centuries the wealthiest city in Mexico, its mines pouring out silver and gold in prodigious quantities. Today it presents a remarkable sight: emerging from the surrounding hills you come upon the town quite suddenly, a riot of colonial architecture dominated by the bluff (and rather ugly) bulk of the university, tumbling down hills so steep that at times it seems that the floor of one building is suspended on the roof of the last. Declared a UNESCO World Heritage Zone in 1988, Guanajuato is protective of its image: there are no traffic lights or neon signs here, and the topography ensures that there's no room for new building.

There's an old-fashioned, backwater feel to the place, reinforced by the students' habit of going serenading in their black capes, the brass bands playing in the plazas, and the refusal to make any very special effort to accommodate the flood of tourists. It's also an extremely enjoyable place to visit, peaceful, yet with plenty of life in the streets (especially in term), lots of good places to eat and drink, and plenty to see. Unmistakeably Mexican, there's also an almost European feel and look to Guanajuato.

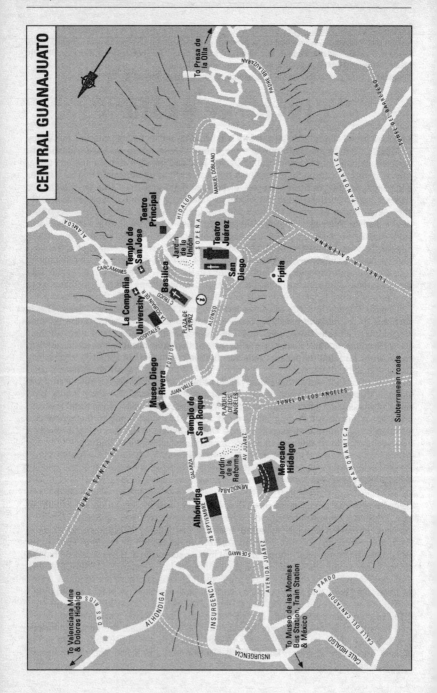

CENTRAL GUANAJUATO

Orientation

Maps of Guanajuato don't always help, but in practice it's not in the least difficult to find your way around. The streets run in close parallel along the steep sides of the valley, while an underground roadway passes almost directly beneath the town's main road, Av. Juárez. This, the **Subterraneo Miguel Hidalgo**, was originally built as a tunnel to take the river under the city and prevent the periodic flooding to which it was liable – and in the process to provide a covered sewer. The river now runs deeper below ground; its former course, with the addition of a few exits and entrances, has proved very handy in preventing traffic from clogging up the centre entirely, and more tunnels have since been added to keep the traffic flowing. If you're interested, some bus routes go through the tunnels, or you could take a drive through in a taxi.

When walking – the only way to get around the city – it's enough to know that **Av. Juárez** runs straight through the heart of town along the ravine floor and that everything of interest is either on it, or just off it on the lower slopes. Should you get lost, simply head downhill and you'll get back to Juárez. The town has two alternative centres: the western end is somewhat rougher, focused on the plaza outside the **Mercado Hidalgo**, where there is always plenty of action in the bars and cheap cafes; while to the east, where Juárez becomes Sopeña, the city is calmer, focusing on the **Jardín de la Unión**, with its shaded restaurants, happy tourists and neatly clipped trees.

Arrival

The **bus station**, with a small tourist information booth, *guardería* and long-distance phones, lies 6km west of the city. Regular local buses ("Centro–Central") shuttle into town in about fifteen minutes, stopping for a while in the triangular plaza outside the Mercado Hidalgo before continuing along Juárez and right through the centre. **Trains** pull in at the west end of Juárez, just where it leaves town. It's not too far to walk in, or get on any bus to the centre.

Before setting off in search of a place to stay it's worth checking out the **tourist office** at Plaza de la Paz 14 (Mon–Fri 9am–7.30pm, Sat & Sun 10am–2pm; ☎473/2-00-86). They'll give you a **free map**, and more importantly have up-to-date information on **hotels**; a board outside lists most of them and their official prices. There are also lots of private information booths throughout town, including at the bus station, offering tours and hotel reservations. One excellent way to get to see some of the less obvious parts of Guanajuato, and get a feel for the town, is to join an organized **Callejoneada** – walking tours wandering through the side streets and back alleys. They leave from behind the Jardín de la Union on Friday and Saturday nights at 9pm (more frequently in high season) – get details of these, and of *Estudiantines* when you can accompany a student minstrel group, at Juárez 210 or from any of the information booths. The **post office** (Mon–Fri 8am–8pm, Sat 8am–1pm) is at the eastern end of Positos, behind the Jardín de la Union, where there's a *Telmex* office (Mon–Fri 9am–8pm, Sat 8am–1pm) for **phone**, fax and telegram services; there are plenty of other *larga distancia* places, including one at Juárez 110. **Banks** can be found along Juárez, including *Banamex* and *Internacional* on the Plaza de la Paz.

Accommodation

Rooms in Guanajuato can at times be hard to come by – especially on Mexican public holidays, at Christmas, *Semana Santa* and during the **International Cervantes Festival** (2–3 weeks in October) – and at these times it's worth trying to book ahead. Budget options are ranged at the western end of Juárez (those just off the main drag are quieter) and around the train station, but by far the best place to stay is around the **Jardín de la Unión**.

Near the Mercado Hidalgo

Alhóndiga, Insurgencia 49 (☎473/2-05-25). Small, very friendly place a short walk north of the centre, with its own small restaurant. ⑤.

Central, Juárez 111-A (☎473/2-93-30). Dark but clean, the best of the cheap hotels around the Jardín Reforma. ③.

Gran Hotel, Alhóndiga 35 (☎473/2-40-88). Some way from the centre, but pleasant and comfortable. ④.

Hacienda de Cobos, Padre Hidalgo 3 (☎473/2-01-43). Comfortable, motel-style rooms around a large parking lot; good if you have a car. ⑥.

Insurgente, Juárez 226 (☎473/2-31-92; fax 2-69-97). Central hotel with 85 clean, carpeted, comfortable rooms, but overpriced. ⑥.

Posada San Francisco, Juárez and Gavira, beside the market (☎473/2-20-84; fax 2-24-67). Central and large; the simple, spotless rooms all have private bathrooms. ④.

Reforma, Juárez 113 (☎473/2-04-69). Again fairly clean, basic and cheap. ③.

Socavón, Alhóndiga 41-A (☎473/2-48-85). Small, friendly place on the road to Valenciana, a short walk from the centre. ⑤.

On and around the Jardín de la Unión

Casa Kloster, c/de Alonso 32, reached from Juárez down the Callejon de la Estrella at its entry to Plaza de la Paz (☎473/2-00-88). Best budget deal in town, hugely popular with backpackers. Clean, simple rooms around a flower-filled courtyard – avoid those by the street – and communal bathrooms with good hot showers. Management prefers couples to be married. ②.

Hosteria del Frayle, Sopeña 3 (☎473/2-11-79). Lovely colonial-style building with luxury rooms. ⑥.

Posada de la Condesa, Plaza de la Paz 60 (☎473/2-14-62). Small, scruffy rooms with showers at very reasonable prices. Best bet in this area if you're travelling in a group. ②.

Posada Santa Fé, Jardín de la Unión (☎473/2-00-14; fax 2-46-53). Very comfortable old hotel right in the heart of the city. ⑦.

San Diego, Jardín de la Unión (☎473/2-56-26). Fine colonial building in the very centre, with great views from its front rooms. ⑦.

Farther out

Parador San Javier, Plaza Aldama 92, 1km from centre on road to Valenciana (☎473/2-06-26; fax 2-31-14). Beautiful hotel set in magnificent grounds of former colonial hacienda. ⑧.

Posada Molino del Rey, Padre Belaunzavan and Sancho Panza (☎473/2-22-23). At the east end of town, very reasonably priced but some distance from buses. ⑤.

The City

There must be more things to see in Guanajuato than in virtually any town of its size anywhere – churches, theatres, museums, battlefields, mines, mummified corpses. To get to some of these, you'll need to take the bus, but most places are laid out along Juárez: if you start your explorations from the Mercado Hidalgo and walk east, you'll be able to see much of what Guanajuato has to offer in a day. Wandering through the maze of narrow alleys that snakes up the side of the ravine is a pleasure in itself, if only to spot their quirky names – Salto del Mono (Monkey's Leap), for example, or c/de las Canterranas (Street of the Singing Frogs).

Mercado Hidalgo to the Plaza de la Paz

The first building of note as you head east up Juárez from the bus station, the **Mercado Hidalgo** is a huge iron-framed construction reminiscent of British Victorian railway-station architecture, crammed with goods of every description. Beyond the market, to the left and through the **Jardín de la Reforma**, with its fountain and arch, you get to the lovely, quiet **Plaza San Roque**. A small, irregular, flagged space, the plaza has a distinctly medieval feel, heightened by the raised facade of the crumbling Iglesia de San Roque that towers over it. It is a perfect setting for the city's lively annual **International Cervantes Festival** (see p.229). The Callejon de los Olleros leads back down to Juárez, or you can cut straight through to the livelier Plazuela San Fernando with its stalls and restaurants. Return to Juárez from here and you emerge more or less opposite the **Plazuela de los Angeles**. In itself this is little more than a slight broadening of the street, but from here steps lead up to some of Guanajuato's steepest, closest alleys. Just off the plazuela is the **Callejon del Beso**, so called because it is so narrow that residents can lean out of the upper-storey windows to exchange kisses across the street – naturally enough there are any number of *Canterbury Tales*-style legends of cuckolded husbands and star-crossed lovers associated with it.

The **Plaza de la Paz** lies east of the Jardín de la Reforma, beyond a number of banks on Juárez. For a while here, Juárez is not the lowest road – Alonso cuts down to the right, to rejoin Juárez a little farther along. Plaza de la Paz itself boasts some of the town's finest **colonial buildings**, among which the late eighteenth-century mansion of the Condes de Rul y Valenciana, owners of the richest mine in the country, stands out as the grandest. It was designed by Eduardo Tresguerras, undoubtedly the finest Mexican architect of his time, and played host briefly to Baron Alexander Von Humboldt, the German naturalist and writer on Mexico, an event commemorated by a plaque. The **Casa de Gobierno**, a short way down towards the Jardín de la Unión, is another fine mansion, this time with a plaque recording the fact that Benito Juárez lived there in 1858, when Guanajuato was briefly his provisional capital. On the far side of the plaza is the honey-coloured **Basilica de Nuestra Señora de Guanajuato**, the Baroque parish church that houses the patroness of the city – an ancient image of the Virgin. This wooden statue, which now sits surrounded by silver and jewels, was given to Guanajuato in 1557 by Philip II in gratitude for the wealth that was pouring from here into the Spanish royal coffers. Even then it was very old and miraculous, having survived more than eight centuries of Moorish occupation hidden in a cave near Granada in Spain.

Around the Jardín de la Unión

From the Plaza de la Paz you can cut up to the university, but just a short distance farther east on Juárez is the **Jardín de la Unión**, Guanajuato's zócalo. It's a delightful little square – or rather triangle – set back from the street, shaded with trees, surrounded by tables outside the cafes, and with a bandstand in the centre from which the town band regularly adds to the early evening atmosphere. This is the best time to sit and linger over a drink, enjoying the passing spectacle of the evening *paseo*, when it seems that everyone in town turns out for a stroll.

Facing the Jardín across Juárez is the Baroque church of **San Diego**, inside which are old paintings and interesting chapels and altars: one in particular is dedicated to the infant Jesus and mawkishly filled with toys and tiny children's shoes left as offerings. Next door is the imposing Neoclassical frontage of the **Teatro Juárez** (Tues–Sun 9.15am–1.45pm & 5–7.45pm; $2). The interior of the theatre is fabulously plush – all red velvet, gilt and chandeliers – as befits its period: built at the end of the last century, it was opened in 1903 by the dictator Porfirio Diaz himself. Behind the theatre, at Constancia 7, is a little **Casa de Artesanías** (Mon–Sat 10am–3pm & 5–8pm), where all the craft works displayed are for sale, though they're not cheap.

Beyond the Jardín, Juárez becomes Sopeña, a short way down which the pretty pink church of San Francisco marks the Plazuela San Francisco. Here too is the **Museo Iconográfico del Quijote** (Tues–Sat 10am–3pm; free), an extraordinary little collection devoted entirely to Don Quijote: mainly paintings of him, but also a Dalí print, a copy of a Picasso drawing, murals, tapestries, sculptures, busts, miniatures, medals, plates, glassware, chess sets, pipes, cutlery, postage stamps, you name it. Beyond here, Sopeña begins to climb the hill behind, eventually becoming the Paseo de la Presa. A walk of thirty minutes or so takes you through some of Guanajuato's fancier residential districts before ending up at the Presa de la Olla and the Presa San Renovato, two small green and rather unimpressive **reservoirs**. This is a popular picnic spot, and you can rent rowing boats or sit out at a restaurant by the Presa de la Olla. There's a bus out here (look for "La Olla" or "Presa"), which goes through town on the underground street – steps near the church of San Diego will take you down to a subterranean bus stop.

Pípila

The **Monumento al Pípila**, on the hillside almost directly above the Jardín de la Unión, affords fantastic views of Guanajuato. You seem to be standing directly on top of the church of San Diego, and if there is a band playing in the plaza it can be clearly heard up here. It's an especially wonderful spot when darkness is falling and the lights start to come on in town – the 45 minutes or so between the sun going behind the hills and the light disappearing altogether. The steep climb takes about twenty minutes going up, ten minutes coming down: the bottom half is lit but the top isn't, so don't wait for total darkness before you descend. There are several possible routes up through the alleys – look for signs saying "al Pípila" – including up the Callejon del Calvario, to the right off Sopeña just beyond the Teatro Juárez, from the Plazuela San Francisco, or climbing to the left from the Callejon del Beso; the signs run out, but if you keep climbing as steeply as possible you're unlikely to get lost. Along the way there are various viewpoints and romantic nooks. There's also a bus ("Pípila") that takes you round the scenic Carretera Panoramica. Pípila was Guanajuato's own Independence hero: you can walk up into the head of his statue for even more spectacular vistas.

Around the university

At the back of the Jardín de la Unión and on the left, the **Plaza del Baratillo** is a small space with a quiet cafe and a clutch of crafts shops. From here the **Teatro Principal** is down to the right, while curving on round to the left there's the church of **La Compañia** and the **University**. The highly decorated monumental Baroque church is just about all that's left of a Jesuit seminary founded in 1732, an educational establishment that eventually metamorphosed into the State University, now one of the most prestigious in Mexico. The university building is in fact quite modern – only some forty years old – but designed to blend in with the town which, for all its size, it does surprisingly effectively. There's not a great deal of interest inside to the casual observer, but wander in anyway: noticeboards detail local cultural events, and there's often a temporary exhibition of some kind. High on the fourth floor you'll find the **Museo de Historia Natural** (Mon–Fri 10am–2pm & 4–6pm; free), a small collection of beetles, butterflies and assorted beasts, including a small two-headed goat. Next door to the university building, the **Museo del Pueblo de Guanajuato** (Tues–Sat 10am–2pm & 4–7pm, Sun 10am–4pm; $2) is a collection of local art and sundry oddities, housed in the seventeenth-century home of the Marqués de San Juan de Rayas.

Positos leads west from the front of the university to the fascinating **Museo Diego Rivera** (daily 10am–2pm & 4–6pm; $3, free on Sun), which occupies the birthplace of Guanajuato's most famous son. For most of his life Rivera, the ardent Revolutionary and Marxist, went unrecognized by his conservative home town, but with international recognition of his work came this museum in the house where he was raised until he was six. The place is far bigger than it looks from the outside: downstairs it's furnished in nineteenth-century style, with some pieces said to be the Rivera family's, and upstairs are many of Rivera's works, especially early ones, in a huge variety of styles, and a large temporary exhibition space. Although there are no major works on show, the many sketches and small paintings are well worth a look.

The Alhóndiga

The **Alhóndiga de Granaditas**, the most important of all Guanajuato's monuments, lies west of the Museo Diego Rivera, more or less above the market. Originally a granary, later a prison, now a very good regional museum, this was the scene of the first real battle and some of the bloodiest butchery in the long War of Independence. Just thirteen days after the cry of Independence went up in Dolores Hidalgo, Father Hidalgo approached Guanajuato at the head of his insurgent force – mostly peons armed with nothing more than staves and sickles. The Spanish, outnumbered but well supplied with firearms, shut themselves up in the Alhóndiga, a redoubtable fortress. The almost certainly apocryphal story goes that Hidalgo's troops could make no impact until a young miner, nicknamed **El Pípila** (the Turkeycock), volunteered to set fire to the wooden doors – with a slab of stone tied to his back as a shield, he managed to crawl to the gates and start them burning, dying in the effort. The rebels, their path cleared, broke in and massacred the defenders wholesale. It was a short-lived victory – Hidalgo was forced to abandon Guanajuato, leaving its inhabitants to face Spanish reprisals, and was eventually tracked down by the royalists and executed in Chihuahua. His head and the heads of his three chief co-conspirators, Allende, Aldama and Jiménez, were suspended from the four corners of the Alhóndiga as a warning to anyone tempted to follow their example, and there they stayed for over ten years, until Mexico finally did become independent. The hooks from which they hung are still there on the outside walls.

Inside, there's a memorial hall devoted to the Martyrs of Independence and a **museum** (Tues–Sat 10am–2pm & 4–6pm, Sun 10am–4pm; $5, free on Sun). On the staircases are **murals** by local artist Chavez Morado, depicting scenes from the War of Independence and the Revolution, as well as native folklore and traditions. The collection, mainly labelled only in Spanish, spans local history from pre-Hispanic times to this century: the most interesting sections cover the Independence battle and everyday life in colonial times. There are the iron cages in which the rebels' heads were displayed and lots of weapons and flags, as well as a study of Guanajuato's mining industry. There's also plenty of art, especially a wonderful series of portraits of local types by Hermengildo Bustos; and don't miss the small *artesanías* section by the side door, which displays a bit of everything from fabrics and clothes to saddles and metalwork.

La Valenciana

From close by the Alhóndiga on c/Alhóndiga, occasional buses ("Valenciana") wind their way 5km uphill to the mine and church of **La Valenciana**. Near the top of the pass here, overlooking Guanajuato where the road to Dolores Hidalgo and San Miguel heads off north, you'll see the elaborate facade of the church with its one completed tower: the entrance to the mine is across the road. La Valenciana (daily dawn–dusk; free) was for hundreds of years the richest **silver mine** in Mexico, tapping Guanajuato's celebrated Veta Madre (Mother Lode). It just about operates still, though on a vastly reduced level, and you can wander around the top of the workings, see some of the machinery and buy rocks at a small shop.

The reason for a visit is not really the mine, though, but the extraordinarily sumptuous **church** constructed by its owner, the Conde de Rul y Valenciana, and his workers. Built between 1765 and 1788, it's the ultimate expression of Mexico's Churrigueresque style, with a profusion of intricate adornment covering every surface – even the mortar, they say, is mixed with silver ore. Inside, notice especially the enormous gilded retablos around the main altar and in each arm of the cross, and the delicate filigree of the roof vaulting, especially around the dome above the crossing.

If you're a real rock enthusiast, then on your way back to town you might call in at the **Mineralogy Museum** (Mon–Fri 9am–1pm & 4.30–7pm; free), in the mining department of the university, which houses some 25,000 rock samples. The museum is in a university building on your left as you head out of town towards Valenciana, about 3km from central Guanajuato – ask for the "Escuela de Minas y Metalurgia".

The Ex-Hacienda de San Gabriel de Barrera

If the crush of Guanajuato gets too much for you, head west (on any bus going to the Camionera Central) to the **Ex-Hacienda de San Gabriel de Barrera** (daily 9am–6pm; $2), a colonial home now transformed into a modern hotel and museum. The beautifully restored **gardens** of the hacienda range through a bizarre selection of international styles, including English, Italian, Roman, Arabic and Mexican. In addition, a part of the house has been restored in colonial style as a **museum**, which includes some magnificent details of daily life among the wealthy silver barons of nineteenth-century Guanajuato. The ground floor is a display of grand and opulent decoration while upstairs is rich in domestic detail. It's a great place to wander at ease and really brings home the sheer wealth of colonial Guanajuato.

Museo de las Momias

Halfway up the hill on the opposite side of town from La Valenciana, the ghoulish *Panteón*, or **Museo de las Momias** (daily 9am–6pm; $3), offers a very different sort of attraction. Here, lined up against the wall in a series of glass cases, are more than a hundred mummified human corpses exhumed from the local public cemetery. All these bodies had originally been laid out in crypts in the usual way, but here, if after five years the relatives are unable or unwilling to make the perpetuity payment, the remains are removed. Many are found to have been naturally preserved, and the "interesting" ones are put on display – others, not properly mummified or too dull for public titillation, are burned or transferred to a common grave. The wasted, leathery bodies vary from some more than a century old (including a smartly dressed mummy said to have been a French mining engineer) to relatively recent fatalities – a small child wearing a nappy – who presumably have surviving relatives. The burial clothes hang off the corpses almost indecently – others, completely naked, seem far less luridly lewd – and the guides delight in pointing out their most horrendous features: one twisted mummy, its mouth opened in a silent scream, is the "woman who was buried alive"; another, a woman who died in childbirth, is displayed beside "the smallest mummy in the world" – the foetus which cost her her life. All absolutely gross, but nevertheless with a macabre fascination. The hawkers outside selling mummy models and sticks of rock in the shape of mummies are easier to resist. To get to the museum, either walk from the centre of town, following the signs out past the train station, or take the bus ("Panteón" or "Momias") that runs along Juárez and up the hill past the main entrance.

Eating

Finding something to eat in Guanajuato is easy – it's impossible to walk more than a few yards down Juárez without passing some kind of cafe or restaurant. At the bottom end, near the bus station, a whole series of very plain little places serve the standard Mexican staples, many of them also offering inexpensive *comidas corridas*, and the university area too brings plenty of choice. Rather more adventurous, and cheaper still, are the stalls in the modern annexe of the **Mercado Hidalgo**: two floors of delights (and horrors) where you'd be advised to take a careful look at what's on offer – some stalls are distinctly cleaner and more appetizing than others. Guanajuato also has a couple of good **vegetarian** restaurants. For bread and cakes, try *Panadería la Purisima*, Juárez 138, or the *Pastelería la Paz*, by the church on the Plaza de la Paz.

Centro Nutricional Vegetariano, Aguilar 43 near Plaza de la Paz. Low-priced salads, fruit, juices and veggie variations of traditional Mexican meals.

El Ágora del Baratillo, in the alley at the back of Jardín de la Unión. Quiet, open-air courtyard setting, good *comidas*.

El Campañero, Sopeña 10, near Plazuela San Francisco. Juices, *licuados*, *tacos* and *tortas*.

Galeria la Mandarina, Juárez 20 by Posada la Condesa. Tranquil cafe upstairs in a delightful antiques and *artesanías* shop.

Los Alpes Cafeteria y Nevería, in courtyard off Positos near the university. Student hangout, for ice cream, coffee and snacks.

Pinguis, northeast corner of Jardín de la Unión. The best bargain in the Jardín: a buzzing, friendly place for excellent breakfasts, *comidas corridas* and a good menu of Mexican and international food.

Pizza Piazza, branches throughout town, including Plazuela San Fernando, Juárez 67 and Hidalgo 14. Spaghetti, hamburgers and, as you might expect, pizza.

Sakura, c/de Juan Valle 7, near Plaza de la Paz. Guanajuato's only Japanese restaurant, dishing up inexpensive tempura and teriyaki as well as – for some reason – fried chicken and curry.

Tasca de los Santos, Plaza de la Paz. Smart Spanish restaurant with outdoor tables, serving European delights such as *paella*, chicken in white wine and *jamon serrano*. Moderate to expensive.

Tortas la Pulga, Plaza de la Paz 36. Tiny sandwich bar, very popular with students. Either take away or eat in chairs along the corridor. Tasty and cheap.

Truco 7, Truco 7. Beautiful little cafe with a very relaxed student atmosphere. Great moderately priced breakfasts, *comidas*, salads and steaks.

Restaurante Vegetariano, Callejon Calisto 20, a small alley off to the south side of Juárez, just west of Plaza de la Paz. Clean and inexpensive, serving veggie *tacos*, juices, salads and good set meals.

Nightlife and entertainment

Guanajuato is a great spot to sit round knocking back bottles of beer, with a host of superb bars in which to do just that. Things are especially jumping at weekends, when refugees from the bigger cities, including México and León, come here to enjoy themselves. The rougher bars are down on Juárez around Mercado Hidalgo, where the *cantinas* are generally reserved for men and prostitutes.

During the **International Cervantes Festival** in October you can, among other things, see the famous *entremeses*, swashbuckling one-act plays from classical Spanish theatre performed outdoors in Plaza San Roque. You don't need good Spanish to work out what's going on – they're highly visual and very entertaining, even if you can't understand a word. There's a grandstand for which you have to book seats, but it's easy enough to join the crowds watching from the edges of the plaza for free. Groups of students (who perform the *entremeses*) will quite often put on impromptu performances outside festival times, so it's worth wandering up here in the early evening just to see if anything is happening, especially on Saturday nights. For details of the Festival, check with the tourist office. Other events are held in the Teatro Juárez and the Teatro Principal.

For a quieter evening, Guanajuato also has three **cinemas**, usually showing films in English with Spanish subtitles: *Ciné Guanajuato*, on the west side of the university; *Ciné Reforma*, Juárez near Mercado Hidalgo; and *Teatro Principal*, Juárez east of Jardín de la Unión.

Bars and clubs

El Gallo Pitagórico, Jardín de la Unión. One of the cheaper places to linger over a cocktail at a pavement table.

Guanajuato Grill, Alonso 4. The town's main disco, fairly tacky and usually packed with local teenagers doing very little but sweating and listening to the music.

La Dama de las Camelias . . . es el, Sopeña 34 opposite Museo Iconografico. Great, atmospheric bar.

To get to Guanajuato's **bus terminal**, catch a local bus ("Centro–Central") from Juárez. There are regular services to Guadalajara, México, San Luis Potosí and Aguascalientes and almost constant departures for León, Dolores Hidalgo and San Luis de la Paz. There are few buses direct to San Miguel de Allende, for which it's often easier to change in Dolores: if you have any problem getting anywhere else, head for León, which is on the main north–south highway and has much more frequent services. **Trains** to Guanajuato seem in a constant state of flux: for a while the excellent *Constitucionalista* first-class express ran to and from México; if it's not operating, don't bother with any of the agonizingly slow alternatives. There's also an **airport** that serves Guanajuato, about 30km away near the main highway just outside the town of Silao, with flights to major Mexican cities and, on *Continental*, to the USA. It's an expensive taxi ride to get there.

Rincon del Beso, Alonso 21. Trendiest bar in town, with loud live music, particularly at weekends. Lots of small, secretive rooms for people to sin in. Attracts an older, sophisticated crowd; doesn't really hot up until 11pm.
Si Señor, Juárez at the corner of Jardín de la Unión. Popular with tourists and locals. Bar, TV, food and special "happy hour" deals.

Around Guanajuato: León

Buses from Guanajuato run every ten minutes or so (1hr) to **LEÓN**, a teeming, industrial city 60km away. There's a long tradition of leather work here – reflected today in the scores of shoe factories and, in the centre, hundreds of shoe shops: a good place to buy hand-tooled cowboy boots. The bus station is some way out, and most people take one look and get no farther, but if you're changing buses here anyway it's well worth taking a couple of hours to wander round the centre – even if you just spend ten minutes in the bus station you'll see stacks of shoe boxes being loaded into just about every waiting bus.

In town, the **Plaza de los Fundadores** is not at all what the rest of the city would lead you to expect – very spacious, tranquil and elegant, with a fine eighteenth-century cathedral built by the Jesuits and a typically colonial Palacio Municipal. Little else survived a disastrous flood in 1883, but the plaza is surrounded by broad boulevards lined with shops, and there are a couple of churches that deserve a look: the Baroque **Templo de los Angeles** and the extraordinary marble **Templo Expiatorio** on Madero, where you can visit a series of underground chambers.

East of Guanajuato: Dolores Hidalgo

Fifty kilometres or so from both Guanajuato and San Miguel de Allende, **DOLORES HIDALGO** is as ancient and as historically rich as either town. This was Father Hidalgo's parish, and it was from the church in the main plaza here that the historic **Grito de la Independencia** (Cry of Independence) was first issued. Perhaps because of its less spectacular situation, though, or perhaps because there is no university or language school, Dolores hasn't seen a fraction of the tourist development that has overtaken its neighbours, despite the fact that for Mexicans the day trip out here is something of a pilgrimage. It's a good bet, though, for a one-night stopover, and certainly if you can't find accommodation in Guanajuato or San Miguel, this is the place to head; you'll get a better room here for half the cost, and both are easily accessible. True, there is less to see, but it's an elegant little town and thoroughly Mexican: busy, too, as it stands on a traditionally important crossroads on the silver route from Zacatecas.

Just a block or two from the bus station as you walk towards the central plaza, the **Casa Hidalgo** (Tues–Sun 10am–6pm; $5), Hidalgo's home, has been converted into a museum devoted to his life: a bit heavy on copies of letters he sent or received and on written tributes from various groups to the "Father of Independence", but interesting nonetheless. Elsewhere there's a beautifully laid-out plaza, overlooked by the exuberant facade of the famous church, a couple of other graceful churches, and little else but the attraction of the dilapidated old streets themselves. As you wander around, look out for the locally made **ceramics**. They're on sale everywhere and are a very ancient tradition here. The bigger shops are near the Casa Hidalgo.

Practicalities

There's little need to visit the small **tourist office** (Mon–Fri 9am–3pm & 5.30–8pm, Sat & Sun 9am–3pm) on the main plaza by the church, but they can offer advice on where to buy ceramics. Dolores' three **hotels** are all reasonable: *Posada Cocomacan*, Plaza Principal (☎0427/2-00-18; ④); *Hotel Caudillo*, Querétaro 8 (☎0427/2-01-98; ④), and the simple *Posada Dolores*, Yucatán 8 (no phone; ②), easily missed behind a small doorway. There's no need to stray far from the plaza to eat well – the hotels have **restaurants**, or you could sample the *Restaurant Plaza*.

Dolores is connected to both San Miguel and Guanajuato by regular, rapid **buses** to and from the *Flecha Amarilla* terminal on Hidalgo beside the river. *Herradura de Plata* also has a terminal at the corner of Chiapas and Yucatán, from where buses run every thirty minutes south to San Miguel Allende and México, and north to San Felipe.

San Luis de la Paz and San José Iturbide

If you carry straight on through Dolores, after 40km you hit the road between San Luis Potosí and Querétaro at San Luis de la Paz. From here a road runs south, parallel to the main road, 50km to San José Iturbide, which is 35km from San Miguel. Both are typically Mexican provincial towns with one main street, a colonial plaza, and horses tied up alongside farmers' pick-up trucks outside the market. **SAN LUIS** is the larger of the two, a major junction where, if you're travelling between San Luis Potosí and Guanajuato, Dolores or San Miguel de Allende, you'll want to change buses: there are regular connections with all these as well as express services to México passing by on the main road. It's also a good place to buy rugs and *sarapes* at reasonable prices, though most of what is made here is sent off to the markets in larger towns. If you

---

THE GRITO DE LA INDEPENDENCIA

On the night of September 15, 1810, **Padre Miguel Hidalgo y Costilla** and some of his fellow plotters, warned by messengers from Querétaro that their plans to raise a rebellion had been discovered, decided to go ahead immediately. At dawn on the 16th, Hidalgo, tolling the church bell, called his parishioners together and addressed them from the balcony of the church with an impassioned speech ending in the **Grito de la Independencia** – '¡Mexicanos, Viva Mexico!'. That cry is repeated every year by the president in México and by politicians all over the country at midnight on September 15: the starting point for the Independence Day celebrations. September 16 remains the one day of the year when the bell in Dolores Hidalgo's parish church is rung – though the bell you see today is a copy of an original which was either melted down for munitions or hangs in the Palacio Nacional in México, depending on which story you believe.

need to stay there are a couple of small, cheap hotels on the main street just up from the bus terminal.

The road between San Luis and San José passes through **POZOS**, which describes itself as a ghost town. But don't expect swing doors flapping in the breeze and tumbleweed gusting through the streets. For although Pozos – once Real de Pozos, a rich and flourishing mining community – does have vast areas of crumbling masonry inhabited only by the odd *burro*, it is still inhabited by quite a number of people. It's far from dead, and indeed seems recently to have undergone something of a revival in its fortunes.

SAN JOSÉ is distinguished by the behemoth of a Neoclassical church on its plaza, dedicated to Agustín de Iturbide, a local opportunist who started the War of Independence as a general loyal to Spain – inflicting major defeats on Morelos – only to later change sides. Having helped secure Mexico's Independence without any concomitant reform, he briefly declared himself emperor in 1822. The plaque reads, accurately enough, "from the only town in Mexico which still honours your memory". There's a frequent **bus service** between San José and San Luis de la Paz and occasional buses on from San José to San Miguel.

San Miguel de Allende

Set on a steep hillside overlooking the Río Laja, **SAN MIGUEL DE ALLENDE** seems at first sight little different from any other small colonial town, dominated by red rooftops and domed churches. Its character, though, is immediately distinct – there's a very high-profile colony of "artists and writers" here, fleshed out with less ambitious retirees from the US and by flocks of students drawn to the town's several language and arts schools. Like such a community anywhere it's inward-looking, bitchy and gossip-ridden, but it's also extremely hospitable and much given to taking newcomers under its wing.

There are good reasons why this should have happened in San Miguel – chiefly that it's a very picturesque town with a perfect climate and, for the artists, good light throughout the year. What got it started, though, was the foundation in 1938 of the **Instituto Allende**, an arts institute that enjoyed an enormous boost after World War II

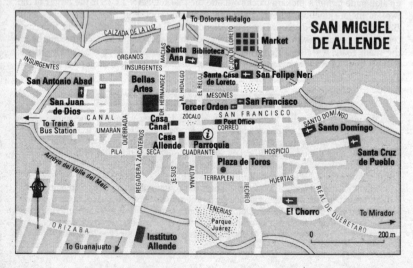

when returning GIs found that their education grants could be stretched much further in Mexico. Its fame established, San Miguel has never looked back, and for all its popularity remains one of the most pleasant places you could pick to rest up for a while in comfort.

There are few sights as such, but the whole town (which has been a National Monument since 1926, hence no new building, no flashing signs, no traffic lights) is crowded with old seigneurial mansions and curious churches. It was founded in 1542 by a Franciscan friar, Juan de San Miguel, and as San Miguel El Grande became an important supply centre for the big mining towns, and a stopover on the main silver route from Zacatecas. The name was changed to honour Ignacio Allende, a native who became Hidalgo's chief lieutenant. The country hereabouts is still ranching territory, though increasingly being taken over by the tourists and foreigners: there is a traditional spa at Taboada, and less lasting attractions nearby – a golf course, water skiing on the new reservoir and horse riding at a couple of dude ranches.

Arrival and information

On the main line from México to Nuevo Laredo, San Miguel has reasonably good **train connections**. A first-class express service heads for the capital via Tula and Querétaro: it leaves here around 1pm, and in the other direction sets out from the capital early in the morning, to arrive here at lunchtime. Fast services to the border tend to pass through in the middle of the night, but there's a departure for Monterrey daily at about 2.30pm. The station is a considerable distance from town, beyond the Camionera: buses marked "Estación" run along c/Canal, but you may well find it quicker and more convenient to take a taxi.

For relatively short journeys it's easier to arrive and leave by bus, although San Miguel has surprisingly poor service; it's often easier to head for San Luis de la Paz or Guanajuato and change there. Regular local buses make the run between the centre and the **bus terminal**, about 2km south, or again there are taxis.

The extremely helpful **tourist office** (Mon–Fri 10am–2.30pm & 5–7pm, Sat 10am–1pm, Sun 10am–noon; ☎465/2-17-47) is in the southeast corner of the zócalo (known variously as Plaza Principal or Jardín de Allende), more or less next door to the Parroquia, tucked in beside *La Terrazza* restaurant. As well as the usual ranks of leaflets and maps, they can provide details of local art classes and language courses. Most other facilities are nearby: you can **change money** right here at *Banamex*, at the corner of Canal, or *Bancomer* and *Comermex* are just off the plaza on San Francisco; the **post office** is a few paces up Correo.

Accommodation

Most of San Miguel's hotels are near the zócalo. Prices tend to be higher here than in other towns in the Bajío, because of its popularity with ex-pats: for the same reason, however, the city also offers **long-stay apartments**, which can work out to be economical. Ask at the tourist office for details, or check noticeboards around town, for example in the Plaza Colonial opposite Bellas Artes. Another option if you want to linger is the *Posada El Mayorazgo*, Hidalgo 8 (☎465/2-10-20), a small, modern building with "suites" around a compact courtyard. Rooms with kitchen, washing machine, cable TV and cooker cost around $400 a month.

Abesón de San Antonio, Mesones 80 (☎465/2-05-80). Rooms around a small garden with a swimming pool. ⑤.

Casa Carmen, Correo 31 (☎465/2-08-44). Very beautiful and intimate little hotel run by US-Mexican couple Horace and Natalie Mooring. Comfortable and totally secure. Rates includes dinner and breakfast. ⑥.

Casa de Huespedes, Mesones 27 (☎465/2-13-78). Beautiful little second-floor hotel: friendly and calm, with clean rooms – some with balconies – and fresh flowers. ④.

Casa de Sierra Nevada, Hospicio 35 (☎465/2-04-15; fax 2-23-37). Built in 1580 and now under Swiss management, this luxury hotel, with rooms around a beautiful colonial courtyard lush with greenery, must rank in the international big league. ⑨.

Hotel Posada Carmina, Cuna de Allende 7 (☎465/2-04-58; fax 2-01-35). Comfortable rooms amid yet more colonial splendour around a beautiful courtyard. ⑥.

Hotel Posada de San Francisco, Plaza Principal 2 (☎465/2-00-72). Lovely colonial building, very calm and sedate, with pretty courtyards. ⑦.

Parador San Sebastian de Aparicio, Mesones 7 (☎465/2-07-07). Cool and calm, with simple rooms around, yes, you've guessed it, a colonial courtyard. ④.

Posada de la Aldea, Ancha de San Antonio (☎465/2-10-22). Enormous hotel opposite the Instituto Allende. Rooms are clean and comfortable with all modern amenities. ⑦.

Posada Allende, Cuna de Allende 10 (☎465/2-06-98). Crumbling old building squeezed in against the Parroquia, run by delightfully chatty old ladies. Basic old rooms but heaps of atmosphere. ④.

Viancy, Aparicio 18 (☎465/2-45-59). Modern, spotless and somewhat faceless. ④.

Villa del Sol, Cuadrante 3 (☎465/2-07-42; fax 2-31-80). Another fine colonial establishment with a pool and gardens overlooking the back of the Parroquia. ⑦.

Youth hostel, Organos 35 (☎465/2-06-74). Cheapest place in town, with fairly basic single-sex dorms ($8). Very clean, very friendly, with breakfast included and kitchen, washing machine and Spanish lessons all available. Rates are lower with a youth hostel or student card. A couple of private rooms too. ③.

The Town

Activity in San Miguel's compact centre focuses on the **zócalo**, and it's here that you should head first. Everywhere else – save for the **Instituto Allende**, south of the centre – is an easy walk from here. The Instituto, also just about in walking distance, though it's a steep climb back up, is an alternative hub, and an especially useful source of information for anyone who wants to stay longer than the couple of days that suffices for sightseeing.

The zócalo

The most famous of the city's landmarks, **La Parroquia** – the parish church – takes up one side of the **zócalo**. This gloriously over-the-top structure, with a towering pseudo-Gothic facade bristling with turrets and spires, was rebuilt towards the end of the last century by a self-taught Indian stonemason, Zeferino Gutiérrez, who supposedly learned about architecture by studying postcards of the great French cathedrals and then drew diagrams in the dust to explain to his workers what he wanted.

Opposite is a block containing the **Palacio Municipal** and the **Galeria San Miguel**, one of the most prestigious of the many galleries showing local artists' work. The remaining two sides of the square are lined with covered *portales*, under whose arches vendors of drinks and trinkets shelter from the sun, with a row of shops behind them – look out for the guy who sells heroic black-and-white postcards of Pancho Villa and Zapata and gloriously lurid images of 1930s Mexican movie stars.

On the zócalo, too, are some of San Miguel's most distinguished mansions, all of them – like almost every home in San Miguel – built in the Spanish style. The **Casa de Don Ignacio de Allende**, on the corner of Allende and Umaran, was the birthplace of the Independence hero: a plaque notes *"Hic natus ubique notus"* – "here was born he who is famous everywhere". On the next corner, Hidalgo and Canal, you can see the **Casa de los Condes de Canal**, with an elaborately carved doorway and elegant wrought-iron grilles over the windows. Near here too, just half a block down Umaran, is the **Casa de los Perros**, its balconies supported by little stone dogs. Forbidding, even grim, from the outside, these mansions mostly conceal patios decked with flowers or courtyards with a fountain playing. If you want to see inside some, and if you think you could take it, the English-speaking community organizes a "**House and Gardens Tour**" every Sunday, leaving the Instituto Allende at noon. You'll see details on posters around the town.

North of the zócalo

Leave the zócalo uphill on San Francisco, and the streets seem less affected by outsiders – Spanish or *norteamericano*. The architecture, it's true, is still colonial, but the life that continues around the battered buildings seems cast in a more ancient mould. Behind the church of **San Francisco**, whose elaborate Churrigueresque facade contrasts sharply with its Neoclassical towers, tiled dome and plain interior (and quite overshadows the modest simplicity of its smaller neighbour, **Tercer Orden**) San Miguel's old **market** area has been refurbished to create a new plaza. The market, which has managed to remain almost entirely traditional – fruit, vegetables, medicinal herbs, pots and pans are all on display, with little specifically for the tourist among the cramped tables with their low canvas awnings – has been moved down the hill to a new site off c/Colegio. Official market day is Sunday, but no one seems to have told the locals and it's pretty busy all week: behind the regular market (with an entrance on the Callejon de Loreto) is a new **Mercado de Artesanías**, where nothing seems very good value. You'll find much more exciting goods in the many crafts shops around town.

Across the new square from San Francisco, up a few steps from the street, the **Oratorio de San Felipe Neri** sits in the centre of a little group of churches and chapels. Its Baroque facade shows signs of native influence – presumably the legacy of Indian labourers – but the main interest lies within in a series of paintings, among them a group depicting the life of San Felipe, attributed to Miguel Cabrera. Next door, off the Callejon de Loreto, you'll find the **Santa Casa de Loreto**, a copy of the Holy House at Loreto, Italy. It was put up by the Conde Manuel de la Canal, and in its gilded octagonal interior there are statues of the count and his wife, below which lie their tombs.

From here you can head down Insurgentes to the **Biblioteca Publica** (Mon–Fri 10am–2pm & 4–7pm, Sat 10am–2pm), a public library which lends **books in English**. There's a substantial collection, with quiet space to sit down and read, and they also sell a number of cheap second-hand books – either duplicates or those deemed too lightweight for preservation in the library. A couple of houses farther down, at Insurgentes 21, is the **Academia Hispano Americana**, one of many local language schools which specialize in high-pressure, total immersion techniques. Less prestigious than the Instituto, but probably better if you want to speak Spanish in a hurry.

Bellas Artes

The **Centro Cultural "El Nigromante"** – also known as **Bellas Artes** – is on Hernandez Macías, just one block downhill from the zócalo. Housed in the beautiful cloistered courtyard of the old **Convento de la Concepción**, it's an arts institute run by the state Fine Arts organization – concentrating on music and dance, but to a lesser extent teaching visual arts too. Mexicans can take courses here for virtually nothing, foreigners pay rather more. Around the courtyard there are various exhibitions, and on the upper floors several murals, including one by David Siqueiros. The church of **La Concepción**, part of the complex, is lovely too, but noted mainly for its tall dome raised on a drum, again said to be the work of the untrained Zeferino Gutiérrez.

Instituto Allende

The famous **Instituto Allende** is down at the bottom of the hill following Hernandez Macías south from La Concepción. On the way, at the corner of Cuadrante, you pass the **Casa del Inquisidor**, an eighteenth-century mansion with a particularly fine facade, now operating as an antiques and *artesanías* shop, so you can take a look inside. Opposite is the old building that served as a jail for the Inquisition. The Instituto itself, on the edges of the old town, occupies a former hacienda of the Condes de la Canal – it was moved here in 1952 when the government recognized its success and it was accredited by the University of Guanajuato. The Institute offers courses in all kinds of arts from painting to sculpture to photography, in crafts like silverwork and weaving, and Spanish-language instruction at every level, all within beautiful, park-like grounds. There's a cafe down here, even a hotel, and the noticeboards are covered with offers of long-term accommodation, requests for and offers of rides through Mexico and up to the States, and information about what's going on in San Miguel.

At the back of the Institute, the refreshing, shaded **Parque Benito Juárez** was created out of the fruit orchards of many of the city's old families. The homes rounda-bout are still some of the fanciest in town. From here it's an uphill walk to **El Chorro**, the little hill whose springs supply the city with water, which was the site of the town originally founded by Juan de San Miguel. There are good views of the town from here, but if you've the energy to climb on higher still to **El Mirador**, the viewing point on the road to Querétaro, you'll find really tremendous panoramas: San Miguel below, the broad plain and the ridge of mountains before Guanajuato in the distance.

Eating, drinking and entertainment

San Miguel is somewhat lacking in low-priced **restaurants**, though there are plenty of cafes, lively with students and ex-pats, and budget snack places: prices are high in the evenings, so check out the many cheap breakfast deals and take advantage of the lunchtime *comidas*. Prices apart, food here can come as a tremendous relief for long-term travellers, with things you may not have tasted for weeks: vegetarians, especially, should take full advantage. **Nightlife** can come expensive too, but again there's lots of it, a refreshing change in itself. The best bet is to gather with everyone else in the zócalo – to take the air, to stroll, and to check out what's going on.

Restaurants

Cafe Correo, Correo 23, just uphill from the plaza. Simple, good-value place for breakfasts and *comidas*.

El Harem, Ancha de San Antonio 18, on the road out to the Instituto Allende. Arabic restaurant serving hummus and stuffed vine leaves at low prices.

Kleins, Hernandez Macías 121, near the Instituto. Veggies, salads, soups and pasta, plus live music at weekends.

Las Musas, in the Bellas Artes complex. Coffee, sandwiches, ice cream and croissants.

Meson de San José, Mesones 38. Lovely patio restaurant in one of the better of the many new shopping courts.

El Otro Café, Mesones 95. Sandwiches, soup and salads, all very reasonably priced. Closed Sat.

Pepe's Pizza, Hidalgo 26. Pizzas, pasta and hamburgers at rock-bottom prices.

La Taberna, Hidalgo 3. Small, simple, inexpensive spot for pizza and pasta.

Restaurant El Infierno, Mesones 25. Very pleasant little Mexican seafood restaurant, serving a good-value *comida corrida*.

Restaurant La Terrazza, next door to the Parroquia. American-style food at quite high prices. You're paying for the location: this is a superb spot to watch the world go by.

Restaurant La Vendimia, Hidalgo 12. Sophisticated little place in lush colonial courtyard, serving salads, trout, steaks, sea bass and the like.

Bars and clubs

Bar Coco, Hernandez Macías and Umarán. Popular bar in the centre of town: local crowd and live music at weekends.

Laberintos, Ancha de San Antonio 7. Lively disco near the Instituto, playing Mexican music alongside popular US hits.

El Ring, Hidalgo 25. Glitzy disco a block from the zócalo, with a couples-only policy.

Around San Miguel: Taboada and Atotonilco

Although as ever there are buses to every village in the vicinity, San Miguel also has dozens of travel agencies and tour operators which, as well as tours of the city, offer many local excursions: try, for example, the *Travel Institute of San Miguel*, Cuna de Allende 11 (☎465/2-00-78), half a block from the plaza. One of the simplest and most enjoyable outings is to **TABOADA**, 8km northwest of San Miguel off the road to Dolores, where the warm thermal waters are ideal for swimming, either in the luxurious surroundings of the *Hotel Hacienda Taboada* or at the public baths just beyond. The hotel puts on a magnificent outdoor buffet three days a week – around $30 but the swimming comes as a free extra; other days there's a small charge ($3–4) for use of the pool. The public area is cheaper, just a short walk from where the bus drops you, beyond the hotel.

ATOTONILCO EL GRANDE, 8km farther in the same direction, is a rural Indian community whose church has come to be a centre of pilgrimage for two reasons – it was founded by Padre Felipe Neri, later canonized, and it was from here that Padre Hidalgo, marching from Dolores to San Miguel, took the banner of the Virgin of Guadalupe that became the flag of the Mexicans in the War of Independence. Allende was married here too. The six chapels of the church, liberally plastered with murals and freely interspersed with poems, biblical passages and painted statues, demonstrate every kind of Mexican popular art, from the naive to the highly sophisticated. There are more warm pools here too.

Querétaro

Most people seem to hammer straight past **QUERÉTARO** on the highway to México, catching sight of only the expanding industrial outskirts and the huge modern bus station. Yet of all the colonial cities in the Bajío this is perhaps the most surprising, preserving at its heart a tranquil colonial core that boasts magnificent mansions and some of the country's finest ecclesiastical architecture. Little more than two hours from México, and at the junction of every major road and rail route from the north, it is also

a wealthy and booming city, one of the fastest-growing in the republic thanks to state encouragement of investment outside the capital.

Some history

There's a history as rich and deep here as anywhere in the republic, starting before the Conquest when Querétaro (rocky place) was an Otomí town subject to the **Aztecs**; many Otomí still live in the surrounding area. In 1531 the Spanish took control relatively peacefully, and under them it grew steadily into a major city and provincial capital before becoming, in the nineteenth century, the setting for some of the most traumatic events of Mexican history. It was here, meeting under the guise of Literary Associations, that the **Independence** conspirators laid their earliest plans. In 1810 one of their number, Josefa Ortiz de Dominguez, wife of the town's Corregidor (or governor – she is known always as *La Corregidora*), found that her husband had learned of the movement's intentions. Although locked in her room, the Corregidora managed to get a message out warning the Revolutionaries, thus precipitating an unexpectedly early start to the struggle for Independence.

Later in the century, less proud events took place. The **Treaty of Guadalupe Hidalgo**, which ended the Mexican-American War by handing over almost half of Mexico's territory – Texas, New Mexico, California and more – to the USA, was signed in Querétaro in 1848. In 1867 the Emperor Maximilian made his last stand here: defeated, he was tried by a court meeting in the theatre and finally faced a firing squad on the hill just to the north of town – the Cerro de las Campañas. The same theatre hosted an important assembly of Revolutionary politicians in 1916, leading eventually to the signing here of the 1917 Constitution, still in force today.

Arrival, orientation and information

Querétaro's **Central Camionera**, at a massive new site south of town, is one of the busiest there is. An endless shuttle of local buses runs to the centre. The **train station** is 3km north of town; again there are buses as well as taxis, or you could walk – straight down Allende and then left on Madero.

For all its sprawl, Querétaro is easy enough to find your way around once you get to the centre, since the core remains confined to the grid laid down by the Spanish. Local buses run anywhere you might want to visit, and taxis are extremely cheap – on the whole, however, walking proves simpler. One very good way of getting to grips with the layout of the old town, and at least a brief glimpse of most of the important buildings, is to join the **walking tour** which sets off from the **tourist office**, Pasteur 17 (Mon–Fri 9am–2pm & 5–8pm; no phone), at 10.30am daily. It's in Spanish and costs only what you have in refreshments along the way. There are several **banks** around the main plaza, the Jardín Obregon, as well as a *casa de cambio* in the *Galerias Gran Hotel* mall, which opens off it; the **post office** is at Arteaga 7; and as well as **phone** booths all around the centre, there are *larga distancia* places at the bus station and at 5 de Mayo 33, just off the plaza.

Accommodation

For **hotels**, head straight for the zócalo and the streets in the immediate vicinity. Streetside rooms may be noisy, but any of the places around here will prove a better bet than those around the old bus station. The **youth hostel**, behind the ex-Convento de la Cruz, about a twenty-minute walk from the centre (☎421/14-30-50; $8), has clean single-sex dorms and an 11pm curfew.

Hidalgo, Madero Pte. 11, just off Jardín Obregon (☎421/12-00-81). Simple but clean rooms, some with balconies and all with bath, around an open courtyard. Good budget option. ③.

Impala, Colón 1 (☎421/12-25-70; fax 12-45-15). Big, modern, overbearing place at the south end of the Alameda; businesslike and soulless. ⑤.

Mesón de Santa Rosa, Pasteur 17 (☎421/14-56-23). Superb luxury hotel, very quiet, calm, beautiful and sophisticated, in an old colonial mansion with a great restaurant. ⑨.

Plaza, Juárez Nte. 25 on the Jardín Obrego (☎421/12-11-38). On the zócalo: clean, but a touch faded and impersonal. All rooms with bath, TV and phone. ⑤.

Posada Juárez, Juárez 29 between Zaragoza and Arteaga (☎421/2-32-32). The most basic place in town, no better than you'd expect for the price, though some rooms do come with shower. ②.

San Francisco, Corregidora Sur 144 (☎421/12-08-58). Amid all the action of this busy street, basic but not unpleasant. ④.

The City

Dominating the Jardín Hidalgo, Querétaro's main square, the church of **San Francisco** was one of the earliest founded in the city. Its beautiful facade incorporates a dome covered in *azulejos* – coloured tiles imported from Spain around 1540 – but for the most part San Francisco was rebuilt in the seventeenth and eighteenth centuries. Adjoining, in what used to be its monastery, is the **Museo Regional** (Tues–Sun 10.30am–4.30pm; $5). The building alone is reason enough to visit – built around a large cloister and going through in the back to a lovely chapel, it's far bigger than you imagine from the outside. Inside the displays are eclectic: the keyhole through which La Corregidora passed on her news; early copies of the Constitution; the table on which the Treaty of Guadalupe Hidalgo was signed; and quantities of ephemera connected with Emperor Maximilian, whose headquarters was here for a while. Then there are the more usual collections relating to local archeology, and a sizeable gallery of colonial art – altogether well worth an hour or two.

South of the museum, the **Plaza de la Constitución**, a raised paved square which used to house the market, is now left bare, without much of a role: there are a few sleazy bars and downmarket restaurants scattered around it. North of the Jardín, the **Teatro de la Republica** (Mon–Fri 10am–2pm & 5–8pm, Sat 9am–noon; free), a grand nineteenth-century structure, has played a vital role in Mexican history: here a court met to decide the fate of Emperor Maximilian, and the 1917 Constitution was agreed. A small exhibition celebrates these events, though the main reason to go in is to take a look at the theatre itself.

Around the Plaza de la Independencia

The little pedestrianized alleys that lead up to the east of the Jardín are some of the city's most interesting: crammed with ancient houses, little restaurants, art galleries and shops selling junky antiques and the opals and other semiprecious stones for which the area is famous. If you buy, make sure you know what you're getting. The first of several little plazas in this direction is the **Plaza de la Independencia** or Plaza de Armas, a very pretty, arcaded open space. In the middle of the plaza stands a statue of Don Juan Antonio Urrutia y Arana, Marques de la Villa del Villar del Aguila, the man who built Querétaro's elegant aqueduct, providing the city with drinking water. Around the square are the **Casa de la Cultura**, with exhibitions of local crafts, and the **Casa de la Corregidora**, now the Palacio Municipal (Mon–Fri 8am–9pm, Sat 9am–2pm; free). It was here, on September 14, 1810, that La Corregidora was locked up while her husband made plans to arrest the conspirators, and here that she managed to get a message to Ignacio Perez, who carried it to San Miguel and Dolores, to Allende and Hidalgo. It's an elegant building, but there's not a great deal to see inside.

The **Jardín Corregidora**, just beyond the Plaza de la Independencia, is another beautiful square, with an imposing statue of La Corregidora and several restaurants and bars where you can sit outside. Just off here on Pasteur, the **Casa de la Artesanía** is worth a look, with a fancy cafe in its patio. Andador Libertad, the pedestrian way that runs from the Jardín Corregidora to the Plaza de la Constitución, has more art galleries and boutiques.

The commercial centre

The commercial centre of Querétaro lies west of the zócalo on and around Av. Madero. This is where you'll find most of the bars and shops, on formal streets lined with stately mansions. At the corner of Madero and Allende, the little Jardín de Santa Clara features a famous **Fountain of Neptune**, designed by Tresguerras in 1797. **Francisco Eduardo Tresguerras** (1765–1833) is rightly regarded as one of Mexico's greatest architects – he was also a sculptor, painter and poet – and was almost single-handedly responsible for developing a native Mexican style diverging from (though still close to) its Spanish roots. His work, seen throughout central Mexico, is particularly evident here and in nearby Celaya, his birthplace. Beside the fountain rises the deceptively simple church of **Santa Clara**, once attached to one of the country's richest convents. Inside it's a riot of Baroque excess, with gilded cherubs and angels swarming all over the profusely decorated altarpieces.

Carry straight on down Madero and you get to the **Palacio de Gobierno** and the **cathedral** , eighteenth-century buildings, neither of which, by Querétaro's standards, is particularly distinguished. Cut down Guerrero, however, and you'll find the **Museo de Arte de Querétaro** (Tues–Sun 11am–7pm; $2, free on Tues) occupying the former **Palacio Federal** on Allende, by the church of San Agustín. Originally an Augustinian monastery (it has also been a prison and a post office in its time), this is one of the most exuberant buildings in a town full of them: at its most extreme, in the cloister, every surface of the two storeys of portals is carved with grotesque figures, no two quite alike, of men and monsters and with abstract designs. The sculptures, often attributed to Tresguerras though almost certainly not by him, are full of religious symbolism which, if possible, you should really try to get someone to explain to you. The large figures supporting the arches, for example, all hold their fingers in different positions – three held up to represent the Trinity, four for the Evangelists and so on. The contents of the museum are good, too: upstairs a brief history of the building and artworks up to the eighteenth century; downstairs there are nineteenth- and twentieth-century art and temporary exhibition spaces. There's some good modern Mexican painting here too. Around the corner at Allende and Pino Suárez, the **Casa de los Perros**, a mansion named for the ugly canine gargoyles that line its facade, is almost as exotic.

The church of **Santa Rosa de Viterbo** is farther out in this direction, at the junction of Arteaga and Montes. Its interior rivals Santa Clara for richness of decoration, but here there is no false modesty on the outside either. Two enormous flying buttresses support the octagonal cupola – remodelled by Tresguerras – and a blue- and white-tiled dome. The needling tower, too, is Tresguerras' work, holding what is said to be the first four-sided public clock erected on the American continent.

Convento de la Cruz

Slightly farther afield, but still in easy walking distance, is the **Convento de la Cruz** (Mon–Sat 9am–2pm & 4–6pm, Sun 9.30am–4.30pm; small donation requested). This monastery is built on the site of the battle between the Spanish and the Otomí in which the Conquistadors gained control of Querétaro – according to legend, the fighting was cut short by the miraculous appearance of Saint James (*Santiago*) and a dazzling cross in the sky, which persuaded the Indians to concede defeat and become Christians. The **Capilla del Calvarito**, opposite the monastery entrance, marks the spot where the first mass was celebrated after the battle. The monastery itself was founded in 1683 by the Franciscans as a college for the propagation of the faith (*Colegio Apostolico de*

Propaganda Fide) and grew over the years into an important centre for the training of missionaries, with a massive library and rich collection of relics.

Because of its hilltop position and hefty construction, the monastery was also frequently used as a fortress – one of the last redoubts of the Spanish in the War of Independence, it was Maximilian's headquarters for the last few weeks of his reign; he was subsequently imprisoned here to await execution. Nowadays you can take guided tours: the proudest exhibit is the **Arbol de la Cruz**, a tree whose thorns grow in the shape of little crosses. The tree grew, according to the story, from a walking stick left behind by a mysterious saintly traveller who slept here one night – certainly it does produce thorns in the form of a cross, but that may not be so rare. The monks, however, appear very excited by the phenomenon and point out that an additional 5 percent of the thorns grow with extra spikes to mark the spots where nails were driven through Christ's hands and feet.

Beyond the monastery you can see the **Aqueduct**, a beautiful series of arches up to 30m high that still brings water into the city from springs nearly 6km away. Spotlit at night, it looks magnificent from a distance, especially as you drive into town.

Cerro de las Campañas

Northwest of the centre, the **Cerro de las Campañas** (Hill of Bells) commands wider, if rather less scenic, views over Querétaro and its industrial outskirts. Maximilian and his two generals, Miguel Miramón and Tomás Mejía, faced their firing squad here. The hill is dominated by a vast stone statue of the victor of that particular war, Benito Juárez, glaring down over the town from its summit. Parts of the new university campus sprawl up one slope too.

Eating and drinking

There's plenty of good food in Querétaro, and some delightful places to sit outside amid the alleys and plazas east of the Jardín Obregón. The zócalo itself has plenty of rather cheaper places. If you want to get together something of your own, head for the **market** – in a huge setting off Calzada Zaragoza, not far from the Alameda.

Bisquets, in *Galerias Gran Hotel*, off Jardín Obregón. Straightforward, inexpensive Mexican place with good breakfasts; also in the mall, *Manolos* has great *comidas*.

Cafe Tulipe, Calzada de los Arcos 3, near the beginning of the aqueduct. Buzzy, studenty place with cheerful art on the walls. Tasty Mexican food and international dishes such as a deliciously gloopy fondue.

La Flor de Querétaro, Juárez on Jardín Obregón. Good *comidas corridas* and straightforward local food.

Fonda del Refugio, Jardín Corregidora. Not too expensive, very elegant place to sit outside, drink, and watch the world go by.

Mesón de Santa Rosa, Jardín Corregidora. Superb restaurant serving Mexican specialities and Spanish food in a beautiful setting, with prices to match.

Ostionería Tampico, Jardín Corregidora. Expensive seafood in a great setting.

Primavera, Corregidora 130 under *Hotel Corregidora*. Good vegetarian restaurant.

On to México

From Querétaro you can race straight into the capital on the highway (Hwy-57, one of the fastest roads in the country). Hundreds of buses a day pass through, and they remain quicker and easier than the train. Many of the buses pull in for a stop at **SAN JUAN DEL RÍO**, 50km or so south of Querétaro. It looks like nothing at all from the highway, but is in fact a major market centre, and a popular weekend outing from the capital. Among the goods sold here are gemstones – mostly local opals but also imported jewels which are polished and set in town – baskets, wine and cheese. If you are going to buy gems, be very careful; it's easy to get ripped off without expert advice. Other purchases are safer, though not particularly cheap on the whole. The best-known wine is *Hidalgo*, a brand name sold all over the country and usually reliable. You can visit their cellars (**Cavas de San Juan**) a short distance out of town on the road to Tequisquiapan. From the Central Camionera, miles to the south on the wrong side of the *Cuota* superhighway from town, take a local bus up Av. Hidalgo to the central Plaza de los Fundadores: the Mercado Reforma is a couple of long blocks north of here up Hidalgo, halfway to the train station. If you decide that you'd like to stay a while to enjoy San Juan's unhurried atmosphere, take your choice of three good **hotels**, all near the centre of town where Juárez crosses Hidalgo: *Estancia*, Juárez 30, friendly, pleasant and comfortable (☎467/2-00-38; ④); the simple and inexpensive *San Juan*, Hidalgo Sur 6 (☎467/2-00-13; ③); or, best of all, *Layseca*, around the corner from the latter at Juárez 9 (☎467/2-01-10; ⑤), an old colonial house with rooms set around a beautiful open courtyard.

Some 20km north of San Juan, along a road lined with factories and workshops, **TEQUISQUIAPAN** is a former Otomí village now overrun by villas catering for escapees from México, who come here to enjoy the springs. It remains very picturesque, if somewhat exclusive, and like San Juan del Río has a big crafts market – especially active on Sundays – one block from the main plaza. At the end of May running into June, Tequisquiapan hosts a major wine and cheese festival, the **Feria Nacional de Queso y Vino**, which is well worth going a bit out of your way for – plenty of free food and drink, and no shortage of other entertainments.

Direct **buses** run from Querétaro to Tequisquiapan (extra ones during the *feria*), and there are local services from San Juan. **Accommodation** in town tends to be overpriced, so it's best to call in for the day and head on. If you do want to stay, you'll certainly have to pay for it: *La Plaza*, Juárez 10, on the plaza (☎467/3-00-05; ⑦), is a perfect luxury hotel, very relaxed, with its own pool; *Casablanca*, 5 de Mayo (☎467/3-00-78; ⑥), is slightly cheaper but still smart, and also has a pool.

Two more places off this route, covered in Chapter Five, are the ancient Toltec capital of **Tula**, and **Tepotzotlán** with its magnificent Baroque architecture. Tula is some way from the motorway and means changing buses, though it is on the railway, while Tepotzotlán is very close to the road, but also so close to México that unless you're driving yourself it's probably easier visited as an outing from there.

fiestas

The Bajío is one of the most active regions in Mexico when it comes to celebrations. The state of Guanajuato, especially, is rich in fiestas: the list below is by no means exhaustive; local tourist offices will have further details.

January

1st NEW YEAR'S DAY widely celebrated. Fair in **Dolores Hidalgo** (Guanajuato).

6th *Feria* begins in **Matehuala** (San Luis Potosí), lasting till the 15th.

20th DÍA DE SAN SEBASTIAN. In **San Luis Potosí** (S.L.P.) the climax of ten days of pilgrimages, in **León** (Gto.) the religious festival coincides with the agricultural and industrial fair.

February

1st **Cadereyta** (Que.), northeast of Querétaro, holds a festival famous for its cockfights – also religious processions, dancing and *mariachi*.

CARNIVAL: the week before Lent, variable Feb-March On the Sunday **Yuriria** (Gto.), between Celaya and Morelia, has real bullfights, processions and dances.

March

First Friday in **San Miguel de Allende** (Gto.) FIESTA DEL SEÑOR DE LA CONQUISTA.

PALM SUNDAY (week before Easter) is the culmination of a week's celebration in **San Miguel de Allende** (Gto.) with a pilgrimage to Atotonilco.

HOLY WEEK is observed everywhere. There's a huge procession, while in **San Miguel de Allende** every family constructs an elaborate altar, proudly displayed in the house.

April

In early April (variable) **Irapuato** (Gto.) holds its FERIA DE LA FRESA (Strawberry Fair) in honour of the region's principal cash crop.

25th FERIA DE SAN MARCOS in **Aguascalientes** (Aguascalientes) runs for around a week either side of this date. One of the largest and most famous in Mexico, there's dancing, bullfights, music, *charrerías* and great wine.

May

24th **Empalme Escobeda** (Gto.), near San Miguel de Allende, has a fiesta lasting until the next Sunday, with traditional dances including that of *Los Apaches*, one of the few in which women take part.

CORPUS CHRISTI (variable – the Thursday after Trinity) is celebrated in **San Miguel de Allende** (Gto.). The following Wednesday sees a very ancient fiesta in **Juchipila** (Zac.), between Zacatecas and Guadalajara, with flowers and dances including the famous *Jarabe Tapatío*, the Mexican Hat Dance.

The FERIA NACIONAL DE QUESO Y VINO in **Tequisquiapan** (Que.) runs from late May through early June.

June

23rd FESTIVAL DE LA PRESA DE OLLA in **Guanajuato** (Gto.).

29th DÍA DE SAN PEDRO. **Chalchihuites** (Zac.), between Zacatecas and Durango, stages a "Battle of the Flowers" in which local kids take part.

July

4th **Acambaro** (Gto.), a very ancient town between Celaya and Morelia, has a fiesta with religious processions, music and many traditional dances.

16th DÍA DE LA VIRGEN DEL CARMEN celebrated in **Celaya** (Gto.).

25th DÍA DE SANTIAGO widely observed. Mass pilgrimages to **San Luis Potosí** (S.L.P); saint's day celebrations in **Santiago Maravatío** (Gto.), near Irapuato; stylized battles between Moors and Christians in **Jesús María** (Ags.), near Aguascalientes.

August

15th DÍA DE LA ASUNCION (Assumption) coincides with the FERIA DE LA UVA in **Aguascalientes** (Ags.) and the FERIA DE LA CAJETA in **Celaya** (Gto.), celebrating the syrupy confection made here.

25th DÍA DE SAN LUIS hugely enjoyed in **San Luis Potosí** (S.L.P) – giant procession and fireworks.

27th In **Zacatecas** (Zac.), battles between Moors and Christians on the Cerro de la Bufa are the highlight of several days' celebrations.

September

1st DÍA DE LA VIRGEN DE REMEDIOS justifies a fiesta in **Comonfort** (Gto.), near San Miguel de Allende. Traditional dances.

8th In **Jerez** (Zac.) the start of a festival lasting till the 15th.

14th Ten days of pilgrimages to the Señora del Patrocinio start in **Zacatecas** (Zac.), coinciding with the FERIA NACIONAL and all sorts of secular entertainments, especially bullfights.

15th–16th INDEPENDENCE CELEBRATIONS everywhere, above all in **Dolores Hidalgo** (Gto.) and **Querétaro** (Que.), where they start several days early.

28th Start of the three-day festival of San Miguel in **San Felipe** (Gto.), north of Dolores Hidalgo, with Otomí dances and battles between Moors and Christians.

DÍA DE SAN MIGUEL (variable, a Friday around the end of Sept) is the most important of **San Miguel de Allende's** (Gto.) many fiestas: two days of processions, concerts, dancing, bullfights and ceremonies.

October

3rd DÍA DE SAN FRANCISCO DE ASIS. Major pilgrimage to **Real de Catorce** (S.L.P.) and festivities in the town.

4th DÍA DE SAN FRANCISCO. **Nochistlán** (Zac.), between Aguascalientes and Guadalajara, starts a *feria* lasting to the end of the month.

23rd **Coroneo** (Gto.), south of Querétaro, begins a three-day *feria*.

November

2nd DÍA DE LOS MUERTOS (All Souls). The famous Day of the Dead is celebrated everywhere.

7th–14th FIESTA DE LAS ILUMINACIONES in **Guanajuato** (Gto.).

Last Sunday Fiesta and crafts markets in **Comonfort** (Gto.).

December

8th DÍA DE LA INMACULADA CONCEPCIÓN. **Dolores Hidalgo** (Gto.) combines a religious festival with a *feria* and traditional dancing.

16th–25th The traditional Christmas Posadas are widely performed. Particularly good in **Celaya** (Gto.). In **Querétaro** (Que.), on the 23rd, there's a giant procession with bands and carnival floats.

travel details

Buses

Relatively densely populated, the Bajío is criss-crossed by thousands of services, locally between towns and villages, and long-distance runs that call in at all major towns on their routes. It can occasionally be difficult to pick up a *de paso* seat on the latter: they're not normally sold until the bus has arrived. As the roads converge on major destinations, so the number of buses increases – there's a constant stream calling in at Querétaro, for example, before the last 2hr 30min stretch to México. In general the fastest and most efficient operators are *Omnibus de Mexico* and *Tres Estrellas de Oro*, though there's little to choose between the first-class companies. *Flecha Amarilla* covers many of the local runs and is fairly reliable – *Estrella Blanca* is better but less frequent. What follows is a minimum, covering the major stops only – it should be assumed that these buses also call at the towns en route.

Aguascalientes to: Guadalajara (9 daily; 6hr); Guanajuato (4 daily; 4hr); León (hourly; 1hr); México (hourly; 7hr); Querétaro (hourly; 6hr); San Luis Potosí (7 daily; 2hr 30min); San Miguel de Allende (daily; 4hr); Zacatecas (hourly; 2hr).

Dolores Hidalgo to: Guanajuato (7 daily; 1hr); México (hourly; 5hr); Querétaro (hourly; 2hr); San Miguel de Allende (every 15min; 1hr).

Guanajuato to: Aguascalientes (4 daily; 4hr); Dolores Hidalgo (every 20min; 1hr); Guadalajara (5 daily; 6hr); León (constantly; 40min); México (7 daily; 4hr); Querétaro (8 daily; 3hr); San Luis de la Paz (5 daily; 2hr 30min); San Luis Potosí (4 daily; 4hr); San Miguel de Allende (7 daily; 2hr).

León to: Aguascalientes (hourly; 1hr); Guadalajara (hourly; 4hr); Guanajuato (constantly; 40min) México (hourly; 5hr); Querétaro (hourly; 2hr).

Querétaro to: Aguascalientes (hourly; 6hr); Dolores Hidalgo (hourly; 2hr); Guadalajara (hourly; 6hr); Guanajuato (8 daily; 3hr); León (hourly; 2hr); México (every 10min; 3hr); San Luis Potosí (hourly; 3hr); San Miguel de Allende (every 30min; 1hr); Zacatecas (hourly; 5hr).

San Luis Potosí to: Aguascalientes (7 daily; 2hr 30min); Guadalajara (9 daily; 6hr); Guanajuato (4 daily; 4hr); México (at least 15 daily; 5hr 30min); Monterrey (hourly; 7hr); Querétaro (hourly; 3hr); Zacatecas (hourly; 2hr 30min).

San Miguel de Allende to: Aguascalientes (daily; 4hr); Dolores Hidalgo (every 15min; 1hr); Guanajuato (7 daily; 2hr); México (every 30min; 4hr); Querétaro (every 30min; 1hr).

Zacatecas to: Aguascalientes (hourly; 2hr); Chihuahua (hourly; 12hr); Ciudad Juárez (hourly; 12–15hr); Durango (hourly; 5hr); Guadalajara (hourly; 6hr); León (hourly; 2hr); México (at least 15 daily; 8hr upwards); Monterrey (hourly; 10hr); Querétaro (hourly; 5hr); San Luis Potosí (hourly; 2hr 30min); Torreón (hourly; 7hr).

Trains

Zacatecas, Aguascalientes and Querétaro are all on the main rail line from México to the border at Ciudad Juárez, while the route from the capital to Monterrey passes through San Luis Potosí. Each of these lines has two long-distance services in each direction. In addition there are first-class only business-oriented services from México to Querétaro, San Luis Potosí, San Miguel de Allende and Guanajuato, leaving the capital early in the morning and returning in the afternoon, and an overnight service in both directions from Zacatecas.

CHAPTER FIVE

MÉXICO AND AROUND

The Valley of México has been the centre of gravity of the Mexican nation since earliest pre-history – long before the concept of such a nation existed. In this mountain-ringed basin – 100km long, 60km wide, 2500m high, dotted with great salt and fresh-water lagoons and dominated by the vast snow-capped volcanic peaks of Popocatépetl and Ixtaccíhuatl – were based the most powerful civilizations the country has seen. Today the lakes have all but disappeared and the mountains are shrouded in smog, but it continues to be the heart of the country: its physical centre, the generator of every political, cultural and economic pulse.

At the crossroads of everything sprawls the vibrant, elegant, choking, crime-ridden fascination of **México**. Arguably the largest city in the world, its lure is irresistible. Beside the mansions of the colonial centre lie excavated pyramids and over them tower the concrete and glass of thrusting development: the city today has fabulous museums and galleries, but above all it's alive – exciting, sometimes frightening, always bewildering – but boldly alive. You can't avoid it, and if you genuinely want to know anything of Mexico you shouldn't try – even if the attraction does sometimes seem to be the same ghoulish fascination that draws onlookers to the site of a particularly nasty accident. Round about there's escape, and interest, in every direction: to the north Tula and Teotihuacán and the magnificent Baroque treasures of **Tepotzotlán**; to the west the market town of **Toluca** and mountainous national parks that are the rural retreat of the wealthy; to the south **Cuernavaca** with its ancient palaces and **Taxco**, where the silver comes from; in the east the volcanoes, **Cholula**, and ultra-colonial, thriving **Puebla**.

It is above all the **Aztecs**, whose warrior state was crushed by Cortés, who are associated with the area today. But they were relative newcomers, forging their empire by force of arms in less than two centuries and borrowing their culture, their science, their arts, even their language from Valley societies that had gone before. **Teotihuacán**, whose mighty pyramids still stand some 50km northeast of the modern city, was the predominant culture of the Classic period and the true forebear of the Aztecs – a city of some 200,000 people whose influence spread throughout the country, south to the Maya lands in the Yucatán and beyond into Guatemala and Central America. Their style, though never so militaristic as later societies, was adopted everywhere: Quetzalcoatl, the plumed serpent, and Tlaloc, the rain god, were Teotihuacán deities.

For all its pre-eminence, though, Teotihuacán was neither the earliest, nor the only settlement in the Valley; the pyramid at **Cuicuilco**, now in the south of the city, is probably the oldest stone structure in the country, and there were small agricultural communities all around the lakes. Nor did the Aztecs, arriving some 500 years after the destruction of Teotihuacán, acknowledge their debt. They regarded themselves as descendants of the **Toltec** kingdom, whose capital lay at **Tula** to the north, and whose influence – as successors to Teotihuacán – was almost as pervasive. The Aztecs consciously took over the Toltec military-based society, and adopted many of their gods: above all Quetzalcoatl who assumed an importance equal to that of their own tribal deity, Huitzilopochtli, the god of war who had brought them to power and demanded human sacrifice to keep them there. In this, in many respects, they were right, for the Toltecs, like the Aztecs themselves, had arrived in central Mexico as a marauding tribe of Chichimeca (sons of dogs) from the north, absorbing the local culture even as they came to dominate it.

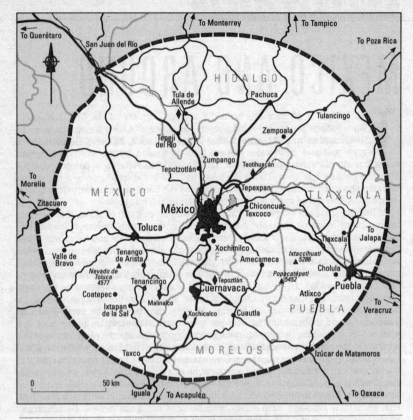

THE CAPITAL

And when we saw all those cities and villages built in the water, and other great towns on dry land, and that straight and level causeway leading to Mexico, we were astounded. These great towns and cues and buildings rising from the water, all made of stone, seemed like an enchanted vision from the tales of Amadis. Indeed, some of our soldiers asked whether it was not all a dream.

Bernal Díaz

It is hardly surprising that Cortés and his followers should have been so taken by their first sight of **Tenochtitlán**, capital of the Aztecs. For what they found, built in the middle of a lake traversed by great causeways, was a beautiful, strictly regulated, stone-built city of 300,000 people – easily the equal of anything they might have experienced in Europe. The Aztec people (or more properly the Mexica) had arrived at the lake, after years of wandering and living off what they could scavenge or pillage from settled communities, in around 1345. Their own legends have it that Huitzilopochtli had ordered them to build a city where they found an eagle perched on a cactus devouring a snake, and this they duly saw on an island in the middle of the lake (the nopal, eagle and snake motif forms the centrepiece of the modern Mexican flag and is seen everywhere, from coins and official seals to woven designs on rugs). The reality was probably more desperate –

driven from place to place, the lake seemed a last resort – but for whatever reasons it proved an ideal site. Well stocked with fish, it was fertile too once they had constructed their *chinampas*, or floating gardens of reeds, and virtually impregnable; the causeways, when they were completed, could be flooded and the bridges raised to thwart attacks (or escape, as the Spanish found to their cost on the *Noche Triste* see p.556).

The **island city** eventually expanded to cover an area of some thirteen square kilometres, much of it reclaimed from the lake, and from this base the Aztecs were able to begin their programme of expansion. First, by a series of strategic alliances, war and treachery, dominating the valley, and finally, in a period of less than a hundred years before the Conquest, establishing an empire that demanded tribute from and traded with the farthest parts of the country. This was the situation when **Cortés** landed on the east coast in 1519, bringing with him an army of only a few hundred men, and began his long march on Tenochtitlán. Three things assured his survival: superior weaponry, and above all the shock effect of horses (never having seen such animals, the Indians at first believed them to be extensions of their riders) and firearms; the support of tribes who were either enemies or suppressed subjects of the Aztecs; and the unwillingness of **Moctezuma II** (Montezuma) to resist openly.

The Aztec emperor, who had suffered heavy defeats in campaigns against the Tarascans in the west, was a broodingly religious man who, it is said, believed Cortés to be the pale-skinned, bearded god Quetzalcoatl, returned to fulfil ancient prophecies. Accordingly he admitted him to the city – fearfully, but with a show of ceremonious welcome. By way of repaying this hospitality the Spanish took Moctezuma prisoner, and later attacked the great Aztec temples, killing many priests and placing Christian chapels alongside their altars. Meanwhile there was growing unrest in the city at the emperor's passivity and at the rapacious behaviour of his guests. Moctezuma was eventually killed – according to the Spanish stoned to death by his own people while trying to quell a riot – and the Spaniards driven from the city with heavy losses. Cortés and a few of his followers, however, escaped to the security of Tlaxcala, most loyal of his native allies, there to regroup and plan a new assault. Finally, reinforced and re-armed, swelled by Indian allies and with ships built in secret, they laid a three-month siege, finally taking the city in the face of suicidal opposition in August 1521.

It is still a harsh memory – Cortés himself is hardly revered, but the Indians who assisted him, and in particular Moctezuma and Malinche, the Indian woman who acted as Cortés's interpreter, are non-people. You won't find a monument to Moctezuma in the country, though Cuauhtémoc, his successor who led the fierce resistance, is commemorated everywhere; Malinche is represented, acidly, in some of Diego Rivera's more outspoken murals. More telling, perhaps, of the bitterness of the struggle, is that so little remains: "All that I saw then", wrote Bernal Díaz, "is overthrown and destroyed; nothing is left standing". The victorious Spanish systematically smashed every visible aspect of the old culture, as often as not using the very stones of the old city to construct the new, and building a palace for Cortés on the site of the Aztec emperor's palace. A few decades ago it was thought that everything was lost; slowly, however, particularly during construction of the Metro and in the remarkable discovery of remains of the **Templo Mayor** beneath the colonial zócalo, remains of Tenochtitlán have been brought to light.

The **new city** developed slowly in its early years, only attaining the level of population that the old had enjoyed at the beginning of this century. It spread far wider, however, as the lake was drained, filled and built over – only tiny vestiges remain today – and grew with considerable grace. In many ways it's a singularly unfortunate place to site a modern city. Pestilent from the earliest days, the inadequately drained waters harboured fevers, and the Indian population was constantly swept by epidemics of European diseases. Many of the buildings, too, simply began to sink into the soft lake bed – a process not helped by regular earthquakes. You'll see old churches and mansions leaning at crazy angles throughout the centre, and evidence of the disastrous earthquake of September 1985 is still apparent.

Visiting the city, though, the horrors that recent growth and industrialization have brought are of more immediate concern. Estimated at around 22 million, the city's **population** is the fastest growing in the world (from fewer than 5 million in 1960) and at present rates will reach 35 million by the end of the century. **Pollution**, churned out by industry but even more by the chaotic traffic, is trapped in the bowl of mountains, hanging permanently in a pall of smog over the city. As you fly in, and often, even, as you arrive by bus over the mountains, you descend from clear blue skies into a thick greyish-yellow cloud: Popocatépetl and Ixtaccíhuatl, the volcanoes on which every visitor used to comment ("Japanese contoured shapes of pastel blue and porcelain snow, and thin formal curls of smoke afloat in a limpid sky", wrote Sybille Bedford in the 1950s) are now rarely visible from the centre. Within hours of arriving your eyes smart and your throat is sore – just breathing is said to be the equivalent of smoking forty cigarettes a day (it's a good place to quit) and chronic bronchitis is endemic among residents. At 2240m, there wasn't much oxygen to begin with. Not surprisingly, Mexico is also the city with the most petty crime in the country, and where you feel least secure walking the streets at night: the centre is safe enough, and the luxurious suburbs, but you should avoid taking risks away from these. None of this should deter you – a certain seaminess amid the elegance of the new quarters and the genteel decay of the old is all part of the city's undeniable charm.

On the whole you won't see the shantytowns, and you'll soon get used to the atmosphere, but it's as well to remember they're there. You'll find the city much easier to take if you acclimatize to the country first – if at all possible try not to spend too long here when you first arrive. Get to know it slowly, and exercise the sort of caution you would in any major city, and you'll enjoy it a lot more.

Orientation

First, forget that you're in Mexico City. As far as a Mexican is concerned you're not, you're in **México**, or possibly *El D.F.* (Day Effé). It's a source of infinite confusion to visitors, but the fact is that the country took its name from the city and México, in conversation, almost always means the latter (in the country it's written Mexico D.F. – the *Distrito Federal* being the administrative zone that contains most of the urban areas). The nation is *La Republica*, or in speeches *La Patria*: very rarely Mexico.

For all its size and the horrors of its traffic, México, once you're used to it, is surprisingly easy to find your way around. Certainly there is more logic in its plan than in any European city and given an efficient and very cheap, if horrendously crowded, public transport system, and reasonably priced taxis, you should have no trouble getting about. Remember the altitude – walking gets tiring quickly, especially for the first day or two.

Traditional centre of the city is the **zócalo**, or Plaza Mayor; the heart of ancient Tenochtitlán and of Cortés' City, it's surrounded by the oldest streets, largely colonial and unmodernized. To the east the ancient structures degenerate rapidly, blending into the slums that surround the airport. Westwards, Avenidas **Madero** and **Juárez** lead to the **Alameda**, the small park that marks the extent of the old city centre. Here is the Palacio de las Bellas Artes, the main post office and the landmark Torre Latino-Americano. Carry straight on past here and you get into an area, between the ugly bulk of the **Monumento a la Revolución** and the train station, where you'll find many of the cheaper hotels. Turn slightly to the left, however, and you're on the elegant **Paseo de la Reforma**, which leads down to the great open space of **Chapultepec Park**, recreation area for the city's millions, and home of the national Museum of Anthropology and several other important **museums**. Off to the left as you head down Reforma is the

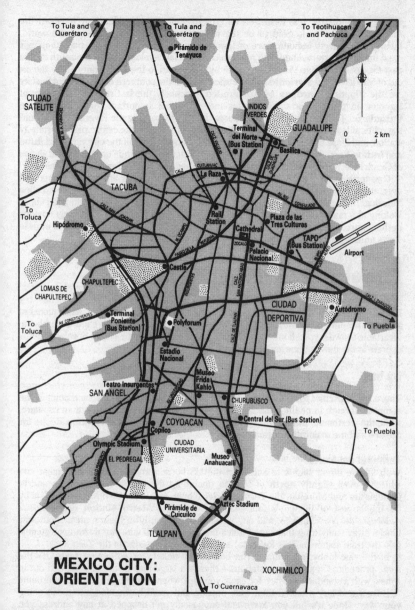

MEXICO CITY: ORIENTATION

To Tula and Querétaro

To Tula and Querétaro

To Teotihuacan and Pachuca

CIUDAD SATELITE

Pirámide de Tenayuca

INDIOS VERDES

GUADALUPE

0   2 km

Terminal del Norte (Bus Station)

Basílica

TACUBA

CALZ

CALZ

La Raza

Plaza de las Tres Culturas

Rail Station

Cathedral

TAPO (Bus Station)

Hipódromo

ZOCALO

Palacio Nacional

Airport

To Toluca

Castle

CHAPULTEPEC

LOMAS DE CHAPULTEPEC

CIUDAD DEPORTIVA

Autódromo

To Puebla

To Toluca

AV. CONSTITUYENTES

Terminal Poniente (Bus Station)

Polyforum

RIO CHURUBUSCO

Estadio Nacional

Museo Frida Kahlo

Teatro Insurgentes

SAN ANGEL

CHURUBUSCO

COYOACAN

Copilco

Central del Sur (Bus Station)

To Puebla

Olympic Stadium

CIUDAD UNIVERSITARIA

Museo Anahuacalli

EL PEDREGAL

Pirámide de Cuicuilco

Aztec Stadium

TLALPAN

XOCHIMILCO

To Cuernavaca

Zona Rosa with its chic shopping streets, expensive hotels, fancy restaurants and constant tourist activity. On the right is a more sedate, upmarket residential area where many of the long-established embassies are based. Beyond Chapultepec, Reforma runs out of the city through the ultra-smart suburb of **Las Lomas**.

The **Avenida de los Insurgentes** crosses Reforma about halfway between the Alameda and the park. Said to be the longest continuous city street in the world, Insurgentes bisects México more or less from north to south. It is perhaps the city's most important artery, lined with modern commercial development. In the south it runs past the suburb of **San Angel** and close by **Coyoacán** to the **University City**, and on out of México by the **Pyramid of Cuicuilco**. Also in the southern extremities of the city are the **Floating Gardens of Xochimilco** – virtually the last remains of the great lagoons. In the outskirts Insurgentes meets another important through-route, the **Calzada de Tlalpan**, which heads back to the zócalo, passing the Rivera Museum and the other side of Coyoacán. To the north, Insurgentes leaves the centre past the railway station, and close by the northbound bus station, to sweep out of the city via **Guadalupe** and **Indios Verdes**. The northern extension of Reforma, too, ends up at the great shrine of Guadalupe, as does the continuation of the Calzada de Tlalpan beyond the zócalo.

One further point to remember is that many **street names** are repeated over and over again in different parts of the city – there must be hundreds of streets called Morelos, Juárez or Hidalgo, and a good score of 5 de Mayos. If you're taking a cab, or looking at a map, you should always be clear which area you mean – it's fairly obvious in the centre, but searching out an address in the suburbs can lead to a series of false starts unless you're clear of the general location or the name of the *barrio*.

Arrival

Arriving unprepared in the vastness of México can be a disconcerting experience, but in fact it's not hard to get into the centre, or to a hotel, from any of the major points of arrival. The only problem is likely to be hauling large items of luggage through the invariable crowds: you should take a taxi if you are at all heavily laden. Special systems operate at the bus stations and the airport.

By bus

There are four chief **long-distance bus stations** in México, one for each point of the compass, though in practice the northbound terminal handles far more than its share, while the westbound one is tiny. All have *guarderías,* and **hotel reservation desks** for México and the major destinations served.

Terminal del Norte

With all the direct routes to and from the US border, and serving every major city which is even slightly **north** of México (including the fastest services from and to Guadalajara and Morelia), the **Terminal del Norte**, Av. de los Cien Metros 4907, is by far the largest of the city's four stations. There's a **Metro station** (*Terminal de Autobuses del Norte*; line 5), and city buses heading south on Insurgentes, about four blocks away – anything that says "Metro Insurgentes" will take you down Insurgentes, past the train station, across Reforma, and on through the edge of the *Zona Rosa*.

In the vast lobby, government-run booths sell tickets for **collective taxis**. It's the same procedure in all the bus stations – there's a large map of the city marked out in zones, with a standard, set fare for each; you pick where you're going (almost certainly "Centro") and buy a ticket, then walk outside and you'll be hustled into a cab going your way. Once it's full you leave and supposedly get dropped at any address you choose within the stated zone. There are just two problems; firstly the driver may drop

---

The **telephone area code** for México is ☎5.

CHECKLIST OF DESTINATIONS FROM MÉXICO'S BUS TERMINALS

TERMINAL DEL NORTE

Aguascalientes	Hermosillo	Querétaro
Chapala	Los Mochis	Saltillo
Chihuahua	Manzanillo	San Miguel de Allende
Ciudad Juárez	Monterrey	Teotihuacán
Colima	Morelia	Tijuana
Durango	Pachuca	Torreon
Guadalajara	Patzcuaro	Tula
Guanajuato	Puerto Vallarta	Zacatecas
Guaymas		

TAPO

Amecameca	Jalapa	San Cristóbal de las Casas
Cancún	Mérida	Tehuacan
Campeche	Oaxaca	Tuxpan
Chetumal	Orizaba	Tuxtla Gutiérrez
Cordoba	Palenque	Veracruz
Cozumel	Popocatepetl	Villahermosa
Fortín de las Flores	Puebla	Zempoala
Ixtaccihuatl		

SUR

Acapulco	Iguala	Taxco
Chilpancingo	Ixtapa	Tepotzlan
Cuautla	Oaxtepec	Zihuatanejo
Cuernavaca		

PONIENTE

Guadalajara	Morelia	Toluca

you a block or two from your hotel rather than take a major detour through the one-way systems (best to accept this unless it's very late at night), and secondly he may demand a large tip, which you're in no way obliged to pay.

TAPO

Eastbound services use the most modern of the termini, the **Terminal de Autobuses de Pasajeros de Oriente**, always known as **TAPO**. Buses for Puebla, for Veracruz, and for places which you might think of as south – Oaxaca, Chiapas and the Yucatán, even Guatemala – leave from here. It's located on Av. Ignacio Zaragoza, out towards the airport, there's a **Metro** station inside the same modern complex (*San Lazaro*; line 1) and regular buses up Zaragoza towards the zócalo and on to Reforma.

Central de Autobuses del Sur

Buses to the Pacific Coast, for Cuernavaca, Taxco, Acapulco and Zihuatanejo in particular, leave from the **Central de Autobuses del Sur**, Av. Taxqueña 1320. It's at the end of Metro line 2 (*Tasqueña*) which is also a big terminus for local buses from the centre – the #7D will take you in to the junction of Juárez and Reforma, or in the streets around the zócalo look for "Metro Tasqueña", "La Villa/Tlalpan", or "La Villa/Xochimilco". If you arrive here by Metro, ignore the signs that point to the *Central de Autobuses* which lead to the city bus stands; the long-distance terminal is immediately obvious when you go out the front of the Metro station.

Terminal Poniente

Finally, for **the west**, there's the **Terminal Poniente**, at the junction of Calles Sur and Tacubaya. The smallest of them, it basically handles traffic to Toluca, but it's also the place to go for the slower, more scenic routes to Morelia and Guadalajara, via Toluca. Hard by the *Observatorio* Metro station, there are also buses heading south on Reforma (look for "Observatorio") or from the stands by the entrance to Chapultepec Park.

By air

The **airport** is some way from the centre, but it is still very much within the city limits and you get amazing views as you come in to land, low over the houses. There are **tourist information** and hotel reservation desks here, and several **banks**, which change money 24 hours a day. As you emerge from Customs and Immigration, or even off an internal flight, you'll be besieged by offers of a taxi into town. Ignore them. By the main exit doors you'll find a booth selling tickets for the *SETTA* airport transit. They used to run a bus, but currently this is no more than a system of official taxis, with a scale of fares posted according to where you want to go. You simply buy a ticket, then take it outside and present it to the driver of one of the waiting white-and-yellow taxis. The system has been set up to avoid rip-offs, and you won't do any better. If you go with an unofficial driver – as often as not it turns out to be a private car – you're very unlikely to pay less, whatever extravagant claims they may make, and there's always the remote possibility that you could find yourself relieved of your money and luggage and dumped by the roadside somewhere. If you're travelling extremely light you could also go in on the Metro (*Terminal Aerea*; line 5, up to the left from the main terminal building – **not** *Aeropuerto*) or walk out to the main road and catch a bus.

By train

All mainline **trains** arrive at the **Estación Central de Buenavista**, just off Av. Insurgentes Nte. about nine blocks from its junction with Reforma. There's no Metro station particularly near, but you'll find a large taxi rank right outside, and buses and taxis heading south on Insurgentes towards Reforma and the *Zona Rosa*, or west on Mosqueta towards the zócalo. Many of the cheaper hotels are in easy walking distance.

City transport

You'll want to walk around the cramped streets of the centre. Heading for Chapultepec, though, or the *Zona Rosa*, you're better off taking the bus or Metro – it's an interesting walk all the way down Reforma, but a very long one. And for the farther suburbs you've clearly got no choice but to rely on taxis or public transport. You'll save a lot of hassle if you avoid travelling during **rush hour** (about 7– 9am & 5–7pm).

Tours that take in the city and often include the surrounding area are available from most of the more expensive hotels, and specialist operators such as *Grey Line*, Londres 166 (☎208-11-63), *London Tours*, Londres 101 (☎533-07-66), and *American Express* at various places around the city (☎514-06-29).

Driving

If you have a car, it's best to choose a hotel with secure parking and leave it there for the duration of your stay, except possibly to do the tour of the south of the city. Driving in the city is a nightmare, compounded by confusing one-way and through-route systems, by the impossibility of finding anywhere to park and by traffic police who can spot foreign plates a mile off and know a potential "fine" when they see one. What is more, as an anti-pollution measure all cars are banned from driving between 5am and 10pm on one weekday depending on the last digit of their number plate: you cannot drive on Monday if your plate ends with 5 or 6, Tuesday 7 or 8, Wednesday 3 or 4, Thursday 1 or 2, or Friday 9 or 0; between 10pm and 5am and at weekends, no ban applies. If you do insist on driving, note that the "Green Angels" that operate throughout the rest of the country (see p.35) do not operate within México: for **breakdown help** call the *AAM* (equivalent of the AA or the AAA) on ☎519-34-36.

The Metro

México's **Metro** (enquiries: ☎709-11-33) has a flat fare of roughly 50¢. Trains run till around midnight every night, later at weekends. Tickets come individually, or slightly cheaper in blocks of five or ten, which save a lot of queueing and messing about with tiny quantities of change. It's a superb modern system, French-built, fast, silent and expanding all the time, but there are problems. Worst of these are the crowds – unbelievable at rush hours when the busiest stations in the centre designate separate entries for women and children only, patrolled by armed guards to protect them from the crush. At such times it can also get unbearably hot, and don't even think of trying to carry anything larger than a briefcase. In theory you're never allowed **luggage** of any size on the Metro, but in practice you can if you board at a quiet station at a quiet time.

Once you've got into the system, there are no maps, just pictographic representations of the line you are on. So before you set off you need to work out where to change, and which way you'll be travelling on each line: these are indicated by the last station in each direction (thus on line 2 you'll want either *Direccion Cuatro Caminos* or *Direccion Tasqueña*), transfers by the word *Correspondancia* and the name of the new line – each has a different colour code to make matters slightly simpler. You may be able to pick up a complete map of the system from the ticket office, but more often than not they've run out.

City buses

Buses in México are unmistakeable, not so much because they're painted yellow as for their deafening roar and the vast plumes of choking black smoke they trail behind them. Some on the central routes have smartened up their acts, but on the whole they're still grimy machines with bone-janglingly hard seats – though also very efficient if you know where you're going. Fares are slightly more than the Metro, but still very cheap.

The two most **useful routes** are along Reforma from Chapultepec to the zócalo, and along Insurgentes, from Indios Verdes in the north, past the Terminal del Norte, the railway station, Metro Insurgentes and eventually on to the University in the south. The former, "Ruta Cien, Expreso Reforma" buses, set off from 16 de Septiembre opposite the *Gran Hotel*, run through the zócalo, down 5 de Mayo and Juárez (past Bellas Artes and the Alameda) and on down Reforma to Chapultepec where some stop, while others continue to Las Lomas or Observatorio – in this direction they're marked "Chapultepec", "Toreo, Lomas Km 13" or "Metro Observatorio"; going back, look simply for "Zócalo". The most useful bus on Insurgentes is #17, which goes all the way from Indios Verdes to San Angel, but many others cover large sections of the route.

The area just by **Chapultepec Metro station** and the entrance to the park is also a major downtown bus terminus, from where you can get to almost any part of the city. Note that during **rush hour** it can be almost impossible to get a bus: once they're full, they simply don't stop to let passengers on.

Colectivos and taxis

Running down the major through-routes, especially on Reforma and Insurgentes, you'll find **peseros** (*colectivos*), which charge more than the bus but far less than a regular

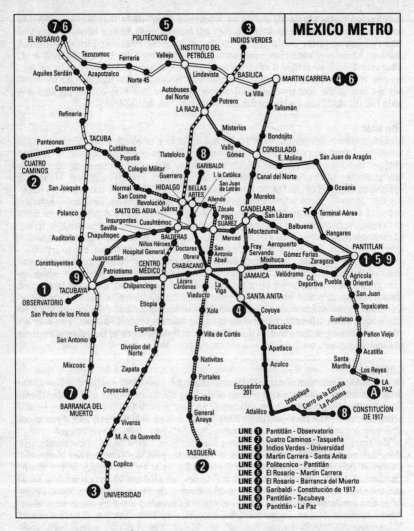

MÉXICO METRO

LINE 1	Pantitlán - Observatorio
LINE 2	Cuatro Caminos - Tasqueña
LINE 3	Indios Verdes - Universidad
LINE 4	Martin Carrera - Santa Anita
LINE 5	Politécnico - Pantitlán
LINE 6	El Rosario - Martin Carrera
LINE 7	El Rosario - Barranca del Muerto
LINE 8	Garibaldi - Constitución de 1917
LINE 9	Pantitlán - Tacubaya
LINE A	Pantitlán - La Paz

taxi, and will let you on and off anywhere along their set route. They're mostly VW vans or large American saloons, usually pale green with a white roof, and have their destination displayed on the windscreen – the driver will cruise by the side of the road holding up a number of fingers to indicate the number of free seats. One of the most **useful routes** is #2, which runs from Chapultepec Park via the Alameda to the zócalo.

Ordinary **taxis** come in a variety of forms. Cheapest and best are the white-and-yellow cabs that cruise the streets looking for custom. These should have a meter (make sure it's switched on) and are extremely good value compared to anywhere in Europe or North America – go for the smaller ones, which seem to charge less and can negotiate the traffic much more easily. Be warned that they can't always adjust taxi meters fast enough to keep up with inflation – there should be a chart to convert the reading into what you actually pay. The orange cabs that wait at *sitios* (taxi ranks) charge slightly more, but in general work in the same way. Look out, though, for *turismo* taxis with their notorious hooded meters, which lie in wait outside hotels and charge rates at least treble those of ordinary taxis. In the normal course of events you should avoid them, but they do have a couple of advantages, namely that they're almost always around and that many of the drivers speak some English. So they can be worth it if, for example, you need to get to the airport in a hurry (for which they charge no more than a *SETTA* cab would) or if you want to go on a tour for a few hours. In the latter case, with some ferocious haggling, you might even get a bargain. If you need to call a taxi, try *Servitaxis* (☎516-60-20) or *Taximex* (☎538-49-66).

Again, it's virtually impossible to get a taxi in the rush hour.

Information

You can pick up information in the booths in the airport and the bus stations; in town there's a **tourist office** at Amberes 54 in the *Zona Rosa* (Mon–Fri 9am–8pm, Sat & Sun 9am–7pm; ☎525-93-80). The *Sectur* office at Presidente Mazaryk 172, Colonia Polanco (Mon–Fri 8am–8pm; ☎520-62-30), is perfectly helpful but a long way from the centre.

Useful **local guides**, **city maps** (the best produced by *Guia Roji*), English-language magazines and pulp paperbacks are sold at *Sanborn's* and in many big hotels, and you can buy English-language **books** and magazines at the *American Book Store*, Madero 25 downtown and Revolución 1570 in San Angel, or at the *Libreria Britanica* at the corner of Mexico and Universidad near Metro *Coyoacán* (there are smaller downtown branches on Serapio Rendon near Parque Sullivan and Río Guadalquivir off Melchor Ocampo). It's also handy to know that you can get **news in English**, and extensive **listings**, from the *Mexico City News*, sold on newsstands throughout the centre, or from the free *Daily Bulletin* which you can pick up in the lobbies of big hotels.

Banks throughout the city are open normal hours, and there are 24-hour branches at the airport. Many will only change money in the morning. Best bet for currency other than dollars are branches of *Banamex*. Most large hotels and shops will **change travellers' cheques** and cash dollars, but the best dollar rates – and the longest queues – are at the *casas de cambio*: you'll find several in the *Zona Rosa*, a couple on Reforma by the *Crowne Plaza*, and a more central one on 16 de Septiembre a block and a half from the zócalo. The main **post office** is at the corner of Lázaro Cárdenas and Tacuba, behind Bellas Artes (Mon–Fri 9am–8pm). Local **calls** can be made from booths throughout the city (and are free of charge if you use the older orange-coloured booths), and in *Sanborn's*. For **international services** look for the blue *Larga Distancia* signs – you can dial direct from most big hotels, but it will cost much more. Useful **casetas de larga distancia** include: Izazaga 20-A, near Metro *Salto de Agua* (Mon–Fri 8am–2pm & 3am–10pm); the train station (Mon–Fri 9am–9pm, Sat & Sun 9am–2pm); Terminal del Norte (daily 7am–10pm); TAPO (daily 7am–10.30pm); and two at the airport (daily 7am–11pm).

Opening hours for most businesses in México are from 10am until 7pm. Some, but increasingly few, close for a siesta from around 2pm to 4pm.

Accommodation

There must be **thousands of hotels** in México. On any street, in any unlikely corner of the city, there seems to be at least one. But in the centre, despite impressions of being spoilt for choice, it can be hard to find anywhere at all that is both well situated and reasonably priced. The vast majority of tourists stay in the expensive modern places of the *Zona Rosa*, or in the even more costly, still flashier hotels overlooking Chapultepec Park.

The avenues around the **Zócalo** are awash with accommodation. Avenida 5 de Mayo is as good a place as any to begin, with a dozen or so fairly good options in close proximity. The hotels in this area are generally older and more established than elsewhere; high ceilings, internal courtyards and some rather dark rooms are common. Most are comfortable, and considering the location – right in the heart of things near many of the sights – excellent value. The area's main drawback is its distance from any good nightlife. Though not the place to head on a tight budget, if you look hard enough you can find luxury accommodation at moderate prices in the **Zona Rosa**. Staying here you'll be spoilt for choice for cafes, posh restaurants, bars and clubs. Between the *Zona Rosa* and the Alameda, in the area centring on the **Revolución monument**, most hotels, like the area itself, are rather humdrum – though you'll find some luxury places at lower rates than in the rest of the city. Those along **Reforma** are expensive.

There's another group of hotels **north of the Alameda**, very convenient if you're arriving or leaving the city by train, but this is a rather less attractive area to stay in on the whole, and can be a little intimidating at night. The hotels around **the Alameda** itself are very good value, though the farther south you go, the less salubrious the area becomes and the cheaper the hotels become.

If you arrive by bus at the **Terminal del Norte** and are concerned only with getting some sleep in silence, head for the good-value *Hotel Brasilia*, Av. de los Cien Metros 4823 (☎587-85-77; ⑤). You can't miss it: it's a modern skyscraper very near the terminus. All rooms have TV, tiled bathrooms, and there's even a decent restaurant. Finally, there's a small group of really cheap hotels near *San Antonio Abad* Metro station, just a couple of stops away from the zócalo: the *Lorenzo* is probably the best of them.

The privately run **accommodation-booking services** at the bus stations charge a commission, but they may be worth a try if you want to avoid wandering the streets looking lost, especially after dark. They're generally reluctant to book the cheaper places, but will if pressed.

Around the zócalo

Azores, Brasil 25 (☎521-52-22). Clean hotel, all rooms with TV and bathroom. ⑤.

Buenos Aires, Motolinia 21 (☎518-21-04). Friendly, if somewhat noisy. The *cantina* next door is overpriced. ④.

Catedral, Donceles 95 (☎518-52-32; fax 512-43-44). All rooms with TV, FM stereo and telephone, and some with jacuzzi. Also a good restaurant, with terrace overlooking the cathedral. Very popular. ⑦.

Concordia, Rep. de Uruguay 13 (☎510-41-00). Quite a walk from the zócalo, so it should always have rooms at busy times. Rooms with bath, TV and phone. ④.

Congreso, Allende 18 (☎518-14-40; fax 512-20-78). All rooms with TV. *Malino*, Allende 30 and *Atlanta*, Allende 31, are fairly similar and charge exactly the same. Secure parking. ⑥.

Gillow, Isabel La Católica 17 (☎510-07-91). Highly recommended luxury hotel with large rooms, in-house travel agency, and a great restaurant. ⑦.

ACCOMMODATION PRICES

All the accommodation listed in this book has been categorized into one of nine price bands, as set out below. The prices quoted are in US dollars and normally refer to the cheapest available room for two people sharing in high season. For more details, see p.37.

① less than $8	④ $18–25	⑦ $50–75
② $8–12	⑤ $25–35	⑧ $75–100
③ $12–18	⑥ $35–50	⑨ more than $100

Gran Hotel, 16 de Septiembre 82 (☎510-40-40). An attraction in itself, this hotel on the zócalo has infinitely more style than the skyscrapers of the *Zona Rosa*. Even if not staying, wander into the lobby and look at its art-deco interior complete with Tiffany stained-glass dome, wrought iron lift-cages and exotic stuffed birds. The rooms are good, too. ⑨.

Isabel, Isabel La Católica 63 (☎518-12-13; fax 521-12-33). Good-value hotel with services – taxis, laundry etc – normally offered at much larger hotels. Restaurant and *cantina*. ③.

Juárez, IER Callejón, 5 De Mayo 17 (☎512-69-29). Quiet hotel on a side street away from the city bustle. Comfortable and good value. ③.

Lafayette, Motolinia 40 (☎521-96-40). Popular, very comfortable place; all rooms with TV. ④.

León, Brasil 5 (☎ 512-90-31). Basic, though all rooms have toilet and shower. The bar downstairs offers live "Afro-Caribbean" music (see "Nightlife"). Popular with travellers. ⑤.

Lido, Brasil 8 (☎512-00-88). Rather foreboding and dark, but the singles are the cheapest in the area. Watch your luggage. ⑤.

Majestic, Madero 73 (☎521-86-00; fax 512-62-62). Luxury hotel on the zócalo. Try the restaurant on the fourth floor for fantastic breakfasts or just a coffee to admire the view. As a luxury hotel it has more character (and is quite a bit cheaper) than the plush *Zona Rosa* establishments. ⑨.

Montecarlo, Uruguay 69 (☎521-25-59). Originally an Augustinian monastery, and later lived in briefly by D.H. Lawrence. It is quiet, comfortable and has a beautiful inner courtyard. ⑤.

París, Rep del Salvador 91 (☎709-50-00). Clean, but dark. All rooms have phones, some have TV. ④.

San Antonio, 2° Callejón, 5 De Mayo 29 (☎512-99-06). Quiet, friendly place on a side street near a branch of *Pizza Hut*. ④.

Unión, Bolivar 67 (☎709-54-00). Rather dilapidated, filled with Mexican visitors. ②.

Washington, 5 De Mayo 54 (☎512-35-02). Clean hotel with cable TV and a shrine in the lobby. Recommended. ④.

Zamora, 5 de Mayo 50 (☎512-82-45). Friendly hotel just two blocks from the zócalo; popular so you may have to book ahead at busy times. ②.

The Zona Rosa

Casa Gonzalez, Rio Sena 69 (☎514-33-02). Good, friendly, comfortable lodgings, with home-cooked food. It is clean and usually full, so book in advance. ⑤.

Century, Liverpool 152 (☎726-99-11). Five-star hotel with all the mod-cons you would expect. ⑨.

El Ejecutivo, Viena 8 (☎566-64-22; fax 705-54-76). Friendly hotel with reasonable prices. ⑦.

Hotel del Principado, Londres 42 (☎533-29-44). Comfortable hotel, all rooms with TV and phone. Laundry service and parking available. ⑥.

Hotel Parador Washington, Dinamarca 42 (☎566-86-48). Centrally located on a pleasant square. Clean, comfortable and attractive rooms. Recommended. ⑤.

Marco Polo, Amberes 27 (☎511-18-39). Beautiful and stylish, this small luxury hotel caters for an artistic Mexican clientele. It has some stunning penthouse suites, should you fancy a honeymoon or something. ⑨.

Royal, Amberes 78 (☎525-48-50; fax 514-33-30). Friendly, modern hotel with excellent Spanish restaurant. ⑨.

Segovia Regency, Chapultepec 328 (☎511-30-41; fax 525-03-91). Reliable place heavily booked with regulars. Reserve ahead. ⑥.

Vasco de Quiroga, Londres 15 (☎546-26-14; fax 535-22-57). Small intimate hotel with piano bar and travel agency. ⑥.

North of the Alameda to Buenavista Station

Buenavista, Bernal Díaz 34 (☎535-57-04). Bottom of the barrel option. Watch your luggage and bring earplugs. ①.

Hotel de Cortés, Hidalgo 85 (☎518-21-81; fax 512-18-63). Just north of the Alameda, the present building dates from the 1780s, although originally it was a sixteenth-century Augustinian wayhouse. The cool, central patio houses a restaurant and a coffee house seemingly a million miles from the bustle of the Alameda. Facilities are generally very good, although perhaps it is a little overpriced. ⑨.

Londres, Plaza Buenavista 5 (☎705-09-10; fax 566-20-26). Beautifully decorated interior on a quiet square. Good restaurant, cable TV and a warm family atmosphere. The very best in the area for the price. ④.

Managua, Plaza de San Fernando 11 (☎512-13-12). Clean, quiet place, in a restful location facing the Jardín de San Fernando, just north of the Alameda. ⑤.

Marconi, Héroes 8 (☎521-28-33). The lobby is nice, the rooms poky and a bit dark. ②.

Polly, Orozco y Berra 25 (☎535-88-81) All rooms with bathroom and FM radio. Safe parking. ④.

South of the Alameda

Bamer, Juárez 52 (☎521-90-60; 510-17-93). Faded grandeur, but big, comfortable old rooms and great position overlooking the Alameda. ⑥.

Monte Real, Revillagigedo 23 (☎521-64-19). Friendly family hotel with its own pharmacy and baby-sitting service. ⑤.

Panuco, Ayuntamiento 148 (☎521-29-16; fax 510-88-31). Good-value hotel in uninspiring surroundings. ④.

San Francisco, Luis Moya 11 (☎521-89-60). Luxury accommodation with a video bar. ⑤.

Sevillano, Ayuntamiento 78 (☎521-67-15). Quiet, airy rooms. ②.

Around the Revolución Monument

Casa de Los Amigos, Ignacio Mariscal 132 (☎705-05-21). Clean and comfortable Quaker-run place in a huge house built for the artist José Clemente Orozco. A great place to meet other travellers and get information on all aspects of the city, as well as details of voluntary organizations. Comfortable rooms, or dorms ($8 per person) with communal kitchen and good-value breakfasts. Minimum stay of two nights, maximum two weeks. House regulations include a no-alcohol rule. ③.

Doral, Sullivan 9 (☎592-20-40; fax 592-27-62). Just on the edge of the *Zona Rosa*. Mid-price hotel with solarium and a restaurant boasting a range of 25 salads. ⑦.

Fontán, Colón 27 and Reforma (☎518-54-60; fax 521-92-40). Close to the Alameda, with good bars and a nightclub; high luxury at a moderate price. ⑧.

Mayaland, Antonio Caso 23 (☎566-60-66; fax 535-12-73). Tall, ugly building with very pleasant rooms. Bar, restaurant and travel agency. ⑥.

Royalty, Jesus Terán 21 (☎566-92-55). Reasonable rates, but rather dark rooms. ③.

Central México

Quite apart from the extraordinary **Aztec remains** in México – chief of which is the **Templo Mayor** on the zócalo – there's a wealth of great colonial buildings, among them the **Cathedral** and **National Palace** around the zócalo and **Maximilian's castle** in Chapultepec. There are superb museums – the **Anthropology Museum** ranks with the world's best, Diego Rivera's **Museo Anahuacalli** with its most bizarre – and art, not only in the galleries but above all in **murals** adorning public buildings everywhere, particularly the startling **University City**. As a backdrop to all México's quite remarkable sightseeing is a diverse, dynamic **street life** unequalled in Latin America.

Around the zócalo: the central zone

The vast paved open space of the **ZÓCALO** – properly known as the Plaza de la Constitución and said to be the second-largest such plaza in the world after Moscow's Red Square – is the city's political and religious centre. It – and by extension every other town square in Mexico – gets its name from a monument to Independence that was planned for the centre of the square by General Santa Ana. Like most of his other plans this went astray, and only the statue's base was ever erected: *el zócalo*, literally, means the plinth. Here stand the great **cathedral**, the **National Palace** with the offices of the President, and the city administration – all of them magnificent colonial buildings. But it also reflects other periods of the country's history. This was the heart of **Aztec Tenochtitlán** too, and in the recently excavated **Templo Mayor** you can see remarkable remains from the magnificent temples on this site. It is a place constantly animated, and for most of the year spectacularly illuminated at night. Among the more certain entertainments is the ceremonious lowering of the national flag from its giant pole in the centre of the plaza each evening at 6pm. A troop of presidential guards march out from the palace, strike the enormous banner, and perform a complex routine at the end of which the flag is left, neatly folded, in the hands of one of their number. You get a great view of this, and of everything else happening in the zócalo, from the rooftop bar in the *Hotel Majestic* at the corner of Madero.

The zócalo, does of course, have its seamier side. México's economic plight is most tellingly reflected in the lines of unemployed who queue up around the cathedral looking for work, each holding a little sign with his trade – plumber, electrician or mechanic – and a box with a few scavenged tools. By them, as often as not, wait a rather shabby group of Indians in wilting headdresses and feathered robes, ready to perform their sad dances for the next group of tourists.

The Cathedral

It's the **Cathedral**, flanked by the parish church of **El Sagrario**, which first draws the eye, with its heavy, grey Baroque facade and squat, bell-topped towers. Like so many of the city's older, weightier structures the Cathedral has settled over the years into the soft wet ground beneath – the tilt is quite plain, despite extensive work to stabilize the building in recent years. The first church on this site was constructed only a couple of years after the Conquest, using stones torn from the Temple of Huitzilopochtli, but the present structure was begun in 1573 to provide México with a cathedral more suited to its wealth and status. The towers weren't completed until 1813 though, and the building incorporates a plethora of architectural styles throughout. Even the frontage demonstrates this; relatively austere at the bottom where work started in a period when the Conquest was still recent, flowering into full Baroque as you look up, and topped by Neoclassical cornices and clock tower. Inside, it was seriously damaged by fire in 1967 and is still not fully recovered – the chief impression is of a vast and rather gloomy space. By contrast, **El Sagrario** seems richer, though that's largely a false impression created by liberal use of gold paint and exuberant Churrigueresque carving.

Palacio Nacional and the Rivera Murals

The other dominant structure is the **Palacio Nacional**, its facade taking up a full side of the zócalo – more than 200 metres. The so-called New Palace of Moctezuma stood here, and Cortés made it his first residence too, but the present building, for all its apparent unity, is the result of centuries of agglomeration and rebuilding. Most recently, a third storey was added in 1927. From 1562 the building was the official residence of the Spanish Viceroy, and later of Presidents of the Republic, and it still contains the office of the President, who makes his most important pronouncements from the balcony – especially on September 15, when the *Grito de Dolores* signals the start of Independence celebrations around the country. Benito Juárez died here in 1872; his living quarters have been turned into a tiny **museum** (Mon–Fri 10am–3pm & 4–6pm; free).

The overriding attraction, however, is the series of **Diego Rivera murals** that decorate the stairwell and upper storey of the main courtyard (there are fourteen courts in all). Those here, which Rivera began in 1929, are classics; ranking with the best of his works anywhere. The great panorama of Mexican history around the **main staircase** combines an unbelievable wealth of detail with savage imagery and a masterly use of space. On the right-hand wall Quetzalcoatl sits in majesty amid the golden age of the Valley of Mexico, with an idealized vision of life in Teotihuacán, Tula and Tenochtitlán going on around him. The main section depicts the Conquest, oppression, war, inquisition, invasion, Independence and eventually Revolution. Almost every major personage and event of Mexican history is here, from the grotesquely twisted features of the Conquistadors, to the heroes: balding white-haired Hidalgo with the banner of

CENTRAL MÉXICO

Independence; squat, dark Benito Juárez with his Constitution and laws for the reform of the Church; Zapata, with a placard proclaiming his cry of *Tierra y Libertad*; Pancho Villa, moustachioed and swaggering. On the left is post-revolutionary Mexico and the future, with Karl Marx pointing the way to adoring workers, and businessmen clustered over their tickertape: a somewhat ironic depiction in the modern city with its skyscraper offices and grim industrial wastes. The surrealist artist Frida Kahlo, Rivera's wife, is depicted too, behind her sister Cristina in a red blouse with an open book.

Around the walls of the **upper storey** are a series of smaller panels originally intended to go all the way round, a project that was probably always over-optimistic. A few sketches are visible on the unpainted walls, while the completed sections mostly depict the idyll of various aspects of life before the Conquest – market day, hunting scenes and so on. The last show the arrival of the Spanish.

Continuing round the zócalo clockwise, the third side is taken up by the city and Federal District administration, the **Ayuntamiento**, while sheltering under the arcades of the fourth is a series of shops, almost all of which sell either hats or jewellery. This practice of giving over a whole street to one particular trade is one that you'll still find to some extent throughout the city: even very near here there are places where you can buy nothing but stationery, other blocks packed exclusively with shoe shops. It's probably the most concrete hangover of Aztec life – their well-regulated markets were divided up according to the nature of the goods on sale, and the practice was continued by colonial planners.

For strange shopping experiences, though, you can't beat the **Monte de Piedad**, at the corner of the zócalo with 5 de Mayo. This huge building, supposedly the site of the palace in which Cortés and his followers stayed as guests of Moctezuma, is now the National Pawn Shop. The most unbelievable variety of stuff put up for hock is displayed here – a better selection than you'd find in the average mail order catalogue and including office machinery, beds, jewellery, artworks, dentists' chairs – anything, in fact, that will go through the doors. From time to time they hold major auctions to clear the place out, but this is really a place to look at – always full of milling crowds – rather than to buy.

DIEGO RIVERA

Diego Rivera (1886–1957) was arguably the greatest of the "Big Three" Mexican artists who interpreted the Revolution and Mexican history through the medium of enormous murals and put the nation's art onto an international footing in the first half of this century. Now very much back in fashion after the international tour of a Rivera exhibition, his works (along with those of José Clemente Orozco and David Siqueiros) remain among the country's most striking sights.

Rivera studied from the age of ten at the San Carlos Academy in the capital, later moving to Paris where he flirted with many of the new trends, and in particular cubism. More importantly, though, he and Siqueiros planned, in exile, a popular, native art to express the new society in Mexico. Almost from the moment of his return he began work, for the Ministry of Education, on the first of his massive, consciousness-raising **murals**: a political art whose themes – Mexican history, the oppression of the natives, post-revolutionary resurgence – were initially more important than their techniques. Many of the early murals are deceptively simple, even naive, but in fact Rivera remained close to the major trends and, following the lead of Siqueiros, took a seriously scientific view of his work, looking to **industrial advance** for new techniques, better materials, fresh hope. The view of industrial growth as a universal panacea (particularly in their earlier works) may have been simplistic, but their use of technology and experimentation with new methods and original approaches often has startling results – look, in particular, at the University City or the *Polyforum Cultural*.

The Templo Mayor

Just off the zócalo, down beside the cathedral, lies the entrance to the site where the **Templo Mayor** (Tues–Sun 9am–5pm; $5, free on Sun; guided evening tours Fri–Sun; ☎542-49-43 or 542-47-84) has been excavated. What you see are the bare ruins of the foundations of the great temple and one or two buildings immediately around it, all highly confusing since, as was normal practice, a new temple was built over the old at the end of every 52-year calendar cycle (and apparently even more frequently here) so that there were a whole series of temples stacked inside each other like Russian dolls. Arm yourself with a cutaway diagram (free from the ticket office) or look at the models and maps in the museum first (see below) and it all makes more sense.

Although it's been known since the beginning of this century that Tenochtitlán's ceremonial area lay under this part of the city, it was generally believed that the chief temple, or Teocalli, lay directly beneath the cathedral. Archeological work only began in earnest in 1978 after workmen uncovered a vast stone disc weighing about eight tons and depicting **Coyolxauhqui**, goddess of the moon. Logic demanded that this must lie at the foot of the temple of Huitzilopochtli, and so the colonial buildings were cleared away and excavation began. Coyolxauhqui was the daughter of Coatlicue, the mother goddess who controlled life and death, who on discovering that her mother was miraculously pregnant, vowed to wipe out the dishonour by killing her. Huitzilopochtli, however, sprung fully armed from the womb (like Athena in Greek mythology), decapitated and dismembered his sister and threw her body down a mountain. He then proceeded to drive off the four hundred other brothers who had gathered to help her: they scattered to become the stars. Coyolxauhqui is thus always portrayed with her head and limbs cut off, and was found here at the foot of the Temple of Huitzilopochtli symbolizing her fall from the mountain. The sacrifices carried out in the temple were in part a re-enactment of this – the victims being thrown down the steps afterwards – and in part meant to feed Huitzilopochtli with the blood he needed as sun god to win his nightly battle against darkness. The Great Temple was also dedicated to Tlaloc, the infinitely more peaceful god of rain, and at its summit were two separate sanctuaries, reached by a monumental double stairway.

Of the seven reconstructions of the temple, layers as far down as the second have been uncovered: of this you see only the top – the bottom is now well below the water table. Confusing as it is trying to work out what's what, it's a fascinating site, scattered with odd sculptures, including some great serpents, and traces of its original bright paintwork. Seeing it here, at the heart of the modern city, brings the ceremonies and human sacrifices that took place all too close to home. The **museum**, entered through the site on the same ticket, helps set it all in context, with some welcome reconstructions and models of how Tenochtitlán would have looked at its height. There are some wonderful pieces retrieved from the site, especially the wall of skulls as you enter, the eagle in room 1 with a cavity in its back for the hearts of sacrificial victims, and of course the huge **Coyolxauhqui stone**, displayed so as to be visible from points throughout the museum. The design is meant to simulate the temple, so you climb through it to reach two rooms at the top, one devoted to Huitzilopochtli, the other to Tlaloc. The only problem is that the whole place is extremely dimly lit; so much so that many of the labels (which are in Spanish only) are illegible. Nonetheless you shouldn't miss it – the best items are towards the top, including some superb stone masks such as the one from Teotihuacán, black with inset eyes and a huge earring, typical of the objects paid in tribute by subject peoples from all over the country. On the highest level are two magnificent, full-size terracotta eagle warriors and numerous large stone pieces from the site. The descent back to ground level concentrates on everyday life in Aztec times – with some rather mangy stuffed animals to demonstrate the species known to the Mexica – along with a jumble of later items found while the site was being excavated.

Calle Moneda

Right beside the archeological zone, on Calle Moneda, is the **Museo Nacional de las Culturas** (Tues–Sun 9.30am–6pm; free), a collection devoted to the archeology and anthropology of other countries. The museum occupies the sixteenth-century Casa de la Moneda, originally the official mint and now immaculately restored, with rooms of exhibits set around a quiet patio. It's more interesting than you might imagine: reflecting Mexico's historical alignment it has a substantial Eastern European section. Calle Moneda itself is one of the oldest streets in the city, and it's fascinating to wander up here and see the rapid change as you leave the immediate environs of the zócalo. The buildings remain almost wholly colonial, but from the prim refurbishment of the museum they gradually become shabbier and shabbier, interspersed with buildings abandoned after earthquake or subsidence damage, blending within four or five blocks into a very depressed residential area. Here you'll find street stalls spreading up from the giant market of La Merced, to the south.

Just a block beyond the museum, the orange dome of the church of **Santa Inés** stands out a mile off. This, though, is its most striking feature, and there's little else to admire apart from the delicately carved wooden doors. Opposite, its entrance in Calle Academia, is the **Academia de San Carlos**. This still operates as an art school, though on a very reduced scale from its nineteenth-century heyday: inside are galleries for temporary exhibitions and, in the patio, copies of classical sculptures. Above them invariably twitter scores of birds, trapped inside the glassed-over courtyard. Further up Moneda, which by this time has changed its name to Emiliano Zapata, the **Templo de la Santisima** boasts one of the city's finest Baroque facades.

North of the zócalo

Calle Seminario (which later becomes Argentina) leads past the Templo Mayor to the **Ministry of Education**, or **SEP** (Mon–Fri 9am–5pm), where Rivera painted his first **murals** on returning from Paris. The inspiration behind them was **José Vasconcelos**, Revolutionary Minister of Public Education but better known as a poet and philosopher, who promoted educational art as a means of instilling a sense of history and cultural pride in a widely illiterate population. As such, he is the man most directly responsible for the murals in public buildings throughout the country. Here, three floors of an enormous double patio are entirely covered with frescoes, as are many of the stairwells and almost any other flat surface. Rivera's work is very simple compared with what he later achieved, but the style is already recognizable: panels crowded with figures, drawing inspiration mainly from rural Mexico, though also from an idealized view of science and industry. The most famous panel on the ground floor is the *Dia de los Muertos*, which is rather hidden away in a dark corner at the back. One suspects that it is its relatively apolitical nature which has made this the main tourist attraction: there are equally striking images on the far wall (*Quema de las Judas* and *La Asamblea*, for example) and the lovely *El Canal de Santa Anita* opposite. On the first floor the work is very plain, mostly in tones of grey – here you'll find the shields of the states of Mexico and such general educational themes as *"Chemistry"* or *"Physics"*, most of it the work of Rivera's assistants. On the second floor are heroes and heroic themes from the Revolution. At the back, clockwise from the left-hand side, the triumphant progress of the Revolution is traced, culminating in the happy scenes of a Mexico ruled by its workers and peasants.

More murals, for which Vasconcelos was also responsible, adorn the **Escuela Nacional Preparatoria** (ENP or National Preparatory School), very nearby in the eighteenth-century Jesuit seminary of San Idelfonso. Turn right out of the SEP and then first left to get there – it's at San Idelfonso 33, with an imposing facade that fills almost a whole block. Many artists are represented, including Rivera and Siqueiros, but the most famous here are the works of José Clemente Orozco, which you'll find on the main staircase and around the first floor of the main patio. As everywhere, Orozco, for all his enthusiasm for the Revolution, is less sanguine about its prospects, and modern Mexico is caricatured almost as savagely as the pre-revolutionary nation. The ENP seems frequently to be closed to the public, but it's worth trying.

To the west (the street changes its name from San Idelfonso to Republica de Cuba) you reach the little plaza of **Santo Domingo**, one of the city's most wholly colonial. There's a fountain playing in the middle and eighteenth-century mansions lining the sides, with the fine Baroque church of Santo Domingo on the site of the country's first Dominican monastery. Under the arcades you'll find clerks sitting at little desks with portable typewriters, carrying on an ancient tradition of public scribes. It's a sight you'll find somewhere in most large Mexican cities – their main function is to translate simple messages into the flowery, sycophantic language essential for any business letter in Spanish, but they'll type anything from student theses to love letters. You'll also probably be accosted by street printers, who'll churn out business cards or invitations on the spot, on antiquated hand presses.

At the far corner of the plaza, on Brasil, the **Museo de la Medicina** (Tues–Sun 9am–6pm; free) was once the headquarters of the Inquisition in New Spain. Free guided tours (Tues–Fri only) let you explore the cells and dungeons where heretics were punished. Although the cruelty of the Inquisition is often exaggerated, their facilities appear gruesome indeed. The museum itself has interesting displays on indigenous medicine, religion and herbalism as well as the progress of western medicine from colonial times to the present. A "wax room" shows full-colour casts of various skin diseases, injuries and truly foul infections.

Avenida Brasil leads from here back to the zócalo, or if you retrace your steps past the ENP you'll arrive at the **Plaza de Loreto**. This too is a truly elegant old square, crowded with pigeons, but unlike Santo Domingo it's entirely unmodernized. On one side the **Templo de Loreto** with its huge dome leans at a crazy angle: inside, where some restoration work is going on, you'll find yourself staggering across the tilted floor. **Santa Teresa**, across the plaza, has a bizarre cave-like chapel at the back, entirely artificial. Behind the Templo Loreto is a large and rather tame covered market, the **Mercado Presidente Rodriguez**, inside which are a series of large murals dating from the 1930s by an assortment of artists including Antonio Pujol and Pablo O'Higgins.

Nearby, the **Museo de la Caricatura**, Donceles 99 (Tues–Sun 10am–6pm; $3) shows a limited selection of work from Mexico's most famous caricaturists. The most bizarre are nineteenth-century prints of skeletal *mariachis* by José Guadalupe Posada, a great influence on the later Muralist Movement. The museum coffee house is a pleasant place to break your journey, its walls decorated with cartoons. From here you can either turn left and go back to Av. Brasil or right to Av. Argentina and back to the zócalo.

Follow Donceles past Argentina – the street name changes to Justo Sierra – and you soon arrive at the rather imposing old school of **San Idelfonso** (Tues–Sun 10am–6pm; free) which has been transformed into a museum with varied temporary exhibitions, and in which you can see some of the first murals by Orozco, Rivera and Siqueiros.

South of the zócalo

Leaving the zócalo to the south, Pino Suárez heads off from the corner between the Palacio Nacional and the Ayuntamiento towards the Museo de la Ciudad. First though, right on the corner of the square, is the colonial-style modern building housing the **Supreme Court** (Suprema Corte de Justicia). Inside are three superb, bitter murals by Orozco – *Proletarian Battles*, *The National Wealth* and *Justice*. The latter, depicting justice slumped asleep on her pedestal while bandits rob the people of their rights, was not surprisingly, unpopular with the judges and powers that be, and Orozco never completed his commission here.

The **Museo de la Ciudad de Mexico** (Tues–Sun 9.30am–7.30pm; free) is a couple of blocks further down, housed in the colonial palace of the Condes de Santiago de

Calimaya. This is a fabulous building, with cannons thrusting out from the cornice, magnificent heavy wooden doors and, on the far side, a hefty plumed serpent obviously dragged from the ruins of some Aztec temple to be employed as a cornerstone. The contents of the museum trace the history and development of the city from prehistoric to modern times, through everything from fossil remains to photographs of Villa and Zapata entering in triumph to architectural blueprints for the future. Perhaps most interesting, though, are the models of Tenochtitlán at its peak, and the old maps and paintings that show the city and the lake as they once were, with the gradual spread of development and disappearance of the water. There are also plans superimposing the map of ancient Tenochtitlán onto the modern streets – giving some idea of its location and extent. On the top storey is preserved the studio of the landscape artist Joaquin Clausell, its wall plastered in portraits and little sketches that he scribbled between working on his real paintings. The museum also presents a multi-media show (in Spanish) describing the city's evolution – supposedly daily at 11am, but cancelled if there are too few customers. Twice weekly **Ballet Folklórico** performances are held here, too (Tues at 8pm, Sun 9.30pm) as well as occasional concerts.

More or less opposite is a small open space and the entrance to **Pino Suárez Metro station**, where a huge Aztec shrine uncovered during construction has been preserved as an integral part of the concourse. Dating from around the end of the fourteenth century, it was dedicated to Quetzalcoatl in his guise of Ehecatl, god of the wind. From here a **subterranean walkway** runs back to the Zócalo Metro station – there are almost always exhibitions down here, or market stalls, and thousands of people.

Before this, though, you should cross the road from the museum for a look at the church and hospital of **Jesús Nazareno**. The **hospital**, still in use and which you're not really allowed to visit, was founded by Cortés himself in 1524 on the site where traditionally he first met Moctezuma. As such it's one of the oldest buildings in the city, if not anywhere in the country, and exemplifies the severe, fortress-like construction of the immediate post-Conquest years. The church, which contains the remains of Cortés, hidden away in an insignificant looking tomb, has been substantially remodelled over the years. Its vaulting was decorated by Orozco with a fresco of the Apocalypse, and around the upper walls with murals relating the Spanish Conquest, but these are all but lost in the gloom of the interior.

Heading east from here on Salvador or Uruguay you get to the giant **market** area of La Merced, passing, on Uruguay, the beautiful cloister that is all that remains of the seventeenth-century **Convento de la Merced**. Westwards you can stroll down some fairly tatty old streets and eventually find yourself approaching the Zona Rosa, passing several smaller markets. It's much more interesting, however, to return to the zócalo and strike down towards the Alameda from there.

A worthwhile detour at this point would be a visit to the **Museo de la Indumentaria Mexicana**, José Maria Izázaga 108 (Tues–Sun 10am–5pm; $3, $1 on Sun), right next to Isabel de la Catolica Metro station. Indigenous costumes from all over Mexico are on display, and a serious attempt is made to decipher the patterns of this colourful and significant art form. Across the road, in a colonial building painted a horrid shade of puce, the **Museo de la Federación de Charros**, Isabel la Catolica 108, is dedicated to all things cowboy, with lots of boots, hats, spurs and saddles, wagons and paintings. The building also houses an atmospheric restaurant (☎709-48-38).

West to the Alameda

The streets that lead down from the zócalo towards the Alameda – Tacuba, 5 de Mayo, Madero, 16 de Septiembre and the lanes that cross them – are the most elegant in the city: least affected by any modern developments and lined with ancient buildings and traditional cafes and shops, and with mansions converted to offices, banks or restaurants. Few of these merit any particular special attention, but it's a pleasant place simply to stroll around, lingering at whatever catches the eye.

Along Madero

On Madero you'll pass several former aristocratic palaces, given over to a variety of uses. At the corner of Bolivar stands the mansion built by mining magnate José de la Borda (see p.315) for his wife, with a magnificent balcony. Close by on Bolivar, the **Spanish-Mexican Club** is a fine example of how the wealthy used to amuse them- selves, and how some apparently still do. If you can talk your way in, the interior is superb – fitted out with Moorish-style dining rooms, vast ballrooms, enormous chande- liers and endless works of art, it's hard to believe it was only built at the beginning of this century: the sort of extreme that led to the downfall of the Díaz regime. Still further down Madero you'll find the **Palacio de Iturbide**, now occupied by *Banamex* and thoroughly restored (the banks seem to have the money for all the best restoration work). Originally the home of the Condes de Valparaiso in the eighteenth century, it was from 1821–23 the residence of the ill-fated "emperor" Augustín de Iturbide.

In the next block, the last before you emerge at Bellas Artes and the Alameda, the Churrigueresque church of **San Francisco** stands on the site of the first Franciscan mission to Mexico. Fragments of the original large complex can be seen behind the church. Opposite is the famous **Casa de los Azulejos**, now a branch of *Sanborn's*. Inside, as well as the usual shopping, you'll find a restaurant in the glassed-over patio. Most remarkable, though, is the exterior – swathed entirely in blue and white tiles from Puebla. The building suffered a gas explosion in August 1994, which did quite a bit of damage; luckily no one was hurt and the more famous parts of the building, including the giant Orozco mural on the staircase, suffered few ill effects.

At the end of Madero you're at the extent of the colonial city centre, and standing between two of the most striking buildings in modern México: the Torre Latino- Americano and the Palacio de las Bellas Artes. Both, though it seems incredible to draw any comparison, are products of this century.

The Torre Latino-Americano

The steel-and-glass skyscraper of the **Torre Latino-Americano** was until very recently the tallest building in Mexico and, indeed, the whole of Latin America. It's now been overtopped by the *Hotel de Mexico* (on Insurgentes Sur) and doubtless by others in South America, but it remains the city's outstanding landmark and a point of reference no matter where you are. In the unlikely event of a clear day, the views from the top are outstanding; if it's averagely murky you're better off going up after dark when the lights delineate the city far more clearly. There's a charge to go up to the top two floors (daily 10am–midnight; $10) where there's a caged-in observation deck, a cafe, perma- nent crowds and, for some bizarre reason, an aquarium – or you can go to the *Muralto* restaurant and bar on the 41st floor for nothing. If you're really mean you could do this, catch the view, study the menu and decide not to eat after all, but if you have a drink you'll be able to sit in luxury and take it all in at your leisure for little more than it costs to get to the *mirador*. On the way up plans explain how the tower is built, proudly boasting that it is the tallest building in the world to have withstood a major earthquake (though since 1985 others may rival the claim). The general principle appears to be similar to that of an angler's float, with enormously heavy foundations bobbing around in the mushy soil under the capital, keeping the whole thing upright.

Bellas Artes

The tower is certainly a more successful engineering achievement than the **Palacio de las Bellas Artes** (Tues–Sun 10am–6pm; $4, free on Sun), which has very obviously subsided. On the other hand Bellas Artes is extremely beautiful, which you certainly couldn't say of the Tower. It was designed in 1901, at the height of the Díaz dictatorship, by the Italian architect Adamo Boari and constructed, in a grandiose Art-Nouveau style, of white marble imported from Italy. Building wasn't actually completed, however, until 1934, with the Revolution and several new planners come and gone. Now it's the headquarters of the National Institute of Fine Arts; venue for all the most important performances of classical music, opera or dance; home of the **Ballet Folklórico**; and a major Art Museum. It's worth getting to some performance in the theatre (preferably the Ballet Folklórico – see "Nightlife and entertainment" on p.294) if only to see the amazing Tiffany glass curtain depicting the Valley of México and the volcanoes. The whole interior, in fact, is magnificent – an art deco extravaganza incorporating spectacular lighting and stylized masks of the rain god, Chac.

The **art collections** are on the upper floors. In the galleries you'll find a series of exhibitions, permanent displays of Mexican art and temporary shows of anything from local art school graduates' work to major international names. Of constant and abiding interest, however, are the great **murals** surrounding the central space. On the first floor are *Birth of our Nationality* and *Mexico Today* – dreamy, almost abstract works by Rufino Tamayo. Going up a level you're confronted by the unique sight of murals by Rivera, Orozco and Siqueiros gathered in the same place. Rivera's *Man in Control of the Universe* (or *Man at the Crossroads*), celebrating the liberating power of technology, was originally painted for the Rockefeller Center in New York, but destroyed for being too leftist. This is Rivera's own copy. It's worth studying the explanatory panels on either side, which reveal some of the theory behind this complex work. Several smaller panels by Rivera are also displayed. These too were intended to be seen elsewhere (in this case on the walls of the *Hotel Reforma*, downtown) but for years were covered up, presumably because of their unflattering depiction of tourists. Themes include *Mexican Folklore and Tourism, Dictatorship*, the *Dance of the Huichilobos* and, perhaps the best of them, *Agustín Lorenzo*, a portrayal of a guerrilla fighter against the French. You get the impression, though, that none of these were designed to be seen so close up. *Catharsis*, a huge, vicious work by Orozco, occupies almost an entire wall, and there are also some particularly fine examples of Siqueiros' work: three powerful and original panels on the theme of *Democracy* and a bloody depiction of *The Torture of Cuauhtémoc* and his resurrection.

The Correo Central and Palacio de Minería

Around the back of Bellas Artes, at the corner of Tacuba and Lázaro Cárdenas, you'll find the **Correo Central**, the city's main Post Office. Completed in 1908, this too was designed by Adamo Boari, but in a style much more consistent with the buildings around it. Look closely and you'll find a wealth of intricate detail, while inside it's full of richly carved wood. Directly behind it on Tacuba is the **Palacio de Minería**, a Neoclassical building completed right at the end of the eighteenth century, and now housing the mining authorities and a school for mining engineers. It makes an interesting contrast with the Post Office and with the National Art Museum (formerly the Palacio de Comunicaciones) directly opposite, the work of another Italian architect, Silvio Contri, in the first years of this century. Behind the mining school on Filomeno Mata is the small **Convento de las Betlemitas**, a seventeenth-century convent that now houses an army museum (Tues–Sat 10am–6pm, Sun 10am–4pm; free) displaying weaponry from the Conquest to the present day.

The Museo Nacional de Arte

The **Museo Nacional de Arte**, Tacuba 8 (Tues–Sun 10am–5.30pm; $4, free on Sun) is set back from the street on a tiny plaza in which stands one of the city's most famous sculptures, *El Caballito*, portraying Carlos IV of Spain. This enormous bronze, the work of Manuel Tolsa, was originally erected in the zócalo in 1803. In the intervening years it has graced a variety of sites and despite the unpopularity of the Spanish monarchy, and of the effete Charles IV in particular, is still regarded affectionately. The latest setting is appropriate, since Tolsa also designed the Palacio de Minería. As for the museum itself, which occupies the second and third floors, it's something of a disappointment. The interest is mainly historical, for although there are more than 1000 works covering Mexican art from pre-Hispanic times to the present, they are on the whole mediocre examples, spiced only occasionally with a really striking work. Come here to see something of the dress and landscape of old Mexico, and also some of the curiosities. The prodigious *Family Tree of San Basilio*, for example, is wonderful – incorporating parents, grandparents and great-grandparents, along with a good scattering of uncles, aunts, sisters and brothers, each of whom were saints in their own right. The naïf *Esta es la Vida* is also a typically Mexican work. As depicted here, life consists almost exclusively of drunkenness and death.

The Alameda

From behind Bellas Artes, Lázaro Cárdenas runs north towards the **Plaza Garibaldi** (see "Nightlife and entertainment") through an area crowded with seedy *cantinas* and eating places, theatres and burlesque shows. Walk on down Tacuba, which here becomes Av. Hidalgo, and you finally reach the **ALAMEDA**. First laid out as a park at the end of the sixteenth century, and taking its name from the *alamos* (poplars) then planted, the Alameda had originally been an Aztec market and later became the site where the Inquisition burned its victims at the stake. Most of what you see now – formally laid-out paths and flowerbeds, ornamental statuary and fountains – recalls the last century when it was the fashionable place to stroll. It's still popular, always full of people, the haunt of ice-cream and sweet vendors, illuminated at night, and particularly crowded at weekends, but it's mostly a transient population – office workers taking lunch, shoppers resting their feet, messengers taking a short cut. The Alameda was one of the areas worst hit by the 1985 earthquake, and one of the few places where you may still, a decade later, get some idea of its scale. A number of buildings still stand in a state of imminent collapse: others have been cleared but not yet replaced.

The Franz Mayer Museum and Museo de la Estampa

On the north side of the Alameda, Hidalgo traces the line of a very ancient thoroughfare. Some of the old buildings on its north side, including the churches of **Santa Veracruz** and **San Juan de Dios**, were severely damaged in the earthquake and have been refurbished as museums. The **Museo Franz Mayer** (Tues–Sun 10am–5pm; $2.50, free on Sun) is dedicated to the applied arts. Occupying the sixteenth-century hospital attached to San Juan de Dios, it's packed with the personal collection of Franz Mayer: colonial furniture, textiles and carpets, watches, Spanish silverwork, religious art and artefacts, a valuable collection of sculpture and paintings, and some fine exhibits of colonial pottery from Puebla. There is also much furniture and pottery from Asia, reflecting Mexico's position on the trade routes, as well as a library with rare antique editions of Spanish and Mexican authors and a reference section on applied arts. Even if this doesn't sound like your thing, it's well worth seeing; a lovely building, beautifully furnished, and offering a tranquil escape from the crowds outside. The coffee bar, too, is a delight, facing a courtyard filled with flowers and a fountain – there's a charge of $4 to drink here without seeing the museum.

The **Museo de la Estampa**, virtually next door in the former church of Santa Veracruz (Tues–Sun 10am–6pm; $3.50, free on Sun), has engravings and printing plates from pre-Columbian times to the modern age, specializing in the nineteenth-century. It's an art form that is taken seriously in Mexico where the legacy of José Guadalupe Posada (see p.212) is still revered; his works are predictably the highlight.

Museo de Artes y Industrias Populares

On Juárez across from the park's semi-circular monument to Benito Juárez, is the **Museo de Artes y Industrias Populares** (Mon–Sat 10am–6pm; free), housed in the chapel of the former convent of Santa Clara. It has displays of craftworks, native art and traditional techniques, some ancient, most contemporary, much of which is also on sale. Further down Juárez, on the opposite side of the road just beyond the park, is a small **crafts shop** run by *FONART*, the government agency that promotes quality arts and crafts and helps the artisans with marketing and materials.

The Pinacoteca Virreinal and a Rivera mural

One of the buildings worst hit by the earthquake was the *Hotel del Prado*, whose Rivera mural *Dream of a Sunday Afternoon in the Alameda* was one of the area's chief attractions. The mural survived and can now be seen in the **Museo Mural Diego Rivera** (Tues–Sun 10am–2pm & 3–6pm; $2; *luz y sonido* Tues–Fri noon & 4.30pm, Sat & Sun 11.30am, 1pm, 4pm & 5pm) at the western end of the Alameda, at the corner of Balderas and Colon. It is an impressive *tour de force* – comprising almost every famous Mexican character from Cortés, his hands stained red with blood, to Rivera himself, portrayed as a child between his mother and daughter, out for a stroll in the park – but one suspects that its popularity with tour groups is as much to do with its relatively apolitical nature as for any superiority to Rivera's other works. A table explains every character in the scene (look out also for caricaturist José Guadalupe Posada, appearing as one of his trademark skeletons), and there are also displays on the history of the mural (the original included a placard with the words "God does not exist", which caused a huge furore and Rivera was eventually forced to paint it out before the mural was displayed to the public) and on the move, which involved picking up the entire wall and transporting it around the Alameda.

Almost next door you'll find the **Pinacoteca Virreinal** at Dr Mora 7 (Tues–Sun 9am–5pm; $2.50, free on Sun), a collection of colonial painting (*Virrey* being the Spanish for Viceroy) in the glorious seventeenth-century monastery of San Diego. The galleries are mostly filled with florid religious works of the seventeenth and eighteenth centuries, but some are exquisitely executed while others are fascinating for their depiction of early missionary work, and all are superbly displayed around the church, chapel and cloister of the old monastery. There are occasional concerts here in the evening – mostly chamber music or piano recitals.

Around the Revolución monument

Beyond the Alameda, Avenidas Juárez and Hidalgo lead on towards the Paseo de la Reforma. Across Reforma, Hidalgo becomes the **Puente de Alvarado**, following one of the main causeways that led into Tenochtitlán. This was the route by which the Spanish attempted to flee the city on the *Noche Triste* (Sad Night), July 10, 1520. Following the death of Moctezuma, and with his men virtually under siege in their quarters, Cortés decided to escape the city under cover of darkness. It was a disaster: the Aztecs cut the bridges and, attacking the bogged-down invaders from their canoes, killed all but 440 of the 1300 Spanish soldiers who set out, and more than half their Indian allies. Greed, as much as anything, cost the Spanish troops their lives, for in trying to take their gold booty with them they were, in the words of Bernal Díaz, "so weighed down by the stuff that they could neither run nor swim". The street takes its name from Pedro de Alvarado, one of the last Conquistadors to escape, crossing the broken bridge "in great peril after their horses had been killed, treading on the dead men, horses and boxes". Recently a hefty gold bar – exactly like those made by Cortés from melted-down Aztec treasures – was dug up here.

Puente de Alvarado: San Fernando and the Museo San Carlos

The church of **San Hipolito**, at the corner of Reforma and Puente de Alvarado, was founded by the Spanish soon after their eventual victory, both as a celebration and to commemorate the events of the *Noche Triste*. The present building dates from 1602, though over the years it's been damaged by earthquakes and rebuilt, and has taken on a distinct list. A little further down is the Baroque, eighteenth-century church of **San Fernando**, by the plaza of the same name. Once one of the richest churches in the city, San Fernando has been stripped over the years like so many others. Evidence of its former glory survives, however, in the highly decorative facade and in the *panteon* or graveyard, crowded with the tombstones of nineteenth-century high society.

Continuing on the same street you'll find the **Museo de San Carlos** (daily except Tues 10am–6pm; $2.50, free on Sun), Puente de Alvarado 50 on the left-hand side, which houses the country's oldest art collection, started in 1785 by Carlos III of Spain, and comprising largely European works of the seventeenth and eighteenth centuries. Travelling exhibitions are also frequently based here. The building itself is a very beautiful Neoclassical design of Manuel Tolsa's, with something of a bizarre history. Its inhabitants have included the French Marshal Bazaine, sent by Napoleon III to advise the Emperor Maximilian – who presented the house to him as a wedding present on his marriage to a Mexican beauty – and the hapless Mexican general and sometime dictator, Santa Ana. Later it served for a time as a cigarette factory.

Along Juárez to the monument

Leaving the Alameda on Juárez, you can see the massive, ugly bulk of the **Monumento a la Revolución** ahead of you. The first couple of blocks, though, are dull enough – commercial streets heavy with banks, offices, travel agents, expensive shops. The junction with Reforma is a major crossing of the ways, and is surrounded by modern skyscrapers and one older one – the marvellous **National Lottery building**. In here, you can watch the winning tickets being drawn each week, although the Lottery offices themselves have been moved to a much duller steel and glass building opposite. Beyond Reforma, Juárez continues in one long block to the **Plaza de la República** and the vast monument. Originally intended to be a new home for the *Cortes* (or parliament) its construction was interrupted by the Revolution and never resumed – in the end they buried a few heroes of the Revolution under the mighty columns (including Presidents Madero and Carranza) and turned the whole thing into a memorial. More recently the **Museo Nacional de la Revolución** (Tues–Sat 9am–5pm, Sun 9am–3pm; free) was installed beneath the monument, with a history of the Revolution told through archive pictures, old newspapers, films and reconstructed life-size scenes. Among the offices and large hotels around the plaza you'll find the **Frontón México** where *frontón* matches are held most evenings (see "Nightlife and entertainment").

Paseo de la Reforma

The **PASEO DE LA REFORMA** is the most impressive street in México. Laid out by Emperor Maximilian to provide the city with a boulevard to rival the great European capitals and as a ceremonial drive from his palace in Chapultepec to the centre, it also provided a new impetus, and direction, for the growing Metropolis. The original length of the broad avenue ran simply from the park to the junction of Juárez, and although it has been extended in both directions, this stretch is still what everyone thinks of as Reforma. Reforma Norte, as the extension towards Guadalupe is known, is almost a term of disparagement – and while the street is just as wide and the traffic just as dense, you won't find people strolling here for pleasure. Real Reforma, though, remains *the* smart thoroughfare – ten lanes of traffic, lines of trees, imposing statues at every intersection. There are perhaps three or four of the original French-style, nineteenth-century houses surviving along its entire extent. Elsewhere even relatively new blocks are constantly torn down to make way for yet newer, taller, more prestigious towers of steel, glass and mirrors.

It's a long walk – some 5km – from the zócalo to the gates of Chapultepec, made more tiring by the altitude and the constant crush, noise and fumes of the traffic. You'd be well advised to take the bus – they're frequent enough to hop on and off at will. The *glorietas*, roundabouts at the major intersections, each with a distinctive statue, provide easy landmarks along the way. First is the **Glorieta Colón**, with a statue of Christopher Columbus (*Cristóbal Colón* in Spanish). Around the base of the plinth are carved various friars and monks who assisted Columbus in his enterprise or brought the Catholic faith to the Mexicans. The Plaza de la Republica is just off to the north. Next comes the crossing of Insurgentes, nodal point of all the city's traffic, with **Cuauhtémoc**, last emperor of the Aztecs and leader of their resistance, poised aloof above it all in a plumed robe, clutching his spear, surrounded by warriors. Bas-relief engravings on the pedestal depict his torture and execution at the hands of the Spanish, desperate to discover where the Aztec treasures lay hidden. **El Angel**, a golden winged victory atop a column nearly 50m high, is the third to look out for – the place to get off the bus for the heart of the *Zona Rosa*.

Zona Rosa

Parallel to Reforma to the south lies the **Zona Rosa** – an area delineated by Reforma and Avenida Chapultepec, the park to the west and spilling across Insurgentes in the east. You can spot it by the street names, famous cities all: Hamburgo, Londres, Genova, Liverpool. . . . Packed into a tiny area here are hundreds of bars, restaurants, hotels and above all shops, teeming with the city's wealthy and would-be elegant, with vast numbers of tourists. You'll also find the highest concentration of beggars and rip-offs anywhere in the city – there are official multi-lingual policemen wandering around specifically to help tourists (they wear little flag emblems to denote which languages they speak) but there are also impressively uniformed unofficial guides whose only task is to persuade you to go to whichever shop or market employs them. You should come and look – for the constant activity, **street entertainers**, especially around the corner of Hamburgo and Florencia, and incredible diversity of shops and places to eat and drink – but remember that everything is very expensive. It's also worth noting that this is no longer where the very best hotels and classiest shops are located. They've generally moved out to **Colonia Polanco**, on the northern edge of Chapultepec.

On the fringes of the *Zona* on Londres 6 there's a **Wax Museum** (*Museo de Cera;* Mon–Fri 11am–7pm, Sat & Sun 10am–7pm; $4), thoroughly and typically tacky, with a basement chamber of horrors that includes Aztec human sacrifices. Also here is the **Museo de lo Increíble** (same hours; joint ticket with the wax museum $9), which displays such marvels as flea costumes and hair sculpture.

On the other side of Reforma, where the streets are named after rivers (Tiber, Danubio etc.) is a much quieter, posh residential area where many of the older embassies are based. You can spot the US embassy (which is actually on Reforma) by the vast queues snaking around it throughout the day. Near the British embassy is the **Museo Venustiano Carranza**, Lerma 35 (Tues–Sat 9am–7pm, Sun 11am–3pm; free). Housed in the mansion which was the México home of the Revolutionary leader and president, shot in 1920, it contains exhibits relating to his life and to the Revolution. Not far away, just north of the junction of Reforma and Insurgentes, the **Parque Sullivan** hosts open air exhibitions and sales of paintings every Sunday: nothing of great quality, but a pleasant holiday atmosphere prevails.

Chapultepec and the National Anthropology Museum

CHAPULTEPEC PARK, or the *Bosque de Chapultepec*, is a vast green area, some 1000 acres in all, dotted with trees, scattered with fine museums – among them the marvellous **anthropology museum** – boating lakes, gardens, playing fields and a zoo. Ultimately it's a resort from the pressures of the city for seemingly millions of Mexicans. On Sundays, when at least a brief visit is all but compulsory and many of the museums are free, you can barely move for the throng. They call it, too, the lungs of the city, and like the lungs of most of the inhabitants, its health leaves a lot to be desired. Large areas, towards the back where it's less frequented, have been fenced off to give them a chance to recover from the pounding they take from the crowds. There has even been talk of sealing the whole place off for three years to give the grass a chance to grow back and the plants to recover their equilibrium. Whatever the hopes or fears of the authorities, though, this is never likely to happen – public outrage at the very suggestion has seen to that. Meanwhile it still manages to look pretty good and remains one of Mexico's most enduring attractions.

Chapultepec Hill

The rocky outcrop of **Chapultepec** (the Hill of the Locust), which lends its name to the entire area, is mentioned in Toltec mythology, but first gained historical significance in the thirteenth century when it was no more than another island among the lakes and salt marshes of the valley. Here the Mexica, still a wandering, savage tribe, made their first home – a very temporary one before they were defeated and driven off by neighbouring cities, provoked beyond endurance. And here they returned once Tenochtitlán's power was established, channelling water from the springs into the city, and turning Chapultepec into a summer resort for the emperor, with plentiful hunting and fishing around a fortified palace. Several Aztec rulers had their portraits carved into the rock of the hill: most were destroyed by the Spanish soon after the Conquest.

The hill, crowned by Maximilian's very peaceful looking "castle", confronts you as soon as you enter. In front of it stands the strange, six-columned monument dedicated to the **Niños Héroes**, commemorating the cadets who attempted to defend the castle (then a military academy) against American invaders in 1847. According to the story, probably apocryphal, the last six flung themselves off the cliff wrapped in Mexican flags rather than surrender. The **Castillo** itself had been built only in 1785 as a summer retreat for the Spanish viceroy – until then it was the site of a hermitage established on the departure of the Aztec rulers. Its role as a military school followed Independence, but the present shape was dictated by Maximilian who remodelled it in the image of his Italian villa. Today it houses the National History Museum.

First, though, as you climb the hill, you pass the modern **Gallery of History** (Tues–Sun 9am–5pm; free) devoted to "the Mexican people's struggle for Liberty". It's known in full as the *Museo Galeria de la Lucha del Pueblo Mexicano por su Libertad*, or colloquially as the *Museo del Caracol* for the snail-like spiral through which you follow the displays. These, with the use of models, maps and dioramas, trace the history of the constant wars which have beset the country – from Independence, through the American and French interventions to the Revolution. There are also murals by Siqueiros and Juan O'Gorman.

Spread over two floors of the castle, the **Museo Nacional de Historia** (Tues–Sun 9am–5pm; $5, free on Sun) is a more traditional collection. The setting is very much part of the attraction, with many rooms retaining the opulent furnishings left behind by Maximilian and Carlota, or by later inhabitants with equally expensive tastes – notably Porfirio Díaz. Rivalling the decor is a small collection of carriages, including the fabulously pompous state coaches favoured by Maximilian. The bulk of the exhibits downstairs, though, follow a straight historical progression, starting with a small

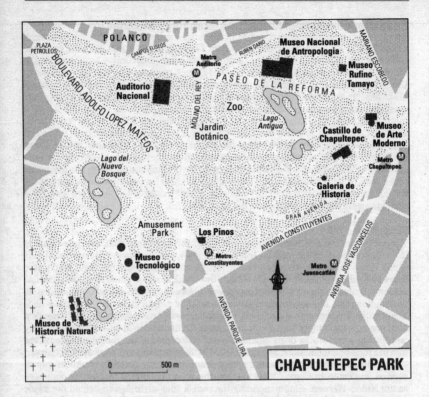

CHAPULTEPEC PARK

collection of pre-Hispanic objects and reproductions of Aztec codices, moving through weapons and paintings of the Conquest and on to documents, pictures, memorabilia and patriotic relics from every era of Mexican development. There are several murals here as well, including a number of works by Orozco and Siqueiros, but the ones by Juan O'Gorman most directly attract attention for their single-minded political message. Upstairs is a more miscellaneous collection of *objets d'art*, jewellery, period costume, furniture, clocks and a host of other bric-a-brac. There should really be wonderful views from here, across the city to Popocatépetl and Ixtaccíhuatl, but of course there never are.

The National Anthropology Museum

The park's outstanding attraction – for many people the main justification for visiting the city at all – is the **Museo Nacional de Antropología** (Tues–Sat 9am–7pm, Sun 10am–6pm; $4.50, free on Sun; ☎553-62-66), beyond doubt one of the world's great museums, not only for its collection, which is vast, rich and diverse, but for the originality and practicality of its design. Opened in 1964, the exhibition halls surround a patio with a small pond shaded by a vast square concrete umbrella supported by a single slender pillar around which splashes an artificial cascade. The halls are ringed by gardens, many of which contain outdoor exhibits.

If you plan to rush it, or to spend most of a day here, you can follow the logical progression round from one room to the next – but each gallery is devoted to a separate period or culture, and all open separately onto the central space, so it's easy enough, and far more satisfactory, to pick one or two to take in on each of several separate visits. Located about half a mile into the park beside the Paseo de la Reforma, you can take the **bus** virtually to its entrance, or walk easily from *Chapultepec* Metro station or any of the other museums at this end of the park. The entrance from Reforma is marked by a colossal statue of the rain god Tlaloc – the story goes that its move here from its original home in the east of the city was accompanied by furious downpours in the midst of a drought.

PRE-CLASSIC

The **Pre-Classic** room covers the development of the first cultures in the Valley of México and surrounding highlands – pottery and clay figurines from these early agricultural communities predominate. Notice especially the **small female figures** from Tlatilco (a site in the suburbs), probably related to some form of fertility or harvest rites, and the amazing acrobat, also from Tlatilco. Later the influence of the growing Olmec culture begins to be seen in art and, with the development of more formal religion, recognizable images of gods appear. Several of these, from Cuicuilco in the south of the city, depict **Huehueteotl**, the Old God or god of fire, as an old man with a brazier on his back. A small model of the circular **pyramid of Cuicuilco** stands in the garden outside.

TEOTIHUACÁN

The next hall is devoted to **Teotihuacán** (see p.300), the first great city in the Valley of México. Growing sophistication is immediately apparent in the more elaborate nature of the pottery vessels and the use of new materials, shells, stone and jewels. There's a full-scale reproduction of part of the **Temple of Quetzalcoatl** at Teotihuacán, brightly polychromed as it would originally have been, and copies of some of the frescoes that adorned the city, including *The Paradise of Tlaloc*, a depiction of the heaven reserved for warriors and ball players who died in action. Many **new gods** appear too – as well as more elaborate versions of Huehueteotl there are representations of Tlaloc, of his companion Chalchiutlicue, goddess of rivers and lakes, of Mictlantecuhtli god of death (a stone skull, originally inlaid with gems) and of Xipe Totec, a god of spring, clothed in the skin of a man flayed alive as a symbol of regeneration.

TOLTEC

The **Toltec room** actually begins with objects from Xochicalco, a city near modern Cuernavaca, which flourished between the fall of Teotihuacán and the heyday of Tula. The large stone carvings and pottery show distinct Maya influence: particularly lovely is the simple stone head of a macaw, similar to ones found on Maya ball-courts in Honduras. Highlights of the section devoted to Tula are the weighty stone carvings, including one of the Atlantean columns from the main temple there, representing a warrior. Also of note are the **Chac-mool**, a reclining figure with a receptacle on his stomach in which sacrificial offerings were placed, symbolizing the divine messenger who delivered them to the gods; the small human figures that acted as flag poles when a standard was inserted into the hole between their clasped hands; the stone relief of a dancing jaguar; and the exquisite **mother-of-pearl and clay mosaic** of a coyote's head with a bearded man emerging from its mouth – possibly a warrior in a headdress.

MEXICA

Next comes the biggest and richest of them all, the **Mexica Gallery**, characterized above all by massive yet intricate stone sculpture, but also displaying pottery, small stone objects, even wooden musical instruments. Many of these objects have been or are being rearranged to make way for new finds from the Templo Mayor. For now,

FINDING YOUR WAY AROUND THE ANTHROPOLOGY MUSEUM

As you come into the **entrance hall** there's a bookshop selling postcards, souvenirs, books in several languages on Mexican culture, archeology and history, and detailed guides to the museum. Some of these are slightly dated (the Mexica room in particular has been rearranged to accommodate new finds from the Templo Mayor, and theories are constantly changing), but they do provide full descriptions of most of the important pieces. Straight ahead is a small circular space with temporary exhibitions, usually devoted to the latest developments in archeology and often very interesting. More of these lie to the right, beyond Rufino Tamayo's mural of a battling jaguar and serpent, and here also are the library and museum offices as well as the small **Sala de Orientación**, which presents an audio-visual overview of the major ancient cultures. The ticket office, and the entrance to the museum proper, is by the huge glass doors to the right. You can buy tickets here too for the regular guided tours – free in Spanish, or for a fee in English, French or German. They're very rushed, but do get you round the whole thing with some form of explanation: labelling inside is meagre and in Spanish only.

The full **tour of the museum** starts on the right-hand side with three **introductory rooms** explaining what anthropology is, the nature of and relationship between the chief Meso-American cultures, and the region's pre-history. Skip or skim them if you're in a hurry. They're followed on the right-hand side by halls devoted to the **pre-Classic**, **Teotihuacán** and **Toltec** cultures. At the far end is the vast **Mexica** (Aztec) room, followed around the left wing by **Oaxaca** (Mixtec and Zapotec), **Gulf of Mexico** (Olmec), **Maya** and the cultures of the north and west. Every hall has at least one outstanding feature, but if you have limited time, the Aztec and the Maya rooms are the **highlights**: what else you see should depend on what area of the country you plan to head on to. The first floor is given over to the **ethnography collections** devoted to the life and culture of the various indigenous groups today: stairs lead up from each side. Downstairs, behind the hall devoted to the cultures of the north and west, is a very welcome restaurant.

though, two of the finest pieces stand at the entrance: the **Ocelocuauhxicalli**, a jaguar with a hollow in its back in which the hearts of human sacrifices were placed (it may have been the companion of the eagle in the Templo Mayor museum; the two were found very close to each other, though over eighty years apart); and the **Teocalli de la Guerra Sagrada** (Temple of the Sacred War), a model of an Aztec pyramid decorated with many of the chief gods and with symbols relating to the calendar. There are hundreds of other powerful pieces – most of the vast Aztec pantheon is represented – and everywhere snakes, eagles, and human hearts and skulls are prominent. Among them is a vast statue of **Coatlicue**, goddess of life and death and mother of the gods. She is shown beheaded, with two serpents above her shoulders representing the flow of blood; her necklace of hands and hearts and pendant of a skull represent life and death respectively; her dress is made of snakes; her feet are eagles' claws. As a counterpoint to the viciousness and hopelessness of most of this, be sure to notice **Xochipilli**, the god of love and flowers, dance and poetry. You'll come across him wearing a mask and sitting cross-legged on a throne strewn with flowers.

The undoubted highlight, though, is the enormous (24-tonne) **Piedra del Sol**, the Stone of the Sun or Aztec Calendar Stone. The latter, popular name is not strictly accurate, for this is much more a vision of the Aztec cosmos, completed under Moctezuma only a few years before the Spanish arrived. The stone was found by early colonists, and deliberately reburied for fear that it would spread unrest among the population. After being dug up again in the zócalo in 1790 it spent years propped up against the walls of the cathedral. You'll pick up the most detailed description on a guided tour, but briefly: in the centre is the sun god and personification of the fifth sun, Tonatiuh, with a tongue in the form of a sacrificial knife and claws holding human hearts on each side, representing the need for human sacrifice to nourish the sun. Around him are symbols for the four previous incarnations of the sun – a jaguar, wind, water and fiery rain; this whole central conglomeration forming the sign for the date on which the fifth world would end (as indeed, with defeat by the Spanish, it fairly accurately did). Encircling all this are hieroglyphs representing the twenty days of the Aztec month and other symbols of cosmic importance, and the whole thing is surrounded by two serpents.

OAXACA

Moving round to the third side of the museum you reach the halls devoted to cultures based away from the highlands of the centre, starting, in the corner of the museum, with the **Zapotec** and **Mixtec** people of Oaxaca. Although the two cultures evolved side by side, the Zapotecs flourished earliest (from around 900 BC to 800 AD) as accomplished architects with an advanced scientific knowledge, and also as makers of magnificent pottery with a pronounced Olmec influence. From around 800 many of their sites were taken over by the Mixtecs whose overriding talents were as craftsmen and artists, working in metal, precious stone and clay. The great site for both is Monte Albán (see p. 403).

Of the Zapotec collection notice above all the fine sense of movement in the human figures: the reproduction of part of the carved facade of the Temple of the Dancers at Monte Albán; a model of a temple with a parrot sitting in it; vases and urns in the form of various gods; and the superb jade mask representing the bat god. Among the Mixtec objects are many beautifully polychromed clay vessels including a cup with a hummingbird perched on its rim, and jewellery of gold and turquoise. Reproductions of Zapotec and Mixtec tombs show how many of the finer small objects were discovered.

GULF OF MEXICO

Next is the **Gulf of Mexico room**, in which are displayed some of the treasures of **Olmec** art as well as objects produced in this region during the Classic period. The Olmec civilization is considered the mother culture of Mexico for its advanced development as early as 1500 BC, which provided much of the basis for later Teotihuacán and Maya cultures. Olmec figures are delightful, but display many puzzling features, in particular their strongly negroid features: nowhere better displayed than in some of the famed **colossal heads** which can be seen in the hall. Many of the smaller pieces show evidence of deliberate deformation of the skull and teeth. Outstanding are the statue known as *The Wrestler* – arms akimbo as if on the point of starting a bout – and the many tiny objects in jade and other polished stones: notice the group of sixteen little figures and six ceremonial axes arranged to represent some religious ceremony. The later cultures are substantially represented, with fine figures and excellent pottery above all. The two most celebrated pieces are a statue of **Huehueteotl**, looking thoroughly grouchy with a brazier perched on his head, and the so-called **Huastec Adolescent**, a young Huastec Indian priest of Quetzalcoatl (perhaps the god himself) with an elaborately decorated body and a child on his back.

MAYA

The hall devoted to the **Maya** is perhaps the most varied of all, reflecting the longest-lived and widest-spread of the Meso-American cultures. In some ways it's a disappointment, since their greatest achievements were in architecture and in the decoration of their temples – many of which, unlike those of the Aztecs, are still standing – so that the found objects seem relatively unimpressive. Nevertheless, there are reproductions of several buildings, or parts of them, friezes and columns taken from them, and extensive collections of jewellery, pottery and minor sculpture. Steps lead down into a section devoted to burial practices, including a reproduction of the Royal Tomb at

Palenque (see p.455) with many of the objects found there – especially the prince's jade death mask. Outside, several small temples from relatively obscure sites are reproduced, the Temple of Paintings from **Bonampak** among them. The three rooms of the temple are entirely covered in frescoes representing the coronation of a new prince, a great battle, and the subsequent punishments and celebrations: very much easier to visit than the originals, and in far better condition.

NORTHERN AND WESTERN SOCIETIES
As a finale to the archeological collections on the ground floor, there's a large room devoted to the north and the west of the country. **Northern** societies on the whole developed few large centres, remaining isolated nomadic or agricultural communities. The small quantities of pottery, weapons and jewellery that have survived show a close affinity with Native tribes of the American Southwest. The **west** was far more developed, but it too has left relatively few traces and many of the best examples of **Tarascan culture** (see p.179) remain in Guadalajara. Among the highlights here are some delightful small human and animal figurines in stone and clay, a Tarascan Chac-Mool, and a copper mask of Xipe Totec representing a flayed human face.

THE ETHNOGRAPHY SECTION
To get to the **Ethnography section**, cross the courtyard back towards the beginning of the museum before climbing the stairs – otherwise you'll go round in reverse order. The rooms relate as far as possible to those below them, showing through photographs, models, maps and examples of local crafts the lifestyle of surviving Indian groups in the areas today. Regional dress and reproductions of various types of hut and cabin form a major part of this inevitably rather sanitized look at the poorest people in Mexico, and there are also objects relating to their more important cults and ceremonies.

The rest of the park and more museums
The enormous success of the Anthropology Museum has led to a spate of other audacious modern exhibition halls being set up in the park. Two are very close by.

The **Museo de Arte Moderno** (Tues–Sun 10am–5.30pm; $3.50, free on Sun) is not far from the entrance to the park between Reforma and the Niños Heroes monument. Two low circular buildings, linked by a corridor, house a substantial permanent collection of twentieth-century Mexican and Latin American art, including works by Rivera, Orozco and Siqueiros, as well as landscapes of the Valley of México by José Velasco (one of Rivera's teachers) and hauntingly surreal canvasses by Frida Kahlo. Often though, it's the temporary exhibitions that prove more arresting. The garden outside, fenced off from the rest of the park, has been turned into a sculpture park.

Nearby, on the other side of Reforma and up towards the Anthropology Museum, another collection of modern art graces the **Museo Rufino Tamayo** (same hours and admission) – this time an internationally based show. It was built by, and stocked with the collection of, Rufino Tamayo, an artist whose work in murals and on smaller projects is far more abstract and less political than the Big Three, but who was nevertheless their approximate contemporary and enjoys an international reputation almost as high. There is much of his own work here, and exhibits of his techniques and theories, but also an impressive collection of European and American twentieth-century art – most of it from Tamayo's private collection. Artists represented include Picasso, Miró, Magritte, Francis Bacon and Henry Moore.

If you're travelling with kids, head for the new **Museo del Papacote** (Mon–Fri 9am–6pm, Sat & Sun 9am–1pm & 2–6pm; free), literally a kite museum. Essentially a museum to childhood, with hands-on exhibits and experiments, at most times it resembles nothing more than a psychopathic kindergarten. Also popular with children, the **Zoo**, on Reforma beyond the Anthropology Museum, retains the distinction of being the only place outside China to have successfully bred Giant Pandas (at least naturally – several others now have test-tube pandas). Indeed there seems to be a veritable production line of the beasts; every time you visit the city there are posters advertising a new baby bear (*Osito Panda*). The zoo has recently undergone a long-awaited landscaping, and the enclosures are now as modern as anywhere in the world. Near here too is a small Children's Zoo, the largest lake, and, a little further up Reforma, the **Botanical Gardens**.

On the far side of the gardens Reforma crosses Molino del Rey, a street named for the major battle here during the Mexican-American War, passes the **Auditorio Nacional** – a major venue for dance, theatre and music events, with a couple of small theatres and the enormous Auditorium – and leaves the park via the Plaza Petroleos, a complex of modern skyscrapers surrounding a monument to the nationalization of the oil industry. Beyond, it heads into Las Lomas, an expensive suburb whose luxury villas are mostly hidden behind high walls and heavy security gates.

Nuevo Bosques de Chapultepec

If you head south on Molino del Rey you approach the new section of the park (*Nuevo Bosques de Chapultepec* or *Chapultepec, Segunda seccion*) which, while considerably less attractive, does offer two more museums, an amusement park and a restaurant that is one of the city's more daring pieces of modern architecture. On Molino del Rey itself though, you first pass the **Presidential Palace**, *Los Pinos*, surrounded by barracks full of presidential guards. This, plus the fact that much of the surrounding park is fenced off to recuperate, makes it extremely difficult to walk from one side to the other, especially when you add the impossibility of crossing the *periferico*. It's much easier to either take the Reforma bus out to the Plaza Petroleos and walk down from there, or to get a bus (#30) from Metro *Chapultepec* along Av. Constituyentes, which skirts the southern edge of the park.

Right by where this bus drops you is the **Museo de Historia Natural** (daily 10am–5pm; free), ten interconnecting domes filled with displays on nature and conservation, biology and geology, and breakdowns of Mexico's mineral wealth, flora and fauna. Modern and well presented, it's particularly popular with kids. From here there's a miniature "railway" that will take you round the new part of the park, or it's not far to walk. Head away from the road and you'll pass the artificial lake; underneath the fountain (the *Fuente Lerma*) is an underwater painting by Rivera. Beyond the lake you can see the roller coaster and giant wheel of the **Amusement Park**, and beside this the **Museo Tecnológico** (Tues–Sat 9am–5pm, Sun 9am–2pm; free).

South to the suburbs

México spreads itself furthest to the south, and here, among a series of old villages swallowed by the urban sprawl, are some of the most enticing destinations outside the centre. The colonial suburbs of **Coyoacán** and **San Angel**, each with a couple of worthwhile museums, make a tranquil respite from the city centre's hustle, and a startling contrast to the ultra-modern bravado of the architecture of the university and the residential area of the Pedregal. There are echoes of ancient Mexico, too, in the archeological sites of **Copilco** and **Cuicuilco**, in the "floating gardens" of **Xochimilco**, final remains of the great valley lakes, and in Diego Rivera's remarkable collection of antiquities in the **Museo Anahuacalli**.

Insurgentes

Insurgentes, the most direct approach to the suburbs, is interesting in its own right: leaving behind the Glorieta de Insurgentes (the roundabout surrounding *Insurgentes*

GETTING TO THE SOUTHERN SUBURBS

It's not at all difficult to get out to any of these sites on **public transport**, but getting from one to the other can be tricky if you're cutting across the main north–south routes. None of the connections are impossible, but it can be worth taking a few short taxi rides – from San Angel to Coyoacán for example, or from Coyoacán to the Rivera Museum. If you're really pushed, and want to see as much as possible in a day or even an afternoon, you could consider getting a **tourist taxi** to take you round the lot. If you bargain furiously this may not be as expensive as it sounds, indeed it sometimes seems that you can barely be paying for the fuel used. Since both the Rivera Museum and the Convento de Churubusco are open late, it can be stretched to a long day's trip. Alternatively, of course, there are **coach tours** run by several of the bigger travel agencies in the *Zona Rosa*.

The main approach is along **Insurgentes Sur**, where you'll find a constant stream of buses and *peseros* heading for San Angel and the University City. Their main destinations should be chalked up, or displayed on a card, on the windscreen – look for "San Angel" or "Ciudad Universitaria" (often simply "C.U." or "UNAM" for Universidad Nacional Autónoma de México) in the first instance. Other **main terminals** for heading south are the bus stands by Metro *Chapultepec* or at Metro *Tasqueña* for services along the Calzada de Tlalpan and to the southwest of the city, above all to Xochimilco.

Metro station) it runs almost perfectly straight all the way out to the university, lined throughout with huge department stores and malls, cinemas, restaurants and office buildings. A little under halfway to San Angel you pass, on the right, the enormous **Hotel de México** and the garish **Polyforum Cultural Siqueiros**. The hotel is the tallest building in the city, and the complex taken as a whole is surely the ugliest, already looking distinctly tatty, despite its modernity.

The Polyforum, designed and decorated by **David Siqueiros**, is certainly way over the top: its exterior plastered in brash paintings designed by Siqueiros and executed by some thirty young artists, the interior containing what is allegedly the world's largest mural (about 4500 square meters of it) painted by Siqueiros alone. If you go in (10am–7pm daily; ☎536-45-22) there's no excessive effort involved in seeing this massive work entitled *The March of Humanity on Earth and Towards the Cosmos* since the floor revolves to let you take it all in. A complete explanation is provided by the daily *Son et Lumière* (at 4pm in Spanish, 6pm in English) which brings out the full impact of the changing perspectives and use of sculptural techniques. Elsewhere, the building also houses visiting art exhibitions and a sizable display of expensive crafts for sale.

Beyond this monster you shortly pass, on the same side, a huge sports centre with the **Estadio Nacional**, a 65,000-seat soccer stadium, and the **Plaza Mexico**, the largest bullring in the world (holding 50,000). Finally, just before San Angel comes the **Teatro de los Insurgentes**, its facade covered in a huge mosaic designed by Diego Rivera depicting the history of Mexican theatre and assorted historical figures: along the top are ranged *Los Insurgentes* (the insurgents of Mexico's War of Independence) Hidalgo and Morelos, along with Benito Juárez and Emiliano Zapata.

San Angel

From the choked traffic of Insurgentes at its junction with Avenida La Paz, a short walk will take you up to the colonial charm of **SAN ANGEL** with its markets and ancient mansions around flower-draped patios. A very exclusive place to live, it's also a highly popular spot to visit (especially on Saturdays for the Bazar Sabado), and is packed with little restaurants and cafes where you can sit outside and watch the crowds go by.

Climb La Paz up to Av. Revolución and you'll find, on the left, the old Carmelite Convent – now the **Museo del Carmen** (Tues–Sun 10am–4.45pm; $3.50, free on Sun). There's a collection of colonial religious paintings and sculpture here, and mummies in the crypt, but the convent itself is the chief attraction, a lovely example of early seventeenth-century architecture with domes covered in multi-coloured (predominantly yellow) tiles and an almost tropical garden in the cloister. Heading up Av. Revolución to the right, past a small flower market, you reach the **Museo de Arte Alvar y Carrillo Gil** (Tues–Sun 10am–6pm; $2.50, free on Sun), a somewhat incongruous and surprisingly good museum of modern art. There are works by Mexicans including Rivera, Orozco and Siqueiros, and an international collection which takes in Rodin, Picasso, Kandinsky and Paul Klee.

If you cross straight over Revolución from the convent and continue up the hill, the centre of San Angel and the oldest mansions lie ahead. **Plaza San Jacinto** is the target, a delightful square that is the centrepiece of the **Bazar Sábado** and animated throughout the week. Initially the Saturday market was based in one of the mansions on the square, which still opens every weekend selling upmarket crafts and artworks, but nowadays there are stalls in all the surrounding streets with fairground rides and freak shows that feature assorted tattooed and bearded ladies. Also on the Plaza is the **Casa del Risco**, sometimes known as the *Centro Cultural Isidro Fabela* (Tues–Sun 10am–2.30pm; free), an eighteenth-century mansion in which is displayed the said Isidro Fabela's collection of antique furniture and paintings, with an extraordinary fountain in the patio made from old porcelain plates and cups, broken and unbroken.

Not far away, on Av. Altavista, is the famous *San Angel Inn*, a luxurious restaurant in the restored **Hacienda de San Angel**. Expensive, and packed with tourists since it's included on many day-trip itineraries, it's nevertheless worth visiting for the lovely gardens and courtyards. The food is very good too. Also on Altavista, on the corner with Diego Rivera, is the **Museo-Estudio Diego Rivera** (Tues–Sun 10am–6pm; $3, free on Sun), where you can see Rivera's studio and personal, rather wonderful, collection of popular and pre-Hispanic art.

El Pedregal

Beyond San Angel it's possible to head south through the **Jardines del Pedregal de San Angel** more often known simply as *El Pedregal*. The Pedregal of the name is actually a vast lava flow that spreads across from here through the University City and on to the south of Coyoacán, but the section south of San Angel is the thickest, the most craggy and dramatic. It was regarded as a completely useless stretch of land, the haunt of bandits and brigands, until in the early 1950s an architect named Luis Barragan began to build extraordinarily imaginative houses here, using the uneven lava as a feature. Now it's filled with the most amazing collection of luxury homes – you're not allowed to build here unless you can afford a sufficiently large piece of land and an architect to design your house – which have become a tourist attraction in themselves. Bus parties ride through in much the same way as they do in Beverly Hills or Hollywood, spotting the homes of the famous. Public transport up here is sparse, though there are buses from San Angel, so if you're really into modern architecture you might try getting a taxi to drive you round for thirty minutes or so.

Coyoacán

On the other side of Insurgentes from San Angel, some distance away, lies **COYOACÁN** – another colonial township that has been swallowed by the city. Even before the Conquest it was a sizeable place, the capital of a small kingdom on the shores of the lake that had been subjugated by the Aztecs in the mid-fifteenth century.

Cortés based himself in Coyoacán during the siege of Tenochtitlán, and continued to live here while the old city was torn down and construction began on the new capital of Nueva España. It remains very peaceful, far less visited than San Angel, and with a couple of lovely, lively plazas. The focus of the area is the spacious **Plaza Central**, which is actually made up of two adjoining plazas – **Plaza Hidalgo** and the **Jardín del Centenario**. Here stand the ancient church of San Juan and a small **Palacio Municipal** (also known as the **Casa de Cortés**) said to have been built by Cortés himself. Inside are two Rivera murals depicting the Conquest and the torture of Cuauhtémoc: the latter is particularly apposite since it was in Coyoacán that the Aztec leader was tortured and finally killed. Nearby, in the small **Plaza de la Conchita**, the **Capilla de la Concepción** has a wonderful Baroque facade. Overlooking the square is the **Casa de la Malinche**, the house in which Cortés installed his native mistress and where he allegedly later murdered his wife shortly after her arrival from Spain. Coyoacán is one of the city's main stomping grounds for artists, artisans and musicians. Activity centres around the *Café el Parnaso*, attached to a bookshop on the corner of the square, and the *Hijo del Cuervo* bar at the opposite side – both good places to check out the latest, as well as to relax and watch the world go by. On Sunday, there's a **market** in the Plaza Central when the whole area is taken up by stalls and various rock, folk and reggae bands. It is far and away the most fun place to buy your souvenirs, though most of the stuff could be found cheaper elsewhere.

Reflecting all this joyous cultural activity, the **Museo de Culturas Populares**, close to the Plaza Hidalgo at Hidalgo 289 (Tues–Sun 10am–6pm; free), has colourful displays on many popular cultural forms including the circus, popular religion, wrestling (for more on which see p.295) and review theatre.

The Museo Frida Kahlo

The **Museo Frida Kahlo** (Tues–Sun 10am–6pm; $3.50, free on Sun) is just a few minutes walk from the centre of Coyoacán, six blocks along Centenario and then down c/Londres to the right – it's painted bright blue and hard to miss. Kahlo was an artist whose morbid, dream-like works reflected the pain of her own life – a polio victim who suffered severe injuries in a drastic bus accident, she spent much of her later life confined to a wheelchair or to bed or in hospital. The products of that experience – grisly, self-absorbed canvasses – almost always feature Kahlo herself: a fixed expression on her face, above a body always sliced open, mutilated or crippled.

The museum occupies Kahlo's family home (she was born here in 1910) where she later returned to live with Diego Rivera from 1929 to 1954. As well as her own paintings – the best of which are frequently off in touring exhibitions – the museum contains early Rivera drawings and many mementoes of their life together and their joint interest in Mexico's artistic heritage. It reflects too, in its extraordinary decoration, littered with pre-Hispanic artefacts and more modern folk items (in particular bizarre papier-maché animals and figures), the coterie of artists and intellectuals of which they were the centre in the 1930s and 40s. Trotsky stayed here for a while and later settled nearby, and D.H. Lawrence too was a frequent visitor to friends in Coyoacán, though he had little political or artistic sympathy with Kahlo – or with Trotsky for that matter. Taken as a whole, the house is a fascinating insight into the social and intellectual background of Mexican art in the aftermath of the Revolution.

Trotsky's House

The *Museo y Casa de Trotsky*, **Trotsky's House** (Tues–Fri 10.30am–2pm & 3–5pm, Sat & Sun 10.30am–4.30pm; $3.50) is not far away at Viena 45 near the corner of Morelos – about three blocks down and a couple to the left. This house is virtually the only memorial to Trotsky anywhere in the world – his small tomb stands in the gardens. Here the genius of the Russian Revolution and organizer of the Red Army lived and

THE ASSASSINATION OF TROTSKY

The **first attempt on Trotsky's life** in his house at Coyoacán, which left more than seventy scars in the plaster of the bedroom walls, came at 4am on the 24 May, 1940. A heavily armed group (led allegedly by the painter David **Siqueiros**, who had been a commander in the Spanish Civil War) overcame the guards and pumped more than two hundred shots into the house, an attack which Trotsky, his wife and son survived by the simple expedient of hiding under their beds. After this the house, already heavily guarded, was fortified still further. But the assassin was already a regular visitor who had been carefully building up contacts for nearly two years: posing as the businessman boyfriend of a trusted Trotskyist who was being slowly converted to the cause, bringing presents for the wife and kids. Although never wholly trusted, it seemed natural when he turned up on the afternoon of August 20 with an article that he wanted Trotsky to look over: Trotsky invited him into the study. About thirty seconds later, the notorious **ice-pick** (the blunt end), which had been concealed under the killer's coat, smashed into Trotsky's skull. He died some 24 hours later, in hospital after an operation. His brain, they say, was vast. The killer, who called himself Frank Jackson and claimed to be Belgian, never explained his actions or even confessed to his true identity – **Jaime Ramon Mercader del Río**.

worked in exile, and here Stalin's long arm finally caught up with him, to stifle the last fears of opposition. The house, with steel gates and shutters, high walls and watchtowers seems at first a little incongruous surrounded by the bourgeois homes of a prosperous suburb, but inside it's a human place, set up as he left it, if rather dustier: books on the shelves, his glasses smashed on the desk, and all the trappings of a fairly comfortable ordinary life. Except for the bullet holes.

Practicalities

You can **get to Coyoacán** from San Angel on buses heading down Altavista by the *San Angel Inn* (or more easily by taxi), or from the centre on buses from Metros *Chapultepec, Insurgentes*, or *Cuauhtémoc*. In each case look for "Coyoacán" or "Colonia del Valle/Coyoacán". There's also a trolley bus that runs down Lázaro Cárdenas (against the flow of traffic) from a stop close by Bellas Artes. Metro line 3, too, passes close by, though note that *Viveros* station is considerably closer to the action than *Coyoacán*: from here walk south on Av. Universidad, then turn left, east, to reach the centre. If you are coming straight from the centre of town down Av. Cuauhtémoc or Av. Lázaro Cárdenas, it makes sense to visit the Kahlo and Trotsky museums first. Get off the bus immediately after passing under Av. Río Churubusco.

The University City and Cuicuilco

Beyond Coyoacán and San Angel, Insurgentes enters the great lava field of the Pedregal. To the left of the road is the **UNIVERSITY CITY** (*Ciudad Universitaria*), dominated by the astonishing twelve-storey **Library**. Each face of this rectangular tower is covered in a mosaic fresco designed by Juan O'Gorman – mostly natural stone with a few tiles or glass to supply colours which would otherwise have been unavailable. It represents the artist's vision of the country's progression through history: on the larger north and south faces are pre-Hispanic and colonial Mexico; on the west wall the present and the University coat-of-arms; on the east the future ranged around a giant atom. It's remarkable how this has been incorporated as an essential feature of the building – at first it appears that there are no windows at all, but look closely and you'll see that in fact they're an integral part of the design, appearing as eyes, mouths or as windows of the buildings in the mural.

More or less beside this are the long, low **administration buildings** (*rectoría*) with a giant mural in high relief (or a "sculptural painting") by Siqueiros, intended to provide a moving perspective as you walk past or drive by on Insurgentes. At the front here too are the University Theatre and the **Museo Universitario de Ciencias y Artes** (Tues–Sun 10am–2pm & 4–9pm; free), a wide-ranging general collection. Behind them spread out the enormous grounds of the main campus, starting with a large esplanade known as the Plaza Mayor, with sculptural groups dotted around a shallow artificial pond. Towards the back are more murals, adorning the Faculties of **Science** and **Medicine**; continue past these to reach another grassy area with the **Botanical Gardens** and several large walls against which the students play *frontón*.

After some forty years of use, parts of the campus are beginning to show their age: certainly it's no longer the avant-garde sensation it was when it opened – but it remains a remarkable architectural achievement. The whole thing was built in just five years (1950–55) under the Presidency of Miguel Alemán, and is now one of the largest universities in the world. It's also the oldest on the American continent. Granted a charter by Philip II in 1551, the University of Mexico occupied a succession of sites in the city centre (including the Hospital de Jesus Nazareno and what is now the Escuela Nacional Preparatoria), was closed down several times in the nineteenth century and was finally granted its status as the *Universidad Nacional Autonoma de México* in 1929.

Directly across Insurgentes from the main buildings is the sculptured oval of the 100,000-seater *Estadio Olímpico*. The main facade is decorated with a mosaic relief by Diego Rivera, representing the development of human potential through sport, and any taxi driver will tell you that the **Olympic Stadium's** curious shape was deliberately designed to look like a giant Mexican sombrero. This, sadly, is not the case, but it is undeniably odd – half sunk into the ground as if dropped here from a great height and slightly warped in the process.

"Ciudad Universitaria" **buses** stop at a terminus right in front of the main complex. You can also get here by the Metro (*Copilco* is closer than *Universidad*) in which case you'll be right at the back of the campus and have to walk all the way through, past the *frontón* courts and medical faculty, to reach the library.

Cuicuilco

To get to the pyramid of **CUICUILCO**, carry on down Insurgentes (buses marked "Tlalpan") to where it crosses the great *periferico* ring-road – the site is just beyond the junction (there are also buses round the *periférico*, look for "Perisur" or "Villa Olimpica"). If you follow the *periferico* round you'll see pieces of sculpture at regular intervals by the roadside – each was a gift from a different country at the time of the 1968 Olympics – and pass the former Olympic Village, now a high-rise residential area. The site itself, however, is dominated by the circular temple clearly visible from the road. This is much the oldest construction of such scale known in central Mexico, abandoned at the time of the eruption of Xitle (the small volcano that created the Pedregal – around 100–300 AD) just as Teotihuacán was beginning to develop. Not a great deal is known about the site, much of which has been buried by modern housing, completing the work of the lava, but other structures have been uncovered, notably at the Olympic Village. The pyramid itself is composed of three sloping tiers (of a probable original five) about 17m high by 100m in diameter, approached by a ramp and a stairway. A small **museum** (daily 9am–5pm; free) displays objects found here and at contemporary settlements.

Xochimilco

The "floating gardens" of **XOCHIMILCO** can provide one of the most memorable experiences in the city and – for all that the canals are heavily polluted, their level dropping alarmingly year by year – remains the most popular Sunday outing for thousands of Mexicans and a place filled every weekend with the most intense carnival atmosphere. It's also the one place with where you get some feel of the ancient city (or at least an idealized view of it) with its waterborne commerce, thriving markets and dazzling colour. **Rent a boat**, its superstructure decorated with an arch of paper flowers, and you'll be punted around miles of canals, continually assaulted by Indian women in tiny canoes selling flowers or fruit, or with a precarious charcoal brazier burning under a pile of *tortillas*, chicken and *chile*, or by larger vessels bearing entire *mariachi* bands in their full finery who, for a small fee, will grapple alongside you and blast out a couple of numbers.

The floating gardens themselves are no more floating than the Titanic: following the old Aztec methods of making the lake fertile, these *chinampas* are formed by a raft of mud and reeds, firmly rooted to the bottom by the plants. As well as amusing the hordes of visitors, the area is still a very important market-gardening and flower-producing centre for the city – if you wander the streets of the town you'll find garden centres everywhere, and wonderful flowers and fruit in the market (though whether it's healthy to eat food raised on these filthy waters is open to question). Off the huge central plaza is the lovely sixteenth-century church of **San Bernardino**, full on Sundays with a succession of people paying homage and leaving offerings at one of its many chapels; in the plaza itself there are usually bands playing, or mime artists entertaining the crowds.

For the easiest **approach to Xochimilco**, take the Metro to *Tasqueña* (line 2) and from there a bus, *pesero* or the red tram. There are also buses direct from the centre, down Insurgentes and around the *periferico* or straight down the Calzada de Tlalpan: on Sundays many extra services are laid on. To get a boat follow the *embarcadero* signs. What you pay depends on the size of the punt, how long you want to go for, and most importantly your skill at bargaining (especially on a weekday when there are few people about). Since you pay by the boat it's much better value to get a group together, and probably more enjoyable too – remember that there are likely to be sundry extras including the cold beers thoughtfully provided by the boatman, and any flowers, food or music you find yourself accepting on your way. While Sunday is by far the most crowded and animated day, Saturdays are lively too, and you can rent a boat any day of the week for a little solitary cruising.

Down the Calzada de Tlalpan

The **Calzada de Tlalpan** is the other main approach to the south, running down more or less from the zócalo to cross the *periferico* not far from Xochimilco. If you want to do the full circuit of the south, head back towards the centre this way: you'll pass the giant **Estadio Azteca** beside the Calzada very close to its junction with the *periferico*. Along the way there are two superb museums – both of them also quite close to Coyoacán.

Museo Anahuacalli

Heading back from Xochimilco towards the centre, you'll pass first the bizarre **Museo Anahuacalli**, c/Museo 15 (Tues–Sun 10am–2pm & 3–5pm; free), designed and built by Rivera to house his own huge collection of pre-Hispanic artefacts. It's an extraordinary structure, inspired by Maya and Aztec architecture, a sombre mass of black volcanic stone atop a hill with magical views: Popocatépetl and Ixtaccíhuatl seem really close here, their snowy peaks glistening on even the smoggiest days. Whether it is altogether a success as a museum is another matter – you can come out thinking more of the building than of the collection. And the ground floor, especially, is appallingly lit: slits in the walls covered in thin sheets of alabaster, scarcely helped by the odd bare bulb lost somewhere in the roof. That said, there are some lovely individual pieces and often a thoroughly imaginative display. One small chamber, for example, contains nothing but a series of **Huehueteotls**, all squatting grumpily in the gloom, their braziers weighing down their heads. In the studio, the one really light place, there's a lively ball-game group and a whole series of wonderfully familiar animals. All the pieces, in fact – none are really big – are exquisite objects, and the place leaves you wondering just why the western cultures have been so neglected.

As a brief guide to what you'll see, the ground floor is devoted to objects from the main cultures of the Valley of Mexico – Teotihuacán, Toltec and Aztec – which provided Rivera with such an important part of his inspiration. On the first floor, rooms devoted to the west of Mexico (arguably the best such collection in the country) surround the huge airy room which Rivera, had he lived, would have used as a studio. It's been fitted out as if he had anyway, with an unfinished portrait on the easel and many sketches and mementoes of the artist lying around. On the top floor are more Aztec objects, along with pottery and small figures from Oaxaca and the Gulf coast. Up here you can also get out onto the roof, for the entrancing views. The museum is on c/Museo, just off Av. Division del Norte: *pesero* "Ruta 29 Xotepingo" passes very near, but it's easier to get a bus or *pesero* heading along Division del Norte, get off at Museo and walk up (a stiff little climb). There's a large restaurant, *Carnitas de Michoacán*, on the corner.

Museo Nacional de las Intervenciones

The **Museo Nacional de las Intervenciones**, 20 de Agosto and General Anaya (Tues–Sun 9am–6pm; $3.50, free on Sun) occupies the old Franciscan **Convento de Churubusco** some 3km to the north. It owes its present role to the 1847 battle in which the invading Americans led by General Winfield Scott defeated a Mexican force under General Anaya – another heroic Mexican defeat in which the outnumbered defenders fought to their last bullet. The exhibits are devoted to the history of foreign military adventures in Mexico and to nationalist expansionism in general. Skeletons in the cupboards of Britain, Spain, France and the USA are all loudly rattled.

First of all, though, you'll notice the building, which is a stunner – especially if you arrive at the end of the day as darkness is falling and the lights are coming on in the gardens. The exhibits themselves may not mean a great deal unless you have a reasonable grasp of Mexican history; they're labelled only in Spanish and not very fully even in that. You start with an introduction to Imperialism and an exhibition – changed monthly – on some aspect of it. The museum proper, on the upper floors, is devoted largely to the Mexican-American wars and the loss of 2,500,000 square kilometres of Mexican territory. It's a very different perspective from that of the Alamo. Spanish and French interventions are covered too, as is the role of western finance generally in upholding the Díaz regime. Fascinating as all this is, you're yet again likely to remember the monastery buildings and grounds at least as well as their contents.

The museum is on General Anaya between the Calzada de Tlalpan and Av. Division del Norte, very close to *General Anaya* Metro station: turn right as you leave the museum and you'll see the trains passing at the end of the road. From the Rivera Museum take a *pesero* up Division del Norte and get off at the large *Pemex* station just before the underpass which carries Av. Río Churubusco. From Coyoacán it's just about walking distance – east on Hidalgo from the plaza and fork left on General Anaya.

North of the centre

There's less to see north of the centre of México, but there are two sites of compelling interest – the great **Basilica of Guadalupe** and the emotive **Plaza de las Tres Culturas** – which well deserve the afternoon it takes to cover both. Further out, and harder to get to, you'll find the pyramids of **Tenayuca** and **Santa Cecilia**, the two most dramatically preserved remains of Aztec architecture in the city.

Plaza de las Tres Culturas

Site of the ancient city of **Tlatelolco**, the **PLAZA DE LAS TRES CULTURAS** will be your first stop. Today a lovely **colonial church** rises in the midst of the excavated ruins, which are in turn surrounded by a **high-rise housing complex**: all three great cultures of Mexico side by side.

You can get to the Plaza de las Tres Culturas either on the Metro (*Tlatelolco*) which continues to Guadalupe, or by bus. It lies between Insurgentes Nte. and Reforma Nte.: on the former take any bus north ("Indios Verdes") and get off shortly before the black A-shaped skyscraper that marks the **Monumento a la Raza**; on the latter "La Villa" buses pass within about three blocks on their way to Guadalupe.

The ruins

Tlatelolco was a considerably more ancient city than Tenochtitlán, based on a separate but nearby island in the lake. For a long time, under independent rule, its people existed in close alliance with the Mexica of Tenochtitlán and the city was by far the most important commercial and market centre in the Valley – even after its annexation into the Aztec empire in 1473 Tlatelolco retained this role. By the time the Spanish arrived much of the swampy lake between the two had been filled in and built over: it was to Tlatelolco that Cortés and his troops came to marvel at the size and order of the market. Cortés estimated that 60,000 people, buyers and sellers, came and went each day, and Bernal Díaz wrote (after several pages of detailed description):

> *We were astounded at the great number of people and the quantities of merchandise, and at the orderliness and good arrangements that prevailed . . . every kind of goods was kept separate and had its fixed place marked for it . . . . Some of the soldiers among us who had been in many parts of the world, in Constantinople, in Rome, and all over Italy, said that they had never seen a market so well laid out, so large, so orderly, and so full of people.*

In 1521 the besieged Aztecs made their final stand here, and a plaque in the middle of the plaza recalls that struggle: "On the 13th of August 1521", it reads, "defended by the heroic Cuauhtémoc, Tlatelolco fell under the power of Hernan Cortés. It was neither a triumph nor a defeat, but the painful birth of the mixed race that is the Mexico of today." The ruins are a pale reflection of the original, whose temples rivalled those of Tenochtitlán itself: some idea of their scale can be gained from the size of the bases. The chief temple, for example, had by the time of the Conquest reached its eleventh rebuilding – what you see now corresponds to the second stage, and by the time nine more were superimposed it would certainly have risen much higher than the church which was built from its stones. On top, probably, was a double sanctuary like that on the Great Temple of Tenochtitlán. The smaller structures include a square **tzompantli**, or Wall of Skulls, near which nearly two hundred human skulls were discovered, each with holes through its temples – presumably the result of having been displayed side by side on long poles around the sides of the building.

The church

The **church** on the site was erected in 1609, replacing an earlier Franciscan monastery. Parts of this survive, arranged about the cloister. Here, in the early years after the Conquest, the friars established a college at which they instructed the sons of the Aztec nobility in European ways, teaching them Spanish, Latin and Christianity:

Bernardino de Sahagun was one of the teachers, and it was here that he collected and wrote down many of the customs and traditions of the Indians, the most important existing record of daily Aztec life.

The modern buildings

The **modern buildings** that surround the plaza – mostly a rather ugly 1960s housing project but including the Ministry of Foreign Affairs – represent the third culture. The current state of Mexico was rather more brutally represented on October 2, 1968, when troops and tanks were ordered to fire on almost a quarter of a million students demonstrating here. It was the culmination of several months of student protests over the government of the day's social and educational policies, which the authorities were determined to subdue with only ten days left before the ceremonial opening of the Olympic Games in the city. Estimates of deaths vary from an official figure at the time of thirty to student estimates of more than five hundred, but it seems clear that hundreds is closer than tens. The Mexican philosopher Octavio Paz saw it all as part of the cycle of history – a ritual slaughter to recall the Aztec sacrifices here – but it's perhaps better seen as an example of at least one thread of continuity between all Mexico's civilizations: the cheapness of life and the harsh brutality of their rulers. More recently, parts of the housing complex suffered severe earthquake damage.

Basilica de Nuestra Señora de Guadalupe

The **Basilica de Nuestra Señora de Guadalupe** is in fact a whole series of churches, chapels and shrines, set around an enormous stone-flagged plaza and climbing up the rocky hillock where the miracles that led to its foundation occurred. The Virgin of Guadalupe, Mexico's first indigenous saint, is still her most popular – the image recurs in churches throughout the country, and the Virgin's banner has been fought under by both sides in almost every conflict the nation has ever seen: most famously when Hidalgo seized on it as the flag of Mexican Independence. According to the legend, a christianized Indian, **Juan Diego**, was walking over the hill (formerly dedicated to the Aztec earth goddess Tonantzin) on his way to the monastery at Tlatelolco one morning in December 1531. He was stopped by a brilliant vision of the Virgin who ordered him, in Nahuatl, to go to the bishop and tell him to build a church on the hill. Bishop Juan de Zumarraga was unimpressed until, on December 12, the Virgin reappeared, ordering Diego to gather roses from the top of the hill (in December!) and take them to the bishop. Doing so, he bundled the flowers in his cape, and when he opened it before the bishop he found the image of the dark-skinned Virgin imprinted into the cloth. The cloak today hangs above the altar in the gigantic modern Basilica: it takes its name from the celebrated (and equally swarthy) Virgin in the Monastery of Guadalupe in Spain.

The **first church** was built in 1533, but the large Baroque basilica you see now was completely reconstructed in the eighteenth century and again remodelled in the nineteenth and twentieth. Impressive mostly for its size, it is anyway closed to the public while being shored up – around the back you can go into a small **museum** (Tues–Sun 10am–6pm; $4) which contains some of the Virgin's many treasures of religious art and a large collection of ex-votos. To the left of the great plaza is the **modern home of the image** – a huge church with space inside for 10,000 worshippers and for perhaps four times that when the great doors all round are thrown open to the crowds. It's always crowded and there seems to be a service permanently in progress. The famous cloak hangs above the main altar, and to avoid constant disruption there's a passageway round behind the altar which takes the devout to a spot right underneath – strips of moving walkway are designed to prevent anyone lingering too long here, but they never seem to be working.

From the plaza you can walk round to the right and up the hill past a series of little chapels associated with the Virgin's appearance. Loveliest is the **Capilla del Pocito**, in which is a well, said to have sprung forth during one of the apparitions. Built in the eighteenth century, it consists of two linked elliptical chapels, a smaller and a larger, with colourful tiled domes and magnificently decorative interiors. On the very top of the hill, the **Capilla de las Rosas** marks the spot where the miraculous roses grew.

Around all this, there swirls a stream of humanity – pilgrims, sightseers, priests and salesmen offering candles, souvenirs, pictures of the Virgin, snacks, any number of mementoes that make Guadalupe a vast industry as well as a religion. On December 12, anniversary of the second apparition, their numbers swell to hundreds of thousands. Many cover the last miles on their knees in an act of penance or devotion, but for others it is more of a vast fiesta, with dancing, singing and drinking throughout the day.

Tenayuca and Santa Cecilia – two Aztec pyramids

In the extreme north of the city, just outside the boundaries of the Distrito Federal, lie the two most wholly preserved examples of Aztec-style architecture. They're hard to get to by public transport but, if you have a strong interest in the Aztecs, they thoroughly repay the effort involved. **Tenayuca** is just off the Av. de los Cien Metros, some 6km north of the Terminal del Norte. Take the Metro to *Basílica* or *La Raza* and catch a bus to Tenayuca. From there walk up the hill past the bridge over the river (very busy roads) and past the square to the museum site. To **Santa Cecilia** there's a bus that runs past the east side of Tenayuca, but it's also just about within walking distance, or a short taxi ride. Some bus tours take both in on their way to Tula and Tepotzotlán.

Tenayuca
TENAYUCA (Tues–Sun 10am–5pm; $3.50, free on Sun) is another site that predates Tenochtitlán by a long chalk, indeed there are those who claim that it was the capital of the tribe that destroyed Tula. In this its history closely mirrors almost all the other valley settlements: a barbarian tribe from the north invades, conquers all before it, settles in a city and becomes civilized borrowing much of its culture from its predecessors – and is in turn overcome by the next wave of migrants. There's little evidence that Tenayuca ever controlled a large empire, but it was a powerful city and provides one of the most concrete links between the Toltecs and the Aztecs. The pyramid that survives dates from the period of Aztec dominance and is an almost perfect replica – in miniature – of the great temples of Tlatelolco and Tenochtitlán. Here the structure and the monumental double stairway are intact – only the twin sanctuaries at the top and the brightly painted decorations would be needed for it to open for sacrifices again tomorrow. This is the sixth superimposition; five earlier pyramids (the first dating from the early thirteenth century) are contained within it (and revealed in places by excavation), while originally there was a seventh layer built on top, of which some traces remain.

The most unusual and striking feature of Tenayuca's pyramid is the border of interlocking stone **snakes** that must originally have surrounded the entire building – well over a hundred of them survive. Notice also the two coiled snakes (one a little way up the north face, the other at the foot of the south) known as the "turquoise serpents": their crests are crowned with stars and aligned with the sun's position at the solstice.

Santa Cecilia Acatitlán
A poor road leads north to **SANTA CECILIA ACATITLÁN** (Tues–Sun 10am–5pm; free) where there's a second pyramid – much smaller and simpler but wholly restored and remarkably beautiful with its clean, very modern looking lines. Originally, this was a temple with a double staircase very similar to the others, but it was discovered during

excavation that one of the earlier structures inside was almost perfectly preserved. The ruined layers were stripped away to reveal what, after some reconstruction, is the only example of a sanctuary more or less as it would have been seen by Cortés. It's a very plain building, rising in four steps to a single roofed shrine approached by a broad ramped stairway. The studded decorations around the roof represent either skulls or stars. You approach the pyramid through a small museum in a colonial house, whose displays and grounds are both well worth a look.

Eating and drinking

Since eating out seems to be the city's main pastime, there are restaurants, cafes, *taquerías* and juice stands on every block, many of them very reasonably priced, even in the heart of the *Zona Rosa*, or along Reforma, or just off the zócalo. As throughout the country, you should make your main meal a late lunchtime *comida* if you want to eat cheaply and well.

México abounds in **rosticerías**, roast chicken shops, serving tasty set meals and crispy chicken with beer in a jolly atmosphere. There are a couple on 5 de Febrero. For fruit shakes, sodas, ice cream, fruit salads and *tortas*, try a **jugo** shop such as *Jugos California*, which has branches all over the country. **Pasterías** or cake shops sell cheap pastries and bread rolls for economical breakfasts: *Pastería Madrid*, 5 de Febrero 25 is good and also has its own restaurant. A typical **taquería**, offering standard Mexican *antojitos* including *tacos*, *quesadillas* and *enfrijolidas* (*tacos* covered in *frijol* sauce), is *Taquería el Tapatío* on c/Palma 15. If you've got a sweet tooth, make for the *Dulcería de Celaya*, 5 de Mayo 39 – a wonderful **sweet shop**, with candied fruit *comates* and *dulce de membrillo*.

There are also several **chains** with branches throughout the city – dull on the whole but reliable. *Sanborn's* is the best known, not particularly cheap but good for a breakfast of coffee and *pan dulce* or for reasonably authentic Mexican food tailored to foreign tastes: chief outlets are in the *Zona Rosa* on Hamburgo; just off Reforma next to the Sheraton and on the street leading up to the Plaza de la República; the House of Tiles by Bellas Artes; 16 de Septiembre just down from the zócalo; and in San Angel. *VIPs* is cheaper and serves a filling *comida corrida* as well as standard Mexican and American dishes – there are branches just off the Plaza de la Republica and in the *Zona Rosa*. For palatable, authentic *tacos*, *El Portón* (*Zona Rosa* at the corner of Hamburgo and Niza and in the Plaza de la Republica) is a safe bet, while *Tacos Beatriz* (at the train station and on Londres in the *Zona Rosa* among others) has a less sanitized atmosphere. Burger places are on the whole to be avoided – if you must have American food try the overpriced *Denny's* (on Londres in the *Zona Rosa* and on Reforma near Colon).

The choice elsewhere is almost limitless, ranging from traditional coffee houses to fast-food lunch counters and taking in Japanese, French, Spanish, expensive international and rock-bottom Mexican cooking along the way. There's even a small Chinatown, of sorts, south of the Alameda where a cluster of **Chinese restaurants** line c/Dolores. As well as the possibilities listed below there are the traditional food stalls in **markets** throughout the city. Merced is the biggest, but not a terribly pleasant place to eat: at the back of the **Plaza Garibaldi** there's a market hall given over to nothing but food stands, each vociferously competing with its neighbours.

Mexican

Cafe Cinco de Mayo, 5 de Mayo 57. Classy nineteenth-century café with good food and coffee. A little expensive, but the food is very good, especially the *comida corrida*.

Cafe Lucky, Articulco 123 no. 35. Cheap, quiet cafe with a cheap *comida corrida.*

Cafe Paris, 5 de Mayo 10. Traditional cafe/restaurant.

Cafe el Popular, 5 de Mayo 52. Cheap place, serving simple food 24hr a day. Surly, overworked staff and cramped conditions make it somewhere not to linger.

Cafe Tacuba, Tacuba 28. Good coffee and reasonable food. One of the country's top bands is sponsored by the café and thus bears its name.

Flash Taco, Monte de Piedad 13. Video bar overlooking the zócalo, serving good, somewhat expensive, *tacos.*

Panchos, Uruguay. Small restaurant offering set meals only. Breakfasts are generous and huge.

Parrilla, Leonesa Bolivar 29-A; another at Insurgentes Sur 86. Smart clean restaurant offering good Mexican grills.

San Angel Inn, Las Palmas 56, San Angel. Very popular, upmarket restaurant; book in advance.

El Tajín, Miguel Angel de Quevedo 687, Coyoacán. Veracruz specialities; the fish dishes such as *huachinango à la Veracruz* and *mojarra al mojo del ajo* are exquisite.

Chinese, Japanese and Indian

Bombay Palace, Amberes 34 (☎525-38-66). Expensive Indian gourmet food.

Chez Wok, Tennyson 117 (☎281-34-10). High-class Chinese food.

Comida Chen, Allende 26. Mexican and Chinese food, and a *comida corrida.*

Kam Ling, 5 de Mayo 14 (☎521-56-61). Chinese food to eat in and take away. Set dinner for two people around $10; the Mexican menu is cheaper.

Pabellon Coreano, Estocolmo 16 (☎525-25-09). Expensive, sophisticated Korean restaurant.

Sushi Tako, Mexico 180. Reasonably priced vegetarian Japanese near *Coyoacán* Metro.

Wok and Roll, Londres 104, *Zona Rosa.* Chinese restaurant and video bar.

European and International

Angus, Copenhague 31, *Zona Rosa.* Best steaks in town.

Champs Elysees, Amberes 7, *Zona Rosa* (☎514-04-50). The city's top French restaurant: truly excellent food, but you don't want to know how much it costs.

La Guardía del Gaucho, Mino 214. Good-value Argentine food, with barbecue and roast meat.

Mauna Loa, San Jerónimo 240 (☎548-68-84). Polynesian restaurant.

Piccadilly Pub, Copenhague 23, *Zona Rosa.* Nothing like an English pub – for a start, the food is good – otherwise rather tacky, with expensive beer.

Shirley's, Reforma 108, and Londres 102-B. Good, American-style afternoon buffet.

La Taberna Griega, Insurgentes Sur 1391, Centro Armand (☎611-69-58). Good-value Greek food and dancing.

Spanish

Camino Real Hotel, Maliano Fercobedo 700, near *Chapultepec* Metro (☎203-21-21). Excellent tapas bar and more formal restaurant.

Restaurante Centro Castellano, Uruguay 16 (☎510-14-16). Huge restaurant occupying three floors, dishing up great, hearty meals with lots of seafood.

Restaurante Centro Catalán, Bolivar 31. Good barbecued meats, especially lamb and rabbit paella. Set lunches for around $10.

Meson del Perro Andaluz, Copenhague 26, *Zona Rosa* (☎533-53-06). Very popular Spanish restaurant with a lively atmosphere.

Seafood

Danubio, Uruguay 3 (☎512-09-12). Established restaurant that has specialized in seafood in all its guises for the last 50 years.

El Marisquito, Donceles 12-B, right next to the Senate House. Join the politicos in eating good-quality shellfish and stews.

Vegetarian

Centro Naturista, Dolores 10, south of the Alameda. Very cheap, with Macrobiotic choices.

Restaurante Vegetariano Karl, Amberes 57, *Zona Rosa*. Expensive wholefood restaurant catering for the many tourists in the *Zona*.

Restaurante Vegetariano Yug, Varsovia 3, *Zona Rosa*. Worthy bookshop and contact point for vegetarians and vegans.

El Vegetariano, Filomeno Mata 13, between Madero and 5 de Mayo. Very tasty vegetarian food in the centre of town.

Vegetariano Lindavista, Insurgentes Nte. 1892. Gives classes on vegetarian food preparation.

Vegetarian Restaurant, Motolinia 31. Friendly place with a good-value set menu.

Cantinas

Bars in México, as in the rest of the country, are very much a male preserve, but here at least things are beginning to change. Even so it's safer for women to stick to hotel bars (most of which are in the centre anyway) or to the established night spots (see "Entertainment" below) and tourist enclaves. One traditional watering hole, which is quite tame – though still predominantly male – is the *Bar L'Opera* on 5 de Mayo near Bellas Artes. It's worth going in just to see the magnificent *fin-de-siècle* decor – ornate mahogany panelling, a brass-railed bar and gilt-framed mirrors in the booths. *Harry's Bar* on Amberes in the *Zona Rosa* is a popular tourist hang-out with a good atmosphere.

Markets and shopping

The big advantage of **shopping** in México is that you can get goods from all over the country: the disadvantage is that they will be considerably more expensive here. By far the greatest concentration of tourist shops can be found in the **Zona Rosa** – pricey leather goods, jewellery, clothes, handicrafts and souvenirs abound, and there's a roaring trade in fake designer labels. Gucci and Lacoste are particularly popular, sold everywhere and very rarely genuine. These places are worth a look, but certainly don't offer good value by Mexican standards.

For anything you really need – clothes and so on – you're better off going to one of the big **department stores**. *Liverpool* and *El Palacio de Hierro* both have branches on 20 de Noviembre just off the zócalo. *Sanborn's*, good for books, sells quantities of tacky souvenirs, too, and every branch has a sizable pharmacy. Much the best **crafts** outside the markets are sold at the various government-run *FONART* shops – branches include Av. Juárez opposite the Alameda, Londres 136 in the *Zona Rosa*, and Av. de la Paz 37 in San Angel. You should come here anyway to get an idea of price and quality before venturing into any serious bargaining in the markets.

Every area of the city has its own **market** selling food and essentials, and many others operate for just one day a week with stalls set up along a suburban street.

Markets

Centro Artesanal de San Juan, about five blocks south of the Alameda along Dolores. Modern tourist-oriented complex: one of the best places for crafts (silver in particular) and for haggling. Near *Salto de Agua* Metro (west on Arcos de Belen and second right). Daily 6am–6pm.

Coyoacán Markets. There are two interesting markets in Coyoacán. The daily markets three blocks up from Plaza Hidalgo are typically given over to food, while on Sunday a craft market converges on the Plaza itself. There you can buy any manner of *típico* clothing and that essential souvenir, the Marcos doll, made in Chiapas by the Maya.

Flower Markets, very close to San Juan, at the corner of Luis Moya and E. Pugibet. Small market selling nothing but flowers – loose, in vast arrangements and wreaths, growing in pots, even paper and plastic. Similar markets can be found in San Angel and Xochimilco.

La Lagunilla, Rayon, a couple of blocks north of the Plaza Garibaldi. Comes closest to rivalling *La Merced* in size and variety, but is best visited on a Sunday when the Thieves' Market takes over the surrounding streets. Get there on buses ("La Villa") heading north on Reforma.

Mercado de Sonora, three blocks from La Merced on Av. Fray Servando Teresa de Mier. This market is famous for its sale of herbal medicines, medicinal and magical plants and the various *curanderos* (traditional medicine men) who go there. Metro *La Merced*.

La Merced, *La Merced* Metro. The city's largest market, a collection of huge modern buildings which for all their size can't contain the vast number of traders who want to set up here. Sells almost anything you could conceive of finding in a Mexican market; fruit, vegetables and other foods take up most space. Daily 6am–6pm.

Nightlife and entertainment

There's a vast amount going on in México, which is the nation's cultural and social centre just as much as its political capital. A lot of the obvious **nightlife**, though, is rather tame in its attempt to be sophisticated – Mexicans themselves favour discos with a diet of American music, while for the tourists they lay on piano bars or "typical" Mexican bands, Herb Alpert style. Two events, however – the *mariachi* music in the **Plaza Garibaldi** and to a lesser extent the **Ballet Folklórico** – transcend this; although both are unashamedly aimed at tourists, they have an enduring appeal, too, for Mexicans. Finding other forms of **live music** in the capital is an unpredictable business, full of disappointments but with occasional delights. Much of the best modern action is to be found in the south, towards Coyoacán and San Angel. Most places play rock and Latin; good **jazz** is virtually non-existent.

Listings for current cinema, theatre and other **cultural events** can be found in the English-language *México News* or to a lesser extent in the *Daily Bulletin*; local newspapers in Spanish will have more detail (certainly for films), or you could try the weekly magazine *Tiempo Libre*. While Mexican theatre tends to be rather turgid, there are often excellent classical music **concerts** and performances of **opera** or **ballet** by touring companies. Bellas Artes and the Auditorio Nacional are again the main venues, but other downtown theatres as well as the Polyforum and the Teatro de los Insurgentes may also have interesting shows. On most Sundays there's a free concert in Chapultepec Park near the lake.

There are at least ten **cinemas** along Reforma, which show all the latest releases. Movies, at least in the city centre, are almost always in English with Spanish subtitles (assuming, that is, they were made in English in the first place); major films open here up to a year before they reach Europe and are sometimes released even before they've been seen in the US. If you go to the cinema arrive early, as popular screenings frequently sell out.

Mariachi

Entertainment in the **Plaza Garibaldi** is not for those of nervous disposition. Here in the evenings gather hundreds of competing *mariachi* bands, all in their tight, silver-spangled *charro* finery and vast sombreros, to play for anyone who'll pay them among the crowds wandering the square and spilling in and out of the bars that surround it. A typical group consists of two or four violins, a brass section of three trumpeters standing some way back so as not to drown out the others, three or four men on guitars of varying sizes, and a vocalist – though the truly macho serenader will rent the band and do the singing himself. They take their name, supposedly, from the French word *mariage* – it being traditional during the nineteenth-century French intervention to rent a group to play at weddings. You may also come across *norteño* bands from the border areas with their Tex-Mex brand of country music, or the softer sounds of *marimba* musicians from the south. Simply wander round the square and you'll get your fill – should you want to be individually serenaded, pick out a likely looking group and negotiate your price. At the back of the square is a huge market hall in which a whole series of stalls serve simple food and vie furiously for custom. Alternatively there are a number of fairly pricey bar/restaurants around the square.

The Plaza Garibaldi is on Lázaro Cárdenas about five blocks north of Bellas Artes. There's a Metro stop, *Garibaldi*, on the new line 8, or you could walk, through a thoroughly sleazy area of cheap bars and cafes, streetwalkers, grimy hotels and several brightly lit theatres offering burlesque and strip shows. As the night wears on and the drinking continues it can get pretty rowdy around the square and pickpockets are always a threat: despite a high-profile police presence you'd be better off not coming laden down with expensive camera equipment or an obviously bulging wallet. The last Metro leaves at 12.30am and you'd be advised to be on it.

Ballet Folklórico

The **Ballet Folklórico** is a total contrast: a long-running, internationally famed compilation of traditional dances from all over the country, elaborately choreographed and designed and interspersed with Mexican music and singing. That said – and despite the billing – there's nothing very traditional about the Ballet. Although it does include several of the more famous native dances, they are very jazzed up and incorporated into what is, in effect, a regular musical that wouldn't be out of place on Broadway.

The best place to see the Ballet Folklórico is in the original setting of the Palacio de Bellas Artes, where the theatre is an attraction in itself. There are performances (usually) on Sunday at 9.30am and 9pm, and Wednesday at 9pm. Tickets, however, can be hard to come by and pressure of other events occasionally forces a move to the Auditorio Nacional in Chapultepec Park. You should try to book at least a couple of days in advance – either from the Bellas Artes box office (☎512-36-33) or through the *Boletrónico* ticket agency that has booths throughout the city, including inside Bellas Artes. If it's sold out, you can always try at reception in one of the big hotels or go with an organized tour, for either of which you'll pay a considerable premium. A rival troupe, every bit as good, performs on Sundays and Tuesdays in the *Teatro de la Ciudad*, Donceles 36, just round the corner from the Bellas Artes.

Live music and bars

Arcauo, División del Monte 2713, Parque San Andres, Coyoacán (☎689-82-73). Jazz club featuring live music most nights. Recommended. Daily 8.30pm until late; no cover on Mon or Tues.

Bar Guau, Pedro Luis de Ogazón 89, San Angel (☎661-29-14). Literary/theatre evenings. Tues–Sat; cover $10, $20 at weekends.

Bar León, Brasil 5 (☎510-30-93). Live Afro-Caribbean music. Mon–Sat 9pm–3am; cover $10.

Butterflies, Izáazaga 9, near *Salto del Agua* Metro. Gay disco; cover $10.

Café Amor, Versailles and Marsella, Juárez (☎566-42-62). Live folk/protest music. Mon–Thurs from 6.30pm.

La Casa del Canto, Local 4, Glorieta de Metro Insurgentes, Juárez. A rock venue with live bands most nights. Unusually for Mexico, it has wheelchair access. Daily 6pm onwards; cover varies.

Clandestine Disco Bar, Colón 1, near Alameda (☎518-19-91). Gay bar; daily from 8pm.

La Guadalupana, Higuera 14, Coyoacán. Good food and imported beer and spirits. Mon–Sat 11am–midnight.

El Hábito, Madrid 13, Coyoacán (☎659-63-05). Quirky venue with a Tango night on Tues, "Beatles" night on Thurs.

El Hijo del Cuervo, Jardín Centario 17, Coyoacán (☎659-89-59). Hip and arty venue with occasional theatre impros and poetry readings. Recommended. Right on the Jardín, next to *Sanborn's*.

Humboldt 34, Humboldt 34 (☎521-22-93). Seedy looking place with stacks of atmosphere. Live music Mon–Sat 9pm–3am; no cover.

Rochotitlán, Insurgentes Sur and Nápoles, Juárez (☎687-78-93). Rock venue; cover $8–15.

Salon Colevia, Manuel M Flores 33, Obrero (☎575-06-19). Live danzón music. Free transport service from *San Antonio Abad* Metro. Daily 6–11.30pm.

Salón Luz, Gante 23 (☎512-26-56). Buzzy bar with live music Wed–Sat, Mon–Sat 10am–11pm, Sun 11am–7pm.

Zotanós, Revillifeuo 20 (☎518-40-37). Great place to hear *salsa*, mambo and rock. Daily 8pm–4am.

Sport

Sport is probably the city's biggest obsession, and **football**, throughout its winter season, the most popular. The big games are held at the *Estadio Azteca* (capacity 108,500; shared between *América*, the nation's most consistently successful club side, *Cruz Azul* and *Necaxa*), the *Estadio Mexico* (65,000; home of the university side *UNAM*) and the *Ciudad de los Deportes* (45,000; home team *Atlante*) – check local papers for fixture details. The **biggest games of the season** are generally those between México sides and those from Guadalajara; they tend to be "grudge" matches and are thus far

---

WRESTLING

After football, *lucha libre* or **wrestling** is Mexico's most popular spectator sport. Over a dozen venues in México alone host fights six nights a week for a fanatical public. Magazines, comics, photonovels and films recount the real and imagined lives of the rings' heroes and villains. The main bouts are shown daily on TV, which can be a good way to absorb the finer points of the Mexican version of the sport.

Mexican wrestling is generally faster, with more complex moves, and more combatants in the ring at any one time than you would normally see in an American or British bout. This can make the action hard to follow for the uninitiated. More important even than the moves is the maintenance of stage **personas**, most of whom, heroes or villains, wear masks. The *rudos* (baddies) indulge in sneaky, underhand tactics to foil the opposition, while the *técnicos* (goodies) try and win fair and square. This cod battle between good and evil requires a massive suspension of disbelief: crucial if you want to join in the fun.

One of the most bizarre features of wrestling in recent years has been the emergence of wrestlers as political figures. Perhaps the most famous of all, **Superbarrio** ("superneighbourhood") arose from the struggle of México's tenant associations for fair rents and decent housing after the 1985 earthquake. He has since become part of mainstream political opposition, regularly challenging government officials to step into the ring with him, and acting as a sort of unofficial cheerleader at opposition rallies. Other wrestlers have espoused political causes, such as Jalapa's **Superecologista** ("superecologist") who campaigns on environmental issues including the demanded closure of Laguna Verde nuclear power station.

The most famous wrestler of all time, however, was without doubt **El Santo** ("the Saint"). Immortalized in more than twenty movies with titles such as *El Santo vs the Vampire Women*, he would fight, eat and drink and play the romantic lead without ever removing his mask, and until after his retirement, he never revealed his identity. His reputation as a gentleman in and out of the ring was legendary, and his death in 1984 was widely mourned, especially by the poor. His funeral was allegedly the second-best attended in Mexican history after that of President Obregón. His son fights under the name of **hijo del Santo** ("son of Santo") and fights regularly at the legendary Coliseo venue at Peru 77, Col. Centro.

more exciting than most. Having adopted the American Football system of mini-leagues leading to play-offs, the league competitions can be rather dull until the fight for play-off positions begins. *América*, which is owned by Emilio Azcárraga, who also owns the *Televisa* TV monopoly, is viewed by opponents and most neutrals as the government's "official" team, which gives their fixtures a certain edge.

Throughout the year you can watch **frontón** (*pelota* or *jai alai*) right in the city centre: it's a pretty dull game unless you're betting – and losing popularity even among locals – but you can wander in and out freely throughout the evening sessions (Mon–Sat). Games are held at the *Frontón Mexico* on the Plaza de la Republica. There's **horse racing**, too, throughout the year (Tues, Thurs & afternoons Sat & Sun) at the *Hipodromo de las Americas*: buses and *peseros* heading west on Reforma will take you there – look for "Hipodromo". More exciting horsey action is involved in the *charreadas*, or **rodeos**, put on by amateur but highly skilled aficionados most weekends; venues and times vary, but these are usually worth witnessing, so check the press to find out what's going on. Finally, there are **bullfights** every Sunday afternoon in the winter season at the giant *Plaza Mexico*, largest bullring in the world. Any bus heading south on Insurgentes will pass close by.

Listings

Airlines The main ones are *Aeroflot*, Insurgentes Sur 569 (☎687-91-22); *Aeroméxico*, Reforma 445 (☎762-40-22); *Air France*, Reforma 404 (☎571-32-06); *American*, Reforma 300 (☎399-92-22); *Aviacsa*, Insurgentes Sur 1261 (☎590-95-22); *British Airways*, Reforma 10, 14° (☎628-05-00); *Continental*, Andrés Bello 45 (☎203-11-48); *Delta*, Reforma 381 (☎202-16-08); *Iberia*, Reforma 24 (☎705-07-16); *KLM*, Paseo de las Palmas 735 (in Las Lomas, ☎202-44-44); *Lufthansa*, Paseo de las Palmas 239 (☎202-88-66); *Mexicana*, handiest office at corner of Juárez and Balderas (☎660-44-44); *Northwest*, Reforma 390 (☎207-05-15); *United*, Hamburgo 61 (☎627-02-22); *US Air*, Reforma 322 (☎208-13-35).

Airport enquiries ☎571-36-00 or 748-48-11. For national flights ext 2259 or 2303; for international flights ext 2288 or 2341.

Ambulance *Cruz Roja* (☎557-57-57); mobile paramedic unit at *Unidad Movil de Terapia Intensiva*, Querétaro 58, Col. Roma (☎598-62-22).

American Express Clients' mail service at Reforma 234 in the *Zona Rosa* (☎533-03-80). Six offices throughout the city. Other services from Campos Eliseos 204, Col. Polanco (☎203-40-20, ext 8940).

Car rental Thousands of agencies throughout the city – small local operations are often cheaper than the big chains. Try *Avis* (airport: ☎762-36-88; city: ☎511-22-88); *Budget Rent-A-Car* (airport: ☎784-30-11; *Zona Rosa*: ☎533-04-50); *Coyoacán Rent*, Av. Coyoacán 47 (☎536-50-14); *Hertz* (*Zona Rosa*: ☎533-24-33; Col. Juárez: ☎592-60-82) or *Limousines Tolteca* (☎531-97-51).

Cultural institutes *US*: *Instituto Mexicano Norteamericano de Relaciones Culturales*, Hamburgo 115 in the *Zona Rosa*; *UK*: *Instituto Anglo-Mexicano de Cultura*, Antonio Caso 127. Both organize film shows, lectures and concerts, run language courses in Spanish and English, and have library facilities. They can be useful places for contacts, and if you're looking for work or long-term accommodation or travelling companions their noticeboards are good places to start.

Embassies *Australia*: Jaime Balmes 11, Torre B (☎395-99-88); *Canada*: Schiller 529 (☎724-79-00 or 254-32-88); *Germany*: Lord Byron 737 (☎280-54-09); *Ireland* (honorary consul): Av. San Jeronimo 790-A (☎595-33-33); *Italy*: Av. Las Palmas 2030 (☎596-82-88); *Netherlands*: Montes Urales 635 (☎202-82-67); *New Zealand*: Homero 229 (☎250-59-99); *Spain*: Edgar Allan Poe 91 (☎280-45-08); *Sweden*: Blvd. Manuel Avila Camacho 1 (☎540-73-93); *Switzerland*: Hamburgo 66, (☎207-48-20); *UK*: Rio Lerma 71 (☎207-24-99); consular service at Río Usumacinta 30 (☎511-48-80); *USA*: Reforma 305 (☎211-00-42).

Emergencies Police emergency number is ☎06, regular enquiries on ☎588-51-00. *Locatec* gives information on missing persons and vehicles, medical emergencies, emotional crises and public services (☎658-11-11).

Hospital The *British-American Cowdray Hospital* (ABC) is at c/Sur 136 (☎272-85-00). Embassies should be able to provide a list of multi-lingual doctors if necessary.

Language schools Many places run Spanish courses: the *Casa de los Amigos*, Av. Ignacio Mariscal 132 keeps lists and details of language schools in Mexico and central America.

Laundry Self-service launderettes are surprisingly rare in México, but most hotels should be able to point one out for you. Options include: *Lavandería Automatica*, Edison 91; *La Eficaz*, Antonio Caso 100; *Lavanet*, Chapultepec 463.

Pharmacies *Sanborn's* offers a wide range of products at most of its branches, as well as dispensing some prescription drugs. Other options include *El Fenix*, Isabel la Catolica and 5 de Mayo; *Paris*, Isabel la Catolica and 5 de Feberero; *Farmacia Homeopática Nacional*, Guatemala 16-3 offers homeopathic curatives.

Tourist cards Should you lose yours, or want an extension, you should officially apply to the *Secretaria de Gobernacion* at Juárez 92, or its *Subdireccion de Inmigrantes* at Insurgentes Sur 1385 (9am–1.30pm). It's generally easier, however, to go to *Inmigracion* at the airport. Any of these will require proof of enough money to support yourself.

Travel agencies *American Express*, see above; *Tourismo Flammel*, Alvara Obregón 143, Col. Roma (☎207-16-92); *Viajes Bojorquez*, Pestalozzi 83, Col. del Valle (☎523-90-10); *Wagonslits Viajes*, Juárez 88 (☎518-11-80).

Visas Needed for onward travel to certain Central American countries. *Costa Rica*: Río Po 113 (☎525-77-64); *El Salvador*, Galileo 17 (☎531-79-95); *Guatemala*: consulate, Explanada 1025 in Lomas de Chapultepec (daily 9am–2pm; visas issued on the spot for a fee; ☎546-48-76); *Honduras*, Juárez 64 (☎512-06-20).

Women's groups *La Casa los Amigos* have details of women's groups and support women's development projects.

Work Very hard to come by – there's some chance of finding a job teaching English, maybe au pair-type work. Look in the *México News* classifieds, or advertise your services to give private lessons in one of the Spanish papers.

MOVING ON FROM THE CITY

By far the most comfortable way to get out of México is **to fly**; especially worth it if you have limited time in the country and wish to visit the Yucatán. The two main Mexican carriers, *Mexicana* and *Aeroméxico*, cover more than fifty destinations between them. To get **to the airport** it's easiest to take a regular taxi, but you can also phone SETTA the day before (☎571-93-44) to arrange to be picked up from your hotel.

All México's **bus stations** are used by hordes of competing companies, and the only way to get a full idea of the **timetable** for any given destination is to check out every one – different companies may take different routes and you can sometimes waste hours by choosing wrongly. We've given a checklist of destinations from each one on p.251. Though it's rare not to be able to get on any bus at very short notice, it can be worth booking in advance for long-distance journeys or for express services to popular destinations – that way you'll have a choice of seat and be sure of getting the fastest service. If you're uncertain which bus station you should be leaving from, simply get into a taxi and tell the driver what your ultimate destination is – he'll know where to take you. You'll find places to eat, and stalls selling food and drink for the journey, in all the termini.

If you're planning to leave by **train** you should get your tickets as far in advance as possible. Certainly don't leave it to the last minute as you often have to queue for hours. The ticket offices are theoretically open from 6am to 10pm daily, but they have a tendency to close for siestas or whenever else they feel the urge.

For details of **destinations, frequencies and journey times** of public transport from México, see the "Travel Details" at the end of this chapter.

AROUND THE CITY

Breaking out of the capital in any direction, there are targets of interest within a couple of hours' drive. First, and the one day trip which everyone seems to take, are the massive pyramids and ancient city of **Teotihuacán**, about 50km northeast. Directly north, on the road to **Querétaro** and the colonial cities, lies **Tula**, the centre that succeeded Teotihuacán as the valley's great power. Its site is perhaps slightly less impressive, but imposing nonetheless, and on the way you can stop in **Tepotzotlán**, with some of the finest Baroque and colonial art in the country.

To the west, **Toluca**, on the old road to Morelia, hosts a colossal market every Friday, and the country surrounding it is full of mountain retreats where Mexicans go to escape the pressures of their city. **Cuernavaca** has long been a sought-after refuge – packed with colonial mansions and gardens, it's also close to several important archeological sites, while beyond it lies the road to Acapulco and the tourist mecca of **Taxco** with its silver jewellery. East towards the Gulf Coast, **Puebla** stands on the plain behind the great **volcanoes**, one of the most colonial towns in the country but also one of its most crowded, and a major industrial centre. Nearby **Tlaxcala** and **Cholula** were important allies of the Aztecs when Cortés marched this way from the coast. Tlaxcala is now a wonderfully quiet colonial town, while at Cholula is the rubble of the largest pyramid in Mexico. Here the Conquistadors claimed to have erected a church on the site of each pagan temple, and there's said to be a chapel for every day of the year.

San Juan Teotihuacán

It seems that every visitor to México heads out to **Teotihuacán** at some stage: there's a constant stream of tours, buses and cars heading this way, and the site itself is crawling with people, increasingly so as the day wears on. On the way you pass a

THE RISE AND FALL OF TEOTIHUACAN

The **rise and fall** of Teotihuacán is almost exactly contemporary with Imperial Rome. From around 600BC there was evidence of small agricultural communities in the vicinity and by 200BC a township had been established on the present site. From then until 1AD (the period known as **Teotihuacán I**) the population began to soar, and the city assumed its most important characteristics: the great Pyramids of the Sun and Moon were built, and the Calle de los Muertos laid out. Development continued through **Teotihuacán II** (0–350AD) with more construction, but most importantly with evidence of the city's influence (in architecture, sculpture and pottery) occurring at sites throughout modern Mexico and into Guatemala and Honduras. From 350 to around 650 (**Teotihuacán III**) it reached the peak of population and power, with much new building and addition to earlier structures. Already by the end of this period, however, there were signs of decline, and the final period (**Teotihuacán IV**) lasted at most a century before the city was sacked, burnt and virtually abandoned. This presumably, was the result of attack by northern tribes, probably the Toltecs, but the disaster may in the end have been as much ecological as military. Vast forests were cut down to build the city (in columns, roof supports, door lintels) and huge quantities of wood burnt to make the lime plaster that coated the buildings: the result was severe soil erosion that left the hillsides as barren as they appear today. In addition, the agricultural effort needed to feed so many people (with no form of artificial fertilizer or knowledge of crop rotation) gradually sapped what land remained of its ability to grow more.

Whatever the precise causes, the city was left, eventually, to a ruination that was advanced even by the time of the Aztecs. To them it represented a holy place from a previous age, and they gave it its present name, which translates as "The Place where Men became Gods". Although Teotihuacán features frequently in Aztec mythology, there are no written records – what we know of the city is derived entirely from archeological and artistic evidence so that even the original name remains unknown. What you see at the site, too, is to some point conjecture, for everything has been dug up and at least partly reconstructed.

couple of places which, if you're driving, are certainly worth a look, but barely merit the hassle involved in stopping over on the bus. First, at **TEPEXPAN**, is a museum (Tues–Sun 10am–5pm) housing the fossil of a mammoth dug up in the surrounding plain (then marshland). There is also a skeleton known as the "Tepexpan Man", once claimed to be the oldest in Mexico but recently revealed as less than 2000 years old. This whole area is a rich source of such remains – the Aztecs knew of their existence, which is one of the reasons they believed that the huge structures of Teotihuacán had been built by a race of giants. The museum is a fifteen-minute walk from the village, near the motorway toll booths, where any second-class bus will drop you: the village itself is attractive, with a good cafe on c/de los Reyes, just off the main square. A little farther on lies the beautiful sixteenth-century monastery of **SAN AGUSTIN ACOLMAN** (daily except Fri). Built on a raised man-made terrace (probably on the site of an earlier, Aztec temple), it's a stern-looking building, lightened by the intricacy of its sculpted facade. In the nave and around the cloister are preserved portions of early murals depicting the monks, while several of the halls off the cloister display colonial religious painting and pre-Hispanic artefacts found here. **CHICONCUAC** is rather more of a detour, but on Tuesday when there's a large market (specializing in woollen goods, sweaters and blankets) it's included in the itinerary of many of the tours to the pyramids. Again this is hard to do on a regular bus and if you want to visit the market it's easier to do so as an entirely separate trip – buses, again, from the Terminal del Norte.

The site

TEOTIHUACÁN is not, on first impression, the most impressive site in Mexico – it lacks the dramatic hilltop setting or lush jungle vegetation of those in the south – but it is a city planned and built on a massive scale, the great pyramids so huge that before their refurbishment one would have passed them by without a second glance, as hills. At its height this must have been the most imposing city ever seen in pre-Hispanic America, with a population approaching 200,000 spread over an area of some 156 square kilometres (as opposed to the four square kilometres of the ceremonial centre). Then, every building – grey hulks now – would have been covered in bright polychrome murals.

Street of the Dead

From the main entrance you emerge at the bottom of the restored Calle de los Muertos (which originally extended 1.5km farther south) opposite **La Ciudadela**, the Citadel. This enormous sunken square, surrounded by stepped platforms and with a low square altar in the centre, was the city's administrative heart, with the houses of its chief priests and nobles arranged around a vast meeting place. Across the open space stands a tall pyramid construction inside which, during excavation, was found the **Templo de Quetzalcoatl**. With the back of the newer pyramid demolished, the elaborate (Teotihuacán II) temple structure stands revealed. It rises in four steps (of an original six), each sculpted in relief and punctuated at intervals by the stylized heads of Quetzalcoatl, the plumed serpent, and **Tlaloc**, the rain god. Traces of the original paint can be seen in places. This theme – with the goggle-eyed, almost abstract mask of Tlaloc and the fanged snake Quetzalcoatl, its neck ringed with a collar of feathers – recurs in later sites throughout the country.

The **Calle de los Muertos** (Street of the Dead) forms the axis around which the city developed. A broad causeway linking all the most significant buildings, it was conceived to impress, with the low buildings that flank most of its length serving to heighten the impact of the two great temples at the northern end. Other streets, leading off to the rest of the city, originally intersected it at right angles, and even the

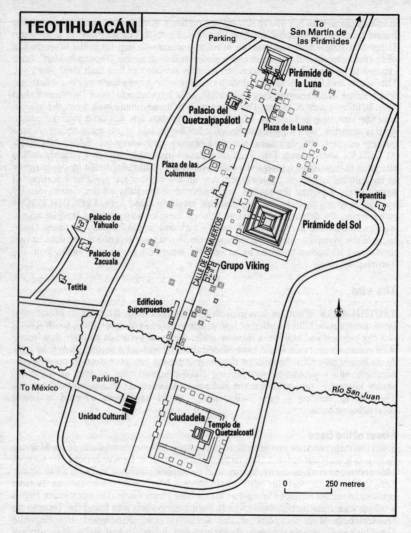

TEOTIHUACÁN

To San Martín de las Pirámides

Parking

Pirámide de la Luna

Palacio del Quetzalpapálotl

Plaza de la Luna

Plaza de las Columnas

Tepantitla

Palacio de Yahualo

Pirámide del Sol

Palacio de Zacuala

Tetitla

CALLE DE LOS MUERTOS

Grupo Viking

Edificios Superpuestos

Parking

To México

Río San Juan

Unidad Cultural

Ciudadela

Templo de Quetzalcoatl

0   250 metres

river San Juan, which you cross just beyond the Citadel, was canalized so as not to disturb the symmetry (the bridge that then crossed it would have extended the full width of the street). Its name is something of a misconception, since it is neither a simple street – rather a series of open plazas linked by staircases rising some 30m between the Citadel and the Pyramid of the Moon – nor in any way linked with the dead. The Aztecs believed the buildings that lined it, then little more than earth-covered mounds, to be the burial places of kings. They're not, and although the exact function of most remains unclear, all obviously had some sacred significance. The design, seen in the many reconstructions, is fairly uniform: low, three- or four-storey platforms consisting of vertical panels (*tableros*) supported on sloping walls.

In many cases several are built on top of each other – nowhere more clearly demonstrated than in the Edificios Superpuestos (**superimposed buildings**) on the left-hand side shortly beyond the river. Here you can descend a metal staircase to find excavated structures underneath the present level. They may have been the living quarters of Teotihuacán's priests.

Pyramids of the Sun and Moon

The great **Pirámide del Sol** (Pyramid of the Sun) is Teotihuacán's outstanding landmark, a massive structure second in size only to Cholula of Mexico's ancient buildings (Cholula is a total ruin). Its base is almost exactly the same size as that of the great Pyramid of Cheops, but since this is not a true pyramid it is very much lower. There are wonderful views from the top nonetheless, and the bulk is all the more remarkable when you consider the accuracy of its alignment*, and the fact that the 2.5 million tons of stone and earth used in its construction were brought here without benefit of the wheel or any beast of burden, and shaped without use of any metal tool. The pyramid you see was reconstructed by Leopoldo Batres in 1908, in a thoroughly cavalier fashion. He blasted, with dynamite, a structure that originally abutted the south face, and stripped much of the surface in a search for a more complete building under the present one. In fact the Pyramid of the Sun, almost uniquely, was built in one go at a very early stage of the city's development (about 100AD), and there is only avery small older temple right at its heart. As a result of Batres's stripping the stone surface, the temple has eroded considerably more than it might otherwise have done. He also added an extra terrace to the original four.

You approach by a short staircase leading to the right off the Calle de los Muertos onto a broad esplanade where stand the ruins of several small temples and priests' dwellings. The main structure consists of five sloping layers of wall divided by terraces – the large flat area at the top would originally have been surmounted by a sanctuary, long disappeared. Evidence of why this massive structure came to be raised here emerged in 1971 when archeologists stumbled on a tunnel (closed to the public) leading to a clover leaf-shaped **cave** directly under the centre of the pyramid. This, clearly, had been some kind of inner sanctuary, a holy of holies, and may even have been the reason for Teotihuacán's foundation and the basis of its influence. Theories abound as to its exact nature, and many fit remarkably with legends handed down through the Aztecs. Perhaps most likely the cave was formed by a subterranean spring, and came to be associated with Tlaloc, god of rain but also a bringer of fertility, as a sort of fountain of life. Alternatively, it could be associated with the legendary "seven grottoes", a symbol of creation from which all later Mexican peoples claimed to have emerged, or have been the site of an oracle, or associated with a cult of sacrifice – in Aztec times the flayed skins of victims of Xipe Totec were stored in a cave under a pyramid.

At the end of the Street of the Dead rises the **Pirámide de la Luna** (Pyramid of the Moon), a smaller structure built slightly later (but still Teotihuacán I and one of the oldest you see) whose top, thanks to the higher ground on which it's built, is virtually on a level with that of the Pyramid of the Sun. The structure is very similar, four sloping levels approached by a monumental stairway, but for some reason this seems a very much more elegant building: perhaps because of the smaller scale, perhaps as a result of the approach, through the formally laid-out **Plaza de la Luna**. The top of this pyramid offers the best overview of the site and its layout, looking straight back down the length of the central thoroughfare.

---

*On two days a year, May 19 and July 25, the sun is directly over the pyramid at noon: the main west facade faces the point at which the sun sets on these days. This alignment just off the cardinal points determined the line of the Calle de los Muertos and of the entire city.

Lesser structures

The **Palacio de Quetzalpapálotl** (Palace of the Quetzal-butterfly) lies to the left of the Plaza de la Luna, behind the low temples that surround it. Wholly restored, it's virtually the only example of a roofed building in Central Mexico and a unique view of how the elite lived at Teotihuacán. The rooms are arranged around a patio whose elaborately carved pillars give the Palace its name – their stylized designs represent birds (the brightly coloured Quetzals, though some may be owls) and butterflies. In the galleries around the patio several frescoes survive: very formalized and symbolic, with the themes reduced almost to geometric patterns. **Mural art** was clearly very important in Teotihuacán, and almost every building has some trace of decoration, though much has been removed for preservation and restoration. Two earlier buildings, half buried under the Palace, still have substantial remains: in the **Palacio de los Jaguares**, jaguars in feathered headdresses blow conch shells from which emerge curls of music, or perhaps speech or prayers to Tlaloc (who appears along the top of the mural); in the **Temple of the Plumed Shells** you see a motif of feathers and sea shells along with bright green parrots. Other murals, of which only traces remain, were found in the temples along the Street of the Dead between the two pyramids.

Such art was not reserved for the priesthood – indeed some of the finest frescoes have been found in outlying "apartment" buildings. At **Tepantitla**, a residential quarter of the old city across the road from the back of the Pyramid of the Sun, the famous *Paradise of Tlaloc* mural (reproduced in the National Museum of Anthropology, see p274) was discovered. Only a part of it survives here, but there are others in the complex depicting a procession of priests and a ball game. All have great vitality and an almost comic-strip quality, with the speech bubbles emerging from the figures' mouths, but their themes always have a religious rather than a purely decorative intent. More can be seen at **Tetitla**, to the west of the main site, and **Atetelco**, a little further west, just off the plan.

Practicalities

To **get to** Teotihuacán, buses head every thirty minutes or so (6am–8pm; 1hr) from the Terminal del Norte. Head to the second-class (left-hand) side of the bus station and look for the *Autobuses Teotihuacán* stand. It's worth getting an early start to arrive before the worst of the crowds. A road, the Carretera de Circunvalacion, surrounds the main structures at **the site** (8am–5pm; $5, free on Sun), with parking spaces at intervals and several restaurants. At the principal entrance there's a **museum**, a restaurant, several shops and market-type stalls. This is said to be the site of the original market, and from here the Calle de los Muertos, chief thoroughfare of the ancient city, leads north through the ceremonial centre to the great pyramids. To see the whole site and its outlying buildings could take a full day, but the most important structures can be looked over in a few hours; this involves a lot of climbing and walking, and can be exhausting at such an altitude. Teotihuacán's **son et lumière** is held between August and May (7pm in English, 8.15pm in Spanish).

Tula

In legend at least, the mantle of Teotihuacán fell on Tollan, **TULA**, as the next great power to dominate Mexico. History, legend and archeological evidence, however, are here almost impossible to disentangle, and often flatly contradictory. The Aztecs regarded their city as the descendant of Tula and hence embellished its reputation – the streets, they said, had been paved with gold and the buildings constructed from precious metals and stones; the Toltecs were the inventors of every science and art. In reality it seems unlikely that this was ever as large or as powerful a city as Teotihuacán had been – or as Tenochtitlán was to become – and its period of dominance (about 950 to 1150AD) was relatively short. Yet all sorts of puzzles remain about the Toltec era, and in particular the extent of their influence in the Yucatán – at Chichén Itzá much of the architecture is clearly Toltec (see p.513). Few people believe that the Toltecs could actually have had an empire stretching so far: however warlike (and the artistic evidence is that Tula was a grimly militaristic society, heavily into human sacrifice), they would have lacked the manpower, resources, or any logical justification for such expansion. Nevertheless, they were there.

The answer lies, perhaps, in the legends of **Quetzalcoatl** that surround the city. Adopted from Teotihuacán, the plumed serpent attained far more importance here in Tula, where he is depicted everywhere. Again the facts and legends are almost impossible to extricate, but at some stage Tula certainly had a ruler regarded as Quetzalcoatl who was driven from the city by the machinations of the evil god Texcatlipoca. In legend Quetzalcoatl fled to the east where he either burnt himself to become the morning star or sailed across the ocean on a raft of snakes, promising one day to return (a prophecy that Cortés turned skilfully to his advantage). What may actually have happened is that the ruler was defeated in factional struggles within Tula and, in exile with his followers, eventually reached Maya territory where they established a new Toltec regime.

The site

Of **the site** (daily 10am–5pm; $5, free on Sun) itself, only a small part is of interest: though the city spreads over some considerable area only some has been excavated, and the outlying digs are holes in the ground, meaningful only to the archeologists who created them. The ceremonial centre, however, has been partly restored. Centrepiece is the low five-stepped pyramid of the **Templo de Tlahuizcalpantecuhtli** (Morning Star), atop which stand the famous **Atlantes**. These giant, five metre-tall figures originally supported the roof of the sanctuary: they represent Quetzalcoatl in his guise as the morning star, dressed as a Toltec warrior. They wear elaborately embroidered loincloths, sandals, and feathered helmets, with ornaments around their necks and legs – for protection, sun-shaped shields on their backs and chest pieces in the form of a stylized butterfly. Each carries an *atlatl*, or spear-thrower, in his right hand and a clutch of arrows or javelins to use in them in the left.

Other pillars are carved with more warriors and gods, and these relief carvings are one of the constant themes in Tula: the entire temple was originally faced in sculpted stone, and although this was pillaged long ago you can see some remnants from an earlier incarnation of the temple – prowling jaguars and eagles, symbols of the two great warrior groups, devouring human hearts. In front of the temple is a great L-shaped colonnade, where the partly reconstructed pillars originally supported a huge roof under which, perhaps, the priests and nobles would review their troops or take part in ceremonies in the shade. Part of a long bench (or *banquette*) survives, with its relief decoration of a procession of warriors and priests. More such benches survive in the **Palacio Quemado** (Burnt Palace – it was destroyed by fire), next to the temple on the western side. In the middle of its three rooms, each a square roofed area with a small central patio to let light in, is the best preserved of them, still with much of its original paint, and two Chac-mools.

The main square of the city stood in front of the temple and palace, with a low altar platform in the centre and the now ruinous pyramid of the Templo Mayor to the left. The larger of two **ball courts** in the central area delineated a third side: although overgrown, this is one of the closest links between Tula and Chichén Itzá – of identical shape and orientation to the great ball court there, and displaying many of the same features. To the north of this plaza, behind the temple, stands a wall known as the **Coatepantli** (Serpent Wall), elaborately carved in relief, and beyond this, across an open space, a second ball court, smaller but in better order.

Practicalities

Buses run from México's Terminal del Norte (*Autobuses del Valle de Mezquital*; less than 1hr 30min) to the modern town of **Tula de Allende** in the valley just below the ruins. Tula is also on the rail line from Mexico to Querétaro, and there's a station right by the site served by the first-class-only *Constitucionalista*, with breakfast en route (older, slow trains will probably still take you to the town station). The **entrance to the site** is on the far side from the town, a considerable walk all the way round the perimeter fence. Either get off the bus just as it enters the town by a bridge and the railway lines, where the road (signed "Parque Nacional") branches off to the right towards the entrance, or take a taxi from the zócalo. There's a small modern **museum** (Tues–Sun 10am–5pm), with assorted statues, artefacts and displays on the Toltecs, just inside the gate.

To get back to town from the site, follow one of the broader tracks that heads down the hill (slightly to the left) from the chief monuments. At the bottom you should find a hole in the fence, or a gate, which local people use to get in and out: much quicker than going back via the entrance (where there's little chance of finding a taxi unless you've asked one to wait or pick you up). In Tula itself it's worth taking a few minutes to look over the impressive, fortress-like **Franciscan monastery and church** (built around 1550). There are several good cafes and **restaurants** around the main square.

Tepotzotlán

Logically, **TEPOTZOTLÁN** lies en route from Tula to the capital, but if you're relying on public transport the problem will be getting from one to the other. It may be easiest to visit the two separately – Tepotzotlán is easily close enough to the city to be a morning's excursion, though once you're there you may find the place seduces you into staying longer. The town is small and thoroughly Mexican-colonial, and the clear air, trees, hills and views make a wonderful antidote to the big city blues. Though somewhat touristy, commercialization is still low-key, and the majority of visitors are Mexican: on Saturdays it's particularly enjoyable, with a holiday atmosphere but no crowds.

Getting to Tepotzotlán

To get to Tepotzotlán from México take the Metro to *Tacuba* (lines 2 and 7) and walk round the back of the station, across the railway lines – through a bit of a shantytown – to a small bus station. The area around **Tacuba** is interesting in itself, full of raucous street life. In an alley of market stalls close to the Metro station there's a great old store, *El Molino de Chile*, selling all sorts of ground *chiles* and spices from huge earthenware bowls, with little packets of powdered *mole*. The bus to Tepotzotlán is very slow, rattling its way round the suburbs for what feels like hours (though the total journey is actually little over an hour) before it finally leaves the city. Alternatively, you can take the Tula bus, or a second-class service to Querétaro, from the Terminal del Norte and get off at the first motorway tollbooths. From here it's about a twenty-minute walk to Tepotzotlán, west on a minor road, and there's a good chance of being able to hitch or catch a local bus. You can also get off here if you want to visit Tepotzotlán on the way back from Tula, or follow the process in reverse to continue to Tula or get back to the city, but it can prove hard to flag down a bus (and sometimes harder to work out which one you should be flagging down).

The Town

Atmosphere apart, there's just one thing that brings people to Tepotzotlán: the magnificent Baroque **Colegio de San Francisco Javier** and the **Museo Nacional de Arte Virreinal** that it houses. These, though, are attraction enough. The church was founded by the Jesuits, who arrived in 1580 with a mission to convert the local Otomí Indians. Most of the huge complex you see today was established during the following century, but constantly embellished right up to the expulsion of the Jesuits in 1767. The facade of the church – considered one of the finest examples of Churrigueresque architecture in the country – was completed barely five years before this. The wealth and scale of all this gives some idea of the power of the Jesuits prior to their ouster: after they left it became a seminary for the training of regular priests until the late nineteenth century when the Jesuits were briefly readmitted until 1914, when the Revolution led to its final abandonment.

Colegio de San Francisco Javier

The main entrance to the **Colegio de San Francisco Javier** (Tues–Fri 10am–5pm, Sat & Sun 10am–6pm; $5, free on Sun) leads into the **Claustro de los Aljibes**, with a well at the centre and pictures of the life of Ignacio Loyola (founder of the Jesuits) around the walls. The entrance to the church is off the cloister, but the main flow will take you round the museum first before leading back here. Directly off the cloister is the **Orfebrería** (the store of precious metals), packed with a treasure of beautiful silver reliquaries and crucifixes, censers, custodia, vestments and even a pair of silver sandals. In the **Botica**, or pharmacy, are bottles, jars, pestles and mortars, and all the other equipment of an eighteenth-century healer. The **Capilla Doméstica** also opens off the cloister, a whirl of painted and gilded Roccoco with a magnificent gilded retablo full of mirrors and little figures.

Descending a level, the **Claustro de los Naranjos** is planted with orange and lemon trees, with a fountain in the middle. Around it are displays of wooden religious statuary; Balthazar and Caspar, two of the three kings, are particularly good. Other rooms contain more miscellaneous colonial art – lacquer work, furniture (especially an inlaid wooden desk) and clothes. Outside is the walled **Huerta**, or garden, some three hectares of it still beautifully maintained, with lawns, shady trees and flower displays, and also with vegetables and medicinal herbs cultivated as they would have been by the monks. On a sunny winter's day it can feel almost like an English garden in summer, and after a few days in the city it's incredibly refreshing: you can feel your lungs start to clear. Dotted around are various architectural pieces and large sculptures, including the original eighteenth-century **Salto del Agua** that stood in México at the end of the aqueduct bringing water from Chapultepec (a replica stands in the city now, near Metro *Salto del Agua*).

Back inside, as you continue round the cloister, there's a room devoted to arms and armour, a substantial collection including an amazing giant penknife that opens into a sword. The **upper storey** around the cloister is mainly devoted to the Spanish trade with Asia, which was trans-shipped via Mexico: there's Chinese porcelain; statuary; intricate *taracea* (marquetry or inlaid work) in various materials, especially mother-of-pearl, and various furnished rooms.

Heading towards the exit, you'll pass the way down to the interior of the **church**. If the facade is spectacular, it's still barely preparation for the dazzling interior. Dripping gold, and profusely carved with a bewilderment of saints and cherubim, it strikes you at first as some mystical cave of treasures. In the main body of the church and its chapels are five huge gilded retablos, stretching from ceiling to floor, each more gloriously flourished and curlicued than the last. Their richness, which already seems unnaturally golden, is enhanced by the soft yellow light penetrating through the alabaster that covers the windows. This, though, is only the start, for hidden to one side is arguably the greatest achievement of Mexican Baroque, the octagonal **Camarín de la Virgen**. It's not large, but every inch is elaborately decorated and the hand of native craftsmen is clearly evident in the exuberant riot of carving – fruit and flowers, shells and abstract patterns crammed in between the angels. There are mirrors angled to allow visitors to appreciate the detail of the ceiling without straining their necks. The Camarín is reached through the **Capilla de la Virgen de Loreto**, inside which is a "house" faced in *azulejos*: supposedly a replica of Mary's house, the house in which Jesus grew up.

Eating and drinking

You'll find plenty of places to **eat and drink** around the plaza, and at weekends there'll probably be *mariachi* musicians playing. The *Hostería del Convento*, in the seminary's grounds, is fairly pricey but has excellent Mexican food. Of the places overlooking the zócalo, the *Galeon*, *El Periquito* and *Casa Blanca* are slightly better value than the *Restaurant Virreyes*. Cheaper still are a couple of small places around the back: the *Cafeteria Colibrí* for *tortas*, the *Santa Elena* (next to the town barber) for a simple *comida*. The *pastorelas* (**nativity plays**) staged here in the week before Christmas are very famous – and booked up long in advance; at other times you may well catch a concert in the church or cloisters.

Toluca

TOLUCA DE LERDO, capital of the state of México and at nearly 2800m the highest city in the country, is today a large modern industrial centre with few attractions in terms of buildings or atmosphere. It is, however, surrounded by beautiful mountain scenery – dominated by the white-capped Nevado de Toluca – and the site of what is allegedly the largest single **market** in the country, despite being recently halved in size by the city's government. This, held every Friday (and to a lesser extent throughout the week), is the overriding reason to visit, attracting hordes of visitors from the capital. It is so vast that there can be no question of its being overwhelmed by tourists – quite the opposite: many outsiders find themselves crushed by the scale of the place, lost among the thousands of stalls and crowds from the state's outlying villages. There's a substantial selection of local crafts – woven goods and pottery above all – but also vast areas selling more humble everyday domestic items. For an idea of what quality and prices to expect, head for the *Casa de Artesanias*, Paseo Tollocan 700 Ote., a few blocks east of the market.

A patent relief after the noise and crush of the market, Toluca's **botanical gardens** (Tues–Sun 9am–4.30pm; $2, free on Sun) by the Plaza España are housed in an enormous Art-Nouveau greenhouse. Downtown, the **Museo Jose Maria Velasco** on Lerdo (Tues–Sun 10am–6pm; free) displays a goodly collection of nineteenth-century paintings, while the **Museo de Bellas Artes**, Santos de Gollada (Tues–Sun 10am–6pm; $2, free on Sun) shows off the best fine arts in the state.

Some 10km out of town there's also the **Centro Cultural Mexiquense**, where several museums (all Tues–Sun 10am–6pm; $2, free on Sun) are scattered in park-like grounds. Among them are the **Museo Regional**, devoted to the archeology and history of the state, a small **Museo de Arte Moderno** and, perhaps the most interesting, the **Museo de Artes Populares**, a collection of local crafts, ancient and modern, in a restored hacienda. Attached to this latter is the **Museo de la Charrería**, full of cowboy equipment and folklore. Although local buses run out there, you really need your own transport to explore the place fully.

Practicalities

An almost uninterrupted stream of **buses** leaves México's Terminal Poniente for Toluca throughout the day; the journey takes about an hour. The modern **Central Camionera**, right by the market, includes a restaurant and its own hotel. If you arrive during the day, you can get a bus to the city centre from the station or on the highway to the left of the station; after 8.30pm you'll be reliant on taxis. Disregard those at the bus station entrance; they charge roughly double the price of the ones that run along the main road at the side of the station building. The information booth in the bus terminal appears to be permanently closed; head instead for the extremely helpful **tourist office** on Edifico Oriente, Plaza Toluca, third floor. *Banamex* and *Serfin* on the Portal Maderro **change dollars**.

There are plenty of places to eat and some **grotty hotels** around the market, but there's little point in staying in Toluca unless you plan to stop over Thursday night, get to the market early, and continue west – if you do this, be warned that on Thursdays it can be hard to find a room. On the terminal itself *Terminal* (☎72/17-45-88; ⑥) is good, despite its grotty surroundings, or try *Albert*, halfway between the city centre and bus station at Rayon Nte. 213 (☎72/14-95-77; ⑤). All rooms have TV and FM radio. Best option in the city centre is the *Colonial*, Hidalgo Ote. 103 (☎72/15-97-00; ⑥), a quiet, cosy place with a good restaurant, bar and live music. *San Francisco*, Rayon Sur 104 (☎72/13-31-14; ⑦) is more luxurious, with its own pool, bar and restaurant.

As usual the markets and outlying areas are the places to go for **budget food**, while around the Portales there are some good, pricier options. *Fonda Rosita*, in a corridor between Portal Madero and the cathedral has a nightclub above it, while *Restaurante Impala*, Portal Madero, does a good *comida corrida*.

The bus terminal at Toluca offers frequent services to México, Cuernavaca, Zincatan, Morelia, Ixtapan and Malinalco during the day (at night the terminal appears to close and services are much sparser). Buy the ticket direct from the driver at the appropriate rank. *Estrellas de Oro* runs daily services farther afield including (once a day) Mazatlán, Tijuana and Mexicali.

Around Toluca

Although most villages around Toluca do have a bus service – if only once or twice a day – this region is easiest explored by car. One trip you will definitely miss out on unless you drive is to the volcano, the **Nevado de Toluca** (or Xinantécatl, 4690m). A rough dirt road – not practicable during the rainy season or in mid-winter – leads all the way to two small lakes (the **Lagos del Sol** and **de la Luna**) in the heart of the crater. From its jagged lip the views are breathtaking: below you the lakes; eastwards a fabulous vista across the Valleys of Toluca and Mexico; and to the west a series of lower, greener hills ranging towards the peaks of the Sierra Madre Occidental. You need a tough vehicle to get up here, and healthy lungs to take even a short climb at 3000m.

Easier, closer to Toluca and accessible by local bus (from Av. Adolfo López Mates), is a visit to the archeological site of **Calixtlahuaca** (Tues–Sun 10am–5pm; $3, free on Sun) just north of the city. This was the township of the Matlazinca people, inhabited from prehistoric times and later subjugated by the Aztecs, who established a garrison here in the fifteenth century. Calixtlahuaca was not a willing subject, and there were constant rebellions; after one, in 1475, the Aztecs allegedly sacrificed over 11,000 Matlazinca prisoners on the Temple of Quetzalcoatl. This, several times built over, is the most important structure on the site. Dedicated to the god in his role as Ehecatl, god of wind, its circular design is typical, allowing the breezes to blow freely around the shrine. See also the remains of the pyramid devoted to Tlaloc, and the nearby *tzompantli* (skull rack), both constructed of the local pink and black volcanic stone. You can also get to the site by taxi from Toluca, which costs around $5.

West from Toluca, the road towards Morelia and the state of Michoacán is truly spectacular. Much of this wooded, mountainous area – as far as Zitacuaro – is given over to villas inhabited at weekends by wealthy refugees from the capital, and nowhere more so than **VALLE DE BRAVO**, reached by turning off to the left about halfway. Set in a deep pine-clad valley, the town sits on the eastern shore of an artificial lake, the **Presa Miguel Aleman**. There's everything here for upmarket relaxation: boat trips, sailing, swimming and water-skiing on the lake; riding, hiking and even golf on dry land. It's expensive, but does make for a very relaxing break – especially if you come during the week, when fewer people are about. There's a reasonable bus service from México via Toluca.

South towards Taxco

A strange thing about the route west is that as you descend from Toluca, so the country becomes more mountainous: where Toluca is on a very high plateau, broken only by the occasional soaring peak, the lower country to the west is constantly, ruggedly hilly. It's also warmer, and far more verdant. Much the same happens as you head south, although here you head across the plateau for some way until you start to go down into the mountains. There are four or five buses a day along this road, and several places of interest on the way. The first village, less than 10km out of Toluca, is **METEPEC**, famed as a pottery-making centre. Brightly coloured local wares can be found at craft shops throughout the country; supposedly the figures were originally inspired by the saints on the facade of Metepec's sixteenth-century Franciscan monastery, and in this century Diego Rivera taught the villagers new techniques of colouring and design. There's a market here on Mondays. After some 25km you pass **TENANGO DEL VALLE**: nearby, you can visit the excavated remains of the large fortified Malatzinca township of **Teotenango** (Tues–Sun 9am–4.30pm; $2, free on Sun). There's a small museum on site.

TENANCINGO, the next village of any size, is perhaps more interesting, and here there are a couple of small hotels – try the *Hotel Jardín* in an old mansion on the zócalo (☎2-01-30; ②) – that make a quiet alternative to Toluca or Taxco. Liqueurs made from the fruit that grows in abundance on the surrounding plain, and finely woven traditional *rebozos* (shawls) are sold here, many of them produced at the lovely monastery of El Santo Desierto. The chief reason to stop, however, is the proximity of the amazing Aztec ruins at Malinalco (see opposite), which can be reached by hourly buses (actually four-wheel-drive jeeps) heading for Chalma.

Continuing on the main road, the next possible stop is **IXTAPAN DE LA SAL**, a long-established spa whose mineral-rich waters are supposed to cure a plethora of muscular and circulatory ills. You can swim in the pools here – cheaper in the old town, where *Balneario Municpal* on Allende (daily 7am–6pm) charges $2, but more elegant at the *Balneario Ixtapan*, towards the outskirts on Benito Juárez. Bathing here costs $8 and includes entrance to the aqua park (with fairground rides). Several reasonably priced hotels offer very good all-inclusive deals; among them *Guadalajara*, Allende 3 (☎714/3-03-57; ①–④), a friendly, basic place where all rooms have hot water. At the excellent-value *Casa Sarita*, Morelos 9 (☎714/3-01-72; ③–⑤), full board includes a trip to the cavern of Cacahuamilpa. For more luxury, try the *Avenida*, Juárez 614 (☎714/3-02-41; ⑥–⑦), a three-star hotel near the *Baleneria Ixtapan*. All rooms have TV, phone, FM radio, and own swimming pool. Alternatively, around Morelos you will find various *casa de huéspedes* whose prices vary between $10 and $20 a night. Most lock you in after 11pm (or out, if you stay out too late).

Farther south, and almost at Taxco, you pass close to the vast complex of caves known as the **grutas de Cacahuamilpa** (daily, guided tours hourly 10am–3pm). This network of caverns, hollowed out by two rivers, extends for some 70km – although the guided tour (obligatory) obviously takes in only a fraction. Among the graffiti you're shown a rather prim note by the Empress Carlota, wife of Maximilian –."Maria Carlota reached this point". Alongside, Lerdo de Tejada, who became president in 1872 five years after Maximilian's execution, has scrawled "Sebastian Lerdo de Tejada went further". There's a swimming pool by the entrance to the caves, as well as a restaurant and several food stalls, and buses on to Taxco or Cuernavaca.

Malinalco and Chalma

Though the Aztec site of **MALINALCO** is small – still incomplete at the time of the Conquest – and relatively unfrequented, it is undeniably one of the most evocative of its kind to survive. Carved in part from the raw rock of a steep mountainside, this was the setting for the sacred **initiation ceremonies** by which Aztec youth became members of the warrior elite. The village itself is a lovely little place surrounded by rich villas – many of them, complete with swimming pools, the weekend retreat of the capital's privileged few – and centred on the huge Augustinian church of Santa Monica. You'll be dropped in the plaza in front of the church, from where **the site** (daily 10am–4.30pm; $5, free on Sun) is some thirty minutes' walk up a very steep, stepped path.

Looking back over the village and valley, the **ruins** may be small, but they are undeniably impressive among the crags, the main structures and the stairways up to them part cut out of the rock, part constructed from great stone blocks. The most remarkable aspect is the circular inner sanctuary of the **Templo Principal** (House of the Eagle), hewn entirely from the face of the mountain. You approach up a broad staircase on either side of which sit stone jaguars – in the centre the broken human statue would have held a flag. To one side of the entrance, a broken eagle warrior sits atop Quetzalcoatl, the feathered serpent: guarding the other side are the remains of a jaguar warrior, representative of the second Aztec warrior class. The doorway of the sanctuary itself, cut through a natural rock wall, represents the giant mouth of a serpent – you walk in over its tongue, and around the entrance traces of teeth are still visible. Right in the centre of the floor lies the figure of an eagle, and on the raised horseshoe-shaped bench behind are two more eagles and the pelt of a jaguar, all carved in a single piece from the bedrock. Behind the first eagle is a hole in the ground where the hearts of human sacrificial victims would be placed, supposedly to be eaten still beating as the final part of the initiation into warriorhood.

Other structures at the site include a small circular platform by the entrance, unfinished at the time of the Conquest, and a low pyramid directly in front of the main temple. Beyond this lie two larger temples. The first, Edificio III, again has a circular chamber at the centre, and it is believed that here Aztec warriors killed in battle were cremated, their souls rising to the heavens to become stars. Edificio IV was originally a temple of the sun: much of its structure went into the construction of the church in the village. Outside the site, visible from about halfway up the steps to the ruins, you can see another prehistoric building nestling among the mountains. It is still used by the locals as a place of pilgrimage, serving both a Christian saint and an Aztec altar-goddess.

There are several places to **stay in Malinalco**. Handiest is the *Hotel Santa Mónica*, Av. Hidalgo 109 (☎714/7-00-31; ②), just below the plaza on the way to the site: if there is no one in attendance, the owner runs a shop on the plaza. On the edge of the village sit *Las Cabañas* (☎714/7-01-01; ⑤), a group of some twenty cabins run by the state government. Each sleeps five and has basic cooking facilities: there's also a pool and the place is excellent value if you gather enough people to fill a cabin (reservations from the Estado de Mexico tourist office in the city, but rarely necessary). There are also a couple of good trailer park/campsites nearby.

Getting to the site: Chalma

Malinalco may seem on the face of it to be somewhat isolated, but in practice it's not difficult to reach by public transport. Though Tenancingo offers one possible approach, the easiest way in is via the tiny village of **CHALMA**, on good roads all the way. There are direct buses to Chalma from México's Terminal Poniente, and also from Toluca and from Cuernavaca via Santa Marta (this is a slightly rougher ride: if you're driving, avoid the direct road signed from Chalma back to Cuernavaca, which rapidly deteriorates to a frightening, mountainous single track). From Chalma *colectivo*s leave for Malinalco every few minutes. They set off from the main street by the taxi sign, downhill from where most buses stop.

Chalma is so well served by bus because it's an important centre of **pilgrimage**, attracting vast crowds every Sunday, and at times of special religious significance (especially the first Friday in Lent, *Semana Santa* and September 29) so many people that it's impossible to get anywhere near the church. The permanent population is only a few hundred, but at such times pilgrims camp out for miles around to take part in the rituals, a fascinating mix of Christian and more ancient pagan rites: before the Spanish arrived the deity Oztocteotl, god of caves, was venerated in a natural cave here, but he was "miraculously" replaced by a statue of Christ when the first missionaries arrived. In the seventeenth century this crucifix was moved to a new church, the **Santuario de Chalma**, now the place of pilgrimage and of miraculous appearances of a Christ-like figure. As well as paying their devotions to Christ the pilgrims bathe in the healing waters that flow from the cave. Despite all this, and the fact that the town is surrounded by impressive craggy peaks, it has to be added that Chalma is a complete dump, its filthy, muddy streets lined with stalls offering tacky souvenirs of the pilgrimage. Nearby **Ahuehuete** also has a shrine visited by many pilgrims, at a spot where a miraculous spring issues from the roots of a huge old tree. Many people stop here first (it's before Chalma coming from México), and some proceed the last few kilometres to Chalma on foot.

Cuernavaca and around

The old road to Acapulco ran out from the capital via Cuernavaca and Taxco, and although the modern route skirts the former and gives Taxco a wide berth, both remain firmly established on the tourist treadmill. The journey starts well: a steep, winding climb out of the Valley of México into refreshing pine forests, and then gently down, leaving the city pollution behind. It's a fast road too, and, smog permitting, offers lovely views back over the D.F.

CUERNAVACA has always been a place of escape from the city – the Aztecs called it *Cuauhnahuac* ("place by the woods") and it became a favourite resort and hunting ground for their rulers. Cortés seized and destroyed the city during the siege of Tenochtitlán, but he too ended up building himself a palace: the Spanish corrupting the name to Cuernavaca ("cow horn") for no better reason than their inability to cope with the original. The fashion then established has been followed ever since – among others by the Emperor Maximilian and the deposed Shah of Iran – but for the casual visitor the modern city is in many ways a disappointment. Its spring-like climate remains, but as capital of the state of Morelos, Cuernavaca is rapidly becoming industrialized and the streets in the centre are permanently clogged with traffic and fumes. The gardens and villas that shelter wealthy Mexicans and ex-pats are almost all hidden behind high walls, or so far out in the suburbs that you won't see them: it seems an ill-planned and widely spread city, certainly not easy to get about on foot. Food and lodging, too, come relatively expensive, in part thanks to the large foreign contingent, swelled by tourists and by students from the many language schools. On the other hand, the town is attractive enough and makes a good base for heading north to the village of **Tepoztlán**, with its raucous fiesta, or south to the ruins of **Xochicalco**. It may also be worthwhile taking a trip to **Cuautla**, if you are at all interested in Mexican history. Emiliano Zapata is buried here in the Jardín Revolución del Sur.

Arrival and information

Buses run every few minutes to Cuernavaca from México's Central del Sur: of the three lines you can take, *Flecha Roja* is probably the best since its Cuernavaca terminal, on Morelos, is central and easy to find. *Pullman de Morelos* also stops quite close to the centre, at the corner of Abasolo and Netzahualcoyotl; simply walk up the latter and you find yourself at the heart of things. The first-class *Estrella de Oro* terminus is a long way south of the centre on Morelos – worth getting to, though, if you're continuing on the long ride south to Acapulco and the coast.

You should head as soon as possible for the state **tourist office**, south of the Jardín Borda on Morelos Sur 802 (☎73/14-38-60) to pick up a map, since Cuernavaca can be very confusing. They also have information on buses and excursions. The Federal office in the Palacio de Gobierno on the main plaza is handier, but less well stocked.

Accommodation

Cuernavaca's tourist offices have long lists of **hotels** and contact addresses for families offering rooms (a service aimed at students attending local language schools – the schools themselves and their noticeboards are also good sources for such accommodation). Many of the cheaper options are just north of the centre, on Matamoros and the streets that connect it with Morelos: you'll pass several if you walk in from the *Flecha Roja* bus station.

América, Aragón y Leon 111 (☎73/18-61-27). Basic place; rooms with bath are more expensive. ③.

Iberia, Rayon 9 (☎73/12-60-40). Large rooms and friendly staff. Parking available. ④.

La Pal, Aragón y Leon (☎73/18-07-21). Popular and inexpensive, if somewhat noisy. ②.

Las Mañanitas, Ricardo Linares 108 (☎73/14-44-66). One of the best luxury hotels in Cuernavaca, with popular restaurant and bars. ⑨.

Motel Royal, Matamoros 19 (☎73/18-64-80). One of a number of similar places along Matamoros; comfortable rooms with bath, and space for parking. ④.

Papagayo, Motolina 13 (☎73/14-17-11). With its swimming pool and children's area this place can get raucous, but the rooms are good value. ⑤.

Roma, Matamoros 404 (☎73/18-87-78). All rooms with TV and bath. ④.

The Town

Right on the zócalo, which is, as ever, the heart of the city, the **Palacio de Cortés** (Tues–Sun 9.30am–5pm; $5, free on Sun) houses the **Museo Regional**

Cuauhnahuac. Building began as early as 1522 when, although Tenochtitlán had fallen, much of the country was still not under Spanish control, and the fortress-like aspect of the earlier parts reflect this period: over the centuries, though, it's been added to and modified substantially – first by Cortés himself and his descendants, later by the state authorities to whom it passed. What you see today is very much a palace. The museum is a good one, covering local archeology and history, with a substantial collection of colonial art, weaponry and everyday artefacts, including a reproduction of a modern Tlahuica Indian hut. The highlight, though, is the series of Diego Rivera murals* around the gallery. Depicting Mexican history from the Conquest to the Revolution, they concentrate in particular on the atrocities committed by Cortés and on Emiliano Zapata – the Revolutionary who was born in nearby Cuautla, raised most of his army from the peasants of Morelos, and remains something of a folk hero to them. From the balcony here, if you're lucky, there are wonderful views to the east, with Popocatépetl in the far distance. Around the main entrance, you can see excavated traces of the Aztec pyramid that originally occupied this site.

Right next to the Palace, on the right as you face it, is a small *FONART* craft shop – the best of many catering to the tourists here – and around the twin plazas you'll find a series of **cafes** where you can sit outdoors. Head out of the zócalo on Hidalgo and you'll reach the **Cathedral**, founded by Cortés in 1529. Bulky and threatening from the outside (at one stage there were actually cannons mounted along the battlemented roof line), it has been remarkably tastefully refurbished within: stripped almost bare and painted in plain gold and white. Traces of murals, discovered during the redecoration, have been uncovered in places – they have a remarkably Oriental look and are believed to have been painted by a Christian Chinese or Filipino artist in the days when Cuernavaca cathedral was the centre for missions to the Far East. The main Spanish trade route then came through here, with goods brought across the Pacific to Acapulco, overland through central Mexico, and on from Veracruz to Spain. The present bishop of Cuernavaca is one of the country's most liberal and, apart from doing up his cathedral, is renowned for his outspoken sermons, and for the Mariachi Mass that he instituted here. Every Sunday morning at 11am, this service is conducted to the accompaniment of traditional Mexican music and usually attracts large crowds.

A few metres beyond the cathedral is the entrance to the **Jardín Borda** (Tues–Sun 10am–5pm; $5, free on Sun), a large formal garden laid out by the Taxco mining magnate José de la Borda (see p.315) in the eighteenth century. Both the gardens and Borda's mansion are in a rather sorry state but they remain delightfully tranquil and a reminder of the haven Cuernavaca once was – and no doubt still is behind the walls of its exclusive residences. Maximilian and Carlota adopted Borda's legacy as their weekend home, but Maximilian also had a retreat in Cuernavaca that he shared with his Indian mistress, "La India Bonita". Officially named *La Casa del Olindo*, this house was popularly known as *La Casa del Olvido* since the builder "forgot" to include quarters for Carlota. Rather more distant – too far to walk – if you're into gardens it's worth taking a taxi to see the grounds and the collection of medicinal plants in the **Museo de la Herbolaria**.

Other sites scattered in the further fringes of the city include the sole significant reminder of the pre-colonial period, the **Pyramid of Teopanzolco** (daily 10am–5pm; $3, free on Sun). Even this was so effectively buried that it took an artillery bombardment during the Revolution to uncover it. To the northeast of the centre beyond the train station (which is what the gunners were aiming at), it's a small temple in which two pyramids can be seen, one built over the other.

---

*More murals, by David Siqueiros, can be seen in the *Hotel Casino de la Selva*, Leandro Valle 1001, and you can also visit his studio at Venus 7 (Mon–Fri 10am–2pm & 4–6pm). Both are a taxi ride away from the centre – in opposite directions.

Eating and drinking

You don't need to wander far from the centre to find good **places to eat**: there's a particulary fine group around the zócalo.

Bar Cuernavaca Jacón, on the zócalo. Typical Mexican place with a lively atmosphere.

Cafe Parroquia, on the zócalo. Perhaps the best in the city, certainly with the cheapest beer in the centre.

Los Pasteles de Vienes, Lerdo de Tejada 302. Sophisticated restaurant for continental-style coffee, cakes and entrées.

Pollo y Más, Galeana 4. Opposite the zócalo, serving tasty roast chicken, *enchiladas* and *antojitos*.

Tepoztlán

One of the most interesting side trips from Cuernavaca is to **TEPOZTLÁN**, just 20km away but, until recently at least, an entirely different world. In a narrow valley spectacularly ringed by volcanic mountains, the village was an isolated agrarian community, inhabited by Nahuatl-speaking Indians whose life can have changed little between the time of the Conquest and the beginning of this century. It was on Tepoztlán that Oscar Lewis based his classic study of *Life in a Mexican Village*, and the effects of the Revolution on it: the village was an important stronghold of the original Zapatista movement. New roads and a couple of luxury hotels have changed things, but the stunning setting survives, as does a reputation for joyously boisterous fiestas (especially the drunken revelry of the night of September 7).

On the zócalo, where the market is held on Sundays and Wednesdays, stands the massive, fortress-like **Dominican Monastery**. It was indeed a fortress for a while during the Revolution, but is now in a rather beautiful state of disrepair. Around the back, part of the church has been given over to a museum (Tues–Sun 10am–6pm; $1) with a remarkably good archeological collection. Several pre-Hispanic temples have been found on the hilltops roundabout and you can reach one, atop the artificially flattened **Cerro del Tepozteco**, with an exhausting climb of an hour or so along a well-signposted path from the village. The pyramid here was dedicated to Tepoztecatl, a god of *pulque* and of fertility, represented by carvings of rabbits. There were so many *pulque* gods that they were known as the four hundred rabbits: the drink was supposedly discovered by rabbits nibbling at the agave plants from which it is made. This one gained particular kudos when the Spanish flung the idol off the cliffs only for his adherents to find that it had landed unharmed – the big September fiesta is in his honour.

Practicalities

Frequent buses leave Cuernavaca for Tepoztlán, which many people visit as a day trip. There's all of three hotels in town: cheapest is *La Cabaña,* on the main road near where the bus stops (no phone; ④). The *Posado del Tepoxteco* and *Hotel Tepoztlán* (both ⑦) offer more comfort for higher prices. There's a *Bancomer* for **currency exchange** near the bus stop and plenty of **restaurants**, the best of which is the *Luna de Mextli* on the road heading down to the monastery. You may also choose to stop for a beer at the *Restaurant Coquis* nearby, where you can have your photo taken with a life-size Marcos model.

Xochicalco

Not much further from Cuernavaca, this time to the south, lie the ruins of **XOCHICALCO** (daily 10am–4.30pm; $4, free on Sun). While not much is known of the history of this site or the peoples who inhabited it, it is regarded by archeologists as one of the most significant in Central Mexico, forming as it does a link between the

Classic culture of Teotihuacán and the later Toltec peoples. Xochicalco flourished from around the seventh to the tenth century AD – thus overlapping with both Teotihuacán and Tula – and also shows clear parallels with Maya and Zapotec sites of the era.

The setting, high on a bare mountain top, is reminiscent of Monte Albán (see p.403), the great Zapotec site near Oaxaca and, like Monte Albán and the great Maya sites (but unlike Tula or Teotihuacán), Xochicalco was an exclusively religious and ceremonial centre rather than a true city. The style of many of the carvings, too, recalls Zapotec and Maya art. Their subjects, however, and the architecture of the temples, do seem to form a transition between Teotihuacán and Tula: in particular Quetzalcoatl first appears here in human guise, as he was to feature at Tula and almost every subsequent site, rather than simply as the feathered serpent of Teotihuacán. The ball court is almost identical to earlier Maya examples, and similar to those that later appeared in Tula. For all these influences, however, or perhaps because there are so many of them, it's almost impossible to say which was dominant: some claim that Xochicalco was a northern outpost of the Maya, others that it was a subject city of Teotihuacán that survived (or perhaps precipitated through revolt) the fall of that empire.

In any case, much the most important surviving monument is the **Pirámide de Quetzalcoatl** on the highest part of the site. Around its base are carved wonderfully elaborate plumed serpents, coiling around various seated figures and symbols with astronomical significance – all clearly Maya in inspiration. On top, part of the wall of the sanctuary remains standing. Not far from here, to the left and slightly down the hill, you'll find the entrance to the **Subterranean Passages**, a couple of natural caves which have had steps and tunnels added to them by human hands. In one a shaft in the roof is so oriented as to allow the sun to shine directly in at times of equinox: any other time you'll need a torch to make out remains of frescoes on the walls. You may have to persuade the guard to unlock the passages for you. There's a new site museum on the next hilltop.

Practicalities

Two first-class buses leave Cuernavaca for Xochicalco. If you're driving, or if you go with a tour, you can continue down the road beyond Xochicalco to the caves of Cacahuamilpa (see p.309) from where Taxco (see below) is only a short distance: alternatively it's about an hour's walk from the site back to the main road where you should be able to flag down a passing bus in either direction.

Taxco

Silver has been mined in **TAXCO** since before the Conquest, and although the sources have long been virtually exhausted, silver is still the basis of the town's fame and its livelihood. Nowadays, though, it's in the form of jewellery: made in hundreds of workshops to be sold throughout the country, and in a bewildering array of shops (*platerías*) catering to the tourists in Taxco itself. It's an attractive place, a mass of narrow cobbled alleys lined with red-roofed, whitewashed houses straggling steeply over the hills. At intervals the pattern is broken by some larger mansion, by a courtyard filled with flowers, or by the twin spires of a church rearing up – above all the famous Baroque wedding cake of **Santa Prisca**.

Taxco's development, though it might seem a prosperous place now, has not been a simple progression – indeed on more than one occasion the town has been all but abandoned. Although the Spaniards came running at the rumours of mineral wealth here (Cortés himself sent an expedition in 1522), their initial success was short-lived, and it wasn't until the eighteenth century that **José de la Borda** struck it fabulously rich by discovering the San Ignacio vein. It is from the short period of Borda's life that most of what you see dates – he spent one large fortune on building the church of Santa Prisca, others on more buildings and a royal lifestyle here and in Cuernavaca – but by his death in 1778 the boom was already over. In 1929 a final revival started with the arrival of the American William Spratling who set up a jewellery workshop in Taxco, drawing on the town's traditional skills and designs. With the completion of a new road around the same time the massive influx of tourists was inevitable, but the town has handled it well, becoming rich without losing too much of its charm.

Arrival and information

Both **bus stations** are on Av. J F Kennedy, the main road that winds around the side of the valley below the town. To get in from *Flecha Roja* (near which are a couple of hotels handy for late arrivals) turn left up the hill and then left again to climb even more steeply past the church of Veracruz to the zócalo, **Plaza Borda**. From *Estrella de Oro* head straight up the steep alley directly across from you until you come, on your right, to the Plazuela San Juan, and from there down Cuauhtémoc to the zócalo.

There's a small **tourist office** more or less opposite the *Estrella de Oro* terminal (daily 9am–7pm; ☎762/2-07-98), and you can **change money** at the *casa de cambio* on the Plazuela de San Juan, which offers good rates and civilized opening hours (Mon–Fri 9am–2pm & 4–8pm, Sun 9am–2pm).

Accommodation

Taxco has some excellent **hotels**, and when most of the day-trippers have left the place settles into a calmer mode. There are plenty of inexpensive places near the zócalo; at the higher end of the scale you're swamped with choices, in particular some lovely colonial buildings restored to make comfortable, popular hotels.

Agua Esondida, on the zócalo (☎762/2-07-26). Can be noisy due to the night-time reveleries on the square. ⑥.

Los Arcos, Juan Ruiz de Alarcón 2 (☎762/2-18-36). Good-value rooms, some with attics, in a pretty colonial building a couple of blocks east of the zócalo. ⑤.

Casa Grande, off Cuauhtémoc (☎ and fax 762/2-11-08). Run-down but friendly place which you'll find by going through to a courtyard behind the cinema on the Plazuela San Juan. ④.

Melendez, Cuauhtémoc 6 (☎762/2-00-06). Large hotel with formal atmosphere – its restaurant is reasonable, and especially good for breakfast. ⑤.

Posada de los Castillo, Juan Ruiz de Alarcón 7 (☎762/2-13-96). Lovely colonial hotel, near the zócalo, with rooms decorated in bright tiles and antique wood. ⑥.

Santa Prisca, Cena Oscuras 1 (☎762/2-00-80). Attractive converted colonial building; rates include breakfast. ⑥.

The Town

Just south of **Plaza Borda** you'll find Taxco's one outstanding sight: the church of **Santa Prisca**, a building so florid and expensive that it not surprisingly arouses strong feeling. Aldous Huxley in his journey *Beyond the Mexique Bay*, regarded the town, and the church in particular, with less than affection:

> *In the eighteenth century, Borda, the mining millionaire, built for Taxco one of the most sumptuous churches in Mexico – one of the most sumptuous and one of the most ugly. I have never seen a building in which every part, down to the smallest decorative detail, was so constantly ill proportioned. Borda's church is an inverted work of genius.*

But that is the minority view – most would follow Sacheverell Sitwell (who loved anything frilly) in his view that:

its obvious beauties in the way of elegance and dignity, and its suitability to both purpose and environment are enough to convert those who would never have thought to find themselves admiring a building of this kind.

Which is probably enough said about the church. Its hyper-elaborate facade towers over the zócalo, and inside there's a riot of gilded Churriguresque altarpieces and other treasures including paintings by Miguel Cabrera, a Zapotec Indian who became one of Mexico's greatest colonial religious artists. On the zócalo itself, the **Museo de Platería** (daily 10am–6pm; free), houses not only silver but a variety of temporary exhibitions. The **Museo Pineda** next door (same times; $1) is another place to admire silverwork, and has a state-run crafts shop devoted to the stuff.

The **Museo Guillermo Spratling** (Tues–Sat 10am–5pm, Sun 10am–3pm; $5, free on Sun), which houses William Spratling's personal collection of antiquities and a small display devoted to the history of Taxco, can be found by going round to the back of the church on c/Veracruz. It's an interesting miscellany, impressively displayed over three floors. Not far from here on Juan Ruiz de Alarcon, the street parallel to Veracruz, is the **Casa Humboldt**, an old staging inn named for the German explorer baron who spent one night here in 1803. A beautiful colonial building, it now houses a small **art museum** (Tues–Sat 10am–5pm, Sun 10am–3pm; $4, free on Sun).

In the other direction, above the zócalo, you'll find the **Casa Figueroa** (Mon–Sat 10am–1pm & 3–7pm), another fine mansion converted into a small art gallery and museum. It was originally known as the *Casa de las Lágrimas* (House of Tears) because the magistrate who built it employed the forced labour of Indians unable to pay the fines he imposed on them.

Beyond these few sights the charm of Taxco is to be found in simply wandering the streets, nosing about in the *platerías*, stopping occasionally for a drink. If you're **buying silver** you can be fairly sure it's the real thing here (check for the hallmark – .925 or "sterling"), but prices are much the same as they would be anywhere and quality and workmanship can vary enormously: there's everything from mass-produced belt buckles and cheap rings to designer jewellery that will set you back thousands of dollars. Whatever you buy, the shops off the main streets will be cheaper and more open to bargaining. A section in the **market**, down the steps beside the zócalo, is given over to the silver hawkers and makes a good place to start. Otherwise it seems to specialize in rather tacky tourist goods.

Eating and drinking

Finding somewhere to **eat** in Taxco is no problem at all, though the enticing places around the zócalo do tend to be expensive. For rock-bottom food the **market** has a section given over to food stalls which are better than they look, or carry on right through to emerge on the street below, where you'll find a couple of reasonable local restaurants. All except the cheapest of the hotels, too, have their own dining rooms.

In the evening everyone gathers around the zócalo to see and be seen, to stroll in front of the church, or to sit outdoors with a coffee or a drink. You can join in from one of the famous bars – *Berta's*, the traditional place to meet right next to the church, or *Paco's*, more fashionable nowadays, across the square.

Puebla

East of the capital, a fast new road climbs steeply, past glorious views of the snow-decked heights of Popocatépetl and Ixtaccíhuatl (the best are looking back, for the last wisps of smog are only left behind at the very brow of the pass) to **PUEBLA**. Little more than an hour on the bus – *ADO, Cristóbal Colón* or *Estrella Roja* from the TAPO

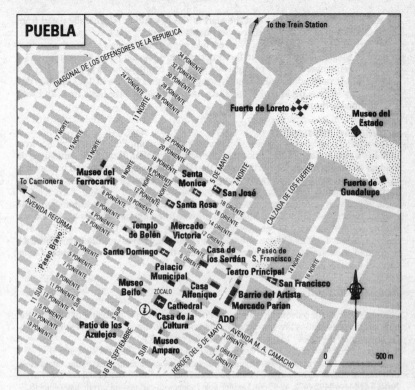

PUEBLA

To the Train Station

DIAGONAL DE LOS DEFENSORES DE LA REPUBLICA

34 PONIENTE
32 PONIENTE
30 PONIENTE
28 PONIENTE
26 PONIENTE
24 PONIENTE

Fuerte de Loreto

Museo del Estado

22 PONIENTE
20 PONIENTE
18 PONIENTE

17 NORTE
15 NORTE
13 NORTE
11 NORTE

Museo del Ferrocarril

To Camionera

Santa Monica

San José

Fuerte de Guadalupe

AVENIDA REFORMA

8 PONIENTE
6 PONIENTE
4 PONIENTE
2 PONIENTE

9 NORTE
11 NORTE

16 PONIENTE
12 PONIENTE
10 PONIENTE

5 DE MAYO
2 NORTE

Santa Rosa

18 ORIENTE
16 ORIENTE

CALZADA DE LOS FUERTES

Paseo Bravo

Templo de Belén

Mercado Victoria

14 ORIENTE
12 ORIENTE

Santo Domingo

Casa de los Serdán

Paseo de S. Francisco

6 ORIENTE

Palacio Municipal

Teatro Principal

14 NORTE
16 NORTE

3 PONIENTE
5 PONIENTE
7 PONIENTE
9 PONIENTE
11 PONIENTE
13 PONIENTE
15 PONIENTE
17 PONIENTE
19 PONIENTE

1 SUR
3 SUR

Museo Bello

Casa Alfeñique

ZÓCALO

San Francisco

Barrio del Artista

Mercado Parian

Cathedral

Casa de la Cultura

ADO

Patio de los Azulejos

Museo Amparo

16 DE SEPTIEMBRE
2 SUR

HEROES DEL 5 DE MAYO

3 ORIENTE
5 ORIENTE
7 ORIENTE

AVENIDA M. A. CAMACHO

0   500 m

terminal – this is the Republic's fourth-largest city, and one of its hardest to pin down. On the whole it's a disappointment, with the initial impression of industrial modernity imparted by the huge Volkswagen works on the outskirts never quite dispelled in streets that are permanently clogged with traffic, raucous and rushed. There are few good places to stay, with rooms expensive and often booked up. Yet this is as historic a city as any in Mexico, and certainly in the centre there's a remarkable concentration of interest – a fabulous **cathedral**, "hidden" convent, museums and colonial **mansions** – while the mountainous country roundabout is often startlingly beautiful. Nevertheless, Puebla is unlikely to tempt you into staying particularly long, and in a packed day both the city and nearby Cholula can be seen, either returning to México or continuing westwards overnight.

The city was founded by the Spanish in 1531 and, rare for this area, was an entirely new foundation – preferred to the ancient sites of Cholula and Tlaxcala because there, presumably, the memories of Indian power remained too strong. It rapidly assumed great importance as a staging point on the journey from the capital to the port at Veracruz, and for the trans-shipment of goods from Spain's Far Eastern colonies, delivered to Acapulco and transported across Mexico from there. Wealth was brought, too, by the reputation of its ceramic and tile manufacture (still very much in evidence) which was in part due to the abundance of good clays, in part to its settlement by Spaniards from Talavera who brought traditional skills with them. The city did well out of colonial rule, and perhaps not surprisingly it took the wrong side in the War of Independence, preserving to this day a name for conservatism and traditional values not dispelled even by the fact that the start of the Revolution is generally dated from the assassination of Aquiles Serdan in his Puebla home.

Military defeat, too, seems to play an even larger part in Puebla's history than it does in most of Mexico – the city fell to the Americans in 1847 and to the French in 1863 – but what's remembered is the greatest victory in the country's history, when a force of some 2000 Mexicans defeated a French army three times its size in 1872. To this day the 5 of May (**Cinco de Mayo**) is commemorated with a massive fiesta here, and with a public holiday throughout the country.

Arrival and information

Puebla's **Central Camionera**, known by the acronym CAPU (Central de Autobuses de Puebla) lies miles out in the northwest of the city. There's a frequent local bus service to and from the centre. You'll need to get out here for local or second-class journeys (to Tlaxcala or Cholula, for example).

At the corner of 16 de Septiembre with 5 Ote., the **tourist office** (Mon–Sat 8am–8.30pm, Sun 9am–2pm; ☎22/46-12-85) can provide free maps and details of city tours – worth taking if you want to see everything in a hurry. The **post office**, on 2 Ote. 411, has an efficient *Lista de Correos* and telegram facilities. **Banks** – on Reforma there's a *Serfin* and a *Banamex* – will change money, and there is a **casa de cambio**, *Dollar Express*, in an arcade off the zócalo.

Accommodation

Finding somewhere reasonable **to stay** in Puebla can be a real problem, but at least the bulk of the possibilities are not far from the zócalo, mostly just to the west and north. On the whole, the closer to the zócalo, the higher the price.

Avenida, 5 Pte. 336 (☎22/32-21-04). Basic but friendly and relatively quiet. No hot water. ①.

Colonial, 4 Sur 105 (☎22/46-42-92). Luxury in a beautiful colonial building next to the Autonomous University of Puebla. All rooms have TV and phone and there's a fine restaurant and bar. ⑥.

June, 5 de Mayo 1402 (☎22/42-05-86). Comfortable rooms with carpets and private bathroom. ③.

Reforma 2000, 4 Pte. on the corner of 11 Nte. (☎22/42-33-63). Carpeted spacious rooms with TV and phone. Nice bar. ⑤.

Regio, 5 de Mayo 1004 (☎22/32-47-74). Some rooms with private bath; the communal bathroom only has hot water 6–10am. ②.

Royalty Centro, Portal Hidalgo 8 (☎22/42-47-40). Luxury on the zócalo; satellite TV, room service, parking and telephone and fax facilities. The restaurant overlooking the zócalo is good too. ⑦.

San Agustín, 3 Pte. 531 (☎22/32-50-89). Parking, two good restaurants, cable TV. ⑤.

Victoria, 3 Pte. 306 (☎22/32-89-92). Next to Bello Museum. Basic, all rooms with bath. ③.

The Town

Any tour of the city must start in the **zócalo**, centre of the numbering system for the ancient grid of streets, where stands the great **Cathedral**, second-largest in the Republic. Under construction from 1562 until the middle of the following century, its ornamentation – especially the interior, decked out in onyx, marble and gilt – is amazing. There are frequent free guided tours and if the tower is open, exceptional panoramas from the top. Near the tourist office behind the cathedral, the old Archbishop's Palace, converted to a library in the seventeenth century (the *Biblioteca Palafoxiana*; reputed to be the oldest library in the Americas), now houses the original collection of ancient books and manuscripts on the upper floor, with the city's **Casa de la Cultura** hosting regular exhibitions of local arts and crafts downstairs (Tues–Sun 10am–5pm; free, $1.50 for the library).

The best museum in Puebla is the modern **Museo Amparo,** on 2 Sur and 9 Ote. (daily except Tues 10am–6pm; $4, free on Mon), which features art from pre-Hispanic, Colonial and modern Mexico. The pre-Columbian era is particularly well represented, detailed on computer screens and in English and Spanish audio-cassette tours.

North of the zócalo

Head north from the zócalo along 5 de Mayo and you reach the church of **Santo Domingo** at the corner of 4 Pte. Its *Capilla del Rosario* is, even in comparison to the cathedral, a quite unbelievably lavish orgy of gold leaf and Baroque excess; a constant hushed, shuffling stream of devotees lights candles and prays for miraculous cures to its revered image of the Virgin. Next door is the **Pinacoteca Bello y Zetina** (daily except Tues 10am–5pm; free) which displays the paintings and furniture of the wealthy Bello household during the nineteenth century. Puebla's main **market**, the Mercado Victoria, lies just north of here on 5 de Mayo. On 6 Ote., east of the market, the **Casa de los Serdán** (Tues–Sun 10am–4.30pm; $1.50, free on Sun) records the liberal struggles of the Serdan family against the dictatorship of Porfirio Díaz. The assassination of Aquiles Serdan in this house was one of the most important steps in the fall of Díaz: the date of Serdan's death, November 18, 1910, is in the absence of any firmer indicators generally recognized as marking the start of the Revolution. In the house the bullet holes have been lovingly preserved, even down to a huge smashed mirror, still hanging on the wall where it appears in contemporary photos of the carnage.

Nine blocks north of the zócalo you'll find the remarkable "hidden" convent of **Santa Monica** (Tues–Sun 10am–5pm; $2.50). Here, from the suppression of the church in 1857 until their discovery in 1934, several generations of nuns lived hidden from the public gaze behind a smokescreen of secret doors and concealed passages. Just how secret they were is a matter of some debate – many claim that the authorities simply turned a blind eye – and certainly several lay families were actively supportive, providing supplies and new recruits. But it makes a good story, embellished by the conversion into a museum that preserves the secret entrances along with many religious artworks and a beautiful cloister. In the same general direction, at 3 Nte. and 14 Pte., is the convent of **Santa Rosa** (Mon–Sat 10am–4pm; $1.50, free on Sat), whose main claim to fame is that the great *Mole Poblano* was invented in its kitchens. You can sample this extraordinary sauce – made of chocolate, *chile*, and any number of herbs and spices – in the kitchens at Santa Rosa, and it's also served with chicken or turkey at every restaurant in Puebla.

East of the zócalo

The rest of the interest is mostly concentrated east of here, northeast of the zócalo. On 2 Nte., just off the zócalo, the **Museo Universitallo** (Tues–Sun 10am–5pm; $2, including tour) displays the history of education in Puebla, along with a collection of colonial furniture and paintings. At the end of 4 Ote. lie the **Mercado Parian** – mostly given over to rather tawdry tourist souvenirs – and the **Barrio del Artista**, traditionally the artists' quarter, now selling work aimed squarely at the tourist market. The **Teatro Principal**, nearby, is a fine eighteenth-century theatre, said to be the oldest on the continent, which still hosts occasional performances. Walking back to the zócalo, you can stop in at the **Casa del Alfeñique**, an elaborate old mansion covered in Puebla tiles, which now houses the regional museum (Tues–Sun 10am–4pm; $1.50). There are period furnishings, Puebla ceramics, a small archeological section, and an excellent display of colonial art.

Further afield, the historic forts of **Guadalupe** and **Loreto**, and the modern **State Museum**, crown a hill to the northwest. They mark the site of the constant battles and sieges of the nineteenth century, and the Fuerte Loreto contains a small military museum; the State Museum is largely devoted to the area's archeology and ethnology.

You'll also find the **Natural History Museum** and a **Planetarium**. To get there take a local bus (marked "Fuertes") from 16 de Septiembre at its junction with 9 Ote.

Eating, drinking and nightlife

Eating in Puebla is no problem, and you should really try a *pollo con mole poblano* at one of the restaurants on the zócalo or at any of the many *fondas típicas* around the central area. For cheaper food, head for the area around the Mercado Victoria, or if you crave the familiar there's a *Sanborn's* on Av. 2 Ote., just off 5 de Mayo. The best-known – and most touristy – restaurant in town is *Fonda de Santa Clara*, a couple of blocks west of the zócalo at 3 Pte. 307, which serves local food with an upmarket twist in a pretty room decorated with Mexican art.

Nightlife in Puebla centres round the *Zona Esmeralda* ten blocks east of the zócalo, where there's a string of bars and clubs to keep you going. Closer to the centre, *Cafe-bookshop Teorema*, 7 Nte., has live music from 9pm until midnight (though it closes after 1am most nights). It serves good food, beer and spirits and excellent cappuccino. Cover is $3. Otherwise, many people head out to **Cholula** to join the lively studenty atmosphere there; buses back to Puebla run until 4am.

Cholula

The ruins of **CHOLULA**, and the largest pyramid in Mexico, are just 15km from Puebla. A rival of Teotihuacán at its height, and the most powerful city in the country between the fall of Teotihuacán and the rise of Tula, Cholula was at the time of the Conquest a vast city of some four hundred temples, famed as a shrine to Quetzalcoatl and for the excellence of its pottery (a trade dominated by immigrant Mixtecs). But it paid dearly for an attempt, inspired by its Aztec allies, to ambush Cortés on his march to Tenochtitlán: the chieftains were slaughtered, their temples destroyed and churches built in their place. The Spanish claimed to have constructed 365 churches here, one for each day of the year, but although there are a lot, the figure certainly doesn't approach that. There may well, though, be 365 chapels within the churches, which is already a few hundred more than the village population could reasonably need. The great multi-domed **Capilla Real** on the Plaza Principal (daily 8am–2pm & 4–6pm) is the most interesting, along with the Convento de San Gabriel next door. Most of the rest, like the colonial glories of Cholula itself, seem to have been left quietly to crumble away. It's a pleasantly tranquil place to decay, at least, and there are a couple of basic cafes on the zócalo where you can sit and join the endless inactivity.

If you want to explore some of the churches roundabout, **ACATEPEC**, easily reached by local bus, is the place to head. The village church here, San Francisco, has a superb Baroque facade entirely covered in glazed bricks and *azulejos* of local manufacture. It's not particularly large, but it is beautifully proportioned, and quite unexpected in this setting. The interior is fairly spectacular too, but just a kilometre away in the village of **Tonatzintla**, the plain facade of the church of Santa Maria conceals an even more elaborate Baroque treasury. Here local craftsmen covered every available inch in ornament, interspersing bird, plant and Indian life with the more usual Christian elements. Acatepec lies on the road from Puebla to Izúcar de Matamoros, so you should be able to pick up a bus heading directly back.

The site

To get an impression of the city as it once looked, head first for Cholula's site **museum,** not far from the entrance (daily 10am–5pm; $5, free on Sun; ticket includes both the museum and the site). Even the **Great Pyramid** is not much to look at these days – at least as a building. Still covered in earth, it makes a not inconsiderable hill; a stiff climb that will take you to the church of **Nuestra Señora de los Remedios** and a viewing position from which you can attempt to count the churches. Within the pyramid/hill a series of tunnels dug during excavations can be explored: more than eight kilometres of them in all wind through the various stages of construction, but only a small proportion is open to the public, poorly lit but fascinating. Emerging at the end of the tunnel, you'll find a small area of open-air excavations, where part of the great pyramid has been exposed alongside various lesser shrines.

Practicalities

Buses leave Puebla for Cholula every thirty minutes or so: pick them up from 4 Pte. and 11 Nte. or from CAPU. In Cholula they drop at 12 Pte. and 5 de Mayo; head down 5 de Mayo to get to the centre of town. From the zócalo follow Morelos past the railway track to the pyramid.

There are a couple of hotels in Cholula, the most economical being the *Reforma,* Morelos and 4 Nte. (☎22/47-01-49; ③). On the outskirts, there is a trailer park – *Trailer Park las Americas* (☎22/47-01-34) where you can pitch a tent for $8 or park your trailer for $12. As the site of the Universidad de las Americas campus Cholula has become the **nightlife capital** of the Puebla region. Discos and bars cluster around 14 Pte. and 5 de Mayo. *Paradise* (open after 10pm; no cover) is probably the most lively.

Heading onwards you can get a slow, stopping, second-class bus straight to México, though it might actually save time to go via Puebla.

Tlaxcala

TLAXCALA, capital of the tiny state of Tlaxcala, is about 30km from Puebla. As Cortés' closest ally in the struggle against the Aztecs, the town suffered a very different fate from that of Cholula, but one that in the long run has led to an even more total disappearance of its ancient culture. For although the Spanish founded a town here – now restored and very beautiful in much of its original colonial glory – to the Mexicans Tlaxcala was a symbol of treachery, and to some extent it still is (in much the same way as Malinche is bitterly remembered in the commonly used insult *"hijo de la chingada"* son of the whore). Siding with Spain in the War of Independence didn't help greatly either, and whether for this reason, or for its genuine isolation, development has largely passed Tlaxcala by.

Tlaxcala today sits in the middle of a fertile, prosperous-looking upland plain surrounded by rather bare mountains and dominated, as you approach, by the **Santuario de Ocotitlán** on a height to the east. At the centre you'll discover an exceptionally pretty and very much rehabilitated colonial town, comfortable but in the final analysis fairly dull. Most of the interest lies very close to the zócalo, laid out with fountains and an ancient bandstand, populated by pigeons and squirrels. One entire side is taken up by the **Palacio de Gobierno** (daily 8am–6pm) whose patterned brick facade is broken by ornate windows and doorways. The building incorporates parts of a much earlier structure, erected soon after the Conquest, and inside boasts a series of brilliantly coloured murals by Desiderio Hernandez Xochitiotzin (a contemporary of Rivera's) dating from the early 1960s. Recently restored, these depict the history of the Tlaxcalan people from their migration from the north to their alliance with Cortés. The panels above the arches depicting rural life and the cultivation of maize and maguey are particularly good. Also on the zócalo the **Palacio de Justicia** has a giant clock, illuminated at night, which actually keeps time.

From a second, smaller plaza south of the zócalo, a broad flagged path leads up to the ex-Convento de San Francisco. Here, around the cloister, the **Museo Regional de**

Tlaxcala (daily 10am–5pm; free) covers local life from prehistoric times to the present day: an unexceptional collection but well displayed in a series of bare, whitewashed rooms. The church next door is also relatively plain, though it has a beautiful vaulted wooden ceiling and choir, decorated in *artesonado* style. The colourful *azulejos* inlaid in the floor echo a popular local fashion. One large chapel, more richly decorated than the rest, contains the font in which Xicohténcatl and the three other Tlaxcalan leaders were baptized in the presence of Cortés. Opposite, another small chapel shows traces of ancient frescoes.

Some 17km from Tlaxcala lies the ancient site of **Cacaxtla** (daily 10am–5pm; $5, free on Sun) where a series of murals, depicting battle scenes which are clearly Maya in style, continue to baffle archeologists. Two kilometres west of Cacaxtla, the ruins of **Xochitecatl** (daily 10am–5pm; $5, free on Sun) have three impressive pyramids and monolithic stones. Every Sunday the tourist office runs **guided tours** to both sites for $10. You're picked up outside the *Hotel Posada San Francisco* at 10am and dropped off at 1pm.

Practicalities

There is an almost constant stream of **buses** between Tlaxcala and Puebla or México, as well as many local services to nearby villages (both the brown *camionetas* roaming round town, and the real thing from the Camionera). Arriving, you can walk from the bus station to the zócalo in about ten minutes, downhill almost all the way, though you'll have to check directions. At the back of the Palacio de Gobierno there's a helpful

---

CLIMBING POPO AND IXTACCIHUATL

As long as you are acclimatized, adequately equipped and the weather conditions are right (see all below), anyone in reasonable physical condition can manage the **climb to the crater rim** – from where Cortés' men were repeatedly lowered to gather sulphur for gunpowder – and on to the summit. But even so it is not to be undertaken lightly – to be safe you need to make the traditional 3am start and expect to be out for around twelve hours. Ideally you should aim to join up with experienced climbers; easy enough to do, especially at weekends, as everyone stays at the refuge, but you might consider getting in touch with a **mountaineering club** beforehand. The *Club de Exploratiónes de México*, Juan Mateos 146, México 8 D.F., or the *Mountain Rescue Club*, San Juan de Letran 80, México D.F., should be able to put you in touch with someone, or you could try *Grey Line*, 166 Londres, México(☎5/208-11-63), a commercial operator who run all-inclusive trips for around $200 each.

The **Las Cruces** trail is the simplest and most easily followed of the half-dozen accepted routes, and one that you could feasibly do independently. A broad sandy path leaves from behind the refuge at Tlamacas, cutting left across the face of Popo to Las Cruces at 4480m. A 3am start should find you here around dawn, with Orizaba silhouetted on the horizon and the lights of the capital gradually disappearing behind their blanket of smog. From Las Cruces the path doubles back right up a 30° snow field to the crater rim at 5100m, from where it skirts right to the summit. Return by the same route.

Other routes up Popo require more finely honed mountaineering skills, some involving nights in very crude shelters high on the sides of Popo's secondary cone, Ventorillo (5000m). More details are available in the Tlamacas refuge.

Ixta is a more serious proposition, chiefly because it requires a night or two with all your gear at very high altitude (needing even more acclimatization) and involves a technical three-kilometre-long ridge traverse (often requiring ropes) to reach the highest point. It is also more difficult to get to; the trailhead is at La Joya some 12km from Tlamacas, beyond the microwave station visible on the side of Ixta. Again, more specialized informa-

tourist office (Mon–Fri 9am–7pm, Sat & Sun 10am–6pm; ☎246/2-00-27) where you can pick up useful free maps.

Just beyond the zócalo on Juárez, the *Maison Xicohténcatl*, Juárez 15 (☎246/2-19-00; ⑤) is a reasonable **place to stay**; farther out, the *Frontera* on Guillermo del Valle 82 (☎246/2-12-26; ②) has more character. Most other facilities – banks, post office, places to eat (there's something of a shortage of restaurants in Tlaxcala) – cluster round the zócalo. To return to the bus station, take the *camioneta* that stops on the corner by the church just off the zócalo.

Popocatépetl and Ixtaccíhuatl

Although you get excellent views of the snowy volcanic peaks of Popocatépetl and Ixtaccíhuatl from almost anywhere west of the capital, actually climbing the volcanoes, or at least spending some time in the national park that encompasses their lower slopes, is an exceptional experience. "Popo", at 5452m, is the taller of the two and though it hasn't had a full-throated eruption since 1802 has been rumbling and fuming away since September 1994: evacuation procedures are posted throughout surrounding towns. "Ixta", 5285m, is the more challenging climb for serious mountaineers and ranks third in height after the Pico de Orizaba and Popo.

The names stem from an Aztec Romeo and Juliet style legend. **Popocatépetl** (Smoking Mountain) was a warrior, **Ixtaccíhuatl** (White Lady) his lover, the beautiful daughter of the emperor. Believing Popocatépetl killed in battle, she died from grief,

tion is available locally or from Hilary Bradt's *Backpacking in Mexico and Central America*, or much more fully from R J Secor's *Mexico's Volcanoes* (see "Books" in *Contexts*).

EQUIPMENT AND CONDITIONS

Popo is snow-capped year-round and extremely cold, so any activity requires the right **equipment**: a hat, scarf, thick gloves, warm sweater, wind-proof jacket and dark sunglasses are the minimum. In addition you'll want to rent strong boots (*botas*; $6) on which to strap crampons (*crampones*; $6): both available at the refuge, though check the quality carefully. An ice axe (*piolet*; $6) and some knowledge of how to use it in an emergency is strongly advised.

What **season** you choose to climb counts for a lot. The best time is usually from October to January, when the snow is firm, and the storms common in February and March haven't yet set in. During the rainy season, from April to September, the mountain is covered in soft snow, making it even heavier work than normal.

ACCLIMATIZATION AND ACUTE MOUNTAIN SICKNESS

Even under ideal conditions, climbing Popo is a strenuous business, made all the more difficult by failure to take seriously the altitude increase. Some people manage to come up to the refuge from México, spend one night there then make a successful pitch for the summit the next morning. It is far more common, though, for aspirants to have to turn back through exhaustion or the early signs of **Acute Mountain Sickness** (aka Altitude Sickness): nausea, double vision and headaches – even fit people used to high altitude can be struck. If you experience any of these symptoms, the only solution is to descend immediately until the symptoms go away. It is far better to progress to altitude slowly, ideally spending a few days in México first, followed by a minimum of two nights at the refuge taking short walks up the mountain each day. Remember too that at high altitude you **dehydrate** quickly: take frequent breaks for food and drink at least two litres of liquid during the day.

and when he returned alive he laid her body down on the mountain, where he eternally stands sentinel, holding a burning torch. From the west, Ixta does somewhat resemble a reclining female form and the various parts of the mountain are named accordingly – the feet, the knees, the belly, the breast, the neck, the head, the hair.

Even if you have no aspirations to climb either mountain, a trip to the **Tlamacas** refuge (3940m), at the upper limit of the pine forests on the flanks of Popo makes a great break from the dirt and noise of the city. At weekends you'll be joining hundreds of Mexicans from the capital, taking in the cool air and strolling the trails around the Paso de Cortés, where a monument on the saddle between the two mountains remembers the spot where the Conquistadors caught their first glimpse of Tenochtitlán. Tlamacas is also the base for climbing Popo (see below).

To get to the **Parque Nactional de Volcánes**, take either a "Cristóbal Colón" or a "Servicio Volcánes" bus from TAPO (every 10min; 5.30am–10pm) to **AMECAMECA** (usually just Ameca) a lovely little town an hour south of México. Dramatic views of the mountain peaks are bizarrely framed by the palms of the zócalo around which you'll find a couple of good, inexpensive hotels and shops to stock up on supplies. From here a tarmac road leads 29km up to the Tlamacas refuge, but **buses** only head up there on Saturday and Sunday mornings (roughly every 20min; 6am–noon) returning later in the afternoon: catch them on 5 de Febrero on the corner of the square by the grain silos. Taxis to Tlamacas charge around $18 from Ameca ($45 from México). You could also take the bus (same stop) the 5km to San Pedro then hitch. When there's a heavy snowfall – most likely from December to February – the last 5–10km of the road can be impassable, otherwise the refuge is below the snow line.

There's nothing at Tlamacas except the **refuge** (check-in 8am–9.30pm; $3, bedding included), formerly an expensive hotel, which now provides year-round **dorm accommodation** for a hundred people. At weekends it is often full but, although you can reserve a place (☎515/553-58-96 in México, or call at Río Elba 20, ninth floor) bookings frequently get misplaced and you're better off just turning up; at worst they'll find you a mattress on the floor. Catering here is limited to tea, coffee and bottled water, so you should bring all the provisions you need and, if possible, cooking equipment.

fiestas

January

6th DÍA DE LOS SANTOS REYES (Twelfth Night). The Magi traditionally leave presents for children on this date: many small ceremonies include a fiesta with dancing at **Nativitas** (Distrito Federal), a suburb near Xochimilco, and at **Malinalco** (México state).

17th BENDICION DE LOS ANIMALES. Children's pets and peasants' farm animals are taken to church to be blessed. A particularly bizarre sight at the Cathedral in **México** and in **Taxco** (Guerrero), where it coincides with a fiesta running over into the following day.

February

2nd DÍA DE LA CANDELARIA is widely celebrated, especially in **Cuernavaca** (Morelos).

CARNIVAL (the week before Lent, variable Feb–Mar.) is especially lively in **Cuernavaca** (Mor.) and nearby **Tepoztlán** (Mor.). Also in **Chiconcuac** (Méx.) on the way to Teotihuacán. In **Xochimilco** (D.F.), for some reason, they celebrate Carnival two weeks after everyone else.

March

On the Sunday following March 9th a large *feria* with traditional dances is held at **San Gregorio Atlapulco**, near Xochimilco (D.F.)

PALM SUNDAY (the week before Easter) sees a procession with palms in **Taxco** (Gro.), where representations of the Passion continue through Holy Week.

HOLY WEEK itself is observed everywhere. There are very famous passion plays in the suburb of

Itzapalapa (D.F.), culminating on the Friday with a mock-crucifixion on the *Cerro de la Estrella*, and similar celebrations at **Chalma** (Méx.) and nearby **Malinalco**. In **Cholula** (Puebla), with its host of churches, the processions pass over vast carpets of flowers.

April

Cuernavaca's (Mor.) flower festival, the FERIA DE LA FLOR, usually falls in early April.

May

1st May Day, a public holiday, is usually marked by large marches and demonstrations in the capital. In **Cuautla** (Mor.) the same day sees a fiesta commemorating an Independence battle.

3rd DÍA DE LA SANTA CRUZ is celebrated with fiestas, and traditional dancing, in **Xochimilco** (D.F.) in **Tepotzotlán** (Méx) and in **Valle de Bravo** (Méx.)

5th Public holiday for the battle of Puebla – celebrated in **Puebla** (Pue.) itself with a grand procession and re-enactment of the fighting.

15th DÍA DE SAN ISIDRO. Religious processions and fireworks in **Tenancingo** (Méx.), and a procession of farm animals through **Cuernavaca** (Mor.) on their way to be blessed at the church.

On the third Monday of May there's a large religious festival in **Tlaxacala** (Tlax.) as an image of the Virgin is processed around the town followed by hundreds of pilgrims.

CORPUS CHRISTI (variable – the Thursday after Trinity). Thousands of children, rigged out in their Sunday best, gather in **México's** zócalo to be blessed.

June

29th DÍA DE SAN PEDRO observed with processions and dances in **Tepotzotlán** (Méx.) and traditional dancing in **San Pedro Actopan** (D.F.), on the southern outskirts of México.

July

16th DÍA DE LA VIRGEN DEL CARMEN. Dancers, and a procession with flowers to the convent of Carmen in **San Angel** (D.F.).

25th DÍA DE SANTIAGO particularly celebrated in **Chalco** (Méx.), on the way to Amecameca. The following Sunday sees a market and regional dances at the **Plaza de las Tres Culturas** (D.F.) and dances too in **Xochimilco** (D.F.).

29th DÍA DE SANTA MARTA in **Milpa Alta** (D.F.), near Xochimilco, celebrated with Aztec dances and mock fights between Moors and Christians.

August

13th Ceremonies in **México** commemorate the defence of Tenochtitlán, with events in the Plaza de las Tres Culturas, around the statue of Cuauhtémoc on Reforma and in the zócalo.

15th DÍA DE LA ASUNCION (Assumption) honoured with pilgrimages from **Cholula** (Pue.) to a nearby village, and ancient dances in **Milpa Alta** (D.F.).

September

8th A very ancient ceremony in **Tepoztlán** (Mor.), a Christianized version of homage to the Pyramid of Tepozteco, and more usual candle-lit religious processions in **Cuernavaca** (Mor.).

15th–16th INDEPENDENCE CELEBRATIONS everywhere, above all in the zócalo in **México** where the President proclaims the famous *grito* at 11pm on the 15th.

21st DÍA DE SAN MATEO celebrated in **Milpa Alta** (D.F.).

29th DÍA DE SAN MIGUEL provokes huge pilgrimages to both **Taxco** (Gro.) and **Chalma** (Méx.)

October

4th DÍA DE SAN FRANCISCO sees a *feria* in **Tenancingo** (Méx.), with much traditional music-making, and is also celebrated in **San Francisco Tecoxpa** (D.F.), a village on the southern fringes of the capital.

12th In **Tlaxacala** (Tlax.), a fiesta centring around one of the ancient churches.

November

1st–2nd DÍA DE LOS MUERTOS (All Souls) is observed by almost everyone and the shops are full of chocolate skulls and other ghoulish foods. Tradition is particularly strong in **San Lucas Xochimanca** (D.F.) and **Nativitas** (D.F.), both to the south of the city.

22nd DÍA DE SANTA CECILIA. Santa Cecilia is the patron saint of musicians, and her fiesta attracts orchestras and *mariachi* bands from all over to **Santa Cecilia Tepetlapa** (D.F.), not far from Xochimilco.

December

1st FERIA DE LA PLATA – the great silver fair in **Taxco** (Gro.) lasts about ten days from this date.

12th DÍA DE NUESTRA SEÑORA DE GUADALUPE – a massive pilgrimage to the **Basilica of Guadalupe** (D.F.) runs for several days round about, combined with a constant secular celebration of music and dancing.

CHRISTMAS. In the week leading up to Christmas *posadas* – nativity plays – can be seen in many places. Among the most famous are those at **Taxco** (Gro.) and **Tepotzotlán** (Méx.).

travel details

The capital is the centre of the nation to such an extent that any attempt at a comprehensive list of the comings and goings would be doomed to failure. What follows is no more than a survey of the major services on the main routes: it must be assumed that intermediate points are linked at least as frequently as those mentioned.

Buses

Literally thousands of buses leave México every day, and you can get to just about any town in the country, however small, whenever you want. The *Terminal del Norte* in particular serves as a base for a bewildering number of companies. Those below are a bare minimum of the main road routes.

Terminal del Norte

to: Aguascalientes (hourly; 7hr); Ciudad Juárez (hourly); Dolores Hidalgo (hourly; 5hr); Guadalajara (every 30min; about 9hr); Guanajuato (7 daily; 4hr); Hermosillo (4 daily); León (every 30min; 5hr); Los Mochis (4 daily); Matamoros (6 daily); Morelia (10 daily; 6hr); Nuevo Laredo (every 2hr); Patzcaro (hourly; 7hr); Querétaro (frequently; 1hr 30min–3hr); Saltillo (9 daily); San Luis Potosí (frequently; 5hr 30min); San Miguel Allende (every 30min; 4hr); Tepic (9 daily); Tuxpan (12 daily); Uruapán (9 daily; 6hr); Zacatecas (at least hourly; 8hr).

Terminal de Autobuses de Pasajeros de Oriente (TAPO)

to: Campeche (3 daily; 12+hr); Cancún (3 daily; 30+hr); Jalapa (every 30min; 6hr 30min); Mérida (6 daily; 28hr); Oaxaca (at least hourly; 9hr); Orizaba (16 daily); Palenque (2 daily); Playa del Carmen (3 daily; 30+hr); Puebla (every 5min; 2hr); Puerto Escondido (2 daily; 12hr); San Cristóbal (4 daily; 24hr); Tehuacan (hourly; 4hr); Tehuantepec (7 daily; 12hr); Tuxtla Gutiérrez (12 daily; 18hr); Veracruz (every 30min; 8hr); Villahermosa (hourly).

Terminal de Autobuses del Sur to: Acapulco
(hourly; 6–9hr); Chilpancingo (hourly; 3hr 30min); Colima (12 daily; 11hr); Cuernavaca (every 5min; 1hr 30min); Ixtapa (4 daily); Puerto Vallarta (6 daily; 14hr); Taxco (7 daily; 3hr 30min); Topoztlan (hourly); Zihuatanejo (6 daily; 9hr).

Terminal Poniente to: Morelia (every 20min);
Pátzcuaro (12 daily); Toluca (every 5min; 1hr 30min).

Cuernavaca to: Acapulco (10 daily; 6hr); Taxco
(12 daily; 2hr).

Puebla to: Oaxaca (10 daily; 7hr); Veracruz (12
daily; 6hr 30min)

Taxco to: Acapulco (2 daily; 5hr).

Toluca to: Morelia (8 daily; 4hr).

Trains

Smart, first-class-only services run daily from México to Guadalajara, Zacatecas, San Luis Potosí and San Miguel de Allende. There are ordinary first-class trains to Tijuana via Guadalajara, Ciudad Juárez, Monterrey, Veracruz, Oaxaca and points en route. Second-class services run on the same lines, but in general are to be avoided.

Planes

México has a busy international and domestic airport, with constant departures for points within the Republic. The following summarizes the major services:

Mexicana fly **México** to: Acapulco (7 daily; 1hr 55min); Guadalajara (14 daily; 1hr 5min); Mérida (6 daily; 1hr 45min); Monterrey (10 daily; 1hr 20min); Puerto Vallarta (4 daily; 1hr 20min); Tijuana (3 daily; 2hr 20min); Veracruz (5 daily; 50min).

Aeroméxico fly **México** to: Acapulco (8 daily; 1hr 55min); Guadalajara (21 daily; 1hr 5min); Mazatlán (3 daily); Monterrey (16 daily; 1hr 20min); Tijuana (12 daily; 2hr 20min).

CHAPTER SIX

ACAPULCO AND THE PACIFIC BEACHES

T he 800km stretch of coast between Puerto Vallarta and Punta Maldonada, where the Sierra Madre reaches out to the ocean to form a string of coves, bays and narrow stretches of sand, is lined with some of Mexico's most popular resorts. **Acapulco** – the original, the biggest, and still for many the best – is a steep-sided, tightly curving bay that for all its excesses of high-rise development remains breathtakingly beautiful, from a distance at least. This is still the stamping ground of the wealthy, whose villas, high around the wooded sides of the bay, offer

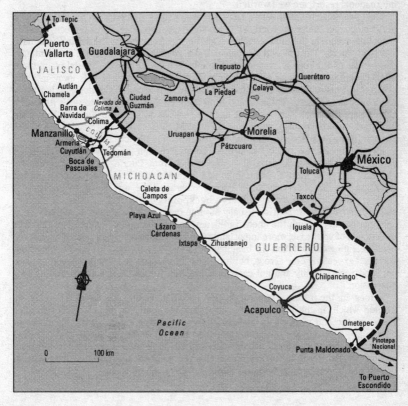

isolation from the packaged enclaves below. It's pricey, but not ridiculously so, and despite the tourists, the city itself remains very Mexican: run-down and often rather tawdry, as befits its status as a working port.

Puerto Vallarta, second in size and reputation, feels altogether smaller, more like the tropical village it claims to be, while in fact spreading for miles along a series of tiny beaches. More chic, younger, more overtly glamorous and certainly far more single-mindedly a resort, it lacks Acapulco's great sweep of sand but makes up for it with cove after isolated cove. Heading south from here, **Barra de Navidad** is still relatively little-known by foreigners, a lovely crescent of sand, backed for once by flatlands and lagoons, with a village at either end. By contrast **Manzanillo**, also well-connected with Guadalajara, is first and foremost a port and naval base – its pitch for resort status seems something of an afterthought. **Zihuatanejo** and its purpose-built neighbour **Ixtapa** are the most recently developed: Ixtapa so much so that there's nothing there but brand new hotels. Zihuatanejo is more attractive: almost, to look at, a mini-Acapulco, with magnificent villas mushrooming on the slopes overlooking the bay.

All along this coast, between the major centres, you'll find **beaches**: some completely undeveloped; others linked to a village with a few rooms to rent and a makeshift bar on the sand; and the odd few with an isolated, maybe even luxurious, hotel. The ocean breakers can be wild, positively dangerous at times, and there are minor discomforts – unreliable or nonexistent water and electricity supplies, vicious mosquitoes – but the space and the simplicity, often just an hour's drive from a packed international resort, are well worth it.

Most people arrive on the new, fast – and expensive – *Autopista del Sol* from México to Acapulco, but the **coast road**, whatever some old maps may say, is perfectly feasible – if a little rough in the final stretches – all the way from the US border to Guatemala. Between Puerto Vallarta and Acapulco, it's a good modern highway; unrelentingly spectacular as it forces its way south, sometimes over the narrow coastal plain, more often clinging precariously to the fringes of the Sierra where it falls away into the ocean. Most buses heading down from **Mazatlán** turn inland to Guadalajara, but many also continue to **Puerto Vallarta**, and from there on down Hwy-200 towards Acapulco. Guadalajara itself has very frequent bus connections with Puerto Vallarta, **Barra de Navidad** and **Manzanillo**, while from central Michoacán you can head down to the coast at **Lázaro Cárdenas**. **Zihuatanejo** has direct bus services from México.

Plentiful buses also run between these resorts, though you may have to change if you're travelling long-distance. It's easy to get from Puerto Vallarta to Barra de Navidad, and from there to Manzanillo and from Manzanillo to Lázaro Cárdenas, but there are few direct services from Puerto Vallarta all the way down. In the state of Guerrero there are occasional **military checkpoints** on the roads, where all traffic is stopped and searched. Tourists usually assume that this is for drugs, which may be at least partly true, though the check rarely amounts to more than a peremptory prod at the outside of your case; more importantly the hills remain wild and relatively undeveloped, retaining a reputation for banditry and guerrilla activity. This is not something you need expect to come across, but travelling these roads you should keep your passport and papers handy and not carry anything you wouldn't want discovered in your possession.

Prices in the resorts, particularly for accommodation, are dictated largely by **season** which, in the bigger places, stretches from early or mid-December to after Easter or the end of April. In high season the swankier hotels on the Pacific coast charge about double the off-season rates and need to be booked in advance. Budget hotels vary their rates less but costs are still 20–30 percent down outside the peak season. Smaller beach towns catering exclusively to Mexicans have a shorter season, usually just December and **Semana Santa**, but the same rules apply.

Puerto Vallarta

By reputation the second of Mexico's beach resorts, **PUERTO VALLARTA** is smaller, quieter and younger than Acapulco. In its own way it is actually every bit as commercial – perhaps more so, since here tourism is virtually the only source of income – but appearances count for much, and Puerto Vallarta, while doing all it can to catch up, appears far less developed. Its hotels are scattered along several miles of coast, the greatest concentration in **Nuevo Vallarta**, north of the town and sliced through by an eight-lane strip of tarmac, but there are no tall or obviously modern buildings in the centre; and the tropical village atmosphere, an asset assiduously exploited by the local tourist authorities, does survive to a remarkable degree.

The town's relative youth is undoubtedly a contributing factor. Until 1954 Puerto Vallarta was a small fishing village where the Río Cuale spills out into the Bahía de Banderas; then *Mexicana* airlines, their hand forced by *Aeroméxico*'s monopoly on flights into Acapulco, started promoting the town as a resort. Their efforts received a shot in the arm in 1964, when John Huston chose Mismaloya, 10km south, as the setting for his film of Tennessee Williams' play **The Night of the Iguana**, starring Richard Burton. The scandalmongering that surrounded Burton's romance with Elizabeth Taylor – who was not part of the cast but came along anyway – is often attributed to putting Puerto Vallarta firmly in the international spotlight: "a mixed blessing" according to Huston, who stayed on here until his death in 1987, and whose bronze image stands on the island in town.

The package tourists stay, on the whole, in the beach hotels around the bay; but are increasingly penetrating the town centre to shop in the pricey boutiques and malls on the streets leading back from the beachfront, and to eat in some of the very good restaurants both on the malecón and downtown. Nevertheless, what could be a depressingly expensive place to visit turns out to be liberally peppered with good-value hotels and a few budget restaurants, especially during the low season (Aug–Nov).

Arrival

The **Río Cuale**, spanned by two small bridges, divides Puerto Vallarta in two. Most of the town – the main square, official buildings, market, and the bulk of the shops and restaurants – lies on the north side. South you'll find the bus stations, the town beach, and the cheaper hotels. It's a very small place, hemmed in by the ocean and by the steep slopes behind – downtown, you can walk just about anywhere. Frequent buses run around the edge of the Bahía de Banderas to the north, towards the hotel zone (buses marked "Hoteles"), and, rather less efficiently, south to the smaller beaches.

The **airport** lies 7km north of the centre on the coastal highway, and is linked to the city by local buses which stop a few steps outside the perimeter fence. Airport taxis go right to the door but are, as ever, expensive: if you can find a *colectivo* it should be around a third of the price.

For years there has been talk of a centralized **Camionera** for Puerto Vallarta, though at the time of writing no site had been chosen. For the moment all the bus companies have offices within a few blocks of each other south of the river (see p.335), from where it's a short walk to the essential facilities and most of the hotels.

Remember that **if you've come south** from Tepic, San Blas, Mazatlán or points north along the coast, you need to advance your watch an hour: the time zone changes at the state border, just north of Puerto Vallarta's airport.

Information

The tolerably helpful **tourist office** (Mon–Fri 9am–9pm, Sat 9am–1pm; ☎322/2-02-42) is in the municipal palace just across the zócalo from the main *Banamex* (which will **change cheques** 9am–2pm). Numerous **casas de cambio** line the nearby streets: some offer criminal exchange rates but those at *Su Casa*, around the corner on Morelos, aren't bad and it stays open until 9pm (6pm on Sun). **American Express**, Morelos 660 at Abasolo (☎322/3-29-55), holds mail and changes cheques at poor rates. The main **post office**, Mina 188 (Mon–Fri 8am–7.30pm, Sat 9am–1pm), is two blocks north, just off the malecón; you can **phone long-distance** from either the *Tres Estrellas* or *Transportes del Pacifico* bus terminals.

For up-to-date, though promotional, information on what's going on in town, pick up the daily *Vallarta Today* (free, in gringo hangouts). If you find yourself in any sort of trouble or just need advice, approach one of the people dressed in white uniforms and pith helmets – these are the **tourist police**.

Accommodation

With the exception of the long lines of big package hotels along the beach, Puerto Vallarta's **places to stay** are within easy walking distance of each other. Most of the affordable options lie south of the Río Cuale, though there are a couple of places worth considering north of the river. The **budget accommodation** is concentrated along Madero – slightly seedy at night – but remember, too, that the pricier places can transform into bargains during the low season, when prices drop by 30–50 percent. For groups of up to six, fully equipped **apartments** can be very good value.

The town's only formal **campsite** is the grassy *Puerto Vallarta Trailer Park* (☎322/2-28-28; $9), several kilometres north of the hotel zone. Free camping on any of the more popular beaches around the middle of the bay is out, but if you're reasonably well provisioned and protected against mosquitoes you could try hiking out to **Punta Mita**, at the northern end of the bay, or south to **Boca de Tomatlán** (where the main road turns inland), each of which from time to time sees small communities establishing themselves on the sand. At **Yelapa**, a southern beach to which there are boat trips from town (see below), there's a small but rather pricey hotel, or you might be able to rent a hut or find somewhere to sling a hammock.

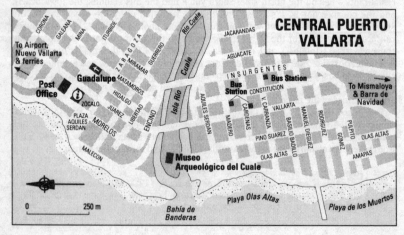

South of the Río Cuale

Apartmentos Posada Olas Altas, Olas Altas 356 at Basilio Badillo (no phone). Dingy but good-value apartments for up to four people, with simple kitchenettes. ③.

Hotel Posada Castillo, Madero 272 at Constitución (☎322/3-14-38). Very basic, but clean, rooms. Good rooftop views from top floor. ②.

Hotel Posada Río Cuale, Serdán 242 at Vallarta (☎322/2-09-14). One of the best-designed of the central hotels, with rooms staggered around gardens to give an open feel. Comfortable a/c rooms with balconies and a decent bar-restaurant beside the pool. ⑤.

Hortencia, Madero 336 at Insurgentes (☎322/2-24-84). Spacious, light quarters that justify the extra cash over the real cheapies. ③.

Lina, Madero 376, east of Insurgentes (☎322/2-16-61). Simple, clean, but slightly gloomy rooms around a courtyard. ②.

Mayo, Basilio Badillo 300 at Constitución (☎322/2-06-39). The ordinary rooms are nothing special but the *cabañas* – self-contained apartments with terraces – are far better. Enclosed parking. *Cabañas* for five cost $45. ④.

El Molino de Agua, Vallarta 130 (☎322/2-19-07). Fully in keeping with Puerto Vallarta's tropical village image, with cabins dotted around a pool in big, tranquil gardens where the Río Cuale meets the sea. ⑧.

Playa Los Arcos, Olas Altas 380 at Diéguez (☎322/2-15-83). The best of the beachfront hotels, with well-appointed a/c rooms around a large pool. ⑤.

Posada de Roger, Basilio Badillo 237 at Vallarta (☎322/2-06-39). Fairly modern, spacious, colonial-style hotel. Attractive rooms set around a shady courtyard where excellent breakfasts are served. Only a couple of blocks from the beach, and with a small pool. Rooms for up to five cost $42. ④.

Villa del Mar, Madero 440 at Jacarandas (☎322/2-07-85). Relaxed, long-time favourite of budget travellers. All rooms have bathrooms, the larger (slightly more expensive) ones also have small balconies. Some two-person apartments available. ④.

Yasmin, Basilio Badillo 168 (☎322/2-00-87). Clean rooms with fans, around a verdant courtyard one block from the beach. ③.

North of the Río Cuale

Casa Kimberley, Zaragoza 445 (☎322/2-13-36). Time-warped small hotel in the house Richard Burton bought for Liz Taylor's birthday in 1964. Except for the Liz memorabilia, the decor is little changed from when she sold it ten years later. Rooms are comfortable enough, with access to kitchenette and free breakfasts, but this is really a place for Liz freaks. Prices drop by 50 percent in low season. ⑦.

La Casa del Puente, Insurgentes just north of the river behind *Restaurant La Fuente del Puente* (☎322/2-07-49). A real home from home: spacious, elegantly furnished rooms (overlooking the river), and extremely attentive staff. Only three rooms: two "apartments" (with fully equipped kitchens), and one double, so book early. ⑨–⑦.

The Town

Apart from the **beaches**, and the tourist shops that pack the centre of town, there's not a great deal to do in Puerto Vallarta; certainly nothing in the way of sights or architecture. You could fill an hour or two, though, wandering around the area between the two plazas and on the island in the river. The **zócalo**, where everyone gathers in the evenings and at weekends, is backed by the **Church of Guadalupe**, its tower a city landmark, topped with a huge crown modelled on that of Maximilian's wife, Carlota, in the 1860s. Just down from here on the malecón, the old seafront, is the **Plaza Aquiles Serdan**, with a strange little amphitheatre looking out over the sea, and 100m off to the north another Puerto Vallarta icon, the seahorse statue.

On the **Isla Río Cuale** a small park surrounds a clutch of shops and restaurants. At the seaward end there's a tiny, irregularly open, local **archeology museum** (daily around 10.30am–3pm & 5–8pm), with half a dozen cases of local discoveries and a couple of benches overlooking the ocean – the best place in town to watch the sun set. Farther inland, expensive restaurants and **galleries** – including *Galeria Vallarta*, which sells and may swap second-hand English-language books – line the middle of the island towards the Insurgentes Bridge, where enterprising young boys make a few pesos posing for photos with their huge sun-baked iguanas. Beyond, past **John Huston's statue**, there's a park, a children's playground and a patch of river where women come to do the family washing, all overlooked from the hillsides by the fancy villas of "Gringo's Gulch".

Beaches in and around Puerto Vallarta

Puerto Vallarta's **beaches** vary in nature as you move round the bay: those to the north, out near Nuevo Vallarta and the airport, are long, flat stretches of sand often pounded by surprisingly heavy surf; south, a series of steep-sided coves shelter tiny, calm strands. The town beach, **Playa de los Muertos** (Beach of the Dead), or Playa del Sol, as the local tourist office would like it known, falls somewhere between the two extremes: not very large and reasonably calm, yet facing apparently open water. This is the most crowded of all, with locals, Mexican holidaymakers and foreign tourists, and in many ways it's the most enjoyable – plenty of people and activities on offer, food and drink close at hand. But don't leave anything of value lying about.

To the **north**, the best beaches tend to front the big hotels, which, since they all have pools and poolside bars, leaves the sand virtually deserted. However, it only really makes sense to make a special journey out here if you plan to sneak in and use the pool – easily enough done – since on all but the calmest days there's sand blowing around and waves that are great for surfers but not so good for swimming. The beaches can be rather dirty too, except right in front of the fancier hotels, where staff keep a patch cleared.

The smaller stretches of sand to the **south** are far more popular, and though the bus service in this direction is less regular there's no real problem in getting out to them. Buses leave from near the junction of Vallarta and Basilio Badillo, but the best bet is to climb up to the highway as it heads south out of town and start hitching – there's a fair amount of traffic and if the bus comes past it will stop for you. There are small beaches every few hundred metres, difficult to get to unless you are staying at one of the hotels or condos that back them, but the best-known and most convenient is **Mismaloya**, some 10km out of Puerto Vallarta. Here John Huston filmed *The Night of the Iguana*, building his film set on the southern side of a gorgeous bay at the mouth of what was once a pristine, jungle-choked gorge. Plans to turn the set and crew's accommodation into tourist cabins never came to anything, and now the huge and expensive *La Jolla de Mismaloya* hotel (⑨) completely dominates the valley. There's still a great beach though, and you can wander out to the point and the ruins of the film set. A string of identical *palapa* restaurants sell beer and seafood cocktails, and boats are on hand to take you snorkelling at **Los Arcos**, a federal underwater park and "eco-preserve" around a group of offshore islands, some formed into the eponymous arches. A superb array of brightly coloured fish – parrot, angel, pencil, croaker and scores of others – negotiate the rock walls and the boulder-strewn ocean floor 5m below. In addition to

---

TRIPS FROM PUERTO VALLARTA

There are **boat trips** out to Mismaloya from Puerto Vallarta; and for the beaches farther round in this direction – Playa Los Animas, Quimixto and Yelapa are the most common destinations – a boat is the only means of access. Travel agents all over town tout a variety of excursions, most of which leave from the new marina. Compare prices and what's on offer in the way of food and drink – if meals are not included it's worth taking your own food along. At **Yelapa** there's a small "typical" village not far from the white sand beach, and a waterfall a short distance into the jungle. It's no longer really deserted – there's a hotel and several tourist cabins – nor is it cheap, but with luck you might be able to rent a hut for very little, or at least you can always find somewhere to sleep out. To get there more cheaply, try going down to Puerto Vallarta dock early in the morning, when supply boats might give you a ride.

The others – Quimixto, Las Animas and so on – are beaches pure and simple. If you want to go **snorkelling** or **scuba diving** at either of them, tours are led by *Chico's Dive Shop*, Díaz Ordaz 770-5 (daily 9am–9pm; ☎322/2-18-95). You can rent gear here, too ($9 a day for the mask, snorkel and fins; $35–40 for the full scuba rig, including tank). It is usually too stiflingly humid to consider anything as energetic as **mountain biking**, but *Mountain Bike Adventures*, Guerrero at Miramar, just north of the upper river bridge (☎322/3-16-80), rents out bikes ($30 a day) and organizes tours into the jungly slopes behind the town and beyond.

---

the scheduled ninety-minute trips from the beach, boats are rented to groups for unlimited periods: if you're feeling adventurous, you could even rent snorkelling gear in Puerto Vallarta beforehand, get off the bus almost as soon as you see Los Arcos, and swim out to the islands; they're less than 300m offshore.

The stream running across Mismaloya beach flows down from **El Eden** – where the movie *Predator* was filmed – passing *Chino's Paradise*, a **restaurant** by a waterfall with a natural pool in which you can swim. Somewhat confusingly, there's also *Chico's Paradise* (daily 11am–6pm), a beautifully set but expensive restaurant, a farther 10km beyond Mismaloya on the main highway south, just after it turns inland. Below the restaurant, the Río Tuito tumbles over a jumble of smoothed rocks or, in drier times, forms cool, clear pools perfect for whiling away an afternoon. There's no formal **accommodation**, but there are sites for fully equipped campers. The *Indian Paradise* restaurant, immediately upstream in the small village of Las Juntas y Los Veranos, is more of the same, but if anything even more spectacular, with wooden walkways out to the huge rocks midstream.

Eating and drinking

Finding somewhere to eat in Puerto Vallarta is no problem – tourist restaurants offering cocktails by candlelight abound – but eating cheaply is rather less easy. As always, the area around the bus station is a good bet for plain, fast food, and as usual the market – on the north bank of the river by the upper bridge – has a few cheap *comedors* tucked away upstairs, overlooking the river, well away from the souvenir stalls that fill the rest of the building. *Taco* and hot-dog stands line the streets, while kids on the beach offer freshly caught fish, roasted on sticks. For a **fast-food** fix, head for the *McDonald's*, *KFC* and glut of pizza places on the malecón and north into the hotel zone. *Gutiérrez Rizo Supermarket*, at Serdán and Constitución, sells **picnic** supplies.

On the whole, for reasonable, straightforward **restaurants** you're better off on the north bank in the centre of town, although south of the Río Cuale along Av. Olas Altas, and particularly on Basilio Bodillo between Suárez and Insurgentes, several restaurants bridge the gap between out-and-out tourist traps and plainer eating houses.

Of **more expensive places** you can really take your pick: most offer some form of music or entertainment, or at least a good view while you eat, and almost all display their menus outside, so you know what you're letting yourself in for.

South of the Río Cuale

Archie's Wok, Francisco Rodríguez 130 near Playa de los Muertos (☎322/2-04-11). Superb, freshly prepared and reasonably priced Indonesian, Thai and Chinese food whipped up by the former private chef to John Huston.

Casa de los Hotcakes, Basilio Badillo 289. Ridiculously named tent-like affair serving good pancakes, waffles and blintzes to a tourist crowd.

El Palomar de los Gonzáles, Aguacate 425 (☎322/2-07-95). Elegant, mainly Mexican and seafood restaurant, high on the hill to the south of the centre with fine views over the city. The place to take your credit card for that romantic candlelit dinner. Evenings only; closed Sun.

El Torito, Vallarta 290 at Carranza. Bar and restaurant for sports jocks with satellite coverage of everything from *Serie A* to the Superbowl. Ribs a speciality.

El Tucán, Vallarta 332 at Basilio Badillo. Very good-value Mexican and continental breakfasts, omelettes and pancakes until 2pm, served in the cool courtyard of the *Posada de Roger* hotel.

Karpathos Taverna, Gómez at Playa de los Muertos (☎332/3-15-62). Airy dinner-only restaurant delivering a fairly standard Greek menu. The prices aren't too bad though, and the food's great.

King's Head Pub, Vallarta 229 at Carranza. British beer (occasionally draught), darts, fish and chips and sometimes decent music.

Los Tres Huastecas, Olas Altas 444 at Francisco Rodrígues. Bargain Mexican and seafood restaurant, right near Playa de los Muertos, with top-value *comidas corridas*.

Natural, Madero 325, east of Insurgentes. Bright and breezy snack bar with great *tortas*, *tacos* and *licuados*.

Pizza Joe, Basilio Badillo 269 (☎322/2-24-77). Mediterranean dining, al fresco beside a tinkling fountain. Very good pastas, pizza, and Italian desserts come with attentive service. Closed Sun.

Quino's, Serdán 438 (☎322/2-12-15). Away from most of the crowds, this excellent, upmarket seafood restaurant lies on a quiet street opposite the top end of Isla Río Cuale.

Vallarta Paradise, Lázaro Cárdenas 341, east of Insurgentes. Nothing but straightforward good Mexican food. About the cheapest decent breakfasts and *comidas corridas* around.

Viejo Ingles, Vallarta 179 at Serdán. Moderately priced restaurant with rooftop terrace serving English staples: shepherd's pie, ploughman's lunches and, of course, fish and chips.

North of the Río Cuale

Café Cristóbal, Corona 172. Relaxing spot to sip a flavoured coffee or cappuccino while flicking through their stock of magazines. Cakes and light snacks, too.

La Chata, Malecón 708 at Dominguez (☎322/3-16-84). Typically tasty Jaliscan food, lightly spiced. Enliven it with whatever you fancy from the stuff on the table. Occasional live music and happy hour almost all afternoon.

Le Bistro Jazz Café, Isla Río Cuale, just east of Insurgentes (☎322/2-02-83). Sophisticated, predominantly seafood dining in black-and-white surroundings, soothed by cool jazz. On the expensive side but a great place to wind down. Open from 8am for breakfast too.

Ocean Bar, Malecón 538. Not too pricey bar and restaurant – a good place to watch the sunset.

Nightlife and entertainment

Most of the **drinking** in Puerto Vallarta is done in the restaurants, though many of the places along the malecón specialize in creating a high energy party-time atmosphere. Old favourites like the *Hard Rock Café* and *Carlos O'Brian's* are here, along with local contenders *Zoo*, *No Name Café* and *Cactus Club*. All open onto the malecón and none has a cover charge, making it easy to wander along and take your pick of the **happy hours**.

Nightclubs are a different matter, charging up to $15 for entry, though by asking around you'll come across free nights early in the week, should find half-price coupons (try the timeshare touts), and can always try talking your way in. *Christine's*, at the *Hotel Krystal* way up in the hotel zone, is lively, expensive and pretentious; *Diva*, Vallarta 268, south of the river, is more human and cheaper.

Sunday tends to be quiet – some places close – except on the zócalo where, from around 6pm, huge crowds gather around the dozens of *taco* and cake stands and listen to the brass band. And there's always the **pool hall** at Madero 279.

Listings

Airlines *Aero California* (☎322/4-14-99); *Aeroméxico* (☎322/1-10-97); *Alaska* (☎322/3-03-50); *American* (☎322/3-62-70); *Continental* (☎322/1-10-25); *Delta* (☎322/1-10-32); *Mexicana* (☎322/2-50-00); *Taesa* (☎322/1-15-21).

Consulates *Canada*, Hidalgo 226 (Mon–Fri 9am–noon, until 1pm in winter; ☎322/2-53-98); *USA*, Parian del Puente 12-A, right by the Insurgentes river bridge (Mon–Fri 9am–1pm; ☎322/2-00-69).

Doctor English-speaking medics at *CMQ Clinic*, Basilio Badillo 365 between Insurgentes and Aguacate (☎322/2-51-41). Also *Cruz Roja* (☎322/2-15-33).

Laundry *Lavanderia Blanquita*, Madero 407, east of Aguacate (Mon–Sat 8am–8pm). There's also a full-service place just up from here at Madero 430 (8am–8pm).

Pharmacy *CMP*, Basilio Badillo 367 (☎322/2-29-41), next to *CMQ* Clinic, is open 24hr; *Lux*, Insurgentes 169 (☎322/2-19-09).

MOVING ON FROM PUERTO VALLARTA

Until the construction of Puerto Vallarta's proposed **Central Camionera**, buses will continue to leave from several locations south of the river. **Elite** and **Tres Estrellas de Oro** (☎322/3-11-17) first-class services leave from the corner of Basilio Badillo and Insurgentes to destinations including Acapulco, Guadalajara, Mazatlán and México. **ETN** (☎322/3-29-99) and **Primera Plus** (☎322/2-69-86) buses leave from Lázaro Cárdenas 258 between Constitución and Vallarta. *ETN* run super-deluxe services to Guadalajara and México, while *Primera Plus* first-class buses go to Barra de Navidad, Colima, Guadalajara and Manzanillo.

Second-class services, run by *Autocamiones del Pacifico* and *Transportes Cihuatlán* (both ☎322/2-34-36), leave from the corner of Madero and Constitución for Guadalajara (2 daily; 9hr), Manzanillo (9 daily; 5–7hr) and Tepic (every 30min; 2hr 30min). The station has a *guardería*.

Puerto Vallarta is well served by **flights** to other Mexican cities and North America. Prices vary dramatically with season and availability but, organized from this end, tend not to be cheap. You can contact the **airport** (☎322/1-12-98) for further details, or call the **airlines** direct. Travel agents such as *SAET Travel Service*, in the Centro Commercial at the corner of Morelos and Rodríguez (Mon–Fri 9am–2pm & 4–7pm, Sat 9am–2pm; ☎322/2-18-86), or any of the many agencies north of the river, can provide up-to-date information and advice.

North of Puerto Vallarta – Punta Mita

North of Puerto Vallarta, over the state line in Nayarit, the **Bahía de Banderas** arcs out to Punta Mita, some 30km away. A summer preserve for Mexicans from Guadalajara and a winter retreat for RVers from the north, these gorgeous beaches offer facilities in just a couple of spots – **Nuevo Vallarta** and **Bucerías** – leaving miles of secluded strand for free camping. To get out there from Puerto Vallarta, the best bet is to board a second-class, Tepic-bound *Autocamiones del Pacifico* bus from the depot, and alight at Bucerías. To continue, hitch or flag down any Punta Mita-bound bus. *Autotransportes Medina*, Brasil 1279 near the *Buenaventura Hotel* in the hotel zone, also runs a daily service to Punta Mita.

Nuevo Vallarta and Bucerías

The embryonic development of **NUEVO VALLARTA**, 9km north of Puerto Vallarta's airport, is a planned mega-resort that has yet to fruit. As you might expect, the beach is great and there's the *Club-Med*-style Jack Tar Village, where $40-odd will buy you a day frolicking with all the watersports gear. Here too is the arty-crafty **Museo Regional Bahía de Banderas** (daily 9am–2pm; free). **Bahía Azul**, a couple of kilometres farther along the same fine sand beach, is a mainly Mexican strand with facilities limited to one shop on the main road.

It is better to push on to another great beach at **BUCERÍAS**, the last of the bay resorts on Hwy-200, with views across the water to Puerto Vallarta from the seafront restaurants. *Adriano's* in particular is superb, if pricey. There's a smallish town here, several apartment-type places, *Motel Marlyn* (⑦) and the *Bucerías Trailer Park*.

Keeping to the coast, you leave the main highway for Punta Mita, passing the beach-free fishing village of **Cruz De Huanacaxtle** and **Playa Manzanillo**. Just over the headland, the coral sand **Piedra Blanca** has a nice relaxed atmosphere, apartments (☎361/7-60-31; ⑦) and an adjacent trailer park. The Punta Mita road continues through jungly terrain, small roads dipping down to secluded beaches, the two *enramadas* at **Destiladeras** being the only facilities. Camping on the beach is great but you need to bring everything. If you're lucky, though, you may find the freshwater seepage on the beach that gives the place its name.

Punta Mita is more developed. You have to camp if you want to stay, but at least there's a grocery store, and you can spend the day snorkelling or boogie boarding with gear rented from the same people who run sport fishing trips and cruises out to the offshore wildlife sanctuary of **Islas Las Marietas**.

Bahía de Navidad

There's not a great deal to delay you in the 200-odd kilometres south from Puerto Vallarta to Barra de Navidad. For much of the way the road runs away from the coast, and where it finally does come in striking distance of the ocean it's either for a fabulously expensive resort development, as at **Costa Careyes**, or a beach, such as **Tenacatitla**, which is easily outshone by those on the Bahía de Navidad. The most tempting-looking beaches are approximately halfway at **Chamela**, a small resort stretched around the wide Bahía de Chamela, with a couple of trailer parks and simple facilities.

Better to press on to the twin towns of **Barra de Navidad** and **San Patricio-Melaque**, among the most enticing destinations on this entire stretch of coastline. They're not undeveloped or totally isolated – indeed, families from Guadalajara come here by their hundreds, especially at weekends – neither are they at all heavily commercialized: just small, simple, very Mexican resorts. The entire bay, the Bahía de Navidad, is edged by fine sands and, if you're prepared to walk, you can easily leave the crowds behind. Regular buses and *colectivos* connect the two communities, or you can walk it along the beach in around half an hour.

Barra de Navidad

Lying towards the southern end of the bay, where the beach runs out and curves back round to form a lagoon behind the town, **BARRA DE NAVIDAD** is the more appealing of the Bahía de Navidad communities. A couple of kilometres north, San Patricio-Melaque, at the other end of the same beach, is slightly less attractive and more commercial, but if you can't find a room in Barra, it makes a good second choice and the range of budget hotels there is considerably wider.

Things look set to change around here after the opening of the *Gran Bahía* hotel, golf course and marina complex across the channel from Barra de Navidad. Undoubtedly there will be an increase in the boat services – either the *cooperativo*, or the less expensive service from outside the *Restaurant Manglito* near the jetty – which currently run across the channel (every 30min 7am–7pm; 50¢) and, less frequently, to the beaches on the other side. Beach-restaurant-backed **Colimilla** ($10 return), across the Laguna de Navidad, is the most popular destination, chiefly for the seafood and as a base for the two- or three-kilometre walk over to the rough Pacific beach of Playa de Cocos. The *cooperativo* also offers fishing trips, lagoon tours and water skiing.

Practicalities

Buses arrive in Barra at either of two terminals almost opposite each other on Av. Veracruz, the town's main drag. The services you are likely to need – post office, *larga distancia* phones and hotels – are all close by: in any case, it only takes twenty minutes to walk around the whole town. The one shortcoming is that there is **no bank** or *casa de cambio*: Cihuatlán, fifteen minutes' bus ride away, has the nearest bank with an ATM and other facilities, or there's a *casa de cambio* in San Patricio. The **tourist office** (Mon–Fri 9am–7pm, Sat 9am–1pm; ☎335/5-51-00) is tucked away in some outbuildings of a private club just back from the beach at the north end of town. They can advise on anything happening locally – usually not much – though you can probably obtain more useful information from Bob, who runs *Bob's Bookswap* at Mazatlán 61, one room absolutely packed with English-language paperbacks: bring one and take one, no charge.

Barra has a couple of small cheap **hotels** and some classier options. Free camping is also a possibility along the beach to the north of town. It is easiest to follow the beach, rather than the road, up to a point where you feel comfortable, as beach access is limited. The best budget option in town is *Posada Pacífico*, inland at Mazatlán 136 (☎335/5-53-59; ③), a simple, friendly place with clean airy rooms, some with balconies. Slightly run-down, *Bungalows Karelia*, on López de Legazpi by the central plaza (☎335/5-53-84; ⑤), has a nice seafront verandah and apartments with simple kitchens. *El Delfín*, Morelos 23 (☎335/5-50-68; ⑤), is a multistorey hotel with spacious clean rooms, a small pool, and sea views from the upper floors. Good value for groups, with rooms that sleep up to five people, the *Tropical*, López de Legazpi 196 (☎335/5-50-20; ⑦), is a slightly worn hotel right by the sea, with a pool and decent bar-restaurant. Some of the large fan-ventilated rooms have balconies.

The junction of Veracruz and Jalisco is the first stop for **restaurants**. Here you'll find *Restaurant Patty*, the best of a number of similar budget places serving excellent *ceviche*, fresh fish and meaty Mexican staples. Next door, *Ivette* dishes up good pizza, while diagonally opposite, *Café Ambar* is renowned for its crêpes, salads and vegetarian dishes. Early in the day, the *Hotel Delfín* does a good continental breakfast with either *huevos al gusto* or banana pancakes, and you can try their Bavarian grilled sausage. Exclusively **seafood restaurants** crowd Legazpi and Morelos down towards the point: *El Manglito* is one of the best. **Nightlife** is limited to playing pool and drinking at *Giff's Barra* on Legazpi – not as seedy as it sounds – listening to live music at *Rocky's Café*, Jalisco 70, and dancing at *El Galeón* disco.

San Patricio-Melaque

SAN PATRICIO-MELAQUE seems much more of a real Mexican town, with its zócalo, church, largish market, and substantial bus station at the junction of Carranza and Gómez Farías. Opposite, in the Pasaje Commercial, you'll find the town's only **casa de cambio** and *larga distancia* (Mon–Sat 9am–2pm & 4–7pm, Sun 9am–2pm): rates are poor. The **post office** is hidden on Orozco, a block seaward and two blocks east of the zócalo.

There's no **tourist office**, but you can find out all you need to know by talking to Phil at *Los Pelicanos*, one of the restaurants at the northern end of the beachfront. She is rightly renowned for her excellent food and always seems ready to talk. In addition to the identikit restaurants along the same strip, you could try the cheaper *comidas* on the streets beachside of the zócalo and around the market on c/Corona.

Free **camping** is an option on the patch of wasteland at the northern end of the beach beyond the restaurants, and there's a full facility campsite right by the beach, *Trailer Park Playa*, Gómez Farías 250 at López Mateos (☎333/5-50-65; $11), but if you want a roof over your head, walk along Gómez Farías, parallel to the beach. *San Patricio*, Gómez Farías 413 (☎333/7-02-44; ③), is the best of the budget places, with outside kitchens and a communal dining area; some apartments (sleeping up to eight) have kitchenettes. There's safe parking, too. In the same vein, *El Marquez*, Gómez Farías 407 (☎333/5-52-13; ⑥), is more luxurious and considerably more expensive. *Posada Pablo de Tarso*, Gómez Farías 408 (☎333/7-01-17; ⑥), has comfortable and nicely furnished rooms, with TV and phone, around a verdant courtyard, and a good pool. Apartments ($52–90) sleep between three and six people. Note that during **Semana Santa**, even the high-season rates quoted here can double.

Manzanillo

Two roads head **inland to Guadalajara** from this part of the coast. The direct-looking route from Barra de Navidad is indeed reasonably fast (although any route has to tangle spectacularly with the Sierra Madre) but it's also very dull, with just one town of any size, the dusty, provincial and untempting community of Autlán. The journey along the coast to **Manzanillo** and inland via **Colima** is considerably more interesting, not only for the towns themselves but also for the spectacular snowcapped volcanoes that come beyond.

Just an hour down the road from the Bahía de Navidad, **MANZANILLO** is a very different sort of place: a working port where tourism – although highly developed – very definitely takes second place to trade. Downtown, it has to be said, is not at all attractive: crisscrossed by railway tracks, rumbling with heavy traffic and surrounded by a bewildering array of inner harbours and shallow lagoons that seem to cut the place off from the land. You can easily imagine that a couple of hundred years ago plague and pestilence made sailors fear to land here, and it's not surprising to read in an 1884 guide to Mexico that "the climate of Manzanillo is unhealthy for Europeans, and the tourist is advised not to linger long in the vicinity". Few tourists do stay even now – most are concentrated in the hotels and club resorts around the bay to the west – but although the streets are still narrow and none too clean, the town is healthy enough and there's a certain shabby romance in staying in the centre. Certainly it's a lot more interesting than the sanitized resort area, and cheaper too. Buses out to the beach are frequent and efficient, but if you are kicking your heels in the centre, you could climb one of Manzanillo's **hills** for a better view of the bay, or leap on one of the sunset cruises (5pm daily; $14), that leave from near *La Perlita* restaurant (see below).

Arrival and information

Manzanillo's **bus station** is inconveniently sited more than 1km east of town, and though there are buses (marked "Centro") these are slow and avoid the zócalo, where you really want to be. Better to walk or take a taxi, most likely passing the **train station** on Morelos, which receives one Guadalajara train per day. Manzanillo's commercial core centres on its zócalo, the **Jardín Alvaro Obregón**, right on the harbourfront opposite the main outer dock. All the hotels, restaurants, banks and offices are a˛very short walk away. *Banamex* and *Bancomer* **banks** (both with ATMs) are next to each other on Av. México at c/10 de Mayo, there's a *larga distancia* booth (8am–10pm; collect calls) on the Jardín Obregón at Dávalos 27, and the **post office** is a block east at Juárez and 5 de Mayo.

Accommodation

Finding a place to stay is no problem in Manzanillo; there's a range of budget to moderately priced hotels, though nothing special, close to the centre. Prices at all but the cheapest drop by about 25 percent outside the July, August, Christmas and *Semana Santa* **high season**. Close to the bus station, *Casa de Huéspedes del Puerto*, Manuel Alvarez 3 (☎333/2-36-95; ②), is basic and inexpensive: turn left beside the bus station and second right. In town the cheapest bet is the friendly *Casa de Huéspedes Petrito*, Allende 20 (☎333/2-01-87; ②), with small, clean rooms and shared showers. Just off the zócalo, the *Emperador*, Dávalos 69 (☎333/2-23-74; ③), has decent rooms with hot showers and fans, and a cheap *comedor* too: far better value than some of the pricier places nearby. If you have the money, though, head straight for *Colonial*, Av. México 100 (☎333/22-10-80; ⑤), where attractive rooms with TV are set around a Moorish-style courtyard with Andalucian *azulejos* and a cooling fountain. If you want to be by the sea, try *Motel Playa San Pedrito*, José Azueta 3 (☎333/2-06-35; ⑤), a rambling place around a pool and tennis court, backing onto **Playa San Pedrito**, about 1km east of the centre (twenty minutes' walk from the zócalo along the waterfront). Spacious and well-equipped apartments sleep six and cost $70 in high season. This beach is probably your best bet for camping, too: Manzanillo has no trailer park and all the other beaches are pretty built up.

Eating and drinking

Places to eat are concentrated around the zócalo, with several good cafes overlooking the Jardín Obregón itself. *Chantilly* on Juárez (closed Sat) and *Roca del Mar*, diagonally opposite, both serve a huge range of decent meals, top-value *comidas corridas* and good espresso and cappuccino. Between the two, *Portofino*, Juárez 116 (☎333/2-42-93), is mainly a pizza delivery place but you can eat in too. Heading east along Morelos, parallel to the waterfront, you come to *La Perlita*, which dishes up *antojitos* and seafood on shaded tables close to the water and, a little farther along, *Lychee*, Niños Héroes 397 (closed Sun), which serves not bad, moderately priced Chinese food. If you head down México, Manzanillo's main commercial and shopping street, you'll find a whole series

---

MOVING ON FROM MANZANILLO

Half a dozen **bus** companies provide services from the Central Camionera along the coast and inland to Colima and Guadalajara. Both *Transportes Sur de Jalisco* and *Soc. Coop de Transportes* run to Colima (6 an hour between them; 2hr), the former also serving Tecomán (every 20min; 1hr), Guadalajara (7 daily; 5–6hr) and Lázaro Cárdenas (6 daily; 6–7hr). *Autobuses de Occidente* runs first-class *Primera Plus* buses to Colima (every 30min; 1hr 30min) and Guadalajara (every 30min; 6hr). *Pacifico/Cihuatlán* serve Barra de Navidad (1hr 30min) and Puerto Vallarta (6hr) with hourly second-class and two first-class buses a day, and *Tres Estrellas* runs first-class to Acapulco (12hr) and all points to Tijuana (38hr).

The sad legacy of Porfirio Diaz's grand designs to link Guadalajara and Manzanillo by **train** is two shabby carriages (one first-class, one second-) leaving Manzanillo at 11.10pm. Tickets (bought from the station an hour before departure) cost two-thirds of the cheapest bus fare in first-class, half that in second-class. When they finish fixing the tunnels (maybe late in 1995, maybe not), the timetable may (or may not) revert to a 6am departure from Manzanillo.

of further possibilities, from take-away *taquerías* and the tiny vegetarian *Yacatecuhtli* at 249, to the fancy restaurant in the *Hotel Colonial*. At the other end of the scale, there are several very cheap places – grimy and raucous on the whole – around the Mercado Francisco Madero, five blocks down México, and at the bottom end of Juárez by the railway tracks.

The coast

While locals might go **swimming** from the tiny harbour beach of San Pedrito and in the Laguna de Cuyutlán behind the town, both are thoroughly polluted. Far better to head for beaches around the bay proper, where the tourist hotels are. The nearest of these, at **LAS BRISAS**, are in fact very close to town, just across the entrance to the inner harbour, but to get there by road you have to go all the way round the Laguna de San Pedrito, before turning back towards Manzanillo along the narrow strip of land that forms Las Brisas. Frequent buses from the centre (marked "Las Brisas") run all the way along the single seafront drive; it's a rather strange area, as much suburb as resort, and the beach, steeply shelving and often rough, is perhaps not as good as those round the bay in the other direction. As the original seaside strip, Las Brisas offers a number of older, and consequently cheaper, hotels and restaurants, but – except when it's flooded by holidaymakers from Guadalajara – the whole place has a depressing, run-down feel. If you want to stay by the beach, take the bus out here and have a look around – *Las Brisas*, Lázaro Cárdenas 1243 (☎333/3-27-17; ④), and the marginally better equipped *Star*, Lázaro Cárdenas 1313 (☎333/3-25-60; ⑤), are among the cheapest. Several places offer **cabins or apartments** for larger groups, but none is particularly good value: *Bungalows Angelica*, Lázaro Cárdenas 1578 (☎333/3-29-82), with a pool and apartments for up to six people for $82, is about the best but not by much. If you can afford it, continue to *La Posada*, Lázaro Cárdenas 201 (☎333/3-18-99; ⑦), a delightful small hotel with huge breakfasts included.

Better and more sheltered swimming can be found along the coast farther round, where the bay is divided by the rocky Peninsula de Santiago. "Miramar" buses run all the way round to the far side of the bay, past the settlements of **Salahua** and **SANTIAGO** and a string of beaches. The best are around the far edge of the peninsula (get off the bus at Santiago). Here you'll find the excellent-value **hotel** *Maria Cristina*, 28 de Augusto 36 (☎333/3-24-70; ⑥), two blocks inland from Santiago's zócalo, with a pool, pleasant garden and rooms which can take four people for much the same price. There are several restaurants here, too, both in the village and down on the beach: *Juanito's*, on the highway, is a long-standing favourite with North Americans and locals alike.

If you're prepared to walk a little way out onto the peninsula, you can reach the beautiful cove of **La Audiencia**, with calm water and tranquil sand. From here, if you're feeling reasonably energetic and looking smart enough to get past the guards, you can climb over the hill to **Las Hadas** (☎333/3-00-00; ⑨) – the amazingly flashy, glistening white hotel-villa complex where Dudley Moore and Bo Derek frolicked in *10*. It's worth seeing even if you can't afford a drink at any of the many bars. There's more flash and glitz at the *Club Maeva* (☎333/3-01-41; ⑧), farther round the bay on the **Playa Miramar**, but on the whole the hotels in the vicinity are thoroughly average, and **nightlife**, such as it is, is confined to a few discos strung out along the coast road.

South from Manzanillo

If all you need is a heaving ocean and a strip of beach backed by a few *enramadas* (restaurants under *palapas*), then you're better off skipping Manzanillo altogether in favour of a series of infinitely preferable, though tiny, resorts that adorn the shoreline

50–80km beyond. Easily accessible by bus, **Cuyutlán**, **Paraíso** and **Boca de Pascuales** boast great beaches that draw Mexican holidaymakers, but none is in any way elaborate, each equipped with very few facilities. To get to Cuyutlán and Paraíso from Manzanillo, catch a bus (every 15min) 50km to the inland market town of Armería. The town has a bank, post office, a long-distance bus stop on the main street, and, three blocks to the north outside the *Camino Real* restaurant, a stand for local buses to the beaches, Buses leave from here to Cuyutlán (every 30min; 20min) and Paraíso (every 45min; 15min), a few kilometres further south. For buses to Boca de Pascuales (every 30min until 6pm; 25min) you'll need to take a direct bus from Manzanillo and change at the market town of **Tecomán**, 20km south of Armería. Buses also run from here to Colima and Lázaro Cárdenas, and there are banking facilities.

Cuyutlán

CUYUTLÁN, the largest of the three coastal resorts some 12km southwest of Armería, is perhaps the most appealing, backed by an immense coconut grove that stretches along a narrow peninsula from here almost to Manzanillo. The old town around the zócalo is sleepy, its inhabitants idling away the day on wooden verandahs under terracotta roofs. Life in the hotels by the beachfront malecón isn't much faster, except in the Christmas, *Semana Santa* and August high season, when things liven up considerably and you should book ahead if you want to stay.

In spring, the coast both here and farther south is subject to the **Ola Verde**: vast, dark green waves up to 10m high that crash down on the fine grey sand. Theories to explain their green hue vary widely – from the angle of the sun refracting off the wave to algal bloom – but whatever the reason, the Ola Verde has entered Cuyutlán mythology. Apparently, however, it has been mysteriously absent the last few years. At other times of the year the surf is impressive but easier to handle.

Outside the high season, **hotels** are affordable (rates usually per person in low season) and all clustered within a block or two of the junction of Hidalgo and Veracruz. If you need to book, call the *larga distancia* office (☎332/4-18-10) in town and ask for the hotel extension number quoted. The ones to go for are *Morelos*, Hidalgo 185 (ext. 107; ④), with good clean rooms, fans and hot water; and the fifty-year-old *Fenix*, Hidalgo 201 (ext. 147; ④ full board), which has some great old-fashioned rooms opening onto spacious communal verandahs. *San Rafael*, Veracruz 46 (ext. 108; ⑤ full board), is only marginally better and probably not worth the extra cost. Rates quoted are all high season. All three hotels have good **seafood restaurants**.

To get to Cuyutlán, you can take the bus from Armería, or drive on either Hwy-200 (signed turn-off 5km before Armería) or the new and little-used Manzanillo–Colima *autopista* that runs along the coast parallel to the train line. The train from Manzanillo will stop on request – ask the conductor before you board – but on the current timetable will drop you 1km from the beach at around midnight.

Paraíso

With your own vehicle you can reach **PARAÍSO** directly from Cuyutlán, but by bus you'll have to return to Armería. From there it is 8km to this tiny place that gives the impression that it is only just hanging on, with a few neglected buildings either side of the dust and cobble street. The beach is fun, though, with banks of crashing surf, and a few *enramadas* behind. Only at *Hotel Paraíso*, right on the seafront (mobile ☎331/8-10-09; ⑤), is the feeling of dilapidation dispelled. The older rooms have character, the new wing is more comfortable; everyone uses the pool and watches the sunset from the bar. If you **camp** on the beach they'll let you use a shower, especially if you buy a drink. About the only other place to stay is the plain *Posada Valencia* (☎331/2-29-10 and ask for *Posada Valencia*; ④).

Boca de Pascuales

Smaller still, **BOCA DE PASCUALES**, 13km from Tecomán, is little more than a bunch of *palapa* restaurants and a beach renowned for huge waves. Swimming can be dangerous but otherwise it's a fine place to hang out for a few days. Beach **camping** is the order of the day; the *Estrella de Sur* (③), on the way in, is poor value. The best **restaurant**, the expensive *Hamacas del Mayor*, serves top-notch seafood.

Colima

COLIMA, the state capital, 100km from Manzanillo, is a distinctly colonial city, and a very beautiful one, too: famed for its parks and overlooked by the perfectly conical **Volcan de Colima** and, in the distance, the Nevado de Colima. It doesn't offer a whole

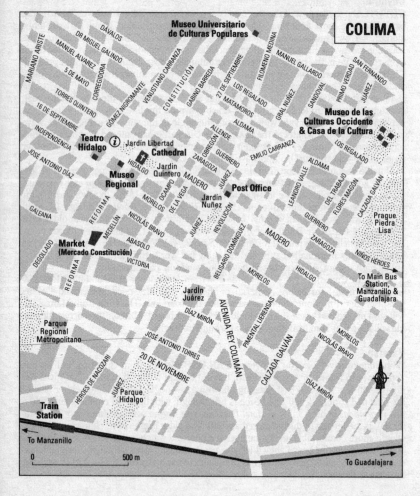

lot in the way of excitement, but it is a pleasant place to stop over for a night or two: cooler than the coast, but never as cold as it can get in the high mountains, and with some good-value hotels and restaurants to boot.

Archeological evidence – much of it explained in the city's museums – points to three millennia of rich cultural heritage around Colima, almost all of it wiped out with the arrival of Cortés' lieutenant Gonzalo de Sandoval who, in 1522, founded the city on its present site. Four years later Cortés decreed that Colima – named after Cilimán, a former ruler of the local Nahua Indians – should be the third city of New Spain after Veracruz and México. However, Acapulco's designation as the chief Pacific port at the end of the sixteenth century deprived Colima of any strategic importance and, combined with a series of devastating earthquakes, left it with few grand buildings to show for its former glory. The town makes up for that with a chain of shady formal **plazas** and a number of attractive **courtyards**, many of them now used as restaurants and cafes, wonderfully cool places to catch up on writing postcards – though the selection of these is uniformly awful.

Arrival and information

Some 2km east of the centre, Colima's **main bus station**, the Central de Autobuses (often referred to as Central Nuevo), handles frequent first- and second-class buses from Guadalajara, Lázaro Cárdenas, Manzanillo, México and farther afield. Taxis and city buses marked "Centro" run towards the central plaza. Most second-class Manzanillo buses and all local services operate from the **Terminal Suburbana** (confusingly known as Central Camionera), 2km out on the opposite, western, periphery and also served by city buses.

Information
Colima's willing but practically useless **tourist office**, Portal Hidalgo 20 (Mon–Fri 9am–3pm & 6–9pm, Sat 9am–1pm; ☎331/2-43-60), lies on the western side of the zócalo – the **Jardín Libertad**. The most useful **bank**, *Banamex* (exchange Mon–Fri 9am–1.30pm), is nearby on Hidalgo between Medellín and Ocampo, and has an ATM, but the Majapara *casa de cambio*, Juárez and Morelos (Mon–Fri 9am–2pm & 4–6.30pm, Sat 9am–2pm), offers better rates for both cash and cheques. *Su Casa*, Madero 150 (Mon–Sat 9am–7pm, Sun 9am–2pm), has reasonable rates and longer hours. The **post office** is at Madero 247, and you can keep in touch through the *Computel larga distancia*, Morelos 234 (daily 7am–10pm; collect calls), at the opposite end of the Jardín Núñez.

Accommodation

Colima boasts plenty of reasonable hotels within a few blocks of the centre. Rates don't vary much year round, but places do fill up rapidly during the San Felipe and Todos los Santos fiestas in early to mid-February and late October to early November.

América, Morelos 162 (☎331/2-03-66). Colima's swankiest hotel, a pretty characterless, international-style place with all the facilities – but no pool. ⑦.

Ceballos, Portal Medellín 12 (☎331/2-44-44). Colonial hotel right on the Jardín Libertad, with wonderfully spacious halls and not bad, but less impressive, rooms. ④.

La Merced, Hidalgo 188 (☎331/2-69-69). Lovely old hotel with fan-ventilated rooms around a central patio and some less attractive, newer a/c rooms. TV and parking. ③.

Núñez, Juárez 88 (☎331/2-70-30). Reliable budget place on Jardín Núñez, ranged around a central courtyard. Large rooms with showers are almost twice the price of small ones without. Parking. ①.

San Cristóbal, Reforma 98 at Independencia (☎331/2-05-15). About the cheapest in town; central with clean basic rooms, some with private bathroom. ①.

San Lorenzo, Cuauhtémoc 149, two blocks west of the cathedral then three south (☎331/2-20-00). Best value of the budget places. Excellent clean rooms with soap and towels provided. ②.

The Town

As in all these old cities, life in Colima centres on the **zócalo**, where you'll find the government offices (take a quick look at the distinctly second-rate murals in the Palacio de Gobierno) and the unimpressive Neoclassical cathedral. Quite out of character for this part of Mexico, however, the town actually boasts a few things to see, too: chiefly a couple of really good **museums**.

The most central of these, Colima's **Museo Regional de Historia** (Tues–Sat 10am–2pm & 4–8pm; free), stands across the street from the Palacio de Gobierno in a lovely old building that also houses the university art gallery. Move swiftly through the stuff on **local crafts** – though the animal and diabolical masks used in traditional dances are interesting – and make for the later rooms, chock-full of **pre-Hispanic ceramics**: gorgeous figurines with superbly expressive faces, fat Izcuintli dogs and people working on mundane, everyday tasks. Though characteristic of western Mexican culture, these examples are specific to Colima, many of them found in *tumbas de tiro*: well-like tombs up to 16m deep, more commonly found in South America and the Pacific Islands. The cultural parallel isn't well understood, but explanatory panels (all in Spanish) show the different styles.

More widely trumpeted than the regional museum, the **Museo de Las Culturas del Occidente** (Tues–Sun 9am–7pm; free), 1km northeast of the Jardín Núñez, holds another substantial collection of local archeology. You'll see the same kind of thing here as in the former, but more figurines: dogs with litters fighting, people blowing conch shells, playing musical instruments and dancing, even a man in a caiman mask whose dances were said to avert hurricanes. There's also a more detailed explanation of the rural agricultural society that produced such well-preserved tombs; again, all in Spanish. In the same park as the museum, an auditorium hosts occasional concerts and films. Look for posters advertising what's on.

With more time to spare, wander eight blocks north of the zócalo to the **Instituto Universitario de Culturas Populares** (Mon–Fri 9am–2pm & 4–7pm, Sat 9am–2pm; free), which has a good but poorly explained collection of masks, a few old photos of some spectacular dances, and a small musical instrument collection including a violin made from scrap wood and a Modelo beer can. Reproductions of some of the ceramic pieces shown at the other two museums are made outside under the banyan tree.

On a hot day, you can cool off in one of two parks, the **Parque Piedra Lisa** to the east – the "sliding stone" in the name referring to a rock that is said to ensure your return if you slide on it – and the **Parque Regional Metropolitano** (dawn–dusk) to the southwest. The latter has a small, depressing zoo, a boating lake with boats for rent, and a swimming pool (daily 10am–4.30pm).

MOVING ON FROM COLIMA

To get to the **Terminal Suburbana**, catch bus #2 on Morelos; for the **Central de Autobuses** take either #4 on Zaragoza, #6 on Revolución or Jardín Núñez, or #18 on Medina at Zaragoza. Dozens of buses head **inland to Guadalajara** or down to **Manzanillo**, but heading south you may find it quicker to leap on the first bus to Tecomán (every 15min; 45min) and change there for Lázaro Cárdenas.

There is also one daily **train** each to Manzanillo (2hr) and Guadalajara (6hr) from the train station ten blocks south of the centre on Héroes de Nacozari. Tickets can be bought from the station thirty minutes before the train departs, though long-term line maintenance has made schedules unreliable.

Eating and drinking

For a town of its size, Colima has a great range of places to eat, from restaurants serving **Oaxacan** and local specialities to the region's best **vegetarian** food.

Ah que Nanishe, 5 de Mayo 267, west of Mariano Arista (☎331/4-21-97). Surprisingly inexpensive courtyard restaurant specializing in dishes from the owner's native Oaxaca. Well worth the walk out from the centre.

Café la Arábica, 162 Guerrero, west of Juárez. The smell of roasting Colimense beans heralds this tiny coffee shop. *Americano*, espresso or cappuccino made from excellent locally grown, roasted and ground coffee, but little else.

Lakshmi del Centro, Madero at Revolución. Mainly a wholefood shop and bakery producing great banana and carrot bread, but with a restaurant area for vegeburgers and nutritious drinks.

Los Naranjos, Gabino Barreda 34, north of Madero (☎331/2-00-29). Slightly upmarket restaurant with live piano music to go with the mainly meat dishes. *Machaca norteña* is a speciality, and you can get a substantial *comida corrida* for around $10.

Los Portales, Hidalgo on the Jardín Libertad. Nice place on the zócalo, great for sitting outside watching the world go by. Reasonably priced *antojitos* and seafood dishes.

El Trebol, 16 de Septiembre and Degollado. Comfortable and very cheap place, just off the zócalo, for egg dishes, *tortas* and light meals.

Restaurant Vegetariano Samahdi, Filomeno Medina 125. Sit at tables around the banana-shaded colonnade and feast on something inexpensive and delicious from the varied (almost entirely

---

CLIMBING THE NEVADO DE COLIMA

The **Parque Nacional Nevado de Colima** comprises two beautiful volcanoes, snowcapped in winter, rising north of Colima. The Volcán de Colima (3900m), also known as Volcán de Fuego, is officially still active and still smokes from time to time, though there seems little imminent danger. It is far less frequently climbed than its larger and less active brother, the **Nevado de Colima** (4335m), which is popular sport for local mountaineers during the clear, dry winter months. Unless there's a lot of snow – in December and January crampons and an ice axe are essential – and provided you are fit and can get transport high enough, it's less of a climb than a relatively easy **hike** up to the summit. The problem is getting someone to take you up to the cabin at La Joya (3500m) – from where it is also possible to make an assault on Volcán de Colima – or on to the microwave station a little way beyond, from where it is a stiff but non-technical walk. Hitching isn't an option; the logging roads up here are rough, requiring high clearance or four-wheel drive vehicles, and see very little traffic. Your best bet is to set three days aside, take a sleeping bag and waterproofs, pack enough food and water for the trip, and plan to walk from the highway.

To get there, take a bus to Tonaya from the Central de Autobuses in Colima, or one of the more frequent buses to Ciudad Guzmán and change for Tonaya. Ask the driver to drop you off on the highway, where an unpaved side road leads 3km to Fresnito. About 300m along the main highway past this junction, a vehicle track leads off on the left towards a house, then veers to the left. Follow this – it soon becomes a path – and keep going on the most obvious path heading up and you should arrive (in about 6–8hr) at the La Joya hut, just below the tree line. An alternative is to follow the dirt road into Fresnito, where there are very limited supplies, and ask for the road to La Joya. Take this and keep right until the route becomes obvious. This rough service road for the microwave station leads up through cow pastures and goes right past the hut, again about six to eight hours walking. Following this you do at least have a chance of hitching. You can tank up from the supply of running water here, but don't expect to stay in the hut, which is often locked, and even if open may be full as it only sleeps six. You should plan on a day from La Joya to the summit and back, then another to get back to Colima, though a very fit walker starting before dawn could make the trip back to Colima, or at least Ciudad Guzmán, in a day.

veggie) menu, including vegeburgers, crêpes, delicious *licuados* and wonderful value *comidas corridas* served from 1 to 4pm. Daily 8am–10pm, Thurs until 5pm.

Around Colima – Comala

The best time to be in Colima is on a clear winter day when the volcanoes in the **Parque Nacional Nevado de Colima** dominate the views to the north. Climbing them, while not that difficult, needs some planning (see p.345). You can get a closer look, however, by spending an afternoon at **COMALA**, 10km north of Colima. Not only do you get a fantastic view of the mountains from the town's colonial plaza but you can sip a beer or margarita while competing *mariachi* bands pitch for your business. Four **restaurants**, huddled together under the zócalo's southern portal, each try to outdo the other by producing better *botanas* – plates of snacks, dips and *tacos* – free with drinks until about 6pm. Of course drinks are expensive, but stay for an hour or so and you won't need a meal. There's little to choose between them, so, if you can face the roving *mariachis*, a restaurant crawl might be an idea. Find a place where one band dominates, otherwise you find yourself trying to disentangle the sound of three. Friday and Saturday are the liveliest times, when you can mingle with day-tripping, predominantly middle-class Mexicans; on Sundays and Mondays there are craft markets in the square. **Buses** come out here from Colima's Terminal Suburbana (every 15min; 20min).

South to Lázaro Cárdenas

Beyond the state of Colima you run into a virtually uninhabited area: there are occasional beaches, but for the most part the mountains drop straight into the ocean; spectacular, but offering no reason to stop. Moving into Michoacán, **CALETA DE CAMPOS**, some 70km short of Lázaro Cárdenas, is the first and in many ways the best place to stop. It's a small village, barely electrified and with distinctly dodgy plumbing, but with two lovely beaches and an impressive ocean view. The streets are still dirt, and horses stand tied to hitching posts alongside the campers of dedicated American surfers and the fancy new cars belonging to visitors from the city. Yet there's one good **hotel**, *Yuritzi* (℡753/6-01-92; ④), with its own generator and water supply, and a string of makeshift bar-restaurants down at the beach. For much of the year it's virtually deserted, but in winter, when the Californian beach boys come down in pursuit of sun and surf, and at weekends, when families pile in from Lázaro Cárdenas, it enjoys a brief season. If the hotel is full, which at such times it can be, beg a hammock under the thatch of one of the beach bars: most are happy enough as long as you eat there too, though you may be bitten by voracious mosquitoes.

In any case the beach should definitely be seen at night, when, if the conditions are right, the ocean glows bright, luminous green. This is not a product of the excellent local beer, or of the Acapulco Gold that allegedly grows in the surrounding mountains, but a naturally illuminated, emerald-green plankton: go swimming in it and you'll come out covered in sparkling pinpoints. The phenomenon is common to much of this coast, and also seen in Baja California – but is nowhere as impressive as here. One word of warning: the second beach, cut off by a narrow, rocky point, looks like an unspoilt paradise (which it is), but you can only get there by boat or a stiff climb over the rocks. Try to swim round and you'll be swept out to sea by a powerful current – locals are well used to picking up tourists who suddenly find themselves several hundred metres offshore.

In addition to the occasional long-distance services, local buses make the trip from Caleta de Campos to **LÁZARO CÁRDENAS** several times a day. But there's little reason to go there except to get somewhere else – it's strictly industrial, dominated by a huge, British-funded steelworks. You'll find several small **hotels** around the bus terminals, which are next to each other in the centre. From the station served by *Galeana, Sur de Jalisco* and *Parhikuni*, walk out the front, turn right, right again and second right to get to the station served by *Tres Estrellas, Estrella Blanca* and others. The **train station** is on the outskirts, the sole daily train leaving at noon for Morelia twelve hours away. On the whole, it is better to press on or catch a local bus from The *Galeana* station to Playa Azul.

Playa Azul

Once a small-time, slow-moving beach not far removed from Caleta de Campos, **PLAYA AZUL** has been rather overrun by the growth of the city, but there are still numerous reasonably priced hotels and not a bad beach, backed by scores of *palapa* restaurants. Aside from lying on the sand, all there is to do is walk 2km north to see the rusting hulk of the *Betula*, a Norwegian sulphuric acid carrier that foundered in 1993. All the acid has gone now.

The road in crosses four streets, parallel to the beach and running down to the vast plaza at the southern end. Along these streets you'll find the *Hotel Playa Azul* (☎753/6-00-24; ④), where the best rooms have a/c and a pool view. You can also camp here ($9), though the campground is little more than a patch of dirt behind the hotel. The pool, though, is a better prospect: $6 for non-guests, it is free if you eat (at least $6 worth) in the decent hotel restaurant. For somewhere a little cheaper, try the clean but basic *Del Pacifico* (☎753/6-01-06; ③) at the northwestern corner of the plaza; the considerably better *Maria Isabela* (☎753/6-00-30; ④), on the far side of the plaza, which has a pool; or *Bungalows de la Curva* (☎753/6-00-58; ③), which isn't spotless but does have rooms with cooking equipment. Most people, though, sleep on the beach or, better still, in hammocks strung out at a beachfront bar. The **beachfront restaurants** satisfy most cravings, and *Coco's*, one street back, is good for breakfasts, burgers and pizza.

Zihuatanejo

Although it's only about 7km from Ixtapa to Zihuatanejo, the two places could hardly be more different. **IXTAPA**, a purpose-built, computer-planned paradise resort, is quite simply one of the most soulless towns imaginable – to say nothing of being one of the most expensive. Twenty years down the line, it still hasn't begun to mellow or wear itself in, and its single coastal drive still runs past a series of concrete boxes of varying heights. These completely cordon off Ixtapa's sole attraction from the road, forcing those who can't afford the hotels' inflated prices to trespass, or even use the hotels' facilities. You might want to visit one of the clubs in the evening, but you will definitely not want to stay.

ZIHUATANEJO, on the other hand, for all its growth and popularity in recent years, has at least retained something of the look and feel of the village it once was – what building there has been is small-scale and low-key. Nevertheless, as soon as you arrive you know you are in a resort: taxi drivers are forever touting for custom, trinket and tacky T-shirt shops are abundant, and as likely as not there'll be a cruise ship moored out in the bay. But at least here there are a fair number of small, reasonably priced hotels (though noticeably more expensive than the lowest rates in Acapulco) and some inexpensive restaurants. For some it's the ideal compromise, quiet – almost dead by night – yet with the more commercial excitements of Ixtapa in easy reach. The one real problem is its popularity – with strictly controlled development, rooms can be hard to find in the centre of Zihuatanejo, a region of barely ten small blocks hemmed in by the main roads into town, the yacht marina and the beach.

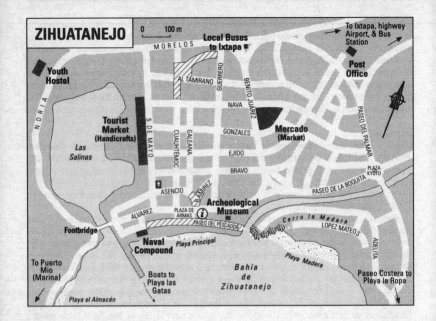

Arrival and information

Buses arrive at Zihuatanejo's brand new station (with *guardería*) about twenty minutes' walk from the centre of town. There are plenty of taxis outside and if you walk a couple of hundred metres to the left you can pick up passing "Zihuatanejo" buses, which will generally drop you off at the top of Juárez, the place where the Ixtapa minibuses leave (6am–10pm; every 10min). Buses marked "Noria" go straight past the youth hostel and *Casa de Huéspedes Nancy. Combis* making the thirty-minute run between Zihuatanejo and the airport, 20km south (and only 2km off the highway to Acapulco), drop and pick up just outside the mercado. To get **back to the bus station**, hop on an Ixtapa-bound bus and ask the driver to drop you off. Although **buses** prove perfectly adequate for getting you around, rented **scooters** from *Michelle*, Galeana 4 (☎743/4-31-99), give you extra freedom and scope for exploring. They're not cheap, though, working out at around $50 a day ($16 an hour) for a 50cc bike capable of carrying one person and $55 a day ($20 an hour) for a more beefy two-person (80cc) model.

Information

Zihuatanejo's facilities are widely scattered. The moderately helpful **tourist office** (Mon–Fri 9am–3pm & 6–8pm, Sat 9am–3pm; ☎743/4-20-01, ext 120) is right by the Plaza de Armas on Alvarez; the **post office** (Mon–Fri 8am–8pm, Sat 9am–1pm) is on a street with no name at the northeastern corner; and the most useful **bank**, *Bancomer* (foreign exchange 9am–1.30pm), lies between the two at the corner of Juárez and Bravo. The **casas de cambio** don't generally offer good rates, but *Central de Cambios Guiball*, on Galeana west of Bravo, is open until 8.30pm daily and has a *larga distancia* pnone for inexpensive collect calls.

Accommodation

Zihuatanejo's high season is fairly long, from mid-November or earlier to the end of April. Outside those times some of the slightly more expensive hotels drop their rates to those of the budget places – which tend to vary their prices less. Rates are generally charged per person, not per room, so there's little advantage for groups. Just ten minutes' walk from the centre, the **youth hostel**, Paseo de las Salinas (☎743/4-46-62; $5), is one of the better examples of its kind, with four-bed single-sex rooms.

Playa la Madera, while part of Zihuatanejo, has a different feel, slightly removed and a touch exclusive – though not necessarily more expensive. **Playa la Ropa**, more than a kilometre from the centre, feels a world apart; at its southern edge, *Los Cabañas Trailer Park* (☎743/4-47-18; $9) is a small, clean campsite and trailer park that is more like someone's back garden. You can also camp officially at the north end of Playa Linda, north of Ixtapa.

Central Zihuatanejo

Casa Bravo, Nicolás Bravo 11 (☎743/4-25-48). Good little hotel; most rooms with fans, TV and private bath. All day hot water and towels provided. ④.

Casa de Huéspedes Elvira, Alvarez 8 (☎743/4-20-61). Small rooms with basic bathrooms around a verdant courtyard and right by the beach. ③.

Casa de Huéspedes Nancy, Paseo del Cantil 6 (☎743/4-21-23). Clean and tidy guesthouse with hammocks on the roof and a peaceful location, but still only ten minutes' walk from the waterfront over the lagoon footbridge. Buses marked "Noria" pass the door. ③.

Casa de Huéspedes Tulipanes, Pedro Ascencio 3 (☎743/4-26-69). Little more than clean concrete cells but with fans, and towels and soap provided. ②.

Posada Michel, Ejido 14 (☎743/4-74-23). Bright hotel right in the centre. Particularly good value off-season. ⑤.

Raúl Tres Marias (Town), Alvarez 52 (☎743/4-29-77). The classier of the two branches of this hotel, but not a lot of character. Shiny and spotless, with some sea views, a/c and bathrooms with hot water all day. ⑤.

Raúl Tres Marias (Lagoon), Noria 4 (☎743/4-21-91). Just across the wonderfully rickety lagoon footbridge from its sister hotel and close to the centre. This is the budget option, with clean basic rooms opening onto flower-filled terraces. ④.

Susy, Alvarez 3 (☎743/4-23-39). Well-run hotel with pleasant, modern rooms with small balconies, fans and shower. Some more expensive with TV and a/c. ④.

Playa la Madera and Playa la Ropa

La Casita, Esciencia on the headland between Playa la Madera and Playa la Ropa (☎743/4-45-10). Front rooms have a great view of the bay from the hammocks swinging on the balcony outside. The rooms are all well furnished and excellent value, but a long way from the beach. ⑤.

Palacios, Adelita, Playa la Madera (☎743/4-20-50). Good, spacious clean rooms, tiled bathrooms and sea views from the balconies. Small pool too. Rooms with a/c cost 20 percent more. ⑤.

APARTMENT HOTELS AT PLAYA LA MADERA

A variety of **apartment hotels** at Playa la Madera cater for groups travelling together. *Bungalows Ley*, López Mateos (☎743/4-40-87; ⑤), has a/c but no pool and charges $33–40 for four people. *Bungalows Allec* (no phone) is better appointed and has rooms for two (⑥) and apartments for four ($45–60), while *Brisas del Mar* (☎743/4-21-42) has more spacious rooms and a pool and charges $45–60 for apartments that sleep up to six. **Bungalows Sotelo**, López Mateos (☎743/4-63-07; ⑥), is in a different class altogether, with deluxe apartments with a/c, jacuzzi, satellite TV and great sea views. Cheapest apartments for four are $60–90.

Villa del Sol, Playa la Ropa (☎743/4-22-39). Claims to be the best small beach hotel in Mexico. Lush gardens of hibiscus and bougainvillea hide spacious luxury suites all with terraces and some with small private pools. Of course there's a big pool too, a private patch of beach and flunkies everywhere. Expensive even off-season but great if you can stretch to it. ⑨.

Villas Miramar, Adelita, Playa la Madera (☎743/4-21-06). Beautiful hotel with rooms on both sides of the road. Those with sea views and a small pool cost more than others set in luxuriant gardens around a large pool. Also a penthouse suite with kitchen for four people ($70–110). ⑦.

The Town

Zihuatanejo has a few things to distract you from lying on the beach. Quite apart from jetskiing, parascending and getting dragged around on a huge inflatable banana, you could arrange to go **fishing** for dorado, yellowtail, bonito or big game. Trips, run by *Lanchas de Pesca* (☎743/4-37-58), leave from the pier in Zihuatanejo. Prices vary according to the size of the boat. **Scuba diving** courses are organized by *Zihuatanejo Scuba Centre*, Cuauhtémoc 3 (☎743/4-21-47). A full-day resort course with one dive costs $70 and reef dives for certified divers will set you back $45 for one, $70 for two. Full certification takes six days and costs $350.

Just behind the beach you'll find the **Museo Arqueologico de la Costa Grande** (Tues–Sun 10am–6pm; $1.50): small, simple and not deserving more than twenty minutes, though it does its best to tackle the history of what has always been a fairly insignificant region.

The beaches

Four beaches surround Bahía de Zihuatanejo. **Playa Principal**, in front of Zihuatanejo, is unspectacular, but interesting to watch when the fishermen haul in their catch early in the morning and sell much of it there and then. A narrow footpath heads east from the end of the beach across the normally dry outlet of a drainage canal, then winds around a rocky point to the calm waters of **Playa la Madera**, a broad golden strand with a couple of restaurants, and hotels and condos rising up the hill behind. Climb the steps between the condos to get to the road if you want to continue a kilometre or so over the headland, past the mirador with great views across the bay, to **Playa la Ropa**, which takes its name – "Clothes Beach" – from the silks washed up here when one of the *Nao de China* (see p.353) was wrecked here. This is Zihuatanejo's finest road-accessible beach, palm fringed for more than a mile with a variety of beachfront restaurants and hotels. You can walk a further fifteen minutes beyond the end of Playa la Ropa to **Playa las Gatas**, the last of the bay's golden beaches, its crystalline blue water surrounded by a reef, giving it the enclosed feel of an ocean swimming pool. This makes it safe for kids, though the sea bottom is mostly rocky and tough on tender feet. Nonetheless, the clear waters are great for snorkelling: you can rent gear from vendors among the rather pricey *palapa* restaurants. Las Gatas is directly opposite the town and accessible by launches (daily 8am–4pm, last return 5pm; 15min; $2 return) run by *Lanchas de Pesca* (see above). Buy tickets at the entrance to the pier.

The long sweep of **Ixtapa**'s hotel-backed **Playa de Palmar** is fine for volleyball or just relaxing, but often too rough for easy swimming, and plagued by the inevitable jetskis. Powered watersports are also in evidence at the inappropriately named **Playa Quieta**, some 5km north of Ixtapa. The water here is wonderfully clear and the surrounding vegetation magnificent, but you won't get anything to eat or drink unless you pay handsomely to enter the confines of Ixtapa's *Club Med*. Boats leave Playa Quieta for **Isla Ixtapa** (9am–5pm; $2 return), a small island a couple of kilometres offshore with two swimming beaches, a spot reserved for diving, watersports gear rental, and a few restaurants – but nowhere to stay. You can also get there on a daily launch from Zihuatanejo, which leaves at 11.30am (1hr; $7). The boat returns at 4.30pm.

The names of Playa Quieta and the next beach on, **Playa Linda**, should be swapped; the latter is by far the more relaxed, with generally safe swimming, though under the right conditions it receives good surf.

Eating, drinking and nightlife

You can barely move for restaurants in Zihuatanejo: the waterfront Paseo del Pescador is the place for fresh fish, expensive drinks and atmosphere; the cheapest place, as ever, is the **market** on Juárez. There isn't much **nightlife** in town, however: for that people head over the hill to Ixtapa and the clubs in the big hotels. A typical Ixtapa night out starts at *Carlos 'n' Charlie's* and progresses to the trendy and expensive *Christine's* at the *Hotel Krystal*. Buses to Ixtapa run until about 10pm; after that you'll need a taxi.

Las Brasas, Cuauhtémoc next to *Cafe NZ*. Simple but very cheap breakfasts and *comidas corridas* served in this cavernous restaurant that runs through to Galeana.

Café Marina, Paseo del Pescador. Cosy little place on the waterfront serving pizza, *tortas* and home-made yoghurt through the high season, and great spaghetti dishes on Wednesday night. English-language book swap too.

Cafetería Nueva Zelanda, Cuauhtémoc 23. You pay slightly over the odds for the good *licuados*, *tortas*, breakfasts and cappuccinos in this often busy cafe.

Cenaduria Artelia, down a small alley off Nicolás Bravo. A great little spot to sit outdoors and eat *tacos*, *quesadillas* and the like until gone 11pm.

Marisco El Acacio, Ejido at Guerrero. Simple seafood restaurant, much cheaper – though considerably less atmospheric – than those on Paseo del Pescador.

Panaderia Francesa, Galeana and Gonzales. The name might be wishful thinking, but they do produce good sesame-topped wholemeal bread, croissants and pastries.

La Sirena Gorda, Paseo del Pescador. Fairly expensive but well-sited, right where evening strollers can watch you dine on succulent tuna steaks and seafood cocktails in the balmy night air.

Splash Bar, Guerrero at Ejido. Coloured bulbs illuminate this dim bar, where people lurk in corners playing chess or backgammon to the accompaniment of constant surf and ski videos. Open 5pm–1am with two-for-one drinks 7–8pm.

On to Acapulco

From Zihuatanejo to Acapulco – along Hwy-200, a fast road with regular buses – the aspect of the coast changes again: becoming flatter, more heavily populated and regularly cultivated. At **PAPANOA**, 50km on, there's a beautiful beach, some 15km long, overlooked from the point at its far end by the *Hotel Club Papanoa* (☎742/7-04-50; ⑤). Obviously someone's plan for a luxurious, *Club Med*-style development, it never quite panned out – there's still considerable comfort, a pool, and a stairway down to the beach through manicured gardens, but the place has a distinctly run-down air. It's not exactly cheap, but nor is it in the high luxury bracket, and a double room is easily large enough for four. You could, too, camp out quite easily on this stretch of sand, getting supplies from the nearby village of **El Morro De Papanoa**. The hotel restaurant is also good value, and the staff friendly.

Beyond Punta Papanoa the road again leaves the coast for a while – although with sturdy transport of your own, there are several places where you could find your way down to a surf-pounded beach – not to rejoin it until shortly before Acapulco itself. Of little interest otherwise, **COYUCA DE BENITEZ**, the last village of any size, has some pleasant restaurants overlooking the Río Coyuca, and you can arrange boat trips downriver into the Laguna de Coyucán. Nearby you could certainly find somewhere to camp or sling a hammock at **PLAYAS DE SAN JERONIMO**, but again it's an exposed, windswept and wavy stretch of sand. You could also get a minibus from Coyuca to the beach at **El Carrizol**, where it's possible to rent a reasonably priced bungalow.

Acapulco

Everyone – even if they've not the remotest idea where it is – has heard of **ACAPULCO**, but few people know what to expect. Truth is that, as long as you don't yearn to get away from it all, you'll find almost anything you want here, from magnifi-

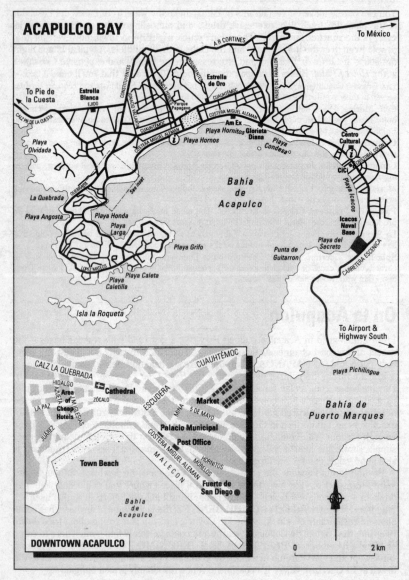

ACAPULCO BAY

To México

A R CORTINES

To Pie de
la Cuesta

Estrella
Blanca
EJIDO

Estrella
de Oro

CONSTITUYENTES

INSURGENTES

PASEO DEL FARALLON

CUAUHTÉMOC

Parque
Papagayo

CALZ PIE DE LA CUESTA

COSTERA MIGUEL ALEMAN

Am Ex

Centro
Cultural

CRISTOBAL COLON

Playa
Olvidada

COSTERA MIGUEL ALEMAN

Playa Hornitos
Playa Hornos

Glorieta
Diana

Playa
Condesa

CICI

Playa Icacos

*Bahía
de
Acapulco*

QUEBRADA

La Quebrada

See inset

Playa Honda

Icacos
Naval
Base

Playa Angosta

Playa
Larga

Playa del
Secreto

LOPEZ MATEOS

Playa Grifo

Punta de
Guitarron

CARRETERA ESCENICA

Playa Caleta

Playa
Caletilla

Isla la Roqueta

To Airport &
Highway South

Playa Pichilingue

*Bahía de
Puerto Marques*

CALZ LA QUEBRADA

CUAUHTÉMOC

HIDALGO
Area
of
Cheap
Hotels

ZÓCALO

Cathedral

ESCUDERA

MINA

Market

5 DE MAYO

LA PAZ

IGLESIAS

JUAREZ

Palacio Municipal
Post Office

COSTERA MIGUEL ALEMAN

HORNITOS

MORELOS

Town Beach

M A L E C O N

*Bahía
de
Acapulco*

**Fuerte de
San Diego**

DOWNTOWN ACAPULCO

0   2 km

N

cent beaches by day to clubs and discos by night. That said, however, the manicured and sanitized hotel zone, where everything is geared towards North American package tourists, can be thoroughly off-putting, as can some of the restaurants and clubs, which exhibit a snobbery seldom seen elsewhere in Mexico. In the old town the grime, congestion and exhaust fumes are the most apparent aspects of the city's **pollution problem**, which peaks in the rainy season when everything from plastic bags to dead dogs get washed off the streets and back alleys into the bay.

What Acapulco undoubtedly has going for it, however, is its stunning **bay**: a sweeping scythe-stroke of yellow sand backed by the white towers of the high-rise hotels and, behind them, the jungly green foothills of the Sierra. And, though there are hundreds of thousands of people here throughout the year – the town itself has a population approaching one and a half million and even out of season (busiest months are Dec–Feb) most of the big hotels remain nearly full – it rarely seems oppressively crowded. Certainly there's always space to lie somewhere along the beach, partly because of its sheer size, partly because of the number of rival attractions from hotel pools to parasailing and "romantic" cruises. **Hawkers**, too, are everywhere. Most of them are easy enough to handle – there's no need to go shopping in Acapulco, simply lie on the beach and a string of goods will be paraded in front of you – but they can become irritating and at times heavy. For women, and women alone in particular, the constant pestering of would-be gigolos can become maddening, and for anyone the derelict downtown backstreets can be dangerous at night – remember that this is still a working **port** of considerable size and in the midst of all the tourist glitz real poverty remains: don't leave things lying about on the beach or too temptingly displayed in hotel rooms.

Though there's little to show for it now beyond the star-shaped Fuerte de San Diego and a few rusty freighters tied up along the quayside, Acapulco was from the sixteenth century one of Mexico's most important ports, the destination of the famous *Nao de China*, which brought silks and spices from Manila and returned laden with payment in Mexican silver. Most of the goods were lugged overland to Veracruz and from there shipped onwards to Spain. Mexican Independence, Spain's decline and the direct route around southern Africa combined to kill the trade off, but for nearly 300 years the shipping route between Acapulco and the Far East was among the most prized and preyed upon in the world, attracting at some time or other (if you believe all the stories) every pirate worth the name. In one such raid, in 1743, Lord Anson (the "Father of the British Navy") picked up silver worth as much as £400,000 sterling from a single galleon and altogether, with the captured ship and the rest of its cargo and crew, collected booty worth over a million even then. With the death of its major trade, Acapulco went into a long, slow decline, only reversed with the completion of a road to the capital in 1928. Even so, but for tourism it would today be no more than a minor port.

Arrival and orientation

Most **buses** arrive at the Central de Autobuses on Ejido, 3km northwest of the zócalo, from where you can pick up buses marked "Centro" or "Caleta" to get to the area where the cheaper hotels are located. *Estrella de Oro* buses from México and Zihuatanejo arrive at their own terminal, 3km west of the zócalo, again connected by "Caleta" city buses. Both stations have a *guardería*. The **airport**, 30km east of the city, is linked only by expensive taxis and the *Tranportaciones Aeropuerto* shuttle service. If you intend to leave by plane (see p.360) it saves money to buy a return ticket for the shuttle when you arrive.

Orientation

Acapulco divides fairly simply into two halves: the **old town**, which sits at the western end of the bay, with the rocky promontory of **La Quebrada** rising above it and curv-

---

ADDRESSES ALONG COSTERA

Finding places along Costera can be tricky, as the numbering system is completely meaning-less: 50 could be followed by 2010, which is next door to 403. The best **landmarks**, apart from the big hotels, are (moving east from the zócalo) Parque Papagayo, the roundabout with the Diana Glorieta statue and the *CiCi* waterpark. An additional difficulty is the construction of a new ring road, which is disrupting some bus routes. The descriptions given here are as accurate as possible, but check routes locally when travelling by bus.

---

ing round to protect the most sheltered anchorage; and the new **resort area**, a clump of hotels and tourist services following the curve of the bay east. A single seafront drive, the **Costera Miguel Aleman** – usually just "Costera" – stretches from the heart of the old town right around the bay, linking almost everything of interest. You can reach everywhere near the zócalo on foot, but to get farther afield, frequent **buses** (look for "Cine Río/La Base", "zócalo" or "Caleta directo") run all the way along Costera. From the east these travel past all the big hotels, then turn inland onto Cuauhtémoc, where they pass the *Estrella de Oro* **bus station** and the **market** before rejoining the Costera just before the zócalo. "Caleta" buses continue round the coast to Playa Caleta.

Information

Most of the things you need cluster around the zócalo. The **post office** (Mon–Sat 8am–8pm for most services, Sun 8am–1pm for stamps) is on Costera, two blocks east of the zócalo, just past the *Banamex* **bank** (exchange Mon–Fri 9am–2pm), which has the best rates and hours. Nearby on Costera there's a *casa de cambio* but rates are poor. If you miss the bank it is far better to head to the hotel zone along Costera, where several places offer good rates for US and Canadian dollars and much worse ones for European currencies: try *Consultoria Internacional* (Mon–Thurs 8.30am–8pm, Fri 8.30am–9pm, Sat 9am–9pm) near the *Fiesta Americana* hotel. The **American Express** office (Mon–Sat 10am–7pm; ☎74/69-11-22), at Costera 1628 between Parque Papagayo and Diana Glorieta, will hold mail, but has awful exchange rates. Long-distance and collect **phone calls** can be made from *Telplus* (daily 7am–10pm), just east of the post office.

Acapulco has two **tourist offices**: the **Guerrero state** tourist office (Mon–Fri 9am–2pm & 4–7pm, Sat 9am–2pm; ☎74/86-91-64), Costera 4455 at Niños Héroes, just before Parque Papagayo, and the **city** office (daily 9am–7pm; ☎74/84-44-16) at Centro Acapulco, a block west of *CiCi*. Unless you strike lucky and encounter an enthusiastic staff member, you're likely to come away from both with little but an armful of brochures and Acapulco's **free magazines** – *Info Acapulco, Adventure in Acapulco*, and the glossy *Acapulco Magazine* – all full of thinly disguised advertising. For more edify-ing reading matter, try the **book swaps** at some of the budget hotels (see below), browse through the selection at the bigger hotels and at *Sanborn's*, just west of the zócalo, or check the second-hand books in the postcard shop on Azueta near the junc-tion with La Quebrada. You can reach the tourist police on ☎85-04-90.

Accommodation

As with everything in Acapulco, hotel rooms are far less expensive in the **old town**. Head for the streets immediately to the west and slightly inland of the **zócalo**, in the calles La Paz and Teniente José Azueta, and particularly on Calzada La Quebrada where it leads up the hill. In contrast to most of Mexico, the hotels in this area tend to charge by the person rather than by the room.

You won't find places as cheap out along Costera but, if you want to stay out by the tourist beaches and the clubs, there are a few reasonably priced options, especially off-season, when even some of the fancier hotels along Costera become quite competitively priced. For **longer stays**, perhaps a better choice is to make for the smaller beaches of Caleta and Caletilla, a ten-minute bus ride from the centre. Hotels here are rather older, mostly patronized by Mexican families, and often booked up in advance. The best plan is to start off in the centre and from there work out where you'd ideally like to be based.

Still farther out there's **Pie de la Cuesta** (see p.358) a quiet out-of-the-city alternative 15km north of Acapulco. This is the only place with official year-round **camping**, at *Acapulco Trailer Park* (☎748/60-00-10; $8), and, with discretion, you could free camp.

Acapulco's **high season** lasts longer than most, from late November or early December through to the end of April.

In the centre

Asturias, La Quebrada 45 (☎74/83-65-48). Reasonable budget option, but with no pool. ④.

Coral, La Quebrada 56 (☎74/82-07-56). Perhaps the best of the many budget places along this road. Clean rooms with wide streetside balconies, a pool and cheap breakfasts downstairs. ④.

Las Glorias, La Quebrada (☎74/83-11-55). Though you pay for the location – right above the rocks where the divers plummet, this is still a fine hotel with cottage-like rooms with kitchenettes ranged along the clifftop. Three pools. ⑨.

Misión, Felipe Valle 12 (☎74/82-36-43). The best hotel in the centre. An old colonial-style house, formerly the American consulate and later a Wells Fargo office, with attractive rooms spread out around a mango-shaded patio. Continental or Mexican breakfasts; book swap. ⑥.

Sagmar, La Quebrada 51 (☎74/83-65-48). From the same mould as *Coral* and *Asturias*, but with the addition of a suite ($36–50 for four) with a stove and fridge but no utensils. ④.

Santa Lúcia, Av. Adolfo López Mateos 33 (☎74/82-04-41). Recently decorated fan-ventilated rooms with TV, private bathrooms and towels provided. Good value. ④.

Sutter, José Azueta 10 (☎74/82-02-09). Plain but clean and spacious rooms with fans and bathrooms. Rear rooms are quieter. ③.

Along Costera

Due to the confusing nature of Costera's numbering system (see p.354), the following hotels are listed in order of their distance along Costero from the zócalo.

Hamacas, Costera 239, 1km east of the zócalo (☎74/83-77-46). The closest international-standard hotel to the zócalo. Swimming pool, tennis court and comfortable rooms with cable TV. ⑧.

Jacqueline, Gonzalo Gomez Espinoza 6, opposite the eastern entrance to Parque Papagayo on Costero (☎74/85-93-38). Basic but good, clean rooms with a/c and shower with 24hr hot water. ⑤.

Del Valle, Gonzalo Gomez Espinoza 150, next door to *Jacqueline* (☎74/85-83-36). Better value than *Jacqueline*, with more spacious, modern rooms (some with a/c) and a pool. ⑤.

Embassy, Costera 50, opposite *CiCi* (☎74/844-02-73). Best value in this part of town with a small pool and mostly a/c rooms. Some have seen better days, so look at a couple before deciding. ⑥.

Quinta Mica, Cristóbal Colón 115 (☎74/84-01-21). Slightly run-down but good-value hotel with a pool and squash court. A/c rooms with equipped kitchenettes. Six-person "bungalow" costs $78 off-season, $150 peak. ⑦.

Suites Selene, Cristóbal Colón 175 (☎74/84-36-43). Similar though slightly less well kept than *Quinta Mica*. Suites for four people $72 off-season, $93 peak. ⑦.

Days Hotel Romano, Costera 2310, past *CiCi* (☎74/84-53-32). A sky-scraping *Holiday Inn* with large pool. The a/c rooms with TV and – at least from the upper floors – great views along the bay are surprisingly good value. Rates are identical for one to four people. ⑧.

Caleta and Caletilla

Boca Chica, on the point at the western end of Caletilla (☎74/83-63-88). Beautifully sited hotel with a pool and some great views, especially from the Junior Suites (off-season $60; peak $72). The smaller rooms are considerably less good. ⑦.

Nao, east end of Caleta (☎74/83-87-10). Faded but acceptable hotel with a pool, usually full of Mexican families. Fan-cooled rooms with shower, some considerably better than others. ④.

Playa Linda, Costera 1, as you reach Caleta (☎74/82-08-14). Recently renovated hotel with nicely decorated rooms, some with balconies. A few rooms (sleep up to four) have kitchenettes. ⑦–⑧.

Pie de la Cuesta

The following hotels are listed in order of distance from Hwy-200. All are right by the beach and reduce their prices dramatically out of season.

Villa Nirvana (☎748/60-16-31). Delightful place with spacious rooms around an attractive garden and great pool. ④.

Ukae Kim (☎748/60-21-87). Huge luxurious rooms with separate sitting area, some with balconies and sea views. Beachside pool. ⑦.

Casa de Huéspedes Playa Leonor (☎748/60-03-48). Simple but clean rooms, breezier on the upper floor. Prices drop considerably in the off season. ④.

Bungalows María Cristina (☎748/60-02-62). Suites for up to five people with fully equipped kitchens and balconies ($75) are the main attraction here, though the rooms are fine too. ⑤.

The Town

No one comes to Acapulco for the sights. By day, if people aren't at the beach or asleep, they're mostly scouring the expensive shops. If you only do one thing in Acapulco, though, make sure you see its most celebrated spectacle, the leap of the daredevil **divers**.

Acapulco's divers

Acapulco's famed **high divers** (*clavadistas*) plunge some 35m from the cliffs of La Quebrada into a tight, rocky channel, timing their leap to coincide with an incoming wave. Mistimed, there's not enough water to stop them hitting the bottom, though the chief danger these experts seem to face is getting back out of the water without being dashed against the rocks. It could easily be corny, but it's undeniably impressive, especially when floodlit at night. The posted rota of dives is unreliable, but the times – 12.45pm, 7.30pm, 8.30pm, 9.30pm and 10.30pm – are rigidly adhered to. A typical display involves three exponents, one or two taking the lower (25m) platform, the remainder diving from the upper level after first asking for the Virgin's intervention at the cliff-top shrine. The final diver in the last show carries a pair of flaming torches. From the road you can see the spectacle for nothing, but you'll get a much better view if you go down the steps to a **viewing platform** ($1.50) more or less opposite the divers. Get here early for a good position. Alternatively, you can sit in the bar at the *Playa Las Glorias* hotel ($10 cover includes two drinks) or watch from the expensive *La Perla* restaurant ($30 buffet including two drinks). To get there, simply climb the Calzada La Quebrada from the town centre, about fifteen minutes' walk from the zócalo.

Fuerte de San Diego and Costera

About the only place in Acapulco that gives even the slightest sense of the historic role the city played in Mexico's past is the **Museo de Acapulco** (Tues–Sun 10.30am–4.40pm; $4, free on Sun) inside the **Fuerte de San Diego**, an impressive, if heavily restored, star-shaped building built in 1616 to protect the Manila galleons from foreign corsairs. The fort's limited success is charted inside the museum, where displays also extend to the spread of Christianity by the proselytizing religious orders and a small anthropological collection. Air-conditioned rooms make this a good place to ride out the midday heat, and you can pop up on the roof for superb views over Acapulco. The **Centro Cultural** (Mon–Sat 10am–8pm; free) has a library, an art gallery and crafts store and also hosts a regular programme of cultural events with a regional bias. Check out the timetable. Surrounded by beautiful gardens (daily 9am–6pm), the ultra-modern

---

TOURS IN ACAPULCO

Anything from a two-hour trip around the town to a day trip to México can be seen on **guided tour** from one of Acapulco's hundreds of travel agents or any large hotel. Unless you're very short of time, however – or desperately bored – it's not worth dishing out the sums charged for the privilege.

Boat trips are more appealing. You can rent your own – inevitably very expensive – cruiser along the malecón to go sea-fishing or diving (haggle fiercely), or try one of the assorted bay cruises or outings in glass-bottomed boats. You'll see details and prices posted up all over town; you can book in any big hotel or simply go down to the quayside – either opposite the zócalo or a few hundred metres west – at departure time. Night-time excursions are particularly appealing, illuminated by the lights of the town shining out from all around the bay. After dark, too, most of the boats lay on some kind of entertainment as they cruise: the huge *Yate Hawaiano*, for example, boasts three bars and dance floors. Prices vary with the length of the trip and what is offered, but $20 for a couple of hours with a free bar is typical at night, $12 with no free bar during the day.

Centro Acapulco convention centre is packed with upmarket shops, pricey restaurants and a futuristic disco.

Geared up for bored kids, the **Parque Papagayo** offers boating, roller skating, gondola rides and the like, all easily accessible from Playa Hornos, as Costero dives through a tunnel at this point. Farther east round the bay near the Centro Acapulco, the **Centro Infantil CiCi** (daily 10am–6pm; $10, children $8) offers dolphin shows (noon, 2.30pm & 5pm) and water-based rides.

The beaches

To get to the best of the **sands around Acapulco Bay** from the centre of town, you're going to have to get on the bus: there is a tiny beach right in front of the town but it's not in the least inviting, with grey sand made greyer by pollutants from the boats moored all around it.

Caleta, Caletilla and La Roqueta
Playas Caleta and **Caletilla** (any "Caleta" bus from Costera) have a quite different atmosphere from those in the main part of the bay. Very small – the two are divided only by a rocky outcrop and breakwater – they tend to be crowded with Mexicans (the foreign tourists who once flocked here have since decamped east), but the water is almost always calm and, by Acapulco's standards, the beach is clean. Most enticingly, you can sit at shaded tables on the sand, surrounded by Mexican matrons whose kids are paddling in the shallows, and be brought drinks from the cafes behind; not particularly cheap, but considerably less than the same service would cost at the other end of the bay. There are showers here too and, on the rock, the **Magic Mundo Marina** (daily 9am–7pm; $6, kids $4.50), a watersports complex similar to *CiCi* with a predictable aquarium and sea-lion show, decent waterslides and a choice of the pool or the bay to swim in.

From outside the complex, small boats ply the channel to the islet of **La Roqueta**, where there are more and yet cleaner beaches, a small zoo (Mon & Wed–Sun 10am–5pm; $1) and beer-drinking *burros*, one of the town's less compelling attractions. Catch the direct launch (frequently until 5.30pm; $5) and keep your ticket for the return journey, or take the glass-bottomed boats (same hours; $7.50) that detour past the submerged one-tonne nickel and bronze statue of the Virgin of Guadalupe. Whether you are off to La Roqueta or only going to Caleta, leave early (especially at weekends) for the best of the sun and at least a sporting chance of getting a beach chair or a patch of sand. Behind the beach a group of moderately priced restaurants and cheaper *loncherias* offer good breakfasts and fish lunches.

Along Costera and on to Revolcadero

The main beaches, despite their various names – Hamacas, Hornos, Hornitos, Morro, Condesa and Icacos – are in effect a single sweep of sand. It's best to go some considerable distance round to **Playa Condesa** or **Playa Icacos**, in front of hotels like the *Hyatt Continental* and the *Holiday Inn*, or opposite the Centro Acapulco, where the beach is far less crowded and considerably cleaner. Here, too, it's easy enough to slip in to use the hotel showers, swimming pools and bars – there's no way they're going to spot an imposter in these thousand-bed monsters. The *Hyatt*, at the very far end, is the swankiest of the bunch. The beaches around here are also the place to come if you want to indulge in such frolics as being towed around the bay on the end of a parachute, waterskiing, or sailing. Outfits offering all of these are dotted at regular intervals along the beach; charges are standard though the quality of the equipment and the length of the trips can vary.

Beyond this end of the bay to the south are two more popular beaches: **Puerto Marqués** and **Revolcadero**. On the way you'll pass some of the fanciest hotels in Acapulco. *Las Brisas*, overlooking the eastern end of the bay, is probably the most exclusive of all, its individual villas offering private swimming pools and pink jeeps to every occupant. Puerto Marqués (buses marked "Puerto Marqués") is the first of the *playas*, a sheltered, deeply indented cove with restaurants and beach chairs right down to the water's edge. It's overlooked by two more deluxe hotels – very calm, very upmarket, though the beach itself is *not*. You can continue by road to Revolcadero (though only an occasional bus comes this far) or get there by boat down a narrow inland channel. The beach, a long exposed stretch of sand, is beautiful but frequently lashed by a surf that makes swimming impossible.

Pie de la Cuesta

Pie de la Cuesta, around 15km north of Acapulco, is even more open to the vicissitudes of the ocean. Definitely not for swimming – even if it weren't for the massive backbreaking waves that dump on the beach, there are said to be sharks offshore – but as good a place as you can imagine to come and watch the sun sink into the Pacific or to ride horseback along the shore. The sand extends for miles up the coast, but at the end nearer Acapulco, where the bus drops you, there are several rickety bars and some **tranquil places to stay**, away from the hubbub of the city (see p.356).

Behind, and only separated from the ocean by a hundred-metre-wide sandbar on which *Pie de la Cuesta* is built, lies the **Laguna de Coyuca**, a vast freshwater lake said to be three times the size of Acapulco Bay, which only connects with the sea after heavy rains. Fringed with palms, and rich in bird and animal life, the lagoon is big enough to accommodate both the ubiquitous noisy jetskiers and the more sedate three-hour **boat trips** (11.30am, 12.30pm & 1.30pm; $6) that visit the three lagoon islands – stopping on one for lunch (not included) and swimming. The bus ("Pie de la Cuesta") runs east every ten minutes or so past the zócalo along Costera, though major roadworks in late 1994 rerouted it along 5 de Mayo. The last bus back leaves around 8pm.

Eating and drinking

Though it may not seem possible, there are even more restaurants than hotels in Acapulco. To eat cheaply, though, you're confined to the area around the **zócalo**. Places actually on the square tend to be quite expensive but are great for lingering over breakfast at an outdoor table and watching the world go by. Cheaper places nearby are nothing special but you won't go hungry.

Eating by the **beach** – where there's some kind of restaurant at every turn – is of course very much more expensive, and increasingly so as you head east, but, if you have the cash to spare, many of these places, along with the fancy tourist traps between the hotels, are very good. Throughout the tourist zone, especially along Costera, *100% Natural*, a chain of 24-hour "healthy" eating places, serve good salads, fruit shakes, burgers and the like at grossly inflated prices. Less healthily, you can choose from *McDonald's, KFC*, the *Hard Rock Café* and the raucous Mexican fun bars *Iguanas Ranas, Carlos 'n' Charlie's* and *Señor Frog*.

One thing to look out for wherever you are on Thursday is **pozole**, a hearty pork and vegetable stew, served up almost everywhere. No one seems to be able to explain why, but *jueves pozolero* is now an institution.

In the centre

El Amigo Miguel, Juárez 31. Two locations at the junction of Juárez and Azueta, both serving good seafood at reasonable prices in clean, if harsh, surroundings.

Cafetería Asturia, inland end of zócalo. Quiet cafe, cheaper than the *El Flor*, tucked just off the plaza. Good coffee and light meals.

Braseritas, on Costera a block and a half west of the zócalo. The best of a series of cheap restaurants in this and the next block, serving bargain breakfasts and a respectable range of seafood.

Fat Farm, Juárez 10, a block west of the zócalo. Inexpensive tourist-oriented restaurant with a central patio that's good for idling over breakfast, though the food often fails to match expectations. Book swap.

El Flor de Acapulco, on the zócalo. Good for Mexican dishes, cocktails or just a coffee. Not the cheapest on the square but a pleasant spot to linger, and a popular meeting place for travellers.

Restaurant del Puerto, on Juárez a block from the zócalo. Perhaps the best budget restaurant in the area. Good-value *comidas corridas* all day for $3.

Along Costera

Tropicana Copacabana, just east of Parque Papagayo on Costero. One of a series of similar restaurant-bars that tend to play *cumbia, merengue* and *salsa* as much as American rock. Try also *Horizonte* and *Amigo Miguel*.

Pastelería Viena, on Costera just past Diana Glorieta. Tiny place for cake, coffee and great ice cream for much less than the neighbouring *Baskin-Robbins*. Daily until 11pm.

Los Tres Amigos Mexicana, just east of the Diana Glorieta. Just one of many al fresco places in this area which start out as restaurants in the early evening then turn into raucous bars around happy hour. Try also *Taboo* and *Disco Beach*.

Dino's, on Costera just beyond Diana Glorieta (☎74/84-00-37). Fancy, expensive and very good Italian restaurant with pretty much the full range of Italian dishes (minus pizza) and a smattering of international meals.

Doña Blanca, behind *Big Boy Burgers*, opposite Plaza Bahía. Buffet-style place where you help yourself to *almuerzo, comida* and *cena*. There's nothing gourmet, but it is filling.

Cocula, opposite the Centro Cultural. Moderate to expensive restaurant right on Costera, dishing up huge tasty breakfasts and specializing in grilled chicken.

Nightlife

If you were so inclined, and perhaps more importantly, if you were extremely rich, you could spend several weeks in Acapulco doing nothing more than trawling its scores of nightclubs and bars, discos and dinner-dances. There are people who claim never to have seen the town during daylight hours. These places are ridiculously expensive and anywhere with music or dancing will demand a hefty cover charge before they even consider letting you spend money at the bar.

However, prices can drop if you haggle, especially on weeknights and in the off-season when business is slow. This is particularly effective for larger groups. Look out

MOVING ON FROM ACAPULCO

Two stations handle Acapulco's intercity **buses**. The first-class **Estrella de Oro** terminal at the corner of Cuauhtémoc and Wilfrido Masseiu (city buses marked "Cine Río" from opposite the zócalo) handles hourly buses to México (4hr 30min) and three services daily to Lázaro Cárdenas (6hr). The much larger **Central de Autobuses** (aka *Estrella Blanca*; ☎74/69-20-28; city buses marked "Ejido") handles the unified services of several companies; don't be surprised if you find yourself on a bus that doesn't match the company named on your ticket. The "*informes*" booth in the middle of the line of ticket-sellers will point you in the right direction for your particular queue.

Buses to México leave continually day and night in five classes: *Turistar Plus* and *Primera* are the ones to go for, as the spacious seating and free drinks of the expensive executive-style buses fail to justify the extra expense. Second-class, avoiding the *auto-pista*, is very slow. You can also get to **Chilpancingo** and **Taxco**, while first- and second-class buses run to **Zihuatanejo**, half of them continuing on to **Lázaro Cárdenas**. Buses also leave hourly for **Puerto Escondido** until 6pm, after which there are three overnight services, which fill early.

To get to Acapulco's **airport** (☎74/66-94-29 or 34) you can take an expensive taxi or contact the *Transportaciones Aéropuerto* shuttle service, Costera 284 (☎74/85-93-60), though this works out cheapest if you have bought a return ticket upon arrival at the airport. Frequent flights leave Acapulco for México and numerous other Mexican and US destinations. For up-to-date details, contact any of the many travel agents that intersperse the hotels along Costera. About the nearest to the zócalo is *Las Hamacas* (☎74/84-68-87), about 1km east.

too for **"Ladies Free" nights** which, when offered at a place that normally has a "free bar", means women get in for half price.

Virtually all the clubs and discos are out along **Costera** in the hotel district, beyond *CiCi* – they move in and out of fashion with such bewildering rapidity that recommendations are virtually impossible. Some, like *Baby-O*, try to maintain a spurious exclusivity by turning people away at the door, but most can afford to do this only at the height of the season. Look for queues outside to see what's flavour of the month. Among the more consistently popular discos are *Baby-O*, *D'Paradise* and *Atrium* in the same area, *Bey's Rock* and *News* a little farther west and, way up on the hill beyond the naval base, the huge, glitzy and extremely expensive *Extravaganza*, *Fantasy* and *Palladium*. *Relax*, opposite the *El Presidente* hotel, is one of the better **gay hangouts**. If you're not easily intimidated you could also try some of the **downtown bars and cantinas**: you'll find a couple that aren't too heavy around the bottom of Azueta – *La Sirena*, for example – but these aren't recommended for women on their own. More traditional entertainment can be found at the *Hyatt Continental*, just in front of Playa Icacos, which features nightly performances by a troupe of the **Ballet Folklórico**. Although the admission is a bit steep, and the waiters persistent, the large-scale show – around sixty singers/dancers/musicians plus full regalia – is undeniably impressive.

If you prefer a quieter time, walk up behind the cathedral on the zócalo to where a few regulars play **chess** in the evening. You're welcome to have a game ($1) and can order soft drinks.

Listings

Airlines *Aeroméxico* (☎74/86-70-24; airport: 66-91-09); *American* (☎74/84-04-61; airport: 66-92-60); *Delta* (☎74/66-94-82); *Mexicana* (☎74/84-68-90; airport: 66-92-60); *Saro* (☎74/81-27-92); *Taesa* (☎74/84-45-76; airport: 66-93-93).

Car rental A car is more of a liability than a help in Acapulco but for heading along the coast or shooting up to Taxco it may be worthwhile. Try *Avis* (☎74/85-89-47); *Budget* (☎74/81-05-92); *Dollar* (☎74/84-30-66); *Express* (☎74/84-00-32); or *Hertz* (☎74/85-89-47).

Consulates *Canada, Club del Sol Hotel* (☎74/85-66-00); *France*, Costa Grande 235 (☎74/82-33-94); *Germany*, Antón de Alaminos 46 (☎74/84-74-37); *UK, Las Brisas Hotel* (☎74/84-66-05). Also *Austria, Spain, Finland, Netherlands, Norway* and *Sweden*: consult telephone directory or the tourist office.

Laundry *Ghost Cleaners*, José María Iglesias 9, near the zócalo (Mon–Fri 8am–2pm & 4–8pm, Sat 8.30am–2pm).

Medical emergency *Cruz Roja* (☎74/81-41-00 or 01); *Emergency IMSS Hospital* (☎74/86-36-23 or 87-00-75); *Sociedad de Assistencia Medico Turistica* (☎74/85-59-59 or 85-58-00) in *Condominium Capri* on Costera near Acapulco Plaza, and in the *Camino Real* hotel.

Pharmacy Plenty of 24hr places in the hotel zone along Costero; *Super Flash*, Costera and 5 de Mayo, just east of the fort.

Chilpancingo

Nestled in a bowl in the Sierra Madre Occidental, 130km north of Acapulco, **CHILPANCINGO**, Guerrero's modest state capital, makes a cool – it is higher than 1000m – and restful stop-off on the trip inland to the capital. Well off the tourist circuit, it is lent a youthful tenor by the large student population of the state university: activity focuses on the stately zócalo, a pristine traffic-free area.

The modern **Ayuntamiento** and **Palacio de Gobierno** combine a harmonious blend of Neoclassical and colonial influences. The latter is adorned with a huge bronze sculpture, "El Hombre Hacia el Futuro"; there's more monumental metalwork, along with busts of famous Guerrerans, in the Alameda three blocks east along Juárez.

Directly opposite its replacement, the former Palacio de Gobierno houses frequently changing exhibitions in the **Instituto Guerrerence de Cultura** and the excellent little **Museo Regional de Guerrero** (both Tues–Sun 11am–6pm; free). Well laid-out displays – some labelled in English – record the history of the state's native peoples from their migration from Asia across the Bering land bridge 30,000 years ago to the Maya and Teotihuacán influences on their pottery and *stelae*. With the coming of the Spaniards, the region benefited from the Manilla galleons that put into Acapulco and from Chilpancingo's location on the *Camino de China* from the coast to México. But the city's most dramatic chapter – vividly depicted on murals around the internal courtyard – came with the Independence struggle. After Hidalgo's defeat in the central highlands it was left to the southern populist movement, fuelled by the spread of land-grabbing haciendas and led by the skilled tactician José Maria Morelos, to continue the campaign. With almost the whole country behind them, they forced the Spanish – who still held México – to attend the Congress of Chilpancingo in 1813, where the Declaration of Independence was issued and the principles of the constitution – chiefly the abolition of slavery and the equality of the races – were worked out. Ultimately the congress failed and within two years the Spanish had retaken Guerrero and executed Morelos.

Practicalities

Buses from México and Acapulco arrive at either the *Estrella Blanca* terminal 1km east of the zócalo on 21 de Marzo – turn right then right again along Juárez – or the *Estrella de Oro* station on Juárez 53, five blocks east of the zócalo. Minibuses run into town along Juárez and back out along the parallel Guerrero. Madero crosses these two streets just before the zócalo and it is around here you'll find all the essential services.

Easily the best **place to stay** is *Posada Meléndez*, opposite the *Estrella de Oro* bus station at Juárez 50 (☎747/2-20-50; ⑤), its vast corridors immaculately tiled with individually painted inserts and furnished with heavy colonial-style chairs. Rooms with double beds all have balconies, and it's worth paying a little extra for a suite with separate sitting room. There are a couple of less expensive places near the zócalo: the colonial *Hotel Cardeña*, Madero 13 (no phone; ③), with overpriced en suite rooms and cheaper bathless ones around a courtyard, and *Hotel Chilpancingo*, Alemán 8 (☎747/2-24-46; ②), with primitive but serviceable cells.

You can **eat** light meals or cake with an espresso at *El Portal*, beside the cathedral on Madero, or find more substantial meals at *Marthita*, Guerrero 6B, and *La Parroquía*, off the north side of the zócalo. The cafe in the *Casino del Estudiantes* on Guerrero near Madero is cheap and good, and the best place to ask if there is anything happening in the way of **nightlife**.

South of Acapulco: the Costa Chica

It is hardly surprising that most tourists zoom straight through the stretch of Hwy-200 south of Acapulco: there's little in the way of facilities between here and Puerto Escondido – a good seven hours on the bus. However, if you have your own transport, it's worth taking some time out to explore this occasionally bizarre coastline, not least for the few great **beaches**.

The people who inhabit the area towards the border of Oaxaca are for the most part either Amuzgo Indian or black – the descendants of African Bantu slaves who escaped and settled here. And the look of the land is vaguely reminiscent of Africa – flat grazing country in which many of the villages consist of thatched huts. In **Coajinicuilapa** the impression is reinforced by the predominance of round constructions, though these are in fact as much a local Indian tradition as an African one. From here a road runs some 20km down to the coast at **Punta Maldonada**, which, along with nearby San Nicolas, has some beautiful beaches but virtually no facilities, and only one or two buses a day. Above all it's famed for glass-clear water and perfect skin diving and snorkelling – most people come down in campers to take advantage.

If you want to break your journey in rather more comfort, there are two possibilities. **OMETEPEC**, an old gold-mining town a few kilometres inland of the main road before it reaches Coajinicuilapa, has several small hotels. Although it's off the highway, there are hourly buses to Acapulco, so it's easy enough to get back to the junction and pick up transport heading south from there. The second option is **PINOTEPA NACIONAL**, across the border in the state of Oaxaca, where again there are a number of basic places to stay. Pinotepa's Sunday market is one of the best in the region, a meeting place for local Amuzgo, Mixtec and Chatino Indians.

fiestas

January

NEW YEAR'S DAY is celebrated everywhere. In **Cruz Grande** (Guerrero), on the coast road about 120km east of Acapulco, the start of a week-long *feria*.

2nd Tuesday DÍA DE JESÚS AGONIZANTE is marked in **Colima** (Colima) by a mass pilgrimage to a nearby hacienda.

26th In **Tecomán** (Col.), on the coast road, a colourful religious procession.

February

2nd DÍA DE LA CANDELARIA (Candlemas) celebrated in **Colima** (Col.) and **Tecomán** (Col.) with dances, processions and fireworks. Similar events in **Zumpango del Río** (Gro.), on the road from Acapulco to México, and particularly good dancing in **Atzacualoya** (Gro.), off this road near Chilpancingo.

5th Fiesta Brava – a day of bullfights and horse races – in **Colima** (Col.).

CARNIVAL (the week before Lent: variable Feb–March). **Acapulco** (Gro.) and **Manzanillo** (Col.) are both famous for the exuberance of their celebrations; rooms can be hard to find.

March

6th Local fiesta in **Zumpango del Río** (Gro.) lasts through the night and into the following day – traditional dances.

10th Exuberant FIESTA DE SAN PATRICIO in **San Patricio** (Jal.) continues for a week.

19th DÍA DE SAN JOSÉ is the excuse for fiestas in **Tierra Colorada** (Gro.), between Acapulco and Chilpancingo, and **San Jeronimo** just outside Acapulco.

HOLY WEEK is widely observed: the Palm Sunday celebrations in **Petatlán** (Gro.), just south of Zihuatanejo, are particularly fervent.

May

3rd DÍA DE LA SANTA CRUZ. Saint's day festival in **Cruz Grande** (Gro.).

5th The victorious battle of Cinco de Mayo commemorated – especially in **Acapulco** (Gro.).

8th In **Mochitlán** (Gro.), near Chilpancingo, the Festival de las Lluvias has pre-Christian roots: pilgrims, peasants and local dance groups climb a nearby volcano at night, arriving at the summit at dawn to pray for rain. Also a local fiesta in **Azoyu** (Gro.), just off the coast road south of Acapulco.

15th DÍA DE SAN ISIDRO provokes a week-long festival in **Acapulco**. Celebrations too in **San Luis Acatlán** (Gro.), south along the coast, where you might see the rare *Danza de la Tortuga* (Dance of the Turtle), and in **Tierra Colorada** (Gro.).

31st **Puerto Vallarta** (Jal.) celebrates its Founder's Day.

June

1st DÍA DE LA MARINA (Navy Day) in the ports, particularly **Manzanillo** and **Acapulco**.

13th DÍA DE SAN ANTONIO. A *feria* in **Tierra Colorada** (Gro.).

3rd Sunday. Blessing of the Animals at the church of Jesús Agonizante outside **Colima** (Col.).

July

25th At **Coyuca da Benitez** (Gro.), very near Acapulco, festival of the patron saint. A colourful fiesta too in **Mochitlán** (Gro.).

August

6th A fiesta in **Petatlán** (Gro.) distinguished by dances and a mock battle between Indians and Spaniards.

23rd DÍA DE SAN BARTOLOMÉ. In **Tecpán de Galeana** (Gro.), between Acapulco and Zihuatanejo, religious processions the preceding night are followed by dancing, music and fireworks.

September

15th–16th INDEPENDENCE CELEBRATIONS almost everywhere.

28th DÍA DE SANTIAGO celebrated in several villages immediately around **Acapulco** (Gro.).

29th DÍA DE SAN MIGUEL exuberantly exploited in **Azoyu** (Gro.) and **Mochitlán** (Gro.).

November

First week **Colima**'s major *feria* runs from the last days of October until November 8th.

2nd DAY OF THE DEAD is widely observed, with picturesque traditions in **Atoyac de Alvarez** (Gro.), just off the Acapulco–Zihuatanejo road.

December

12th DÍA DE NUESTRA SEÑORA DE GUADALUPE, patroness of Mexico. In **Atoyac de Alvarez** (Gro.) and **Ayutla** (Gro.) there are religious processions and traditional dances, while **Acapulco** enjoys more secular celebrations. In **Manzanillo** (Col.) the celebrations start at the beginning of the month, while in **Puerto Vallarta** (Jal.) they continue to the end of it.

travel details

Buses

Bus services all along the coast are frequent and fast, with the possible exception of the stretch between Manzanillo and Lázaro Cárdenas and there are almost constant departures on the major routes heading inland. The southern sector – Acapulco and Zihuatanejo – is served largely by *Estrella de Oro* (first-class) and *Flecha Roja* (second-class). In the north there's more competition, but since everywhere of size – except, for the moment, Puerto Vallarta – has a unified Central Camionera, this is rarely a problem. *Tres Estrellas de Oro, Transportes del Pacifico* and *Omnibus de Mexico* are the first-class standbys, while *Autobuses de Occidente, TNS* and *Flecha Amarilla* are the most widely seen second-class outfits. The following list covers **first-class services** and some local second-class services. On most routes there are as many, if not more, second-class buses, which take around 20 percent longer.

Acapulco to: Chilpancingo (hourly; 2hr); Cuernavaca (7 daily; 6hr); Guadalajara (3 daily; 17hr); Lázaro Cárdenas (8 daily; 6–7hr); Manzanillo (5 daily; 12hr); México (60 daily; 5–9hr); Puerto Escondido (10 daily; 7hr); Puerto Vallarta (2 daily; 10hr); Salina Cruz (7 daily; 12–13hr); Taxco (4 daily; 4hr); Tijuana (3 daily; 35hr+); Zihuatanejo (every 30min; 4–5hr).

Barra de Navidad to: Cihuatlán (every 30min; 15min); Colima (1 daily; 2hr 30min); Guadalajara (10 daily; 6–7hr); Manzanillo (3 daily; 1hr 30min); Puerto Vallarta (2 daily; 5hr).

Chilpancingo to: Acapulco (hourly; 2hr); México (hourly; 3hr 30min).

Colima to: Barra de Navidad (1 daily, 2hr30min; 15min); Comala (every 15min; 20min); Guadalajara (hourly; 3hr); Lázaro Cárdenas (6 daily; 6–7hr); Manzanillo (every 30min; 1hr 30min); México (12 daily; 11hr); Puerto Vallarta (1 daily; 6hr); Tecomán (every 15min; 45min).

Lázaro Cárdenas to: Acapulco (8 daily; 6–7hr); Colima (6 daily; 6–7hr); Guadalajara (3 daily; 6hr); Manzanillo (9 daily; 6hr); México (5 daily; 11–14hr); Morelia (10 daily; 7–8hr); Pátzcuaro (1 daily; 7hr); Puerto Vallarta (3 daily; 12hr); Uruapán (5 daily; 6hr); Zihuatanejo (hourly; 2hr).

Manzanillo to: Acapulco (5 daily; 12hr); Barra de Navidad (3 daily; 1hr 30min); Colima (every 30min; 1hr 30min); Guadalajara (every 30min; 5–

6hr); Lázaro Cárdenas (9 daily; 6hr); Puerto Vallarta (11 daily; 5–7hr); Tijuana (3 daily; 38hr).

Puerto Vallarta to: Acapulco (2 daily; 10hr); Barra de Navidad (2 daily; 5hr); Colima (1 daily; 6hr); Guadalajara (at least hourly; 6–7hr); Lázaro Cárdenas (3 daily; 12hr); Manzanillo (11 daily; 5–7hr); Mazatlán (2 daily; 8hr); México (6 daily; 14hr); Tepic (every 30min; 2hr 30min).

Zihuatanejo to: Acapulco (every 30min; 4–5hr); Ixtapa (continuously; 15min); Lázaro Cárdenas (hourly; 2hr); Mazatlán (6 daily; 7–8hr); Salina Cruz (2 daily; 17–18hr).

Trains

The main rail line in the region links **Manzanillo** to **Colima** and **Guadalajara**. The tunnels are currently being renovated so the present schedule may change once this work is complete sometime in 1996. For the moment the single daily train leaves Manzanillo at 11.10pm, arriving at Colima at 1am and at Guadalajara at 7.35am. Returning, it leaves Guadalajara at 8pm arriving Manzanillo at 4.15am. A second line links **Lázaro Cárdenas** and **Morelia**, the daily train leaving at noon and arriving in Morelia at midnight.

Planes

This section of Mexico's coast is well served by **flights**, with international services to Acapulco, Puerto Vallarta and Zihuatanejo and domestic flights to various points in between. Guadalajara and México are accessible from Manzanillo, Ixtapa/Zihuatanejo and Acapulco; Acapulco also has flights to US cities including Chicago, Dallas, Houston and Los Angeles.

Puerto Vallarta is one of the busiest air hubs in Mexico, with flights to: Chicago (1 daily); Dallas (1 daily); Denver (1 daily); Detroit (1 daily); Guadalajara (8 daily); Houston (1 daily); Los Angeles (4 daily); Los Cabos (2 a week); México (6 daily); San Diego (1 daily); San Francisco (1 daily); and Seattle (1 daily).

CHAPTER SEVEN

VERACRUZ

T he central Gulf coast is among the most distinct, atmospheric areas of Mexico. From the capital you descend through the southern fringes of the Sierra Madre Oriental, past the country's highest peaks, to a broad, hot, wet, lush and jungly coastal plain. In this fertile tropical zone the earliest Mexican civilizations developed, and it remained densely populated throughout the pre-Hispanic era. Cortés

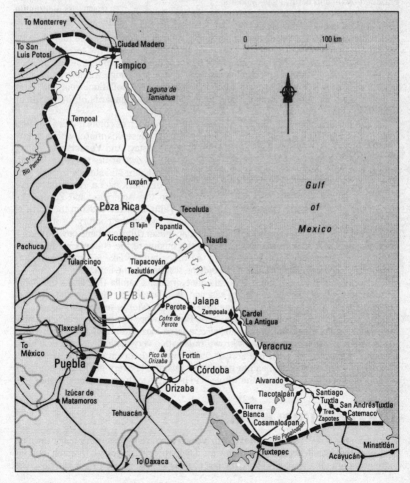

himself began his march on the capital from Veracruz, and the city remains, as it was throughout colonial history, the busiest port in the country. Rich in agriculture – coffee, vanilla, tropical fruits and flowers grow everywhere – the Gulf coast is further enriched by oil and natural gas deposits.

Few tourists come here, and those who do are mostly passing through. In part, at least, this is because the area doesn't need them and makes no particular effort to attract them; in part the **weather** can be blamed – it rains more often and more heavily here than just about anywhere else. Yet even in the rainy season the torrential downpours are shortlived, and within a couple of hours of the rain starting, you can be back on the steaming streets in bright sunshine. There are long, windswept Atlantic **beaches** all down the coast, and although many suffer pollution from the busy shipping lanes and the oil industry, and none is up to the standards of the Pacific or Caribbean shores, enough remain to make a real attraction.

On the eastern slopes of the Sierra Madre are a number of colonial cities worth a look in passing: **Jalapa**, seat of the state government, deserves more, with a balmy climate and a superb archeological museum to repay a stay. And **Veracruz** is among the most welcoming of Mexican cities – too busy with its own affairs to create a separate life for visitors, you're drawn instead into the atmosphere of a steamy tropical port with strong echoes of the Indies. Within a couple of hours lie **La Antigua**, where Cortés established the first Spanish government in the Americas, and **Zempoala**, ruined site of the first civilization he subdued. **El Tajín**, near the coast in the north of the state, is one of the most important archeological sites in the country – surrounded now by oilfields, it's also in an area where Totonac Indian culture retains powerful influence. South, **Lake Catemaco** again reflects the mixing of the cultures: middle-class Veracruzanos have their villas overlooking the water, but the lake is also renowned as a meeting place for Indian *brujos* and *curanderos*, witches and healers.

The **food**, too, is great – not only local coffee, fruit and vanilla (Mexicans inevitably take home a plastic bottle of vanilla essence as a souvenir), but also the seafood. *Huachinango a la Veracruzana* (red snapper Veracruz style) is served throughout the country, and is of course on every menu here. But there are many more exotic possibilities, from langoustines and prawns to *jaiba*, a large local crab; look out for anything made with *chile chipotle*, a hot, dark brown *chile* with a very distinctive (and delicious) flavour – *chilpachole de jaiba* is a sort of crab chowder that combines the two. Sweet *tamales*, too, are a speciality, and to go with all this, the brewery at Orizaba produces several local beers – cheaper on the whole, and better, than the big national brands.

The route from México

If you take the direct bus **from México to Veracruz** you'll bypass every major town en route on the excellent new toll highway; if you're driving yourself, watch out for extremely high tolls. If time is short, the fast route is a blessing – Veracruz and the coast are very much the outstanding attractions – but there are at least three cities in the mountains that merit a stop if you're in no hurry. This is, however, the rainiest area of all, and while it brings bounties in terms of great coffee and a luxuriance of flowers, downpours can become a problem. Particularly irritating – especially in October and November – is what the locals call *chipichipi*: a persistent fine drizzle caused by warm airstreams from the Gulf hitting cooler air as they reach the eastern face of the Sierra. When it's not raining this is among the most beautiful drives in Mexico. As Ixtaccíhuatl gradually disappears behind you, the snow on the Pico de Orizaba comes into view, and the plains of corn and maguey in the west are supplanted on the eastern slopes by woods of pine and cypress, and by green fields with fat and contented cows out to pasture.

Orizaba

ORIZABA, first major town in the state of Veracruz, some 150km from Puebla, is largely an industrial city in spite of its colonial centre. What Orizaba lacks in innate charm, though, it makes up for by being positioned at the foot of the **Pico de Orizaba** (or *Citlaltépetl*), a perfectly formed volcano and, at 5700m, the highest peak in Mexico.

There's further comfort in that the most important industry here is brewing, with the giant *Cervecería Moctezuma* producing some of the best **beer** in the republic – ask at the tourist office for details of tours. Seeing the town need only take a couple of hours even so, and there are more attractive places to spend the night farther down the road at Fortín and Córdoba. If, however, you plan to tackle the Pico de Orizaba – and the climb, outlined in detail in R J Secor's *Mexican Volcanoes*, is only for serious mountaineers – you should change here for the second-class bus to the villages of Serdán or Tlachichuca, from where the main trails start.

Practicalities

The **tourist office** (Mon–Fri 10am–1pm & 5–7pm, Sat 10am–1pm), on Norte 1 between Poniente 2 and 4, right behind the Palacio Municipal, can help with further information. Should you need **to stay**, the *Gran Hotel de France*, Oriente 6 no. 186 at Sur 5, near the *ADO* bus station (☎272/5-23-11; ⑤), offers rooms with a degree of class; there's cheaper accommodation along Norte 4, including the *San Cristóbal* (☎272/5-11-40; ②).

Fortín de las Flores

FORTÍN DE LAS FLORES (Fortress of the Flowers), where a beautiful minor route cuts across country to Jalapa, lies on the old road to Córdoba, 12km away. For once, its name is singularly appropriate, for here more than anywhere in the state there are flowers all over the place – in the plaza, in the hotels, on the hillsides all around. Rain, which is frequent from May to December, and the constant muggy warmth ensure their growth – with the coming of the rains in May wild orchids bloom freely.

The fortress of the name has all but disappeared, but you can visit the **Hacienda de las Animas**, once a residence of Maximilian and Carlota, now part of the luxurious *Fortín de las Flores* (☎27/13-00-55; ⑥), at Av. 2 between calles 5 and 7. Rooms here are reasonable considering the facilities: there's a huge swimming pool and the gardens are exquisite. A few kilometres out of town, the **Barranca de Matalarga** exemplifies the luxuriance of the vegetation: above the ravine you see plantations of coffee and fruit trees, while the banks of the torrent itself are thick with a stunning variety of wild plants, and with hummingbirds and insects. It's a small town, but there are a number of inexpensive **places to stay**: try the *Bugambilias* (☎27/13-05-22; ③), not far from the *Fortín de las Flores* on Av. 1 between calles 7 and 9; several other cheap places to stay and to eat are nearby on Av. 1, and the *Bugambilias* itself has a decent restaurant.

Córdoba

Second-class buses take the mountain road from Fortín to Jalapa fairly regularly, but on towards the coast it's only a few kilometres farther to **CÓRDOBA**, the centre of the local coffee trade, a busy modern town grown up around a somewhat decaying colonial centre. Founded in 1618 by thirty Spanish families – and so also known as the City of the Thirty Knights – its main claim to fame is that here, in 1821, the last Spanish viceroy, Juan O'Donoju, signed a treaty acknowledging Mexican Independence with General Iturbide, soon to become emperor. This took place in the Palacio de los Condes de Zeballos – known as the **Hotel Zevallos**, though it's not a hotel – on the zócalo. There's not a great deal to do beyond sitting in the zócalo, sampling the coffee under the arcades and listening to the music, but it's a pleasant enough place to do that: the *Café Parroquia* occupies part of the Hotel Zevallos.

Practicalities

There are two **bus** terminals in Córdoba: the *AU* terminal, ten minutes' walk from the zócalo at Av. 7 and c/9, is permanently crowded and confused. You're more likely to get a seat on the main routes at the quieter *ADO* first-class terminal, Av. 3 at c/4. Buses to Fortín de las Flores leave every ten minutes or so from the corner of c/3 and Av. 5 and take about fifteen minutes. The **post office** (Mon–Fri 8am–8pm, Sat & Sun 9am–1pm) is in the Palacio Municipal on Av. 3, half a block from the plaza towards the *ADO* station.

As well as the more pricey **hotels** around the zócalo, you'll find plenty of cheap places scattered about, especially along Av. 2. Closest to the action are the *Virreinal*, by the side of the cathedral at the corner of Av. 1 and c/5 (☎27/12-23-77; ④), and the *Mansur*, in the same block of Av. 1, which is quiet, though not cheap (☎27/12-60-00; ④). Slightly farther out are the pleasant *Iberia*, Av. 2 no. 919 (☎27/12-13-01; ③), and the *Marina*, Av. 2 at c/11 (☎27/12-26-00; ③), which has a restaurant. **Places to eat** are in the same areas. In the zócalo, the cafes are good but pricey: the *Restaurant El Cordobés* has a varied menu, huge *comidas*, and an excellent Sunday buffet. There's also a good restaurant at the *Virreinal*. Cheaper options are along Av. 2. For breakfast and heaps of fresh fruit, the *ADO* bus station cafe, is unbeatable.

Jalapa

Although it's a slower route, a number of buses go from México to Veracruz via **JALAPA** (or Xalapa, as locals and bus companies frequently spell it). The state capital, Jalapa is remarkably attractive despite its relative modernity, and set in countryside of sometimes breathtaking beauty. The city sprawls across a tumbling hillside below the volcanic peak of the Cofre de Perote (4282m), and enjoys a richness of vegetation almost the equal of Fortín's (with which it also shares a warm, damp climate). In addition to these natural advantages, Jalapa has been promoted by its civic leaders as a cultural centre, and frequent music festivals, or other events, may well add to your stay. Home of the **University of Veracruz**, it's a lively place, enjoyable even if you're doing no more than hanging around watching life pass by.

Arrival and information

Jalapa's modern **bus station**, with every facility including a **tourist information** kiosk where you can book rooms, is a couple of kilometres east of the centre on 20 de Noviembre. If you manage to get past the taxi drivers vying for your custom, there are buses to take you downtown: look for "Centro". Buses back to the bus station are marked "CAXA" (Central de Autobuses de Xalapa). If you're heading on **from Jalapa to Veracruz** you'll pass through Zempoala (p.376), and if you have a couple of hours it's well worth breaking the journey here to visit the ruins.

There's another **tourist office** (Mon–Fri 8am–3pm & 6–9pm, Sat 9am–1pm; ☎28/18-72-02) a long way northwest of the centre on Av. M A Camacho, but it's barely worth the long trek out. To **change money**, try *Banco Serfin* at Zamora and Mata (Mon–Fri 9–11.30am), or the *casa de cambio* nearby at Zamora 36-A (Mon–Fri 9am–1pm & 4–6pm, Sat 10am–1pm). The **post office** (Mon–Fri 7am–6pm) is on the corner of Diego Leño and Zamora.

Accommodation

Most of the cheaper **hotels** are along Av. Revolución, which runs north from the zócalo, Parque Juárez, towards the market area, and there's a congregration of more expensive options on Zaragoza, east of the Parque.

Continental, Zamora 4 (☎28/17-35-30). Shabby but popular colonial-style hotel, a couple of blocks east of the Parque. Rooms at the back aren't too noisy; those at the front are. ③.

Hotel del Bosque, Revolución 163 (☎28/17-69-80). One of the better budget hotels. ②.

Limón, Revolución 8, in the final block before the zócalo (☎28/17-22-04). Comfortable but noisy. ②.

Maria Victoria, Zaragoza 6 (☎28/18-60-11). Luxury option with all the facilities you'd expect for the price. ⑤.

Posada Santiago, Ursulo Galván 89, near the Parque Juárez (☎28/18-63-33). Clean and friendly, family-owned place. ②.

Principal, Zaragoza 28 (☎28/17-64-00). Large, comfortable rooms. ③.

Salmones, Zaragoza 24 (☎28/17-54-31). Colonial-style hotel with carpeted rooms and a good restaurant. ③–④.

The Town

Downtown, the small colonial area around the Parque Juárez, is the main attraction – the eighteenth-century **Cathedral** and **Palacio de Gobierno** (with murals by the Chilean artist José Chaves Morado) both deserve to be seen, and, at dusk, the trees around the zócalo are filled with extraordinarily raucous birds. Jalapa's lively arts crowd meets up at the **Agora de la Ciudad**, a cultural centre in the Parque; and just west on Av. M Avila Camacho is the **Teatro del Estado**, home to the state orchestra – for more on both of these see "Nightlife", p.370.

If you're feeling energetic, you could also climb **Macuiltepec**. At 1590m, this is the highest of the hills on which the town is built, and from its *mirador* – if you're lucky – you might catch a glimpse of the Gulf. About thirty minutes' walk from the centre (or a ride on the "Tepic" bus), Macuiltepec also boasts an Ecological Park at its base, with a specially designed barbecue and picnic area. Entrance is from c/Tepic or Volcán de Colima (Tues–Sun 6am–5pm).

Jalapa's outstanding sight, however, is the **Archeology Museum** (Tues–Sun 9am–5pm; $3.50) located on the outskirts of town – take any bus marked "Xalapa" along Dr Lucio. They say it's the second-best archeological museum in the country (for the best, of course, you should head for México), and for good reason. Certainly the collection itself can rival any outside the capital in both extent and quality, and the building that houses it, flowing down the hillside in a series of spacious marble steps, may well be the finest in Mexico. It's a wonderful introduction to the various pre-Hispanic cultures of the Gulf coast. You start at the top of the hill, where the first halls deal with the **Olmecs**. There are several of the celebrated colossal stone heads, a vast array of other monumental statuary and some beautiful masks. Later cultures are represented mainly through their pottery – lifelike human and animal figurines especially – and there are also displays on the architecture of the major sites: El Tajín, Zempoala and so on. Finally, with the Huaxtec culture come more giant stone statues. Some of the larger, less valuable pieces are displayed in the landscaped gardens outside. There's a cafe on the first floor, and also a shop selling fantastic, though expensive, masks.

Around Jalapa

With more time on your hands, a number of worthwhile **excursions** can be made into the jungly country around Jalapa. Just a couple of kilometres south of the city, on the road to Coatepec (local bus), is the **Jardín Botanico Francisco Clavijero** (Tues–Sun 10am–5pm; free), a collection of plants native to the state, from jungle to mountain forest. Farther out in this same direction, the villages of **Coatepec** itself and **Teocelo** are also worth a visit, mainly for their beautiful setting. Nearby is the spectacular **Cascada de Texolo**, a triple waterfall that can be admired from an ancient iron bridge. Many of the scenes in the film *Romancing the Stone* were shot around these villages and waterfalls, and there are more sets from the film around the village of **Naolinco**, north of Jalapa. All can be reached by local bus; further details from the tourist office. To get to the Cascada de Texolo, take a bus from the *ADO* station to Xico (about 20min), and get off at the outskirts of the village, by a tiny church. Then ask the way – it's forty minutes' hot walk along a paved road through banana and coffee plantations, but worth it. On the road to Veracruz, 10km outside the city, is the **museum of El Lencero** (Tues–Sat 10am–5pm): a colonial hacienda that was once the property of the controversial general and president, Antonio López de Santa Anna. It is preserved in its full nineteenth-century splendour, and the grounds and surrounding countryside are stunning too. The Chilean poet Gabriela Mistral stayed here in 1949, and wrote about the fine view of the coast.

Eating and drinking

Good **food** is abundant in Jalapa; the city is home to the *jalapeño* pepper, which you'll probably taste at all main meals. Another one of the great pleasures here is local coffee served with *pan dulce* in a traditional cafe. Several of these, including the very popular *La Parroquia*, can be found on Zaragoza, the street just below the zócalo; they serve good full meals too. Or head for the small but excellent *Café Latino*, at the bottom of Zamora, near the post office. Inexpensive full meals can as ever be found around the market, but more appetizing restaurants, and some good *jugo* and *torta* places, are concentrated around Av. Enriquez (the continuation of Camacho on the other side of the zócalo). The Callejón dell Diamante, an alley leading uphill off Enriquez by the *Hotel Regis*, has several good-value, Mexican family restaurants, popular at lunch, including *La Fonda*, *La Sopa* and the excellent *El Mayab*, which serves a huge, fresh *comida*. The cheapest **breakfast** in town can be had at *Terraza Jardín*, on Enriquez overlooking Parque Juárez. For **vegetarians**, *El Champiñion* at Allende 78 has excellent food and a noticeboard for contacts.

Nightlife

Jalapa is a city of great creative energy, boosted by a large **student community**, a number of good **theatres** and an excellent **orchestra**. The main attraction after dark, however, is the number of *peñas* and **bars** offering folk music, theatre and poetry. Cover charges are rare, beer is reasonably priced, and, refreshingly, there's little or no intimidating macho atmosphere. A free fortnightly listings sheet, *La Farándula*, is available from cafes, museums and galleries, and provides useful information on where to go and what to see.

Agora de la Ciudad, Parque Juárez. Thriving arts centre with a cinema, theatre, gallery, bookshop and coffee shop. Tues–Sun 8.30am–9pm.

La Guarida, Ursulo Galván 2. A *peña* right next to the Parque Juárez. Live music most nights. It's a very small narrow space, which fills up quickly with students and arty types. Thurs–Sat 8pm–1am.

Los Molinos, Ursulo Galván 57. Near *La Guarida*, this restaurant-bar offers a wide selection of spirits as well as free live entertainment at weekends. Mon–Sat 8pm–1am.

El Tapanco, Hidalgo 18. Video bar offering live music too. Wed–Sun 8pm–1am.

La Tasca del Cantor, Xicotencatl 76. Live music and occasional art exhibitions. The owner is friendly, and the crowd a pleasant mix of local bohemians. Wed–Sat 8pm–1am.

Teatro del Estado, at the corner of M. Avila Camacho and c/de la Llave. The Orquesta Sinfónica de Jalapa gives regular performances here, with some free off-season concerts (June–Aug); also dance and theatre.

Veracruz

VILLA RICA DE LA VERACRUZ was the first town founded by the Spanish in Mexico, a few days after Cortés' arrival on Good Friday, 1519.

> *As soon as we had made this treaty of alliance with the Totonacs . . . we decided with their ready help at once to found the city of Villa Rica de la Veracruz. So we planned a church, a marketplace, arsenals and all the other features of a town, and built a fort.*

This first development – little more than a wooden stockade – was in fact some way to the north, later being moved to La Antigua (see p.376) and subsequently to its present site in 1589. But the modern city is very much the heir of the original; only recently, for the first time since its foundation, has Veracruz begun to lose its position as the most important port in Mexico (to Tampico and Coatzacoalcos), and its history reflects every major event from the Conquest on. "Veracruz", states Paul

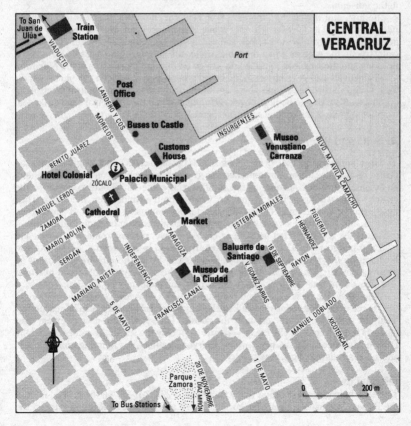

Theroux, "is known as the 'heroic city'. It is a poignant description: in Mexico a hero is nearly always a corpse."

And if the modern city is far from dead, then certainly its past has been a series of "invasions, punitive missions and local military defeats . . . humiliation as history". This started even before the Conquest was complete, when Panfilo Narvaez landed here on his ill-fated mission to bring Cortés back under the control of the governor of Cuba, and continued intermittently for the next 400 years. Throughout the sixteenth and seventeenth centuries Veracruz, and the Spanish galleons that used the port were preyed on constantly by English, Dutch and French buccaneers. In the War of Independence the Spanish made their final stand here, holding the fortress of San Juan Ulúa for four years after the country had been lost. In **1838** the French occupied the city, demanding compensation for French property and citizens who had suffered in the years following Independence; in **1847** US troops took Veracruz, and from here marched on to capture the capital; in **1862** the French, supported by Spanish and English forces that soon withdrew, invaded on the pretext of forcing Mexico to pay her foreign debt, but ended up staying five years and setting up the unfortunate Maximilian as emperor; and finally in **1914** US marines were back, occupying the city to protect American interests during the Revolution. These are the *Cuatro Veces Heroica* of the city's official title, and form the bulk of the history displayed, with a certain bitterness, in the museums.

The first, and the lasting, impression of Veracruz, however, is not of its history or bitterness, but of its life now. The city is one of the most enjoyable places in the republic in which simply to be, to sit back and watch – or join – the daily round. This is especially true in the evening when the tables under the *portales* of the plaza fill up, and the drinking and the *marimba* music begin – to go on through most of the night. **Marimba** – a distinctively Latin-Caribbean sound based around a giant wooden xylophone – is *the* local sound, but at peak times there are *mariachi* bands too, and individual strolling crooners, all striving to be heard over each other. When the municipal band strikes up from the middle of the square, confusion is total.

Arrival and information

The **bus stations**, both *ADO* first-class and *AU* second-class, are a long way from the centre on Av. Díaz Mirón (the entrance to second-class is actually on the street behind, La Fragua). Any bus heading to the right as you come out should take you to the centre – most will have "Díaz Mirón" or "Centro" on the windscreen; if not, ask. They head straight to the end of Díaz Mirón, round a confusing junction at the Parque Zamora, and then take a variety of routes that mostly end up on Independencia as it runs past the zócalo. To get back, head for 5 de Mayo, parallel to Independencia, and take any bus marked "Camionera". The **train station** is very central, only about five blocks from the zócalo along the dock-front. If you fly in, the **airport** is 10km or so south of the city; *Transportacion Aeropuerto* runs the usual system of official *colectivos* and taxis downtown – for a pick-up to the airport, call them on ☎29/32-35-20.

Although Veracruz is a large and rambling city, the downtown area, once you've got to it, is relatively straightforward and small – anywhere farther afield can be reached by local bus from somewhere very near the **zócalo**. This, to an even greater extent than usual, is the epicentre of city life in Veracruz – not only the site of the cathedral and the Palacio Municipal, but the place where everyone gathers, for morning coffee, lunch, afternoon strolls and night-time revelry.

Information

There's a helpful **tourist office** (daily 9am–9pm; ☎29/32-19-99) on the ground floor of the Palacio Municipal right on the zócalo; there's also a **hotel-booking service** at the airport souvenir shop. **Changing money**, the quickest service is at the *casa de cambio*, Juárez 112, a block from the port (Mon–Fri 9am–2pm & 4–7pm, Sat 9am–1pm). The queues may be shorter, though, at *Comermex*, corner of 5 de Mayo and Juárez, or at *Bancomer* and *Banamex*, around the corner in Independencia, all of which change travellers' cheques. The **post office** (Mon–Fri 8am–8pm, Sat & Sun 9am–noon) is on the Plaza de la Republica, a couple of blocks north of the zócalo.

Accommodation

There's a **hotel** right next to the first-class bus station, and several very cheap and rather grim places around the back of the second-class bus terminal, but unless you've arrived very late at night there's no point in staying this far out. The other cheap places are mostly within a couple of blocks of the zócalo, often around the market; they're nothing to write home about, and noise can be a real problem, but at least you should find a clean room with a fan. There are also a few more expensive options on the zócalo itself. Alternatively, you could try staying out by the beach, where there are some reasonable Mexican family hotels and a number of **campsites**. Take the "Boca del Río" bus and get off when you see something promising.

Amparo, Serdán 482 (☎29/32-27-38). One of a cluster of cheap places, behind the zócalo near the market. ③.

Baluarte, Canal 265 at Av. 16 de Septiembre (☎29/32-60-42). Well-kept hotel with pool, TV, a/c and views of the Baluarte de Santiago, though not the friendliest of places. ④.

Cielo, S Perez Abascal 580 (☎29/37-23-67). Pleasant enough but inconvenient unless you've arrived late at the second-class bus terminal. ③.

Colonial, Lerdo 105 (☎29/32-01-93). Right on the plaza at the heart of the action, the best-value of the places here. Variety of rooms and prices; the tempting ones with balconies over the plaza can be noisy at night. ⑤.

Mar y Tierra, M Avila Camacho at Figueroa (☎29/32-02-60). A/c rooms in the old (at the front) and new buildings are very different, so look first: some have sea views. Overpriced restaurant. ④.

Marisol de Veracruz, Díaz Mirón 1242 (☎29/32-53-99). Three blocks from the *ADO* terminal. Clean rooms with fan or a/c; quieter than the nearby *Central*. ③.

Oriente, Lerdo 20 (☎29/31-24-90). Handy for the zócalo – walk past the side of the Palacio Municipal and into a small park facing the Customs House (*Aduana Maritima*) and other port authority buildings and it's on your right. Smallish a/c rooms. ⑤.

Rex, Morelos 225 (☎29/32-54-36). Past the *Oriente*, more or less opposite the post office on the Plaza de la Republica. A former convent with spacious rooms around a flower-filled courtyard, but it has definitely seen better days. ②.

Royalty, M Avila Camacho and Abasolo (☎29/36-14-90). Clean and friendly, with a/c rooms plus some cheaper ones with a fan, TV and small balcony. Far enough away from the noise but close enough to get everywhere on foot. ⑤.

Veracruz, Independencia and Lerdo, overlooking the zócalo (☎29/31-22-33). Pick of the upmarket places, if only for its position. Thoroughly refurbished; seventh-floor pool. ⑦.

Villa Rica, M Avila Camacho 7 (☎29/32-07-82). A little way out, just past Doblado, but close to the water. Small, simple rooms with fan. ③.

The City

The outstanding sight in Veracruz is the **Castillo de San Juan de Ulúa** (Tues–Sun 9am–5pm; $4), the great fortress that so signally failed to protect the harbour. In most cases this was hardly the fault of its defenders, since every sensible invader landed somewhere on the coast nearby, captured the town and, having cut off the fort by land and sea, called for its surrender. Certainly the fortifications are impressively massive despite their dire state of disrepair, and from the walls there are superb views over the harbour and city. A bus runs out regularly (it's a very long walk, through parts of town you would not want to explore alone) past the busiest part of the docks and along the great harbour bar that joins the mainland to the former reef on which the castle stands. Catch it on Av. Landero y Cos, in front of the tacky souvenir stands that line the dockside.

The fortress is thoroughly run-down – watch out for unguarded ten-metre drops and take a torch if you really want to penetrate the dingy, dripping depths – but fascinating nonetheless, and a fitting location for the climactic chase scene in *Romancing the Stone* that was shot here. You can still see the gun emplacements on the great walks around the ramparts, today overseeing a busy modern port; and, within the defences, the arsenals (some still with a few rusty cannons lying around), barracks and dungeons, partially submerged at high tide. For more on the fort's history, take a look inside the small **museum**.

Back in town there are two museums worth seeing. The **Museo de la Ciudad** (Mon–Sat 9am–4pm; $3) covers local history and folklore from the earliest inhabitants to the 1914 US invasion. Inevitably, it's rather a potted version, and many of the exhibits go completely unexplained, but there's some beautiful Olmec and Totonac sculpture, including one of the giant Olmec heads; fascinating photographs of more recent events; and relics of the city's various "heroic defenders".

The Museo de la Ciudad occupies an old mansion on Zaragoza, about five blocks from the Palacio Municipal, and from here it's an easy walk, down past the market, to the malecón at the side of the harbour. Here the **Museo Venustiano Carranza** is in the old *faro* (lighthouse), alongside the huge *Banco de México* building on Insurgentes. Venustiano Carranza established his Constitutionalist government in Veracruz in 1915 (with the support of US President Woodrow Wilson, whose troops then occupied the town), living in the Castillo de San Juan and running his government – and the war against Villa and Zapata – from this lighthouse building. There's a fine statue of Carranza outside, looking exactly as John Reed describes him in *Insurgent Mexico*: "A towering, khaki-clad figure, seven feet tall it seemed . . . arms hanging loosely by his side, his fine old head thrown back." Inside are gathered assorted memorabilia of his government's term here, and you can view Carranza's bedroom and living room. Opening hours (officially Tues–Fri 9am–1pm & 4–6pm, Sat & Sun 9am–noon; free) seem to be at the whim of the navy, whose local headquarters the building also houses.

Two blocks south and three west from the Carranza museum, you can't miss the **Baluarte de Santiago**, a seventeenth-century fort between Av. 16 de Septiembre and Gómez Faria. Originally one of nine forts along a 2650-metre long wall, the Baluarte is now the only survivor – it's hard to imagine that the sea reached this far when the fort was built in 1635. You can go inside for a wander around the small museum (daily 9am–5pm; $4.50, free on Sun).

The city's newest attraction is the **Acuario de Veracruz** (Mon–Fri 10am–7pm, Sat & Sun 9am–7pm; $5, children half-price), in the shopping centre next to the *Hotel Villa del Mar* on Blvd. M Avila Camacho. Designed by a Japanese architect, the aquarium isn't exactly huge but it is impressive, with waterturtles and other aquatic beasts enjoying the natural-looking surroundings.

Veracruz beaches

You wouldn't make a special trip to Veracruz for its **beaches** – although for Mexicans from the capital it's a relatively cheap and handy resort, and there are hotels catering to them for miles to the south – but for an afternoon's escape to the sea they're quite good enough. Avoid **Villa del Mar**, which is the closest, most crowded and least clean, and head instead to **Mocambo** or **Boca del Río**. Buses (marked "Boca del Río") head out to both from the corner of Zaragoza and Serdán; or get a lift in one of the vans marked "Playas", which leave regularly to Mocambo from every corner along the malecón, arriving twenty minutes later at the *Hotel Mocambo* (☎29/21-39-90; ⑦), a former grand hotel now somewhat faded. From here, follow the street down to the wide sandy beach, where the water is warm and calm – though from time to time it can be pretty filthy. As its name suggests, the small village of Boca del Río is located at the mouth of a river – watch out for the persistent boat trip touts. In the village's tiny centre is the cheap *Hotel San Juan* (no phone; ③), with plenty of basic **rooms**.

An alternative, but more expensive, beach option is to take a boat trip out from the dock to the **Isla de Sacrificios** (10am–4pm hourly; $15). The island was named by Juan de Grijalva, whose expedition sailed up this coast a full year before Cortés arrived. Bernal Diaz explains that, on landing:

> *We found two stone buildings of good workmanship, each with a flight of steps leading up to a kind of altar, and on those altars were evil-looking idols, which were their gods. Here we found five Indians who had been sacrificed to them on that very night. Their chests had been struck open and their arms and thighs cut off, and the walls of these buildings were covered with blood.*

Hence the name.

Eating and drinking

"A la Veracruzana" is a tag you'll find on menus all over the country, denoting a delicious sauce of onions, garlic, tomatoes, olives, *chiles* and spices, served with meat or fish. And not surprisingly there are seafood **restaurants** all over Veracruz, although by no means all are particularly good value. The zócalo itself is ringed by little bars and cafes, but these are really places to drink, and though most do serve food, or at least sandwiches, it's generally overpriced and not up to much.

One place you should definitely try is the **Café La Parroquia**, just off the zócalo on Independencia, opposite the cathedral, which claims its locally grown coffee is the best in the country. Certainly the *lechero* (white coffee) is extremely good, and the cafe, though cavernous inside, is permanently packed. If you can fight your way to a table you'll be presented with a menu, but most people simply drink the coffee – maybe, at breakfast time, with a *pan dulce*. Ordering coffee here is something of a fine art – you have to tap your empty glass with a spoon in order to attract the attention of the waiter, who wanders around with two kettles (one of coffee, one of milk). He doesn't respond to any other command, so waiting politely will get you ignored, and competition for service, even at quieter moments, can be fierce. Less crowded and almost as good, especially for breakfast, is the restaurant of the *Hotel Diligencia*, on the zócalo. Or try the huge, cheap breakfast, or the *comida corrida* at the *Cocina Economica*, at Mariano Escobedo and Xicoténcatl, past Blvd. M Avila Camacho.

For more substantial meals there are a whole series of small **fish restaurants** around the market, and the top floor of the market building itself is given over to cooked food stalls. Between here and the zócalo (leave the square through the passageway, Portales Miranda, behind the cathedral) is another small square with a group of restaurants. *La Gaviota* serves good *comidas* and plain meals 24 hours a day (can be useful after an evening in the zócalo bars), and next to it are two small places that serve nothing but **fruit** – fruit salads, fruit drinks, fruit cocktails, fruit juices. Try a *jaiba rellena* – half a melon stuffed with fresh seasonal fruit and ice cream. These are all just off Zaragoza at its junction with Molina. For seafood in slightly less frenetic surroundings, head up Zaragoza towards the museum, where you'll find *El Tiburón* and *El Pescador*, good places to sample a *coctel* of real *jaiba* (crab).

Hard to find, but worth it for the delicious, cheap *comida*, is the *Restaurant Acuario*, above a small grocery store at Abasolo and 21 de Febrero. Or, if you feel like a change of cuisine, try the **Italian-Canadian** *Restaurant Chastev*, on the malecón between the hotels *Villa Rica* and *Royalty* – it also serves as a gallery for Mexican artists.

La Antigua and Zempoala

Heading north from Veracruz, there's a short stretch of highway as far as Cardel, junction of the coastal highway and the road up to Jalapa. **LA ANTIGUA**, site of the first real Spanish town in Mexico, lies just off this road. Although it does see an occasional bus, you'll find it much easier and quicker to take one heading for Cardel (about every 30min from the second-class terminal in Veracruz) and get off at the toll-booths. From here it's only about twenty minutes' walk up a signed road.

For all its antiquity, there's not a great deal to see in La Antigua; however, it is a beautiful, broad-streeted tropical village on the banks of the **Río La Antigua** (or Río Huitzilapan), and at weekends makes a popular excursion for Veracruzanos, who come to picnic by the river and to swim or take boat rides. Lots of seafood restaurants cater to this local trade. In the semi-ruinous centre of the village stand a couple of the oldest surviving Spanish buildings in Mexico: the **Edificio del Cabildo**, built in 1523, housed the first *Ayuntamiento* (local government) to be established; the **Casa de Cortés**, a fairly crude construction of local stone, was built for Cortés himself a few years later; and the parish church too dates from the mid-sixteenth century, though it's been altered and restored several times since. On the riverbank stands a vast old tree – the *Ceiba de la Noche Feliz* – to which, according to local legend, Cortés moored his ships when he arrived here.

Zempoala – the site

That Cortés came to this spot at all, after first landing near the site of modern Veracruz, was thanks to the invitation of the Totonac Indians of **ZEMPOALA** (or Cempoala), then a city of some 25,000 to 30,000 inhabitants. It was the first native city visited by the Conquistadors ("a great square with courtyards", wrote Bernal Diaz, "which appeared to have been lime coated and burnished during the last few days . . . one of the horsemen took the shining whiteness for silver, and came galloping back to tell Cortés that our quarters had silver walls . . . ") and quickly became their ally against the Aztecs. Zempoala, which had existed in some form for at least 800 years, had been brought under the control of the Aztec empire only relatively recently – around 1460 – and its people, who had already rebelled more than once, were only too happy to stop paying their tribute once they believed that the Spanish could protect them from retribution. This they did, although the "Fat Chief" and his people must have begun to have second thoughts when Cortés ordered their idols smashed and replaced with crosses and Christian altars.

Cortés left Zempoala in August 1519 for the march on Tenochtitlán, taking with him 200 Totonac porters and 50 of the town's best warriors. The following May he was forced to return in a hurry by the news that Panfilo Narvaez had come after him with a large force, on a mission to bring the Conquistadors back under the control of the governor of Cuba. The battle took place in the centre of Zempoala, where, despite the fact that Narvaez's force was far larger and had taken up defensive positions on the great temple, Cortés won a resounding victory: the enemy leaders were captured and most of the men switched sides, joining in the later assaults on the Aztec capital.

The **archeological site** (daily 8am–6pm; $3.50, free on Sun) dates mostly from the Aztec period, and although obviously the buildings have lost their decorative facings and thatched sanctuaries, it's one of the most complete examples of an Aztec ceremonial centre surviving – albeit in an untypically tropical setting. The pyramids with their double stairways, grouped around a central plaza, must have resembled those of Tenochtitlán, though on a considerably smaller scale. Apart from the main, cleared site, consisting of the **Templo Mayor** (the largest and most impressive structure, where Narvaez made his stand), the Great Pyramid and the Templo de las Chimeneas, there are lesser ruins scattered throughout, and around, the modern village. Most important of these are the Templo de las Caritas, a small temple on which a few carvings and remains of murals can still be seen, in open country just beyond the main site, and the Templo de Ehecatl, on the opposite side of the main road through the village. You need a couple of hours to explore the site.

Getting there: Cardel

There are **buses** (second-class) to Zempoala from both Veracruz and Jalapa, but it's quicker – certainly if you plan to continue northwards – to go back to **CARDEL** and change there for a first-class service. Coming **from La Antigua**, you can go back to the main road, get a bus on to Cardel and go on from there. From Cardel there are plenty of green-and-white taxis to the site, but the minibuses that leave every thirty minutes from the south side of the plaza are cheaper. Cardel itself is not of much interest, but has several seafood restaurants and a couple of small **hotels** around the plaza. They're rather expensive, though the *Plaza*, Independencia 25 Pte. (☎2-02-88; ④), just opposite the *ADO* bus stop, may let you bargain off-season. Best value is the friendly *Maty*, Carretera Nacional, on the outskirts of town opposite the hospital (☎2-02-67; ②), which has a good restaurant. From Cardel you can head down to a good beach at **Chachalacas** (another short bus journey), a small fishing village with a luxury hotel and some excellent seafood.

North to Tuxpán

Continuing north up the coast, there's very little in the long stretch (some 4hr on the bus) from Cardel to Papantla. The village of **Quiahuitzlán**, about 70km from Veracruz, bears the name of a fortified Totonac town visited by Cortés, but the ruins lie unexcavated nearby. At **Laguna Verde** there's a controversial nuclear power station*, and at **Nautla** you pass the largest town en route, surrounded by coconut groves. Although there are long, flat stretches of sand much of the way, they are pretty uninviting – desolate, windswept, and raked by heavy surf. Only in the final stretch does the beach offer much temptation, with several (expensive) motels dotted between Nautla and **TECOLUTLA**, a low-key resort a few miles off the main road. If you crave the beach you can stay here (try the *Playa* or the *Tecolutla*, both ③) and still get to Papantla and El Tajín with relative ease.

Tlapacoyan

Some 50km southwest of Nautla, bounded to the south by the Río Bobos and to the north by the Río Maria de la Torre, **TLAPACOYAN** is surrounded by jungly hills and

---

*Construction took more than fifteen years, with the plant finally brought on-line in early 1989, despite bitter local opposition, fuelled by the fact that the design had been heavily criticized in the US (where similar plants had closed on safety grounds), by Chernobyl, and by Mexico's appalling industrial safety record. The reactor, which supplied less than 3 percent of Mexico's electricity at twice the cost of conventional plants, is at present out of service – eco-conscious Mexicans hope it will remain closed forever.

pre-Columbian ruins. Most important of these is the massive undeveloped site of **Filo Bobos**, inaugurated in 1994 as part of a plan to turn the area into a major tourist destination. The town itself is still largely unspoilt, a friendly place going about its main business as a centre of citrus fruit production. Captured briefly by the Aztecs on a raid from the port of Nauhtla (Nautla), in 1865 Tlapacoyan was taken by Austrian troops loyal to Emperor Maximilian, and after a long siege it finally fell to imperial troops in November. One of the republican commanders, Colonel Ferrer, distinguished himself in the battle and was elevated to the rank of general. Today his statue stands in the main square.

Regular **buses to Tlapacoyan** run from Jalapa, Papantla and Puebla. *ADO* buses drop off in the centre of town. Turn left at 5 de Mayo and walk up Héroes de Tlapacoyan for the main square. Second-class services to Nautla leave from the terminal opposite *ADO*. **Hotels** are thin on the ground, but in the centre there are a few quiet, good-value choices. Try the *Melagrejo*, Gutiérrez Zamora 399 (☎231/5-00-57; ④); and on the square itself, the *Hotel Plaza* (☎231/5-05-20; ④) and the *San Agustín* (☎231/ 5-00-23; ④), which also has the best restaurant in town.

Filo Bobos

Opened to the public in 1994, the **"Filo Bobos project"** has still to take off. Archeological work is continuing, there's no infrastructure to speak of, and the information office in Tlapacoyan is generally reticent on the subject. Obviously as time goes by this situation will improve, though how fast is hard to tell. For now, though, its rawness is all part of the charm. There are no formal opening hours, so you can come and go as you please, entrance is free, and you'll probably have the site to yourself. Although details are sketchy about who actually lived here, it is agreed that Filo Bobos reached its peak during the Classic period (300–900 AD) and declined soon after.

The site itself is set in a steep-walled valley, divided into two halves by the flow of the river. The first section you come to is **Santa Elena**, better known as **El Cuajilote**. At present only half the structures have been uncovered and excavated, showing platforms constructed with rounded river-stones. The rest have been left as uncovered green mounds, some of which sport tangerine trees from the surrounding plantations (the fruit is deliciously sweet, and no one really minds if you pluck the odd one for refreshment along the way).

EL BAILE DE LOS NEGRITOS

Popular at festivals in the state of Veracruz, the frenetic **Baile de los Negritos** is a Totonac dance dating back to colonial times, when black slaves were imported in numbers into the plantations of Veracruz, often living and working alongside Indian labourers. Stories abound as to the origin of the dance; the most popular version has it that a female African slave and her child escaped from a plantation near Papantla, and lived in the dense jungle with the local indigenous groups. After her child was poisoned by a snake bite, the mother, using African folk medicine, began to dance herself into a trance. The Totonacs around her found the spectacle highly amusing and, it is said, began to copy her in a spirit of mockery.

The costumes of the dance are influenced by colonial dress, and the dancers wear a snake motif around the waist. The dance is directed by a "Mayordomo", the title given to plantation overseers in the colonial era. If you're in Tlapacoyan for the **Feast of Santiago** (July 25), dedicated to the town's patron saint, or the **Day of the Assumption** (August 16), you'll see the dance at its best and most spectacular; at other times it's held on a smaller scale in other village festivals in the area.

Arranged around a main plaza measuring 31,500 square metres, the surrounding buildings mirroring the shape of the valley, are what appear to be a series of temples dedicated to the **fertility cult**. At Shrine A, a *stela* related to the cult was discovered, and at Shrine A4 more than 1500 phallic figurines were found. None of these remains on site today. You can also make out a ball-court.

Four kilometres away, linked to El Cuajilote by a series of paths and bridges over the river, the site of **Vega de la Peña** covers some 8000 square metres of protected parkland. There's little doubt that structures buried beneath the lush greenery extend farther than that; some archeologists believe they may have stretched as far as Nautla. If true, this would radically alter the accepted conception of Mexican and Mediterranean pre-Columbian history, placing this coast in a far more prominent position than previously thought. What you see here today are small buildings, with more palatial dwellings than at El Cuajilote.

A few companies offer **river trips to Filo Bobos** and the Antigua River. Two of the more reliable, both based in Jalapa, are *Veraventuras*, Morelos 76 (☎281/8-95-79), and *Far-Flung Adventures*, Roble 85 (☎281/1-88-17; in the US: 1-800/359-4138), which run comprehensive, all-inclusive packages for around $50 a day.

Papantla

PAPANTLA is by far the most attractive town on the route north, flower-filled and straggling over an unexpected outcrop of low, jungly hills. It's one of the most important centres of the Mexican **vanilla** industry – the sweet, sticky odour frequently hangs over the place, and vanilla products are on sale everywhere – and also one of the surviving strongholds of **Totonac** Indian life. You'll see Totonacs wandering around in their loose white robes and bare feet, especially in the market; but, more significantly, Papantla (with El Tajín) is the one place where you can regularly witness the amazing **dance-spectacle** of the *Voladores de Papantla* (see below).

First-class **buses** use the *ADO* terminal on Juárez, some way out of town; you can just about walk, climbing straight up Juárez until you meet Enriquez, where you turn right for the centre of town, but it's easier to take a taxi. It can be hard to get a bus out, as most are *de paso*: book ahead for a local service, or take second-class, at least as far as Poza Rica, from where there's much more choice. The chaotic second-class *Transportes Papantla* terminal is more central on 20 de Noviembre – again, walk straight up to the zócalo. Buses **to El Tajín** via Chote (where you change) run from here, or there are direct minibuses from alongside the cathedral at fifteen minutes past each hour; details from the **tourist office** in the Palacio Municipal (theoretically open Mon–Fri 9am–3pm, Sat 9am–1pm). Both *Banamex* and *Bancomer*, on Juan Enriquez south of the *Hotel Premier*, **change travellers' cheques**, though it can be a very slow process.

There are several reasonably priced **hotels** in Papantla. Most obvious, and most expensive, is the *Premier*, Juan Enríquez 103 (☎784/2-26-00; ⑥), with pleasant modern rooms facing the zócalo. Comfortable alternatives include the *Tajín*, J J Núñez 104 (☎784/2-10-62; ④), and the *Totonacapan*, 20 de Noviembre at Olivio (☎784/21-22-00; ④). **Restaurants** are cheap and plentiful, though most are fairly ordinary. From the first floor of the *Totonacapan*, the *Cafe La Terraza* overlooks the plaza and is a lively place from which to watch the evening action. It's open daily, from noon to midnight, and serves good regional specialities. The *Café Cordral* next to the cathedral makes excellent coffee and *pan dulce* and is good for a light breakfast, while behind the cathedral cheap restaurants include *Bolognos, Pizza Parlour* on c/Obispo, and *Cenaduría* for local specialities.

THE VOLADORES DE PAPANTLA

The dance of the **Voladores** is performed every Sunday and on holidays (weather permitting) from the huge pole by the church. It involves five men: a leader who provides music on flute and drum, and four performers. They represent the five earthly directions – the four cardinal points and straight up, from earth to heaven. After a few preliminary ceremonies, the five climb to a small platform atop the pole, where the leader resumes playing and directs prayers for the fertility of the land in every direction. Meanwhile the four dancers tie ropes, coiled tightly around the top of the pole, to their waists and at a signal fling themselves head first into space. As they spiral down in ever-increasing circles the leader continues to play, and to spin, on his platform, until the four hit the ground (or hopefully land on their feet, having righted themselves at the last minute). In all they make thirteen revolutions each, symbolizing the 52-year cycle of the Aztec calendar. Although the full significance of the dance has been lost – originally the performers would wear bird costumes, for example – it has survived much as the earliest chroniclers reported it, largely because the Spanish thought of it as a sport rather than a pagan rite. In Papantla and El Tajín (where performances take place more frequently) it has become, at least partly, a tourist spectacle – though no less hazardous for that – as the permanent metal poles attest. If you can see it at a local village fiesta, there is still far more ceremonial attached, particularly in the selection of a sufficiently tall tree and its erection in the place where the dance is to be performed. Modernity has, however, impinged so far that the Papantla dancers now boast their own trade union and have been known to strike. At El Tajín they perform the ceremony specifically for tourists, but charge $10 to let you watch.

El Tajín

However charming and peaceful Papantla may be, the main reason anyone comes here is to visit the ruins of **EL TAJÍN**, by far the most important archeological site on the Gulf coast, and a much more interesting and impressive collection of buildings than the more recent remains of Zempoala. The city flourished – extending to occupy an area of some ten square kilometres – during the Teotihuacán or Classic period, 300–900 AD, and above all in the Postclassic (900–1100 AD), before eventually suffering the fate of most of its contemporaries, being invaded, burned and abandoned some time before 1200. By the time of the Conquest it had been forgotten, and any knowledge of it now comes from archeological enquiries since the accidental discovery of the site in 1785. Although it is generally called **Totonac**, after the present inhabitants of the region, few experts believe that it was the Totonacs who created El Tajín – though none can agree on just who did.

For all the years of effort, only a small part of the huge site has been cleared, and even this limited area is constantly in danger of being once more engulfed by the jungle: stand on top of one of the pyramids and you see green mounds in every direction, each concealing more ruins. The temptation to go and discover one of these for yourself is a powerful one, but should be resisted, as one look at the rogue's gallery of poisonous **snakes and insects** in the site museum will doubtless convince you. Stick to the cleared areas and paths and, if you do wander into the longer grass or into the jungle, make sure that your feet and legs are well covered: Totonac trousers lace at the ankle for added protection. A more charming feature of the wildlife here is the profusion of multicoloured butterflies that flutter through the greenery.

The ruins

The site (daily 9am–5pm; $5, free on Sun) divides broadly into two areas: Tajín Viejo, the original explored area centring on the amazing Pirámide de los Nichos, and Tajín Chico, a group of administrative buildings built on an artificial terrace. From the entrance (where, as well as the museum, there's a cafe and bar) a track leads through a small group of buildings, and into Tajín Viejo. Before you reach the square in front of the pyramid you pass several **ball-courts**, the most important, on your left, being the South Court or **Juego de Pelota Sur**. There are seventeen such courts, possibly more, and the game must have assumed an importance here far greater than at any other known site: we know little of the rules, and courts vary widely in size and shape, but the general idea was to knock a ball through a ring or into a hole without the use of the hands. Clearly, too, there was a religious significance, and at El Tajín the game was closely associated with human sacrifice. The superb bas-relief sculptures that cover the walls of the South Court show aspects of the game, and include portrayals of a decapitated player, and another about to be stabbed with a ritual knife by fellow players. These bas-reliefs are another constant feature of the site, adorning many of the ballcourts and buildings, with more stacked in the museum, but those in the South Court are the most striking and best-preserved.

The unique **Pirámide de los Nichos** is the most famous building at El Tajín, and indeed one of the most remarkable and enigmatic of all Mexican ruins. It rises to a height of about 20m in six receding tiers, each face punctuated with regularly spaced niches; up the front a steep stairway climbs to a platform on which the temple originally stood. If you total up the niches, including those hidden by the stairs and those, partly destroyed, around the base of the temple, there are 365 in all. Their exact purpose is unknown, but clearly they were more than mere decoration: perhaps each would hold some offering or sacrifice, one for each day of the year, or they may have symbolized caves – the dwellings of the earth god. Originally they were painted deep red, with a blue surround, to enhance the impression of depth.

Around the plaza in front of the pyramid stand all the other important buildings of **Tajín Viejo**. Opposite is Monumento 3, a similar pyramid without the niches, and behind it Monumento 23, a strange steep-sided bulk, one of the last structures to be built here. To the right of the Pirámide de los Nichos, Monumento 2, a low temple, squats at the base of Monumento 5, a beautiful truncated pyramid with a high decora-

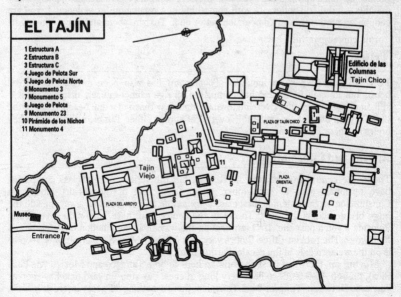

EL TAJÍN

1 Estructura A
2 Estructura B
3 Estructura C
4 Juego de Pelota Sur
5 Juego de Pelota Norte
6 Monumento 3
7 Monumento 5
8 Juego de Pelota
9 Monumento 23
10 Pirámide de los Nichos
11 Monumento 4

Edificio de las Columnas
Tajín Chico

PLAZA DE TAJÍN CHICO

Tajín Viejo

PLAZA ORIENTAL

PLAZA DEL ARROYO

Museo

Entrance

tive pediment broken by a broad staircase; on the left, Monumento 4 is one of the oldest in El Tajín, and only partly restored.

From the back of Monumento 4 the path continues, past the **Juego de Pelota Norte** with its worn relief sculptures, up onto the levelled terrace of **Tajín Chico**. Originally this raised area was supported by a retaining wall, part of which has been restored, and reached by a staircase opposite the ball-court. Only parts of the buildings now survive, making a rather confusing whole. **Estructura C**, and the adjoining Estructura B, are the most impressive remains: Estructura C has stone friezes running around its three storeys, giving the impression of niches. In this case, they were purely decorative, an effect that would have been heightened by a brightly coloured stucco finish. It has, too, the remains of a concrete roof – originally a huge single slab of poured cement, unique in ancient Mexico. **Estructura A** also had a covered interior, and you can still get into its central terrace via a narrow staircase, the entrance covered by a false arch of the type common in Maya buildings. On the hill above Tajín Chico stood the **Edificio de las Columnas**, which must have dominated the entire city. Here El Tajín's governor, 13 Rabbit, lived – bas reliefs on columns here recorded his exploits, and some of these are now on show in the museum. The building is little restored, but you can clamber to the top for a fine view over the site.

Getting there and moving on

To get to El Tajín from Papantla, take one of the *camionetas* that leave from near the cathedral at fifteen minutes past each hour; alternatively a bus from the second-class terminal will take you to **Chote**, where you change (ask, because buses to numerous destinations pass through this crossroads village). From Chote it's another 5km through oil-rich country – nodding-donkey wells dot the skyline – to the entrance of the ruins. Assuming the buses connect, the entire journey takes only about twenty minutes. There are also buses direct from El Tajín, or from Chote, to **POZA RICA** (marked "El Chote" and "San Andrés"), where you can connect with services to México as well as up or down the coast. In itself, though, Poza Rica is not a place of any delights – a dull, oil-boom city with something of a reputation for violence. If you are continuing northwards you'd be much better off in Tuxpán, about an hour up the coast.

Tuxpán

TUXPÁN (or Tuxpam, pronounced Toosh-pam) has also been swollen by the oil boom, but its tank farms and half-completed oil rigs cannot entirely disguise what is still, in places, a beautiful riverside town. Within easy reach of a fine beach 12km to the east, Tuxpán offers a far preferable overnight stay to either Tampico, three and a half hours north, or Poza Rica.

Arrival and information

There's no central **bus station** in Tuxpán, but the various second-class companies have terminals near to each other, about 600m east of the zócalo, mostly on Constitución or Cuauhtémoc; first-class *Omnibus de México* is not far away, beside the huge bridge across the river. To get to the centre from here, follow the river along Reforma – you'll pass the *ADO* terminal on the way, near the junction of Reforma and Rodriguez. The **tourist office** (hours vary, but officially Mon–Sat 9am–1pm & 4–6pm) is on the western side of the zócalo, Parque Juárez.

Moving on, there's at least one **bus** an hour to both Tampico and México (via Poza Rica), though *ADO* tends to have very long queues; buy your onward ticket as soon as you can. **Between Tuxpán and Tampico** there's nothing of great interest: a slow, bumpy and sweaty road across a plain whose thick tropical vegetation quickly becomes monotonous. Only the ferry crossing of the Río Panuco, just before Tampico, livens things up a little – and you'll miss even that if your bus takes the longer, inland route via Tempoal, as most seem to do.

Accommodation

Most of Tuxpán's **hotels** are a block or two from the waterfront, along the main street, Juárez, or on Morelos. As well as the usual budget dives right by the bus terminals, there are plenty of good mid-range choices, too.

Florida, Juárez 23 (☎783/4-02-22). Takes up a whole block on Juárez with small, good-value rooms. Communal balcony and a cafeteria with a great view of the plaza. ④.

El Huasteco, Morelos 41, just behind the *Tuxpán* (☎783/4-18-59). A/c rooms here are definitely worth trying: small but good value. ③.

Reforma, Juárez 25 (☎783/4-02-10). Comfortable rooms with a/c and TV. Parts of the hotel date from the boom years of the early 1900s. ⑤.

Posada San Ignacio, Melchor Ocampo 29 (☎783/4-29-05). Quiet and reasonable, with motel-like rooms set around a narrow courtyard. ③.

Tuxpán, Juárez at Mina (☎783/4-41-10). Best value cheapie in town, but check the rooms. ③.

The Town

While Tuxpán has no great historical monuments to inspire you, there are a couple of museums, and the **Parque Juárez** buzzes with life until late in the evening. Cafes surround the central bandstand, and there's a small archeological museum near the tourist office. The marketplace, where rows of stalls display vast amounts of inexpensive fruit, spills over onto the nearby waterfront of the Río Tuxpán. Small boats, known as **esquifes**, shuttle constantly across the river, allowing you to visit the house where Fidel Castro spent a year planning his revolutionary return to Cuba. The **Museo de la Amistad Mexico–Cuba** (Mon–Sat 8am–4.30pm, Sun 8am–3pm; free) focuses on Castro, Che Guevara and Spanish imperialism in the Americas in general. The revolutionaries sailed from Tuxpán in December 1956 in the *Granma*, almost sinking on the way, and arrived to find Batista's forces waiting. A replica of the *Granma* stands on the river bank. To get there, walk inland a couple of blocks to Obregón then turn right, heading back to the river at the end of the street.

The beaches

Tuxpán's real attraction are the beaches at **Barra de Tuxpán**, by the river mouth: **buses** (marked "Playa") run all day along riverside Reforma, past fishing boats and tankers, and arrive twenty minutes later at a vast stretch of sand. There are restaurants and changing rooms here, a couple of basic rooms in the first restaurant on the right, and any number of shaded hammocks under little *palapas* – or sling your own under the trees behind the beach. As long as the wind keeps up to drive the worst of the insects away – and it's usually fairly breezy – you could sleep out or **camp** here, no problem. There are plenty of showers around that you can use for a few pesos.

Eating and drinking

Cheap **restaurants** line Juárez, with the 24-hour *Café Mante*, on the corner opposite the *ADO* terminal, offering a great selection of Mexican dishes. The *Nuevo 303* on Pipila, leading down from Juárez to the river, is a favourite with families and often packed – a sure sign of its value. Other places serving **seafood** are plentiful, and virtually all the hotels have adequate, if unexciting, restaurants attached.

South of Veracruz

Leaving Veracruz to the south, Hwy-180 traverses a long expanse of plain, a country of broad river deltas and salt lagoons, for nearly 150km, until it hits the hills of the **Sierra Tuxtla**. Beyond, there's more low, flat, dull country all the way to Villahermosa (p.465). Though few tourists come this way, it is a heavily travelled route, with plenty of buses and trucks thundering through. In the first stretch there are a few interesting fishing towns, and in the Sierra some really attractive scenery and a welcome dose of cool, fresh air: a definite incentive for an overnight stop before the tedious haul that follows. This was **Olmec** country, the first real civilization of Mexico, but Olmec sites are virtually impossible to get to without your own transport, and largely disappointing when you do. Unless you've some special reason, it's best to reserve your studies for museums and the reproduction of the site of La Venta in Villahermosa.

Alvarado and Tlacotalpan

ALVARADO is the first stop, an extraordinary town on a narrow strip of land between the sea and the Laguna de Alvarado, some 70km from Veracruz. It's a working fishing port, and as such a real slice of old-fashioned Mexico: as soon as the bus pulls in to the raucous main street, it's invaded by people selling the most extraordinary variety of food, drink and souvenirs. There are plenty of hotels in sight, but it's not somewhere you'd want to stay long. You might, however, be tempted to stop for a meal – the fishing fleet is enormous and there are lots of good fish **restaurants** along the front. Alvarado's Port Authority restaurant, especially, is famed for its excellence and is also cheap, since it is genuinely used by port workers and fishermen.

If you want somewhere small, quiet, and entirely off the tourist circuit to stay, try instead **TLACOTALPAN**, some twenty minutes away on the spectacular road that heads inland towards Tuxtepec and eventually Oaxaca. Still on the edges of the Río Papaloapan, close to the lagoon, it's a very pretty village, and although there's absolutely nothing laid on you can rent boats on the river, and fish or swim. There are a couple of small hotels on the main street near where the buses stop.

Los dos Tuxtlas

Once the mountains start (in a region that Alexander von Humboldt described as "the Switzerland of Veracruz", an overblown and overused claim), things become much more interesting, and the cooler climate is an infinite relief. The two townships of **Santiago Tuxtla** and **San Andrés Tuxtla** are the region's hub, each with several hotels and surrounded by attractive hill country.

San Andrés Tuxtla

SAN ANDRÉS TUXTLA is the larger of the two Tuxtlas, and the one where most buses will drop you (many long-distance services pull in here for a brief stop). The majority of buses stop at the top of the hill where the highway passes by – first-class *ADO* and second-class *AU* are more or less opposite each other here at the top of Juárez, which leads straight down to the zócalo – though some other second-class buses will drop you by the market: the centre is within easy walking distance of either.

Local buses run from here to Santiago Tuxtla and Catemaco, but there are a couple of more local attractions. **La Laguna Encantada** is a volcanic lake about 2km from the town and a popular local swimming spot. It can be reached in less than an hour on foot: follow Belisario Dominguez to the top where it crosses the highway, turn right (towards Catemaco), and after a couple of hundred metres a signed path leads up to the left. The **Salto de Eyipantla** is a little farther afield, but served by local buses that leave from around the market – frequently at weekends. This series of three waterfalls, reached down 244 worn steps from a car park, is worth a look, though, and also you can swim in calmer pools nearby. It's a beautiful spot, but can get packed out in summer.

Most **accommodation** and other facilities are very close to the zócalo or on Juárez: the *Catedral* (☎294/2-02-37; ①) on Pino Suárez (reached via the alley beside the church) is clean and reasonably priced, or you could try the *Colonial* (☎294/2-05-52; ①) or *Figueroa* (☎294/2-02-57; ②), one block away at the corner of Suárez and Belisario Dominguez. All are very basic, but good value for the money. A number of fancier hotels are visible from the square: the *San Andrés* at Madero 6 (☎294/2-06-04; ④) is the most reasonable of them, the *Hotel de los Pérez* (☎294/2-07-77; ⑤–⑥), Rascon 2, a little classier and pricier. **Food** options include cafes on the zócalo, a number of reputable fish and seafood restaurants along Madero, past the *San Andrés – Mariscos Chazaro* at no. 12 is good – and others up by the *ADO* terminal. There's an excellent market, too.

Santiago Tuxtla and Tres Zapotes

SANTIAGO TUXTLA is considerably quieter, and requires something more of an effort to visit, since it lies a little distance from the highway and many buses simply ignore the place – though there are very frequent connections with San Andrés. A giant Olmec head stands in the centre of the zócalo, on one side of which is a small museum of local archeology and ethnography (Tues–Sat 9am–6pm, Sun 9am–3pm; $3). Although Santiago is itself a beautiful spot, the main reason people come here is to visit the important Olmec site of **Tres Zapotes**, a little less than an hour away by local bus. Frankly, the journey is barely worth it, a painfully slow ride by unreliable bus (or taxi) to what is basically just a **museum** (daily 9am–4pm; $2) containing little that is not duplicated elsewhere. Its main interest lies in a series of *stelae* inscribed with Olmec glyphs. Of the site itself, nearby, virtually nothing can be seen.

There are a couple of small **hotels** in town, including the remarkably good *Castellanos* (☎294/7-03-00; ⑤), right on the zócalo with all facilities, as well as cheaper places – and plenty of **restaurants** and cafes, again around the zócalo.

Catemaco

CATEMACO is a more attractive place to stay than either Santiago or San Andrés. Squatting on the shore of a large, mountain-ringed lake – by tradition a centre of Indian witchcraft – it would be hard to envisage a more picturesque spot to break the journey before the long leg south. Veracruzanos arrive in force at weekends and holidays, but it's little spoiled for all that – although hotels can be expensive. Watch out for the touts, though, who'll try and persuade you to attend an Indian spiritual purification ceremony or to visit the place where Sean Connery's *Medicine Man* was filmed.

There isn't a great deal to do in Catemaco – haggle at the dock over the price of a boat trip round the lake or to one of the islands; visit the local waterfall (*Salto de Teoteapan*) or one of the lake beaches – but it's an ideal place not to do a great deal. The only tourist sight is the **Basilica de Nuestra Señora del Carmen**, decorated with multicoloured tiles. The original statue of the Virgen del Carmen can be seen in a narrow grotto in El Tegal, around twenty minutes' walk around the lakeshore. A local bus from the plaza (marked "La Margarita") goes round much of the shore, passing a couple of beaches and the beautiful Río Cuetzalpan.

Practicalities

Catemaco is slightly off the main road, and although there are some direct **buses** from Veracruz there's no need to make a special effort to get one, as local services from San Andrés cover the short journey regularly. **Moving on**, second-class buses depart the *AU* terminal on 2 de Abril for all the main towns in western Mexico; try to buy tickets a day in advance, since seats are numbered. On the zócalo, *Comermex* **bank** (Mon–Fri 10am–1pm, changes travellers' cheques, while the **post office** is just round the corner towards the *Hotel Juros*.

On the whole, **hotels** right on the lake are expensive, though out of season prices do drop. Otherwise, there are several places a couple of streets inland, just down from where the buses stop: people may try to accost you as you arrive to take you to a hotel, but rooms are easy enough to find without help. On the lakeside very close to the centre, *Julita* (☎294/3-00-08; ②), Av. Playa 10, offers simple, clean rooms with fans and is probably the best value in town; farther along at no. 14, *Juros* (④) has a fantastic roof-top swimming pool, but be sure to check the room and price. The hotels away from the lakeshore include *Los Arcos* (☎294/3-00-03; ④), at Madero 7 and Mantillo, which has pleasant rooms with fans and TV; and *Catemaco* (☎294/3-00-45; ④), on the zócalo oppo-site *Comermex*, where facilities include a/c, TV, a pool and restaurant. *Hotel del Lago* (④), Av. Playa and Abasolo, at the edge of the village on the Tuxtla road, is a secure, friendly place with small, clean rooms with a/c, a palm-ringed pool and restaurant.

Seafood **restaurants** abound on the shore and around the zócalo, most offering the local speciality, *mojarra* (small perch from the lake), best sampled when cooked *a la tachagobi* – with a delicious hot sauce. One of the best deals is the *comida corrida* in the *Restaurant Aloha*.

Coatzacoalcos and Acayucán

The **northern shore** of the Isthmus is even less attractive, with a huge industrial zone stretching from the dirty concrete town of Minatitlán to **COATZACOALCOS** (formerly Puerto México, the Atlantic railway terminus), dominated by a giant oil refinery. If you have to stop here Coatzacoalcos is definitely the better choice: big enough to have a real centre and with plenty of hotels and restaurants around the Camionera. Coatzacoalcos also boasts a spectacular modern bridge – known as Coatzacoalcos II – by which the main highway bypasses the town. If you're on a bus heading downtown you'll cross the Río Coatzacoalcos by an older, lesser suspension bridge. In legend, Coatzacoalcos is the place from which Quetzalcoatl and his followers sailed east, vowing to return.

Crossing the north of the Isthmus you'll also inevitably pass through **ACAYUCÁN**, where the coastal highway and the trans-Isthmus highway meet. The enormous bus station and equally giant market cater for all the passing travellers; there's little other-wise but mud or dust. Make your visit a short one and, if you have any choice at all, press straight on through to Villahermosa (see p.465). If you do need to **stay**, go for the *Joalicia*, at Zaragoza 4 on the zócalo (☎924/5-08-77; ③), or the more luxurious *Kikadu*, Ocampo Sur 7 (☎924/5-04-10; ⑥), just off the zócalo.

fiestas

January

In the last week of January **Tlacotalpan** has a fiesta with dances, boat races and bulls let loose in the streets.

February

2nd DÍA DE LA CANDELARIA. Colourful Indian fiesta in **Jaltipán** on the main road south of Catemaco, which includes the dance of *La Malinche* (Malintzin, Cortés' Indian interpreter,

known to the Spanish as Malinche, is said to have been born here), recreating aspects of the Conquest. Also the final day of celebrations in **Tlacotalpan**.

4th Agricultural festival in **Otatitlán**, near the Oaxaca border off the road from Alvarado to Oaxaca, where many Indians attend a midnight mass to bless their crops.

CARNIVAL (the week before Lent, variable Feb–March) is celebrated all over the region, most riotously in **Veracruz**.

March

On the first Friday, the FERIA DEL CAFE in **Ixhualtán**, a coffee-growing town near Córdoba – both trade fair and popular fiesta.

18th–19th FIESTAS DE SAN JOSÉ. In **Naranjos**, between Tuxpán and Tampico, a fiesta with many traditional dances celebrates the local patron saint. Similar events in **Espinal**, a Totonac village on the Río Tecolutla, not far from Papantla and El Tajín, where with luck you can witness the spectacular *Voladores*.

HOLY WEEK is widely observed, and in this area recreations of the Passion are widespread. You can witness them in **Papantla** – where you'll also see the *Voladores* – in **Coatzintla**, a Totonac village near Tajín, in **Cotaxtla**, between Veracruz and Córdoba, and in **Otatitlán**. **Naolinco**, a beautiful village near Jalapa, stages a mock crucifixion on Good Friday. Also celebrations in **Catemaco** – and in the port of **Alvarado** – a far more ribald Fish Fiesta following hard on the heels of the Veracruz Carnival.

April

15th–17th (approx.) FERIA DE LAS FLORES. Flower festival in **Fortín de las Flores**.

May

3rd Hundreds of pilgrims, mostly Indian, converge on **Otatitlán** to pay homage to the village's *Cristo Negro*.

27th DÍA DEL SAGRADO CORAZON – the start of four days of festivities in **Naranjos**.

CORPUS CHRISTI (variable, the Thursday after Trinity) sees the start of a major four-day festival in **Papantla** and in particular regular performances by the *Voladores*.

June

13th DÍA DE SAN ANTONIO. Fiesta in **Huatusco**, between Córdoba and Veracruz.

24th DÍA DE SAN JUAN celebrated in **Santiago Tuxtla**, with dancing, and in **Martinez de la Torre**, on the road inland from Nautla, where the *Voladores* perform.

July

15th DÍA DE LA VIRGEN DEL CARMEN – a massive pilgrimage to **Catemaco**, accompanied

by a fiesta which spills over into the following day.

24th DÍA DE SANTIAGO is celebrated with fiestas in **Santiago Tuxtla** and **Coatzintla**; each lasts several days. In **Tlapacoyan** you can see the bizarre *Baile de los Negritos*.

August

14th **Teocelo**, a village in beautiful country between Jalapa and Fortín, celebrates an ancient fiesta with dance and music.

15th In **Tuxpán**, a week-long *feria* begins – dancing and *Voladores*.

16th In **Tlapacoyan**, the *Baile de los Negritos* is held to commemorate the Day of the Assumption.

24th **Córdoba** celebrates the anniversary of the signing of the Treaty of Independence.

September

15th–16th Independence celebrations take place everywhere.

21st DÍA DE SAN MATEO sees secular as well as religious celebration in **Naolinco**.

30th **Coatepec**, between Jalapa and Fortín, celebrates its patron's day – processions and dances.

October

7th FIESTA DE LA VIRGEN DEL ROSARIO, patroness of fishermen. In **La Antigua** she is honoured with processions of canoes on the river, while **Alvarado** enjoys a more earthy fiesta, filling the first two weeks of the month.

November

2nd DAY OF THE DEAD is honoured everywhere – the rites are particularly strictly followed in **Naolinco**.

30th Fiestas in **San Andrés Tuxtla**, carrying on into December 1.

December

12th DÍA DE LA VIRGEN DE GUADALUPE widely observed, especially in **Huatusco**, **Cotaxtla**, and **Amatlán de los Reyes**, near Córdoba.

24th Christmas, of course, celebrated in **Santiago Tuxtla** with a very famous festival that lasts until Twelfth Night – January 6th.

travel details

Buses

First-class buses are mostly operated by *Autobuses del Oriente* (*ADO*) – remarkably slick and efficient. Second-class is dominated (at least on long hauls) by *Autobuses Unidos* (*AU*), more of a mixed bag. The following is a brief rundown of the routes, and should be taken as a minimum.

Jalapa to: México (6hr 30min); Veracruz (12 daily; 2hr 30min).

Poza Rica to: México (8 daily; 5hr); Tuxpán (frequently; 1hr); Veracruz (10 daily; 4hr 30min).

Tuxpán to: Poza Rica (frequently; 1hr); Tampico (10 daily; 5hr).

Veracruz to: Coatzacoalcos (10 daily; 5hr 30min); Córdoba (15 daily; 2hr 30min); Jalapa (12 daily; 2hr 30min); México (15 daily; 8hr); Oaxaca (4 daily; at least 8hr); Orizaba (15 daily; 3hr 30min); Papantla (10 daily; 4hr); Poza Rica (10 daily; 4hr 30min); San Andrés Tuxtla (10 daily; 3hr); Villahermosa (10 daily; 7hr).

Trains

The main line from **Veracruz to México** via Córdoba and Orizaba has two trains daily in each direction: the comfortable overnight *El Jarocho* leaves in both directions around 9.30 at night, arriving early the next morning; the daytime service is slower and much less luxurious.

Planes

There are regular flights to México from Veracruz, and three a week from Poza Rica.

CHAPTER EIGHT

OAXACA

T he state of **Oaxaca** (pronounced "wa-há-ka") marks the break between North American central Mexico and Central America. Here the two chains of the Sierra Madre converge, to run on as a single range right through into South America and the Andes. The often barren landscapes of northern Mexico are left firmly behind, replaced by thickly forested hillsides, or in low-lying areas by swamp and jungle. It is all very much closer to a Central American experience than anything that has gone before, a feeling compounded by the relative lack of development – the "Mexican miracle" has yet fully to transform the south.

Indigenous traditions and influence remain powerful in this area. The old tongues are still widely spoken, and there are scenes in the villages that seem to deny that the Spanish Conquest ever happened. For the colour and variety of its markets, and the fascination of its fiestas, there is no rival in Mexico. Less enticingly, but arising out of the same traditions and geographical accidents, the region has witnessed considerable political disturbance in recent years, though protest has never been as manifest as in its more troubled neighbour.

The laid-back city of **Oaxaca** itself is the prime destination, close enough to México and the mainstream to attract large numbers of tourists to its fine crafts stores and markets, seemingly constant fiestas, and occasionally bizarre mix of colonial buildings and Indian street life. From the earliest times the valley of Oaxaca was inhabited by the same Zapotec and Mixtec Indians who form the bulk of its population now. Their ancient sites – at **Monte Albán, Yagul** and **Mitla** – are less well known than their contemporaries in central and eastern Mexico, but every bit as important and impressive. The growing Pacific resorts of **Puerto Escondido, Puerto Ángel** and **Huatulco** are also easily reached from the city. Their reputation for being unspoilt beach paradises is no longer entirely justified – Escondido in particular is a resort of some size, with an international airport, and there's another huge resort under construction at Huatulco. That said, both Puerto Ángel and its much touted hedonistic neighbour, **Zipolite**, are pretty small-scale, and along this coast you'll discover some of the emptiest and best Pacific beaches in Mexico, easily reached from the main centres.

The resorts are all around 250km from Oaxaca, reached via spectacular mountain roads that take a minimum of six hours to traverse. Although there are regular **buses** to **Pochutla**, just inland from Puerto Ángel, and thence on to Puerto Escondido, it's a slow and occasionally heart-stopping journey. Many people prefer to **fly** down, either with *Aeromorelos* from Oaxaca to Escondido – an experience in itself – or with *Mexicana* direct from México to Escondido or Huatulco. There are also regular bus connections along the coast, from Acapulco in the north or Salina Cruz in the south, and a direct overnight service between México and Puerto Escondido.

Getting there from México

There are a number of ways of approaching Oaxaca. The brand new *cuota* **toll road** north from Oaxaca now links to the México–Puebla–Córdoba *autopista*, reducing the México–Oaxaca road time from ten hours to around five. Undoubtedly the buses will soon start using this road, but at the time of writing the majority (*ADO* or *Cristóbal Colón* from the TAPO terminal) were still using the Pan-American Highway (Hwy-190) via Puebla and Izúcar de Matamoros. You can also get to this road by heading south of

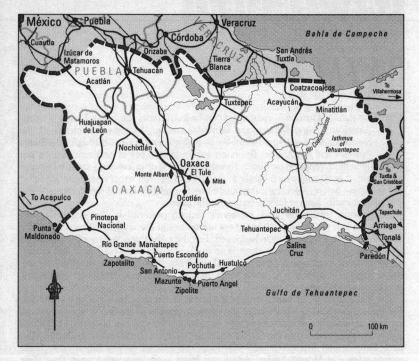

the capital to **Cuautla**, birthplace of Emiliano Zapata and a spa town with a climate similar to Cuernavaca's. Either way, it's a ride of at least ten hours through some impressive mountain scenery – cactus and scrub in the early stages giving way to thicker vegetation as you approach Oaxaca. Most people do this non-stop, which is in all honesty the best policy, though Acatlán – almost exactly halfway – does produce beautiful black pottery, on sale throughout the town. Some 50km farther on you enter the state of Oaxaca near. Huajuapan de León – a town of no great interest in itself, but marking the beginning of *mescal* producing territory, with spiny, bluish-green maguey cactuses cultivated all around the road. On the side road that leads from here to the spa town of Tehuacán, you pass through one of the largest and most impressive **cactus forests** in the republic. The route from the capital to Oaxaca via **Tehuacán** (Hwy-150 and 131) is also served by plenty of buses and is, if anything, even more spectacularly mountainous.

To reach Oaxaca from Acapulco it is probably quicker to go through México, but there are relatively frequent buses up from the Pacific coast at Pinotepa Nacional; more frequently, and equally uncomfortably, from Puerto Escondido or Pochutla, the service town for Puerto Ángel. That said, if you are travelling along the Pacific coast, it seems a pity to miss out on the region's excellent beaches just to get to Oaxaca fast.

Tehuacán

With the recent completion of a new *autopista*, and fast bus services, there is little need to break the México to Oaxaca journey. And on the whole there's nowhere worth stopping except **TEHUACÁN**, the source of the bulk of the bottled mineral water (*Agua de*

Tehuacán), consumed throughout Mexico. A spa town of some antiquity, relaxing, easy-paced, temperate in every sense of the word, its centre is dotted with buildings from the town's early twentieth-century heyday. The tiled arcade-fronted house on the zócalo, with its Moorish flourishes, was obviously designed with Vichy or Evian in mind and bears a plaque to Señor Don Joaquim Pita, who first put the water in bottles. Take a look, too, at the underside of the colonnade for highly graphic murals depicting the five regions that make up Tehuacán district. A more pedestrian introduction to the region fills the halls of the **Museo del Valle de Tehuacán** (Tues–Sun 10am–5pm; $2) at Reforma Nte. 200 in the elegant ex-Convento de Carmen, featuring a brightly coloured tiled dome that dominates the skyline in this part of town. A tiny collection of prehistoric relics shores up the thinly illustrated story of maize in Mesoamerica and particularly in the Tehuacán valley, which was the first place to truly cultivate (rather than simply harvest) the crop some 6000–7000 years ago; ample evidence that this was one of the earliest inhabited areas in Mexico.

All this can be seen in a couple of hours, but if you decide to stay in town you can fill the time by heading out to the **springs** on the outskirts to sample the clean-tasting water, or take a dip at **Balneario Ejidal San Lorenzo** (daily 6.30am–6pm; $3), a large complex of sun-warmed pools (including one Olympic-sized affair), most of which use the local springs. Catch a bus from the *Autobuses Unidos* bus station to San Lorenzo, a suburb 5km west of the centre.

Practicalities

Most **long-distance buses** arrive at the *ADO* station on Independencia, two blocks west of the zócalo. Second-class buses from México, Oaxaca and elsewhere arrive at the *Autobuses Unidos* station near the junction of c/5 Ote. and c/5 Sur, on the opposite side of the centre. Independencia runs all the way out to the suburb of San Lorenzo, past *ADO* and the **train station** (☎238/2-11-34), seven blocks from the centre: services to Oaxaca leave at 3am and 10am, to Puebla at 1.30am and 3pm, the former continuing to the capital.

The best-value **place to stay** in Tehuacán is the *Hotel Montecarlo* (☎238/3-19-41; ④), five blocks out at Reforma Nte. 400, with a pool, parking and large clean rooms around a huge garden. *Hotel México*, Independencia at Reforma, one block west of the zócalo (☎238/2-25-19; ⑤), is considerably more luxurious, and there's a good budget choice, the *Hotel Madrid*, c/3 Sur 105 (☎238/3-15-24; ①), with gardens, a parrot and somewhat overpriced en suite rooms; go for those without bathrooms. **Banks** (with ATMs) and other services are mostly on Reforma.

Oaxaca

The city of **OAXACA**, capital of the state, sprawls across a grand expanse of deep-set valley, 1600m above sea level, some 500km southeast of México. Its colour, its folklore, the huge extent of its Indian market and its thoroughly colonial centre combine to make this one of the most popular, and most rewarding, destinations for travellers. Even the increase in package tourism and the pedestrianization of Macedonia Alcalá, the main thoroughfare from the zócalo to the cathedral, a street now lined with high-class handicraft and jewellery shops, have done little to destroy the city's gentle appeal.

Increasingly, it's becoming an **industrial** city – the population is well over 200,000, the streets choked and noisy – yet it seems set to remain easy to handle. In the centre, thanks to strict building regulations, the provincial charm is hardly affected and just about everything can be reached on foot. Provincial it remains, too, in its habits – the big excitements are dawdling in a cafe, or gathering in the plaza to stroll and listen to the town band; by eleven at night the city is asleep.

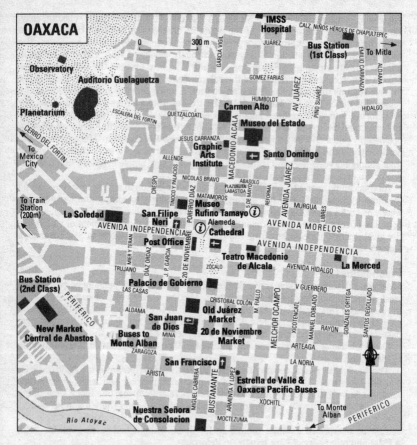

Once central to the **Mixtec** and **Zapotec** civilizations, the city later took a lesser role. Cortés, attracted by the area's natural beauties, took the title of *Marques del Valle de Oaxaca* and until the Revolution his descendants held vast estates hereabouts. But for practical purposes Oaxaca was of little interest to the Spanish, with no mineral wealth and no great joy for farmers (though coffee was grown). The indigenous population was left to get on with life far more than was generally the case, with only the interference of a proselytizing Church to put up with. The city's most famous son, **Benito Juárez**, is commemorated everywhere in Oaxaca, a privilege not shared by **Porfirio Díaz**, the second most famous *Oaxaqueño*, whose dictatorship most people choose to forget.

Arrival, information and city transport

Both **bus stations** in Oaxaca are a good way from the centre – at least twenty minutes' walk. First-class (where there is a *guardería*) is on Calzada Niños Héroes de Chapultepec, north of the centre, from where your best bet is to get a taxi in: if you're absolutely determined to walk, turn left along the main road about four blocks to Av. Juárez, left again for nine or ten blocks to Independencia or Hidalgo, then right to the zócalo. On Juárez you can start to pick up city buses. The second-class terminal – where you'll find a **casa de cambio** with good rates (daily 9am–7pm) and a *guardería* (6am–9pm) – is west of the centre by the new market buildings: walk past these, across the railway lines and the *Periferico*, and on up Trujano towards the centre. The **train station** is still farther out, but from here there is a good bus service ("Colonia Reforma"/ "Santa Rosa"/"Centro") that will take you right into the centre. From the **airport** a *colectivo* service (*Transportacion Terrestre Aeropuerto*) will drop you right by the zócalo. On **leaving** (see p.401) you should buy tickets in advance wherever possible – especially for early morning departures on popular routes, to México or to San Cristóbal.

BENITO JUÁREZ

Despite the blunder and poor judgement of his later years, **Benito Juárez** ranks among Mexico's greatest national heroes and as *the* towering figure of nineteenth-century Mexican politics. His maxim *"El respeto al derecho ajeno es la paz"* – the respect of the rights of others is peace – has been a rallying cry for liberals ever since. A Zapotec Indian, he strove against nineteenth-century social prejudices and, through four terms as president, successfully reformed many of the worst social remnants of Spanish colonialism, earning a reputation for honesty and fair dealing.

Juárez was born outside the city at San Pablo Guelatao in 1806. His parents died when he was three, and he grew up speaking only Zapotec; at the age of twelve he was adopted by priests and moved to Oaxaca, where he was educated. Turning his talents to law, he provided his legal services free to impoverished villagers, and by 1831 had earned a seat on Oaxaca's municipal council, lending voice to a disenfranchised people. Juárez rose through the ranks of the city council to become **state governor** from 1847 to 1852, on a liberal ticket geared towards improving education and releasing the country from the economic and social stranglehold of the Church and aristocracy. In 1853 the election of a conservative government under Santa Ana forced him into eighteen months of exile in the USA.

Liberal victory in 1855 enabled Juárez to return to Mexico as minister of justice and lend his name to a law abolishing special courts for the military and clergy. His support was instrumental in passing the **Ley Lerdo**, which effectively nationalized the Church's huge holdings, and bills legalizing civil marriage and guaranteeing religious freedom. In 1858, President Ignacio Comonfort was ousted by conservatives enraged by these reforms and Juárez, as the head of the Supreme Court, had a legal claim to the presidency. However, he lacked the military might to hold México and retired to Veracruz, returning three years later, victorious in the War of Reform, as **constitutionally elected president** for further attempts to reduce the power of the Church. Hog-tied by an intractable Congress and empty coffers, Juárez suspended all debt repayments for two years from July 1861. To protect their investments, the British, Spanish and French sent their armies in, but when it became apparent that Napoleon III had designs on control of Mexico the others pulled out leaving France to install Hapsburg Archduke **Maximilian** as puppet emperor. Juárez fled again, this time to Ciudad Juárez on the US border, but by 1867 Napoleon III had buckled under Mexican resistance and US pressure, and Juárez was able to return to the capital and his army to round up and execute the hapless Maximilian.

Juárez was returned as president at the **1867 elections** but alienated much of his support by unconstitutional attempts to use Congress to amend the constitution. Nevertheless, he was able to secure another term in the 1870 elections, spending two more years trying unsuccessfully to maintain peace before dying of a heart attack in 1872.

Information

Oaxaca's chief **tourist office** (Mon–Fri 9am–3pm & 6–8pm, Sat 9am–2pm; ☎951/6-38-10) is inside the Palacio Municipal, on Independencia opposite the Alameda, with another branch (daily 9am–8pm; ☎951/6-48-28) at 5 de Mayo 200, on the corner of Morelos. Both are extremely helpful, with piles of maps, leaflets and other handouts, including two free monthly English-language newspapers, the *Oaxaca Times* and *Oaxaca*, both of which have topical features and useful events listings.

Casas de cambio litter the centre of town – the ones on the zócalo, at Hidalgo 820 and at Alcalá 100-A all give near identical rates to the banks and also open longer hours (usually daily 8am–8pm). Some of them change European currencies but at insulting rates. Most **banks** have ATMs and are open for foreign exchange from 9am to 12.30pm. The **American Express** office, on the zócalo at the corner of Hidalgo and Valdivieso (Mon–Fri 9am–2pm & 4–8pm; ☎951/6-27-00), generally offers poor rates.

The **post office** (Mon–Fri 9am–7pm, Sat 9am–1pm), also on Independencia, by the Alameda, shelters a row of **Ladatel phones** for collect calls. There are plenty more all over Oaxaca, and a *Computel* place at Trujano 204, just west of the zócalo. You can get a reasonable selection of new and second-hand **English-language books** (including some on local history) from the *Librería Universitaria*, Guerrero 108, just off the zócalo (Mon–Sat 9.30am–2pm & 4–8pm), but it's probably better to consult (or borrow for a joining fee of around $10) the books at the *Biblioteca Circulante de Oaxaca*, Alcalá 305 (Mon–Fri 10am–1pm & 4–7pm, Sat 10am–1pm), between Matamoros and Bravo, or the excellent, predominantly arts library at the *Graphic Arts Institute*, Alcalá 507.

City transport

Because Oaxaca is so compact, walking is the best way of getting around. The **bus** routes are byzantine in their complexity and once you've hopped on the right one the traffic is so slow that you could have taken a pleasant stroll to your destination in half the time. **Taxis** are a better bet; they can be flagged down or found on Independencia near the cathedral.

Getting out to the sites around the valley is a different matter. Buses from the second-class bus station are fairly frequent though slow; *colectivos* – cars which leave when full – from outside the new market depart more frequently and are only a little more expensive. **Car rental** is as expensive here as everywhere in the country, but if you are planning extensive exploration of the valley may prove worthwhile, allowing you to trade a week of long waits for a couple of days of independence. In town, try *Dollar*, Matamoros 100-C (☎951/6-63-29), and *Hertz* at *Hotel Margarita*, Labastida 115 (☎951/6-24-34); or, at the airport, *Budget* (☎951/1-52-52) or *Hertz* (☎951/1-54-78). One alternative is to cycle: *Bicicletas Martinez*, J P García 509 (☎951/4-31-44), **rents mountain bikes** for around $2 an hour or $12 a day in high season, a little less off-season, and roadsters are cheaper still.

Accommodation

Although there are hundreds of **hotels** in Oaxaca, there are thousands of visitors, and if you arrive late you may well have difficulty finding a room. Under such circumstances it's best to take anything that's offered, and look for something better the next morning. Alternatively call at the main tourist office and consult their list of **families** who take in guests on a daily basis (usually around $10 per person), or try the 5 de Mayo branch for a list of **apartments**, many of them fairly central, which also charge around $10 per person.

The bulk of the **cheaper places** are south of Independencia, especially between the old market and c/Trujano: Trujano, Díaz Ordaz, García and Aldama all have a multi-

---

ACCOMMODATION PRICES

All the accommodation listed in this book has been categorized into one of nine price
bands, as set out below. The prices quoted are in US dollars and normally refer to the
cheapest available room for two people sharing in high season. For more details, see
p.37.

① less than $8	④ $18–25	⑦ $50–75
② $8–12	⑤ $25–35	⑧ $75–100
③ $12–18	⑥ $35–50	⑨ more than $100

---

tude of possibilities. Closer to the **zócalo** and to the north, both prices and quality tend
to be rather higher, though there are surprisingly good-value places among the credit
card establishments. Prices in general drop by 10 to 20 percent outside the Christmas,
Semana Santa, July and August high season.

The only **campsite** anywhere near town is *Trailer Park Oaxaca* (☎951/5-27-96; $10),
just over 3km north of the centre at the corner of Heroica Escuela Naval Militar and
Violetas: follow Niños Héroes east five blocks from the first-class bus station and turn
left up Ruíz. Camping is also possible in the grounds of **Tourist-Yú'ù** (see p.396),
which makes a great, relaxed alternative to staying in the city.

Around the zócalo
Antonio's, Independencia 601 (☎951/6-72-27). Tastefully decorated hotel with attractive smallish
rooms with TV around two stone-paved courtyards. Very good value considering the location. ⑤.
Francia, 20 de Noviembre 212 (☎951/6-48-11). Faded but still respectable colonial hotel where D H
Lawrence spent some time in 1925. Bathrooms and fittings are better in the newer section but the
high-ceilinged older rooms are more in the spirit of the place. ⑤.
Monte Albán, Alameda de León 1 (☎951/6-27-77). Beautiful colonial-style hotel right opposite the
cathedral. Excellent value with some lovely external rooms and less good internal ones. ⑤.
Pombo, Morelos 601 (☎951/6-26-73). Oddball but central, with plain rooms, some spacious and
airy, others little more than cupboards. Some showers have stoves in which you burn rolled up
paper and wood shavings when you want hot water. ②.
Las Rosas, Trujano 112 (☎951/4-22-17). Surprisingly peaceful and spacious white rooms all around
a colonnaded courtyard where tea and coffee are available and there are magazines to read. At the
lower end of this price category. ⑤.
Youth Hostel (CREA), Fiallo 305, south of Guerrero (☎951/6-12-87). One of the most popular in
the country, though rather cramped. Backpackers get washing and cooking facilities, mixed dorms
(non-members $7, members $6) or private rooms. ①.

North of Independencia
Calesa Real, García Vigil 306 (☎951/6-55-44). *Azulejo*-tiled corridors, a small pool and attractive
tile-floored rooms with locally made rugs make this one of the best of the central top-end places. ⑦.
Camino Real Oaxaca, 5 de Mayo 300 (☎951/6-06-11; in US: ☎1-800-722-6466). Oaxaca's top hotel
by a long stretch and the ultimate place to stay – the beautifully converted sixteenth-century ex-
convento de Santa Catalina with ornate fountains, jasmine-scented gardens and a swimming pool in
the cloister. Worth visiting if only to look around. ⑨.
Casa Arnel, Aldama 404, Colonia Jalatlaca (☎951/5-28-56). Welcoming small hotel built around a
verdant courtyard and geared to the budget traveller, though it is neither especially cheap nor
central. Basic rooms have private bath and there are facilities to wash, cook and phone home. ⑤.
Las Golondrinas, Tinoco y Palacios 411 at Allende (☎951/6-87-26). Relaxed hotel with personal
service. Clean, tastefully decorated rooms, all with private bath, are arranged around a series of
banana-filled patios. Rates include breakfast. ④.
Posada Margarita, Labastida 115 (☎951/6-28-02). Almost in the shadow of Santo Domingo, this is
about the best of the budget hotels with some spacious high-ceilinged older rooms and smaller
modern affairs, all with private bath. ③.

TOURIST-YÚ'Ù: LOW-COST ACCOMMODATION IN THE OAXACA VALLEY

In 1994 SEDETUR and the *Secretaria de Turismo* opened the first batch of **Tourist-Yú'ù** – Zapotec for house – nine small self-contained houses scattered through the villages of the Oaxaca valley. An attempt to jump on the ecotourism bandwagon, they are supposed to help bring income to the local village while minimizing the disruptive effects of mass tourism. You can judge their success for yourself by staying at one for a night, a week or longer.

Normally sited on the edge of a small village – currently Abasolo, Papalutla, Teotitlán del Valle, Benito Juárez, Tlacolula, Quialana, Tlapazola, Santa Ana del Valle, and Hierve el Agua – Tourist Yú'ùs are detached houses (painted a distinctive but ugly teal colour) designed to sleep up to five people, with a bedroom, a fully equipped kitchen with stove and refrigerator, an *artesanía* shop, and an outside shower and toilets which can also be used by people camping in the grounds. Each Tourist Yú'ù has a custodian who attends the shop during the day and collects $10 per person ($7 for students) up to a maximum of $33 for five, and $3 for campers.

Bookings – preferably a few days in advance, especially for the more accessible sites – can be made through the *Secretaria de Desarrollo Turistico Oaxaca* (☎951/6-01-23 or 6-09-84), in the same building as Oaxaca's main tourist office.

Principal, 5 de Mayo 208 (☎951/6-25-35). Colonial-style place with a central courtyard and good rooms with private bathrooms. A good deal less of a splurge than the *Camino Real*. ⑤.

South of Independencia

Cabaña, Mina 203 (☎951/6-59-18). Decent rooms, surprisingly quiet for this part of town. ②–③.

Hotel del Valle, Aldama 517 (☎951/6-49-11). Grotty from the outside and in a shabby part of town but with clean, adequate rooms, some with private bath, and hot water all day. Very cheap *comedores* round about. ②.

Lupita, Díaz Ordaz 314 (☎951/6-57-33). The best of a number of budget places in this area. ③.

Mesón del Angel, Mina 518 (☎951/6-66-66). Soulless hotel with some ugly Sixties rooms and a more tasteful modern wing, huge pool, parking, TVs and phones. ⑥.

Mina, Mina 304 (☎951/6-49-66). Cell-like rooms but good, clean and with 24-hour hot water in the communal bathrooms. ②.

Vallarta, Díaz Ordaz 309 (☎951/6-40-67). Though built around an unpleasant modern courtyard, above average for this area, with good, clean, well-furnished rooms, towels and soap provided. ④.

Yagul, Mina 103 (☎951/6-27-50). Spacious clean rooms around a huge plant- and caged-bird-filled courtyard. Well-priced, though rooms with a double bed are more expensive than twins. ③.

The City

Simply being in Oaxaca, absorbing its life and wandering through its streets, is an experience, especially if you happen to catch the city during a fiesta (they happen all the time – the most important are listed at the end of the chapter), but you should definitely take time out to visit the **State Museum** and the **Museo Tamayo**, the **market** (shopping in Oaxaca is quite simply some of the best in the entire country), the **churches** of Santo Domingo and La Soledad, and to get out to Monte Albán and Mitla. All in all it could be a long stay.

Around the zócalo

The **zócalo**, closed to traffic and constantly animated, is the place to start. Beggars, hawkers, businesspeople, tourists and locals pass through, and on Sundays and many weekday evenings there's a band playing in the centre. On the south side, the

Neoclassical, *Porfiriano* **Palacio de Gobierno** features historical murals, second-rate by Mexican standards; you reach the **Cathedral** from the northwest corner, opposite. Begun in 1544, its construction was only completed in the eighteenth century, since when it has been repeatedly pillaged and restored: as a result, despite a fine Baroque facade, it's not the most interesting of Oaxaca's churches. It is impressively big, though, with a heavy *coro* blocking the aisle in the heart of the church.

Walk past the cathedral and the Alameda, then right onto Independencia, and you reach the **Teatro Macedonio de Alcalá** in a couple of blocks. Still operating as a theatre and concert hall, it is typical of the grandiose public buildings that sprang up across Mexico around the turn of the century – the interior, if you can see it (try going to a show, or sneaking in before one), is a magnificent swathe of marble and red plush.

North of the zócalo

Heading north from the zócalo, Valdivieso crosses Independencia to become Macedonio Alcalá, the city's pedestrianized shopping street, a showcase for the best Mexican and Oaxacan **crafts**. This is the place to come for exquisitely intricate silver designs, finely executed, imaginative textiles, and the highest prices: check the quality here before venturing out to the villages where they are made. Four blocks up Alcalá stands the church of **Santo Domingo** (daily 7am–1pm & 4–8pm; no sightseeing during mass; free). Considered by Aldous Huxley to be "one of the most extravagantly gorgeous churches in the world", this sixteenth-century extravaganza is elaborately carved and decorated both inside and out, the external walls solid, defensive and earth-quake-proof, the interior extraordinarily rich. Parts – especially the chapels, pressed into service as stables – were damaged during the Reform Wars and the Revolution, but most have been restored. Notice especially the great gilded main altarpiece, straight ahead, and, on the underside of the raised choir above you as you enter, the family tree of the Dominican order, in the form of a vine with leafy branches and tendrils, busts of leading Dominicans and a figure of the Virgin right at the top. Throughout there must be tons of gold leaf, beautifully set off in the afternoon by the golden light flooding through a predominantly yellow window. Looking back from the altar end you can appreciate the relief scenes high on the walls, the biblical events depicted in the barrel roof, and above all the ceiling of the choir, a vision of the heavenly hierarchy with gilded angels swirling in rings around God. The adjoining **Capilla del Rosario** is also richly painted and carved: the Virgin takes pride of place in another stunning altarpiece, all the more startlingly intense in such a relatively small space.

Behind the church, the old Dominican monastery has been restored to house the **Museo Regional de Oaxaca** (Tues–Sat 10am–6pm, Sun 10am–5pm; $5, free on Sun) in a series of beautiful chambers on two floors around two adjoining cloisters. This, too, was used as a barracks, and part of the complex still is; the rest looks pretty battered. The majority of the interest is upstairs, where beyond an ethnographic display devoted to the state's various Indian groups – their art, crafts and costumes – you reach the archeological collection, and above all one room containing the magnificent **Mixtec jewellery** discovered in Tomb 7 at Monte Albán (see p.403). What you see here constitutes a substantial proportion of all known pre-Hispanic gold, since anything the early Spanish found they plundered and melted down. Highlights include a couple of superbly detailed gold masks and breastplates. There are also smaller gold pieces, and objects in a wide variety of precious materials – mother-of-pearl, obsidian, turquoise, amber and jet among them.

Across the road the **Graphic Arts Institute** (Mon & Wed–Sun 10.30am–8pm; free) displays changing exhibits of works by nationally renowned artists. It is worth popping in just to amble around the small rooms of what was once a rather grand colonial house and to spend an hour in the excellent art library. The **Casa Juárez**, nearby on García Vigil, is currently closed.

West of the zócalo

Four blocks back down Alcalá then three blocks to the right lies the **Museo Rufino Tamayo** (Mon & Wed–Sat 10am–2pm & 4–7pm, Sun 10am–3pm; $3), a private collection of pre-Hispanic artefacts, gathered by the *Oaxaqueño* abstract artist who ranks among the greatest Mexican painters of the century. In many ways this museum is more interesting than the bulk of the regional museum, though it's not really fair to compare them. Rather than set out to explain the archeological significance of its contents, this classy collection is deliberately laid out as an art museum, showing objects as aesthetic forms, and includes truly beautiful items from all over Mexico. Aztec, Maya and western cultures all feature strongly, while there's surprisingly little that is Mixtec or Zapotec.

Around the corner on J P García, the **Iglesia de San Felipe Neri** is mostly Baroque with a Plateresque facade and a wonderful gilt Churrigueresque altarpiece, but what really makes it unusual is its interior decor. The church was used as barracks during the Revolution and, by the 1920s, needed to be repainted: which it was in an unusual Art Nouveau–Art Deco style. This is also where Benito Juárez got married.

The **Basilica de Nuestra Señora de la Soledad**, not far away to the west along Independencia, contains an image – the *Virgen de la Soledad* – that is not only Oaxaca's patron saint, but one of the most revered in the country. The sumptuously decorated church, late seventeenth-century with a more recent facade, is set on a small plaza surrounded by other buildings associated with the Virgin's cult. This is where the best ice cream in town – if not the whole of Mexico – is sold (see p.400), and the adjoining **Plaza de la Danza** is a setting for outdoor concerts, *folklórico* performances, or specialist craft markets. A line of ramshackle stalls behind the ice-cream vendors sells gaily coloured religious icons. Just below the church there's a small **museum** (Mon–Sat 10am–2pm, Sun 11am–2pm; 30¢) devoted to the cult. It's a bizarre jumble of junk and treasure – native costumes displayed on permed blonde 1950s dummies; *ex-voto* paintings giving thanks for miracles and cures – among which the junk is generally far more interesting. The museum also explains how the church came to be built here, after the image miraculously appeared, in 1620, in a box on the back of a mule.

South of the zócalo: shopping in Oaxaca

The only local church to compare with La Soledad, in terms of the crowds of worshippers it attracts, is the ancient **San Juan de Dios**, right in the heart of the old market area. Here villagers who've come to town for the day and market traders drop in constantly to pay their devotions – often in curiously corrupted forms of Catholic ritual.

Saturday, by tradition, is **market day** in Oaxaca and although nowadays the markets operate daily, Saturday is still the time to come if you want to see the old-style *tianguis* at its best. Indians flood in from the villages in a bewildering variety of costumes, and Mixtec and Zapotec dialects replace Spanish as the lingua franca. The majority of this activity, and of the serious business of buying and selling everyday goods, has moved out to the **new market** by the second-class bus station, but the old **Mercado Benito Juárez**, downtown, still sells the bulk of village **handicrafts** as well as plenty of fruit and veg. Be warned that it's very touristy – you're harassed far more by the vendors and have to bargain fiercely – and the quality of the goods is also often suspect. **Sarapes**, in particular, are often machine-made from chemically dyed artificial fibres: these look glossy, and you can also tell real wool by plucking out a thread – artificial fibres are long, thin and shiny, woollen threads short, rough and curly. If you hold a match to it a woollen thread will singe and smell awful, an artificial one will melt and burn your fingers. There's a *Fonart* shop at the corner of García Vigil and Bravo that will give you a good idea of the potential quality, and there are many more expensive craft shops scattered about, as well as a small handicrafts market just beyond the main section around 20 de Noviembre and Zaragoza.

Despite Oaxaca's many crafts stores, if it's quality you're after, or if you intend to buy in quantity, visiting the **villages** from which the goods originate is a far better bet. Each has a different speciality (**Teotitlán del Valle**, for example, for *sarapes*, or **San Bartolo Coyotepec** for black pottery; see p.408) and each has one market a week. Though there's no guarantee that you'll be able to buy better or more cheaply, you will be able to see the artesans in action, you may be able to have your own design made up, and quite apart from all that, a village market is an experience in itself.

MONDAY **Miahuatlan**: *mescal*, bread, leather.

TUESDAY **Santa Ana del Valle**: general.

WEDNESDAY **Etla**: meat, cheese, flowers.

THURSDAY **Zaachila**: meat, nuts; **Ejutla**: *mescal*, embroidered blouses.

FRIDAY **Ocotlán**: flowers, meat, pottery, textiles.

SATURDAY **Oaxaca**: everything.

SUNDAY **Tlacolula**: ceramics, rugs, crafts; **Tlaxiaco**: leather jackets, blankets, *aguardiente*.

Out from the centre

Although it is fairly easy to find your bearings in the centre of town, to get a fix on Oaxaca's relation to the rest of the valley and Monte Albán, take a hike (about 45min from the zócalo) up **Cerro del Fortín**, on the northwestern edge of the city. It is steep but the views are rewarding and in the evening you can call in on the **Planetario Nundenui** (45min shows in Spanish only: Wed, Fri & Sat at 7pm, Sun 6pm & 7pm; $2). The road up here passes the **Auditorio Guelaguetza**, the venue for the annual festival known as **"Lunes del Cerro"** (Monday of the Hill), primarily because the folk dances take place on the first two Mondays after July 16. Around Christmas, many of Oaxaca's boisterous celebrations also take place here.

Eating and drinking

Food is good in Oaxaca, and readily available on almost every street corner. The cheapest places to eat are in the **markets** – either a section of the main market around 20 de Noviembre and Aldama, or the new one by the second-class bus station – where you'll find excellent **tamales**. More formal but still basic restaurants are to be found in the same areas as the cheaper hotels, especially along Trujano. The **zócalo** is ringed by cafes and restaurants where you can sit outside: irresistible as ever and not as expensive as their position might lead you to expect; and there are plenty of simple places for everyday meals in the streets round about.

Around the zócalo

Cafetería Chips, Trujano 116, just west of the zócalo. Basic, inexpensive cafe with a good range of *tortas*, *licuados* and *jugos*. Try especially the *Torta Italiana*.

El Jardín, on the zócalo. One of the best cafes for watching life go by, but little to choose between it and *Mario's Terranova*, *La Primavera* or *El Asador Vasca* – though the last does serve excellent Spanish-style food.

Restaurant Quickly, Alcalá 100, just north of the zócalo. Touristy menu with huge portions and lots of green vegetables. Inexpensive.

Del Vitral, Guerrero 201, east of Bustamente (☎951/6-31-24). Oaxaca's finest restaurant – and one of Mexico's best – in an amazing seigneurial hall with chandeliers, fireplaces and a series of French

FOOD AND DRINK IN OAXACA

Oaxaca is a wonderful city for gourmands: local specialities worth trying are **tamales** – in just about any form, and often better from street or market vendors than in restaurants – **mole oaxaqueño**, which is not significantly different from *mole* anywhere else, but good nonetheless, and very special home-made **ice cream**. The place to go for ice cream is the plaza in front of the church of La Soledad, full of rival vendors and tables where you can sit and gorge yourself while watching the world go by. Flavours are innumerable and often bizarre, including *elote* (corn), *queso, leche quemada* (burnt milk; even worse than it sounds), *sorbete* (cinnamon-flavoured sherbet) and rose, exotic fruits like *mamey, guanabana* and *tuna* (prickly pear, a virulent purple that tastes wonderful), as well as more ordinary and less good varieties such as chocolate, nut and *coco*.

It's something of a leap from here to **mescal** (or *mezcal*), which is *the* local drink, sold everywhere in bottles that usually have a dead worm in the bottom. This creature lives on the maguey cactus and is there to prove it's genuine: you don't have to drink it, though few people are in any state to notice by the time they reach the bottom of the bottle, and no one seems to come to much harm, at least not from the worm. Basically, *mescal* is a rougher version of tequila, and developed at the same time, when the Spaniards introduced distillation after the Conquest. It is drunk the same way, with a lick of salt and lime. **Specialist shops** all around the market – try *El Fornoso*, J P García 405, and *El Flor de Maguey*, 20 de Noviembre 606 – sell *mescal* in various qualities (including from the barrel), and most also sell it in souvenir pottery bottles, which are amazingly cheap.

At the south side of the market, your nose will lead you to c/Mina, which is lined with **spice** vendors, selling plump bags of the *chile*-and-chocolate powder that makes up Oaxacan *mole*. Cinnamon-flavoured **chocolate** powder is also available, for cooking or making into drinking chocolate.

fin-de-siècle glass panels of a Louis Quinze patio and fountain. *Oaxaqueño* and international cuisine with a hint of *nouvelle*, and you can still walk away with change from $30 after three courses. Open 8am–11pm with live piano music in the afternoon and evening.

North of Independencia

Flor de Loto/Plaza Gourmet, Morelos 509 at Díaz. Relatively pricey, predominantly vegetarian restaurant with a broader menu than *El Manantial*, including pasta, pizza and some meat dishes. Good *comida corrida*.

Hipotesis, Morelos 519 at Díaz. Tiny bohemian cafe/bar: all wood beams and impromptu folk music (especially at weekends). Light snacks and good coffee. Daily except Sun 1pm–1am.

El Manantial Vegetariano, Díaz at Morelos. Inexpensive vegeburgers, fruit shakes and meat-free Mexican breakfasts are the order of the day at this small wholefood restaurant. Closes 8pm.

Morgan, Morelos 601 by *Hotel Pombo*. Small Italian-run restaurant with a limited range of very good cheap pasta, Mexican breakfasts, some of the best coffee in town and what must be one of the world's most out-of-date noticeboards. Daily except Sun 7.30am–1pm & 5.30–10pm.

Los Olmas, Alcalá 301, north of Matamoros. An unprepossessing doorway opens into a large courtyard with a few rough tables normally surrounded by everyone from local businesspeople to language students eating *antojitos regionales*. Clean, quick, informal and very inexpensive.

Plaza Garibaldi, Alcalá 303, north of Matamoros. Striking colonnaded nightspot (see also "Nightlife") with white-painted alcoves, some bearing faded frescoes. You pay for the location but the Oaxacan-Mexican food isn't too expensive.

La Sol y La Luna, Alcalá 109, west of Alcalá (☎951/4-81-05). An appealing cluster of small, dimly lit rooms and an open courtyard make up this well-priced restaurant. The soups, salads, pasta, steaks and deep-pan pizza are reliable, the choice of background music less so.

El Topil, Plazuela Labastida opposite *Posada Margarita*. Simply decorated restaurant specializing in Oaxacan dishes, including *tamales* in *mole* and a cheese fondue that bears no relation to the Swiss dish. The service isn't what the white shirts and bow ties would lead you to expect. Moderate.

South of Independencia

Alex, Díaz Ordaz 218 at Trujano. Pleasant place to sit over good-value food, especially the excellent breakfasts and $3 *comidas corridas*. Mon–Sat 7am–9pm, Sun 7am–noon.

Las Chalotes, Fiallo 116 south of Independencia (☎951/6-48-97). French menu that runs from couscous and fondue to terrines and stuffed quail: the surroundings are cosy enough to make you want to linger. Tues–Sun 2–11pm.

Nightlife

If you're not content sitting around the zócalo over a coffee or a beer, whiling away a balmy night to the accompaniment of *mariachi* or brass bands, don't expect too much of evenings in Oaxaca. The **folk dances** at the *Camino Real Oaxaca* and *Monte Albán* hotels are another possibility, but there's nothing much more lively even at weekends. Weeknights are quieter still, though there is usually some kind of cultural activity at 6pm on Wednesday outside the Santo Domingo church.

Centro Cultural Juan Rulfo, Independencia 300 at Mier y Terán. Tucked in the back of an *artesanía* shop this privately run showcase for local talent puts on music from 8pm to around midnight Wed, Thurs and Sat, along with Sat afternoons from around 2pm are the best bets, though the schedule varies, as does the quality of the acts. Occasional small cover charge.

MOVING ON FROM OAXACA

Unless you need to get to Puerto Escondido in a hurry, the **bus** is, as usual, the best way to travel on from Oaxaca. From the **first-class** bus station on Chapultepec, *Cristóbal Colón* and *ADO* between them run regular first-class and pullman services to México, Puebla, Puerto Escondido, Pochutla, San Cristóbal, Tehuacán and Villahermosa. *Cristóbal Colón* has a downtown **ticket office** at 20 de Noviembre 204-A (Mon–Sat 9am–2pm & 4–7pm) and *ADO* has one inside the *American Express* office, on the zócalo at the corner of Hidalgo and Valdivieso (Mon–Fri 9am–2pm & 4–8pm). Slower, cheaper, more frequent and less comfortable services leave from the **second-class bus station** near the new market, to México (mostly overnight), Puerto Escondido, Pinotepa Nacional, Pochutla, Salina Cruz, Tuxtla Gutiérrez and other destinations.

If you are prepared to take the risk of having stuff stolen while you sleep, the **overnight train to México** is unusually convenient and phenomenally cheap at around $14 in first-class and $8 in second-class (the latter about a third of the bus fare). The train (which no longer has sleepers) leaves at 7pm, arriving in México about 10am: an equivalent overnighter follows the same timetable in the opposite direction. A second train (no first-class) runs only as far as **Puebla**, leaving Oaxaca at 7.30am, while another arrives from Puebla at around 6pm. To get to the station, catch buses marked either "Colonia Reforma" or "Santa Rosa", or walk twenty minutes west along Independencia.

Numerous **flights** leave Oaxaca, predominantly for México (5 daily with *Mexicana*, 2 daily with both *Aeroméxico* and *Aviacsa*, and 1 daily with *PAL*), but also to Puerto Escondido (6-seater *Aerovega* and *Aeromorelos*), Huatulco (*Aeromorelos*), and Cancún via Tuxtla Gutiérrez, Villahermosa and Mérida (*Aero Caribe* and *Aviacsa*). Prices increase dramatically during Mexican holiday times, but as a rough guide expect to pay $50–100 to México, $90 to Puerto Escondido and $160 to Mérida. Oaxaca's **airport** is about 10km south of the city on the road to San Bartolo Coyotepec and Ocotlán. Buses between Oaxaca and these two towns (from the second-class bus station) pass within a kilometre or so of the airport but it is far easier to contact *Transportacion Terrestre Aeropuerto*, on the Alameda (☎951/4-43-50), who, if you contact them the day before your flight, will pick you up at your hotel and charge around $3.

Rather than deal with the individual airlines, enquire and book flights through a **travel agent** such as the *Universal Travel Centre*, c/Fiallo 117 on the first floor (Mon–Sat 9am–9pm, Sun 9am–1pm; ☎951/4-70-39 or 4-69-43), which has good deals and some English-speaking staff.

Eclipse, Díaz 219. Very young disco with mainstream American dance music. Thurs–Sat until 2pm, expensive drinks and a $10 cover (negotiable) at the weekend.

London, Hidalgo 1002 at Fiallo. A (very loosely) Beatles-themed bar – apparently there's a twin called *Liverpool* somewhere out in the suburbs – with live music daily (10pm–1am). No cover and reasonably priced drinks, but the attempt at a British-pub atmosphere fails dismally.

Plaza Garibaldi, Alcalá 303 (☎951/6-79-33). *Salsa* on Fri and Sat from around 9pm. Cover charge.

Principal, 20 de Noviembre 110. Club catering to a mid to late-twenties crowd. Some Latin tunes but mostly American. Free on Thurs; $5–10 cover at weekends.

Listings

Airlines *Aeroméxico*, Hidalgo 513 (☎951/6-71-01); *Aeromorelos*, Macedonia Alcalá 501-B (☎951/6-09-74); *Aviacsa*, Calzada Díaz 102 (☎951/3-18-01); *Mexicana* and *Aero Caribe*, Fiallo 102 at Independencia (☎951/4-72-48); *PAL*, Morelos 602 (☎951/4-69-13).

Consulates *Canada*, Liceaga 119-8 (9am–2pm; ☎951/3-37-77 or 5-21-47); *USA*, Alcalá 201 Int 204 (9am–2pm, ☎951/4-30-54, emergency ☎4-14-04). For *French*, *Spanish* and *Italian* consulates ask at the tourist office.

Medical emergencies English-speaking doctor, Francisco Hernandez (☎951/6-93-71); *Cruz Roja* (☎951/6-44-55); *IMSS hospital*, Niños Héroes 621 (☎951/5-20-33).

Laundry *Azteca Laundry*, 404-B Hidalgo (Mon–Sat 8am–8pm, Sun 10am–2pm).

Photographic supplies Numerous places on 20 de Noviembre south of Independencia. *Figueroa*, Hidalgo 516 at 20 de Noviembre, is the cheapest and best.

Police ☎6-27-26.

The Zapotec and Mixtec heartland

The Valley of Oaxaca, or rather the three valleys that abut each other here, saw the development of some of the earliest and most accomplished civilizations in Mexico. Small and relatively peripheral regional powers, to be sure, but ones that survived in a degree of peace far longer than any other, and whose craft skills – in pottery and metal-working – were unrivalled. There is evidence of settled population in the valleys dating back to several millennia BC, but the earliest concrete remains are at **Monte Albán**, founded around 700 BC. Its impractical, mountain-top site raises several problems: pre-eminently, why should the **Zapotecs** have abandoned the fertile valley that supported them? In all probability, the bulk of the population never did, and Monte Albán reflects rather the growing sophistication of their society: it was a religious and political centre, physically dominating all three valleys from a neutral vantage point. Until about 700 AD Monte Albán was clearly the most important town in the region – trading over long distances with both Teotihuacán and the Maya, waging war where necessary to preserve its hegemony.

After 700, though, Monte Albán was suddenly deserted. This, probably, was a knock-on effect of the fall of Teotihuacán – in the period of uncertainty that followed, and especially with the loss of an important trading partner, the non-productive elite simply became too much of a burden. At the same time, incursions of mountain-dwelling **Mixtecs** began to disturb the life of the valleys, as through war and intermarriage Mixtec influence grew and eventually came to dominate. The style of **Mitla**, successor to Monte Albán, is Mixtec, although whether it was inhabited by Mixtecs or by Zapotecs under Mixtec control is impossible to say. They maintained control right through to the fifteenth century, developing above all the arts of the potter and the goldsmith to new heights. Moctezuma is said to have eaten only off plates made by Mixtec craftsmen – Aztec forces having conquered (although by no means pacified) the area in the years before the Conquest. The road to Mitla from Oaxaca passes close by several lesser sites – notably **Dainzu**, **Lambityeco** and **Yagul**, all three deserted and eerily fascinating. Along the way, too, are several villages with **craft specialities** that merit a detour, and, right by the road, the mighty **Arbol de Tule**, an enormous tree that everyone stops to admire.

Monte Albán

> *Imagine a great isolated hill at the junction of three broad valleys; an island rising nearly a thousand feet from the green sea of fertility beneath it. An astonishing situation. But the Zapotecs were not embarrassed by the artistic responsibilities it imposed on them. They levelled the hill-top; laid out two huge rectangular courts; raised pyramidal altars or shrines at the centre, with other, much larger, pyramids at either end; built great flights of steps alternating with smooth slopes of masonry to wall in the courts; ran monumental staircases up the sides of the pyramids and friezes of sculpture round their base. Even today, when the courts are mere fields of rough grass, and the pyramids are buried under an obscuring layer of turf, even today this high place of the Zapotecs remains extraordinarily impressive . . . Monte Albán is the work of men who knew their architectural business consummately well.*
>
> Aldous Huxley, *Beyond the Mexique Bay*

In the sixty years since Aldous Huxley visited, little has changed at **MONTE ALBÁN**. The main structures have perhaps been cleared and restored a little more, but it's still the great flattened mountain-top (750m by 250m), the overall lay out of the ceremonial precinct and the views over the valley that impress more than any individual aspect. Late afternoon, with the sun sinking in the valley, is the best time to see it.

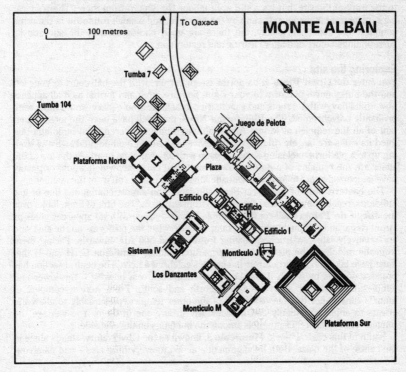

It seems almost madness to have tried to build a city here, so far from the obvious livelihood of the valleys and without even any natural water supply (in the dry season water was carried up and stored in vast urns). Yet that may have been the point – to demonstrate the Zapotecs' mastery of nature. Certainly, the rulers who lived here must have commanded a huge workforce, first to create the flat site, later to transport materials and keep it supplied. What you see today is just the very centre of the city – the religious and political heart later used by the Mixtecs as a magnificent burial site. On the terraced hillsides below lived a population that, at its peak, reached over 25,000: craftsmen, priests, administrators and warriors, all, presumably, supported by tribute from the valleys. Small wonder that so top-heavy a society was easily destabilized.

Getting to Monte Albán

Monte Albán (daily 8am–5pm; $5, free on Sun) is just 9km from town, up a steeply switchbacking road. *Autobuses Turisticos* operating from the *Hotel Mesón del Angel* (see p.396) hold a monopoly on **buses from Oaxaca to Monte Albán** ($2.50 return). In peak season buses depart very frequently but usually they leave at 8.30am (returning at 11am), 9.30am (back at noon), and hourly until 3.30pm (returning at 5.30pm), giving at best two hours at the site, which is barely enough to see it even quickly. If there is space you can return on a later bus, but will have to pay half the fare again. It's sometimes possible to hitch a ride or find a taxi (which for four or five people is not much more expensive than the bus), and walking back is also a realistic option: more than two hours, but downhill almost all the way. Get a guard or one of the kids selling "genuine antiquities" to show you the path. The **bus from Zaachila** (see p.409) passes close to the front of the site, but it's a stiff walk (about 1hr 30min) from there. There's a car park, restaurant and souvenir shop by the entrance, and a small **museum** in the same complex: the collection is tiny, but there are good photographs of the site and its surroundings before and after clearing and restoration.

Exploring the site

You enter the **Great Plaza** at its northeastern corner, with the ball-court to your left and the bulky north platform to your right. Sombre, grey and formal as it all appears now, in its day, with its roofs and sanctuaries intact, the whole place would have been brilliantly polychromed. The **Plataforma Norte** may well have been the most important of all the temples at Monte Albán, although now the ceremonial buildings that lined its sides are largely ruined. What survives is a broad monumental stairway leading up to a platform enclosing a square patio with an altar at its heart. At the top of the stairs are the remains of a double row of six broad columns, which would originally have supported a roof to form a colonnade, dividing this plaza off from the main one.

The **eastern side** of the Great Plaza consists of an almost continuous line of low buildings, reached by a series of staircases from the plaza. The first of them looks over the **Juego de Pelota** (ball-court), a simple I-shaped space with no apparent goals or target rings, and obviously an early example. Otherwise, the platforms on the east side are relatively late constructions dating from around 500 AD onwards. Facing them from the middle of the plaza is a long tripartite building (**Edificios G, H** and **I**) that must have taken an important role in any rites celebrated here. The central section has broad staircases by which it can be approached from east or west – the lower end temples have smaller stairways facing north and south. From here a complex of tunnels runs under the site to several of the other temples, presumably to allow the priests to emerge suddenly and miraculously in any one of them. You can see the remains of several of these tunnels among the buildings on the east side.

South of this central block, **Montículo J**, known as the Observatory, stands alone in the centre of the plaza. Both its alignment – at 45° to everything else – and its arrow-shaped design mark it out from its surroundings. Although the orientation is almost certainly for astronomical reasons, there's no evidence that this was actually an observatory; more likely it was built (around 250 AD, but on the site of an earlier structure) to celebrate a military victory. Relief carvings and hieroglyphs on the back of the building apparently represent a list of towns captured by the Zapotecs. In the vaulted passage that runs through the heart of the building, several more panels carved in relief show *danzante* figures (see below) – these, often upside down or on their sides and in no particular order, may have been reused from an earlier building.

The southern end of the mountain-top is dominated by its tallest structure, the **Plataforma Sur**. Unrestored as it is, this vast square pyramid still offers the best overview of the site. Heading back from here up the western side of the plaza, you'll pass just three important structures – the almost identical **Monticulo M** and **Sistema IV**, with the great Dancers Group between them. Monticulo M and Sistema IV, which are probably the best preserved buildings on the site, both consist of a rectangular platform reached by a stairway from the plaza. Behind this lies a small sunken square from which rises a much larger pyramid, originally topped by a roofed sanctuary.

The gallery and building of **Los Danzantes** (the Dancers) are the most interesting at Monte Albán. A low wall extending from Monticulo M to the base of the Danzantes building forms the **gallery**, originally faced all along with blocks carved in relief of Olmec or negroid-featured "dancers". Among the oldest (around 500 BC) and most puzzling features of the site, only a few of these *danzantes* remain in situ. Quite what the nude male figures represent is in dispute. Many of them seem to have been cut open and may represent sacrificial victims or prisoners; other authorities suggest that the entire wall was a sort of medical textbook, or that the figures really are dancers, or ball-players, or acrobats. Whatever the truth, they show clear Olmec influence, and many of them have been pressed into use in later buildings throughout the site. The Danzantes **Building** itself is one such, built over and obscuring much of the wall. It's a bulky, relatively plain rectangular platform with three temples on top – tunnels cut into the structure by archeologists reveal earlier buildings within, and more of the dancing figures.

Several lesser buildings surround the main plaza, and although they're not particularly interesting, many contained tombs in which rich treasures were discovered (as indeed did some of the main structures themselves). **Tumba 104**, reached by a small path behind the Plataforma Norte or from the car park area, is the best preserved of them. One of several in the immediate vicinity, this vaulted burial chamber still preserves excellent remains of murals. **Tumba 7**, where the important collection of Mixtec jewellery now in the Oaxaca Museum was found, lies a few hundred metres down the main road from the site entrance. Built underneath a small temple, it was originally constructed by the Zapotecs towards the end of Monte Albán's heyday, but was later emptied by the Mixtecs, who buried one of their own chiefs here along with his magnificent burial trove.

The road to Mitla

Mitla, some 45km from Oaxaca, just off the Pan-American Highway as it heads towards Guatemala, involves a slightly longer excursion. It's easy enough to do, though: buses leave from the second-class terminal every thirty minutes or so throughout the day. On the way are several of the more easily accessible **Indian villages**; if you want to stop at one, check with the tourist office which one has a market on the day you're going – there will be more buses and much more of interest once you get there. Also en route are a couple of smaller, lonelier ancient sites. If you rent a car in Oaxaca, you can take in all of this in a single day.

Santa María del Tule

At **Santa María del Tule** you pass the famous *Arbol del Tule* in a churchyard by the road. This mighty tree, said to be at least 2000 years old (some say 3000), is a good 40m round and slightly fatter than it is tall. A noticeboard gives all the vital statistics: suffice it to say that it must be one of the oldest living (and flourishing) objects on earth, and that it's a species of cypress (*Taxodium mucrunatum*) that has been virtually extinct since the colonial era. An extremely tacky souvenir market takes advantage of the passing trade, and there are various food and drink stalls, but if you're on the bus (left-hand side heading for Mitla) you get a good enough view as you pass.

Dainzu

Twelve kilometres farther on, **DAINZU**, the first significant archeological site, lies about 1km south of the main road (daily 8.30am–6pm; $2.50, free on Sun). A Zapotec centre broadly contemporary with Monte Albán, Dainzu stands only partially excavated in a harsh landscape of cactus-covered hills. The first structure you reach is **Edificio A**, a large and rambling construction, with elements from several epochs, set around a courtyard. The highlight of this building is a tomb with a jaguar doorway. Nearby is the ball-court, only one side of which has been reconstructed, and higher up the hill **Edificio B**, the best preserved part of the site. Along the far side of its base a series of dancer figures can be made out, similar to the Monte Albán dancers except that these clearly represent ball players.

Lambityeco

A couple of kilometres beyond Dainzu, **LAMBITYECO** (daily 10am–5.30pm; free) is an even smaller site, but its remains are considerably more stimulating, with some wonderfully vivid carved friezes and faces. If you are coming by bus, it has the additional advantage of being right on the main road – though since you can see the lot in just a few minutes, you may face a long wait for the next bus to stop.

The site was occupied for only a relatively short period around the eighth century AD, the very final period of occupation at Monte Albán, before being abandoned for the relative safety of Yagul. Nowadays, just a small portion is excavated and fenced off. Entering this area, climb the small pyramid directly ahead and you can look down over the two palace courtyards that are the site's main interest: one open, with an altar in the middle, the other closed off and surrounded by friezes. Beneath the latter is the entrance to a tomb on which are carved two wonderfully life-like faces of its occupants, thought to be the last rulers of Lambityeco – since you can only see these from a distance, it's worth getting the free handout on the site (available from the Oaxaca tourist office), which has a good photograph. On the cover of this leaflet you'll see the superb facade of the altar to the god Cocijo: two stylized jaguar faces with plumed headdresses, holding the force of the wind and sun in their hands. This is around the back of the pyramid.

Teotitlán del Valle

Almost opposite Lambityeco, a road leads 4km to **TEOTITLÁN DEL VALLE**, a town dedicated to weaving. All over town you see bold-patterned and brightly coloured **rugs** and **serapes**, some vaguely following traditional designs, others copying European cubists. Most are the product of cottage industry: even if you're not buying, poke your head into the compounds with rugs hanging outside. When dropped off the bus, you'll probably be pointed along a street to the left which leads to the **mercado de artesanías**. You'll see the widest range here, and some nice pieces if you ask to rummage in the back, but steel yourself against the urgent sales patter. Prices are unlikely to be much cheaper than in Oaxaca but the choice is wider. There are direct buses out here every hour or so; the last returns at around 5pm.

Tlacolula and Santa Ana del Valle

Just a few kilometres beyond Teotitlán del Valle, **TLACOLULA** is well worth a stop, featuring a large Sunday market and a beautiful sixteenth-century church, about 1km to the south of the main road.

A road leading north from the junction at Tlacolula goes to two villages: make sure you catch the bus to **SANTA ANA DEL VALLE**, smaller than Teotitlán but also specializing in rugs. One very high quality firm, *Casa Martinez*, has a wide selection – or place orders for your own designs – and you can see the production from beginning to end. One side of the small central square is devoted to the **Shon-Dany Archeological Museum** (daily 10am–2pm & 3–6pm; $2). Its name is Zapotec, meaning "foot of the hill", and it marks the exact spot where a couple of tombs were discovered in the 1950s and more recently excavated. Probably contèmporary with Dainzu and Monte Albán, the Zapotec site here produced some fine glyphs. Excavations have also been carried out beneath what are now basketball courts outside, enough pots and stones being recovered to fill the small but impressive co-operatively run museum. The local weaving industry is also covered and, though panels are all in Spanish, the gist is clear enough.

Yagul

The site of **YAGUL** lies to the north of the main road after about 35km – a couple of kilometres uphill from where the bus stops. It's a much larger area, spread expansively across a superb defensive position, and although occupied by the Zapotecs from a fairly early date, its main features are from later on (around 900–1200 AD, after the fall of Monte Albán) and shows strong **Mixtec** influence. On the lowest level, is the **Patio de la Triple Tumba**, where the remains of four temples surround an altar and the entry to the **Triple Tomb**, whose three chambers show characteristically Mixtec decoration. Immediately above the patio you'll see a large and elegantly simple ball-court, and a level above this, the maze-like **Palacio de los Seis Patios**. Probably a residential complex, this features six small courtyards surrounded by rooms and narrow passages. Climbing still higher towards the crest of the hill and the fortress, you pass several lesser remains and tombs, while from the fortress itself there are stunning views of the valley, and a frightening rock bridge across to a natural watchtower.

Mitla

The town of **MITLA** (Place of the Dead), where the bus finally drops you, is some 4km off the main road and just ten minutes' walk from the site of the famous ruins. It's an unattractive, dusty little place where you'll be harassed by would-be guides and vendors of handicrafts (there's also a distinctly second-rate crafts market by the ruins). As some consolation, however, there's a good **archeological museum** (the *Museo Frissel de Arte Zapoteca*; daily 9am–5pm; free), and next door to it the *Posada La Sorpresa*, which serves tasty *comidas* and has a few comfortable rooms. Cheaper accommodation can be found at the *Hotel Mitla* (②) or *La Zapoteca* (④), in town on the way to the ruins.

The **history of Mitla** is a complicated one, and still far from agreed among archeologists. The Mixtec-style buildings date probably from as late as the thirteenth century: the area, though, is a Zapotec one, inhabited by Zapotecs before the Mixtecs arrived, and inhabited by them again (by now under Aztec domination) when the Spanish came. It may well be that the population of Mitla was always Zapotec, but that the most important buildings were constructed under Mixtec direction, or in a period when Zapotec culture had been totally swamped.

Exploring the site

The site itself (daily 8.30am–6pm; $5, free on Sun) may seem disappointing on first sight: it's relatively small, and in the middle of the day overrun with visitors. But on closer inspection the fame of the place becomes more justifiable. Pure Mixtec in style, the palace complexes are magnificently decorated with elaborate stone mosaics. You'll see it at its best if you arrive towards closing time, when the low sun throws the patterns into sharp, shadowed relief, and the bulk of the visitors have left.

The **Grupo de las Columnas**, the best-preserved and most impressive of the palace complexes, is the obvious place to head from the entrance. The only other site that these long, low, fabulously decorated buildings recall in any way is Uxmal in the Yucatán (see p.504), which, along with other evidence, suggests that there may have been some contact between Mixtec and Maya. At Uxmal, though, pyramids rise among the palaces and much of the decor has a clearly religious significance. Here – where the designs are purely geometric patterns (or "petrified weaving", as Aldous Huxley saw them) – there is no evidence of the buildings having any spiritual importance.

The first large courtyard is flanked by constructions on three sides – its central **Templo de las Columnas** is magnificent, precision engineered and quite overpowering in effect. Climbing the broad stairway and through one of three entrances in its great facade, you come to the **Salon de las Columnas**, named after the six monolithic, tapered columns of volcanic stone that supported its roof. A low, dark and very narrow passageway (probably deliberately restricted so as to be easily defensible) leads from here into the small **inner patio** (*Patio de las Grecas*), lined with some of the most intricately assembled of the geometric mosaics. Four dark rooms that open off it continue the patterned mosaic theme. The second courtyard of the Columns group, adjoining the southwestern corner of the first, is similar in design though perhaps less impressive in execution. Known as the **Patio de las Tumbas**, it does indeed contain two cross-shaped tombs – long since plundered by grave robbers. In one the roof is supported by the **Columna de la Muerte** (Column of Death); embrace this, they say, and the gap left between your outstretched fingers tells you how long you have left to live.

The **Grupo de la Iglesia**, a short distance north, is so called because the Spanish built a church over, and from, much of it. Two of its three original courtyards survive, however, and in the smaller one the mosaic decoration bears traces of the original paint, indicating that the patterns were once picked out in white from a dark red background.

Three other groups of buildings, which have weathered the years less well, complete the site. All of them are now right in the modern town, fenced off from the surrounding houses: the **Grupo de los Adobes** can be found where you see a chapel atop a pyramid; the **Grupo del Arroyo** is very nearby; and the **Grupo del Sur** lies right beside the road to the main site.

South of Oaxaca

The two roads that run almost due south of Oaxaca don't have the same concentration of interesting villages and sites as the Mitla road, but there is plenty to occupy a day or so. Again, you can travel around the area by **public transport** on market days – by far the best time to go – but cycling on rented bikes from Oaxaca isn't as arduous as it might sound, especially if you keep out of the midday heat.

San Bartolo Coyotepec and Ocotlán

Fifteen kilometres south of Oaxaca on the main highway to Puerto Ángel lies **SAN BARTOLO COYOTEPEC**, as unprepossessing a town as you could imagine, famed only for its shiny black pottery – **barro negro brillante** – a purely ornamental material found in crafts shops all around Oaxaca, but made only at the small factory here. From the bus stop a road, one side awash with black pottery vendors, leads to the pottery where, in 1934, Doña Rosa developed the manufacturing technique. Her family still run the sole "factory", now very tourist-oriented, with pieces ranging from beautifully simple amphorae to ghastly clocks and breast-shaped mugs. Prices are supposed to be fixed, and at the factory they probably are, but places down the road will haggle; just remember your piece has to get home and the stuff is fragile. **Buses** to San Bartolo Coyotepec leave Oaxaca's second-class bus station (gate 24) every thirty minutes.

The same buses continue to **OCOTLÁN**, chiefly noted for the **painted ceramic figures** crafted by the Aguilar sisters. On the approach into town, look out on the right for the adjacent workshops of Guillermina, Josefina and Irene, each producing slightly different figures, though the distinctive Aguilar style, originated by their mother, shows through them all. Again, you can find examples in Oaxaca, but a trip out here allows you to see the full range: animals, men and women at work and play, and even nativity scenes are all considered fair game, often gaudily decorated in polka dots or geometric patterns. Try to make it on a Friday when the weekly **market** takes place not far from the **Parroquia de Santo Domingo de Guzmán**, with its newly restored facade and multiple domes richly painted with saints. Take a peek in at the gilded south transept.

Arrazola, Culiapan and Zaachila

The other major region of interest in this area is along, or beside, the road to Zaachila that runs southwest from Oaxaca past the foot of Monte Albán. **ARRAZOLA**, an easy cycle ride 5km off to the right from this road, is the home of the local woodcarvers and painters who produce the delightful boldly patterned animals from copal wood that you'll see for sale in Oaxaca and all over Mexico. Carvers from other villages are catching on to the popularity of these whimsical, spiky figures and producing the polka-dot, hooped or expressionist examples themselves, but few, if any, are better than in Arrazola.

The village of **CULIAPAN**, 14km from Oaxaca (buses from Gate 29 at the second-class bus station), seems insignificant beneath the immense sixteenth-century hulk of the Dominican **ex-Convento de Santiago Apóstol** which, though badly damaged, is still an impressive place to wander around, with a Renaissance twin-aisled nave and largely intact vaulting. One section is still roofed, and mass is said here amid the clangs and echoes of ongoing restoration work. The real interest, however, lies around the back in the **cloister** (daily 10am–6pm; $2.50), which features a few faded frescoes on the wall. Look out for the sign pointing to the back wall, where Vincente Guerrero was executed by firing squad after spending his captivity here.

Buses from Oaxaca to Culiapan continue 5km to **ZAACHILA**, which has a colourful Thursday market. Come here on that day and you've got the best chance of being able to get into the **zona arqueologica** (nominally Mon–Fri 9am–6pm, Sat & Sun 9am–4pm; $2.50, free on Sun) up behind the multi-domed church. There's not a great deal to see, but you can step down into the two opened tombs – of what is probably a much larger site – and, when your eyes become accustomed to the gloom, pick out detailed bas-relief geometric figures on the lintel and owls guarding the entrance. Inside, two marvellous glyphs show who was interred here: Señor Nine Flower, probably a priest, depicted carrying a bag of copal for producing incense.

Puerto Escondido

PUERTO ESCONDIDO is no longer the hippy hangout it was twenty-odd years ago. With direct flights from the capital and an already widespread reputation, it has firmly established itself as a mainstream resort, with the strings of souvenir shops and constantly spiralling prices that all this entails. Escondido still has a lot going for it, though, with beaches stretched out around the bay for miles in each direction and an

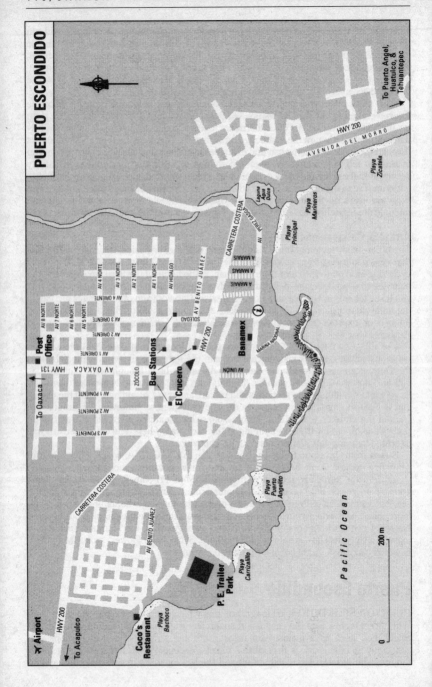

PUERTO ESCONDIDO

atmosphere that remains, against all the odds, small-town. There are no really big hotels, and most of the visitors are young, with surfing a major attraction.

Indeed, it is along the surf beach, **Zicatela**, less than a kilometre away from the centre, that most of the recent changes have taken place. Where once stood just a few weatherbeaten huts, there's now a thriving community with several good hotels – most with pools, since the sea is almost always too rough for swimming – and great restaurants. Everything revolves around surfing and being outdoors: you can get your hair cut while watching the boys (and one local girl) on the boards, or watch a video of the morning's action in one of the hotels. Non-surfers have cottoned on to the relaxed pace, and Zicatela is now as much a destination as Escondido town itself, especially between August and November. At either end of this season Escondido is packed for the **surf tournaments**: a locally sponsored event in late August and an international one – possibly due for inclusion on the professional tour – in late November. Despite its laid-back atmosphere, however, it is in Zicatela that the rumours of **muggings** in Puerto Escondido originate – mostly they're overstated but everyone advises against walking on the beach at night. The road by the hotels is fine.

Arrival, orientation and information

Puerto Escondido can be loosely divided into three zones; all contiguous but with completely different characters. The **old town** sprawls across the hill behind the bay, with the newer **tourist zone** spilling down towards the water and concentrated along Av. Peréz Gasca. **Zicatela** beach runs east then south from here.

The four **bus stations** are all near each other in the old town on the hill near El Crucero, the junction where the main road between the old town and the tourist zone crosses the Carretera Costera (Hwy-200). From here it's best to take a taxi to your hotel, especially if you're planning on staying in Zicatela: there's a minimum fare of around \$2.50. **Flights** from Oaxaca and México arrive at the airport 3km north of town, from where taxis (around \$10) and a cheaper minibus run into the centre.

Information

Although there's a **tourist office** (Mon–Fri 9am–2pm & 6–8pm, Sat 9am–1pm; ☎958/2-01-75) out on Hwy-200 to the north of town, the best source of information and maps is the **information booth** (Mon–Fri 9am–2pm & 5–7pm, Sat 9am–1pm) near the western end of the pedestrianized section of Peréz Gasca, the town's main thoroughfare. In the pedestrianized section, where there are several **Ladatel** phones (free collect calls), there's also a *larga distancia* office next door to the **casa de cambio** (daily 9am–2pm & 5–8pm). The rates at the latter aren't great; better to make it just up the hill to the often busy *Banamex* (exchange Mon–Fri 9am–noon), which also has an ATM. There's a self-service **laundry** (daily 8am–8pm) next door.

The **post office** (Mon–Fri 9am–6pm, Sat 9am–noon) is in the old town at c/7a Nte., though you can get stamps from postcard vendors (at a half-peso premium) and chance your luck with the mail boxes along Peréz Gasca. Out in Zicatela there are few facilities: the *Puerto y Bahías* **casa de cambio** is supposed to be open from 9am to 2pm and 4pm to 7pm daily, but seldom is, and never out of season.

Accommodation

Finding somewhere to stay in Puerto Escondido can be a problem, especially over Christmas or during the major surfing contests, when prices, seldom very low, are pushed up higher still. At any other time you'll have a wide choice of good hotels. Standards are high across the board, from simple *cabañas* to tasteful rooms. For

campers the best bet is the *Puerto Escondido Trailer Park* (☎958/2-00-77; $8–15), a spacious and grassy full-facility site with a pool, out on the west side of town above Carrizalillo beach. *Trailer Park Neptune*, by the eastern end of Playa Principal (☎957/2-03-27; $6), is less good: a tatty but reasonably shady and well-located ground with cabins for the same price as pitching a tent; rates quadruple in December, however.

In town

Aldea Marinero, c/del Morro, Playa Marinero (no phone). Slightly grotty rooms around a tiny courtyard. Fans and hammocks cost extra. ②.

Central, Oaxaca at Hidalgo (☎958/2-01-16). Poor-value hotel far from the beach but close to the bus stations and acceptable for just one night if you arrive late. ③.

Flor de María, c/del Morro, Playa Marinero (☎958/2-05-36). One of the best-value places in town; its design and decor showing the hand of the Italian owner. Fan-cooled rooms with beautifully tiled bathrooms, and a rooftop pool with restaurant and great views. ⑤.

Loren, Peréz Gasca 507 (☎958/2-00-57). High standard hotel away from the sea but with a good pool and impressively low off-season prices, which can be slashed by up to 50 percent. ⑥.

Mayflower, Andador Libertad, off Peréz Gasca (☎958/2-03-67). Well-kept American-run hotel with clean rooms, some with sea views, and dorm beds for $5. Plants all around and fridges for everyone's use. ④.

Zicatela beach

The hotels listed below are in **order of distance from Puerto Escondido**.

Santa Fe (☎958/2-01-70). Puerto Escondido's top hotel, catering to an older crowd, with very comfortable balconied rooms and a villagey feel. Next door, they have similar standard a/c "bungalows" ($90) for four; each has a private pool. ⑦.

Cabo Blanco. Rustic rooms for rent in this popular seafood restaurant (see p.414) and live music venue; unsurprisingly, it can be quite noisy. ③.

Casas de Playa Acali (☎958/2-02-78). Wooden-floored *cabañas* and well-appointed a/c bungalows, all with cooking equipment, tumble down the jungly hillside between the two pools. Upper rooms get great views along the beach, though the lower ones are more convenient. Helpful staff, too. ④.

Arcoiris (☎958/2-04-22). One of the classier places on the beach with none of the surf-city feel you get elsewhere. Luxuriant gardens and a secluded pool hide behind a block of spacious, comfortable rooms, some with fully equipped kitchen, some without. ⑤.

Beach Hotel Ines (☎958/2-07-92). Hammocks around the palm-shaded pool and the restaurant-bar are the centre of (in)activity here. Rooms range from simple *cabañas* – one Robinson Crusoe affair up among the coconuts – to cool, white-painted rooms, some with kitchen and fridge. The atmosphere is a little more formal than some of its neighbours, but it's relaxing nonetheless. ②–⑥.

Rockaway Surfer Village (☎958/2-06-68). Aptly named hotel where dedicated surfers hole up for the entire season. Simple but nice *cabañas* (with hammocks but no showers) around the pool sleep up to four. Surf shop and volleyball court. Prices halved in the low season. ⑥.

Villa María del Mar (☎958/2-10-91). *Cabaña*-like rooms with fan, hammock and private bath scattered around a compound with a pool. 400m beyond the end of the paved Zicatela road, so out of season, when the restaurant is closed, you'll appreciate being able to cook your own food here. ④.

The beaches

There's absolutely nothing to do in Escondido but swim, surf, laze on the beach and eat and drink. In most places you needn't move all day, as you'll be regularly approached by ice-cream carts, people trying to sell cold drinks or hot snacks, and vendors of T-shirts and trinkets. The choice of beaches even within a couple of kilometres of town is impressive: take your pick from the town strand, with the convenience of shops and bars nearby, pounding surf beaches or secluded coves ideal for snorkelling.

There are three main beach areas: the **town beach**, which stretches round to the east and south from the town centre; the surfing Mecca of Zicatela; and the trio of small coves to the west. The sand directly in front of town is perhaps a little overused, and shared, too, with the local fishermen and the activities of the port. A little to the east, beyond where the Laguna Agua Dulce occasionally reaches the sea, **Playa Marinero** is quieter, sometimes graced with gentle surf. But the real big stuff is southeast, beyond the little headland, where **Zicatela** stretches 2km to the point. One of the world's top surf beaches, Zicatela regularly receives perfectly formed beach breaks of 4m for days on end and occasionally a seven- or eight-metre monster stirred up by south Pacific storms between August and November. Surf- and boogie-boards can be rented from a number of places along Zicatela beach. When it is pumping, consider your strength and swimming fitness before venturing into the waves: they're very powerful, there's a significant rip and even experienced surfers occasionally drown.

Everything is much calmer in the coves to the west of the town. **Puerto Angelito** is the closest, divided in two by a rocky outcrop. It's about twenty minutes' walk from town, either by a track which leads to the left off Peréz Gasca, or direct from the highway on a signed road leading down opposite the *El Padrino* restaurant (the two paths meet above the beach). An alternative is the recently completed concrete footpath that sets out from the western end of the town beach, dipping and turning over the coastal rocks and eventually climbing up to a road. Follow this inland, then turn left along another road, which turns into steps onto the beach. Both the little inlets have small beaches and excellent **snorkelling** among the rocks, but you'll have to bring your own gear or rent some at great expense from the handful of makeshift restaurants.

The next bay, **Carrizalillo**, is reached along the same track, following signs to the *Puerto Escondido Trailer Park*. At the end you have to scramble down over the rocks to reach the sand, guaranteeing that there won't be too many other people around. **Bacocho Bay** is farther, following the highway out towards the airport and then cutting through the new hotel zone. Small boats will bring you round here from town, which is a great deal easier than walking and usually cheaper than a taxi; you can also arrange boat rides to beaches farther afield. There aren't many hotels here yet, so Bacocho offers good, secluded swimming; though again, caution is needed, as this beach is open to the ocean. *Coco's Bar and Restaurant* serves good, if pricey, **food**; eat, and you can use their pool for free.

Eating, drinking and nightlife

It doesn't cost much to eat well in Escondido: many of the **restaurants** and cafes are laid-back, low-key affairs with plenty of natural light and a cool breeze. The **seafood** is always fresh, and you can vary your diet with **vegetarian** food, excellent **bread and cakes** and **Italian food** from the inordinately large number of Italian restaurants. Most of the restaurants double as bars, and some even host live music. The large Italian contingent can usually be found glued to the Italian film *Puerto Escondido* – which is more about drug running from Real de Catorce than high intrigue in a beach resort – shown nightly at *Spaghetti House*.

There are more **films** on show at *Cine Club Ariel* (nightly Tues–Sun; $3; ☎958/2-02-44), this time art-house, usually in English or with subtitles. The screen is just by the *Villa María del Mar* hotel, about 400m beyond the rest of the hotels at Zicatela. Shows start at 9pm and occasionally at 7pm. Otherwise, nightlife is concentrated in the **bars** along Peréz Gasca.

In town

Barfly, Peréz Gasca. One of a couple of neighbouring places with early evening happy hours and usually live music until late. Unusually for Escondido, the taped music sometimes runs for over thirty minutes without a Bob Marley or U2 track.

La Gota de Vida, Peréz Gasca at the bottom of the hill. Reasonable vegetarian place serving yoghurt, granola, soya burgers and hummus during the day.

La Patisserie, c/del Morro, Playa Marinero. Croissants and pastries from *Carmen's* at Zicatela, plus sandwiches, fruit salads and yoghurt served in a quiet palm hut with a book swap.

El Sol y La Rumba, Andador Mar y Sol, off Peréz Gasca. *Salsa* bar with a tiny dance floor where gringos fail to imitate the locals. Some *cumbia*, *merengue* and reggae. Opens around 10pm.

Spaghetti House, just off the eastern end of Peréz Gasca. About the best Italian place in town. Not expensive and great food, with a tatty video of *Puerto Escondido* playing in the background.

Zicatela beach

The restaurants below are listed in **order of distance from Puerto Escondido**.

Cabo Blanco. The best seafood on the beach at reasonable prices. Fish or shrimps dressed with a choice of delicious sauces: Thai curry or lime, wine and cream. Live music most nights draws a lively crowd.

Carmen's. Tiny pavement bakery with great espresso, *pain au chocolat, pain aux raisins* and spinach rolls. After 4pm they have the day's *The News*, México's English-language daily.

Bruno's. Rightly popular open-fronted *palapa* restaurant. A great place for breakfasts, burgers and *burritos* through the day, and seafood in the evening. Check out the daily specials and two-for-one drinks 5.30–7pm.

Art and Harry's Surf Inn. Favourite evening spot where surfers and their acolytes come to watch the sun go down and drink two-for-one beers, staying on to play pool and look over that morning's surf photos on the noticeboard. Tasty, good-value salads, seafood and burgers served all day.

Around Puerto Escondido – the lagoons

Though most people find it almost impossible to drag themselves off the beaches of Puerto Escondido, there are a couple of boat trips worth making. **LAGUNA MANIALTEPEC**, about 15km west of Puerto Escondido, is cut off from the sea most of the year, forming a freshwater lake unfeasibly rich in wildlife. You can easily spot fifty-odd species in a day, among them several types of heron, ibis, egret, duck and cormorant, along with lily walkers and parrots. **Buses** run out here from El Crucero, or you can go with an organized tour through one of the travel agencies in Puerto Escondido.

With more time to spare – preferably a couple of days so you can stay over – the wildlife of the **LAGUNAS DE CHACAHUA** and the beach at the far end make a more interesting venture. Catch a bus from El Crucero (every 20min) to **Río Grande**, 50km west of Puerto Escondido on Hwy-200, then change on to one of the frequent minibuses to the one-time cacao and cotton port of **Zapotalito**. The road does continue a short way from here to the beach and *palapa* restaurants at Cerro Hermosa, but it is

---

MOVING ON FROM PUERTO ESCONDIDO

Of the four **bus stations**, *Estrella Blanca*, at Oaxaca and Benito Juárez (☎958/2-00-86), is the most useful, with first- and second-class buses to Acapulco, Huatulco, México and Salina Cruz. *Estrella del Valle*, Hidalgo at c/3 Ote. (☎958/2-00-50), runs to **Oaxaca** in three classes: deluxe (at 10.30pm; 6hr), first-class (2 daily; 6hr) and second-class (6 daily; 8hr). *Transportes Oaxaca Istmo*, Hidalgo at c/1 Ote, operates second-class to Salina Cruz (5 daily; 5hr), with one a day continuing to Tuxtla Gutiérrez (10hr); finally, *Cristóbal Colón*, Hidalgo at c/2 Pte., runs one overnight first-class bus to Oaxaca via Salina Cruz (11hr).

Three daily **flights** currently leave for Oaxaca: an *Aeromorelos* 40-seater at 8.30am and an *Aerovega* 6-seater at 7.30am and 10.30am. There's also one daily *Mexicana* flight to México. You can save money on taxis by engaging the services of *Transportes Aeropuerto y Turistico* (☎958/2-01-23), whose office is in town at the foot of the hill of Peréz Gasca. For more information contact *Erikson* travel agents (☎958/2-03-89) on Peréz Gasca at Andador Libertad.

better to take a *lancha* to Playa Chacahua – you could also rent one to tour the lagoon, but unless you have a special interest in tangled webs of mangroves you might as well make straight for the beach. There's a restaurant and some scruffy **rooms** (①) by the water, and more just across the lagoon: *cabañas* (②) and a huge beach, calm enough in parts but with some good surf. There's also space to camp and a row of outdoor seafood **restaurants** where you could hang a hammock.

Puerto Ángel and around

Though it's pretty well-known these days, **PUERTO ÁNGEL** still goes about its business as a small fishing port with little fuss. Everything remains resolutely small-scale, and you'll find pigs and chickens mingling with the visitors on the streets. Set around a sheltered bay ringed by mountains, it has two beaches: one right in front of town, the other opposite, beyond a rocky promontory and the mouth of a small stream. There is no bank, one *larga distancia* place, just back from the pier, near the **post office**, no police – though you may encounter a heavily armed patrol from the naval base on the beach – and very few shops. Small hotels, rooms and simple places to sling a hammock, however, are abundant, some of the most promising on the road between the main village and the second beach (Playa del Panteón).

Locals are always fishing off the huge concrete dock in Puerto Ángel – which never seems to be used for anything else – catching Yellowtail Tuna and other gamefish with a simple rod and line. Not surprisingly there's superb **seafood** everywhere.

Of the **beaches**, the Playa del Panteón, reached by road or a path around the base of the cliffs to the west, is the cleaner and quieter, with interesting snorkelling round the rocks. By the afternoon, though, it's in shade, so most people wander round to the town beach. With just a little more effort you can visit one of the far better beaches either side of Puerto Ángel. To the west is the even more primitive **Zipolite**, while to the east, about fifteen minutes' walk up the Pochutla road and then down a heavily rutted track to the right, you'll find **Estacahuite**. Here there are three tiny, sandy coves, divided by outcrops of rock. The rocks are close in, so you can't swim far, but there's wonderful snorkelling and rarely more than a couple of other people around. In a pleasantly breezy *palapa* overlooking the first of the coves, the *Club Playa Estacahuite* (fancy name, simple place) serves amazingly good food.

Practicalities

Puerto Ángel's **hotels** are a bit scattered and in general you can't phone to check availability, but the village is small enough that you should be able to find someone to mind your bags while you look around. The places listed below represent only a third of the total, but you'll find little better. **Restaurants** are all the way along the waterfront in town, where *Restaurant Las Espress* is always popular for Mexican and Italian dishes, while on the road to Playa del Panteón, *Beto's* is hard to beat. *El Tiburón Dormido*, near the naval base, serves high-quality seafood.

Accommodation

Casa de Huéspedes Capy, on the road to Playa del Panteón. Not as good as the nearby *Puesto del Sol*, it is nevertheless a bit cheaper and the rooms with private bath aren't bad. ②.

Casa de Huéspedes Gundí y Tomas, up some steps opposite the naval base in the centre. Friendly atmosphere, open-sided lounge area with views of the bay, and decent meals. The cheaper rooms leave a bit to be desired. Hammock space for a couple of dollars. ③.

Posada Cañon del Vata, inland from the far end of Playa del Panteón (☎958/7-09-02). Simple but beautifully furnished rooms – seats carved from huge logs and neat tile details – spread through a jungly hillside behind Playa del Panteón, most of them barely visible from the others and reached on winding paths. You'd think you were miles from a beach. There's a *palapa* with hammocks and a rooftop bar for guests to relax and watch the sunset, meat-free communal meals ($6) each evening, and even a place to wash clothes. Perfect for recharging batteries. ④.

Puesta del Sol, on the right as you head to Playa del Panteón. The pick of the cheaper hotels. Not much in the way of a view but clean, airy rooms, a place to wash clothes and communal space lined with photos taken by the husband of the congenial, knowledgeable owner. Breakfast. ②.

Rincón Sabroso, on the hill, up steps near the *Restaurant Las Espress*. Pleasing rough-tiled rooms with fans, *baños* and hammocks outside make this hotel a steal. ③.

Zipolite

Though some people rave about Puerto Ángel, others are ecstatic about **ZIPOLITE**, 3km along the road north, whose reputation as the ultimate in relaxed beach resorts has become legendary. The travellers' grapevine is alive with tales of the widely available hallucinogens, low living costs and liberal approach to nudity: rumours which are largely well-founded. Certainly nude bathing – predominantly at the northern end – is sanctioned by the local military, who patrol the area as light-handedly as men in big jackboots can. Keep cover handy for trips to the restaurants, though. As for **drugs**, grass, mushrooms and acid are as illegal as – though more prevalent than – anywhere else in Mexico and unscrupulous dealers are not above setting people up. Theft, too, is rife, but seems in no way to detract from the lure of a few days of complete abandonment.

The **beach** itself is magnificent, long and gently curving, pounded by heavy surf with a rip that requires some caution: drownings are depressingly common. All the way along, *palapa* huts cater for simple needs. **Seafood** and egg dishes are everywhere, rentable **hammocks** are strung from every rafter and many places offer simple **rooms**: share, if only to store your gear safely.

Practicalities

The most organized **places to stay** are at the far end of the beach, where a few rocks offer a little shade and privacy. The *Posada Shambhala* (②; aka *Casa de Gloria*) enjoys a spectacular setting on a rocky hillside. One of the main attractions here is the very good and reasonably priced vegetarian **restaurant**, with fabulous views back along the beach. It's a great place to spend a good part of the day, accompanied by impromptu outbursts of acoustic music at busier times, though alcohol isn't served and drugs are strongly discouraged. *Shambhala* looks quite fancy but isn't: *cabañas* are only marginally better than the simple rooms, and hammocks ($2) are all strung close together, but no one seems to mind. Nearby at the back of the beach is *Lo Cosmico*, smaller but otherwise very similar; and farther along there's *Rosa Blanca* with bargain hammocks, camping space at the back and good rooms (②). About halfway down the beach *Gemini's Pizza* helps vary the diet, and beyond it there's what passes for a **disco**.

For anything other than the simplest needs you'll have to catch the **buses** that run to Puerto Ángel and on to Pochutla (every 20min, until around 8pm). **Taxis** are plentiful, or you can walk in around thirty minutes.

Mazunte

Rounding the headland north of Zipolite you come to **San Agustinillo**, another fine beach backed by a few *palapa* restaurants with hammock space, followed by the tiny village of **MAZUNTE**, once notorious as the site of a turtle abattoir that at its most gruesome slaughtered 3000 head a day. In 1990 the Mexican government, bowing to international environmental pressure, effectively banned the industry overnight, removing in one fell swoop the livelihood of the village. Ironically, ecotourism has been encouraged in its place. Mazunte is certainly an attractive place, with a beautiful beach and a relaxed atmosphere very different to that in Zipolite. Already there's the **Centro Mexicano de Tortuga** (Tues–Sat 10.30am–4.30pm, Sun 10.30am–2.30pm; $3), where a guide, who may speak English, leads a thirty-minute tour of tanks full of turtles at various stages of development. You can **stay** too, either camping on the sand, in cabins rented locally or at superb *cabañas* (⑥) at the western end of the beach, which can be rented through the *Agencial Municipal* on the main road.

Getting to Mazunte from Puerto Escondido, you can save going through Pochutla and Puerto Ángel by getting dropped off at **San Antonio**, just a few houses and a restaurant, from where you can hitch or take a taxi the 5km to Mazunte. Buses from Mazunte go to Zipolite, Puerto Ángel and Pochutla (every 30–40min).

Pochutla

Anyone visiting Puerto Ángel and the beaches either way along the coast comes through **POCHUTLA**, a dull place 2km north of Hwy-200, some 12km from Puerto Ángel. Apart from catching a bus to the coast there's little reason to come here, though long stayers will need to return to change money – there are no banks at the beaches – and perhaps to visit the market for provisions.

The **bus stations** – the new second-class *Estrella del Valle* and the first-class *Garcela* and *Cristóbal Colón* – are close to each other on Cárdenas, which runs from Hwy-200 into the centre of town. Farther along Cárdenas the *Bancomer* will **change money** (9–11am) at a half-decent rate. Of the **hotels**, *Hotel Pochutla*, Madero 102 (☎958/4-00-33; ③), on the central plaza, is comfortable and spacious, while *Hotel Santa Cruz*, Lázaro Cárdenas 88 (☎958/4-01-16; ②), near the bus stations, is much poorer with noisy front rooms.

Buses frequently head down to Puerto Ángel, along with *colectivo* or *especial* taxis; *especial* costs well over five times as much, so go *colectivo*: you should rarely have to wait long for fellow passengers. In Puerto Ángel, the taxis drop off at the rank by the dock. If you want to go farther, over to Playa del Panteón for example, make this clear as you set out or you'll be charged an outrageous amount for the last part of the journey (you probably will be anyway, but at least you'll be prepared).

Huatulco and around

Heading **east from Puerto Ángel towards Salina Cruz**, there's 170km of coast that until recently was quite untouched. It's a slow, hot drive – but an enjoyable one – along a jungly coastal strip regularly cut by small rivers and giving frequent tantalizing glimpses of fabulous-looking beaches. All of these are extremely tough to get to, however, and few are as idyllic as they appear: quite apart from the total lack of facilities, they're marred by strong winds, tricky currents, and, as you approach Salina Cruz, increasing oil pollution.

At **Huatulco**, some 35km from Puerto Ángel, where previously you'd have found only a couple of fly-blown villages and nine stunning sandy bays, the latest of Mexico's purpose-built resorts is well underway. By the late 1980s there was an airport, four large hotels including a *Club Med* and a *Sheraton*, and an expectation of rapid expansion. More recently, however, progress has slowed: probably a blessing as it gives FONATUR – the government tourist development agency whose baby Huatulco is – a chance to carry out its professed intention to preserve **ecological zones** among the hotels and to ensure the infrastructure (especially sewage treatment plants) is working in time. For the moment, only two of the nine bays have been developed, though new roads mean that there is now access to eight of them. The long-term effects of this remain to be seen, but this is a large area and it may be years before the outlying bays are spoilt. Until then they're not far from the paradise that the brochures describe, though the lack of budget accommodation remains a problem.

Huatulco is the all-encompassing name of the resort, with **SANTA CRUZ HUATULCO**, the village on the coast, as its focus. It's been cleaned up in expectation of becoming an "authentic Mexican village", something it patently fails to be, comprising a marina, handicraft stalls, a few relatively inexpensive seafood restaurants and a handful of condos. There's no reason to stay here – and nowhere reasonably priced to do so – but at the *embarcadero* you can organize horseback rides to **Maguey Beach**, fishing and diving trips, or catch boats which (on demand) ply the coast to the more remote bays. All of these have at least some sort of *enramada* and **SAN AGUSTÍN**, one of the most developed, is lined with seafood restaurants.

Access to the beach at **TANGOLUNDA**, 5km northeast over the headland, is almost completely cut off by the aforementioned international hotels and the swanky homes of the likes of Julio Iglesias and ex-Mexican president Salinas. The only public access is by the road leading to *Club Med* and, of course, you can sneak into the *Sheraton* for a swim in the pool, but there's little else to do and the restaurants are grossly overpriced.

Crucecita

The purpose-built town of **CRUCECITA** (also, confusingly, known as **Santa Cruz**, especially by the bus companies), 2km inland from Santa Cruz Huatulco, serves both bays. Though designed to house the 10,000 Mexicans needed to support the bayside hotels, it is now becoming a tourist centre in its own right, probably helped along by the slow progress elsewhere. Certainly it boasts a zócalo, shops and various businesses, along with pizza joints, costly stores and an outpost of the *Carlos 'n' Charlie's* fun bar chain, a sure sign of resort status. Nevertheless, in its dozen years of existence, it has matured well to become a thriving and enjoyable place.

Finding a budget **place to stay** in Crucecita, while easier than around the bays, is still a problem, though outside the high season (Dec, *Semana Santa*, July & Aug) prices drop by around 30 percent. The cheapest **hotel** is the basic *Hospedaje Gloriluz* (☎958/7-01-60; ④) on Pochote, near the entrance to town between Gardenia and Bugambilia, which run parallel down to the zócalo. Much better is *Grifer* (☎958/7-00-48; ⑤), at the corner of Guamachil and Carrazil, near the start of the road to Santa Cruz Huatulco, which has comfortable, attractive rooms with balconies but no a/c.

The bulk of the **restaurants** surround the zócalo, among them *Oasis*, on the corner of Bugambilia and Flamboyan, which serves up reasonably priced *tortas* as well as excellent sushi. For something simpler and cheaper, try *El Típico*, on the corner of Bugambilia and Macuil. All these places, and everywhere else in Crucecita, lie within easy walking distance of the bus stations that line Gardenia. The **post office** is a bit farther out on the road to Santa Cruz Huatulco, where you'll also find a number of **banks** (with ATMs).

On to the Isthmus

The **Isthmus of Tehuantepec**, where the Pacific and the Atlantic are just 210km apart and the land never rises to more than 250m above sea level, is the narrowest point of Mexico. For years – until Panama got there first – there were plans to cut a canal through here: as it is, the coast-to-coast railway (still a link in the line to Guatemala) was, in the late nineteenth century, an extremely busy trade route, the chief communication link between the American continent's east and west coasts. It's a hot and steamy region, long run-down and not in any way improved by the trappings of the

1980s oil boom, and one where the only good reason to stop is if there's a **fiesta** going on – they're among the most colourful in the country. Otherwise you can go straight through – from Oaxaca to **Tuxtla Gutiérrez** and from there on to **San Cristóbal** – in a single, very long, day. Only if you plan to head straight for the Yucatán is there any particular reason to cross the Isthmus: it's considerably quicker to stick to the lowlands, though a lot duller than the route through highland Chiapas.

Historically the **Indians** of this region, especially in the south, have always had a matriarchal society. But though you'll still find women dominating trade in the markets, this is a tradition that is dying faster than most others in macho Mexico. Nevertheless, at least some elements remain: the women are spectacularly colourfully dressed, and draped with gold jewellery; it's still the mother who gives away her child at a wedding (and occasionally still the eldest daughter who inherits any land); and on feast days the women prove their dominance by climbing to the rooftops and throwing fruit down on the men in the *Tirada de Frutas*.

Salina Cruz

SALINA CRUZ, 130km east of Huatulco on the coast, was the Pacific terminus of the trans-Isthmus railway and the port through which everything was shipped. Nowadays, again exporting oil in large quantities, it's a sprawling, unattractive place, with a reputation for crime and brawling violence. **Buses** all arrive and leave from terminals close to each other 2km from the centre on the northern outskirts, so changing from trans-Isthmus to coastal buses should present no problem, nor any need to head downtown.

If you do get stuck here for the night, head for the plaza and c/5 de Mayo, leading off it, where you'll find the *Hotel Fuentes* (☎971/4-02-93; ③) at Camacho 114, the basic but comfortable *Hotel Magda* (☎971/4-01-07; ③), two doors away, and, best of all, the *Posada del Jardin*, Camacho 108 (☎971/4-01-62; ③).

LA VENTOSA, the nearby beach village, reached by bus from the side of the plaza, may once have been picturesque, but it's now spoilt by the oil refinery backdrop. As windy as its name implies, and polluted too, it's a run-down place, where most of the seafront restaurants seem in danger of dissolving into the sea. The best **hotel**, conveniently the first one you reach, is the *Posada Rustrian* (③), which has a courtyard and a garden.

Tehuantepec

The modest town of **TEHUANTEPEC**, 14km north of Salina Cruz, preserves the local traditions of the Isthmus most visibly, has some of the best of the fiestas, and is also an extremely pleasant place to stop, with a fine zócalo and several inexpensive hotels around it. In the evening, the zócalo really comes alive, with people strolling and eating food from the many stalls set up by the townswomen, who proudly wear the traditional flower-embroidered *huipil* and floor-length velvet skirt of the Zapotec – a costume adopted by the artist Frida Kahlo in some of her self-portraits. Tehuantepec is a tiny place where a walk of ten blocks in any direction will take you out into the countryside. Despite this – or perhaps because it's so concentrated – the town is extraordinarily noisy, the constant din of passing buses made worse by the motor tricycles (*motos*) that locals use as taxis. There's really no reason to stay long, and the number of second-class buses makes it extremely easy to leave, but if you do stop awhile pop into the **Casa de Cultura** (Mon–Fri 4–9pm, Sat 9am–2pm; free), where dance, music and art workshops are held in the remains of the Dominican ex-Convento Rey Cosijoní, started in 1544 at the behest of Cortés and named after the incumbent Zapotec king. You can wander around and take a look at the few remaining frescoes by taking Hidalgo from the north side of the zócalo and following it right as it becomes Guererro.

The ruins of Guiengola

The hill-top fortress of **GUIENGOLA**, 15km north of Tehuantepec, was the Zapotec stronghold on the Isthmus, and in 1496 its defenders successfully fought off an attempt by the Aztecs to gain control of the area, which was never fully incorporated into their empire. It continued to be a centre of resistance during the early years of the Conquest and was a focus of Indian revolt against Spanish rule throughout the sixteenth and seventeenth centuries.

At the site you'll see remains of pyramids and a ball-court, but the most striking feature is the massive **defensive wall**. By definition, Guiengola's superb defensive location makes it somewhat inaccessible and it's probably best to take a taxi, though buses to Oaxaca do pass the turn-off to the site, 8km from Tehuantepec on the main road (look out for the "Ruinas Guiengola" sign). From here it's a hot, 7km uphill walk. The site is open daily and if the caretaker is around you may be asked to pay a small fee, though you'll almost certainly have the place to yourself.

Tehuantepec practicalities

Buses stop at several stations near each other at the northern edge of town on Hwy-190, a twenty-minute walk or a short *moto* ride from the centre. Some local services also pause at the end of 5 de Mayo, 100m west of the zócalo. There's a **post office** and **bank** on the north side of the square; on 5 de Mayo itself you'll find a *Bancomer* with good rates and an ATM, and a **caseta de larga distancia** (7am–10pm). **Hotels** aren't far away: *Donaji* (☎971/5-00-64; ③–⑤) at Juárez 10, a block south of the zócalo, is marginally the best, overlooking the Parque Juárez and with a rooftop view over the town. The simple *Casa de Huéspedes Istmo*, Hidalgo 31 (☎971/5-00-19; ②), is better value for money.

Calle Juana, south from the zócalo, has two of the best **places to eat**: *El Portón* serves extremely cheap sandwiches and regional *antojitos*; *Café Colonial*, at no. 66, stays open later (until 10pm) and dishes up good local food, including chicken prepared in almost every way imaginable. On the zócalo itself, *Jugos Hawaii* is good for *tortas* and *licuados*, and be sure to try some of the corn bread that local women hawk insistently to everyone arriving on the bus.

While Tehuantepec is a major stopping point en route to Oaxaca or the Chiapas coast, few buses originate here, so **moving on**, you may find it easier to take one of the constant stream of buses to **Juchitán**, 26km away (see below), and continue from there. The main long-distance routes, operated by first-class *Cristóbal Colón* and *Autobuses Unidos*, serve Oaxaca, México, Tuxtla Gutiérrez, Coatzacoalcos and Villahermosa, and there are also buses to San Cristóbal and Puerto Escondido; you can buy tickets in advance. Several second-class companies also operate between the main towns on the Isthmus, and there are constant departures for Salina Cruz.

Juchitán

JUCHITÁN, just 26km east of Tehuantepec and the point where the road meets the railway to Guatemala, is not much more attractive than Salina Cruz. It does, however, enjoy Indian traditions and fiestas similar to those of Tehuantepec, a good market and a rather sleazy tropical port atmosphere. The town is best known in modern Mexico, however, for having somehow managed to elect a reforming socialist government in the early 1980s. The PRI didn't take kindly to their activities, and eventually the state governor found a pretext to remove local officials from power and replace them with party faithfuls. The political trouble – and violence – that followed has largely blown over, but local events still occasionally make the front pages, and Juchitán's fiestas have a tendency to become political demonstrations.

The **bus** stations line the highway and you won't have long to wait, whichever direction you're heading. If you do need to stay the night, Tehuantepec is a much better base. The fanciest **place to stay** is the overpriced *Hotel La Mansión* (☎971/1-20-55; ⑤), Prolongacion 16 de Septiembre 11, a couple of blocks towards town from where most of the buses stop. Better to press on 2km along 16 de Septiembre, past several poor-value hotels, to the adequate *Casa de Huéspedes Echazarreta* (no phone; ②) on the **zócalo**. Here you'll also find the **post office**, a **Banamex** and some good **places to eat**, notably the *Casa Grande*, which serves reasonably priced seafood in an elegant cool atrium.

fiestas

January

1st NEW YEAR'S DAY is celebrated everywhere, but is particularly good in **Oaxaca** (Oaxaca) and **Mitla** (Oax.).

14th Fiesta in **Niltepec** (Oax.), on the Pacific coast road.

20th DÍA DE SAN SEBASTIAN Big in **Tehuantepec** (Oax.), **Jalapa de Díaz** (Oax.), near Tuxtepec, and in **Pinotepa de Don Luis** (Oax.), near the coast and Pinotepa Nacional.

February

2nd DÍA DE LA CANDELARIA. Colourful Indian celebrations in **Santa María del Tule** (Oax.) and in **San Mateo del Mar** (Oax.), near Salina Cruz.

22nd–25th *Feria* in **Matias Romero** (Oax.), between Juchitán and Coatzacoalcos.

CARNIVAL (the week before Lent – variable Feb–March) is at its most frenzied in the big cities – especially **Oaxaca** (Oax.) – but is also celebrated in hundreds of villages throughout the area.

21st **Gueletao** (Oax.), near Oaxaca, celebrates the birthday of Benito Juárez, born in the village.

25th Fiesta in **Acatlán** (Puebla), with many traditional dances.

March

HOLY WEEK is widely observed – particularly big ceremonies in **Pinotepa Nacional** (Oax.) and nearby **Pinotepa Don Luis** (Oax.), as well as in **Jamiltepec** (Oax.).

May

3rd DÍA DE LA SANTA CRUZ celebrated in **Salina Cruz** (Oax.), the start of a week-long *feria*.

8th DÍA DE SAN MIGUEL. In **Soyaltepec** (Oax.), between Oaxaca and Huajuapan de León, festivi-

ties include horse and dog races, as well as boating events on a nearby lake.

15th DÍA DE SAN ISIDRO sees peasant celebrations everywhere – famous and picturesque fiestas in **Juchitán** (Oax.)

19th *Feria* in **Huajuapan de León** (Oax.).

CORPUS CHRISTI (variable – the Thursday after Trinity) sees a particularly good *feria* in **Izúcar de Matamoros** (Pue.).

June

24th DÍA DE SAN JUAN falls in the midst of festivities (22nd–26th) in **Tehuantepec** (Oax.).

July

On the first Wednesday of July, **Teotitlán del Valle** (Oax.), near Oaxaca, holds a fiesta with traditional dances and religious processions.

23rd *Feria* in **Huajuapan de León** (Oax.).

25th DÍA DE SANTIAGO provokes widespread celebration – especially in **Izúcar de Matamoros** (Pue.), **Niltepec** (Oax.) and **Juxtlahuaca** (Oax.).

In **Oaxaca** itself, the last two Mondays of July see the famous festival of GUELAGUETZA (or the *Lunes del Cerro*), a mixture of traditional dancing and Catholic rites on the Cerro del Fortín. Highly popular; tickets for the good seats are sold at the tourist office.

August

13th–16th Spectacular festivities in **Juchitán** (Oax.) and lesser fiestas in **Nochixtlán** (Oax.), between Oaxaca and Huajuapan de León, and on the 15th in **Tehuantepec** (Oax.).

24th Fiesta in **San Bartolo Coyotepec** (Oax.), near Oaxaca.

31st Blessing of the animals in **Oaxaca** – locals bring their beasts to the church of La Merced to be blessed.

September

3rd–5th **Juchitán** (Oax.) once again hosts a series of picturesque celebrations.

8th Religious ceremonies in **Teotitlán del Valle** (Oax.), in **Putla** (Oax.), on the road inland from Pinotepa Nacional, and in **Tehuantepec** (Oax.).

25th FIESTA DE SAN JERONIMO in **Ixtepec** (Oax.) lasts until October 2nd.

29th DÍA DE SAN MIGUEL is celebrated in **Soyaltepec** (Oax.).

October

1st Several *barrios* of **Tehuantepec** (Oax.) have their own small fiestas.

On the first Sunday in October, the DÍA DE LA VIRGEN DEL ROSARIO is celebrated in **San Pedro Amuzgos** (Oax.). On the second Sunday there's a large· *feria* in **Tlacolula** (Oax.), near Oaxaca, and on the second Monday the FERIA DEL ARBOL based around the famous tree in **Santa María del Tule** (Oax.).

18th Indian fiesta in **Ojitlán** (Oax.), near Tuxtepec, with a formal, candlelit procession.

24th In **Acatlán** (Pue.), a fiesta with processions and traditional dances.

November

2nd DAY OF THE DEAD is respected everywhere, with particularly strong traditions in **Salina Cruz** (Oax.) and in **San Gabriel Chilac** (Pue.), near Tehuacán.

25th Patron Saint's day in **Mechoacán** (Oax.), on the coast near Pinotepa Nacional.

29th DÍA DE SAN ANDRES celebrated in **San Juan Colorado** (Oax.), on the coast road near Pinotepa Nacional.

December

8th DÍA DE LA INMACULADA CONCEPCIÓN is widely observed – especially with traditional Indian dances in **Juquilla** (Oax.), not far from Puerto Escondido, and **Zacatepec** (Oax.), on the road inland from Pinotepa Nacional.

16th–25th The pre-Christmas period is a particularly exciting one in **Oaxaca**, with *posadas* and nativity plays nightly. The 18th is the FIESTA DE LA VIRGEN DE LA SOLEDAD, patroness of the state, with fireworks, processions and music. The 23rd is the FIESTA DE LOS RABANOS (Radishes), when there's an exhibition of statues and scenes sculpted from radishes. On Christmas Eve there's more music, fireworks and processions before midnight mass. Throughout it all, **buñuelos** – crisp pancakes that you eat before smashing the plate on which they are served – are dished up at street stalls.

travel details

Buses

The following frequencies and times are for first-class services. Scores of second-class buses usually cover the same routes, taking 10–20 percent longer.

Huatulco to: Acapulco (10 daily; 10–11hr); Pochutla (hourly; 1hr); Salina Cruz (7 daily; 2hr 30min).

Oaxaca to: México (at least hourly; 9hr); Pochutla (4 daily; 8hr); Puebla (8 daily; 7hr); Puerto Escondido (3 daily; 10hr); San Cristóbal (2 daily; 12hr); Tehuacán (15 daily; 6hr); Tehuantepec (hourly; 4–5hr); Villahermosa (2 daily; 12hr.

Pochutla to: Acapulco (hourly; 8hr); Huatulco (hourly; 1hr); Oaxaca (4 daily; 8hr); Puerto Escondido (hourly; 1hr); Salina Cruz (hourly; 4hr); San Cristóbal (2 daily; over 12hr).

Puerto Ángel to: Pochutla (every 20min; 20min); Zipolite (every 20min; 10min).

Puerto Escondido to: Acapulco (at least hourly; 7–8hr); Huatulco (hourly; 2hr); México (2 daily; 12hr); Oaxaca (3 daily; 10hr); Pochutla (hourly; 1hr); Salina Cruz (7 daily; 5–6hr); Tehuantepec (1 daily; 5–6hr).

Salina Cruz to: Acapulco (7 daily; 11hr); Huatulco (7 daily; 2hr 30min); Oaxaca (4 daily; 5hr); Pochutla (hourly; 4hr); Puerto Escondido (7 daily; 5–6hr); Tehuantepec (every 30min; 20min).

Tehuacán to: Córdoba (every 30min; 3hr); México (hourly; 4hr); Oaxaca (15 daily; 6hr); Veracruz (every 30min; 4hr).

Tehuantepec to: Coatzacoalcos (10 daily; 6hr); México (7 daily; 12hr); Oaxaca (hourly; 4–5hr); Puerto Escondido (1 daily; 5–6hr); Salina Cruz (every 30min; 20min); San Cristóbal (2 daily; 8hr); Tuxtla Gutiérrez (7 daily; 5hr); Veracruz (3 daily; 9hr).

Trains

One train, with first- and second-class carriages, runs daily in each direction between México and Oaxaca; another, second-class only, runs between Puebla and Oaxaca.

Planes

Oaxaca to: Cancún (9 weekly); Huatulco (1 daily); Mérida (9 weekly); México (10 daily); Puerto Escondido (3 daily); Tuxtla Gutiérrez (9 weekly); Villahermosa (9 weekly).

Puerto Escondido to: México (1 daily); Oaxaca (3 daily).

CHIAPAS AND TABASCO

E ndowed with a stunning variety of cultures, landscapes and wildlife, **Chiapas**, Mexico's southernmost state, has much to tempt visitors. Deserted Pacific beaches, rugged mountains, ruined cities buried in steamy jungle and powerful tropical rivers offer a bewildering choice, added to which the observation of **indigenous traditions** continues – albeit with a struggle – almost everywhere.

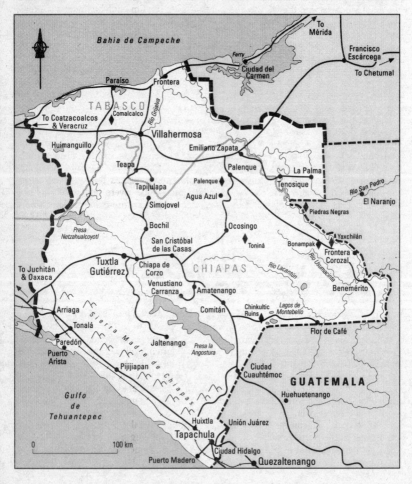

Chiapas was actually administered by the Spanish as part of Guatemala until the early nineteenth century, when it seceded to join newly independent Mexico, and today it is second only to Oaxaca in the proportion of Indians in its population: 750,000 out of a total of three and a half million. The villages around **San Cristóbal de las Casas**, in the geographic centre of the state, are the stronghold of Indian culture. A visit here is an entry to another age and, though tolerated, your presence is barely acknowledged. There is, of course, a darker side to this: picturesque as their life may seem to tourists, the indigenous population has long been bypassed or ignored by the political system, their land and their livelihood under constant threat from modernization, or straightforward seizure.

Long before open revolt broke out on New Year's Day 1994 (see below), a revived **Zapatista** peasant movement had carried out attacks on army patrols, and despite official denials of armed insurrection the army had raided training camps in search of "subversives": news of such happenings was successfully suppressed, however, until the situation burst into the world's consciousness. At the time this book went to press, tourists were continuing to visit Chiapas in safety, but the situation remains sensitive, and it is crucial that you get as much information as you can beforehand and check locally and with other travellers. Although there is a heavy army presence around the area from San Cristóbal to Palenque and from San Cristóbal to the Lagos de Montebello, in general the area controlled by the Zapatistas is well outside of the usual tourist routes, and their tactics involve no urban guerrilla campaigns.

Tabasco is less obviously attractive than its neighbour – steamy and low-lying for the most part, with a major oil industry to mar the landscape. Recently, however, the state has been seeking to encourage tourism, above all pushing the legacy of the **Olmecs**, Mexico's earliest developed civilization. The vibrant, modern capital, **Villahermosa**, has a wealth of parks and museums, the best-known of which, the **Parque La Venta**, displays the original massive Olmec heads. In the extreme southwest, bordered by Veracruz or Chiapas, a section of Tabasco reaches into the mountains up to 1000m high. Here, in a region almost never visited by outsiders, a low-impact tourism initiative allows you to splash in pristine rivers and waterfalls and explore the astonishing ruins of **Malpasito**, a city of the **Zoque** culture, about whom little is known. Tabasco is also the starting point for river trips into **Guatemala**.

CHIAPAS

Despite the rebellion of 1994, tourists continue to come to Chiapas, though in slightly smaller numbers than before; some, indeed, come specifically to witness the unfolding events. Before visiting, however, you should get **up-to-date advice**: though travel was apparently safe at the time of writing, in a volatile situation such as this things can change quickly.

The terrain of Chiapas ranges from the Pacific coastal plain, backed by the peaks of the Sierra Madre de Chiapas, through the mainly agricultural Central Depression, irrigated by the Río Grijalva, rising again to the highlands, **Los Altos de Chiapas**. Beyond the highlands the land falls away again: in the north to the Gulf coast plain of Tabasco, while to the east a series of great rivers, separated by the jungle-covered ridges of the **Lacandón rainforest**, flow into the Río Usumacinta, which forms the border with Guatemala.

The **climate**, too, can vary enormously. In one theoretical day you could be basking on the beach at Puerto Arista in the morning, and spending the night by a fireside in the old colonial capital of San Cristóbal de las Casas. Generally the lowlands can be almost unbearably hot and humid, with heavy afternoon rainfall in summer, making a

THE ZAPATISTA REBELLION

On **January 1, 1994**, the day the NAFTA treaty came into effect, several thousand lightly armed rebels, wearing their uniform of green or black army-style tunics and black balaclavas, occupied San Cristóbal de las Casas, the former state capital and Chiapas' major tourist destination. From the balcony of the Municipal Palace, **Subcomandante Marcos**, the Zapatistas' enigmatic leader, or at least main spokesperson, read *La Declaración de la Selva Lacandóna*, declaring war on the "seventy-year-old dictatorship . . . of traitors", and demanding the resignation of the Mexican president and the state governor, and an overhaul of the country's archaic political structure. Simultaneously, in a series of bold, carefully executed strikes, the rebels occupied the towns of San Cristóbal , Las Margaritas, Ocosingo and Altamirano, making the same demands.

After a thirty-hour occupation, during which they destroyed government equipment and municipal records, the EZLN withdrew from San Cristóbal on January 2. The next day, the army began its furious counterattack with ground troops and aircraft. Dozens of civilians and Zapatistas were killed as the army retook **Ocosingo**; a series of isolated attacks by groups claiming to support the rebellion led the army to believe there was a serious possibility of a nationwide revolution, and for several days journalists were kept away from the conflict zone.

Meanwhile, erudite, witty and penetrating communiqués signed by Marcos, sent from a secret destination in the Lacandón rainforest and published in the Mexican and international press, became a major feature of the battle to keep the struggle in the world spotlight. The war was waged by the Zapatistas with the pen and the **Internet** – and they were winning. Reports of widespread human rights abuses committed by the army – including summary execution of suspected rebels and terrorizing civilians – caused an international outcry, and on January 8, President Carlos Salinas proposed a **ceasefire**, which took effect five days later. In the meantime, dozens of *campesino* and indigenous organizations in Chiapas formed a representative body (**CEOIC**), calling for an end to human rights abuses and the start of peace negotiations.

Manual Camacho Solís, Mexico's foreign minister, was appointed the government negotiator, while **Bishop Samuel Ruiz** of San Cristóbal agreed to mediate for the CEOIC. When negotiation began on February 22, the EZLN president presented a list of

dip in the sea or river (or pool) a daily necessity. Days in the highlands can also be hot, and you'll need to carry water if you're hiking, but by evening you may need a sweater.

For its size Chiapas is said to have the greatest **biological diversity** in North America. A visit to the **zoo** in the state capital of **Tuxtla Gutiérrez**, which houses only animals native to the state, will whet your appetite for the region's natural wonders. In the huge **Montes Azules Biosphere Reserve**, reached from Palenque, a section of the last remaining rainforest in North America has been preserved. This is also the home of the **Lacandón Maya**, who retreated into the forest when the Spanish arrived, and shunned contact until fifteen years ago. There's **cloud forest** in the south, protected in the **El Triunfo Biosphere Reserve** and, far easier to visit, the beautiful lakes and hills of the **Lagos de Montebello National Park**.

The Classic period Maya site of **Palenque**, on the northern edge of the highlands, is one of Mexico's finest ancient sites and has been the focus of much recent restoration work. The limestone hills in this area are pierced by crystal-clear rivers, creating exquisite waterfalls – most spectacularly at **Agua Azul**. Palenque is also the best starting point for a trip down the **Usumacinta valley**, to visit the remote ruins of **Bonampak** and **Yaxchilán**. The Frontier Highway pushes on south beyond these sites to the growing town of Benemérito, where you can get a boat to **Guatemala**, or head on around the border on an arduous circuit to the Lagos de Montebello and back to San Cristóbal.

34 demands, including their recognition (under the Geneva Convention) as a belligerent force, the resignation of President Salinas and the withdrawal of the army from Chiapas. At first talks appeared to go well, but on March 23, the **assassination of Luis Donaldo Colosio**, the PRI presidential candidate – effectively the next Mexican president – sparked conspiracy theories and halted the peace process. The EZLN withdrew, believing the army was preparing an attack, but continued to consult with communities in the area, and in June announced a rejection of the proposals. Soon after, both Camacho Solís and Bishop Ruiz resigned.

Mexico's **general election** on August 21 passed relatively quietly, though when the results were announced the main left-wing opposition party, the **PRD**, accused the PRI of fraud and organized a series of demonstrations and marches in Chiapas. When the PRI candidate took office, the opposition candidate – who claimed to have survived an assassination attempt – assumed the role of parallel governor, establishing with the support of the Zapatistas a **"Rebel Government in Transition"**. On September 28, the assassination of Ruiz Massieu, General Secretary of the PRI, heightened tension, and the situation fell into stalemate as the army waited at the ends of the roads leading to Zapatista-controlled areas.

Within days of the new president, Ernesto Zedillo, taking office in **December 1994**, the Zapatistas made their first major foray through the army cordon, briefly occupying several towns. Despite the provocation, Zedillo's response was restrained, and no major offensive was ordered, though reports of rebels on the move sent panic through Mexico's financial markets, leading to a massive **devaluation of the nuevo peso**.

At the time of writing the Zapatistas still control much of the land they took at the beginning of the conflict and count on the support of much of the population. In México demonstrations are held in support of Marcos and souvenirs are sold emblazoned with his masked features. No end to the conflict was in sight, though **talks** resumed in May 1995 amid an agreed ceasefire. Little progress was being made, however, and, though the de facto peace may hold, it was hard to see how the entrenched positions of the two sides could be reconciled. If you have access to the Internet, the latest news is available on the **EZLN home page**, and (in Spanish only) from the pages of *La Jornada*, a Mexican newspaper.

Travelling around Chiapas is not difficult: the main cities are connected by a network of good, all-weather roads and the **Pan-American Highway** passes through some of the most spectacular scenery in the state. In the south the coastal highway offers a speedy route from **Arriaga**, near the Oaxaca border, right through to **Tapachula**, almost on the frontier with Guatemala. In the out of the way places, particularly in the jungle, travel is by dirt roads, which, though generally well maintained, can cause problems in the rainy season.

The Chiapas coast

Hwy-200, much of it recently upgraded, provides a fast route from the Oaxaca border to Tapachula: if you plan on getting **to Guatemala** as quickly as possible, this is the road to take. It traverses the steamy coastal plain of the **Soconusco**, running about 20km inland, with the 2400m peaks of the **Sierra Madre de Chiapas** always in view. These little-visited mountains, protected by National and Biosphere Reserve status, are penetrated by roads only at their eastern and western extremities. The plain itself is a fertile agricultural area, mainly given over to coffee and bananas, though there are also many *ranchos*, where cattle grow fat on the lush grass; the excellent local **cheese** is celebrated in the *Esposicion de Quesos*, held in Pijijiapan the week before Christmas.

ACCOMMODATION PRICES

All the accommodation listed in this book has been categorized into one of nine price bands, as set out below. The prices quoted are in US dollars and normally refer to the cheapest available room for two people sharing in high season. For more details, see p.37.

① less than $8   ④ $18–25   ⑦ $50–75
② $8–12   ⑤ $25–35   ⑧ $75–100
③ $12–18   ⑥ $35–50   ⑨ more than $100

Arriaga

ARRIAGA, the first town on the Chiapas coast road, is a dusty, uninteresting place, but its location at the junction of Hwy-195 (the road over the mountains to Tuxtla Gutiérrez) means you may have to change buses here. The new **Central de Autobuses** is on the main road, south of the train tracks, about a kilometre from the zócalo. Unusually for a Mexican bus station, there isn't a huge sign advertising its presence; if you're coming from the town centre, follow c/1a Sur for three blocks, turn left and after three blocks look for a large yellow building with dark windows on your right. At least half a dozen companies operate from here: the main first-class company is *Cristóbal Colón*, serving México, Oaxaca, Tuxtla, Villahermosa and Tapachula, with a daily bus to San Cristóbal de las Casas. The main second-class companies are *Sur*, *Autotransportes Tuxtla Gutiérrez* and *Transportes Oaxaca-Istmo*, which serve the same destinations more frequently. Microbuses for Tonalá leave constantly from just south of the zócalo, passing (though not stopping at) the bus station en route.

Hotels in Arriaga aren't recommended; if you get stuck, try *Hotel Iris* (③), signposted from the bus station, or the *Colonial* (②), across the train tracks from the bus station.

Tonalá

Larger and marginally more inviting than Arriaga, **TONALÁ** is just a thirty-minute microbus ride away down Hwy-200 which, as Av. Hidalgo, forms the town's main street. All the bus companies terminate along Hidalgo: *Cristóbal Colón* and *Autotransportes Tuxtla* pull in about 1km west of the zócalo; *Sur* and others to the east.

Everything you need in Tonalá is either on the **zócalo** – Parque Esperanza – or within a couple of blocks. The central feature of the park is the **Estela de Tlaloc**, a large standing stone carved by the Olmecs, depicting the rain god Tlaloc. Several good **restaurants** ring the zócalo: the *Fiesta Jardín*, next to the *New York* disco is farthest from the traffic. If you're stuck for something to do, you could always visit the **Museo Arqueologico**, on Hidalgo across from *Cristóbal Colón*, though the Olmec and Maya exhibits here appear to have been abandoned. The museum has few visitors, so anyone there may be surprised to see you. Next door is the *Centro de Producción Artesanal*, where artists and students make ceramics using both traditional and modern methods.

Practicalities

The **tourist office**, on the ground floor of the Palacio Municipal (Mon–Fri 9am–3pm & 6–8pm, Sat 9am–2pm), isn't an essential stop, though it does have information about local beaches. The constant traffic noise makes staying in Tonalá rather uncomfortable. The *Tomás* (no phone; ②), on Hidalgo east of the centre, is worth trying, as is the *Tonalá* (☎966/3-04-80; ③), Hidalgo 172, in the opposite direction about halfway between *Cristóbal Colón* and the zócalo, which has some a/c rooms – ask for one away from the street. The *Faro* (☎966/3-00-33; ②), at the corner of 16 de Septiembre and

Matamoros, has a reasonable restaurant. Slightly more upmarket, though still a little shabby, is the *Galilea* (☎966/3-02-39; ④), on the zócalo, or try the *Hotel Grajandra* (☎966/3-01-44; ③), next to the *Cristóbal Colón* stop at Hidalgo 204.

Leaving Tonalá, most buses are *de paso* and you may have to wait until the bus arrives to see if there's a seat; alternatively, you could catch a microbus to Arriaga and buy your ticket there. *Combis* to **Puerto Arista** leave hourly from the corner of 5 de Mayo and Matamoros, in the **market** area, where the streets are crammed with fruit and vegetable stalls. *Transportes Rudolfo Figueroa* also operates buses to Puerto Arista and, less frequently, to Boca del Ciego, 15km farther down the coast.

Puerto Arista

Although this quiet village may not be everyone's idea of a perfect beach resort, **PUERTO ARISTA**, with its miles of clean sand and invigorating surf, does offer a chance to escape the unrelenting heat of the inland towns. There's certainly nothing to see, and you have to stay under the shade of a *palapa* near the shore to benefit from the breezes, but it's a worthwhile stop if you've been doing some hard travelling. While the waves are definitely refreshing, you need to be aware of the potentially dangerous **rip tides** that sweep along the coast – never get out of your depth.

The road from Tonalá joins Puerto Arista's only street at the lighthouse. Here you're in the centre of town: walk a kilometre left or right and you'll be on a deserted shoreline; ahead lies the beach, with hotels and restaurants packed closely together. You won't feel crowded though, unless you arrive in *Semana Santa*, as there seem to be at least as many buildings abandoned or boarded up as there are occupied.

Practicalities

There are many **hotels** in Puerto Arista but few customers: prices are difficult to determine since most places will try to overcharge outrageously. The best bet is to have a *refresco* or a cold beer at a restaurant and ask if you can leave your bags while you have a good look around. The cheaper places are basic and not particularly good value; bargain with the owner and you may be able to knock the price down. The more established hotels, such as *La Puesta del Sol* (④), the nearby *Brisas del Mar* (④) and the *Agua Marina* (turn right at the lighthouse; ④), are all clean and well run, but best of all is *Arista Bugambilias* (☎966/3-07-67; ⑤), with a pool and private garden on the beach.

There are a couple of dozen beachfront *palapa* **restaurants**, serving basic seafood, but only five or six ever open at any one time. Most will rent you a hammock or let you sling your own for a couple of dollars. And you can always **camp** on the beach for free.

Tonalá to Tapachula

With your own vehicle you can explore some of the side roads leading from Hwy-200 in the 220km between Tonalá and Tapachula: either up into the mountains, where the heavy rain gives rise to dozens of rivers and waterfalls, or down to almost deserted beaches. Most coastal villages are actually on the landward side of a narrow lagoon, separated from the ocean by a sandbar. These sandbars block many rivers' access to the sea, causing marshes to form and providing a superb wetland habitat, the highlight of which is an **ecological reserve** protecting 45km of coastline near **Acacoyagua**.

Travelling **by bus**, it's much more difficult (though still possible) to take in destinations off the main road, and you need to be prepared to hitch and camp. At **HUIXTLA**, 42km before Tapachula, Hwy-211 snakes over the mountains via Motozintla to join the Pan-American Highway near Ciudad Cuauhtémoc and the Guatemalan border at La Mesilla. This boneshaking road offers stupendous mountain views and is covered by buses running between Tapachula and Comitán and San Cristóbal de las Casas.

Tapachula

Though most travellers see it as no more than an overnight stop en route to or from Guatemala, **TAPACHULA** does actually have something to offer, being a gateway to both the coast and the mountains, with a lovely setting at the foot of the 4000m Volcán Tacaná. A busy commercial centre, known as the capital of the Soconusco, it grew in importance with the increasing demand for coffee and bananas in the nineteenth century. Being a border city, it has a lively cultural mix, including not just immigrants from Central America, but also small German and Chinese communities. The **Museo Regional de Soconusco** (Tues–Sun 8am–5pm; 50¢), in the same building as the tourist office, tells their story, as well as displaying scraps of excavated finds from local ruins.

Arrival and information

The **tourist office** (daily 9am–3pm & 6pm–9pm; ☎962/5-54-09) is on the ground floor of the old Palacio Municipal, on the west side of the zócalo. The helpful staff will give you city maps and also offer reasonably priced tours to Unión Juárez and Izapa.

The town's layout is confusing, for while the streets are laid out in the regular numbered grid common to towns in Chiapas, the zócalo, **Parque Hidalgo**, is not at its centre. It's not too far away, though: c/Central meets Av. Central three blocks east and a block south of the zócalo. All the **bus stations** are north of the centre; the various second-class companies have their terminals within walking distance of the zócalo, while first-class *Cristóbal Colón* is farther out at c/17 Ote. between Av. 3 Nte. and Av. 5 Nte., about a twenty-minute walk. The **post office** (Mon–Fri 8am–6pm, Sat 8am–1pm) is a long way southeast of the zócalo at c/1 Ote., between 7 and 9 Nte. The main **banks** are one block east of the zócalo but for changing cash and travellers' cheques you'll get a much quicker service from *Cambios Tapa* at the corner of Av. 4 Nte. and c/3 Pte. (Mon–Sat 8am–7.30pm, Sun noon–7.30pm).

If you need a visa to cross into Guatemala, the **Guatemalan consulate** is at c/2 Ote. 33, between Av. 7 and 9 Sur (Mon–Fri 8am–4pm; ☎962/6-12-52), the **El Salvadorean** at c/8 Ote. 12-A (☎962/6-48-22).

Accommodation

There's at least one **hotel** near any of the bus stations, but the ones around the second-class terminals are often sleazy. Calle 11 also has a few, and there's a whole clutch on Av. 8 Nte., between 11 and 13 Pte. Some rather desperate-looking places can be found around the **market**, which straggles down the hill west of the zócalo.

Carballo, Av. 6 Nte. 18, off the southwest corner of the zócalo (☎962/6-43-70). One of the cheapest in town. ①.

Colonial, Av. 4 Nte. 31 (☎962/6-20-52). Two blocks east of the zócalo, this is excellent value; rooms have private bath and there's a garden. Friendly owners. ③.

Fénix, Av. 4 Nte. 19, near the corner of c/1 Pte. (☎962/5-07-55). Good value: some rooms have a/c and there's a cooling fountain in the courtyard. ④.

Michell, c/5 Pte. 23-A (☎926/6-88-74). Modern hotel half a block east of the zócalo; all rooms have a/c and doubles have balconies. ⑤.

Pakal-Na, Av. 16 Nte. (☎962/6-60-46). Almost at the edge of town, though only four blocks west of the zócalo, past the market. Very comfortable rooms with a/c, private bath and TV. Parking. ⑤.

Santa Julia, c/17 Ote. 15, across from the *Cristóbal Colón* depot (☎962/6-31-40). A cut above the norm in both facilities and price. ④.

Eating and drinking

There are more than enough **restaurants** around the zócalo to satisfy all tastes. Most are on the south side, where *Doña Leo* has the best-value breakfast and *comida corrida*, together with *tortas* and *tacos*; *Los Comales* is similar, but a bit more expensive. The

---

MOVING ON FROM TAPACHULA

The main second-class **bus** operators are *Sur*, at 9 Pte. and 14 Nte., for the coast as far as Salina Cruz; *Autobuses Paulino Navarro*, 7 Pte. between 2 and Central Nte., for the coast road, Ciudad Hidalgo and Puerto Madero; *Autotransportes Motozintla* and others run services to Comitán and San Cristóbal from the same address. The most frequent service to San Cristóbal is with *Lombardo* (second-class) at 11 Ote. and 3 Nte., with hourly services between 4am and 8pm (7hr 30min). *Union y Progreso*, 5 Pte. between 12 and 14 Nte., runs *combis* to the Talisman Bridge for the **Guatemalan border**. Tapachula's **airport** (☎962/6-22-91), 18km south on the road to Puerto Madero, is served by *Aeroméxico* (☎962/6-20-50), *Aviacsa* (☎962/6-14-39), *Taesa* (☎926/6-37-32) and several smaller commuter airlines.

---

restaurant at the *Hotel Don Miguel*, c/1 Pte., off the southeast corner of the zócalo, is pretty fancy but does a great-value breakfast. As usual there are cheap places to eat and some fine *panaderías* to be found around the market area, beginning on 10 Av. Pte., a block west of the zócalo.

Unión Juárez

The small town of **UNIÓN JUÁREZ**, high on the flank of the Tacaná volcano, 43km from Tapachula, offers a chance to escape the heat of the lowlands. The journey from Tapachula follows the valley of the Río Suchiate, which forms the border with Guatemala, taking you through cacao and coffee plantations. At **CACAHOATÁN**, you change to a *combi* run by *Transportes Tacana*. Unión Juárez is almost on the border and hikers can obtain permission here to cross into Guatemala on foot at Talquian, 10km north. There are also some excellent day hikes to waterfalls and, with a guide, you can even reach the volcano's summit, at 4092m the highest point in Chiapas. This is a two- to three-day trip, with a cabin to sleep in at the top, though you'll need to bring a sleeping bag at least.

Practicalities
Buses for Unión Juárez leave several times a day from the *Union y Progreso* station in Tapachula. There are just two **places to stay**: the budget but comfortable *Posada Alijoad*, half a block off the west side of the plaza (☎962/2-02-25 ext 37; ③), which has hot water and a good inexpensive restaurant, and the good-value *Hotel Colonial Campestre*, which you pass as you enter the town from the south (☎962/2-02-25; ask for *Campestre*; ④–⑦). Rooms in the hotel are all recently modernized and have hot water, while impressive A-frame cabins, reached by an underground passage, sleep six. On the north side of the plaza the *Carmelita* and *La Montaña* are good, inexpensive **restaurants**. *Combis* leave for Cacahoatán from the east side of the plaza (every 30min until 4pm).

The ruins of Izapa

Though the road to the border passes right through the archeological site of **IZAPA**, few visitors bother to stop, which is a pity, since as well as being easy to get to, the site is large – with more than eighty temple mounds – and important for its evidence of both the Olmec and early Maya cultures. Izapa culture, in fact, is seen as a transitional stage between the Olmecs and the glories of the Classic Maya period; here you'll see early versions of the rain god Chaac and others in elaborate bas relief on the stone facings of the temples. Founded as early as 800 BC, Izapa continued to flourish throughout the Maya Preclassic period, until around 300 AD; most of what remains is from the later period, perhaps around 200 AD.

The **northern side** of the site (left of the road as you head to the border) is more cleared and accessible than the southern half. There's a ball-court, and several *stelae*, which, though not Olmec in origin, are carved in a recognizable Olmec style, similar to monuments at other early Maya sites. The **southern side**, down a track about 1km back along the main road, is a good deal more overgrown, but you can spot altars with animal carvings – frogs, snakes and jaguars – and several unexcavated mounds.

There's a caretaker at Izapa and you'll be charged a small fee. To **get there**, take any bus or *combi* to the Talisman border and ask the driver to drop you at the site, which is signposted from the road.

The Guatemalan border: the Talismán bridge and Ciudad Hidalgo

Both of these southern crossing points are easy places to enter Guatemala, but the **Talismán bridge** is closer to Tapachula and better for onward connections. From Tapachula *combis* (*Union y Progreso*) run frequently (taking about 30min), passing the *Cristóbal Colón* bus station on the way.

In theory there's a small toll to pay to cross the bridge, but the **immigration procedure** is generally pretty slack and trouble-free. At present US citizens and nationals of EC states (apart from Ireland) don't need visas and must simply get a Guatemalan tourist card. This should be free but officials often illegally ask for money. How you get out of this depends on your attitude (and that of the immigration official) – if you go expecting to be ripped off, you will be. For those who need a visa there are **Guatemalan and El Salvadorean consulates** in Tapachula. Changing money is best done in Tapachula, but there's no shortage of moneychangers at the border and you'll only get a slightly less favourable rate.

There are several **hotels** and **restaurants** at the border, some technically in Mexico, some in Guatemala, but almost all of them over the bridge in the no-man's land between the two border posts. None is particularly good value, but the *Buenavista* and the *Handall* hotels (②–③) are the best of the bunch. Heading **onward**, Guatemala City is about five hours away: there's usually a bus waiting, but if not, take a bus or van to **Malacatán** and continue from there. There's also an early morning **bus to San Salvador** run by *Transportes El Condor*. Travelling into Mexico, you'll probably have your passport checked many times along Hwy-200, so be prepared. *Cristóbal Colón* runs some services directly to México for those keen to press on, and there's no shortage of *combis* to Tapachula.

CIUDAD HIDALGO is a very busy road crossing and the point where the train enters Guatemala, but it's less convenient if you're travelling by bus. There's a **casa de cambio** at Central Sur and 2 Av. Ote., and several nondescript, overpriced **hotels**; the ones over the border in Ciudad Tecúm Umán are cheaper. Plenty of willing locals offer to pedal you across the Puente Rodolfo Robles but it's an easy walk. *Cristóbal Colón* runs a **bus** from Ciudad Hidalgo to México daily at 7pm, but it's much easier to take a bus or *combi* to Tapuchula (45min) and change there. There's almost always one waiting by the *casa de cambio*.

The Chiapas highlands

There is nowhere in Mexico so rich in scenery or indigenous life as inland Chiapas. Forested uplands and jungly valleys are studded with rivers and lakes, waterfalls and unexpected gorges, and flush with the rich flora and fauna of the tropics – wild orchids, brilliantly coloured birds and monkeys. Even now the network of roads, though growing, is skeletal, and for much of its history the isolation of the state allowed its **indigenous population** to carry on their lives little affected. In the villages you'll see the trappings of Catholicism and of economic progress, but in most cases these go no deeper than the surface: daily life is still run in accordance with ancient customs and beliefs.

Strong and colourful as the traditions are – away from the big towns Spanish is still very much a second language – the economic and social lot of the Indians remains greatly inferior to that of *ladinos*. The **Zapatista rebellion**, centred in this area, did not appear from nowhere. The oppressive exploitation of the *encomienda* system remained powerful here far longer than in parts of Mexico more directly in the government eye (there were local rebellions, quickly suppressed, in the early eighteenth and late nineteenth centuries), and despite some post-revolutionary land redistribution, most small villages still operate at the barest subsistence level. Not surprisingly, many of the customs are dying fast, and it's comparatively rare to see men in traditional clothing, though many women still wear it. Conversely, such traditions as do survive are clung to fiercely and you should be extremely sensitive about **photography** – especially of anything that might have religious significance – and donning **native clothing**, the patterns on which convey subtle social and geographic meaning.

Tuxtla Gutiérrez

TUXTLA GUTIÉRREZ, the capital of the state, does its best to deny most of Chiapas' attraction and tradition – it's a fast-growing, modern and crowded city. However, it is also a major transport hub, and you may well end up having to stay the night. It's not a bad place – there's a fascinating **zoo** and some excellent **museums** to fill some time –

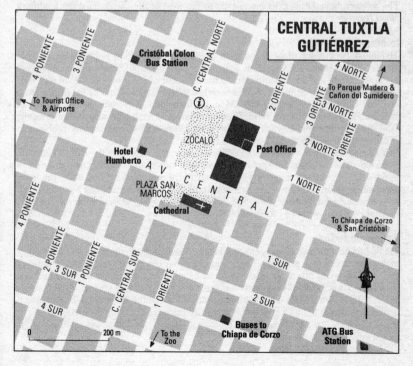

CENTRAL TUXTLA GUTIÉRREZ

but there's no call to stay longer than necessary, and if the timing is right your best bet is to carry straight on through to San Cristóbal.

Arrival and orientation

Tuxtla has two **airports**. The main one, **Aeropuerto San Juan**, near Ocozocautla on a hill top often shrouded in fog, 28km to the west of town, is used by *Mexicana* (☎961/3-49-21). To get into the city, buy a *colectivo* ticket from the booth upstairs, which also gives out a limited amount of **tourist information**. **Aeropuerto Terán** (or Aeropuerto Francisco Sarabia) is a more convenient 7km west of the city and served by *Aviacsa* (airport: ☎961/5-05-97; office: Av. Central Pte. 1144 ☎961/2-68-80) and *Aerocaribe* (airport: ☎961/5-15-30; office: in *Hotel Bonampak* ☎961/2-20-32). Taxis or *colectivos* will bring you into the centre; call ☎961/1-17-35 for pick-up. First-class **buses** pull in to the *Cristóbal Colón* station on Av. 2 Nte. at c/2 Pte.: to reach the centre (you can leave luggage at the juice bar opposite), turn left from the entrance onto Av. 2 and left again when you reach Av. Central. The main second-class terminal, used by *Autotransportes Tuxtla Gutiérrez* (*ATG*) and a couple of smaller companies, takes up half a block of 3 Sur, near 7 Oriente, 1km southeast of the centre: for the zócalo, follow 2 Sur west past the market area until you hit c/Central Sur, then turn right.

The centre of town is arranged in the usual Chiapas **grid of numbered streets** fanning out from Av. Central, which runs east–west, and c/Central, which runs north–south; often you'll see the streets named not just as Av. 3 Nte., but as Av. 3 Nte. Pte., which defines which quarter of the city you're in – it can be extremely confusing if you're looking for the junction of 3 Nte. Pte. with 3 Pte. Nte. **Avenida Central** (also known as 14 de Septiembre) is the town's focus, with the **zócalo** right at the centre. The modern business district lies mostly to the west of the zócalo, past the landmark *Hotel Humberto*.

Information

The most convenient place to pick up maps and information is at the **municipal tourist office** (Mon–Fri 9am–3pm & 6–9pm; ☎961/03-76-90), conveniently located at c/Central Norte and Av. 2 Norte Ote. Tuxtla's **tourist office** proper is a good way west of the zócalo, across from the *Hotel Bonampak* in the *Edificio Plaza de las Instituciones* at Blvd. Belisario Domínguez 950 (Mon–Fri 9am–3pm & 6–9pm; ☎961/2-55-09). In addition, **Margarita Ruíz**, a former senior member of staff who now works privately (and speaks excellent English), will help travellers who encounter any problem in Chiapas with free advice; call her on ☎961/1-32-21.

You may be able to obtain **topographic maps** of the state from the *INEGI* (*Instituto Nacional de Estadística, Geografía y Información*) office, on 1 Norte Ote., just east of the zócalo – useful if you're travelling in out of the way places. Next door, the main **post office** (Mon–Fri 8am–7pm, Sat 9am–1pm), just off the zócalo, has a reliable *Lista de Correos*. As for **banks**, you'll find *Banamex* on 1 Sur Pte. and *Bancomer* on Av. Central Pte., both within a couple of blocks of the zócalo.

Accommodation

Tuxtla has no shortage of inexpensive **places to stay**, though finding a halfway decent budget room can be a problem. Though inexpensive, the hotels near the **bus stations** or facing the road are noisy. Most of them have hot water, but there are occasional shortages. Check, too, if your hotel has pure drinking water. If you want the convenience, with less noise, head a few blocks east (left out of the first-class bus station and across the zócalo) to find a clutch of hotels in all price ranges along **2 Norte Ote**.

Balun Canan, Av. Central 944 (☎961/2-30-50). Best hotel in this price range with very comfortable rooms, a garden and good restaurant. ⑤.

Bonampak, Belisario Domínguez 180 (☎961/3-20-50). Fourteen blocks west of the zócalo, where Av. Central becomes Blvd. Domínguez, this hotel belongs to the *Best Western* chain. Rooms are all a/c and there are private *cabañas* in the gardens, a pool and a restaurant. It's worth dropping in for a look at the Bonampak mural reproductions (see p.461). ⑦.

Casablanca, 2 Norte Ote. 25 (☎961/1-03-05). Good-value a/c rooms with TV. ③.

Catedral, 1 Norte Ote. 367 (☎961/3-08-24). The best budget hotel in the city. Clean rooms, tiled bathrooms, even a bedside light. Drinking water available. ②.

Faro, 1 Norte Ote. 1007 (☎961/2-26-61). Some way east of the centre, but handy for Parque Madero, this very quiet hotel has good-sized rooms. Water available. ③.

Fernando, 2 Norte Ote. 515 (☎961/3-17-40). The best value in this area: large, comfortable rooms and helpful staff. ②–③.

Hotel Posada Del Rey, c/1 Oriente Nte. 310 (☎961/2-29-11). Luxury tower overlooking the zócalo. Comfortable rooms with a/c and TV. ⑥.

Hotel Trailer Park La Hacienda, Blvd. Belisario Domínguez 1197 (☎961/2-78-32). Motel-like place on the western edge of town, 3km from the centre, with lots of parking. Rooms are spacious but bare, with bath, TV and phone. Good, inexpensive restaurant. ⑥.

La Mansión, 1 Poniente Nte. 221 (☎961/2-21-51). Only a block west of the zócalo and a block from *Cristóbal Colón*, this comfortable, affordable hotel has a good-value restaurant. ④.

Mar-Inn, 2 Norte Ote. 341 (☎961/2-27-15). Some a/c rooms near the *Cristóbal Colón* station. ③.

María Teresa, 2 Norte Pte. 259, directly across from the *Cristóbal Colón* station (☎961/3-01-02). Convenient but noisy. ②.

Plaza Chiapas, 2 Norte Ote. 299 (☎961/3-83-65). New hotel with great prices. All rooms have private bath, some have balcony. ③.

Regional San Marcos, 2 Oriente 176 at 1 Sur (☎961/3-19-40). Good-value modern hotel, a block south of the zócalo and a block east of the cathedral. Rooms are clean, with private shower, some with a/c, plus there's drinking water on all floors. ③.

San Antonio, 2 Av. Sur Ote. 540 (☎961/2-27-13). Clean, friendly, inexpensive hotel near the *ATG* terminal. Good budget restaurant next door. ③.

The City

Sights downtown are few: the **zócalo**, known as the Plaza Cívica, is the chief of them, recently refurbished with much ostentatious marble, fountains, and a very restrained, whitewashed **Cathedral**. Its bell tower is one of the leading local entertainments: every hour it plays a different tune while a mechanical procession of the twelve apostles goes through a complicated routine. At the side of the cathedral, the **Plaza San Marcos** is full of life, its ever-growing **handicraft market** bustling with vendors from all over Chiapas. In the main plaza, across Av. Central, there is often free live music, especially at weekends. Also worth seeing is the **Hotel Bonampak**, whose lobby has copies of the Maya murals from Bonampak (see p.461) – a great deal easier to get to than the real thing.

Slightly farther afield, you could also head out to the **Parque Madero**, northeast of the centre, where the small **Museo Regional de Chiapas** (Tues–Sun 9am–4pm; donation requested) displays artefacts and maps detailing the pre-Columbian groups living in Chiapas. Highlights include intricately carved human fencers from the ruins of Chiapa de Corzo (see p.437). Botanical gardens and an *Orquideario* full of blooms native to the Chiapas jungle are in the same complex, reached along a shaded walkway. To get there, head north from the zócalo and then turn right onto 5 Norte Ote. for 1km; or take a *combi* marked "Parque Madero" along Av. Central.

If you do have half a day to kill, however, it's far more worthwhile to spend it at the **Zoológico Miguel Alvárez del Toro** or *ZOOMAT* (Tues–Sun 8.30am–5.30pm; free), on a forested hillside south of the city. There's a **bus** out there, marked "Cerro Hueco", which you can catch on 1 Oriente between 6 and 7 Sur, a bit of a walk from the centre, but it's very slow and roundabout – a taxi is a great deal easier and on the way back you may find people to share. The zoo claims to have every species native to Chiapas, from spiders to jaguars, and by Mexican standards it's excellent, with good-sized cages, complete with jungle and freshwater streams, and a conservationist approach. There is, for example, one dark cage with a label that announces the most destructive and dangerous species of all: peer in and you're confronted with a reflection of yourself. A number of animals, including *guaqueques negros* – rodents about the size of a domestic cat – and some very large birds, are free to roam the zoo grounds. Occasionally you'll witness bizarre meetings, as these creatures confront their caged relatives through the wire. This is particularly true of some of the pheasants – *ocofaisan* and *cojalita* – where the descendants of the caged birds are freed but make no attempt to leave because they naturally live in family groups. People of nervous disposition should avoid the *Vivario*, which contains a vast and stomach-turning collection of all the insects and spiders you might meet on your travels.

Eating and drinking

The centre of Tuxtla has dozens of **restaurants**, and you need never wander more than a block or so either side of Av. Central to find something in every price range. Juice bars are everywhere and there are also some great bakeries along Av. Central. The very **cheapest** places are on 2 Sur, while between the second-class bus area and the centre you'll pass several tiny, family-run restaurants, each serving an excellent-value *comida corrida*. More cheap places to eat can be found around the market.

All the larger hotels have a restaurant attached, and these are often good value. Otherwise, the *Restaurant del Cheff*, right by the *Hotel Humberto*, is handy and open long hours; and *Gringo's Chicken*, on 2 Ote. just south of Av. Central, may satisfy a longing for cooking *estilo Americano*, though the combination of southern-fried chicken with *chile*, *tortillas* and southern-fried potatoes is uniquely Mexican. If you're heading for the Yucatán, then the inexpensive *El Nuevo Yucatán*, just off the west side of the zócalo, may give you a taste of things to come. Most popular for socializing and people-watching are the swish restaurants behind the cathedral, always packed with smartly dressed locals. Prices for the Mexican food at *La Parroquia* are not too high and there's a good breakfast buffet. Next door, the *Trattoria San Marco* serves good portions of pizza, Mexican food, and great gateaux at slightly higher prices. For **vegetarian** food try *Nah Yaxal*, just off Av. Central at 6 Poniente Nte., west of the zócalo. It's clean and modern, though a little pricey. Opposite there's a good bread and cheese shop.

MOVING ON FROM TUXTLA

ADO, *Rapidos del Sur* and *Maya de Oro* buses all depart from the *Cristóbal Colón* station. Generally *ADO* run to México, Veracruz and Oaxaca; *Rapidos del Sur* serve the Chiapas coast; and *Maya de Oro* run luxury services to Mérida and Cancún. *Cristóbal Cólon* has luxury *plus* services to most destinations. The various **second-class terminals** are dotted around the city. The main terminal, used by *Autotransportes Tuxtla Gutiérrez* (*ATG*), serves Oaxaca, via Juchitán, Villahermosa, Mérida and Palenque. There's even a service to Chetumal, Playa del Carmen and Cancún. Getting to **San Cristóbal** is extremely easy: *combis* leave from 3 Sur, near *ATG*, whenever they have a full load, and from only a block away on 8 Ote., between 2 and 3 Sur, *Transportes Nha-Bolom* also runs a frequent and inexpensive service. A shared **taxi** to San Cristóbal (four people) will cost only $5 each.

To get to **Aeropuerto San Juan**, buses from the city leave from the downtown *Mexicana* office, Av. Central Pte. 206 (☎961/2-00-20); or call ☎961/2-15-54 for a pick-up. Taxis and *combis* run to Aeropuerto Téran.

Tuxtla to San Cristóbal

Driving east from Tuxtla towards San Cristóbal, you'll catch occasional glimpses of the lower reaches of the **Cañon del Sumidero**. Through this spectacular cleft the Río Grijalva runs beneath cliffs that in places reach almost 1500m in height. To appreciate it better, take the road that runs north from Tuxtla past a series of *miradores*, in a National Park that includes all the most scenic sections of the canyon. The best views are from the *mirador* known as **La Coyota**, or at the end of the road near the restaurant *La Atalaya*. The only public transport from Tuxtla is an expensive *colectivo*, from 1 Av. Norte Ote., near the corner of c/3 Oriente Nte., a couple of blocks east of the zócalo. A group of six should be able to get a tour, with a brief stop at the top, for around $30 per van. You could also take a "Km 4" *colectivo* heading north along 11 Oriente Nte., past the Parque Madero, and get off at the turnaround point. From here it's a 25-minute walk to the first *mirador*, **La Ceiba**, for stunning views of the canyon and river. There's usually sufficient traffic to make hitching a possibility, though be sure to take water along.

For better views still, take a **boat ride** through the canyon. Regular boat trips run from **Cahuaré**, where the highway crosses the river, or the small colonial town of **Chiapa de Corzo** (see below), for much the same price of around $70 per boat. Joining up with people is usually easy enough if you wait at the *embarcadero* in Chiapa in the morning. The trip lasts a couple of hours, passing several waterfalls (best during the rains) and entering caves in the cliffs, enlivened by commentary that points out such detail as the spot where hundreds of Indian warriors flung themselves off the cliff rather than submit to the Spanish. The river is dead calm since a dam was constructed not far beyond the canyon.

Chiapa de Corzo

CHIAPA DE CORZO is an elegant little town overlooking the river, barely twenty minutes by bus from Tuxtla. An important centre in Preclassic Maya times, it's the place where the oldest Long Count date, corresponding to December 7, 36 BC, has been found on a *stela* (the remaining ruins are on private land behind the Nestlé plant, beyond the far end of 21 de Octubre). There are at least a dozen **places to eat** on the riverside here, and plenty to see: the small **museum of regional handicrafts** next to the cathedral, in a cobbled courtyard surrounded by ancient brick arches (Tues–Sun 10am–4pm; 50¢), which features the local painted and lacquered gourds; an amazingly elaborate sixteenth-century fountain, shaped like the Spanish crown, in the zócalo; fine murals depicting local history in the Palacio Municipal; and a small **market** around the cathedral. The two **hotels** in town are both overpriced. The basic *Los Angeles*, on the southeast corner of the zócalo (③), is often full, while the new **Hotel La Ceiba**, Domingo Ruíz 300 (☎961/6-07-73; ⑦), three blocks west from the zócalo, is a luxury place, very quiet and comfortable: all rooms have a/c and there's a small pool.

To get to Chiapa, hop on one of the *colectivos* that leave every ten minutes from the *Transportes Chiapa–Tuxtla* office at 3 Oriente and 3 Sur in Tuxtla. It's easy enough to get back: *combis* and microbuses leave from the northeast corner of the zócalo. You could also continue on to **San Cristóbal**: more than a dozen buses a day leave from Chiapa's small bus station on 21 de Octubre, just east of the zócalo.

The ruins of Chiapa de Corzo

Strategically located on an ancient trade route high above the Río Grijalva, the ruins of **Chiapa de Corzo** comprise some 200 structures scattered over a wide area of private property, shared among several different owners and sliced in two by the Pan-American Highway. Mound 32, a small flat-topped pyramid, is clearly visible at the road junction as you head east of town. This is the longest continually occupied site in

Chiapas, beginning life as a farming settlement in the early Preclassic period (1400–850 BC). By the late Preclassic (450 BC–250 AD) it was the largest centre of population in the region, trading with all Mesoamerica. What you see today are mainly low pyramids, walls and courtyards.

To **get to the site** from town, take any microbus heading east and get off at the junction with Hidalgo and follow the signs. After about ten minutes you'll come to an unmarked gate in a fence on the right; go to the house (officially closed Mon) and pay the $1 **fee** to the family who farm among the ruins. **Walking**, it's about 3km northeast from the zócalo in Chiapa de Corzo, passing the beautifully located sixteenth-century church ruin of San Sebastian on the way.

Simojovel and Bochil

Just beyond Chiapa de Corzo, the **road to Villahermosa** – a spectacular wind down to the Gulf plain – cuts off to the north. Few tourists take this route, since ahead the Pan-American Highway continues to the far more enticing destination of San Cristóbal. Off the side road, however, lies **SIMOJOVEL**, source of most of the amber you'll find sold in local markets. Should you want **to stay**, the *Casa de Huéspedes Simojovel*, one block south of the plaza, on Independencia (no phone; ①), has basic rooms round a flower-filled courtyard.

The road climbs at first through mountains wreathed in cloud to **BOCHIL**, some 60km from Tuxtla, where some buses pull over for a rest stop. It's a pleasant small town, a centre for the **Tzotzil Maya**, and a good base from which to explore the surrounding hills and villages. Most people still wear the traditional dress or *traje*: the women in white *huipiles* with red embroidery, pink ribbons in their hair and dark blue skirts, and maybe a few men in the white smock and trousers rolled up to the knee. You'll be stared at, usually covertly, and, as always, should be *very* wary of **taking photographs**: not merely out of simple courtesy but because you may be taken for a government agent – these towns protested very strongly at the election result in August 1994 and in December 1994 were briefly occupied by the Zapatistas, who destroyed public records. There are a couple of simple **places to stay**, including the *Posada San Pedro* (②), whose basic rooms are set out around a courtyard on 1 Poniente Nte., a block from the plaza: head for *Banamex* at the top of the plaza and turn right.

Combis run regularly up the minor road to Simojovel, 40km away, and Bochil also has a frequent second-class bus service to Tuxtla, with *Autotransportes Tuxtla–Bochil*. Five kilometres beyond Bochil at **Puerto Cate**, a side road to the right leads down to **San Andrés Larráinzar**, a Tzotzil village 23km down the dirt track. Trucks cover the route and from San Andrés you can reach **San Juan Chamula**, 18km away, which is well connected by *combis* to San Cristóbal. This makes for an interesting route to or from San Cristóbal – but you'll need to check the current political situation and set off fairly early.

Jaltenango

Completely unused to visitors, the small town of **JALTENANGO**, jumping-off point for the **Reserva Biosfera El Triunfo**, is just a three-hour bus ride south of Tuxtla. Also known as **Angel Albino Corzo**, it lies at the junction of three rivers and is surrounded by coffee *fincas* on the slopes of the Sierra Madre de Chiapas. The highest peaks of the reserve, a refuge for Chiapas' tropical wildlife, are covered in dense **cloud forest**.

Of the two **hotels** here, the *Hotel Esperanza* (①), one block east of the plaza, is by far the better; there are also a couple of basic **restaurants** and a bakery. Apart from the main road, the streets are unpaved. Tracks lead up to the hills and if you're a wild-life enthusiast you could easily spend a few days exploring the area, though to get the best out of a visit you need to camp and use a local guide. **Buses** leave Tuxtla several times a day from the *Cuxtepeques y Anexas* station at 10 Oriente and 3 Norte, running via Jaltenango to Cuxtepec, high up at the head of a forested valley. The same company also operates an hourly service from Comitán.

San Cristóbal de las Casas

Just 80km from Tuxtla Gutiérrez, **SAN CRISTÓBAL DE LAS CASAS** is almost 1700m higher – a cool place with an unrivalled provincial colonial charm. Its low, whitewashed red-tiled houses seem huddled together on the plain as if to keep out enemies – indeed, the town was designed as a Spanish stronghold among an often hostile indigenous population; the attack by Zapatista rebels in January 1994 was the latest in a long series of uprisings. It took the Spanish four years to pacify the area sufficiently to establish a town here in 1528. Officially named San Cristóbal, it was more widely known as *Villaviciosa* (evil city) for the oppressive exploitation exercised by its colonists. In 1544 Bartolomé de las Casas was appointed bishop, and promptly took an energetic stance in defence of the native population, playing a similar role to that of Bishop Vasco de Quiroga in Pátzcuaro (see p.184). His name – added to that of the town – is still held in something close to reverence by the Indians. Throughout the colonial era San Cristóbal was the capital of Chiapas, then administered as part of Guatemala, and it lost this rank in 1892 only as a result of its reluctance to accept the union with Mexico.

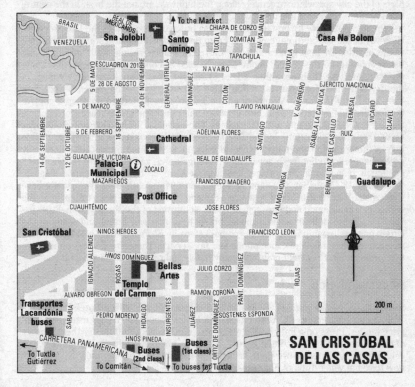

Though it's the local crafts and the indigenous way of life that draw people to San Cristóbal, this romanticization is not always appreciated by the *indigenos* themselves, who not surprisingly resent being treated as tourist attractions or objects of amateur anthropology. Nevertheless, the life of the town depends on the life of the people from surrounding villages, who fill its streets and dominate its trade. Many of the salespeople are **expulsados**: converts to evangelical Protestantism expelled by the villages, now living in shanties on the edge of town and unable to make a living from farming. The women making crafts to sell to tourists soon took advantage of the publicity generated by the Zapatistas; the most popular souvenirs are now **Marcos dolls**, complete with ski mask, rifle and bandoliers – there's even a female Zapatista doll of Romana, who is reputed to be in a position of command in the movement.

Despite being the main focus of the Zapatista attack, the town was only occupied for thirty hours, and no tourists were harmed; many, in fact, took advantage of the opportunity to be photographed with the rebels. For the time being, San Cristóbal remains one of the most restful and enjoyable places in the republic to spend a few days doing very little, with an infrastructure set to cater for its predominantly young, European visitors.

Arrival and information

The road from Tuxtla Gutiérrez to San Cristóbal is one of the most spectacular in Mexico, twisting through the mountains and climbing constantly, breaking through the cloud into pine forests. First impressions of San Cristóbal itself, as the modern parts of the city sprawl unattractively along the highway, are not the best. In the centre, though, there is none of this unthinking development.

Whether you arrive by first- or second-class **bus**, you'll be just off the Pan-American Highway at the southern edge of town. From the *Cristóbal Colón* **first-class terminal**, at the junction of Insurgentes and the Carretera Panamericana, walk straight along Insurgentes up to the zócalo, about seven blocks. **Second-class** services stop along the Pan-American Highway either side of *Cristóbal Colón*. Many hotels supply maps of the city and the helpful **tourist office** (Mon–Sat 8am–8pm, often closed 2–4pm, Sun 8am–2pm), in the Palacio Municipal on the zócalo, is well stocked. Pick up a copy of the free listings magazine *Aqui San Cristóbal* and check the noticeboards for information on hotels, restaurants and excursions. The excellent *Mapa Turistico de Chiapas* (1:400,000 scale, 4km:1cm) is available at most of the bookstores in town and some hotels, though not at the tourist office. **Banks**, mostly around the zócalo, will usually do exchange, including cash advances (mornings only), and some have ATMs. You'll get much better, quicker service, however, at *Casa de Cambio Lacantún*, Real de Guadalupe 12 (Mon–Sat 8am–2pm & 4–8pm, Sun 9am–1pm); they also usually have Guatemalan Quetzales. Many restaurants change dollars. The **post office** is at the corner of Cuauhtémoc and Crescencio Rosas, southwest of the zócalo (Mon–Fri 8am–7pm, Sun 8am–1pm); in addition, most hotels have *Mexipost* boxes and many of the larger ones sell stamps. The *La Pared* bookstore in *El Puente* (see p.444) also sells **stamps** and has a long-distance phone and **fax** service. There are *Ladatel* **phones** on the zócalo and in *Cristóbal Colón*, and many hotels and restaurants have *casetas*.

Accommodation

San Cristóbal boasts some of the best-value **budget and mid-price hotels** in Mexico. Walking up Insurgentes from the bus station to the zócalo, you'll pass examples in all price ranges. Press on a little farther along Real de Guadalupe, off the northeast corner of the zócalo, and you'll find many more. Nights can be pleasantly cool in summer, but cold in winter, so make sure there are enough blankets. All but the most basic places now have hot water, though not necessarily all the time.

For **longer stays**, check out the many noticeboards in the bus stations and popular cafes, where you'll find rooms and even whole houses for rent. The closest official **campsite** is at *Rancho San Nicolás* (see below).

Bungalows at the Posada Los Morales, Ignacio Allende 17 (☎967/8-14-72). Whitewashed stone cabins with living room with fireplace, bath (generally with hot water) and stove, in a hillside garden five blocks west of the zócalo. Authentic colonial atmosphere, right down to the ancient wooden furniture and flagstoned floor. Good for groups. ⑥.

Casa de Huéspedes Margarita, Real de Guadalupe 34 (☎967/8-09-57). Long-standing budget favourite. Rooms are bare but comfortable (no private showers, but communal ones are clean) and the dorms are a bargain. Good, inexpensive restaurant in the blue-and-white tiled courtyard, and live music most nights. Horse-riding and other trips can be arranged. ①–③.

Casa Na Bolom, Vicente Guerrero 33 (☎967/8-14-18; fax 8-55-86). Staying in this famous museum and research centre was formerly possible only for invited scholars and archeologists – now it's open to anyone. Comfortable rooms with fireplaces, decorated with village artefacts. Residents can eat here if they book ahead – or just turn up for breakfast 7.30–10am, or Sunday brunch from 10.30am to 2.30pm. ⑥.

Ciudad Real, Plaza 31 de Marzo 10 (☎967/8-04-64). Colonial mansion, superbly located overlooking the zócalo. Most rooms rise above the covered courtyard (now a dining room, adorned with potted palms); quieter ones are at the back. Friendly, helpful staff. Popular with upmarket European tour groups. ⑤.

Don Quijote, Cristóbal Colón 7; turn left where Colón crosses Real de Guadalupe (☎967/8-09-20; fax 8-03-46). Newish hotel on a quiet street. Comfortable, well-lit, carpeted rooms with shower and constant hot water. The lobby is decorated with costumes from Chiapas villages. Free morning coffee. English and French spoken. ④.

Español, 1 de Marzo 15, corner of 16 de Septiembre (☎967/8-04-12). Two blocks north of the zócalo, this is the oldest hotel in town, little changed since Graham Greene stayed in 1938. The best rooms open onto the peaceful garden, where there's a fountain, but the furnishings are plain. ⑤.

Posada Capri, Insurgentes 54, near the bus terminal (☎967/8-30-18; fax 8-00-15). Excellent-value, clean rooms, some with balconies. Good pizza restaurant. Not to be confused with the other hotel of the same name, farther up on the opposite side. ④.

Posada Casa Blanca, Insurgentes, on the right just before the zócalo (no phone). One of the best-value budget hotels, conveniently located. Rooms are basic but clean; private showers with hot water. ①.

Posada Casa Real, Real de Guadalupe 51 (☎967/8-00-24). Lovely, friendly hotel with a flower-filled courtyard. Large rooms all with very comfortable double beds and a place for washing and drying clothes on the sunny rooftop terrace. No private baths, but there is hot water. ③.

Posada del Barón, Belisario Domínguez 2 (☎ and fax 967/8-08-81). Well-run new hotel one block east of the zócalo. Each room has a spotless tiled bathroom with plenty of hot water. You can make international calls, and there's someone who speaks English. ③.

Posada Diego de Mazariegos, 5 de Febrero 1 (☎967/8-18-25). San Cristóbal's top historic hotel, in two colonial buildings, either side of General Utrilla. Many rooms feature a fireplace and antique furniture; bathrooms are beautifully tiled. Often busy with tour groups. ⑦.

Posada Santo Domingo, 28 de Agosto 3 (☎967/8-22-46). Excellent, family-run place, north of the centre, a block before the Santo Domingo church. ②.

Rancho San Nicolás, 2km east of the centre, on the extension of Francisco León (☎967/8-00-57). Primarily a campsite and trailer park, but also has a few rooms in a pleasant country setting. ②.

Real de Valle, Real de Guadalupe 14 (☎967/8-06-80). Highly recommended, only half a block from the zócalo. Large rooms with bath and constant hot water. Friendly English- and French-speaking staff. Cafe, laundry, parking and bike rental. Trips can be organized. ③.

Rincon del Arco, Ejercito Nacional 66, corner of Vicente Guerrero (☎967/8-13-13; fax 8-15-68). Lovely luxury hotel with rooms round a courtyard or in delightful gardens. About 1km northeast from the zócalo, it's just a block from Casa Na Bolom and affords gorgeous views of the surrounding hills. Comfortable rooms with beautifully tiled bathrooms. Restaurant and parking. ⑦.

Santa Clara, Insurgentes 1, corner of the zócalo (☎967/8-11-40). In the former home of Diego de Mazariegos, the Conquistador de Chiapas, the large rooms have antique furniture, and public areas are adorned with colonial weapons and suits of armour. Heated pool and good restaurant. ⑤.

The City

There aren't that many specific things to do in San Cristóbal: the true pleasures lie in simply wandering the streets and in getting out to some of the nearby villages. As always the **zócalo**, Plaza 31 de Marzo, is worth seeing, not so much for the relatively ordinary sixteenth-century cathedral (though it does have a nice *artesonado* ceiling and elaborate pulpit) as for some of the colonial mansions that surround it. The finest is the **Casa de Mazariegos**, now the *Hotel Santa Clara*, which was built by the town's founder and has a very elaborate doorway around the corner on Insurgentes. In the middle of the zócalo there's a bandstand, which now incorporates a cafe, but even when no band is playing the city authorities provide piped music (Frank Sinatra and classical jazz) for people strolling here.

If you haven't already come across them, this is probably where you'll first encounter some of San Cristóbal's insistent **salespeople**, mostly women and girls from the villages, traditionally dressed and in no mood to take no for an answer. You must either learn to say no as if you really mean it, or else accept that they'll break your resistance eventually. Bear in mind that they really do need the income: many have been expelled from their villages for converting to Protestantism and live in desperate hardship.

Templo del Carmen
From the zócalo, Hidalgo leads south to the **Templo del Carmen**, by the Moorish-style arch across the road. The church is not particularly inspiring architecturally, but it's worth a visit to see the adjoining cultural complex, with the Casa de la Cultura and **Instituto de Bellas Artes**. Considering the amount of artistic activity in and around San Cristóbal, these are pretty disappointing – especially since a serious fire in 1993 destroyed several eighteenth-century religious paintings – but sometimes there's an interesting temporary exhibition, concert or recital.

The museums and Santo Domingo
In the other direction, General Utrilla leads north from the zócalo towards the market. At no. 10 (Plaza Siván), the small **Museo del Ambar** (daily 10am–6pm; free) displays amber found in the Simojovel Valley; you can buy pieces here too. **Santo Domingo**, farther up, is perhaps the most intrinsically interesting of San Cristóbal's churches, with a lovely pinkish Baroque facade embellished with Hapsburg eagles. Inside it's huge and gilded everywhere, with a wonderfully ornate pulpit – see it in the evening, by the dim light of candles, and you can believe it's all solid gold. Being so close to the market, Santo Domingo is often full of traders and Indians. Appropriately, then, part of the former *convento* next door has been converted into a craft co-operative (*Sna Jolobil*) selling textiles and other village products. The quality here is generally good, and prices correspondingly high. A block behind the church, in another part of the monastery, the **Museo Etnografía y Historia** – or *Centro Cultural de los Altos de Chiapas* – (Tues–Sun 10am–5pm; $3.50) has gorgeous displays of textiles as well as vivid portrayals of how the Indians fared under colonial rule. For scholars the **library** at the rear is a fascinating place to study old books and records of Chiapas, and the gardens are a relaxing place to rest.

The market
San Cristóbal's **market** lies beyond Santo Domingo along General Utrilla, and trades every morning except Sunday, when most of the villages have markets of their own. It's a fascinating place, if only because here you can observe Indian life and custom without causing undue offence. What's on sale is mostly local produce and household goods, although there are also good tyre-soled leather *huaraches* and rough but warm sweaters, which you might well feel the need of. The market is far bigger than at first you

suspect, so make sure you see it all (though beware that the main covered part is full of really gross, bloody butchers' stalls). Wander through the covered parts, including the section selling clothes, then up and down the hill behind. At the top there's a pleasant square and the *Café la Terraza del Cerrillo*, unfortunately open evenings only.

For most **crafts** you'd actually be better off at one of the stores in town, especially on Real de Guadalupe – those farthest from the zócalo, like *Artesanías Real* at 44, and *Artesanías Chiapanecas* at 51-A, are the best.

Casa Na Bolom

Opposite Santo Domingo, Chiapa de Corzo leads east towards the **Casa Na Bolom** at Vicente Guerrero 33, a private home, museum and library of local anthropology (Tues–Sun 9am–1pm), devoted especially to the isolated Lacandón Indians (see p.460). This was the home of Danish explorer and anthropologist Frans Bolom, and is still run by his widow as a centre for the study of the region. The **Museo Moxuiquill** (tour in English or Spanish Tues–Sun 4.30pm; $3.50 including film; mini tours in Spanish only at 10am, $2) exhibits discoveries from the site as well as an excellent map. Every evening after the tour, *La Reina de la Selva,* a film about the destruction of the Lacandón forest, is shown, and sometimes a video on Lacandón agriculture. Na Bolom also hosts some volunteer cultural projects. Write or call for details (see p.441).

Guadalupe and San Cristóbal

Farther afield, two churches dominate views of the town from their hill-top sites: **Guadalupe** to the east and **San Cristóbal** to the west. Neither offers a great deal architecturally, but the climbs are worth it for the views – San Cristóbal, especially, is at the top of a dauntingly long and steep flight of steps. Be warned, though, that women have been subjected to harassment at both of these relatively isolated spots (especially San Cristóbal): don't climb up here alone or after dark.

Eating, drinking and entertainment

There's a huge variety of good **restaurants** along Insurgentes and in the streets immediately around the zócalo, especially Madero. Where San Cristóbal really scores, however, with a small university of its own, a permanent population of young American outcasts, a popular language school, and a constant stream of travellers, is in lively places that cater to this disparate, somewhat bohemian crowd. Lots of them are vaguely arty, with a coffee-house atmosphere and interesting menus that feature plenty of vegetarian options.

As for **nightlife**, in the evenings many of these same places host **live music**, when they may impose a cover charge. Happy hours, with two drinks for the price of one, have become a feature of several bar-restaurants. There are even a couple of **discos** in the big hotels: one at the *Posada El Cid* on the Pan-American Highway, another at the *Hotel Rincon del Arco,* towards the Casa Na Bolom at Ejercito Nacional and Guerrero.

San Cristóbal also boasts three **cinemas**: the *Cine Las Casas,* Guadalupe Victoria 21, and the *Cinemas Santa Clara,* 16 de Septiembre 30, show mainly Mexican films, while *El Puente,* Real de Guadalupe, screens other Latin American and foreign films.

Cafes and restaurants

El Bazar, Flavio Paniagua 2. Live and recorded music, good, inexpensive wholefood, dominoes and backgammon make this a popular hangout. Open until 11pm.

Cafe Altura, 1 de Marzo 60, near the corner with 20 de Noviembre. Best of several coffee shops around here, serving organic coffee and natural foods. The owner leads ecological tours around San Cristóbal and to the farm in the mountains where the coffee is grown. Phone and fax service.

Café Restaurant Los Candiles, Insurgentes 79c. Opposite the *Cristóbal Colón* terminal. Very good little restaurant with the best-value breakfasts this side of town.

Café El Puente, Real de Guadalupe 55. Excellent cafe serving good inexpensive salads, soups, sandwiches and delicious cakes; also acts as a cultural centre, with newspapers and magazines, lectures, film shows and a good noticeboard. Closed Sun.

Cafe San Cristóbal, Cuahtémoc 2, near the corner with Insurgentes. This tiny coffee house has changed little in decades, which is the way the patrons who come to play chess and read the newspapers like it.

Cafetería La Troje, Cuauhtémoc 11, next to the post office. A good place for cheap breakfasts; it's also an atmospheric coffee house and juice bar, with magazines to read.

Casa de Pan, Dr Navarro 10. Superb range of vegetarian food and baked goods, including bagels, made with locally grown organic ingredients. A little more expensive than most, but during Friday evening happy hour you can fill up on the "all you can eat" pasta special.

El Faisán, Madero 2, just off the zócalo. Pricey but excellent French food.

La Galería, Hidalgo 3, just south of the zócalo. Increasingly sophisticated restaurant where international food is served in the refined atmosphere of a colonial mansion, surrounded by some fairly expensive art. Still has traces of its hippy origins, though.

Guelaguetza, Diego Mazariegos, near Allende. Oaxaqueño specialities.

Madre Tierra, Insurgentes 19, corner of Hermanos Domínguez. European-style restaurant in a colonial house, often with live *salsa* or classical music. Great, healthy food: home-made soup, salad, pasta and cappuccino. The next-door bakery sells wholewheat bread and carrot cake until 8pm.

El Mirador II, Madero 16. The best cheap Mexican restaurant on Madero; good *comidas corridas*.

La Pavilla, corner of Belisario Domínguez and Dr Navarro, on a tiny square. Specializing in grilled meats, including *alambres al queso*, similar to a kebab with melted cheese, they also serve great pizza. Sit on one of the saddles used as bar stools to enjoy the atmosphere and great views.

Paris-Mexico, Madero 20. Superb authentic French and Mexican cuisine, expertly cooked and not overpriced – try the daily lunch special, a three-course meal of soup, *crêpe* and dessert, always with a vegetarian option.

La Pergola, 20 de Noviembre 6, 1 block north of the plaza. Good Mexican food, pizza, spaghetti, and a daily special. Espresso and a 7–8pm happy hour on Mexican beer.

Plaza Mirador, Plaza 31 de Marzo 2. Surprisingly inexpensive considering the location overlooking the zócalo, and serving tasty filling meals, usually with a vegetarian choice.

Restaurante Campestre, 3km out of town on the road to Chamula. Good Mexican food in a rustic setting, with garden and great hill views. You can also camp here, but it's not particularly cheap.

Restaurante Normita II, corner of Juárez and José Flores, 1 block south east of the plaza. A great little restaurant, serving Jaliscan specialities and inexpensive breakfasts.

Restaurante Tuluc, Insurgentes 5. Justifiably popular, with a good *comida corrida* and dinner specials, this the first place to open in the morning (6am); ideal if you have to catch an early bus.

La Salsa Verde, 20 de Noviembre 7. Established place serving the best, priciest *tacos* in town.

La Selva, Real de Guadalupe 73. Pizza, pasta and Mexican *antojitos* at good prices, along with free live music nightly and a 6–8pm happy hour. Great breakfasts, too.

El Teatro Café, 1 de Marzo 8. Superb, moderately priced French and Italian food.

Listings

Bike rental An enjoyable way to get out to the surrounding villages. *Hotel Real de Valle*, Real de Guadalupe 14 (☎967/8-06-80), charges around $2.50 per hour, $12 a day. *Los Pinguinos*, 5 de Mayo 10–13, has well-maintained bikes for about $2–5 per hour, $12 per day, and takes tours to local attractions.

Bookstores Casa Na Bolom, Vicente Guerrero 33, has an excellent library and sells some books and maps of the Lacandón forest. *Casa Utrilla*, on General Utrilla near Dr Navarro, has a wide selection including academic and educational books; also topographic maps of Chiapas. *Librería Soluna*, Real de Guadalupe 13B, offers a fair choice of books, including guides, in English; try also *Librería La Quimera*, Real de Guadalupe 24B, and *Librería La Pared*, located in the *Centro Cultural El Puente*, Real de Guadalupe 55, which has new guidebooks and an excellent selection of secondhand English-language titles.

Car rental *Auto Renta Ricci Dieste*, 5 de Mayo 6 (☎967/8-09-88); *Budget*, Diego Mazariegos 36 (☎967/8-18-71).

Ecology and the environment Out of town, the biological station *Pronatura* has a reserve with a 2km trail climbing the side of Huitepec mountain (Tues–Sun 9am–5pm; donation appreciated; ☎967/8-06-97). To get there, take a *combi* to Chamula and ask the driver to drop you at the entrance, 3.5km from town.

Language courses *Centro Bilingue*, in *Centro Cultural El Puente*, Real de Guadalupe 55 (☎ and fax 967/8-37-23), is the best and longest-established language school in San Cristóbal, offering courses at various levels, and can arrange accommodation with local families.

Laundry *Lava Sec*, Crescencio Rosas 12; *Lavorama*, Guadalupe Victoria 20A; *Lavendaría Mixtli*, corner of 1 de Marzo and 16 de Septiembre; and several more.

Travel agencies Travel agencies in San Cristóbal are really tour agencies and can arrange only domestic flights; to buy international tickets you'll need to go to Tuxtla. Try *Futura Viajes*, 5 de Mayo 6 (☎967/8-09-88); *Viajes Lacantun*, Madero 18 (☎967/8-25-88); and *Viajes Pakal*, Cuauhtémoc 6B (☎967/8-28-18; fax 8-28-19).

MOVING ON FROM SAN CRISTÓBAL

San Cristóbal is pretty well connected, and you can get directly to most destinations in the state and throughout the Yucatán. The **tourist office** maintains an accurate and up-to-date list of *all* bus times – check first. **Tuxtla Gutiérrez** (2hr) is served by most companies: *Cristóbal Colón* and *Transportes Nha Bolom* on the Pan-American Highway, just west of the junction with Insurgentes, run comfortable services hourly from 5.30am to 7.30pm. **Villahermosa** is not so well served, though there are a couple daily with *Cristóbal Colón* and *Maya de Oro* (7hr). For **Palenque**, *Cristóbal Colón*, *Maya de Oro*, *ATG*, *Pullman de Chiapas* (day and night departures), and *Transportes Lacandónia*, on the Pan-American Highway, east of the junction with Hidalgo, run a variety of services (5hr). All buses going to Palenque call at **Ocosingo** (2hr 30min), and in addition there's plenty of passenger van traffic: just go to the highway and someone will call out to you. Several first-class buses head for Ciudad Cuauhtémoc on the **Guatemalan border**: *Cristóbal Colón* takes 3hr 30min, while *Transportes Lonardo*, on the Pan-American Highway to the east of the junction with Insurgentes, runs services beginning at 4.30am, most of which continue to **Tapachula** (7hr 30min).

For **Mérida** and **Campeche**, *Transportes Lacandónia* has a second-class bus at 1.15pm (15hr); while *Maya de Oro*'s first-class service leaves at 7.30pm, calling at Chetumal (13hr 30min) and Cancún. For **Oaxaca**, best get to Tuxtla first. The first-class companies all have at least one daily service to **México** (20hr).

Around San Cristóbal

Excursions to the villages around San Cristóbal should be treated with extreme sensitivity. Quite simply, you are an intruder, and will be made to feel so – be very careful about taking photographs, and certainly never do so inside churches (theoretically you need a permit from the tourist authorities in Tuxtla Gutiérrez for any photography in the villages; in practice you should always get permission locally). There's a well-worn travellers' tale, true in its essentials, of two gringos being severely beaten up for photographing the interior of the church at San Juan Chamula. You should also be careful about what you wear: cover your legs, and don't wear native clothing – it may have some meaning or badge of rank for the people you are visiting.

The best time to make your visit is on a Sunday, when most villages have a market, or during a fiesta. At such times you will be regarded as having a legitimate reason to come, and you'll also find some life – most villages are merely supply points and meeting places for a rural community and have only a very small permanent population. In recent years, some families have been driven out of the villages for abandoning traditional religion for evangelical Protestantism – they live in poverty on the outskirts of the city.

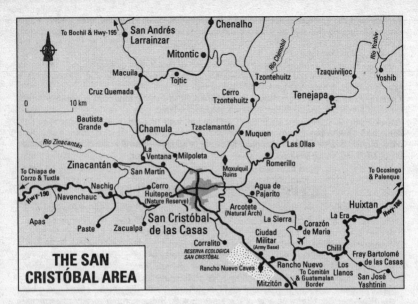

To Bochil & Hwy-195 · San Andrés Larrainzar
Chenalho
Mitontic
Macuila
Tojtic
Tzontehuitz
Tzaquiviljoc
Yoshib
Cruz Quemada
Cerro Tzontehuitz
Tenejapa
Río Chenalhó
Río Yashiv
Bautista Grande
Chamula
Tzaclamantón
0   10 km
Río Zinacantán
La Ventana · Milpoleta
Muquen
Las Ollas
Zinacantán
San Martín
Moxuiquil Ruins
Romerillo
To Chiapa de Corzo & Tuxtla
Nachig
Cerro Huitepec (Nature Reserve)
Agua de Pajarito
To Ocosingo & Palenque
Hwy-190 · Navenchauc
Arcotete (Natural Arch)
La Sierra
Huixtan
La Era
Hwy-190
Apas
Paste · Zacualpa
San Cristóbal de las Casas
Corazón de María
Corralito
RESERVA ECOLÓGICA SAN CRISTÓBAL
Ciudad Militar (Army Base)
Chilil
Fray Bartolomé de las Casas

THE SAN CRISTÓBAL AREA

Rancho Nuevo Caves
Rancho Nuevo
To Comitán & Guatemalan Border
Los Llanos
San José Yashtinin
Mitzitón

Some kind of trip out of San Cristóbal is definitely worth it, though, if only for the ride into the countryside, even if on finally reaching a village you find doors shut in your face and absolutely nothing to do (or, conversely, are mobbed by begging kids). The Indians in the immediate vicinity of San Cristóbal and to the west are generally **Tzotzil** speaking, those a little farther to the east **Tzeltal**, but each village has also developed its own trademarks in terms of costumes, craft specialities and linguistic quirks: as a result, the people are often subdivided by village or groups of villages and referred to as Chamulas, Zinacantecos, Huistecos (from Huistán) and so on.

The **tourist office** has a good display on the villages, with pictures of the local dress in each and details about them (including tours and bus timetables where relevant).

Transport and tours

Inexpensive *combis* leave frequently for Chamula and Zinacantán, less often for other villages, from Utrilla, just north of the market in San Cristóbal. If you'd rather take an **organized tour**, there are several to choose from. Among the best are Alex and Raul's "Culturally Responsible Excursions", which leave from outside the tourist office at 9.30am (☎967/8-37-41; about $11), and the groups led by Mercedes Hernández Gómez, travelling on foot and by public transport (around $10; meet by the kiosk in the zócalo at 9am; she'll be carrying her distinctive umbrella). Mercedes grew up in Zinacantán and her knowledge is so extensive that she never gives the same tour twice. Staff at the Casa Na Bolom also organize visits, departing from Na Bolom at 10am.

From the tourist office you can also get details on **horseback tours** into the surrounding area. The *Posada Margarita* is one of several places organizing riding tours, or you can simply hire a horse and set off on your own. Many of the organized tours go to the **Grutas de San Cristóbal** (daily 9am–5pm; $1), an enormous cavern extending deep into a mountain about 10km away. This is quite far enough to get saddle sore if you're not used to riding, though the horses are placid enough even for total beginners. Make sure you agree your itinerary before setting off: some guides expect you to turn round and head home as soon as you reach your destination. The caves can also be reached by bus since they're barely half a kilometre from the main road to Comitán. Look for the *Rancho Nuevo* sign on the right. A track leads for about 1km from the road through a park with hiking trails often used by the army. If you want to go by bike it's about a fifty-minute ride, uphill most of the way from San Cristóbal.

Another favourite trip is to **El Arcotete**, a large, natural limestone arch that forms a bridge over a river. To get there, follow Real de Guadalupe out of town, past the Guadalupe church, where it then becomes the road to Tenejapa; El Arcotete is down a signed track to the right about 3.5km past the church.

San Juan Chamula

SAN JUAN CHAMULA is the closest of the villages to San Cristóbal and the most frequently visited. It's also the most commercialized – prices in the market are certainly no bargain and local kids will pester you for "presents" the whole time. To get the most out of a visit you need to go on one of the organized tours (see above); questions are answered honestly and in full.

Chamula is little more than a collection of civic and religious buildings with a few huts – most of its population actually lives on isolated farms or *ejidos* in the countryside. Protestant converts among the villagers were driven out thirty years ago and only some of the Catholic sacraments are accepted. The rituals practised in the **church** at Chamula, a mixture of Catholic and traditional Maya practice, are extraordinary, and the church itself is a glorious sight, both outside and in, where worshippers and tourists shuffle about in the flickering light of a thousand candles. Before you enter, though, be sure to obtain permission (and buy a ticket; 75¢) from the "tourist office", to the right-hand side of the plaza as you face the church. Do *not* take **photographs** inside, or even write notes. In the *cantina* in Chamula you can buy *Pox* (posh), a wickedly strong cane alcohol used as offerings in the church and also simply to get celebrants blind drunk.

There are fairly regular **buses** from San Cristóbal's market to Chamula, and frequent *colectivo* departures for the Sunday market. If you take a bus or taxi up, the 10km back is an easy and delightful walk, almost all downhill.

Zinacantán

ZINACANTÁN is also reasonably close, some 15km, and accessible on public transport. It's an easy walk from Chamula (about 1hr 30min), slightly harder in the other direction: if you reach Zinacantán early enough on Sunday morning you'll have time to look around, visit the market, and still walk to Chamula before the market there has packed up (Chamula's stays open longer than the others, presumably in honour of its foreign visitors). Zinacantán also has a new **museum**, called *Museo Ik'al Ojov* ("our great Lord"), with displays of costumes from different hierarchical groups and a tableau of a house interior (daily 8am–6pm; donation).

Other villages

A number of other villages can be reached by early morning buses from the market area, although you may have difficulty getting back. **TENEJAPA**, about 28km northeast of San Cristóbal through some superb mountain scenery, is the closest easily accessible Tzeltal village, and has a particularly good Sunday market: there's even a *pensión* here, though no particular reason to stay. *Combis* leave for Tenejapa from Bermudas, an unmarked side street running east from the market, near the corner with Yajalon, about hourly or when full (1hr). Last one back to San Cristóbal leaves Tenejapa at 3pm.

HUISTÁN, some 36km out, just off the road to Ocosingo, is Tzotzil, and with more than the usual amount of villagers in traditional dress. **SAN PEDRO CHENALHO**, in a valley 36km north, is harder to get to, but again it has a *pensión* (②) and, perhaps because of fewer visitors, seems friendlier than most.

Moxviquil

MOXVIQUIL, a completely deserted ruined **ancient site**, is a pleasant excursion of a few hours on foot; it's best, however, to study the plans at the Casa Na Bolom first, as all you can see when you get there are piles of rough limestone. To get there, find Av. Yajalon, a few blocks east of Santo Domingo, and follow it north to the end (about 30min) at the foot of tree-covered hills, in a little settlement called Ojo de Agua. Head for the highest buildings you can see, two timber shacks with red roofs. The tracks are at times indistinct as you clamber over the rocks, but after about 300m a lovely side valley opens up on your left – suitable for camping. The main path veers gradually to the right, becoming quite wide and leading up through a high basin ringed by pine forest. After 3km you reach the village of **Pozeula**; the ruins are ahead of you across a valley, built on top of and into the sides of and a hill.

San Cristóbal to Guatemala: Comitán and Montebello

Beyond San Cristóbal, the Pan-American Highway continues to the border through some of Chiapas' most scintillating scenery. **Amatenango del Valle** is a Tzeltal-speaking village with a reputation for good unglazed pottery, but **Comitán** is the only place of any size – jumping-off point not only for **Guatemala** and for the **Lagos de Montebello National Park**, but for the Classic period **Maya sites** of Junchavín and Tenam Puente.

Comitán and around

An attractive town in its own right, **COMITÁN** is spectacularly poised on a rocky hillside and surrounded by country in which wild orchids bloom freely. Once a major **Maya centre** of population (Bonampak and Yaxchilán, even Palenque, are not far away as the parrot flies across the jungle), Comitán was originally a Maya town known as Balún Canán, renamed when it came under Aztec control. The final place of any note before the border (the inaptly named Ciudad Cuauhtémoc is no more than a customs and immigration post with a collection of mean shacks), today it has a **Guatemalan consulate** and a collection of reasonable **hotels**, and is a good place to rest if you've some hard travelling through the Lacandón forest or into Guatemala ahead of you.

Arrival and information

Buses stop along the Pan-American Highway, a long nine or ten blocks from the centre. Only *Cristóbal Colón* has a terminal; all the others just pull in at the roadside.

Comitán's layout can be a little confusing at first; pick up a free map from the **tourist office** in the Palacio Municipal on the zócalo (Mon–Sat 9am–8.30pm, Sun 9am–2pm). They will also have the latest information on who needs Guatemalan visas. The **consulate** itself is at the corner of c/1 Sur Pte. and 2 Poniente Sur, a couple of blocks southwest of the zócalo (Mon–Fri 8am–4.30pm; ☎ and fax 933/2-26-69; $10 fee). Also on the zócalo is a *Bancomer* for **currency exchange** plus dollar cash advances. The **post office** is one and a half blocks south on Central Sur (Mon–Fri 8am–7pm, Sat 8am–1pm).

Moving on from Comitán, there are plenty of buses to the border, San Cristóbal and Tuxtla. Heading for the Lagos de Montebello, *combis* leave about every thirty minutes from 2 Poniente, between 2 and 3 Sur, about five blocks from the zócalo. Otherwise, you can just wait for one to come along on the highway heading south.

Accommodation

Comitán has plenty of hotels, especially good value in the budget range. Nights are much cooler than days, so you'll need at least one blanket.

Hospedaje Montebello, 1 Poniente Nte. 10, a block northwest of the zócalo (☎933/2-17-70). Great budget hotel. Large, clean rooms around a courtyard, some with private bath, and the communal shower is really hot. Clothes washing facilities. ①.

Hospedaje Primavera, c/Central Pte. 4, just west from the zócalo (no phone). Basic but clean rooms round a courtyard, with several budget places to eat nearby. ②.

International, Av. Central Sur 22, a block south of the zócalo (☎933/2-01-11). Popular, comfortable business hotel, central and secure. Fills up quickly. ⑤.

Lagos de Montebello, on the Pan-American Highway at the junction with 3 Norte Pte. (☎933/2-06-57). Modern, comfortable rooms round a shady courtyard. Convenient if you're travelling by car. ⑤.

Pensión Delfín, Av. Central 19-A, right on the zócalo (☎933/2-00-13). Good value, with modernized rooms and dependable hot water. Rooms with windows are much better than those without. ④.

Río Escondido, 1 Poniente Sur 7 (no phone). Very basic hotel with a decent restaurant. ①.

The Town

Comitán's zócalo, on several levels and with plenty of shady places to rest, is surrounded by the municipal buildings, cathedral, shops and the theatre. Opposite the tourist office, the **Casa de la Cultura** (daily 9am–8pm; free) features exhibits on local history and archeological finds from sites in the area, while the splendid little **Museum of Archeology** (Tues–Sun 10am–5pm; free) presents an easily understandable chronological sequence on local Maya sites.

Just half a block away you can also visit the **Museo Belisario Domínguez** (Tues–Sat 10am–6pm, Sun 9am–1pm; free), a collection of mementoes in the former home of the local doctor and politician who was assassinated in 1913 for his outspoken opposition to Huerta's usurpation of the presidency.

Eating and drinking

Apart from in the hotels, most of the best **places to eat** in Comitán are on the **zócalo** – for really good-value Mexican food served in clean surroundings, try the *Restaurant Nevelandia*. There's a good market two blocks east of the zócalo, with lots of fruit stands and some very good *comedores*.

Junchavín and Tenam Puente

JUNCHAVÍN (daily 7am–5pm; free) is about a 45-minute walk north from Comitán's zócalo: follow Av. Central Nte. for about 2km until you reach the Church of Santa Teresita on the right, recognizable by its two tall bell towers. The road immediately past the church to the right, signposted Quija, will lead you out of town into hilly farming country. The entrance to the site is on the left after 1500m. Hundreds of steps lead up to a small flat-topped pyramid about 5km high, flanked by two smaller structures. The best time to visit is early or late in the day to avoid the heat. Views are superb and it is said you can see Chinkultic, 45km to the southeast. *Combis* from the zócalo run along the road to Quija; ask at the tourist office for times.

TENAM PUENTE is a much larger site, a few kilometres off the Pan-American Highway, 15km to the south of Comitán. A bus leaves for the *ejido* of **Francisco Sarabia** from 3 Oriente Nte. in Comitán at 8.30am, but you can take any bus heading south and get off at the junction, 11km on the right, then hitch or walk the 3km to the village. People here are friendly and will direct you to the ruins, which lie a kilometre beyond the school and playground. The path is difficult to find among the bushes and cornfields, but you'll soon see stone terraces and moulds, and eventually several large structures, including a 20m pyramid. There are several pleasant walks in the forested hills around here, but you'll need to take water.

Lagos de Montebello and the Frontier Highway

The **Parque Nacional Lagos de Montebello** stretches along the border with Guatemala down to the southeast of Comitán, beautiful wooded country in which there are more than fifty lakes, sixteen of them very large. The combination of pine forest and lakes is reminiscent of Scotland or Maine, with miles of hiking potential: for the less energetic, roadside viewpoints provide glimpses of many of the lakes, including the Lagunas de Siete Colores, each one lent a different tint by natural mineral deposits and the surroundings. You could see quite a bit of the park in a long day trip – buses cover the route all day from about 6am, with the last bus leaving the park entrance around 7.30pm – but to really enjoy the beautiful lakes and forest, and to visit the small but spectacular **ruins of Chinkultic**, you're better off staying in the park.

If you intend to head off the beaten track, you'll need to get hold of a good **map** before you arrive. The restaurant at the park headquarters displays an excellent topographic map of Chiapas, copies of which are sometimes available at the **tourist offices** in Comitán or San Cristóbal.

Park practicalities

The road leading to the National Park turns off the Pan-American Highway 16km from Comitán at the village of **La Trinitaria**, with the park entrance 36km farther on. The most comfortable of the several **places to stay** along the road is the *Parador Museo Santa María*, about 18km along on the right (☎967/8-09-88; ⑤). A former hacienda, it's a lovely place furnished with antiques and oil paintings. Don't expect too many mod cons, though: the rooms are lit with oil lamps.

Another 12km brings you to the best **budget accommodation** on the road, the *Hospedaje and Restaurant La Orquidea* (②), better known simply as *Doña María's*. Here there are half a dozen simple cabins with electric light, and hot showers in a separate building. It's a very *simpatico* place, run by Doña María Domínguez, who has given much help and support to Guatemalan refugees – you may find volunteers staying here. It's certainly very peaceful, set among the pines, just a short walk from the Chinkultic ruins, with a restaurant serving good helpings of simple food; buses stop right outside. A couple of kilometres farther on, the *Hotel Restaurant Bosque Bello* (☎933/2-17-02; ③) also has cabins, though these have TVs and are made of concrete, with consequently less atmosphere than *Doña María's*.

ARMY AND ZAPATISTA CHECKPOINTS ON THE FRONTIER HIGHWAY

At the time this book went to press, there was a major **Mexican army checkpoint** at the **La Trinitaria junction**. If you're travelling to or from the Lagos, you'll have to get off the bus here and have your passport (and possibly your luggage) examined. Searches are usually speedy, efficient and above all polite, but do expect delays and be prepared for the chance that you won't be allowed beyond the National Park. If you are one of the few going farther, note that the **Zapatista** checkpoint is about 50km beyond Tziscao at Amparo Agua Tinta. There you will be stopped and searched by members of the EZLN at least as thoroughly as by the army, and probably allowed to proceed. Of course the situation may have completely changed by the time you read this, so try to get as much information as you can – which is difficult. The **tourist office** is not able to help much but buses run daily, so check with *Transportes Lagos de Montebello* in Comitán to see if their services are continuing along the Frontier Highway.

Inside the park, the paved road ends a few kilometres beyond the entrance at the **park headquarters**, after passing some of the more accessible and picturesque lakes. There's a free lakeshore **campsite** and some simple *cabañas* (①) and a **restaurant**, the *Bosque Azul*, overlooking the lake of the same name. Small boys will greet you and offer to guide you to the nearby *grutas*; though you won't really need their help, they are friendly and do have a genuine interest in showing the caves to visitors. **Horses** are available for hire here.

The ruins of Chinkultic
Just before *Doña María's* on the Lagos de Montebello road, a 2km track leads off to the left to the Classic period Maya ruins of **CHINKULTIC** ($3). So far only a small proportion of the site has been cleared and restored, but it's well worth a visit for the setting alone. Climb the first large mound and you're rewarded with a view of a small lake, with fields of maize beyond and forested mountain ridges in the background. Birds, butterflies and dragonflies abound, and small lizards dart at every step. A ball-court and several *stelae* have been uncovered, but the highlight is undoubtedly the view from the top of the tallest structure, **El Mirador**. Set on top of a steep hill, with rugged cliffs dropping straight down to a *cenote*, the temple occupies a commanding position; though peaceful now, this was clearly an important centre in ancient times.

Tziscao and the Frontier Highway
Near the entrance to the park, the Frontier Highway, unpaved but in good condition, turns off to the right. Still inside the park boundaries, it passes the village of **TZISCAO**, a tiny settlement on the shore of Laguna Tziscao. On the lakeshore here is the *Albergue Tziscao*, an unofficial youth **hostel** (no membership needed). While its location is great, and you can rent boats to paddle on the lake, the three-tiered concrete bunks ($8) give you the impression of being in a cave and you'll almost certainly need a sleeping bag. Food and cold beer is available. To follow the trail around the lake, go back to the junction beyond the church and turn right. Along the way you pass Laguna Internacional, where the border is marked by a white obelisk at either end of the lake. **Entering Guatemala** here is not recommended. You could always try asking at the International Border Commission in Tziscao, or at the tourist office in Comitán, for the latest information on new border posts. There was one due to open on the road near *La Orquidea*, but the Zapatista uprising has postponed this indefinitely.

Beyond Tziscao, the Frontier Highway continues for another 70km through mountains and jungle with some spectacular views and precipitous drops, to the end of the line at Flor de Café. The largest settlement along the road is **Las Maravillas de Tenejapa**, a lovely village with a restaurant but no accommodation, about three and a half hours from Tziscao.

Flor de Café stands at the foot of a steep limestone ridge formed by a finger of the Sierra la Colmena. Though the road goes no farther, there is a track over the ridge connecting with the village of **Peña Blanca**, two hours away, a neat, clean *ejido* where you can get food, drinking water and, if you want, a guide to **Nuevo San Andrés** on the Río Lacantún, which has a weekly boat downstream to **Ixcán** and **Pico de Oro**. At Pico de Oro there are buses to **Bememérito** (for Bonampak and Yaxchilán, see p.461) and Palenque (p.455). To make this journey you'll need camping equipment and should be prepared to wait for connections.

Ciudad Cuauhtémoc and the Guatemalan border

A visit to the Lagos de Montebello is a good introduction to the landscapes of Guatemala, but if you want to see the real thing it's only another 60km or so from the

REFUGEES IN CHIAPAS

Some 50,000 Guatemalans are estimated to have fled across the border during the 1980s, and many of them remain in **refugee camps** on the fringes of the park and along the border. For the Mexican government, the camps have always been a major headache. Not only do they fear that association with the "problems" of Central America might tarnish their international image (in the 1980s there were several Guatemalan army operations against their occupants), but also the refugees have strong **support in Chiapas** – Indian groups on either side of the border are closely related. The first reaction was to relocate the camps in the Yucatán – but this was met with strong resistance from the refugees themselves, backed by **Samuel Ruiz**, bishop of San Cristóbal. So most of the camps remain, but in an atmosphere where the two main relief agencies, government-backed COMAR and the Church, refuse to co-operate with each other.

Some of the camps – one near the hamlet of **Benito Juárez**, for example – have been established for as long as thirteen years. Yet conditions remain primitive, usually with no power and a single water tap for the entire camp. What little land they can rent from Mexican landowners costs so much that it's uneconomic to farm their subsistence crops, and working (unofficially) for *patrones* or *finqueros* (large landowners) earns them around US$2 per day (even this precarious cash income is threatened by Mexico's worsening economic situation). Most, then, are reliant on the relief agencies, who can afford to supply only the barest subsistence diet.

Many of the refugees are desperate to return home and have formed **action committees** (*Comisiones Permanantes*, or *CPs*) to negotiate with the UNHCR and the Guatemalan government. An accord signed in October 1992 set out the conditions under which groups should return to Guatemala; the first convoy of buses carried the initial *retornados*, some 2000 people, to Ixcán in January 1993. Over the next two years 6000 people were repatriated in the organized returns, many airlifted back in an operation funded by the UN and Guatemalan government and accompanied by international observers. Smaller numbers have also returned in small groups without taking part in the international operation.

Still only a fraction of those wanting to leave the camps in Mexico have been repatriated. In January 1995, about 23,000 remained in camps in Chiapas, with a further 20,000 in Campeche and Quintana Roo – a far cry from the original CP estimate that 76 percent would have returned by the end of 1994.

The main stumbling block to full repatriation is the lack of available land for the *retornados* to farm. Much of the best land is owned by a small number of large landowners, and the land the refugees left often has several claimants. Sometimes these include internal refugees who fled to remote areas of Quiché and the Petén, establishing civil communities ("Communities of Population in Resistance") in some cases on land abandoned by fleeing refugees. The Guatemalan government and URNG, representing the guerrilla groups, have been negotiating, and apparently making progress, but at the time of writing no firm peace treaty had been signed.

La Trinitaria junction (plenty of passing buses) to the Mexican border post at **CIUDAD CUAUHTÉMOC**. There's nothing here but a few houses, the immigration post, a restaurant and the *Cristóbal Colón* bus station; a couple of **hotels** have recently opened – nothing special, but if you need to stay try the *Camino Real*, above the *Cristóbal Colón* station (②), which has clean rooms with fans.

The **Guatemalan border** post is at La Mesilla, a 3km taxi ride away; there's a charge of about $1 per person to cross. As always, the crossing is best attempted in daylight. The border is open until at least 10pm, but onward transport will be difficult if you leave it this late. If you need a **visa** (North Americans and EC citizens are exempt) you should really have one by now: chances are you'll be let in if you agree to pay the entry charge ($10) plus a bit more for a **tourist card** (around $5). Officially, if you have a visa or tourist card (or are British, in which case you need neither), there is **no charge** for entering Guatemala. However, the La Mesilla border post is the worst in the country for exacting illegal charges from tourists, with the customs officers sometimes joining in with demands for *inspección aduanal*. If you think you've been charged too much – anything over US$1 – politely but firmly refuse to pay or, failing that, demand a receipt and, if you feel up to it, report the incident.

Buses on to Huehuetenango, Quezaltenango and Guatemala City wait just over the border, leaving every hour or so until about 4pm. The **money changers** will give you reasonable rates for travellers' cheques or dollars, not so good for pesos. There are a couple of adequate **bars** on the Guatemalan side, and several hotels up the street from the border: the *Calins* is clean, inexpensive and has a good restaurant, or try the *Marisol*.

Getting back into Mexico is much easier: the Mexican tourist card should be issued free, though you'll have to pay an exit tax, usually of at least 5 quetzales. Vans or buses will be waiting to take you to Comitán (passing La Trinitaria junction), or there are several services to Tuxtla and a bus to México at 12.30pm. The last direct bus to San Cristóbal is the *Cristóbal Colón* at 6.30pm (4hr).

San Cristóbal to Palenque

Heading from San Cristóbal to the Yucatán, the best route takes you **to Palenque**, via Ocosingo, on a good paved road that is frequently used by buses and *colectivos* (a journey of around 5hr). Ocosingo and the surrounding area was the heartland of the **Zapatista** rebellion, so check on security before stopping in any of the villages along here, and be prepared to be searched by the Mexican army on the road. Although the going can be a bit rough in the rainy season, at any time it's an impressive and beautiful drive, through jungly mountains lush with streams and greenery. In the largely Tzeltal villages around Ocosingo, all of the women, if none of the men, are in traditional garb, and there are lots of Indians on the buses too – given a hard time by everyone.

Ocosingo

All things being equal (which they may not be), **OCOSINGO** makes a good place to escape the tourist crowds of San Cristóbal or Palenque. It's not as pretty as San Cristóbal but it's certainly a great deal more attractive than Palenque, its streets lined with single-storey, red-tiled houses and thick with the scent of wood smoke. It's a town that has stayed close to its country roots, with plenty of cowboys in from the ranches in their stetsons and pick-ups; it is also the most convenient base for a trip to the Maya site of **Toniná**.

Buses all stop on or near the main road: walk down the hill and you can hardly miss the zócalo. It's surrounded by elegant *portales* and a big old country church, as well as an *Ayuntamiento* with a thoroughly incongruous modern first floor, complete with tinted-glass office windows. The best of the **hotels**, the *Hotel Central* (☎967/3-00-24; ④), sits under a modern section of the *portales* by the *Restaurante La Montura*. Other hotels include the *Margarita* (☎967/3-00-48; ④), down the side street by the *Montura*; the *Hospedaje San José* (☎967/3-00-39; ②), off to the left at the bottom of the zócalo; and *Hotel San Jacinto* (☎967/3-03-79; ②), on Av. Central towards the market. Several other restaurants face the square – *Los Portales* is good but shuts very early. The **food market**, straight down Av. Central from the zócalo, sells locally produced cheeses, including a round waxy variety and delicious cream cheese. **Leaving Ocosingo** is easy enough until mid-evening: *Transportes Yaxnichil* run frequent microbuses to San Cristóbal, and the last *ATG* buses to San Cristóbal and Palenque leave at 7.30pm – likely to be later as they're *de paso*.

Toniná

Considering how little-known it is, the Classic period Maya site of **TONINÁ** (daily 9am–4pm; $3), some 15km east of Ocosingo, is surprisingly big, and restoration is uncovering many more buildings. It centres on an enormous grassy plaza, once surrounded by buildings, and a series of seven artificial terraces climbing the hillside above it. At the bottom are two restored ball-courts and an overgrown pyramid mound; as you climb the hill, passing corbel-arched entrances to two vaulted rooms on the right, you begin to get an impression of Toniná's vastness. The sixth and seventh terraces each have a number of small temples, while beyond are more huge mounds, awaiting excavation. There are also tombs on both the fifth and sixth levels, one of which contains an enormous mask of the Earth Monster, a powerful force in Maya cosmology. From the top there are fine views of the surrounding country.

The easiest way **to get to Toniná** from Ocosingo is in a taxi out along the unpaved road and back; it costs around $25. Alternatively, you should be able to get some kind of early morning transport – bus, *colectivo* or truck – from the market area along the road that passes close by the ruins (towards Guadalupe and Monte Libano). Hitching a lift with one of the archeologists' trucks is not too difficult. Walking takes more than three hours; if you're determined, take c/1 Ote. south from the church. The ruins are actually right by *Rancho Toniná*, where the site guardian (and guide) lives: there's a small open-air "museum" at the ranch, where some of the most interesting carved pieces have been gathered behind barbed wire.

Agua Azul

The chief attraction of the road beyond Ocosingo is the series of beautiful waterfalls on the Río Tuliá, in the Parque Nacional at **AGUA AZUL**, about 4km down a track from the road, 54km before Palenque. It's now a major tour bus destination, and there are microlight flights over the falls, or horse-riding tours for the less foolhardy. If you come by bus it will drop you at the crossroads, from where it's 45 minutes' walk down the track, and an hour's sweaty hike back up. At the end of the track you pay to enter the park (35¢), and there are several restaurants and a campsite (with hammock space): you can eat better at *Comedor & Camping Casa Blanca* at the top of the main fall, where there are also beds and hammock space in a large barn-like building (①), and the owners hire out horses. Of course, you can camp free almost anywhere if you walk upstream a way: the best spot is a tiny beach by the entrance to a magnificent gorge. There's a difficult trail leading up and over the top. Be sure to keep a close eye on your belongings, though, and be warned that muggings have been reported. If you do plan to stay, bring some food of your own, since the restaurants are expensive.

You should walk upstream anyway, where perilous-looking bridges cross the river at various points, for this really is an area of exceptional beauty, with hundreds of lesser falls (at least if you count the really tiny ones) above the developed area. At the right times of year, the river is alive with butterflies. Higher up the swimming is safer, too – though watch out for signs warning of dangerous currents as there are several tempting but extremely perilous spots, and people drown here every year. At **Misol-Ha**, 20km from Palenque, a 30m waterfall provides a stunning backdrop to a pool that's safe for swimming (75¢). It's an easy 1500m walk from the road, signposted on the left, with accommodation at a campground with some beautiful wooden *cabañas* (☎ and fax 934/5-04-72; ④) owned and run by the *ejido* of **San Miguel**.

Palenque

Set in thick jungle screeching with insects, **Palenque** is for many people the most extraordinary of the major Maya sites. It's not large – you can see everything in a morning – but it is hauntingly beautiful, strongly linked to the lost cities of Guatemala while keeping its own distinctive style. Some people choose to visit as a day trip from Villahermosa, but this seems a strange way of going about things: the laid-back **Palenque village**, with its wide choice of hotels and restaurants, makes an ideal jumping-off point for the ruins.

The village

Quite apart from being the best base for any detailed exploration of the ruins, **PALENQUE** (officially Santo Domingo de Palenque) is less oppressively hot than the coast, with a couple of fine swimming holes and waterfalls in the nearby hills. Most popular of these are **Nututum** and the small waterfall of **Motiepa** (reached by a signed path off the road about 1km from the ruins).

Arrival and information

Arriving by bus, you'll be on Juárez, where the highway comes into town, between the centre and the road to the ruins. The *ADO* station is about 100m farther into town, just off Juárez on 20 de Noviembre. The morning *ADO* service from Villahermosa continues from the village to the site, but you have to get off and buy a ticket for this extra section – if you plan to leave the same day, get your onward or return ticket at the same time. The

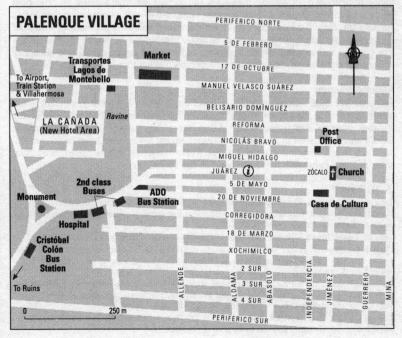

PALENQUE VILLAGE

PERIFERICO NORTE
5 DE FEBRERO
Market
Transportes Lagos de Montebello
12 DE OCTUBRE
To Airport, Train Station & Villahermosa
MANUEL VELASCO SUÁREZ
BELISARIO DOMÍNGUEZ
LA CAÑADA (New Hotel Area) *Ravine*
REFORMA
NICOLÁS BRAVO
Post Office
MIGUEL HIDALGO
JUÁREZ ⓘ
ZÓCALO ✝ **Church**
2nd class Buses
5 DE MAYO
ADO Bus Station
20 DE NOVIEMBRE
Monument
Casa de Cultura
CORREGIDORA
Hospital
18 DE MARZO
Cristóbal Colón Bus Station
XOCHIMILCO
To Ruins
2 SUR
3 SUR
4 SUR
ALLENDE
ALDAMA
ABASOLO
INDEPENDENCIA
JIMÉNEZ
GUERRERO
MINA
0   250 m
PERIFERICO SUR

TOURS AND TRAVEL AGENCIES IN PALENQUE

The surge in the numbers of tourists visiting Palenque has encouraged at least a dozen **travel agencies** to offer tours to the surrounding attractions. Any of them can take you to the **waterfalls** at Agua Azul and Misol-Ha (see p.454) and farther afield to the ruins of **Bonampak** and **Yaxchilán**, but none can sell you an international air ticket. Trips on the Río Usumacinta and guided horse-riding are also on offer, and some can organize **rafting**, light aircraft and **river trips to Guatemala**. Sample **prices** are: around $30 for four to five hours' horse-riding; $7 per person for an all-day *combi* trip to Misol-Ha and Agua Azul; $65 for a day trip to Yaxchilán; and $100 for an overnight trip that involves **camping** at Yaxchilán, then a guided walk to Bonampak. To visit both sites by **plane** will cost around $160.

The most experienced of Palenque's **tour agents** is *ATC Tours and Travel*, Allende (☎934/5-11-30; fax 5-02-10), next to *Colectivos Chambalu*. Other recommended agencies include: *Viajes Aventura Maya*, Juárez 122 (☎ and fax 934/5-08-16); *Viajes Misol-Ha*, Juárez 48 (☎ and fax 934/5-04-88); *Tonina Travels*, Juárez 105 (☎934/5-03-84); and *Viajes Yax-Ha*, Juárez 123 (☎ and fax 934/5-07-67).

---

train station is 6km north of town in a dusty settlement called Pakal Nal – if you're lucky there'll be a bus or taxi, though since the trains never run on time (and consequently often arrive in the early hours of the morning) this cannot be guaranteed.

Palenque's three **main streets**, Av. Juárez, 5 de Mayo and Hidalgo, all run parallel and lead straight up to the zócalo, the Parque Central. For a **map** and lots of useful information, call in at the helpful **tourist office** in the Plaza de Artesanías on Juárez, a block west of the zócalo. The staff know all the bus times and give out plenty of free leaflets. There's also a **noticeboard** for leaving messages and to find out what's going on. The **post office** is on Independencia, a block from the plaza; and there's a **laundry** on 5 de Mayo, opposite the *Hotel Kashlan*. The **banks** on Juárez are well used to changing travellers' cheques but service is as slow as ever. *El Rodeo* restaurant (see below) changes travellers' cheques without commission, and many of the **travel agencies** will change money or cheques; commission varies but it's considerably quicker than at the banks.

Accommodation

Palenque has seen a massive boom in hotel construction in recent years. There are plenty of places in the streets leading from the **bus stations** to the zócalo, especially Hidalgo (though the traffic noise makes these best avoided); the **La Cañada Rainforest Area**, west of the town centre, set among the relative quiet of the remaining trees, is generally more upmarket. You'll also find a host of new places, in addition to the *Mayabel* **campsite**, lining the **road to the ruins**.

IN TOWN

Casa de Huéspedes Los Portalitos, Mañuel Velasco Suárez, near the *Transportes Lagos de Montebello* bus station. Very ordinary place with rather less ordinary concrete beds, more comfortable than they sound. Private showers. ②.

Casa de Pakal, Juárez 10, below the zócalo (☎934/5-01-02). Good hotel with a/c and TV. ⑤.

Chan Kah, corner of Juárez and Independencia (☎934/5-03-18). A touch of luxury right on the zócalo, this very comfortable small hotel is owned by the same people as the *Chan Kah Resort Village* near the ruins. ⑥.

La Croix, Hidalgo, on the corner of the zócalo (☎934/5-00-14). A long-established favourite and, though past its best, still worth trying. Rooms are arranged around a plant-filled courtyard whose walls are decorated with murals of Palenque. Popular with motorcyclists. ③.

Posada Can Ek, 20 de Noviembre 43 (☎934/5-11-13). One of the best-value new hotels, with large, bright rooms, private bath and good views from the balcony. ③.

Posada Shalom, Juárez 156 (☎934/5-09-44). New hotel, with clean rooms and tiled private bathrooms. ③.

Regional, Juárez 119 (☎934/5-01-83). Halfway up Juárez, this friendly, well-run place is popular with European groups. Rooms are basic but clean, with showers and constant hot water. The courtyard is a good meeting place. You can safely store luggage here. Triple rooms available. ④.

Vaca Vieja, 5 de Mayo 42 (☎934/5-03-77). A couple of blocks beyond the zócalo, this is a comfortable hotel with private bathrooms, hot water and a decent restaurant. ④.

Yaxchilán, Manuel Velasco Suárez, two blocks east of the *Transportes Lagos de Montebello* terminal (☎934/5-14-66). New hotel with large comfortable rooms; very good value. ④.

LA CAÑADA RAINFOREST AREA

La Cañada, Merle Green 14 (☎934/5-01-02). Regular hotel rooms and cottages in the tree-shaded grounds; some fans, some a/c. ⑤.

Maya Tulipanes, Merle Green 6 (☎934/5-02-01). Off the road, in shady grounds; some a/c. ⑤.

La Posada Cañada, behind the *Maya Tulipanes* (☎934/5-04-37). A friendly place, popular with backpackers, *La Posada* is good for information about trips into the jungle. Eight rooms in the grounds, with private showers, hot water and a fridge for cold drinks. ③.

ON THE ROAD TO THE RUINS

The following hotels are listed in **order of their distance from town**.

Villas Kin-Ha, 2.5km along on the right. Large oval thatched *cabañas*, swimming pool and restaurant. There's also a trailer park. ⑤.

Chan Kah Resort Village, 6km along on the left, next to the National Park entrance (☎934/5-03-18; fax 5-04-89). Luxury *cabañas* in a lovely forest and river setting, humming with bird life. Swimming pool and restaurant. ⑦.

Mayabel Camping and Trailer Park, 2km from the site entrance. A great favourite with backpackers, *Mayabel* now has a number of vehicle pads with electricity and water, and some *cabañas* (with hot water), in addition to *palapa* shelters for hammocks and tents. The site isn't crowded, and you can usually get a space. The path to the ruins through the back of the campsite is now closed but magic mushroom aficionados continue to scour the fields in the morning mist. Hammock $2, tent $4, vehicle $9; *cabañas* ④–⑤.

Eating and drinking

Palenque has several budget **places to eat** between the bus stations and the zócalo. On Juárez the *Restaurant Ixchel* serves good cheap breakfasts and *comidas corridas*, as does *El Herradero*, near the *Banamex*. A more "international" menu is available at *Piccolino's Pizza* – good pizza but not particularly cheap – or try the hamburgers at *El Rodeo*. *Las Tinajas*, on 20 de Noviembre, is a very pleasant, family-run restaurant, with good food at fair prices.

In the Cañada area all the hotels have their own restaurants and there are several more expensive places, such as *El Fogon de Pakal*, which sports a **video bar** and **live music**, as well as a large, cool dining room beneath a thatched roof. Most of the restaurants along the road to the ruins are huge thatched places, built in the expectation of vast numbers of customers being delivered by the tour buses; they certainly couldn't hope to survive on the passing trade.

The site

Palenque's style is unique. Superficially it bears a closer resemblance to the Maya sites of Guatemala than to those of the Yucatán, but its **towered palace** and **pyramid tomb** are like nothing else, and the **setting**, too, is remarkable. Surrounded by hills covered in impenetrable jungle, Palenque is at the same time right at the edge of the great Yucatán plain – climb to the top of any of the structures and you look out, across the dark green of the hills, over an endless stretch of low, pale-green flatland. The city

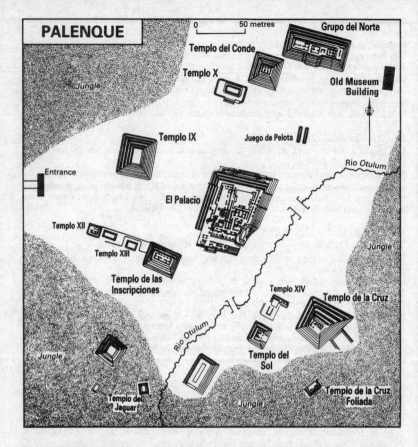

PALENQUE

0   50 metres

Grupo del Norte

Templo del Conde

Templo X

Jungle

Old Museum Building

Templo IX

Juego de Pelota

Entrance

Rio Otulum

El Palacio

Templo XII

Templo XIII

Jungle

Templo de las Inscripciones

Templo XIV

Templo de la Cruz

Rio Otulum

Templo del Sol

Jungle

Templo del Jaguar

Templo de la Cruz Foliada

Jungle

flourished during the Classic period from around 300 to 900 AD, but its peak apparently came during a relatively short period of the seventh century, under two rulers – **Pacal** and **Chan-Bahlum**. Almost everything you can see (and that's only a tiny, central part of the original city) dates from this era.

Practicalities

Getting to the site from the village is no problem. The most regular *combi* service is operated by *Colectivos Chambalu*, at the corner of Allende and Hidalgo, and you'll never have to wait more than fifteen minutes. The *combis* will stop anywhere along the road, useful if you're at one of the new hotels or the *Mayabel* campsite, but they stop running at 6pm. After that it's either walk or take a taxi.

The ruins are in a **national park** (daily 8am–6pm; archeological zone 8am–5pm; free except to vehicles). Arrive early if you want to avoid the worst of the heat and the crowds. There's a small cafe by the entrance, where for a fee you can leave bags while you explore, and a toilet by the ticket office. At the entrance to the site there are ranks of souvenir stalls and you'll usually find a group of Lacandón Indians in white robes (and gold watches) selling arrows and other artefacts. The huge new **museum**, also by the entrance, contains a good number of carved panels removed from various parts of the site, and modern, interactive displays with explanations in Spanish, English and Chol, the language spoken by modern Maya in this part of Chiapas.

Visiting the site

As you enter **the site**, the great palacio, with its extraordinary watch-tower (closed to visitors), stands ahead of you. To the right, and first, comes the **Templo de las Inscripciones**, an eight-stepped pyramid, 25m high, built up against a thickly overgrown hillside. The broad, extremely steep stairway up the front, and paths up to the hill, lead to a sanctuary on top that contains a series of stone panels carved with hieroglyphic inscriptions relating to Palenque's history. Most remarkable, though, is the **tomb** that lies at the heart of this pyramid. Discovered in 1952, this was the first such pyramid burial found in the Americas, and is still much the most important and impressive. The smaller objects – the skeleton and the jade death mask – have been moved to the Anthropology Museum in México, but the crypt itself is still here, as is the massive, intricately carved stone sarcophagus. The **burial chamber**, and the narrow, vaulted stairway leading down to it (10am–4pm), are uncomfortably dank and eerie, but well worth the steep, slippery descent. You may not feel able to linger long at the bottom, however, as a long line of hot, claustrophobic visitors waits impatiently behind you. The deified king buried here was Pacal, and, in order that he should not be cut off from the world of the living, a hollow tube, in the form of a snake, runs up the side of the staircase from the tomb to the temple.

In June 1994 another remarkable tomb was discovered, in **Templo XIII**, in a pyramid similar to the Temple of the Inscriptions, located just to the west. This burial, of a man around forty years of age, is considered by archeologists to be very similar chronologically to that of Pacal. In addition to a number of jade and obsidian grave goods and food and drink vessels to sustain the deceased on his way to *Xibalba*, the Maya Underworld, the sarcophagus also contained the remains of two females, one adult and one adolescent. At present the tomb is not open to the public.

The centrepiece of the site, **El Palacio**, is in fact a complex of buildings constructed at different times to form a rambling administrative or residential block. Its square **tower** (whose top was reconstructed in 1930) is quite unique, and no one knows exactly what its purpose was – perhaps a look-out post or an astronomical observatory. Bizarrely, the narrow staircase that winds up inside it starts only at the second level. Throughout you'll find delicately executed relief carvings, the most remarkable of which are the giant human figures on stone panels in the grassy courtyard.

From here, the lesser buildings of the **Grupo del Norte**, and the **Juego de Pelota** (ball-court), are slightly downhill across a cleared grassy area. On higher ground in the

---

MOVING ON FROM PALENQUE

Leaving Palenque on the **bus**, there are surprisingly few direct services to Mérida: *ADO* has one at 9pm (and a direct service to México at 6pm), and *Transportes DAG-DUG* have a second-class service to Mérida (9hr) at 5pm, calling at Campeche. To Tuxtla there are many services: *ATG* runs first- and second-class at least hourly, also calling at San Cristóbal. *ADO* has plenty of buses to Villahermosa during the day and a service to Cancún via Chetumal at 9.30pm (12hr). *Transportes Comitán y Lagos de Montebello*, on Velasco Suárez, just past the market, has services down the Usumacinta Valley. If you have problems, however, there are second-class departures to Catazaja on the main highway every couple of hours, and you should be able to pick up a *de paso* bus there. If you're taking the boat from **La Palma** to **El Naranjo**, Guatemala, catch the 8am *Libertad* bus, from 20 Noviembre, near Allende, and change at **Emiliano Zapata** and **Tenosique**; this will get you there in time for the 2pm boat.

other direction, across the Río Otulúm – lined with stone and used as an aqueduct in the city's heyday – that runs through the site, and half-obscured by the dense vegetation around them, lie the **Templo del Sol**, the **Templo de la Cruz** and the **Templo de la Cruz Foliada**. All are tall, narrow mounds surmounted by a temple with an elaborate stone roof-comb. Each, too, contains carved panels representing sacred rites – the cross found here is as important an image in Maya iconography as it is in Christian, representing the meeting of the heavens and the underworld with the land of the living. The **Templo del Jaguar** is reached by a small path that follows the brook upstream – a delightful shaded walk. Downstream, there's a small pool just beyond the old museum building and, although swimming is theoretically forbidden, it's often used by Mexican families for bathing. A path leads down from here, past more mounds under excavation, along a gorgeous series of pools and cascades, eventually coming out on the main road.

If you want to penetrate a bit farther, follow the path along the stream behind the Templo de las Inscripciones and you're in the real jungle – or at least a pleasantly tame version of it. Tarzan creepers hang from giant trees, while all around there's the din of howler monkeys, strange bird calls and mysterious chatterings. The path doesn't go anywhere much (it leads to an *ejido* a little over an hour's walk away, which is why it's there), but it's easy to believe you're walking over unexcavated pyramids. The ground is very rocky and some of the stones certainly don't look naturally formed.

The Usumacinta valley

Palenque is the obvious starting point for trips to the sites of **Bonampak** and **Yaxchilán**. Formerly an option open only to those who could afford to rent a plane – still one way of doing it – several agencies in Palenque now offer overland trips to the sites, or you can easily organize your own. If you do decide to head out on your own, you'll need to be prepared to walk, to camp and, above all, be resourceful. Even with the slightly easier option of an organized trip, you'll have to do just as much walking and camping, with perhaps a little less time to enjoy the ruins.

THE LACANDÓN

You may already have encountered the impressively wild-looking **Lacandón Indians** selling exquisite (and apparently effective) bows and arrows at Palenque. Still wearing their simple, hanging white robes and with their hair uncut, the Lacandón were until recently the most isolated of all the Mexican tribes. The ancestors of today's Lacandónes are believed to have migrated to Chiapas from the Petén of Guatemala during the eighteenth century. Prior to that the Spanish had enslaved, killed or relocated the original inhabitants of the forest. The Lacandón refer to themselves as *Hach Winik* (true people); "Lacandón" was a label used by the Spanish to describe any group of Indians outside colonial control who lived in the Usumacinta valley and western Petén. Appearances notwithstanding, some Lacandón families are quite wealthy, having sold timber rights in the jungle, though most of the timber money has now gone. This has led to a division in their society and now most Lacandón live in one of two main communities: **Lacanjá Chansayab**, near Bonampak, where the villagers are developing low-impact tourism facilities (see below); and **Nahá**, where a small group still attempt to live a traditional life.

The best source of information on the Lacandón is the **Casa Na Bolom** in San Cristóbal de las Casas (see p.443), where you can find a manuscript of *Last Lords of Palenque* (Little Brown & Co, 1982) by Victor Perera and Robert Bruce.

The Usumacinta valley is Mexico's last frontier, with new towns and farms carved out from the rainforest: the **Frontier Highway** (**Carretera Frontera**) provides access to a number of new settlements whose inhabitants are rapidly changing the rainforest to farmland. The road is not yet complete all the way along the frontier, despite what some maps indicate, but it has gone beyond where the Usumacinta enters Mexico and may well have reached Chajul on the Río Lacantún by now. Plans for a series of **hydro-electric dams** on the Usumacinta, which would have inundated many archeological sites (as well as several new townships), appear to have been shelved, hopefully for good.

Exploring this route presents other options beyond Bonampak and Yaxchilán. From the fast-expanding town of Benemérito you can get a ride on a trading boat upstream to Sayaxché, on the Río de la Pasión **in Guatemala**. Or to visit the Lagos de Montebello (see p.450), you can continue along the road to Pico de Oro and then take a boat up the Río Lacantún to Ixcán; from here a day's walk takes you to Flor de Café, at the end of the Frontier Highway leading in from Comitán (see p.451). The interior of this remote corner of Chiapas is the home of the **Lacandón Maya** and fortunately has some form of protection as the Montes Azules Biosphere Reserve.

Bonampak

It's always best to get an early start and the *Transportes Lagos de Montebello* **bus** company, on Velasco Suárez in Palenque, has several departures to destinations along the Frontier Highway between 4.30am and midday, and even some overnight services. Although the road is constantly being maintained, it's a long and bumpy ride.

For **BONAMPAK** you need to get off the bus at **San Javier** (about 6hr), where there's a whitewashed government control hut on the left and on the right a hut where you can buy drinks, though you really need to bring your own food. Take the track bearing right to Lacanjá Chansayab (it may be signposted), and after 5km, at a right-hand bend in the road, fork left. This is as near to Bonampak as most vehicles can get, though villagers from Lacanjá offer rides on their Honda four-wheelers if you can't face the two- to three-hour walk. The road continues a few more kilometres to the Lacandón village, where you'll find several purpose-built **camping shelters**; there are also hammocks available. Ask for Kin Bor or Chan Bor, who will also be able to fix you up with knowledgeable Lacandón guides to lead you through the forest. There are several waterfalls in the area and you can reach the **Lacanjá ruins** in under two hours or Bonampak in three. If you can, pick up an information sheet in the **Casa Na Bolom** in San Cristóbal before you set off.

Lacandón boys may offer to guide you to the ruins and, though it's perfectly possible to follow the track on your own, you'll have a less apprehensive trip through the forest if you accept – and it won't cost much. From here it's about two or three hours' walk to the ruins, crossing streams on slippery log bridges: wonderful in the dry season (Jan–April), calf-deep in mud in the rain.

After taking the **entrance fee** ($5), the guard will probably not let you out of his sight. Day-trippers make their way back after a short visit but the guards, who supplement their wages by selling cold drinks, will let you **camp** here, or possibly stay in one of the huts. Once you've seen the ruins, head back to San Javier junction, where there's a **bus** to Palenque at around 11am and one to Benemérito at 11.30am; several others pass by throughout the day and the road sees enough traffic to make hitching possible.

The site

The outside world first heard of the existence of Bonampak in 1946, when Charles Frey, an American conscientious objector taking refuge in the forest, was shown the site by some Lacandón Indians, who apparently still worshipped at the ancient temples. The setting, deep in the rainforest, is superb and the highlight is the famed **Temple of the Frescoes**. In three separate chambers, on the temple walls and roof, are depicted vivid scenes of haughty Maya lords, splendidly attired in jaguar-skin robes and quetzal-plume headdresses, their equally well-dressed ladies, and bound prisoners, one with his fingernails ripped out, spurting blood. Musicians play drums, pipes and trumpets in what is clearly a celebration of victory. Though time and early cleaning attempts have taken their toll on the murals, recent work has restored some of their glory. However, it has to be said that you'll get a better impression of the whole scene from the repro-ductions in the National Museum of Anthropology in México or, much nearer, at the *Hotel Bonampak* in Tuxtla Gutiérrez (see p.435).

Frontera Corozal and Yaxchilán

Twenty kilometres beyond San Javier, the turning for **FRONTERA COROZAL** (some-times referred to as Frontier Echeverría) is marked by a *comedor* and shop selling basic supplies. Corozal, another 20km down the little-travelled side road, on the bank of the Usumacinta (bus from Palenque at 9am, returning at 5am), is where you need to catch a boat to get to Yaxchilán. Facilities are limited, but there are a couple of shops and a cheap *comedor* and you can **camp**.

There's a Mexican **immigration post** here and visitors to Yaxchilán will always be asked to show their passports, despite the fact that the site is in Mexico. **Entering Guatemala** is relatively easy as there's plenty of river traffic to Co-op Bethel, a few kilo-metres upstream on the opposite bank, where there's a new Guatemalan immigration post. A couple of buses leave Bethel daily for Flores (for Tikal), an exhausting ride of at least five hours along a dirt road.

To reach the site, you need to get a ride in a boat heading downstream – ask around at the waterfront. It shouldn't prove too difficult as these are the boats used by tours from Palenque and the boatmen will be pleased to make some extra money; bargain carefully, though, since you need to be picked up again. The trip takes about an hour and, unless you have to charter your own boat, should cost less than $10 per person. **Admission** is $5. There's an open-sided shelter on the edge of the airstrip for camping and you may be able to get a meal at the hut used by tour groups.

Yaxchilán – the site

A much larger site than Bonampak, **YAXCHILÁN**, strategically built on a bend in the river, was an important Classic period centre. Its most famous kings, identified by their name glyphs, were Shield Jaguar and his son Bird Jaguar, who ruled at the beginning of the city's rise to power, around 700 AD. Under their command Yaxchilán began the campaign of conquest that extended its sphere of influence to include the Usumacinta centres and alliances with Tikal (in Guatemala) and Palenque.

The first groups of numbered buildings and those around the **main plaza** are easy to view. The temples bear massive honeycombed roofs, now home to bats, and every-where there are fine stucco carvings. Some of the very best lintels have been removed to the British Museum in London, but plenty of well-preserved carvings remain. A path behind Building 42 leads through the jungle, over several unrestored mounds, to three more tall temples. The guards won't always take you back here, as it's out of their way (and they insist you begin to return well before the 4pm closing time), but the climb is worth the effort for the view of distant mountain ridges, in solitude. There's a real sense of a lost city as you explore the ancient, moss-covered stones, watched from the trees by toucans and monkeys. Butterflies flit around the forest glades, as, unfortu-nately, do mosquitoes.

On from Yaxchilán

Heading **downstream from Yaxchilán** is really only practicable as part of an organized whitewater rafting expedition, as the river speeds through two massive canyons, the **Cañon de San José**, with fearsome rapids between cliffs 300m high, then the slightly less dramatic **Cañon de las Iguanas**.

Below the rapids lie the ruins of **Piedras Negras**, which, though possibly as large as Tikal, are scarcely visited due to their inaccessibility. An easier way to visit is to take an organized trip from Tenosique (see p.476).

The southern Usumacinta

Continuing south a further 25km brings you to **BOCA LACANTÚN**, where a bridge carries the road over the Río Lacantún and there's a Mexican **immigration post**; make sure you get your passport stamped if you've entered Mexico from anywhere upstream. You can expect any bus along this road to be stopped by immigration officials or army checkpoints, so keep your passport handy. At the confluence of the Lacantún and Usumacinta rivers is an unusual Maya remain, the **Planchon de Figuras**, a great limestone slab of unknown origin, carved with Maya glyphs, birds, animals and temples. If you're travelling by river, the beautiful **Chorro cascades** are just downstream.

Benemérito

The sprawling frontier town of **BENEMÉRITO**, 1km beyond Boca Lacantún, is the largest settlement in the Chiapas section of the Usumacinta valley, fast becoming an important centre for both river and road traffic. There's a hospital, market, shops, restaurants and a few basic hotels. The highway is the town's main street and in the centre, at the *Farmacía Arco Iris*, is the main road leading to the river, less than 2km away. **Arriving by boat**, you'll find a restaurant, a shop and some none too cheap rooms by the dock. The other **hotels**, on the main street, are hardly any better: the *Hospedaje Montañero* (②) has rough beds with mattresses that feel like you're sleeping on a ploughed field, but there is electric light.

Getting back to Palenque is no problem: there are at least seven buses a day, several in the early morning, and a regular stream of trucks and pick-ups. **Heading south**, a couple of buses a day go as far as the end of the road, which at the time of writing was Nuevo Jerusalem (3hr).

By river to Guatemala

If you hope to get **from Benemérito to Sayaxché** by boat, you'll need a good deal of money or patience. **Trading boats** are the cheapest method, but with no proper schedule you just have to ask. To reach Sayaxché in one day you'll need to leave early. Fast boats are now making the trip, stopping at the various sites en route, but they're only chartered to groups and cost at least $150, though the journey takes less than three hours.

Entering Guatemala, the immigration post is at Pipiles, on the Río de la Pasión. There's no Mexican immigration here (or at Benemérito), but if you're leaving this isn't a problem. If you're **entering Mexico**, you'll be stopped either on the road or at the post at Boca Lacantún.

Upstream from the junction with the Río de la Pasión the Usumacinta becomes the **Río Salinas**, continuing to form the border as far as the Mexican town of Flor de Cacao, also accessible by bus. Boats do travel up this far and even go up to and beyond Playa Grande in Guatemala, but this is an isolated area, with nothing like the traffic between Benemérito and Sayaxché.

Pico de Oro and onward

A side road branching off southwest 8km beyond Benemérito leads to **PICO DE ORO**, an amazingly clean, pleasant village on the south bank of the Lacantún. There are a couple of **restaurants**, the best of which is *El Marqués*, a few blocks up from the dock, but no hotels; it's possible to **camp** above the dock. At least two **buses** a day leave for Palenque, at 10am and 6pm.

Across the river the huge **Montes Azules Biosphere Reserve** stretches for miles along the opposite bank and you can hear the howler monkeys roaring. There is some boat traffic upstream from Pico de Oro to Chajul, where there's a research station, and to **IXCÁN**, almost on the Guatemalan border at the confluence of the Río Ixcán. From Ixcán, a trail leads over the mountains to Flor de Café, at the end of the road from Comitán – a five- or six-hour walk (see p.451).

TABASCO

The state of **Tabasco**, crossed by numerous slow-moving tropical rivers on their way to the Gulf, is at last making determined efforts to attract tourists. These rivers were used as trade highways by the ancient **Olmec** and **Maya** cultures and the state boasts dozens of **archeological sites**. Few of these pre-Columbian cities have been fully excavated, though **Comalcalco**, north of Villahermosa, has been expertly restored and is certainly worth a visit.

Tabasco's **coast**, alternating between estuaries and sandbars, salt marshes and lagoons, is off the beaten track to most visitors. A road runs very close to the shore, however, enabling you to reach the deserted **beaches**. As yet these have somewhat limited facilities – even the main coastal town, **Paraiso**, is a tiny place.

Much of inland Tabasco is very flat, consisting of the flood plains of a dozen or so major rivers; indeed, most of the state's borders are waterways. Enterprising tour operators are running **boat trips** along the main rivers, the Grijalva and the Usumacinta, which are the best way to see remote ruins and to glimpse the region's abundant bird life. You can also travel by river into the Petén in **Guatemala**, leaving from La Palma, near Tenosique, in the far eastern corner of the state.

In the far south of the state, around **Teapa** and Villa Luz, the Chiapas highlands make their presence known in the foothills called the **Sierra Puana**. Overlooking the vast Gulf coast plain, these hills offer a retreat from the heat and humidity of the lowlands. Waterfalls spill down from the mountains and a few small spas (*balnearios*) have developed. Village tracks provide some great **hiking trails** and, despite the proximity to Villahermosa, the capital, you can enjoy a respite from the well-travelled tourist circuit. Nearby, in the remote **Sierra Huimanguillo**, southwest of Villahermosa, the **Agua Selva Project** is a superb example of eco-tourism, aiming to bring small groups of visitors to enjoy these pristine mountains.

Villahermosa itself, the state capital and an almost unavoidable stop, has in recent years undergone an amazing transformation, with oil wealth financing the creation of spacious parks and several museums – the city at last lives up to its name. One excellent example is the **Parque Museo La Venta**, an outdoor archeological exhibition on the bank of a lagoon, which provides a glimpse of the otherwise barely accessible **Olmec** civilization.

A brief history

Little is known about the **Olmec culture**, referred to by many archeologists as the mother culture of Mesoamerica. Its legacy of the Long Count calendar, glyphic writing, a rain god deity – and probably also the concept of zero and the ball game – informed all subsequent civilizations in ancient Mexico, and the fact that it developed and flourished in the unpromising environment of the Gulf coast swamps 3200 years ago only adds to its mystery.

The Spanish Conquistador **Hernan Cortés** landed at the mouth of the Río Grijalva in 1519, and at first easily defeated the local Chontal Maya. However, the town he founded, Santa María de la Victoria, was beset by Indian attacks and then by pirates, eventually forcing a move to the present site and a change of name to Villahermosa de San Juan Bautista in 1596. For most of the colonial period Tabasco remained a relative backwater, since the Spanish found the humid, insect-ridden swamps distinctly inhospitable. **Independence** did little to improve matters as local leaders fought among themselves, and it took the **French invasion** of 1862 and Napoleon III's imposition of the unfortunate Maximilian as Emperor of Mexico to bring some form of unity, with Tabasco offering fierce resistance to this foreign intrusion.

The industrialization of the country during the dictatorship of Porfirio Díaz passed agricultural Tabasco by, and even after the **Revolution** it was still a poor state, dependent on cacao and bananas. Though **Tomás Garrido Canabal**, Tabasco's governor in the 1920s and 30s, is still respected as a reforming socialist whose implementation of laws regarding workers' rights and women's suffrage were decades ahead of the rest of the country, his period in office was also marked by intense **anticlericalism**. Priests were killed or driven out and all the churches were closed, many of them, including the cathedral in Villahermosa, torn down. The region's **oil**, discovered in the 1930s but not fully exploited until the 1970s, provided the impetus to bring Tabasco into the modern world, enabling capital to be invested in the agricultural sector and Villahermosa to be transformed into the cultural centre it is today.

Villahermosa

VILLAHERMOSA, capital of the state, is a major and virtually unavoidable road junction: sooner or later you're almost bound to pass through here on the way from central Mexico to the Yucatán or back, especially if you hope to see Palenque (see p.455). It's a

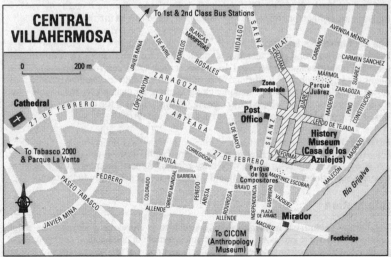

CENTRAL VILLAHERMOSA

0   200 m

Cathedral

To Tabasco 2000
& Parque La Venta

To 1st & 2nd Class Bus Stations

Zona Remodelada

Post Office

History Museum (Casa de los Azulejos)

Parque de los Compositores

Mirador

Río Grijalva

To CICOM (Anthropology Museum)

Footbridge

large and prosperous city – expensive, too – and at first impression it can seem as bad a case of urban blight as any in Mexico. But the longer you stay, the more compensations you discover – quite apart from the **Parque La Venta**, there are the attractive plazas and quiet ancient streets, impressive ultra-modern buildings, and sudden unexpected vistas of the broad sweep of the Río Grijalva. In the evening, as the traffic disperses and the city cools down, it begins to look really appealing, and strolling the pedestrianized streets around the zócalo, where everything stays open late, becomes a genuine pleasure.

Arrival and orientation

Things are pretty hectic where you arrive, as the highway thunders through the concrete outskirts and past the bus stations. The centre is a vast improvement. The two **bus stations** are pretty close to each other – second-class a ramshackle affair actually on the highway, first- (always known simply as *ADO*) an ugly but efficient modern building just off the highway on Javier Mina. You'd be well advised to buy your outward ticket on arrival, partly because it can be hard to get on to departing buses (especially late afternoon and early morning ones to Palenque or Mérida), partly to avoid having to come back here more often than necessary.

The ADO terminal
There's a *guardería* at *ADO* (7am–11pm). To **get to the centre**, take a *colectivo* taxi from outside the front of the terminal. There are also *combis* aplenty – look out for those labelled "Parque Juárez" or "Malecón". Otherwise, it's at least twenty minutes' walk to town: head up Merino or Fuentes, opposite the station, for six or seven long blocks, and then turn right at Madero, which will eventually get you to the zócalo (Plaza de Armas), past most of the cheap hotels. Venustiano Carranza, the street west of Madero, will also take you to the centre; the first part of it has three or four *larga distancica* **telephone** booths, then it becomes a pedestrianized shopping street, changes its name to Juárez, and heads straight for the zócalo.

To get **from ADO to the second-class terminal**, turn left on Mina, walk three blocks down to the highway, Blvd. Adolfo Ruíz Cortines, and cross it on the overpass – the terminal is 100m or so to your right on the left-hand side of the road.

The second-class terminal
Villahermosa's second-class terminal is much more crowded than *ADO*, with constant buses to main destinations. To **get into the centre**, cross the road and turn left, to follow the highway by the footbridge to its junction with Madero. Local **buses** and *peseros* are plentiful – you want one heading along Madero, for example, or to CICOM – but it's not easy to work out where they're going. Asking a local is the only way to find out. **Taxis** are around too, but not always as easy to find as at *ADO*.

Arriving by air
The **Aeropuerto Carlos A Rovirosa**, Carretera Villahermosa–Palenque Km 13 (☎93/12-75-55), east of the centre, is a very busy regional airport, the nearest to Palenque. *Combis* (buy a ticket from the booth) and taxis (more expensive) run to the centre.

Information

Villahermosa's **tourist information** infrastructure is developing slowly. The small booths at the airport and at *ADO* can offer only a jumble of hotel leaflets, but you might be able to get hold of some excellent booklets and maps at the main state and federal

tourist office, out at the modern **Tabasco 2000** shopping and business complex (Mon–Fri 8.30am–5pm; ☎93/16-35-06 or 16-35-07). It's not clearly signposted; look for the SEFICOT sign on the large concrete building on the right at the entrance to the complex opposite the Palacio Municipal. There have been plans afoot to install new information booths in the **Zona Remodelada** (the town's pedestrianized centre, also known as the **Zona Luz**) for some time now; if they're still not there, you should at least be able to pick up a copy of the free bimonthly *Amigo Tips* magazine.

Branches of all major **banks** are in the *Zona*, on Madero or Juárez, and at the airport, where you can easily change travellers' cheques – though for some reason changing cash is very difficult. *Banamex*, on the corner of Reforma and Madero, does *Visa* cash advances. The best place to go for **currency exchange** is the *Casa de Cambio Blahber*, 27 de Febrero 1537, on the corner of c/1 (Mon–Fri 8.30am–6.30pm, Sat 8.30am–3pm; ☎93/13-34-19). It's some distance from the centre; to get there, take any *combi* going along 27 Febrero or Paseo Tabasco from the centre, get off where they meet and go 500m south, along 27 de Febrero then left on c/1, around 30m from the landmark clock with three faces – *Reloj con tres caras* – which some *combis* have written on the windscreens. The main **post office** is in the *Zona Remodelada* at the corner of Saenz and Lerdo (Mon–Fri 8am–7.30pm).

Accommodation

There are plenty of budget hotels along Constitución and, if you look around carefully, you can find somewhere both comfortable and reasonable in the pedestrianized *Zona Remodelada*, on Madero, Lerdo de Tejada, or Reforma, close to the zócalo. In the downtown area it's possible to find rooms for very little: the very cheapest are distinctly dodgy. The most upmarket hotels are around the *Tabasco 2000* complex.

Calinda Viva Villahermosa, Paseo Tabasco 1201 at Ruíz Cortines (☎93/15-00-00). A low-rise ultra-modern hotel, across the road from Tabasco 2000. Rooms set around the pool. ⑧.

Casa de Huéspedes San Martin, Constitución 908, near the corner with Fuentes (☎93/12-99-85). Clean, bare rooms with private, basic bathrooms, round a narrow courtyard. ②.

Cencali, Paseo Tabasco and Juárez (☎93/15-19-99; fax 15-66-00). Set in luxuriant gardens on the shore of a lagoon, this has a quiet location and a large inviting pool. ⑦.

Don Carlos, Madero 422 (☎93/12-24-92; fax 12-46-22). Thoroughly modern, comfortable a/c rooms that aren't outrageously expensive. Good restaurant and bar. ⑥.

Howard Johnson, Aldama 404 (☎ and fax 93/14-46-45) Just what you'd expect from the chain; comfortable rooms with a/c and TV. Great views from the rooftop terrace. The pavement cafe right in the *Zona Remodelada* is a luxurious place to read the papers. ⑦.

Madero, Madero 301 (☎93/12-05-16). The city's best value in this range; ask for a room away from the street. Private showers and some a/c rooms. ③.

Madan, Pino Suárez 105 (☎93/12-16-50). Well-priced a/c rooms in a clean, modern hotel. There's another entrance on Madero, near the *Don Carlos*, through the dining room. ⑥.

Miraflores, Reforma 304 (☎93/12-00-22; fax 12-04-86). Excellent value on a pedestrian street in the heart of the *Zona Remodelada*. Colour TV and phone; a balcony cafe for people-watching; plus a restaurant and bar. Car rental in the lobby. ⑥.

Oviedo, Lerdo de Tejada 303, between Juárez and Madero (☎93/12-14-55). The best of the choices in this cluster, with some a/c rooms. ③.

Pakaal, Lerdo 106, corner of Constitución (☎93/14-46-48). Clean, modern hotel with immaculate bathrooms, half a block from the malecón. Small, comfortable rooms with a/c and TV. ⑥.

Palomino Palace, across from *ADO* (☎93/12-84-31). Decent hotel right by the bus station. Usually plenty of rooms available with fan, private shower and TV. Bar and restaurant. ④.

Teresita, Constitución 224 (☎93/12-34-53). Easily the nicest budget accommodation along here, quite basic but friendly. Some rooms have private bath; the best are at the back, overlooking the river. ②.

The City

Though most visitors quite rightly head straight out to the **Parque La Venta**, the centre of Villahermosa warrants some exploration. The pedestrianized **Zona Remodelada**, with some vestiges of the colonial city, is as good a place as any to start your wandering. At its northern end, opposite the Parque Juárez, at the junction of Madero and Zaragoza, the **Centro Cultural de Villahermosa** (daily 10am–9pm; free) has changing exhibitions of art, photography and costume, as well as being a venue for films and concerts. The cafe here is excellent. The zócalo, **Plaza de Armas**, with its river views, is a pleasant places to while away some time, especially in the cool of the evening. The new footbridge at the corner of the Plaza de Armas allows you to stroll over the river and watch the fireflies glow in the bushes on the bank, and has an enormous *mirador* for splendid views.

The history museum and CICOM complex

Villahermosa's small **history museum**, at the corner of 27 de Febrero and Juárez (daily 9am–6pm; $1), gives a quirky, detailed account of Tabasco's history, illustrated by such diverse objects as an early X-ray machine, archeological pieces from Comalcalco, and the printing press of *El Disidente* newspaper from 1863. The turn-of-the-century museum building, which used to be a hotel, is popularly known as the *Casa de Azulejos* – and indeed there are tiles everywhere, forming an optical illusion in the lobby, with examples of patterns from all over Europe and the Middle East. The bakery across from the entrance on Juárez sells delicious French-style pastries and baguettes.

An easy walk along the river from the *Zona Remodelada* brings you to Villahermosa's cultural centre, **CICOM** – *Centro de Investigaciónes de las Culturas Olmeca y Maya*. At a couple of places small ferry boats cross the river. The complex includes a concert hall, a beautiful theatre, a research library and a fine restaurant, along with the **Centro de Estudios y Investigación de los Belles Artes** (Tues–Sun 10am–4pm; free), which hosts art and costume displays. The highlight for most visitors is undoubtedly the **Carlos Pellicer Cámara Regional Anthropology Museum** (daily 9am–8pm; $3), with artefacts and models displayed on four levels, proceeding chronologically downwards. In addition to the Olmec and Maya displays, you can also view a reproduction of the Bonampak murals. Carlos Pellicer, a poet and anthropologist born in Villahermosa, and the driving force behind the rescue of the stone carvings from the original La Venta, is commemorated by a bronze statue outside the complex. His house, at c/Narciso Sáenz 203, in the *Zona Remodelada*, has also been turned into a museum – the **Casa Museo Carlos Pellicer** (daily 9am–8pm; free).

Parque La Venta

Soon after they were discovered by Pemex engineers draining a marsh, most of the important finds from the Olmec site of La Venta – some 120km west of the city, at the border with Veracruz state – were transferred to the **Parque La Venta** (Tues–Sun 9am–5pm, tickets sold 9am–4pm; $1, $1.70 including the *Museo de Historia Natural*). Although hardly the exact reproduction it claims to be, La Venta does give you a chance to see a superb collection of artefacts from the earliest Mexican civilization, in the beautiful jungly setting of the Parque Tomás Garrido Canabal. The most significant and famous items are, of course, the three gigantic **basalt heads**, which present such a curious puzzle with their flattened, negroid features. There's a whole series of other Olmec stone sculptures, too, along with a less mystifying **zoo** and boating lake. In their zeal to re-create an authentic jungle setting, the designers have deer, monkeys and anteaters wandering around freely, while alligators, a jaguar and others exist in miserably small pits. The mosquitoes are an authentic but unplanned touch. Also in the park, near Av. Ruíz Cortines, the excellent **Museo de Historia Natural** (daily 9am–8pm; joint ticket with the park) has displays on geography, geology, animals and plants.

Buses run to the park from Madero in the city centre ("Tabasco 2000", "Circuito 1", "Parque Linda Vista" among others) and also along the highway from the second-class bus terminal. Beyond La Venta, many of the buses continue to *Tabasco 2000*.

Yumká

Villahermosa's latest ecological attraction, **Yumká** (daily 9am–5pm; $5), is an ambitious combination of safari park and environmental studies centre, focusing on Tabasco's jungle and wetland habitats. Its formal name, *Centro de Interpretación y Convivencia con la Naturaleza*, is a bit of a mouthful, so most people simply call it Yumká, after the Chantal Maya god, a dwarf who looks after jungles. The park is huge, covering more than 100 hectares, so after a guided walking tour of the Tabasco jungle, complete with crocodiles, you board a train for a tour round enormous paddocks representing the savannahs of Africa and Asia. Elephants, rhinos, giraffes and antelopes are rarely displayed in Mexico and almost never in such spacious surroundings. After a stop at the restaurant and souvenir shop, you're taken on a boat tour of the lagoon, where, in addition to hippos and monkeys, there are good bird-watching opportunities.

Yumká is 14km from the centre of Villahermosa, on the road to the airport. The **free minibus** decorated with a colourful jungle theme departs from the car park near the restaurant *Las Blancas Maiposas* in Parque La Venta, just before the entrance to the museum on Av. Ruíz Cartines.

Eating and drinking

The number of **restaurants** in Villahermosa has grown over the last few years, and some of the new ones are truly cosmopolitan. Most of the better hotels have improved their own dining rooms and, if you're staying near *Tabasco 2000*, your hotel restaurant will be among the best in the city. One drawback of the oil boom is that there aren't any really budget places: even the *taco* stands on Madero are more expensive than usual.

Both **bus stations** have plenty of food joints nearby: inside the second-class there are juice and coffee bars, a good bakery and a less good restaurant; across the street from *ADO* there's a row of inexpensive places. The *Bar Neptuno*, half a block from *ADO* down Fuentes, is great to while away some time if you're waiting for a bus. The sign on the door says "Turistico" but the atmosphere is distinctly Mexican, with live music and slow service. Women are admitted though it's probably best not to go alone. As ever, the **market** is good for fruit, bread and cheap *tacos*: you'll find it several blocks east of the *Zona Remodelada*, at Pino Suárez and Zozoya. *Aquarius*, Zaragoza 513, behind the Parque Juárez, is an excellent **vegetarian restaurant** and **health food shop**, with delicious fresh wholemeal sandwiches and daily specials.

At the northern end of the *Zona,* which at night really lives up to its **Zona Luz** soubriquet, the Parque Juárez is lively in the evenings as crowds swirl around watching the street entertainers. The pedestrian area fills with window-shoppers enjoying frozen yoghurts or eating out at open-fronted restaurants or one of the many *coctelerias*; a cheap alternative is the **torta and taco bar** on Reforma, opposite the *Hotel Miraflores*. The best place here for an inexpensive, filling meal is *Chilangos Snack Bar*, where tables spill out into the street onto the little plaza known as the Parque de los Compositores, near the fountain dedicated to Vicente Guerrero, between the west side of the *Zona Luz* and the Plaza de Armas. Also worth trying are the *Paris*, Reforma 410, and the *Café Casino* on Pino Suárez.

Beyond here, at the junction of Paseo Tabasco and the malecón, there are several **taco restaurants**, some of them quite fancy. More restaurants line Paseo Tabasco at

MOVING ON FROM VILLAHERMOSA

Villahermosa being the state capital, you should have no problems getting an **onward bus**. From the first-class station there are handy *ADO* (☎93/12-89-00) departures **to Palenque**, the most popular at 8am, another at 2pm and the last at 6.30pm – and there are also the more luxurious *Plus* services. Between them, *ADO* and *Cristóbal Colón* (☎93/14-36-45) operate services to all the main destinations: Tuxtla, Veracruz, Tenosique, México, Mérida, Cancún, Chetumal, Campeche, Playa del Carmen, San Cristóbal, Oaxaca, the US border and Pacific coast. You can also easily get to Palenque from the second-class terminal, from where there are constant departures to all the same destinations, plus Comalcalco, Paraiso and Frontera.

intervals all the way up to the junction with Mina. Head up this way if you want to sample the best of *comida Tabasqueña* at the *Guaraguao*, on the corner of 27 de Febrero and Javier Mina (☎93/12-56-25). Specialities from the coasts and rivers of Tabasco include *pejelargarto*, a type of alligator, and great seafood. It closes early, though, about 8.30 or 9pm.

Listings

Airlines *Aeroméxico* (CICOM: ☎93/12-43-89; airport: ☎93/12-15-28); *Aviacsa* (airport: ☎93/14-47-55); *Litoral* (airport: ☎93/14-36-14); *Mexicana* (*Inter*), D'Atocha Mall, in *Tabasco 2000* (☎93/16-31-32; airport: ☎93/14-46-95). Check with a travel agent for details of charter airlines.

Car rental At the airport and in all the big hotels. Try *Budget* (☎93/14-37-90); *Dollar* (☎93/16-00-80); *Hertz* (☎93/12-11-11); *National* (☎93/12-03-93); or *Usumacinta* (☎93/15-19-97).

Travel agents Another boom industry, with dozens in the *Zona* and the bigger hotels, all of them arranging flights and trips to Palenque. Downtown, *Viajes Villahermosa*, 27 de Febrero 207 (☎93/12-54-56; fax 14-37-21), is one of the best; at *Tabasco 2000* try *Viajes Tabasco*, Galerias Tabasco (☎93/16-40-88; fax 16-40-90), which runs river trips up the Usumacinta.

Comalcalco and the coast

The journey from Villahermosa along **the coast**, west to Veracruz or east to Campeche, is in many ways extraordinarily beautiful: the road hugs the shore so closely that in some places it's been washed away by storms, and it's never hard to find deserted beaches and lagoons. New bridges have replaced all but one of the ferries that used to cross the broad river mouths; the only one left is an ageing vessel carrying vehicles and passengers between Zacatal and **Ciudad del Carmen**, at the western end of the huge Laguna de Terminos.

Undeniably attractive as the coastal route is, almost no tourists travel it, preferring the inland route to the Yucatán in order to visit Palenque en route. Even if this is your intention, you'll be well rewarded by spending a day north of Villahermosa, visiting **Comalcalco** in the morning and perhaps spending the afternoon on one of the beaches near **Paraiso**.

Comalcalco

The Classic period site of **COMALCALCO** (daily 8am–5pm; $4.50) is an easy and worthwhile trip from Villahermosa and you can be fairly sure of having the carefully tended ruins virtually to yourself. Comalcalco, the westernmost Maya site, was occupied around the same time as Palenque, with which it shares some features, and may even have been ruled by some of the same kings.

The area's lack of building stone forced the Chontal Maya to adopt a distinctive, almost unique, form of construction – kiln-fired brick (the site's name means "house of bricks" in Náuhatl). As if the bricks themselves were not sufficient to mark this site as different, the builders added mystery to technology: each brick was stamped with a geometric or representational design before firing and the design was deliberately placed facing inwards, so that it could not be seen in the finished building.

Visiting the site

There's a small **museum** at the site, and a restaurant. Take water with you, though, since humidity is extremely high. If you're going to venture into the long grass or bushes, insect repellent is a must. Though there are dozens of structures, only around ten or so of the larger buildings have been subjected to any restoration. The first one you come to is the main structure of the **North Plaza Cluster**: Temple I, a tiered pyramid with a massive central stairway. Originally the whole building (along with all of the structures here) would have been covered with stucco, sculpted into masks and reliefs of rulers and deities, and brightly painted. Now only a few of these features are left, the exposed ones protected from further erosion by thatched shelters, while some are deliberately left buried.

Opposite Temple I is the **Great Acropolis**: more mounds, mainly grass-covered, though there's a fine stucco mask of Kinich Ahau, the Maya sun god. Due to the fragile nature of the brick you're not allowed to climb most of the temples, but if you walk to the far end of the complex you'll come to **El Palacio**, where you can climb the mound and get a close view of the brickwork. There's a series of small arches here, faintly reminiscent of English Victorian railway architecture. You'll also get a good overview of the whole site, including many other mounds in the surrounding forest and farmland. **Cacao**, used as money by the Maya, is grown in the area, and you'll pass cacao bushes on the way in, their huge green bean pods sprouting straight from the trunk.

Practicalities

The **bus from Villahermosa** takes an hour and a quarter: *ADO* has several departures a day, and *Transportes Somellera* runs a service every thirty minutes from the second-class station. Both bus stations in Comalcalco are on Gregorio Méndez; walk the 150m back to the highway and catch a *combi* heading north (left) towards Paraiso. The ruins are on the right (signposted) after about five minutes. Some *combis* go all the way there; otherwise, the site is fifteen minutes' walk up the track, past some houses and a cacao plantation. If you get stuck in Comalcalco there are a few **hotels** near the bus stations – the *San Agustín* (②) is the closest.

Paraiso and the coast west

To cool off after sweating it out at the ruins, catch one of the frequent buses passing the Comalcalco turn-off to **PARAISO**, a sleepy place thirty minutes away on the banks of the Río Seco. Everything you need is close to the pleasant, modern zócalo. Paraiso's *ADO* **bus station**, at the corner of Juárez and 2 de Abril, is just two blocks south of the zócalo. The second-class, with far more departures, is less than fifteen minutes' walk north of the centre and well served by *combis*. If you're walking from the second-class to the centre, head south (left) and aim for the cathedral tower. Of the **hotels**, *Sabina*, on the zócalo (☎933/3-00-16; ④), is the least expensive, but it's not particularly good value and only the a/c rooms have hot water. You're better off trying the *Hotel Hidalgo* (☎933/3-00-07; ⑤) on Degollado 206, at the corner of 2 de Abril, which has good, clean rooms with a fan, private bathrooms with hot and cold water, and drinking water. There are plenty of juice bars in and around the zócalo and a couple of decent, moderately priced **restaurants**: *La Galeria* serves inexpensive *comedores*, while *La Señorial* is a little more upmarket. The **post office** is north of the zócalo, along Méndez, and there's a **travel agency**, *Viajes Estupenda*, on Juárez, four blocks south of the zócalo across the river bridge. The **market** is five blocks north, along 5 de Mayo.

The beaches

The nearest Gulf coast beach, **Playa Limon**, is a twenty-minute *combi* ride north of Paraiso. East and west are more *playas* with thatched shelters and tiny seafood restaurants but, frankly, the beaches are a bit of a disappointment. The sand is grey-brown and, though generally clean, you've always got the oil refinery in sight to the east. There are no hotels along this stretch, but plenty of spaces for camping – though you'll be attacked by swarms of mosquitoes and sandflies. Heading farther **west** along the coast, you pass a few more tiny, rustic "resorts", some of them exhibiting signs of desolate poverty. **Sánchez Magallanes** is the only town in the next hundred kilometres but it's hardly worth staying here: the beaches aren't that clean, and there's only one hotel, the *Casa de Huéspedes Delia* (②), along with lots of dilapidated seafood restaurants. From here the road heads away from the coast towards La Venta, forty minutes away.

La Venta

The small town of **LA VENTA**, on the border between Tabasco and Veracruz, would be of little interest were it not for the **archeological site** (daily 10am–4.30pm; $4.50, free on Sun) where the huge Olmec heads displayed in Villahermosa were discovered. In the **museum** at the entrance, models show where the site was located, in a swamp surrounded by rivers, while glass cases are filled with unlabelled bits of pottery. Information panels on the wall give a good explanation of Olmec culture and history. The site itself has a few weathered *stelae* or monuments, but the highlight is the huge grass-covered mound, about 30m high, clearly a pyramid. The climb up is worth the effort for the views and the breeze. Paths below take you through the jungle; fascinating for plants and butterflies but haunted by ferocious mosquitoes.

La Venta is served by a steady stream of **buses** to Villahermosa and Coatzalcoalcos, so there's no need **to stay**; the *Hotel del Sol* (③) on the corner of the small plaza is a friendly, pleasant option if you get stuck.

Frontera and the coast road east

East of Paraiso the road crosses several lagoons and rivers before reaching the junction with Hwy-180. Dirt roads head off left to numerous palm-shaded *playas*, each about 5 or 6km from the highway. If you're travelling light you could easily camp at any of these and get back to the main road in the morning. About 25km beyond Paraiso the bus will drop you in **FRONTERA**, a pleasant if uninspiring working town and port, little changed since Graham Greene landed here in 1938:

> *Shark fins glided like periscopes at the mouth of the Grijalva River . . . three or four aerials stuck up into the blazing sky from among the banana groves and the palm-leaf huts; it was like Africa seeing itself in a mirror across the Atlantic. Little islands of lily plants came floating down from the interior, and the carcasses of old stranded steamers held up the banks. And then round a bend in the river Frontera . . . the Presidencia and a big warehouse and a white blanched street running off between wooden shacks.*

The scene on the waterfront would be familiar to Greene but there's now a huge bridge over the Grijalva and the plaza, the Parque Quintin Arauz, has been tastefully modernized. **Arriving** by second-class bus, turn left out of the bus station and walk two blocks along Madero to get to the Parque or, from the first-class bus station, left along Zaragoza, then right, and walk three blocks down Madero from the other direction. Everything you'll need is around the plaza. For **rooms**, *Hotel San Agustín*, at the corner of Pino Suárez and Juárez 100 (☎2-07-85; ⑤), on the opposite side of the plaza to Madero, has some a/c; *Hotel Maya del Grijalva* (☎2-00-58; ③–⑤), also on the plaza on the corner of Madero and callejón Nte., is slightly more upmarket. For a tasty shrimp **dinner** or a good-value *comida corrida* try *El Conquistador*, in an old colonial building, Juárez 8. Right by the wharf is a restaurant where the dock workers have their coffee served in tin mugs; as a visitor you'll get the chipped china cup and saucer but the coffee's great. **Bars** in Frontera can exude a somewhat cosmopolitan atmosphere when the crew from a foreign ship is in port.

Thirteen kilometres away at the mouth of the river, on the eastern bank, is the run-down fishing settlement of **EL BOSQUE**. The beach is great for a lone, windswept walk, but is mainly left to the pelicans, except for on Sundays when it gets busy with holidaying Mexicans. The dirt road out here goes through lagoons and protected swamps, inhabited by a multitude of wildlife. *Colectivos* from Frontera are supposed to operate every ten minutes between 7am and 5pm but they aren't reliable. If you get stranded, start to walk back along the dirt road. The farther you walk, the more you improve your chances of catching a ride with someone heading back into town.

Buses leave Frontera for Villahermosa or Ciudad del Carmen every one or two hours during daylight hours and four buses daily go to Veracruz.

The Sierra Huimanguillo and the Agua Selva Project

More than 100km southwest of Villahermosa, between the borders of Veracruz and Chiapas, a narrow triangle of Tabasco thrusts into the mountains. Known as the **Sierra Huimanguillo**, from the town in the lowlands just to the north, this little-visited corner of the state is the focus of the **Agua Selva Ecotourism Project**. Designed to bring the benefits of small-scale tourism to the *ejidos* of the area by building *cabañas* and *albergues* in the villages, the project aims to bring economic benefits without sacrificing the abundant natural attractions. The mountains here are not that high, only up to 1000m, but they are rugged, and to appreciate them at their best you have to hike; not only to caves, canyons and waterfalls, but also to the **Zoque** ruins of Malpasito, with their astonishing **petroglyphs**. So far, this is the only site easily accessible by public transport from Huimanguillo, but check with the tourist office in Villahermosa (see p.467) before setting out; things are changing here all the time and new *albergues* are planned.

Huimanguillo to Malpasito

Visiting the Aqua Selva Project, you'll have to pass through **HUIMANGUILLO**, a mid-sized town 75km west of Villahermosa. Buses leave Villahermosa frequently during the day; if there isn't a direct one, go second-class to **Cárdenas** and change there. *ADO* buses stop right in the centre, on Escobar, half a block south of the plaza. Second-class buses arrive at the terminal on Gutiérrez, near the market, five blocks west along Libertad from the town centre. The bus for Malpasito leaves at 1pm (2hr 30min).

In the centre of town, the *Hotel del Carmen* on Morelos 39, two blocks south of the plaza (☎ and fax 937/5-09-15; ④), offers **accommodation** and **information**, with large well-furnished rooms, all with private bath. Downstairs the *Cafetería Orquidias* serves good Mexican food and you can eat surrounded by photographs of the mountains and waterfalls in the *sierra*. The owner, George Pagole del Valle, a leading light in the Aqua Selva project, will be able to supply information and may even give you a lift if he's heading to Malpasito. There are a couple of other hotels in town: the *Guyucan*, Allende 124 (☎937/5-05-77; ⑤), and the very basic *Maya*, Allende 34 (no phone; ①).

Malpasito

Beyond Huimanguillo the road to Malpasito heads south, following the valley of the **Río Grijalva** (here called the Mezcalapa) for 60km, crossing the Chiapas at one point, before heading west onto a dirt road for 15km to reach the *ejido*.

By now you can see the peaks, with the great jungle-covered plateau of El Mono Pelón (the bald monkey) dominating the skyline. This is the highest point in Tabasco and the sheer sides look impossible to climb. In **MALPASITO** you can stay right by the river, in the simple, three-room *Albergue Ecológico* (②) managed by the Peréz Rincón family; you can eat with them or at the table by the river. Drinking and cooking water is piped in from a spring, pure and fresh, but you bathe in the river. Higher up, and nearer the waterfalls, the plusher *Albergue La Pava* (⑦, including meals) consists of large, oval thatched *cabañas* with bamboo sides, some with two storeys, giving you a bird's-eye view into the surrounding forest. This is an utterly beautiful, tranquil place, perfect for enjoying the abundant wildlife. The dirt road from Malpasito comes to within half a kilometre of the *cabañas*, then it's a 45-minute walk over a suspension bridge and along the side of a gorge between moss-covered boulders. The **bus to Huimanguillo** departs at 5am.

The Zoque ruins of Malpasito

A walk of just over 1km from the *albergue* in Malpasito brings you to the Postclassic **Zoque** ruins of the same name, overlooked by jagged, jungle-covered mountains and reminiscent of Palenque (see p.455). Though the ruins look similar, the Zoque were not a Maya group, and little is known about them today. On the way in you pass terraces and grass-covered mounds, eventually leading to the unusual **ball-court**. At the top of the stone terraces forming the south side of the court a flight of steps leads down to a narrow room, with stone benches lining either side. Beyond this, and separate from the chamber, is a square pit more than 2m deep and 1.5m square. This room may have been used by the ball players, or at least one team, to effect a spectacular entrance as they emerged on to the top of the ball-court. Beyond the ball-courts a grass-covered plaza leads to two flights of wide steps with another small plaza at the top, with stunning views of mountains all around.

Perhaps the most amazing feature of this site are the **petroglyphs**. More than three hundred have been discovered so far: animals, birds, houses and presumably religious symbols etched into the rock. One large boulder has the most enigmatic of all: flat-topped triangles surmounted by a square or rectangle, and shown above what look like ladders or steps. Stylized houses or launching platforms for the chariots of the gods? The trail leads on to a clear pool beneath a 12m waterfall; too good to miss if the hike around the ruins has left you hot and dirty. More trails lead up into the mountains; one relatively easy one leads to the base of La Pava, on almost perpendicular pillars of rock, the top of which is said to resemble the head of a turkey.

Francisco J Mujica and the Cascada Velo de Novia

Another *ejido* in the Agua Selva Project, **Francisco J Mujica**, 18km northeast of Malpasito, has simple accommodation at the *Cabaña Raizes Zoque* (③). At the moment there's no public transport (though this could change soon), but it's connected by dirt road to Hwy-187 south from Huimanguillo and you could get directions there or in Malpasito. When you arrive ask for Antonio Dominquez de Dominquez.

The hills around here are superb for walking and scrambling around canyons, but to venture to the most scenic parts you'll need a guide – easily arranged by the *ejido*. An hour-long hike from Mujica takes you over several rivers, beyond the *milpas*, to **Cascada Velo de Novia** (Bridal Veil Falls) and to the edge of an enormous canyon.

The hike entails descending about 300m down an extremely steep slope – the guide will have a rope, but you'll still need to clutch at tree roots for support – then walking along a narrow rock ledge at the side of the river to get beneath the thundering cascade. Below the falls the river winds between huge boulders before plunging over the edge of a sheer-sided, semicircular **gorge**. The only way out is to clamber up the way you came in. Few outsiders have ever been here and you'll also have a chance to explore the hills, which are full of caves, many containing petroglyphs.

Teapa and the southern hills

An hour's bus ride through banana country to the south of Villahermosa, the small, friendly town of **TEAPA** is a lovely base for the spas and caves nearby. *Cristóbal Colón* **buses** leave Villahermosa for Tuxtla every couple of hours, calling at Teapa, though buses back are *de paso* and it may be difficult to get a seat. Though some second-class buses stop at the terminal on Méndez, right in the centre, most pull in at the **market** (plenty of good fruit stalls) near the edge of town. To get to the centre, walk a couple of blocks down the hill and turn left at the green clock onto Méndez, which takes you past the hotels and onto the plaza.

Teapa's **hotels** are good value: try the *Casa de Huéspedes-Miye* (②), a clean, family-run place with private showers and hot water, with rooms round a tiny plant-filled court-yard, or the very comfortable *Jardín* (③), both on Méndez. At the top of the street is the *Plaza Independencia* (⑤), facing the park from which it takes its name – more expensive than the other two and not really worth the extra.

There's **swimming** in the Río Teapa here but it's better at the *balneario* on the Río Puyacatengo, a few kilometres east (walk or take the bus for Tacotalpa). Six kilometres west of Teapa, almost on the Chiapas border, is the **El Azufre Spa**, where for a small fee you can bathe in clear pools or take the waters in the sulphur pool. **Camping** is free and there's a small restaurant. Again you can get here on foot, or catch a second-class bus towards Pichucalco. *Colectivos* run from the plaza in Teapa to the spectacular **Grutas de Coconá** (daily 8am–4pm; $1). Eight chambers are open to tourists, and some for spelunking only. A stroll through the caves takes about 45 minutes; in one chamber there's a supposedly miraculous representation of the face of Christ, carved by nature into the rock. You could also walk (45min) to the caves from Teapa; from Méndez, head for the Pemex station and turn right, following the sign. When you get near the forested hills, the road divides; head left over the railway track.

The Sierra Puana: Tapijulapa and Oxolotán

East from Teapa, you can get farther away from the humidity of the lowlands by taking day trips up the valley of the Río Oxolotán to Tabasco's "hill country". This is an extraordinarily picturesque area, with unspoilt colonial towns set in beautiful wooded valleys, and a turquoise river laden with sulphur cascading over terraced cliff. You'll need to get a fairly early start to make the most of the day. The 6.30am bus to **Tacotalpa** from the second-class station on Méndez in Teapa (20min) connects with one to **TAPIJULAPA**, the main settlement (45min), in time to have breakfast in the *Restaurant La Indomable*, overlooking the shady plaza. The village is tiny, with narrow cobbled streets, red-tiled roofs, and no accommodation; turn right at the end of the main street, Av. López Portillo, where steps lead down to the Río Oxolotán. Here you'll find boats to take you upstream to visit the **Parque Natural Villa Luz**, with its spa pools, rivers, cascades and caves, all for free.

In the park, signed trails lead to caves, but the outstanding feature – not least for its powerful aroma – is the river, which owes its colour to dissolved minerals, especially sulphur. The river exits from a cave and meanders for 1km or so until it reaches the cliff marking the valley of the Río Oxolotán. Here it breaks up into dozens of cascades and semicircular pools. Thousands of butterflies settle on the riverbanks, taking nourishment from dissolved minerals, and jungle trees and creepers grow wherever they find a foothold: a truly primeval sight. The **caves** are not really open to the public, but you can peer into their precipitous entrances; in Maya cosmology the openings are believed to lead to the Underworld (*Xibalba*) and abode of the Lords of Death. Beyond the caves are a couple of open-air **swimming pools** said to have therapeutic properties.

Trucks and *combis* frequently make the trip (25min) from Tapijulapa to **OXOLOTÁN**. Here the ruins of a seventeenth-century Franciscan monastery host performances by the *Teatro Campesino y Indigena* (The Peasant and Indian Theatre), a company that has taken part in cultural festivals throughout Mexico and abroad. If you're in the area when a performance is scheduled it's worth making an effort to go. **To get there from Tapijulapa**, climb the hill to the church, then descend to the road beyond, where there's a bus stop. The last bus back leaves at 6pm, but you're probably better off catching the 3pm bus if you're heading to Teapa.

East to the Usumacinta and Guatemala

Heading east from Villahermosa, Hwy-186 cuts across a salient of northern Chiapas before swinging north into **Campeche** to Francisco Escárcega, then east again as the only road across the base of the Yucatán peninsula to Chetumal. At Catazajá, in Chiapas, 110km from Villahermosa, is the junction for **Palenque** (see p.455). If you've been there and want to see **Tikal** in Guatemala's Petén, the most direct route is via **Tenosique** and La Palma, then by boat up the Río San Pedro to El Naranjo. Several travel agencies in Palenque run minibuses to La Palma but it's very easy to do it yourself, though the journey can be uncomfortable either way and always involves at least one very early start.

Coming from either Palenque or Villahermosa, you'll pass through the dull town of **EMILIANO ZAPATA**, hopefully only to change buses. The **bus stations** are in the same building on the edge of the town and there are plenty of first- and second-class services to Villahermosa and Tenosique, tailing off rapidly in the evening. If you do get stuck, try the *Hotel Ramos* (☎934/3-07-44; ④), opposite the bus station, which is at least comfortable and saves you going into town. It also has the only proper **travel agent** for a long way: *Creatur* (☎934/3-07-99; fax 3-01-22).

Tenosique

The Río Usumacinta is crossed by the road and railway at Boca del Cerro, a few kilometres from **TENOSIQUE**, where the now placid river leaves some pretty impressive hills. The **bus and train stations** are close to the highway, just out of town. Inexpensive *colectivos* run frequently to the centre; get off when you see a large church on the right of the main street, c/26 (also known as Pino Suárez). If you have **to stay**, the *Azulejos* (②), opposite the church, has friendly staff; slightly better is the *Rome* (☎934/2-01-51; ③), on the corner of calles 28 and 2.

Once you've exhausted what limited sightseeing Tenosique has to offer (such as visiting the house where Pino Suárez was born and admiring his bust and monument), you'll want to head for the zócalo and calles 26 and 28, the main areas for shopping and **eating**. The juice bar on the corner of the plaza prepares good *licuados*; there's also a coffee shop just past the zócalo on c/28. *La Palapa* restaurant overlooks the broad river, where the boat traffic heads constantly back and forth.

If you're going to Guatemala you'd be wise to stock up on provisions: there's a good **bakery** opposite the *Hotel Roma* and fruit stalls everywhere. The banks in Tenosique aren't interested in changing **money**; for **Guatemalan quetzales** ask around in the shops, where you should find someone who will give better rates than the boatmen. **Moving on**, there are plenty of bus services to Villahermosa during the day, a first-class service to México at 5pm and a 6pm bus to Escárcega and points east.

Pomoná and Piedras Negras

The valley of the Río Usumacinta upstream from Tenosique abounds with archeological sites, few of them regularly visited by tourists. **POMONÁ** is only about 15km west of Tenosique by river but twice that distance by road. The restored structures date from the Late Classic period; the site's largest building is a stepped pyramid with six levels and there are several smaller ones, too, with others still being cleared, as well as an interesting little free museum. **Getting there** is not easy, however, and a visit is really only for the dedicated; if you can't go by boat, the entrance is 30km from Tenosique on the road to Zapata, then 4km down a signed track.

A much more exciting prospect is a visit to the ruins of **PIEDRAS NEGRAS**, over the border in Guatemala. The site is difficult to reach from either direction, entailing a rough river trip. However, the Tabasco state tourist office is making an effort to open up this remote part of the Usumacinta valley. From Tenosique, a good dirt road leads south, through hills and jungle, to the small town of **NIÑOS HÉROES**, where you can camp, continuing on to **Madero del Río** to board the boat for the site. It's easier this way than going downstream from Yaxchilán (and it's also possible to continue upstream) but you still get to experience the forest and river wilderness. For prices and **information**, contact the tourist office in Villahermosa (see p.467) or *Trek Mexico*, at Havre 67-305, Colonia Juárez, CP 06600, México (☎91/525-68-13).

La Palma and the Río San Pedro to Guatemala

Buses for **LA PALMA** leave Tenosique from by the mercado at the corner of c/51 and c/50, six blocks from the main street (hourly 4am–5pm). They head due east through flat farming and ranching country and after an hour reach the Río San Pedro.

There's a choice of two speeds (and prices) from here for the **boat trip to El Naranjo**: fast (1hr 30min) or slow (4hr 30min). The usual departure time is 8am, returning at 1pm from El Naranjo: with a large enough group you can charter your own boat. There are some basic **rooms** at La Palma; ask at *Restaurant Parador Turistico*, by the dock.

Border formalities are hardly rigorous, though your luggage will probably be searched on leaving Mexico, at El Pedregal, about halfway through the journey, and possibly again by the Guatemalan army on arrival at **EL NARANJO**. It's generally dark when you arrive and your passport will be stamped and a fee (usually $5) demanded. There's a small, basic hotel and restaurant, the *Quetzal* (②), overlooking the river in El Naranjo, and 1km upstream from the ferry in the town proper, the *Posada San Pedro* has rustic bungalows (⑤); alternatively, no one will mind if you **camp**. Just up from the riverbank are some large, overgrown **ruins** with the bigger pyramids surmounted by machine gun posts. At least four daily **buses** leave El Naranjo for **Flores** (4hr 30min); catch the 6am departure and you can reach Tikal the same day.

The ruins of Reforma

If you get a chance to **continue downstream** from La Palma, take it: there are ruins on almost every bend. The rivers of Tabasco were highways for the Maya and the sheer number of mounds and pyramids lining their banks present a graphic image of the extent and duration of Maya civilization. There's a rail and road crossing at **San Pedro**, about 40km downstream; just upstream of these modern bridges a curiously straight line of rapids may indicate the remains of a **Maya bridge**. Farther down, at **REFORMA**, the river spills over a series of beautiful but unnavigable **cascades**. There's a picnic site and the remains of a restaurant but the site is hard to reach unless you charter a boat of your own. Set back from the bank, the **ruins of Reforma** cover a huge site, with half a dozen very tall pyramids. Restoration work is only just beginning, however, so only a couple of them are cleared. Some of the *stelae* and altars found here can be seen in the **museum** at **BALANCAN**, 20km west on the Usumacinta. The town is well off the tourist track but it's accessible by bus from Villahermosa (2hr). There are a couple of small **hotels**, the *Delicias* and the *Usumacinta* (both ②). Ask around in the town hall and the museum and you may meet a boatman heading upstream; this sleepy part of Mexico would welcome more visitors.

fiestas

The states of Chiapas and Tabasco are extremely rich in festivities. Local tourist offices should have more information on what's happening in your vicinity.

January

1st NEW YEAR'S DAY **San Andres Chamula** (Chiapas) and **San Juan Chamula** (Chis.), both near San Cristóbal, have civil ceremonies to install a new government for the year.

19th At **Tenosique** (Chis.) the *El Pochó* dancers perform, dressed as jaguars and men to represent the struggle of good and evil. The celebration concludes on SHROVE TUESDAY with the burning of an effigy of El Pochó, god of evil.

20 DÍA DE SAN SEBASTIAN sees a lot of activity. In **Chiapa de Corzo** (Chis.) a large fiesta with traditional dances lasts several days, with a re-enactment on the 21st of a naval battle on the Río Grijalva. Big too in **Zinacantán** (Chis.), near San Cristóbal.

February

2nd DÍA DE LA CANDELARIA. Colourful Indian celebrations at **Ocosingo** (Chis.)

11th Religious fiesta in **Comitán** (Chis.).

27th In **Villahermosa** (Tabasco), a fiesta commemorates the anniversary of a battle against the French.

CARNIVAL (the week before Lent – variable Feb–March) is at its most frenzied in the big cities – especially **Villahermosa** (Tab.) – but is also celebrated in hundreds of villages throughout the area. **San Juan Chamula** (Chis.) has a big fiesta.

March

1st Anniversary of the foundation of **Chiapa de Corzo** (Chis.) celebrated.

HOLY WEEK is widely observed – particularly big ceremonies in **San Cristóbal de las Casas**. **Ciudad Hidalgo** (Chis.), at the border near Tapachula, has a major week-long market.

April

1st–7th A *feria* in **San Cristóbal de las Casas** (Chis.) celebrates the town's foundation. A Spring Fair is generally held here later in the month.

In the second half of the month **Villahermosa** (Tab.) hosts its annual *feria*, with agricultural and industrial exhibits and the election of the queen of the flowers.

29th DÍA DE SAN PEDRO celebrated in several villages around San Cristóbal, including **Amatenango del Valle** and **Zinacantán**.

May

3rd DÍA DE LA SANTA CRUZ celebrated in **San Juan Chamula** (Chis.) and in **Teapa** (Tab.), between Villahermosa and San Cristóbal.

8th DÍA DE SAN MIGUEL. Processions and traditional dances in **Mitontic** (Chis.), near San Cristóbal.

15th DÍA DE SAN ISIDRO sees peasant celebrations everywhere – famous and picturesque fiestas in **Huistán** (Chis.), near San Cristóbal.

Also there's a four-day nautical marathon (variable dates) **from Tenosique to Villahermosa** (Tab.), when crafts from all over the country race down 600km of the Usumacinta.

June

13th DÍA DE SAN ANTONIO celebrated in **Zimojovel** (Chis.), near San Cristóbal, and **Cárdenas** (Tab.), west of Villahermosa.

24th DÍA DE SAN JUAN is the culmination of several days' celebration in **San Juan Chamula** (Chis.).

July

7th Beautiful religious ceremony in **Comitán** (Chis.), with candlelit processions to and around the church.

20th Heavily Indian festivities in **Las Margaritas** (Chis.), near Comitán.

25th DÍA DE SANTIAGO provokes widespread celebration – especially in **San Cristóbal de las Casas** (Chis.), where they begin a good week earlier (17th is Día de San Cristóbal), and in nearby villages such as **Tenejapa** and **Amatenango del Valle**.

August

6th Images from the churches of neighbouring villages are brought in procession to **Mitontic** (Chis.), for religious ceremonies there.

10th FIESTA DE SAN LORENZO in **Zinacantán** (Chis.), with much music and dancing.

22nd–29th *Feria* in **Tapachula** (Chis.).

24th Fiestas in **Venustiano Carranza** (Chis.), south of San Cristóbal.

30th DÍA DE SANTA ROSA celebrated in **San Juan Chamula** (Chis.).

September

14th–16th Throughout Chiapas, celebration of the annexation of the state to Mexico, followed by Independence celebrations everywhere.

29th DÍA DE SAN MIGUEL is celebrated in **Huistán** (Chis.).

October

On the first Sunday in October, the DÍA DE LA VIRGEN DEL ROSARIO is celebrated in **San Juan Chamula** and **Zinacantán** (Chis.).

3rd DÍA DE SAN FRANCISCO in **Amatenango del Valle** (Chis.).

November

2nd DAY OF THE DEAD is respected everywhere, with particularly strong traditions in **Chiapa de Corzo** (Chis.).

29th DÍA DE SAN ANDRES celebrated in **San Andres Chamula** (Chis.).

December

12th DÍA DE LA VIRGEN DE GUADALUPE is an important one throughout Mexico. There are particularly good fiestas in **Tuxtla Gutiérrez** and **San Cristóbal de las Casas** (Chis.), and the following day another in nearby **Amatenango del Valle** (Chis.).

17th–22nd **Pijijiapan** (Chis.), on the road to Tapachula, holds a *feria* and cheese expo.

travel details

Buses

Palenque to: Campeche (3 daily; 5hr); Mérida (3 daily; 8hr); San Cristóbal (9 daily; 5hr–6hr 30min); Tuxtla Gutiérrez (hourly; 8hr); Villahermosa (8 daily; 2hr 30min).

San Cristóbal to: Ciudad Cuauhtémoc, for Guatemala (8 daily; 3hr); Comitán, for Lagos de Montebello or the Guatemalan border (at least hourly; 2hr); México (4 daily; 24hr); Palenque (9 daily; 5hr–6hr 30min); Tapachula (2 daily; 9hr); Tuxtla Gutiérrez (constantly; 2hr); Villahermosa (6 daily; 9hr).

Tapachula to: Arriaga (9 daily; 3hr); México (10 daily; 18hr); Oaxaca (1 daily; 12hr); San Cristóbal (2 daily; 9hr); Tuxtla Gutiérrez (15 daily; 7hr); Veracruz (1 daily; 14hr); Villahermosa (2 daily; 13hr).

Tuxtla Gutiérrez to: Ciudad Cuauhtémoc, for Guatemala (2 daily; 4hr); Comitán, for Lagos de Montebello or the Guatemalan border (hourly; 3hr 30min); México (at least 9 daily; 18hr); Palenque (hourly; 8hr); San Cristóbal (constantly; 2hr); Tapachula (15 daily; 7hr); Tonalá (hourly; 3hr 30min); Villahermosa (9 daily; 7hr).

Villahermosa to: Campeche (12 daily; 8hr); Palenque (8 daily; 2hr 30min); San Cristóbal (6 daily; 9hr); Tapachula (2 daily; 13hr); Tuxtla Gutiérrez (9 daily; 7hr); Veracruz (10 daily; 7hr).

Trains

At the time of writing all train services in this area had been suspended: in any case they are a slow and uncomfortable alternative to the bus.

Planes

Villahermosa has several daily flights to the capital, but there are also daily direct services from Tuxtla Gutiérrez, Ciudad del Carmen, Coatzacoalcos and Tapachula. Several local companies operate light planes – from Palenque or San Cristóbal to Yaxchilán or Bonampak, for example.

CHAPTER TEN

THE YUCATÁN

B oth physically and historically, the three states that comprise the **Yucatán peninsula** – Campeche, Yucatán and Quintana Roo – are distinct from the rest of Mexico. The interminably flat, low-lying plain is one of the hottest and most tropical-feeling areas of the country, but in fact it lies farther north than you might imagine – Mérida is actually north of México. Until the 1960s, when proper road and train links were completed, the Yucatán lived out of step with the rest of Mexico – there was almost as much contact with Europe and the US as with the centre. Now tourism has made major inroads, especially in the north around the great **Maya sites** and on the route from **Mérida** to the "super-resort" of **Cancún**, and new investment has brought it closer to the heart of things. But a unique character remains, and in the south, where townships are sparsely scattered in thick, jungly forest, there's still a distinct pioneering feel.

The modern boom is, in fact, a reawakening, for this has been the longest continuously civilized part of the country, with evidence of Maya inhabitants as early as 2500 BC, producing good pottery and living in huts virtually identical to those you see in the villages today. **The Maya** are not a specifically Mexican culture – their greatest cities, indeed, were not in Mexico at all but in the lowlands of modern Guatemala, Belize and Honduras – but they did produce a unique style in the Yucatán and continued to flourish here long after the collapse of the "Classic" civilizations to the south. This they did in spite of natural handicaps – thin soil, heat, humidity and lack of water – and in the face of frequent invasion from central Mexico. And here the Maya peasantry still live, remarkably true to their old traditions and lifestyle, despite the hardships of the intervening years: ravaged by European diseases and forced to work on vast colonial *encomiendas*, or later, through the semi-slavery of debt peonage, on the *henequen* plantations or in the forests, hauling timber.

The florescence of Maya culture, throughout their extensive domains, came in the **Classic period** from around 300 to 900 AD: an age in which the cities grew up and Maya science and art apparently reached their height. The Maya calendar, a complex interaction of solar, astronomical and religious dates, was far more complicated and accurate than the Gregorian one, and they also developed a sophisticated mathematical and (still largely undeciphered) hieroglyphic system. In the ninth century, though, the major cities were gradually abandoned – the result perhaps of revolt by a population from whom the elite had become too remote, their knowledge too arcane, and provoked by some natural disaster. Whatever the reason, in Guatemala and Honduras the sites were never to be repopulated. In the Yucatán the abandonment was less total, and in many places short-lived. Instead there was a renaissance stimulated by contact with central Mexico: initially perhaps through trade, later by a direct Toltec invasion. A new society sprang up that fused the Toltec emphasis on militarism, and new gods, with Maya traditions. Its ultimate achievement was at **Chichén Itzá**, dominant until the twelfth century.

From the twelfth century on, **Mayapán** became the new centre of power, controlling the entire peninsula in an era when artistic and architectural standards went into sharp decline. By the time the Spanish arrived Mayapán's power, too, had been broken by revolt and the Maya had splintered into tribalism – although still with coastal cities and

ACCOMMODATION PRICES

All the accommodation listed in this book has been categorized into one of nine price bands, as set out below. The prices quoted are in US dollars and normally refer to the cheapest available room for two people sharing in high season. For more details, see p.37.

① less than $8	④ $18–25	⑦ $50–75
② $8–12	⑤ $25–35	⑧ $75–100
③ $12–18	⑥ $35–50	⑨ more than $100

long-distance sea trade that awed the Conquistadors. It proved the hardest area of the country to pacify. Despite attempts to destroy all trace of the ancient culture, there was constant armed rebellion against the Spanish and later the Mexican authorities – the last the **Caste Wars** of the nineteenth century, during which the Maya, supplied with arms from British Honduras, gained brief control of the entire peninsula. Gradually, though, they were again pushed back into the wastes of southern Quintana Roo, where the final pockets of resistance held out until the beginning of this century.

CENTRAL YUCATÁN: THE GREAT MAYA SITES

There's really only one route around the Yucatán: the variation comes in where you choose to break the journey or to make side trips off the main trail. Whether from Palenque or by road and ferry along the beautiful coast from **Ciudad del Carmen**, Hwy-180 heads up to **Campeche**, from there to **Mérida**, and on via **Chichén Itzá** to the Caribbean coast. From Mérida the best of the **Maya sites** – Uxmal, Chichén Itzá and a trove of smaller, less visited ruins – are in easy reach. Most people head there first, avoiding Campeche altogether. This is strongly to Campeche's advantage (even if locals don't see it that way), for while the attractions in and around the city can't compare with Mérida's, it is at least spared the blight of tourist overkill.

The road across the south of the peninsula, from **Francisco Escárcega** to Chetumal, is relatively new, passing through jungle territory rich in Maya remains, several of which have recently been opened to the public for the first time. Though largely unexplored, these are beginning to see a trickle of visitors as access improves; you can get accommodation and tours at **Xpujil**, a village named after the nearby archeological site, on the border between Campeche and Quintana Roo states.

Campeche

CAMPECHE, capital of the state that bears its name, is something of a bizarre mixture of ancient and ultra-modern. At its heart, relatively intact, lies a colonial port still surrounded by hefty defensive walls and fortresses; around, the trappings of a city that is once again becoming wealthy. Nowhere is this more obvious than along the seafront. Originally the city defences dropped straight into the sea, but now they face a reclaimed strip of land on which stand the spectacular new Palacio de Gobierno and State Legislature (spectacularly ugly in the eyes of most locals), and the big hotels.

A Spanish expedition under Francisco Hernandez landed outside the Maya town of Ah Kin Pech in 1517, only to beat a hasty retreat on seeing the forces lined up to greet them, and it wasn't until 1540 that Francisco de Montejo founded the modern town,

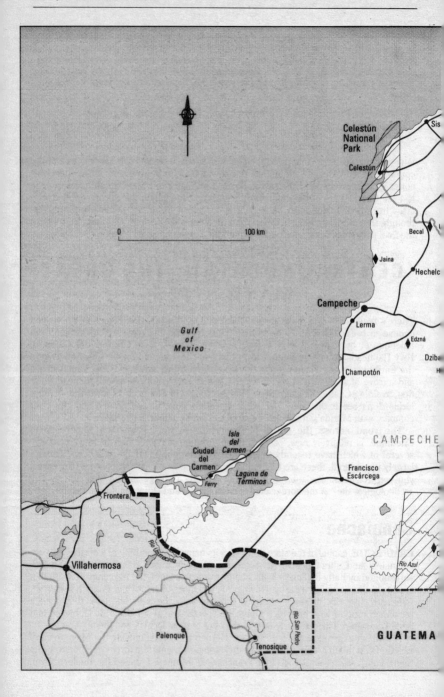

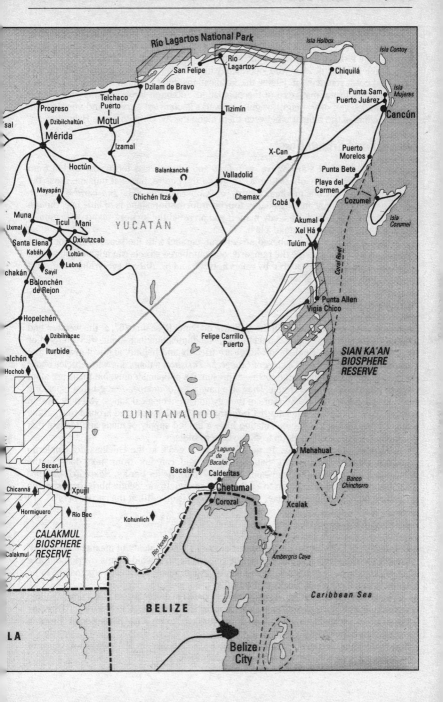

Río Lagartos National Park

Isla Holbox   Isla Contoy

San Felipe   Río Lagartos   Chiquilá

Dzilam de Bravo   Punta Sam   Isla Mujeres

Progreso   Telchaco Puerto   Tizimín   Puerto Juárez   Cancún

sal   Dzibilchaltún   Motul

Mérida   Izamal   X-Can   Puerto Morelos

Hoctún   Balankanché   Valladolid   Punta Bete

Mayapán   Chichén Itzá   Chemax   Playa del Carmen

Muna   Cobá   Cozumel

Ticul   Mani   YUCATÁN   Isla Cozumel

Uxmal   Oxkutzcab   Akumal

Santa Elena   Kabáh   Loltún   Xel Há

chakán   Sayil   Labná   Tulúm

Bolonchén de Rejon   Coral Reef

Hopelchén

Dzibilnocac   Punta Allen   Vigia Chico

alchén   Iturbide   Felipe Carrillo Puerto   SIAN KA'AN BIOSPHERE RESERVE

Hochob

QUINTANA ROO

Becan   Laguna de Bacalar   Mahahual

Chicanná   Bacalar   Calderitas   Banco Chinchorro

Xpujil   Chetumal

Hormiguero   Río Bec   Kohunlich   Corozal   Xcalak

CALAKMUL BIOSPHERE RESERVE   Río Hondo

Calakmul   Ambergris Caye

Caribbean Sea

LA   BELIZE

Belize City

and from here set out on his mission to conquer the Yucatán. From then until the nineteenth century it was the chief port in the peninsula, exporting above all logwood (source of a red dye known as *hematein*) from local forests. It became, too, an irresistible target for the pirates who operated with relative impunity from bases on the untamed coast roundabout. Hence the fortifications, built between 1668 and 1704 after a particularly brutal massacre of the population. Although large sections of the walls have gone, seven of the eight original bulwarks (*baluartes*) survive, and you can still trace the line of the ramparts between them along the Av. Circuito de los Baluartes.

Arrival and orientation

Campeche's **Central Camionera**, with first- and second-class terminals, is 2km from the centre, along Av. Gobernadores. To get to the centre, turn left outside, cross the road and take a city bus marked "Centro" or "Gobernadores". The *guardería* is for first-class passengers only and the nearby **tourist information** stand is of little use, though you may be able to pick up a city map. If you arrive at the **airport**, about 10km southeast of town, you'll have to take a taxi.

Within the city, even-numbered **streets** run parallel with the sea, starting for some reason with c/8, just inside the ramparts; odd-numbered streets run inland. The zócalo, **Parque Principal**, is bordered by calles 8, 10, 55 and 57. Almost everything of interest is gathered within the old walls.

Information

Campeche's **tourist office** is in the Baluarte de Santa Rosa on c/67, at the western end of c/14 (Mon–Fri 9am–9pm, Sat 9am–2pm, sometimes Sun 9am–2pm; ☎981/6-73-64 or 6-55-93). Staff (some English-speaking) are friendly and helpful, and will give out free maps and leaflets. Pick up a copy of *Campeche Turístico*, a magazine with articles about what's going on in and around town – at present it's in Spanish only, but plans are afoot for an English-language version. They also have a list of independent **guides** (speaking various languages) who lead tours of the city and archeological zones; you may have to provide the transport. Other tourist **information booths** scattered around town at the major tourist sites and the bus station have a limited supply of maps and leaflets that you could just as easily pick up from the larger hotels.

The **post office** is on Av. 16 de Diciembre at c/53, in the Oficinas del Gobierno Federal (Mon–Fri 8am–8pm, Sat 9am–2pm); you can **fax** from next door in the *Telecomm* office (Mon–Fri 9am–8pm, Sat 9am–1pm). As for **banks**, *Banco del Atlantico* and *Bancomer* are next door to each other on Av. 16 de Septiembre, opposite the Baluarte de la Soledad; both have ATMs. *Banamex* is on c/10, at the corner of c/53.

Accommodation

Because Campeche is not on the tourist circuit, it boasts plenty of inexpensive **hotels**, though for the same reason they can be rather shabby. Avoid rooms overlooking the street, as Campeche's narrow lanes magnify traffic noise. The best bargains are to be found within a couple of blocks of the zócalo.

The **youth hostel**, on Av. Agustín Melgar (☎981/1-18-08; $4), is clean and bustling, with single-sex dorms. You can also camp in the grounds. Catch a bus ("Directo/Universidad") from the *ADO* station, or one marked "Lerma" or "Playa Bonita" heading west through the old city.

America, c/10 no. 252, between 59 and 61 (☎981/6-45-88). Elegant colonial building with comfortable rooms; the best overlook the courtyard. Very good value. ⑨.

Baluartes, Av. Ruíz Cortines, just south of the *Ramada* (☎981/6-39-11). The *Ramada*'s older and slightly cheaper rival, with modern facilities and more atmosphere. ⑦.

Campeche, c/57 no. 2, opposite the cathedral (☎981/6-51-83). Best value of the budget hotels on the zócalo, in a former colonial mansion seeping faded glory. ③.

Central, Av. Gobernadores 462 (☎981/1-07-66). The name is hardly appropriate, as it's way out opposite the bus stations, but with perfectly adequate rooms. ③.

Posada del Ángel, c/10 no. 307, corner of c/55 (☎981/6-77-18). Modern hotel, centrally located by the corner of the cathedral. Some rooms with a/c. ⑤.

Ramada Inn, Av. Ruíz Cortines 51 (☎981/6-22-33). Comfortable, upmarket hotel with pool, restaurant and nightclub. Also has a travel agency and car rental. ⑨.

Roma, c/10 between 59 and 61 (☎981/6-38-97). In a colonial mansion even more faded than most, this is probably the cheapest hotel you'd actually want to stay in. Very basic; no hot water. ②.

The City

Though your time is really as well spent wandering Campeche's old streets or seafront, you could pass some time at the **Baluarte San Carlos**, which has a small armaments museum (Tues–Sat 9am–1pm & 4–8pm, Sun 9am–1pm; free): there are cannons on the battlemented roof and, underneath, the beginnings of a network of ancient tunnels that undermines much of the town. Mostly sealed off now, the tunnels provided a place of refuge for the populace from pirate raids, and before that were probably used by the Maya. The **Museo de Estelas Mayas** (Tues–Sat 9am–2pm & 3–8pm, Sun 9am–1pm; free) is back around the walls from here, facing the zócalo in the Baluarte de la Soledad. It traces the region's history from early Maya relics – especially from the nearby sites of Edzná and the island of Jaina – to collections of colonial art, weapons and marine trophies. If you want to continue the **tour of the walls**, the "Circuito Baluartes" bus will take you right round, stopping at regular intervals. The Baluarte San Pedro now houses a crafts exhibition and shop, while the Baluarte Santiago is surrounded by a small **Jardín Botanico** (Tues–Sat 9am–8pm, Sun 9am–1pm; free).

Founded in 1540, the **Cathedral**, overlooking the zócalo, is one of the oldest churches on the peninsula – the bulk of the construction, though, took place much later, and what you see is not particularly striking Baroque. The **Museo Regional de Campeche** (Tues–Sat 8am–2pm & 2.30–8pm, Sun 9am–1pm; $6), in one of the old colonial mansions on c/59, is more interesting, with exhibits from the Maya and Olmec civilizations (above all the treasure from the tomb of Calakmul) and the colonial era.

Other sights are a little farther out. About twenty minutes' walk to the right (northeast) along the seafront is **Iglesia de San Francisco**, the only surviving remnant of a sixteenth-century Franciscan monastery. On this site, supposedly, the first mass to be heard in Mexico was celebrated in 1517. Not far beyond lies the **Pozo de la Conquista** (Well of the Conquest), where the same Spanish expedition, under Francisco Hernandez, took on water to fill their leaking casks. In the other direction, again along the waterfront malecón, the **Fuerte de San Miguel** houses Campeche's **archeological museum** (Tues–Sun 9am–2pm & 4–8pm). It's not a particularly large collection, but there are some fine Olmec and Maya pieces and the fort itself, on a low rise just inland of the road, offers great views across the Gulf. Objects from Edzná and Jaina again predominate – some of the delicate Jaina figurines are cross-eyed, a feature that the Maya considered a mark of beauty (and also, presumably, a badge of rank, since it must have been a considerable handicap in most forms of work). As with straightened noses and flattened foreheads, this was often brought about by deliberate deformation – Bernal Diaz noted that the first two prisoners taken by Hernandez were both cross-eyed.

If you're desperate to be by the sea, a "Playa Bonita" bus along the waterfront will take you past the museum and beyond to the **beaches** at **Playa Bonita** and **Lerma**, a fishing village just beyond the city. It's not a terribly attractive prospect however, with the port and lots of factories probably spewing out pollutants.

Eating and drinking

Restaurants abound in the centre of Campeche, especially along calles 8 and 10. **Seafood**, served almost everywhere, is a good bet; try the shark or shrimps in spicy sauce.

El Gato Pardo, c/49, between 10 and 12, just outside the city wall. Pizzeria and video bar, serving excellent pizzas to young rock fans. Nightly until 1am.

Marganzo Regional, c/8 no. 262. Seafood and regional dishes served in relaxed surroundings. Especially busy for the $5 breakfast buffet. Open 7am–midnight.

Restaurant Miramar, c/8 and 61. Campeche's best seafood; pricey, but worth it.

Nutri Vida, c/12 no. 167, near c/59. Good vegetarian restaurant: fresh fruit, granola, yoghurt, juices, vegeburgers and other healthsome food at reasonable prices. Closed Sat evening and Sun.

Restaurant del Parque, c/8 no. 251, corner of 57 on the zócalo. Popular budget place for standard Mexican food. Daily 6am–midnight.

La Parroquia, c/55 no. 8. Traditional, family-run restaurant, good value and very popular with locals. Open 24hr.

Los Portales, c/55 no. 9. Across from *La Parroquia* and in much the same vein. Open 24hr.

MOVING ON FROM CAMPECHE

Regular first-class *ADO* and second-class *Autobuses del Sur* **buses** leave for Ciudad del Carmen, Mérida, Chetumal and Villahermosa. Second-class buses reach all the villages around, with buses direct to Uxmal. *Sur* have departures at 2 and 9pm for Palenque (6hr), and for San Cristóbal at 9pm (9hr). *Aeroméxico* (☎938/6-56-78 or 6-49-25) operates a variety of internal flights; *Calakmul* (☎938/6-31-09 or 1-36-50) flies to México only. A taxi out to the **airport** costs around $8.

The Campeche coast

South of Campeche, Hwy-180 sweeps along the mostly deserted coast, passing several small resorts. Most tourists heading in this direction turn inland at Champotón, following the route southeast to Palenque. If you want to get anywhere reasonably quickly, even if you're heading to Villahermosa and beyond, this is the best option. The oil industry generally has a higher profile than tourism here. There are, however, some pleasant beaches beyond Lerma, admittedly not always accessible by public transport. **Seyba Playa**, a fishing village 33km south of Campeche, has the **Balneario Payucan**, where there are a few *palapas* and seafood restaurants along a clean beach. **Champotón**, 30km farther on at the mouth of the Río Champotón, is a growing fishing and oil port with a few places to stay and several seafood restaurants. At **Isla Aguada** the Puenta de la Unidad, said to be the longest road bridge in Mexico, crosses the eastern entrance to the **Laguna de Terminos**, joining the **Isla del Carmen** to the mainland.

Ciudad del Carmen

CIUDAD DEL CARMEN, the only town of any size on the 35-kilometre long Isla del Carmen, doesn't merit a special trip except during its lively **fiesta** in July. It's not unpleasant, but it is hot and crowded and has much less historical atmosphere than Campeche. The Conquistadors landed here in 1518, but the first settlers were pirates in 1633. Nowadays it's home to a fishing fleet, catching, among other things, giant prawns for export. The oil boom has created new industries and forced prices up, so you'll find no accommodation bargains.

Just west of town is the **ferry dock** for Zacatal, where the road to Frontera (see p.462) continues. Buses don't necessarily make a direct connection. Naturally the Mexican entrepreneurial spirit rises to the occasion and the *Restaurant Red*, a large, thatched open-sided place by the dock in Zacatal, does a brisk trade serving exasperated commuters; there are even strolling musicians to entertain you.

Practicalities

ADO (first-class) and *Sur* (second-class) buses use the same station on Av. Periferica Ote. To get to the centre, take a taxi or *colectivo* (5am–11pm; about 20min). The **tourist office**, in the Palacio Municipal on the corner of calles 22 and 31 (Mon–Fri 8am–3pm), has plenty of information (English and Spanish) on Campeche state, but little about Ciudad del Carmen. The **post office** (Mon–Fri 7am–7pm, Sat 7am–1pm) is tucked away at c/22 no. 57, between c/25 and 27, while *Banamex*, on the corner of c/24 at the edge of the Parque General Ignacio Zaragosa, and *Bancomer*, c/24 no. 42 at the corner with c/29 (both Mon–Fri 9am–1.30pm), have ATMs and *cajeros*.

Most of the **accommodation** is on calles 20, 22 and 24 near the waterfront. At fiesta time places fill up, so book ahead. Five minutes around the corner from the bus station, *Casa de Huéspedes Bugambilias*, Av. Periferica Nte. 4 (☎938/2-49-28; ③), has large clean rooms with baths away from the main road. The *Roma*, c/22 no. 10 (☎938/2-04-10; ②), is a good-value place across a small park from the waterfront; most luxurious of all is the *Hotel de Parque*, on the corner of c/33 between Parque General Ignacio Zaragosa and the waterfront (☎938/2-30-46 or 2-30-66; ⑦), where all rooms have a/c, TV and phone. **Food** in Ciudad del Carmen is a mixture of specialities from the Yucatán peninsula and the state of Tabasco, with a stress on shellfish. Many low-priced restaurants are grouped together along c/33 by the busy Parque General Ignacio Zaragosa, and there are two good places on the seafront opposite the *Roma*: *Cafetería La Fuente*, for basic Mexican snacks, and *La Ola Marina*, next door, which serves expensive, good seafood and shellfish in a relaxed atmosphere.

Edzná and the Chenes sites

Some 60km from Campeche lie the ruins of **EDZNÁ** (daily 8am–5pm; $4.50, free on Sun): not the most impressive in the Yucatán, but beautiful nonetheless, and the only local site practically accessible by bus. Though this is an area where the **Chenes** style of architecture (closely related to the Puuc of Uxmal – see p.502) dominated – *Chen* means "well" and is a fairly common suffix to place names hereabouts – Edzná is far from a pure example of it, also featuring elements of Río Bec, Puuc and Classic Maya design. For the real thing, you have to venture farther south.

Edzná was a large city, on the main trade route between the Maya of the highlands and the coast. By the entrance to the site is a large *stela* carved with the image of a local noble wearing a huge headdress and with Maya glyphs: others have been taken to the museums in Campeche. The most important structure is the great **Templo de los Cinco Pisos** (Temple of the Five Storeys), a stepped palace/pyramid more than 20m high at the highest point of the raised platforms of the acropolis. It's on a base 60m square, topped by a broken roof-comb set at the back of the highest level. Unusually, each of the five storeys contains chambered "palace" rooms: while solid temple pyramids and multistorey "apartment" complexes are relatively common, it is rare to see the two combined in one building. At the front, a steep monumental staircase leads to a three-roomed temple at the top.

Lesser buildings surround the ceremonial precinct. The **Casa Grande**, a palace on the northwest side, and some of the buildings alongside it, were cleared by archeologists in late 1986. Some 55m long, the Casa Grande includes a room used as a steam bath, with stone benches and hearths over which water could be boiled. Near here, too, is a ball-court. The rest of the site – including a large system of drainage (and possibly irrigation) canals – remains unexcavated.

Getting to Edzná by bus is not easy: a second-class bus to **Pich** or **Hool** leaves around noon from the huge market in Campeche (c/53 and Circuito Baluartes Este) and will take you right past the entrance. Getting back is harder; there are passing buses but you may have to hitch. Alternatively, you could join an **organized trip** from Campeche; ask at the tourist office or the larger hotels.

More Chenes sites

The examples of true Chenes style are accessible only with a car or exceptional determination. The chief sites are reached on a poor road from **HOPELCHÉN**, a village about 100km from Campeche on the long route to Mérida. A bus follows this road as far as **Dzibalchen** and **Iturbide**, but it's not much use for visiting the sites as it turns straight round on arrival. If you choose to **stay** in Hopelchén, *Los Arcos*, c/23 on the corner of the plaza, near where the buses stop (☎982/2-00-37; ③), is the only option.

The best of the ruins are some way from the paved road and substantially buried in the jungle. **HOCHOB** has an amazing three-roomed temple (low and fairly small, as are most Chenes buildings) with a facade entirely covered in richly carved, stylized snakes and masks. The central chamber is surmounted by a crumbling roof-comb, and its decoration creates the effect of a huge mask, with the doorway as a gaping mouth. The remains of **DZIBILNOCAC**, 1km west of Iturbide, demonstrate the ultra-decorative facades typical of the Chenes style. Recent work has restored the western temple pyramid to its original condition, making a trip out here well worthwhile.

Francisco Escárcega to Xpujil

Heading south from Campeche on the inland route, Hwy-261 meets the east–west Hwy-186 at **FRANCISCO ESCÁRCEGA** (always referred to as Escárcega – with the emphasis on the first syllable), a hot, dusty town straggling along the road and old train tracks for a couple of kilometres. There's little to detain you in town, but Escárcega does provide a jumping-off point for visits to a number of relatively unexplored Maya sites that are now beginning to be developed for tourism.

The *ADO* bus station is at the road junction; from there, walk 1500m east to the centre and the *Sur* bus station. If you need to **stay**, try the *Posada Escárcega* (☎981/4-00-79; ②), just two blocks from the second-class terminal; turn left and then second left. **Getting out of town** is relatively easy: at least ten buses run daily to Mérida, there's an hourly service to Campeche between 4am and 6pm, a 4.30am second-class bus to Palenque, and a couple to San Cristóbal; in addition, Escárcega is on the *ADO* first-class route between Chetumal and Villahermosa. Services to Xpujil and Chetumal run overnight or in the mornings only – nothing heads out in the afternoon.

Xpujil and the Río Bec sites

The Río Bec style, characterized by long buildings with matching towers at each end and narrow roof-combs, can be seen at a number of sites near Escárcega. **Río Bec** itself is in the jungle to the south, accessible only by dirt road, but the others – **Xpujil**,

Becan and **Chicanná** – are easy enough to get to. Buses run east from Escárcega (2hr 30min) to the crossroads village of Xpujil; there's a handy second-class bus at 7am and all buses to Chetumal stop here briefly. **Heading on to Chetumal** (2hr 30min) by bus or *combi* is relatively simple until late afternoon. The last *ADO* bus is at 5pm.

The sites

Though the sites are all relatively near the road, if you're just visiting for a day then the most accessible is **XPUJIL**, just 1500m back along the highway from the village of the same name, whose towering pyramid dominates for miles. With a few houses, shops, and a couple of restaurants, Xpujil village also boasts a good **place to stay**: the *Restaurant and Cabañas El Mirador Maya*, which has simple, thatched *cabañas* with hammocks, no electricity and shared hot water, or bungalows with hot showers, electricity and fans (☎982/4-03-71; ②–④). **Expeditions** to the more remote sites in the area are led from here, either on foot or using four-wheel drive vehicles (see below). You could also **camp** ($3.50) at the trailer park.

BECAN, 6km west of Xpujil then 500m north on a signed track, is unique among Maya sites in being entirely surrounded by a dry moat, 15m wide and 4m deep. This moat and the wall on its outer edge form one of the oldest known defensive systems in Mexico, and have led some to believe that this was the site of Tayasal, capital of the Itzá, rather than present-day Flores in Guatemala. **CHICANNÁ** lies 3km farther to the west, south of the highway, and hosts the luxurious *Ramada Eco Village Resort* (☎91/535-24-66; ⑨). The buildings at the site recall the Chenes style in their elaborate decoration and repetitive masks of Chac – the great doorway in the **House of the Serpent Mouth** is especially impressive.

Though to see all the scattered buildings of **RÍO BEC** you need to go on an organized expedition, you can see one small group independently: head east 13km from Xpujil, then south 6km to the *ejido* of 20 de Noviembre. The site is protected within the **Reserva de Fauna U'Luum Chac Yuc**, so you need to sign in at the small museum that acts as the reserve headquarters (☎982/4-03-73), who will fix you up with a guide from the village. You'll see that the "steps" on the twin towers were never meant to be climbed: the risers actually angle outwards.

Serge (known to everyone as Checo) at *Cabañas El Mirador* leads expeditions to **Hormiguero**, southwest of Xpujil, and to the huge site of **Calakmul**, two days' hard walking south from the highway, or just two hours and thirty minutes on a new dirt road from Xpujil. Here, in the heart of the enormous Calakmul Biosphere Reserve, is the most massive Maya pyramid of all: the base covers five acres, and from the top it's possible to see the tallest Maya pyramid, **Danta** at El Mirador in Guatemala.

From Campeche to Mérida

From Campeche to Mérida there's a choice of two routes. First-class buses, and all *directo* services, take the shorter road via **Hwy-180** – the colonial Camino Real, lined with villages whose plazas are laid out on the traditional plan around a massive old church. **HECELCHAKAN**, about 80km from Campeche, has a small **archeology museum** on the main square (Mon–Sat 9am–6pm; free), with figures from Jaina and objects from other nearby sites. **BECAL** (35km farther) is one of the biggest centres for the manufacture of basketware and the ubiquitous Yucatecan **Jipis**, or "Panama" hats (real panama hats, as everyone knows, come from Ecuador). There's a *Centro Artesanal* by the road where you can buy them, but it's more interesting to go into the village and watch this cottage industry at work.

The longer route **via Hopelchén and Muna** is much better if you have the time, passing the great sites of **Sayil**, **Kabáh** and **Uxmal** (see p.503). With a car you could easily visit all three, perhaps stopping also at **BOLONCHÉN DE REJON**, with its nine wells (*Bolonchén* means nine wells), and the nearby **Grutas de Xtacumbilxunan**, 3km south, and still get to Mérida within the day. By bus it's slightly harder, but with a little planning – and if you set out early – you should be able to get to at least one. Kabáh is the easiest since its ruins lie right on the main road.

Mérida

Even if practically every road didn't lead to **MÉRIDA**, it would still be an inevitable stop. The "White City", capital of the state of Yucatán, is in every sense the leading town of the peninsula, and remarkably calm and likeable for all its thousands of visitors. Every street in the centre boasts a colonial church or mansion, while the plazas are alive with market stalls and free entertainment. You can live well here and find good beaches within easy reach, but above all it's the ideal base for excursions to the great Maya sites of Uxmal and Chichén Itzá.

CENTRAL MÉRIDA

Museo de Antropologia

CALLE 43

PASEO MONTEJO

CALLE 45

Santa Ana

CALLE 47

CALLE 49

CALLE 66
CALLE 64
CALLE 62
CALLE 60
CALLE 58
CALLE 56
CALLE 54
CALLE 52
CALLE 50
CALLE 48

CALLE 51

CALLE 53

Santa Lucia

Train Station

CALLE 55

Teatro

CALLE 57

Contreras

University

Iglesia de Jesus

Parque Carrillo Puerto

La Mejorada

Museo de Arte Popular

Palacio de Gobierno

CALLE 59 PLAZA HIDALGO

Casa de Artesanías

Arco Dragones

CALLE 61

Cathedral

PLAZA MAYOR

Palacio Municipal

CALLE 63

Museo de Arte Contemporaneo

Casa de Montejo

CALLE 46

Arco del Puente

CALLE 65

Post Office

Market

CALLE 67

CALLE 69

0   200 m

To Bus Station

Parque San Juan

Arrival and orientation

Mérida is laid out on a simple **grid** of numbered streets: even numbers run north–south, odd from east to west, with the zócalo, **Plaza Mayor**, bounded by calles 60, 61, 62 and 63. Mérida's **bus stations** lie around the corner from each other on the west side of town. The brand new first-class **Cameon**, c/70 no. 55, between c/69 and 71, is sparkling and air-conditioned, with a *guardería*. Some short-haul buses use minor terminals, but you're almost bound to arrive at the busy **second-class** terminal, on c/69 between c/68 and 70. Inside is a **tourist information** counter, hotel reservations desk and phones; and you'll find a small **post office** at the side on c/70, and a *Banpais* **bank** (Mon–Fri 9am–1.30pm) on the nearby corner.

City buses don't go all the way from the bus stations to the Plaza Mayor. To walk (about 20min), turn right outside the second-class bus station and you'll be on the corner of c/68 and 69 at the northeast corner. The Plaza Mayor is three blocks north and four blocks east. If you're **coming from Ticul** or some of the other smaller places off the main highways, the *colectivo* will drop you in Plaza de San Juan, on c/69 between c/62 and 64. To get to the Plaza Mayor, leave Plaza de San Juan by the northeast corner and walk three blocks north up c/62.

Mérida's *Manuel Cresencio Rejón* **airport** is 7km southwest of the city. There's a **tourist office** (daily 8am–8pm), post office, long-distance phones and car rental desks. To get downtown, take a *colectivo* (buy a ticket at the desk) or bus #79 ("Aviación"), which drops off at the corner of calles 67 and 60.

Information

Mérida's main **tourist office** is in the *Teatro Peón Contreras*, on the corner of calles 60 and 57 (daily 8am–8pm; ☎99/24-92-90). Pick up a copy of *Yucatán Today*, in English and Spanish, to find out what's going on in and around town. *Discover Mérida of Yucatán* offers information about the areas outside Mérida, while *Restaurants of Yucatán* gives detailed reviews. There are also plenty of leaflets available and you'll usually find some English-speaking staff. The **federal tourist office** is in the pink building marked *Gobierno del Estado Secretaria de Desarollo Economico*, c/59 no. 514, between calles 62 and 64 (Mon–Fri 8am–2pm).

Mérida's main **post office**, on c/65, between 56 and 56-A (Mon–Fri 7am–7pm, Sat 9am–1pm), has a reliable *Lista de Correos* that keeps mail for ten days. Most of the **banks** are around c/65 between calles 60 and 64, and are open from 9am to 1.30pm. *Banco Atlantico*, c/65 no. 515, opens an hour earlier, and stops doing foreign exchange at 1pm. Of the many **casas de cambio** around the centre, try *Canto*, c/61 no. 468, between calles 54 and 52 (Mon–Fri 8.30am–1.30pm & 4.30–7.30pm, Sat 8.30am–1pm), or *Del Sureste*, c/56 no. 491, between calles 57 and 59 (Mon–Sat 9am–5pm). *Finex*, c/60 and 59, in the corner of the Parque Hidalgo, is open longest (daily 8.30am–8pm).

For **telephone calls**, head for one of the many *casetas* dotted around town: *Caseta Condesa*, c/59 near c/62; *Computel*, Paseo de Montejo on the corner with c/37; or *TelPlus*, c/61 no. 497, between calles 58 and 60.

THE PUUC ROUTE BUS

While at Mérida's second-class bus terminal you may want to buy a ticket for a transport-only day trip by bus around the **Puuc Route**, which can be inaccessible without your own transport. Look for the counter for *Autotransportes del Sur*. The trip costs $10 and leaves at 8.30am every morning, visiting Uxmal, Labna, Sayil, Kabáh and Xlapak. You get just long enough at each site to form a general impression, but there's no guide or lunch included in the price.

City transport

As traffic in Mérida is so congested, and most of the places of interest are within walking distance, it really isn't worth the bother of using public transport to get around in the centre – though it can be fun to hop onto one of the **horse-drawn carriages** that trot up and down the Paseo de Montejo (see p.495). However, to get out to some of the more far-flung sites (the Museum of Anthropology and History, for example), you may need to catch a bus. A number of buses leave from c/59 just east of the Parque Hidalgo; fares are around 50¢. **Taxis** can be hailed all around town and from ranks at Parque Hidalgo, the post office, Plaza de San Juan and the airport. **Car rental** offices abound in Mérida, both at the airport and in the city (see "Listings" on p.498).

Accommodation

There are hundreds of **hotels** in Mérida, many in lovely colonial buildings very near the **centre**, so that although the city can get crowded at peak times you should always be able to find a room. The expensive places fill up first. The cheapest hotels are concentrated **near the bus station**, a noisy and grimy part of town, while at the other end of the scale there's a string of upmarket hotels along the elegant boulevard, **Paseo de Montejo**, just north of the centre.

Rainbow Maya **trailer park**, Km 8 on the road to Progreso (☎99/28-04-48; fax 24-77-84; $6–14), has about 100 hook-ups, water and electricity. The head office is in the *Canto Farmacía*; to book ahead, write to c/61 no. 468.

Near the bus station

Alamo, c/68 no. 549, corner of c/71 (☎99/28-62-90). Clean but basic with private baths. ③.

Cortez, c/68 no. 545-A, between 69 and 71 (☎99/24-48-43). More character and marginally less expensive than the other hotels in the area. Restaurant with cabaret until 1am. ②.

San Jorge, c/69 no. 563-F, between 68 and 70 (☎99/24-91-44). The most expensive of the hotels near the bus station, but still basic and without character. ④.

In the centre

Caribe, c/59 no. 500, Parque Hidalgo (☎99/24-90-22; fax 24-87-33; toll free: in Mexico ☎800/2-00-03, in USA: ☎1-800/826-6842). In a small plaza just a block from the Plaza Mayor. Justifiably popular, with bargain non-a/c rooms and a good-value full-board package. Lovely patio restaurant and views of the cathedral and plaza from the rooftop pool. Travel agency; parking. ⑥.

Casa Becil, c/67 no. 550-C, between 66 and 68 (☎99/24-67-64). Friendly and convenient for the bus station. Popular with North Americans. ③.

Casa Bowen, c/66 no. 521-B, between 65 and 67 (☎99/28-61-09). A travellers' favourite for years, this restored colonial house is set around a bright, pleasant courtyard. Spartan, acceptable rooms have bath (some with a/c), and there are two apartments with kitchens. Book exchange. ③–⑤.

Casa de Huéspedes Peniche, c/62 no. 507, just off the zócalo (☎99/28-55-18). Shambling place in a former colonial house, with original oil paintings and huge, bare rooms. The shared bathroom looks much as it must have done a century ago. Cheapest place in the centre, and a good meeting place for backpackers. ②.

Dolores Alba, c/63 no. 464, between 52 and 54 (☎99/28-31-63). Good value, with comfortable public areas, shady courtyard and pool. All rooms are well furnished and have private bath; some have a/c. Restaurant and parking. You can book here for the *Dolores Alba* at Chichén Itzá. ④.

Flamingo, c/58, corner of 59 (☎99/24-77-55). One of the cheapest in town with a pool. *Restaurant Tikal* has good set meals. ③.

Gran Hotel, c/60 no. 496, Parque Hidalgo (☎99/24-77-30; fax 24-76-22). Colonnades and fountains, palms and statues ensure that the *Gran* lives up to its name. Rooms, all with private shower, are well furnished, often with antiques. No pool, but still good value. ⑥.

Hotel del Parque, c/60 no. 495, Parque Hidalgo (☎99/24-78-44; fax 28-19-29). Lovely old building just off the main plaza. Some rooms need improvement; those at the back are quieter. Dine in intimate little balconies in the resaurant, *La Bella Epoca*. ⑥.

Margarita, c/66 no. 506, between 61 and 63 (☎99/23-72-36). Budget favourite; small but clean rooms and good rates for groups. ②.

Mucuy, c/57 no. 481, between 56 and 58 (☎99/28-51-93). Quiet, well-run and pleasant hotel, with clean, good-value rooms. English-speaking staff and a selection of books in English. ④.

Posada del Ángel, c/67 no. 535, between 66 and 68 (☎99/23-27-54). Better quality than most in this area, and more expensive. Quiet and comfortable, with parking and restaurant. ⑤.

Posada Toledo, c/58 no. 487 (☎99/23-16-90 or 23-22-56). Superb, beautifully preserved nineteenth-century building. Rooms, all with private shower and some a/c, are filled with antiques and the courtyard is a delight. Good food served in the historic dining room. ⑥.

Reforma, c/59 no. 508 (☎99/24-79-22; fax 28-32-78). Long-established, recently restored hotel in a colonial building. Rooms arranged around a cool courtyard and there's a relaxing poolside bar. Parking and good prices on guided day trips to Uxmal and on the *Ruta Puuc*. ⑤.

San José, c/63 no. 503-C (☎99/28-66-57). Cheap, no-frills place just off the corner of the plaza. Some private baths. Enter through the cafe (handy for inexpensive meals). ②.

Santa Lucía, c/55 no. 508, Parque Santa Lucía (☎99/28-26-72; fax 28-26-62). Good-value, mid-sized hotel with a/c rooms and a pool. One of the best features is the location, on one side of a park that hosts a free weekly performance of Mexican folk music (see p.497). ⑤.

Trinidad, c/62 no. 46, between 55 and 57 (☎99/23-20-33). Wide range of rooms and a plant-filled courtyard. Decorated with modern paintings and antiques. Guests can use the pool at its sister hotel, the *Trinidad Galería* (☎99/21-09-35), nearby on the corner of 60 and 51. ③.

Luxury hotels

Calinda Panamericana, c/59 no. 455, corner of 52 (☎99/23-91-11; fax 24-80-90). Turn-of-the-century elegance and modern luxury four blocks from the plaza. Imposing entrance opens onto a beautiful tiled courtyard, with a balcony supported by Corinthian columns. Large rooms all have a/c, some in a modern wing. Nightclub, travel agency, car rental, parking. ⑧.

Hotel Casa del Balam, c/60 no. 488, corner of 57 (☎99/24-88-44; fax 24-50-11; in US: ☎1-800-624-8451). Luxury, ambience and beautifully furnished rooms, all with a/c, in a central location make this mid-sized hotel very popular. The particularly pleasant bar has *mariachi* crooners in the evening. Travel agency and car rental; parking. ⑨.

Montejo Palace, Paseo de Montejo 483-C (☎99/24-76-44; fax 23-03-88; toll free in Mexico: ☎800 2-00-12; in US: ☎1-800/437-9607). Eight-storey hotel with fully equipped rooms, including satellite TV, in an upmarket location. Restaurant, cafeteria and pool. ⑧.

Paseo de Montejo, Paseo de Montejo, opposite *Montejo Palace* (☎99/23-90-33; toll free in Mexico: ☎800 2-00-12; in US: ☎1-800/437-9607). Same management as the *Montejo Palace*, with comfortable rooms in an older building. Restaurant, cafeteria and pool. ⑦.

The City

Founded by Francisco de Montejo (the Younger) in 1542, Mérida is built over, and partly from, the ruins of a Maya city known as **Tihó**. Although, like the rest of the peninsula, it had little effective contact with central Mexico until the completion of road and rail links in the 1960s, trade with Europe brought wealth from the earliest days. In consequence the city looks more European than almost any other in Mexico – many of the older houses, indeed, are built with French bricks and tiles, brought over as tradeable ballast in the ships that exported *henequen* (or sisal). Until the advent of artificial fibres, a substantial proportion of the world's rope was manufactured from Yucatecan *henequen*, a business that reached its peak during World War I.

In 1849, during the Caste Wars, the Maya armies besieging Mérida came within a hair's breadth of capturing the city and thus regaining control of the entire peninsula, when the Indian peasants left the fight in order to return to the fields to plant corn. It was this event, rather than the pleas of the inhabitants for reinforcements, that saved the elite from defeat and brought Yucatán under Mexican control. Around the turn of the century Mérida was an extraordinarily wealthy city – or at least a city that had vast numbers of extremely rich landowners riding on the backs of a landless, semi-enslaved peonage – a wealth that went into the grandiose mansions of the outskirts (especially along the Paseo de Montejo) and into European educations for the children of the *haciendados*. Today, with that trade all but dead, it remains elegant and bustling, its streets filled with Maya going about their daily business.

Plaza Mayor

Any exploration of Mérida begins naturally in the **Plaza Mayor**. The hub of the city's life, it's ringed by some of Mérida's oldest buildings, dominated by the **Cathedral of San Idelfonso** (daily 6am–noon & 5–8pm), built in the second half of the sixteenth century. Although most of its valuables were looted in the Revolution, the **Cristo de las Ampillas** (Christ of the Blisters), in a chapel to the left of the main altar, remains worth seeing. This statue was carved, according to legend, from a tree in the village of Ichmul that burned for a whole night without showing the least sign of damage; later, the parish church at Ichmul burned down and the statue again survived, though blackened and blistered. The image is the focal point of a local fiesta at the beginning of October. Beside the cathedral, separated from it by the Pasaje San Alvarado, the old bishop's palace has been converted into shops and offices.

Next door to the cathedral is the new **Museo de Arte Contemperáneo Arteneo de Yucatán** (daily 9am–5pm; $3, free on Sun), the finest art museum in the state, with permanent displays of the work of internationally acclaimed Yucatecan artists such as Fernando Castro Pacheco, Gabriel Ramírez Aznar and Fernando García Ponce. Temporary exhibitions include ceramics from around the region, Yucatecan embroidery and metallic art. On the south side of the plaza stands the **Casa de Montejo**, a palace built in 1549 by Francisco de Montejo himself and inhabited until 1980 by his descendants. It now belongs to *Banamex*, and much of the interior is open to the public (Mon–Fri 9am–5pm): the facade is richly decorated in the Plateresque style, and above the doorway Conquistadors are depicted trampling savages underfoot. The **Palacio Municipal**, on the third side, is another impressive piece of sixteenth-century design with a fine clock tower, but the nineteenth-century **Palacio de Gobierno** (daily 8am–10pm), completing the square, is more interesting to visit. Inside, murals depict the history of the Yucatán and, on the first floor, there's a small historical chamber devoted to the same subject.

North of the Plaza Mayor

Most of the remaining monuments in Mérida lie north of the zócalo, with c/60 and later the Paseo de Montejo as their focus. Calle 60 is one of the city's main commercial streets, lined with several of the fancier hotels and restaurants. It also boasts a series of colonial buildings, starting with the seventeenth-century Jesuit **Iglesia de Jesús**, between the Plaza Hidalgo and the Parque de la Madre. Beside it on c/59 is the **Cepeda Peraza Library**, full of vast nineteenth-century tomes; a little farther down 59, the **Pinacoteca Virreinal** houses a rather dull collection of colonial artworks and modern sculptures in a former church. Continuing up c/60, you reach the **Teatro Peón Contreras**, a grandiose Neoclassical edifice built by Italian architects in the heady days of Porfirio Díaz and recently restored. The **University** is opposite.

The **Museo de Arte Popular** (Tues–Sat 8am–8pm, Sun 8am–2pm; free) in the former monastery of La Mejorada, c/59 between 50 and 48, displays a fine collection of the different styles of Indian dress found throughout Mexico. The rich wood and glass cases show *huipiles* (the long white dresses embroidered with colourful flowers at the neck, worn by Maya women), jewellery and household items, while old black-and-white photos provide glimpses of village life and ceremonials. At the rear of the museum you can stock up on souvenirs at the really good *artesanía* shop.

One block north of the *Teatro Peón Contreras*, the sixteenth-century **Iglesia Santa Lucía** stands on the elegant plaza of the same name – a colonnaded square that used to be the town's stagecoach terminus. Finally, three blocks farther on, there's the **Plaza Santa Ana**, a modern open space where you turn right and then second left to reach the Paseo de Montejo.

Paseo de Montejo

The **Paseo de Montejo** is a broad, tree-lined boulevard lined with the magnificent, pompous mansions of the grandees who strove to outdo each other's style (or vulgarity) around the turn of the century. In one of the grandest, the Palacio Canton at the corner of c/43, is Mérida's **Museo de Antropología** (Tues–Sat 8am–8pm, Sun 8am– 2pm; $5, free on Sun). The house was built for General Canton, state governor at the turn of the century, in a restrained but very expensive elegance befitting his position, and has been beautifully restored and maintained. Given the archeological riches that surround the city, the collection is perhaps something of a disappointment, but it's a useful introduction to the sites nonetheless, with displays covering everything from prehistoric stone tools to modern Maya life. Obviously there are sculptures and other objects from the main sites, but more interesting are the attempts to fill in the background and give some idea of what it was like to live in a Maya city; unfortunately, most labels are only in Spanish. Topographic maps of the peninsula, for example, explain how *cenotes* are formed and their importance to the ancient population; a collection of skulls demonstrates techniques of facial and dental deformation; and there are displays of jewellery, ritual offerings and burial practices, as well as a large pictorial representation of the workings of the Maya calendar. The **bookshop** has leaflets and guidebooks in English to dozens of ruins in Yucatán and the rest of Mexico.

The walk out **to the museum** is quite a long one – you can get there on a "Paseo de Montejo" bus from c/59 just east of the Parque Hidalgo, or take a *calesa* (**horse-drawn taxi**) instead. This is not altogether a bad idea, especially if you fancy the romance of riding about in an open carriage, and if times are slack and you bargain well it need cost no more than a regular taxi. Take some time to head a little further out on the Paseo de Montejo, to a lovely and very wealthy area where the homes are more modern and interspersed with big new hotels and pavement cafes. The **Monumento a la Patria**, about ten long blocks beyond the museum, is a titan, covered in neo-Maya sculptures relating to Mexican history – you'll also pass it if you take the bus out to Progreso. Really to do the Grand Tour you should visit the **Parque de las Americas**, on Av. Colón, which is planted with trees from every country on the American continent, and get back to the centre via the **Parque Centenario**, Av. de los Itzaes and c/ 59, where there's a zoo, botanical gardens and a children's park.

Markets and handicrafts

Mérida's **market**, a huge place between calles 65, 67, 56 and 54, is for most visitors a major attraction. As far as quality goes, though, you're almost always better off buying in a shop – prices are no great shakes, either, unless you're an unusually skilful and determined haggler. Before buying anything, head for the **Casa de Artesanías** in the Edificio de Manjas, on c/63 west of the zócalo, where you'll get an idea of the potential quality and price of the goods. Run by the government-sponsored *Fonapas* organization, it sells crafts from the peninsula – consistently high quality, right down to the cheapest trinkets and toys.

The most popular purchase is a **hammock** – and Mérida is probably the best place in the country to buy one – but if you want something you can realistically sleep in, exercise a degree of care. There are plenty of cheap ones about, but comfort is measured by the tightness of the weave (the closer-packed the threads the better) and the breadth: since you're supposed to lie in them diagonally, in order to be relatively flat, this is far more crucial than the length (although obviously the central portion of the hammock should be at least as long as you are tall). A decent-sized hammock (*doble* at least, preferably *matrimonial*) with cotton threads (*hilos de algodon*, more comfortable and less likely to go out of shape than artificial fibres) will set you back at least $20 – more if you get a fancy multi-coloured version.

If you'd rather not mess about with vendors in the market, head for a **specialist dealer**. *Tejidos y Cordeles Nacionales* is one of the best, very near the market at c/56 no. 516-B. More of a warehouse than a shop, it has hundreds of the things stacked against every wall, divided up according to size, material and cost. Buy several and you can enter into serious negotiations over the price. Similar hammock stores nearby include *El Campesino* and *El Aguacate*, both on c/58, and *La Poblana* at c/65 no. 492.

Other good **buys** include tropical shirts (*guayaberas*), panama hats (known here as *jipis*) and *huipiles*, which vary wildly in quality, from factory-made, machine-stitched junk to hand-embroidered, homespun cloth. Even the best, though, rarely compare with the antique dresses that can occasionally be found: identical in style (as they have been for hundreds of years) but far better made and very expensive.

Eating

Good **restaurants** are plentiful in the centre of Mérida, though those on the Plaza Major can be quite expensive. Best head for the historic and atmospheric area around the **Plaza Hidalgo**, just north, along c/60 between calles 61 and 59, where you'll find half a dozen or more good restaurants and pavement cafes, lively with crowds of tour groups and locals. Farther afield, on **Paseo de Montejo**, the more expensive and sophisticated restaurants include lots of upmarket places popular with young locals.

There are a number of less expensive places around the junction of calles 62 and 61, at the northwest corner of the Plaza, but cheapest of all are the *loncherías* in the **market**, where you can get good, filling *comidas corridas*. Around the Plaza Mayor several wonderful **juice bars** – notably *Jugos California* – serve all the regular juices and *licuados*, as well as more unusual local concoctions: try *mamey* or *guanabana*. Other branches are dotted about the city. Combine these with something from the **bakery** *Pan Montejo*, at the corner of calles 62 and 63, to make a great breakfast.

Los Almendros, c/50, between 57 and 59, in the Plaza Mejorada. One of Mérida's most renowned restaurants, popular with locals and visitors. Delicious, moderately priced Yucatecan food, especially on Sunday lunchtime. The original *Los Almendros*, in Ticul, claims to have invented *poc-chuc*.

Restaurante Amaro, c/59 no. 507, between 60 and 62. With some vegetarian menus, this offers a welcome change for veggies who are tired of endless *quesadillas*. In a lovely stone-flagged courtyard with a fountain and shaded by trees.

La Bella Epoca, in the *Hotel del Parque*. Intimate dining in a building full of period ambience.

YUCATECAN CUISINE

Typical **Yucatecan specialities** include *puchero*, a stew of chicken, pork, carrot, squash, cabbage, potato, sweet potato and banana chunks with a delicious stock broth, garnished with radish, cilantro and Seville orange; *poc-chuc*, a combination of pork with tomatoes, onions and spices; *sopa de lima* (not lime soup, exactly, but chicken broth with lime and tortilla chips in it); *pollo* or *cochinita pibil* (chicken or suckling pig wrapped in banana leaves and cooked in a *Pib*, basically a pit in the ground, though restaurants cheat on this); *papadzules* (*tacos* stuffed with hard-boiled eggs and covered in red and green pumpkin-seed sauce); and anything *en relleno negro*, a black, burnt-*chile* sauce. Little of this is hot, but watch out for the *salsa de chile habanero* that most restaurants have on the table – pure fire.

Cafetería Pop, c/57 no. 501, across from the university between 60 and 62. Inexpensive and popular student hangout; a/c and open until midnight.

Lonchería Milly, c/59 no. 520, between 64 and 66. Tiny cafe serving basic, inexpensive dishes to a largely local crowd. Open daily 7am–11am & noon–5pm.

El Louvre, c/62 no. 499, corner of c/61. Popular eating place with tasty *comidas corridas*.

Las Mil Tortas, c/62, between 67 and 65. Great Mexican-style sandwiches and *tortas*.

El Patio Español, c/60, Parque Hidalgo. Historic restaurant inside the *Gran Hotel*. Good, surprisingly well-priced food, and great service. As the name indicates, Spanish dishes are a speciality.

Pizzería de Vito Corleone, c/59 no. 508, corner of c/62. Takeway pizza and inexpensive restaurant.

El Rincón, in the *Hotel Caribe*, c/60 in the corner of Parque Hidalgo. Both this and the cheaper *Cafetería El Meson*, in the same building, are good, central places to eat in pleasant surroundings.

Tiano's, next to the *Hotel Caribe* on Plaza Hidalgo. A favourite street cafe, with wrought-iron tables and chairs spread out on the square. Great place to relax over a coffee or a beer while you read the *México News* from the newsstand opposite. Moderately priced, and often has live music.

Entertainment and nightlife

Mérida is a lively city, and every evening you'll find the streets buzzing with revellers enjoying a variety of **free entertainment**. To find out what's happening, pick up a free copy of *Yucatán Today* from the tourist office or any hotel. **Venues** include the plazas, the garden behind the *Palacio Municipal*, the *Teatro Peón Contreras* (next to the tourist office) and the *Casa de la Cultura del Mayab*, c/63 between 64 and 66. Things can change but typical performances might include energetic and fascinating **vaquerías** (vibrant Mexican folk dances, featuring different regional styles, to the rhythm of a *jaranera* band); Glen Miller-style **Big Band** music; the **Ballet Folklórico de la Universidad de Yucatán**, which performs a spectacular interpretation of Maya legends; **marimba** in the Parque Hidalgo; **classical music** concerts; and the very popular **Serenata Yucateca**, an open-air performance of traditional songs and music.

Perhaps the best time to see the Plaza Mayor and the surrounding streets is **Sunday**, when vehicles are banned from the area and day-long music, dancing, markets and festivities take over – a delight after the usual traffic roar. Street markets are set up along c/60 as far as the Plaza Santa Ana and there's a **flea market** in the Parque Santa Lucía.

There's plenty to do of a more commercial nature too, from **mariachi nights** in hotel bars to **Maya spectaculars** in nightclubs. Those aimed at tourists will be advertised in hotels, or in brochures available at the tourist office. Less obviously there are **video bars** and **discos** in most of the big hotels.

Apart from the hard-drinking *cantinas* (and there are plenty of these all over the city – including a couple of good ones on c/62, south of the Plaza), many of Mérida's **bars** double as restaurants.

Bars, discos and live music

Bin-Bon-Bao, c/29 no. 97, near c/18 – along Prolongación Paseo de Montejo. One of Mérida's biggest and most popular discos, playing dance and *salsa* music. Take a taxi. Cover charge, though women may get free drinks on Friday.

Carlos 'n' Charlie's, Prolongación Paseo de Montejo 447. One in the popular "fun bar" chain; gallons of beer and *tortilla* chips and superfast service. Daily specials and early happy hour.

La Ciudad Maya, c/84 no. 502, corner of c/59 (☎91/24-33-13). Floor shows with Yucatecan and Cuban music. Daily 1–10pm.

La Conquista, inside the *Paseo de Montejo* hotel, c/56 no. 482, near c/41. Quiet, dark, romantic disco.

Estudio 58, c/58, between 55 and 57, next to and underneath the *Hotel Maya Yucatan*. Central disco and nightclub with no cover charge. Live music and a happy hour 9.30–10.30pm.

Los Juglares, c/60 no. 500. Live jazz, blues and rock until 3am.

Kalia Rock House, c/22 no. 282, near c/37. Flavour of the month disco; noisy and fun; 9pm–3am.

Pancho's, c/59, opposite the *Hotel Reforma*. A steak restaurant with a pricey Tex-Mex menu and a later disco, *Pancho's* is a magnet for Americans homesick for "Mexican" food. The fun theme, with giant photos of Mexican Revolutionaries and bandolier-draped waiters in sombreros is ridiculously over the top. Try to hit the happy hour, 6–9pm.

La Prosperidad, c/56, corner of c/53. Earthier than the "touristy" bars, though becoming ever more popular. It's in a huge *palapa*, with live rock music in the afternoons and evenings. The beer's not cheap but it does come with substantial tasty snacks.

Listings

Airlines *Aerocaribe/Aerocozumel/Mexicana Inter*, Paseo de Montejo 500 (☎99/24-95-00; airport: ☎99/46-13-66); *Aeroméxico*, Paseo de Montejo 460 (☎99/27-94-55; airport: ☎99/46-14-00); *Aviacsa*, c/ 30 no. 130 (☎99/26-90-87; airport: ☎99/46-13-78); *Aviateca*, c/58 between 49 and 51 (☎99/24-94-77; airport: ☎99/46-12-96); *Continental*, at the airport (☎99/46-13-90); *Mexicana*, Paseo de Montejo 493 (☎99/24-66-33; airport: ☎99/46-13-92); *Taesa*, c/60 no. 468 (☎99/28-69-50; airport: ☎99/46-18-26).

American Express Paseo de Montejo 95, between c/43 and 45 (Mon–Fri 9am–2pm & 4–5pm, Sat 9am–noon; ☎99/28-42-22).

Bookstores English-language guidebooks are sold at *Dante Touristic Bookstore* on the corner of c/ 57 and 60. The *Holiday Inn*, Av. Colón near the junction with Paseo de Montejo, has a small supply of English-language novels.

Car rental *Avis*, Paseo de Montejo 500, near c/47 (☎99/28-28-28; airport: ☎99/84-21-34); *Better Car*, c/57 no. 491, between 58 and 60 (☎99/23-96-48); *Budget*, Paseo de Montejo 497 (☎99/27-27-08; airport: ☎99/46-13-80); *Easy Way*, c/59 no. 501-A (☎99/28-15-60); *Executive*, c/60 no. 446 between 49 and 51 (☎99/23-37-32; airport: ☎99/46-13-87); *Hertz*, c/55 no. 479, near c/54 (☎99/24-28-34; airport: ☎99/24-94-21); *Max*, c/60 no. 48, between 55 and 57 (☎99/24-76-06; fax 24-30-82).

Consulates Opening hours are likely to be fairly limited, so it's best to phone ahead and check. *Belize/UK*, c/53 no. 498 (☎99/28-61-52); *Canada*, Av. Colón 309-D, at the corner of 62 (☎99/25-62-99); *Cuba*, c/60 no. 285, at the corner of 23 and 25 (☎99/25-64-19); *Denmark*, c/32 no. 30 (☎99/25-45-99); *Switzerland*, c/56 no. 482, at the corner of 41 (☎99/23-90-33); *USA*, Paseo de Montejo at Av. Colón 453 (☎99/25-50-11).

Laundry If your hotel doesn't do laundry, try *Lavamatica*, c/59 no. 508 (Mon–Fri 8am–6pm, Sat 8am–2pm), which offers full-service washes.

Travel agencies Mérida boasts dozens of travel agencies. *Buvisa Travel*, c/56-A no. 475 (☎99/27-79-33); *Ecoturismo Yucatán*, c/3 no. 325 (☎99/25-21-87; fax 25-90-47); *IMC Travel*, Prolongación

---

VISITING CUBA

Many travel agents in Mérida promote **trips to Cuba** – on which, incidentally, Cuban immigration officers obligingly omit stamping the passports of US visitors. The recent lifting of restrictions on the possession of US dollars by ordinary Cubans should go some way to easing exchange problems; hotels, shops and businesses can now accept US dollars, and do so willingly. Fuel and food shortages still make life difficult for ordinary Cubans, however, and you'll frequently be approached by "guides" and hustlers. Despite economic problems, most Cubans are friendly to foreigners and will happily talk to you.

Havana, founded in 1515, is one of the oldest cities in the New World, and boasts a wealth of colonial buildings. The old city, **ciuda vieja**, has been declared a **World Heritage Site** by UNESCO, enabling much-needed refurbishment to be carried out. **Tours** of the city always take in at least one museum; you can also visit a **cigar factory** or a **rum distillery**, and leave with excellent souvenirs at great prices. Hemingway fans can visit the room at the *Hotel Ambros Mundos* where he lived for ten years in the 1930s.

A typical **package** of three nights from Mérida will cost around $300–360, which includes return airfare to Havana, a room in a "tourist-class" hotel with breakfast and dinner, and a city tour. Week-long packages cost about $100 more. **Operators** in Mérida include *Cubamex*, c/61 no. 499 (☎99/24-07-77), and *Taino Tours*, Paseo de Montejo 496, near c/45 (☎99/23-23-96; fax 23-17-84).

MOVING ON FROM MÉRIDA

Mérida is a major transport hub, especially if you're travelling on **by bus**. Most major destinations are served from the main first- and second-class stations, but some places are better served from the multitude of different little stations dotted around town.

From the first-class **Cameon**, the most important routes run by **ADO** are to Campeche (6am–11.30pm), México (10am–7.15pm), Palenque (8am & 10pm) and Villahermosa (7.30am–11.30pm). **Caribe Express** (☎99/24-42-75) provides a comfortable, a/c service with videos to Campeche and Villahermosa, as well as Cancún, Escárcega, Playa del Carmen and a number of other destinations. There are also services to Akumal, Villahermosa, Tulum and Playa del Carmen run by **Autotransportes del Caribe**. Both *Caribe Express* and *Autotransportes del Caribe* also have desks in the main first- and second-class buildings.

Buses from the **second-class** station, on c/69 between c/68 and 70, leave for **Campeche** (*Autotransportes de Sureste*; frequent; 4hr); **Cancún** (*Expreso de Oriente*; 6am–midnight; 6hr); **Escárcega** (*Autotransportes de Sureste*; 9 daily; 6hr); **Palenque** (*Autotransportes de Sureste*; 1 daily; 10–11hr); **Playa del Carmen** (*Expreso de Oriente*; 6.30am–11.45pm; 6 daily; 7hr); **Tuxtla Gutiérrez** (*Autotranportes de Sureste*; 1 daily; 20hr); **Valladolid** (*Expreso de Oriente*; 6.15am–midnight; 5 daily; 3hr); and **Villahermosa** (*Autotransportes de Sureste*; 1 daily; 10hr).

Of Mérida's **smaller bus stations**, c/50 on the corner with c/67 serves *Autobuses de Occidente en Yucatán*, for destinations west of Mérida, and *Lineas Unidos del Sur de Yucatán*: buses leave for **Celestún** (5am–8pm; every 1hr 30min–2hr; 2hr), **Oxkutzcab** (hourly) and **Sisal** (5am–7pm; every 1hr 30min–2hr; 2hr). *Autobuses del Noreste en Yucatán* leave from c/50 no. 529, between c/65 and 67, for **Río Lagartos** (6.45am, 4.30pm & 5.30pm; 6hr), San Felipe (4.30 & 5.30pm; 7hr) and Tizimín (6.45am–8pm; 8 daily; 4hr). Directly opposite, *Autotransportes de Oriente* leave for **destinations inland and east of Mérida**, with hourly buses to Cancún (5am–9pm; 6hr) and to Izamal, Piste and Valladolid.

In addition, **colectivos** depart Plaza de San Juan, c/69 between 62 and 64, for Dzibilchaltún, Oxkutzcab and Ticul, among other destinations. On the northern side of the plaza there are departures to Progreso (5.20am–9.20pm; every 20–40min; 1hr) and to Dzibilchaltún, Sierra Papacal, Komchén and Dzita.

Flights from Mérida leave for most Mexican cities and some international destinations; to get out to the airport, catch bus #79 ("Aviacion") going east on c/67.

Paseo de Montejo 74 (☎99/26-00-37; fax 26-35-98; in US: ☎1-800/331-6666); *Mayaland Tours*, Av. Colón 502 (☎99/25-22-46; in US: ☎1-800/235-4079); *Yucamex*, c/59 no. 498 (☎ and fax 99/24-42-52); *Yucatán Trails*, c/62 no. 482, between 57 and 59 (☎99/28-52-82; fax 24-49-19).

North to the coast: Dzibilchaltún and Progreso

From Mérida to the port of **Progreso**, the closest point on the coast, is just 36km – thirty minutes on the bus. The drive out of the city follows Paseo de Montejo through miles of wealthy suburbs and shopping malls before reaching the flat countryside where the *henequen* industry seems still to be flourishing. On the outskirts of Mérida there's a giant Cordemex processing plant, and a nearby shop run by the same company sells goods made from the fibre.

The ruins of **DZIBILCHALTÚN** (daily 8am–5pm; $3.50, free on Sun) lie about half-way to the coast, a few kilometres off the main road. Their importance for archeologists – there's evidence of settlement here from 1000 BC right through to the Conquest, the longest continuous occupation of any known site – is hardly reflected in what you actually see, but it's a very easy excursion from Mérida and an interesting stop on the way to the ocean. What's more, you can swim in the **cenote** at the very middle of the ancient city, which is fed with a constant supply of fresh water from a small spring.

Dzibilchaltún was, apparently, an extremely large city – more than eight thousand structures have been mapped and its major points were linked by great causeways – but little has survived, in particular since the ready-dressed stones were a handy building material, used in several local towns and in the Mérida–Progreso road. In addition to providing the ancient city with water, the 44-metre-deep **Cenote Xlacah** was of ritual importance to the Maya: more than six thousand offerings – including human remains – have been discovered in its depths. A causeway leads from the *cenote* to a ramshackle group of buildings around the **Templo de las Siete Muñecas** (Temple of the Seven Dolls). The temple itself was originally a simple square pyramid, subsequently built over with a more complex structure. Later still, a passageway was cut through to the original building and seven deformed clay figurines (dolls) buried, with a tube through which their spirits could commune with the priests. In conjunction with the buildings that surround it, the temple is aligned with various astronomical points and must have served in some form as an observatory. It is also remarkable for being the only known Maya temple to have windows and for having a tower in place of the usual roof-comb. The dolls, and many of the finds from the *cenote*, can be seen in a small museum by the site entrance. Around Dzibilchaltún, 540 hectares have been declared an **Eco-Archeological Park**, partly to protect a unique species of fish found in the *cenote*. Nature trails take you through the surrounding forest and it's a great place for bird-watching.

Buses from Mérida leave for Dzibilchaltún village (4 daily; 1hr) from a small terminal on c/62 between 65 and 67, or from the small office on the northern side of Plaza San Juan. The ruins are ten minutes' walk from the bus stop: to or from the main road, you face a walk of thirty minutes or so.

Progreso

First impressions of **PROGRESO**, a working port with a vast (6.5km) concrete pier, are unprepossessing; but penetrate to the beach and its image changes. Along the shorefront are ranged the mansions of the old *henequen* exporters, modern holiday villas, and a fair smattering of small hotels and restaurants – and there's a beach that stretches for miles in each direction. The water may not be the cleanest, and visually this can't compare with the Caribbean sands of the eastern Yucatán, but it's a pleasant day out from Mérida. Good for kids too, as the sand shelves away unbelievably gently (which is why the pier's so long), and always crowded at weekends with day-trippers. There are changing rooms and showers, and excellent seafood to be had everywhere.

There are plans to expand Progreso's tourism potential, and some hopeful new construction but, apart from in the key months of July and August, it's fairly quiet, and during the winter you'll find a mournful sight, with the hotels locked and boarded up.

Practicalities

It's easy enough to see Dzibilchaltún and Progreso in one trip from Mérida: **buses** to Progreso leave from the same terminal as those to the ruins. Head out to the ruins early and from there either walk, hitch or wait for the lunchtime bus back to the main road, where you can flag down a Progreso bus.

Streets in Progreso are confusingly numbered using two overlapping systems: one has numbers in the 70s and 80s, the other in the 20s and 30s. However, it's a small place, and not difficult to find your way around. There are a few moderately priced **places to stay** on Av. Malecón, which runs along the seafront between the beach and the hotels. The less expensive hotels are a few roads back. Best bets include *Posada Juan Carlos*, c/74 no. 148, between 29 and 81 (☎993/5-10-76; ③); *Hotel Miralmar*, c/27 no. 124, on the corner of c/76 (☎993/5-05-52; ③); *Real del Mar*, Av. Malecón, near c/20 (☎993/5-07-98; ④), which has clean simple rooms with bathrooms; and *Tropical Suites*, Av. Malecón 143 (☎993/5-12-63; ④), which has some suites with kitchen and refrigerator. As for **eating**, try the seafood snacks served at *Sol y Mar*, Av. Malecón at c/80, or buy **picnic food** at the market on c/27 and 80.

Beaches and resorts near Progreso

There are beautiful stretches of beach in either direction from Progreso and, though this coast is the focus of much new tourism development, it's never crowded. Indeed, in winter, when the holiday homes are empty (and the rates come down), you'll have miles of sand to yourself. Check the numbers posted outside the villas and you may find bargain **long-term accommodation**.

Heading east from Progreso, a ten-minute bus ride brings you to **PUERTO CHICXULUB**, a small, busy fishing village, with boats scattered all along the picturesque beach. Calle 19 is the main road, a couple of blocks back from the beach; here you'll find the **zócalo** where the **buses** stop. There's a busy **market** and a **post office**, but no bank. An amiable enough place to join Mexican holidaymakers for a day or two, Puerto Chicxulub has just two **places to stay**, both of which are likely to be full during Mexican holidays. The *Vistalmar*, c/29 no. 29 (no phone; ④), on the beach not far from the zócalo, is run-down and characterless but conveniently placed. A better bet, *Hotel and Restaurant Chujuc Maria*, c/25 no. 124-A, near c/28 (no phone; ④), has been recently refurbished and extended but is quite a walk from the main square: head west along c/21 and take the left about 50m before the cemetery, a good fifteen-minute walk. *Restaurant Bar Moctezuma*, c/19 near c/16, serves a variety of Mexican **food** to a lively crowd. You could also try along c/20, which is lined with places to eat and boasts the village **disco**, *Hysteria*.

The road continues east, skirting practically empty beaches and shallow lagoons, past Telchac Puerto, one hour from Progreso, and the luxury resort of **Nuevo Yucatán**, to **Chabihau**, where there's a small, unnamed **hotel** (①). With more time and a little perseverance, it's possible to get even farther east, to **DZILAM DE BRAVO**, a remote fishing village at the end of the road, with no beach because of its ugly, though functional, sea defence wall. Here the *Hotel Los Flamencos* (③), on the main road about ten minutes' walk west of the main square, offers basic rooms. You can rent boats (at least $65) at the dock to visit **Bocas de Dzilam**, 40km away in the **San Felipe Natural Park**. Set in 62,000 hectares of coastal forests, marshes and dunes, the *bocas* (Spanish for mouths) are freshwater springs on the seabed; the nutrients they provide help to encourage the wide biological diversity found here. Bird and wildlife-watching is superb: you'll see turtles, tortoises, crocodiles, spider monkeys and dozens of bird species.

A more direct way to get to Dzilam de Bravo is to catch a second-class bus in Mérida from the *Autobuses del Noreste* terminal. Four buses daily pass through on their way to and from Tizimín and Progreso, and one bus daily leaves for Izamal at 1pm.

Heading west, there are a number of new hotels and holiday homes along the road to **Yucalpetén**, a busy commercial port and naval base 4km from Progreso. Farther west, the small but growing resorts of **Chelem** and **Chuburná**, respectively fifteen and thirty minutes from Progreso – and easy day trips from Mérida – have clean, wide beaches and a few rooms and restaurants. It's hard to believe that the semi-deserted pueblo of **SISAL** was in colonial times Mérida's chief port. Change is in the air though, as Sisal is earmarked for tourism; at present just a few North American duck-hunters come for the shooting in winter, staying at the *Club de Patos*; the only other accommodation as yet is a couple of basic **budget hotels**, the *Los Corsarios* (②) and the *Felicidades* (②). Beyond here the coast road is barely practicable, but there are empty beaches all the way round to Celestún.

Celestún

CELESTÚN, at the end of a sandbar on the peninsula's northwest coast, would be little more than a one-boat fishing village were it not for its amazing bird-filled lagoon that boasts a large flock of flamingoes. To see them – as well as the blue-winged teals and shovellers that migrate here in the winter to take advantage of the plentiful fish in these warm, shallow waters – rent one of the boats from the bridge on the main road into Celestún. Get your bus driver to drop you off, as it's a twenty-minute walk from the main square. Launches cost $33 and take up to six people. Bring your bathers with you as you may get the chance to swim in the rich red waters among the mangroves.

Nominally protected by inclusion in the 60,000-hectare **Celestún Natural Park**, the flamingoes are nevertheless harassed by boats approaching too close in order to give visitors a spectacular flying display, disturbing the birds' feeding. Try to make it clear to your boatman that you don't wish to interrupt the birds' natural behaviour; you will get good photos if the boat is poled to within a respectable distance, particularly if you have a telephoto lens.

Practicalities

Buses leave Mérida for Celestún and Sisal from the terminal on c/50, corner of c/67. There are half a dozen **lodgings** in the village: the *Hotel Gutiérrez*, c/12 no. 107 (☎992/28-01-60; ④–⑤), which has some a/c rooms, and *Hotel Marel Carmen*, c/12 no. 111 (☎992/28-03-13; ④), are both on the beach not far from the main square. Farther along the beach to the north is the *Hotel San Julio*, c/12 no. 93-A (no phone; ③), more basic than the others but clean and comfortable. Several **seafood restaurants** can be found on the dusty main street and on the beach – the *ceviche* in Celestún is invariably good – and there's also a market, a bakery, a **bank** and a **filling station**.

South of Mérida: Uxmal and the Ruta Puuc

About 80km south of Mérida in the **Puuc hills** lies a group of the peninsula's most important archeological sites. **Uxmal** (pronounced Oosh-mal) is chief of them, second only to Chichén Itzá in size and significance, but perhaps greater in its initial impact and certainly in the beauty and harmony of its extraordinary architectural style. Lesser sites include **Kabáh**, astride the main road not far beyond; **Sayil**, nearby down a rough side track; and **Labná**, farther along this same track. Though related, each site is quite distinct from the others, and each is dominated by one major structure. From Labná you could continue to **Oxkutzcab**, on the road from Muna to Felipe Carillo Puerto.

Getting to the sites

Obviously it's impractical to do more than a fraction of the sites by bus, unless you're prepared to spend several days and endure a lot of waiting around. Uxmal and Kabáh are perfectly feasible, but getting to both in a single day requires an early start and careful conning of the timetable. An **organized tour** from Mérida is well worth considering – it may not give you as long at the sites as you'd like, but at least you'll see them. For around $30, most take in Uxmal in the morning (with lunch and a chance to swim at one of the hotels there), and one or more of Kabáh, Sayil and Labná in the afternoon. Any tour agency or large hotel in Mérida can arrange the trip. The budget version is the **"Tura Puuc" day-trip bus** run by *Autotransportes del Sur* from the bus station in Mérida (see p.491).

It's better still to **rent a car**: in two days you can explore all the key sites, either returning overnight to Mérida or finding a room in Muna, Ticul or, more expensively, at Uxmal itself. This way you could even include the Uxmal *son et lumière* – better than the one at Chichén Itzá. For details of car rental agencies, see p.498.

If you are driving, one stop you might consider on the way to Uxmal is the **Hacienda Yaxcopoil** (Mon–Sat 8am–6pm, Sun 9am–1pm; $1). This former *henequen* hacienda has been opened to the public, and you can tour the house and the processing sheds. The ornate furnishings and formal gardens convey an impression of the privileged lifestyle enjoyed by the wealthy *hacendados* – in complete contrast to the abject poverty endured by their Maya serfs. Don't be taken in by the kids who stand at the gates pretending to be guards – pay inside and get a ticket.

Uxmal

UXMAL – "thrice-built" – represents the finest achievement of the **Puuc architectural style**, in which buildings of amazingly classical proportions are decorated with broad stone mosaic friezes of geometric patterns, or designs so stylized and endlessly repeated as to become almost abstract. As in every Maya site in the Yucatán, the face of **Chac**, the rain god, is everywhere. Chac must have been more crucial here than almost anywhere, for Uxmal and the other Puuc sites, almost uniquely, have no *cenote* or other natural source of water, relying instead on artificially created underground cisterns, jug-shaped and coated with lime, to collect and store rainwater. In recent years these have all been filled in, to prevent mosquitoes breeding.

Little is known of the city's history, and what can be gleaned from Maya chronicles is not only confusing and contradictory, but in direct opposition to the archeological evidence. What is clear is that the chief monuments, and the city's peaks of power and population, fall into the **Late Classic period** (600–900 AD) and that it was probably founded only slightly earlier than this. Later, the **Xiu dynasty** settled at Uxmal, which became one of the central pillars of the League of Mayapán, and from here in 1441 the rebellion originated that finally overthrew the power of Mayapán and put an end to any form of centralized Maya authority over the Yucatán. All the significant surviving structures, though, date from the Classic period.

The site

Entering **the site** (daily 8am–5pm; $7), the back of the great **Pirámide del Adivino** (Pyramid of the Magician) rises before you. The most remarkable-looking of all Mexican pyramids, it soars at a startling angle from its oval base to a temple some 30m above the ground, with a broad but terrifyingly steep stairway up either side. It takes its name from the legend that it was magically constructed in a single night by a dwarf, though in fact at least five stages of construction have been discovered – six if you count the modern restoration, which may not correspond exactly to any of its earlier incarnations. Two of the older structures are entirely buried within the pyramid, visible only through tunnels punched in the facade; two others form an integral part of what you see.

The rear (east) stairway leads, past a tunnel which reveals Templo III, directly to the top, and a platform surrounding the temple that crowns the pyramid. Even with the chain to help you, the climb up the high, thin steps is not for the unfit, nor for anyone who suffers from vertigo: standing near the unguarded edges on top is a sure recipe for heart failure (especially on windy days), and coming down is even worse. The views,

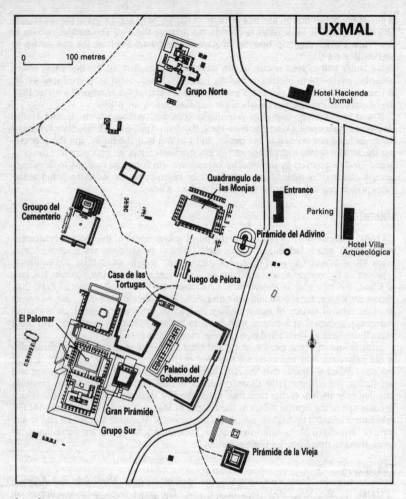

UXMAL

0 —— 100 metres

Grupo Norte

Hotel Hacienda Uxmal

Quadrangulo de las Monjas

Entrance

Parking

Pirámide del Adivino

Hotel Villa Arqueológica

Groupo del Cementerio

Casa de las Tortugas

Juego de Pelota

El Palomar

Palacio del Gobernador

Gran Pirámide

Grupo Sur

Pirámide de la Vieja

though, are sensational, particularly westward over the rest of the site and the green unexcavated mounds that surround it. Here you're standing at the front of the summit temple, its facade decorated with interlocking geometric motifs. Below it, the west stairway runs down either side of a second, earlier sanctuary in a distinctly different style. Known as the **Edificio Chenes** (or Templo IV), it does indeed reflect the architecture of the Chenes region, the entire front forming a giant mask of Chac. At the bottom of the west face, divided in half by the stairway, you'll find yet another earlier stage of construction (the first) – the long, low facade of a structure apparently similar to the so-called "Nunnery".

The **Quadrangulo de las Monjas** (Nunnery Quadrangle), a beautiful complex of four buildings enclosing a square plaza, is one of many buildings here named quite erroneously by the Spanish, to whom it resembled a convent. Whatever it may have been, that wasn't it; theories range from it being a military academy to a sort of earthly paradise where intended sacrificial victims would spend their final months in debauchery. The four buildings are in fact from different periods and, although they blend superbly, each is stylistically distinct. The **north building**, raised higher than the others and even more richly ornamented, is probably also the oldest. Approached up a broad stairway between two colonnaded porches, it has a strip of plain stone facade (from which doors lead into the vaulted chambers within) surmounted by a slightly raised panel of mosaics: geometric patterns and human and animal figures, with representations of Maya huts above the doorways. The **west building** boasts even more varied themes, and the whole of its ornamentation is surrounded by a coiling, feathered rattlesnake with the face of a warrior emerging from its jaws. All four sides display growing Maya architectural skills – the false Maya vaults* of the interiors are taken about as wide as they can go without collapsing (wooden crossbeams provided further support), and the frontages are slightly bowed in order to maintain a proper horizontal perspective.

An arched passageway through the middle of the south building provided the square with a monumental entrance directly aligned with the **ball-court** outside. Nowadays a path leads through here, between the ruined side walls of the court, and up onto the levelled terrace on which stand the Palacio del Gobernador and the **Casa de las Tortugas** (House of the Turtles). This very simple, elegant building, named for the stone turtles (or tortoises) carved around the cornice, demonstrates well another constant theme of Puuc architecture: stone facades carved to appear like rows of narrow columns. These probably represent the building style of the Maya huts still in use today – walls of bamboo lashed together. The plain bands of masonry that often surround them mirror the cords that tie the hut walls in place.

It is the **Palacio del Gobernador** (Governor's Palace), though, that marks the finest achievement of Uxmal's builders. John L Stephens, arriving at the then virtually unknown site in June 1840, had no doubts as to its significance: "if it stood this day on its grand artificial terrace in Hyde Park or the Garden of the Tuileries," he later wrote, "it would form a new order . . . not unworthy to stand side by side with the remains of the Egyptian, Grecian and Roman art". The palace faces east, away from the buildings around it, probably for astronomical reasons – its central doorway aligns with the column of the altar outside and the point where Venus rises. Long and low, it is lent a remarkable harmony by the architect's use of light and shade on the facade, and by the strong diagonals that run right through its broad band of mosaic decorations – particularly in the steeply vaulted archways that divide the two wings from the central mass, like giant arrow-heads aimed at the sky. Close up, the mosaic is equally impressive, masks of Chac alternating with grid-and-key patterns and with highly stylized snakes. Inside, the chambers are, as ever, narrow, gloomy and unadorned; but at least the great central room, 20m long and entered by the three closer-set openings in the facade, is grander than most. At the back, rooms have no natural light source at all.

Behind the palace stand the ruinous buildings of the **Grupo Sur** (South Group), with the partially restored Gran Pirámide (Great Pyramid), and El Palomar (Dovecote or Quadrangle of the Doves). You can climb the rebuilt staircase of the **Gran Pirámide** to see the temple on top, decorated with parrots and more masks of Chac, and look across at the rest of the site. **El Palomar** was originally part of a quadrangle like that of the "Nunnery", but the only building to retain any form is this, topped with the great wavy, latticed roof-comb from which it takes its name.

---

*The Maya never discovered the art of building a true arch supported by a keystone; instead they relied on a corbel vault, or false arch, in which each stone slightly overlaps the one below, but is entirely supported by it. Thus doorways and interiors were always extremely narrow.

Of the outlying structures, the **Pirámide de la Vieja** (Pyramid of the Old Woman), probably the earliest surviving building at Uxmal, is now little more than a grassy mound with a clearly man-made outline. The **Grupo del Cementerio** (Cemetery Group), too, is in a state of ruin – low altars in the middle of this square bear traces of carved hieroglyphs and human skulls.

Practicalities

Several **buses** a day run direct from Mérida to Uxmal, and any bus heading down the main road towards Hopelchén (or from Campeche to Mérida on the longer route) will drop you just a short walk from the entrance. Note that none runs late enough to get you back to Mérida after the *son et lumière*. At the modern **entrance to the site** (daily 8am–5pm; $7, free on Sun) the **tourist centre** includes a small museum, a snack bar and a shop with guides to the site, souvenirs, film and such like. Uxmal's **son et lumière** (daily except Mon) is at 7pm in Spanish ($2.50), 9pm in English ($3); the commentary is pretty crass, but the lighting effects are undeniably impressive.

There are three expensive **hotels** nearby: the *Club Med*-run modern *Villas Arqueológicas* (Nov–April only; ☎992/4-70-53; in US: ☎1-800/258-2633; ⑦), right at the entrance, has a/c rooms, a pool and a good library on the Maya; better value, the *Hacienda Uxmal* (☎992/4-71-42; in US: ☎1-800/235-4079; ⑧) is a gorgeous colonial-style hotel with undoubtedly the best restaurant and pool; and 1km up the road to Mérida is the *Misión Uxmal* (☎ and fax 992/4-73-08; in US: ☎1-800/223-4084; ⑧), which provides transport to the ruins. **Lunch** at any of them is costly (least so at the *Hacienda*) but it does give you a chance to cool off in a pool. A little farther away (4km north, towards Muna), the *Rancho Uxmal* (☎999/2-02-77; ⑤) is a comfortable, less expensive alternative that also has its own restaurant: rooms have a fan and private bath and you can **camp** for $3.

Travelling from Uxmal to Kabáh, you'll pass the **Sacbe campsite and trailer park** ($2.50–8). It's about fifteen minutes' walk south from the main square in the village of Santa Elena; if you're travelling by bus, ask the driver to drop you off at the entrance. Run by a Mexican–French couple, who have maps and can provide accurate information about the area, the site is a haven for backpackers, with tent sites dotted among the shady fruit trees. There are also some new *cabañas* (②), and limited space for your own hammock. There's nowhere to **eat** here or in Santa Elena, so bring supplies.

Kabáh

Some 20km south of Uxmal, the extensive site of **KABÁH** (daily 8am–5pm; $3.50, free on Sun) stretches across the road. Much of it remains unexplored, but the one great building, the **Codz Poop** or Palace of Masks, lies not far off the highway to the left. The facade of this amazing structure is covered all over, in ludicrous profusion, with goggle-eyed, trunk-nosed masks of Chac. Even in its present state – with most of the long, curved noses broken off – this is the strangest and most striking of all Maya buildings, decorated so obsessively, intricately and repetitively that it seems almost insane. Even the steps by which you reach the doorways and the interior are more Chac noses. There are a couple of lesser buildings grouped around the Codz Poop, and on the other side of the road an unusual circular pyramid – now simply a green, conical mound. Across the road a sort of triumphal arch marks the point where the ancient causeway from Uxmal entered the city.

Leaving Kabáh, you may have to virtually lie down in the road to persuade a bus to stop for you – ask the guards at the site for the bus times. Hitching a ride with other visitors, though, is generally pretty easy, and with luck you may even meet someone touring all the local sites.

Sayil

A sober, restrained contrast to the excesses of Kabáh, the ruined site of **SAYIL** (daily 8am–5pm; $3.50, free on Sun) lies some 5km along a minor road heading east from the highway 5km farther on. It is again dominated by one major structure, the extensively restored **Gran Palacio** (Great Palace), built on three storeys, each smaller than the one below, and some 80m long. Although there are several large masks of Chac in a frieze around the top of the middle level, the decoration mostly takes the form of bamboo-effect stone pillaring – seen here more extensively than anywhere. The interiors of the middle level, too, are lighter and airier than is usual, thanks to the use of broad openings, their lintels supported on fat columns. The upper and lower storeys are almost entirely unadorned, plain stone surfaces with narrow openings.

Few other structures have been cleared. From the Gran Palacio a path leads to the right to the large temple of **El Mirador**, and in the other direction to a *stela*, carved with a phallic figure and now protected under a thatched roof. On the opposite side of the road from all this, a small path leads uphill, in about ten minutes, to two more temples.

Xlapak and Labná

The minor road continues, paved but in poor condition, past the tiny Puuc site known as **XLAPAK** (daily 8am–5pm; $3, free on Sun). Its proximity to the larger sites of Labná and Sayil means that Xlapak (Maya for "old walls") is seldom visited, but if you have the time, stop to see the recently restored buildings with their carvings of masks and yet more Chac noses. About 3km farther on lies the site of **LABNÁ** (daily 8am–5pm; $4, free on Sun). Near the entrance to this ancient city is a palace, similar to but less impressive than that of Sayil, on which you'll see traces of sculptures including the inevitable Chac, and a crocodile (or snake) with a human face emerging from its mouth – symbolizing a god escaping from the jaws of the underworld. Remnants of a raised causeway lead from here to a second group of buildings, of which the most important is the **Arco de Labná**. Originally part of a complex linking two great squares, like that of the "Nunnery" at Uxmal, it now stands alone as a sort of triumphal arch. Both sides are richly decorated: on the east with geometric patterns; on the west (the back) with more of these and niches in the form of Maya huts or temples. Nearby is El Mirador, a temple with the well-preserved remains of a tall, elaborate roof-comb.

Oxkutzcab

From the village of **OXKUTZCAB**, also known as Huerta del Estado, you can head north back to Mérida via Ticul and Mani. Though there's little reason to overnight in Oxkutzcab, it's as good a place as any to stop for a while, with a huge **fruit market**, bustling and lively in the mornings, selling most of its produce by the crate or sack. Calles 51 and 50 edge the main park and the mercado, with a large Franciscan church cornering them.

Buses arrive from and leave for Mérida, via Ticul, about every hour (2hr). A few each day take the route past Mayapán. The **bus station** is at the corner of calles 56 and 51; *colectivos* come and go from beside the mercado on c/51. Of the two basic hotels, *Hospedaje "Trujeque"*, c/48, opposite the park (☎997/5-05-68; ②), is cleaner and more comfortable, though *Hospedaje Rosalia*, c/54 no. 103 (☎997/5-03-37; ②), has the advantage of being just around the corner from the bus station. The *Banamex* **bank** on c/50, opposite the park, can only exchange US dollars cash – not travellers' cheques. **Restaurants** and cafeterias skirt the market, but if you fancy a long, lazy lunch, try a few blocks back at the *Restaurante Su Cabaña Suiza*, c/54 no. 101, where *comidas* are served in the tranquillity of a spacious open-sided *palapa*.

The Grutas de Loltún

Hidden away near the minor road from Labná, the **Grutas de Loltún** (daily 9am–5pm; $7, $2 on Sun), studded with stalactites and stalagmites (one in the shape of a giant corn cob), were revered by the Maya as a source of water from a time long before they built their cities. At the entrance, a huge bas-relief of a Jaguar Warrior guards the opening to the underworld, and throughout there are traces of ancient paintings and carvings on the walls. Nowadays the caves are lit, and there are spectacular guided tours (officially at 9.30am, 11am, 12.30pm, 2pm & 3pm; in practice it depends on who turns up, and when). The surrounding jungle is visible through the collapsed floor of the last gallery and tree roots 10m long find an anchor on the cavern floor. The *Restaurante Guerrero*, by the entrance to the caves, is welcome but expensive.

There's very little transport to the caves **from Oxkutzcab**: taxis exploit their monopoly by charging well over the odds for the short run. *Colectivos* and trucks that pass the caves leave from c/51 next to the market; if you get there by 8.30am you may be able to catch the truck taking the cave employees to work. Getting back is less easy, as the trucks are full of workers and produce, but, if you wait, something will turn up.

Ticul

Conveniently located 80km south of Mérida, **TICUL** makes an excellent base for exploring the Puuc region. The town is an important pottery-producing centre, full of shops selling reproduction Maya antiquities, mostly too big to carry home. Visitors are welcome at the *fabricas* to watch the manufacturing process. The footwear trade is big here too, with almost as many shoe shops as ceramic outlets. Despite this, Ticul lives life at a slow pace, with more bicycles (and passenger-carrying *triciclos*) than cars.

On the main road between Mérida and Felipe Carrillo Puerto in Quintana Roo, Ticul is an important transport centre, well served by **buses** to and from Mérida and with services to Cancún. If you're arriving **by bus from Mérida**, you'll be dropped in c/24 on the corner with c/25, behind the church. Buses from Campeche don't go through Ticul so you'll have to get off at Santa Elena to catch one of the *colectivos* that leave from the main square between about 6am and 7pm. The trip takes about thirty minutes.

Even-numbered roads run north to south, odd numbers east to west. Calle 23 is the main street, with the plaza at its eastern end at c/26. Half a block from the plaza, the *Sierra Sosa*, c/26 no. 199-A (☎997/2-00-08; ④), has basic **rooms**, with shower and fan (upstairs is better), and a few new a/c rooms with TV. The English-speaking manager, Luis Sierra, is a good source of information, and you can make international calls from the reception. Alternatives include the plusher *Motel Cerro Inn*, c/ 23 no. 292, at the western edge of town (☎997/2-02-60; ③), in its own tree-shaded spacious grounds with an on-site *palapa* restaurant; and the newer *Hotel Bugambilias*, c/23 between 44 and 46 (☎997/2-07-61; ③), slightly closer to town than the *Cerro*, but with less character.

The best of the **restaurants** is the original *Los Almendros*, c/23 no. 207, which serves superb local dishes in pleasant surroundings. The *Restaurant Colorín*, next door to *Hotel Sierra Sosa* on c/26, does an inexpensive *comida*, or, if you fancy a large satisfying pizza, try *La Gondolia Pizzeria*, c/23 on the corner of c/26. As usual, the least expensive places are the *loncherías* near the bus station. **Trucks** for Oxkutzcab and surrounding villages set off when they're full from the side of the plaza next to the church; **combis** for Mérida leave from farther down the same street.

Mayapán and Mani

MAYAPÁN was, from the eleventh to the fifteenth century, the most powerful city in the Yucatán. Its history is somewhat vague but, according to Maya chronicles, it formed (with Chichén Itzá and Uxmal) one of a triumvirate of cities that as the **League**

of **Mayapán** exercised control over the entire peninsula from around 987 to 1185*. This broke up when the **Cocom** dynasty of Mayapán attacked and overwhelmed the rulers of Chichén Itzá, establishing themselves as sole controllers of the peninsula. Mayapán became a huge city by the standards of the day, with a population of some 15,000 in a site covering five square kilometres, in which traces of more than 4000 buildings have been found – here, rulers of subject cities were forced to live where they could be kept under control, perhaps even as hostages. This hegemony was maintained until 1441 when Ah Xupan, a Xiu leader from Uxmal, finally led a rebellion that succeeded in overthrowing the Cocom and destroying their city – thus paving the way for the disunited tribalism that the Spanish found on their arrival, which made their Conquest so much easier.

What can be seen today is a disappointment – the buildings anyway were crude and small by Maya standards, at best poor copies of what had gone before. This has led to its widespread dismissal as a "decadent" and failing society, but a powerful case can be made for the fact that it was merely a changing one. Here the priests no longer dominated – hence the lack of great ceremonial centres – and what grew instead was a more genuinely urban society: highly militaristic, no doubt, but also far more centralized and more reliant on trade than anything seen previously.

After the fall of Mayapán, the Xiu abandoned Uxmal and founded **MANI**. It's hard to believe that what is now simply a small village was, at the time of the Conquest, the largest city the Spanish encountered. Fortunately for the Spanish, its ruler, Ah Kukum Xiu, converted to Christianity and became their ally. Here, in 1548, was founded one of the earliest and largest **Franciscan monasteries** in the Yucatán. This still stands, surrounded now by Maya huts, and just about the only evidence of Mani's past glories are the ancient stones used in its construction. In front of the church, in 1562, Bishop Diego de Landa held the notorious *auto-da-fé* in which he burned the city's ancient records (because they "contained nothing in which there was not to be seen the superstitions and lies of the devil"), destroying virtually all surviving original Maya literature.

Chichén Itzá

Chichén Itzá, the most famous, the most extensively restored, and by far the most visited of all Maya sites, lies conveniently astride the main road from Mérida to Cancún and the Caribbean, about 120km from Mérida and a little more than 200km from the coast. There's a fast and very regular bus service all along this road, making it perfectly feasible to visit as a day's excursion from Mérida, or en route from Mérida to the coast (or even as a day out from Cancún, as many tour buses do). The site, though, deserves better, and both to do the ruins justice and to see them when they're not entirely overrun by tourists, an overnight stop is well worth considering – either at the site itself or, less extravagantly, at the nearby village of **Pisté** or in Valladolid.

The country you pass through is not of any outstanding interest – monotonously flat plain with only the occasional pueblo, the larger of them marked by the inevitable colonial church and, as often as not, by a semi-ruinous hacienda complete with abandoned *henequen* processing factory. If you rent a car in Mérida and take the back roads, you'll pass through an amazing number of once prosperous villages and towns, each place equipped with a huge crumbling church – an indication of Yucatán's wealth just one century ago.

---

*These dates, based on surviving Maya chronicles, are controversial, since archeological evidence suggests that Mayapán was not a significant settlement until the thirteenth century. The rival theory has Mayapán founded around 1263, after the fall of Chichén Itzá.

If your trip to Chichén Itzá is fairly leisurely, **IZAMAL,** 72km from Mérida, is the one place that does merit a detour. Though still a large town, Izamal is something of a quiet backwater whose colonial air is denied by its inhabitants' allegiance to their traditional dress and lifestyle. It was formerly an important Maya religious centre, where they worshipped **Itzamna,** mythical founder of the ancient city and one of the gods of creation, at a series of huge pyramid-temples. Most are now no more than low hillocks in the surrounding country, but two survive in the town itself. One, **Kinich Kakmo** (daily 8am–8pm; free), just a couple of blocks from the central plaza and dedicated to the sun god, has been partly restored. The other had its top lopped off by the Spanish and was replaced with a vast monastery, the **convent of St Anthony of Padua** (daily; free), painted pale yellow, like much of the town. The porticoed atrium, or square, in front of this church encloses a vast 8000 square metres, and inside is the Virgen de Izamal, patron saint of the Yucatán.

There are two simple **hotels** in Izamal, next to each other on the main square. The *Kabul* (☎995/4-00-08; ③) is marginally more comfortable than the *Canto* (no phone; ②), though both offer rooms with fans and bath. Don't get caught out with no money in Izamal as there isn't a bank, though there is a **post office** on the main square. *Restaurant Portales* on the main square serves good Mexican **food**, as does the *Cafe Restaurant Los Norteños*, next to the bus station, one block back from the main square.

Buses to Izamal run from the main second-class bus station in Mérida, and there are several onward services to Valladolid, passing Chichén Itzá. To continue eastwards you have to get a Mérida bus back as far as Hoctun, on the main road, and pick up a mainline bus from there.

Practicalities

Arriving at Chichén Itzá you'll find that the highway, which once cut straight through the middle of the ruins, has been re-routed around the site. If you're on a through bus it may drop you at the junction of the by-pass and the old road, about ten minutes' walk from the entrance – most, though, drive right up to the site entrance. Although blocked off by gates at each side of the fenced-in site, the old road still exists, conveniently dividing the ruins in two: **Chichén Viejo** (Old Chichén) to the south, **Nuevo Chichén** (New or Toltec Chichén) to the north.

The main **entry to the site** (daily 8am–5pm, though the process of getting everyone out starts at least an hour earlier; $7, at least $7 extra with video camera or tripod, free on Sun) is to the west, at the Mérida end. Keep your ticket, which permits re-entry, and check the timetable for admissions to the various buildings – most open only for a couple of hours each day, and you'll want to plan your wanderings around their schedules. There are bus and car parks here, and a huge **visitors centre** (open until 10pm) with a museum, restaurant, and shops selling souvenirs, film, maps and guides (best are the *Panorama* series). **Guided tours** of the ruins can be arranged at the visitors centre. Group tours (9am–3.30pm) are for six to eight people, in Spanish or English, and cost around $8 per person. Private tours (8am–2.30pm) cost around $33 per guide. There's a nightly **son et lumière** in English (9pm; $6) and Spanish (7pm; $4): worth seeing if you're staying nearby – it's no great shakes, but there's nothing else to do in the evening.

You can also buy tickets and get in at the **smaller eastern gate** by the *Hotel Mayaland* (see p.512), where there are fewer facilities. Book at the hotel reception for two-hour **horseback riding trips** around Chichén Viejo.

To make your way to the Caribbean coast from Chichén Itzá, it's best to take any bus you can as far as Valladolid (see p.516), and if necessary change there for a first-class service.

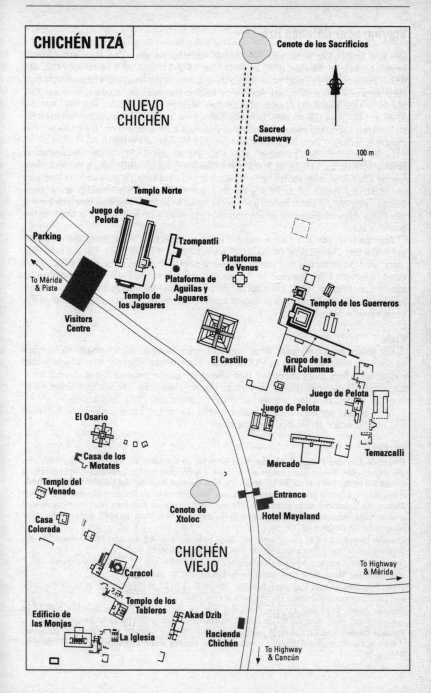

CHICHÉN ITZÁ

Cenote de los Sacrificios

NUEVO CHICHÉN

Sacred Causeway

0   100 m

Templo Norte

Juego de Pelota

Parking

Tzompantli

Plataforma de Venus

To Mérida & Piste

Plataforma de Aguilas y Jaguares

Templo de los Jaguares

Visitors Centre

El Castillo

Templo de los Guerreros

Grupo de las Mil Columnas

Juego de Pelota

Juego de Pelota

El Osario

Casa de los Metates

Temazcalli

Templo del Venado

Mercado

Casa Colorada

Cenote de Xtoloc

Entrance

Hotel Mayaland

CHICHÉN VIEJO

To Highway & Mérida

Caracol

Templo de los Tableros

Akad Dzib

Edificio de las Monjas

La Iglesia

Hacienda Chichén

To Highway & Cancún

Staying near Chichén Itzá

Chichén Itzá boasts some excellent hotels virtually **on site**. The *Hacienda Chichén* (☎985/1-00-45; in Mérida: ☎99/24-88-44, fax 24-50-11; in US: ☎1-800/624-8451; ⑧), which has a couple of small ruins within its grounds, is the best; unfortunately it is only open between November and April. For written reservations, contact c/60 no. 488, Mérida 97000. The *Hotel Mayaland*, Carretera Mérida–Puerto Juárez Km 120 (☎985/1-01-29 or 1-00-77; in US: ☎1-800/235-4079; ⑨), is also beautiful, with a gorgeous colonial-style dining room and rooms in luxurious thatched huts dotted about the gardens. You can book packages here with *Mayaland Tours* in Mérida (see p.499).

Least aesthetically pleasing, but still pretty good, is *Villas Arqueologicas* (☎985/1-00-34; fax 1-00-18; in México: ☎5/254-7077; fax 255-3164; ⑧), a modern place run by *Club Med*, with rooms set out round a patio enclosing a pool and cocktail bar: by night, its library of archeological and architectural tomes doubles as a disco (usually empty). All three hotels have pools, open to anyone who eats lunch there – in the *Villas Arqueologicas* you could probably get away with just having a drink at the poolside bar.

Alternatively, you can take a taxi in the **other direction** (east) from the ruins and get to the tiny *Dolores Alba* (☎985/21-37-45; in Mérida: ☎99/28-31-63; ⑤), just over 2km away, with a restaurant and rooms around a pool – the best value here if you don't mind being stuck by the road in the middle of nowhere (but still much less than an hour's walk from the site). The staff are very helpful and friendly and will provide transport to the site (but not back). Rooms can be booked in advance at the hotel of the same name in Mérida (see p.492).

Pisté

About **thirty minutes' walk west** from the ruins, along a rather overgrown footpath beside the road, the village of **PISTÉ** is the place to stay cheaply near Chichén Itzá; rooms are a little more expensive than elsewhere on the peninsula, but at quiet times it's worth bargaining. **Buses** pass every thirty minutes for Mérida and about every hour for Valladolid. There are also services to Cancún and Playa del Carmen.

Most **hotels** are on the main road, between the village and the ruins; the following are listed in order of distance from the ruins.

HOTELS

Piramide Inn and Trailer Park, 2km from the ruins, on Carretera Mérida–Valladolid (☎985/1-01-15). Reasonable, though some rooms are in need of decoration and the proximity to the main road means it's pretty noisy at night. However, it's near the bus stop and the western entrance to the ruins, there's a decent pool open to non-residents, and a tennis court. Home of *The Explorers Club of Mexico*, it's decorated with accounts of the members' exploits, and they offer tours to several remote ruins and *cenotes*. There's camping in the grounds, away from the road, and room for a few hammocks ($5 per person). ⑤.

Posada Novelo, next to the *Oriente* bus stop. New place under the same management as the *Stardust Inn*, whose rather unimpressive pool residents can use. ④.

Stardust Inn, Carretera Mérida–Puerto Juárez Km 118 (☎985/1-01-22). Modern, a/c rooms. ⑥.

Posada Chac Mool. New, basic and friendly, just beyond the *Stardust*. ④.

Hotel Misión Chichén Itzá Park Inn, Km 118 (☎985/1-00-22; in Mérida: ☎99/23-95-00, fax 23-76-75). Laid-back atmosphere and the best pool in Pisté. ⑧.

Posada Maya, c/41 and 42, 20m down the road by the sign to Tizimín. Another new basic, concrete hotel, away from the village centre, with hammock space ($5) for about five people. ③.

Posada Olalde, c/6, off the main road; coming from the bus terminal, turn left by *El Guayacan Artesenía*. Basic, clean and friendly; rooms with fans and hot water. The village itself is 100m or so beyond. ④.

RESTAURANTS

Pisté also offers a number of **restaurants**, most of them on the main road near the hotels. Their prices, like those of the hotels, are a little higher than similar places elsewhere, but if you have a full day at the ruins it works out economical to eat at Pisté and re-enter the site later. Closest to the ruins, the *Piramide Inn*, on the eastern edge of Pisté, offers a $10 *comida corrida*, while opposite, the huge *Restaurant Bar Pueblo Maya* caters for tour groups, with a $10 buffet from 11am to 4.30pm (vegetarian dishes on request); at *Restaurant Xaybeh*, also aimed at the tour group market, you can eat a buffet lunch then take a dip in the pool. At the opposite end of the scale, *Mr Taco Pizzeria*, opposite the *Misión Chichén*, sells pizza and Mexican food. For an evening meal, *Restaurant los Pàjaros* is the most popular choice, with laid-back surroundings and reasonable prices.

The Site

Though in most minds the image of **CHICHÉN ITZÁ** *is* the image of the Maya, in reality it is its very divergence from Maya tradition that makes it so fascinating, and so important to archeologists. For at Chichén Itzá the stamp of an outside influence – that of the **Toltecs** – is clearly marked across all the most famous structures.

The site's **history** is a curious and hotly disputed one, but its broad outlines are accepted by most authorities. A city was founded around the fifth century, and flourished along with all the great Classic Maya sites until about 900 AD: much of Chichén Viejo reflects this era. Thereafter it appeared, like many Maya centres, to decline – but at Chichén there was a startling renaissance in the following century. New and magnificent buildings clearly employed the themes and style of central Mexico: new gods, a new emphasis on militarism and, apparently, human sacrifice on an unprecedented scale. The city had, it seems, been conquered and taken over by the Toltecs under their god-king **Quetzalcoatl** (Kukulkán to the Maya), and a dynasty established in which Maya and Toltec art were fused into a new synthesis. There are all sorts of problems with the theory – some claim that Tula, the Toltec capital, was a Maya colony from the start, others point to similar tales of an invasion by the **Itzá**, who may or may not have been the same people as the Toltecs – but it fits remarkably well with both Maya and Aztec accounts of the banishment of Quetzalcoatl from Tula in 987 and his subsequent journey to the east, and with a good deal of the archeological evidence.

Chichén Nuevo

If it's still reasonably early, head first for **El Castillo** (or the Pyramid of Kukulkán), the structure that dominates the site. This should allow you to climb it before the full heat of the day, and get a good overview of the entire area. It is a simple, relatively unadorned square building, with a monumental stairway climbing each face (though only two are restored), rising in nine receding terraces to a temple at the top. The simplicity is deceptive, however, as the building is in fact the **Maya calendar** made stone: each staircase has 91 steps, which, added to the single step at the main entrance to the temple, amounts to 365; other numbers relevant to the Maya calendar recur throughout the construction. Most remarkably, at sunset on the spring and autumn equinoxes, the great serpents' heads at the foot of the main staircase are joined to their tails (at the top) by an undulating body of shadow – an event of just a few hours that draws spectators, and awed worshippers, by the thousand.

Inside the present structure, an earlier pyramid survives almost wholly intact. An entrance has been opened at the bottom of El Castillo, through which you reach a narrow, dank and claustrophobic stairway (formerly the outside of the inner pyramid) that leads steeply to a temple on the top. In its outer room is a rather crude chac-mool, but in the **inner sanctuary**, now railed off, stands one of the greatest finds at the site: an altar, or throne, in the form of a jaguar, painted bright red and inset with jade "spots" and eyes – the teeth are real jaguar teeth. This discovery created endless problems for archeologists, since these are clearly Toltec relics yet the temple apparently predates their arrival. Most would say now either that the original dating was wrong, or that the Toltecs discovered the original pyramid just as modern investigators have done. The interior is open for just a couple of hours in the middle of the day, starting at 11am (but check the current times).

THE TOLTEC PLAZA

The Castillo stands on the edge of the great grassy plaza that formed the focus of Nuevo (Toltec) Chichén Itzá: all its most important buildings are here, and from the northern edge a *sacbe*, or sacred causeway, leads to the great **Cenote de los Sacrificios**. The **Templo de los Guerreros** (Temple of the Warriors), and the adjoining **Grupo de las Mil Columnas** (Group of the Thousand Columns), take up the eastern edge of the plaza. These are the structures that most recall the great Toltec site of Tula (see p.302), both in design and in detail – in particular the colonnaded courtyard (which would originally have been roofed with some form of thatch) and the use of "Atlantean" columns, representing warriors in armour, their arms raised above their heads. Throughout, the temple is richly decorated with carvings and sculptures (originally with paintings, too) of jaguars and eagles devouring human hearts, feathered serpents, Toltec warriors and, the one undeniably Maya feature, masks of Chac. On top are two superb **chac-mools**: offerings were placed on the stomachs of these reclining figures, representing the messengers who would take the sacrifice to the gods, or perhaps the divinities themselves.

Once again, the Templo de los Guerreros was built over an earlier temple, in which (during set hours) some remnants of faded **murals** can be made out. The "thousand" columns alongside originally formed a square, on the far side of which is the building known as the **Mercado**, although there's no evidence that this actually was a marketplace. Near here, too, is a small, ruinous ball-court.

Walking across the plaza towards the main ball-court, you pass three small platforms. The **Plataforma de Venus** is a simple, raised, square block, with a stairway up each side guarded by feathered serpents. Here, rites associated with Quetzalcoatl in his role of Venus, the morning star, would have been carried out. Slightly smaller, but otherwise virtually identical in design, is the **Aquilas y Jaguares** platform, on which you'll see relief carvings of eagles and jaguars holding human hearts. The jaguar and the eagle were symbols of the Toltec warrior classes, one of whose duties was to capture sacrificial victims. Human sacrifices may even have been carried out here, judging by the proximity of the third platform, the **Tzompantli**, where victims' skulls were hung on display. This is carved on every side with grotesquely grinning stone skulls.

THE BALL-COURT

Chichén Itzá's **Juego de Pelota** (ball-court), on the western side of the plaza, is the largest known in existence – some 90m long – and again its design recalls Tula: a capital I shape surrounded by temples, with the goals, or target rings, halfway along each side. Along the bottom of each side wall runs a sloping panel decorated in low relief with scenes of the game and its players. Although the rules and full significance of the game remain a mystery, it was clearly not a Saturday afternoon kick-about in the park. The players are shown processing towards a circular central symbol, the symbol of death, and one player (presumably the losing captain – just right of the centre) has been decapitated, while another (to the left, surely the winner) holds his head and a ritual knife. Along the top runs the stone body of a snake, whose heads stick out at either end of this "bench".

At each end of the court stand small buildings with open **galleries** overlooking the field of play – the low one at the south may simply have been a grandstand, that at the north (the **Templo Norte**, also known as the Temple of the Bearded Man, after a sculpture inside) was almost certainly a temple – perhaps, too, the umpires' stand. Inside, there are several worn relief carvings and a whispering gallery effect that enables you to be heard clearly at the far end of the court, and to hear what's going on there.

The **Templo de los Jaguares** also overlooks the playing area, but from the side; to get to it, you have to go back out to the plaza. At the bottom – effectively the outer wall of the ball-court – is a little portico supported by two pillars, between which a stone jaguar stands sentinel. Inside are some wonderful, rather worn, relief carvings of Maya priests, Toltec warriors, and animals, birds and plants. Beside this, a very steep, narrow staircase ascends to a platform overlooking the court and to the **Upper Temple** (restricted opening hours), with its fragments of a mural depicting battle scenes – perhaps the fight between Toltec and Maya for control of the city.

The **Cenote de los Sacrificios** lies at the end of the causeway that leads off through the trees from the northern side of the plaza – about 300m away. It's a remarkable phenomenon, an almost perfectly round hole in the limestone surface of the earth, some 60m in diameter and more than 40m deep, the bottom half full of water. It was thanks to the presence of this natural well (and perhaps another in the southern half of the site) that the city could survive at all, and it gives Chichén Itzá its present name "At the Edge of the Well of the Itzá". Into the well the Maya would throw offerings – incense, statues, jade and especially metal disks (a few of them gold), engraved and embossed with figures and glyphs – and also human sacrificial victims. People who were thrown in and survived emerged with the power of prophecy, having spoken with the gods. A new cafeteria now overlooks the well, a distraction for anyone contemplating the religious and mystical significance of the *cenote*.

Chichén Viejo

Buildings in the southern half of the site are not, on the whole, in such good condition. Less restoration work has been carried out here so far, and the ground is not so extensively cleared. A path leads from the road opposite El Castillo to all the major structures, passing first the pyramid known as **El Osario** (aka the High Priest's Grave), currently undergoing restoration. Externally it is very similar to El Castillo but inside, most unusually, was discovered a series of **tombs**. A shaft, explored at the end of the last century, drops down from the top through five crypts, in each of which was found a skeleton and a trap door leading to the next. The fifth is at ground level, but here too there was a trap door, and steps cut through the rock to a sixth chamber that opens onto a huge underground cavern – the burial place of the high priest. Sadly the shaft and cavern are not open to the public.

Near here, also very ramshackle, are the **Templo del Venado** (Temple of the Deer) and the **Casa Colorada** (Red House), with a cluster of ruins known as the Southwest Group beyond them. Follow the path round, however, and you arrive at **El Caracol** (the Snail, for its shape; also called the Observatory), a circular, domed tower standing on two rectangular platforms and looking remarkably like a twentieth-century observatory in outline. No telescope, however, was mounted in the roof, which instead has slits aligned with various points of astronomical observation. Four doors at the cardinal points lead into the tower, where there's a circular chamber and a spiral staircase leading to the upper level, from where sightings were made.

El Caracol is something of a Maya-Toltec mix, with few of the obvious decorative features associated with either: the remaining buildings are pure Maya. The so-called **Edificio de las Monjas** (the Nunnery) is the largest and most important of them – a palace complex showing several stages of construction. It's in rather poor condition, the rooms mostly filled with rubble and inhabited by flocks of swallows, and part of the facade blasted away by a nineteenth-century explorer, but is nonetheless a building of grand proportions. Its **annexe** has an elaborate facade in the Chenes style, covered in masks of Chac which combine to make one giant mask, with the door as a mouth. **La Iglesia** (the Church), a small building standing beside the convent, is by contrast a clear demonstration of Puuc design, with a low band of unadorned masonry around the bottom surmounted by an elaborate mosaic frieze and a roof-comb. Hook-nosed masks of Chac again predominate, but above the doorway are also the figures of the four **bacabs**, mythological creatures that held up the sky – a snail and a turtle on one side, an armadillo and a crab on the other.

Beyond Las Monjas, a path leads in about fifteen minutes to a further group of ruins – among the oldest on the site, but unrestored. Nearer at hand is the **Akad Dzib**, a relatively plain block of palace rooms which takes its name ("Obscure writings") from some undeciphered hieroglyphs found inside. There are, too, red palm prints on the walls of some of the chambers – a sign frequently found in Maya buildings, whose significance is not yet understood. From here you can head back to the road past El Caracol and the Cenote de Xtoloc.

Valladolid and around

The second town of Yucatán state, **VALLADOLID** is around 40km from Chichén Itzá, still close enough to beat the crowds to the site on an early bus, and of interest in its own right. Although it took a severe bashing in the nineteenth-century Caste Wars, the town has retained a strong colonial feel, and centres on a pretty, peaceful zócalo. The most famous of the surviving churches is sixteenth-century **San Bernardino**, 1km southwest of the zócalo (daily 9am–11pm; mass daily at 6pm). Built over one of the town's **cenotes**, Sis-Ha, the church is currently under restoration: the buildings are very impressive, but there's little left inside as, like so many of the Yucatán's churches, San Bernardino was sacked by the local Indians in the Wars. Valladolid's other *cenote*, **Zací**, on c/36 between 39 and 37 (daily 8am–6pm; $2), has become a tourist attraction, with a museum and an open-air restaurant at the entrance.

Arrival and information

Valladolid's **bus station** is located on c/37 between 54 and 56, seven blocks to the west of the zócalo. *De paso* buses run at least hourly to both Mérida and Cancún and there are at least ten daily departures for Playa del Carmen, a few of which take the road past Cobá and call at Tulum. Some local second-class buses begin their journey here, too, for the above destinations and the smaller towns, including Tizimín, for Río Lagartos.

To get to the centre from the bus station takes about ten minutes. Turn left onto c/37, then right after a couple of blocks, then left again, following c/39 to the pretty zócalo; you'll pass some of the cheaper **hotels** on the way. The **tourist office** is on the southeastern corner of the zócalo (daily 9am–noon & 4–6pm). Though in theory there's plenty of information available, including free maps of Valladolid, you'll be lucky to find the office attended. Best to head for **El Bazaar**, a collection of inexpensive restaurants on the corner of c/39 and 40 on the zócalo; the souvenir shop here has maps and current information. The **post office** is on the zócalo, near the corner of c/39 on c/40 (Mon–Fri 8am–2.30pm), as is *Bancomer*, which changes travellers' cheques between 9.30am and 12.30pm. For national and international **telephone calls** there are *Computel casetas* at the bus station and on the zócalo (daily 7am–10pm). You can **rent bikes** from the little shop *Refaccionaría de Bicicletas Paulino Sliva*, c/44 no. 191, between 39 and 41, for $3 an hour.

Accommodation

Valladolid's budget hotels lie between the bus station and the centre, but for more atmosphere it's worth splashing out a bit to stay in colonial style on the zócalo.

María de la Luz, c/42, on the zócalo (☎985/6-20-71). Rooms are less luxurious than the lobby, but comfortable and good value, with a/c. The restaurant opens onto the zócalo, and there's a pool. ⑤.

María Guadalupe, c/44 no. 198 (☎985/6-20-68). Clean, well-kept rooms with bath. ④.

Maya, c/41 no. 231, four blocks west of the zócalo (no phone). The best-value cheap hotel, with rooms around a courtyard. ③.

El Mesón del Marqués, c/39 no. 203, on the zócalo (☎985/6-20-73 or 6-30-42; fax 6-22-80). Lovely hotel in a former colonial mansion overlooking a courtyard with fountains and lush plants. There's a wonderful palm-fringed pool, and one of the best restaurants in town. ⑦.

Mendoza, c/39 no. 204, corner of c/46 (☎ and fax 985/6-20-02). The sole advantage of this place is its proximity to the bus station; you'll find better quality if you press on towards the centre. ②–⑤.

San Clemente, c/42, corner of c/41 (☎985/6-22-08). Just off the zócalo, this very comfortable hotel has similar prices and better facilities than the *María de la Luz*. Restaurant and pool. ④–⑤.

Zací, c/44 no. 193, between 39 and 37 (☎985/6-21-67). Pleasant hotel with lovely, plant-filled courtyard and a small pool. Rooms have either a fan or, for a few dollars more, a/c and cable. ⑤.

Eating and drinking

Whatever your budget, to eat well in Valladolid you don't have to stray farther than the zócalo, where you can get inexpensive snacks or treat yourself without going into debt.

El Bazaar, northeastern corner of the zócalo, c/39 and 40. Inexpensive *loncherías* and pizzerias, always busy and open until late.

Casa de los Arcos, c/39 between 38 and 40 (☎985/6-27-20). Mid-priced restaurant recommended for its Yucatecan specialities.

El Mesón del Marqués, c/39 no. 203, on the zócalo. Tranquillity in the centre of town with tables around the fountain of the hotel courtyard, where you can eat Yucatecan specialities such as lime soup and *poc-chuc*. Probably Valladolid's best restaurant.

Restaurante San Bernardino de Siena, c/49 no. 227, two blocks from Convento San Bernadino (☎985/6-27-20). Locally known as *Don Juanito's* and frequented mostly by Mexicans, this highly recommended, mid-priced restaurant is a great place for a lazy lunch or dinner away from the hustle and bustle of the town centre.

Around Valladolid

From Valladolid the vast majority of traffic heads straight on to Cancún and the Caribbean beaches. There are a few places worth taking time out to explore, however, and, if you have more time, an alternative is to head north via Tizimín to **Río Lagartos** or **San Felipe**. You'll need to make an early start if you want to co-ordinate your buses, go on a flamingo trip and get back to Valladolid in the same day – the last bus for Tizimín from Río Lagartos leaves at 5.30pm and the last bus for Valladolid leaves Tizimín at 7pm. You'll have to return to Valladolid to head on to the Caribbean coast.

Balankanché

Six kilometres from Chichén Itzá on the way to Valladolid, you can visit the **Caves of Balankanché**, where in 1959 a sealed passageway was discovered leading to a series of caverns in which the ancient population had left offerings to Tlaloc, the Toltec equivalent of Chac. "Guided tours" (in English daily 11am, 1pm & 3pm; $7, $2.50 on Sun) – in reality, a taped commentary – lead you past the usual stalactites and stalagmites, an underground pool and, most interestingly, many of the original Maya offerings still in situ. Be warned that in places the caves can be cold, damp and thoroughly claustrophobic. Charles Gallenkamp's *Maya* (see "Books" in *Contexts*) has an excellent chapter devoted to the discovery of the caves, and to the ritual of exorcism that a local *h-man* (traditional priest) insisted on carrying out to placate the ancient gods and disturbed spirits. Buses between Valladolid and Mérida will drop you at *las grutas*.

Cenote Dzitnup

Seven kilometres west of Valladolid, the remarkable **Cenote Dzitnup** or X'Keken (daily 8am–5pm; $1.50) is reached by descending into a cave, where a nearly circular pool of crystal-clear, turquoise water is illuminated by a shaft of light from a opening in the roof. A swim in the ice-cold water is a fantastic experience, but take a sweater as the temperature in the cave is noticeably cooler than outside.

Any westbound second-class bus will drop you at the turn-off, 5km from Valladolid, then it's a 2km walk down a signed track. You could also take a taxi or, best of all, cycle from Valladolid.

Río Lagartos and Las Coloradas

Travelling by bus from Valladolid north to Río Lagartos, you have to change at the elegant colonial town of **TIZIMÍN**, 51km from Valladolid. There's little to see, but the small **Parque Zoológico de la Reina** has animals from all over the peninsula, and the pretty plaza is peaceful enough for whiling away a few hours. The best of the modest but overpriced hotels in the centre is *María Antonia*, c/50 (☎986/3-23-84; ④). Tizimín also has direct bus services to and from Mérida and Cancún.

RÍO LAGARTOS, 100km north of Valladolid, stands on a lagoon in marshy coastal flatland, inhabited by vast colonies of **pink flamingoes**. There's talk of turning the area into a new tourist centre, but so far it remains a backwater fishing village, with just one hotel and a couple of *cabañas*. The overpriced *Hotel María Nerfertiti* on c/40 (⑩) is reached by turning left from the bus station, right at the junction and then left onto c/17. The very comfortable *Cabañas dos Hermanos*, at the back of a family home, by the beach, are better. Each can sleep two or three people, with private bathrooms and pay-as-you-view cable TV. From the bus station, turn right and continue on to the water's edge. You can also **camp** on the lagoon shore almost anywhere near town. A boat trip over to the seaward shore of the spit that encloses the lagoon will bring you to a couple of **beaches**, but they're not up to much, and in the end it's the flamingoes alone that make a visit worthwhile.

The *María Nerfertiti* is a good starting point for finding a guide to take you to the flamingoes, though you're likely to be swamped by offers as soon as you get off the bus or out of your car. A **boat** to visit the many feeding sites costs around $45, with a maximum of seven people, but the price and length of the trip are infinitely negotiable. Make sure that your guide understands that you don't want to harass the flamingoes, as some will get too close if they think their passengers would prefer to see some action. If you want to be certain that you are getting a knowledgeable guide, controlled by the syndicate that protects the flamingoes, prearrange a trip with Adrian Marfil, c/16 no. 100 (☎3-26-68), or from Cancún with *EcoloMex Tours* (☎98/84-38-05; fax 84-38-49). Incidentally, you're unlikely to see any of the crocodiles for which Río Lagartos was named as they have been hunted to virtual extinction.

The most spectacular colony is at **Las Coloradas**, on the narrow spit that separates the lagoon from the sea about 16km east of Río Lagartos. There's a small village and salt factory here, but you'll need your own transport, as the bus timetable does not give you a chance to stay long enough to see anything. So for bird-watching without a car, you're again at the mercy of the *María Nefertiti*, or try the *Restaurante Economico*, opposite, where local fishermen may be prepared to take you out.

San Felipe

If it's beaches you're after, **SAN FELIPE**, 12km west of Río Lagartos, is a much better bet – many of the buses from Valladolid to Río Lagartos come out here. There are a few cheap rooms for rent, above the *Marufo* cinema, and at least one good restaurant, the *El Payaso*. But most people get a boat across to the offshore spit to set up **camp** on one of a number of beaches. At Mexican holiday times these are positively crowded, the rest of the year quite deserted. If you do camp, be sure to bring protection against mosquitoes; if not, it's easy enough to arrange for the boat to collect you in the evening.

Isla Holbox

Although most traffic between Mérida and the coast heads directly east to Cancún, it is possible to turn north at Valladolid or Nuevo X-Can to **Chiquilá**, where you can board the ferry for **ISLA HOLBOX**, a 25-kilometre-long island near the easternmost point of the Gulf coast. Sometimes touted as a new beach paradise to fill the place that Isla Mujeres once had in travellers' affections, it's by no means as attractive: the water is murkier than on the Caribbean coast and the sea can be rough. However, there are miles of empty beaches to enjoy, and anyone who's come from the more touristy resorts will find the island's relaxed, laid-back pace – and the genuinely warm welcome – something of a relief.

Practicalities
Buses for Chiquilá leave Valladolid (2hr 30min) and Tizimín (1hr 30min) a couple of times a day. Catch an early bus to make sure you get the afternoon ferry. Coming from the east, get a bus to the road junction just before Nuevo X-Can and wait for a *colectivo* ($1.50) to Kantunilkin, about halfway to Chiquilá, where you can pick up the bus. The **Chiquilá ferry** for Holbox leaves twice a day, at 8am and 1pm (1hr; $2), and returns at 5am and noon. Holbox is also served by a **car ferry**, leaving Chiquilá at 10am (daily except Thurs & Sun) and returning at 6am. Make sure you don't miss the boat: Chiquilá is not a place you want to get stranded. There's a restaurant and a store but little else; if you need to stay the night in order to get the early ferry, you could camp under the *palapa* by the basketball court – mosquito netting is essential.

Isla Holbox has a few simple and inexpensive **hotels** (to contact any, call ☎988/7-16-68 and ask for the hotel by name or by its extension number). The first hotel you see, the *Posada Flamingo* (ext 102; ②), just to the right of the dock, has basic clean rooms with hot showers. It's handy for the early ferry and the friendly owners **rent scooters** and organize **boat trips**. To get nearer the **beach** you'll have to walk across the island, which takes about ten minutes. Here you'll find the *Posada Los Arcos* (②) on the plaza (ask at the *Tienda Dionora*), and, even nearer the sea, the *cabañas* at the *Posada Dingrid* (②). You'll also spot **houses for rent**, which can be worth it if you plan to stay a while. A couple of shops provide basic supplies and there are some good **seafood restaurants** but little in the way of entertainment; have a drink and a chat with a fisherman and you may get a chance to go fishing.

QUINTANA ROO AND THE CARIBBEAN COAST

The coastal state of **Quintana Roo** was a forgotten frontier for most of modern Mexican history – its lush tropical forests exploited for their mahogany and chicle (from which chewing gum is made), but otherwise unsettled, a haven for outlaws and pirates and for Maya living beyond the reach of central government. Tourism, however, has brought a dramatic upsurge of interest: in the 1970s the first highways were built, new townships settled, and the place finally became a full state (as opposed to an externally administered Federal Territory) in 1974. In an attempt to promote development Quintana Roo was initially a duty-free zone, and sales tax is still far lower

---

REEF BEHAVIOUR

Coral reefs are the richest and most complex ecosystems on earth but they are also very fragile. The colonies grow at a rate of only around 5cm per year, so they must be treated with care and respect if they are not to be damaged beyond repair. Remember to follow these **simple rules** while you are snorkelling, diving or in a boat.

- Never touch or stand on corals, as the living polyps on their surface are easily damaged.
- Avoid disturbing the sand around corals. Quite apart from spoiling visibility, the cloud of sand will settle over the corals and smother them.
- Don't remove shells, sponges or other creatures from the reef and avoid buying reef products from souvenir shops.
- Don't use suntan lotion in reef areas, as the oils remain on the surface of the water.
- Don't anchor boats on the reef: use the permanently secured buoys instead.
- Don't throw litter overboard.
- Check where you are allowed to go before going fishing.
- If you are an out-of-practice diver, make sure you revise your diving skills away from the reef first.

---

here than in the rest of Mexico. The most recent development has been the new, very fast, **cuota** road between Cancún and Mérida, a toll road running just north of the old road.

Nevertheless, most of the state remains very sparsely populated and much of the jungle-covered interior is relatively inaccessible. The stretch of coast beween Cancún and the beautifully located ruins of **Tulum** is the most heavily visited – and the focus of much recent, rapid hotel construction – but even here it's easy enough to escape the crowds. Modern development is centred on the mega-resort of **Cancún** in the north and the islands of **Isla Mujeres** and **Cozumel. Chetumal**, the state capital and a bustling modern city with a growth rate almost as phenomenal as that of Cancún, is of chief importance as a gateway to and from Belize. The southern coast, while rewarding for naturalists and adventurers, is difficult to visit: only a couple of roads offer access, and public transport is minimal.

The entire Caribbean coast is lined with stunning palm-fringed white-sand **beaches**, while its magnificent offshore **coral reefs** form part of the second-longest barrier reef system in the world. **Maya ruins** are dotted all along the coast, most spectacularly at Tulum, and dozens more lie hidden in the dense forests, though at the moment the only interior sites regularly open to visitors are **Cobá**, near Tulum, and **Kohunlich**, reached from Chetumal. However, the Mexican government is spending a good deal of time and money on restoring other sites in the south and it's worth checking with tourist offices for the latest situation.

Cancún

Hand-picked by computer, **CANCÚN** is, if nothing else, proof of the rise and rise of Quintana Roo, and of Mexico's remarkable ability to get things done in a hurry if the political will is there. In 1970 there was nothing here but an island sand-spit and a fishing village of some 120 people. Now it's a city with a resident population of half a million and with almost two million visitors a year.

To some extent the computer selected its location well. Cancún is marginally closer to Miami than it is to México, and if you come on an all-in package tour the place has a

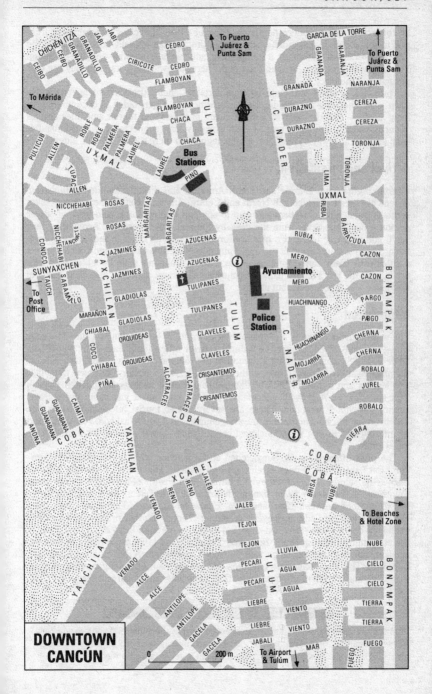

DOWNTOWN CANCÚN

lot to offer: striking modern hotels on white beaches; high-class entertainment from golf to scuba-diving; and much of the rest of the Yucatán is easily accessible. For the independent traveller, though, it is expensive, and can be frustrating and unwelcoming. You may well be forced to spend the night here, but without pots of money the true pleasures of the place will elude you.

There are, in effect, two quite separate parts to Cancún: the *zona commercial* downtown – the shopping and residential centre which, as it gets older, is becoming genuinely earthy – and the *zona hotelera*, a string of hotels and tourist amenities around "Cancún island", actually a narrow strip of sandy land connected to the mainland at each end by causeways. It encloses a huge lagoon, so there's water on both sides.

Arrival and orientation

Charter flights from Europe and South America, and direct scheduled flights from dozens of cities in Mexico and North and Central America, land at the **airport**, 15km south of the centre. *Colectivos* take you to any part of town for a fixed price of $8 per person – buy your ticket from the desk by the exit. Taxis cost $22. Arriving by bus, you'll pull in at one of the two **bus stations**, next to each other in the heart of downtown, just by a roundabout at the major junction of avenidas Tulum and Uxmal; there's a **guardería** (daily 7am–11pm). **Avenida Tulum**, Cancún's main street, is lined with the bulk of the city's shops, banks, restaurants and travel agencies, as well as many of the hotels – up side streets, but in view.

Information

The state **tourist office** is a couple of blocks from the bus station at Tulum 26 (daily 9am–9pm; ☎98/84-80-73). For the **federal tourist office** (daily 9am–9pm; ☎98/84-32-38 or 84-34-38), continue along Tulum until the roundabout at Av. Cobá, turn left and the office is at the furthest corner of the block with Av. J C Nader. Both have free maps and leaflets and copies of the ubiquitous **promotional listings magazines** *Cancún Tips* and *Cancún Nights*: all information you can pick up at just about every travel agency and hotel reception. There are several other tourist information kiosks on Tulum and in the *zona hotelera*; some are genuine, but if you're asked if you want "tourist information" as you pass it's almost certain you're being selected for a **timeshare sales pitch**.

The **post office** is on Av. Sunyaxchen at the junction with Xel-Ha (Mon–Fri 8am–7pm, Sat 9am–1pm). Service is efficient and friendly and there's a reliable *Lista de Correos* (postcode 77501). All the main **banks** – many with 24-hour ATMs – are along Tulum and in the *zona hotelera*; banking hours are 9am to 1.30pm but foreign exchange has to be done between 10am and 1pm. *Banco del Atlantico*, Tulum 15, offers good rates and credit card advances over the counter. There's another branch, with a money exchange booth (Mon–Fri 11am–2pm & 4–9pm), in the *zona hotelera* on the corner of the convention centre at Km 9. *Banamex*, Tulum 19, and in Plaza Terramar in the *zona hotelera*, offers a bad exchange rate but has a convenient ATM, as does *Bancomer*, Tulum 26. The many **casas de cambios** will change cash (including currencies other than US$) and travellers' cheques faster than the banks, but at worse rates.

ADDRESSES IN CANCUN

Downtown street names in Cancún are often followed by the letters **SM** and two numbers. These stand for *Supermanzanas*, or city districts, usually bounded by major thoroughfares. They're shown on all the city maps and do help you to find your way around.

Many hotels arrange **trips to the chief Maya ruins** – most commonly Chichén Itzá, Tulum and Cobá – check with the receptionist about the latest offers.

City transport

Downtown you'll be able to walk just about anywhere, but you need some sort of transport to get around the *zona hotelera*, which stretches for more than 20km. **Buses** marked "Tulum – Hoteles, Ruta 1" run to Av. Tulum every few minutes. There's a fixed fare of $1. Alternatively, **taxis** are plentiful and can be hailed almost anywhere – the trip between downtown and the *zona* costs around $6. A car affords you more scope and makes day trips as far as the ruins at Cobá perfectly feasible; **rental firms** are represented at most hotels and at the airport. Try *Avis*, Mayfair Plaza (☎98/83-08-03; airport: ☎98/86-02-22), or *Budget*, Tulum 214 (☎98/84-41-01).

Accommodation

Cancún has plenty of accommodation, most of it very expensive for the casual visitor. **Downtown** holds the only hope of a decent budget room, while the glittering beachfront palaces of the **zona hotelera** offer exclusive luxury, many with extravagant interiors featuring waterfalls and cascades of tropical vegetation. All have excellent service, with colour TV and minibars in rooms, at least one immaculate pool, glitzy bars and restaurants, and, more often than not, shops and a travel agency. Many will also have a show in the evening, a disco, or both. Of course, this is all rather expensive if you just drop by, but very much more reasonable as part of a **package**, and prices may be reduced considerably in the summer.

At the other end of the spectrum there is a 600-bed **youth hostel** out on the beach at the beginning of the *zona* on Av. Kukulkán (☎98/83-13-37; $10). Single-sex dorms have bunks and lockers; the beach isn't great here, but there's a pool.

Downtown hotels

Caribe Internacional, Yaxchilán 36, on the corner with Sunyaxchen (☎98/84-39-99; fax 84-19-92). Large hotel, popular with tour groups. Restaurant, bar, small pool and a travel agency. ⑥.

Casa de Huéspedes Punta Allen, c/Punta Allen 8, off Yaxchilán, near the junction with Uxmal (☎98/84-02-25). Quiet, friendly, family-run hotel with comfortable rooms (some a/c) and restaurant. ⑤.

Coral, Sunyaxchen 30, near Grosella (☎98/84-05-86; fax 84-45-69). Very reasonably priced for Cancún; away from the busiest traffic, clean rooms, some with a/c, and a pool. ④.

Hacienda, Sunyaxchen 39 (☎98/84-36-72; fax 84-12-08). Good location and good value; rooms all have a/c and colour TV and there's a pool, cafe, travel agency and beach club. ⑥.

Novotel, Tulum 27, corner of Azucenas and across from the bus station (☎98/84-29-99; fax 84-31-62). Centrally located, clean and secure; the best hotel in its class. Rooms with fan or a/c are very comfortable; try to get one at the back. The cool patio restaurant overlooks a small garden. ⑥.

Parador, Tulum 26, just south of the bus station (☎98/84-19-22; fax 84-97-12). Large, modern hotel with comfortable rooms offering surprisingly good value for the price. Parking. ⑥.

Piña Hermanos, c/7 Ote. (☎98/84-21-50). The best of three budget hotels in a row, and one of the city's best deals; from the bus station, head north along Tulum (by bus or about 15 minutes' walk) almost to the junction with Av. López Portillo. Turn right at c/10 Ote., then take the third on the right. Clean rooms with hot showers. ③.

Posada Luis Fernando, near the corner of López Portillo and c/25 Nte., SM63 (☎98/84-33-86). Basic rooms in a pleasant, family-run hotel. Locked courtyard for safe parking. Head west along Uxmal from the bus station. ③.

Tropical Caribe, c/Cerdo 30, five blocks north along Tulum from the bus station (☎98/84-14-42). Large place with plenty of basic but clean rooms with hot showers. Good budget option. ③.

Beach hotels

Club Las Vegas, Blvd. Kukulkán, Km 3.5 (☎98/83-22-22; fax 83-21-18; in US: ☎1-800/223-9815). Overlooking the Nichupté Lagoon, this all-inclusive resort (meals and drinks, sports and evening entertainment) somehow manages to retain a village atmosphere. ⑨.

Kin Há, Blvd. Kukulkán, Km 8 (☎98/83-23-77; fax 83-21-47). Beautiful rooms and suites with spacious balconies. Near the main shopping and entertainment centres. All the facilities and a great buffet breakfast at a reasonable price. ⑨.

Krystal Cancún, Blvd. Kukulkán, Km 9 (☎98/83-11-33; fax 83-17-90; in US: ☎1-800/231-9860). Definitely in the top league, even by Cancún standards. Full-service rooms, superbly decorated, and absolutely everything for a luxury holiday: sports facilities, fantastic swimming pools, two of the best restaurants around, and a justly famed disco. ⑨.

Presidente Cancún, Blvd. Kukulkán, Km 7.5 (☎98/83-02-00; fax 83-25-15; in US: ☎1-800/468-3571). Luxury, first-class hotel with superb service. All rooms overlook the sea, and there are two pools and a jacuzzi. ⑨.

El Pueblito, Blvd. Kukulkán, Km 17.5 (☎98/85-08-49 or 85-07-97; fax 85-07-31; in US: 1☎-800/325-2525). One of the best-value hotels on the beach, affordable even if you simply turn up. Built on high ground, the low-rise rooms are arranged in terraces around one of five pools (linked by the only waterslide in Cancún), and all have a balcony or patio. The beach is uncrowded this far up, and immaculately clean. Good-value poolside bar and restaurant. ⑦.

The Town

There's little to see in **downtown Cancún**; most visitors head straight for the *zona hotelera* and the **beaches**. Though you're free to go anywhere, some of the hotels do their best to make you feel like a trespasser, and staff will certainly move you off the beach furniture if you're not a guest. To avoid being eyed suspiciously by hotel heavies, head for one of the dozen or so **public beaches**: all are free but you may have to pay a small charge for showers. Entertainment and expensive watersports are laid on all around the big hotels; if you venture farther, where more sites await construction, you can find surprisingly empty sand and often a small group of nude sunbathers.

To catch a bit of culture while you're out here, the *Sheraton* boasts a small Maya ruin in its grounds, above the pool, while the **Museo de Antropología**, located behind the convention centre (Tues–Fri 9am–7pm, Sat & Sun 10am–5pm; $3, free on Sun), has a small but absorbing outline of Mesoamerican and Maya culture and history, with information in English and Spanish. Cancún's largest Maya remains, the **Ruinas del Rey** (daily 8am–5pm; $3, free on Sun), are at Km 17, overlooking the Nichupté Lagoon. They're not especially impressive – and, if you decide not to take one of the guides at the entrance, there's no information available to explain them – but the area is peaceful and very good for bird – and iguana – watching.

The best **snorkelling** in Cancún is at Punta Nizuc, next to *Club Med* territory. You aren't allowed to cross the grounds unless you're staying there, so you have to get off the bus at the *Westin Regina Resort*, cross their grounds to the beach, then turn right and walk for about twenty minutes until you reach the rocky point. Walk across the rocks and snorkel to your heart's content. To join a **snorkelling tour** or go **diving**, contact *Aqua Tours* (☎98/83-04-33) or *Fortunal* (☎98/86-13-98 or 85-13-96). Rates range from a one tank dive at about $45 to a full PADI open water certification course, which costs around $375. To view the colourful underwater life in a more leisurely fashion, take a trip on *Nautibus* (☎98/83-35-52 or 83-21-19; $25), a **glass-bottomed boat** that leaves from Playa Linda every ninety minutes from 8am until 3.30pm.

Eating

Cancún's **restaurants** outnumber hotels many times over, and competition is fierce. The bulk of the **tourist restaurants** line Av. Tulum and its side streets: eat here and you can enjoy "fun" disco sounds with your meal. Though seafood and steak form the mainstay of many menus, you can also eat Arabic, Yucatecan, Italian, Chinese, French, Cajun and Polynesian, not to mention international fast food plus some local chains. All the hotels in the *zona* have at least one **formal restaurant**, some of which are very elegant indeed, surrounded by tropical foliage with fountains and music. Many also feature a more relaxed and relaxing beach or **poolside** dining room.

For **budget food**, follow the locals and make for the markets. From the bus station, walk a few blocks north along Tulum, turn down Flamboyan or Cerdo and you'll come to the **Mercado Municipal**, with plenty of food stalls and tiny restaurants. Farther along, at the junction of Tulum and López Portillo, is a small plaza, complete with fountain, at the edge of another market. The little cafes here are packed with Mexican families and it's the nearest Cancún comes to having a zócalo.

Downtown

100% Natural, Sunyaxchen 26, at the junction with Yaxchilán. Not entirely vegetarian, but serves fruit drinks, salads, yoghurt and granola, as well as Mexican dishes, seafood and burgers. A pleasant enough place, if a little overpriced. There's also a branch in the Plaza Terramar in the *zona hotelera*.

Los Almendros, Bonampak 60, opposite the Plaza de Toros. This is the Cancún branch of the famous restaurant that originated in Ticul, and is justly renowned for its good-value Yucatecan specialities.

Gory Tacos, Tulipanes 26. Don't be put off by the name: this spotless and very friendly place serves good, inexpensive Mexican food, steaks, hamburgers and sandwiches, and a range of vegetarian meals.

La Habichuela, Margaritas 25, in front of the Parque Las Palapas. Long-established and fairly expensive restaurant set in a walled garden. The menu is excellent, featuring such dishes as *cocobichuela*: half a coconut filled with lobster and shrimp in a curry sauce, accompanied by tropical fruits. Live jazz adds to the atmosphere.

La Placita, Yaxchilán 12. Highly recommended Mexican restaurant. *Tacos*, steaks and the like served in fairly authentic style.

El Tacolote, Cobá 19, across from the hospital. Popular with Mexicans and offering a wide range of good-value *tacos*.

Taquería Yoly, Uxmal 42, near the corner with Yaxchilán. Inexpensive charcoal-grilled snacks in simple surroundings.

Las Tejas, Uxmal 26. The best place to enjoy charcoal-grilled meat *norteño* style, with hand-made *tortillas* at reasonable prices. Delicious *tacos*, too.

The zona hotelera

Doña Yola, between Plaza Caracol and Plaza Mayfair, opposite the *Fiesta Americana* hotel. Bargain all-you-can eat breakfast for $4; the rest of the American-style menu is more expensive.

Faro's, Plaza Lagunas. Famed for fresh fish, lobster, shrimp, crab, mussels and clams; also serves steaks, pasta and *tapas*.

Mr Papa's, Terramar Plaza. Giant baked potatoes with dozens of fillings for around $7.

Entertainment and nightlife

Since Cancún's whole rationale is to encourage almost two million visitors each year to "have fun", the entertainment scene is lavish – or remorseless, depending on which way you look at it. There's everything from sports and gambling **bars** to romantic piano bars and fun bars, even just plain drinking bars: enough choice to ensure that you can find a place to have a good time without being ripped off. Most of the **nightclubs**, on the other hand, are pricey, with a "no shorts or sandals" dress code. A couple of **cinemas** show new American releases subtitled in Spanish: the largest downtown is the multi-screen *Cine Royal* on Tulum opposite the bus station; in the *zona*, *Cinema Kukulkán* is in the Plaza Kukulkán .

Bars and nightclubs

La Boom, Blvd. Kukulkán Km 3.5 at the front of the *Hotel Aquamarina Beach* (☎98/83-16-41). High-tech disco in an "English setting" with continuous videos. No cover charge on Mon; check *Cancún Tips* and *Cancún Nights* for other events.

Cats, Yaxchilán 12. Downtown club with live Jamaican bands. Daily 9pm–5am.

Christine's, in the *Krystal*, Blvd. Kukulkán Km 9 (☎98/83-11-33, ext. 499). The most sophisticated and expensive nightclub in town, famed for its light show. Thurs is 1970s and 80s night: look in the free magazines or phone to check other weekly events. Don't turn up in shorts, jeans, sandals or without a shirt.

Daddy'o, Blvd. Kukulkán Km 9, opposite the convention centre. A 21st-century nightclub with a high-tech sound system and a light and laser show. Casual dress but no shorts.

Fat Tuesday, Blvd. Kukulkán Km 6.5, and in the Terramar Plaza in the *zona hotelera* (☎98/83-26-76 or 83-03-91). Restaurant-bar with an outside dance floor and a choice of 60 flavours of frozen drinks. Cover charge after 9pm; open until 4am.

Pat O'Brien's, Flamingo Plaza in the *zona hotelera* (☎98/83-08-32). Live rock, blues and jazz in a larger than life version of the famous New Orleans bar. Three bars: a piano bar, a video lounge or an outdoor patio. Open until 2am.

MOVING ON FROM CANCÚN

Hwy-307 skirts the coast all the way down to **Tulum**, where a dirt track leads down to Punta Allen in the Sian Ka'an Biosphere Reserve. **Heading west** to Valladolid, Chichén Itzá and Mérida, you have a choice between the **old road** (*viejo*) or the new **cuota** highway, running a few kilometres north of the old road for most of its length. Drive north on Av. Tulum then turn left to join López Portillo: after a few kilometres you will have the choice of which road to join. You pay in advance, at the booths on the highway, for the sections you intend to travel along. The trip all the way to Mérida costs $30.

The first- and second-class **bus stations** are next to each other on the corner of Tulum and Uxmal. For **Mérida**, choices include the *ADO* Mercedes Benz; *UNO*; first-class, *directo* or second-class (5am–9pm; hourly). The journey takes between six and seven hours. Other destinations include **Campeche** on the deluxe *ATS Plus* (daily; 9.30am; 9hr); **Chetumal** on first-class (6.30am–midnight); first-class to **México** (6pm); **Playa del Carmen** on *ADO* Mercedes Benz (8am–7.45pm; 3 daily; 1hr); first-class (6.30am–midnight; 5 daily; 1hr) and second-class (5am–5.45pm; every 30–45min; 1hr); **Tizimín** on first-class (6.30am–6.30pm) and second-class (5am–7pm; 6 daily; 4hr); **Tulum** on first-class (6.30am–midnight; 5 daily; 2hr) and second-class (6.45am–2.15pm; 5 daily; 2hr); **Valladolid** on *ADO* Mercedes Benz (7.30am–6.30pm) and second-class (2am–8pm; hourly; 3hr).

International **flights** leave regularly from Cancún; from downtown and the *zona hotelera* a taxi to the airport costs about $16.

THE FERRY TO ISLA MUJERES

The **passenger ferry** for **Isla Mujeres** (see p.527) officially leaves from **Puerto Juárez** every thirty minutes between 8am and 8pm, the fast ferry (15min) on the hour and the slow ferry (30min) at 30 minutes past. However, in reality they simply leave when full, often at the same time. To get to the ferry terminal, catch a bus ("Puerto Juárez" or "Punta Sam") heading north from the stop on Tulum, opposite the bus station (20min), or take a taxi from Tulum (around $3).

The **car ferry** ($10 for car, plus $2 for each passenger) leaves from **Punta Sam**, another few kilometres north of Puerto Juárez. There are six departures daily between 7.15am and 8.15pm, returning from Isla Mujeres between 6am and 7.15pm. However, it is hardly worth taking a car over to the island, which is small enough to cycle around and has plenty of bicycles and mopeds for rent.

Señor Frogs, Blvd. Kukulkán Km 5.5. Live reggae bands and karaoke nights.

Tequila Rock, in the *Party Centre*, Blvd. Kukulkán Km 9 (☎98/84-81-32 or 90-98-45). Pop, rock and disco music with high-tech effects. Check for the daily events – open bar, two-for-one drinks, ladies night and the like. Casual dress, shorts allowed.

Dinner with live music

Ballet Folklórico Nacional de México, at the *Continental Villas Plaza Hotel* in the *zona hotelera* (☎98/85-14-44 or 83-10-22, ext 5706 & 5690). Buffet dinner nightly at 7pm with a professional ballet featuring 35 artists. Tickets cost around $35.

La Fisheria, Plaza Caracol. Fresh seafood and pizza accompanied by live Caribbean music.

Iguana Wana, Plaza Caracol. Lively cafe with Mexican and seafood specialities. Live music every evening, happy hour from 5 to 7pm. Open until 2am.

Los Rancheros, Flamingo Plaza. Another Mexican restaurant with a lively atmosphere, *mariachi* and *marimba* music every night.

Dinner cruises

Cancún Queen, Blvd. Kukulkán Km 10.5 (☎98/83-30-07 or 83-17-63). Fish and chicken dinner on a traditional Mississippi paddle boat. Live music followed by a fiesta and a variety of party games with prizes. Two daily departures at 6.30pm and 9.30pm; returning ninety minutes later.

Columbus, from the Royal Maya Marina at Blvd. Kukulkán (☎98/83-32-68 or 83-32-71). Romantic cruise with lobster and steak dinners. Daily 4–7pm and 7.30–10.30pm.

Listings

American Express Tulum 208, next to *Hotel America* (☎98/84-19-99; fax 84-69-42).

Consulates *Canada*, Plaza Mexico 312, Av. Tulum (Mon–Fri 10am–2pm; ☎98/84-37-16); *Germany*, Punta Conoco 36, SM24 (Mon–Fri 10am–1pm; ☎98/84-18-98); *Italy*, La Mansión Costa Blanca Shopping Centre (Mon–Fri 9am–2pm; ☎98/83-21-84); *Sweden*, Yaxchilán 71, SM25 (Mon–Fri 9am–2pm; ☎ and fax 98/84-80-48); *UK, The Royal Caribbean, zona hotelera* (Mon–Fri 9am–5pm; ☎98/85-11-66, ext. 462); *US*, Edificio Marruecos 31, Av. Nader 40 (Mon–Fri 9am–2pm & 3–5.30pm; ☎98/84-24-11 or 84-63-99; fax 84-82-22).

Laundry *Lavendería Las Palapas*, on Gladiolas at the far side of the park (Mon–Sat 7am–8pm, Sun 8am–2pm); *Lavendería Alborada*, Av. Nader, just south of City Hall.

Travel agents There's a superabundance of tour operators, and travel agency desks at most hotels. These can easily fix you up with the standard trips to Xel-ha, the main ruins or sell tickets for a cruise. For something different, visit *Marand Travel*, Plaza Mexico, Av. Tulum 200, Suite 208 (☎98/84-38-05; fax 84-38-49). Owned by Martha and Richard Uscanga who run *EcoloMex Tours*, this is the best travel agency if you want to see the wildlife of the Yucatán.

Isla Mujeres

ISLA MUJERES, just a couple of kilometres off the easternmost tip of Mexico in the startlingly clear Caribbean sea, is an infinitely more appealing prospect than Cancún. Its attractions are simple: first there's the beach, then there's the sea. And when you've tired of those, you can rent a bike or a moped to carry you around the island to more sea, more beaches, a coral reef and the tiny Maya temple that the Conquistadors chanced upon, full of female figures, which gave the place its name. Unfortunately, however, Mujeres is no longer the desert island you may have heard about, and its natural attractions have been recognized and developed considerably in the last few years: there are several large hotels and regular day trips from Cancún. Inevitably, prices have risen and standards (in many cases) have fallen. All that said, it can still seem a respite to those who've been slogging their way down through Mexico and around the Yucatán – everyone you've met along the way seems to turn up here eventually.

Arrival, information and getting around

The passenger **ferry** arrives downtown, at the main pier at the end of Av. Morelos on Av. Rueda Medina, which runs northeast to southwest; the car ferry comes in farther east on Medina at the end of Bravo. Avenida Madero, one block north from the passenger ferry dock, cuts northeast straight across the island; as you walk away from the dock, the first street you cross is Juárez, the second Hidalgo and the third Guerrero, both of which lead north to the North Beach and south to the zócalo. There's also a more expensive **hydrofoil**, which leaves from Playa Linda in Cancún's *zona hotelera* a few times a day, returning about an hour later. *Aerocaribe* and others also occasionally fly out in light planes to Cancún or Cozumel.

The zócalo is skirted by Morelos, N Bravo, Guerrero and Hidalgo. The friendly **tourist office** (Mon–Fri 9am–2.30pm & 7–9pm; ☎987/7-03-16) is on the Hidalgo side, opposite the church. Here you can pick up leaflets, maps and copies of the magazine *Islander* (in Spanish and English). The **post office** (Mon–Fri 8am–7pm, Sat 9am–1pm) is at the corner of Guerrero and Mateos, about ten minutes' walk from the centre; mail is held at the *Lista de Correos* for up to ten days (postcode 77400). There are **long-distance phones** on Av. Medina 6-B (9am–9pm). **Banks** are few: *Banco del Atlantico*, Medina 3 (Mon–Fri 9am–1pm), does currency exchange between 10am and noon, but to avoid the queues you could use the **casa de cambio** (daily 9am–9pm) on Hidalgo, opposite *Rolandis* restaurant between Madero and Abasolo.

The best way of getting around the island is by **moped or bicycle**: the island is a very manageable size with few hills. *Cardenas*, Guerrero 105 (☎987/7-00-79), rents out mopeds and golf carts, while *Sport Bike* (Mon–Sat 8am–5pm, Sun 8am–2pm & 5–5.30pm), on Morelos near the corner with Juárez, rents bicycles for around $5 per day and **snorkelling** equipment for $4 per day.

Accommodation

Isla Mujeres is short on good-value **budget places to stay**, and, though prices are lower than at Cozumel, so is the quality. Most of the reasonably priced options are on the northern edge of the island. Here, about fifteen minutes' walk from the ferry, the modern whitewashed Poc Na, Matamoros 15 (☎987/7-00-90; $5), near the junction with Carlos Lazo, is a kind of private youth **hostel**, with small rooms with bunks and hammock space. It's a great place for meeting people, and has a reasonable restaurant. Rates include mattress and sheet or hammock.

There is no official **campsite** on Isla Mujeres but you can pitch your tent or hang your hammock under one of the *palapas* ($2 per person paid to the restaurant) on Playa Indios, towards the southern end of the island, shortly before reaching El Garrafón National Park.

El Caracol, Matamoros 5 (☎ 987/7-01-50; fax 7-05-47). Two blocks from North Beach, rooms with or without a/c and a restaurant serving typical Mexican food. ④–⑤.

Caribe Maya, Av. Francisco I Madero 9 (☎987/4-49-17). More character than the average budget hotel and good value. Some a/c rooms. ③–⑤.

Hotel Cabañas María del Mar, Av. Carlos Lazo 1 (☎987/7-02-13 or 7-01-79; fax 7-01-73). Next to North Beach, with deluxe *cabañas* on the beach or hotel rooms with a/c, refrigerator and private balcony or terrace. ⑧.

Posada del Mar, Medina 15-A (☎987/7-00-44 or 7-03-00; fax 7-02-66). Spacious rooms or bungalows with a/c. There's a restaurant, and a pool with its own bar. ⑥.

María José, Madero 25 (☎987/70-24-44 or 70-24-45). Well-kept family-run hotel. Some of the back rooms open onto next door's roof, where you can hang your hammock. ③.

Osorio, Madero: turn left from the ferry, take the first right, and the hotel is on your left (☎987/7-00-18). Rooms take up to five for $3 extra per person, although they can get crowded. ③.

Las Palmas, Guerrero 20 (no phone). The cheapest option on the island, basic but fine. ③.

Perlas del Caribe, Madero 2 (☎987/7-01-20 or 7-05-07; fax 7-00-11). At the opposite side of town to the ferry, one of the smartest hotels on the island, with a pool, restaurant and sea-view rooms with verandahs. ⑧.

Posada del Mar Hotel, Medina 15-A (☎987/7-00-44; fax 7-02-66). Spacious a/c hotel rooms or bungalows. There's a restaurant and pool with bar. ⑥–⑦.

Roca Mar, corner of Guerrero and Bravo, behind the church next to the zócalo (☎987/7-01-01). One of the island's oldest hotels, well maintained, with a restaurant overlooking the Caribbean. ⑥.

Xul-ha, Hidalgo 23 Nte. (☎987/7-00-75 or 7-00-39). Recently rebuilt next to the old hotel, this new hotel is clean and comfortable. ④.

The Island

Isla Mujeres is no more than 8km long, and, at its widest point, barely a kilometre across. A lone road runs its length, past the dead calm waters of the landward coast – the other side, east-facing, is windswept and exposed. There's a small beach on this side in the town, but the currents even here can be dangerous. The most popular beach, just five minutes' walk from the town plaza, is **Playa Los Cocos** – at the northern tip of the island but protected from the open sea by a little promontory on which stands what was the lone luxury hotel, the *El Presidente Zazil-Ha*. The hotel now stands abandoned, ravaged by one of the hurricanes that periodically wreck this coast. The beach takes its name from the tall coconut palms that until recently stood in ranks behind it; sadly, most of these are now dead, killed by a disease (brought from America, say the locals) that has swept not only the island but much of this Caribbean coast. New strains have been planted but most are still young and even when full-grown lack the sweeping majesty of the towering originals.

If you've had enough of the beach, windsurfing and wandering round town (the Grand Tour takes little more than thirty minutes), rent a bike or moped to explore the south of the island. **El Garrafón National Park** (daily 8am–5pm; $3), a tropical reef teeming with fish, just a few metres offshore, is the most obvious destination. To see it at its best you should set out early: by 11am the day-trip launches from Cancún have arrived and, although this doesn't seem to worry the fish, it can get unpleasantly crowded. There are an enormous number of completely tame, fabulously coloured tropical fish swimming about here (and waterproof underwater fish-spotting guides are on sale to help you recognize them), which can be seen even by non-swimmers wading in the shallows. If you rent a snorkel and mask it's quite extraordinary – indeed, at times it seems you need the equipment not so much to help you find the swarms of Mohican-styled parrot fish, as to dodge them. Small and commercialized as El Garrafón is, you shouldn't miss it. The cheapest way to get to El Garrafón and back is by taxi, but **moped rental** rates are better by the day than they are by the hour, so make it part of a day's exploration. Rent mask and flippers in town too, since they cost the same as at El Garrafón and you'll be able to use them all day.

El Garrafón is almost at the southern end of the island – beyond, the road continues to the lighthouse, and from there a short rough track leads to the **Maya Temple** at the southernmost tip. It's not much of a ruin, but it is very dramatically situated, on low rocky cliffs below which you can often spot worryingly large fish basking.

On the way back, stop at **Playa Lancheros**, a palm-fringed beach that is virtually deserted except at lunchtimes when the day-trippers pile in. There's a small restaurant here, specializing in seafood, and a clutch of souvenir stalls. Inland, in the jungly undergrowth, lurk the decaying remains of the **Hacienda Mundaca**: an old house and garden to which scores of romantic (and quite untrue) pirate legends are attached.

You could also take a day-long boat trip to the island bird sanctuary of **CONTOY** (some, with special permission, stay overnight), where you can see colonies of pelicans and cormorants and occasionally more exotic sea birds, as well as a sunken Spanish galleon. Or, with more sang froid, you can take the scuba-diving trip to the **"Cave of the Sleeping Sharks"**. In these underwater caverns bask groups of nurse sharks, lulled into a semi-comatose state by the heavily oxygenated, almost fresh water. Apparently they don't bite, but even so, this close encounter with the sharks is not, as the local guide puts it, an adventure for "neophyte aquanauts".

Eating

The area along and around Hidalgo between Morelos and Abasolo, lined with **restaurants** and crafts shops, is the best place to spend an evening on Isla Mujeres. Simply wander through the laid-back music-filled streets and see what takes your fancy. For inexpensive, basic Mexican food and great low-priced fruit salads, head for the **loncherías** opposite *Las Palmas* hotel.

Ciros Lobster House, Matamoros near Guerrero. The name is self-explanatory and the menu is expensive. Civilized and relaxing ambience, away from the main centre.

Restaurant Gomar, Hidalgo 5 on the corner with Madero. Good seafood and chicken but not much atmosphere – and a very loud TV – in this rather expensive restaurant.

Mexico Lindo, Hidalgo, between Madero and Morelos. Sets the atmosphere for this stretch with loud reggae music and reasonably priced Mexican food.

Miramar, Medina, next to the pier. Attractive place on the seafront, away from the centre. Seafood and meat dishes, a little on the expensive side.

Pizza Rolandis, Hidalgo, between Madero and Abasolo. One of a chain serving pizza, lobster, fresh fish and other Italian dishes with salads.

Tonyno's Pizza and Pasta, Hidalgo, between Madero and Morelos, opposite *Mexico Lindo*. The lowest-priced pizzas, delicious too.

The east coast: Cancún to Playa del Carmen

Resort development along the spectacular white sand beaches south from Cancún to the marvellous seaside ruins of Tulum proceeds rapidly as landowners cash in on Cancún's popularity. The **Caribbean Barrier Reef** begins off Puerto Morelos, a quiet town with a working port that also boasts excellent beaches and good-value accommodation. Farther south, the phenomenal growth of **Playa del Carmen**, the departure point for boats to **Cozumel**, has transformed a village with a ferry dock into a major holiday destination.

Despite the building boom, finding a relatively deserted stretch of beach is fairly easy. Transport along Hwy-307 is fast and frequent, and many visitors based in Cancún rent a car to explore the coast. Although a moped is feasible as far as Puerto Morelos, where the divided highway ends (and there's a filling station), it's a long trip for the underpowered bikes, and bus and truck drivers show scant respect as they pass. The bus service is so good and cheap that renting one is not worth the effort.

Puerto Morelos

Leaving Cancún behind, the first town on the coast is **PUERTO MORELOS**, 20km south. Formerly of little interest except as the departure point for the car ferry to Cozumel, in recent years Puerto has seen a surge in popularity, becoming a base for tours and **diving trips**. The taxi ride from Cancún airport to Puerto Morelos is slightly cheaper than to Cancún itself, and many visitors on international flights bypass the city altogether, making this their first stop. And it's as good a place as any to hang out for a while: despite a rash of new hotel and condo construction, it is certainly a relaxing, laid-back alternative to the bustle of Cancún, with some lovely beaches and exceptionally fine watersports.

Arrival and information

Interplaya **buses** leave Cancún's bus station every thirty to forty-five minutes between 5am and 10pm. Some stop by the plaza, others will drop you at the highway junction, where taxis wait to take you the 2km into town. There's a **long-distance telephone** by the police station on the corner of the plaza, a number of small shops, a supermarket and a **bank** (Mon–Fri 9.30am–1pm) that will cash travellers' cheques. The **car ferry to Cozumel** operates daily, at 6am every day except Tuesday, when it goes at 9am, and Thursday, when it goes at 5am. On Monday there's an extra ferry leaving at noon. You need to get to the terminal around three hours early to be sure of getting a space. The ferry returns from Cozumel at 2pm daily except for Monday, when it leaves at 10am and 5pm.

Accommodation

Hotels in Puerto Morelos are generally very good value and almost all of them are right on the beach. You can **camp free** on the sand as long as you're not directly in front of a house or hotel; the *Acamaya Reef Trailer Park* (☎987/1-01-32) is a couple of kilometres away from the centre, down the first turning on the left, 2km after the turn-off from the main highway, near the entrance to Crococun.

Amor Inn, north of the plaza, 500m along the seafront (☎987/1-00-26). Pretty rooms and *cabañas* with kitchenettes around a shaded garden. ④–⑤.

Caribbean Reef Club, fifteen minutes south of the plaza, beyond the car ferry dock (☎987/1-01-62). Luxury accommodation right on the beach, around a pool. Every room has a sea view. Guests have free use of sailboats and windsurf boards. Prices soar in December and January. ⑤–⑨.

Hacienda Morelos, on the front, south of the plaza (☎ and fax 987/1-00-15). Bright, airy rooms. ⑦.

Ojo de Agua, north of the plaza (☎987/1-00-27). Sixteen beachfront rooms and a pool. ⑥.

Posada Amor, Rojo Romez, just south of the plaza (☎987/1-00-33). The least expensive option, not on the beach, but friendly and comfortable, with plenty of character. ④.

Rancho Libertad, fifteen minutes south of the plaza, beyond the car ferry dock (☎987/1-01-81; in USA: ☎1-800/305-5225). Two-storey thatched *cabañas* in a superb beach and garden setting. The upper rooms are more expensive, but all have private hot showers and beds that are suspended from the ceiling by thick ropes: relaxing if you're lying still but with a tendency to swing alarmingly if you make any movement. Rates include substantial fruit and cereal breakfasts but no other meals. Snorkel rental and scuba instruction is available and guests can rent bicycles. No children. ⑦.

The Town

The turn-off from Hwy-307 ends at the small, modern **plaza** in the centre of Puerto Morelos: the only proper streets lead north and south for a few blocks, parallel to the beach. Ahead lies the **beach**, a wooden **dock** (the car ferry terminal is a few hundred metres south) and the **lighthouse**. There's a small wooden tourist booth in the plaza minded – sometimes – by Fernando during the mornings. You'll see signs advertising rooms, snorkelling, scuba diving, and catamaran trips ($40 per day, including lunch): with the reef only 600m offshore and in a very healthy condition, Puerto Morelos is a great place to learn to **dive**. *Rancho Libertad* (see above) offers a resort course for $70 and PADI certification for $325; snorkel equipment rental is $8 per day or $40 per week. If you want to learn more about the **natural and social history** of the area, contact Sandra Drayton (☎987/1-01-17; or leave a message in the restaurant at the *Posada Amor*) who, in conjunction with a team of biologists, runs *Maya Echo Tours*, which emphasizes environmental conservation.

Just south of the turn-off for the *Acamaya Reef Trailer Park* (see above), the **Jardín Botanico Dr Alfredo Barrera** (daily 9am–5pm; $2.50) features the native flora of Quintana Roo, with exhibits labelled in Spanish and English. Trails lead to a small Maya site and a reconstruction showing how chicle was tapped from the sap of the sapodillo tree before being used in the production of chewing gum. Definitely worth a visit if you have the time, and guides are available that describe the medicinal uses of the plants.

Eating

Most of the town's **restaurants** are around the plaza. *Los Pelicanos* and *Las Palmeras* are good for seafood, and the *Maison del Tiburon* serves vegetarian meals. The cosy restaurant at *Posada Amor* offers very good value in a friendly, informal atmosphere. It's also a great place to pick up information about what's going on in town.

Punta Bete

Tucked away between the more touristed resorts of Puerto Morelos and Playa del Carmen, the sedate **PUNTA BETE** is little more than a beach, a restaurant and a few *cabañas*. Just a few visitors – day-trippers, most of them – use the long, white and palm-fringed beach; wonderful for **snorkelling** when the sea is calm. You can rent equipment from the **restaurant** *Xcalacoco*, which dishes up reasonably priced basic Mexican food and superb fish from 7.30am until 8pm. To get there, it's a slow, careful drive or a hot, dusty four-kilometre walk down the untarmacked and pot-holed dirt track from the highway. There's room for around 30 people in the **cabañas** (⑤), and **campers** with tents or trailers are welcome ($3 per person), although there are no water or electricity hook-ups. You're also welcome to string your hammock ($2 per person) in one of the beach *palapas* once the diners have gone. The showers are for everyone.

Playa del Carmen

Tourism is mushrooming in **PLAYA DEL CARMEN**, once a soporific, very Mexican fishing village. To the south, the huge *Playacar* resort seems a little out of place in a town full of small hotels and restaurants, while to the north, where the *Blue Parrot Inn* used to stand out on its own, marking the edge of town, the gaps are rapidly being filled in. For the time being, however, Playa retains its laid-back atmosphere and, unlike Cozumel, has plenty of budget food and accommodation options. Most of what happens happens on the **beach**, where the sea is gloriously clear and the sand unfeasibly white; inland, the main centre of activity is one block back on Av. 5, pedestrianized across five blocks from *Playacar* to c/6. Here, a multitude of dive shops offer diving and **snorkelling trips** to some of the best spots on this coast, and you can stock up on clothes, crafts and exquisite jewellery from all over Mexico and Guatemala – at a price.

Arrival and information

Buses pull in at the corner of Av. 5 and Av. Juárez, the main street running east–west from the highway to the beach; some second-class buses stop one or two blocks farther inland on Juárez. For **tourist information**, head for the wooden booth in the corner of the plaza (Mon–Sat 7am–midnight) at the end of Juárez. It's run by the multi-lingual Ramón Nuñez Díaz, who is there every day except August 31, when the booth is closed in celebration of his birthday. Pick up a copy of the useful *Destination Playa del Carmen*, which has a map, hotel and restaurant listings. Beware the other tourist information booths scattered around town, as they're mostly tied up with some ulterior motive – selling timeshares, for example. There's a tiny **post office** (Mon–Fri 9am–

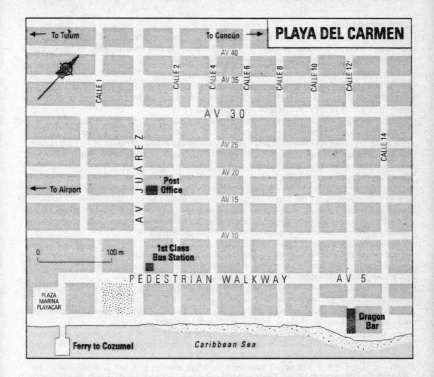

7pm, Sat 9am–4pm) on Juárez, four blocks back from the beach, mainly geared to dealing with tourists and with a stamp machine outside. The *Lista de Correos* (postcode 77710) keeps mail for ten days. If you're heading south for Tulum, where there's no **bank**, you should change enough money here to get you through. *Banco del Atlantico* (Mon–Fri 8am–1pm), on Juárez between avenidas 10 and 15, a competitive rate on foreign exchange, with unusually fast service, while *Bancomer* (Mon–Fri 9am–1.30pm), on Juárez between avenidas 25 and 30 has a 24-hour ATM. There are a few **casas de cambio** around town but they offer no better rates than the hotels. Phones are a recent luxury in this part of Mexico, but there are already a number of places where you can call **long distance**, among them the convenient *Computel caseta* (daily 7am–10pm) next to the bus station. You can also make long-distance and international calls at *La Tiendita*, on Av. 5 between calles 2 and 4.

Getting around and tours

The best way to get around Playa is on foot. To make trips farther afield you can rent a **bike** from *Ciclissimo Sport* ($8 per day; Mon–Sat only), opposite the ice factory on Juárez, near Av. 30, or at *Copacabaña*, Av. 5 between calles 10 and 12. **Car rental** is provided by *National* (☎987/3-01-36 or -34), in the foyer of the *Molcas* hotel. The small airstrip handles short jaunts, chiefly to Cozumel, but also to Chichén Itzá and other key Maya sites – operators include *Aeroferinco* (☎987/3-03-36), *Aeroméxico* (☎987/3-03-50) and *Saab* (☎987/3-05-01). *Eurotravel* at *Rincon del Sol*, Av. 5 near c/8, or the travel agency at *Molcas* can organize **tours to Maya ruins**, along with horse riding, boat trips, and national and international **flights**.

Accommodation

There are plenty of hotels in Playa, the cheapest of them inland. If you want to stay on the beach you're looking at paying $10–15 more. Prices rise in July, August and December, but outside these busy periods you're sure to find a room.

The **youth hostel** is in a quiet part of town, ten minutes' walk from the centre, on Av. 30 near c/8. It's mainly aimed at young Mexicans, with only a few foreign visitors passing through. Bunks in tightly packed dorms cost $5 per person, with a 10 percent discount with an IYH card. Lockers are provided.

Albatros, corner of c/8 Nte. and Av. 5 (☎987/3-00-01; fax 3-00-02; in USA: ☎1-800/538-6802). Two-storey hotel on the beach with a *palapa* roof and hammocks swinging around the garden. Complimentary coffee and *panecillos* in the reception at breakfast time. ⑦.

Banana Cabañas, c/6 Nte. between Av. 5 and 10 (☎987/3-00-36). Comfortable *cabañas* surrounding a leafy garden. Mosquito nets provided. ⑤.

Blue Parrot Inn, on and slightly back from the beach (☎987/3-00-83; fax 3-00-49). Wide range of *cabañas* and rooms; the new *Tucan* annexe has suites with one or two bedrooms and kitchenettes. Can be noisy at night when the hugely popular beachfront *Dragon* bar is hopping. ④–⑨.

Cabañas/Rooms Tuxatah, Av. 10 on the corner with c/1 Sur (☎987/3-00-25; fax 3-01-48). Quiet establishment tucked away by the edge of the *Playacar* development. Clean, basic rooms and a shaded garden with owners who speak German, English and French. ⑤.

Campamiento La Ruina, c/2 Nte., between Av. 5 and the sea (☎987/3-04-05). Playa's most sociable and economical place to stay, on the beach with its own ruin in the grounds. There are a variety of options: a few hook-ups; *cabañas* with or without private bath; camping space ($3 per person), and a huge *palapa* with lockers and room for 34 hammocks ($5; rental $2). ③.

Casa de Gopala, c/2 between Av. 10 and 15 (☎ and fax 987/3-00-54). Small hotel with spacious, comfortable rooms; far enough from Av. 5 to get some peace, but close enough to take part. ⑤.

Condotel El Toucan, Av. 5 between c/14 and 16 (☎987/3-04-17 or 3-04-77). New mini-apartments with terraces and kitchenettes; some with separate dining area and living room. ⑥.

Copa Cabaña, Av. 5 between c/10 and 12 (☎987/3-02-18). *Cabañas* with private bath, and hammocks around the garden. Bikes and snorkelling equipment for rent and boat trips arranged for small groups. Reception open 7am–2pm & 5–7pm. ⑥.

Costa del Mar, c/1 Nte., half a block back from the beach between c/10 and 12 (☎987/3-00-58; fax 2-02-31; in USA: ☎1-800/329-8388). Comfortable hotel rooms or *cabañas* with or without a/c, with a pool and small garden leading out onto the beach. Restaurant, bar and dive shop. ⑤–⑦.

Delfin, Av. 5 on corner with c/6 Nte. (☎ and fax 987/3-01-76; in USA: ☎718/297-6851). Relatively new hotel; rooms with fans and private bathrooms. ⑤.

Da Gabi, c/1 Nte., on the corner with c/12 (☎987/3-00-48). Small Italian-run hotel with a variety of rooms, some with verandahs and mosquito nets. Popular pasta restaurant. ⑥.

Hotel Posada Lily, Juárez, between Av. 5 and 10 (☎987/3-01-16). Good budget option just one block back from the beach. ②.

Hotel Posada Sian Ka'an, corner of Av. 5 and c/2 Nte. (☎987/3-02-02 or 3-02-03; fax 3-02-04). Small hotel built around a dried-up *cenote*. Clean and comfortable rooms, some with kitchenette, others with private terraces. ③–⑦.

Maya Bric, Av. 5 between c/8 and 10 (☎987/3-00-11). Set around a leafy garden with a small pool, and a restaurant for the sole use of residents. ⑥.

Molcas, south side of the main square (☎987/2-04-77 or 2-05-88; fax 2-17-18). Comfortable a/c rooms around a pool. ⑧.

Yax-ha, c/10 Nte., on the beach (☎987/3-02-58; fax 3-02-57). Four well-equipped *cabañas* with kitchenette and bathroom, for three or four people each. You can arrange diving and snorkelling trips and maybe a visit to *Yax-ha's* beachside ranch in the Sian Ka'an Biosphere Reserve. ⑥.

Eating

Playa del Carmen is heaving with **restaurants**, whether you want a romantic candlelit dinner or a low-priced traditional Mexican meal. The pedestrianized section of **Avenida 5** is edged end-to-end with dining tables where you can eat pizza, pasta, French food, burgers and chips, veggie – you name it. Probably the nicest places, though, are the **beach restaurants** and bars, where your can sift sand between your toes while eating fresh fish and sipping icy margaritas. Keep an eye open for the various happy hours.

Alejan, on the beach near the corner of c/6. Basic Mexican food; the setting hikes the prices a bit.

Chile Morran, Juárez, near the beach on the north side of the plaza. Laid-back Mexican restaurant with live music.

Da Gabi, c/12, half a block from the beach near the *Blue Parrot Inn*. Italian-run restaurant serving delicious fresh pasta and pizza. A little pricey but recommended.

Deli Cafe, Av. 5, between c/4 and 6. Fresh juices, pastries, ice cream, burgers and other snacks. Great place for an inexpensive breakfast or to satisfy late-night munchies. Open all night.

Karen's, Av. 5, between c/2 and 4. Busy, moderately priced pizza restaurant in the heart of the pedestrianized zone. Live music on stage most nights and a happy hour between 7 and 9pm.

Limones, Av. 5, on the corner with c/6, just past the end of the pedestrianized area. Yucatecan and international specialities in romantic, leafy surroundings. Daily 6–11pm.

Mascaras, Juárez, near the beach. Thin-crust pizza, home-made pasta and seafood. Sip margaritas during the happy hour between noon and 6pm.

Media Luna, Av. 5, opposite Plaza Rincon del Sol, near c/8. Vegetarian and seafood restaurant with delicious pasta and veg dishes. Hot crusty bread with fresh herb and garlic butter served with every meal. Small and popular; get there early. Daily except Tues; opens around 7pm.

Molcas, next to the pier. Pleasant setting for an expensive restaurant with an extensive menu. Live music Fri and Sat 6–9pm.

Sabor, Av. 5, between c/2 and 4. Great place for fresh juices, scrumptious cakes and vegetarian food at reasonable prices. The soya *tortas* are delicious.

Sergios, Av. 5, on the corner of c/2. Good basic Mexican food in simple surroundings but still within the buzzy atmosphere of Av. 5. Low prices for this part of town.

El Tacolote, Juárez, near the beach at the north edge of the plaza. Moderately priced restaurant serving barbecued meat with melted cheese.

El Torton, Juárez, between c/10 and 15, opposite *Banco del Atlantico*. Good-value, basic Mexican food in a simple, untouristy restaurant.

Bars and nightlife

You can wander through Playa del Carmen well into the night, following the happy-hour trail and listening to all sorts of music from *salsa* and reggae to 1970s classic. Drinks aren't cheap if you pay the full price, but the atmosphere is unbeatable.

Caribe Swing Bar and Restaurant, on the beach near c/4. Totally laid-back. Swing in a hammock on the beach while listening to live reggae, calypso and soca. 9pm–12.30am.

MOVING ON FROM PLAYA DEL CARMEN

Playa is pretty well connected by bus. **First-class buses** leave from the station at the corner of Av. Juárez and Av. 5, serving Mérida, direct or via Valladolid or Cobá. Buses also leave for México and Villahermosa. At 6.30pm every day a bus leaves for Palenque, San Cristóbal de las Casas and Tuxtla Gutiérrez. *Grupo Caribe* (☎987/3-03-66) has an office just around the corner in Juárez and operates more luxurious services to Mérida, Cancún, Tulum and Chetumal. **Second-class** buses leave for Cancún and Tulum every thirty minutes, the former from beside the *Grupo Caribe* office, the latter from beside *Banco Atlantico*.

Buying a ticket for a **ferry to Cozumel** can be a frustrating experience. Various booths around town, particularly around the plaza, are staffed by enthusiastic young men shouting special offers "just for you". To avoid ending up with the feeling that you aren't being taken very seriously, or being treated with respect, bear in mind that there are two types of passenger service to Cozumel: the aerodynamic **fast** boat (30min; $10 return) with tinted-glass windows and comfortable seats, and the **slow** boat (1hr; $7) with open sides and wooden seats. Ferries leave every one to two hours, between 5am and 8.45pm; returning to Playa, they leave between 4am and 8pm. Check at the pier for the current timetable.

Dragon Bar, at the *Blue Parrot Inn. The* place to be as the evening turns into night. Live bands on stage and swing seats at the bar. Two beers or cocktails for the price of one during happy hours, 2–8pm and 10pm–midnight.

New Calypso House Bar, Av. 5, between c/4 and 6. Live Caribbean music on Fri and Sat, 5–11pm. Cosy atmosphere and a busy dance floor.

Ziggy's Disco, Juárez, near the beach. Patchily popular disco that doesn't get going till after midnight. No cover charge most nights, except Saturday ($5) and Wednesday when $15 buys unlimited drinks. Open 10pm–4am.

Cozumel

ISLA COZUMEL is far larger than Mujeres, and has been developed for much longer – up to, and beyond, its potential. Initially overshadowed by the rise of Cancún in the 1980s, it is now a major port of call for Caribbean cruise ships and promoted as a **diving** destination. Before the Spanish arrived, Cozumel appears to have been a major Maya centre, carrying on sea trade around the coasts of Mexico and as far south as Honduras and perhaps Panama; after the Conquest it was virtually deserted for four hundred years. This ancient community – one of several around the Yucatán coast that survived the collapse of Classic Maya civilization – is usually dismissed as being the decadent remnant of a moribund society. But that was not the impression the Spanish received when they arrived, nor is it necessarily the right one. Architecture might have declined in the years from 1200 to the Conquest, but large-scale trade, specialization between centres and even a degree of mass production are all in evidence. Cozumel's rulers enjoyed a less grand style than their forebears, but the rest of an increasingly commercialized population were probably better off. And Cozumel itself may even have been an early free-trade zone, where merchants from competing cities could trade peaceably.

Whatever the truth, you get little opportunity to judge for yourself. A US air base built here during World War II has erased all trace of the ancient city, and the lesser ruins scattered across the roadless interior are mostly unrestored and inaccessible. The airfield did, at least, bring new prosperity – converted to civilian use, it remains the means by which most visitors arrive. The miles of **offshore reefs**, with crystal-clear water all the way down, are the draw for diving enthusiasts – **bird-watchers** will also find a visit worthwhile, as Cozumel is a stopover on migration routes and has several species or variants endemic to the island.

Arrival and information

Arriving by boat, you'll be right in the centre of town (officially **San Miguel**, but always known simply as Cozumel) with the zócalo just one block inland along Juárez; from the airport you have to take the VW *combi* service. The **tourist office** (Mon–Fri 9am–1pm) is upstairs inside the *Plaza del Sol* shopping centre on the zócalo; but there's nothing here that you can't get at hotels, restaurants and shop counters throughout the island. *Cozumel Tips* and the *Free Blue Guide to Cozumel* are crammed with discount cards and vouchers; the tabloid-sized, one-sheet *Insider's Guide to Diving and Snorkelling* can also be useful. The **post office** (Mon–Fri 8am–8pm, Sat 8am–5pm, Sun 9am–1pm) is about fifteen minutes' walk from the centre, on Av. Melgar at the corner with c/7 Sur; for *Lista de Correos* use the postcode 77600. Cozumel has many **banks** (Mon–Fri 9am–1.30pm), most of them with ATMs; currency is exchanged between 10am and 12.30pm. Outside these hours, *Banco del Atlantico* on the southeast corner of the zócalo has a money exchange counter (Mon–Fri 9am–8pm) separate from the main banking hall, and there's also a **casa de cambio** on the south side of the main square (daily 9am–8pm).

Getting around

Cozumel town has been modernized and is easy enough to get around on foot – there's even a pedestrian zone. There's a distinct lack of buses, however, so to get farther afield you'll have to go on a tour, take a taxi or rent a vehicle. **Cycling** is feasible on the tarmacked roads, but it can be a bit of an endurance test if you aren't used to long-distance pedalling, and positively unpleasant if you get caught in a sudden storm, likely from around July to October. **Mopeds** give you a bit more freedom and are easier to handle, and **jeeps** are available from numerous outlets (be sure to check the restrictions of your insurance if you want to go onto the dirt tracks). Prices vary little, but it's worth shopping around for special offers. Bikes cost around $5 for 24 hours, mopeds three times that much, and jeeps around $45 for a twelve-hour day.

Try *Rentadora Cozumel,* Av. 10 Sur 172 (daily 8am–8pm; ☎987/2-11-20 or 2-14-29), and in the lobby of *Hotel Flores,* Salas 72, which offers a full range of vehicles, or *Rentadora Aguila,* Melgar 685 (Mon–Sat 8am–8pm, Sun 8am–7pm; ☎987/2-07-29 or 2-13-75), on the waterfront between c/3 and 5, which has consistently good-quality models. *Less-Pay,* at the *Barracuda Hotel,* Melgar 628 (daily 8am–8pm; ☎987/2-47-44 or 2-19-47), has a range of jeeps and cars.

Accommodation

Hotels in Cozumel are not cheap, most of them geared to divers. The affordable places are some way from the beaches, and you can find some bargains in the town centre, but the only budget option is to camp on the sands.

Aguilar, c/3 Sur 98, near the corner of Av. 5 Sur (☎987/2-03-07; fax 2-07-69). Quiet rooms away from the road around a garden with pool and paddling pool. Fridges and cable TV cost extra. ⑤.

Bahía, Av. Melgar, near the corner of c/3 Sur (☎987/2-02-09 or 2-40-34; fax 2-12-87). Good modern a/c rooms with kitchenette, TV and telephone. Some sea views. ⑥.

Suites Colonial, Av. 5 Sur 9, Aptdo 286 (☎987/2-05-42 or 2-05-06). A/c rooms with baths, kitchenettes, cable TV and phones. ⑥.

Flores, Salas 72 (☎987/2-14-29). Basic rooms, fine for the price, and moped and bike rental in the lobby. ③.

Posada Letty, c/1 Sur, on the corner with Av. 15 Sur (☎987/2-02-57). Cheapest of the lot, with clean, basic rooms; very light and airy on the first floor. ②.

El Marques, Av. 5 Sur 180 (☎987/2-06-77; fax 2-05-37). Comfortable a/c rooms with refrigerator, close to the zócalo. ⑤.

Maya Cozumel, c/5 Sur 4 (☎987/2-00-11; fax 2-07-81). Less expensive than the seafront hotels, but just as good, with spacious garden and pool. The a/c rooms have TV, refrigerators and phones. ⑥.

Pepita, Av. 15 Sur, on the corner with c/1 Sur (☎987/2-00-98). Basic option with a small pool. ④.

Pirata, Av. 5 Sur 3-A (☎987/2-00-51 or 2-00-89). Big clean rooms with fan or a/c and cable TV. ⑤.

Saolima, Salas 268 (☎987/2-08-86). Rooms away from the road around a plant-filled courtyard. ③.

Villablanca Garden Beach Hotel, about 2km east of the zócalo (☎987/2-01-30 or 2-45-88; fax 2-08-65). More spacious than the town hotels, with a pool, tennis court and dive shop. Dive packages offered and good snorkelling from just across the road. ⑥.

Vista del Mar, Melgar 45, near the corner with c/5 Sur (☎987/2-05-45; fax 2-04-45). Comfortable, modern a/c rooms with sea view, private terraces and refrigerator. Small pool, restaurant, cafeteria, bar, private parking, diving shop and car or scooter rental on the premises. ⑥.

The Island

Downtown Cozumel is almost entirely devoted to tourism, packed with restaurants, souvenir shops, tour agencies and "craft markets". **Black coral,** a rare and beautiful product of the reefs, is sold everywhere: until Jacques Cousteau discovered it off the island about twenty years ago, it was thought to be extinct. Even now there's not a great deal (it grows at little more than an inch every fifty years), so it's expensive and heavily protected – don't, under any circumstances, go breaking it off the reefs. A recent addition to the tourist attractions on the island is the **Archeological Park** (daily 8am–6pm; $9) on Av. 65 on the inland, southern edge of town. The fee includes a guided tour that lasts around an hour, depending on your own pace and interest, leading you along a shady path through a garden filled with replicas of relics from the various ancient Mesoamerican cultures. You can also see demonstrations of hammock- and *tortilla*-making, in a replica of a Maya home, by Mayans in traditional dress.

Cozumel's eastern shoreline is often impressively wild but, as on Isla Mujeres, only the west coast is really suitable for **swimming**, protected as it is by a line of reefs and the mainland. The easiest **beaches** to get to are north of the town in front of the older resort hotels. Far better, though, to rent a vehicle and head off down to the less exploited places to the south.

Heading **south**, you pass first a clutch of modern hotels by the car ferry dock; offshore here, at the end of the Paraiso Reef, you can see a rather alarming wrecked airliner on the bottom – it's a movie prop. There's accessible snorkelling by *Hotel Barracuda* and farther along opposite the *Villablanca Garden Beach Hotel*. Carry on to the **Parque Chankanaab** or "Little Sea", recently designated a **National Park** (daily 7am–5.30pm; $5), a beautiful if rather over-exploited lagoon full of turtles, lurid fish surrounded by botanical gardens. There's a beach and a tiny reef just offshore; also changing rooms, showers, diving and snorkelling equipment for rent ($5–500), an expensive restaurant, and a protected children's beach. Farther south, **Playa San Francisco** is the best spot for lounging and swimming, while at the southern tip the **Laguna de Colombia** offers interesting snorkelling.

From here you can complete a circuit of the southern half of the island by following the road up the windswept eastern shoreline. There are a couple of good restaurants at **Punta Chiqueros** and **Punta Morena** and, on calm days, excellent deserted sands. The main road cuts back across the middle of the island to town, but if you have a jeep (not a moped, which probably won't have enough gas anyway) you could continue up a rough track to the northern point – off here is the small ruin of **Castillo Real**.

More accessible – halfway across the island from town, on the northern side of the road – the only excavated ruin on the island, **San Gervasio**, was built to honour Ixchel, the god of fertility. On the southern part of the island, the village of **CEDRAL** has a tiny Maya site near the old Spanish church; turn inland on the road shortly after passing San Francisco beach. If your vehicle is insured to go on dirt tracks, you can get to **Tumba de Caracol**, near the Punta Celarin Lighthouse on the southernmost point of the island. It may have been built by the Maya as a lighthouse, and is worth visiting to hear the music produced when the wind whistles through the shells encrusted in its walls.

If you want to do any serious **diving**, you'll need to go with an organized group from any of the dive shops around the docks in town. The better reefs are all some distance offshore (**Arrecife Palancar** is the most popular) and most are protected, so supervision is compulsory. Rather more easily and cheaply, you can sail over the reefs in a **glass-bottomed boat** – ask at the docks for details.

Eating

Eating tends to be expensive wherever you go on Cozumel, but there's plenty of choice if you've got money to spend. Most of the restaurants are downtown and along the west coast, but for a more laid-back atmosphere you can enjoy long, lazy lunches in the **palapas** dotted every few kilometres along the rugged eastern coast. Keep your eyes peeled for **discount vouchers** such as the Promo Tips Card given away with *Cozumel Tips*.

La Choza, corner of Av. 10 and c/Salas. Busy and popular, mid-priced restaurant serving Mexican home cooking. Good service and a buzzing atmosphere.

El Foco, Av. 5 Sur 13, near c/Salas. Long-established, busy restaurant, serving moderately priced Mexican dishes.

Joe's Lobster Pub, Av. 10, between c/Salas and c/3. Touristy restaurant serving Mexican food; the house speciality is lobster in garlic sauce. Nightly live music. Open 6pm–2am.

La Laguna, inside Parque Chankanaab. Busy, expensive restaurant with an extensive menu including superb seafood, typical Mexican dishes and cocktails. The park closes at 5.30pm.

Las Palmeras, on the zócalo (☎987/2-05-32). Seafood and Mexican cuisine by the main pier. Busy but mediocre considering the prices. Open 7am–11pm.

Mi Chabelita, Av. 10, between c/1 and Salas. One of the few lower-priced restaurants left near the downtown area. A basic Mexican menu in simple surroundings.

Paradise Cafe. *Palapa*-roofed restaurant/bar in the middle of nowhere, dishing up moderately priced Mexican food to the accompaniment of reggae. Good place to swing in a hammock, sipping a margarita. On an anticlockwise circuit of the island, it's where the tarmac road meets the east coast. Daily 10.30am–6.30pm.

Pepe's Grill, Av. Melgar and c/Salas (☎987/2-02-13). Seafood and steak in an elegant and relaxed atmosphere. Expensive but worth it. Daily 5–11pm.

Pizza Rolandi, Melgar 23. The best pizza on the island. Good service and great sangria.

Las Tortugas, Av. 10 Nte., near c/2 Nte. Seafood, steaks and *fajitas*, as well as West Indian dishes, away from the hustle and bustle of the centre. Daily 11am–11pm.

From Playa south to Tulum

South of Playa del Carmen are any number of exquisite **beaches**, mostly undeveloped, often with no access by road. The first of note, 6km south of Playa, is **Xcaret**, tagged the "Incredible Eco-Archeological Park" but in fact a huge, somewhat bizarre **theme park** (daily April–Sept 8.30am–6pm; Oct–March 8.30am–5pm; $25, free for children under 5). There's a museum, tropical aquarium, aviary, "Maya village", botanical garden, small archeological ruins, pools and beaches, and more than a kilometre of subterranean rivers down which you can swim, snorkel or simply float – along with scores of others – with the help of neon rubber rings.

Puerto Aventuras, 20km south of Playa, was originally planned to complement Cancún, with the five-star hotels, tennis and golf clubs and first-class service to show for it. There's a wide white-sand beach, a marina and a dive centre, but little worth stopping for apart from the **Cedam Museum**, which gives an insight into the lives of the ancient mariners and pirates of this coast, displaying artefacts from ships wrecked on the reefs in the 1700s. Five kilometres south, the small fishing village of **Xpu-ha** is known for its spectacular fresh-water lagoons **El Cenote Azul** and **El Cenote**, both of which are popular swimming spots.

Akumal – "the place of the turtles" – is 11km on: another resort area with high-class accommodation and top-notch facilities. As you enter from the highway, you're greeted by an arch across the road, to the right of which is the reception for the swanky *Hotel Club Akumal Caribe Maya Villas* (☎987/3-05-96; from USA: ☎1-800/351-1622; ⑦–⑨). Apart from this, there's a variety of accommodation around the bay, ranging from beachfront bungalows to suites and condos. There are a couple of good, if expensive, restaurants and bars, limited shopping and a dive shop, *The Akumal Dive Shop* (☎987/4-12-59; fax 7-31-64). **Aventuras Akumal**, slightly farther south, is dominated by the *Oasis Akumal* (☎987/2-28-28; fax 2-28-87; ⑧), an all-in resort with every facility you can think of. Also here is the *Villa de Rosa* (Postal 25, Tulum, Quintana Roo, 77780; ☎ and fax 987/4-12-71) which specializes in **cave and cavern diving trips** along the Caribbean coast. A seven-night all-inclusive package starts at $850 per person for a minimum of five people.

Keen snorkellers should make their way to the idyllic bay of **Chemuyil** ($3 fee), about 4km south of Akumal. This beach is popular with holidaying Mexicans, who pitch tents, and there's quite a party atmosphere at night. Facilities are limited to the **snack bar** (10am–6pm), communal showers and ten or so *palapas* on the sand: during the day these provide welcome shade, while at night you can hang your hammock in them ($7 per *palapa*). Try to get one without too many holes in the flyscreen, as the mosquitoes around here are ferocious. There's parking space for trailers, but no hook-ups.

Two kilometres away is another beautiful beach at **Xcacel** ($2 fee), from where you can walk ten minutes south to a clean, cool *cenote* with a wooden platform for easy access (remember not to wear suntan lotion). Turtles lay their eggs here from May to September, when tourists are not encouraged: outside these times, you can see a few of the gentle creatures at the **turtle sanctuary**. The beach fills up occasionally with day-trippers from Playa del Carmen and Cancún, who flock to the large, expensive **restaurant** at the top of the beach (daily 10am–8pm), but otherwise this is a tranquil place to pitch your tent or park your trailer (no hook-ups), with clean showers and plenty of shade.

Xel-Ha Lagoon National Park (daily 8am–5.30pm; $5), 13km north of Tulum, is somewhat overexploited, with expensive restaurants and souvenir shops, and a comments book full of complaints from disgruntled Mexicans who feel that too much of the information is in English rather than Spanish. That said, it's a beautiful place, great for snorkelling, with amazingly tame and colourful fish – get there early, as after 9.30am you'll be fighting for space. You can rent snorkelling equipment on the spot and lockers are available. Across the other side of the highway, the small and only partly excavated **ruins** of Xel-Ha are of little interest but for the Temple of the Birds, where faded paintings are still visible in places.

Tulum

TULUM, 130km south of Cancún, is one of the most picturesque of all Maya sites – small, but exquisitely poised on fifteen-metre-high cliffs above the turquoise Caribbean. When the Spanish first set eyes on the place, in 1518, they considered it as large and beautiful a city as Seville. They were, perhaps, misled by their dreams of Eldorado, by the glory of the setting and by the brightly painted facades of the buildings, for architecturally Tulum is no match for the great cities. Nevertheless, thanks to the setting, it sticks in the memory as no other.

If you want to take time out for a **swim**, you can plunge into the Caribbean straight from the beach on site. There are limitless further possibilities strung out along the sandy road that runs south along the beautiful and deserted coastline. This track continues, though practicable only in a sturdy (and preferably four-wheel drive) vehicle, all the way to Punta Allen at the tip of the peninsula. The beginning of the old road has been blocked to protect the ruins from traffic damage, so you have to join it farther south.

The Site

The site (daily 8am–5pm; $5, free on Sun) is about 1km from the main road – be sure to get off the bus at the turn-off to the ruins and not at the village of Tulum, a few kilometres farther on. **Entrance** is through a breach in the wall that protected the city on three sides; the fourth was defended by the sea. This wall, some 5m high with a walkway around the top, may have been defensive, but more likely its prime purpose

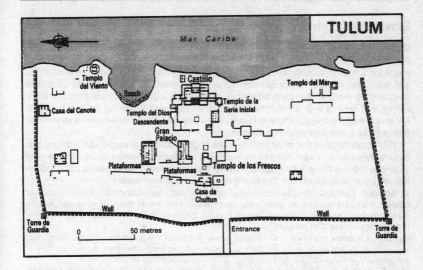

was to delineate the ceremonial and administrative precinct (the site you see today) from the residential enclaves spread out along the coast in each direction. These houses – by far the bulk of the ancient city – were mostly constructed of perishable material, so little or no trace of them remains.

As you go through the walls, the chief structures lie directly ahead of you, with the Castillo rising on its rocky prominence above the sea. You pass first the tumbledown **Casa de Chultun**, a porticoed dwelling whose roof collapsed only in the middle of this century, and immediately beyond it the **Templo de los Frescos**. The partly restored murals inside the temple depict Maya gods and symbols of nature's fertility: rain, corn and fish. They originally adorned an earlier structure and have been preserved by the construction around them of a gallery and still later (in the fifteenth century) by the addition of a second temple on top, with walls which, characteristically, slope outwards at the top. On the corners of the gallery are carved masks of Chac, or perhaps of the creator god Itzamna.

The **Castillo**, on the highest part of the site, commands imposing views in every direction. It may have served, as well as a temple, as a beacon or lighthouse – even without a light, it would have been an important landmark for mariners along an otherwise monotonously featureless coastline. You climb first to a small square, in the midst of which stood an altar, before tackling the broad stairway to the top of the castle itself. To the left of this plaza stands the **Templo del Dios Descendente**. The diving or descending god – depicted here above the narrow entrance of the temple – appears all over Tulum as a small, upside-down figure. His exact meaning is not known: he may represent the setting sun, or rain or lightning, or he may be the Bee God, since honey was one of the Maya's most important exports. Opposite is the **Templo de la Serie Inicial** (Temple of the Initial Series) – so called because in it was found a *stela* (now in the British Museum) bearing a date well before the foundation of the city, and presumably brought here from elsewhere. Right below the castle to the north is a tiny cove with a beautiful white beach, and on the promontory beyond it the **Templo del Viento** (Temple of the Wind), a small, single-roomed structure. This is reflected by a similar chamber – the **Templo del Mar** – overlooking the water at the southern edge of the site.

Staying near Tulum

South of the ruins, scattered along the coast road to Punta Allen, especially in the first few kilometres, are groups of **cabañas** and **campsites** where you can rent huts or find space for a tent or a hammock. Most are plagued by mosquitoes, have no electricity, and some overcharge, but in the end the setting is worth it. Even with the increased numbers of visitors, the gorgeous white-sand beach along this coast remains fairly empty, and the sea is deliciously warm and clear. Although **camping on the beach** in Mexico is free, camping very near to one of the *cabaña* places could cause aggravation: best pay the small fee or move farther away.

The places nearest the ruins are the most lively, with **restaurants**, and a **disco bar** at *Don Armando's*. There have been a number of **thefts** recently, so be sure to give your valuables in for safe keeping and check the sturdiness of your *cabaña*. The following are listed in order of their distance from the ruins, going south.

El Mirador Cabañas, 1km from the ruins along the old Punta Allen road. Basic sandy-floor *cabañas* with hammock hooks only: bring your own or rent one of theirs. Shower *palapa* with running water. The restaurant is perched on the cliff, giving an idyllic view and wonderful cooling breezes. Snorkelling trips arranged. ①.

Santa Fe Cabañas, next door to *El Mirador*. Lively place with restaurant-bar. *Cabañas* have a bed and a hammock but no showers; you have to dredge your washing water from the well and toilets are primitive. Watch your valuables. Camping $2.50. Snorkelling trips arranged. ①–③.

Don Armando's Cabañas, next door to *Santa Fe* (Aptdo Postal 44, Cabañas de Don Armando, Tulum, Quintana Roo; ☎987/4-45-39 or 4-38-56). The most popular of the inexpensive places near the ruins, with sturdy, sandy-floored *cabañas* and security guards. Get there early or, better still, book ahead. There's a three-minute maximum for a shower. Camping $3. ③.

Mar Caribe Cabañas, next to *Don's*. Rickety old *cabañas* for hammocks; only intended for use by a fishing co-op but there are plans to improve them. The restaurant does great fresh fish. ①.

Los Gatos Cabañas, 2km from the ruins. More laid-back than places nearer the ruins; well-built thatched *cabañas* with mosquito-netted doubles and hammocks. A relatively private, shady spot, with a beach for superb swimming and snorkelling. Horseback riding can be arranged. Electricity in the restaurant and shower, and some *cabañas* have feeble battery light. ④.

La Perla Cabañas, the next along. Four basic *cabañas* and a restaurant with bar. ③.

Que Fresco, next to *La Perla*. Nice new *cabañas*, restaurant and a shower with hot and cold water. ④.

Osho Oasis, 7km from the ruins (PO Box 99, Tulum, Quintana Roo; ☎ and fax 987/4-27-72). A comfortable retreat/resort with four standards of *cabaña*, some luxurious and spacious with private bath. The restaurant does a delicious veggie buffet, with fish by order. Electricity until about midnight. There's a meditation room and yoga classes, massage sessions, Zen sittings, Kundalini meditation, and a TV with video for occasional film shows. ⑤–⑧.

Los Arrecifes, 500m farther south along the road. One of the oldest places on this coast, established twenty years ago, with a restaurant. *Cabañas* with or without private bath in an idyllic setting with its own stretch of palm-fringed beach. ④.

Ana y José, a little farther south (call Cancún for reservations: ☎98/80-60-21; fax 80-60-22). A variety of comfortable rooms with bathrooms, some close to the beach with hot and cold water, others set back slightly with cold water only. Good restaurant with a sedate and intimate atmosphere. You can rent bikes and organize day trips into the Sian Ka'an Biosphere Reserve. ⑥.

Cabañas Tulum, the last of the places on this stretch (call Mérida for reservations: ☎99/25-82-95). All rooms on the beach, with their own bath and verandahs with hammocks. The restaurant is the cheapest on this part of the coast, offering good Mexican food, and there's a table tennis table. ⑤.

Cobá

Set in muggy rainforest dotted with lakes, 50km northwest of Tulum, **COBÁ** is a fascinating, if little-visited site. Still only partly excavated, its most surprising characteristic is a resemblance not to the great ruins of the Yucatán, but to those of the Maya in lowland Guatemala and Honduras. This was clearly a very important centre in the Late

Classic period (600–800 AD), and its remains, scattered between two lakes, are linked by more causeways than have been found at any other site. Seeing it all requires at least a couple of hours' wandering in the jungle, along sparsely signed paths. Most important of the structures is the part-restored **Pyramid of Nocoh Mul**, the tallest in the Yucatán and strikingly similar, in its long, narrow and precipitous stairway, to the famous Guatemalan ruins of Tikal.

Practicalities

Heading inland on the road from Tulum to Cobá is easy enough if you're **driving**, in which case you can see the ruins and continue past them to come out on the Cancún–Valladolid road at the village of X-Can, completing the tour from there. If you want to get to Cobá by **bus**, you'll have more problems: there are theoretically two buses along the road daily, from Tulum to Valladolid (via X-Can), but in practice these are unreliable and sometimes don't turn up for days. When they do run, they leave Tulum at 6am and noon, passing Cobá ninety minutes later, and in the other direction depart Valladolid at 4am and 2pm, reaching the ruins after two hours. If you manage to get to Cobá by bus and then find yourself stranded, there is a lone taxi that will bring you back (for a heavy fee). More securely, you may be able to negotiate a good price for a return **taxi** ride from Tulum.

The **village** of Cobá, where the bus stops, is little more than a collection of shacks a few hundred metres from the site entrance. Should you be in the mood to blow a lot of money, you could do little better than **stay** at the *Villas Arqueologicas* (☎98/84-25-74; in US: ☎1-800/528-3100; ⑨), the only hotel anywhere near the site, and a wonderful bit of tropical luxury complete with swimming pool and archeological library. On the less expensive side, there are basic rooms to be had at *El Bocadito* (②), which also has a decent restaurant. Otherwise, you have little choice but to grab a drink and something to eat from one of the stalls by the entrance, and press on.

The Sian Ka'an Biosphere Reserve

Created by presidential decree in 1986, the 528,000-hectare **SIAN KA'AN BIOSPHERE RESERVE** is one of the largest protected areas in Mexico. The name means "the place where the sky is born" in the Maya language, and seems utterly appropriate when you experience the sunrise on this stunningly beautiful coast. It's a huge, sparsely populated region, with only around 1000 permanent inhabitants, mainly fishermen, *chicleros* and *milpa* farmers.

Approximately one-third of the area is **tropical forest**, one-third **fresh and salt water marshes and mangroves**, and one-third is marine environment, including a section of the longest **barrier reef** in the western hemisphere. The coastal forests and wetlands are particularly important feeding and wintering areas for North American migratory birds. Sian Ka'an contains examples of the principal ecosystems found in the Yucatán peninsula and the Caribbean: an astonishing variety of flora and fauna. All five species of Mexican **cat** – jaguar, puma, ocelot, margay and jaguarundi – are present, along with spider and howler **monkeys**, tapir, deer and the West Indian manatee. More than 300 species of **birds** have been recorded, including flamingo, roseate spoonbill, white ibis, crested guan, wood stork, osprey, and fifteen species of heron. The Caribbean beaches provide nesting grounds for four endangered species of **marine turtle**: the green, loggerhead, hawksbill and leatherback, while Morelet's and mangrove **crocodiles** inhabit the swamps and lagoons.

The Biosphere Reserve concept, developed since 1974 by UNESCO, is an ambitious attempt to combine the protection of natural areas and the conservation of their genetic diversity with scientific research and sustainable development. Reserves consist of a strictly protected **core area**, a designated **buffer zone** used for non-destructive activities, and an outer **transition zone**, merging with unprotected land, where traditional land-use and experimental research take place. The success of the reserve depends to a great extent on the co-operation and involvement of local people and the Sian Ka'an management plan incorporates several income-generating projects, such as improved fishing techniques, ornamental plant nurseries and, of course, tourism.

Although you can enter the reserve on your own (and at present there is no entrance fee), by far the best way to explore is on a **day trip** with the **Amigos de Sian Ka'an**, a Cancún-based, non-profit organization formed to promote the aims for which the reserve was established. The *Amigos* support scientific research and produce a series of guide and reference books on the natural history of Sian Ka'an. You can either be picked up at your hotel **in Cancún** or at *Ana y José Cabañas* **in Tulum**. The trip, led by bilingual Mexican biologists, begins at *Boca Paila Lodge*, where you will board a small launch and motor across the lagoon and upstream along through the mangroves canalized by the Maya. It's an amazing trip, with excellent opportunities for bird-watching and spotting crocodiles or manatees. At the inner lagoon you'll be shown where fresh water percolates up through the sandy lagoon floor. You'll also be given the choice to snorkel back along the channels through the mangroves, drifting with the current – that is, after a short talk on what to do if you meet a crocodile. Some day trips include a visit to **Chunyaxche ruins** (see below), walking from the lagoon through the rainforest to the site. Ask when you're booking your trip; it's more likely if it starts in Tulum rather than Cancún. To arrange a trip, for information on the work of the *Amigos*, or for details of how to receive their bulletin, call in at their office in Cancún at Av. Cobá 5 between Nube and Brisa, on the third floor of the Plaza America (☎98/84-95-83; fax 87-30-80), or write to Apartado Postal 770, Cancún 77500, Quintana Roo, Mexico.

Chunyaxche

Heading south from Tulum through the reserve brings you after 25km or so to the little-visited site of **CHUNYAXCHE** (daily 8am–4pm; $3, free on Sun). Despite its size – probably the largest on the Quintana Roo coast – and proximity to Hwy-307, Chunyaxche is hardly developed for tourism, and you'll probably have the place to yourself. Some day trips to the reserve (see above) include a trip to the ruins; to **get there independently**, catch any second-class bus heading between Tulum and Chetumal and ask to be dropped at the entrance. A sign on the left of the highway points to a *palapa* that will one day be a visitor centre: for now you pay the caretaker.

The Site

Archeological evidence indicates that Chunyaxche (also known as Muyil) was continuously occupied from the Preclassic period until after the arrival of the Spanish in the sixteenth century. There is no record of the inhabitants coming into direct contact with the Conquistadors, but they were probably victims of depopulation caused by introduced diseases. Most of the buildings you see today date from the Postclassic period, between 1200 and 1500 AD. The tops of the tallest structures, just visible from the road, rise 20m from the forest floor. There are more than one hundred mounds and temples, none of them completely clear of vegetation, and it's easy to wander around and find dozens of buildings buried in the jungle; climbing them is forbidden, however.

The centre of the site is connected by a *sacbe* – a Maya road – to the small **Muyil lagoon** 500m away. This lagoon is joined to the large Chunyaxche lagoon and ultimately to the sea at **Boca Paila** by an amazing **canalized river**: the route used by Maya traders. If you travel along the river today you'll come across even less explored sites, some of which appear to be connected to the lagoon or river by **underwater caves**.

Leaving the site, particularly if you're making your way up to Tulum, should be easy enough provided you don't leave it too late; continuing south could prove a little more difficult.

Punta Allen

Right at the tip of the peninsula, with a lighthouse guarding the northern entrance to the **Bahía de la Ascensión**, the Maya lobster-fishing village of **PUNTA ALLEN** is not a place you'd stumble across by accident. Some tourists from Cancún do get down this far in rented cars, but if you've only got one day virtually all you can do is turn around and head back.

Despite having a population of just four hundred, Punta Allen is the largest village within the reserve and is a focus of initiatives by both government departments and non-governmental organizations promoting sustainable development. *Earthwatch* volunteers (see p.53 in *Basics*) stay in the village during the summer and assist scientists gathering data.

Practicalities

Entering the village, past the tiny naval station on the right and beached fishing boats on the left, you come to the first of the **accommodation** options: the *Cuzan Guest House* (☎983/4-03-58; ④), where *Earthwatch* volunteers stay in tall conical *cabañas* and teepees, some with hot water. There's a **bar** and **restaurant** with information about the reserve, though you'll need to book meals if you're not staying there. On the beach, the *Let It Be Inn* (⑤) has three *cabañas* with private bath and a separate large thatched *cabaña* with a self-catering kitchen and dining room. *Chen Chomac Resort* (in Playa del Carmen: ☎987/2-20-20; fax 2-41-20; ⑤), a few kilometres north of the village, has some comfortable, modern thatched *cabañas* on the beach.

In theory there's a **long-distance phone** in the village shop, the *Tienda Lili*, but it can't be relied upon. A couple of small **restaurants**, the *Punta Allen* and the *Candy*, serve food. A **mobile shop** travels the length of the peninsula on Saturdays, selling meat, bread, fruit and vegetables, reaching Punta Allen about 2pm: useful if you're camping. Although there's no **dive shop**, the hotels generally have some form of watersport equipment for their guests and may let non-residents rent it. Fishermen can be persuaded to take you out into the reserve for a fee; they also go across the bay to the even tinier village of **Vigia Chico**, on the mainland.

From Tulum to Chetumal

A little under halfway along the inland road from Tulum to Chetumal lies **FELIPE CARRILLO PUERTO**, a major crossroads for the routes to Valladolid and Mérida, but otherwise a town of strikingly little interest. You could find yourself stuck here overnight if you intend to circle back towards Mérida, in which case you'll have the choice of several reasonable **hotels** around the main plaza – try the *Chan Santa Cruz* (☎983/4-01-70; ④), named after a cross, much venerated by the Maya in the nineteenth century, which allegedly spoke and gave orders during the Caste Wars. Farther south, the **Laguna Bacalar** is a vast and beautiful lake some 35km north of Chetumal. Near the village of Bacalar there's a semi-ruinous **fort**: built by the Spanish for protection against British pirates from Belize (then British Honduras), it became a Maya stronghold in the Caste Wars, and was the last place to be subdued by the government, in 1901. There are several lakeshore restaurants and, nearby, the **Cenote Azul**, an inky-blue "bottomless" well that is crowded with swimmers and picnickers at weekends.

Chetumal

Unless you're heading south to Belize or Guatemala, there's little reason to stop in **CHETUMAL**, capital of the state of Quintana Roo. After decades of virtual stagnation (and sulkily jealous of Cancún) the city is beginning to assert itself, but there are still no "sights" to speak of. Even the new **Museo de la Cultura Maya** (Tues–Sun 9am–

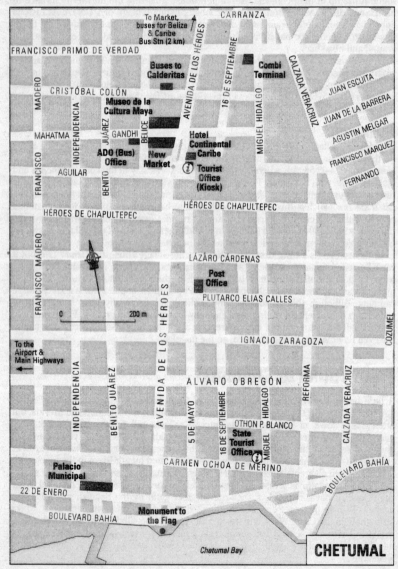

CHETUMAL

7pm; $3) on Héroes, near the corner of Mahatma Gandi, isn't up to much: after a dispute with INAH, the Mexican archeological authority, it was deprived of many of its exhibits. On the bright side, the courtyard often hosts free exhibitions, and there's a good **bookshop** selling guides and maps. Otherwise the broad, modern streets (the town was levelled by Hurricane Janet just over thirty years ago) are lined with rather dull, overpriced hotels and restaurants, and with shops doing a brisk trade in **low-duty goods** – Dutch cheese, Taiwanese Hi-Fi, American peanuts, reproduction Levis from the Far East, Scotch whisky – to be smuggled into Belize or back into Mexico. Chetumal's surroundings, however, do offer the opportunity for some beautiful excursions, and the **waterfront**, enlivened by free music in the plaza, has a certain sleazily tropical charm.

Arrival

The three **bus stations** are all some way north of the centre, and not well served by *combis*, though *colectivos* are easy to find. *Autotransportes Peninsulares*, serving Mérida, Ticul and Carrillo Puerto, and *ADO*, from México, Villahermosa, Campeche and Veracruz, share a small terminal a long way northwest of the centre at the far end of Insurgentes. *Autotransportes Caribe*, the main company, lies 2km farther east, on Insurgentes near the junction with Belice, and just three blocks from the buses to Belize. Buses **from Belize** arrive in front of the Mercado Lázaro Cárdenas. Chetumal's **airport** is only 2km west of the centre, at the end of Av. Revolución.

Information

Avenida de los Héroes, the town's main street, runs down from a big electricity generating plant to the waterfront. Though open irregularly, the **information kiosk** (look for the small glass pyramid opposite the museum) has a few maps and can give information on Belize. The **state tourist office**, on the corner of Hidalgo and Carmen de Merino, is one block from the sea (Mon–Fri 8.30am–4.30pm). There's a **Guatemalan consulate** on Héroes 354 (Mon–Fri 9am–4pm; ☎983/2-65-65), which issues visas (not necessary for citizens of the EC or the USA).

Accommodation

Most of Chetumal's hotels are on Héroes, especially around the information kiosk and at the junction with Obregón. One of the best in town, with private showers and a good restaurant, is the *Hotel Ucum*, Mahatma Gandi 167 (☎983/2-07-11; ③), while the nicest

---

MOVING ON FROM CHETUMAL

The increase in tourism along the Quintana Roo coast means that you can get up to Cancún fast and frequently by **bus**. *Caribe* runs services – including one express – calling at Playa del Carmen and Tulum. There are also plenty of departures to Mérida, Campeche and Villahermosa (9hr), and one to San Cristóbal de las Casas at 9pm (12hr). *ADO* runs the long-haul routes to México (23hr), Veracruz (15hr) and Villahermosa; they have an **office** in town at Gandi and Belice. For Flores and Tikal in **Guatemala**, a minibus leaves the *Caribe* terminal at 1.30pm (8–9hr). Buses **to Belize City** and northern Belize depart from Mercado Lázaro Cárdenas hourly from 4am to 6pm: *Venus* in the morning and *Batty's* in the afternoon.

Taesa, *Aviacsa* and *Aeroméxico* have daily **flights** to Mérida, Cancún and México; if you want to fly to Belize you'll have to cross to Corozal, twenty minutes from the border, and take an internal flight. **Crossing into Belize** is straightforward: hand in your Mexican tourist card at the immigration office at the border and walk over the bridge to Belizean immigration. There's no charge. Money changers at the border take US dollars or travellers' cheques, and offer fair rates.

luxury option is the *Continental Caribe*, Héroes 171 (☎983/2-13-71; ⑦), which has a/c rooms, a pool and a travel agency. Obregón, which cuts east–west along Héroes, also has some good deals – the *María Dolores*, Obrégon 206 (☎983/2-05-08; ③), for example, which has one of the best budget restaurants in town, and the *Jacaranda*, opposite (☎983/2-14-55; ④), where rooms have showers and some a/c.

Eating

Chetumal has nothing special in the way of restaurants, though there are **places to eat** all along Héroes, especially around Obregón – try *Sosilmar* at the *María Dolores* for good meat and fish. *Pantoja*, next to the *Hotel Ucum*, serves a good *comida corrida* – a favourite with the locals. For budget food, stick to the area around the markets, or eat in one of the stalls in the market opposite the museum. There's a good **bakery** next to the *María Dolores*.

Around Chetumal

Near Chetumal are any number of refreshing escapes from the heat and dull modernity. At weekends, the town descends en masse on **CALDERITAS**, a small seaside resort just 6km north around the bay; there's a good campsite on the beach here, at *Amanacer en El Caribe*: they also have thatched *cabañas*, some with cooking facilities (⑤), and a trailer park. *Combis* run from Chetumal to the **remote Caribbean beaches** of Xcalak and Punta Herrero, at the southern end of the Sian Ka'an Biosphere Reserve. Also good for swimming, **Laguna Milagros**, off the road towards Francisco Escárcega, is less spectacular than Bacalar but emptier, and superb for bird-watching.

Local buses and *combis* run out to all of these frequently from the terminal at the junction of Verdad and Hidalgo, four blocks northwest of the information kiosk on Héroes. Buses to Calderitas leave from Cristóbal Colón, near the junction with Héroes. Travelling around this area, keep your passport and tourist card with you – as in all border zones, there are checkpoints on the roads.

Kohunlich

The most direct route from Chetumal back towards central Mexico is across the bottom of the peninsula via Francisco Escárcega. This, on the whole, is virgin forest dotted only by sparse settlements with a desperately pioneer air, but in the Classic Maya era it was relatively populous. With a car you could visit several **sites** along the way – first, and most impressive, is **KOHUNLICH**, set in rainforest 60km from Chetumal, then another 9km off the road (daily 8am–5pm; $4, free on Sun). Like Cobá, Kohunlich owes more to the traditions of Maya Guatemala than to the Yucatán. The ruins, dating from the late Preclassic to Early Classic (100–550 AD) are characteristic of sites in southern Campeche and Quintana Roo, featuring enormous monumental masks of deities. Its most impressive structure is the **Temple of the Masks**, with great sculpted faces of the Maya sun god. At present there is no transport to the ruins, but plans are afoot to start a local bus from Chetumal; check with the tourist office.

fiestas

January

The first week of January sees the festival of the Magi in **Tizimín** (Yucatán), an important religious and secular gathering.

6th FIESTA DE POLK KEKEN in **Lerma** (Campeche), near Campeche, with many traditional dances.

21st In **Dzitas** (Yuc.), north of Chichén Itzá, an ancient festival with roots in Maya tradition.

In **Temax** (Yuc.), between Mérida and Tizimín, the last Sunday of the month is celebrated with a fiesta – the culmination of a week's religious celebration.

February

CARNIVAL (the week before Lent, variable Feb–March) is at its most riotous in **Mérida**, though it's celebrated too in **Campeche** and **Chetumal** and on **Isla Mujeres** and **Cozumel**.

March

20th FERIA DE LAS HAMACAS in **Tecoh** (Yuc.), a hammock-producing village near Mérida.

21st EQUINOX Huge gathering to see the serpent shadow at **Chichén Itzá**.

April

13th The traditional festival of honey and corn in **Hopelchén** (Cam.) lasts until the 17th.

May

3rd DÍA DE LA SANTA CRUZ is the excuse for another fiesta in **Hopelchén** (Cam.); also celebrated in **Celestún** (Yuc.) and **Felipe Carrillo Puerto** (Quintana Roo).

12th–18th Fiesta in **Chankán Veracruz** (Q.R.), near Felipe Carrillo Puerto, celebrating the Holy Cross which spoke to the Maya here.

20th FERIA DEL JIPI in **Becal** (Cam.), the town where many of these hats are made.

June

14th–16th Fiestas for the patron saint of **Ciudad del Carmen** (Cam.).

26th–30th The Festival of San Pedro and San Pablo celebrated on **Cozumel** and in **Panaba** (Yuc.), north of Tizimín.

July

At **Edzná** (Cam., date variable) a Maya ceremony to the god Chac is held, to encourage, or celebrate, the arrival of the rains.

August

10th–16th *Feria* in **Oxkutzcab** (Yuc.).

September

14th DÍA DE SAN ROMAN. In **Dzan** (Yuc.), near Ticul, the end of a four-day festival with fireworks, bullfights, dances and processions – in **Campeche** (Cam.) the Feria de San Roman lasts until the end of the month.

21st EQUINOX Another serpent spectacle at **Chichén Itzá**.

29th DÍA DE SAN MIGUEL is celebrated with a major festival in **Maxcanu** (Yuc.), on the road from Mérida to Campeche.

October

The first two weeks of October in **Mérida** see processions and celebrations associated with the miraculous statue of Cristo de las Ampillas.

18th A pilgrimage centred on **Izamal** (Yuc.) starts ten days of celebration, culminating in dances on the night of the 28th.

November

1st–2nd DAY OF THE DEAD celebrated almost everywhere.

8th–13th *Feria* in **Tekax** (Yuc.), on the road from Mérida to Felipe Carrillo Puerto, with dances and bullfights.

December

3rd–8th Popular fiesta with traditional dances in **Kantunilkin** (Q.R.).

8th DÍA DE LA INMACULADA CONCEPCIÓN is widely celebrated, but especially in **Izamal** (Yuc.) and **Champotón** (Cam.), each of which has a fiesta starting several days earlier.

travel details

Buses

There aren't many places that you can't get to by bus on the peninsula. Sometimes the timetabling isn't totally convenient but the service is generally efficient. The most useful services are between Mérida and Cancún and those provided by *Interplaya*, which run at least every thirty minutes between Cancún, and Tulum. Some places aren't served by first-class buses, but second-class buses and *combis* will get you around locally and to the nearest major centre. Such places include: Oxkutzcab, Progreso, Ticul and Tizimín. The following frequencies and times are for first-class services. Second-class buses usually cover the same routes running 10–20 percent slower.

Campeche to: Cancún (1 daily; 8hr); Chetumal (1 daily; 6hr); Ciudad del Carmen (5 daily; 2hr 30min); Cordoba (3 daily; 12hr); Escárcega (1 daily; 2hr); Mérida (every 30min; 3–4hr)); México (3 daily; 22hr+); Palenque (2 daily; 5hr); San Cristóbal de las Casas (1 daily; 10hr); Villahermosa (5 daily; 6hr).

Cancún to: Campeche (1 daily; 8hr); Chetumal (5 daily; 6hr); Mérida (frequently; 5–6hr); México (1 daily; 30hr+); Playa del Carmen (frequently; 1hr); Puerto Morelos (at least every 30min; 1hr); Tizimín (3 daily; 3hr); Tulum (at least every 30min; 2hr); Valladolid (6 daily; 2hr); Villahermosa (1 daily; 14hr).

Chetumal to: Campeche (1 daily; 6hr); Cancún (5 daily; 6hr); Mérida (7 daily; 9hr); Playa del Carmen (5 daily; 5–8hr); Tulum (6 daily; 4–5hr); Valladolid (3 daily; 5hr).

Mérida to: Campeche (every 30min; 3–4hr); Cancún (frequently; 5–6hr); Chetumal (7 daily; 9hr); México (6 daily; 28hr+); Palenque (2 daily; 10–11hr); Playa del Carmen (7 daily; 8hr); Progreso (frequently; 45min); Tizimín (3 daily; 4hr); Tulum (3 daily; 6hr); Uxmal (13 daily; 2hr); Valladolid (hourly; 3hr); Villahermosa (6 daily; 10hr).

Playa del Carmen to: Cancún (frequently; 1hr); Chetumal (5 daily; 5–8hr); Cobá (3 daily; 2hr); Mérida (7 daily; 8hr); México (3 daily; 30hr+); Palenque (1 daily; 12hr); San Cristóbal de las Casas (1 daily; 14hr); Tulum (frequently; 1hr); Tuxtla Gutiérrez (1 daily; 16hr); Valladolid (3 daily; 4hr); Villahermosa (4 daily; 13hr).

Tizimín to: Mérida (3 daily; 4hr); Río Lagartos (5 daily; 1hr); Valladolid (hourly; 1hr).

Tulum to: Cancún (at least every 30min; 2hr); Chetumal (6 daily; 4–5hr); Cobá (3 daily; 1hr); Mérida (3 daily; 6hr); Playa del Carmen (frequently; 1hr); Valladolid (2 daily; 4hr).

Valladolid to: Cancún (6 daily; 2hr); Chetumal (3 daily; 5hr); Cobá (2 daily; 2hr); Mérida (hourly; 3hr); Playa del Carmen (3 daily; 4hr); Tizimín (hourly; 1hr); Tulum (2 daily; 4hr).

Planes

Mérida, Cancún and Cozumel all have busy **international airports** with several daily flights to México and regular connections to Miami and many other cities in the southern USA. Campeche and Chetumal also have daily direct services to México. Around the Caribbean coast various small companies fly light planes – very frequently between Cancún and Cozumel, less often from these places to Isla Mujeres, Playa del Carmen and Tulum.

Ferries

There are frequent competitive ferry services to **Isla Mujeres** and **Cozumel**. On both routes there is a choice between a low-cost slow boat or a more luxurious fast boat, which generally halves the crossing time. Although there is a car ferry to Isla Mujeres, it is hardly worth taking a vehicle over as the island is so small.

Passenger Ferries

Chiquilá to: Isla Holbox (2 daily; 1hr).

Playa del Carmen to: Cozumel (every 1–2hr; 30min–1hr).

Punta Juárez to: Isla Mujeres (every 30min; 15–30min).

Car Ferries

Chiquilá to: Isla Holbox (1 daily, except Thurs & Sun; 1hr).

Puerto Morelos to: Cozumel (1 daily, 2 on Mon; 2hr 30min).

Punta Sam to: Isla Mujeres (6 daily).

PART THREE

THE

CONTEXTS

THE HISTORICAL FRAMEWORK

Mexico as we know it, with its present borders, has been in existence for less than 150 years. Real history, and a political entity known as Mexico, can be traced back before that, to the Spanish Conquest – but anything which predates the sixteenth century is largely a matter of oral histories recorded long after the events, and of archeological conjecture, for the Spanish were assiduous in their destruction of every trace of the cultures which preceded them.

Such cultures were not confined to Mexico, but must instead be considered as part of **Meso-America**, which extends from the mid-north of Mexico well into Central America. To the north of this imaginary line the Indian tribes were essentially akin to those of North America, never abandoning their nomadic, hunter-gatherer existence; in the south, the Maya were spread all the way from south-eastern Mexico into what is now Honduras. Within Meso-America some of the world's most extraordinary societies grew up, creating – without the use of metal tools, draft animals or the wheel (used only in toys) – vast cities controlling millions of people, superb statuary and sculpture, and a mathematical and calendrical system more advanced than those known in the "civilized" world.

The **prehistory** set out below is a synthesis of the theories which are generally, but by no means universally, accepted. There are still major puzzles – especially concerned with the extent and nature of the contact between the societies and their influence on each other – which, should they be solved, may overturn many existing notions. And there remain those determined to prove some of the theories first coined in the eighteenth century when serious investigation began – that Mexico is Atlantis, or that its cities were founded by Egyptians, Assyrians or Indians (or more recently space travellers). Mormon expeditions, for instance, continue to dig for proof that ancient Mexicans were in fact the lost tribes of Israel.

PREHISTORY

The **first inhabitants** of the Americas crossed the Bering Straits around 50,000 BC, and successive waves of nomadic, Stone-Age hunters continued to arrive for the next 40,000 years, pushing their predecessors gradually farther south. In central Mexico, the earliest evidence of human life dates from about 20,000 BC. In the period known as **Archaic**, from around 5000–1500 BC, come the first signs of settled habitation: the cultivation of corn, followed by the emergence of crude pottery, stone tools and even of trade between the regions. But the first real civilization was established in the **Pre-Classic** era (1500 BC– 300 AD) with the rise of the Olmecs.

Still the least known of all the ancient societies, **Olmec** cities flourished in the low-lying coastal jungles of Tabasco and Veracruz. They are regarded by many as the inventors of almost every aspect of the cultures which are recognizably Meso-American, including the first calendar and hieroglyphic system in the western hemisphere, and a religion, based around the jaguar god, which was spread by their traders throughout central and southern Mexico. Above all, though, and what you see of them in the museums today, is a magnificent artistic style exemplified in their sculpture and in the famous colossal heads. These, with their puzzling negroid (or "baby-faced") features, were carved from monolithic blocks of basalt and somehow transported over ninety kilometres from the quarries to their final settings – proof in itself of a hierarchical society commanding a sizeable workforce.

CLASSIC CIVILIZATIONS

The Olmec centres were already in decline by the end of the pre-Classic period – **La Venta**, the most important site, seems to have been abandoned about 400 BC, and the rest followed in the next few hundred years – but by this time other cities were growing up throughout central Mexico. The early phases of **Monte Albán**, near Oaxaca, show particularly strong Olmec influence. And in and around the great **valley of México** itself (where México now stands; an area known in pre-Hispanic times as Anahuac) many small cities grew up. **Tlatilco** concealed a great hoard of Olmec objects, and all of them must have had contact with the Olmecs through trade at least. Meanwhile there were hints of more important things to come; **Cuicuilco** (now in the capital's suburbs) was an important city until it was buried by a volcanic eruption around the beginning of the first century AD, and at the same time the first important buildings of **Teotihuacán** were being constructed.

Teotihuacán dominated the **Classic Period** (300–900 AD) in central Mexico as the first truly great urban society, and its architectural and religious influences are seen as far south as the Maya heartlands of Guatemala. Even today the city, with its great Pyramids of the Sun and Moon, is a vast and chillingly impressive testimony to an urban-based society ruled by a demanding religious elite. Here for the first time appear many of the familiar gods – in particular **Tlaloc**, god of rain (and fertility), and **Quetzalcoatl**, the plumed serpent who brought civilization to man. Historically, there's not a great deal to be said about Teotihuacán, for in the absence of written records we know almost nothing of its people or rulers, or even its true name (Teotihuacán was coined by the Aztecs – it means "the place where men became gods"). What is certain is that the city's period of greatness ended around 650 AD, and that within a century it had been abandoned altogether. Societies throughout Meso-America, and in particular the Maya, seem to have been disrupted at much the same time, and many other important sites were deserted.

The great **Maya** centres had also reached the peak of their artistic, scientific and architectural achievements in the Classic period, above all in their cities in the lowlands of Guatemala and Honduras. These survived longer than Teotihuacán, but by around 800 AD had also been abandoned. In the Yucatán the Maya fared rather better, their cities revived from about 900 by an injection of ideas (and perhaps invaders) from central Mexico. The famous structures at **Chichén Itzá** mostly date from this later phase, around 900–1100 AD.

In general, the Classic era saw development everywhere – other important centres grew up on the Gulf Coast at El Tajín and in the Zapotec areas around Monte Albán – followed by very rapid decline. There are numerous theories to account for this – and certainly the fall of Teotihuacán must have affected its trading partners throughout Mexico severely – but none are entirely convincing. In all probability, once started, the disasters had a knock-on effect, and probably they were provoked by some sort of agricultural failure or ecological disaster which led to a loss of faith in the rulers, perhaps even rebellion.

TOLTECS AND AZTECS

At the same time, the start of the **post-Classic** era (900–1520 AD) saw the first of a series of invasions from the north which must have exacerbated any problems. Wandering tribes would arrive in the fertile valley of México, like what they saw, build a city adopting many of the styles and religions of their predecessors in the area, enjoy a brief period of dominance, and be subdued in turn by a new wave of Chichimeca. In general, all such tribes were known as **Chichimec**, which implies barbarian (even if many of them were at least semi-civilized before they arrived), and all claimed to have set out on their journeys from the legendary seven caves of Chicomoztoc. Many cities were founded in the valley, and many achieved brief ascendancy (or at least independence), but two names stand out in this new warlike era – the Toltecs and the Aztecs.

The **Toltec** people, who dominated the central valleys from around 950–1150 AD, were among the first to arrive – indeed some say that it was a direct attack by them which destroyed Teotihuacán. They assumed a mythical significance for the Aztecs, who regarded them as the founders of every art and science and claimed direct descent from Toltec blood. In fact, the Toltecs borrowed almost all their ideas from Teotihuacán, and their influence can never have been as pervasive as that city's (for the probabilities of Toltec invasions at Chichén Itzá, see p.509).

Nevertheless there were developments under the Toltecs, and in particular the cult of **Quetzalcoatl** assumed new importance: the god is depicted everywhere at Tula, the Toltec capital (where he may have been embodied as a king or dynasty of kings), and it was from here that he was driven out by the evil god Texcatlipoca. The prediction of his return was later to have fatal consequences. The structure of Toltec society, too, was at least as militaristic as it was religious, and human sacrifice was practised on a far larger scale than had been seen before.

When the **Aztecs** (or Mexica) arrived in central Mexico around the end of the twelfth century they found numerous small city-states, more or less powerful, but none in anything like a position of dominance. Even so it wasn't until 1345 – a period spent scavenging and raiding, often in semi-slavery to local rulers or working as mercenaries – that they found sufficient peace and the prophesied sign (an eagle perched on a cactus devouring a snake) to build their own city.

This, **Tenochtitlán**, was to become the heart of the most formidable of all Mexican empires, but its birth was still not easy. The chosen setting, an island in a lake (now México) was hardly promising, and the new city was at first a subject of its larger neighbours. By forming reed islands anchored to the lake bed by trees, the Mexica became self-sufficient in agriculture and expanded their base; they rebelled successfully against their former rulers, and around 1429 formed a triple alliance with neighbouring Texcoco and Tlacopán to establish the basis of the **Aztec empire**. Its achievements were remarkable – in less than a hundred years the Aztecs had come to control, and demand tribute and taxes from, the whole of central and southern Mexico. Tenochtitlán became huge – certainly the invading Spanish could not believe its size and grandeur – but however it grew, the gods continued to demand more war: to suppress rebellious subjects, and to provide fresh victims for the constant rituals of human sacrifice.

Meanwhile, other societies had continued much as before. In Oaxaca the Zapotecs were subjected to invasions by **Mixtecs** from the mountains in much the same way as was

happening in central Mexico. By war and alliance the Mixtecs came eventually to dominate all their lands – developing the crafts of the potter and goldsmith as never before – and fell to the Aztecs only in the last years before the Spanish Conquest. In the Yucatán, the **Maya** were never conquered, but their culture was in decline and any form of central authority had long since broken down. Nevertheless, they carried on trade all around the coasts, and Christopher Columbus himself (though he never got to Mexico) encountered a heavily laden boat full of Maya traders, plying between Honduras and the Yucatán. On the **Gulf Coast** Aztec dominance was total by the time the Spanish arrived, but they were still struggling to subdue the **West**.

THE SPANISH CONQUEST

Hernan Cortés landed on the coast near modern Veracruz on April 21, 1519 – Good Friday. With him there were just 550 men, a few horses, dogs and a cannon; yet in less than three years they had defeated the Aztecs and effectively established control over most of Mexico. Several factors enabled them to do so. First was Cortés himself, as ruthless a leader as any in history: he burned the expedition's boats within days of their arrival, so that there was literally no turning back. In addition his men had little to lose and much to gain, and their metal weapons and armour were greatly superior to anything the Indians had (although many Spaniards adopted Aztec-style padded cotton, which was warmer, lighter and almost as protective). Their gunpowder and cannon could also wreak havoc with opposing armies – if mainly psychologically. The horses, too, terrified the Indians as well as affording greater manoeuvrability, and the attack dogs, trained to kill, were almost as effective. None of these, though, in the end counted a fraction as much as Cortés' ability to form alliances with tribes who were fretting under Aztec subjugation and whose numbers eventually swelled his armies at least tenfold.

Even so, **Moctezuma**, had he chosen to do so, could certainly have destroyed the Spanish before they left their first camp, since his spies had brought news of their arrival almost immediately. Instead he sent a delegation bearing gifts of gold and jewels which he hoped would persuade them to leave in peace.

They served only to inflame the imaginative greed of the Spanish. By all accounts Moctezuma was a morose, moody and indecisive man, but his failure to act against Cortés had deeper roots: he was also heavily influenced by religious omens, and the arrival of Cortés coincided with the predicted date for the return of **Quetzalcoatl**. The invaders were fair-skinned and bearded, as was Quetzalcoatl, and they had come from the east, whither he had vanished – moreover it seemed they bore a peaceful message like that of the god, for one of their first acts was always to ban human sacrifice. So although he put obstacles in their way, tried to dissuade them, and even persuaded his allies to fight them, when the Spanish finally reached Tenochtitlán in November 1519, Moctezuma welcomed them to the city as his guests. They promptly repaid this hospitality by making him a prisoner within his own palace.

This "phony war", during which Spanish troops skirmished with a number of other Indian tribes and made allies of many – most significantly the **Tlaxcalans** – lasted for about a year. In April 1520 news came of a second Spanish expedition, led by Panfilo Narvaez, which was under orders to capture Cortés and take him back to Cuba (the mission had always been unofficial, and many others hoped to seize the wealth of Mexico for themselves). Again, though, Cortés proved the more decisive commander – he marched back east, surprised Narvaez by night, killed him, and persuaded most of his troops to switch allegiance.

Meanwhile the Spaniards left behind in Tenochtitlán had finally provoked their hosts beyond endurance by killing a group of priests during a religious ceremony, and were under siege in their quarters. Cortés, with his reinforcements, fought his way back into the city on June 24, only to find himself trapped as well. On June 27, Moctezuma (still a prisoner) was killed – according to the Spanish, stoned to death by his own people while attempting to appeal for peace. Finally Cortés decided to break out on the night of the 30th – still commemorated as the **Noche Triste** – when the Spanish lost over half their number on the causeways across the lake. Most of them were so weighed down with gold and booty that they were barely able to move, let alone swim in the places where the bridges had been destroyed.

Once more, though, the Aztecs failed to follow up their advantage, and the Spanish survivors managed to reach the haven of their allies in Tlaxcala where they could regroup. The final assault on the capital began in January 1521, with more fresh troops and supplies, and more and more Indians throwing their lot in with the Spanish. Tenochtitlán was not only besieged (the Spanish built ships which could be sailed on the lake) but ravaged by an epidemic of smallpox among whose victims was Moctezuma's successor, Cuitlahuac. They held out for several more months under **Cuauhtémoc** – the only hero of this long episode in Mexican eyes – but on August 13, 1521 Tenochtitlán finally fell to the Spanish.

Although much of the country remained to be pacified, the defeat of the Aztec capital made it inevitable that eventually it would be.

COLONIAL RULE

By dint of his success, Cortés was appointed Governor of **Nueva España** (New Spain) in 1522, although in practice he was watched over constantly by minders from Spain, and never therefore had much real freedom of action. There followed three hundred years of direct Spanish rule, under a succession of 61 viceroys personally responsible to the king in Spain. By the end of the sixteenth century the entire country had been effectively subjugated, and its boundaries stretched by exploration from Panama to the western states of the USA (although the area from Guatemala down, including the Mexican state of Chiapas, was soon under separate rule).

The first tasks, in the Spanish mind, were of reconstruction, pacification and conversion. Tenochtitlán had already been destroyed in the war and subsequently pillaged, burned and its population dispersed. To complete matters – a conscious policy of destroying all reminders of Aztec power – the remaining stones were used to construct the new city, México. At first there was quite remarkable **progress**: hundreds of towns were laid out (on a plan, with a plaza surrounded by a grid of streets, as laid down in Spain); thousands of churches built, often in areas which had been sacred to the Indians, or on top of their pyramids (there were over 12,000 in Mexico by 1800); and with the first Franciscan monks arriving in 1524, mass conversions were the order of the day. In a sense the indigenous peoples were used to all this – the Aztecs and their predecessors had behaved in a similar manner – but they had never experienced a slavery like that which was to follow.

When the Spanish arrived the **native population** of central Mexico was at least 25 million; by the beginning of the nineteenth century the total population of Nueva España was just six million, and at most half of these were pure-blooded Indians. Some had been killed in battle, a few as a result of ill treatment or simply from being left without homes or land to live on, but the vast majority died as a result of sucessive epidemics of European diseases to which the New World had no natural immunity. The effects were catastrophic, and not only for the Indians themselves. The few survivors found the burden of labour placed on them ever increasing as their numbers dwindled – for certainly no white man came to Mexico to do manual work – and became more and more like slaves.

At the same time **the Church**, which at first had championed indigenous rights and attempted to record native legends and histories and educate the children, grew less interested, and more concerned with money. Any attempt to treat the Indians as human was in any case violently opposed by Spanish landowners, to whom they were rather less than machines (cheaper than machinery, and therefore more expendable). By the end of the colonial era the Church owned more than half of all the land and wealth in the country, yet most Indian villages would be lucky to see a priest once a year.

In a sense Mexico remained a wealthy nation – certainly the richest of the Spanish colonies – but that sense would only have been understood by the rulers, or by those back home in Spain. For the governing philosophy was that "what's good for Spain is good for Mexico", and to that end all **trade**, industry and profit was exclusively aimed. No local trade or agriculture which would compete with Spain was allowed, so the cultivation of vines or the production of silk was banned; heavy taxes on other products – coffee, sugar, tobacco, cochineal, silver and other metals – went directly to Spain or to still poorer colonies, and no trade except with Spain was allowed. Since the "Spanish Galleon" (actually more of a convoy) sailed from Veracruz just once a year and was even then subject to the vagaries of piracy, this was a considerable handicap.

It didn't prevent the growth of a small class of extraordinarily wealthy **hacendados** (owners of massive haciendas) and mineowners – whose growing confidence is shown in the architectural development of the colonial towns, from fortress-like huddles at the beginning of the colonial era to the full flowering of baroque extravagance by its end – but it did stop the development of any kind of realistic economic infrastructure, even of decent roads linking the towns. Just about the only proper road in 1800 was the one which connected Acapulco with México and Veracruz, by which goods from the Far Eastern colonies would be transported cross-country before shipment on to Spain.

Even among the wealthy there was growing **resentment**. Resentment which was fuelled by the status of Mexicans: only *gachupines*, Spaniards born in Spain, could hold high office in the government or church. There were about 40,000 of them in Mexico in 1800 out of the six million population, and some three million Indians – the rest were *criollos* (Creoles, born in Mexico of Spanish blood) who were in general educated, wealthy and aristocratic; and *mestizos* (of mixed race) who dominated the lower ranks of the church, army and civil service, and worked as shopkeepers, small ranchers or even bandits and beggars.

INDEPENDENCE

By the beginning of the **nineteenth century** Spain's status as a world power was in severe decline. In 1796 British sea power had forced the Spanish to open their colonial ports to free trade, and in 1808 Spain itself was invaded by Napoleon, who placed his brother Joseph on the throne. At the same time new political ideas were transforming the world outside, with the French Revolution and the American War of Independence still fresh in the memory. Although the works of such political philosophers as Rousseau, Voltaire and Paine were banned in Mexico, the opening of the ports made it inevitable that their ideas would spread – especially as it was traders from the new United States who most took advantage of the opportunities. Literary societies set up to discuss these books quickly became centres of political dissent.

The spark, though, was provided by the French invasion of Spain, as colonies throughout Latin America refused to recognize the Bonaparte regime (and the campaigns of Bolivar and others in South America began). In Mexico, the *gachupin* rulers proclaimed their loyalty to Ferdinand VII (the deposed king) and hoped to carry on much as before, but creole discontent was not to be so easily assuaged. The literary societies continued to meet, and from one, in Querétaro, emerged the first leaders of the Independence movement: Father **Miguel Hidalgo y Costilla**, a creole priest, and **Ignacio Allende**, a disaffected junior army officer.

When their plans for a coup were discovered, the conspirators were forced into premature action, with Hidalgo issuing the famous *Grito* (cry) of Independence – *Mexicanos, viva Mexico!* – from the steps of his parish church in Dolores on September 16, 1810. The mob of Indians and *mestizos* who gathered behind the banner swiftly took the major towns of San Miguel, Guanajuato and others to the north of the capital, but their behaviour – seizing land and property, slaughtering the Spanish – horrified the wealthy creoles who had initially supported the movement. In Spring 1811, Hidalgo's army, huge but undisciplined, moved on the capital, but at the crucial moment Hidalgo threw away a clear chance to overpower the royalist army. Instead he chose to retreat, and his forces broke up as quickly as they had been assembled. Within months, Hidalgo, Allende and the other ringleaders had been captured and executed.

By this time most creoles, frightened at what had been unleashed, had rejoined the ranks of the royalists. But many *mestizos* and much of the indigenous population remained in a state of revolt, with a new leader in the *mestizo* priest **José María Morelos**. Morelos was not only a far better tactician than Hidalgo – instituting a highly successful series of guerrilla campaigns – he was also a genuine radical. By 1813 he controlled virtually the entire country, with the exception of the capital and the route from there to Veracruz, and at the **Congress of Chilpancingo** he declared the abolition of slavery and the equality of the races. But the royalists fought back with a series of crushing victories, Morelos was executed in 1815, and his forces, under the leadership of Vicente Guerrero, were reduced to carrying out the occasional minor raid.

Ironically, it was the introduction of liberal reforms in Spain, of just the type feared by the Mexican ruling classes, which finally brought about **Mexican Independence**. Worried that such reforms might spread across the Atlantic, many Creoles once again switched their positions. In 1820 **Agustin de Iturbide**, a royalist general but himself a mestizo, threw in his lot with Guerrero; in 1821 he proposed the **Iguala Plan** to the Spanish authorities, who were hardly in a position to fight, and Mexico was independent. With Independence, though, came none of the changes which had been fought over for so long – the church retained its power, and one set of rulers had simply been changed for another, native, set of rulers.

FOREIGN INTERVENTION

In 1822 Iturbide had himself proclaimed emperor; a year later he was forced to abdicate, a year after that he was executed. It was the first of many such events in a century which must rank among the most confused – and disastrous – in any nation's history. Not only had Independence brought no real social change, it had left the new nation with virtually no chance of successful government: the power of the Church and of the army was far greater than that of the supposed rulers; there was no basis on which to create a viable internal economy; and if the state hadn't already been bankrupted by the Independence struggle, it was to be cleaned out time and again by the demands of war and internal disruption. There were no less than 56 governments in the next forty years. In what approaches farce, the name of General **Santa Ana** stands out as the most bizarre figure of all, becoming president or dictator on eleven separate occasions and masterminding the loss of more than half of Mexico's territory.

Santa Ana's first spell in office followed immediately on Iturbide – he declared Mexico a Republic (although he himself always expected to be treated as a king, and addressed as His Most Serene Majesty) and called a constitutional convention. Under the auspices of the new constitution, the Republic was confirmed, the country divided into thirteen states, and **Guadalupe Victoria**, a former guerrilla general, elected its first president. He lasted three years, something of a record. In 1829 the Spanish attempted a rather half-hearted invasion, easily defeated, after which they accepted the fact of Mexican Independence. In 1833 Santa Ana was elected president (officially) for the first time, the fifth thus far.

In 1836 a rather more serious chain of events was set in motion when **Texas**, Mexican territory but largely inhabited by migrants from the USA, declared its independence. Santa Ana commanded a punitive expedition which besieged **the Alamo** in the famous incident in which Jim Bowie and Davy Crockett, along with 150 other defenders, lost their lives. Santa Ana himself, though, was promptly defeated and captured at the battle of San Jacinto, and rather than face execution he signed a paper accepting **Texan Independence**. Although the authorities in México refused to accept the legality of its claim, Texas was, de facto, independent. Meanwhile, in 1838, the French chose to invade Veracruz, demanding compensation for alleged damages to French property and citizens – a small **war** which lasted about four months, and during which Santa Ana lost a leg.

In 1845 the United States annexed Texas, and although the Mexicans at first hoped to negotiate a settlement, the redefinition of Texas to include most of Arizona, New Mexico and California made yet another war almost inevitable. In 1846 clashes between Mexican troops and US cavalry in these disputed western zones led to the declaration of the **Mexican-American War**. Following defeat for the Mexicans at Palo Alto and Resaca, three small US armies invaded from the north. At the same time General Winfield Scott took Veracruz after a long bombardment, and commenced his march on the capital. Santa Ana was roundly defeated on a number of occasions, and in September 1847, after heroic resistance by the Niños Heroes (cadets at the military academy) México itself was captured. In 1848, by the **Treaty of Guadalupe Victoria**, the US paid $15 million for most of Texas, New Mexico, Arizona and California, along with parts of Colorado and Utah: in 1854 the present borders were established when Santa Ana

sold a further strip down to the Rio Grande for $10 million.

REFORM

Mexico finally saw the back of Santa Ana when, in 1855, he left for exile in Venezuela. But its troubles were by no means at an end. A new generation had grown up who had known only an independent Mexico in permanent turmoil, who had lived through the American humiliation, and who espoused once more the liberal ideals of Morelos. Above all they saw their enemy as **the Church**: vast, self-serving, and far wealthier than any legitimate government, it had further sullied its reputation by refusing to provide funds for the American war. Its position enshrined in the constitution, it was an extraordinarily reactionary institution, bleeding the peasantry for the most basic of sacraments (few could afford official marriage, or burial) and failing to provide the few services it was charged with. All education was in church schools, which for 95 percent of the population meant no education at all.

Benito Juárez, a Zapotec Indian who had been adopted and educated by a priest, and later trained as a lawyer, became the leader of this liberal movement through several years of civil war in which each side became more bitterly entrenched in increasingly extreme positions. When the liberals first came to power following Santa Ana's exile they began a relatively mild attempt at reform: permitting secular education, liberating the press, attempting to distance the Church from government and instituting a new democratic Constitution. The Church responded by obstruction and by threatening to excommunicate anyone co-operating with the government. In 1858 there was a conserative coup, and for the next three years **internal strife** on an unprecedented scale. With each new battle the liberals proclaimed more drastic reforms, churches were sacked and priests shot; while the conservatives responded by executing anyone suspected of liberal tendencies.

In 1861 Juárez emerged, at least temporarily, triumphant. Church property was confiscated, monasteries closed, weddings and burials became civil affairs, and set fees were established for the services of a priest. It wasn't until 1867 that most of these **Reform Laws** were to be fully enacted – for the conservatives had one more card to play – but most are still in force today. Priests in Mexico, for example, are forbidden to wear their robes in public.

The conservatives' final chance was to appeal for outside help. At the end of the civil war, with the government bankrupt, Juárez had suspended payment of all foreign debts, and in 1861 a joint British, Spanish and French expedition occupied Veracruz to demand compensation. It rapidly became clear, however, that the French were after more than mere financial recompense. Britain and Spain withdrew their forces, and Napoleon III ordered his troops to advance on México. The aim, with the support of Mexican conservatives, was to place **Maximilian**, a Habsburg archduke, on the throne as emperor.

Despite a major defeat at Puebla on May 5, 1862 (now a national holiday), the French sent for reinforcements and occupied Mexico City in 1863. The new emperor arrived the following year. In many ways, Maximilian cuts a pathetic figure. He arrived in Mexico with almost no knowledge of its internal feuds (having gleaned most of his information from a book on court etiquette), expecting a triumphal welcome. Proving to be a liberal at heart – he refused to repeal any of Juárez's reforms – he promptly lost the support of even the small group which had initially welcomed him. While his good intentions seem undeniable, few believe that he would have been capable of putting them into practice even in the best of circumstances. And these were hardly ideal times. With Union victory in the US Civil War, the authorities there threw their weight behind Juárez, providing him with arms and threatening to invade unless the French withdrew (on the basis of the Monroe doctrine: America for the Americans). Napoleon, already worried by the growing power of Bismarck's Prussia back home, had little choice but to comply. After 1866, Maximilian's position was hopeless.

His wife, the **Empress Carlota**, sailed to Europe in a vain attempt to win fresh support, but Napoleon had taken his decision, the Vatican refused to contemplate helping a man who had continued to attack the church, and the constant disappointments eventually drove Carlota mad. She died, insane, in Belgium in 1927. Maximilian, meanwhile, stayed at the head of his hopelessly outnumbered troops to the end – May 15, 1867 – when he was defeated and captured at Querétaro. A month later, he faced the firing squad.

Juárez reassumed power, managing this time to ride the worst of the inevitable bankruptcy. The first steps towards economic reconstruction were taken, with the completion of a railway from Veracruz to the capital, encouragement of industry, and the development of a public education programme. Juárez died in office in 1872, havng been re-elected in 1871, and was succeeded by his vice-president Lerdo de Tejada, who continued on the same road, though with few new ideas.

DICTATORSHIP

Tejada was neither particularly popular nor spectacularly successful, but he did see out his term of office. However, there had been several Indian revolts during his rule and a number of plots against him, the most serious of them led by a new radical liberal leader, **Porfirio Díaz**. Díaz had been a notably able military leader under Juárez, and in 1876, despite the re-election of Tejada, he proclaimed his own candidate president. The following year he assumed the presidency himself, and was to rule as dictator for the next thirty-four years. At first his platform was a radical one – including full implementation of the Reform Laws and a decree of no re-election to any political office – but it was soon dropped in favour of a brutal policy of modernization. Díaz did actually stand down at the end of his first term, in 1880, but he continued to rule through a puppet president, and in 1884 resumed the presidency for an unbroken stretch until 1911.

In many ways the **achievements** of his dictatorship were remarkable: some 10,000 miles of railway were built, industry boomed, telephones and telegraph were installed, and major towns, reached at last by reasonable roads, entered the modern era. In the countryside, Díaz established a police force – the notorious *rurales* – which finally stamped out banditry. Almost every city in Mexico seems to have a grandiose theatre and elegant public buildings from this era. But the costs were high: rapid development was achieved basically by handing over the country and its people to **foreign investors**, who owned the vast majority of the oil, mining rights, railways and natural resources. At the same time there was a massive policy of land expropriation: formerly communal village holdings being handed over to foreign exploitation or simply grabbed by corrupt officials.

Agriculture, meanwhile, was ignored entirely. The owners of vast haciendas could make more than enough money by relying on the forced labour of a landless peasantry, and had no interest in efficiency or production for domestic consumption. By 1900 the whole of Mexico was owned by some 3–4 percent of its population. Without land of their own, peasants had no choice but to work on the haciendas or in the forests, where their serfdom was ensured by wages so low that they were permanently in debt to their employers. The rich became very rich indeed; the poor had lower incomes and fewer prospects than they had a century earlier.

Once the *rurales* had done their job of making the roads safe to travel, they became a further burden – charging for the right to travel along roads they controlled and acting as a private police force for employers should any of their workers try to escape. In short, slavery had been reintroduced in all but name, and up to a quarter of the nation's resorces came to be spent on internal security. The press was censored, too, education strictly controlled, and corruption rife.

REVOLUTION

With the onset of the **twentieth century**, Díaz was already old and beginning to lose his grip on reality. He had evey intention of continuing in power until he dropped; but a real middle-class opposition was beginning to develop, concerned above all by the racist policies of their government (which favoured foreign investors above native ones) and by the lack of opportunity for themselves – the young educated classes. Their movement revived the old slogan of "*no reelección*", and in 1910 **Francisco Madero** stood against Díaz in the the presidential election. The old dictator responded by imprisoning his opponent and declaring himself victor at the polls by a vast majority. Madero, however, escaped to Texas where he proclaimed himself president, and called on the nation to rise in his support.

This was an entirely opportunist move, for at the time there were no revolutionary forces,

but several small bands immediately took up arms. Most important were those in the northern state of Chihuahua, where **Pancho Villa** and **Pascual Orozco** won several minor battles, and in the southwest, where **Emiliano Zapata** began to arm Indian guerrilla forces. In May 1911 Orozco captured the major border town of Ciudad Juárez, and his success was rapidly followed by a string of Revolutionary victories. By the end of the month, hoping to preserve the system if not his role in it, Porfirio Díaz had fled into exile. On October 2, 1911, Madero was elected president.

Like the originators of Independence before him, Madero had no conception of the forces he had unleashed. He freed the press, encouraged the formation of unions and introduced genuine democracy, but failed to do anything about the condition of the peasantry or the redistribution of land. Zapata prepared to rise again.

Emiliano Zapata was perhaps the one true Revolutionary in the whole long conflict to follow, and his battle cry of *Tierra y Libertad* (Land and Liberty) and insistence that "it is better to die on your feet than live on your knees" make him still a revered figure among the peasants. By contrast, the rest were mostly out for personal gain: **Pancho Villa**, a cattle rustler and bandit in the time of Díaz, was by far the most successful of the more orthodox generals, brilliantly inventive, and ruthless in victory. But his motivation, though he came from peasant stock, seems to have been personal glory – he appeared to love fighting, and at one stage, when a Hollywood film crew was travelling with his armies, would allegedly arrange his battles so as to ensure the best lighting conditions and most impressive fight scenes.

In any case Madero was faced by a more immediately dangerous enemy than his own erstwhile supporters – **US business interests**. Henry Lane Wilson, US ambassador, began openly plotting with **Victoriano Huerta**, a government general, and Felix Díaz, a nephew of the dictator, who was held in prison. Fighting broke out between supporters of Díaz and those of Madero, while Huerta refused to commit his troops to either side. When he did, in 1913, it was to proclaim himself president. Madero was shot in suspicious circumstances (few doubt an assassination sanctioned by Huerta) and opponents on the right, including Díaz, either imprisoned or exiled. The new government was promptly recognized by the United States and most other foreign powers, but not by the important forces within the country.

CONSTITUTION VS. CONVENTION

Villa and Zapata immediately took up arms against Huerta, and in the north Villa was joined by **Alvaro Obregón**, governor of Sonora, and **Venustiano Carranza**, governor of Coahuila. Carranza was appointed head of the Consititutionalist forces, though he was always to be deeply suspicious of Villa, despite Villa's constant protestations of loyalty. At first the Revolutionaries made little headway – Carranza couldn't even control his own state, although Obregón and Villa did enjoy some successes raiding south from Chihuahua and Sonora. But almost immediately the new US president, Woodrow Wilson, withdrew his support from Huerta and, infuriated by his refusal to resign, began actively supplying arms to the Revolution.

In 1914, the **Constitutionalists** began to move south, and in April of that year US troops occupied Veracruz in their support (though neither side was exactly happy about the foreign presence). Huerta, now cut off from almost every source of money or supplies, fled the country in July, and in August Obregón occupied the capital, proclaiming Carranza president.

Renewed fighing broke out straight away, this time between Carranza and Obregón, the Constitutionalists, on one side, and the rest of the Revolutionary leaders on the other, so-called **Conventionalists** whose sole point of agreement was that Carranza should not lead them. The three years of fighting which followed were the most bitter and chaotic yet, with petty chiefs in every part of the country proclaiming provisional governments, joining each other in factions and then splitting again, and the entire country in a state of anarchy. Each army issued its own money, and each press-ganged any able-bodied men they came across into joining. By 1920 it was reckoned that about one eighth of the population had been killed.

Gradually, however, Obregón and Carranza gained ground – Obregón defeated Villa several times in 1915, and Villa withdrew to carry out border raids into the United States, hoping to provoke an invasion (which he nearly did: US troops pursued him across the border but were never able to catch up, and following defeat in a skirmish with Carranza's troops they withdrew). Zapata, meanwhile, had some conspicuous successes – and occupied México for much of 1915 – but his irregular troops tended to disappear back to their villages after each victory. In 1919 he was tricked into a meeting with one of Carranza's generals and shot in cold blood; Villa retired to a hacienda in his home state, and was assassinated in 1923.

THE END OF THE REVOLUTION

Meanwhile Carranza continued to claim the presidency, and in 1917 set up a **Constitutional congress** to ratify his position. The document they produced – the present constitution – included most of the Revolutionary demands, among them workers' rights, a mandatory eight-hour day, national ownership of all mineral rights, and the distribution of large landholdings and formerly communal properties to the peasantry. Carranza was formally elected in May 1917 and proceeded to make no attempt to carry out any of its stipulations, certainly not with regard to land rights. In 1920 Carranza was forced to step down by **Obregón**, and was shot while attempting to escape the country with most of the contents of the treasury.

Obregón, at least, was well intentioned – but his efforts at real land reform were again stymied by fear of US reaction: in return for American support, he agreed not to expropriate land. In 1924 **Plutarco Elias Callés** succeeded him, and real progress towards some of the ideals of the Revolutionary Constitution began to be made. Work on large public works schemes began – roads, irrigation systems, village schools – and about eight million acres of land were given back to the villages as communal holdings. At the same time Calles instituted a policy of virulent anticlericalism, closing churches and monasteries, and forcing priests to flee the country or go underground.

These moves provoked the last throes of a backlash, as the Catholic **Cristero movement** took up arms in defence of the Church. From 1927 until about 1935 isolated incidents of vicious banditry and occasional full-scale warfare continued, eventually burning themselves out as the stability of the new regime became obvious, and religious controls were relaxed. In 1928 Obregón was re-elected, but assassinated three weeks later in protest at the breach of the "*no reelección*" clause of the Constitution. He was followed by Portes Gil, Ortiz Rubio and then Abelardo Rodriguez, who were controlled behind the scenes by Calles and his political allies, who steered national politics to the right in the bleak years of the 1930s depression.

MODERN MEXICO

By 1934 Mexico enjoyed a degree of peace, and a remarkable change had been wrought. A new culture had emerged – seen nowhere more clearly than in the great murals of Rivera and Orozco which began to adorn public buildings throughout the country – in which native heroes like Hidalgo, Morelos, Juárez and Madero replaced European ideals. Nowadays everyone in the Republic would claim Indian blood – even if the Indians themselves remain the lowest stratum of society – and the invasion of Cortés is seen as the usurpation of the nation's march to its destiny, a march which resumed with Independence and the Revolution. At the same time there was a fear in these early days that Calles was attempting to promote a dynasty of his own.

With the election of **Lázaro Cárdenas** in 1934, such doubts were finally laid to rest. As the spokesman of a younger generation, Cárdenas expelled Calles and his supporters from the country, at the same time setting up the single broad-based party which still rules today as the **PRI** (Party of the Institutionalized Revolution). Cárdenas set about an unprecedented programme of reform, redistributing land on a huge scale (17 million hectares during his 6-year term), creating peasant and worker organizations to represent their interests at national level, and incorporating them into the governing party. He also relaxed controls on the church to appease internal and international opposition.

In 1938 he nationalized the **oil** companies, an act which has proved one of the most significant in shaping modern Mexico and bringing about its industrial miracle. For a time it seemed as if yet more foreign intervention might follow, but a boycott of Mexican oil by the major consumers crumbled with the onset of World War II (apart from Neville Chamberlain, who cut off diplomatic relations and lost Great Britain an important investment market as a result), and was followed by a massive influx of money and a huge boost for Mexican industry as a result of the war. By the time he stood down in 1940, Cárdenas could claim to be the first president in modern Mexican history to have served his full six-year term in peace, and handed over to his successor without trouble.

Through the war **industrial growth** continued apace under Avila Camacho, and Mexico officially joined the Allies in 1942. Miguel Aleman (1946–52) presided over still faster development, and a further massive dose of public works and land reform – major prestige projects, like the University City in the capital, were planned by his regime. Over the next thirty years or so, massive oil incomes continued to stimulate industry, and the PRI maintained a masterly control of all aspects of public life without apparently losing the support of a great majority of the Mexican public. Of course it is an accepted fact of life that governments will line their own pockets first – a practice which apparently reached its height under **Lopez Portillo** (1976–82) – but the unrelenting populism of the PRI, its massive powers of patronage, and above all its highly visible and undoubted achievement of progress, maintained it in power with amazingly little dissent.

All this is not to say that there were no **problems**. The year 1959 saw the repression of a national railway strike where 10,000 workers lost their jobs and their leaders were placed in jail, and in **1968** hundreds of students were massacred in Tlatelolco square in México to stem an active pro-democracy student movement which threatened Mexico's image abroad as the Olympic games neared (Mexico's were the first Olympics to be held in the "Third World" and were seen as an opportunity to promote the regime abroad). The PRI was unable to buy off the students due to their rotating leadership, and unwilling to negotiate for fear of losing face. Although the massacre did put an end to student unrest, or at least any public manifestation of it, from Tlatelolco on the Mexican system lost a great deal of its legitimacy as the opposition saw fewer reasons for working within the system; guerrilla movements sprang up in Guerrero state, for example. The PRI was still, however, very much in control and had snuffed these movements out by the mid-seventies. The government, who ran the union movement and the peasant organizations and delivered steady economic growth, appeared to have an unassailable hold on power as well as being genuinely popular across a wide spectrum of the population. In the mid-1990s, however, their sixty-year reign seems far less secure.

ECONOMIC CRISIS

The government of **Miguel de la Madrid** (1982–88) found itself faced with economic crisis on a national and international scale. Mexico's vast foreign debt (of almost \$100 billion) had been run up in the heady days of the oil boom. Already a severe burden on the economy, the debt was greatly exacerbated by falling oil prices and revenues and rising international interest rates. At the same time the PRI seemed to be losing its populist touch: the twelve previous years, known as the "Docena Trágica" or tragic dozen, had seen flourishing corruption and economic mismanagement destroy the hopes brought about by the development of the oil industry. Also, de la Madrid was a US-educated financier who adopted severe **austerity measures**. Such policies won widespread acclaim from international bankers (Jesus Silva Herzog was voted "finance minister of the year" after his first year in office) but at home produced massive unemployment and drastically reduced standards of living – the average wage earner lost 50 percent of his or her purchasing power – while struggling to keep inflation down to 100 percent a year. An exploding population only adds to the problems, and even the huge level of illegal emigration to the US can have little impact on it. The business community suffered too. Outraged by the nationalization of the banks in 1982, they were further hit by a series of bankruptcies and by devaluation which made

imported materials almost impossible to afford. With no sign of economic recovery, some of the vast panoply of interests covered by the PRI – from the all-powerful unions to the top businessmen – began to split off.

This movement against the PRI was exacerbated in 1985, when a huge **earthquake** hit the capital. The quake revealed widespread corruption, as the government attempted to prevent ordinary people from organizing their own rescue attempts to try and hide the inadequacy of official efforts. Furthermore, many of the buildings which collapsed were government-owned and although supposedly built to withstand earthquakes, turned out to have been constructed using inferior materials, with the profits siphoned off to construction companies and government officials. International relief aid was also diverted as the quake's victims were abandoned by the authorities.

From the experience of the earthquake, many grass-roots organizations were formed. Independent tenant groups, neighbourhood and women's groups, and small scale trade unions began to press the government for specific rebuilding programmes and on wider social concerns such as lack of housing, basic services, police corruption and pollution.

Opposition also grew outside the capital. The right-wing opposition **PAN** won a string of minor election victories in the north (and were cheated out of the state governorship of Chihuahua by blatant fraud), while in the south a socialist/peasant alliance held power for a while in Juchitán (Oaxaca) before being ousted with traditional strong-arm tactics. These episodes highlighted a further danger – the increasing **polarization** of the country. In the north, life is heavily influenced by the USA and business and ranching interests hold sway. In the south, where peasants continue to press for more land redistribution, opposition is far more radical and left-wing: alternately inspired and intimidated by events in Central America.

De La Madrid's unpopularity was demonstrated at the 1986 World Cup final, when the crowd – mainly middle-class Mexicans – booed and jeered at him as he took his seat. Considering the traditional reverence which is usually accorded to the figure of the president, this was an unprecedented show of disrespect.

The **1988 election** was certainly dramatic, and may yet prove one of the most significant since the Revolution. Predictably, the PRI candidate, **Carlos Salinas de Gortari**, won. The extent of the opposition however, was significant, and into the traditional contest between PRI, PAN and a number of tiny splinter groups, a formidable new challenger emerged in the form of **Cuauhtémoc Cárdenas**, son of the legendary and much loved Lázaro. Cárdenas split from the PRI a year before the election and succeeded in uniting the Mexican left behind him (under the banner of the National Democratic Front, or FDN) for the first time since the Revolution.

The success of the **FDN** was spectacular, Cárdenas officially winning 32 percent of the vote, although the results took a week to appear after the "breakdown" of the electoral computer at a point when Cárdenas was clearly in the lead. Ballot rigging, voter intimidation and vote buying (typical of all Mexican elections), reached new heights. Cárdenas and his supporters claimed that he had won, and also claimed to have figures to support them. Salinas emerged from the tarnished contest with 50.36 percent of the vote and the PAN leader, Manuel Clouthier (previously the only serious challenger), came third with 17 percent Opposition parties won seats in the Senate for almost the first time since the PRI came to power.

Salinas undertook to pave the way for a new multi-party democracy in Mexico. As a relatively young, untried, internally chosen candidate, he had little in the way of a following either within the PRI itself or the country as a whole, and began by announcing a clean-up **campaign against corruption**. On Salinas' orders, the head of the official PEMEX oil workers' union (a notoriously corrupt figure known as "La Quina") was arrested. He also created a human rights commission to investigate abuses, and ended direct government control over PIPSA, the official monopoly newsprint supplier. Salinas also upheld mid-term electoral triumphs by the opposition PAN in the states of Baja California and Guanajuato, despite opposition from local PRI activists.

Early signs were thus encouraging. Despite the death in mysterious circumstances of the PAN leader Manuel Clouthier in **1989** and controversial victories by the PRI in various state elections, Salinas managed to secure widespread support through the radical nature of his economic programme, as well as through

traditional political patronage. Initially Salinas maintained the economic policy of his predecessor, strategically timing Mexico's privatization programme to maximize revenue, tightening up on tax avoidance and the black economy, and reducing the foreign debt by almost half in three years through restructuring and co-operation with the IMF and private banks.

A compliant **television** media also helped foster the image of the president. This was not a new phenomenon, but Salinas benefited media barons through deregulation of the media and the sale of the state-owned station (now Televisión Azteca) and their support helped the PRI to sweep the board during the 1991 mid-term elections. Economic growth, falling inflation and a large influx of foreign capital seemed to confirm the success of the government's agenda.

In the meantime the opposition had been trying to mount a coherent challenge to the PRI. Cuauhtémoc Cárdenas, building from his success in 1988, founded a party to harness his popular support. The **PRD** (Party of the Democratic Revolution) had a very radical platform, reflecting much of its support base, but has moved increasingly to the centre, no longer opposing privatization in principle, and accepting the need for reform of the *ejido* system (see below). The PAN, with the PRI moving to the right, found its support base being eroded although it enjoyed unprecedented electoral gains.

The long-term consequences of the Salinas policy, however, were much less positive. **Social polarization** became even more extreme. By 1993, forty million Mexicans were living below the official poverty line (about half the population), while 24 Mexicans were listed in the Forbes list of the 500 richest men in the world. Most of these billionaires had acquired their wealth through buying privatized utilities. Salinas was committed to reducing the public debt and encouraging private investment, which he achieved by drastically cutting public spending and encouraging foreign companies by holding down wage levels. This involved expanding the "*maquiladora*" programme, which allowed foreign companies to set up assembly plants along the US-Mexican border (enjoying substantial tax concessions), a ban on union activity and relaxed health and safety and environmental requirements; and pushing through the North American Free Trade Area (**NAFTA**) which creates a free market between Canada, the USA and Mexico. This agreement has many opponents. Theoretically, a free market should increase trade levels to a degree which would benefit all the participants, spurring the Mexican economy to expand to the level of its partners and allowing Mexico to enter the "First World". Most Mexicans, with good reason, suspected that the agreement would provide little benefit, allowing US companies to offload polluting industries in Mexico and to take advantage of cheap Mexican labour. Fears also existed about NAFTA in the US (where they were exploited by Ross Perot), largely concerned with loss of jobs and immigration.

Salinas' response to the problems was to intensify his programme of reform, while at the same time introducing a social programme to ameliorate the effects of his economic programme. The **national solidarity programme**, or PRONASOL, directed a billion-dollar budget towards self-help programmes for the poor. Communities would typically supply free labour, while PRONASOL would provide materials and technical expertise for such projects as supplying basic amenities – electricity, piped water, street lighting – or making up for cuts in other government services such as school and hospital building. PRONASOL was supported by a huge advertising campaign, and its logo (like the PRI insignia, in Mexico's national colours) was painted upon every available surface to advertise the achievements of the programme – and by implication of the PRI – in the community. Most of the PRONASOL budget went to areas with strong PRD support such as México, the southern states and Cárdenas' home state of Michoacán, in an attempt to buy off opposition and co-opt self-help groups.

Another plan of the Salinas strategy was to modify much of Mexico's Revolutionary legacy. Diplomatic relations with the Vatican, severed during the Revolution, were re-established, allowing the pope to visit Mexico for the first time. The national oil company PEMEX was split into smaller units to improve productivity, and foreign oil companies were allowed to prospect for new deposits, although the PEMEX monopoly was still more or less intact at the time of writing. The most important change in this direction was the Amendment to article 27 of the Constitution, which deals with land reform.

Land reform, as enshrined in the original article of the Constitution, owed much to the legacy of Zapata. Land redistributed after the Revolution was parcelled out in communal holdings, known as "**ejidos**", which could not be sold as they belonged to the state. At a local level the land was held in common, divided up by the communities themselves, following the pre-hispanic and Colonial tradition. Salinas changed all that by allowing the sale of *ejido* lands. Many peasants and indigenous communities feared that their landholdings were now vulnerable to speculators, especially as many poor communities exist in a state of almost permanent debt, and believed that their land would be seized to cover outstanding loans, worsening their economic plight still further.

Despite, and maybe because of, these unpopular moves, Salinas began to be seen as a strong presidential figure, with a dynamic agenda for change. The successful negotiation of the NAFTA treaty, on which he had staked his reputation, went smoothly despite having to deal with two very different US presidents (Bush and Clinton), and this enhanced his reputation as a statesman. Even the opposition had to concede that economic progress had been made, and that Salinas had a clear agenda for Mexico and would leave the presidency in a much better state than he found it, giving the PRI a new lease of life.

There seemed little doubt that the PRI would go on to win the presidential election scheduled for 1994 with a minimum of fuss. In many areas, it wouldn't even have to resort to fraud. The crisis and upheavals of earlier days finally seemed to have been left behind. . ..

POLITICAL CRISIS

All this changed on New Year's Day 1994, when an armed guerrilla movement known as the **Zapatista Army of National Liberation** (EZLN), took control of the town of San Cristóbal de las Casas, the second-largest in the southernmost state of Chiapas, and four other municipalities. The guerrillas were mainly indigenous villagers: they demanded an end to the feudal system of land tenure in Chiapas, free elections, the repeal of NAFTA and the restoration of Article 27 of the Constitution.

The army reacted with predictable use of force, committing human rights abuses along the way that included the bombing of civilians and the murder of prisoners. Long hidden from the world, the repressive side of the Mexican state – together with the plight of the indigenous peoples of Mexico – were suddenly front-page news throughout the world. To Salinas' credit, he rapidly prepared the ground for peace negotiations by ordering a cease-fire.

Negotiations progressed with remarkable speed to begin with. The government representative, Manuel Camacho Solís, ex-mayor of México and at one time potential PRI candidate for the presidency, made concessions to the guerrillas and upstaged the presidential candidate, Luis Donaldo Colosio, who remained silent about the conflict. Camacho was assisted by the Bishop of San Cristóbal de las Casas, Samuel Ruiz, a champion of Indian rights in Chiapas and an advocate of liberation theology. (Many on the right have since accused the diocese of San Cristóbal of fostering the subversion, though with little apparent evidence: the Vatican even attempted to recall him in the middle of negotiations to explain himself and calls by the right have insisted on his excommunication.) The real star of the negotiations was **Subcomandante Marcos** of the EZLN, the main spokesperson for the guerrillas. His speeches and communiques were full of literary allusions and passionate rhetoric and also revealed a strong sense of humour. The balaclava-clad, pipe-smoking guerrilla soon became a cult hero and was later voted Mexico's sexiest man. Talks ended in March, when an accord was put together. The EZLN then sent the accord back to its community bases for them to vote upon it. The EZLN are unique among guerrilla movements in that they act according to the wishes of the communities from which they are drawn: individual villages will discuss proposals, send delegates to committees and reach collective agreement which they then implement. Decisions regarding whether to fight or negotiate follow this time-consuming method, aggravated by the many different languages and dialects spoken and the inaccessibility of many villages. The full text of the accord had thus to be translated, carried to each community, discussed, voted upon and the results collated centrally. In this case the results were not ready until June. An uneasy truce between army and guerrillas was maintained, and Mexicans were given ample time to dwell upon events in Chiapas.

As the Mexican saying goes, "Nothing happens in Mexico. . . until it does." Something happened on March 23, when the presidential candidate for the PRI, Luis Donaldo Colosio, was shot dead on the campaign trail in the border city of Tijuana. This was the first **assassination** of such a prominent government figure since 1928. The assassin, a former policeman, was allowed by Colosio's bodyguards to shoot him from almost point-blank range, fuelling conspiracy theories about the murder on a scale similar to the John F Kennedy murder north of the border.

Despite the unexpected nature of the assassination, political violence in Mexico has a long history. This has been aggravated in recent years by a surge in **drug-related crime** among the Mexican cocaine cartels. In 1993, the archbishop of Guadalajara, Juan Jesús Ocampo was shot dead at Guadalajara airport. He was reportedly caught in the crossfire between warring drug gangs, and some allege that drug cartels were also involved in the assassination of Colosio. Whatever the truth, and neither murder has been satisfactorily cleared up at the time of writing, it is clear that a huge amount of drugs are making their way across the Mexican border into the US, and that drug money has corrupted many in Mexican law enforcement and political circles. Although violence is nowhere near as widespread as in Colombia, say, the danger exists that the situation may deteriorate.

Another group suspected of carrying out the murder are elements within the PRI itself. The so-called "**dinosaurs**" within the party, those committed to maintaining the status quo, felt threatened by moves to democratize the political system, which had been galvanized by the Chiapas negotiations. Colosio had pledged himself to democratization, and was apparently building a power base among not only the PRI reformers, but also talking to the PRD and PAN, promising to include the opposition in his cabinet. The murder was thus calculated to remove the threat to the established system posed by the reformers. Subsequent events back up this theory. Colosio's successor, **Ernesto Zedillo Ponce de León**, was a minor apparatchik who owed his position to Hank Gonzalez, a billion-aire dinosaur allied to the Salinas ruling cadre. The assassination of another prominent reformer in September 1994, José Francisco Ruiz Massieu (general secretary of the PRI), who was gunned down in México, seems also to have served as a warning against anyone trying to modify the system.

In this climate of insecurity and violence, the **elections of August 1994** did not augur well. In June the EZLN rejected the accord with the government, and in July the PRD candidate for the governorship of Chiapas, Amado Avendaño Figueroa, met with a suspicious "accident" when a truck with no number plates collided with his car, killing three passengers. Avendaño lost an eye as a result of the crash. It was no surprise when the PRI again triumphed in the presidential elections: Zedillo gained 48 percent of the vote, Diego de Cevallos, the PAN candidate, 31 percent and Cárdenas for the PRD only 16 percent. The PRI also won all the senatorial races and the governorship of Chiapas. The scale of the vote (75 percent of voters participated, contrasting with tradition-ally high levels of absenteeism) and the pres-ence of foreign observers at an election for the first time left little doubt that the PRI had managed yet again to defy all attempts to remove them; and despite high levels of fraud, it was clear that the governing party really had obtained popular backing. The Left were left in disarray as over 75 percent of Mexicans had voted for the PRI and the PAN.

Zedillo, despite the rare accolade of a popu-lar mandate, has so far appeared weak and bereft of ideas to tackle the worsening situa-tion. A deal seems to have been struck with the PAN opposition, who gained a seat in the cabi-net: the powerful but risky office of official prosecutor, whose most important task is the resolution of the assassinations of Posada, Colosio and Ruiz Massieu.

The results announced, the situation began almost immediately to deteriorate. In **Chiapas** the defeated Avendaño declared himself "**rebel governor**" after denouncing the elec-tions as fraudulent. As many as half the munici-palities in the state backed him, refusing to pay taxes to the official government, and both the PRD and the EZLN also supported his move. The EZLN warned that if the PRI candidate Eduardo Robledo was sworn in, the truce with the government would be at an end. Chiapas

was anyway in a state of virtual civil war. Ranchers and landowners, who had long enjoyed the use of hired muscle to intimidate the peasantry, organized death squads to coun-ter a massively mobilized peasantry. Land seizures and road blocks by one side were met with assassinations and intimidation by the other in a rapidly polarizing atmosphere. A build-up of Mexican troops in the state exacer-bated the situation as Chiapas began to appear like an occupied Central American republic rather than a part of Mexico.

Post-electoral conflicts also developed after the governorship contests in **Veracruz** and **Tabasco**, both won in controversial circum-stances by the PRI. Tabasco followed Chiapas' lead by declaring a "governor in rebellion". PRD supporters temporarily took over the centre of the state capital Villahermosa, and numerous PEMEX oil installations. In Veracruz, the PRD again claimed fraud in many of the municipali-ties in the south of the state. The PAN won in most of the urban centres, including the port of Veracruz itself.

On January 8, 1995, Zedillo attended the swearing in of the PRI governor of Chiapas. Ten days later, the EZLN deployed their forces, breaking the army cordon surrounding their positions and moving in to 38 municipalities (they had previously been confined to four). They did it virtually undetected and later retreated, again without detection or a shot being fired. The ease of movement of the guer-rillas, even under the watchful eyes of govern-ment troops, showed their familiarity with the terrain, the discipline of their troops and the folly of the "surgical strike" option contem-plated by many in the military to wipe out the guerrillas. It was now clear that the govern-ment would face a Vietnam-type situation if hostilities broke out on a wider scale, and both sides resumed their positions more wary than ever.

The symbolic value of the EZLN action, combined with the apparent failure of the government to cope with either the worsening political or economic situation, triggered a massive **devaluation of the peso**. Foreign capital started to flood out of the country, and at a stroke Mexican wages were cut by almost half in real terms. Meantime, higher interest rates hit Mexican business hard, unemploy-ment rose drastically, and IMF austerity measures were again imposed on Mexicans to pay for a debt run up by their government. Not surprisingly, public anger turned to the government, and especially Carlos Salinas, who was now said to have kept the peso artificially high to hide economic problems from view. On this tide of discontent, the PAN prosecutor arrested Raúl Salinas, brother of the president, in February, and Ruiz Massieu's brother Mario later in the year. Both were accused of complicity in the murder of José Francisco Ruiz Massieu.

In March 1995, apparently under pressure from the US, Zedillo launched an **offensive against the EZLN**. Subcomandante Marcos was unmasked as Rafael Guillén, a veteran of the 1970s guerrilla movements, ex-"brigadista" with the Sandinistas in Nicaragua and former media studies lecturer. A small-arms cache was uncovered in Veracruz, and supposed members of the EZLN were arrested. An army offensive followed, but the EZLN retreated and major confrontation was avoided.

This was a high-risk strategy for Zedillo, and one that didn't really come off: the EZLN enjoyed considerable public sympathy, especially in view of their largely non-violent methods, while unmasking Marcos failed to affect his popularity – indeed, cries of "Guillén for president" became common at opposition rallies. In a rapid U-turn, the government called off the army and set up **new negotiations**, which were under way at the time of writing. Meanwhile support for the government seemed to be slipping away, with PAN winning the governorship of the state of Jalisco in relatively clean elections, and the state of Guanajuato by a landslide in May.

Clearly Mexico is undergoing a period of unparalleled **instability**, which shows little sign of abating. Whether the PRI can hold out against the tide of opposition is uncertain, although they have overcome more than their share of problems in nearly seven decades in power. What seems certain is that the PRI will face ever greater pressures to reform, both from internal factions and as a consequence of NAFTA. Whether those reforms bring with them a democratic transition or a backlash remains to be seen.

MONUMENTAL CHRONOLOGY

20,000 BC	First waves of Stone-Age migrants from the north.	Earliest evidence of man in the central valleys.
C6–C2 BC	Archaic period.	First evidence of settlement – cultivation, pottery and tools in the Valley of México.
1500 BC –300 AD	Pre-Classic period. Rise and dominance of the **Olmecs**.	The first simple pyramids and magnificent statuary at their Gulf Coast sites – San Lorenzo, La Venta and Tres Zapotes. Olmec influence on art and architecture everywhere, especially Monte Albán. Early evidence of new cultures in the Valley of México – Cuicuilco (buried by volcano) and Teotihuacán.
300–900 AD	Classic Period. **Teotihuacán** dominates Central Mexico, with evidence of its influence as far south as Kaminaljuyu in Guatemala. **Maya** cities flourish in the highlands of Guatemala and Honduras, as well as Mexican Yucatán.	Massive pyramids at Teotihuacán, decorated with stucco reliefs and murals. Monte Albán continues to thrive, while El Tajín on the Gulf Coast shows a new style in its Pyramid of the Niches. All the great sites – Uxmal, Palenque, Chichén Itzá, Edzná, Kabah – at their peak. Puuc, Chenes and Río Bec styles are perhaps the finest pre-Hispanic architecture.
900–1500 AD	Post-Classic. In Central México, a series of invasions by warlike tribes from the north.	**Toltecs** make their capital at Tula (c.900–1150), new use of columns and roofed space – chac-mools and Atlantean columns in decoration.
987	Toltec invasion of the Yucatán?	New Toltec-Maya synthesis especially evident at Chichén Itzá.
C10	**Mixtecs** gain control of Oaxaca area.	Mixtec tombs at Monte Albán, but seen above all at Mitla.
C11	League of Mayapán.	Maya architecture in decline, as Mayapán itself clearly demonstrates.
C13	Arrival of the Mexica in Central Mexico, last of the major "barbarian" invasions.	Many rival cities in the Valley of México, including Tenayuca, Texcoco and Culhuacán.
1345	Foundation of Tenochtitlán – rapid expansion of the **Aztec Empire**.	Growth of all the great Aztec cities, especially Tenochtitlán itself. In the east, cities such as Cholula and Zempoala fall under Aztec influence, and in the south, the Mixtecs are conquered. To the west, Purepecha (or Tarascan) culture developing, with their capital at Tzintzuntzan. Maya culture survives at cities such as Tulum.

1519	**Cortés** lands.	
1521	Tenochtitlán falls to Spanish.	Spanish destroy many ancient cities. Early colonial architecture is defensive and fortress-like; churches and mansions in México and elsewhere, monasteries with huge atriums for mass conversions. Gradually replaced by more elaborate renaissance and plateresque styles – seen above all in churches in the colonial cities north of the capital.
1524	First Franciscan monks arrive.	
1598	**Conquest** officially complete.	
C17–C18	**Colonial** rulers grow in wealth and confidence.	Baroque begins to take over religious building – great cathedrals at México and Puebla, lesser ones at Zacatecas. Towards the end the still more extravagant Churri-gueresque comes in: magnificent churches around Puebla and at Taxco and Tepotzotlán.
1810	Hidalgo proclaims **Independence**.	The development of the Neoclassical style through the influence of the new San Carlos art academy, but little building in the next fifty chaotic years.
1821	Independence achieved.	
1836	Texas declares independence – battles of the Alamo and San Jacinto.	
1838	Brief French invasion.	
1845	Texas joins USA – **Mexican-American War**.	
1847	US troops occupy México.	
1848	Half of Mexican territory ceded to US by treaty.	
1858-61	**Reform Wars** between liberals under Benito Juárez and Church-backed conservatives.	Many churches damaged or despoiled.
1861	Juárez triumphant; suspends payment of foreign debt. France, Spain and Britain send naval expedition.	
1862	Spain and Britain withdraw – invading French army defeated on May 5.	
1863	French take México. **Maximilian** becomes emperor.	Brief vogue for French styles. Paseo de la Reforma and Chapultepec Castle in the capital.
1866	French troops withdrawn.	

1867	Juárez defeats Maximilian.	
1876	**Porfirio Díaz** accedes to power.	The Porfiriano period sees a new outbreak of Neo-classical and grandiose public building. Palacio de las Bellas Artes and Post Office in México. Theatres and public buildings throughout the country.
1910	Madero stands for election, sparking the **Revolution**.	Another period of destruction rather than building.
1911	Díaz flees into exile.	
1911-17	Vicious revolutionary infighting continues.	
1920 on	Modern Mexico.	Modern architecture in Mexico is among the world's most original and adventurous, combining traditional themes with modern techniques. Vast decorative murals are one of its constant themes. The National Archeology Museum and University City in the capital are among its most notable achievements.

WILDLIFE

The vast size of Mexico (over 760,000 square miles) and the diversity of its natural environment make it an ideal location for the visiting naturalist, irrespective of expertise. The wildlife interest exists in a wide variety of forms, but specific highlights include: the **gray whale** migrations off the west coast of Baja California (at their best in January and February; see p.78); the arid interior plains of northern Mexico and their diverse collection of **cacti**; the semi-tropical forests which line the Gulf coast near Veracruz, and the remaining populations of **monkeys** and **large cats**; the Yucatán Peninsula, with its fabulous collection of migrating birds, including large flocks of **greater flamingo**; the coastal islands in the Caribbean Sea, where the snorkelling reveals shoals of brilliantly coloured **fish**; the lush tropical forests of the Chiapas uplands, full of rare and beautiful **orchids** and vividly coloured **parakeets** and **toucans**; the impressive colonies of sea birds along the southern Pacific coastline, including **frigate birds** and **boobies**.

Unfortunately, as in many third-world countries where economic hardship remains the prime concern, much of this natural beauty is under threat either from direct hunting or the indirect effects of deforestation and commercialization. It is imperative that we, as paying visitors, show a **responsible attitude** to the natural environment where it remains and endeavour to support the vital educational programmes which are seeking to preserve these remnants.

It should be stressed that not only is it extremely irresponsible, but it is also **illegal** to buy, even as souvenirs, any item which involves the use of wild animals or flowers in its production. This applies specially to tortoiseshell, black coral, various species of butterfly, mussels and snails, stuffed baby crocodiles, cat skins and turtle shells. Trade in living animals, including tortoises, iguanas and parrots (often sold as nestlings) is also illegal, as is the uprooting of cacti.

CLIMATE AND LAND USE

The distinct geographical pattern seen in Mexico, in conjunction with the climatic variation from north to south, creates a series of isolated **biomes**, each with their individual flora and fauna.

The predominant geographical features of Mexico tend to be southward continuations of North American counterparts; the **Sierra Madre Oriental** range which lies to the east is an extension of the Rocky Mountain range, and the **Sierra Madre Occidental** range to the west is an extension of the Sierra Nevada range. The interlying highlands and intermontane basins form the lofty **Northern Plateau**, which extends from México to the western tablelands of the United States.

Further south (between latitudes 18 and 20 degrees north) lies the range of volcanoes which delineate the southern extent of North American influences. The range rises in altitude towards its southern edge and runs from the Pacific coast, almost as far as the Gulf of Mexico; it is known as the **Sierra Volcanica Transversal**. The lands south of this range are extensive coastal plains and plateaus (the low-lying Yucatán), with intermittent higher ranges, such as the **Oaxaca** and **Chiapas Uplands**.

The country is divided laterally by the **Tropic of Cancer** which, at sea level, places half inside and half outside the tropics. The influence of the territorial highlands however, tends to a "vertical" rather than longitudinal climate. Most of the landmass is subject to the prevailing **trade winds** which blow from the northeast out across the Gulf of Mexico.

Local physiography significantly modifies the roles of longitude, elevation and prevalent wind direction; the cool water currents tending to keep the Pacific coastline cooler and drier than the Atlantic, while the sharp escarpments of the Sierra Madre Oriental, creating a vast rain shadow, contribute to the aridity of the northern plateau.

Rainfall is variable across the landmass, scant in the arid deserts of the north Pacific and interior sierras and extremely heavy in the tropical cloud and rain forests of the southeastern slopes of the **Sierra Madre del Sur** and sections of the Gulf coast (the rainy season itself extends from late May to October or November).

VEGETATION

The influence of long-term **deforestation** for charcoal cutting or slash-and-burn agriculture has substantially denuded the original forest which covered large areas of Mexico. Today the northern mountains contain tracts of conifer, cedar and oak, especially around **Durango** where the largest pine forest reserves are to be found. At lower altitudes, the grass-covered **savannahs** are interrupted by the occasional palm or palmetto tree, and the riverbanks are graced with poplar and willow.

The tropical rainforests which border the Gulf of Mexico form a broad band which extends southward from **Tampico** across the base of the Yucatán peninsula and the northern part of Oaxaca, containing mahogany, cedar, rosewood, ebony and logwood, but these reserves are being ever reduced. Seasonal tropical forest and dry scrub cover the remaining areas of the Gulf coast and the lowlands of the Pacific coast. One particularly notable tree is a single **ahuehuetl** (or giant cypress) tree, believed to have a bore of more than 50m in circumference and rumoured to be the oldest living thing in the Americas (see p.406).

The flatter lands of the north, the north Pacific, portions of central Mexico and the **Isthmus of Tehuantepec** are characterized by dry scrub and grassland. The most conspicuous of the vegetation in these drier areas however are the **cacti**. Various species of cacti adorn these flat grasslands; the **saguaro** is a giant, tree-like growth which can exceed 15m in height, whereas the columns of the **cereus** cactus stand in lines, not dissimilar to fence posts, and can reach 8m in height. Another notable variety is the **prickly pear** (or *nopal*)

which produces a fruit (*tuna*) that can either be eaten raw or used in the production of sweets. Other harvested varieties include the pulpy-leaved **maguey** cactus (one of the Agave family), whose fermented juice forms the basis of tequila, mescal and pulque, and **henequen** (another Agave), which is grown extensively on the Yucatán Peninsula and used in the production of fibre.

The extensive **temperate grasslands** are composed primarily of clumped bunch grass and wiry, unpalatable Hilaria grass. Low-lying shrubs which are also found amongst these grassy expanses include the spindly ocotillo, the creosote bush, the palm-like yucca with low-lying mesquite and acacia bushes in the more sheltered, damper areas. Such savannahs have few trees, either tropical or sub-tropical, but cover extensive parts of coastal central Mexico and the south Pacific, and combine with scattered **mangrove** thickets around the Bay of Campeche.

Flowers are commonplace throughout Mexico and form an integral part of day-to-day life. Two flowers, **frangipani** and **magnolia**, were considered to be of such value that they were reserved for the Aztec nobility. Today the blue blossoms of **jacaranda** trees and purple and red **bougainvillea** still adorn the walls of cities and towns during their spring and summer blooms. Even the harsh arid deserts of the north are carpeted with wild flowers during the brief Spring blooms which follow the occasional rains; the cacti blooms are particularly vivid. Many of these floral species are indigenous to Mexico, including cosmos, snapdragons, marigolds, dahlias and several species of wild **orchid** (over 800 species have been classified from the forests of Chiapas alone).

The **tropical forests** of Mexico provide supplies of both **chocolate** (from the cacao trees of the Chiapas) and vanilla, primarily for export. Also harvested is **chicle**, used in the preparation of chewing gum, from the latex of the sapodilla tree and wild rubber and sarsparilla. Herbs, used in medicinal or pharmaceutical industries, include digitalis from wild foxgloves and various barks used in the preparation of purges and disinfectants. One plant, unique to Mexico, is *Discorea composita*, which is harvested in Veracruz, Oaxaca, Tabasco and Chiapas, and is used in the preparation of a vegetable hormone that forms an essential ingredient of the contraceptive pill.

INSECTS

Insect life is abundant throughout Mexico but numbers and diversity reach their peak in the tropical rain forests, particularly to the south of the country. Although not immediately apparent, except in the clearings around tree falls where sunlight may penetrate, the forest floors contain a myriad of species engaged in their daily activities. These openings in the tree canopy attract a variety of colourful **butterflies**, gnats and locusts which swarm in abundance. For the most part, insect life makes itself known mainly through the variety of bites and sores incurred whilst wandering through these areas! **Mosquitoes** are a particular pest, with malaria still a risk in some areas.

Within the forests themselves, long columns of **leafcutter ants** criss-cross the floor in their search for food and surrounding tree trunks provide ideal shelter for the large, brown nests of **termites**. One particularly abundant species is *Coptotermes niger* which can cause significant damage to pine plantations in particular. Other serious pests of *Pinus caribaea* are the **scolytid bark beetles**, of which the species *Dendroctonus frontal* is particularly harmful, due to infection by the fungus *Ceratocystis*, which it transmits.

Further north in central Mexico, **army ants** have a direct bearing on the agricultural cycle; early cynicism by agronomists about the reluctance of peasant farmers to plant corn during certain phases of the moon, has been forgotten with the realization that it is at these times that the ants are on the march. One species of ant, local to **Tlaxcala**, provides for seasonal labour not once but twice each year; firstly during the egg stage when it is harvested to produce a highly prized form of caviar and secondly during the maggot stage, when it frequents the maguey cactus, which provides an equally prized food source.

The **garrapata** is a particularly tenacious tick, found in the northern deserts, which also form the ideal habitat for a range of **scorpions** whose sting can vary from extremely painful to definitively lethal. Their renown is highlighted in the region of Durango, where local craftsmen use these creatures as decorations, embedding them in glass ashtrays and jewellery.

The most spectacular insect migration can be seen in winter in eastern **Michoacán**, where thousands of **monarch butterflies** hatch from their larval forms en masse, providing a blaze of colour and movement (see p.194).

FISH, AMPHIBIANS AND REPTILES

The diversity of Mexican inland and coastal habitats has enabled large numbers of both marine and freshwater species to remain largely undisturbed. Among the freshwater species, rainbow and brook **trout**, silversides and catfish are particularly abundant (as are European carp in certain areas, where it has been introduced). The most highly regarded is a species of **whitefish** found in **Lake Chapala** and **Lake Patzcuaro**, where it forms the basis of a thriving local fishing industry.

Offshore, Mexican waters contain over one hundred marine species of significance, including varieties of tropical and temperate climates, coastal and deep waters, surface and ground feeders and sedentary and migratory lifestyles. Among the more important Gulf and Caribbean species are shrimp, oyster, jewfish, croaker, swordfish, snapper, pompano, king mackerel, snook, mullet, sea bass and haddock. In Pacific waters, the most important are shrimp, crayfish, spiny lobster, sardine, croaker, tuna, skipjack, sea bass, hake and anchovy. The marine fishing grounds on the **Pacific coast** are at their best off the coast of Baja California, where the warmer southern waters merge with sub-arctic currents from the north. Similarly, deep ocean beds and coastal irregularities provide correspondingly rewarding fishing in the waters of the **Campeche** bank on the Gulf of Mexico.

Amphibian life is similarly abundant; varieties include salamanders, several types of frog (including one tree-climbing species in the southern forests) and one marine toad that measures up to 20cm in length.

Reptiles are, if anything, even more widely represented throughout Mexico. The lower river courses that flow through the southern forests are frequented by **iguana**, **crocodile** and its close relative, the **cayman**. Some of the southern rivers and streams have small populations of **alligator** and resident lizards range from the tiny nocturnal lizards along the

Gulf coast to the tropical iguanas, which can reach up to 2m in length. The giant **sea turtle**, though sadly reduced through the hunting of both adults and eggs, is still found off the shores of Baja California and much of the Pacific shore.

Several kinds of **rattlesnake** are common in the deserts of northern Mexico, and farther south the rainforests hold a substantial variety of other snakes, including the **palanca**, **fer-de-lance**, **bushmaster** and the small **coral snake**.

BIRDS

After insects, the most diverse group of animals to be found in Mexico are the birds. More than five hundred species of tropical birds are known to exist in the rain and cloud forests of southern Mexico alone. Among these are resplendent **macaws**, **parrots** and **para-keets,** which make a colourful display as they fly amongst the dense tree canopy. In the lower branches, one can see large-billed **toucans** and on the ground, amongst the dense vegetation, it is also possible to see the occasional larger game birds, such as **curassow**, **crested guan**, **chachalaca** and **ocellated turkey**.

Particularly noticeable are the brilliantly coloured trogons, including the renowned **quetzal**. This magnificent bird once inhabited the cloud forests from the Chiapas to Costa Rica but, since the days of the Maya when it was first hunted for its long, showy feathers which were used in priestly headdresses, its numbers have been significantly reduced and its current status is severely endangered. The cereal-feeding habits of the Parrot family have not endeared them to local farmers either, and for this reason (and their continuing capture for sale as pets) their numbers have also been seri-ously depleted in recent times.

To the east, the drier tropical deciduous forests of northern Yucatán, the Pacific coastal lowlands and the interior lowlands provide an ideal habitat for several carnivorous birds including owls, hawks and the ubiquitous carrion-eating **black** and **turkey vultures**. The Yucatán is also one of the last remaining strongholds of the small **Mexican eagle**, which features in the country's national symbol. The most familiar large bird of Mexico however is the **zopilote** (a form of turkey buzzard) which is a highly successful scaven-ger, often seen soaring in large groups.

Large numbers of coastal lagoons provide both feeding and breeding grounds for a wide variety of **aquatic birds** – some of them winter visitors from the north – including ducks, herons and grebes.

In the north of Mexico, the harsher and drier environment is less attractive; outlying towns and villages form a welcome sanctuary from this harshness for a variety of doves and pigeons and the areas with denser cover have small numbers of quail and pheasant. These drier zones, in addition to other areas further south, form attractive migration stopover sites for large flocks of North American species, including wildfowl and waders. Foremost amongst these are the substantial flocks of graceful **flamingo** which can be seen at selected sites along the western and northern coasts of the Yucatán peninsula.

MAMMALS

Zoologists divide the animals of the Americas into two categories; the Nearctic region of the mid-latitudes in which the native animals are of North American affinity, and the Neotropical region of the lower latitudes, in which the fauna is mainly South American. The Isthmus of Tehuantepec marks the border between these two regions, serving as a barrier to many larger mammalian species.

The northern Nearctic faunal region is predominantly composed of open steppe and desert areas and higher altitude oak and pine forests. Relatively few large mammals inhabit the highland forests, although one wide-spread species is the white-tailed deer, which is still overhunted as a source of food. The northern parts of the Sierra Madre Occidental mark the southernmost extent of several typi-cally North American mammals, such as mountain sheep and black and grizzly **bears**. A large array of smaller rodents, and their natural predators, the **coyote** and the **kit fox**, are also widespread throughout the forests. Brown bears live in the **Cumbres de Monterrey National Park** and wild horned sheep can be seen at the **San Pedro Martír National Park** in Baja California. There are several other varieties of deer, puma, lynx, marten, grey fox, mule sheep, porcupine, skunk, badger, rabbit and squirrel.

The steppes and deserts of northern Mexico, including both the coastal lowlands and the interior plateaus, contain a diverse and flourishing fauna. Nowadays the extensive grassland plains are frequented only by sporadic herds of white-tailed deer; the days of the pronghorn antelope and even the bison have long passed under the burden of overhunting. Within the desert scrub, the **peccary** is still widely hunted and rodents, as ever, are in abundance forming an ample food supply for the resident **bobcats** and **ocelots**.

Baja California forms an outstanding wildlife sanctuary for marine mammals. **Guadalupe Island** is one of the few remaining breeding sites of the endangered **elephant seal** and the only known mating and nursery sites of the **gray whale** are around **Guerrero Negro** (p.78). **Dolphins** can also still be seen off the coasts of the peninsula.

Some southern species have also succeeded in breaching the Tehuantepec line, and now thrive in northern Mexico and the southern United States. Particularly successful colonizers include the **opossum** and **armadillo**. On the whole, though, the Neotropical region holds a very different collection of mammals. The relationship between these species and the lush vegetation of the tropical rain forest and highland cloud forests is particularly apparent. Many species are arboreal, living amongst the expansive tree canopies: these include spider and **howler monkeys**, opossums, tropical squirrels, racoon-like coati, **cacomistle** and **kinkajou**.

Because of the paucity of grass on the shaded forest floors, ground-dwelling mammals are relatively scarce. The largest is the **tapir**, with its characteristic pied coat and ungainly snout. Amongst this ground fauna, there are two species of peccary, which wander the forest floors in large groups seeking their preferred foods (roots, palm nuts and the smaller brocket deer). There are also large rodents, such as the South American water rat (or **agouti**) and the spotted **cavy**, which live in abundance along the numerous streams and river banks. These are hunted by the resident large cats, including **jaguar** and **puma**.

Similar animals inhabit the drier tropical deciduous forests of northern Yucatán, the Pacific coastal lowlands and the interior basins. The increased sunlight that is enjoyed by the floors of these drier forests, however, produces a more varied ground cover of shrubs

and grasses which supply food for the abundant small rodents (including the **spiny tree rat**) and the white-tailed deer which in turn provide food for a variety of predators such as the ocelot, tiger cat, **maragay**, **jaguarundi**, bobcat and Nearctic coyote.

Other large herbivores which can still be found in small numbers are large and small **anteaters**, opossums, armadillos and the elusive **paca**. Further south, the rainforests which lie along the border with Belize also have smaller numbers of **gibnut**, peccary and **warrie** (wild pigs), **quash**, anteaters (of the *Tamandua* species) and opossums (of the genera *Didelphis* and *Marmosa*).

The coastal lagoons which run along the eastern edge of the Yucatán have small colonies of the large aquatic sea cow (or **manatee**) and occasional sightings of West Indian **seal** are a possibility in the coastal waters.

WILDLIFE SITES

It would be almost impossible to compile a comprehensive list of sites of wildlife interest in Mexico, particularly as so much can be seen all over the country. The following is a selection of some of the outstanding areas, particularly ones that are easily accessible or close to major tourist centres.

BAJA CALIFORNIA

Easily accessible from the west coast of the United States, the peninsula of **Baja California** is a unique part of the Mexican landmass. Its exceptional coastline provides sanctuaries for a wide variety of marine mammals, including the major wildlife attraction of the area, the migratory **gray whale** (see box overleaf). The lagoons where the whales gather can also offer superb views of **dolphins** and **sea lions** and a variety of sea birds, including pelicans, ospreys and numerous waders such as plovers and sanderlings. The sparse vegetation provides roosting sites for both **jaegers** and **peregrines** and even the occasional coyote may be seen wandering over the sandy shores. The whole area is worthy of lengthy inspection but little can match the views (best during February and March) of the magnificent gray whales, spouting and breaching in the shallow waters, quite oblivious of the abundant human onlookers.

GRAY WHALE MIGRATION

It is the **gray whales** and their well-documented migrations off the west coast of the peninsula which remain the outstanding spectacle of the region and continue to attract an estimated 250,000 visitors each year. Times have not always been so peaceful for these graceful leviathans; less than 150 years ago, the secret breeding grounds of the whales were discovered by Charles Melville Scammon. The Laguna Ojo de Liebre (renamed in recent times after the infamous whaler) was rapidly denuded of almost all of these magnificent beasts and it wasn't until the establishment of Scammon's Bay as the world's first whale sanctuary in 1972 that their numbers began to recover. The population in the area is currently estimated at about 20,000 – a dramatic recovery within the time span.

The whale's **migratory route** runs the length of the American Pacific seaboard, from Baja to the Bering Sea and back; this is a round trip of some 20,000km, which remains the longest recorded migration undertaken by any living mammal. They remain in the north for several months, feeding on the abundant krill in the high Arctic Summer, and building up body reserves for the long journey south to the breeding lagoons. The migration begins as the days begin to shorten and the pack ice starts to thicken, some time before the end of January.

Nowadays the human interest in the whales is purely voyeuristic, whale watching being a million-dollar industry, and in 1988 the Mexican government extended the range of the protected area to include the nearby San Ignacio Lagoon, forming the all-embracing National Park, the **Biosfera El Vizcaíno**. The San Ignacio Lagoon offers a daunting entrance of pounding surf and treacherous shoals, but once inside, its calmer waters flatten and spread inland for 15km towards the distant volcanic peaks of the Santa Clara mountains. Accessible points for land-based observation lie further north in the **Parque Natural de Ballena Gris** ("Gray Whale Natural Park"), 32km south of Guerrero Negro.

Offshore, there are several small islands whose protected status has encouraged colonization by highly diverse animal communities. Furthest north is the island of **Todos Santos** where the sandy beaches, festooned with the remnants of unfortunate shellfish, are used as occasional sunning spots by the resident **harbour seals**. The atmosphere is rife with an uncommon blend of guano, kelp and Californian sagebrush. The Pacific swell frequently disturbs the resting cormorants, which bask in the hot sunshine, and the skies are filled with wheeling western gulls, whose appearance is not dissimilar to the more familiar European lesser blackback gull. These gulls form breeding pairs in February and March amongst the thriving colony which forms on the island.

Farther south lies the island of **San Benito**, which lies just to the northeast of the much larger island of **Isla Cedros**. The island provides ideal nesting grounds for migrating **ospreys**, which travel south from the United States. The hillsides are covered by the tall **agave** (century plants) whose brief, once-in-a-lifetime blooms add an attractive splash of colour to the surrounding slopes. These towering succulents produce a broad rosette of golden florets, which provide a welcome supply of nectar for resident **hummingbirds** and ravens. The island, along with Isla Cedros, also provides a winter home to thousands of **elephant seals**, now happily recovering after years of overhunting.

A more important site for these impressive beasts is the distant **Isla Guadalupe**, now a Biological Reserve. The large adult males arrive in December and the pebbly coves are soon crammed with the noisy and chaotic colony of mothers, calves and bachelor bulls, ruled by one dominant bull (or beach master) which can weigh up to two tonnes. The males make a terrible spectacle as, with necks raised and heads thrown back, they echo their noisy threats to any would-be rival who challenges the mating rites within their harem.

The interior of the peninsula has several areas of wildlife interest, many of which now have the protected status of nature reserve. Most significant of all are the National Parks of the **Sierra San Pedro Martir** and the **Desierto Central**. Here the **chapparal**-covered hills cede to forests of Jeffrey pine and meadow tables, indispersed with granite picachos and volcanic mesas. The **Constitución de 1857** National Park is another green oasis amongst the arid lowlands, where the coniferous woodlands form a picturesque border to the central **Laguna Hanson**. These sierras are renowned for the numerous palm-filled canyons which cut deep into the eastern escarpment; they make spectacular hiking areas with their minature waterfalls, Indian petroglyphs, caves, hot springs and groves of **fan palms**.

DURANGO

Durango lies within a dry, hilly area where the intermittent oak and pine woodland is surrounded by large expanses of low-lying scrub. These areas are frequented by large numbers of **birds**, whose presence is an extension of their North American range. Typical species include red-tailed hawk, American kestrel and mockingbird. The denser, wooded areas provide the necessary cover for several more secretive varieties such as Mexican jay, acorn woodpecker, Hepatic grosbeak, American robin and the diminutive Mexican chickadee. This is also an occasional haunt of the mountain lion (or puma) and another "immigrant" from the United States, the coyote. In the dry scrub, **scorpions** abound. Other nearby sites worthy of investigation include El Salto and El Palmito.

THE MAZATLÁN ESTUARY

The **Mazatlán estuary** is an extensive area of estuarine sands with marshy margins: ideal feeding grounds for a variety of **waders and wildfowl**, including marbled godwit, greater yellowlegs and willet. Large numbers of herons and egrets feed in the shallow waters (including little green and Louisiana heron and snowy and cattle egret), while further out to sea passage birds include laughing gull, gull-billed tern and olivaceous cormorant. Most spectacular of all are the aptly named magnificent frigate birds, who make a dramatic sight with their long wings, forked tails and hooked bills, as they skim over the water's surface, in their search for fish.

The rocks offshore provide a suitable breeding site for both brown and blue-footed **booby** and the pools at the northern end of the town, behind the large hotels, have some interesting ducks, including **jacana**, ruddy duck and canvasback.

SAN BLAS

Immediately around **San Blas** are lagoons with wildlife very similar to that found in the Mazatlán estuary; boat tours from San Blas take you out to see herons, egrets and much more, with the possibility of a **cayman** the big attraction. Farther out the landscape forms areas of thicker scrub and dense forest at higher altitudes. Amongst this lower-lying scrub, it is possible to see the purplish-backed jay, gila woodpecker and **tropical kingbird**, whilst the skies above have the patrolling white-tailed kite. At higher altitudes, the bird life includes the locally named San Blas jay, white-crowned **parrot** and **cinnamon hummingbird**. The town itself provides sufficient scraps for scavengers such as black and grey hawk and various unwanted rodents.

VERACRUZ AND THE GULF COAST

The eastern coastline of Mexico has particular attractions of its own, and none are more rewarding to the visiting naturalist than the final remaining tract of **rainforest** on the Mexican Gulf coast, southeast of Veracruz. The surrounding vegetation is lush, the tended citrus orchards yielding to rolling tropical forest, with its dense growth of **ficus**, mango and banana trees and the occasional coconut palm. These trees provide cover for a colourful underlying carpet including **orchids**, lemon trees, camellias, fragrant **cuatismilla** and gardenias. Even the roadsides are lined with banks of **hibiscus**, oleander and the pretty, white-flowered shrub, known locally as "cruz de malta". At the centre of the whole area, **Lake Catemaco** is outstandingly beautiful.

The surrounding forest has suffered much in recent times and many of the larger mammals, such as **spider monkey**, jaguar, Baird's tapir and Mexican white-tailed deer, are no longer found in the region. One sanctuary which remains amongst this destruction is the ecological research station of **Los Tuxtlas**. Although the Institute's holding is fairly small, it adjoins a much larger state-owned reserve of some 25,000 acres on the flank of the San Martín volcano. Despite the problems of poaching and woodcutting, the area has the last remaining populations of brocket deer, **black howler monkey**, ocelot, **jaguarundi**, **kinkajous** and coati. It also boasts 92 species of reptile, fifty amphibians, thousands of insects and over three hundred species of birds.

With patience, it is possible to see such outstanding varieties as **keel-billed toucan**, black-shouldered kite, gold-crowned warbler, red-throated ant tanager, white-throated robin, plain-breasted brush finch, **red-lored parrot**, ivory-billed woodpecker and the magnificent **white hawk**, to name but a few.

PALENQUE AND THE CHIAPAS UPLANDS

In the **Chiapas uplands,** the absence of climatic moderation by lower altitudes and coastal breezes creates dense, lush vegetation that is truly worthy of the name of tropical rainforest. The **Sierra Madre de Chiapas** is of particular interest to visiting naturalists, particularly the Pacific slope at altitudes between 1500 and 2500 metres, as these are the last sanctuary of the endangered **horned guan** and **azure-rumped tanager**. El Triunfo, at 1800 metres in the very southeastern corner of the country, less than 50km from the Guatemalan border makes an excellent base camp for exploration of the area. The cloud forest is dense in this locality and the tall epiphyte-laden trees grow in profusion on the slopes and in the valleys, in the humid conditions which occur after the **morning fogs** have risen (generally by early afternoon).

Another area of interest in this part of the Chiapas is the **Lagos de Montebello** National Park (p.450). The area is not easily accessible and the insects are almost intolerable outside the winter months, but the more determined bird-watcher may be rewarded with views of azure-hooded jay, **barred parakeet** and even the illustrious **quetzal**. Human encroachment has substantially reduced the number of large mammals in the area, but small numbers of **howler monkey**, tapir and jaguar (known locally as "el tigre"), are a reminder of bygone days. Another speciality of the region is the vivid and diminutive **tree frog**, whose precise camouflage ensures that it is more often heard than seen.

At the archeological site of **Palenque** you're back among the tourists, but if you can drag yourself away from the ruins, a little time will be amply rewarded. The two most promising areas lie just to the north of the ruins and due south of the river. The birding is unrivalled and local specialities include chestnut-headed oropendola, **scaled ant pitta** and white-whiskered puffbird at the former site and slaty-tailed trogon, green shrike vireo and **masked tanager** at the latter; the area also offers a wide variety of more approachable birds to suit the less dedicated ornithologist. In the area of marshland around the Río Usumacinta about 25km east of the junction between the main Palenque road and Highway 186, **pinnated bittern**, everglade kite and the rare **lesser yellow-headed vulture** have all been recorded.

THE YUCATÁN PENINSULA

The vegetation of the **Yucatán peninsula** is influenced by the lower altitudes, and thus drier and warmer climate than the surrounding areas, and the ameliorating effects of its extensive coastline which bring more frequent rain and winds. In the north it's predominantly dry scrub and bush, although large areas have been cleared for the cultivation of crops such as maize, citrus fruits and henequen. To the south are lusher tropical and sub-tropical forest, where the effects of agriculture are less obvious and the dense forest of **acacia**, **albizias**, widespread **gumbo limbo** and **ceiba** is in parts almost impenetrable. These form an ideal shelter for scattered populations of both the white-tailed and brocket deer. The whole peninsula is a unique wildlife area, with the bird life being particularly outstanding. Two specific sites worthy of thorough investigation are the archeological sites of **Cobá** and **Chichén Itzá**.

Cobá (p.542) makes an ideal centre for a tour of the area which lies between X-Can and Tulum. The roads here provide numerous points where it is possible to pull over and make a trek on foot into the forest, while the site itself is barely cleared. The abundant and spectacular birds which fill the treetops include squirrel cuckoo, **citreoline trogon** and **Aztec parakeet**, whilst circling in the skies above are the resident birds of prey such as bat falcon, snail kite and the ever-present black and turkey **vultures** (these can be distinguished, even at great heights, as the wings of the latter are clearly divided into two bands — the darker primaries and the lighter secondaries being quite distinct). It is also possible for the more patient, and fortunate, observer to see all three species of Mexican **toucan**; collarded aracari, emerald toucanet and the spectacular keel-billed. The denser areas of forest also hold a small remnant of the original **black howler monkey** population.

The village of Cobá borders a lake with extensive reed margins along its eastern edge, which attracts a variety of water birds. Typical visitors, either migratory or resident, include the grebe, the elusive spotted rail, ruddy crake, northern **jacana** and the occasional **anhinga** – a spectacular bird which captures its primary food source of fresh fish by spearing them with its dagger-like bill. The reed beds provide cover for several more secretive species, including mangrove vireo, ringed **kingfisher** and blue-winged warbler, as well as several varieties of Hirundine such as mangrove swallow and grey-breasted martin.

Chichén Itzá (p.509) is a must on the list of any visitor, but save a little time at the end of the day for an exploration of the forested areas which lie to the south of the "nunnery". The drier climate and lower altitude in this part of the peninsula encourages a sparser vegetation, where the oaks and pines are less obvious. Other colours amongst this greenness come from a variety of splendid flowers, such as the multicoloured **bougainvillea**, the aromatic **frangipani** and the eye-catching blue and mauve blooms of the **jacaranda** tree. Occasional splashes are added by the striking red flowers of the **poinsettia** (or Christmas flower) and the brilliant yellows of **golden cups**, during their spring and summer blooms.

The resident birds appear oblivious to the busy tourist traffic, and amongst the quieter areas, to the south and southwest of the main site, the abundant bird life includes **plain chachalaca** (surely a misnomer), ferruginous pygmy owl, cinnamon hummingbird, **turquoise-browed motmot** and numerous brilliant vireos, orioles and tanagers. The display is both vivid and spectacular.

COZUMEL AND THE CARIBBEAN COAST

A series of offshore islands and coastal sites in Yucatán are worthy of special mention. **Natural Parks and nature reserves** include the Parque Natural Flamenco Mexicano de Celestún, on the west coast about 70km from Mérida and Río Lagartos Park, 40km north of Tizimín (both with spectacular flocks of migratory **flamingos**, which stay the winter here in the milder climes see p.502 and p.518); the Isla Contoy bird sanctuary off the northeastern tip of the peninsula; and above all the **Sian Ka'an Biosphere Reserve** (p.543), which includes reef, coast and forest and possibly the widest range of flora and fauna in the whole of Mexico.

Two more easily accessible and still rewarding sites are the islands of Cozumel and Mujeres. **Cozumel** can be reached by frequent ferries from Playa del Carmen and the hour-long journey produces occasional sea birds of note, such as royal and Caspian terns, **black skimmer**, frigate birds and Mexican sheartails. Playa del Carmen is also frequented by various wetland species including American wigeon. On the island, the most rewarding sites are a couple of kilometres inland on the main road that runs across the island. The sparse woodland and hedgerows provide shelter for many typical endemics, such as Caribbean dove, lesser night-hawk, Yucatán vireo, Cozumel vireo, the splendid **bananaquit** and a variety of tanagers. Elusive species which require more patient exploration (best through the **mangroves** which lie 3km north of San Miguel along the coast road) are the mangrove cuckoo, **yellow-lored parrot**, Caribbean ealania and Yucatán flycatcher.

Further north, even **Cancún** itself has wildlife possibilities: the lagoons which line the outskirts have a variety of birds (such as great-tailed grackle and melodious blackbird) and **lizards** which disappear miraculously from their basking spots into the thorny scrub at the slightest disturbance. These wetland wastes form an ideal breeding ground for a number of brilliantly coloured **dragonflies** and **damselflies**, and the offshore scuba diving and snorkelling is quite stunning. The most important element of these extensive and spectacular reefs are the limey skeletons, secreted by dozens of species of **coral**. The diversity of shape and form is spectacular, with varieties such as star, lettuce, gorgonian, elkhorn and staghorn being particularly widespread. The reefs provide food and shelter for over four hundred species of fish alone, including the **parrotbill** (which browses on the coral), butterfly fish, beau gregories, rock beauties and porkfish; the blaze of colour and feeling of abundance is unforgettable.

The coral also provides protection for several other residents, such as **sea urchins**, crabs and tentacled **anenomes**, but this fragile environment requires cautious exploration, if the effects of snorkellers and boat anchors are not to destroy the very thing that they seek to enjoy.

Puerto Juárez, where the ferries to Isla Mujeres leave from, and Isla Mujeres itself, offer a slightly less "touristy" environment in which to appreciate the natural beauty of the area. The bird life is also quite spectacular, with frequent views of frigate bird, **brown noddy**, laughing gull, rufus-tailed hummingbird, tropical kingbird and the ubiquitous bananaquit.

Chris Overington

MEXICAN MUSIC: MORE THAN MARIACHI

Mariachis – those extravagantly passionate bands, with their sly rhythms and natty hats – have been shorthand symbols for Mexico in a thousand low-budget films and television episodes. However, they are only the best-known example from a country rich in traditional musics: *bandas, cumbia Mexicana, norteño* ballads, and *huapango* – the music that gave the world "La Bamba".

When foreigners run away to Mexico, they tend to bury themselves in bars and – to the sound of local ballads – weep over the hopelessness of love. Mexicans who run away to the United States tend to take their music with them. They complain that gringos don't know how to throw a party, they indulge in nostalgia through their **ranchera** songs, and they finance extravagant tours so that they can see their favourite stars in person.

Considering that its border with the US stretches for 2000 miles, Mexico has put up a remarkable resistance to American **rock**. Yet Mexico's own music is very hard to define. As well as American sounds, musics from Spain, Argentina, Colombia and Britain have all arrived in Mexico and been assimilated and reworked to local taste. All of them are given a treatment that is more romantic, more emotional and more danceable. Thus recycled, they are sold as Mexican music and dispersed by satellite all over the Americas from Alaska to Patagonia.

Mexican versions don't respect their sources and nor are they much bothered by international music fashions. Rap songs become love songs with a bit of cumbia thrown in. **Danzones** and **boleros** are now far removed from the original versions from Cuba, where both styles have almost died out, but are still the most popular requests at barrio parties in México. Young Mexicans still dance the **chachachá**, too, along with a Mexican variant of **mambo**. And in the 1990s, the country has seen an extraordinary craze for brass bands – **bandas** – playing everything from salsa to ballads.

CUMBIA MEXICANA

Cumbia is now more popular in Mexico than in its native Colombia. In its new home it has become simpler, more direct and danceable. For a long time, a national radio station used to call out "¡Tropi. . .Q!" – the last letter a "cooooooh" that could unblock traffic jams – and then launch into the latest cumbia hit, which was played without reprieve for a month and then forgotten. A song about cellular telephones replaced "No te metes con mi cucu" (Don't Mess With My Toot Toot), which in turn had taken over from a song about fried chicken and chips – a thinly disguised treatise on how a macho likes his bird.

The flirtatious, addictive cumbia was the most popular music in Mexico in the 1980s, until bandas came along, and it remains a force throughout the country. Outside the capital it tends to take on a more mellow, romantic tone: a sound closely associated with the band **Los Bukis**, whose album "Me volvi a acordar de ti" sold 1.5 million legal copies and an estimated four million more in bootleg cassettes.

Although Los Bukis come from Michoacán in central Mexico, their biggest market – like that of other Mexican bands – is north of the border in California and Texas, among the new Mexican immigrant communities. Most of these migrants come from rural Mexico and, facing racism and alienation, the communities hold firmly onto the music that they identify with back home. This means principally the *cumbia* and *norteño*.

NORTEÑO

Norteño, which is known north of the border as Tex-Mex, has its roots in the *corrido* ballads that retold the battles between Anglos and Meskins in the early nineteenth century. The war turned out badly for Mexico, which lost half of its territory, and Mexicans living in what is now California, Arizona, New Mexico and Texas found themselves with a new nationality.

The late 1920s was the golden age of the **corrido**, when songs of the recent Revolution were recorded in the hotels of San Antonio, Texas, and distributed on both sides of the border. The accordion, which had arrived with Bohemian immigrants who came to work in the mines in the late nineteenth century, was introduced into the originally guitar-based groups by Narciso Martinez and **Santiago Jimenez** (father of the famous Flaco) in the 1930s, and the sound that they developed became the essence of *corrido* ensembles on both sides of the border.

When the **accordion** appeared, it brought the polka with it, and by the 1950s this had

---

**Cruce el Rio Grande
(I Crossed the Rio Grande)**

I crossed the Rio Grande
Swimming, not giving a damn!
The Border Patrol threw me back . . .
I disguised myself as a gringo
And tinted my hair blonde
But since I didn't know English
Back I go again

Popular *norteño* ballad

---

blended with the traditional duet singing of northern Mexico and with salon dances like the waltz, mazurka and the *chotis* (the central European schottische that travelled to Spain and France before arriving in northern Mexico) to produce the definitive *norteño* style. The accordion had already pepped up the songs with lead runs and flourishes between the verses, but the *conjuntos norteños* needed to round out their sound to keep up with the big bands and so added bass and rolling drums — the basis of today's **conjuntos**.

El Gato Felix (Felix the Cat)

I'm going to sing a *corrido*
About someone who I knew
A distinguished journalist
Feared for his pen
From Tijuana to Madrid

They called him Felix the Cat
Because the story goes that
He was like those felines
He had seven lives
And he had to see them through

He came from Choi, Sinaloa
That was the place he was born
He stayed in Tijuana
Because it took his fancy
And he wanted to help in some way
With what he wrote in the paper

He made the government tremble
He went right through the alphabet
A whole rosary of threats
He made his paper Zeta popular
With his valiant pen

He pointed to corruption
He always helped the people
And more than two presidents
Had their eyes on him

In a treacherous way
the Cat met his end
Death, mounted on a racehorse
A real beast
Rode him down

Now Felix the Cat is dead
They are carrying him to his grave
He will be another one on the list
Of brave journalists
That they've wanted to silence

Candles burn for Felix Miranda
To you I dedicate my song
But don't you worry
There will be other brave people
To take your place

Enrique Franco

Unlike most other regional styles, *norteño* is popular throughout the country. At a party in an isolated mountain community in central Mexico, the host takes out his accordion and plays *norteño corridos* until the dawn breaks. In an ice-cream parlour on the Pacific coast, the piped music is a *norteño* waltz. And waiting for darkness to cross the border at Tijuana, *norteños* are again the musical backdrop.

This country-wide popularity is most likely due to the **lyrics**. *Norteño* songs speak to people in words more real and interesting than the cozy pseudo-sophistication of Mexican pop music. The ballads tell of antiheroes: small-time drug runners, illegal "wet-back" immigrants, a small-time thief with one blond eyebrow who defied the law. *Norteño* reflects the mood of a country that generally considers the government to be big-time thieves and hence has a certain respect for everyday people with the courage to stand up to a crooked system.

Groups like **Los Tigres del Norte** and Los Cadetes del Norte take stories from the local papers and convert them into ballads that usually begin "Voy a cantarles un corrido" (I'm going to sing you a *corrido*) before launching into a gruesome tale sung in a deadpan style as if it were nothing to go to a local dance and get yourself killed. One of the most famous *corridos*, "Rosita Alvírez", tells the story of a young girl who struck lucky: only one of the three bullets fired by her boyfriend hit and killed her.

Los Tigres are by far the most successful of all *norteño* groups – superstars, in fact – having won a Grammy and subsequently been adopted by the (generally bland) Mexican TV company, Televisa. They recorded their last album in Miami – a sign of the power of the US Mexican market. Quite early in their career, the band modified the traditional line-up by adding a sax and mixed the familiar rhythms with *cumbias*; however, their nasal singing style and the combination of instruments identifies the music very clearly as *norteño*.

RANCHERA

There is absolutely nothing deadpan about **ranchera** music: a style that is again hugely popular. *Ranchera* songs are loaded with melodramatic passion and characterized by cries of "¡ay ay ay ay ay!" – joyous exclamations that come from singer and audience alike.

Ranchera is essentially nostalgic and pessimistic – the lament of a people who have left their land and are lost in a strange city or in a different country. The American singer **Linda Ronstadt**, who recorded a fine album of *ranchera* songs, said she was simply following what her father, a Mexican immigrant, used to sing in their home in Tucson, Arizona. The late **José Alfredo Jimenez**, the greatest *ranchera* singer of all time, raised pessimism to a high art, and wrote his own epitaph in his much-loved song, "La vida no vale nada" (Life is worth nothing). His was a world where only the tequila bottle is faithful, where love is violent and jealous, and where a man who dies in a duel is a man who has lived.

The music calls heavily on various regional styles but is essentially an urban phenomenon. The songs began life at the beginning of this century and – as well as their unconcealed emotion – are distinguished by the way that singers stretch out the final note of the line and add a glissando. Today, with the exception of TV star **Vicente Fernandez**, most of the top singers are women: María de Lourdes, Lola Beltran, Lucha Villa, and – the hottest property – **Chavela Vargas**. Vargas has found an audience among Mexico's radical chic, who pay a vast cover charge to hear the same songs that were once the favourites of their mothers' maids.

MARIACHI

The regional style that has contributed most to *ranchera* is *son jaliscience*, the traditional music of Jalisco, in western Mexico. The *son* is the musical form that grew out of the mestizo mix of Spanish and indigenous cultures, a style popularized by the **mariachi bands** who came originally from Jalisco state.

Mariachi bands were popular at wedding ceremonies around the turn of the century and some say their name is a corruption of the French word *mariage*. One version of *mariachi* history tells how, in 1907, Mexico's last dictator, General Porfirio Díaz, organized a garden party for a visiting US secretary of state. Since he wanted to include Mexican music, a quartet from Jalisco were contracted – and told to change their white cotton trousers for the *charro* suits worn by the men who owned the haciendas where they worked as servants. A quartet, even in their fancy dress, still seemed too poor for the occasion, so eight musicians and two dancers were contracted. The Jaliscan son was never the same again, and *mariachi*, along with its costume, was born.

The early *mariachis* played violins, guitars, a harp and the enormous *guitarrón*, an acoustic bass guitar; trumpets were added later while the harp has generally been dropped. From the 1920s on, when the legendary (and still flourishing) **Cantina Tenampa** opened with a resident band in México, *mariachi* bands have played mainly in taverns. They are employed today all over the country, as well as across the border, where they make better money playing to homesick field workers.

Since most bands are paid by the song, the leader identifies likely customers in a seedy Texas or California bar and the trumpeter grabs a seat at their table, launching himself into a classic piece from the badly missed home country. As the drinkers indulge their sadness, the singer utters the cry, the violins wail and the trumpeter prepares to slide straight into the next song so that, by the end of the evening, a week's wages can easily have been spent on music.

Although *mariachis* began with a repertoire of *sones* from Jalisco, today they play *cumbias*, polkas, waltzes, ballads and an incredible range of popular songs on request. With only two hundred songs, you might as well stay at home in the village, one *mariachi* told me. Like most of his colleagues, he could play around 1500 pieces on demand.

The **golden age of mariachi** was the 1950s, when the *ranchera* music they played accompanied a series of Hollywood films, with Mexican matinee idols serenading their lovers. Many of the greatest films featured **Mariachi Vargas**, a group that was founded in the 1930s and is still considered to be the best in Mexico. Virtually all the original members have died but the band replaces old stars with the pick of the younger generations and they remain very hot. It was Mariachi Vargas, notably, who Linda Ronstadt chose as backing on her "Canciones" album of *ranchera* classics.

Most of the *mariachi* songs are old-established classics, although some of the more adventurous and technically accomplished bands will perform songs by the remarkable **Juan Gabriel**. Gabriel is a rare phenomenon in Mexico, an enormously talented composer, arranger, singer and TV star with an excellent understanding of Mexican regional music. He writes and performs *canciones*, *norteñas* and *sones* as well as commercial ballads and soft rock. He plays with *mariachis* and with a symphony orchestra and his concert seasons all over the country sell out months in advance. For years he was excluded from radio and TV on account of being gay – but his talent eventually won through.

THE BANDA BOOM

The enormous success of Los Tigres del Norte and their updated *norteño* sound resulted in a phenomenon that has changed the face of Mexican music in the 1990s: **banda music**. This is a fusion of the *norteño* style with the brass bands that have played at village fiestas all over the country for the last century. There are now hundreds of *bandas* in Mexico – ranging from four to twenty musicians, and all playing brass and percussion, with just an occasional guitar. Their repertoire includes *norteño* polkas, *ranchera* ballads, *cumbia*, *merengue* and *salsa* – all arranged for brass.

The most exciting of these groups is a fiery orchestra from Mazatlán, Sinaloa – the **Banda del Recodo**. This is not a new band. Indeed, its leader, Don Cruz Lizárraga, has been in the business for half a century, starting out in a traditional *tambora* marching band (the *tambora* is the huge carried side drum) that played a straight repertoire of brass-band numbers. However, Don Cruz has always had an eye for musical fashions, adapting his material to merengue, *ranchera* – whatever anyone wanted to hear. His great banda hit was a version of Cuban bandleader Beny Moré's classic "La Culebra".

The *banda* boom currently dominates the TV music programmes and more or less all points of the country, except for the capital, where *cumbia* and *salsa* stay top of the bill. Elsewhere, it is the *bandas* that fill the stadiums and village halls, and it is their names you'll see painted in enormous multi-coloured letters on any patch of white wall along the roads. The craze has brought with it a series of new dances, too, including the **quebradita** – a gymnastic combination of lambada, polka, rock'n'roll, rap and *cumbia*, which is danced with particular skill in all points north of Guadalajara.

HUAPANGOS AND HARPS

In the central Bajío region and along the Gulf coast of eastern Mexico, **huapangos** give *banda* a run for its money. These are basically variants on *son* and divide into three main regional types: the *huapango huasteco*, *arribeño* and *veracruzano*.

The **huapango huasteco** is played on violin with a guitar and small *jarana* guitar and is usually sung in falsetto. Although its repertoire is limited, it requires improvised lyrics that change according to the occasion, and it is distinguished by musical flourishes that mean no *son* sounds the same twice over. There are dozens of *huapango huasteco* bands, appearing at the fiestas, weddings and parties, bars and brothels of states from Tamaulipas to Hidalgo and Puebla. Several of them feature on locally produced cassettes, where they often add *rancheras*, paso dobles and *corridos*, which are given a fiery violin treatment but no falsettos. One of the best groups – who have made it onto CD and the World Music festival circuit – are **Los Camperos de Valles**, a trio from Ciudad Valles in San Luis Potosí.

Farther inland, the **huapango arribeño** places more emphasis on the verse, which is improvised in *décimas*, the old Spanish form. A top group here are Guillermo Velazquez's **Los Leones de Xichu**.

The third of the *huapangos*, **veracruzano**, is instantly recognizable thanks to Ritchie Valens' rearrangement of a famous local number, "La Bamba". The traditional *huapango veracruzano* – or **son jarocho** as it is better known – is played on guitars, harp and percussion. To hear it you need to head for Veracruz, where bands vie for business under the arches in the central square and down at the port's seafood restaurants. Outstanding musicians among them include the legendary **Don Nicolás Sosa**, now in his nineties; **Graciana Silva**, who plays solo harp and sings in a style inherited from generations past; and the bands **Boca del Rio** and **Mandinga**.

Other regional styles of *son* thrive to the blissful ignorance of just about everyone who lives outside their patch. They include the *sones calentanos* of the hot lands of western Mexico; the big harp music of Apatzingán; the less frantic *sones istmeños* from Oaxaca; and the Purépecha dance music from Michoacán, itself heavily influenced by the *calentanos*. A recent compilation CD, "Anthology of Mexican Sones", provides an excellent introduction to these styles, all of which have an intensity that sets them apart from their commercial counterparts, modified for radio and cassettes.

Mary Farquharson

The original version of this article appears in the *Rough Guide to World Music*.

DISCOGRAPHY

Mexican recordings are widely available in the US – less so in Europe. A label to look out for is Corason, who are recording and releasing consistently excellent CDs and cassettes of traditional sounds from all over the country. They are distributed in the US by Rounder and by Topic in Britain.

COMPILATIONS

Various, *Anthology of Mexican Sones* (Corason, Mexico). This 3-CD set is the definitive survey of Mexican traditional music, featuring wonderful recordings of rural bands. Excellent accompanying notes plus lyrics in Spanish and English.

Various, *Mexico – Fiestas of Chiapas & Oaxaca* (Nonesuch Explorer, US). Atmospheric recordings from village festivities in southern Mexico. Marimba *conjuntos*, brass bands, some eccentric ensembles and great fireworks on the opening track. The next best thing to being there.

Various, *Mexique – Musiques Traditionnelles* (Ocora, France). For the more folklorically inclined, music from the many little-known indigenous communities of Mexico.

SONES AND MARIACHI

Conjunto Alma Jarochos *Sones Jarochos* (Arhoolie, US). A fine disc, the first in a series of regional Mexican releases, featuring *sones* from Veracruz with harps and *jaranguitas*.

Los Camperos de Valles *Sones de la Huasteca and El Triumfo* (Corason, Mexico). The Huasteca *sones* are considered by many to be the most beautiful music in Mexico. Played on violin, guitar and the small *vihuela* guitar, an important element is the falsetto singing of love songs that are both rowdy and romantic.

Mariachi Coculense de Cirilo Marmolejo, *Mexico's Pioneer Mariachis Vol 1* (Arhoolie, US). Wonderful archive recordings from the 20s and 30s of one of the seminal groups. The disc also includes the first ever *mariachi* recording, from 1908.

Mariachi Reyes del Aserradero, *Sones from Jalisco* (Corason, Mexico). An excellent *mariachi* band from Jalisco state play the original *sones* from this region where *mariachi* was born.

Mariachi Tapatió de José Marmolejo, *The Earliest Mariachi Recordings: 1906–36* (Arhoolie, US). Archive recordings of a pioneer *mariachi* band, featuring the great trumpet playing of Jesús Salazar.

Mariachi Vargas, *20 Exitos* (Orfeon, Mexico). Big-band style *mariachi* from Silvestre Vargas, who has managed to stay at the top of his field for over fifty years. Always flexible, his band released one disastrous album of *mariachi*-rock but has otherwise had hits all the way. They work much of the year in the US.

Los Pregoneros del Puerto, *Music of Veracruz* (Rounder, US). Rippling *sones jaroches* from the Veracruz coast, where harp and *jarana* guitars still dominate. An enchanting album.

RANCHERA AND NORTEÑO

Flaco Jimenez, *Ay te dejo en San Antonio* (Arhoolie, US). The best of Flaco's many recordings; he's a huge name in the Tex-Mex world north of the border.

José Alfredo Jimenez, *Homenaje a José Alfredo Jimenez* (Sony Discos, US). Jimenez was the king of *ranchera* and embodied the best and worst of Mexican machismo. As he predicted in one of his songs, everyone in Mexico missed him when he died.

Santiago Jimenez, Snr *Santiago Jimenez Snr* (Arhoolie, US). One of the great accordion players, recorded in 1979 with son Flaco on *bajo sexto*. Earthy, authentic sound.

Los Lobos, *La Pistola y El Corazón* (Warner, US). The East LA band's brilliant 1991 tribute to their Mexican roots, with David Hidalgo pumping the accordion on their blend of *conjunto* and rock'n'roll.

Narciso Martínez, *Father of the Tex-Mex Conjunto* (Arhoolie, US). The title says it all: a collection of 1940s and 1950s numbers, some

instrumental, others featuring the leading vocalists of the day.

Los Pingüinos del Norte, *Conjuntos Norteños* (Arhoolie, US). This album pairs up Tex and Mex *conjuntos*: Los Pingüinos, singing *corridos*, live in a *cantina* in northern Mexico, and Fred Zimmerle's Trio from San Antonio, Texas, performing typical polkas and *rancheras*.

Linda Ronstadt, *Canciones de mi Padre* and *Más Canciones* (Asylum, US). *Ranchera* classics sung very convincingly by the Mexican-American rocker, accompanied by Mariachi Vargas.

Los Tigres del Norte, *Corridos Prohibidos* (Fonovisa, US). A collection of *corridos* about Mexican low life and heroism from one of the best *norteño* groups in the business.

CUMBIA

Los Bukis, *Me Volvi a Acordar de Ti* (Melody, Mexico). The sound of soft *cumbia* – and the most popular Mexican record ever.

Sonora Dinamita, *Mi Cucu* (Discos Fuentes, Colombia). Mexican *cumbia* performed by a breakaway group of artists who took the name of the Colombian originals. Their lyrics, full of double meanings, are performed with a zest that has brought huge success in Mexico.

OTHERS

Agustín Lara, *Agustín Lara* (Orfeon, Mexico). The legendary crooner, the man who idolized prostitutes and married for love twelve times. One of Mexico's greatest composers of popular music, specializing in bolero ballads and music from Veracruz.

Juan Reynoso, *The Paganini of the Mexican Hotlands* (Corason, Mexico). The title is fair dues: Reynoso is Mexico's greatest country violinist, eighty years old now, but still in fine form on this recording, backed by vocal, guitars and drum.

Various, *New Mexico: Hispanic Traditions* (Smithsonian Folkways, US). A good ethnographic recording from the Mexican diaspora in the US. Dances, songs, *corridos* and religious music in rustic style.

Various, *Pure Purépecha* (Corason, Mexico). A gem that brings together three duets of Purépecha peoples from Michoacán, singing sweet *pirecua* love songs, and some rowdy *abajeño sones* from Conjunto Atardecer.

BOOKS

Mexico has attracted more than its fair share of famous foreign writers, and has inspired a vast literature and several classics. Until very recently, however, Mexican writers had received little attention: even now, when many new translations are being made available through small US presses, few are well known. Most big US bookshops will have an enormous array of books about, from, or set in Mexico, plus a few novels. In the rest of the English-speaking world there's far less choice, though the best known of the archeological and travel titles below should be available almost anywhere. In the lists below, the US publisher is followed by the UK one; where only one publisher is listed it's the same in both places, or we've specified. O/p means a book is out of print, but may still be found in libraries or secondhand bookstores.

For the less mainstream, and especially for contemporary Mexico, there are a couple of useful **specialist sources**. In the US, the *Interhemispheric Education Resource Center* produces a wide range of publications: for a catalogue and information about the quarterly *Bulletin* ($5 annually) contact *The Resource Center*, PO Box 4506, Albuquerque, New Mexico 87196 (☎505/842-8288; fax 505/246-1601). Many of the *Resource Center's* publications are available in the UK from the *Latin America Bureau*, 1 Amwell St, London EC1R 1UL (☎0171/278-2829; fax 0171/278-0165), which also publishes in its own right books covering all aspects of the region's society, current affairs and politics. Supporters (£15/£7.50 concessions) receive a 25 percent discount off *LAB* books (and many *Resource*

Center ones), access to the library and a quarterly copy of *Latin America Outlook*.

If you're travelling to the **Maya areas** of Mexico or Guatemala and require in-depth information and advice based on recent experience of the region the best place to call at in London is *Maya – The Guatemalan Indian Centre*, 94A Wandsworth Bridge Rd, London SW6 2TF (Wed, Thurs & Sat 9am–6pm; closed Jan & July; ☎0171/371-5291). The Centre's director, Krystyna Deuss, is the acknowledged English authority on Guatemalan life, dress and contemporary Maya rituals, and will make you welcome at the monthly events and film shows held at the Centre. Members (£5 annually) have access to the library and video collection and receive a discount on admission to events. There is a particularly fine textile collection.

TRAVEL

Sybille Bedford *A Visit to Don Otavio* (NAL-Dutton, o/p/Eland). An extremely enjoyable, often hilarious, occasionally lyrical and surprisingly relevant account of Ms Bedford's travels through Mexico in the early 1950s.

Frances Calderon de la Barca *Life in Mexico* (University of California). The diary of a Scotswoman who married the Spanish ambassador to Mexico and spent two years observing life there in the early nineteenth century.

Tom Owen Edmunds *Mexico: Feast and Ferment* (Viking Penguin/Hamish Hamilton). A coffee-table book of photographs, and a particularly good one, full of marvellous and unexpected images including the one on the cover of this book.

Charles Macomb Flandrau *Viva Mexico!* (Eland). First published in 1908, Flandrau's account of life on his brother's farm is something of a cult classic. Though attitudes are inevitably dated in places, it's extremely funny in others.

Thomas Gage *Travels in the New World* (University of Oklahoma Press). Unusual account of a Dominican friar's travels through Mexico and Central America between 1635 and 1637, including some fascinating insights into colonial life and some great attacks on the greed and pomposity of the Catholic Church abroad.

Graham Greene *The Lawless Roads* (Penguin). In the late 1930s Greene was sent to

Mexico to investigate the effects of the persecution of the Catholic church. The result (see also his novel below) was this classic account of his travels in a very bizarre era of modern Mexican history.

Katie Hickman *A Trip to the Light Fantastic: Travels with a Mexican Circus* (Flamingo, UK). Enchanting, funny and uplifting account of a year spent travelling (and performing) with a fading Mexican circus troupe.

Aldous Huxley *Beyond the Mexique Bay* (Academy Chicago, o/p/Grafton). Only a small part of the book is devoted to Mexico, but the descriptions of the archeological sites around Oaxaca, particularly, are still worth reading.

DH Lawrence *Mornings in Mexico* (Peregrine Smith/Penguin). A very slim volume, half of which is devoted to the Hopi Indians of New Mexico, this is an uncharacteristically cheerful account of Lawrence's stay in southern Mexico, and beautifully written.

John Lincoln *One Man's Mexico* (Century, o/p). Lincoln's travels in the late 1960s are an entertaining and offbeat read – travelling alone, often into the jungle, always away from tourists.

Patrick Marnham *So far from God. . .* (Penguin). A rather jaundiced view, but nevertheless a humorous and insightful one, as Marnham travelled from the US to Panama in 1984. About half the book is occupied with his journey through Mexico.

James O'Reilly and Larry Habegger, eds *Travelers' Tales Mexico* (O'Reilly, US). An anthology of Mexican travel writing. Disappointing considering the riches that are available: many here are reprinted magazine articles. Nonetheless there's something for everyone somewhere.

Nigel Pride *A Butterfly Sings to Pacaya* (Constable, UK, o/p). The author, accompanied by his wife and four-year-old son, travels south from the US border in a Jeep, heading through Mexico, Guatemala and Belize. Though the travels took place over fifteen years ago the pleasures and privations they experience rarely appear dated.

John Lloyd Stephens *Incidents of Travel in Central America, Chiapas, and Yucatán* (Dover). Stephens was a classic nineteenth-century traveller. Acting as American ambassador to Central America, he indulged his own enthusiasm for

archeology. His journals, told with superb Victorian pomposity punctuated with sudden waves of enthusiasm, make great reading. There have been many editions of the work: many include fantastic illustrations by Catherwood of the ruins overgrown with tropical rainforest; the Smithsonian edition combines some of these with modern photographs.

Paul Theroux *The Old Patagonian Express* (Pocket/Penguin). The epic journey from Boston to Patagonia by train spends just three rather bad-tempered chapters in Mexico, so don't expect to find out too much about the country. A good read nonetheless.

John Kenneth Turner *Barbarous Mexico* (University of Texas). Turner was a journalist, and this account of his travels through nineteenth-century Mexico exposing the conditions of workers in the plantations of the Yucatán, serialized in US newspapers, did much to discredit the regime of Porfirio Díaz.

Ronald Wright *Time Among the Maya* (H Holt & Co/Bodley Head, o/p). A vivid and sympathetic account of travels from Belize through Guatemala, Chiapas and Yucatán, meeting the Maya of today and exploring their obsession with time. The book's twin points of interest are the ancient Maya and the recent violence.

MEXICAN FICTION

Mariano Azuela *The Underdogs* (University of Pittsburgh). The first novel of the Revolution (finished in 1915), *The Underdogs* is told through the eyes of a group of peasants who form a semi-regular Revolutionary armed band: the story concerns their escapades, progress and eventual betrayal, ambush and massacre. Initially fighting for land and liberty, they end up caught up in a cycle of violence they cannot control and descend into brutal nihilism. The novel set many of the themes of post-revolutionary Mexican writing.

Carmen Boullosa *The Miracle Worker* (Jonathan Cape). One of Mexico's most promising contemporary writers, Boullosa's work focuses on traditional Mexican themes, often borrowing characters from history or myth. *The Miracle Worker* explores Mexican attitudes to Catholicism through the eyes of a messianic healer and her followers. The story can be seen as a parable on the Mexican political system, where ordinary Mexicans petition a distant and incomprehensible government machinery for favours, which are granted or refused in seemingly arbitrary decisions.

Laura Esquivel *Like Water for Chocolate* (Doubleday/Black Swan). Adapted to film, Laura Esquivel's novel has proved a huge hit in Mexico and abroad. The book is even better: sentimental (schmaltzy, even) it deals with the star-crossed romance of Tita, whose lover Pedro marries her sister. Using the magic of the kitchen, she sets out to seduce him back. The book is written in monthly episodes, each of which is prefaced with a traditional Mexican recipe. Funny, sexy, great.

Carlos Fuentes *The Death of Artemio Cruz* (Farrar, Straus & Giroux/Penguin o/p), *The Old Gringo* (HarperCollins/Picador). Fuentes is by far the best-known Mexican writer outside Mexico, influenced by Mariano Azuela and Juan Rulfo, and an early exponent of "magic realism". In *The Death of Artemio Cruz* the hero, a rich and powerful man on his deathbed, looks back over his life and loves, from an idealist youth in the Revolution through disillusion to corruption and power; in many ways an indictment of modern Mexican society. Some of his other books are harder work: they include *Distant Relations* (Farrar, Straus & Giroux/Abacus, o/p), *Where the Air is Clear* (Farrar, Straus & Giroux/ Deutsch), *A Change of Skin* (Farrar, Straus & Giroux/Deutsch) and *Terra Nostra* (Farrar, Straus & Giroux/Penguin).

Sergio Galindo *Otilia's Body* (University of Texas, US). This prize-winning novel, published in Mexico as *Otilia Rauda*, traces the story of Otilia's passionate, tragic affair with an outlaw in post-revolutionary Mexico. Somewhat let down by an over-literal translation.

Jorge Ibargüengoitia *The Dead Girls, Two Crimes* and others (all Avon/Chatto, o/p). One of the first modern Mexican novelists translated into English, Ibargüengoitia was killed in a plane crash in 1983. These two are both blackly comic thrillers, superbly told, the first of them based on real events.

Octavio Paz, ed *An Anthology of Mexican Poetry* (Riverrun/John Calder). Edited by Paz (perhaps the leading man of letters of the post-revolutionary era) and translated by Samuel Beckett, this is as good a taste as you could hope for of modern Mexican poets. Some of Paz's own poetry is also available in translation.

Juan Rulfo *Pedro Páramo* (Grove Atlantic/ Serpent's Tail). Widely regarded as the greatest Mexican novel of the twentieth century and a precursor of magic realism. The living and spirit worlds mesh when, at the dying behest of his mother, the narrator visits the deserted village haunted by the memory of his brutal patriarch father, Pedro Páramo. Dark, depressing and initially confusing but ultimately very rewarding. Rulfo's short-story collection *The Burning Plain and Other Stories* (University of Texas), is rated by Gabriel García Marquez as the best in Latin America.

FOREIGN FICTION

There must be hundreds of novels by outsiders set in Mexico, all too many in the sex-and-shopping genre: apart from those below, others to look out for include a whole clutch of modern Americans, especially **Jack Kerouac's** *Desolation Angels* (Berkeley/Granton) and several of **Richard Brautigan's** novels. And of course there's **Carlos Castaneda's** *Don Juan* series (Pocket Books/Penguin) – a search for enlightenment through peyote.

Tony Cartano *After the Conquest* (Secker and Warburg, UK) An extraordinary fictional account of a fictional author who believes he is B Traven's son and sets out to discover the truth about his father (see below). A psychological thriller which is also full of Mexican history and politics.

Eduardo Galeano *Genesis* and *Faces and Masks* (both Pantheon/Quartet). The opening parts of a trilogy by a Uruguayan writer, these anthologies of Indian legends, colonists' tales and odd snatches of history illuminate the birth of Latin America. Not specifically Mexican, but wonderful, relevant reading nonetheless.

Graham Greene *The Power and the Glory* (Penguin). Inspired by his investigative travels, this story of a doomed whisky priest on the run from the authorities makes a great yarn. It was a wonderful movie too.

Gary Jennings *Aztec* (Avon, US). Sex and sacrifice in ancient Mexico in this gripping best seller. The narrator travels around the Aztec empire in search of his fortune, chancing upon almost every ancient culture along the way, and sleeping with most of them, until finally the Spanish arrive. Perfect beach or bus reading, and informative too.

DH Lawrence _The Plumed Serpent_ (McKay/ Penguin). One of Lawrence's own favourites, the novel reflects his intense dislike of the country which followed on the brief honeymoon period of _Mornings in Mexico_. Fans of his heavy spiritualism will love it.

Haniel Long _The Marvelous Adventure of Cabeza de Vaca_ (Dawn Horse Press, US). Two short stories in one volume – the first the account of a shipwrecked Conquistador's journey across the new continent, the second the thoughts and hopes of Malinche, Cortés' interpreter.

Malcolm Lowry _Under the Volcano_ (NAL-Dutton/Pan). A classic since its publication, Lowry's account of the last day in the life of the British Consul in Cuernavaca – passed in a Mescal-induced haze – is totally brilliant. His _Dark as the Grave Wherein my Friend is Laid_ is also based on his Mexican experiences.

James A Michener _Mexico_ (Random House/ Mandarin). Another doorstop from Michener. Fans will love it.

B Traven Traven's true identity is still unknown but he wrote a whole series of compelling novels set in Mexico. Among the best known are _Treasure of the Sierra Madre_ (Farrar, Straus & Giroux/Picador) and _The Death Ship_ (L Hill Books/Picador, o/p), but of more direct interest if you're travelling are such works as _The Bridge in the Jungle_ and the six books in the Jungle series: _Government, The Carreta, March to the Monteria, Trozas, The Rebellion of the Hanged_ and _General from the Jungle_ (all I R Dee/Allison & Busby, some o/p). These latter all deal with the state of the peasantry and the growth of Revolutionary feeling in the last years of the Díaz dictatorship, and if at times they're overly polemical, as a whole they're enthralling. Will Wyatt's _The Man who was B. Traven_ (Cape, o/p in UK, published by Harcourt Brace in the US as _The in UK Secret of the Sierra Madre_) is the best of the books on the quest for the author's identity.

HISTORY

The sources below are all entertaining and/or important references: more standard **general histories** include Henry Bamford Parkes' _History of Mexico_ (Houghton Mifflin); _Fire and Blood: a History of Mexico_ by TR Fehrenbach (Da Capo, US); _A Concise History of Mexico from Hidalgo to Cárdenas_ by Jan Bazant (CUP); and Judith Hellman, _Mexico in Crisis_ (Holmes & Meier).

Inga Clendinnen _Ambivalent Conquests: Maya and Spaniard in Yucatán 1517 to 1570_ (CUP). A product of meticulous research which documents the methods and consequences of the Spanish conquest of the Yucatán. The ambivalence in the title reflects doubts about the effectivness of the conquest in subjugating the Maya; over three hundred years after the conquest the Maya rose in revolt, and almost succeeded in driving out their white overlords, while in January 1994, Maya peasants in Chiapas stunned the world and severely embarrassed the Mexican government by briefly capturing and controlling cities in the southeastern area of the state.

Hernan Cortés _Letters from Mexico_ (Yale UP). The thoughts and impressions of the Conquistador, first hand. Less exciting than Díaz, though.

Bernal Díaz _The Conquest of New Spain_, translated by JM Cohen (Linnet Books/Penguin). This abridged version is the best available of Díaz's classic _Historia Verdadera de la Conquista de la Nueva España_. Díaz, having been on two earlier expeditions to Mexico, accompanied Cortés throughout his campaign of Conquest, and this magnificent eye-witness account still makes compulsive reading.

Adolfo Gilly _The Mexican Revolution_ (Routledge, Chapman & Hall/Verso). Written in México's notorious Lecumberri jail (Gilly was later granted an absolute pardon), this is regarded as the classic work on the Revolution. Heavy-going and highly theoretical though.

Michael Meyer and William Sherman _The Course of Mexican History_ (OUP). Comprehensive and up-to-date general history.

William Prescott _History of the Conquest of Mexico_ (Corona). Written in the mid-nineteenth century, and drawing heavily on Díaz, Prescott's history was the standard text for over a hundred years. It makes for pretty heavy reading and has now been overtaken by Thomas' account.

John Reed _Insurgent Mexico_ (International Publications). This collection of his reportage of the Mexican Revolution was put together by Reed himself. He spent several months in 1913 and 1914 with various generals of the

Revolution – especially Villa – and the book contains great descriptions of them, their men, and the mood of the times. It's far more anecdotal and easy to read than the celebrated *Ten Days that Shook the World*.

Hugh Thomas *Conquest: Montezuma, Cortés, and the Fall of Old Mexico* (Simon & Schuster, US); *The Conquest of Mexico* (Pimlico, UK). Same book, different title, but either way a brilliant narrative history of the Conquest by the British historian previously best known for his history of the Spanish Civil War. A massive work of real scholarship and importance – much of the archive material is newly discovered – but also humorous and readable, with appendices on everything from Aztec beliefs, history and genealogy to Cortés' wives and lovers.

James W Wilkie and Albert L Michaels, eds *Revolution in Mexico* (University of Arizona Press). A fascinating anthology of contemporary and more recent writing on the Revolution and the years which followed.

ANCIENT MEXICO

There are thousands of studies of ancient Mexico, most of them extremely academic and detailed, plus any number of big, highly illustrated coffee-table tomes on individual sites. Those below are of more general interest, and any of them will have substantial bibliographies to help you explore further.

Ignacio Bernal *Mexico Before Cortés* (Doubleday, US, o/p). The leading Mexican archeologist of the century, and one of the inspirations behind the National Museum of Anthropology, Bernal did important work on the Olmecs and on the restoration of Teotihuacán, and has written many important source works. This book covers much the same ground as Davies', though in less detail and more dated, but it has the advantage of being widely available in Mexico. A more scholarly version is available in *A History of Mexican Archeology: the Vanished Civilizations of Middle America* (Thames and Hudson, o/p).

Warwick Bray *Everyday life of the Aztecs* (P Bedrick/Batsford). A volume full of information about Aztec warfare, music, games, folklore, religious ritual, social organization, economic and political systems and agricultural practice. Although the book is now showing its age, and some of its conclusions are a bit dubious, its attractive comprehensiveness more than makes up for this. An excellent general introduction.

Inga Clendinnen *Aztecs: an interpretation* (CUP). A social history of the Aztec empire that seeks to explain the importance – and acceptance – of human sacrifice and other rituals. Fascinating, though best to know something about the Aztecs before you start.

Michael D Coe *The Maya* (Thames & Hudson/ Penguin). The updated fifth edition is the best available general introduction to the Maya: concise, clear and comprehensive. Coe has also written several more weighty, academic volumes. His *Breaking the Maya Code* (Thames & Hudson), a history of the decipherment of the Maya glyphs, owes much to the fact that Coe was present at many of the most important meetings leading to the breakthrough, demonstrating that the glyphs actually did reproduce Maya speech.

Nigel Davies *The Ancient Kingdoms of Mexico* (Penguin). Although there's no single text which covers all the ancient cultures, this comes pretty close, covering the central areas from the Olmecs through Teotihuacán and the Toltecs to the Aztec Empire. An excellent mix of historical, archeological, social and artistic information, but it doesn't cover the Maya. Davies is also the author of several more detailed academic works on the Aztecs and Toltecs including *The Aztecs, A History* (University of Oklahoma).

MS Edmonson, trans *The Book of Chilam Balam of Chumayel* (Aegean, US). The Chilam Balam is a recollection of Maya history and myth, recorded by the Spanish after the Conquest. Although the style is not easy, it's one of the few keys into the Maya view of the world.

Charles Gallenkamp *Maya* (Penguin, o/p in UK). Gallenkamp's now slightly dated account takes a historical view of the development of Mayanism, from the earliest discoveries to more recent theories. Anecdotal and easy to read.

Norman Hammond *Ancient Maya Civilization* (Rutgers UP/CUP). An excellent introductory summary of current knowledge on the Maya.

George Kubler *Art and Architecture of Ancient America* (Yale UP/Penguin). Exactly what it says: a massive and amazingly comprehensive work, covering not only Mexico but Colombia, Ecuador and Peru as well.

Diego de Landa *Yucatán Before and After the Conquest* (Dover). A translation edited by William Gates of the work written in 1566 as *Relación de las Cosas de Yucatán*. De Landa's destruction of almost all original Maya books as "works of the devil" leaves his own account as the chief source on Maya life and society in the immediate post-conquest period. Written during his imprisonment in Spain on charges of cruelty to the Indians (remarkable itself, given the institutional brutality of the time) the book provides a fascinating wealth of detail for historians.

Ellen Miller *The Art of Mesoamerica: From Olmec to Aztec* (Thames & Hudson, UK). An excellent survey of the artisanship of the ancient cultures of Mexico, whose work reflects the sophistication of their civilizations.

Mary Miller and Karl Taube *The Gods and Symbols of Ancient Mexico and the Maya: An Illustrated Dictionary of Mesoamerican Religion* (Thames and Hudson). A superb reference on ancient Mexican gods and beliefs, written by two leading scholars. Taube's *Aztec and Maya Myths* (British Museum Press) is exactly what it says, a short, accessible introduction to Mesoamerican mythology.

Jeremy A Sabloff *The New Archeology and the Ancient Maya* (WH Freeman). In this highly readable book Sabloff explains the "revolution" which has taken place in Maya archeology since the 1960s, overturning many firmly held beliefs and assumptions on the nature of Maya society. Also worth checking is his *The Cities of Ancient Mexico* (Thames and Hudson).

Linda Schele and David Freidel *A Forest of Kings: The Untold Story of the Ancient Maya* (William Morrow). The authors are in the forefront of the "new archeology" and have been personally responsible for decoding many of the glyphs. This book, in conjunction with *The Blood of Kings* (by Linda Schele and Mary Miller; Braziller/Thames and Hudson), shows that far from being governed by peaceful astronomer-priests, the ancient Maya were ruled by hereditary kings, lived in populous, aggressive city- states, and engaged in a continuous entanglement of alliances and war.

Dennis Tedlock, trans *Popol Vuh* (Simon & Schuster). Translation of the Maya Quiché bible, a fascinating creation myth from the only ancient civilization to emerge from rainforest terrain. The Maya obsession with time can be well appreciated here, where dates are recorded with painstaking precision.

J Eric S Thompson *The Rise and Fall of Maya Civilization* (University of Oklahoma, o/p/ Pimlico). A major authority on the ancient Maya during his lifetime, Thompson produced many academic works; *The Rise and Fall...*, originally published in 1954, is one of the more approachable. Although more recent researchers have overturned many of Thompson's theories, his work provided the inspiration for the postwar surge of interest in the Maya, and he remains a respected figure.

Richard F Townsend *The Aztecs* (Thames & Hudson). Companion in the series to Coe's Maya book, this is a good introduction to all aspects of Aztec history and culture.

SOCIETY

Tom Barry, ed *Mexico: A Country Guide* (Interhemisperic Education Resource Center). A comprehensive and up-to-date study of contemporary Mexico: Barry and ten other contributors impart their expertise to make this probably the best single volume survey on the issues facing Mexico in the 1990s.

Harry Browne *For Richer, For Poorer* (Interhemispheric Education Resource Center/ Latin America Bureau). An analysis of the background to NAFTA and the effects of and prospects for closer economic integration between the US and Mexico. Heavy going.

Miguel Covarrubias *Mexico South* (Routledge, Chapman & Hall/KPI). The people and popular culture of Veracruz and the Isthmus of Tehuantepec by the well-known Mexican artist and anthropologist. A good read, well illustrated.

Augusta Dwyer *On The Line* (Latin America Bureau). A painstakingly detailed account of conditions on the US/Mexico border, where many of the most environmentally damaging factories on the continent poison lands and people on both sides of the frontier. This is the only place in the world where the rich north directly borders the poorer south, and Dwyer documents the consequences of this economic discrepancy in case studies of *maquila* workers, legal and illegal immigrants and both victims and members of the US Border Patrol.

Oscar Lewis *The Children of Sanchez* (Vintage/Penguin, o/p). These oral histories of a working-class family in the México of the 1940s are regarded as a seminal work in modern anthropology. The book is totally gripping, though, and doesn't read in the least like an anthropological text. Lewis' other works, including *Pedro Martinez* (Vintage, o/p/ Penguin, o/p), *A Death in the Sanchez Family* (Vintage, US, o/p) and *Five Families* (Basic Books/Souvenir, o/p), use the same first-person narrative technique. All are highly recommended.

Octavio Paz *The Labyrinth of Solitude* (Grove Atlantic/Penguin). A series of philosophical essays exploring the social and political state of modern Mexico.

Elena Poniatowska *Until We Meet Again Sweet Jesus* (Pantheon, US). A pioneer in the field of testimonial literature, Poniatowska turns her attentions to Jesusa, her cleaning lady. Jesusa's story of her marriage, involvement in the Revolution and postwar period include her views on life, love and society. Narrated in the first person, the text is compelling, lively and at times ribald: Jesusa herself is now a celebrity on the literary circuit. Poniatowska is one of Mexico's best-known essayists and journalists: other works available in English include *Massacre in Mexico* (University of Missouri, US), first-hand accounts of the 1968 student massacre; *Dear Diego* (Pantheon, US); and *Tinisima* (Faber & Faber/Farrar, Straus & Giroux).

Gregory G Reck *In the Shadow of Tlaloc* (Waveland/Penguin, o/p). Reck attempts a similar style to that of Oscar Lewis in his study of a Mexican village, and the effects on it of encroaching modernity. Often seems to stray over the border into sentimentality and even fiction, but interesting nonetheless.

Alan Riding *Mexico: Inside the Volcano* (IB Tauris, UK). In-depth analysis of modern Mexico by the British correspondent for the *New York Times*. Enlightening, though gloomy.

Chloë Sayer *The Arts and Crafts of Mexico* (Chronicle/Thames and Hudson). Sayer is the author of numerous books on Mexican arts, crafts and associated subjects (see below); most of them worth reading.

Mariana Yampolsky *The Traditional Architecture of Mexico* (Thames and Hudson). The enormous range of Mexico's architectural styles, from thatched peasant huts and vast *haciendas* to exuberant Baroque churches and solid, yet graceful public buildings is encompassed in this inspired book. While most of Mariana Yampolsky's superb photographs are in black and white, a chapter on the use of colour emphasizes its importance in every area of life; the text by Chloë Sayer raises it above the level of the average coffee-table book.

LOCAL & WILDLIFE GUIDES

Carl Franz *The People's Guide to Mexico* (John Muir). Not a guidebook as such, more of a series of anecdotes and words of advice for staying out of trouble and heading off the beaten track. Perennially popular, and deservedly so.

C Kaplan *Coral reefs of the Caribbean and Florida* (Houghton Mifflin). Useful handbook on the abundant wildlife off the coasts off the Yucatán peninsula.

RT Peterson and EL Chalif *Mexican Birds* (Houghton Mifflin). The premier ornithological guide to Mexico. The text is excellent, but drawings are limited to indigenous examples only; migratory species are included in additional (North American) guides, which can be frustratingly impractical.

DG Schueler *Adventuring along the Gulf of Mexico* (Sierra Club Books, US). An entertaining read, with much general info on plants and animals along the Gulf coast.

RJ Secor *Mexico's Volcanoes* (Mountaineers). Detailed routes up all the big volcanoes, and full of invaluable information for climbers.

In Mexico itself, the best and most complete series of guides is that published by *Guias Panorama* – they have small books on all the main archeological sites, as well as more general titles ranging from *Wild Flowers of Mexico* to *Pancho Villa – Truth and Legend*.

LANGUAGE

Once you get into it, Spanish is the easiest language there is – and in Mexico people are desperately eager to understand and to help the most faltering attempt. English is widely spoken, especially in the tourist areas, but you'll get a far better reception if you at least try to communicate with people in their own tongue. You'll be further helped by the fact that Mexicans speak relatively slowly (at least compared with Spaniards in Spain) and that there's none of the difficult lisping pronunciation here.

The rules of **pronunciation** are pretty straightforward and, once you get to know them, strictly observed. Unless there's an accent, words ending in d, l, r and z are **stressed** on the last syllable, all others on the second last. All **vowels** are pure and short.

A somewhere between the A sound of back and that of father

E as in get

I as in police

O as in hot

U as in rule

PHRASEBOOKS AND DICTIONARIES

Although we've listed a few essential words and phrases here, if you're travelling for any length of time some kind of dictionary or **phrasebook** is obviously a worthwhile investment – the Rough Guide Spanish phrasebook will be supplemented shortly after publication of this book by the *Rough Guide to Mexican Spanish*. One of the best small, Latin-American Spanish dictionaries is the University of Chicago version (Pocket Books), widely available in Mexico. If you're using a **dictionary**, bear in mind that in Spanish CH, LL and Ñ are traditionally counted as separate letters and are listed after the Cs, Ls and Ns respectively. This has recently changed, but many dictionaries won't have caught up.

C is soft before E and I, hard otherwise: *cerca* is pronounced serka

G works the same way, a guttural H sound (like the *ch* in loch) before E or I, a hard G elsewhere: *gigante* becomes higante.

H is always silent

J the same sound as a guttural G: *jamon* is pronounced hamon.

LL sounds like an English Y: *tortilla* is pronounced torteeya.

N is as in English unless it has a tilde (accent) over it, when it becomes NY: *mañana* sounds like manyana.

QU is pronounced like an English K.

R is rolled, RR doubly so.

V sounds more like B, *vino* becoming beano.

X is slightly softer than in English – sometimes almost S – except between vowels in place names where it has an H sound – i.e. México (Meh-Hee-Ko) or Oaxaca (Wa-ha-ka).

Z is the same as a soft C, so *cerveza* becomes servesa.

BASICS

Yes, No	*Si, No*	Open, Closed	*Abierto/a, Cerrado/a*
Please, Thank you	*Por favor, Gracias*	With, Without	*Con, Sin*
Where, When	*Donde, Cuando*	Good, Bad	*Buen(o)/a, Mal(o)/a*
What, How much	*Que, Cuanto*	Big, Small	*Gran(de), Pequeño/a*
Here, There	*Aqui, Alli*	More, Less	*Mas, Menos*
This, That	*Este, Eso*	Today, Tomorrow	*Hoy, Mañana*
Now, Later	*Ahora, Mas tarde*	Yesterday	*Ayer*

GREETINGS AND RESPONSES

Hello, Goodbye	*Ola, Adios*	I don't speak Spanish	*(No) Hablo Español*
Good morning	*Buenos dias*	What (did you say)?	*Mande?*
Good afternoon/ night	*Buenas tardes/noches*	My name is...	*Me llamo...*
How do you do?	*Qué tal*	What's your name?	*¿Como se llama usted?*
See you later	*Hasta luego*	I am English	*Soy Ingles(a)*
Sorry	*Lo siento/disculpeme*	...American*	*Americano(a)*
Excuse me	*Con permiso/perdon*	...Australian	*Australiano(a)*
How are you?	*¿Como esta (usted)?*	...Canadian	*Canadiense(a)*
Not at all/You're	*De nada*	...Irish	*Irlandes(a)*
welcome		...Scottish	*Escoses(a)*
I (don't) understand	*(No) Entiendo*	...Welsh	*Gales(a)*
Do you speak English?	*¿Habla (usted) Ingles?*	...New Zealander	*Neo Zelandes(a)*

*Mexicans are Americans too, so describing yourself as American can occasionally cause offence. But there's no easy alternative; Norteamericano, Gringo, Yanqui. . ...none really work.

NEEDS – HOTELS AND TRANSPORT

I want	*Quiero*	How do I get to...?	*¿Por donde se va a...?*
Do you know...?	*¿Sabe...?*	Left, right, straight on	*Izquierda, derecha,*
I'd like	*Querria*		*derecho*
I don't know	*No se*	Where is...?	*¿Donde esta...?*
There is (is there)?	*Hay (?)*	...the bus station	*...el camionera central*
Give me...	*Deme...*	...the railway station	*...la estacion de*
(one like that)	*(uno asi)*		*ferrocarriles*
Do you have...?	*¿Tiene...?*	...the nearest bank	*...el banco mas*
...the time	*...la hora*		*cercano*
...a room	*...un cuarto*	...the post office	*...el correo (la oficina*
...with two beds/	*...con dos camas/cama*		*de correos)*
double bed	*matrimonial*	...the toilet	*...el baño/sanitario*
It's for one person (two	*Es para una persona (dos*	Where does the bus	*¿De donde sale el*
people)	*personas)*	to... leave from?	*camion para...?*
...for one night (one	*...para una noche (una*	Is this the train for	*¿Es este el tren para*
week)	*semana)*	Chihuahua?	*Chihuahua?*
It's fine, how much is it?	*¿Esta bien, cuanto es?*	I'd like a (return) ticket	*Querria un boleto (de*
It's too expensive	*Es demasiado caro*	to...	*ida y vuelta) para...*
Don't you have anything	*¿No tiene algo mas*	What time does it leave	*¿A que hora sale (llega*
cheaper?	*barato?*	(arrive in...)?	*en...)?*
Can one...?	*¿Se puede...?*	What is there to eat?	*¿Que hay para comer?*
...camp (near) here?	*¿...acampar aqui*	What's that?	*¿Que es eso?*
	(cerca)?	What's this called in	*¿Como se llama este en*
Is there a hotel nearby?	*¿Hay un hotel aqui cerca?*	Spanish?	*Espanol?*

NUMBERS AND DAYS

1	*un/uno/una*	13	*trece*	90	*noventa*	third	*tercero/a*
2	*dos*	14	*catorce*	100	*cien(to)*	fifth	*quinto/a*
3	*tres*	15	*quince*	101	*ciento uno*	tenth	*decimo/a*
4	*cuatro*	16	*diez y seis*	200	*doscientos*		
5	*cinco*	20	*veinte*	500	*quinientos*	Monday	*Lunes*
6	*seis*	21	*veintiuno*	700	*setecientos*	Tuesday	*Martes*
7	*siete*	30	*treinta*	1000	*mil*	Wednesday	*Miercoles*
8	*ocho*	40	*cuarenta*	2000	*dos mil*	Thursday	*Jueves*
9	*nueve*	50	*cincuenta*	1996	*mil novecientos*	Friday	*Viernes*
10	*diez*	60	*sesenta*		*noventa y seis*	Saturday	*Sabado*
11	*once*	70	*setenta*	first	*primero/a*	Sunday	*Domingo*
12	*doce*	80	*ochenta*	second	*segundo/a*		

A GLOSSARY OF COMMON MEXICAN TERMS AND ACRONYMS

AHORITA diminutive of *ahora* (now) meaning right now – usually a couple of hours at least.

ALAMEDA city park or promenade; large plaza.

AYUNTAMIENTO town hall/government.

AZTEC the empire that dominated the central valleys of Mexico from the thirteenth century until defeated by Cortés.

AZULEJO decorative glazed tile, usually blue and white.

BARRIO area within a town or city; suburb.

CAMIONETA small truck or van.

CANTINA bar, usually men-only.

CENOTE underground water source in the Yucatán.

CENTRAL CAMIONERA bus station.

CHAC Maya god of rain.

CHAC-MOOL recumbent statue, possibly a sacrificial figue or messenger to the gods.

CHARRO a Mexican cowboy.

CHURRIGUERESQUE highly elaborate, decorative form of Baroque architecture (usually in churches).

COMEDOR cheap restaurant, literally dining room.

CONVENTO either convent or monastery.

CTM Central Union organization.

CUAUHTÉMOC the last Aztec leader, commander of the final resistance to Cortés, and a national hero.

DESCOMPUESTO out of order.

DON/DOÑA courtesy titles (sir/madam), mostly used in letters or for professional people or the boss.

EJIDO communal farmland.

EZLN the Zapatista Army of National Liberation.

FERIA fair (market).

FINCA ranch or plantation.

FONART government agency to promote crafts.

GRINGO not necessarily insulting, though it does imply North American – said to come from invading US troops, either because they wore green coats or because they sang "*Green grow the rushes oh!...*"

GUAYABERA embroidered shirt.

GÜERA/O blonde – very frequently used description of Westerners, especially shouted after women in the street; again, not intended as an insult.

HACIENDA estate or big house on it.

HENEQUEN hemp fibre, grown mainly in Yucatán, used to make rope.

HUIPIL Maya women's embroidered dress or blouse.

HUITZILOPOCHTLI Aztec god of war.

I.V.A. 15 percent sales tax.

KUKULCAN Maya name for Quetzalcoatl.

LADINO applied to people, means Spanish-influenced as opposed to Indian: determined entirely by clothing (and culture) rather than physical race.

MALECÓN seafront promenade.

MALINCHE Cortés' Indian interpreter and mistress, a symbol of treachery.

MARIACHI quintessentially Mexican music, with lots of brass and sentimental lyrics.

MARIMBA xylophone-like musical instrument, also used of the bands based around it and the style of music.

MAYA tribe who inhabited Honduras, Guatemala and southeastern Mexico from earliest times, and still does.

METATE flat stone for grinding corn.

MIRADOR lookout point.

MIXTEC tribe from the mountains of Oaxaca.

MOCTEZUMA Montezuma, penultimate Aztec leader.

MUELLE jetty or dock.

NAFTA the North American Free Trade Agreement including Mexico, the USA and Canada.

NAHUATL ancient Aztec language, still the most common after Spanish.

NORTEÑO literally northern – style of food and music.

PALACIO mansion, but not necessarily royal.

PALACIO DE GOBIERNO headquarters of state/federal authorities.

PALACIO MUNICIPAL headquarters of local government.

PALAPA palm thatch. Used to describe any thatched/palm-roofed hut.

PALENQUE cockpit (for cock fights).

PAN *Partido de Accion Nacional*, conservative opposition party, allied to the US Republicans; has gained several local election victories in the north.

PASEO a broad avenue, but also the ritual evening walk around the plaza.

PEMEX the Mexican national oil company, a vast and extraordinary wealthy corporation, rumoured to be riddled with corruption, as is the powerful oil workers' union.

PLANTA BAJA ground floor – abbreviated PB in lifts.

PLATERESQUE elaborately decorative renaissance architectural style.

PORFIRIANO the time of Porfirio Díaz's dictatorship – used especially of its grandiose neoclassical architecture.

PRD Party of the Democratic Revolution, the new left-wing coalition formed by Cuauhtémoc Cárdenas.

PRI *Partido Revolucionario Institucional*, the ruling party for the past eighty years.

QUETZALCOATL the plumed serpent, most powerful, enigmatic and widespread of all ancient Mexican gods.

SACBE Maya road.

STELA free-standing carved monument.

TENOCHTITLÁN the Aztec capital, on the site of México.

TEOTIHUACÁN ancient city north of the capital – the first major urban power of central Mexico.

TIANGUIS Nahuatl word for market, still used of particularly varied marketplaces.

TLALOC Toltec/Aztec rain god.

TOLTEC tribe which controlled central Mexico between Teotihuacán and the Aztecs.

TULA Toltec capital.

TZOMPANTLI Aztec skull rack or "wall of skulls".

VIRREINAL from the period of the Spanish viceroys – i.e. colonial.

WETBACK illegal Mexican (or any Hispanic) in the US.

ZAPOTEC tribe which controlled the Oaxaca region to about 700 AD.

ZÓCALO the main plaza of any town.

INDEX

HELP US UPDATE

We've gone to a lot of effort to ensure that this edition of the *Rough Guide to Mexico* is up-to-date and accurate. However, things do change, and any suggestions, comments or corrections would be much appreciated. We'll send a copy of the next edition (or any other *Rough Guide* if you prefer) for the best contributions. Please mark letters "Rough Guide to Mexico update" and send to:

Rough Guides, 1 Mercer St, London WC2H 9QJ

or Rough Guides, 375 Hudson St, 3rd floor, New York NY 10014

DIRECT ORDERS IN THE UK

Title	ISBN	Price
Amsterdam	1858280869	£7.99
Andalucia	185828094X	£8.99
Australia	1858280354	£12.99
Barcelona & Catalunya	1858281067	£8.99
Berlin	1858280338	£8.99
Brazil	1858281024	£9.99
Brittany & Normandy	1858281261	£8.99
Bulgaria	1858280478	£8.99
California	1858280907	£9.99
Canada	185828130X	£10.99
Classical Music on CD	185828113X	£12.99
Corsica	1858280893	£8.99
Crete	1858281326	£8.99
Cyprus	185828032X	£8.99
Czech & Slovak Republics	185828029X	£8.99
Egypt	1858280753	£10.99
England	1858280788	£9.99
Europe	185828077X	£14.99
Florida	1858280109	£8.99
France	1858280508	£9.99
Germany	1858281288	£11.99
Greece	1858281318	£9.99
Greek Islands	1858281636	£8.99
Guatemala & Belize	1858280451	£9.99
Holland, Belgium & Luxembourg	1858280877	£9.99
Hong Kong & Macau	1858280664	£8.99
Hungary	1858281237	£8.99
India	1858281040	£13.99
Ireland	1858280958	£9.99
Italy	1858280311	£12.99
Kenya	1858280435	£9.99
London	1858291172	£8.99
Mediterranean Wildlife	0747100993	£7.95
Malaysia, Singapore & Brunei	1858281032	£9.99
Morocco	1858280400	£9.99
Nepal	185828046X	£8.99
New York	1858280583	£8.99
Nothing Ventured	0747102082	£7.99
Pacific Northwest	1858280923	£9.99
Paris	1858281253	£7.99
Poland	1858280346	£9.99
Portugal	1858280842	£9.99
Prague	185828015X	£7.99
Provence & the Côte d'Azur	1858280230	£8.99
Pyrenees	1858280931	£8.99
St Petersburg	1858281334	£8.99
San Francisco	1858280826	£8.99
Scandinavia	1858280397	£10.99
Scotland	1858280834	£8.99
Sicily	1858280370	£8.99
Spain	1858280818	£9.99
Thailand	1858280168	£8.99
Tunisia	1858280656	£8.99
Turkey	1858280885	£9.99
Tuscany & Umbria	1858280915	£8.99
USA	185828080X	£12.99
Venice	1858280362	£8.99
Wales	1858280966	£8.99
West Africa	1858280141	£12.99
More Women Travel	1858280982	£9.99
World Music	1858280176	£14.99
Zimbabwe & Botswana	1858280419	£10.99

Rough Guide Phrasebooks

Title	ISBN	Price
Czech	1858281482	£3.50
French	185828144X	£3.50
German	1858281466	£3.50
Greek	1858281458	£3.50
Italian	1858281431	£3.50
Spanish	1858281474	£3.50

Rough Guides are available from all good bookstores, but can be obtained directly in the UK* from Penguin by contacting:

Penguin Direct, Penguin Books Ltd, Bath Road, Harmondsworth, West Drayton, Middlesex UB7 0DA; or telephone our credit line on 0181-899 4036 (9am–5pm) and ask for Penguin Direct. Visa, Access and Amex accepted. Delivery will normally be within 14 working days. Penguin Direct ordering facilities are only available in the UK.

The availability and published prices quoted are correct at the time of going to press but are subject to alteration without prior notice.

* For USA and international orders, see separate price list

DIRECT ORDERS IN THE USA

Title	ISBN	Price
Amsterdam	1858280869	$13.59
Andalucia	185828094X	$14.95
Australia	1858280354	$18.95
Barcelona & Catalunya	1858281067	$17.99
Berlin	1858280338	$13.99
Brazil	1858281024	$15.95
Brittany & Normandy	1858281261	$14.95
Bulgaria	1858280478	$14.99
California	1858280907	$14.95
Canada	185828130X	$14.95
Classical Music on CD	185828113X	$19.95
Corsica	1858280893	$14.95
Crete	1858281326	$14.95
Cyprus	185828032X	$13.99
Czech & Slovak Republics	185828029X	$14.95
Egypt	1858280753	$17.95
England	1858280788	$16.95
Europe	185828077X	$18.95
Florida	1858280109	$14.95
France	1858281245	$16.95
Germany	1858281288	$17.95
Greece	1858281318	$16.95
Greek Islands	1858281636	$14.95
Guatemala & Belize	1858280451	$14.95
Holland, Belgium & Luxembourg	1858280877	$15.95
Hong Kong & Macau	1858280664	$13.95
Hungary	1858281237	$14.95
India	1858281040	$22.95
Ireland	1858280958	$16.95
Italy	1858280311	$17.95
Kenya	1858280435	$15.95
London	1858291172	$12.95
Mediterranean Wildlife	0747100993	$15.95
Malaysia, Singapore & Brunei	1858281032	$16.95
Morocco	1858280400	$16.95
Nepal	185828046X	$13.95
New York	1858280583	$13.95
Nothing Ventured	0747102082	$19.95
Pacific Northwest	1858280923	$14.95
Paris	1858281253	$12.95
Poland	1858280346	$16.95
Portugal	1858280842	$15.95
Prague	1858281229	$14.95
Provence & the Côte d'Azur	1858280230	$14.95
Pyrenees	1858280931	$15.95
St Petersburg	1858281334	$14.95
San Francisco	1858280826	$13.95
Scandinavia	1858280397	$16.99
Scotland	1858280834	$14.95
Sicily	1858280370	$14.99
Spain	1858280818	$16.95
Thailand	1858280168	$15.95
Tunisia	1858280656	$15.95
Turkey	1858280885	$16.95
Tuscany & Umbria	1858280915	$15.95
USA	185828080X	$18.95
Venice	1858280362	$13.99
Wales	1858280966	$14.95
West Africa	1858280141	$24.95
More Women Travel	1858280982	$14.95
World Music	1858280176	$19.95
Zimbabwe & Botswana	1858280419	$16.95

Rough Guide Phrasebooks

Czech	1858281482	$5.00
French	185828144X	$5.00
German	1858281466	$5.00
Greek	1858281458	$5.00
Italian	1858281431	$5.00
Spanish	1858281474	$5.00

Rough Guides are available from all good bookstores, but can be obtained directly in the USA and Worldwide (except the UK*) from Penguin:

Charge your order by Master Card or Visa (US$15.00 minimum order): call 1-800-253-6476; or send orders, with complete name, address and zip code, and list price, plus $2.00 shipping and handling per order to: Consumer Sales, Penguin USA, PO Box 999 – Dept #17109, Bergenfield, NJ 07621. No COD. Prepay foreign orders by international money order, a cheque drawn on a US bank, or US currency. No postage stamps are accepted. All orders are subject to stock availability at the time they are processed. Refunds will be made for books not available at that time. Please allow a minimum of four weeks for delivery.

The availability and published prices quoted are correct at the time of going to press but are subject to alteration without prior notice. Titles currently not available outside the UK will be available by July 1995. Call to check.

For UK orders, see separate price list

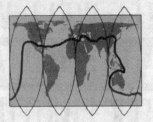

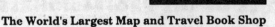

You are A STUDENT

You travel THE WORLD

You want TO SAVE MONEY

Here's how

The International Student Identity Card

Available at Student Travel Offices Worldwide.

Entitles you to discounts and special services worldwide.